JEWS

and the

FRENCH REVOLUTIONS

of

1789, 1830 and 1848

By

ZOSA SZAJKOWSKI

KTAV PUBLISHING HOUSE, INC.

NEW YORK

1970

Library of Congress Catalog Card Number: 71-86313
Manufactured in the United States of America

TABLE OF CONTENTS

VI

III. *THE REVOLUTION OF 1789*

VIII

INTRODUCTION

This book is not a history of Jews during the French Revolutions of 1789, 1830, and 1848. It contains only a collection of my studies on these subjects. Nor should this introduction be considered as a guide for such a history. It consists mostly of summaries and conclusive paragraphs adopted from my earlier studies. (The notes relating to the aformentioned studies, which give full documentation and the sources upon which they are based are, however, not reproduced in this introduction.)

I was sometimes asked why I did not write a general history on those subjects, particularly on the Revolution of 1789. My reply was that I was not yet prepared to undertake such a task. In almost all of my studies I dealt with themes that are basic for any general, regional or local history of the periods, such as nationalized properties, paper money, taxation, émigrés, demography, etc. Such themes were usually ignored by most historians of French Jews who were interested mostly in the political and legislative history of Jewish emancipation. Many important aspects of Franco-Jewish history of the period of the First French Republic should be investigated in detailed monographs before entering upon the writing of a general, definitive history. The tendency to publish "definitive, conclusive" books on Jewish emancipation in France without preliminary monographs can, unfortunately, be misleading. Of course, not everyone can or must wait until a sufficiency of monographs be made available in order to initiate the writing of a general history. But then, under such circumstances, sermon-like conclusions must be shunned.

Too many historians have formed an opinion concerning the events of the various Revolutions solely on the basis of popular pamphlets and official laws. They have completely and utterly disregarded the mass of other materials, for example, documents of a judicial character. Both published and unpublished briefs (*factums*), memoranda, and legal opinions written by lawyers and judges had a great influence on the struggle for Jewish emancipation. To cite but one example: the speech by an unnamed jurist at a conference held by the Strasbourg Magistrates on February 14, 1781, in Wasselonne, in connection with the counterfeit receipts, was probably one of the most liberal speeches in favor of the Jews before 1789. The jurist pointed out that even in trials involving Jews justice must always reign. One had to be especially careful, he said, in cases involving the possibility of passing sentences in the spirit of the Strasbourg statute on Jews, because the statute was of a criminal rather than civil character. Jurists always disliked and distrusted passing sentences leading to the confiscation of property. According to the Roman tradition of jurisprudence, the judge in such cases usually tended to favor the accused. If Jewish creditors were not guilty of breaking the law the court should defend them against the debtors, who could otherwise easily refuse to repay their debts and threaten the Jews with the eventual confiscation of the debts by the courts. The anonymous jurist cited an example of a similar trial: a Christian paid a Jewish merchant for the purchased merchandise with a promissory note. This was—according to the jurist—

a legal transaction, usurious rates were not involved, but the Jew was still brought to the law court. Should cases of falsified receipts be judged in the spirit of confiscation, justice would surely suffer.

The study of some themes is hampered by a defensive attitude, taken by many authors. They all come, for example, to the same apologetic conclusion: large numbers of Jews fought in the armed forces of France and were ready to die for their country. I tried to take a different position, as for example: many Jews avoided military service, but then this was a common practice among non-Jews as well. On the other hand, in spite of the Jews' traditional distrust of the army and the aversion of many non-Jews toward protecting the Republic together with Jews, Jews, as a whole, participated in the armed forces of the Revolution.

*   *   *

Some readers may regard the introduction to this collection of my papers as the expression of a strictly partisan view, full of enthusiasm for both the Revolution of 1789 in general and its attitude toward Jews. If so, then so be it. The historiosophical battle for or against the Revolution of 1789 is not yet over. Accounts are still being settled between partisans and adversaries of 1789. If my admiration for the Revolution of 1789, which emancipated the Jews, is not contradicted by serious research then so much the better. I believe that the honor due the 1789 Revolution will survive the books and articles by a few scholars, and many pseudo-scholars, who are trying to revise the historiography of that Revolution by uncritically judging 1789 by moral standards of 1969 and by their own present-day prejudices.

Of late, the French Revolution of 1789 has become a scapegoat which is being condemned for many evils— for the rise of nationalism, for secularism, and for the disregard of rights of minorities. Writers who are unable to explain our contemporary wrongs, and their own feelings of guilt, are only too eager to find fault with the Encyclopaedists and the Jacobins for all the unresolved disadvantages of Jewish life, including modern anti-Semitism. In doing so they often unwillingly join the old fashioned reactionary critics of 1789; they discover liberalizing tendencies in Louis XVI's attitude towards Jews, and conveniently forget the role which the Catholic Church —as well as the Protestants—played in the struggle against Jews long before Voltaire's name became known. Until the very end of the old regime Jews obtained, not general reforms liberalizing their status, but only privileges— rather, renewals of old privileges—for which they had to pay large sums of money.

No doubt, to a certain extent Jews were tolerated at that time because they were living in the age of mercantilism. But the usefulness of Jews in the mercantile scheme of things was rarely appreciated by local authorities. More often than not, Jews were able to exist only by virtue of the protection offered them by the King and his representatives, for whom the Jews' usefulness was sometimes more important than local anti-Jewish tendencies and their own traditional anti-Jewish feelings. For example, in the seventeenth century, Jews participated in a substantial way in clearing swampland around Arles, and at the beginning of the eighteenth century, in controlling the Durance River. Yet, even then, they were not allowed to reside in these areas. Also, the King's protection was given only on rare occasions. Moreover, whatever service the Jews rendered in commerce did not always entitle them to the right of residence or to exist as a Jewish community recognized by law. Only a long legal battle combined with large bribes for high officials and even for the King, were finally effective in securing for the Jews the right to settle anywhere in France. And even where such rights were attained, the authorities permitted the Jewish communities to function not for the fulfillment of religious, educational, social, legal and other needs, but rather in order to have easy control over them, particularly for the purpose of tax collection.

The policies of the royal administration in Alsace and in neighboring provinces where the Ashkenazic Jews resided, can be summarized as follows: royal administration sought to protect the Jews from local persecution, since it received from them special taxes and in times of war the Jews were in a position to provide horses, grain and even some cash. The Alsatian and neighboring noblemen and city administrations were not particularly satisfied with this state of affairs; hence, controversies frequently ensued between the royal French administration and the local authorities. The kings of France inherited the German rulers' rights regarding the Jews, while the municipalities retained their own rights. Alsace was divided into countless, more or less independent, small states and cities rivaling one another. These entities sometimes consisted of a city, an entire region, or a group of towns, or even a single village, with traditions of their own, separate jurisdiction, and specific political and economic interests. This condition made the assimilation of Alsace as a French province very difficult. Indeed, the situation of the Alsatian Jews was further complicated by the fact that on the eve of the 1789 Revolution the 182 cities and villages where they were permitted to live belonged to no less than sixty-one different owners: the King, the Church authorities, and various noblemen, and each of them pursued his own interests at the Jews' expenses. In the final count one has to conclude that until the Revolution of 1789, Alsace was an occupied province with a strange language, a strange culture, divided into a series of local political entities and interests, undermined by intrigues. France was able to assert her authority there only by force of her military and the royal civil administrators. The Alsatian Sovereign Council also officially represented the King, yet it was more flexible than the royal administrators, since it was composed of

Alsatian personalities and was more influenced by local events and interests. Thus the Council was frequently the scene of conflicts between the interests of the monarchy and their own local interests, and also of differences between the Council and the King's two direct representatives in Alsace, the military Commandant and the Intendant. Conditions in Alsace were approximately the same as in Metz, even though the opposition of the Metz Parliament to the King was stronger than that of the Alsatian Council. In studying the condition of the French Ashkenazic Jewry these general circumstances of political life in Alsace and neighboring Provinces must be borne in mind.

There is no reason to minimize the significance of the privileges accorded the Sephardim. The fundamental point is to refrain from seeking a consistent line in the policy of the crown and of the city of Bordeaux with regard to the Sephardim. Despite all the persecutions, for example, the Bordeaux Parliament, on August 14, 1719, liberated a Spanish-Jewish merchant, who had been arrested for having defaulted on a debt in Malaga, after he had testified that his family had been wiped out by the Inquisition. By and large, the Sephardim were hardly any more privileged than were the Avignonese or Ashkenazic Jews. All pretense of French Sephardim to such privileges was but an expression of their claim to superiority over other non-Sephardic Jews. The Marranos—and later the Sephardim who followed—resided in a region which gave them the opportunity to engage in many economic activities in which the Ashkenazim of Alsace, Metz and the province of Metz, and Lorraine could not engage. The commerce and industries of the latter regions were simply much less developed than in the territory under the jurisdiction of the Bordeaux Parliment.

In June 1776, Louis XVI renewed the old privileges that had been granted since 1550 to the Marranos who had arrived from Spain and Portugal and who, since 1723, had lived openly as Sephardic Jews. In the previous privileges—including the Letters Patent of 1723—the right of residence for the Sephardim was limited to the territory within the jurisdiction of the Bordeaux Parliament. Thus, even the privileged Sephardic Jews could not move freely. They were driven from many large commercial centers, such as Dijon, Poitiers, Orléans, Pau, Cognac, Rochfort, Saintes, and other places. A memorandum submitted as late as 1788 by the Sephardic Jews to the Minister, Chrétien Guillaume de Lamoignon de Malesherbes, contained a plea for the right of residence in the whole of France and in the French colonies. The restriction of residence to the territory of the Bordeaux Parliament was omitted from the 1776 renewal of privileges, and this fact was used by other communities which tried to gain legal status by registering the Letters Patent of 1776 with the Parliaments of the provinces in which they were settled. It was in this way that the Jewish community of Marseilles obtained legal status, though not until many years later and in the face of numerous difficulties. On February 12, 1788 the letters patent of 1776 were registered by the Parliament of Provence in whose territory the city of Marseilles was located. According to one source the Jews of Marseilles paid the sum of 6,000 livres to have these letters registered, thereby securing for themselves the right of residence not only in Marseilles but in all of Provence. To achieve their purpose the Jews of Marseilles had to declare themselves a community of Sephardim, for the letters patent of 1776 were granted to Sephardim only. But this was only a legal subterfuge for, in reality, the Jewish community of Marseilles at that time was composed of Jews of varied origin and only a few were Sephardim.

Moreover, the Sephardim had not acquired their privileges gratis. They had to pay substantial sums for the privileges of 1550 and for each renewal as in 1723, when they paid over 100,000 livres. Like the Ashkenazim and the Jews in Avignon and Comtat Venaissin, they were compelled to pay huge taxes, to make forced loans, to

present many gifts, and the like. Their privileges notwithstanding, the Sephardim suffered from all sorts
of restrictions. Essentially, they were confined to trade,
and barred from all other occupations, no less than the
Ashkenazim. In his memoirs, Salomon Lopes Dubec related that he studied arithmetic and banking methods,
since only Christians were permitted to engage in crafts.
Medicine was closed to Jews. To be sure, one finds a very
sizable number of Sephardic names among the physicians
of Bordeaux, as in all of southern France, and even in
Paris. These were, however, with few exceptions, until
the eve of 1789, Marranos or even faithful Christians. Jews
engaging in medicine were penalized. Even in trade there
were innumerable limitations imposed on Sephardim. They
were, for example, excluded from the Bordeaux Chamber
of Commerce. Christian firms constantly sought to restrict
the rights of Jews. In the city of Bayonne, Jews were not
allowed to engage in trade of any sort. The production
of chocolate had been introduced there by Jews. Nonetheless, attempts were made to prohibit them from engaging
in this enterprise.

In the approximately fifteen-year period preceding the
Revolution of 1789, a number of events occured that ought
to be considered the forerunners of the emancipation of
Jews. During this period many liberal voices advocated
the improvement of the Jews' status. These years laid the
groundwork for the act of emancipation itself. Yet it appears that the old anti-Jewish sentiments prevailed in the
pre-Revolutionary Provincial Assemblies as well as in
other local and central government agencies. The new
liberal feelings toward the Jews failed to penetrate the
Provincial Assemblies, whose views were traditionally anti-
Jewish. The Body Toll had been abolished in January
1784, but the much praised Letters Patent of July 10,
1784 were not a preemancipation act. They comprised
a series of very severe ordinances directed against the
Jews of Alsace, making life for these Jews even more
miserable.

Less than three years before the outbreak of the Revolution, in November 1786, Louis XVI suggested that the Jewish creditors of Alsace be allowed to request only one-fifth of their debts. This meant that the Alsatian Jews would be dispossessed of four-fifths of their properties. On January 10, 1787, the King's proposal was confirmed by the Council of Alsace, but in August of the same year this decision was the subject of many changes. The decision of January was a very dangerous precedent; both the King and the Council became afraid of the possible consequences of such an act, and the debtors were granted only the right of term payments of debts.

The text of some articles in the Edict of November 1787 in favor of Protestants could easily have been applied to Jews. Malesherbes favored the inclusion of Jews in the general law regulating the *état-civil*. This would have favored the struggle for Jewish emancipation, but the idea was not carried out. In places where Jews were— on the basis of the Edict of November 1787 in favor of Protestants—registered together with the latter, this was done only in an administrative manner, without taking a position on the broader problem of Jewish emancipation. The Decree of the National Assembly of December 28, 1789, which completed the emancipation of the Protestants —"without intending to prejudge relative to Jews on whose status the Assembly intends to pronounce itself"— definitely sanctioned the official interpretation that the Edict of 1787 was not applicable to Jews.

Moreover, the pre-Revolutionary advocates of Jewish emancipation were not completely free of missionary tendencies. Malesherbes expressed a desire to reduce the hatred against the Jewish people by hoping to have Christians content to detest only the Jewish religion. Malesherbes' main reason for adopting a more favorable attitude toward the Jews was his conviction that such a change would contribute greatly toward their conversion. In fact, Malesherbes was then one of those pro-Jews who favored the emancipation of the Jews as a means toward their conversion to Christianity. It is known that a similar opinion was expressed by the great fighter for Jewish emancipation, Abbé Henri Grégoire. The French-Jewish historian Léon Kahn correctly summarized the policy of Louis XVI toward the Jews as follows: "There could be no question of granting them the full rights enjoyed by other citizens. The Jews did not dare to request that much; Malesherbes and the King did not wish to grant them that much. Later, the Church pretended that in the Act of Emancipation of the Jews, the Revolution of 1789 only carried out the initiative and acted upon the proposal of the Church. This was a willful misrepresentation . . . Louis XVI gave the Jews a . . . mask of liberty . . . The Revolution was more generous and displayed considerably more justice." Yet historians and Jewish leaders have not always properly presented the policy of Louis XVI and his regime toward the Jews in this manner. Gradually a legend was created that Louis XVI started the emancipation of the Jews. This legend may well date from the post-Napoleonic Restoration years, when the Jews, too, had to praise the Bourbon family and to relate the virtues of the "martyr" Louis XVI and "his" emancipation of the Jews. This was, in part, a Jewish reaction to Napoleon's anti-Jewish Decrees of May 30, 1806 and March 17, 1808.

Despite the liberal sentiments in France nothing might have been done to better the Jews' status, and had the Revolution of 1789 not come Jewish emancipation might not have been realized till a much, much later date. Until the very last days of the old regime, the Jews were an oppressed, barely tolerated group. All the liberal voices favorable to the Jews were unable to achieve any practical improvement in their status. It took a far more important event to accomplish this—the Revolution of 1789. The small and persecuted Jewish minority was not in a position to share the impatience of the French people, but when the latter proclaimed Liberty, Equality, Fraternity, when they chanted the Marseillaise and the Carmagnole, Jews became free human beings.

In the eyes of the generation of Jews which was emancipated by the Revolution the new regime was just and beneficent to them. Olry Terquem (Tsarphati), the nineteenth century leader of the proponents of a reform of Jewish religious practices, in 1843 called the new regime *notre sainte révolution*. There were, of course, exceptions: the Franco-Jewish philosopher, Adolphe Frank, advocated love for the old regime. But in general, even the Jewish bourgeois was not always reactionary, because French reaction was too closely connected with the old regime.

The influence of the Encyclopaedists, who disliked Judaism as the source of Christianity, may clearly be seen among the Jacobins. However, a few facts must be remembered. Albert Mathiez has pointed out that the Jacobins were not ideological nonbelievers. They did not fight religion as a matter of principle but were primarily opposed to the Catholic Church for its association with the counterrevolution. Dechristianization of the population meant saving the Revolution. The venom of atheism was provoked by a very real and dangerous pact between the Church and the enemies of the Revolution.

The influence of the Encyclopaedists' view of the Jewish source of the Church did not provoke an anti-Jewish movement among Jacobins. Persecution of Jews was not a result of a Jacobin policy directed from Paris. Although the idea of having minorities was repugnant to the Revolution, there was no need for drastic action against Jews as a group because they—and most Protestants—were not as dangerous to the Revolution as was the large and counterrevolutionary Catholic Church. Robespierre himself was one of the first to demand citizenship for the Jews. The persecution of rabbis and Sabbath observers, the confiscation of synagogues and Jewish cemeteries, etc. should not be understood as acts of a specifically anti-

Jewish character because these acts were part of a general antireligious drive against what the Jacobins considered to be fanaticism. Catholic priests and Protestant ministers were arrested and so were rabbis. The antireligious policy was directed chiefly against the powerful Catholic Church which helped organize the campaigns against the new regime. The action against the Protestants and Jewish religious minorities should be regarded only as small by-products of an uproar. Jews and Protestants were not as powerful or dangerous to the Republic as the Catholics and, in most cases, they were considered friendly to the new regime. Still, there was the question of principle—the fight against all religious symbols, without exception. It was impossible to close churches and allow the Jews to keep their synagogues open. (This situation could be compared to the atheist policy of Soviet Russia before the advent of official anti-Semitism in the late 1930's.) There is a story about a revolutionary meeting in Saint-Esprit-lès-Bayonne, during which Jews applauded a speaker who criticized the Christians, and the latter applauded a speaker who criticized the Jews.

Sometimes local Jacobins did single out Jews in the drive against religions, but this was done against the will of Robespierre and his close friends. However, it would be impossible to prove that such local anti-Jewish feelings were influenced not by the traditionally anti-Jewish Church, but rather by the recent Encyclopaedists. Surely, Voltaire's influence was greater in the cosmopolitan port of Bordeaux than in Bayonne, yet Jews suffered more in the latter city.

*   *   *

Of course, one cannot judge the Revolution of 1789 by evaluating only its attitude towards Jews. Too often Jewish historians of the Franco-Jewish emancipation period treated it not from the perspective of the totality of general events, but in isolation, as a purely Jewish occurence, and they disregarded the general, organic atmosphere of the period. On the other hand, one should not ignore the fact that neither during the reign of Terror nor during the Thermidor was a Jew executed because he was a Jew. In cases of arrests and fines anti-Jewish discrimination was of a purely local and not federal origin. In a few of my studies I proved that historians who wrote about Jews who were executed because they were Jews were not familiar with the actual facts. According to Abraham Fustado's diary, during the Terror the people of Bordeaux requested a *Jewish* victim. They saw men and women of all classes being guillotined, but no Jew. Even in this great Girondist center Jews were only arrested or fined; not one was guillotined. Even in Alsace and the neighboring departments, where well-organized local propaganda against Jews on charges of economic speculation was conducted, the number of Jews sentenced to death for major crimes against the Revolution was very small. In Moselle—two Jews for speculation with assignats; in Meurthe a Jew was sentenced (in 1798) as a thief; not one Jew in the Upper Rhine and only one in the Lower Rhine.

In the atmosphere of anti-Jewish pressure in traditionally anti-Jewish regions Jews were able to exist and not be exterminated only because of the attitude from Paris. This was true for both the old regime, with its policy of using the Jews for the monarchy's needs, and the sympathetic attitude of the federal revolutionary authorities during the Republic.

I am not trying to say that the Terror was justified in all its activities and that the tragic dissensions were unavoidable, or that only the Terror could have saved the Revolution. But, while writing on victims of the Terror one must not forget that the active counterrevolution was not a myth. Those trying to judge the 1789 Revolution by later philosophical standards may be reminded that during the tragic period of 1793-1794 fewer people were executed than during the few days at the end of May 1871, when the Commune of Paris was defeated by Adolphe Thiers.

*   *   *

The account of anti-Jewish persecutions during the period of the Terror was told by chroniclers, and later accepted as fact by historians. Legends were even circulated of how Jews were miraculously saved from the Terror. Hanna Jacques Brunschwig-Padagay, daughter of Joel Padagay of Dornach (Upper Rhine), related that her father was warned to escape to Mulhouse because the Terrorists would arrest him. While leaving the house an old man came along, asked for food, and blessed him. When Joel came back during the Thermidor he found the key in the keyhole and everything inside the house in perfect order. The old man was none other than Elijah the Prophet who had kept the house clean.

What was the status of the Jews during the Thermidorian reaction which followed the tragic era of the Terror? Some adverse policies of previous revolutionary periods were continued during the Thermidor (the refusal to nationalize the debts owed by former Jewish communities to Christian creditors). But the statement of the historian Raphael Mahler that "the propaganda against the remains of Robespierre's party took on in some newspapers an air of anti-Semitic propaganda" and that "whoever dared to say a good word about the previous regime was called a Jew," is greatly exaggerated. One of the strongest attacks against Jews from the rostrum of a legislative body during the Revolution was delivered on May 7, 1799 by the deputy François Balthazar Darracq at the Council of Five Hundred. His tirade was directed against the Jews of Bordeaux, who refused to permit their cemetery to become nationalized property. However, his speech could hardly be taken as an expression of the feelings of the Council of Five Hundred. In fact, the Council refused to follow him, and the cemetery was given back to the Jews. On an earlier occasion Darracq was censured for his anti-Jewish remarks. It would be very difficult to point out special anti-Jewish restrictions or other kinds of persecution that resulted from the general developments during the Thermidorian reaction. There were many cases of anti-Jewish propaganda, even of the plundering of Jewish property but, as during the Terror, such instances did not take place on the order or under the influence of federal authorities. Jewish emancipation in France was already well established. Of course, it was not yet accepted by the entire Christian population. A story was told about a Jew who visited a deputy. Still accustomed to the good old days of fraternization, he acted in a familiar manner toward him. This the deputy took as an insult. The Thermidorian period may perhaps be characterized as a period of struggle by the Jews to retain the rights secured by them in the first years of the Revolution. But the entire French nation was engaged in a similar struggle. Be that as it may, the Thermidorian period—or the previous Terror period— did not produce measures directed against Jews as a specific group. The Terror dealt evenhandedly with the Jews as a group, and the same can be said of the Thermidor and the Directoire, and even of the Consulate. The historian Simon Dubnow was correct in writing that "during the ten years between the Directoire and Napoleon's Empire nothing important happened in the life of the French Jews." Even Napoleon's anti-Jewish policy came in a later period, in 1806. Surely his appeal of 1799 to the Jews, in which he promised to restore Jerusalem to them, was in direct contrast to his later attitude toward Jews in 1806 and 1808.

In one study I attempted to show that during all periods of the Revolution of 1789 Jews were sometimes singled out for compulsory taxation and other drastic economic exigencies. Although in some instances even Paris representatives pursued such a policy, economic chicanery, too, against Jews was inspired by local anti-Jewish sentiments and not by any policy directed from Paris. There was no official revolutionary levy against Jews as a collective body. In this respect the Revolution was even more liberal than the later regimes at the beginning of the nineteenth century, when Jews of the Alsatian departments were singled out as a collective body and forced to pay heavier taxes than were Christians, and were even forced to make special contributions.

* * *

According to Judd L. Teller "Voltaire must be regarded as the progenitor of the secular anti-Semitism which still lingers on in liberal movements. . . . The first signs of this trend were evident in the French Revolution which suddenly unveiled the Jew to his fellow Frenchmen." Henri Grégoire "apparently" inherited his friendly attitude toward Jews "from Christian, not secular sources" (*Scapegoat of Revolution,* 1954, pp. 21-22, 26). Recently the same idea was repeated in more detail by Rabbi Arthur Hertzberg. "Modern anti-Semitism Traced By |Hertzberg| to Rise of Intellectuals, 18th-Century Enlightment in France Linked to Cultural Arrogance of the West"—such was the title of an interview in *The New York Times* (April 18, 1968) with Rabbi Hertzberg, author of *The French Enlightment and the Jews* (1968). Indeed, Rabbi Hertzberg states in the introduction to his book: "Modern, secular anti-Semitism was fashioned not as a reaction to the Enlightment and the |1789| Revolution, but within the Enlightment and Revolution themselves" (p. 7). His conclusion is: "The liberal age in Europe was, indeed, made by the new intellectuals who first appeared in power in the French Revolution. It was to be devastated by the heirs and successors to the anti-Jewish intelligentsia that appeared in the very midst of these events" (pp. 367–368).

Such undocumented statements naturally arouse misgivings about the reliability of other assertions, but they still make serious scholarship more difficult because rebuttals are sometimes unavoidable and they take up much valuable time.

The richness of available material makes it possible to describe even in detail an imaginary anti-Jewish revolutionary society, especially among the intelligentsia. This is what some authors have tried to do. One can always cite a casual anti-Jewish expression by Jean-Paul Marat or another Jacobin, but conveniently omit Robespierre's strong statement in favor of Jews. My own studies contain hundreds of examples of both pro- and anti-Jewish statements by Jacobins and other partisans of the Revolution. In the traditionally anti-Jewish Alsace and neighboring departments Eulogius Schneider and other Jacobins needed much courage in order to defend the Jews against their anti-Jewish minded political friends. The question is: What was the source of the latter's anti-Jewish convictions? In my opinion, it was the entire Christian anti-Jewish tradition. Those who think otherwise, who want to discover a secular source, should prove it by more than a mere similarity between the arguments of Voltaire and the anti-Jewish elements in Alsace.

The Revolution occured in a country which had one of the most vicious anti-Jewish legislations in Europe, and which dated not from the Encyclopaedists but from much earlier.

*   *   *

In discussing Voltaire's role one must not forget the background of the pamphlets published in reply to his anti-Jewish assertions. Isaac de Pinto's replies to Voltaire's attacks against the Jews were by no means the result of a courageous stand against a Judeophobe, but were rather the product of the hostile relations between one group of Jews and another. Voltaire's sharp criticism of Jews aroused the Sephardim, because he had failed to distinguish between them and Ashkenazim. Pinto berated Voltaire for not having been aware of the difference between the "good" Sephardim and the "bad" Ashkenazim. Sparing no detail, he discussed the contempt in which the Ashkenazim —he stated—were held by the Sephardim. The differences between the two groups were not merely in customs and rituals, but in moral standards. Sephardim were finer and more honest. They had no criminals, ursurers, or swindlers

among them. (Being unaware of 1969 moral standards
Pinto did not mention the role of Sephardim in the trade
of slaves.) To whichever land they came, they brought
only wealth and prosperity. The low moral standards of
the Ashkenazim resulted from the persecutions which they
suffered, whereas the Sephardim had always been privileged. Pinto's violent attack on the Ashkenazim aroused
dissatisfaction even among Christians. A London monthly
of 1763 chided Pinto for besmirching the Ashkenazim.
He replied with a pamphlet (in 1766) in which he reiterated his condemnation of the Ashkenazim. In a pamphlet
written by a Christian in reply to Pinto (in 1768) the
author argued that even if the claimed distinctions between
Sephardim and Ashkenazim were true, Pinto would have
done better to pass over them in silence. The attacks against
the Ashkenazim were repeated in the introductions to the
collections of privileges of Sephardim in France, published
by the Bordeaux Jewish community in 1765 and 1777.
The very language is almost identical with that in Pinto's
pamphlet. At about this time (1767) the Parisian merchants corporation printed a brief, prepared by the lawyer
Goulleau, opposing the right of Jews to live in Paris.
Goulleau did not spare the Sephardim. In an open letter,
dated September 4, 1767, Jacob Rodriguez Péreire accused
him of transposing Pinto's attacks on the Ashkenazim to
attacks on the Sephardim. Goulleau responded immediately
that it would be most interesting to know what other
Jews thought of the Sephardim. He concluded that, inasmuch as Jews themselves despised each other greatly, it
was hardly surprising that Christians were unable to
tolerate Jews. Péreire's reply to this was contained in a
second letter, replete with new attacks on the Ashkenazim.

The question as to whether Pinto's reply to Voltaire
did have an influence on the struggle for Jewish emancipation is still open for discussion. It contained more attacks
on non-Sephardic Jews than on Voltaire. But the other
replies to Voltaire, especially the widely read Antoine

Guenée's *Lettres,* were the most important pro-Jewish pamphlets of the period and even of later years. Thus, Voltaire's anti-Jewish writings boomeranged and provoked a chain reaction in favor of Jews.

The emancipation of Jews was delayed not only by Christian opposition, but also by internal conflicts among the various Jewish groups. The Ashkenazim and Sephardim were hardly on speaking terms. This subject was analyzed in my study "The Diaries of the Delegations of the Bordeaux Jews to the Malesherbes Commission, 1788, and the National Assembly, 1790" (*Zion,* xviii, 1951, pp. 31-79, in Hebrew, not included in the present volume). This study is based on newly discovered documents concerning French Jews on the eve of the 1789 Revolution and during the first struggles in the National Assembly to achieve full citizenship. The diary of the delegation of the Bordeaux Jews to the National Assembly (January-February 1790), notes by Lopes Dubec, who was a member of these delegations, and other documents in various public and private archives give a picture of the internal conflicts among the Jews in France during the emancipation period. The "aristocratic" Sephardim were interested mainly in preserving their own privileges and in not being confused with the Ashkenazic Jews of north-eastern France. Because of this attitude, their delegations fought all projects favoring equally all the Jews of France. This policy of the Sephardic Jews was one of the reasons for the failure of the Malesherbes Commission to achieve amelioration of the status of the Jews on the eve of the Revolution and of the National Assembly's failure immediately to emancipate all the Jews of France. (See also my "Relations among Sephardim, Ashkenazim and Avignonese Jews in France from the 16th to the 20th Centuries, "*Yivo Annual,* 1955, 165-196.)

It is a fact that the decree of January 28, 1790, bestowing citizenship upon the "privileged" Jews, endangered the entire struggle for the emancipation of the Ashkenazic

Jews. It took great courage and patience to overcome this danger, and in the struggle for citizenship for all the Jews of France the Sephardim had no share whatsoever. Relations between the various Jewish groups did not change for the better during the First Empire. During this period new developments occurred. In the first post-Revolutionary attempts made to organize Jewish communities in France (in 1805) it was difficult to achieve unity between Sephardim and Ashkenazim. On February 4, 1805, the government queried a number of Jewish leaders from Paris on their attitude toward reorganizing the religious Jewish administrations. Jewish community life in Bordeaux was at the time conducted by a philanthropic society (*Société de Bienfaisance*) which had been reorganized on June 29, 1803. At a meeting held on March 4, 1805, to consider the government inquiry of February 4th the tendency of the Sephardim to dispense with the formation of official communities and to restrict organization to philanthropic societies was manifested. On March 10, 1805, the *Société* protested against the supposed fact that the commission to reorganize the Jewish religious administration was dominated by Ashkenazim who were intent upon placing the Jews again "under the rabbinical yoke." Eessentially, the fear of forming communities derived from their realization that, under the Napoleonic regime, this would ultimately lead to a centralization of all communities in France. Then Sephardim and Ashkenazim would be forced to cooperate. This was expressed in unmistakable terms by David Gradis at a meeting of the *Société* held on June 7, 1806. A week earlier, on May 30, 1806, Napoleon I had issued the decree concerning a Jewish Assembly, and the "danger" of the establishments of communities in a centralized body had increased. Gradis came out most forcefully in favor of restricting organization to charitable societies, and for perpetuating the separation between Sephardim and Ashkenazim. During the time of the Jewish Assembly, during the Sanhedrin period, and in the years in which Napoleon's

anti-Jewish decrees were issued (1806-1808) the Sephardim once again devoted all their energies to intrigues
against the Ashkenazim. They still attempted to salvage
a communal administration of Sephardim which would
be distinct from that of the Ashkenazim.

*   *   *

Many politicians, historians and others tried to find a
materialistic reason for the emancipation of Jews by the
Revolution. According to Bernard Lazare, the Revolution
did so because the bourgeoisie was vitally interested in
liberating those who were particularly fitted for the role
of pioneers of industry and finance. Even earlier, a similar
opinion had been expressed by Eugène Rodrigues, a Saint-
Simonian. Such theories are, however, very much open
for discussion. Although the usefulness of Jews was so
often used as an argument during the struggle for Jewish
emancipation, one must not always look for purely materialistic considerations in the various acts of the Revolution. Is it not possible that the leaders of the Revolution
acted so as a result of purely humane and brotherly
feelings toward the persecuted Jews?

*   *   *

One of my studies, which deals in detail with the anti-
Jewish riots in Alsace during the Revolutions of 1789,
1830, and 1848, was published in Hebrew (*Zion*, xx,
1955, 82-102), and is not included in the present
collection. In 1789 the riots broke out in about twenty
Jewish communities of Sundgau (Upper Alsace) immediately after the first news of the events in Paris had reached
Alsace. Many Jews escaped to the neighboring Basel
(Switzerland) and Mulhouse, which was then an independent republic. Jews who escaped from Alsace then formed
the Jewish community of Dijon. The Parisian and Alsatian
authorities suppressed the riots, which were directed not
exclusively against Jews but also against wealthy non-
Jewish landowners and administration and Church officials.
My study further analyzes the anti-Jewish activities in

Alsace between 1789 and the outbreak of the Revolution of 1830 and subsequent events, which again, were inaugurated in Alsace with anti-Jewish riots. The authorities openly accused the Church of being responsible for the attack on Jews. In 1832 the Catholics tried to provoke anti-Jewish and anti-Protestant riots as part of a general uprising against the accomplishments of the Revolutions of 1789 and 1830. The Alsatian riots on the eve and during the Revolution of 1848 were of an economic character and were not directed exclusively against Jews, but during pogroms in over sixty communities Jews suffered more than the non-Jewish population. The study analyzes in detail the responsibility of various groups for the pogroms, the Jewish reaction, and the influence of the event on the Jewish community and general Alsatian politics.

*   *   *

It would be difficult to find a common rule for all the French Protestant denominations in their respective attitudes towards Jews. We do not know of any active anti-Jewish movement among Bordeaux Protestants during the Revolution; but in Alsace the Protestants joined their enemies, the Catholics, in a common fight against Jewish emancipation. Both (Jews and Protestants) were persecuted in Bordeaux during the old regime, but being busy with the persecution of the Protestants, the Catholic Church sometimes neglected its anti-Jewish policy. In some respects the situation of the Protestants there—but not in Alsace and neighboring provinces—was even worse than that of the Jews.

"L'émancipation des Israelites est un fait anti-catholique" ("The emancipation of the Jews is an anti-Catholic act"), the physician and communal Jewish leader, Michel Lévy, wrote in 1836. In a special study I tried to prove the veracity of such a conclusion, that the Jewish emancipation in France came in spite of the opposing efforts of the Catholic Church. This is especially important in view of a contemporary tendency to blame not the Church but secular elements for the struggle against Jewish emancipation and for later day anti-Semitism. The vehement Catholic propaganda against the Jews had a double objective: to oppose the emancipation of the Jews and, at the same time, to discredit the new regime. God would punish those responsible for the emancipation of the Jews, became a popular byword. Of course, the Jews also had many sincere friends among Catholics. These Catholics, moreover, supported the new regime and openly opposed the counterrevolutionary activities conducted by their Church.

Basically, any act of the Revolution directed against the Catholic Church as a body was a step toward a more complete emancipation of the religious minorities, the Protestants and the Jews. Such, for example, was the law of September 20, 1792, which secularized the *état-civil*. But for many reasons Jews distrusted the new law. This was part of a much broader picture. After the outbreak of the Revolution, the much persecuted Cagots in many localities destroyed the *état-civil* records, which contained separate records of Cagots. It was a symbolic act on their part expressive of their emancipation: there were no more separate records, and nobody would know who was a Cagot. No special act in favor of their emancipation was required; in a natural manner they became an integral part of the population, although anti-Cagot discrimination continued to exist. Such a transformation was impossible for Jews; the Cagots were Catholics, easily assimilable, while the Jews were of a different religion to which non-Jews continued to be hostile. Moreover, the practice of Judaism was, to a very large degree, connected with the existence of separate Jewish communities with many functions of a civil character, which the Jews were not yet willing to give up, but which was contrary to the spirit of the Revolution.

* * *

The 1830's saw the beginning of an anti-Jewish movement among utopian Socialists, which was later to be

taken over by the French disciples of Karl Marx. In my
book *Anti-Semitism in the French Labor Movement, from
the Fourierist Movement until the Closing of the Dreyfus
Case 1845-1906* (1948, in Yiddish with an English summary) I wrote: "Searching for formulas and catchwords
which the masses would accept quickly and unthinkingly,
Socialists were also among those who helped to spread
the notion of Rothschild as the Jewish king, and of him and
the Jewish nation as the symbols of capitalism. Later,
during the Dreyfus trial, the Socialist, Eugène Fournière
wrote: 'We ascribed a human name to every idea, to every
passion. We had our god—Marx, and our devil—Rothschild.' The desire to make Rothschild as a Jew into a
symbol of capitalism was neither a spontaneous popular
trend nor a senseless impulse. Some Socialist circles sought
in this manner to win over anti-Semitic groups for the
Socialist camp. Since anti-Semitism drew followers from
among the masses, it therefore paid to subscribe to anti-
Semitic propaganda in order to win the masses for Socialism."

Where is the link between the nineteenth-century Socialist anti-Semitism and the so-called anti-Jewish tradition of
the 1789 Revolution? In many cases the bases of Socialist
feelings against Jews were similar to the Catholic motives.
The following is but one example: The Alsation abbot
and anti-Semitic historian, Charles Hoffman, wrote that
the Revolution had exerted a negative influence on agriculture in general. He disliked Jews for their role in helping
in the parceling of land confiscated from the Church. In
the nineteenth century, the Church, the rich classes, the
local administrative bodies, even the utopian Socialist,
Charles Fourier—all of these, with few exceptions, opposed the parceling of the land into small holdings. The
reactionary circles saw in the fractionalization of the land
a revolutionary tendency; some liberals, later utopian-
Socialists, and still later French disciples of Karl Marx
viewed it as a reactionary move. The truth is that even

though the small peasant was used, at certain times, by the reactionary groups, he represented in the main a liberal force. Thus, for instance, during the post-Napoleonic Restoration, the government dared not annul the sales of Church and émigrés' properties confiscated during the Revolution because it had to consider the peasant who had since bought these properties—and that was certainly a liberal victory over the reactionaries.

For a very long time the Alsatian historiography was—and in many cases still is—Catholic, and she could forgive the Jews neither the fact of emancipation nor the role of the Jews in the parceling of land. Exactly the same way, Alsatian historiography has been pervaded with a fervent love for the *ancien régime* and with hatred of the Revolution. In the last generation there made their appearance several good Alsatian historians of pronounced republican leanings, but there is still a bridge which connects most of them with the avowedly reactionary Alsatian historiographers—their common hatred of the Jews. But why wonder? Even Jewish historians began to believe in Jewish usury as a fact; or were they misled by their reformist hatred of the Orthodox Jews of Alsace? The historian François Alphonse Aulard justly remarked that in his book Robert Anchel treated Napoleon far more leniently in his conclusions than when analyzing the particular.

In my "The Jewish Saint-Simonians and Socialist Anti-Semites in France" I noted the similarity between the radical anti-Jewish feelings and the Catholic opposition, for some time, to the growth of industry in which Jews played an important role.

* * *

From all points of view the case of counterfeit receipts in Alsace was the most important event on the eve of the 1789 Revolution, and a study of this case is included in this book. Toward the end of 1777, and particularly during 1778, Alsace was inundated by a mass of counterfeit receipts signed in Hebrew characters, purportedly by

Jewish creditors. When the Jews requested the payment of debts owed them by Gentile debtors, they were presented with these falsified receipts for sums allegedly paid them in partial or full payment of the debts. It immediately became apparent that a well-organized group had persuaded the Christian debtors, mostly the peasant-debtors, not to repay their debts. The unusual affair, which endangered the economy of the entire French province, brought about the economic ruin of the Jews, threatened their very existence, and even influenced the struggle for the Jewish emancipation during the Revolution of 1789. The case of the counterfeit receipts instigated a whole series of very important events in the history of the Jews in France: the aggravation of the conflict between the Jewish leader Herz Cerfberr of Medelsheim and the city of Strasbourg; the abolition of the body toll; the publication of Dohm's book on the emancipation of Jews; the Letters Patent of July 10, 1784; the census of Alsatian Jews and the danger of expulsion for many Alsatian Jewish families; etc. The case of the counterfeit receipts was never properly resolved. At the outbreak of the 1789 Revolution the debts were not yet paid off; legally, the debtors had still many terms for the payment of their debts. In a memorandum of 1790 the Jews asked not to use the case of the receipts against their struggle for citizenship, because they were prepared to respect the terms granted to the debtors.

On September 27, 1791, full citizenship was granted to the Jews, and in a decree dated the following day, September 28th, the National Assembly ordered the Alsatian Jews to present a list of debts owed them by peasant-debtors, and directed that a way of paying these debts be worked out. On September 28th the anti-Jewish elements had their revenge; they tried to emasculate and minimize the value of the decree of September 27th. There was no real opposition to such an act, which was organized by the Alsatian deputies. The National Assembly was tired of the long discussion of the Jewish question and at first the new decree did not seem to be in opposition to the emancipation of Jews. In 1806, the anti-Jewish pamphleteer, Louis Poujol, wrote that emancipation was given to Jews conditionally. The great historian of the French Revolution, Albert Mathiez, noted correctly that both events, the decree of September 27, 1791 and Napoleon I's decree of May 30, 1806 convening the Jewish Assembly (and later the Sanhedrin), were tied to decrees directed against Jewish creditors. Although historians paid very little attention to the decree of September 28, 1791, there can be no doubt that after analyzing the facts the act of emancipation looks a little less glorious.

Yet, the decree of September 28th was never adhered to. The Jews refused to present the required list of debts and they were not forced to comply with it. The Alsatian Jews stated that the decree, which spoke not about all "capitalists" (i.e., creditors) but only Jewish ones, was contradictory to the decree of the previous day. The immediate Jewish protests and the fact that the legislators did not anticipate any punishment for violating the decree of September 28th, prevented any punishment for the Jews' refusal to present a list of debts. In petitions prepared by the attorney, Chauveau de la Garde, they stated that the decree and a decision taken in this spirit by the General Council of Upper Rhine (December 7, 1791) were a result of anti-Jewish hatred; anticonstitutional, and a combination of anti-Jewish and counterrevolutionary forces of Alsace; that such means were unpractical, etc. Officially, Jewish creditors were able to ask repayment of the debts through the courts. The situation was saved because the creditors were repaid by their peasant debtors in *assignats*.

Many people tried to safeguard the real value of their possessions by making quick investments and paying debts with *assignats*. Those who held *assignats*, which were shrinking in purchasing power, tried to get rid of them by exchange for any conceivable asset of fixed value. One of the results of the increase in the currency which the revolutionary government printed freely was the race of debtors to repay in *assignats* debts which they had incurred in hard money. In the first years of the Revolution many peasants enjoyed increased incomes, part of which they used to repay their debts with paper money. The number of such repayments to Jewish creditors was certainly large enough to enable us to conclude that the decree of September 28, 1791 which ordered the Jews of Alsace to present a list of the debts owed to them, was not put into effect because the debtors repaid their debts in *assignats*.

It is, of course, difficult to speculate on the theme of what would have happened if a list of Alsatian Jewish creditors would have been presented. The decree of September 28, 1791, was a clever manoeuvre schemed up by the Alsatians and other adversaries of Jewish emancipation at the National Assembly. It made the decree of the previous day, September 27th, an act of a conditional emancipation of Jews, leaving the door open for a possible repeal of the emancipation act. Perhaps it would have brought upon Jews measures such as were enacted only later, during the First Empire.

My study about the decree of September 28, 1791, was published in Hebrew (*Zion,* xvii, 1952, 84-100) and is not included in the present book. This study also analyzes the general aspect of credit and *assignats* in relation to Jews during the Revolution. The paper money created a difficult problem for all of France, but in Alsace and neighboring departments it became one of those misfortunes for which somebody had to be blamed, and again the Jews became the scapegoat. There, the Jews were blamed for discrediting the national money. However, in the overall picture of France Jews did not speculate or discredit *assignats* more than non-Jews. They simply were not numeorus enough nor strong enough economically to do so.

*   *   *

There was a large number of Jewish merchants; some of them were also active in banking. But there were no really big Jewish bankers able to influence the financial and other economic policies at the beginning of the Revolution, during the Terror or the Thermidor. Swiss and other bankers were then the most active. Only eight of 150 important financiers during the Revolution of 1789, as listed by the historian Edmond Soreau, were Jews. Nor were these Jews the most important financiers, and some of them could hardly be called Jews. But the tradition of the Jews' economic usefulness, the idea that the Jews could accomplish great things in this field, still persisted and was used by both enemies and friends of Jews. In some regions the Jews took over the often disliked occupation of contractors for the government. They were disliked as speculators by the administrations which, in the end, had to pay for the supplies and by the peasants who were not always too happy to sell their products, especially if they were paid with paper money.

Wealthy Jews suffered much as a result of the events, but in most cases not more than non-Jews; surely not to the extent of completely pauperizing the Jews and making it impossible for them to play a certain role in the economic life of the Revolution, at least in the provinces where they resided. Further research may prove or disprove the following conclusions:

Historiography may have greatly exaggerated the wealth of Jews and their economic role in France during the old regime. This may be the result of a comfortable methodology of drawing conclusions on the basis of scattered examples instead of detailed monographs. It is, for example, easy to cite a long list of Marranos and Sephardic Jews who were active in the field of maritime insurance. However, on the basis of such lists one can only draw the conclusion that Jews were active in this field. Any conclusion as to the extent of such activity can be drawn only after finding out what percentage of Jews were active in this field. Even such data cannot be conclusive without first obtaining documentation on the percentage of Jewish capitals involved in such transactions, at least during a short period. In 1790, eight of the eleven Bordeaux money changers were still Jews. But what was the percentage of the total capital involved in their operations?

A similar system—compiling lists of mortgaged debts owed to Jews, without giving the percentage which they comprised of the total number of debts—was used in the preparation of many anti-Jewish restrictions, including the decree of September 28, 1791, and Napoleon's Decree of March 17, 1808. Following is an example of how studies of details can prove or disprove the moral and legal basis of anti-Jewish propaganda and legislation in connection with money. Figures about the number of Jewish creditors and sums owed to them were never given in comparison with similar figures involving non-Jewish creditors. However, of 1,704 mortgages in the aggregate sum of 7,091,549 francs registered in the Strasbourg office of mortgages between November 4, 1798 and April 5, 1799, only 210 in the sum of 215,548.66 francs were held by Jewish mortgagees against Christian mortgagors. Of 741 mortgages in the sum of 1,164,034.06 francs registered in the Saverne office between May 22 and June 14, 1799, only 121 for 89,554.81 francs were held by Jews against Christians. Of 787 mortgages valued at 2,244,126.46 francs, registered in the Metz office between June 3 and June 18, 1799, only forty-six valued at 87,838 francs were held by Jews against Christians. Of 312 mortgages of the value of 890,431.09 francs, registered in the Nancy office between March 13 and March 27, 1799, only seven of the value of 24,442.20 francs were in favor of Jews against Christians. According to my analysis of 62,149 mortgages of the value of 115,543,561.27 francs in Alsace and neighboring departments in 1799-1865, 52,710 mortgages of the value of 107,088,668.98 francs were held by non-Jewish creditors. (See my *Agricultural Credit* . . .)

Numerically, the Jews were not important enough. Saint-Esprit-lès-Bayonne, a suburb of Bayonne, was an exception. Because of their large number in this suburb of Bayonne, the Jews played an important role in the local events; the "Jewish" Surveillance Committee was faithful to Paris while Bayonne was a sanctuary of counterrevolutionaries. Yet, the number of Jews was too small to be used in case of a military operation. In spite of their attachment to the Revolution during the Terror, not even one Jew of Saint-Esprit was appointed to an important office on a departmental or national level. Perhaps because the "Jewish" Jacobins of Saint-Esprit never became excessive extremists, the guillotine was never brought to Saint-Esprit or to any other community under the jurisdiction of the "Jewish" Jacobins.

The secular cultural undernourishment, the lack of secular Jewish intellectuals, made it even more difficult for Jews to play a leading role in the Revolution.

The results of limitations imposed during the old regime did not disappear overnight and handicapped Jewish activities even after the outbreak of the Revolution. This was especially true in regions where traditional anti-Jewish animosities continued to exist.

The large migration of Jews, particularly of the wealthy ones, from former ghettos and restricted areas to the interior of France (especially from the former papal province of Avignon and Comtat Venaissin) made their economic expansion difficult.

*   *   *

Should one conclude that the Jews of France were partisans of the Revolution which emancipated them and that they were willing to defend the new regime? Each region and period must be judged separately. Jacob Pereyra of Bordeaux wrote on the "ingratitude" of Bordeaux Jews who did not assist the anti-Girondists. The Jews of Saint-Esprit-lès-Bayonne were Jacobins while many Sephardic Jews of Bordeaux were active Girondists. Yet, such an of-

fensive pamphlet against the Terror as the one published by
an Alsatain Jew, Seligman Alexandre, the son-in-law of
Cerfberr, was not published by any Sephardic Jew. Surely,
the lot of the Jews of Avignon and Comtat Venaissin depended upon the fate of a centralized France. But in the
neighboring Nîmes, Jassé Carcassonne, a peddler of Carpentras origin, was guillotined together with others for trying to weaken the national authority of Paris.

Historians are justified to judge the attitude of Jews to
the Revolution by their trust or distrust in the economic
policies of the Revolution, for example, buying or avoiding
to buy nationalized properties. Indeed, Jews did not follow
the economic policies of the Revolution. Unlike Protestants,
their role in buying nationalized properties was limited and
then mostly for the purpose of resale.

Politically, the most important factor of the Jewish participation in the finances of the Revolution was the role of
the Strasbourg Jewish banker Marx Berr [Cerfberr] as one
of the tree heads of the Purchasing Directory, which was
created on November 4, 1791. Berr's activities were restricted to contracting business and in this field Jews did
play an important role, not so much because of their own
large funds as through their skill in such transactions developed through the old regime.

*   *   *

The Revolution of 1789 did not occur only in the few
French provinces where Jews resided. All actions in which
Jews participated or did not participate, for which they
were praised or criticized, occurred also in provinces where
no Jews resided. Even where Jews resided, nothing done by
non-Jews was not to some degree done also by Jews, and
vice versa. Buying or avoiding buying nationalized properties; serving in the armed forces of the Republic or evasion
of service; trust in paper money or speculation with it; following the enemies of the Republic on emigration or remaining in the country under the new regime; remaining
faithful to old religious beliefs and traditions or following

the secular revolutionary spirit, etc., were not particular either to regions where Jews resided nor to Jews alone in regions where they lived.

In a way, the attitude of Jews to the Revolution was similar to the attitude of another minority, the Protestants. In many provinces the Protestants were, of course, the best partisans of the new regime. Still, the French Protestants of all denominations did not as a body and on a national scale endorse the Revolution, its principles, its fight against the anti-Revolutionary Catholic Church, etc. Alsatian Protestant leaders were suspected as aristocrats and traitors by the Strasbourg Jacobins.

A study on Jewish émigrés makes it clear that many Jews did not favor the Revolution and even opposed it, despite their gain of citizenship and equality. A small number of Jews openly favored the old regime. Some were connected with the army of Condé as purveyors or spies. Others became agents of émigrés. Many Jews without forethought followed the non-Jewish exiles. However, all possible excuses cannot hide the fact that there were Jews among the émigrés and other adversaries of the Revolution.

There is enough proof for many contradictory conclusions. In many places Jews were active Jacobins, yet in other places they were also suspected of being enemies of the Revolution. Some Jews were Girondists, but they were distrusted by the Thermidorian regime. The fact is that it is impossible to observe a monolithic Jewish attitude. The vast majority of Jews did favor the new regime, but because of their economic and regional attachments, and other factors, Jews were active not in one but all factions of the Revolutionary regime.

* * *

In the course of the debate on emancpiation the Jews had to listen to the views of the physiocrats among the Christians and the *maskilim* among the Jews on the "productivity" or "unproductivity" of certain occupations. They could not have imagined the change of opinion that was

to come almost 150 years later. For the period when Jews
were legally able to change their occupations judgment
cannot be rendered on the basis of Jewish workers, employers, or merchants, i.e., on the percentage of Jews who
were proletarian. Such a judgment would ask of Jews
more than of others. At the time when Jews were permitted
to enter "productive" occupations, many of them were
too old to give up money lending, peddling, horse trading,
etc., to which they had previously been restricted. In the
country at large widespread industrialization had not yet
begun. Productivity was no longer conceived as inherent
only in the status of a worker. The trend away from the
life of a poor agrarian laborer in favor of ownership of
a piece of land, away from the village and to the city,
toward entering into business for oneself, away from the
life of a poor worker in favor of ownership of a small
factory or a store, had already started.

Although emancipation widened the range of economic
pursuits open to Jews, this great benefit was in part offset
by unfavorable developments affecting economic activities
in general. Most Jews continued to live in misery. In
spite of the much publicized role of Jewish merchants,
there were almost no Jews among the big financiers of
the Revolutionary period. The Revolution did not enrich
the Jews. On the contrary, Jews as well as Frenchmen
were often ruined by the economic policies of the Revolution. Most Jews happened to live in centers that were
slow in becoming industrialized. Metz was still known
for its famous army center, and industry in Moselle did
not start until seventy years later. Strasbourg was more
a trade than an industrial center. This applies to Alsace
in general, with the exception of Mulhouse and a few
smaller places, mostly where Protestants pioneered in
local industries. It was impossible, even by the Revolutionary standards of 1789, to change, overnight, the occupational status of a minority long kept down by economic
restrictions. In 1818, the Central Jewish Consistory, in a

petition against the renewal of Napoleon I's anti-Jewish
decree of March 17, 1808, stated: "It is not in the nature
of things that mores established over centuries can be
uprooted within just a few years." Some historians in
commenting on the occupational status of the Jews during
the Revolutionary period, were more severe in their
judgments than the Revolutionary politicians and pamphleteers. Typical of this group was the historian Rodolphe
Reuss, who while in general very favorably disposed toward Jews, stated that in respect to their choice of occupations, only a small number of them justified the good will
of the legislature.

It is true that, upon the aboltion of the old regime,
many Jews failed to seize the opportunity to give up
their old occupations. The slow Jewish response to the
possibility of shifting to productive activities can best be
seen in the limited Jewish acquisition of national property
(*biens nationaux*), such as Church and other properties
confiscated and sold by the Revolutionary government.
It stands to reason that Jews should have been active
purchasers of national property, as this was their first legal
opportunity to own land and houses outside the former
ghettos. However—as already noted—unlike the Protestants, who became large landowners, the number of Jews
who bought national property was very small and they
purchased it primarily for resale. Needless to say, there were
many reasons for the Jews' reaction. The Catholic Church
spread the word that the Jews would desecrate former
churches. Many Jewish creditors were often afraid to ask
for payment from the nationalized properties of émigrés
of debts owed to them. At the same time it should be
remembered that the purchase of national property was
viewed as an act of revolutionary patriotism.

The Marxist historian, Dr. Raphael Mahler, stated that
the French Revolution did absolutely nothing to industrialize the Jews or to make them take up agriculture
so that they might achieve economic equality with the

rest of the population (*History of the Jewish People.
Modern Times*, I, 1957, p. 67, Yiddish edition). He did
not elaborate on how this could have been done. Did he
expect the Revolution of 1789 to force a change in the
occupational status of the Jews, such as occurred during
the Russian Revolution of 1917? Love of manual work
during the Revolution of 1789 was not based on such
methods. In fact, Mahler's statement shows only that he
tried to apply a twentieth-century yardstick to eighteenth-
century events. The French Revolution was liberal in its
attitude toward the occupational status of the Jews, and
once they were emancipated, it was up to them to maintain
or change their occupational status. Additional opportunities were given to them, such as the right to buy nationalized property, of which they did not avail themselves.
Surely any force applied in this case by the Revolutionary
regime would have been rightly denounced as an exceptional policy directed exclusively against the Jews.

The liberal attitude of national and even of some local
leaders of the new regime towards the occupational status
of the Jew can best be illustrated by their treatment of Jewish émigrés who left France in the wave of largely anti-
revolutionary emigration. The law of January 11, 1795,
permitted the return of those émigrés who, at the time of
their departure from France, had manual occupations:
peasants, workers, artisans, etc. But since agriculture and
all other productive pursuits were closed to Jews during the
old regime, how could a Jewish émigré prove that he made
a living by working with his hands? In many cases the authorities decided that Jewish émigrés who were peddlers,
merchants, and the like should benefit from the law because during the old regime they were forced to make a
living at dishonest occupations. In other cases the authorities declared that Jewish peddlers and traders in second-
hand goods, horses and cattle were useful to the local
population. Some Jewish émigrés stated that they were so
poor that they could rightly be called hard-working people.

                    *   *   *

The Revolution introduced significant demographic changes in French Jewry. In spite of restrictions which continued to exist in the beginning of the new regime, entire Jewish communities immigrated to other places in France. However, former ghettos continued to exist for many years as Jewish quarters. Although I have already discussed this problem in my studies, much more remains to be done in this field, especially on the economic changes related to the internal migrations.

After the emancipation, while officially the Jews were almost entirely free to immigrate to new communities, they continued to live in the old ghettos or in adjacent streets. Possibly in some instances they still felt safe only there. On December 29, 1790 the district of Benfeld (Lower Rhine) requested the restriction of Jewish inhabitants to ghettos with locked gates. From 1793 to 1806 only twenty-nine Jewish families had left the ghetto of Metz and settled in other parts of the city. Even after 1830, the other parts of the city were called *Mâqôm* by the Jews. In 1808, almost all the Jews of Nancy lived around the synagogue, in a sort of freely formed ghetto. Only after the Revolution of 1830 did Carpentras Jews begin to settle outside the ghetto. During the Revolution Armand Lunel's grandfather moved from Carpentras to Saint-Andiol, but in the time of the Restoration of 1814 he was forced to return to the Carpentras ghetto. In the eighteen-twenties the Jews of Saint-Esprit-lès-Bayonne, a suburb of Bayonne, were still not tolerated in Bayonne itself .

The story of Dijon (Côte-d'Or) is one of the most striking examples of the creation of a large Jewish community after the emancipation period. No Jews had been allowed to live there during the old regime. In 1790, a few Alsatian Jews from communities where anti-Jewish riots had occurred at the beginning of the Revolution, requested permission to settle in Dijon and "to exercise their religion, to have their cemetery and to be listed as active citizens." In 1798, there were twenty-eight Jewish families in Dijon; one hundred and ten out of 233 Jews according to a Dijon census of 1809, were born in Dijon itself. It seems that most of the Alsation Jews who settled in Lyons (Rhône) during the Revolution also came from communities that had suffered anti-Jewish riots.

Of the large amount of wealth possessed before the Revolution by the Jews of Comtat, particularly those of Carpentras, nothing remained in the Department of Vaucluse. In 1786, one Jew of Carpentras had possessed a fortune of 100,000 livres, another of 150,000 livres, while a third had made a bequest of 792,000 livres. Similarly, in 1789, a local Jew had left as much as 600,000 livres, and a year later another assessed his wealth at 728,000 livres, while in 1794, there were still three Jews who ranked among the twenty wealthiest residents of the city. By 1812, however, there was not a single Jew among the hundred highest taxpayers of the city.

Above all, the apologetic approach to minimize the number of immigrated Jews should be avoided. Writing in 1843, Samuel Cahen, editor of *Archives Israélites,* was able to affirm roundly that the majority of the Jews then living in Lyons were immigrants from Alsace-Lorraine and had not even been born in France. Similarly, in Marseilles, the bulk of the Jewish community was of foreign extraction, even the rabbi speaking with a marked accent. Nearly half a century later, in 1896, when the anti-Semitic Phillippe Sapin drew up his list of Jewish enterprises which he believed ought to be boycotted, we find that out of 415 economically active heads of households (1,010 persons) cited for Lyons, the bulk of those whose birthplaces are given were of foreign provenance; as against forty-eight born in the city itself, eleven in Paris and thirty-nine in various other French departments, there were 108 who were natives of Alsace and thirty-nine of foreign countries, the latter consisting mainly of Alsatians who had entered through Switzerland.

The Napoleonic regime restricted the right of Alsatian

Jews to move freely to other places. Some villages and
cities remained closed to Jews even in later periods of the
nineteenth century. As late as 1815 it was still impossible
for a Jew to reside in Oloron (Basses-Pyrénées). In 1844,
Archives Israélites reported that Sélestat, Rouffach and
other Alsatian towns tolerated Jews who came there to
do business only on a day-to-day basis, and would not
permit them to settle.

* * *

The fact that the Ashkenazim were, at first, not too happy
with the idea of giving up the autonomous rights of their
communities in favor of emancipation is well known. In
some of my studies I noted that the Sephardim also tried
to retain their communal organizations under new forms.

Some Jewish historians have argued that in giving up
their autonomous communities the Jews paid too high a
price for their emancipation; that this was the beginning of
a complete renunciation of Jewish life. It is, however,
doubtful whether the Jews could have retained the pre-
revolutionary status of their communities, even if they
had resigned themselves to doing so without civil rights.
In the long run a status of non-citizens for the Jews would
have been incompatible with the ideology and the very
existence of the new regime. Clermont-Tonnerre, who
fought for Jewish emancipation in the National Assembly,
stated on December 23, 1789, that, should the Jews refuse
to dissolve their communities and become citizens, they
should be banished. There was no alternative for the
Revolution but to integrate the Jews with the French
people. This attitude sprang not only from humanitarian
feelings toward the Jews, but also from an urgent need to
amalgamate all segments of France's population. Of course,
it was difficult, indeed almost impossible, for the Jews
suddenly and completely to abandon their millennia-old
traditions and principles. On the other hand, there was
nothing particularly anti-Jewish in the attitude of the revolutionary leaders against separate Jewish communities.

This would have implied the existence of even more than privileged communities: it would have required autonomy with its own judicial system, inheritance laws, *état-civil*, etc.; not one but three or more separate antonomies for the various regional groups of Jews, and this the Revolution could not have tolerated. As Graetz remarked, the Revolution emancipated the Jews without asking them to renounce even one iota of their religion. However, as I have noted in one of my studies, due to inconsistent policies of the Revolution the Jewish communities were never completely disoslved.

* * *

The Revolution of 1789 induced the Jewish leaders to adopt democratic procedures for governing the Jewish communities. In Bordeaux, all taxpayers participated in the meetings of the philanthropic society which took over the functions of the former *Nation*. As late as 1836, S. Mayer-Dalmbert opposed the use of the term *syndics* in communal Jewish life, reflecting the tradition of distrust by Jews of their syndics prior to the Revolution of 1789.

Very little is known about the struggles among various elements in the Jewish communities during the Revolution of 1789 and in the very beginning of the First Empire, before the creation of the Consistories by Napoleon I. In my *Autonomy and Communal Jewish Debts . . .* I draw attention to such conflicts between the communal leaders and the "young Jews" of Metz and Avignon.

It is interesting to observe that whereas at the outbreak of the Revolution and for some time afterwards a system of progressive taxation had operated in the Four Communities of the former papal province (i.e., the wealthier the person, the more he paid), this later gave way to one of regressive taxation (i.e., the wealthier the individual, the smaller the proportion of payment). The wealthy Jews had complained that besides taxes they were also obliged to give alms. It was for their benefit, therefore, that a proportionally regressive system of taxation was instituted.

Five taxpayers, who possessed a joint total of 70,100 francs, paid between them 228.95, or fifty centimes for every hundred francs (0.5 percent). Another 121, having a total of 977,600 francs, paid 1,684.55 francs or 1.75 per thousand (0.26-0.16 percent). Five others with a total wealth of 980,000 francs paid 551 francs and 25 centimes (from 0.60 to .05 percent).

Perhaps in some cases the continuation of Jewish communities was often a deliberate anti-liberal act directed primarily against the poor Jewish masses, a means for wealthy Jews to get more influence for themselves and keep the poor Jews in isolation, pretending that this separation is part of their religion (H. E. G. Paulus, 1831, according to Hannah Arendt, *The Origins of Totalitarianism,* 1951, p. 33). Napoleon's system of Jewish Consistories was almost a perfect example of such a system. Only much later, with the rise of Zionism, Socialism, and other movements among Jews were workable plans for Jewish autonomy on liberal principles worked out and even realized after the fall of the Czarist regime in Russia in 1917.

Of course, Reform Judaism and assimilation became a major problem. The intellectual changes which took place among France's Jews as a result of the Revolution of 1789 can best be illustrated by the fact that, due to the emancipation, the language spoken by the Jews of Avignon and Comtat Venaissin went out of existence even before it had managed to reach the status of a more or less developed written language (see my *The Language of the Jews in the Four Communities . . .,* 1948. On other languages see my "The Struggle Against Yiddish in France," *Yivo Bleter,* xiv, 1939, 46-77, and "Notes on the Languages of the Marranos and Sephardim in France," *For Max Weinreich* . . . ., 1964, pp. 237-244).

In one of my studies I concluded that the loosening of the ties of the Jewish religion and the mixed marriages as a result of the Revolution probably influenced Jews toward conversion. Yet, it was not visible during the Revolution, but only in the later years, beginning with the First Empire. The introduction of Reform Judaism from Germany started even before the emancipation and conversions took place, long before 1789. The Revolution came too late to save the Marranos from complete integration within the Catholic population. Almost all first generations of Marranos who arrived from Spain and Portugal were lost to the Jewish communities. Those who remained Jewish were Marranos who arrived during the last century prior to the Revolution, and their number was small in comparison to those who had arrived earlier and remained Christians (see my "Population Problems of Marranos and Sephardim in France, from 16th to the 20th Centuries," *Proceedings of the American Academy for Jewish Research, xxvii,* 1958, 83-105, and "The Marranos and Sephardim of France," *The Abraham Weiss Jubilee Volume,* 1964, pp. 106-127).

* * *

The Jews requested that the debts contracted by the Jewish communities during the old regime to pay oppressive taxes be nationalized and repaid by the government. This was a justifiable demand because all other autonomous *corporations* had been dissolved, their properties confiscated, and the debts owed by them assumed by the government. The Christian creditors of the Jews, fearful that the government would refuse to repay them, fought bitterly against the Jews' demand.

Prior to the Revolution of 1789 the legal status of the Jews was not clearly defined. This opened the way for many interpretations that were prejudicial to the Jews, not only during the old regime, but even during the Revolution. Thus, while Jews were criticized for their separatist tendencies, François-Balthazar Darracq, in a strong attack against the Jews delivered on March 7, 1799, at the Council of the Five Hundred, pressed the argument that the Jews—as foreigners—could not have been organized in communities which were in the category

of those dissolved by the new regime. The debts owed by the
Jewish communities were not taken over by the government, partly as a result of this propagandistic statement
that during the old regime the Jews were considered
legally as aliens. The government's reluctance to pay the
debts from public funds forced the Jews to continue to
exist as communal groups. The Jewish commissions appointed for the liquidation of the debts helped to retain communal ties among the Jews to preserve their group existence,
until the official reconstitution of Jewish communities
during the First Empire. The newly formed bodies for the
liquidation of the debts were not designated as *communities, nations* or *carrières,* but as *commissions* to liquidate
the debts. However, the functions of these commissions
were much broader than their names indicated. They not
only had to levy taxes, prosecute tax delinquents, and pay
the debts. These commissions also were in charge of all
communal Jewish properties and activities and conducted
many religious and social activities of the disolved *corporations.* However historians and partisans of the Revolution
must view the government's action as incompatible with
the aspirations of the new regime. For this error only the
authorities—and not the Jews—are blameworthy. The
Jews argued eloquently for the nationalization of the debts
and thus for the complete abolition of their officially dissolved communities. But they lost. The Revolution thus
followed the pattern of the old regime and of many other
countries: on the one hand, it dissolved autonomous Jewish
communities, and on the other, it forced them to remain
in existence for taxation and other administrative purposes.

* * *

French Jewry during the First Empire was discussed
in my book *Agricultural Credit and Napoleon's Anti-
Jewish Decrees* (1953). The Restoration period was discussed in my "The Jews in the Post-Napoleonic Restoration
in France, 1814-1815" (*The Jews in France,* i, 1942,
190-204, in Yiddish).

In spite of many anti-Jewish acts during the Restoration, the mass of Jews did not oppose it actively, for they remembered the anti-Jewish restrictions of Napoleon I. On the other hand, they did not engage in sharp criticism of Napoleon. Except for a few individual cases, the Jews as a group participated neither in the republican opposition of the 1820's, nor in the Revolution of July 1830, nor in the Republican opposition to the July Monarchy. In my study on French Jews during the Revolution of 1830 and the July Monarchy I analyzed the motives for such an attitude. The only exception to the minor political role of Jews was the movement of Saint-Simonism. Although many recent studies were published on the subject, my own paper was included in the present volume because I tried to prove that the Jewish Saint-Simonians were more Christian than Jewish.

The law of February 8, 1831, declaring that members of the Jewish clergy were civil servants and should be salaried by the government, and which was considered to be the final act of Jewish emancipation, was not a gracious concession to Jews but was hard won. Nor did the July Monarchy solve important Jewish problems, such as the debts owed by the Jewish communities. The oath *more judaïco* was abolished not by action of the King or the legislature, but after a long battle in the courts.

The small world of French Jewry during the July 1830 regime was a microcosm of the life of the country, without any sharply defined political attitudes. There were many liberals, many opportunists, some confused people, and they were to be found among Jews, too. There was one exception to this generalization: French Jewry had few outright monarchistic reactionaries. This political inclination was reserved almost entirely for Catholics.

In the first half of the nineteenth century there was much political inconsistency within the first generation of emancipated Jews in France. Some Jews became leading republican figures. Others, however, easily adapted themselves to changes of regimes. Michel Berr, for example, praised Napoleon I's *Acte additional* during the Hundred Days. Then, immediately at the beginning of the second Restoration, he declared himself in favor of Louis XVIII. After the events of July 1830, he glorified Louis Philippe.

The Simon Deutz case was a striking example of political confusion, of the lack of independent political conviction and religious and moral balance on the part of the Central Consistory, the organized body representing French Jewry. On November 7, 1832, the Duchesse de Berry was arrested for preparing a conspiracy of the Legitimists against Louis Philippe and his regime of the July Monarchy. She was denounced by Simon Deutz, who was a converted Jew, the son of the Chief Rabbi of France. Emanuel Deutz. Although Deutz thus helped to save France from a civil war, he was denounced by the press, pamphleteers, chroniclers and later historians—even republicans—as a "Jewish traitor." His father was persecuted by the Central Consistory because he refused to denounce the "shameful" act committed by his son.

The Revolution of 1848 helped to democratize the leadership of the Jewish communities by introducing universal suffrage. This was accomplished at the insistence of the Orthodox, who organized a Democratic Club of the Faithful in Paris, which was liberal in politics and conservative in religious observance. However, in the final analysis the events of 1848 brought about no great changes in French Jewry. The new electoral system was not sufficiently utilized by the democratic elements in the communities. The social struggle did not transcend the bounds of the synagogue interests. If there came into being a revolutionary element among the Jewish population, it generally and completely withdrew from communal affairs, and devoted itself to the general political struggles of the country. The contests in the congregation over issues of communal tax, burial plots, seats and "honors" in the synagogues, could not satisfy such an element. The com-

munities remained the same as before 1848. Even the one
achievement of the revolutionary days, the democratic
electoral system, did not succeed in really democratizing
the regime in the communities, and the rulers remained
practically the same as therefore. The official Jewish
community went the way of the entire regime in the country.
After the enthusiasm of the first days of the Revolution
of 1848 came political opportunism; the Second Republic
was succeeded by the Second Empire under the regime
of Napoleon III. Jewish life was and remained a miniature
of the general political life in the country.

The consequences of the introduction of universal suffrage in the Consistories and later struggles for the democratization of communal Jewish life were analyzed in my
studies "Di kamfn arum der val system in di yidishe
kehiles in frankraykh, 1850–1880" ("The Struggles in
Connection With the Electoral System in the Jewish Communities in France, 1850–1880," *Yivo Bleter,* vol. xxxv,
1951, 139-764, in Yiddish) and "Vi azoy dos optayln
di kirche fun der melukhe in 1905 ot bavirkt di yidishe
kehiels in frankraykh ("How the Seperation of the Church
from the State in 1905 Influenced the Jewish Communities
in France," *Davke,* No. 21, 1954, 382-392, in Yiddish).
See also my "Struggles between Orthodox and Reform
Jews in France," *Horev,* xiv, 1960, 253-292, in Hebrew.

The 1830's saw large scale participation by French Jews
in finance, commerce and industry, and the political attitude of Jews often followed the existing regime. Jewishness
did not any longer determine the philosophy or political
attitude of French Jews. Although Adolphe Crémieux in
1840 spoke in London in the name of "the emancipated
Jews in France" in favor of the abolition of slavery, the
Gradis family of Bordeaux was against the emancipation of
Negroes even in 1848. It is even not always easy to clarify
the political attitudes of Jews according to their economic
and social status. Michel Goudchaux and Marx Théodore
Cerfberr were both wealthy; both came from eminent Jewish families of the same milieu, both were active in communal Jewish life, yet their political affiliations were far

apart. While Goudchaux fought as a republican leader, Cerfberr was elected in Alsace as a conservative deputy.

* * *

Franco-Jewish historiography seldom considered Jewish poverty in the nineteenth century. According to most historians, poverty among Jews in France first appeared with the mass immigration from Eastern Europe. Rothschild became the symbol of French Jewry. This book contains excerpts from my book *Poverty and Social Welfare Among French Jews, 1800–1880* (1954), in which I tried to show an entirely different picture; to prove that there was great poverty and want among the native Jewish population of France before the mass immigration from Eastern Europe, which began in 1881–1882.

French Jewry during the Second Empire was also discussed in my papers "New Material on Altaras and His Colonization Plan," *YIVO Bleter,* xxi, 1943, 47-70,. in Yiddish; "The Struggle for Jewish Emancipation in Algeria After the French Occupation," *Historia Judaica,* xviii, 1956, 27-40; "Di grindung fun der parizer alians, 1860" ("The Founding of the Aliance Israélite Universelle, 1860"), *YIVO Bleter,* xviii, 1941, 1-21, in Yiddish).

Perhaps this book should also have included my study in Hebrew on Jews and the 1871 Commune of Paris (Tel Aviv, 1956). It was a patriotic and social revolution in which many Jews participated. While the fate of Jews as a collective body was connected with the Revolutions of 1789, 1830, and 1848, it was not anymore so in 1871. By 1871, Jews fought on both sides of the barricades, with the official Jewish leadership on the right. However, my study of the Commune was not included in this volume, because only my papers published in Latin characters are produced here.

I am grateful to the editors and publishers of the journals in which my studies were originally published for their permission to include them in the present book.

Zosa Szajkowski
September, 1969

POPULATION PROBLEMS OF MARRANOS AND SEPHARDIM IN FRANCE, FROM THE 16TH TO THE 20TH CENTURIES

I

An estimate of the number of Marranos who arrived from Spain and Portugal and settled in France would not be more than a guess. In this study we would like to pose only a few problems which are connected with this subject.

There is no doubt that a large number of Marranos became an integral part of the Christian population. Others remained faithful to their Jewish religion and founded the Sephardic communities — called *Nations* — of Bordeaux, Saint-Esprit-lès-Bayonne, Bidache, Dax, Peyrehorade and a few other places. The Marranos — known as New Christians — were permitted by the King's Letters patent of 1550 to settle in the territory of the Bordeaux Parliament. These Letters were renewed in 1574, 1656, 1723 and 1776. But only in the Letters patent of 1723 were the Marranos first mentioned as Jews and allowed to live openly as such.

The number of Sephardic Jews in Bordeaux was estimated at about 150 families (500 persons) in 1718; 132 families (500 persons) in 1722; 115 families (500 persons) in 1729. There were 327 families (1,598 persons) in 1752, not including

The following abbreviations were used in the notes: AdG — Departmental archives of Gironde: AdSeine inf. — Departmental archives of Seine inférieure; AmBa — City archives of Bayonne; AmBx — City archives of Bordeaux; AmDax — City archives of Dax; AmNantes — City archives of Nantes; AmRouen — City archives of Rouen; Amsterdam — Archives of the Sephardic community of Amsterdam; Jerusalem — Jewish Historical General Archives of Jerusalem; JTS — The Library of the Jewish Theological Seminary, New York, N. Y.

Originally published in *Proceedings of the American Academy for Jewish Research*, vol. XXVII (1958).

Avignonese, Ashkenazic and Italian Jews, who then resided in Bordeaux. In 1772 the Church authorities estimated the number of inhabitants in Bordeaux at 40,000 and the number of Jews in the parish of St.-Eulalie, which was the Jewish center of Bordeaux, at 4,000. But this was much exaggerated. According to the census of December 5, 1806, 2,131 Jews lived in Bordeaux. 1,651 of them were Sephardim, 336 Ashkenazim and 144 Avignonese. According to consistorial censuses there were 2,248 Jews in the regional consistory of the Gironde in March 1897 (2,110 in Bordeaux, 20 in Arcachon, 23 in Blaye, 4 in Gujan-Mestras, 36 in Langon, 9 in Panillac, 2 in La Teste); and only 2,088 in 1900 (1, 940 in Bordeaux itself). During World War II Bordeaux became a center for many Jewish refugees. When the Jews were ordered to register for a special census, 2,119 declarations were made in Bordeaux which involved 5,722 persons. 5,177 of them declared themselves as Jews and 545 as non-Jews. 722 had come to Bordeaux from the interior of France, 153 from Alsace-Lorraine and 112 from North Africa. (70 of the latter were French Jews from Algeria, 3 from Tunisia and 10 from Morocco. 5 were Tunisian Jews and 16 Morocco Jews. 8 were foreign Jews who had resided in Tunisia and Morocco.) 1,132 were foreign Jews of whom only 316 were naturalized French citizens. Only 542 out of the 2,119 declarations were made by French Jews of Bordeaux or of otherwise South-Eastern origin, and they represented only 1,198 out of the 5,722 Jews. Between July 18, 1942 and February 1944, 1,279 Jews were deported from Bordeaux, among them 214 Sephardim from long-established families.[1]

The historian Henry Léon noted twenty-four families of Saint-Esprit-lès-Bayonne who disappeared from 1693 to 1788 and forty-seven from 1791 to 1883. According to one source there were 1,100 Jews in Saint-Esprit in the 16th century, the

---

[1] A. Nicolaï, *La population de Bordeaux au XVIIIe siècle, 1700–1800* (Paris — Bordeaux, 1909), 29–44, 77, 178; George Cirot, *Recherches sur les Juifs Espagnols et Portugais à Bordeaux* (Bordeaux, 1908), 184–88; T. Malvezin, *Histoire des Juifs à Bordeaux* (Bordeaux, 1875), 199–286; Censuses of the Bordeaux Jews, Dec. 5, 1806, March 1897 and 1900 (Jerusalem); Census of the Bordeaux Jews during World War II (at the Prefecture of Gironde).

same number in 1728, and 3,500 in 1762, which number is considerably exaggerated. The estimate of 1,100 Jews and 900 Christians in 1723 is more reliable. There were 1,173 Jews in 1809. In 1808–1810 the names of 1,096 Jews were registered there, but another 124 did not register then. There were 1,166 Jews on June 15, 1812. In 1846 the general population of Saint-Esprit was 7,324, including 1,012 Jews. Bayonne had then a general population of 17,546, including 298 Jews who had moved in from Saint-Esprit. (Saint-Esprit became later a part of Bayonne.) There were 794 Jews in 1872; 706 — in 1886; 632 — in 1896; 606 — in 1901; 527 — in 1906; 515 — in 1911; 427 — in 1921. According to a consistorial census of 1890, 890 Jews lived then in Bayonne, 28 in Dax, 5 in Monceaux, 18 in Mont-de-Marsan, 52 in Perpignan, 16 in Peyrehorade, 16 in Tartes. Only a handful of Jewish families lives in Bayonne now.[2]

The general population of the region and its large cities increased constantly. The population of the Gironde department rose from 481,221 in 1781 to 735,242 in 1876. From 1780 till 1876 the general population of Bordeaux increased by 156.12% (from 84,000 to 215,140).[3] But the number of Jews in the Sephardic communities either dropped or remained the same only thanks to the large number of newly arrived Ashkenazic, North-African and other Jews.

Only a few Sephardic families settled in the four Jewish communities of the Papal possession of Avignon and Comtat Venaissin (Avignon, Carpentras, Cavaillon and L'Isle-sur-Sorgue). A municipal order dated as early as June 15, 1493, prohibited the entry of foreign Jews into Avignon, lest more

[2] H. Léon, *Histoire des Juifs de Bayonne* (Paris, 1893), 49, 210; Pierre Genevray, "Les Juifs de Landes sous le Premier Empire." *REJ*, LXXIV (1922), 28; Register of the names of the Bayonne Jews, 1808–1810 (AmBa) and copy of the same register (Jerusalem); Census of the Jews in Saint-Esprit, Peyrehorade and Mont-de-Marsan, 1809 (Jerusalem); Censuses of the Bayonne Jews, copied from general censuses in 1808–1810, 1812, 1886, 1896, 1901, 1906, 1911 and 1921 (Jerusalem); Census of the Bayonne Jews, 1890 (Jerusalem).

[3] Nicolaï, 86; E. Féret, *Statistique générale . . . de Gironde* (Bordeaux, 1889), I, 29, 286.

refugees from Spain arrive.[4] In Paris the Jews did not exist
officially. They were tolerated there only as persons passing
through the capital. The historian Léon Kahn analyzed 258
reports of the Paris police concerning Jews pertaining to the
period 1755 to 1759. Only in one case was it noted that the Jew
came from Spain; in five cases — that they came from Bayonne;
in 35 cases — from Bordeaux; but most of them were Avignonese
who had resided in Bordeaux. In six other cases it was noted
that the Jews were *espagnols*, or *portugais*. The same historian
noted the names of eighty families (308 persons) of Portuguese
and Spanish Jews in Paris in 1809 (out of a total number of
2,733 Jews). Or, twenty-three families (84 persons) out of the
eighty were Avignonese who had settled first in Bordeaux and
later emigrated to Paris. According to an official government
census of 1872, there were 23,434 Jews in Paris at the time.
A consistorial census of the same year indicated 16,535 Jews in
the arrondissements 1–3 and 5–20, including information on the
place of birth of 10,185 Jews. Of this number only 288 were
born in Bordeaux, 31 in Bayonne and 2 in Spain.[5]

The Letters patent of 1550, 1574, 1656 and 1723 were all
limited to the territory of the Bordeaux Parliament. The Letters
patent of June 1776 did not mention a restricted area there by
allowing the Sephardim to dwell anywhere in France. This
authorization was only theoretical, for all efforts made to have
these Letters recognized by the Paris Parliament and in the
colonies were in vain. In the interior provinces of France the
Jews from Bordeaux and Saint-Esprit were simply barred.
Marranos were persecuted in Rouen and Nantes. The Jews of
Bordeaux and Saint-Esprit were driven out from Bayonne,

[4] M. de Maulde, *Les Juifs dans les Etats français du Saint-Siège au moyen
âge* (Paris, 1886), 7; Z. Szajkowski, "Relations among Sephardim, Ashkenazim
and Avignonese Jews in France from the 16th to the 20th Centuries." *Yivo
Annual of Social Science*, X (1955), 177.

[5] Léon Kahn, "Les Juifs de Paris de 1755 à 1759," *REJ*, XXXXIV (1904),
120–45; *Idem, Les Juifs à Paris depuis le VIe siècle* (Paris, 1889), 235–37;
Z. Szajkowski, *Poverty and Social Welfare Among French Jews* (New York,
1954), 75, 87.

Blaye, Dijon, Cognac, Pau, Poitiers, Rochefort, La Rochelle and from many other large cities and commercial centers.[6]

Altogether the number of Sephardim in France was never larger than about 3,500.

II

We already mentioned that a large number of Marranos became an integral part of the Christian population of Bordeaux and of other cities. Their exact number is not known, but a detailed study could give us some idea of the extent to which these New Christians contributed to the overall increase of the general population. One source of material for such a study is the *état-civil* (registries of baptism, marriages and deaths); but this task would require a lifetime.[7] In the registries of the *état-civil* the New Christians could easily be recognized from their characteristic family names. Moreover, in most cases they are listed as *portugais, marchand portugais, portugais de nation,* or other characterizations which were used to identify New Christians and, in the later period, Sephardim, i. e. those who lived legally as Jews. In the later period, they could also be easily recognized by their first names. A large number of Sephardim had two first names, one non-Jewish and another Jewish. Teilles, the syndic of the Bordeaux *Nation* in 1745 had the first names Blaise Abraham. As a rule, those with Christian and Jewish first names were baptised. The Jewish first names were adopted when they later returned to the Jewish faith.[8]

---

[6] Z. Szajkowski, "The Jewish Status in Eighteenth-Century France and the 'Droit d'Aubaine.' " *Historia Judaica,* XIX (1957), 148–49.

[7] Following are but a few examples picked from registries of baptism in the Bordeaux parish of the Church of *Saint-Croix*: June 13, 1571, Arnau, son of Elye Mendes and Helène Nones; Apr. 1, 1574, Louis, son of Diegue Mandes; Oct. 12, 1589, Jehan, son of Manuel Brandon; Aug. 17, 1590, François, son of Dominique Dies and Eleonre Cotigne; Sept. 27, 1590, Françoise, daughter of Philippe Dies and Izabeau Perier (AmBx, GG 177, Nos. 4374, 5162, 9474, 9940, 9973).

[8] L. Cardozo de Béthencourt, "Le Trésor des Juifs Séphardim." *REJ,* XXVI, (1893), 242. *Portugais, portugaise* figures also in Jewish records, e. g.

In the register of baptism of the Bordeaux parish of Saint-André during the period of August 31, 1603 — 1605 we noted forty cases where the father of a new-born child was indicated as *marchand portugais*.[9] A large number of other cases in the same register also concern Marranos; this can be easily inferred from the names of the children and their parents. But we did not consider them because the parents were not registered as *marchands portugais*. In the register of baptism of the same parish for the period February 24, 1625 to May 10, 1627 we noted thirteen similar cases.[10] In the register of baptism for the period August 12, 1631 to October 5, 1638 we noted at least thirty-two cases of Marranos because of their characteristic names,[11]

in the register of the deceased in the Bordeaux Nation (AmBx, GG 790, Nos. 185, 193, 226, 293, 367, 550, etc.).

[9] Michel (son of Domengues Loppes), Frañ (Balthesard de Marthes), Louys (Louys de Léon), Yzabeau (Anthony Vas), Anthoyne (Elissientiade Francisco Gommes), Yzabeau (Symon Rodrigues), Blanche (Francisco Ortis), André (Diego Francisco), Pierre Gonssal (Diougue Martys), Yzabeau (Altonsse [Alfonsse?] Sainctes), Yzabeau (Diegou Fernãdes), Gabriel (Frañ de Valbelde), Loys (Melchiol Mommes), Marie (Gabriel de Villiologier), Jacques (Thomas Fernandes), Anne (Sébastien Medines), Ysabeau (Alvorou Gommes), Jacques (Bras Dies), Emanuel (Loys Loppes), Dominique (Paule Gommes), Ysabeau (Jehan Castera), Loys (Gabriel Bache), Claire (Simon Gommes), Pascal (Louys de Léon), Dominique (Anthony Mendes), Alfonse (Pey Rodrigues), Cathérine (Manuel Francoysonna), Dominique (Diogue Martin Derebeyre), Catherine (Diogue Vas), Leone (Anthoyne Fernandes), Philippes (Manuel Fernandes), Ldenis [?] (Fernandes Dalbes), Marie (Michel Gomes), Alfon[s?]e (Anthony Loppes), Jehane (Francisque Mendes), Rodrigues (André Rodrigues Loppes), Blanche (Douard Prera), Francoys (Manuel Arnales), Jacques (Lionnel de Chaues), Jacques (Bras Dies). AmBx, GG 15.

[10] Pierre (son of Alphõse Rodrigues), Guymarde (Francoys Jehan), Antoine (Belchor Loppes), Anne (Georges Rodrigues), Philippe (Manuel de Seres) Baithar (Francoys Dies), Blanche (Pierre Lopes), Marie Rachel (Pasquel Lopes), Louyse (Anthoine Henriques de Mores), Marie (Louys Gommes), Jean (Manuel de Seres), Esperanse (Louys Gommes Chacon), Jehan (Rouy Loppes). AmBx, GG 26.

[11] Yzabeaux Guomes, Bartholome de Lopes, Diegue Cardose, Sébastien Dies, Diegue Cardosse, Diou Rodrigues, Anne Mendes, Rodrigues Fernandes, Francoys Simon Goumes, Philipe Dies, Dominique Lopes, Fernandes Rodrigues, Violante Rodrigues, Beatrix Cardose, Francoys Bas, Beatrix Rodrigues, Francoys Mendes, Francoyze de Lopes, Heymard Mendes, Jacques Dies, Henric Mendes, Beatrix Mendes, Blanche Rodrigues, Beatrix Lopes,

and in the register for 1654–1658 at least 44 names, many of them mentioned as *marchand portugais*.[12]

In the register of baptism in the Bayonne parish of Saint-Etienne d'Arribe-Labourd (to which Saint-Esprit belonged) for the years 1632–1657 we recognized — according to their characteristic names — at least 103 cases of Marranos. But their number was probably much larger.[13] In the register of the same parish for the years 1657–1674 we noted at least 158 cases of

Fernande (Frañ Cardoze Leynes), Eleonor Dias, Clare Nunes, Marguerite Mendes Peichotes, Anthoine Lopes, Benoit Cardose, Izabel Mendes Dies. AmBx, GG 28.

[12] AmBx, GG 1, Nos. 66, 215, 240, 437, 441, 476, 613, 638, 659, 834, 1095, 1254, 1325, 1361, 1672, 1692, 2025, 2106, 2179, 2362, 2363, 2568, 2644, 2665, 2728, 2740, 2780, 3032, 3071, 3086, 3224, 3264, 3414, 3522, 3528, 3568, 3908, 4014, 4303, 4312, 4334, 4369, 4508, 4563.

[13] Jehan Mendes, Bernard de Rodrigues, Joseph Alues Frades, Jacques de Ladesma, François de Martin Gomes, Marie de Lopes de Léon, Manuel de Mendes, Joseph d'Henriques, Marie d'Alues, Cathérine de Carnero, Anne Henriques Mendes, Jacques Alues Frade, Antoyne Nunes, Dolyuero, Marie Fernandes Gommes, Léone de Ledesma, Cathérine de Martin Gommes, Joseph de Mendes, Anne de Castres, Elizabet Lopes, Marie Rodrigues, Agne Rodrigues, Jacques Mendes, Beatrix Lopes, Agne Rodriguez Pereira, Françoise de Sarmento (Rodrigues Lopes), Jean Nunes, Helène Sidereal (Rodrigues Pereyra), Jeane de Lopes, Sara de Gou[n]sales, Pierre Goummes, Rodrigues Ydaigne, Ester Rodrigues Cardoza, Jean Louis Nunes, Anne Mendes, Denis Lopes, Gorge Cardose, Gorges Fernandous (Cardose), Leonor Rodrigues, Simon de Pas, Louis Peres (de Pas Mendes), Jacques Rodrigos, Samuel Louis Nones, Izabeau Cardoze, Cathérine de Rodrigues, Beatrix Car[dose], Martin de Nonis, Raphaël de Saramentou (Rodrigues), Gaspart Francisquo Dacoste, Jacques de Pas, Violante Lopes, Francois Rodrigos, Dvarte de Fonseque, Cardose Rodrigues, Blanque de Carmento, Antonio Doarte (Rodrigues-Perere), Philipe de Soase, Antoine Fernandes Castre, Cathérine Rodrigues, Ester Cardose, Leonor Rodrigos Lopes, Jan de Cardose, Philipe de Soure (Lopes Dies), Isabeau Fernandes (Cardose), Anthony de Louys Bas Couillou (Lacoste Rodrigues), Saubadine de Cossens [name of a house] (Gomes), Pascoual Gomes, Marie de Penna (Enriques), Barthélémy de Lugat [name of a house] (Rodrigues), Manuel Ferro, Anthoine de Caurence, Samuel de Pas, Jan Sarmento, Claire de Gomes, Pierre Enriques, Pierre Nonne, Laurence Nones, David Lopes, Samuel Cardose, Jeanne de Fernandes, Beatrix Roudrigues, Anne de Laborde (Fonsèque), Izabeau de Gommes, Marie Rodrigos, Marie de Pas, Manuel Carbaillo (Dacoste Nunes), Jacques de Loupes de Pas, Gracy Gommes, Janne Rodrigos, Antoine Lopes de Castro, Jan de Sarmentou (Lopes Rodrigos), Louys Destandau [name of a house] (Albarez),

Marranos.[14] The historian, Moïse Schwab, noted 28 listings of deaths which showed the remark *de la nation portugaise* in the register of deaths in the same Bayonne parish for 1633–1656. To take another example: In the same register 69 cases of deaths would, on the basis of their names, be identified as Marranos, on 14 pages of the 56-pages register.[15]

Another source of information are the great number of various legal documents, e. g. the notarial acts.[16]

Daniel Enriques, Manuel Chimenes Cardose, Samuel Delbaillez, Antoine Petcheque (Peichequeotto), Raquel du Jardin [name of a house] (Henriques), Raquel de la Raset [name of a house] (Cardose), Francisque de Valentin [?], Raquel du Jardin [name of a house] (Loupes), Izabeau de Pas, Fernando Lopes de Castres, Philipe de Mesquite (Dias), Marthe Nones, Joseph Lopes de Pas, Beatrix de Sosa, Leonor de Castres, Janne B[R]odrigues, Jeanne L[N]ones. AmBa, GG sup. 2.

[14] AmBa, GG sup. 4.

[15] AmBa, GG sup. 3, pp. 4, 6–8, 43–45, 49–54, 56; Moïse Schwab, "Rapport sur les inscriptions heraïques de la France." *Nouvelles archives des missions scientifiques et littéraires*, XII–3 (1905), 369–70.

[16] Following are but a few examples of such acts in Bordeaux in which persons were designated as *marchands portugais* (AdG, E). Notarial acts of Lafite: Jean Dacosta Fortade (fol. 443, July 28, 1630), Dominique Abres de Crastre, of Rouen (fol. 501, Aug. 18, 1630), Antonys da Costa Cortissos (fol. 508, Aug. 20, 1630), Alfonso Custado (fol. 602, Oct. 2, 1630), Louis Fernandes Viere (fol. 605, Oct. 5, 1630), Ant? Anriques de Mora (fol. 608, Oct. 7, 1630), Marie Sarra, widow of Antoine Luis (fol. 628, Oct. 18, 1630), Henriques Nunes Saravia (fol. 639, Oct. 22, 1630), Alonso Romero (fol. 729, 1630), Diego Montezinos (fol. 844, 1630); Louis Fernandes Viere (fol. 43, Jan. 17, 1631), Diegue Castacque (fol. 67, Jan. 28, 1631), Manuel Peres (fol. 115, Feb. 19, 1631), Pierre Sisneres (fol. 175, March 12, 1631), Dominique Nunes Sabes (fol. 1120, Nov. 5, 1631), Guillen de Sotto (fol. 1120, Nov. 5, 1631), Jean Loppes Telles (fol. 83, Feb. 1, 1632), Lopez Saraunia (fol. 91, Feb. 14, 1632), Joũo de Porto (fol. 111, Feb. 9, 1632), Pierre Sisneros (fol. 266, Apr. 18, 1632), Diogue Cardoso Dazebedo (fol. 273, Apr. 20, 1632). In the minutes of the notary P. Bancherau: François Vaz Isidre (3 E 152, Oct. 2, 1635), Peres de Lesmous (3 E 153, June 6, 1637), Pol Gosmes Porte (3 E 154, Aug. 1, 1637), François Bassiadro (3 E 155, Sept. 27, 1639), Jean Buson and François Martin (3 E 157, Apr. 18, 1643), Francisque Albes Frare (3 E 159, May 1, 1644), Diego de Tabora (3 E 159, May 15, 1644), Diego Vaz Faro (3 E 159, June 1, 1644).

III

After a study of many available demographic sources we have concluded that the majority of the first Marranos who came to France at the end of the 15th century, during the entire 16th century, and some even of those who came at the beginning of the 17th century, remained Christians. Very few of them came back to Jewish life. The Sephardic Jewish population of Bordeaux, Saint-Esprit, Peyrehorade, Bidache and a few smaller communities in the 18th century was composed of new Marranos, who had come from Spain and Portugal in the 17th century and, to a large extent, during the 18th century. Already in 1636 only five of the thirty-six heads of family officially listed in the Bordeaux *Nation* were born in France. All others were newly arrived New Christians; six of these had obtained French citizenship by individual naturalizations.[17] According to one historian, a person registered in the *état-civil* or other documents as a *portugais* had, in fact, come from Portugal.[18] But it seems that this is a much exaggerated statement.

The Bordeaux *Mohalim* Jacob and Abraham Mezes registered nineteen circumcisions in 1706–1707, six of them concerned adult, newly arrived Marranos. The same applies to four out of the twenty circumcised in 1716–1717, seven out of twenty-five in 1726–1727, seven out of twenty-six in 1746–1747. 757 circumcisions were registered by the Bordeaux *Mohel* Jacob de Mezes in the years 1742 to 1793. Only 617 were circumcised at the normal age. Thirteen of the remaining 140 were circumcised at the age of 1 to 7 months, thirteen — from 1 to 5 years, nine — from 6 to 10 years, sixteen — from 11 to 15 years, eighteen — from 16 to 20 years, forty-five — from 21 to 40 years, twenty-one — from 41 to 60 years; and five from 65 to 68 years. To mention a few characteristic individual cases: In 1723 Abraham Fajardo [Faxardo] Delbaille arrived from Spain with his family

[17] Béthencourt, XXV, 96.
[18] G. Cirot, "Notes sur les Juifs portugais à Bordeaux" *Miscelãnea de estudos en homa de D. Carolina Michaëlis de Vasconcellos . . .* (Cointra, 1930), 6.

and was circumcised together with his four sons. Louise Marie
Bernarde (Sara), born in 1712 in Spain, the widow of François
Henriques Raba, who died in December 1742, arrived on June
24, 1763 in Bordeaux from Spain together with her eight children
and her niece Esther Fereyra. All her sons were circumcised
and the entire family adopted Jewish names.[19] (In other countries, too, Marranos who arrived during the 18th century, or
earlier, were circumcised at advanced ages.[20])

The register of deaths in the Bordeaux *Nation* for 1739–1792
contains 1,949 deaths. A large part of the 242 death cases
registered between April 13, 1788 and December 23, 1792 (Nos.
1707–1949) contain information on the place of birth of the
deceased or of their parents. Thus, seven of the 242 were born
in Spain or Portugal, ten in Bayonne, one in the colonies and
six in various other countries. In thirty-eight cases it was noted
that one or both parents of the deceased came from Spain or

---

[19] Béthencourt, XXVI, 254; Cirot, 175–76. The names of the fathers of the
circumcised boys are rarely omitted in the register. Only in those cases where
the circumcised persons were adults were the fathers' names omitted. Some
Marranos, who did not have themselves circumcised after their escape from
Spain or Portugal, were circumcised only after their death. In Bordeaux three
such cases were registered in 1706–1709 (Cirot, 47). Morelz (or Morel)
Flores was brought from Lisbon to Bidache at the age of 8 or 9 to be circumcised. He later died in a prison of the Portuguese inquisition. C. Roth, "Les
Marranes de Guyenne et l'Inquisition." *REJ*, XCII (1932), 169.

[20] Following are a few of such cases from Amsterdam: In the *pinkhas* of the
mohel Jacob, son of Dias Coutinho, the circumcision in 1699 of Ishak Avila
(at the age of 24) and in 1700 of Ishak Brandas (at the age of 64). The
pinkhas of Nosso Pay Mosseh Abraband shows in 1725 the circumcision of
Ishak Almeida, 27. The *pinkhas* of Abm. Semeh Aboab lists the following:
"98. Em 16 hesvan 5490 [1730] circumsidey a hum repas vindo de Espanha
chamouse Ab^m Carillo Sardanha," "117. Em 27 tebeth 5494 [1734] circumsidey
a humde portugal chamouse Semeul henriques chaves;" "126. Em 4 adar
5496 [1736] circumsidey a hum mosso de 27 annos vindo de Espanha chamouse
David dias Coitinho." In the *pinkhas* of another Amsterdam *mohel*, Moseh,
son of David Henriques Castro, are noted: "14 (5526) Em tersa feira 13 Kisleu
26 novembro [1766] circoncidei a hum mosso vindo de Lisboa o qual se chamava
Franco Machado Cardozo & tomou o nomen de Jacob da idad de 24 anos 11
dias." Francisco Lopes was circumcised in 1768 at the age of 32½ (Amsterdam).

Portugal, in thirty-two cases — from Bayonne or Bidache, in sixteen cases — from various countries.[21]

The register of births in the Bordeaux *Nation* (1738–1792) was started by a decision of the *Nation* on December 7, 1738. 152 cases out of 198 registered during the period of April 1788 — August 15, 1791 (Nos. 1535–1732) contain information on the origin of the grand-fathers. In twenty-one of these 152 cases both grand-fathers were born in Spain or Portugal. In twenty-nine cases one grand-father was born in Portugal or Spain and the other in Bordeaux or Bayonne. In seven cases one grand-father was born in Spain or Portugal and the other in Avignon, Metz, Italy, Germany or Morocco. In seven cases both grand-fathers were born in Bayonne, in twenty-three cases in various countries and in one case in the colonies. In fifteen cases one of the grand-fathers was born in Bordeaux and the other in Bayonne, Bidache, or Amsterdam. In six cases one was born in Bordeaux and the other in other French cities (Avignon, Metz, Lorraine). In twenty-one cases one of the grand-fathers was born in Bordeaux and the other in England, Holland or in another foreign country. Only in twenty-two cases were both grand-fathers born in Bordeaux itself. To summarize: in 57 out of these 152 cases one or both of the grand-fathers were born in Spain or Portugal, and in fifty-six cases in Bordeaux, Bayonne or Bidache.[22]

The register of marriages in the Bordeaux *Nation* contains fifty-four cases (Nos. 121–177), between April 20, 1788 and September 30, 1792, and contains also information on the place of birth of the couples and of their parents. Thus, in seven cases the groom or bride — or both of them — came from Bayonne, in one case from the colonies and in three cases from other countries. In eighteen cases the fathers of the grooms or of the brides — or both of them — came from Spain or Portugal, in

[21] AmBx, GG 845. Sometimes the death of Marranos who had died in Spain or Portugal was registered in Bordeaux, e. g.: "Sara Ximenes, veuve d'Abraham Ximenes, mort en Espagne, mourut le 12 janvier 1739., agée de 58 ans" (AmBx, GG 790, fol. 1, No. 2).

[22] AmBx, GG 844.

eleven cases — from Bayonne and Bidache, and in fourteen cases — from other places.[23]

The register of names of the Bordeaux Jews in 1808–1810 contains 2,063 declarations. Nine (mostly heads of families) stated that they were born in Spain, forty three in Portugal, twenty-two in the colonies, seven in the United States, two hundred and thirty in Saint-Esprit and thirty-one in Bayonne. Many others were born in other parts of France or in various foreign countries. Some of them had arrived from Spain or Portugal only on the eve of the Revolution of 1789.[24]

For many other Marranos from Portugal and Spain Bordeaux was only a point of transit on their way to other countries.[25]

It should be noted that during that late period mostly wealthy Marranos could afford to leave Spain and Portugal. Anyway, most of those who arrived in France during the 18th century were rich. An official report of 1772 spoke of Jewish refugees who arrived in Bordeaux during the past ten years from Spain and Portugal, all of them rich. So did a document on taxes of 1774.[26] Jaques Rodrigues saved from the inquisition 600,000 livres and Carlos Rodrigues over 200,000 livres.[27]

IV

Here should be mentioned the role of the *Nation*, the organized community of the New Christians, and later of those who lived openly as Jews. The membership of the Bordeaux *Nation* was small: on December 4, 1636 it consisted of 260 persons. There is no doubt that the number of New Christians in Bordeaux was considerably larger. It should be noted that even these 260

---

[23] AmBx, GG 850.

[24] AmBx, GG 799. Leonor Abigail Pereyra and Binjamin Posso arrived in the 1780's (*Ibid.*, Nos. 896, 1133).

[25] Z. Szajkowski, "Jewish Emigration from Bordeaux During the Eighteenth and Nineteenth Centuries." *Jewish Social Studies*, XVIII (1956), 119.

[26] "toutes riches ou très aisées" (Cirot, 41); "nombre considérable de leurs coreligionaires dernièrement venus à Bordeaux d'Espagne et de Portugal, dont la plupart sont de très riches familles" (AdG, C2851).

[27] Me. Lamothe, *Précis du procès . . . entre Francisco Dasilva Correa Alpalhao, juif portugais . . .* (Bordeaux, 1768), 4.

lived then officially as New Christians and not as Jews. The number of those who lived openly as Jews was much smaller: only one family was listed for the period from 1656 till 1668, two families from 1668 till 1676, nine families from 1676 till 1686, seventeen families from 1686 till 1700.[28] But the number of New Christians organized in the *Nation* was limited. There are no documents to prove that this was due to a policy imposed upon the *Nation* by the authorities. On the contrary, all the documentary evidence points to the conclusion that this was a self-imposed policy of the *Nation* and that the majority of New Christians was not accepted into this body. The *Nation* was largely responsible for the trend of a large number of Marranos to abandon Judaism completely. In many instances this was the result of the *Nation's* fight against poor and other "undesirable" Sephardic elements.

Historians have heretofore portrayed Bordeaux and Saint-Esprit Sephardim as communities of wealthy merchants. But, there is no doubt that a large proportion of Sephardim were paupers. On a list of the *Portugais* presented on December 4, 1636 to the Bordeaux authorities the names of 167 persons of thirty-six wealthy families and of ninety-three paupers are mentioned. In 1735, the Bordeaux *Nation* decided to assist only eighty poor families, but the number of the needy was really much larger. It would not be an exaggeration to say that almost every second Sephardic family was poor.[29]

[28] Béthencourt, XXV, 109.

[29] Ad. Detcheverry, *Histoire des Israélites de Bordeaux* (Bordeaux 1850), 59, 62; Cirot, 32. On Aug. 4, 1649 the City of Bordeaux granted "215 [livres] à quelques pauvres Portugais" (AmBx CC 16).

Among the Bordeaux permits for burials of non-Catholics issued in 1737–1780 we noted a large number of such permits which pertained to poor Sephardim (*pauvre portugais*); most of them were issued at the request of Abraham Gradis, the *Nation's syndic des pauvres*. Of the 695 permits granted during the years 1737–1750 (AmBx, GG 810) the following, among others, concern poor Sephardim: Nos. 408, 497, 499, 507, 509, 517, 526, 529, 538, 550, 553, 568–69, 575, 579, 585–86, 614, 622, 627, 636–37, 665. In another file containing the permits for the years 1737–1780 we found 29 cases of poor Jews. As late as 1911, 428 out of the 1,640 Jews listed in Bordeaux (Jerusalem) were registered as poor.

From the minutes of a meeting of fifty-two Sephardim, who gathered in Bordeaux on June 24, 1764, to protest against the *Nation's* syndics, we learn that two thirds of those who arrived in Bordeaux after the expulosin from Spain were impoverished; that in the early period, the wealthy were most charitable, even paying the taxes of the indigent Marranos.[30] But that changed soon. The *Nation*, from its very inception, was headed by a number of wealthy families, who jealously used the *Nation* for their own legal and economic interests. The *Nation* became a closed circle restricted to a limited number of members. When in danger to become too large the *Nation*, for fear of competition, found ways to expel large numbers of Sephardim. One way to do so was to send poor Sephardim to other communities, or abroad. In 1711, the *Nation* of Bordeaux decided to help newly arrived Sephardim to emigrate. In 1719 an entire family from Portugal, with small children, obtained a passport from London on condition that they would never return to France.[31]

But more often the *Nation's* leaders took more drastic steps and obtained from the authorities the expulsion of large numbers of Sephardim, not only of the poor. In 1597 all the New Christians who had resided in the city for less than ten years, were expelled from Bordeaux. The renewed exile of Jews from France on April 23, 1615 did not affect the New Christians of Bordeaux, but the *Nation* took advantage of this occasion and saw to it that no more of them should be permitted to settle there, and that many of them, including some who had been living in Bordeaux for twenty years, should be expelled. On November 20, 1684, ninety-three families of New Christians were expelled from

---

[30] AdG, E. Notarial acts of Rauzan, 34. June 24, 1764.

[31] The family of Abraham Nunes, which left Bordeaux on Nov. 29, 1713 (AdG, 6 B 45, fol. 2); Cirot, 36–37.

The same policy was applied in other Jewish communities. Between May 27, 1759 and Nov. 14, 1802, the Sephardic community of Amsterdam helped 404 poor families or single persons to emigrate, mostly to London, Surinam, Jamaica, etc. It seems that in most cases people were forced by the community to leave the country. Joseph Levy Flores was to leave for London on July 8, 1759 and he was given 200 florins. But when it was discovered in September that he was still in Amsterdam Flores was arrested and released only to board a ship for Surinam. ("Registro dos despachos," 202 folios, Amsterdam.)

Bordeaux, Saint-Esprit, Dax, Bidache and Peyrehorade. In 1730, 1744 and 1753 the Bordeaux *Nation* obtained new expulsions.[32]

Even in such large cities as Bordeaux it was often hard for poor Marranos to remain faithful to their Jewish religion. In 1622 Pierre de Lancre noted that poverty often forced Marranos to abandon their practice of Judaism.[33] In the less friendly atmosphere of the smaller places, where the New Christians were hardly accepted, it was often impossible for the expellees to remain Jews even secretly.

V

The New Christians registered their births, marriages and deaths in parochial Catholic registries. According to one source the New Christians of Saint-Esprit stopped to have their children baptized already in 1686, while still not being allowed to live openly as Jews. Even earlier, in 1633, they had their own cemetery. In Bordeaux this happened much later. Soon, the Jews introduced their own official *état-civil* (registries of births, circumcisions, marriages and deaths). According to one source, the last marriage registered by a Sephardic Jew of Bordeaux in a Catholic parish was on August 9, 1753. Although rabbis performed marriage ceremonies and delivered *cartes nuptiales* even before that date, the *Nation* started its register of marriages only on December 24, 1775. This means that during a period of more than twenty years marriages of Sephardim in Bordeaux were not registered, except in notarial acts.[34]

[32] Detcheverry, 51, 64; Szajkowski, Relations, 177–78. In 1744 the Bordeaux *Nation* requested the expulsion of thirty-five families, including Jehuda Raba, Salomoin Yfla, Jacob Soria, David Torrès, Izaac Torès and other Sephardim (Minutes of the *Nation*, No. 110, fol. 26–27, AdG).

[33] "Encore que la pauvrété leur ait fait relascher beaucoup de leur cérémonies & religion." P. de Lancre, *L'Incredvlité et mescréance du sortorilège plainement convaincue* (Paris, 1622), 470.

[34] Léon, 23; Cirot, 163–65. According to Alex. Ducourneau, the baptism of Jewish children was not registered after 1682. But this is not exact. *Essai sur l'histoire de Bordeaux* (Bordeaux, 1844), 275. According to the historian Beaufleury, the last Jewish marriage entered in a parochial register was in 1706. This is also inexact. Detcheverry, 116.

Or, even after the Sephardim of Bordeaux were permitted to live openly as Jews (in 1723) and they had introduced their own registries of the *état-civil*, a large number of names characteristic for the New Christians appear in the Catholic parochial registries of baptism, marriages and deaths. This is another proof that many New Christians remained good Christians after publication of the Letters patent of 1723. Many of the people registered in the Catholic registries were mixed couples, i. e. Marranos married to Christian women. But many others were still listed in the parochial registries as *marchand portugais*; or as having been married according to the Jewish law (*selon les usages et coutumes des portugais*).[35] Even newly arrived Marranos from Spain and Portugal were often entered in the parochial registries and not in those of the *Nation*.[36] Very few of these were cases of double entry, i. e. people who had registered with both Catholic parish and the *Nation*.[37]

[35] Following are a few examples of this type from registries of baptism: Sept. 23, 1750. Dominique, son of the merchant Jean Loppes de Pas and Magdelaine St. Germain (AmBx, GG 92, No. 637); June 5, 1753. Jeanne, daughter of the musician Gabriel Nones and Marguerite Lafe[u]rière (GG 95, No. 515); Dec. 1, 1769. Guillaume, son of David Cardove and Thérèse Fort (GG 108, No. 222); May 4, 1784. Jeanne, daughter of André Benoit Mendes and Mrgtite Lavergne (GG 122, No. 437); Dec. 22, 1786. Pierre, son of Joseph Albarès Corréa and Madelaine Courregelongue (GG 252, No. 122); Jan. 9, 1789. Jean, son of Joseph Mendes and Louis Rogeat [Roget] (GG 127, No. 28); Aug. 10, 1789. Armand, son of Joseph Mendes, "sacriste des religieuses Carmélites de l'Assomption" and Louise Rogeat [Roget] (GG 123, No. 759). On March 24, 1754, was patised "une nègresse, native de Guinée, agée d'environ 13 ans, appartenant à Raphael Mendes, juif de cette ville" (GG 96, No. 281). Earlier, on Nov. 29, 1724, was baptised in Bordeaux "Nicolas, garçon nègre, natif de Arada en Guinée, âgé d'environ 20 ans, appellé auparavant Jupiter, appartenant à M. Ignace Pereire, négociant de l'isle de la Goideloupe" (GG 70, No. 1056). Following are a few examples from registries of deaths: Dec. 21, 1773. Suzanne Elizabeth, daughter of Antoine Henriques and Elizabeth Lopes (GG 628, No. 170); Aug. 4, 1780. Antoine Nones, son of Gabriel Nones and Marie Laspinasse (GG 404, No. 315); Apr. 12, 1788. Bernard Felix Mendes, son of Joseph Mendes and Marie de Anabe [?] (GG 495, No. 401).

[36] In 1766, the Bordeaux parish of Sainte-Eulalie registered two such marriages, those of Gaspard Lopes Henriques de Chaves to Leonore de Miran (both from Portugal) and of Joseph Antoine de Carvallo de Chaves to Marie Madeleine de Moraine (both from Portugal also) (GG 387, Nos. 205–206).

[37] In other cases, too, births or deaths of Jews were not registered with the

VI

The traces of Marranos disappeared also from other French cities where they were not allowed to live as Jews prior to the Revolution of 1789. There is no doubt that many Marranos lived in Nantes. A considerable amount of information on them is available in the registries of the *état-civil* and other local documents.[38] A large number of Marranos married there into well known Catholic families.[39] But no trace of local Sephardim is to be found among the twelve Jewish families who resided in Nantes in 1809.[40] The presence of Marranos in Rouen is

Nation. But this concerned entries during the last years of the old regime and only in city records, but not the parochial registries. Following are a few cases of this kind: Nov. 13, 1792, the birth of David, son of Izac Foy and Rachel Roget; Nov. 15, 1792, the birth of Lucile, daughter of Abraham Peixotto; Dec. 17, 1792, the birth of Moize, son of Abraham Iflah and Sara Chimene (GG 418, Nos. 259, 418, 531). Nov. 16, 1788, the death of the ninety-years-old "juif" Britin de Carcassonne; Feb. 15, 1790, the death of Astruc; Apr. 7, 1790, the death of Lyere Lévy, "juive" (GG 815, Nos. 56, 103, 106). It is worth noting the case of eight-days-old son of Jacques Joseph Ephraïm, "juif," who was baptized on Jan. 30, 1781 by his *nourrice* (AmBx, GG 405, No. 788).

[38] E. g.: the baptism on Oct. 12, 1593 of Alphous, son of H. P^nes André Vaz and Agnès Cardoze, who came from Portugal (AmNantes, GG 177); the baptism on Apr. 12, 1639 of Fr^ois Dandrade (GG 361); the baptism on May 8, 1644 of Pierre, son of H. H. Louis Rodrigue and Perrine Dies (GG 186); the marriage on Jan. 20, 1593 of the above mentioned H. P. Me André Vaz and Agnès Cardoze, both from Portugal (GG 195); the marriage on March 31, 1636 of F^ois Lopez and Marie, daughter of Henriques Cuneca and Blache d'Andrade (GG 347); the death on Jan. 26, 1608 of Anthoine Vaz, born in Portugal (GG 203). On Aug. 30, 1569 Phelippes Martines, *marchand portugais* was fined by the courts (FF 56). But in Nantes, not only Jewish refugees from Spain and Portugal were called *New Christians*. A document of 1561 refers of Protestants as *nouveaux chrestiens* (CC 300).

[39] To cite one such case: On June 11, 1663 Isabelle Lopes, daughter of Jean Loppes and Jeanne Diais, was married in Nantes to Germain Laurencin, surely a non-Marrano (AmNantes, GG 310). On Feb. 19, 1688 B. Elisabeth Despinose was married to the Count G.-Sébastien de Rosmadec (*Idem*, GG 403). The bride was, most probably, of the family of the Amsterdam philosopher, whose grandfather Abraham d'Espinoza, had come to Amsterdam from Nantes. J. Mathorez, "Notes sur l'histoire de la colonie portugaise à Nantes." *Bulletin Hispanique*, XV (1913), 320.

[40] AmNantes.

also well known.[41] The records of *Lettres de naturalité* (naturalization letters), e. g. contain much information on them.[42] But no trace of the Marranos is to be found on the records of Jews during the First Empire. Sixty-three Jews were registered in Rouen in 1809. Only twenty-three of them were Sephardim, but all came from Bordeaux and La Rochelle. Seven Jews were born in Rouen itself, but they were of Ashkenazic origin. All others came from Ashkenazic communities.[43] The same could be said about La Rochelle,[44] Dax,[45] Toulouse[46] and other places.

[41] C. Roth, "Les Marranes à Rouen." *REJ*, LXXXVIII (1929), 113–55.

[42] E. g., in Rouen records of such letters in the beginning of the 17th century: Antoine Rodrigues Lamego, Diego Henriques Cardoso; Philippe Henriques, Louis Dias de Lemes, Gracia Denis and her son Dominique Pereira, Antoine Fenseca, Fernande Loppe de Paz, Barthelemy and Martin Rodrigues, Domingo Alvares, Diego Fernandes Penso, Simon Loppes Manuel, Fernande de Castro, Manuel Dacosta Borgès, Alienor Pimentel, Leonor Rodrigez, Antonio and Francois Acosta, Rodrigo de Morais, Henrique Mendez de Quaros, Jérôme Mendes, Antoine Mendez Dacosta, Leonor Rodrigues, Louis Anthonio, Violan Vaes and Marie Mendez, François Acosta de Pas, Elisabeth Mendez, Diego Henriques Lamego, Anthoine Foncea Henriques (Ad Seine inf., C 1245–1248, 1252–1257, 1263, 1268).

[43] Register of names of Jews in Rouen (AmRouen).

[44] Isaac Lameira of La Rochelle was circumcised by a Bordeaux *mohel* on March 27, 1713, when he was fourteen years old. Béthencourt, XX, 289.

[45] Following are a few examples from registries of baptism in Dax (names of the children or of their parents, who, in most cases, were listed as *marchand portugais*): Roudrigues, Isabel Roudrigues, Manuel Roudrigues, Simon Rodigous, Pierre Albaris, Blanche Mendes, Pereyre (Am Dax, GG 1, 1607—Jan. 1613, fol. 13, 25, 67, 23, 40, 39, 75); Jehan Louis, Cathérine de Rodrigues, Alienor Albarez, Plaisance de Gomes, Thomé Louys, Arnaud de Goumes, Ysabeau de Goumes, Daniel Rodrigues, Helaine helianore, daughter of Aexo Gomes; Estienne Goutières (GG 2, 1613–1620).

[46] Toulouse was a center not only of the descendents of the 14th century French Marranos, but also of Marranos from Spain and Portugal. On June 19, 1614 a group of New Christians in Bordeaux signed a contract with Gérauld and Pierre Palauque to take them to Toulouse for the price of 44 livres: "les sieurs Douarte Fonseccà et Dominique Loppes, et toutes leues familhes et au[tr]e nombre de personnes qu'ils vouldront en leur compaignie de nation porthugaisse, avec toutes leues hardes bagaige et balles, tout aultant que leur dict et coural en pourra porter" (AdG, 3 E 7101, Minutes of the notary Isandou, 1614, fol. 401–02).

VII

A study of the family names of the Sephardim proves that a very large number of Marranos remained Christians forever. It proves also that no trace of many Sephardim who in the 18th century lived openly as Jews could be found in the Sephardic communities in the beginning of the 19th century. The censuses of the Sephardic Jews in Bordeaux, Bayonne, Bidache, Peyrehorade and Paris in 1806–1810 contain about three hundred Sephardic family names.[47] Or, from only a very limited number of sources of the 17th–18th centuries we compiled a list of about three hundred characteristically Sephardic family names that do not appear anymore in the censuses of 1806–1810.[48] A detailed study would bring out a much larger number of such names. Undoubtedly, many of the individual names were carried by more than one family. Many of these "lost" names were taken from non-Jewish sources, mostly from the registries of the *état-civil*. But in every case the person was identified as *marchand portugais, portugais de nation*, or by a similar epithet which shows that the person was a New Christian. But most of the other "lost" names were obtained from Jewish sources.

The Letters patent of 1550 in favor of the New Christians were registered by the Bordeaux Parliament on April 19, 1580 at the request of Diego Mendes Dias of Spain and Simon Meira of Portugal. The history of these two families is unknown and no trace of them could be found among the Jewish families in the 18th century. On December 4, 1636 the physician Sébastien Dias and the merchant Henri de Mora submitted to the *Jurats* of Bordeaux a list of the 36 families (167 persons) of New Christians, except another 93 persons who were paupers. The historian L. Cardozo de Béthencourt noted that he could not trace the descendants of seven of these 36 families. But his information on the heirs of the other 29 is based only on a vague similarity

---

[47] The list of these names will be published in a separate study.

[48] The list of the "lost" names, too, will be published in a separate study.

of names.[49] Among the "lost" names are about fifty of the 93 families banished in 1684.[50]

Of course, many "lost" names reappeared later in other countries where Sephardim from France emigrated, e. g. Paiba, Spinosa, Pinto and others in London and Amsterdam.[51] But it seems that their number was not too large.

The Catholic parochial *état-civil* contains a tremendous number of family names characteristic for Marranos. The twelve names Alvarez, Cardoze, Dias, Dacosta, Gomes, Lameyra, Lopes, Mendes, Pas, Pereyre, Rodrigues and Silva were noted 707 times in the Catholic registries of baptism (335 times), marriages (149 times) and deaths (223 times) of nineteen Bordeaux parishes between 1541 and 1792. The name Alvarez appeared 24 times, Cardoze—69, Dias—23, Dacosta—16, Gomes—122, Lameyra—23, Lopes—216, Mendes—99, Pas—10, Pereyra—17, Rodrigues—66, Silva—22. (Curiously, the name Silveyra did not appear even once.)[52] This proves, again, that a large number of Marranos remained Christian.

It should be mentioned that the largest number of the Sephardim living in Bordeaux and Bayonne in the 19th century were descendants of a limited number of family branches. When Ester Cardose Lameyra of Bordeaux died in 1762 at the age of 81 she left fifty-nine descendants. This could also be proven by the limited number of Sephardic family names in the later period. Among the eight hundred Jewish families of Bordeaux

---

[49] Cardozo de Béthencourt thought that the Lameiras had branched off from the Meira family; but he could not cite any source showing a link between the Meiras of an early period and the Lameiras of the 18th century. Béthencourt, XXV (1892), 97–99. A family named Maïr appeared in a case of a child baptized on Jan. 30, 1781 by his *nourrice*: "fils de Jacques Joseph Ephraïm, juif, et de Marie Maïr (AmBx, GG 405, No. 788, see also note 37).

[50] Béthencourt, XXV, 240–41. See note 48.

[51] The parents of Francis Francia emigrated from Bordeaux to London in 1678, because they feared anti-Jewish persecutions. *The case of Mr. Francis Francia* . . . (London, 1716). 12 pp.

[52] According to 15 volumes (10,832 pages) of indexes of the registries GG 34–151, 155–458, 463–669, 673–695, 718–840. For each name were noted the various variations, e. g. Gomez, Guomes, Gommes, Gaumes, etc. were noted for Gomes; Loppes, Lopez, Louppes, de Louppes, etc. for Lopes.

in 1854 forty-nine had the family name Léon, twenty-seven—
Mendes, twenty-five—Rodrigues, nineteen—Lopes, eighteen—
Torrès, fourteen—Dacosta, eleven—Pereyre, eight—Depas,
seven or six each—Delvaille, Fonseque, Ifla, Lameyra, Lopes,
Dias, Lopes Dubec. The Bayonne list of consistorial electors in
1930 included three hundred and one people. Only about forty
family names were of Sephardic origin. The name Gomes was
repeated eighteen times, there were sixteen Delvailles, fifteen
Pereyres, nine Salzedos, eight Possos, seven Frois.[53] This again
seems to prove that the original number of Marrano families
who remained Jewish was small.

VIII

Of course, we must take into consideration the fact that it
was almost impossible for Marranos who lived openly as Christians to become Jews legally. In Saint-Jean-de-Luz a Marrano
woman perished in 1622 at the autodafe. On April 26, 1722 —
only one year prior to the publication of the Letters patent
of 1723 permitting the New Christians to live as Jews, the
authorities of Bordeaux complained to higher authorities
against two women for their practicing Judaism.[54] But on
the other hand a large number of Sephardim was converted to
Catholicism. We noted for France alone about eighty such cases
during the period from the end of the 17th century to the end of
the 18th century, not including those of the French colonies.
The number of conversions among the Sephardim in France was
probably larger than in any other community.[55] Among them

---

[53] Census of the Bordeaux Jews, 1854 (Jerusalem); List of the consistorial
electors in Bordeaux, 1930 (AdG, V); Cirot, 130.

[54] Léon, p. 26; AdG, C 1089 ("deux femmes de Bordeaux anciennes cat[h]o-
liques judaïsoient").

[55] According to one source, only 23 Sephardic Jews, including 16 girls,
were converted between 1695 and 1789. Z. Szajkowski, "Marriages, Mixed
Marriages and Conversions among French Jews During the Revolution of
1789." *Historia Judaica*, XIX (1957), 47. A detailed list of Sephardic conversions will be published in a separate study. 141,562 Jews lived in Prussia in
1821. There were there 763 conversions between 1812 and 1821. A Menes,

were Marranos who came from Spain and Portugal, had adopted
Jewish names in their new Jewish environment, were circumcised
there and remarried according to Jewish law. The majority of
the Sephardim who settled in the French colonies converted to
Catholicism in order to preserve their legal and economic status.
Officially Jews were banned from the French colonies on April 23,
1615. On April 2, 1784 David Silveyra, the Paris representative
of the Bordeaux *Nation* wrote to Bordeaux that many Jews in
the French colonies became baptized in order to be able legally
to leave their properties to their children, as the authorities
tried to declare the Jews as *aubains*, i. e. as alines whose estates
were taken over by the King.[56] It is worth while to mention the
story of the Faxardo family as a characteristic case. Raphaël
Faxardo was born in 1669 in Spain as the son of Dom Pedro
Faxardo (born in 1623 in Toledo). In 1696 he married Haycinthe-
Magdaleine Pinedo Gusman. In Spain Raphaël Faxardo practiced medicine, was enobled by the King and also was a financeer.
In 1702 he was made apostolic notary. He served in the Spanish
army in 1704 and 1705 and in 1721 he became a vice-consul of
France in Taveira (Portugal). In August 1722 he came to France
with his entire family. There he joined the Jewish community.
In 1723 he again remarried his wife according to Jewish law.
They were married under the names of Abraham and Sara. His
five children, too, adopted Jewish names. In France they had
three more children. But the children soon emigrated to the
French colonies, where they were at various times all converted
to Catholicism.[57]

On the other hand, Marranos who reemigrated from the
French colonies often came back to Jewish life. Abraham
Guimardin, who was born on November 23, 1786 in San-Domingo

"Conversion in Prussia in the First Half of the 19th Century." *Historishe
Schriften* I (Warsaw, 1929), 375–404.

[56] ". . . d'après que divers américains m'ont raporté, que plusieurs de nos
juifs français et autres avaient eprouvé le désagrement dévoir que le domaine
s'était emparé de leurs biens, ce que necessairement force beaucoup de nos
gens a abjurer pour conserver leur fortune" (JTS).

[57] Me. Bourbon, *Mémoire pour le Sieur Alexandre Faxardo* . . . (Le Cap,
1780). 60 pp.

and whose parents both came from Portugal, was circumcised in Bordeaux on September 20, 1792. David Astruc who was also born at San-Domingo (an Avignonese Jew according to his name) was circumcised in Bordeaux on May 19, 1793 at the age of sixteen months and twelve days.[58]

In conclusion of this study — which would be considered only as notes and not as a final study — it should be said that almost all first generations of Marranos who arrived from Spain and Portugal were lost to the Jewish communities. Those who remained Jewish were Marranos who arrived at a later period and their number was small in comparison to those who had arrived earlier and remained Christians.

[58] AmBx, GG 798, No. 33; Cirot, 182.

The Marranos and
Sephardim of France

T HE MAJORITY of the first Marranos who came to France at the end of the 15th century, during the entire 16th century, and even at the beginning of the 17th century, became an integral part of the Christian community. Very few of them resumed Jewish affiliation. The eighteenth century Sephardic communities, on the other hand, were composed mostly of recently arrived Marranos.[1] For expressing this view in an earlier article, the present author was strongly criticized by the historian, I. S. Révah, according to whose sentimental approach to the history of Marranos such a conclusion is inadmissable.[2] Let us, then, review the facts on this problem.

The following abbreviations are being used in the notes and Appendixes: AdG—Departmental archives of Gironde; Ba—City archives of Bayonne; Béthencourt—see note 11; Bx—City archives of Bordeaux; Bxreg—Eighteenth century registees of the Jewish *état-civil* in Bordeaux (in Bx); Cirot—*Recherches sur les Juifs Espagnols et Portugals a Bordeaux*, by G. Cirot. Bordeaux, 1908; Dax—City archives of Dax; Factum—*Factums* (briefs) published in connection with lawsuits; Léon—*Histoire des Juifs de Bayonne*, by H. Léon, Paris, 1893; Malvezin—*Histoire des Juifs a Bordeaux*, by T. Malvezin, Bordeaux, 1875; Nantes—City archives of Nantes; Seine inf.—Departmental archives of Seine inférieure; Schwab—*Rapport sur les inscriptions hébraiques* . . . Paris, 1907; 1684—The names of Jews expelled in 1684, according to Béthencourt, XXV, 240-41 (see note 11).

1. Z. Szajkowski, "Population Problems of Marranos and Sephardim in France, from the 16th to the 20th Centuries." *Proceedings of the American Academy for Jewish Research*, XXVII (1958), 91.

2. I. S. Révah, "Les Marranes." *REJ* CXVIII (1959-60), 65-67.

Originally published in *The Abraham Weiss Jubilee Volume* (1964).

Nantes, for example, was a large center of Marranos. However, *all* the Jews who were registered there in 1808-1809 were Ashkenazim. Révah himself confirms the absorption of the Marranos there by the Catholic population.[3] But how about other Marrano centers? A very large number of Marranos lived in Rouen.[4] However, no trace of them is to be found in the Jewish community of Rouen after the emancipation. Sixty-three Jews were registered there in 1809-1810. Twenty-three of them were Sephardim, but all of them had come from Bordeaux and La Rochelle. Seven Jews were born in Rouen itself but they were of Ashkenazic origin. All others came from Ashkenazic communities.[5] In the period after 1810, the Jewish community of Rouen consisted almost entirely of non-Sephardim.[6] According to I. S. Révah in the 1660's only four or five of the Rouen Marranos were integrated into the French-Catholic life of that city. What happened to the remaining Marranos who did not join the Jewish community of Rouen after 1789? Did they *all* at a very early date emigrate to Amsterdam, London, Hamburg, and Italy, as Révah believes?[7] All the ten Jewish families registered in 1808 in Brest were Ashkenazic.[8] No former Marranos of Toulouse were among the members of the Jewish community there after 1789.[9] The same applies to the former Marranos of Montpellier and other large cities. What happened to them? Surely not all of them had left these cities prior to 1789. Neither did they become secular citizens—like Alexander Lambert of Saint-

---

3. J. Mathorez, "Notes sur l'histoire de la colonie portugaise à Nantes." *Bulletin Hispanique*, XV (1913), 316-39; Léon Brunschvicq, "Les Juifs de Nantes . . ." *REJ*, XIX (1889), 303-04; Révah, *op. cit.*, p. 66.

4. Max Grunwald, "Note sur des Marranes à Rouen et ailleurs." *REJ*, LXXXIX (1930), 381-84; C. Roth, Les Marranes à Rouen." *REJ*, LXXXVIII (1929), 43-55.

5. City archives of Rouen, 133e5bis; Deaprtmental archives of Seine inférieure, M, Juifs.

6. In 1846, only three of the 102 families of Rouen registered by the Jewish consistory were Sephardic (according to the 1846 census of the Paris consistory. General Historical Archives of Israel, Jerusalem).

7. Révah, *op. cit.*, p. 65.

8. City archives of Brest.

9. J. Gross, "Les Juifs de Toulouse pendant la Révolution et l'Empire." *Revue des Pyrénées*, XVIII (1906), 250. It is not exact, as Révah states (*op. cit.*, p. 65), that no Marranos lived there after 1685.

Jean-d'Angély—with the advent of the new regime of 1789.[10]

The eighteenth century registries of the Bordeaux *Mohalim*—and also of other sources—contain information on Marranos who were circumcized at advanced ages. However, almost all of them were newly-arrived Marranos from Spain and Portugal and not from other large French centers, such as Nantes, or Le Havre.[11]

Many Marranos continued to live apart from the Jewish Nation, openly as Christians, or on the border between the Jews and Christians, unable to make up their minds about their place; even in Bordeaux, where the attitude toward New Christians was more liberal than in other large cities; and even after 1723 when the New Christians were allowed to live openly as a *Jewish Nation*. Sometimes Marranos took such a step for economic reasons or because of mixed marriages, but often also because they had lost all ties with Judaism. How else should we explain the fact that the Catholic parochial registries of the *état-civil* (births, marriages and deaths) of Bordeaux, for example, contain the names of Marranos at the time when the Jews had their own registries?[12]

Révah seeks to dispose our conclusion by minimizing the number of Marranos in such centers and by relying on reports by officials of the Spanish Inquisition sent to France.[13] Of course, the latter material should not be disregarded, but it cannot always be accepted without reservations and it cannot take the place of more reliable sources. So, for example, an official of the Inquisition reported in 1633 only sixty Judaic families among the New Christians of Saint-Esprit-lès-Bayonne, while, most probably, no New Christians there were ever sincere Catholics. Indeed, those Marranos of Saint-

10. A. Lambert was the author of *Discours de morale, prononcé le 2 décadi, 20 Frimaire l'an 2ᵉ de la République une et indivisible [10 Décembre 1793], au Temple de la Vérité, ci-devant l'église des Bénédictins, à Angély-Boutonne, ci-devant Saint-Jean d'Angély, fait par le citoyen Alexandre Lambert fils, Juif et élevé dans les préjugés du culte judaïque.* Rochefort, n.d. 23 pp. 8°.

11. Registries of the Bordeaux *Mohalim* in the series GG of the city archives of Bordeaux. Isaac Lameira of La Rochelle was circumcised by a Bordeaux *mohel* on March 27, 1713. L. Cardozo de Béthencourt, "Le Trésor des Juifs Séphardim." *REJ*, XX (1890), 289.

12. See Szajkowski, *op. cit.,* p. 98, notes 37-36.

13. Révah, *op. cit.,* p. 66.

Esprit were more openly Judaic than in Bordeeaux. The Bayonne author of a 17th century memorandum complained that some Marranos who professed Christianity in Bordeaux, started to practice Judaism upon their arrival in Saint-Esprit.[14] As long as they remained there, there was no danger of the integration of the Marranos of Saint-Esprit and the Christian population. This was simply the result of the strict restrictions imposed by the city of Bayonne upon the Marranos. There the Marranos were seldom referred to in official documents as *New Christians,* or *Portuguese merchants,* as they were in other centers of Marranos in France. In a large number of Bayonne documents the Marranos were often denoted *marchands Juifs ou Portugais.*[15] The city of Bayonne maintained that as long as the Marranos remained Jews, they could not legally reside in Bayonne.[16] In fact the Marranos were forced to live in a ghetto, in the Bayonne suburb of Saint-Esprit-lès-Bayonne. In 1753 the Intendant noted the great difference between these two Sephardic centers: in Bordeaux the Jews were free, able to reside in various parts of the city, while they were excluded from the city of Bayonne itself.[17] Thus, the ghetto saved many Marranos of Saint-Esprit from mixed marriages and other temptations to remain Christian.

In Letters patent of 1723, renewing the old privileges that had been granted since 1550 to the New Christians, the latter were described for the first time as Jews and thereafter could live undisguized as Sephardic Jews.[18] On the basis of these Letters patent Manuel Degante and Abraham Morelle obtained individually the

14. "Il en avait mesme quelques uns à Bordeaux qui professoient le Christianisme, lorsqu'ils sont retirez aud. Bourg du St. Esprit où ils Judïsent" (Ba, GG229, No. 1).

15. Ba, GG229. See also: *Ordonnance . . . de la Ville de Bayonne, du 23. aoust 1691 . . .* Bayonne, 1692, pp. 1-2, 7 (". . . aux Juifs & Portugais;" "Juifs disans Portugais").

16. ". . . Jacob Alvarez Louis Juif marchand residant au bourg St. Esprit, n'est point bourgeois de la ville, n'y ne peut pretendre a le devenir tant qu'il professera la religion judaïque suivant les statuts reglemens de la Ville . . ." (Ba, GG229, No. 6).

17. Aveillé, *op. cit.,* pp. 11-12.

18. *Lettres patentes du Roy, pour les Portugais des Généralitez de Bordeaux . . . juin 1723 . . .* Bayonne, n.d. 4 pp. Also in other editions.

right to reside in Bordeaux.[19] In 1752, the Intendant stated that in accordance with the Letters patent of 1723, granted "to the Jews" of Saint-Esprit, the latter should not be disturbed in the practice of their religious customs.[20] These Letters patent were not cited by Marranos of other large centers for the purpose of gaining legal status as Jewish individuals or Jewish communities. Of course, in all the Letters patent granted to the Marranos, including the 1723 Letters patent, the right of residence for the Marranos (and, since 1723, for the Sephardim) was limited only to the territory under the jurisdiction of the Bordeaux Parliament.[21] However, in June 1776, King Louis XVI, again renewed the old privileges, omitting the previous restriction of the Sephardim to the territory of the Bordeaux Parliament.[22] On the basis of these new Letters patent the Jewish community of Marseilles gained a legal status, though not until many years later. On February 12, 1788, the Letters patent of 1777 were registered by the Parliament of Provence, where the city of Marseilles was located.[23] According to one source, the Jews of Marseilles paid the sum of 6,000 livres to have these Letters patent registered, thereby securing for themselves the right of residence in Provence.[24] To achieve their purpose the Jews of Marseilles had to declare themselves a community of Sephardim, for the Letters patent of 1776 were granted to Sephardim only. But this was only a legal subterfuge, for in reality the Jewish com-

---

19. Bx, Registre de la Jurade, fol. 94, Dec. 16, 1729 ("conformément aux lettres patentes données à Meudon en juin 1723"); fol. 102, July 17, 1738 ("En conséquence des Lettres patentes . . . de juin 1723").

20. M.H. Aveillé, *L'Intendant d'Etigny et les Juifs de Bayonne d'après sa correspondence.* Auch, 1901, p. 9.

21. Thus, Révah's statement (*op. cit.*, p. 64) that the Letters patent of 1550 were the juridical basis for the establishment of Marranos not only in Bordeaux and [Saint-Esprit-lès-] Bayonne, but also in Toulouse, Nantes, Rouen, Paris, and other places is not correct.

22. *Lettres-patentes du Roi, confirmatives des privilèges, dont les Juifs Portugais jouissent en France depuis 1550 . . . de juin 1776 . . .* n.p., 1781. 4 pp. Also in other editions.

23. Archives départmentales de Bouches-du-Rhône, dépôt d'Aix, fonds du Parlement de Provence, B3465, fol. 29; *Mémoire pour les Sieurs Vidal aîné . . .* Marseille, 1792, pp. 2-3.

24. *Réponse à de nouvelles objections. Pour les Sieurs Vidal et Consorts.* Marseille, 1792, p. 14.

munity of Marseilles at that time was composed of Jews of varied origin and only a few were Sephardim.[25] But the large groups of Marranos in Nantes, Rouen, Le Havre and other commercial centers did not try to gain the legal status of Jewish communities on the basis of the Letters patent of 1776.

It seems that the Letters patent of 1776 were not applied in favor of Marranos in the French colonies. A memorandum, submitted as late as 1788 by the Sephardim to the Minister, Ch. G. L. de Malesherbes, contained a plea for the right of residence in the whole of France and in the French colonies.[26] Moreau de Saint-Méry noted that the Letters patent of 1776 were in fact also legal in the colonies.[27] But the Marranos in the colonies themselves did not seek legal status as a Jewish community on this basis.

Individual Jews, too, obtained many rights, including naturalization, on the basis of the various Letters patent in favor of the Sephardim. In September 1775, the three brothers Léon, Gerson and Eliézer Homberg, and also Joseph Lallemant, merchants of Havre—all of them Jews of Ashkenazic origin—obtained from the King naturalization Letters. Their request was based on the Letters patent in favor of Sephardim and the printed text of their naturalization Letters contains the text of the Letters patent of June 1723.[28] Later, when Jacob de Perpignan, a Bordeaux Jew of Avignonese origin, requested naturalization letters, he referred to the naturalization of the Hombergs and Lallemant.[29] But no individual Marranos of Rouen, Le Havre, Nantes and similar places made such individual requests on the basis of Letters patent in favor of Sephardim.

---

25. Z. Szajkowski, "The Jewish Community of Marseilles at the end of the Eighteenth Century," to be published.

26. In Le Havre only one Jew, David Raphaël, was registered as a Jew in 1809 (The Jewish Historical General Archives, Jerusalem, Zf492).

27. Moreau de Saint-Méry, *Lois et constitutions des colonies françaises d'Amérique sous les Vent.* Paris, 1784-90, V, 715-16 ("Les dispositions de ces Lettres-Patentes ont été adoptées par le Conseil du Cap").

28. *Lettres patentes du Roi, qui accordent aux sieurs Homberg, Frères, & Lallemant, négocians du Havre de Grâce, les droits de Régnicoles & Naturels Francois. Du mois septembre 1775.* n.p., 1776. 11 pp.

29. *Lettres patentes du Roi, qui accordent aux Sieurs Jacob de Perpignan, Juif . . . les droits de Régnicoles . . . Mars 1776,* Paris, 1779 [?] 7 pp.

A decision by the Rouen Parliament of March 11, 1769, forbidding conversion of Jewish children against the will of their fathers, was based on such a privilege granted on July 15, 1728, to Sephardim.[30]

In January 1790, the Sephardic Jews obtained full emancipation.[31] Again this decree was used by other Jews—but not Marranos—in order to gain legal status, *e.g.,* in September 1790, a meeting of the Jewish community of Marseilles pronounced itself a Sephardic community, on the basis of the decree of January 1790;[32] and in October 1790, a Jew from Avignon tried to settle in Toulouse on the basis of the same decree.[33]

From only a very limited number of sources of the 17th and 18th centuries, we compiled a list of about three hundred characteristically Marrano and Sephardic names that do not appear in Sephardic censuses of 1806-1810.[34] These names were taken from Jewish or from non-Jewish sources. But in every case the person was identified as *marchand portugais,* or *portugais de nation,* or by other epithets given to New Christians. Many of the bearers of these "lost" names probably left for other communities, or went abroad. But surely, not all of them. A large number of them remained Christians. Among the lost names are about fifty of the ninety-three Marrano families banished from Bordeaux in 1684.[35]

From the end of the seventeenth to the end of the eighteenth century there were about eighty conversions of French Sephardim to Catholicism.[36] This is, indeed, a very large number for a com-

---

30. *Archives israélites,* XX (1859), 159-70.

31. *Lettres patentes du Roi, sur un Décret de l'Assemblée Nationale, portant que les Juifs, connus en France sous le nom de Juifs portugais, espagnols et avignonais, y jouiront des droits de citoyen actifs. Transcrites en Parlement, en vacations, le 9 février dudit an.* Paris, 1790. 3 pp. 4º. Other editions: Bordeaux (two editions), Aix, Nantes, Lille, Colmar, Metz, Nancy.

32. *Réponses . . .* pp. 36-37 ("Les Juifs Espagnols et Portugais, établis à Marseille, en vertu de leurs Lettres-patentes confirmées par un Décret de l'Assemblée Nationale . . .").

33. Ad. Crémieux, "Pour contribuer à l'histoire de l'accession des Juifs à la qualité de Citoyen français." *REJ,* XCV (1933), 44-53.

34. See Appendixes I and II.

35. Béthencourt, XXV, 240-41.

36. See Appendix III.

munity which was never larger than about 3,500 individuals and can probably be explained in part by the Catholic feelings of the former Marranos.

The number of Sephardim in France between 1723 and 1939 was never larger than about 3,500. In fact, the Sephardic population remained almost the same for over two centuries. For unexplained reasons the death rate was higher among the Sephardic than among Ashkenazic and other non-Sephardic Jewish groups, and also among non-Jews. However, the percentage of old people was strikingly large among Sephardim; much larger than among non-Sephardim and non-Jews. In addition the proportion of large families among Sephardim was above average, certainly not smaller than among the other Jewish groups.[37] The emigration of Sephardim from well-established communities, e.g., from Bordeaux to other countries abroad was not large enough to explain the small size of such Jewish communities.[38] Neither was the interior migration large enough.[39] Further, the number of Marranos—and later of Sephardim—who left France, was always offset by newly-arrived Marranos from Spain and Portugal.[40]

37. Z. Szajkowski, "Notes on the Demography of the Sephardim in France." *Hebrew Union College Annual*, XXX (1959), 217-32.

38. Z. Szajkowski, "Jewish Emigration from Bordeaux during the Eighteenth and Nineteenth Century." *Jewish Social Studies*, XVIII (1956), pp.

39. From 1755 until 1759 the Paris Police reported on 258 Jews. In forty cases it was noted that they came from Bordeaux and Saint-Esprit, but most of them were Avignonese Jews who had settled in Bordeaux. Six other cases noted *espagnols*, or *portugais*. In 1809, 840 Jewish families (2,908 persons) lived in Paris. Eighty families (308 persons) were Sephardim, including 23 families (84 persons) of Avignonese Jews. There is information on the place of birth of 10,185 Jews of Paris in 1872 (out of the total number of 23,434 according to the official census). Of this number only 288 were born in Bordeaux and 31 in Bayonne. See L. Kahn, "Les Juifs de Paris de 1775 à 1759." *REJ*, XLIX (1904), 121-45; *Idem, Les professions manuelles*. Paris, 1885, pp. 72-73; *Idem, Les Juifs à Paris depuis le VIe siècle*. Paris, 1889, pp. 235-37; Z. Szajkowski, *Poverty and Social Welfare among French Jews*. Paris, 1954, pp. 75, 87.

40. For information on Marranos who arrived in the eighteenth century from Spain and Portugal to Bordeaux and Saint-Esprit, based on the Jewish registries of the *état civil*, see Z. Szajkowski, "Population Problems . . .," pp. 91-94.

Révah favors the idea that the Judaism of the Marranos was essentially *potential,* and changed into *real* Judaism, when they lived in a Jewish community.[41] But, the Marranos' Judaism often became just as easily a *potential* Catholicism, changing into a real one if the Marranos lived for a long period in a Catholic environment.

No comparison could be made between the Marranos of Portugal and other countries and those Marranos of France who did not openly join Jewish communities. The latters' integration with Catholics was complete, and no trace of Judaism was left among them at the end of the 18th century. There is also a theological aspect of this problem which we do not discuss here. For example, should a Marrano of Bordeaux continue to be considered one even after marriage into a fully Christian family of Marrano or non-Marrano descent? Historians cannot disregard a theological criterion in designating Marranos.

The entire problem of French Marranos who were lost to the Jewish community should be no surprise to Jewish historians of our own generation, because they witnessed similar situations during and after World War II in Poland and other countries. The lives of many modern Marranos were saved from annihilation by the Germans thanks to their non-Jewish appearance and their ability to pass as Christians and to hide the fact that they were Jews. After the liberation many of them did not rejoin the Jewish community but remained secular Gentiles, if not always Christians.

---

41. Révah, *op. cit.,* p. 55.

APPENDIX I

"Lost" Names of Marranos and Sephardim
of Bordeaux and Saint-Esprit-lès-Bayonne

Names according to Jewish sources are indicated with *.

*Abaad, Aron hijo de Jacob, 1744, 1751 (Léon, 196).
*Aeugna, Jacob, 1706, 1716 (Bxreg).
*Acuner, Isaq Yesurum de, 17th cent. (Léon, 197).
*Agnillar, 1719 (Bxreg).
*Alas, Jacob, 1729 (Bxreg).
*Alascu, 1674 (Schwab).
Aldres, Nones, 1620 (Bx, GG21).
*Alfarim, 1684 (*Factum*).
Alpalhao, Correa (*Factum*, 1768).
Alues, Manuel, 1610 (Bx, GG19).
*Anabia, Daniel & Joseph (Bxreg); Anavia, Daniel, 1748 (Bx, GG810).
Arnales, Manuel, 1685 (Bx, GG15).
Arpailhan, Harpaillan, 1670 (Bx, GG319).
*Arpuget, Samuel, 1731 (Bxreg).
*Asbede, Jacob & Moise, 1749, Riques, 1753 (Bx, GG30); Assebede, Gaspar d', 1669 (Bx, GG10); Assede, David, 1745 (Bx, GG810).
Bache, Gabriel, 1604 (Bx, GG15).
Balbedrey, Francys, 1602 (Bx, GG13).
*Balthasar, Esther (Bxreg).
*Barbada, Abraham Lopes, 1750 (Bx, GG810).
*Barbossa (Béthencourt); Barboze, Jehan, 1624 (Bx, GG25).
Barjaco, Joseph, 1729 (Bx, GG355).
*Barmaiesse, Aaron, 1721 (Bx, GG30).
*Barrabas (1684).
Bas, Diego, 1606 (Bx, GG16).
Bassan, 1767 (Bx, GG291).
Baubelde, Frañ, 1604 (Bx, GG15).

*Bazilay, Marquet (Bx, GG30); Brazilay, 1711 (Bx, GG342).
Bellisari, Francois Mendes, 1669 (Bx, GG10).
*Bergacy (1684).
*Bergary (1684).
*Bigail (1684).
*Bigaye, "juifve," 1751 (AdG, E, Rauzan, Oct. 15, 1751).
*Blanka, 1718 (Bx, GG346).
*Bon Marine, Ribca (Bxreg); Boumaren, Branquet de (1684).
Bourges, Alonae de, 17th cent. (Bx, GG15); Bourgillos, Judique (Bxreg); Burgos (1684).
Brechede, de la, 1710 (Bx, GG342).
*Caillou (1684).
*Caldes, 1743 (Bx, GG789).
*Camin, Esther (Bxreg).
*Capadose, Jacob, 1751 (AdG, E, Rauzan, Apr. 26, 1751).
*Capoone, Abraham (Bxreg).
*Carabal, Sara (Bxreg).
Carille, 1722 (Bx, GG318).
*Carnallo, Rachel, 1761 (Ba, GG-3supl.).
*Casenave, 1733 (Bx, GG295).
*Catino, Jacobi, 1651 (Léon, 195).
Chagues, Anthoyne, 1604 (Bx, GG15).
Chares, Lionel de, 1605 (Bx, GG15).
Chascan, Louis Gomes, 1630 (AdG, E, Lafite, Jan. 15, 1630).
*Choisa, Abraham & Henriques, 1737 (Bx, GG30).
*Coenadlura, Rachel Peña, 1743 (Léon, 196).
*Coitigue (Bxreg).
*Colla, 1794 (Bareg).

*Confiteiro, Jacob Nugues (Bxreg).
*Corsina, Rica (Bxreg).
*Coues, Esther, 1668 (Léon, 195).
Coureges, Dias, 1779 (Bx, GG789);
  Courrege, Ontoine, 1668 (Bx,
  GG9).
Craste, Joseph de, 1672 (Bx,
  GG15).
*Cuna, V. (Bxreg).
Dabendana, Moyze, 1751 (AdG, E,
  Rauzan, March 7, 1751).
*Dacongne (1684); Dacougne, 1789
  (Bx, GG789).
*Dagrusde, 1636 (Detcheverry, 59-
  62).
Dalbes, Fernandes, 1605 (Bx,
  GG15).
Damota, Manuel Peres, 1632 (AdG,
  E, Lafite, 1632, fol. 259).
Daragon, "docteur ez droutz, de
  nation portugaise," 1610 (Bx,
  BB, Jurade, 1610).
Darbes, Fernand, 1688 (Bx, GG16).
*Davente, Mullerqfoy de, 1645
  (Léon, 195).
Dazebede, Fernandes Martines, 1631
  (AdG, E, Lafite, 1631, fol. 703).
Degante, Manuel, 1727 (Bx, BB,
  Jurade, 1727, fol.94).
*Delsotte, Sara, 1747 (Bx, GG30).
Denitoria, Diniuzia, 1630 (AdG, E,
  Lafite, 1630, fol.21).
Derebeyre, Diogue Martin, 1685
  (Bx, GG15).
*Desisneros, 1636 (Detcheverry,
  59-62).
Dessa, 1718 (Bx, GG346).
*Desser, Abigail (Bxreg).
*Dessere, Manuel, 1622 (Bx, GG25).
*Deyossona, David, 1749 (Bx,
  GG30).
Diagbas, 1601 (Bx, GG12).
*Diera, 1636 (Detcheverry, 59-62).
*Dierx, Jacob (Bx, GG30).
Doliuere, Dominique Lopes, 1711
  (Bx, Jurade, 1711, fol.87).
*Domingue, 1716 (Bx, GG291).
*Donartey (1684).

*Escaramelo, Moyse (Bxreg).
*Escoudero, 1718 (Bx, GG346).
Espine, André Rodrigues, 1605 (Bx,
  GG15).
Farlantes, Manuel, 1596 (Bx,
  GG11).
*Fastio Ribca (Bxreg).
*Faxardo (Bxreg).
*Fenis, Mendes de, 1788 (Bx,
  CC1098).
Fenis, Moïse Mendes de, 1761 (Bx,
  Jurade, 1761, fol.47).
*Fenix, Mendes de, 1777 (Bx,
  Jurade, 1777, fol.25).
Fernãdes, Diegou, 1604 (Bx,
  GG15).
*Ficaillou (1684).
*Francoysonna, Manuel, 1605 (Bx,
  GG15).
*Freirerinero, Abraham, 1674 (Léon,
  197).
Fronsette, la, 1710 (Bx, GG342).
*Garsies (1684).
*Gonzales, Lopes, 1789 (Bx,
  GG789).
*Gornez (1684).
Gosmes Silva, Pierre, 1670 (Bx, BB,
  Jurade, 1670, fol.40).
*Gouttières, Ishac, 1765 (Ba,
  GG3sup.).
*Grande (Bxreg).
*Gravis, Jacob (Bxreg).
Gremache, 1686 (Bx, GG155-56).
*Grenouilleau, Banaventure, 1743
  (Bx, GG85, No. 210).
*Guedes, Moïse, 1775 (Ba,
  GG3sup.).
*Hocho, Dias (Bxreg).
*Ibar, 1718 (Bx, GG346).
*Ibarre, 1722 (Bx, GG293).
Jan, Sébastien, 1604 (Bx, GG15).
*Janic, Rodrigues, 1788 (Bx,
  CC1098).
*Jobar (1684).
Jouan, Francisque, 1613 (Bx,
  GG19).
*Lagonue, Rachel, 1745
  (Bx, GG810).

*Lagune, 1792 (Bx, GG797).
Lalures, Manuel, 1604
  (Bx, GG15).
*Lara, Abigail Nunes, 18th cent.
  (Bx, GG844).
Laynes, Manuel Cardose, 1659
  (Bx, BB Jurade, Jan. 1, 1659).
*Laynes, Cardoze, 1719
  (Bx, GG346).
Laze, Louis de, 1598
  (Bx, GG11).
*Leal, 1788 (Bx, GG789).
*Ladesme, 1780 (Ba, GGsup.3).
*Lehatal, Esther (Bxreg).
*Lezi, Jacobi (Bxreg).
*Liala, Abr. & Sarra, 1745
  (Bx, GG810).
*Lombresso (1684).
Louis, Vento, 1626 (Ba, GG7).
*Loxano (1684).
*Machuca (Bxreg).
*Malez (1684).
*Mariguiffe (1684).
Marthes, Balthesard de, 1603
  (Bx, GG15).
*Martin, 1636 (Detcheverry, 59-62).
Martinis, 1686 (Bx, GG155-156).
Martins (1684).
Martys, Diougue, 1604
  (Bx, GG15).
*Maxera, 1703 (AdG, C2700).
*Messe, de (1684).
*Mogata, Léa, 17th cent.
  (Léon, 195).
*Montezines, Izaac, 1745
  (Bx, GG810).
Monthesis, Bartholomi Fernande,
  1622 (Bx, GG25).
Morais, Joseph, 1775 (Bx, Jurade,
  1775, fol.48).
*Morelle, Abraham, 1738
  (Bx, Jurade, 1738, fol.102).
Morene, Michel Rodrigues, 1667
  (Bx, GG8).
Mores, Anthoine Henriques, 1626
  (Bx, GG26).
*Moymanuel, Raquel Imanuel de
  Olivera de, 1683 (Léon, 195).

*Muchagato, Isha Lopes, 1758
  (Ba GG3sup.).
*Muños, Jacob Rodrigues, 1676
  (Léon, 197).
*Nogeira, 1678 (Schwab).
*Nogueira, 1678 (Léon, 197).
*Noguira, Eliau Rodrigues, 1751
  (Ba, GG3sup.).
*Norzi, Rebecca (Bxreg).
*Nugues, Confiteiro, Jacob
  (Bxreg).
Ortis, Francisco, 1604 (Bx, GG15).
*Pachées (1684).
*Paez, François, 1790 (Bx, Jurade,
  1790, fol.53).
Pais, 1694 (Bx, GG331).
*Paiz, Pachéez de (1684).
*Pantoche (1684).
*Paradey (1684).
*Paraneanou (1684).
*Pasque (1684).
*Patto, Miriam, 1719 (Bxreg).
*Payer de Léon, David (Bxreg).
*Payes, Jacob (Bxreg).
*Pays (1684).
*Peloufe (1684).
*Pena, 1675 (Schwab).
*Penamacor, Moize Henriques, 1754
  (Bx, GG30).
*Pensse, Rachel & Salomon, 1749
  (Bx, GG810).
*Pequignes (1684).
*Peremote, 17th cent.
  (Béthencourt,, XXV, 99).
Perez, 1688 (Bx, GG276).
*Pesah, Ab. & Esther, 1745
  (Bx, GG810).
*Pesoa, Rachel, 1770 (Bx, GG30).
*Philip, Riby (Rabbi) Ephraïm
  (Bxreg).
*Pimemole (1684).
*Pinel (1684).
*Poiz, de (1684).
*Pontoche (1684).
Prera, Douard, 1605 (Bx, GG15).
*Primaute, 1727 (AmBx, GG294).
*Puita, Raquel, 1655 (Léon, 195).
*Queyla, Moise (Bxreg).

*Quinchy, Rakel & Jacob, 1748
  (Bx, GG810).
*Raitona, Sara, 1654 (Léon, 195).
*Rames, Izaac, 1742 (Bx, GG30).
*Ramos, Abram, 1742 (Bx, GG810).
*Real (1684).
*Remore, 1636 (Detchevery, 59-62).
*Remoro, 17th cent.
  (Béthencourt, XXV, 98).
*Requene, Mardochée Gutierres d^t,
  1789 (Bx, CC1098).
*Ribeirou (1684).
Rioues, Diege de, 1668 Bx, GG9).
Ripouille, 1679 (Bx, GG325).
*Romeira, Lopes, 17th cent.
  (Bx, GG292).
Romere, Alfonso, 1632 (AdG, E
  Lafite, 1632, fol.259).
Romeres, 1686 (Bx, GG275).
Romerott, Alphonse, 1617
  (Bx, GG6).
*Rouyx, 1790 (Bx, GG346).
*Roze, 1788 (Bx, CC1098).
*Saba, Ester, 1748 (Bx, GG810).
*Sainctes, Alfonse, 1604 (Bx, GG15).
*Salazar, Mendes, 17th cent.
  (Léon, 197).
Saldaigne, Sara & Aaron, 1748
  (Bx, GG810).
*Saldaner, Ribca, 18th cent.
  (Bxreg).
*Samas (1684).
*Sanches, 1705 (Bx, GG337).
*Sapateyrou (1684).
*Seijes [Seches?], 1750 (Bx, GG789).
Serabia & Serabj, Antoine Fernandes,
  1656, 1657 (Bx, GG1).
Serron, 1686 (Bx, GG155-156).
*Sespeds, Isaac Mendes, 1755
  (Ba, GG3sup.).
*Sicaillou (1684).
*Sisneres, Pierre, 1631 (AdG, E
  Lafite, 1631, fol.703).

*Siston, Francois Francia de, 1788
  (Bx, CC1098).
*Soiza, Esther (Bxreg).
*Soria, 1788 (Bx, CC1098, GG789).
*Spaelmans, 1657 (Léon, 195).
Spinosa, Ferdinand, 1708 (Bx,
  Jurade, 1708, fol. 123).
*Taboide, Raphaël & Izaac, 1744
  (Bx, GG810).
*Taives, Sarra & Abraham, 1744
  (Bx, GG810).
*Tasseres, 1788 (Bx, CC1098).
Teilles, 1716 (Bx, GG343).
*Teilles da Costa, Jacob (Bxreg).
*Telles, Jacob, 18th cent., Abraham
  1788 (Bxreg, GG1098).
Theirs, Jeham Loppes, 1625
  (Bx, GG26).
*Tinoque, Rachel, 1744
  (Bx, GG30, 810).
Tinoxo, Nunes (also Timoco), 1707
  (Bx, GG339).
*Tolede, 1721 (Bx, GG293).
*Torgi, de 1719 (Bx, GG292).
Vabelde, Frañ de, 1604
  (Bx, GG15).
*Valère, Joseph (Bxreg).
*Valbery, Juda (Bxreg).
*Vaz, Vas, also Batz (Bxreg).
*Vays de Oliveira, Abraham
  (Bxreg).
*Victoire, Isaac (Bxreg, Bx, BB8).
*Villanueba, Vaz, 1675 (Schwab).
*Villanuela, Isaq Pez, 1675
  (Léon, 197).
*Villar, Sara, 1752 (Léon, 196).
Villialougous (also Villiologier),
  Gabriel de, 1604 (Bx, GG15).
*Vinegre, 1716 (Bx, GG291).
*Vurga, Rachel de (Bxreg).
*Ximenés (Bxreg).

Appendix II

Sephardic Family Names in the Censuses of Bordeaux,
Saint-Esprit-lès Bayonne, Bidache, Peyrehorade and Paris.

1 8 0 6 - 1 8 1 0

(According to the Censuses of Jews and registries of
Jewish names 1806-1810) *

Aguillard
Albuquerque
Alexandre
Almeyda, Franco d'
Alonzo
Alvarès; Alvarès Pignero; Alvarèz de
Léon
Amar
Andrade
Athias; Attias
Avigdor
Azevedo
Baeza; Baiz
Barbude
Bargues
Baroche
Bastide
Benzacar; Benzachar
Bernal; Bernal, Rodrigues
Bizente, Fonseque
Blanche
Bologne
Bonito
Brandam
Brito; Brito, Gomez; Britos, Gommes
Butto, Gommes
Caba
Cabanac, Mendes
Caffre
Campos
Capoche, Léon; Capotte
Carance; Carance, Lopes
Carasco
Cardoso; Cardoso Gaspar; Cardoze

Correges
Carrion
Carvaillo; Carvallito; Carvallo
Casseres; Casseres, Gommes
Castelle
Castro; Castro Mimito
Cava
Cazado, Costa
Cazie
Cenegain
Chacon
Chavés
Chimenés
Chouab
Clava
Colace; Colaco
Costa Cazado
Corcos
Cordova
Corinaldy
Corro, Mendes
Cortigno; Couitigne; Coutigno
Coste
Dacosta; Dacosta Sarranotte
Dalmeyda; D'Almeyda
Dalsem
Delvaille
Dias, Lopes; Dias Pereyra
Dovalle; Duval
Ely, Rodrigues
Esdra; Esra
Fallot; Fallot Gomes
Fastia
Ferreira

---

* Ba; Bx; The Jewish Historical General Archives (Jerusalem).

Fernandes; Fernandez Patto
Ferro
Fonseque; Fonseque Bizente
Foy
Franc
Francia
Franco d'Almeyda
Frois
Furtado; Furtado, Lévy
Garcias; Garcias, Robles; Carcies; Garsias
Gaspar, Cardoso
George
Gomes Fallot; Gomes Talavera; Gomes Vaez; Gomes Brito; Gommez Britos; Gommes Butto; Gommes Casseres; Gommez
Goudrin
Gonzales
Gostallas, Guestalla
Gradis
Guichote
Guimarins
Gutières
Henriques, Rodrigues
Herrere
Hesdra
Iflax
Isidoro, Olivera
Janic, Rodrigues
Julian
Ladesme
Lagoune
Lameyra
Lapés
Lattad de Rose
Laveur
Léal
Léon; Léon, Alvarez de; Léon Boulogne
Lévy; Lévy Furtado; Lévy Martines; Lévy Recio
Lima
Lindo
Lion
Lopes; Lopes Carance; Lopes Dias; Lopes, Nonez; Lopes Pereyra;

Lopes Salvador; Lopes Tabouade; Lopes Capoche
Malendres; Melendes
Mana; Mana, Pas
Marc foy; Marqfoy
Martines, Lévy
Mathis; Mattis; Mattos
Mendes; Mendes Cabanac; Mendes Corro; Mendes Morao; Mendes Morron; Mendes Sola; Mendes Solla; Mendes Vega; Mendes Veiga
Meran
Mesquita; Mesquitta; Mesquitte
Mezes
Mimito, Castro
Moline; Molines
Monis
Monteire
Montes
Moraes; Morão; Morão, Mendes; Morea; Morere
Moran, Rodrigues; Moron, Mendes
Mugés
Navarre
Naxara
Ninor
Nobles
Noé
Nunés; Nunes Payba; Nunes Tavarez; Nunez Nunez, Lopes; Nounes
Norsy
Nouse
Oliveira, Vaez d'; Olivera; Olivera Isidoro; Olivié
Osoris
Oxeda; Oxeda, Silva d'
Pas Mana; Pas, Torrès de
Patto; Patto, Fernadez de
Payba, Nunes
Paz; Paz Pereyre
Peigna; Peigne
Peixotto
Peraire; Pereire; Pereyra, Dias; Pereyra Lopes; Pereyre; Paz; Pereyre Talad
Pessoa
Peynado

Pignero; Pignero, Alvares
Pimentel
Portugaize
Posso
Quiros
Raba
Rabello
Ramon, Tores
Raphaël
Recio, Lévy
Regidor; Reguidor, Rodrigues;
    Requidor
Riveire Ladesme
Robles; Robles Garcias; Robles
    Garcies
Rodrigues; Rodrigues Bernal; Rodri-
    gues Ely; Rodrigues, Henriques;
    Rodrigues Janic; Rodrigues Mo-
    ran; Rodrigues Reguidor; Rod-
    rigues Silva
Rophé
Rose, Lattad de
Rubio
Rubis
Sacerdote
Saci
Salsedo; Salzedo
Salvador, Lopes
Sarranotte, Dacosta
Sasportas

Sazias
Scaramella
Seba
Sèches
Sequeyra
Serano; Serrano
Silva; Silva d'Oxeda; Silva Rodrigues;
    Silvale; Silva Valle
Silveirot
Soa
Sola, Mendes; Solla, Mendes
Soreph
Soria; Soria de
Sosa; Sossa; Soussa; Souza
Souares; Souarez
Sourdis
Tabouade, Lopes
Talad, Pereyre
Talavera; Talavera, Gomes
Tavarés; Tavarez, Nunes
Torès Ramon; Torrès; Torrès de Pas
Totta
Vaez, Gomez; Vaez, d'Oliveira; Vaïz
Valéry
Valle, Silva
Vaz
Vega, Mendes; Veiga, Mendes
Victoria
Villalam; Villalan

APPENDIX III

Conversions of Sephardic Jews in France, 18th century*

1. Brettes[?] d'*Acosta*, born in Lisbon, was converted in 1764 (Cirot, 195).

2. Louis Eugenio del *Aguila*, born in Spain and circumcised in Bordeaux, was converted in 1728 (Cirot, 174).

3. Aaron *Albares Correa*, "juif de nation," the son of Isaac Albarès Correa and Rachel Rodrigue Spereyre, baptized by his parents, converted Jews themselves, and named Joseph Correa in June 1761 (Bx, GG103, No. 538).

4. Joseph Alphonse *Albares* (*A Nosseigneurs de Parlement*. [Signed by Me de Caillavet. Bordeaux, 1720? 5 pp.). His daughter Marie-Anne *Alvarez*,

---

* Unless otherwise indicated, the conversion took place in Bordeaux.

"fille legitime de Sr. Joseph Alphonse Alvarez [Albarès], cy-devant juif et nouveau converty" and of "Mle Bonaventure Grenouilleau," was baptised on Feb. 21, 1743 (Bx, GG85, No. 210).

5. Theres *Albres* [Alvares]," juive de nation," born in Portugal and daughter of Gaspard Alpres and Anne de Vas, was baptized at the age of 16 (Bx, GG38, No. 1604).

6-8. Israël *Bomarin*, "juif d'origine et actuellement Chrétien," was converted in Vannes in 1747 together with his daughters Blanche and Esther and named Anne Jules (AdG, C1087; Malvezin, 163).

9. Anne de *Campo*, was converted in 1721 (Malvezin, 157).

10. "Abjuration du judaïsme par demoiselle *Carbaille*, de Saint-Martin-de-Hinx," at Dax on July 12, 1705 (Dax, GG10).

11. The physician Joseph Cardose, son of Moyse Cardose and Marie Rodrigues of Dax; was converted there on October 10, 1705 (Dax, GG10; Malvezin, 166; *La partie de sieur Joseph Cardose* [Bordeaux, 1742]. 14 pp. Dr. G. Pery, *Histoire de la Faculté de médecine de Bordeaux* (Bordeaux, 1888), 24).

12. Marie Anne *Cardose*, "fille de nation juifve," daughter of David and Eleonore Cardose was converted on June 25, 1710 (Bx, GG60, No. 150).

13. David *Cougue*, sixteen-year-old son of Jacob and Rachel C. was converted on Jan. 25, 1722 and named Louis (Bx, GG68).

14. Claude Marie de *Costa* [Dacosta], son of Blaise D. and Catherine Silva, was converted on Sept. 4, 1738 (Bx, GG80, No. 726).

15. Francoise *Dalpuget*, daughter of Manuel and Marianne D.; she became the wife of R. Perrens (Bx, Delpit).

16. Jeanne-Catherine Salon *Dalpuget*, who probably was the sister of the above mentioned Francoise D., was converted in 1742. She died on May 5, 1781, at the age of 58 (AdG, C1087; Bx, GG392, No. 286; Malvezin, 160-61).

17. Anne *Delcampos*, "juive nouvellement convertie," 1711 (AdG, C1086).

18. Gaspard *Destrade* (Ba, FF190).

19. Louis *Duval*, "né à Bordeaux dans la religion des juifs," brother of a Jew named Delbaille, was converted at the age of 26 in 1749 (AdG, C1087).

20. M le Marg te *Emmanuel*, "juive d'origine," daughter of Abraham Emmanuel and Rachel Bénédic. On April 30, 1782, she was married in Nantes to Antoine Joseph, born in Portugal, and son of Bonaventure Joseph, probably a Marrano (Nantes, GG284).

21. Jacques Joseph Ephraïm, "né depuis environ 8 jours, fils de Jacques Joseph Ephraïm, juif, et de Marie Maïr," was baptized, probably without the knowledge of his parents, by his *nourrice* on Jan. 30, 1781 (Bx, GG405, No. 788).

22. Joseph *Fernandes*, the twenty-year-old son of Moyse F. and Philippe [?] de Soza, "de nation Juifve, natif du diocèze d'Acqz," converted on July 18, 1706 (Bx, GG54).

23. *Fossa* [Sossa?] (AdG, C1087-88).

24. Andrée Elisabeth *Francia*, daughter of Jacques F. and Rachel Pinto.

was converted at the age of 15 on May 5, 1755 (Bx, GG97, No. 490, Delpit).

25. Esther *Francia,* daughter of Abraham and Esther F., was converted in 1757 at the age of 22 (Malvezin, 162-63).

26. Louise-Marie *Francia,* was converted in Versailles in 1757 (AdG, C1087).

27. Marie Joseph Francoise *Francia,* "juive de nation," daughter of Antoine F. and Angélique Médine, was converted on July 8, 1771, when she was about twenty-two years old (Bx, GG109).

28. In 1731, Marie *Furtade,* was forcibly converted in Bayonne and given the name of "Sister of Saint-Charles" (Léon, 135-36).

29. Esther *Garsie* [*Garcie*], daughter of Isaac G. and Esther Campos, was converted at the approximate age of 15 on March 24, 1741, and given the name of Marie Anne. On Nov. 27, 1754, she was married to Jacques de Launay (Bx, 376, No. 250).

30. Therese *Gaspard Albres,* "juifve de nation," daughter of G.A. and Anne Vas, converted on Oct. 30, 1695 (Bx, ii 21, fol.96; GG38, No. 1604; Malvezin, 152; Cirot, 173).

31. Thérèse *Gaspart Laville,* wife of Jérôme Lamouroux, "juive de nation," was converted on July 12, 1721 (Bx, reg. de la Jurade).

32. Jean *Gomez,* was converted in Dax on May 25, 1709, at the age of 30 (Dax, GG10).

33. Rachel *Gomès,* eight-year-old, daughter of Jean G. Delbaille, was converted in 1722 (AdG, C1082, 1086; Malvezin, 153-55).

34. Mathieu *Gonsales,* "juif de nation," 17th century (Ba, GG229, No. 20bis).

35. Esther *Gradis,* daughter of Antoine G., was converted on Sept. 27, 1715, and named Suzanne Urdine (Bx, GG65; AdG, C1086; Malvezin, 158).

36. Suzanne Elizabeth *Henriques* of La Rochelle, was converted in 1714 when she was about twenty (AdG, C1086; Malvezin, 152; Cirot, 195).

37. Hayman *Isaac,* born in London, was converted in Nantes on Jan. 23, 1753 at the approximate age of 71 and received the name of Patrice (Nantes, GG225).

38. "L'ex-juif *Léon*" (Bx, ms. 712, vol. 12, p. 554).

39. Abraham de *Lévi,* was converted on Nov. 21, 1667, and was given the name of François. He may have been of Avignon origin (Bx, GG9, No. 1017).

40. Marie-Louise-Claudine *Linde,* the seventeen-year-old daughter of David Li and Esther Lopes de Pas, was converted in 1759; she was known as "soeur Victoire" (AdG, C1088; Malvezin, 162).

41-45. On Aug. 23, 1729, the five children of Melendez *Lisoba* were converted in Bayonne. The children whose names were Pierre Antoine, Joseph Antoine, Cristobal Antoine, Jean Marie, Marie-Anne-Rose, ranged in age from 11 months to 15 years (Léon, 138).

46. Antoinette *Loppes,* twelve-year-old daughter of Sébastien L. and Izabeau Mendes, was converted in 1706 [?] (AdG, C1088; Malvezin, 160).

47. Isaac *Lopez Raphael,* was converted in Dax on Apr. 28, 1734, at the age of 23 (Dax, GG14).

48. Cadette *Lopes de Pas,* daughter of Joseph Lopes de Pas and

Angélique Francia, "juifs de nation," was converted on June 19, 1761, and received the name of Marie-Augustine (Bx, GG103, No. 575; Malvezin, 161; F. de Lamontaigne, *Chronique bordelaise*. Bordeaux, 1926, 74).

49. Marie-Magdelaine-Charlotte *Lopes de Pas,* daughter of Louis Lopes de Pas and Rebecca Gradis, was converted on Jan. 19, 1770, and was known as "soeur Marie-Angélique." She died on Jan. 15, 1780 (AdG, H, Madelon-nettes 1; Bx, GG403).

50. *"Lopez,* juif rénégat" (Bx, ms. 713-1, vol. 5, p. 355, 1788).

51. Louis *Martial Daguillard,* son of Moïse D. of Port au Prince, was converted on Apr. 15, 1762 at the age of 15 (Bx, GG103, No. 1595).

52. Charles *Mendes,* 1778 (AdG, C99).

53. Charles *Mendes,* son of Moïse M. and Rachel Peixotte, was converted on July 23, 1770, when he was about 32 years of age and was given the name of Charles-Antoine-François-Hyacinthe (Bx, GG108, No. 1117).

54. Jean de *Mendes,* 1776. Known as Blondin. See Z. Szajkowski, in *Historia Judaica*, XVIII (1956), 113.

55. Moise *Mendes,* "un garcon, juif de nation," the twenty-year-old son of Moise Mendes de Finis and Rachel Peixotte, was converted on Apr. 22, 1759, and received the name of Louis-Armand Mendes (Bx, GG101, Nos. 366, 617).

56. Rachel *Mendez,* daughter of Jacob M. (alias Jacolin) and Judith Bas was converted in Saint-Esprit in 1707 (Léon, 138).

57. Rebecca *Mendes,* the thirty-six-year-old daughter of Mardochée Mendes France and Rachel Peixotto and wife of Isaac Peixotto, converted with her father's permission on June 26, 1755(?), and given the name of Françoise-Armande (Bx, GG97, No. 629; AdG, C1087; Malvezin, 163).

58. Moize *Metz* of Bordeaux, converted in 1758 in Versailles; most probably was an Ashkenazic Jew (AdG, C1087).

59. Jeanne *Meses,* fourteen-year-old daughter of Alexandre M. and Blanche Gomes, was converted on Feb. 21, 1730 (Bx, GG74, No. 765).

60. Abigail, Rachel, and Rica *Mezes,* daughters of Alexandre M. were forcibly converted in 1728. They were 14, 12 and 10 years at the time (AdG, C1086; *Ordonnance. Du quinzieme Juillet 1728.* Bordeaux, 1728. 3 pp.; Malvezin, 155-56).

61. *Nonès,* and her two nephews Nonès Pinto were converted prior to 1732 (Malvezin, 164). Probably the same as No. 63.

62. Esther *Nunes Dacosta,* "juifve de nation," was converted on June 17, 1729, at the age of 17 and was given the name of Marie (Bx, GG72, No. 1297).

63. *Nones* and *Pinto,* two Jews from Bordeaux, were converted in Toulouse on July 12, 1732 (*Relation de la cérémonie de baptême, faite dans l'Eglise Métropolitaine Saint-Etienne de Toulouse . . . le 12 Juillet 1732.* n.p., n.d. 4 pp.).

64. Abraham *Paiba,* "juif de nation, né à Londres," nineteen-year-old son of Moise and Rachel de P., was converted on July 18, 1759, and given the name Francois Armand (Bx, GG101, No. 618).

65. Cadette de *Pas,"* "petite juive," was converted in 1758 at the age of 12 (AdG, C1088).

66. Abraham *Passe* (*Exhortation* . . ., par M. [Jean] Bruté. n.p., n.d. 4 pp.).

67. "Marie Peichote, agee de 18 ans, convertie de la religion juifve à la romaine," was the daughter of Mendes, a converted Jew himself. She died on Feb. 16, 1759 (Bx, GG380).

68. Charles *Peixotto* of Bordeaux, converted on Apr. 18, 1781, in Spain (British Museum, ms. 21445, pp. 153-54).

69. Rachel-Marie-Jeanne *Pexiotte*, daughter of Abraham P. and Ricote Lopes. On Feb. 10, 1763, she was married, against her father's will, to the Christian Bertrand-Léon Chevaux (Bx, GG557, No. 683).

70. Claude *Perere*, was converted on Feb. 14, 1721, when he was about 42 years old (Ad Seine inf., D).

71. *Pereyre* aine, converted prior to 1749 (AdG, C1087; Malvezin, 167).

72. Joseph *Nunès Pereyre* (Bx, registre de la Jurade, fol.169, Jan. 26, 1760).

73. Esther *Pexeau de Léon*, "une juifve de nation, cy devant nommée Esther, a qui on a donné le nom de Marie Marguerite," daughter of Joseph Pexeau de Léon and Degrace," portugais de nation, Juifs de religion," was converted on Aug. 3, 1768, at the approximate age of 18 (Bx, GG107, No. 111; AdG, C3774).

74. Esther *Pimentel*, born in Montpellier on Jan. 1, 1756, daughter of Juda P., "juif portugais . . . et d'une femme juive aussi portugaise son epouse dont la dite Esther ne s'est point rappelle le nom," was converted in Rouen on Apr. 18, 1772, and received the name of Marie-Dominique Adelaïde (Ad Seine inf., D).

75. Charles-Honoré *Pinto*, was converted in 1750[?] (Malvezin, 165).

76. Jean *Rodrigue*, converted in Nantes in 1711 (Nantes, HH182).

77. Aaron *Rodrigues*, was converted in Dax on Apr. 4, 1731, when he was about twenty years old (Dax, GG14).

78. Isaac Rodrigues, was converted in Dax on Aug. 30, 1733, at the age of 50 (Dax, GG14).

79. Abigaïl *Romaine*, daughter of Cardose, "de nation juive," was converted on Dec. 23, 1730, at the age of about 18 and received the name of Marie (Bx, GG75).

80. *Salomon*, "juif de profession," son of Abraham and Sara, was converted in Nantes on Jan. 14, 1723. He signed the act of baptism in Hebrew (Nantes, GG497).

81. Catherine *Salon*, most probably of Avignon origin (AdG, C1086-88).

82. Sara *Silves*, daughter of Abraham S. and Rose Loppes, was converted on Dec. 22, 1722, at the approximate age of 21 (Bx, GG110).

83. Moyse *Fernandez*, 48 years old; he married Marguerite de Solze on Sep. 1706 (Bx, GG54, No. 721).

84. Charles *Sossa*, son of Isaac S. and Esther Rodrigues de Léon, converted in 1718 (AdG, C1086).

85. Isaac *Sossa*, born prior to their marriage to the above named Isaac S. and Esther Rodrigues de Léon, was converted in 1718 (Malvezin, 164).

86. Marie-Cathérine-Henriette-Jean-Luc *Sylva*, daughter of the physician Sylvia and his wife Rachel Lopes Dias, "juifs de religion," was converted on June 30, 1778, at the approximate age of 22 (Bx, GG116, No. 512).

87. Moise *Telles Dacosta,* son of Samuel T.D. and Sara Gradis, was converted on Apr. 14, 1768, at the age of 42 and was given the name of François (Bx, GG106, No. 1723; Malzevin, 164).

88. Eléonore *Telles Dacosta,* 6 years old, daughter of the above named converted Jew Moïse T.D., was baptized on Apr. 14, 1768 (Bx, GG106, No. 1724; Malvezin, 164).

89. *Telles Dacosta,* sister of the same Moïse T.D., was converted in 1768 (Bx, GG106, No. 1724).

90. *Telles Dacosta,* son of the above named Moïse T.D., was converted in 1768 (Bx, GG106, No. 1724).

91. Marie-Thérèse Tinoë, was converted in 1731 (Malvezin, 160).

92. X, was converted in Toulouse, again became a Jew in Amsterdam; and later he was sentenced to death in Flandres (Cirot, 57).

THE DEMOGRAPHIC ASPECTS OF JEWISH EMANCIPATION IN FRANCE DURING THE FRENCH REVOLUTION

I

Mobility Restrictions Against Jews During the Old Regime

PRIOR to the Revolution of 1789 the Jews of France, numbering about 40,000, enjoyed no freedom of movement.

There were 95 Jewish communities in Alsace in 1689 (522 families), 129 in 1716 (1,269 families), and 182 in 1784 (19,707 Jews forming 3,913 families). These were for the most part small communities, for Jews were not allowed to live in the largest Alsatian cities. Eighty-seven of the 129 communities in 1716 consisted of 1 to 10 families each and 34 of 11 to 25 families each. In 1784 only 16 communities had 50 or more Jewish families each. Most communities—exactly 111—were comprised 1 to 25 families each.[1] The situation of the Alsatian Jews was further complicated by the fact that the 182 cities and villages where they were permitted to live belonged to no less than sixty-one different owners: the King, the Church authorities, and various

[1] E. de Neyremand, "Dénombrement des familles israélites en Alsace, années 1689 et 1716," *Revue d'Alsace*, X (1859), 564-68; *Dénombrement général des juifs tolérés en la Provice d'Alsace en exécution des lettres patentes... du 10 Juillet 1784* (Colmar, 1785), 386 pp.; *Supplément au dénombrement . . .* [Colmar, 1875], 2 *pp.*; reprinted in *Les Juifs d'Alsace doivent-ils être admis au droit de citoyens* (Paris, 1790), pp. 248-51; G. Hemerdinger, "Le Dénombrement des israélites d'Alsace," *REJ.*, XLII (1901), 253-64; idem, "La Population israélite en Alsace. Recensement de 1784, 1860 et 1895," *Univers israélite*, LVIII, 1 (1902-03).

Originally published in *Historia Judaica*, vol. XXI (1959).

seigniors, and each of them pursued his own interests at the Jews' expense.[2]

In the city of Metz the Jews were continuously forced to defend their right of residence, while in the province of Metz they were hardly tolerated. A few months before the outbreak of the Revolution the governor of the province of Metz permitted Jewish peddlers to reside in Verdun for no more than a few days at a time, but the city officials protested against even this limited concession.[3] In Lorraine only 180 Jewish families were permitted to live in a total of 52 communities.[4]

Even the privileged Sephardic Jews could not move freely. The royal letters patent granted to them were valid only in the territory under the jurisdiction of the Bordeaux Parliament. Sephardic and Avignonese Jewish merchants from Bordeaux and Saint-Esprit-lès-Bayonne and from the papal province were driven out from many large commercial centers, for instance, Dijon, Poitiers, Orléans, Pau, Cognac, Rochefort, Saintes, etc. A memorandum submitted in 1788 by the Sephardic Jews to the Minister, Chrétien-Guillaume Lamoignen de Malesherbes, contained a plea for the right of residence in the whole of France.[5]

In Paris, where they had no legal status, the Jews, who numbered about 700, were only tolerated before 1789. Four Jewish communities existed in the papal province of Avignon and Comtat Venaissin. Their status was often described as good; however, this was more legend than reality. Small

---

[2] See Appendix I.

[3] Z. Szajkowski, *The Economic Status of the Jews in Alsace, Metz and Lorraine, 1648-1789* (New York, 1954), pp. 31-38; *Archives israélites*, XXVII (1866), 1097.

[4] L. Vanson, "Imposition sur les Juifs en Lorraine dans l'ancien régime," *Revue juive de Lorraine*, IX (1933), Nos. 98-99; *idem*, "Curieuses requêtes des Juifs," *ibid.*, X-XI (1934-35), Nos. 109-121.

[5] Szajkowski, "The Jewish Status in Eighteenth-Century France and the 'Droit d'Aubaine'," *Historia Judaica*, XIX (1957), 147-49; H. Léon, *Histoire des Juifs de Bayonne* (Paris, 1893), p. 153. Concerning the Sephardim a curious detail should be noted. A group of Jews of Amsterdam requested the city council of Charleville (in the department of Ardennes after 1789) for permission to settle there. It was granted by the city council on September 27, 1649. Departmental archives of Ardennes, E 677, Charleville, règlements pp. 57-58.

Jewish communities were permitted in Marseilles, Nîmes, Montpellier, Lyons, and a few other cities.[6]

II

RESTRICTIONS AGAINST JEWISH MOBILITY DURING THE REVOLUTION

Not all restrictions against the mobility of Jews were abolished at the outbreak of the Revolution in 1789. The Jews of Alsace and the neighboring departments were surrounded by so many enemies that their elementary right to exist was in jeopardy at the very time they were fighting for full emancipation.

At the beginning of the Revolution a large number of communities, mostly of Upper Alsace, were scenes of anti-Jewish riots.[7] In May, 1790, an Alsatian pamphleteer demanded "an end to their [the Jews'] enormous population which is threatening to engulf the rest of our inhabitants."[8] The Colmar petition of April 25, 1790, which opposed Jewish emancipation and called for the expulsion of Jews, was followed by similar petitions from Soultz, Altkirch, Huningue and eighty of its surrounding villages and other places in Alsace, as well as from the former province of Metz and Lorraine.[9] In August, 1790, the Jews were attacked in

[6]   I. Loeb, *Biographie d'Albert Cohn* (Paris, 1878), p. 27; H. Monin, "Les Juifs de Paris à la fin de l'ancien régime," *REJ.*, XXIII (1891), 85; Szajkowski, "Jewish Motifs in the Folk Culture of Comtat in the 17th-19th Centuries," *Yivo Bleter*, XIX (1942), 337 (Yiddish); S. Kahn, *Notice sur les israélites de Nîmes* (Nîmes, 1901), p. 29; *idem*, "Les Juifs de Montpellier au 18e siècle," *REJ.*, XXXIII (1896), 294-95; Alfred Lévy, *Notice sur les israélites de Lyon* (Paris, 1894), pp. 20-24.

[7]   Szajkowski, "Anti-Jewish Riots in Alsace during the Revolutions of 1789, 1830, and 1848," *Zion*, XX (1955), 82-102 (Hebrew).

[8]   *Avis aux Alsaciens* (no place, [Mai, 1790]), p. 12.

[9]   *Très humble et très respectueuse Adresse . . . de la Commune de Colmar. . . . le 25 Avril 1790* (n.p., n.d.), 4 pp.; *Demütigste und ehrerbietigste Bittschrift an die National-Versammlung* (n.p., n.d.), 8 pp. [by Huningue]; "Notes et documents pour servir à l'histoire de la Révolution en Alsace," *Revue d'Alsace*, XVI (1865), 234-36; Charles Hoffman, *L'Alsace au dix-huitième siècle*, IV (Colmar, 1907), 520-23; M. Ginsburger, *Histoire de la communauté israélite de Soultz* (Strasbourg, 1939), p. 40; departmental archives of Moselle, L 525 (petition of the district of Sarreguemines against

Scherwiller, and in the beginning of 1791, in Marmoutier
(Lower Rhine). In February, 1791, the district of Mutzig
asked the departmental *Directoire* for permission to apply
a statute of 1759 against the Jews.[10]

In 1790 the Jews of Niederenheim (Lower Rhine)
warned that, if the persecutions against them continued,
they would be forced to emigrate abroad.[11] That the Jews
did not easily give up is attested by an incident that Dominicus Schmutz, a Christian of Colmar, noted in his diary.
In 1790 the Christian population of Wintzenheim proposed
to use force to banish a Jew. The latter was not intimidated
and hired for his protection a detachment of the regiment
of Neufbrisach. Because the soldiers were refused permission to attend a local dance of Christian youths, a fight
broke out in the course of which a girl was slain and a man
wounded. Three soldiers were arrested and the Jew was
forced to pay all expenses.[12]

The liberal Alsatian historian Rodolphe Reuss noted in
his introduction to a collection of documents on Jews in the
Lower Rhine during the Revolution that the anti-Jewish
feeling sprang principally, not from religious bigotry, but
from the Jacobins' hatred of speculators. However, most
of the documents cited by Reuss consist of complaints
against Jews for trying to settle in places that had been
forbidden to them during the old regime.[13] In 1790 the
Alsatian Jews still paid protection money to the King and
to local seigniors.[14]

According to the letters patent of July 10, 1784, which

Jews, Sept. 25, 1790); Robert Parisot, *Histoire de Lorraine*, III (Paris,
1924), 22.

[10] Rod. Reuss, "L'Antisémitisme dans le Bas-Rhin pendant la Révolution
(1790-1793), nouveaux documents inédits," *REJ.*, LXVIII (1914), 249,
252-53; 247; P. Hildenfinger, "Actes du district de Strasbourg...," *REJ.*,
LX (1910), 241.

[11] "...au point qu'ils se voient forcés de chercher leur pain sous un
autre ciel"; departmental archives of Lower Rhine, L-1-825 (minute of
October 2, 1790).

[12] Julien Sée, *Hausbuch von Dominicus Schmutz, Bürger zu Colmar*
(Colmar, 1878), p. 94.

[13] Reuss (*supra*, n. 10), 247.

[14] *Pétition des Juifs établis en France adressée à l'Assemblée Nationale
le 28 janvier 1790* (Paris, 1790), p. 100.

aimed at limiting the number of Jews, Alsatian Jews had
no right to marry without express permission from the King.
Newly wedded couples always faced a desperate search for a
place to settle. Very often local authorities prevented Jews
from marrying even when they had royal permits. This
situation persisted until after the outbreak of the Revolution,
for the *cahiers de doléances* of Haguenau-Wissembourg and
other places sought to prevent marriages by Jews.[15] On
August 14, 1789, the city council of Osthoffen complained
that the number of Jewish families there had increased from
three to eighteen. In 1790, Bischeim refused to let Alexandre
Libmann-Lazare establish a home there, although in 1772
he had obtained permission to reside in Alsace, but in another
community (Brumath).

On January 25, 1790, the King granted Nathan Lazard
of Fegersheim permission to marry, but the city council
ordered the rabbi not to perform the marriage ceremony.
Lazard appealed to the higher authorities of the district of
Strasbourg, which had no alternative but to recognize the
royal authorization and, accordingly, on December 11, 1790,
ordered the city council of Fegersheim not to interfere
with Lazard's plans. Fegersheim then raised objections to
the establishment of homes by Jews who were newcomers
and again refused to allow a Jew, Macholem Abraham, to
marry a girl named Bessel from Mutzig. In 1790 also, the
city council of Wintzenheim decided to deny migrant Jews
the right to settle there. Although on December 12, 1788,
Isaac Hirtzel obtained permission to settle in Zelwiller, in
April, 1791, he was ordered to leave the place. Only the
intervention of the district authorities of Upper and Lower
Rhine in many such cases compelled the city councils to
respect the royal permits for Jews to marry.

Among the numerous instances of opposition to formation of new family units by Jews we may mention the cases
of Aaron and Paul Lévy of Thann (September 11, 1790);
Raphaël Ziffy of Mühlheim, who wanted to settle in Bischeim

---

[15] M. Liber, "Les Juifs et la convocation des États Généraux," *REJ.*,
LXIII (1912), 188.

(November 24, 1790); David Meyer of Bolsenheim, who was attacked by a mob of Christians because he wanted to settle in Habsheim (March 2 and April 12, 1791); Jacques Wolf of Obersteinbrunn (September 27, 1790); Abraham Ulmo of the same place, who wanted to settle in Sierentz (June 14, 1791); Meyer Dreyfus and Marc Dreyfus of Uffheim (February 22, and March 3, 1791); Jacques Ditisheim and Schwob of Hegenheim (May 18, 1791). On other occasions the higher district authorities prevented Jews from marrying and settling legally, for instance, in the case of a Jew of Osthoffen on July 31, 1790. On February 15, 1791, the city council of Odratzheim entered a protest against permitting Jewish marriages.

Other city councils levied high taxes on Jewish marriages: In 1790, Jacques Lévy of Mutzig complained that he had been forced to pay 72 livres for the marriage of his son, and Manuel Geschen of Quatzenheim likewise the sum of 120 livres. It was more than two years after the outbreak of the Revolution before these chicaneries were halted by the decree of September 27, 1791, which granted full citizenship to the Ashkenazic Jews. Until then the district and departmental authorities often refused to interfere with lower authorities in favor of Jews on the ground that the National Assembly had ordered them only to protect the Jews, but did not grant the Jews the right to settle freely. The departmental authorities claimed that they had to wait for a clear-cut decision of the National Assembly on the status of Jews. This happened in the cases of Emmanuel Bloch of Hattstatt, who tried to settle in Lingolsheim (November 15, 1790), and of Samson Isaac of Uttenheim who, having obtained a royal permit dated February 25, 1789, tried to marry a girl from Fegersheim and to settle there (May 19, 1790).[16]

[16] Hildenfinger (*supra*, n. 10), 238-43; Reuss, *op. cit.*, 247-55; *idem*, "Arrêtés du Directoire du département du Haut-Rhin..," *REJ.*, LXXV (1922), 45-47, 49, 55, 58, 60-61, 63. It should be mentioned that in his anti-Jewish paper published in *Publiciste* of February, 1806, Bonald (1767-1840) advocated the restrictions of the Jews' right to marry; J. Hours, "Un Précurseur oublié de l'antisémitisme français: le vicomte de Bonald," *Cahiers sioniens*, IV (1956), 165-69.

Even after the Jews were granted full citizenship, on February 1, 1793, the city council of Soultz demanded that a Jew pay 66 livres for residence rights.[17]

No Jews were allowed to reside in Colmar, which was the capital of the province of Alsace during the old regime. In 1789 five single Jews lived there. In 1792, two more single Jews settled in Colmar, and in 1793 the first Jewish couple, Jacob Meyer and his wife Féanne Lévy. In the same year, on April 13, 1793, the district of Colmar accused the Jews of speculation, of preparing food for the German armies in case of an invasion of France, and of proposing to the Pope a joint fight against France. The council requested the expulsion of the Jews. In 1794 two more couples settled in Colmar and in 1795-1798 another thirteen Jews, including some couples, joined the first Jewish settlers in that city. All of them came from the smaller Alsatian places of Bergheim, Buxwiller, Hagenthal, Hattstatt, Jungholz, Ostheim, Rixheim, Wettolsheim, Wintzenheim. With the exception of Herlisheim these were communities of the Upper Rhine department, of which Colmar was the capital. It should be observed that these Jews were all single persons or childless couples. It seems that Jewish families with children were as yet afraid to settle in the unfriendly city. In later years the number of Jews in Colmar rose rapidly: 260 in 1818, 761 in 1841, 1,128 in 1861.[18]

Even after the outbreak of the Revolution the city of Strasbourg sought to oust Jews who had settled there against the city's wishes on the strength of the royal letters patent granted in 1775 to Cerfberr. In May, 1793, the authorities of the Strasbourg district forwarded to the city council a list of Jews who had left Bischeim for Strasbourg, together with an order to keep an eye on them. On December 10, 1793, the military authorities of Strasbourg ordered the expulsion from the city of newly arrived Jewish families. The official reason for such an order was the scarcity of

[17] Ginsburger (*supra*, n. 9), p. 40.
[18] Departmental archives of Upper Rhine, L 645; city archives of Colmar, censuses of Jews.

food and the presumption that these families came to Strasbourg in order to evade the law (*pour se soustraire à la loi*).
In June or in the beginning of July, 1794, the Jews complained that they were not allowed to visit the city of Strasbourg on certain days. Other people made exaggerated
statements about an invasion of the city by a considerable
number of Jews.[19]

During the Alsatian anti-Jewish riots of 1789 Jews took
refuge in Mulhouse, which was a free city in the old regime.
However, they were not allowed to settle there. Only in
1798, after Mulhouse became a French city and Jewish
emancipation was a well-established fact, did Jews settle
there, the first of them being Meyer Hirsch. By 1808 the
number of Jews in Mulhouse reached 165 and in 1822, 400,
in a total population of 9,000.[20] The same situation prevailed
in smaller places. In May, 1791, the city council of Bischeim
resolved that newly arrived Jewish families would not be
permitted to settle there.[21]

III

LATER RESTRICTIONS

During the First Empire Napoleon I's anti-Jewish
policy limited Jewish mobility. Article 16 of the "Ignominious Decree" (*Décret infâme*) of March 17, 1808, prohibited migrant French Jews from settling in Alsace and
foreign Jews from settling in France for other than agricultural work. The local administration refused to register
marriages of Alsatian Jews with women from other departments, and Alsatian Jews were even refused permission to

[19] Szajkowski, "The Jewish Problem in Alsace, Metz and Lorraine on
the Eve of the Revolution of 1789," *Jewish Quarterly Review*, XLIV (1954),
218; city archives of Strasbourg, minutes of the *Corps municipal*, IV, 497-98
(May 4, 1793), 1020-21 (Dec. 10, 1793); *Copie de la pétition par plusieurs
citoyens du Bas-Rhin, à la Convention Nationale* (Colmar, [1794]), 7 pp.
The German Professor Christoph Meiners wrote about 8,000 Jews living in
Strasbourg; *Beschreibung einer Reise nach Stuttgart und Strassburg* (Göttingen,
1803), pp. 149-50.

[20] René Hirschler, *Les Juifs à Mulhouse* ([Mulhouse], 1938), p. 5.

[21] Departmental archives of Upper Rhine, L 645.

move to other departments.[22]   During the Napoleonic wars Ashkenazic Jews were denied permission to settle near the Spanish border.[23]

It is possible that many Jews found ways of evading the restrictions. On the other hand, the Jewish consistories, in discouraging paupers, were in general unsympathetic to newcomers. In 1812, the Paris consistory handed the police a list of thirty penniless Jews marked for expulsion.[24]

Some villages and cities remained closed to Jews even in later periods of the nineteenth century. As late as 1815 it was still impossible for a Jew to reside in Oloron (Basses-Pyrénées). In 1844 the editor of Les Archives israélites reported that Sélestat, Roffach, and other Alsatian towns tolerated Jews who came there to do business only on a day-to-day basis, and would not permit them to settle.[25]

After the emancipation, while officially the Jews were almost entirely free to immigrate to new communities, they continued to live in the old ghettos or in adjacent streets. Possibly in some instances they still felt safe only there. On December 29, 1790, the district of Benfeld (Lower Rhine) requested the restriction of Jewish inhabitants to ghettos with locked gates.[26] In 1806, the prefect of Moselle noted that since 1793 only twenty-nine Jewish families had left the ghetto of Metz and settled in other parts of the city. Even after 1830, the other parts of the city were called *Mâqôm* by the Jews.[27] In Nancy there was no official ghetto during the old regime, but most of the Jews there lived on the *rue Saint François*. In 1808, almost all the Jews of Nancy lived around the synagogue, in a sort of freely formed

---

[22] Robert Anchel, *Napoléon et les Juifs* (Paris, 1928), pp. 336-47.

[23] Pierre Genevray, "Les Juifs des Landes sous le Premier Empire," *REJ.*, LXXIV (1922), 129.

[24] Anchel, *op. cit.*, pp. 234-35.

[25] *Archives israélites,* IV (1843), 93; V (1844), 467.

[26] Js. Foesser, *Meistratzheim* (Strassburg, 1939), p. 363.

[27] S. Posener, "The Immediate Economic and Social Effects of the Emancipation of Jews in France," *Jewish Social Studies,* I (1930), 285; A. Lipman, *Un Grand Rabbin français, Benjamin Lipman* (1819-1866) (Paris, 1923), pp. 5-6. In 1844, 1,929 persons lived in the former ghetto of Metz; 598 of them were Christians. O. Terquem, *Quelques réflexions à propos d'une lettre* (Metz [1845]), 16 pp.

ghetto.[28] Only after the Revolution of 1830 did Carpentras
Jews begin to settle outside the ghetto. During the Revolution Armand Lunel's grandfather moved from Carpentras
to Saint-Andiol, but in the time of the Restoration of 1814
he was forced to return to the Carpentras ghetto. In the
eighteen-twenties the Jews of Saint-Esprit-lès-Bayonne, a
suburb of Bayonne, were still not tolerated in Bayonne
itself.[29]

In such an atmosphere it was a miracle that the Jews
were able to withstand local anti-Jewish pressure and to
increase in numbers. This was possible only because of the
sympathetic attitude of the federal revolutionary authorities
of Paris, although some commissioners sent from Paris to
departmental centers did express anti-Jewish feelings.[30] What
may be called the demographic aspect of Jewish emancipation will be the subject of the following sections.

IV

The Increase of Large Jewish Communities

The Jewish population of Alsace increased from 19,707,
according to the census of 1784, to 26,363 in 1808-1810,
that is, by 24.2 percent. One direct result of the Jewish
emancipation was the formation of large communities.
Whereas, during the old regime, there were no Jewish communities with as many as 500 Jews (Wintzenheim, the largest Alsatian community, had only 430 Jews), in 1808, 5
communities existed with 500 or more Jews each. The growth

[28] J. Godechot, "Les Juifs de Nancy de 1789 à 1795," *REJ.*, LXXVI
(1928), 7; André Gain, "La Population juive de Nancy en 1808," *Revue juive
de Lorraine*, IX (1933), 292; Daniel Kahn, "Le Ghetto de Nancy," *ibid.*, VIII
(1932), 253-56.

[29] City Library of Carpentras, Barjavel's Notes, 1217, fol. 166; Armand
Lunel, *Nicolo Peccavi* (Paris, 1926), pp. 110-111; *Nouvelle chronique de la
ville de Bayonne*, par un Bayonnais (Bayonne, 1827), p. 151.

[30] Alexandre Weill wrote correctly in his memories: "Si le gouvernement
n'eût pas été plus humain, plus libéral, plus tolérant que la population alsacienne,
les Juifs eussent tous été, sinon exterminés, du moins pillés et expulsé"; *Ma
jeunesse*, I (Paris, 1888), 57.

of the Jewish population was even more striking in Lorraine, where 180 families (990 persons) were officially permitted to live in 52 communities by letters patent of 1752. In 1808-1810 the number of Jews there totaled 10,545 in 168 communities. In Nancy the number of Jews rose from about 40 families in 1789 to—according to one census—739 persons. Sixty-eight Jews lived in Strasbourg in 1784 and 1,467 in 1808-1810; in Haguenau, 325 and 639 in the respective years; in Hegenheim, 409 and 639; in Dürmenach, 340 and 460.[31]

According to a register of Jews in Nancy in the years 1808-1810, 175 Jews had settled there prior to 1789 and 454 in the period 1789-1809. The rest of over 700 Jews were born in Nancy itself. Most family heads, however, were not natives of Nancy, while their wives and children formed the bulk of those born in this city. Only in sixty cases was the entire family—husband, wife, and children—born in Nancy.[32] In Lunéville (Meurthe) the number of Jews increased from 11 in 1752 to 322 in 1808. Only 9 out of 57 Jewish family heads of Lunéville were born there; 8 of them were natives of Metz, and the others came from outside communities.[33] In some Lorraine communities the number of Jews remained the same (Mitting, Lahgatt, Deutz), or even diminished as a result of immigration to larger communities.

The story of Dijon (Côte-d'Or) is one of the most striking examples of the creation of a large Jewish community after the emancipation period. No Jews had been allowed to live there during the old regime. In 1790, a few Alsatian Jews from communities where anti-Jewish riots had occurred at the beginning of the Revolution, requested permission to settle in Dijon and "to exercise their religion, to have their cemetery and to be listed as active citizens."

[31] Posener (*supra*, n. 27), 282-83; *idem*, "Les Juifs sous le Premier Empire: les statistiques générales," *REJ.*, XCIV (1933), 157.

[32] City archives of Nancy, 1 F 1-2. Compare with André Gain, who published another register of 855 Jewish declarations of names in Nancy; *Revue juive de Lorraine*, Nos. 100-108 (Register E 31 in the city archives and 2 E 603 in the departmental archives of Meurthe-et-Moselle).

[33] Departmental archives of Meurthe-et-Moselle, V 8.

In 1798 there were 28 Jewish families in Dijon; in 1820, 45; in 1830, 59; in 1840, 65 families. One hundred and ten out of 233 Jews, according to a Dijon census of 1809, were born in Dijon itself.[34] It seems that most of the Alsatian Jews who settled in Lyon (Rhône) during the Revolution also came from communities that had suffered anti-Jewish riots.[35]

Many more places of the eighteenth century Metz province and of Lorraine (which later formed the departments of Moselle and Meurthe), where few Jews lived during the old regime, became large Jewish communities.[36] On the other hand, in many other places where only a few Jews had been tolerated during the old regime no Jews remained in 1806-1808.[37] In the Lower Rhine 5 Jewish communities with a total of 228 Jews, according to the census of 1784, had completely disappeared by 1806, according to a census of August 15 of that year.[38]

The Jews took advantage of their hard-won freedom of movement to settle in new communities, but not in a very large number of new places. In 1784 Alsatian Jews lived in 182 communities and in 1808 in 203 communities. In Lorraine the number of Jewish communities was increased

[34] Departmental archives of Côte-d'Or, L 495; census of Dijon, 1809 (in the General Historical Archives of Israel, Jerusalem); Clément-Janin, *Notice sur la communauté israélite de Dijon* (Dijon, 1879), pp. 67-69; Anchel (*supra*, n. 22), p. 40.

[35] Anchel, p. 40.

[36] *E.g.*, Fenetrange—10 families in 1762, 101 persons in 1808; Forbach— 9 families in 1762, 314 persons in 1831; Gosselming—1 family in 1762, 48 persons in 1808; Lixheim—14 families in 1762, 190 persons in 1808; Loudrefing, 1 family in 1762, 27 persons in 1808; Phalsbourg, 18 families in 1787, 220 persons in 1808; Schalbach—5 families in 1762, 85 persons in 1808; Thionville —2 families in 1788, 306 persons in 1808. According to registries of taxes in the Metz province prior to 1789 (in the Library of the Jewish Theological Seminary, New York, N. Y); the printed lists of Jewish communities permitted to exist in Lorraine, 1753, 1762 and 1775; Moselle census of 1808 (Jewish Theological Seminary Library); Meurthe census of 1808 (General Historical Archives of Israel, Jerusalem).

[37] For example, Achâtel, Alincourt, Anzeling, Burst, Baudrecourt, Boudanges, Chicourt, Domnon-les-Dieuze, Edling, Fameck, Frémestroff, Grening, Halstroff, Imeldange, Lemersdorf, Liauvillé, Malzéville, Méy, Petite-Rhorbach, Solgne, etc. See the sources listed *supra*, note 36.

[38] Berg, Otterswiller, Ottrot-le-Haut, Avenheim, Le Fort-Vauban (departmental archives of Lower Rhine, 7 M 190).

by 117. In 1808 Jews lived in only 18.2 percent of the communes of both Alsatian departments and only in 6.0 percent of the communes of Moselle, Meurthe, Meuse, and Vosges. The tendency was to settle in already well-established communities, or in larger cities where new communities were created.[39] This conclusion was reached on the basis of the number of Alsatian Jewish communities on the eve of the Revolution and during the First Empire. A more detailed analysis on the basis of Jewish population movements in these communities confirms the following finding: Between 1784 and 1806-1808 the number of Jews increased in 116 communities and decreased in 64 communities. In 3 communities the number of Jews remained the same. Seventeen communities disappeared, and Jews settled in 32 new communities, where none had lived before the Revolution.[40]

For economic reasons, and also as a result of greater intolerance toward Jews in smaller settlements, Jews started early to leave the villages for the cities. This touches on the problem of the so-called "productivity" of occupations held by Jews, which is not under consideration here. It should, however, be noted that at the time of the Jewish emancipation, when Jews were for the first time permitted to become landholders, the general tendency to leave the village for the city had already formed.[41]

V

LARGER CENTERS AVOIDED BY JEWS

It is a surprising fact that after the emancipation a number of old, established Jewish communities, some of them in large cities, attracted relatively few Jews. This occurred first in the Sephardic communities of southwestern France.

[39] Posener (supra, n. 27), pp. 286-88.
[40] On the basis of the Alsatian censuses of 1784, 1789 and 1806-1808.
[41] Szajkowski, Poverty and Social Welfare among French Jews, 1800-1880 (New York, 1954), pp. 11, 73-74.

There were, in Bordeaux in 1752, 1,598 Sephardic Jews
(327 families), not including Avignonese, Ashkenazic,
Italian, and other "foreign" Jews. According to a census
of December 5, 1806, 2,131 Jews lived in Bordeaux, and
only 1,651 of them were Sephardim. This means that in
a period of over 150 years the Sephardim in Bordeaux increased by only about fifty persons. The number of Jews
in Saint-Esprit-lès-Bayonne was estimated in 1723 at 1,100.
According to a census of 1809, only 1,173 Jews lived there.
The smaller Sephardic communities of Bidache, Peyrehorade,
Saint-Jean-de-Luz, and other nearby places almost completely disappeared during the revolutionary period. The
natural increase of the Jewish population in these communities was limited. In addition, immigration of new Marranos
from Spain and Portugal, which continued even during the
eighteenth century, had almost completely stopped, while
at the same time a large number of Jews continuously
emigrated from these communities. This emigration explains the seemingly low mortality in some Sephardic communities, e.g., in Peyrehorade, where 119 births and only 30
deaths were noted during the period 1793-1879.

During the revolutionary period traces of Marranos
completely disappeared in such cities as La Rochelle, Nantes,
Rouen. There is no doubt that many of them lived there
prior to 1789 but no trace of them is to be found among
the Jewish families residing there during the First Empire.
They may have emigrated or, if they remained there, isolated
themselves from the Jewish communities that consisted of
newly arrived Jews, mostly from Ashkenazic communities.
This applies to Dax, Toulouse, and other places, where there
is no record of former Marranos during the First Empire.[42]

A substantial number of Jews emigrated from Bordeaux
during the Revolution, some even to foreign countries.
Among them were Sephardim who had escaped from the
French colonies and then tried to settle in American coun-

---

[42] Szajkowski, "Population Problems of Marranos and Sephardim in France,
from the 16th to the 20th Centuries," *Proceedings of the American Academy
for Jewish Research*, XXVII (1958), 83-105. Records of the Jewish population
in Peyrehorade (General Historical Archives of Israel).

tries. In Saint-Esprit-lès-Bayonne, near the Franco-Spanish frontier, a surprisingly large number of Jews applied for permission to leave for Bordeaux and other French cities. For this the Jews of Bordeaux and Saint-Esprit were severely criticized by the revolutionary authorities, although emigration with official approval was not illegal.[43]

The historian S. Posener noted correctly that "following the granting of freedom of movement and settlement, the Jews of Alsace and Lorraine flocked to cities where there already were large numbers of their co-religionists."[44] However, there were many exceptions, for example, in the traditionally large Ashkenazic center of Metz, where the number of Jews did not rise as a result of emancipation in the same proportion as it did in Strasbourg, Nancy, and other large provincial centers. Only 29 new Jewish families settled in Metz between 1793 and 1806. The total number of Jewish families there decreased from 550 (3,025 persons) in 1789 to 503 in 1800 and 456 (2,186 persons) in 1806. The number of marriages also dropped, 21 in 1798-1800 as against 44 in 1787-1789; and the number of births to 182 in 1798-1800 against 199 in 1787-1789. On the other hand, the population of the Jewish communities in the district of Metz increased from 447 families in 1789 to 550 in 1800, in spite of a decrease in the number of marriages and births in the district (21 marriages and 85 births in 1789 as against 25 marriages and 111 births in 1788), and the rise of mortality (62 in 1789 as against 48 in 1788). We may then conclude that during the old regime many Jews lived in Metz because they were not permitted to reside elsewhere. After the emancipation more Jews settled in the smaller communities around Metz than in this departmental capital itself. A very large number of old settled Jews emigrated

[43] Szajkowski, "Jewish Emigration from Bordeaux during the Eighteenth and Nineteenth Centuries," *Jewish Social Studies*, XVIII (1956), 120-121; a register of requests for passports, in the city archives of Bayonne, 58 L—1*; A. Ducaunnes-Duval, *Inventaire sommaire des archives municipales. Période révolutionnaire*, II (Bordeaux, n.d.), 337; Ernest Ginsburger, *Le Comité de surveillance de Jean-Jacques-Rousseau, Saint-Esprit-lès-Bayonne* (Paris, 1934), p. 180.

[44] Posener (*supra*, n. 27), 281.

from Metz, not only to Paris and other large cities, but to small communities as well. According to a tax register for the period March 23, 1795-August 26, 1798, of the 1,036 Jews of Metz origin and of the former Metz province who paid taxes, only 478 of them still lived in Metz proper, and 558 resided in other communities of the former Metz province or in new communities. Eighteen years later, in 1816, only 176 out of 826 descendants of Jews of Metz paying the tax lived in Metz itself.[45]

Jews did not settle in certain large cities from which Jewish merchants had been harshly expelled during the old regime. In Orléans (Loiret) only 7 Jews had settled by 1806 (61 in 1851); in Cognac (Charente), 3 by 1851; in Saintes, La Rochelle, Rochefort (Charente-Maritime), 4, 36, and 27, respectively, by 1851; in Poitiers (Vienna), 24 by 1851; in Narbonne (Aude), 9 by 1851, etc.[46] In 1737 the Christian merchants of Aurillac (later in the department of Cantal) tried to prevent Avignonese Jews from trading there; in 1851 only two Jews lived there.[47] There may have been many reasons for this aversion to settling in these places. The emancipation made it possible for many Jewish merchants to be discriminating in their choice of residence in the interior of France. However, we can test one of the reasons suggested by examining the cases that seem exceptions to it. Dijon, as has been noted, became a large Jewish community. So did Nantes, where a tavern-keeper came under suspicion in 1783-1786 because a Jew lived in his house (in 1846, 146 Jews lived in the city).[48] On the eve of the Revolution the corporations of

[45] V. Colchen, *Mémoire statistique du département de la Moselle* (Paris, an X), pp. 54-55; *Archives israélites*, IV (1843), 640; XXIX (1869), 196; S. Posener, "Les Juifs sous le Premier Empire," *REJ.*, XCIV (1933), 161-63; documents of the Jewish communities in France during the Revolution of 1789; Metz, no. 51, fol. 518 (Library of Hebrew Union College, Cincinnati).

[46] Szajkowski, *Historia Judaica*, XIX (1957), 147-49; *Statistique de France* (census of 1851).

[47] Departmental archives of Puy-de Dôme, C 817.

[48] Léon Brunschvig, "Les Juifs de Nantes et du Pays Nantais," *REJ.*, XVII (1888), 141; census of Nantes, 1846 (General Historical Archives, Jerusalem).

jewellers and dealers in old clothes requested the expulsion of Jews from Montpellier. In 1809, 124 Jews lived there.[49] In Toulouse, where the Jews perished in an auto-da-fé in 1685, there were 107 Jewish inhabitants in 1808.[50] However, it should be noted that in Dijon, Nantes, and even Montpellier and Toulouse the Jews who settled after 1789 were mostly Ashkenazim, as registries show. The conflicts during the old regime on the right of residence of Jewish merchants in these cities involved Sephardim and Jews of the papal province who had settled in Bordeaux. In conclusion, it appears that the Ashkenazim were a more important factor than the Sephardim in producing full geographical emancipation of the Jews. The Jews of the papal province who did not settle in Bordeaux also created large new communities, such as that in Aix (169 Jews in 1809).

Even some new centers of Jews from the former papal province were created with the help of Ashkenazim. In 1788 there were 170 Jews in Nîmes (37 families). Forty out of 224 names mentioned in the Nîmes register of the Jewish *état-civil* (1778-1792) bear the family name Allemand, which indicates that they were of Ashkenazic origin.[51]

Ten Jewish families settled in Lamanche, Neufchâteau, Charmes, and Saint-Dié (in the Vosges) from 1775 until 1789; the number reached 80 in 1808.[52] However, in some isolated areas of the Vosges, where Jews used to visit for business, they settled very late. In Gérardmer, a market center for Jewish horse and cattle dealers, there were only about 25 Jewish families 150 years after the emancipation.[53]

[49] Salomon Kahn, "Les Juifs de Montpellier au XVIIIe siècle," *REJ.*, XXXIII (1896), 294.

[50] J. Gross, "Les Juifs de Toulouse," *Revue des Pyrénées*, XVIII (1906), 267. The event of 1685 will be the subject of a special study.

[51] Szajkowski, "The Reform of the Etat-Civil of the French Jews during the Revolution of 1789," *Jewish Quarterly Review*, XLIX (1958), 73.

[52] Archives nationales, F 19-11010; Anchel, *op. cit.*, p. 39.

[53] Louis Géhin, "Gérardmer à travers les âges," *Bulletin de la Société philomatique vosgienne*, XVIII (1893), 221.

VI

Immigration of Foreign-Born Jews

From the outbreak of the Revolution persecuted men everywhere rallied around the banner of France, and Paris became a center for political refugees dedicated to the liberation of their native countries.[54] In such an atmosphere the Jews could very well point out that by granting them full citizenship France would attract a large number of Jews from abroad, who would enrich the nation's economy. The same argument was made by an English woman, author of a pro-Jewish pamphlet (1790), and by the deputy Charles-François Bouche in his proposal concerning Jews, which he put forth in connection with the annexation by France of the papal province of Avignon and Comtat Venaissin.[55] However, the anti-Jewish elements warned that a consequence of Jewish emancipation would be an influx into France of a multitude of German and Polish Jews. P. Arlés the elder of Lyons wrote to the National Assembly on January 4, 1790, that a million Jews would invade France.[56] In April, 1790, a section of Strasbourg issued a similar warning.[57] On May 4, 1790, the city council of Lixheim viewed with alarm the "bands of German, Polish, Turkish and other Jews, who arrive daily in squadrons."[58]

At the time of the First Empire Jean-Charles-Joseph Laumont, prefect of Lower-Rhine, claimed that since the beginning of the Revolution a large number of Jews had arrived in France. However, this was later contradicted

---

[54] Albert Mathiez, *La Révolution et les étrangers* (Paris, 1918), pp. 4-12.

[55] *Pétition* . . . (*supra*, note 14), pp. 23, 28-30; La Baronne de Vasse, Angloise, *Mémoire à l'Assemblée Nationale* (Paris, 1790), pp. 2-3, 7; Charles-François-Bouche, *De la restitution du Comté Venaissin, des villes et état d'Avignon* (Paris, 1789), p. 38.

[56] Georges Bourgin, "La Fonction économique des juifs," *Souvenir et science*, III (1932), nos. 3-4.

[57] P. Hildenfinger, "L'Adresse de la commune de Strasbourg . . . ," *REJ.*, LVIII (1909), 124. Names of a few foreign Jews are mentioned in the published lists of foreigners, *e.g.*, Nath. Maas and his daughter Rachel: *Tableau des déclarations reçues par le comité de la XIe section . . . des étrangers . . .* [Strasbourg, 1793], broadside.

[58] Bibliothèque Nationale Paris, naf. 22706, fols. 203-204.

by E. Coquebert de Montbret, who stated in a study on Jews in France (1821) that as early as 1789 it had been alleged without proof that a third of all Alsatian Jews had been born abroad.[59]

There is no doubt that a number of foreign-born Jews settled in France during the Revolution, but their number should not be exaggerated. During the Terror Jews were arrested in Paris as suspected foreigners. Some of them proved that they had resided in Paris for over twenty years, or that they had been born in France.[60] In Metz only eight or ten of forty-three Jews who settled there between 1789 and 1808 were foreign-born. Not one of the 306 Jews (56 families) who settled between 1789 and 1808 in Thionville was born abroad. In the entire department of Meurthe (with 3,289 Jews in 1808) only 20 Jewish families from abroad settled there between 1789 and 1800. In 1806, 20 out of 273 Jews of Fegersheim were foreign-born; in Mutzig, 9 out of 313; in Osthoffen, 5 out of 78. However, no details on the dates of their arrival are available.[61] S. Posener states that "not over" 2,000 foreign Jews came to Alsace between 1784 and 1810. This conclusion was not reached on the basis of statistical data but by the following reasoning: From 1784 to 1810 the number of Alsatian Jews rose by about 6,000. As the natural increase—according to Posener—totaled 4,625 in twenty-five years, the remaining increase was a result of immigration.[62]

In the eighteen-seventies foreign-born Jews formed a large percentage of French Jewry. According to an official government census of 1872, there were then in Paris 23,434 Jews. A census of the Jewish consistory of the same year

[59] J.-Ch.-J. Laumond, *Statistique du département du Bas-Rhin* (Paris, an X), p. 198; [E. Coquebert de Montbret], *Notice sur l'état des israélites en France* (Paris, 1821), p. 78.

[60] L. Kahn, *Les Juifs de Paris pendant la Révolution* (Paris, 1899), pp. 109-110.

[61] Anchel, *op. cit.*, p. 39; departmental archives of Lower Rhine, 7 M 190.

[62] Posener, "L'Immigration des Juifs allemands en France sous le Premier Empire," *Univers israélite,* March 10, 16, 23, 1934; *idem,* "Les Juifs sous le Premier Empire: les colporteurs, *ibid,* October 8, 1937; *idem* (*supra,* n. 27), pp. 292-93.

gives the place of birth of 10,185 Jews. Of these 2,333 were born abroad.[63]

VII

INTERNAL MIGRATIONS

As a result of emancipation entire Jewish communities immigrated to other places. A striking example is provided by the district of Altkirch (Upper Rhine). According to official censuses, 3,964 Jews lived there in 26 communities in 1789 and 4,345 Jews in 24 communities in 1807. The total population of Christians and Jews in these communities was 74,474 in 1789 and 94,374 in 1807. In 1807 no Jews resided in Zimmersheim, Struet, Dietwiller, Waltenheim, and Tagolsheim, while 31, 70, 96, 35, and 19 Jews lived in these towns, respectively, in 1789. In 1789 no Jews resided in Altkirch itself, but by 1807, 55 Jews had settled there, and in 1851 the number was 267. (The total population of Altkirch, the main city in the district, was 1,134 in 1789, 2,268 in 1807, and 3,611 in 1851.) In many other communities of the Altkirch district the number of Jews declined: from 121 in 1789 to 115 in 1807 in Hirsingen, from 198 to 195 in Blotzheim, from 320 to 299 in Hagenthal-le-Bas. In most communities where the Jewish population declined between 1789 and 1807 the total population increased: in Zimmersheim, from 384 to 426; in Struet, from 331 to 391; in Dietwiller, from 449 to 500; in Tagolsheim, from 230 to 245, etc.[64] By 1808 (or 1809) the last Jewish family of Dangolsheim (Lower Rhine) had already left the village.[65]

In 1809, of 2,908 Jews (840 families) living in Paris, only 1,324 had been born there. Of the others 273 had lived in Paris for twenty years or more; 206, from ten to twenty years, that is, they had arrived in the French capital during

[63] Szajkowski (*supra*, n. 41), pp. 75, 87.

[64] Departmental archives of Upper Rhine, I M 138a & 1.

[65] L. W., "Histoire de nos communautés, Dangolsheim," *Bulletin de nos communautés*, March-April, 1956.

the revolutionary years; 90 had lived in Paris less than ten years.[66]

In 1809, 4 Jewish families resided in Amiens (Somme). Three of them came from Metz and one from the Upper Rhine. After 1789 a Jewish community was founded in Lille (Nord) by Ashkenazic Jews. It seems that few of the first Jewish settlers remained there; most of them emigrated later to other places. A list of consistorial electors of Lille in 1861 contains the names of 55 Jews aged twenty-five or older, of whom only four had been born in Lille itself. Not one of the 22 Jewish Notables of Nantes (Loire-inférieure) in September, 1848, had been born there.[67]

In the papal province of Avignon and the Comtat Venaissin the exodus of Jews from the four communities of Avignon, Carpentras, Cavaillon, and L'Isle-sur-Sorgue started even before the Revolution. In 1789, 705 Jews (179 families) resided in Carpentras, while 213 Jews (50 families) of Carpentras origin then resided in other communities located in France. At first only wealthy Jews were in a position to leave the papal province. The loss of capital and commerce as a consequence of Jewish emigration weighed heavily on the community. To counteract this development non-Jewish opinion came to favor an improvement in the status of the Jews. The Jews of Carpentras feared that the emigration of rich Jews would impose on those remaining the burden of supporting the poor and paying off the communal debts owed to Christian creditors. On July 17, 1791, they petitioned the city council for permission to arrange a meeting of the Jews of Carpentras origin residing in other communities in order to discuss this problem.[68]

[66] L. Kahn, *Les Professions manuelles et les institutions de patronage* (Paris, 1885), pp. 69-72.

[67] City archives of Amiens, register of declarations of names by the Jews, 1809; departmental archives of Nord, V (list of Jewish electors, February 20, 1861), and of Loire-inférieure, V (list of Jewish notables, September 11, 1848).

[68] *Copie de la supplique . . . des Juifs de la commune de Carpentras . . .* (Carpentras, 1791), 6 pp. See also the two contemporary pamphlets on the emigration of Jews from Carpentras: [J. J. C. V. Raphaël, or Cottier Julian], *l'Enfant du patriotisme* [Carpentras, 1789], 13 pp.; F. R. Ch. J. Cottier, *Dialogue* [Carpentras, 1789], 15 pp.

Of about 2,000 Jews living in the department of
Vaucluse (formed by the former papal province) prior to
the Revolution, only 631 remained in 1808. Twenty-six
of the 109 Jews who settled in Marseilles between 1789 and
1808 came from the former papal province. Forty settled
in the Gard department (mostly in Nîmes) prior to 1789
and 47 later. Only a few wealthy Jews remained in the
former papal province. According to a census of 1809, the
wealth of 539 Jews who remained in the four communities
was estimated at 1,429,900 francs, while that of 169 Jews
who emigrated from these four communities to Aix-en-
Provence was estimated at 1,047,000 francs.[69]

In the time of the Revolution and later, the poor Jews
of the Carpentras ghetto moved to the upper floors of the
houses of rich Jews who had left the ghetto for other parts
of France. On November 7, 1797, Escoffier the elder of
the Carpentras *Directoire*, advocated the destruction of these
upper floors as a menace to public safety. Under the old
regime the Jews found a means of expanding the restricted
area of their ghetto by building the highest houses in town.
During the First Empire half or completely abandoned
houses in the former ghettos of the papal province started
to fall into ruins and the civil authorities warned their former owners that these houses had to be repaired or demol-
ished. Still, poor Jews continued to inhabit them.[70]

Jews emigrated even from rapidly growing communities. Four out of the 2,908 Jews in Paris (in 1809) had
been born in Dijon, 15 in Lyons, 42 in Nancy, 18 in Lunéville. In 1808 a Jew with five children, all of whom had
been born in Dijon, was registered in Nancy. There were

[69] Census of the Jews in the regional consistory of Marseille, 1809
(General Historical Archives, Jerusalem); Archives Nationales, F 19-11008;
Anchel, *op. cit.*, p. 37; H. Chobaut, "Les Juifs d'Avignon et du Comtat et la
Révolution Française," *REJ.*, CI (1937), 11; CII (1938), 38; Szajkowski, "The
Growth of the Jewish Population of France," *Jewish Social Studies*, VIII (1946),
180-83; *idem*, "The Decline and Fall of Provençal Jewry," *ibid.*, IV (1944),
31-54.
[70] City archives of Carpentras, Rév. No. 217, reg. 1, fol. 3-4 (Escoffier's
request); 44, fol. 50 and FF 19, fol. 27 (on the high houses of Carpentras),
48, fol. 18, 42 (on the ruins); city archives of Cavaillon, Corresp. June 12,
1806 (on the ruins of the Cavaillon ghetto).

14 or 15 Jewish families in Orange (Vaucluse) in 1803; only 3 or 4 of them remained in 1806.[71]

VIII

Various Aspects of the Jewish Population Problem

Many Jews were among the emigrés who left France during the Revolution and some also among the anti-revolutionary elements who were deported. Of 3,956 emigrés in the Moselle department in 1791-1800, 31 or 32 were Jews. Names of 226 Jews appear in the printed lists of emigrés from the Lower Rhine; 8 Jews were among the 2,895 listed emigrés of the Upper Rhine. Not all of them were later able to go back to France.[72]

Were the Jews who, after the emancipation, settled in new communities received in a friendly way by the Jews already there? Probably not. In Haguenau they were called *Neuländer,* and they had their own synagogue.[73]

Another unsettled problem concerns the initial date of the emigration of Ashkenazic Jews to Switzerland and to American countries. Did this emigration, which was substantial in later years, start during the emancipation period?[74] The economic status of the Jews during the emancipation period is not the subject of this demographic study, but both problems are clearly interrelated. New Jewish settlers were often pioneers of local industries. For instance, Israël-Hayemsohn Créhange (1769-1844), one of the first Jews to settle in Sedan, opened a textile factory there in 1796.[75]

The division of former provinces into departments often brought out significant demographic and economic

[71] L. Kahn (*supra,* n. 66), p. 72; Gain (*supra,* n. 32), No. 101, 297-98; departmental archives of Vaucluse, V (report on the Jews of Orange, 1806).

[72] Szajkowski, "Jewish Emigrés during the French Revolution," *Jewish Social Studies,* XVI (1954), 319-34.

[73] E. Scheid, "La Synagogue de Haguenau," *Univers israélite,* XXXVIII (1883), 761.

[74] Szajkowski, "Some Facts about Alsatian Jews in America," *Yivo Bleter,* XX (1942), 312-18 (Yiddish).

[75] *Archives israélites,* V (1844), 754.

differences among Jewish communities. Thus, the number
of small Jewish communities was greater in the Lower Rhine
than in the Upper Rhine. The Jews of the Upper Rhine
were considered wealthier than those of the Lower Rhine.
Likewise, in the Sephardic center of southwestern France the
Jews of Landes (most of whom lived in Saint-Esprit) were
considered wealthier than those of Gironde (most of whom
lived in Bordeaux).[76] Only three of the Alsatian communities where Jews were listed for the first time in 1806-1808
were located in the Upper Rhine; all the others were in the
Lower Rhine.[77]

The Jewish migrations had a considerable influence on
the activities of the Jewish communities during the emancipation and in later years. Thus, the Jews of Alsace, Metz
and the Metz province, and of the papal province, or their
descendants who emigrated to other places, were forced by
law to pay taxes in order to liquidate the debts owed by
their former communities to Christian creditors. Adolphe
Crémieux, who was born in Nîmes and later settled in Paris,
was obliged to pay a tax for the liquidation of the Metz
debts because he had married a woman from that community. Over one thousand such cases created a complicated
bond through special taxes between the Jewish emigrants
and their descendants and the communities of their origin.[78]
A large number of communities which, during the old regime, belonged to the Metz province, of which the community of Metz was the largest, were later located in the
territory of the Meurthe department, of which Nancy was
the largest community.

IX

THE DECREASE IN LARGE FAMILIES

The number of large Jewish families began to decrease
during the emancipation period. Three hundred sixty-two

[76] Posener (*supra*, n. 27), p. 283; Szajkowski (*supra*, n. 41), pp. 57, 59.
[77] According to the censuses.
[78] This subject will be treated in a separate study.

out of a total of 3,913 Alsatian Jewish families in 1784 had more than 5 children each; 2,953, from 1 to 5 children each, and the remainder were childless couples.[79] Of 16,398 Jews in Lower Rhine in 1806 there were only 9,849 parents and children, the remaining individuals being childless couples, widowers, and widows.[80] In 1808 there were 51 Jewish families in Lunéville (Meurthe). Ten of them were childless couples; 9 had 1 child each; 16, 2 or 3 children each; 14, from 4 to 6 children each; 6 with 7 children each; 3 with 8 children each; and 3 with 10 or 11 children each. However, Lunéville was a small center with an exceptionally large number of children.[81] While the Jewish community of Metz noted 3,546 births against 2,804 deaths in the forty-two-year period covering 1717-1758, the number of births in the fifty-year period 1759-1808 was almost the same— 3,506—against 3,159 deaths. The number of marriages was larger in the first period (1,715) than in the second (1,641). Some demographic findings demand more study before any conclusion can be drawn from them, for example, the annual total of births and deaths. There were, in Metz, 66 births and 72 deaths in 1783; 64 births and 69 deaths in 1785; 61 births and 47 deaths in 1790; but there were 61 births and 132 deaths in 1784, 79 births and 102 deaths in 1788, 46 births and 106 deaths in 1791. However, the winters of the last three years were exceptionally severe. In a later period, at the end of 1833, there were 2,124 Jews in Metz, with only 1,189 children.[82]

E. Schnurman, who wrote on the Jews of Strasbourg at a much later period, ascribed to the local bourgeois tendency to rear small families the lesser increase in the Jewish population than in the non-Jewish population. This tend-

---

[79] Gabriel Hemerdinger, "Le Dénombrement des israélites d'Alsace." *REJ.*, XLII (1901), 12.

[80] Departmental archives of Lower Rhine, 7 M 190. On the other hand, it should be noted that on October 13, 1823, the Jewish consistory of Lower Rhine called upon poor Jews to think carefully before getting married. Gerson-Lévy of Metz reprimanded poor Jews for having too many children. Szajkowski (*supra*, n. 41), p. 27.

[81] Departmental archives of Meurthe-et-Moselle, V 8.

[82] Coquebert de Montbret (*supra,* n. 59), pp. 79-80; departmental archives of Moselle, V 152.

ency probably existed as early as the emancipation period.
However, Schnurman overlooked other factors, for instance,
emigration.[83]

Often the number of Jewish families rose while the
total number of Jews dropped, probably as a result of a
further migration of grown children. On the eve of the
Revolution seven families (46 persons) lived in the territory
later formed into the district of Uzès (Gard). Ten families
resided there in 1808, but their total number was three less
than before 1789.[84] In Carpentras 22 Jews died in 1780, 43
in 1783; in Avignon, 4 in 1780, 9 in 1783, 18 in 1785; in
Cavaillon, 2 in 1781, 11 in 1782; in L'Isle-sur-Sorgue, 4 in
1781, 18 in 1785. A possible reason for a rise in mortality
during certain years is an increase in the number of births
and deaths of infants: in Carpentras, 25 births in 1780, 33
in 1783; in Avignon, 7 births in 1780, 10 in 1783.[85]

X

Jewish Population Problems of Later Periods

In later periods Jewish population movements were
characterized by most of the trends that were started during
the revolutionary period.[86] On the other hand, many population trends, such as migrations from one department to
another, were not exclusively Jewish.

Despite the fact that they had the right to move freely,
Jews did not begin to settle in large numbers until a very
late date, mostly in the eighteen-seventies, in many important
centers of industry and trade, such as Lille, Roubaix,

---

[83] E. Schnurman, *La Statistique de la population juive de Strasbourg*
(Strasbourg, 1933), 8 pp. M. Ginsburger noted other factors, *e.g.*, the number
of illegitimate children was lower among Jews than among Christians; *Souvenir
et science*, IV, No. 2 (1933), 14.

[84] Departmental archives of Gard, 6 V 43.

[85] City archives of Carpentras, GG 47; of Avignon, GG; of Cavaillon,
GG 29; of L'Isle, GG 23.

[86] Szajkowski, "The Growth of the Jewish Population of France," *Jewish
Social Studies*, VIII (1946), 179-92, 297-318. Also according to a Franco-
Jewish Gazetteer, to be published by the author.

Tourcoing. Departments located in regions from which Jews had been excluded prior to the Revolution remained without a single Jew, according to the census of 1872 (Vendée, Côtes-du-Nord, Corrèzes, Lot, Cantal), or had only a handful of Jews (Basses-Alpes—4 Jews, Cher—7 Jews, Maine-et-Loire—12 Jews). Of 89 departments there were in 1866 4 with no Jews at all, 19 with only 1 to 9 Jews in each, 14 with 11 to 24 Jews in each. Only 9 departments had over a thousand Jews each. The situation in 1866 was almost unchanged from that in 1808. In 1808 there were 14 departments with 100-1,000 Jews in each, 6 with 1,000-10,000, and 1 with over 10,000 Jews. In 1866 there were 21, 6, and 3 departments, in the respective ranges. In 1808, there were 44 departments with no Jews at all, in 1866 only 4. However, the number of small communities (from 1 to 100 Jews in each) rose from 22 in 1808 to 55 in 1866.

The Jews continued to concentrate in large cities. In 1809, 47.7 percent of the Jews in the department of Bouches-du-Rhône, were urban residents; in 1872, 83.03 percent. The total population had 56.3 percent urban residents in 1872. Nevertheless, a large number of small Jewish communities continued to exist at all times, although the percentage of Jews living there was very small. According to the census of 1851 Jews lived in 222 capitals of districts, although 107 of them had only from 1 to 10 Jews each, or a total of 345 Jews. The largest number of Jews continued to live in the departments that had been formed from the provinces where most of the Jews lived during the old regime: Alsace, Metz and Lorraine, Guyenne and Gascogne, Ile-de-France, Provence, Languedoc, Comtat Venaissin (45,520 out of 47,166 Jews in 1808; 68,892 out of 73,975 Jews in 1851).

From the end of the seventeenth century until 1936 Jews resided officially in 896 cities and villages of Alsace, Metz and its province, and Lorraine, which during the Revolution, formed the departments of Upper and Lower Rhine, Moselle, and Meurthe. (Both Rhine departments, Moselle, and Meurthe-et-Moselle after the War of 1870-

1871.) Only in 168 out of these 896 places did Jews still reside in 1936. Prior to 1936, Jews ceased to live in 115 places which they had inhabited before 1789. Of the 38 places where Jews began officially to reside about 1806-1810, only 15 had Jewish inhabitants in 1936.[87]

Further studies are needed before definitive conclusions may be drawn on the Jewish population problem during the French Revolution of 1789. It is clear, however, that in spite of local hostility and maneuvering, the revolutionary regime granted freedom of movement to the Jews even before conferring full citizenship on them.

APPENDIX I

A LIST OF OWNERS OF THE ALSATIAN CITIES AND VILLAGES
INHABITED BY JEWS

Following is a complete list of these owners, together with the number of Jewish communities and the total number of Jews living there in 1784: the King, 9 communities with 1,329 Jews; the King, given *en fief* to Meuse Choiseul, 8—650; the city of Colmar, 1—28; the city of Colmar and the imperial bailiff de Kayserberg, 3—889; Prince Evêque de Strasbourg (i.e., the city of Strasbourg), 16—1,444; Evêque de Spire, 5—291; Abbaye de Neubourg, 2—81; Abbaye de Marmoutier, 2—58; Chapitre Equestral de Mürbach, 3—277; Ordre Teutonique, 1—50; d'Andlau, 7—527; d'Anthès, 1—226; de Behrenfels, 1—409; de Berkheim, 1—152; de Böcklin Böcklinsau, 1—473; Prince de Broglie, 5—442; de Detlingen and others, 2—182; de Deux-Ponts, 3—629; d'Eckbrecht de Dürheim, 4—146; d'Eptingen, 3—759; de Falkenhayon, 1—65; de Falkenstein, 1—59; de Flachsland, 1—340; de Flaxlanden, 4—264; de Gail and de Voltz, 1—94; de Gayling d'Altenheim, 1—71; de Gérardon, 1—181; de Glaubitz, 1—88; de Gohr and others, 1—138; de Gölinitz, 1—41; de Hagenbach, 1—42; de Haindel d'Erlenbourg, 1—206; Landgrave de Hesse-Darmstadt, 21—1,837; Prince de Hohenlohe and others, 6—345; d'Ichtratzheim, 1—72; de Kemfer and others, 1—20; de Klinglin, 3—405; de Krebs and d'Herisheim, 1—163; de Landenberg, 1—162; de Landsperg and others, 3—426; de Meuse Choiseúl, 2—207 (except the 8 communities owned by the King); de Monjoie de Hirsingen, 1—95; Prince de Nassau-Saarbrück, 1—6; d'Oberkirch and others, 1—94; Ocahan, 1—50; de Rath-

---

[87] Not including the departments of Meuse and Vosges, where few Jews lived before 1789.

samhausen, 4—479; de Reichenstein, 1—201; de Reinach, 4—467; de
Rinck, 1—31; Prince de Rohan-Soubise, 6—588; de Schauenbourg,
4—526; de Senozan and others, 7—836; Duc de Valentinois, 5—543;
de Waldner, 4—640; de Wangen, 1—52; de Worstatt, 2—192; Duc
de Würtemberg, 1—92; de Zorn de Bulach, 1—63; de Zu Rhein,
2—162.[88]

APPENDIX II

THE JEWISH ASPECT OF REVOLUTIONARY TOPONYMY

There were revolutionary changes in the Jewish topographical denominations in a large number of cities and villages where names of
streets and other places bore witness to contemporary or past residence
of Jews.[89] During the Revolution many city councils replaced geographical names of the old regime as well as Jewish names of places
with revolutionary names. In 1793 the *rue de Juifs* of Strasbourg
became *rue des Droits de l'Homme*; the *Pont de la Porte des Juifs* became
Pont des Droits de l'Homme; *Porte des Juifs, Porte de l'Egalité*; and
Quartier des Juifs, Quartier des Droits de l'Homme. In Metz *rue* and
quai des Juifs became *rue* and *quai de l'Arsenal*. *Rue Judaïque* in
Bordeaux was changed to *rue de la Délivrance*. In Nice the *rue des
Juifs* was broken up into two parts—*rue de la Régénération* and *rue du
Bonheur*. *Rue des Juifs* in Saint-Malo became *rue de la Fraternité*. The
name of *rue de la Juiverie* in Meaux was changed to *Quartier du Contrat
Social*.[90] But this was not done everywhere. In Lyons, Sélestat,
Haguenau, "Jewish" names of streets were unchanged during all revolu-
tionary periods[91] Nor did such cities as *Villejuif* change their names.[92]

---

[88] Compiled according to the Alsatian Jewish census of 1784, and F.-C.
Heitz, *L'Alsace en 1789: tableaux des divisions territoriales. . . .* (Strasbourg,
1860), 32 pp.

[89] Robert Anchel, *Les Juifs de France* (Paris, 1946), pp. 41-57 ("To-
ponymie juive"). See also the indexes of *L'Intermédiaire des chercheurs et
curieux* ("Rues dites des Juifs").

[90] *Délibération du corps municipal de la commune de Strasbourg. Portant
une nouvelle dénomination des rues* (n.p., n.d.), pp. 8, 9-10; Jean-Julien Barbé,
Metz pittoresque: les rues et places de la cité (Metz, 1930), p. 15; P. Bernardau,
Le Viographe bordelais (Bordeaux, 1844), p. 43; Joseph Combet, *La Révolution
à Nice* (Paris, 1912), pp. 206-207; city archives of Meaux, minutes of the
city council, vol. XXIV, fol. 190; A. Carro, *Histoire de Meaux* . . . (Paris,
1865), pp. 437, 547; Anchel, *Les Juifs de France*, p. 51. In Rovingo (Italy)
the ghetto was given a new name, *Via Libera*, and later *Contrada della Riunione*;
Cecil Roth, *The History of the Jews of Italy* (Philadelphia, 1946), p. 433.

[91] C Riffaterre, *Le Mouvement antijacobin et antiparisien à Lyon* . . . ,
I (Lyon-Paris, 1793), 6, 70, 84, 176-179 ("La Juiverie"); Alexandre Dorlan,
Histoire architecturale et anécdotique de Schlestadt, II (Paris, 1912), 366
(*rue des Juifs*); Scheid (*supra*, n. 73), pp. 759, 761.

[92] Roger de Figuères, *Les Noms révolutionnaires des communes de France
. . .* (Paris, 1901), 125 pp.

The topographical denomination was sometimes used for anti-Jewish propaganda. On May 3, 1791, the *Journal de la Cour* proposed changing the name of *rue de l'Université,* where resided the Bishop Charles-Maurice de Talleyrand-Périgord d'Autun, a partisan of Jewish emancipation, to *rue des Juifs.*[93] It should be mentioned that in later periods the toponymy of the old regime was revised and in many cases a Jewish toponymy was introduced even in places where it had previously not existed.[94]

[93] L. Kahn, *Les Juifs de Paris,* pp. 60-61.

[94] In Ribeauvillé the *Runtzelgasse* became ca. 1861 *Synagogue,* because a synagogue was built there in 1711-1712 and was reconstructed in 1832; departmental archives of Upper Rhine, E 1624; city archives of Ribeauvillé, 269. In 1885 the *Neier Platz* of Ribeauvillé became known as *Place de Juifs* (according to information given by Robert Faller, archivist of Ribeauvillé). In Molsheim the *Petite rue des Juifs* was changed to *Rue Liebermann,* in honor of a converted Jew (information given by Dr. Gerlinger of the city archives). It is worth while mentioning that Rabbi Abraham Andrade was the first to propose to change the name of Saint-Esprit-lès-Bayonne to Jean-Jacques-Rousseau. A Jew of Bordeaux, Tavarez, changed the name of his house from *Le Marquisat* to *Marat*; after the Revolution he reverted to the original name. H. Léon (*supra,* n. 5), pp. 161, 163, 165, 201, 409-410. The well-known Jew, Zalkind Hourwitz, was the author of a project on a revolutionary toponymy for the streets of Paris; Zalkind Hourwitz, "Projet d'une nouvelle carte de Paris," *Journal de Paris,* No. 124, 4 pluviose an VII, pp. 538-40: "La plupart des rues de Paris portent des noms de ci-devant Saints, des noms féodeaux, indécens ou ridicules"; Fr. Bouillier, *Nouvelles études familières de psychologie et de morale* (Paris, 1887), p. 251.

THE GROWTH OF THE JEWISH POPULATION OF FRANCE

The Political Aspects of a Demographic Problem

The historians of French Jewry since the Revolution have been remarkably reticent in respect to population data and trends. It is indeed no simple matter to obtain a reliable estimate of the number of Jews in France (outside of Alsace-Lorraine) during the eighteenth century or later. The emancipation of the Jews in 1789 meant, among other results, that the religious bodies lost their official status. With membership in the Jewish "consistory" placed on a voluntary basis, these communal agencies were no longer in a position to collect reasonably complete information regarding the Jewish population. Nor did the government, in conducting a census, have the power to classify inhabitants as Catholics, Protestants and Jews, except to the extent that each person might choose to specify his religious affiliation. In the midst of successive changes in the French state, accompanied by incessant charges of a "Jewish invasion" and controversies over the size of the Jewish population, various efforts were, nevertheless, made to enumerate this group. These attempts were in the form of a question on religion in the census schedule, enumerations compiled by the Jewish consistories, and studies prepared by professional demographers. It will be shown below how wide was the range of degree of reliability attained by the post-Emancipation efforts to solve this practical problem.

Readers interested in the current discussion in the United States, regarding the need for Jewish population data, will readily recognize many of the situations which arose in 19th-century France. It will be seen that the controversy over the population issue in that country was rather

Originally published in *Jewish Social Studies*, vol. VIII (1946).

more acute, both within the Jewish group and in public life at large.
The material analyzed here is culled both from numerous printed sources,
some of which have been ignored since publication, and from the archives
of various Jewish communities. The period to be covered extends from
the eve of the Revolution to the eighties of the last century, when Jewish
life in France began to be transformed by the influx of East-European
immigrants. It was during this period that the Jewish population spread,
chiefly from Alsace-Lorraine, to all parts of the country, particularly to
Paris.

I

Prior to 1800 the Jewish population within the present-day borders
of France was concentrated chiefly in Alsace, to which their ancestors
had come in the fourteenth century, following their expulsion from the
domain of the French king. The other regions, to be considered in this
study, consist of Lorraine, the southern portion of the old French
kingdom, and the former papal domain.

Between 1637, when the number of Jewish families in Alsace was
estimated as 3,665,[1] and the latter part of the following century there
were at least a dozen estimates of this population, of which no more
than one or two may be considered reliable.[2] The earliest census of the
Jews in this province is that of 1784, which was prompted by the
authorities' determination to check a corrupt practice involving the
issuance of forged tax-receipts. According to this census, there were
19,707 Jews (9,945 males and 9,762 females) distributed in 177 communities.[3] It cannot be assumed, however, that all the Jews registered.
As the historian G. Hemerdinger stated, the enumeration of the Catholics,

[1] Posener, S., "Les Juifs sous le Premier Empire," in *Revue des études juives,* vol. xciii
(1932) 213.

[2] Hoffman, Charles, *L'Alsace au 18e siècle* (Colmar 1907) vol. iv, p. 319; Poujol, *Quelques
observations* . . . (Paris 1806) p. 33; Neyremant, "Dénombrement des familles israélites en
Alsace, 1689 et 1716," in *Revue d'Alsace* (1854) 564; Schnurmann, E., *La Population juive
en Alsace* (Paris 1936) p. 6; Posener, *loc. cit.,* p. 213 f.; Scheid, Élie, *Histoire des juifs
d'Alsace* (Paris 1887) p. 157; Bail, *Des Juifs au dix-neuvième siècle* . . . (Paris 1816) p. viii.

[3] *Dénombrement général des juifs* . . . (Colmar 1785 and Strasbourg 1929) 386 pp. (fol.);
Récapitulation du dénombrement général des juifs d'Alsace fait à la fin de l'année 1784
(Colmar 1785) 2 pp (fol.). Cf. Hemerdinger, G., "Le Dénombrement des israélites d'Alsace,"
in *Revue des études juives,* vol. xlii, 253-264.

Protestants and Jews paved the way for the Emancipation which was proclaimed by the Revolution.[4] The Alsatian Jews, however, regarded the census as an unfavorable measure, which many undoubtedly evaded. As evidence in support of this surmise, we may attempt to estimate the Alsatian-Jewish population on the basis of the contemporary birth and death rates.

S. Posener cites a source which indicates that in 1783 there were recorded 610 births and 425 deaths among the Alsatian Jews; for each 100 births there are said to have been 69.6 deaths.[5] This corresponds closely to the ratio among the Jews in Lorraine, viz., 71.46 deaths to 100 births.[6] According to the census of 1803 in Lorraine, the ratio of births to the number of Jews was 1 to 37 (among Christians 1 to 24) ; the ratio of deaths was 1 to 56.[7] In view of the fact that in the stormy days of the Revolution the birth rate decreased, we may apply the birth and death rates in Lorraine of the year 1803 to the Jewry of Alsace on the eve of the Revolution; it would then follow that there were in Alsace 22,570 or 23,800 Jews, depending on which of the two rates is applied. These figures are, at all events, higher than the total of 19,707 returned by the 1784 census.

With regard to the number in Lorraine, the problem is complicated by the fact that only a fraction of the Jewish population had the right of domicile. Under the law of 1721 a quota of 180 families was fixed,[8] and the extra-legal residents had to wait for vacancies or for an opportunity to purchase or inherit the privilege.[9] Thus, in Nancy, in 1789 the census recognized 40 Jewish families, although there were 97 in the city.[10] It is, indeed, known that in 1808 there were 10,545 Jews in Lorraine, distributed in 168 communities, of which no more than 51 were recognized

---

[4] Hemerdinger, loc. cit., p. 258.

[5] Posener, S., "L'Immigration des juifs allemands en France sous le Premier Empire," in Univers Israélite (1934) 785-87, 821-23, 856-59.

[6] Colchen, Mémoire statistique du dép. de la Moselle (Paris an XI) ; cf. Legoyt, A., in Archives Israélites, vol. xxix (1868) 1094-96.

[7] Idem, loc. cit.; cf. Colchen, op. cit.; Posener, in Revue des études juives, vol. cliv, p. 161-62.

[8] Revue des études juives, vol. xiii (1912) 201.

[9] Posener, loc. cit., p. 158.

[10] Godechot, J., "Les Juifs à Nancy de 1784-95," in Revue des études juives, vol. lxxxvi, p. 2-3.

by the census of 1752.[11] From the census of 1788 it appears that about a fifth of this population (410-420 families) was concentrated in Metz, the capital of this province.[12]

Prior to 1789 there were three important Jewish communities in southern France, two of Spanish-Portuguese origin (in southwestern France) and a third in the papal provinces of Avignon and Comtat-Venaissin (ceded to France in 1791). In 1789 there were approximately 2,000 Jews in this area, chiefly in the ancient communities of Carpentras, Avignon, Cavaillon and Isle-sur-Sorgue.[13] There is a characteristic incident told in the Carpentras *pinkas* (now in the archives of the Yiddish Scientific Institute in New York). In 1763 the son of the local scribe, Elijah Carmi, was forcibly baptized; thereupon many Jews fled to French royal territory, to Nice and to neighboring towns. The bishop of Carpentras subsequently ordered all the refugees to compile a list, and in 1763 the Church at Rome published a decree requiring an exact record of Jewish births, marriages and deaths to be entered in a register in Hebrew and French. This register is still extant in the library of Carpentras. It is, nevertheless, doubtful whether the Jews kept a complete record of vital statistics. The register indicates that there occurred in

[11] Calmet, Don, *Histoire de Lorraine* (Nancy 1757), vol. vi, p. 338. In 1792 the Nancy Jewish community stated that in view of the restrictions imposed on the Jews, no registers were kept; see Vanson, L., in *Revue Juive de Lorraine* (September 1933) 236-36. Regarding numerous similar instances see *idem*, "Curieuses requêtes de juifs tendant à faire partie, au fur à mesure des places disponibles, des quatre-vingt familles juives tolérées en Lorraine, dans l'ancien régime," in *La Revue juive de Lorraine* (1934). Cf. Liber, M., *in Revue des études juives*, vol. lxiii (1912) 195; Gregoire, M., *Essai sur la régéneration des juifs* (Metz 1789) p. 257 ff. Bail, *Des Juifs au dix-neuvième siècle* . . . (Paris 1819) p. 110.

[12] Grégoire, *Essai*, p. 258.

[13] Chobaut, H., "Les Juifs d'Avignon et du Comtat . . . ," in *Revue des études Juives*, vol. ci-cii (1936-37); Mossé, A., *Histoire des juifs d'Avignon et du Comtat Venaissin* (Paris 1934); cf. Szajkowski, Z., "The Decline and Fall of Provençal Jewry," in *Jewish Social Studies*, vol. vi (1944) 31-54. See Carmona-Benveniste, Laurent, "Les Séphardims en France sous l'ancien régime," in *Revue hébdomadaire*, année 48, vol. iii, pp. 469-88; Cirot, G., *Recherches sur les juifs espagnols et portugais à Bordeaux*, vol. xv, p. 135; Genevray, P., "Les Juifs des Landes sous le Premier Empire," in *Comité des travaux historiques et scientifiques. Bulletin de la section de géographie*, vol. xxxvii (1922) 128-29; Anchel, R., *Napoléon et les juifs* (Paris 1928) p. 2.

1780-89, 478 births and 487 deaths in the four major communities.[14] According to the *pinkas* cited above, however, the Jewish population had an excess of births over deaths during the preceding generations, unless a plague prevailed. As for the period 1780-89, it may be assumed that emigration led to a decrease in the number of Jewish births in the papal provinces. It is likely, however, that in order to avoid payment of the head-tax and other charges the Jews often failed to enter births in this register.

As for the small Jewish remainder in southern France, the following data may be noted: Nice 295 (lost during the Restoration but reincorporated in 1861) ; Nîmes 115; Montpellier 100; Lyons about 80;[15] a few in Marseilles, in which the synagogue was re-opened in 1790. (The synagogues of Aix-en-Provence, Arles and Salon remained closed until 1800-1804).[16] Jews had been attracted at an early date to southeastern France, with its large towns situated on important trade routes, in which they were to form large communities. During the period before 1789, however, the Jews were subject to restrictions. Of the 2,300 enjoying the right of domicile, 2,000 were in Avignon and Comtat-Venaissin; Nice was opened to them officially only after the Revolution.

Before 1789 Paris was the only place in central France which had a Jewish community of some size. Isidore Loeb estimated on the basis of the mortality rate that about 700-800 Jews lived in the capital in 1780.[17]

From the foregoing survey it must be concluded that there are no reliable estimates of the Jewish population on the eve of the Revolution in the areas comprised in present-day France. Over 70 percent were concentrated in Alsace and another 20 percent in the south. It is generally held that the Jews numbered about 40,000 at this date,[18] but this estimate

---

[14] Including 255 births and 286 deaths in Carpentras; Chobaut, H., in *Revue des études juives*, vol. ci (1937) 10. On the evasion of registration by non-Catholics, cf. Nicolai, A., "La Population de Bordeaux au 18e siècle," in *Revue économique de Bordeaux*, vol. xv, p. 135.

[15] Emanuel, Victor, *Les Juifs à Nice 1400-1860* (Nice 1905) p. 26, 48, 53; Kahn, S., *Notice sur les israélites de Nîmes* (Nîmes 1901) p. 29; Kahn, S., "Les Juifs de Montpellier au 18e siècle," in *Revue des études juives*, vol. xxxiii; Lévy, Alfred, *Notice sur les israélites de Lyon* (Paris 1894).

[16] Villeneuve, *Statistique du département des Bouches-du-Rhône* (Marseille 1924) vol. ii, p. 702.

[17] Loeb, Isidore, *Biographie d'Albert Cohn* (Paris 1878) p. 27; cf. Hildenfinger, P., *Documents sur les juifs à Paris au 18e siècle* (Paris 1913).

[18] Anchel, *Napoléon et les juifs*, p. 2; Bail, *ibid.*, p. 110 (50,000).

is derived from the later enumerations, with which the present study is primarily concerned.

Jewish Censuses During the First Empire

Under the *ancien régime* there had been no census of the population. Although a law providing for one was passed in 1791, the first census was delayed until 1801 and was followed by a second in 1806. During the first half of the century, until 1851, the Jews as such were not enumerated; the censuses of this period gathered no statistics on religious groups. A police-prefect indeed wrote on May 6, 1806 that it was regrettable that this was not being done.[19] Under Napoleon, when the question of the number of Jews came up, together with the decree regarding the Sanhedrin a circular was sent out on May 7, 1806 to the prefects of police, requiring them to take a count of the number of Jews. The compilation of this questionnaire was undertaken by Coquebert-Montbret, an industrious and sincere man with no anti-Jewish prejudice.[20] He could not, however, do much with the replies he received from the prefects, and therefore submitted a report "merely in order to comply with orders."[21] He gave the number of Jews in the entire French Empire (France and the occupied provinces) as 63,945, but this is not to be taken seriously. For example, in regard to the number of Jews in Alsace, Coquebert-Montbret used the estimates of the geographer Bursching, who in 1750 had given the total number of families as 88,698, including 2,585 Jewish families (2.92 percent). Inasmuch as the Jewish population had increased, it was estimated that it constituted 3 percent of the total, i.e., 11,679 in Bas-Rhin and 14,417 in Haut-Rhin.[22] Such guesswork regarding the number of Jews continued during the entire period of the First Empire.

According to the census of the Jewish consistories in 1808, there were in France (within the borders of 1815) 46,663 Jews.[23] According to

[19] Posener, S., "Les Juifs sous le Premier Empire. Les enquêtes administratives," in *Revue des études juives*, vol. xc (1931) 2.

[20] [de Montbret, E. C.], *Notice* . . . (Paris 1820); cf. Hildenfinger, P., "Un Ami des juifs en 1820, Eugène Coquebert de Montbret," in *Univers Israélite*, vol. lix, pt. 2 (1904) 301-306.

[21] Liber, M., "La Question Juive . . . en 1806," in *Revue des études juives*, vol. lxxii (1911) 136-37.

[22] Posener, *loc. cit.*, p. 3.

[23] *L'Univers Israélite*, vol. v (1849), 191-92.

another source, however, a consistorial census of the same year enumerated 43,237,[24] but the latter probably omitted several *départements*. A higher figure, 48,850 as of 1810, is given by Bail on the basis of a census of 44 *départements* (post-1815 boundaries), but without indicating his source.[25]

The best source for ascertaining the number of Jews at this time would seem to be the lists drawn up under the decree of July 20, 1808, requiring each Jew to register and adopt a family-name. A number of the local lists has been investigated thoroughly, but in respect to the names only. If the National Archives contain copies of these lists, this material might solve the problem. In the meantime, however, we may use the work of Posener.[26] This scholar took, as the basis for his study of the number of Jews during the First Empire, the report submitted by Minister of Interior Montalivet to Napoleon on March 13, 1811. This was the last report regarding the number of Jews compiled by the statistical bureau during the First Empire, and its figures appear to be much more reliable than those contained in the other official reports; Montalivet, moreover, shows close agreement with the reports of the Jewish consistories.

The year 1808 is not to be regarded as the exact date of a Jewish census in France. The figures presented below may, however, be accepted as the estimate of the number of Jews under the First Empire. Herein, to be sure, lies the weakness of this census for, between 1789 and the fall of the First Empire, French Jewry underwent important demographic changes. The Montalivet report of 1811 cites the figure of 141,147 Jews in the French Empire (France and the occupied territories, viz., Belgium, the Netherlands, the German and Swiss provinces, Italy, the Illyrian provinces). As for the number of Jews in the post-1815 borders of France, there were in the 44 *départments* 47,166 Jews, or .16 percent of the total population of 29,107,425 (census of 1808).

If we estimate the number of Jews in 1789 as 40,000, it follows that an increase of 17.8 percent took place during a period of fifteen to twenty years. The picture, nevertheless, becomes altogether different when we attempt to analyze this increase according to the separate provinces. The

[24] *Le Lien d'Israél,* vol. iii (1857) 18-19.

[25] Bail, *op. cit.,* p. 106.

[26] Posener, S., "Les Juifs sous le Premier Empire," in *Revue des études juives,* vol. xciii (1932) 192-214, vol. xciv, p. 157-66; Posener, S., "The Immediate Economic and Social Effects of the Emancipation of the Jews in France," in *Jewish Social Studies,* vol. i (1939) 271-326.

censuses of Alsace-Lorraine in 1752 and 1784 returned a total of 20,697 (19,707 in Alsace and about 990 in Lorraine). According to Montalivet, there were 26,070 in Alsace, an increase of over 30 percent in a space of twenty-four years; in Lorraine there were 10,896, a tenfold increase. In Alsace-Lorraine as a whole there were 36,966 Jews, an increase of 16,356 persons or 79 percent. During the period in question there was an influx of Jews from abroad into Alsace, which, however, was offset by the number who moved to Paris and southern France during the first years after 1789.

It is very unlikely that such a rapid natural increase should have taken place during a period of war and revolution which laid waste so many Jewish settlements in Alsace-Lorraine. It is assumed that this increase is partially due to the immigration from the other side of the Rhine into Alsace-Lorraine during the First Empire. Posener is, however, of the opinion that this influx was minimal and much exaggerated in the consistorial and police reports regarding beggars and itinerant peddlers;[27] according to him, the immigration of Jews into Alsace during the years 1784-1808 added about 1,500 to the Jewish population. It must, however, be pointed out that Jewish emigration from this province and the decline of the rate of natural increase were undoubtedly greater than Posener believes. As for the Jewish increase in Lorraine, this was in large part due to the influx from Alsace. On the other hand, the difference between the 1808 total in both provinces and the figures for the preceding period is too great to be attributed to migration alone; the earlier figures undoubtedly represent underestimates.

The archives of the Yiddish Scientific Institute contain the census of the Marseilles Jewish consistory (eight *départements*) of 1809. This census was undertaken for the purpose of collecting the communal taxes and it must be assumed to have been far more reliable than those conducted by the police officials. Let us compare these figures with those of Montalivet and Bail.

---

[27] Posener, in *Univers Israélite* (1934) 785-87, 821-23, 856-59; cf. Anchel, *Napoléon et les juifs*, p. 66, 77-78, 340-46, 532; Grégoire, *Motion en faveur des juifs* (Paris 1789) p. 9; Liber, M., "Les Juifs et la convocation des Etats Généraux," in *Revue des études juives*, vol. lxv-lxvi (1913) 2; *idem*, "La Question juive devant le conseil d'état en 1806," *loc. cit.*, vol. lxxii (1921) 9-10, 150-51.

TABLE I

THE JEWISH POPULATION IN EIGHT DÉPARTEMENTS
OF SOUTHERN FRANCE, 1809

Département	Consistoire	Montalivet	Bail
Alpes Maritimes	285	303	303
Bouches-du-Rhône	869	942	942
Gard	414	425	425
Hérault	177	141	141
Isère	15	4	4
Rhône	184	195	67
Var	11	14	14
Vaucluse	654	631	631
Total	2,609	2,655	2,527

The official census of 1831 gave the total population as 32,569,223.[28] In a report to the Ministry of Cults of the same year, the Central Consistory estimated the number of Jews in the country as 73,000, an estimate based on reports received from the local consistories.[29] In comparison with Montalivet's report this indicated an increase of 25,834, or over 50 percent, in a twenty-year period. Toward the end of 1845 the Central Consistory carried out a census which indicated the number of Jews to be 85,910,[30] a growth of 12,910 (17 percent) since the previous Jewish census of 1831.

The Censuses of 1851, 1861 and 1866

The question of religion was included for the first time in the census of 1851, under a fourfold classification: Catholics, Protestants, Jews and other non-Christians. While there was no decree requiring the adherence of all Jews to the Jewish consistory, there was a regulation to that effect, in an article in the budget law of July 17, 1819, which was reiterated in subsequent periods; namely, that all Jews had to pay a tax to support the Jewish consistories.[31] A sharp debate broke out over this require-

[28] *Statistique de France,* série 1, vol. i, p. 21.
[29] *Archives Nationales* 11094; cf. Anchel, R., *Notes sur les frais du culte juif en France de 1815 à 1831* (Paris 1928) p. 43.
[30] *L'Univers Israélite,* vol. v (1849) 40, 191-92 (dates the census erroneously in 1835).
[31] Cerfberr, A., *Les Juifs* (Paris 1847) preface

ment:[32] on the one hand there were the antisemites who objected to the state's recognition of the Jewish consistories; on the other was the group of Jews who argued that they were unable to pay the tax. In addition, there were Jews who on principle contended that they were not religious and that "no faith should be forced upon them."[33] The Central Consistory realized the danger in this viewpoint. A number of high government authorities were likewise opposed to this trend and the government, as a matter of fact, did not yield to the Jews who preferred to be without any religious affiliation. Only baptized Jews were stricken from the tax-rolls of the Consistory.

The attempt to gather figures regarding religious groups came at an inauspicious time. The 1851 census took place during a period of serious political struggle, immediately after Napoleon III had seized power and had suppressed the republican opposition. The republicans had a good reason to regard the introduction of the category "religion" in the census as reprehensible and felt justified in fighting such an innovation as an "infraction of the freedom of conscience,"[34] especially since the Church regarded Napoleon III as a godsend.[35]

While the consistorial censuses were undertaken by the Jewish communities and the general censuses during the First Empire involved the aid of the consistories, there was yet no attempt to appoint Jews as census-takers either in 1851 or later. It is true that a ministerial directive provided that rabbis were to be invited to collaborate with the local statistical bureaus.[36] It is not known to what extent this directive was carried out; the number of rabbis in the country (82 in 1872) was in fact too small to enable them to exercise proper control. The return of the census forms to the Ministry of Interior was, moreover, in many instances delayed because of the addition of the new categories. This, according to the report of the Minister, militated against the accuracy of the census.[37] In fact, the results of the census turned out to be quite dubious. The

[32] Anchel, R., *op. cit.*, p. 17-19.

[33] *Ibid.*, p. 22.

[34] "Un grande nombre d'habitants l'ayant considéré [le census] comme une sorte de violence à la liberté de conscience;" Legoyt, A., "Rapport au Congres int. de Florence sur l'état de la statistique en France" in *Journal de la société statistique de Paris* (1868) 55.

[35] Debidour, A., *Histoire des rapports de l'église et de l'état en France de 1789 à 1870* (Paris 1898) p. 518-23.

[36] Uhry, J., *Récueil des lois* (Bordeaux 1903) p. 2.

[37] *Moniteur* (May 14, 1851).

data were inexact and not presented according to *départements;* it was even contemplated to remove the section on religion from the published report altogether.[38] The census gave the number of Jews as 73,975 in a total of 35,787,170 (0.2 percent) . In 1857 the statistician J. Ch. M. Boudin obtained the data on religion according to *départements,* which he published for the purpose of proving the existence of a "Jewish invasion" in some of the provinces.[39]

As a matter of fact, the subsequent census of 1856 omitted the question on religion, which was, however, re-introduced in 1861. In 1866 the section on religion included a subdivision for persons whose religion was unknown[40] and the data were published according to *départements.* In the introduction to this publication it is stated that although this census did not offer the serious difficulties of the census of 1851, the results were again somewhat incomplete and to be accepted with a certain amount of reserve.[41]

The religious data returned by the censuses of 1851, 1861, and 1866 were as follows:[42]

TABLE II

POPULATION OF FRANCE ACCORDING TO RELIGION, 1851, 1861, 1866

Religion	1851	1861	1866
Catholics	34,931,032	36,490,891	37,107,212
Protestants	748,332	802,339	846,619
Jews	73,975	79,964	89,047
Other non-Christian cults	26,348	1,295	1,400
Unknown	3,483	11,824	22,786
Total	35,787,170	37,386,313	38,067,064

According to these data, between 1851 and 1866 the number of Jews

[38] Levasseur, E., *La Population française* (Paris 1889), vol. i, p. 338. The data on religion were, however, given for the *villes chefs-lieux d'arrondissement; Statistique de France,* série 2, vol. ii (1851) 262-79.

[39] Boudin, J. Ch. M., *Traité de géographie et de statistique médicale,* vol. ii (Paris 1857) p. 133-135.

[40] *Statistique de France,* série 2, vol. xvii, p. xxvi. Boudin included such a subdivision in connection with data drawn from the census of 1851, but it is not clear on what basis he did so.

[41] *Op. cit.,* vol. xiii, p. xiv.

[42] Not including the small number in Metz; see Szajkowski, Z. in *Yidn in Frankreich* (New York 1942) vol. i, p. 232.

increased over 20 percent, whereas the total population increased only 6.4 percent. Moreover, when the figures in Montalivet's report are compared with the censuses in question, it would appear that between 1808 and 1851 the growth of the Jewish population was over 85 percent, as against an increase in the total population of only 18.6 percent. Similarly, in the period between 1808 and 1866, the former increased about 90 percent and the latter about 30 percent.

Reliability of the Censuses

The result is quite different when we compare the consistorial with the official enumerations. Between 1831 (consistorial census) and the census of 1851 it appears that the Jewish population increased only 1.3 percent, while the total population increased 8.6 percent. The consistorial figures for 1845, furthermore, indicate a decrease of the Jewish population enumerated in 1851. Thereafter, according to the official census of 1866, the Jewish population increased 13.6 percent during the ensuing period of twenty-one years, as against an increase of 7.5 percent in the total population.

An analysis of the statistics of Jewish voters registered in the consistorial elections indicates, on the other hand, that many Jewish families were not registered. In 1850-52 the Jewish voters numbered 13,859,[42] or 18.7 percent of the number of Jews recorded in the census of 1851. In the total population of France in 1848, however, the voters formed 22.9 percent (census of 1851). In 1900 the consistorial census of the department of Bouches-du-Rhône counted 5,587 Jewish persons and 551 voters, or 9.1 percent, as compared with the ratio of 22.3 percent in the local population as a whole.[43] Again, the Jewish voters in the Paris consistory increased from 2,295 in 1852 to no more than 3,991 in 1900, while the number of Jews grew fivefold during this period.[44] It is clear that a considerable number of Jewish men of voting age (25 and over) failed to register; inasmuch as the communal officials conducted the successive enumerations of the Jews as well as of the voters it follows that the consistorial censuses were inevitably incomplete.[45]

[43] Archives of the Yiddish Scientific Institute; cf. "Bouches-du-Rhône," in *Encyclopédie départmentale*, vol. xiii, p. 352.

[44] Szajkowski, *loc. cit.; Univers Israélite*, vol. lvi (1900-01) 207-9.

[45] *Loc. cit.*, vol. lvii, p. 688-90, 456. On the extra-legal status of religious statistics, see Baugey, Georges, *De la Condition légale du culte israélite* . . . (Paris 1899) p. 72.

It is thus evident that a discrepancy exists between the official and the consistorial censuses. One must therefore assume either that the censuses of 1808, 1831 and 1845 exaggerated the number of Jews, or that the data of the official census of 1851 are incomplete. While the figures of the consistories seem to be closer to the truth, these must be taken with due reserve in view of the fact that the consistories began to lose their hold on the Jews in 1815. It should be observed that the statistical records of the Jewish and other religious bodies had no official status throughout this century. As for the dubious reliability of the Jewish statistics collected by the official census, we may cite two cases in regard to the 1861 census. According to this census, there were in the *département* of Gironde no more than 2,253 Jews, while in the capitals of arrondissements (*chefs-lieux d'arrondissements*) alone there were fully 2,771. Similarly, according to the census of 1872, there were 1,175 Jews in the city of Lyons, or considerably more than the total of 866 indicated for the entire *département* of the Rhône.[46]

Political Aspects

The political aspect of the question of religious statistics may be illustrated by the following incident. In 1856 Georges Darboy, an abbé who later became bishop of Paris, published an official Catholic work in which he estimated the Paris population to be divided as follows: Catholics 1,025,000, Protestants 13,300 and Jews 10,709; others 4,000.[47] The Protestants contended that the Catholic Church had purposely exaggerated the number of its communicants and underestimated that of the Protestants, while Isidore Cahen, editor of *Archives Israélites,* added that Darboy had intentionally "reduced" the number of Jews.[48]

According to the official census of 1851, the local Jewish population was 10,719.[49] The statistician Boudin, however, who set little store on this census, calculated their number as 14,320 in 1846 and 16,512 in 1848,[50] an increase of 2,192 in two years. The consistorial census of 1845

[46] *Statistique de France,* series 2, vol. xiii, p. 84-85, 213; vol. xxi, p. 32, 236.

[47] Darboy, G., *Statistique réligieuse du diocèse de Paris, mémoire sur l'état présent du diocèse* (Paris 1856).

[48] "Il y a tout lieu de croire que certaines évaluations ont été enflées et certaines autres amoindries à dessein;" *Archives Israélites,* vol. xvii (1856) 569.

[49] *Statistique de France,* série 2, vol. ii, p. 276.

[50] Boudin, *op. cit.,* p. 137.

estimated the number as 15,000.[51] On the basis of their mortality rate, Isidore Loeb estimated the Jews of Paris to have numbered 14,938 in 1851 and 26,298 in 1861.[52]

The vociferous antisemitic circles tried to inflate the number of Jews in order to prove their charge of a Jewish "invasion" of France. Thus the deputy of Haut-Rhin, André, declared on December 4, 1830 that there were 400,000 Jews in France,[53] while certain anti-Jewish Catholic circles, on the other hand, regularly underestimated the size of the non-Catholic population in order to prevent them from claiming a proportionate place in public life, as well as to decrease the governmental allocation of funds for the Jewish religion. As a matter of fact, the inclusion in the budget of appropriations for the Jewish religion, beginning in 1831, evoked a number of parliamentary debates[54], with the Ministry of Justice and Cults maintaining that the funds set aside for the Jewish religion were not out of proportion.[55]

While Jews, with few exceptions, refrained from attacking or even criticising Catholicism, the Church included in its program a campaign against Jewry. When in 1842 Auguste Fabius, a Jew in Lyons, printed a sermon which he had delivered, in which he attempted to refute the Catholic faith,[56] the consistory sharply rebuked him.[57] The Catholic Church, however, attacked both Jews and Protestants openly. An example of these attacks is the curious brochure against Jews and Protestants which appeared in Paris in 1815.[58] The Fourierist antisemite and Anglophobe, Toussenel, in a well-known book written in 1845, stated: "When you say Jew you also mean Protestant, and you know it."[59] The two religious minorities, on the other hand, at times united in defense. In Nîmes, a stronghold of Protestantism, Jews and Protestants came together to form the republican opposition.[60] In 1902 the economist Anatole

[51] *Archives Israélites* (1849) 40; cf. *loc. cit.* (1858) 309 (27,000).

[52] Loeb, *Albert Cohn*, p. 28.

[53] *Moniteur* (1830) 1641; Hallez, T., *Des Juifs en France* (Paris 1845) p. 241-42.

[54] Halphen, A. E., *Recueil des lois* (Paris 1851) p. 450, 427.

[55] *Archives Israélites* (1843) 400.

[56] Fabius, Auguste, *Offrande au Dieu de l'univers* (Lyon 1842) 47 pp.

[57] *Archives Israélites* (1843) 13, 257-58, 266-69.

[58] *La Boîte à Pierrette des protestans et des israélites* (Paris 1815). Pp. 8, (12°); cited in *Philobiblion*, no. 64 (1934) 9.

[59] "Et qui dit Juif, dit protestant, sachez le;" Toussenel, A., *Les Juifs, rois de l'époque. Histoire de la féodalite financière* (Paris 1847) vol. i, p. iv.

[60] Posener, S., *A. Cremieux* vol. i (Paris 1933) p. 41, 190-92.

THE GROWTH OF THE JEWISH POPULATION OF FRANCE

(Concluded) *

After 1872

At the International Congress of Demography, which met at Paris in 1878, Professor Emile Worms (1838-1918) of the University of Rennes (a Jew), came out strongly against a section on religion in the census schedule. A census, he argued, must be non-political; not everyone practiced the religion of his parents; and, moreover, added Worms with an air of satisfaction, there was a tendency for races and religious groups to become assimilated, the number of mixed marriages was on the increase, etc. This assimilationist viewpoint was, however, opposed by almost all the other demographers.[87] The question was again debated in 1880 by a committee set up to modify the system of census-taking. On this occasion Arthur Chevrin, the committee reporter, took the position of the democratic wing of the Third Republic: religion was a private affair and no one should be questioned about it, just as one's monarchist or republican leanings should not be the subject of inquiry.[88] The government adopted this view of the matter and, while the complete separation of Church and State was not effected until 1905, no religious statistics were gathered by the census-takers after 1872.

During the ensuing period we find the antisemites greatly exaggerating the number of Jews, citing figures as high as 500,000. As part of this campaign, on October 15, 1889, *L'Intransigéant*, the antisemitic newspaper edited by the former revolutionary, Rochefort, alleged that 35,000

* See vol. viii, no 3, p. 179-96.

[87] Worms, René, "Émile Worms," in *Revue internationale de sociologie*, vol. xxvi (1918), 225 ff.; cf. *Congrès international de démographie*, pp. 33-45.

[88] Chevrin, *op. cit.*, p. 472-78.

[89] Loeb, *Biographie*, p. 28, 602; Kahn, *op. cit.*

foreign Jews had been naturalized for electoral purposes. Such propaganda was, indeed, not limited to areas with a Jewish population. One of the earliest antisemitic newspapers, which helped to prepare the atmosphere of the Dreyfus affair, *L'Anti-Sémite de Mondidier* (1881), appeared in a town which had not a single Jew in it.[89]

During the fifteen-year period after the census of 1872, a number of widely differing estimates of the Jewish population of France were published by more objective persons. The range of these estimates may be seen from the following list:

Author	Date	Estimate
Maurice Bloch[90]	1873	90,000
Emile Levasseur[91]	1879	Under 100,000
Isidore Loeb[92]	1884	63,000
Archives Israélites[93]	1884	74,400
Jonas Weyl[94]	1885	70,000
Emile Levasseur[95]	1887	69,791

II

Throughout the nineteenth century there was a constant movement of Jews from one *département* to another, a trend already observable prior to 1789. There were large portions of France in which few or no Jews lived, and the ratio of the Jewish to the total population of individual *départements* showed a wide range. Until 1789 over 90 percent of the Jewish population was to be found in several provinces comprising no more than a sixth of the country's population (post-1815 boundaries). The fluctuation of the density of the Jewish population during subsequent years may be judged from Tables IV and V (see also the maps, p. 316 [38] f.).

[90] Bloch, M., *Statistique de France* (1873); Lagneau, *Anthropologie* . . . p. 674; *idem*, in *Revue d'anthropologie*, vol. iv (1875) p. 175. A geographer outside of France is cited as estimating the number as only 43,000; *Archives israélites*, vol. xxxvi (1875) 715.

[91] Levasseur, E., *Géographie de la France* (Paris 1879) p. 151.

[92] Loeb, *Juifs*, p. 10-11.

[93] Prague, H., *Annuaire des Archives Israélites, 5645* (Paris 1884).

[94] Weyl, Jonas, "La Population juive dans le monde," in *Bulletin de la société de géographie de Marseille*, vol. ix (1885) 139-40.

[95] Levasseur, *Population*, vol. i, p. 341.

TABLE IV

DENSITY OF THE JEWISH POPULATION OF FRANCE, 1808-1872,
BY GROUPS OF *DÉPARTEMENTS*

Group	Number of *Départements*				
	1808	1851	1861	1866	1872
No Jews	44	2	6	4	7
1-100 Jews	22	57	53	55	48
100-1,000 Jews	14	19	26	21	25
1,000-10,000 Jews	6	5	6	6	6
Over 10,000 Jews	1	3	3	3	1
All groups	87	86	89	89	87

In 1808 the Jews formed about 0.16 percent of the total population
of France, but in 31 *départements* their ratio was less than 0.1 percent.
In 7 *départements* the ratio ranged from 0.2 to 0.9 and in 3 others from
1.7 to 3.2 percent. In the remaining 44 *départements*, which comprised
45.7 percent of the country's population, there were no Jews. In 1866,
on the other hand, the 4 *départements* with no Jewish population comprised only 4.7 percent of the total population. As late as 1872, when the
means of communication in France were quite well developed, there were
still 7 *départements* without any Jews; 2 had one Jew each and 12 had
from 2 to 10 Jews. In 1861, when the Jews formed roughly 0.2 percent
of the population, in 27 *départements* there was less than one Jew to
10,000 of the population; in 1866 this ratio prevailed in 32 *départements*.
In 1861, on the other hand, in 4 *départements* the Jews formed from 1.19
to 3.63 percent of the total (Bas-Rhin, Haut-Rhin, Moselle, Meurthe-et
Seine).

In 1808, 91.7 percent of French Jewry[96] and in 1851, 89.1 percent lived
in the *départements* which were formed from the provinces of Alsace,
Lorraine, Guyenne, and Gascogne (with the cities of Bordeaux, Bayonne,
and Paris). These provincial boundaries, however, had hardly any influence on the internal migration of French Jewry, either before or after
1789. In those provinces where Jews were permitted to live prior to the
Revolution, they were not allowed to move about freely, but were
restricted to certain localities. In the papal provinces of Avignon and Com-

[96] Not including the Vaucluse *département* (under papal rule until 1789).

TABLE V

JEWISH AND TOTAL POPULATION OF FRANCE, 1808 AND 1851,

BY PROVINCE[1]

Province	1808		1851	
	Total population	Jewish population	Total population	Jewish population
Alsace	837,866	26,070	1,081,581	35,757
Lorraine	1,370,394	10,896	1,666,173	15,336
Guyenne-et-Gascogne	3,062,810	3,330	3,250,090	3,351
Ile-de-France	2,222,674	2,960	3,202,541	11,470
Provence	720,274	956	939,016	1,456
Languedoc	2,291,732	677	2,763,758	884
Comtat-Venaissin	205,833	631	264,618	673
Comté-de-Nice [2]	131,266	303	-------	---
Bourgogne	1,457,688	278	1,729,089	582
Lyonnais	658,033	195	1,247,333	487
Flandres	839,533	166	1,158,285	271
Champagne	1,061,916	158	1,238,243	818
Béarn	382,575	127	446,997	394
Franche-Comté	825,144	91	957,447	1,340
Aunis-et-Saintonge	405,592	70	469,992	80
Artois	570,092	63	692,994	157
Normandie	2,575,745	47	2,709,792	287
Auvergne	1,094,270	38	850,226	87
Bretagne	2,298,062	33	2,838,779	165
Limousin	496,219	29	640,243	31
Orléannais	770,063	17	897,813	79
Picardie	494,642	14	570,641	36
Angoumais	327,052	8	382,912	18
Bourbonnais	260,046	5	336,758	12
Dauphiné	849,933	4	1,062,381	89
Others	2,897,971	none	4,385,470	125
Total	29,107,425	47,166	35,783,172	73,975

[1] Pre-1789 boundaries.
[2] Not under French rule in 1851.

tat-Venaissain they were allowed to reside only in 4 towns (Carpentras, Avignon, Cavaillon and Ile-sur-Sorgue). In Alsace-Lorraine they were permitted to live in the cities of Strasbourg, Nancy, etc., in very restricted numbers. We, therefore, get the following picture in 1808: in the 8 *départements* formed within the limits of the former province of Languedoc there were 677 Jews (673 in 4 *départements* and 4 in another). Of the 2,960 Jews in the five *départements* of the former province of Ile-de-France, 92.3 percent lived in Paris; in 2 *départements* there were no Jews at all.

Thus, a comparison of the geographic distribution of the Jewish population in 1808 and in 1851 indicates that it was influenced by the boundaries of the *départements* rather than by the older provincial

boundaries. In provinces which had a relatively small Jewish population
in 1808 no increase occurred during the intervening period.

Let us now consider the distribution of the Jewish population in the
central and frontier *départements,* which must also be taken into account
in relation to the economic situation of French Jewry. In 1808 the maritime *départements* contained 30.7 and in 1866 31.5 percent of the total
population of the country. (Table VI) With regard to the Jewish population the corresponding ratios were, respectively, 2.3 and 3.8 percent.
Thus, both the total and the Jewish population increased somewhat in
these *départements.* In the other frontier *départements,* on the other
hand, the population as a whole decreased from 20 percent of the total
in 1808 to 19 percent in 1866. Within the Jewish population, however,
the ratio dropped from 71.2 to 53.2 percent as a result of the influx of
Jews from Alsace-Lorraine to Paris and to *départements* not situated on
the national borders. In these central *départements* there was in 1808
26.5 and in 1866 43 percent of the total Jewish population.

Internal Migration

The memorandum submitted in 1788 by the emissaries of the
Sephardic Jews of Bordeaux and Bayonne to Minister Malesherbes contained a plea for the right of residence in the whole of France.[97] Thereafter although the Jews received almost complete freedom to settle anywhere they pleased, they nevertheless did not spread over the entire
country but preferred to migrate to localities already settled by Jews or
to neighboring *départements.* There were but few new large Jewish
communities after 1789, located in regions in which Jews had formerly
wished to settle and which were in the vicinity of older groups. By the
close of the nineteenth century there were new Jewish groups elsewhere
as well, but these were mostly small. The internal migrations of the
Jews after 1789 were thus guided by a combination of economic considerations and the traditional tendency toward living in more or less com-
pact groups.

The important industrial center of Northern France (*département
du Nord*), where there had been no Jews prior to 1789, contained 3.8
percent of the total (including Alsace-Lorraine), but only 0.9 percent of

[97] Henry, Léon, *Histoire des juifs de Bayonne* (Paris 1893) p. 153.

the Jewish population. In the town of Tourcoing the population grew from 27,615 to 43,322 in the period of 1851-72, but Jews did not begin to arrive in this important center of industry and trade until the German annexation of Alsace-Lorraine. In 1896 the antisemite P. Sapin reported 43 Jewish-owned enterprises in Roubaix and eight in Tourcoing. The industrial center of Lille, likewise, did not attract Jews until after the German annexation of Alsace-Lorraine. A chief rabbinate was instituted, not because of the large number of Jews, but in deference to Rabbi Lippman, who had left Metz in order to remain a French citizen.

TABLE VI

JEWISH AND TOTAL POPULATION IN THE BORDER *DÉPARTEMENTS*
OF FRANCE, 1808 AND 1866

Region	1808		1866	
	Total population	Jewish population	Total population	Jewish population
Maritime	8,924,631	5,313	12,002,104	9,801
La Manche	3,633,989	190	4,521,154	1,230
Océan	2,297,662	23	2,911,807	218
Golfe de Gascogne	1,571,668	3,999	2,313,637	5,015
Mediterranée	1,421,312	1,101	2,255,506	3,338
Départements bordering on other states	5,835,241	33,600	7,197,820	47,375
Belgium	1,780,897	7,192	2,410,837	8,774
Germany	837,866	26,070	1,106,058	35,814
Switzerland	526,090	86	592,161	995
Italy	1,329,224	18	1,494,710	106
Spain	1,361,174	234	1,594,054	1,686

Several *départements,* in which the population showed a considerable increase since 1806, remained, according to the census of 1872, without a single Jew; e.g., La Vendée, with an increase of 133,002 persons, Côtes-du-Nord (105,867), Corrège (81,159), Lot (106,399) and Cantal (19,565). Other *départements,* in which the population likewise showed a considerable increase, had only a handful of Jews in 1872; e.g., Basses Alpes (4), Cher (7) and Maine-et-Loire (12). All of these were located in regions from which Jews had been excluded prior to the Revolution.

The *départements* on the Atlantic did not attract many Jews. This is again ascribable both to economic reasons and to the previous exclusion. The *départements* containing the ports on the Gulf of Gascony, on the other hand, with the Sephardic communities of Bordeaux and Bayonne, saw an increase in the Jewish population during 1808-1872 of 40.1 percent (in the total population 47 percent). In the larger Jewish centers (Paris, Lyon, Marseille, Strasbourg and Metz), however, the number of Jews increased at a more rapid rate than did the total population. During 1808-1866 the number of Jews in the *départments* bordering on the Mediterranean (the community of Marseille was founded after 1789), increased 67 percent. We may, therefore, infer that one of the reasons for the slower growth of the Sephardic centers was the migration which took place after 1789. It also shows clearly that here, too, the Jews had remained only because they had no choice. Although they contributed in large measure to the development of the port of Bordeaux, after 1789 few Jews were attracted to the southwest. Immediately after the Revolution a handful of Jews from Alsace-Lorraine arrived; when the approximately 2,000 Jews came to register their names in Bordeaux, in accordance with Napoleon's decree of July 20, 1808, there were among them only about 30 Ashkenazim,[98] most of whom had probably lived in Bordeaux before 1789. This situation may also have been influenced by antipathy between the Ashkenazim and the Sephardim, although their relations were not as acrimonious as they had been in the eighteenth century.[99]

Of special interest in this connection is the case of St. Esprit, a suburb of Bordeaux. In the sixteenth century it had a community of about 1,100 Jews and in 1808 of 1,170.[100] Prior to 1789 it was difficult for Jews to settle in the city of Bordeaux proper. During the Empire and the Restoration periods the local reactionary groups were very hostile,[101] but the Jews gradually found it possible to move from St. Esprit to Bordeaux.

The Jewish population of Paris had always been a mixture of Ashkenazim from Alsace-Lorraine, of Sephardim, Comtadines and Jews from

[98]Leroux, A., *La Colonie germanique de Bordeaux* (Bordeaux 1918) vol. i, p. 169.
[99] The Comtadin Jews prohibited marriage with Ashkenazim as late as 1789; Lunel, A., "La Solidarité juive," in *Revue juive de Genève*, no. xxxi, p. 35; cf. Szajkowski, in *Yivo Bleter*, vol. xix (1942) 312; Tcherikover, E., in *Yidn in Frankreich*, vol. i, p. 116-17.
[100] Genevray, Pierre, "Les Juifs des Landes sous le Premier Empire," in *Comité des travaux historiques et scientifiques, Bulletin de la section de geographie*, vol. xxxvii (1922) 128-29.
[101] Henry, *op. cit.*, p. 240.

other countries. One source gives the number of Jews in Paris in 1808 as 2,733, of whom 1,324 had been born in the capital, the others having come from other *départements* and from abroad.[102] According to a list of 1809, there were 2,908 Jews in Paris, of whom only 1,324 were born in the city, while over 1,500 had come from other *départements* and from abroad.[103] Included in the latter category were 311 living in Paris from 10 to 25 years; 90 from 5 to 10 years; 114 from 1 to 5 years and 17 less than a year.

The emigration of Jews from Alsace-Lorraine was especially marked. According to the census of 1808, there were 26,070 Jews in Alsace (Haut-Rhin and Bas-Rhin) or 55.3 percent of French Jewry; the 36,966 Jews of Alsace-Lorraine constituted 78 percent of the total Jewish population. According to the 1851 census, 69.1 percent of French Jewry lived in Alsace-Lorraine; in 1861 the ratio was 62.2 and in 1866 56.9 percent. According to the census of 1872, there remained in the lost provinces 40,812 Jews, forming no more than 45.2 percent of the 90,251 Jews within the former boundaries of the country.

During the period 1789-1808 many Alsatian Jews moved to Lorraine, which, as a result, again became a great Jewish center. A list of Jews of the year 1811, naming those obliged to pay the debts of the old Metz community, comprises 87 families who had left Alsace; five years later a similar list contained 93. A third list of the year 1816 names 60 families who had migrated to *départements* recently annexed by France. In 1843 there were former inhabitants of Metz still paying old debts, while living in the following places: Charleville, Sédan, Troyes, Marseille, Besançon, Valence, Brest, Bordeaux, Tours, Orléans, Chalôns-sur-Marne, Epernay, Rheims and some 50 other towns.[104] The first Jewish inhabitants in Dijon (from which Jews had been excluded prior to the Revolution) as well as of many other towns were likewise from Alsace.[105]

In a number of localities, especially in Alsace, there were attempts, even after 1789, to interfere with the Jews' freedom of settlement. In

[102] Lévy, Louis, "Les Juifs à Paris sous l'Empire et la Restauration," *Univers israélite* (1905-06).

[103] Kahn, Léon, *Les Professions manuelles* . . . (Paris 1885) p. 71-73; cf. Loeb, *Albert Cohn;* Hildenfinger, P., *Documents sur les juifs à Paris au 18e siècle* (Paris 1913).

[104] P. H., "Dette de l'ancienne communauté juive de Metz," in *La Revue juive de Lorraine* (June-September 1934); Anchel, *op. cit.*, p. xxviii, 526.

[105] Clément-Janin, *Notice sur la communauté israélite de Dijon* (Dijon 1879) p. 69.

other places, even during the Revolution, Jewish residents were threatened with expulsion, their funeral cortèges met with interference and the abrogated head-tax was demanded.[106] Napoleon's decree of March 17, 1808 forbade Jewish immigration into Alsace and that of Jews from foreign countries into France; for a time the police made it difficult for Jews to migrate from one *département* to another (especially in Alsace). The Central Jewish Consistory often had to intervene in cases where the administration withheld marriage licenses on the ground that the bride had no right of domicile in the *département* in which the groom lived.[107] It is noteworthy that the Jewish pamphleteers during the First Empire (Furtado, Ber, Isaac-Ber, Cerfbeer, *et al.*), who discussed all other aspects of Napoleon's decree, failed to mention this opposition to the internal migration of Jews in the eastern *départements*. In the west the Jews apparently saw no serious danger in this campaign. At any rate, most Jews who desired to move to another *départment* found a way out and evaded the regime. At the same time the Jewish consistories made such internal migrations more difficult by conducting their campaign against Jewish vagrants. The Paris consistory, for example, exercised quasi-police powers in dealing with such newcomers; in order to settle in Paris a Jew had to secure permission from the consistory. In 1812, the Paris consistory handed the police a list of 30 penniless Jews designated for expulsion.[108] The consistory regarded such measures as a mark of true emancipation: Jews were now capable of shaking off "such unfortunate solidarity."[109]

On the whole the Jews were in a nervous state during the First Empire; Napoleon's decree had placed them in a precarious position. The Parisian Jews were reported to be inclined to sell all their worldly goods so as to be ready to leave the country in case of persecution.[110] Such apprehensions stimulated the internal migration. The strong anti-Jewish sentiment in the provinces, where self-defense was more difficult than in the larger towns, was another serious factor.[111] The editor of *Archives Israélites* reported in 1844 (vol. v, p. 467) that Schelestadt, Rouffach and

[106] Anchel, *op. cit.*, p. 12.
[107] Posener, in *Univers israélite* (1934) 786.
[108] Anchel, *op. cit.*, 534-535.
[109] *Op. cit.*, p. 535.
[110] Posener, S.. "Les Juifs sous le Premier Empire," in *Univers israélite* (1936) 731.
[111] Bing, *Mémoire particulier . . .* (Metz 1789).

other Alsatian towns tolerated Jews who came there to do business only on a day-by-day basis, and would not permit them to settle. Even as late as 1848 there were pogroms in Alsace and the anti-Jewish feeling in that province was destined to persist. It is interesting to note that at a time when Jewish leaders did everything they could to promote agricultural pursuits for Jews, the editors of *Archives Israélites* (1864, p. 598-99) advocated the exodus of Jews from the rural areas. In the villages, they stated, the Jews engaged in peddling and formed a separate group, cut off from the non-Jews while in the city they could engage in trade or some other vocation.

The four ancient communities in the South saw an exodus consisting chiefly of rich Jews, but it was penury which drove the Alsatian Jews to leave. During the entire nineteenth century Alsace suffered from famine, on account of crop failures, from epidemics, etc. Its population was greatly impoverished and there was a continual movement to other parts of France, to Algeria and the United States. Already in 1789 the Jewish leader, Isaiah Beer Bing, wrote that two thirds of the Jewish population of Alsace were on the brink of starvation. Gabriel Schramek, an Alsatian-Jewish soldier who had served under Napoleon, has left a record of how he travelled from one community to another in order to eke out a meager existence.[112] The children came to school without breakfast.[113] Of the 3,000 Jewish families in the regional consistory of Colmar, only 900 could pay taxes (1828), and of the 450 families in Metz, 226 were able to pay.[114] Bands of Jewish beggars and their families were roving about in Alsace-Lorraine; around 1850 there were 200 Jewish families of roving beggars and an additional 600 families lived partly on charity.[115] A student of conditions in Alsace stated that the extent of poverty among Jews in Bas-Rhin was 50 percent greater than among non-Jews.[116] In the '50s there were in the regional consistory of Colmar only 27 communities

[112] Grunwald, M., *Die Feldzuege Napoleons . . .* (Vienna 1913) p. 223-224.

[113] Bloch, M., "L'Oeuvre scolaire de juifs français depuis 1789," in *Revue des études juives,* vol. xxvi.

[114] Szajkowski, in *Yidn in Frankreich,* vol. i, p. 210.

[115] *Extrait du registre des délibérations du Consistoire Israélite de la circonscription de Strasbourg, 24 octobre 1822;* Levy, J., "Les Mendiants juifs en Alsace et en Lorraine," in *Le Lien d'Israël* (1858) 453-39; *Archives israélites,* vol. i (1840) 315-317.

[116] Reboul-Deneyrol, *Paupérisme dans le Bas-Rhin;* Boudin, M., in *Journal de la société de statistique de Paris,* vol. i (1860) 55.

in a total of 53 which had regular budgets (averaging a mere 3.7 francs per person annually). The amount of meat consumed was so small that the income from the tax on kosher meat was less than one franc per person.[117]

Daniel Stauben, in his *Scènes de la vie juive en Alsace,* described the Jewish *colporteurs* (intinerant peddlers) thus: "These unfortunate peddlers may be seen all week long trudging along the roads, stick in hand, their backs bent under the weight of a load of merchandise, representing their entire wealth; they wander over hill and dale, living on black bread and water."[118] This occupation had a strong influence on the internal migrations. The Jewish peddler would start out from Alsace or Lorraine with his pack directly after Passover and did not return until the beginning of the winter. On the way many a peddler would cast about for a place in which to settle with his family. During the First Empire peddling was the chief occupation of Jews. Thus, according to the census of 1808, 20 of approximately 26 Jewish families in Fontainebleu were so engaged; in Versailles, Orléans and Nantes all the Jews were peddlers. In the eastern *départements* a similar situation prevailed into the second half of the century, but in the south the scene differed. In the 8 *départements* forming the regional consistory of Marseilles there were 98 peddlers listed among 641 gainfully occupied Jews; toward the close of the nineteenth century there remained 10 Jewish peddlers. Within the same region there was in 1809 one Jew living on income from investments; in 1844 there were 56.

The migration from one *département* to another was not, however, an exclusively Jewish trend. The census of 1861 shows that for every 10,000 inhabitants in the *département* of Seine (including Paris) only 3,747 were born there. While the annual average increase of the entire French population during the period 1836-61 was 35 for every 10,000, in the *département* of Seine the rate was 306; the difference was essentially the result of migration from other *départements*.[119] In the 'eighties and 'nineties one-fifth of the French population were not natives of the

[117] *Le Lien d'Israël,* vol. iii (1857) 139-146.

[118] Stauben, D. [Auguste Vidal], *Scènes de la vie juive en Alsace* (Paris 1860) ; *Univers israélite* (1863) 224.

[119] Lagneau, G., "Étude de statistique anthropologique sur la population parisienne," in *Annales d'hygiène publique et de médécine légale* (1869) 258.

départements in which they resided.[120] The *département* of Seine grew
370 percent during the period 1801-1886, Rhône (including Lyon) 158
percent, Bouches-du-Rhône (including Marseille) 112 percent.[121]

Upon the annexation of Alsace-Lorraine by Germany in 1871, entire
Jewish communities left.[122] The famous spinning mills of Buischwiller
(Alsace) were transferred to Elbeuf, Nancy, Sédan and towns, which grew
rapidly.[123] Conversely, the population of Buischwiller declined from
11,500 in 1869 to 7,700 in 1874. Its 96 factories, employing 5,000 workers,
dwindled to 21 with 2,000 workers. Jewish businesses in Metz and Strasbourg were transferred to Rheims; within one year the local Jewish group
increased from 180 to 270. By October 1, 1872, the last day for choosing
between German and French citizenship, 180 Jewish families had left
the city of Metz, in addition to the youths who had left earlier.[124]

Among the factors behind this exodus were the German taxation
system, the economic depression in the newly annexed provinces and the
fear of universal military service.[125] It is noteworthy that among the
Jews who emigrated during the early '70s, there were more men than
women. According to the French census of 1866, the Jewish population
of Alsace had a ratio of 95.5 males to 100 females. According to later
German censuses, this ratio fell to 94.9 in 1871 and to 92.2 in 1875, while
among the Jews living in areas under French rule, the ratio was 97.7
females to 100 males. On the other hand, the migration can hardly be
attributed entirely to material causes, for what could a conquered and
ruined France offer the newcomers? Nor did antisemitism in Alsace-
Lorraine become more virulent under German rule. We must, therefore,
endorse the interpretation given by contemporary Franco-Jewish journalists and writers, namely, that the Alsatian Jews left for patriotic reasons.[126]

[120] Levasseur, E., *Questions ouvrières et industrielles* (Paris 1907) p. 277.
[121] Foville, Alfred de, *La France économique* (Paris 1890) p. 11.
[122] Szajkowski, "Some facts about Alsatian Jews in America," in *Yivo Bleter*, vol. xix (1942);
cf. Weill, Alexandre, *Ma Jeunesse*, vol. i (Paris 1870) p. 299.
[123] On the growth of Epinal and Belfort, cf. de la Blache, Vidal P., "Evolution de la
population en Alsace-Lorraine," in *Annales de géographie*, vol. xxv (1916).
[124] Cahen, Isidore, "Les Exiles volontaires," in *Archives israelites* (1872) 332-38, 439-40,
722-24, 754-56; Delahage, Georges [Aaron, Lucien], *L'Exode* (Paris 1914); *Revue israélite*
(1872) 780. On the exodus from Alsace, see in addition to the writings cited above, Szajkowski,
in *Yidishe Ekonomik*, vol. iii (1939) 87-89; Oualid, W., "La Démographie juive en Alsace et
en Lorraine," in *Univers israélite*, vol. lxxxvii (1932) 165; Netter, N., *Vingt siècles d'histoire
d'une communauté juive. Metz et son grand passé* (Paris 1938) p. 448-50.
[125] Delahage, *op. cit.*, p. 2-7, 211.
[126] Bloch, J. R., *... Et Cie* (Paris 1918).

Indeed, two Jews became the symbols of French patriotism in Alsace: the deputy Edouard Bamberger (1825-1910) and Lucien Aron (George Delahache) (1872-1929).

In 1872 there remained in France 49,439 Jews in a total population of 36,002,921 (0.14 percent). According to Lagneau (1882), however, it would appear that, relatively speaking, the number of Catholics in France decreased 1.27 percent during 1866-72 and the Protestants 5.06 percent, while that of Jews actually increased 11.35 percent, as a result of the influx from Alsace-Lorraine. According to the first German census in Alsace-Lorraine (December 1, 1871), there were 40,812 Jews in a total population of 1,549,738 (2.64 percent). In 1875 the Jews numbered 39,002 (2.25 percent of 1,531,801), while by 1890 their number had decreased to 34,645 in a total of 1,603,506 (2.16 percent). According to the census of 1910, there were 30,483 Jews in a total population of 1,874,014 (1.7 percent). Between 1871 and 1910 217,597 emigrated from Alsace-Lorraine (10.4 percent of the population according to the latter census). During this period the total population increased by 324,276 (21 percent), but the number of Jews declined by 10,329 (25.3 percent of the Jewish population in 1871 and 33.4 percent in 1910). Lower Alsace lost 21.6 percent of its Jews, Upper Alsace 36.5 and Lorraine 18.8.

The Jewish Population in the Major Towns

Until 1871 France was divided into 89 *départements*, 363 *arrondissements*, 2,834 cantons, and 37,234 communes. The capital of each *arrondissement* (*chef-lieu d'arrondissement*) was usually its largest town. Let us analyze the statistics for these capitals, as well as for cities with a population of 10,000 and over, and a number of other towns in order to survey the distribution of the Jewish population in the largest and most important towns of France.[127] The data to be presented comprise for the year 1851 222 towns with a Jewish population and 182 with none; for 1861 200 and 209, respectively; for 1872 212 and 193, respectively. This indicates that, according to the official censuses, there were no Jews in about half of the *arrondissements*. If, however, we group the capitals

[127] In the enumeration according to *départements* a smaller number of Jews is given than in the enumeration according to *arrondissements; Statistique de France,* 2nd series, vol. xiii, pp. 84, 85, 213. When the figures for 1851 and 1866 are compared it will be seen that the *arrondissement* figures are correct.

according to size of population, it is evident that Jews were found in the most important towns of this group. In 1851 the population of the 222 capitals of *arrondissements* with a Jewish population totalled 4,943,721, an average of 22,269 per town, whereas the other 182 capitals totalled 1,562,836, an average of 8,587 per town.

In 1851-1861, while among the non-Jews 13.7 percent lived in the capitals of *arrondissements,* among the Jews the ratio was 45.1 percent. In 1872 the respective ratios were 18.2 and 91.7 percent. Thus, the ratio of the Jewish population concentrated in these capitals rose during the period 1851-1872 56.6 percent, as compared with the 4.3 percent rise in the case of the total population.

According to the consistorial census of 1809, 47.7 percent of the Jewish population of the *département* lived in the city of Marseille, increasing to 83.03 percent in 1872 (official census), while of the total population only 56.3 percent lived in the city. According to the 1900 consistorial census, 82.3 percent of the Jews in the *département* lived in Marseille. In 1872 82.8 percent of the Jews in Alpes-Maritimes lived in Nice, as against 26.6 percent of the total population. Further data on the concentration of the Jews throughout the country in urban centers are presented in Tables VII and VIII.

TABLE VII

JEWISH POPULATION IN THE CAPITALS OF
ARRONDISSEMENTS, FRANCE, 1851 AND 1872, BY GROUPS

Group	1851		1872	
	Towns	Jewish population	Towns	Jewish population
1-10 Jews	107	345	106	505
11-100	71	2,400	57	2,089
101-200	21	3,133	20	2,671
201-300	7	2,830	12	3,060
301-400	2	762	7	2,441
401-500	5	2,164	1	489
501-600	none	none	2	1,105
701-800	1	746	2	1,540
801-900	1	849	none	none
901-1,000	1	986	none	none
1,001-3,000	5	9,421	4	8,032
Over 10,000	1	10,719	1	23,424
All groups	222	33,375	212	45,356

In 1851 45 percent of the Jews were distributed in 222 capitals; in 1861 51.2 percent were in 200 such towns. On the other hand, in 1851 there were 40 large towns (total population 346,135) with an average of one Jew in each. The number of such towns fell in 1861 to 27 and to 15 in 1872. During the decade 1851-61 the number of towns with 1,000 or more Jews increased from 6 to 9 (including 4 in Alsace); the same situation prevailed in 1872. In 1872, when the Jews formed 0.14 percent of the total population of France (reduced boundaries), fully 91 percent of them lived in the capitals of *arrondissements,* where they constituted 0.7 percent of the population. After 1872 the tendency of the Jews to concentrate in the cities continued.

It should, however, be pointed out that the degree of urbanization was lower in Alsace-Lorraine than in the rest of France. Table VIII enables us to see this difference in terms of the Jewish population in the capitals of *arrondissements* in 1851 and 1871-72. For the sake of obtaining a truer picture, it was deemed best in preparing the table to be guided, not by administrative boundaries established after the annexation, but by the departmental boundaries of previous years. We shall accordingly not attempt to separate the annexed area of Alsace-Lorraine from the parts which remained French (Meurthe-et-Moselle, Vosges, Meuse, and the Territory of Belfort).

TABLE VIII

TOTAL AND JEWISH POPULATION IN CAPITALS OF
ARRONDISSEMENTS, FRANCE, 1851 AND 1871-72[1]

Region	1851		1871-72	
	Number	Ratio in percent	Number	Ratio in percent
Alsace-Lorraine				
Total population	391,932	14.5	437,221	16.7
Jews	12,490	24.4	14,886	31.06
Remainder of France				
Total population	4,551,789	13.7	6,433,542	18.3
Jews	20,885	91.05	42,244	97.0
France as a whole				
Total population	4,943,721	13.9	6,870,763	18.2
Jews	33,375	45.1	57,130	63.2

[1] Boundaries as of 1870.

In 1851 45.1 percent of French Jewry lived in the capitals of *arrondissements* and in 1872 63.2 percent. This increase of 18.1 percent in 21 years was considerably greater than the 4.3 percent rise (from 13.9 in 1851 to 18.2 in 1872) shown by the total population. In Alsace-Lorraine (in 1851 68.2 percent of French Jewry), however, only 24.4 percent of the Jews lived in these capitals in 1851 and 31.06 in 1872, an increase of 6.6 percent; within the total population the comparable ratios were 14.5 in 1851 and 16.7 in 1872, an increase of 2.2 percent. According to the first German census in the annexed provinces, the Jews numbered 40,812 or 2.6 percent of the total population (1,517,496). The total population living in the towns and villages inhabited by Jews was 752,651, so that the Jews formed 5.4 percent in these localities, a much higher ratio than they formed in the reduced boundaries of France, viz., 0.7 percent.

During the eighteenth century the Jews had, to a considerable degree, lived in the smaller towns and villages of Alsace-Lorraine. Although many moved to the larger towns immediately after 1789, as late as 1939 (when the Jews were evacuated from Alsace-Lorraine) there still remained a rural Jewish population. There were, however, certain difficulties, as exemplified by the fact that in 1802 only 89 Jews lived outside of the Metz ghetto.[128]

For the years 1871-72 we have census figures regarding the size of the local Jewish groups in Alsace-Lorraine and of 91.7 percent of those of France (reduced boundaries). Table IX presents the distribution of these groups according to the number of Jews in each.

In 1871-72 95.4 percent of the Jews were distributed in 615 localities (212 in France and 403 in Alsace-Lorraine), from 1,500 to 3,000 population, as well as in Paris.[129] Of the 212 towns and cities of France proper with some Jewish population, 137 had a total population of over 10,000 each, 47 had 5,000-10,000 and 28 1,500-5,000. In Alsace-Lorraine, on the other hand, of the 403 localities inhabited by Jews no more than 7 had a total population of over 10,000. The remaining 396 were distributed as follows: 3 with 250 or less; 212 with 251-1,000; 169 with 1,001-5,000; 12 with 5,001-10,000.

[128] Liber, M., in *Revue des études juives,* vol. lxxi, p. 129.

[129] *Statistique de France,* 2nd series, vol. ii, p. 22-25. In 1851 there were 2,679 localities with over 2,000 population in a total of 63,835.

TABLE IX

JEWISH POPULATION OF FRANCE AND ALSACE-LORRAINE
BY SIZE GROUP, 1871-72

Number of Jews	Number of localities	
	France	Alsace-Lorraine
1	15	27
2-5	47	68
6-10	44	31
11-25	24	55
26-50	17	43
51-100	16	61
101-250	24	76
251-1,000	20	38
1,001-3,000	4	4
10,00 and over	1	none

Despite the relatively large number of localities in Alsace-Lorraine inhabited by Jews, there were many with no recorded Jewish residents. Thus, in 1808, of the 1,113 towns and villages in Alsace, no more than 203—145 in Bas-Rhin and 58 in Haut-Rhin—had a Jewish population. Of the 2,780 towns and villages in Lorraine Jews lived in 168. All in all, there were Jews in 371 of the 3,893 localities of Alsace-Lorraine.

Of the 177 local Jewish groups in Alsace recorded by the census of 1784, 31 were no longer in existence a century later. By the latter date, however, there were Jews living in 79 localities which had had no Jews in 1784.[130] In 1784 there were few towns with a large number of Jews, most of whom lived in villages lying close to towns which, until 1789, were more or less closed to Jewish residents. Following the Revolution there was an influx of Jews into the towns and the Jewish population tended to concentrate in a number of large centers. The progressive urbanization of French Jewry is clearly reflected in the censuses of 1851 and 1871-72. The census of 1851 returned 73,975 Jews in a total population of 35,783,172. Nine cities—Paris, Bordeaux, Lyon, Marseille, Nancy, Strasbourg, Metz, Colmar, and Mulhouse—contained 5 percent of the total (1,789,753), as compared with 30.2 percent (22,413) of the Jewish population; Paris comprised 2.9 percent of the country's total (1,053,362)

[130] Hemerdinger, G., "La Population israélite d'Alsace," in *Univers israélite*, vol. lviii (1902-1903) 269-273, 304-308.

and 14.5 percent of all Jews. According to the census of 1872, there were 49,439 Jews in France (not including Alsace-Lorraine) in a total population of 36,102,921. The cities of Paris, Bordeaux, Lyon, Marseille and Nancy contained 7.5 percent of the country's total (2,735,106), as compared with 63.6 percent (31,456) of the Jews. In France and Alsace-Lorraine combined there were 90,251 Jews in a total population of 37,620,415.

In 1872 Paris comprised 5.1 percent of the population (1,851,792) of France and Alsace-Lorraine combined, as compared with 47.3 percent (23,424) of the Jewish population. During 1809-1872 the Jewish population of Paris increased eightfold, from 2,908 to 23,424. According to the official censuses of 1851-1872, it increased 118 percent in a 21-year period, while the population as a whole rose 75.8 percent. It must, moreover, again be noted that the censuses understated the number of Jews. This tendency toward concentration in the larger towns, like the migration from one *département* into another, was, however, not limited to the Jews. In 1846 the French population was 75.58 percent rural and 24.42 percent urban; in 1866 69.54 and 30.46 percent, respectively; and in 1886 64.05 and 35.95 percent, respectively.[131]

It is evident that the Jews who flocked to the larger towns were largely persons without occupations or property. According to the census of the regional consistory of Marseille for 1809, only 117 of the 265 Jewish households in the *département* of Bouches-du Rhône had any taxable property and in Lyon only 7 of the 58. In 1838 there were in Paris 1,828 Jews who were supported by a relief committee, even though all except the old and the very young plied a trade. The extent of the poverty among the Jews is indicated by the number buried at communal expense, a practice regarded as highly disgraceful among Jews. In 1838 of the 173 who died, 127 were buried at the cost of the relief committee;[132] in 1841 105 in a total of 190; in 1842 152 in a total of 239; in 1858 247 in a total of 400; in 1862 245 in a total of 477; in 1868 349 in a total of 580, etc.[133] Thus, over 60 percent of the Jews who died in Paris were paupers. Of the burials paid for by the families of the deceased, only half were permanent and the others temporary burials.[134]

[131] Foville, *La France économique*, p. 14.
[132] *Archives israélites* (1840) 89-96.
[133] Kahn, Léon, *Le Comité de bienfaisance* (Paris 1886) p. 129.
[134] *Archives israélites*, vol. xviii (1857) 262-266.

According to the census of 1851, there were 10,719 Jews in Paris; of this number 2,138, or 19.8 percent, were dependent on the relief committee. There were in addition 44 indigent immigrants. Thus, one-fifth of the Parisian Jews were paupers, although not entirely without an occupation (46 were day laborers, 218 merchants, 79 peddlers, 2 locksmiths, etc.).[135] This ratio was undoubtedly higher than that of the paupers among the non-Jews, who likewise flocked to Paris during the second half of the nineteenth century.[136]

[135] *Loc. cit.*, vol. xiii (1852) 432. It should be noted that of the 924 dependent Jewish families in Paris (2,314 persons) in 1850 only 2 lived in the poor quarter (*arrondissement* XI), and 364 in the fashionable *arrondissement* VII; *Univers israélite* (1851) 399. This distribution changed during the subsequent years.

[136] Cheysson, E., *La Question de la population en France et à l'étranger* (Paris 1885) p. 27.

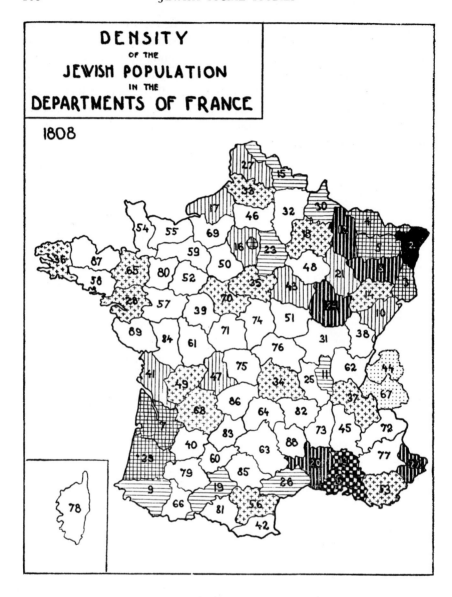

DENSITY
OF THE
JEWISH POPULATION
IN THE
DEPARTMENTS OF FRANCE

1808

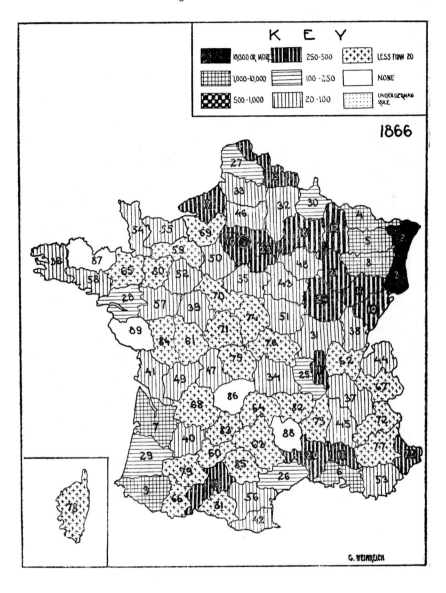

Appendix

DÉPARTEMENTS

in Order of the Size of Their Jewish Population, 1866
(cf. the maps, p. 316 [38] f.)

1.	Seine	21,767	30.	Ardennes	109	60.	Tarn-Garonne ...	16
2.	Bas-Rhin	21,318	31.	Saône-Loire	95	61.	Vienne	13
3.	Haut-Rhin	14,496	32.	Aisne	94	62.	Ain	11
4.	Moselle	7,337	33.	Somme	92	63.	Aveyron	11
5.	Meurthe	5,240	34.	Puy-de-Dôme	85	64.	Cantal	11
6.	B.-du-Rhône	3,161	35.	Loiret	81	65.	Ile-Vilaine	11
7.	Girone	2,618	36.	Finistère	64	67.	Savoie	9
8.	Vosges	1,510	37.	Isère	64	68.	Dordogne	8
9.	Basses-Pyrénées	1,235	38.	Jura	64	69.	Eure	8
10.	Doubs	931	39.	Indre-Loire	56	70.	Loire-Cher	8
11.	Rhône	888	40.	Lot-Garonne	43	71.	Indre	5
12.	Meuse	801	41.	Charente-Inf.	41	72.	Htes-Alpes	4
13.	Vaucluse	615	42.	Pyrénées-Orient.	37	73.	Ardèche	4
14.	Haute-Saône	602	43.	Yonne	37	74.	Cher	4
15.	Nord	527	44.	Hte-Savoie	34	75.	Creuse	4
16.	Seine-Oise	519	45.	Drôme	31	76.	Allier	3
17.	Seine Inf.	441	46.	Oise	30	77.	Basses-Alpes	3
18.	Marne	439	47.	Haute-Vienne	30	78.	Coroe	3
19.	Hte-Garonne	403	48.	Aube	29	79.	Gero	3
20.	Gard	350	49.	Charente	27	80.	Mayenne	3
21.	Haute-Marne	328	50.	Eure-Loire	25	81.	Ariège	1
22.	Alpes Maritimes	270	51.	Nièvre	25	82.	Hte-Loire	1
23.	Seine-Marne	250	52.	Sarthe	24	83.	Lot	1
24.	Côte-d'Or	224	53.	Var	24	84.	Deux Sèvres	1
25.	Loire	199	54.	Manche	23	85.	Tarn	1
26.	Hérault	193	55.	Calvados	22	86.	Corrèze	0
27.	Pas-de-Calais	125	56.	Ande	20	87.	Côtes-du-Nord	0
28.	Loire Inf.	121	57.	Maine-Loire	20	88.	Lozère	0
29.	Landes	110	58.	Morbihan	20	89.	Vendée	0
			59.	Orne	19			

THE DECLINE AND FALL OF PROVENÇAL JEWRY

Ever since the Revolution most of the Jews of France have lived in Alsace-Lorraine and around Paris. It is therefore not surprising that the modern history of French Jewry has been written almost exclusively in terms of those areas and that comparatively little attention has been paid to the smaller communities in the south-east of the country. These, however, are by no means devoid of interest, including as they do such important centers as Marseille and Lyon and reflecting in their story the gradual disruption and decay of the younger Jewish settlements of France. Moreover, this story can now be told in greater detail than heretofore owing to the fact that many of the records of these communities, hitherto all but hidden in local archives, have now at last been made available to scholars.

In the tragic days of 1940, on the eve of the German occupation, the writer was able, by a peculiar combination of circumstances, to salvage much of this material and to bring it for safe keeping to this country, where it has been deposited in the library of the Yiddish Scientific Institute in New York. The present study is based largely on these new sources.[1]

At the beginning of the nineteenth century the Jewish communities of south-eastern France were united for purposes of religious administration in the regional consistory of Marseille. This comprised, in addition to that city and Lyon, the following eight departments: (i) Alpes-Maritimes; (ii) Bouches du Rhône; (iii) Gard; (iv) Hérault; (v) Isère; (vi) Rhône; (vii) Var, and (viii) Vaucluse, besides the four older communities of Carpentras, Avignon, Cavaillon and Lisle-sur-Sorgue, which

---

[1] For a description of the documents see the writer's papers, "Eighteenth Century Documents from the Four Communities" (Yiddish) in *Yiden in Frankreich* (New York 1942), vol. ii, p. 304-09 and "Eighteenth Century Pinkasim from Carpentras" (Yiddish) in *Yivo Bleter*, vol. xxi (1943), 351-55.

Originally published in *Jewish Social Studies*, vol. VI (1944).

had originally formed part of the papal province of Avignon and Comtat Venaissin.

Population
(Table I)

Jews had been settled in this area for some time before the Revolution. In 1791, when Comtat Venaissin was taken over by the French government and transformed into the department of Vaucluse, there were already some two thousand of them in the four older communities mentioned above.

Similarly, when, in the same year, France annexed NICE, that city contained a Jewish community of 295 persons (62 families), 230 of whom (46 families) had already been settled in pre-Revolution times. They were a 'mixed multitude' of Italians and Comtadins (who had a congregation of their own), together with a sprinkling of Sephardim and descendants of an Algerian group which had come from Oran in 1669.[2] In the city of NIMES (Gard), there were at this same period 115 Jews (37 families);[3] in MONTPELLIER, approximately one hundred;[4] and in LYON about eighty.[5] In MARSEILLE (Bouches-du-Rhône) there were at the time of the Revolution merely a few isolated Jews. (The local synagogue was not established until 1790,[6] while the sister edifices at AIX-EN-PROVENCE, ARLES, and SALON date only from the years 1800-04.[7])

Jews had always sought to settle in this part of southern France on account of the commercial opportunities afforded by the larger cities, where communities had been established already in the previous century, when they had been permitted to live there. Later, too, the existence of the four older communities doubtless contributed greatly to the influx of their coreligionists, a fact already noted by the prefect of Marseille, in 1824, in his statistical survey of Bouches-du-Rhône.[8] On the eve of the

---

[2] Emanuel, Victor, *Les Juifs à Nice, 1400-1860* (Nice 1905), p. 26, 48, 53. Those who came after 1792 left again in 1814, when France lost control of the city—a control which she did not regain until forty-seven years later; *ibid.*, p. 55.

[3] Kahn, S., *Notice sur les Israélites de Nîmes* (Nîmes 1901), p. 29.

[4] id., "Les Juifs de Montpellier au XVIIIme siècle," in *Revue des études juives*, vol. xxxv.

[5] Levy, Alfred, *Notice sur les Israélites de Lyon* (Paris 1894).

[6] Villeneuve, *Statistique du départment des Bouches-du-Rhône* (Marseille 1824), vol. ii, p. 702.

[7] *ibid.*

[8] *ibid.*

TABLE I

JEWISH POPULATION IN THE CONSISTORY OF MARSEILLE, 1808-1900

Department	1808 (Posener)	1809-51				1854-72				1893-1900		
		Consistorial Census			1851 National Census	1854 Cons. Census	National Census			Consistorial Census		
		1809	1841	1844			1861	1866	1872	1893	1898	1900
Alpes-Maritimes	303	285	.....	.....	.....	.....	321	270	678	548	536	584
Bouches-du-Rhône	942	869	1,463	1,637	1,371	1,932	2,532	3,161	3,206	2,429	3,811	5,587
Gard	425	414	465	518	494	499	375	350	458	352	352	349
Hérault	141	177	131	116	158	111	171	193	300	161	161	243
Isère	4	15	9	11	20	?	24	64	47	?	?	?
Rhône	195	184	621	797	458	1,092	967	888	866	?	.....	.....
Var	14	11	35	52	79	?	67	24	67	81	81	81
Vaucluse	631	654	865	737	673	816	638	615	620	413	397	359
Total	2,655	2,609	2,646	3,954	3,253	4,584	5,095	5,565	6,242	3,984	5,348	6,385

NOTE: In connection with the above figures it should be borne in mind that in the national census the number of Jews tends to be minimized while, on the other hand, the Consistory could not keep account of every coreligionist. There is thus a certain discrepancy, and a reasonable margin of error must be allowed.

It should be observed also that after 1893 Lyon ceased to be included in the consistorial census for Marseille. On the other hand, however, the townlet of Loire (119 Jews) was added in 1854 and that of Drome (15 Jews) in 1894.

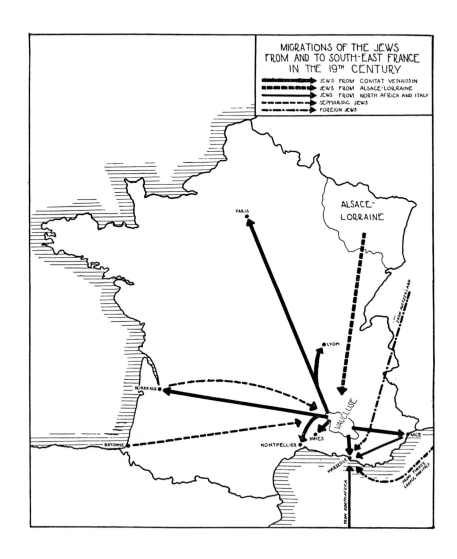

Revolution, however, Jewish residence in this area was restricted to certain specific localities, although here and there, e.g., in ORANGE, AIX, and TARASCON small groups undoubtedly enjoyed illicit residence. In all of the then seven departments—Nice was added only during the Revolution—there were no more than 2,300 legal Jewish inhabitants, and of these about 2,000 lived in the papal province of Comtat Venaissin.

According to Posener, at the time of the first Empire, the department of MARSEILLE possessed 2,656 Jews in a total population of 2,347,928 (0.1 percent). In 1861, however, the national census recorded 5,095 in a total of 3,407,196 (0.1 percent), while in 1872 there were 6,242 in a total of 3,407,196 (0.1 percent). The increase between 1809 and 1900 is assessed by the consistorial figures at 62 percent.

In the department of RHÔNE, the Jewish population increased between 1808 and 1872 by 78.3 percent as against a 49.0 percent rise in the general population. However, since the census statistics are obviously inaccurate—866 Jews are recorded for the whole department in 1872, whereas for Lyon alone 1,175 are recorded—this figure cannot be accepted. Other sources show clearly that the increase was nearer 90 percent.

In BOUCHES-DU-RHÔNE, the Jewish population increased during the same period by 70.6 percent, as against a 47.2 percent rise in the general population; while over the entire span of 1809-1900 the increase, according to the consistorial records, was 84.4 percent as against 60.1 percent in the general population between 1806 and 1901.

Distribution
(Table II)

The Jews lived mainly in the large cities, a fact easily explained. Prior to the Revolution they were permitted to dwell only in the cities, and not in the villages. In the papal province of Avignon and Comtat Venaissin, for example, they could live only in Carpentras, Avignon, Cavaillon, and Lisle-sur-Sorgue and when, following their emancipation, they secured the right of dwelling where they pleased, the concession was, in fact, more nominal than real. In Carpentras, for instance, the poorer elements who had "stayed put" throughout the upheaval, were markedly reluctant to leave the ghetto because they feared the surrounding Christian population.[9] Instead, they improved their economic plight by appropriating the homes of their wealthier coreligionists who had moved out. Moreover, the general population throughout France was drifting at the time from the villages to the larger cities. It would therefore have been unnatural for the Jews to do the opposite, particularly since their entire

TABLE II

DISTRIBUTION OF JEWS IN THE DEPARTMENT OF VAUCLUSE, 1809-1900

City	1809		1841		1844		1854	1893	1896	1900
	Families	Per.	Families	Per.	Families	Per.	Persons			
Apt	9	24	2	7	3	3	......	......	......	......
Avignon	51	106	?) 45	158	61	141	170	149	145	145
Bastide	......	......	2	15	2	2	......	......	......	......
Bédarrides	......	......	3	19	5	19	16	......	......	......
Bollene	......	......	......	......	1	6	......	......	......	......
Cardenet	......	......	1	2	1	3	......	......	......	......
Carpentras	118	364	73	261	79	280	250	151	139	107
Cavaillon	18	52	13	39	8	26	25	20	20	17
Courtheson	......	......	1	3	1	5	5	......	......	......
Entraigues	......	......	1	8	1	11	......	......	......	......
Lagnes	......	......	......	......	1	1	......	......	......	......
Lisle-sur-Sorgues	10	22	13	59	13	64	58	13	13	20
Orange	6	30	40	174	40	145	164	80	80	70
Pertui	8	36	?	......	......	......	......	......	......	
Serignan	1	9	......	......	......	......	......	......	......	......
Sorgues	......	......	1	3	3	12	7	......	......	......
Thor	1	11	1	10	3	13	14	......	......	......
Védennes	......	......	1	7	2	6	9	......	......	......
Total	222	654	206	865	224	737	816	413	397	359

mode of living, forced upon them before the Revolution, had been an urban one. On the other hand, in Alsace-Lorraine, where they had been permitted, even before the Revolution, to dwell in the small towns and villages, many Jews continued to do so, at least until 1936. Even there, however, a drift to the larger cities was perceptible.

[9] *Revue des études juives*, vol. cii (1937), p. 37. In his novel *Nicolo Peccavi* Armand Lunel relates how his grandfather, who had settled after the Revolution in a village outside Carpentras, was virtually driven back, after the Restoration, into the ghetto of that city.

The urbanization of the Jews is evident from the figures of both the national and consistorial censuses. According to the former, for instance, in 1871-2 some 63.2 percent of all the Jews of France (including Alsace-Lorraine) lived in the large administrative centers—the so-called *chefs lieux d'arrondissement*—as against 18.2 percent of the total French population. (Significant, however, is the fact that while in France proper the proportion was as high as 97 percent, in Alsace-Lorraine it was only 31.06 percent.)

These over-all statistics are supplemented by data respecting the individual cities. According to the consistorial records, between 1806 and 1901 some 48 percent of all Jews in the department lived in Marseille; and in 1872 the national census indeed registered the proportion as 56.3 percent, as against 83.03 percent of the general population. By 1900, however (again according to the consistorial figures), it had risen to 82.3 percent. Similarly, of the Jews of Alpes-Maritimes, 82.8 percent lived in Nice in 1872, as against 26.6 percent of the general population.

Significant also was the proportion of the Jews in this area to the total Jewish population of France. In 1808 no more than 5.6 percent of the Jews lived there as compared with 8.06 percent of the total French population; and by 1872, following the cession of Alsace-Lorraine to Germany, the Jewish proportion had risen only to 6.9 percent—not a large increase when compared with the contemporary growth of the Jewish community in Paris.

Emigration

The decline of the Jewish population in south-eastern France was the direct consequence of a large-scale emigration from the four older communities of Carpentras, Cavaillon, Avignon and Lisle-sur-Sorgue which had taken place when the former papal province was annexed by France in 1791 and transformed into the department of Vaucluse. Of the approximately 2,300 Jews who had lived there on the eve of the Revolution, only 631 remained in 1808. In 1851, according to the national census, there were 673; ten years later, the figure dropped to 638; in 1866, there were 615, and in 1872 the number increased by only five. The consistorial records, while they vary in regard to the several figures, present approximately the same general picture. According to this source, only 32.7 percent of the original number remained in 1809. Despite a slight increase in 1854 to 40.8 percent, by 1900 the proportion had reached a low of 17.9 percent,[10] and only half of the department's 359 Jews were then descendants of the old Comtadin element. In other words, the original community, which had served as the stimulus for the later settlements, had shrunk to about one-twelfth of what it had been on the eve of the Revolution.[11]

The exodus had begun already before the Revolution. Isolated 'colonies' and small settlements of Comtadin Jews had existed in Bordeaux since 1674,[12] in Montpellier since 1706,[13] in Nice since the seventeenth[14] and in Paris[15] and Lyon since the eighteenth century. The Comtadin Jews had long entertained commercial relations with the other areas of south-eastern France, and until the time of the Revolution made constant efforts to settle there.[16] It was, indeed, scarcely of their own choice that they remained in the papal province. As soon as the opportunity arose, they left. Nor is it difficult to understand why. The papal province was not, in fact, that 'Jewish paradise' which so many writers and historians would represent it to have been.[17] Even in 1593, during the conflicts between the Catholics and Protestants, it is related (in a well known satire attributed to Pierre Pitou, the public prosecutor of Paris) that the

[10] To be sure, non-Jews also emigrated from the department, but not on so large a scale. Between 1836 and 1881 only 11,120 left, as against 100,000 who entered.

[11] That the Jewish population then consisted largely of émigrés from Alsace-Lorraine is shown clearly by the names which figure in the consistorial censuses. Eloquent of the admixture is the fact that the old Valabrègue family of Carpentras intermarried with a Dreyfus from Alsace—a forbear of Captain Alfred Dreyfus; see Talmeyer, M., "Les Dreyfus de Carpentras," in *Revue hebdomaire*, May 7, 1898.

[12] Cf. Cirot, G., *Recherches sur les Juifs à Bordeaux* (Bordeaux 1908) and the same writer's articles in *Revue historique de Bordeaux*, vols. xxxi-xxxii (1938-39).

[13] Cf. Kahn, S., "Les Juifs de Montpellier au XVIIIme siècle" in *Revue des études juives*, vol. xxxiii (1901), 283.

[14] Cf. Meiss, Honel, *A travers le Ghetto. . .* (Nice 1923).

[15] Cf. Hildenfinger, P., *Documents sur les Juifs au XVIIIme siècle* (Paris 1913); Cerfberr, A., *Les Juifs* (Paris 1847), p. 32.

[16] Roubin, N., "La vie commerciale des Juifs comtadins en Languedoc au XVIIIme siècle" in *Revue des études juives*, vol. xxxiv-xxxvi (1897-99).

[17] The expression occurs in Mistral's *Lou Tresor dou Félibrige* (Paris 1878), vol. ii, p. 477. Similarly, Georges Martin, in his *Neuf et Une* (Paris 1936), p. 140, blandly describes how "under the southern skies, the Pope openly patronized the ghetto, and the New Testament was able to blend with the Old, just as did the vernacular with the Hebrew tongue." In the

Parisians were "more enslaved than the Christians in Turkey or the Jews in Avignon."[18] Indeed, the laws governing the latter were often more severe in the papal province than in France proper; they had, for instance, to wear the yellow hat. Eloquent of this severity is the record of a lawsuit at the end of the eighteenth century between the Comtadin Jew, Mordecai Vidal and a Christian debtor. After the Revolution, Vidal demanded that his case be tried in accordance with the French law, since legislation in the papal province in these matters was much more severe for Jews.[19]

Moreover, there is evidence that Jews did not leave the province for purely economic reasons. A very characteristic incident is recorded in a minute-book from Carpentras. Recording that in 1763 his son Zemah was forcibly converted to Christianity, Elijah Carmi (Crémieux), the writer of this record, adds that at this time many of his local coreligionists fled to Nice and the other neighboring cities of France proper for fear lest a similar fate befall their own children. So great, indeed, was the exodus that the bishop of Carpentras demanded a list of all who departed; and in the same year, an edict from Rome ordered that henceforth an exact register be kept both in Hebrew and French of all births, marriages and deaths in the Jewish community. (This register is now in the writer's possession.) Nor was this example by any means unique. In 1781, the city council of Avignon had already prepared for the bishop a recommendation concerning the improvement of the lot of the Jews, not only on humanitarian grounds but also in the interests of the Christians who hoped thereby to halt the economically injurious emigration. At the last moment, however, the recommendation was not forwarded.[20] A later testimony (1840) tells much the same story, showing once again that in

same vein, a recent Jewish writer, Mordecai Kleiner, paints a glowing picture of how "under the brilliant sunshine of Provence the old-time persecution of the Jews melted away" (*Di Zukunft*, vol. xliii [1938], 476); while according to C. F. Barjavel, when the Comtadin Jews were compelled to listen to conversionist sermons, they actually enjoyed it, especially when the preacher was the erudite Father Justin! Cf. his *Notice sur la vie et les écrits du père Justin* (Carpentras 1859), p. 284.

[18] *Satire Ménipée de la vertu du Catholicon d'Espagne et de la tenue des Estatz de Paris* (Paris 1593).

[19] *Précis pour le Sieur Antoine-Jean-Baptiste-Pierre Pelissier contre le Sieur Mardochée Vidal, Juif* . . . Dec. 3, 1806, p. 10 (MS. Carpentras 16587, p. 7).

[20] Chobaut, H., "Les Juifs d'Avignon et du Comtat," in *Revue des études juives*, vol. ci (1937), 35.

the early days of the Revolution the Comtadin Jew felt more at liberty in France than in the papal province.[21]

At the beginning of the Revolution the exodus tended to slacken off, the Comtadin Jews taking advantage of the general unstable state of affairs. Thus, of 226 Jewish families (923 persons) living in Carpentras in 1788, there were still some 173 (963 persons) by May 19, 1789.[22]

As the Revolution progressed, however, the emigration increased because of the war between Avignon, which had sided with Paris, and Carpentras, which had for some time been in accord with the reaction.[23] It was mainly the wealthier Jews who fled from the Four Communities. In Carpentras matters reached such a state that on March 23, 1791 the Jewish community intervened, requesting the municipal authorities to halt the exodus. The émigrés, it transpired, had sold their property during the previous month and started to move, leaving the entire burden of supporting the community and the poor on the shoulders of the middle classes.[24] In Avignon, the poorer Jews resorted to asking the city council for support, so few were their wealthy coreligionists who still remained.[25] Nor was it only the Jewish community that suffered. The emigration was likewise injurious to the trade of the province. So much, indeed, was this the case that in May 1790, the city of Lisle-sur-Sorgue resolved to ameliorate the situation of its Jews in order to induce them to stay,[26] while the city council of Carpentras adopted a similar resolution for the same purpose.[27]

Few of the émigrés went to Vaucluse. Only in Orange (which had a few Jewish families at the beginning of the nineteenth century) did the Comtadins settle in sufficient numbers to constitute a community with

[21] *Archives Israélites,* vol. i (1840) , 290, 652.

[22] According to one account, there were at Carpentras, at the beginning of the Revolution, 179 Jewish families (705 persons). Some 213 Jews had already left. Of these, 51 went to Montpellier, 96 to Nîmes, 12 to Avignon, 36 to Aix-en-Provence, 17 to Arles, 5 to Lille, 3 to Paris and one to Lyon. See Mossé, A., *Histoire d'Avignon et du Comtat Venaissin* (Paris 1934) , p. 98-100.

[23] Cf. Milhaud's article, "Biographie de feu M. Roquemartine," in *Le Lien d'Israél,* 1857, p. 59; Chobaut, H., in *Revue des études juives,* vol. cii (1938) , 29.

[24] *Livres des verbaux. Exposition et interrogatovies, 1791,* p. 3-4. (Uncatalogued manuscript in the Carpentras library.)

[25] Chobaut, *op. cit.* vol. cii, p. 28.

[26] *Demandes et doléances de la ville de Lille,* May 21, 1790; art. XXIV.

[27] Chobaut, *op. cit.,* vol. cii, p. 6, 11.

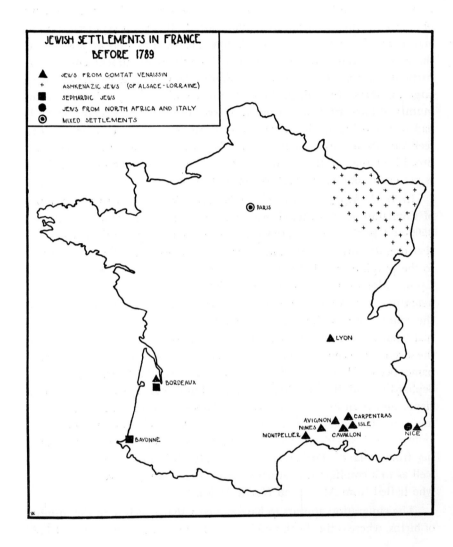

JEWISH SETTLEMENTS IN FRANCE
BEFORE 1789

▲ JEWS FROM COMTAT VENAISSIN
+ ASHKENAZIC JEWS (OF ALSACE-LORRAINE)
■ SEPHARDIC JEWS
● JEWS FROM NORTH AFRICA AND ITALY
◉ MIXED SETTLEMENTS

◉ PARIS

▲ LYON

▲ BORDEAUX
■

AVIGNON ▲ ▲ CARPENTRAS
NIMES ▲ ▲ ISLE
MONTPELLIER ▲ ▲ CAVAILLON ● NICE
■ BAYONNE

their own synagogue and burial ground. In that city they increased from 30 in 1809 to 164 in 1854.[28] Orange, however, was a special case, since it possessed a large horse-market, and the horse trade had been a specialty of the Comtadin Jews from time immemorial. It is not a very rich section, and many of the remaining population, Christian as well as Jew, stayed there not so much out of economic interest as of attachment to this particular sector. To other parts of France, however, the émigrés went in large numbers. Indeed, in the early nineteenth century, when the community of Carpentras was at length forced to liquidate the debts which it had incurred before the Revolution, it was put to considerable pains to seek out its members, scattered as they were through the length and breadth of the country. (An interesting correspondence on the subject is preserved among the archives recently retrieved.)

In 1847, Alphonse Cerfberr, a baptized Jew, estimated the number of Comtadin Jews scattered over Paris and southern France as between 3500 and 4000.[29] The reason why the émigrés settled in those parts was that opportunities for economic development were greater there, owing to the propinquity of the seaport Marseille and the industrial center of Lyon. Moreover, southern France already possessed a nucleus of Ashkenazim from Alsace, reinforced by Sephardim from various parts of the country and by immigrants from North Africa and the Levant who had been coming in through the ports of Marseille and Nice ever since the seventeenth century. In a consistorial census of 1809 typical Comtadin names occur side by side with those of Alsatians, like Levy, Cohen, Cerf; Sephardim and Italians, like Servadio, Tubiyana, Toledano and Veneziano; and Africans like Altaras, Ben Samon, Foa and Galula. Furthermore, in the ledger of the community of Avignon (now in the YIVO archives) it is stated, in 1863-64, that aid had been given to Jews emigrating from Poland, Turkey, Hungary, Italy, Gibraltar and Germany, as well as to a coreligionist returning from Brazil, and, above all, to others who hailed from Alsace and North Africa.

The emigration appears to have caused a sharp decline in the number of births, whereas the death rate increased. Thus, between 1780 and 1789

---

[28] Cf. Mossé, Noémi, "Nouvelle orangeoise," in *La Famille de Jacob*, vols. xxiii-xxiv (1882-83.)

[29] *Les Juifs* (Paris 1847), p. 33.

there were 478 births in the Four Communities, as against 487 deaths; while in Carpentras alone the figures were respectively 255 and 286.[30] In 1737, however, there were 24 Jewish births in that city and 15 deaths, while thirty years later (1767) the former still exceeded the latter bv 35 to 11.[31] In appraising these figures, however, it must not be forgotten that the seeming decline in the birth rate may also be due to the fact that the Jews did not register all births accurately, since the record was kept for the Christian chancellory and they might thus have exposed themselves to higher assessment for taxes.

Economic Status
(Table III)

Writing in 1843, Samuel Cahen (1796-1862) editor of *Archives Israélites*, was able to affirm roundly that the majority of the Jews then living in Lyon were immigrants from Alsace-Lorraine and had not even been born in France. Similarly, in Marseille, the bulk of the Jewish community was of foreign extraction, even the rabbi speaking with a marked accent.[32] Nearly half a century later, in 1896, the antisemitic Phillippe Sapin drew up his list of Jewish enterprises which ought to be boycotted,[33] we find that out of 415 economically active heads of households (1010 persons) cited for Lyon, the bulk of those whose birthplaces are given were of foreign provenance; as against 48 born in the city itself, 11 in Paris and 39 in various other French departments, there were 108 who were natives of Alsace and 39 of foreign countries, the latter consisting mainly of Alsatians who had entered through Switzerland. The influx from Alsace-Lorraine was especially heavy after 1871, when large numbers of Jews from that area migrated to France in order to escape the necessity of becoming German subjects. Many of them established businesses at Lyon and Marseille, trading under such names as: *À la ville de Sedan, Toilerie des Vosges, Aux Emigrés Alsaciens* and the like.

The general economic situation was better in the younger communities, since these consisted mainly of the wealthier elements who had left

[30] Chobaut, H., *op. cit.*, vol. ci (1937), 10.
[31] The figures are taken from the Carpentras minute-book. The only exception to the preponderance of births over deaths occurred during periods of epidemic. In 1748, for instance, when there was widespread disease among the children, 38 births were registered, but 44 deaths.
[32] *Archives Israélites*, vol. iii (1843), 627, 692.
[33] *Indicateur Israélite* (Lyon 1896), p. 289-313.

TABLE III

STATUS AND PROPERTY OF JEWISH FAMILIES IN THE CONSISTORY OF MARSEILLE, 1809

Department	Households	Persons	Persons possessing property			Persons without property									
			Male heads of families	Total of all family properties (in francs)	Average property per family	Widows	Spinsters	Family heads employed but without property	Family heads unemployed and without property	Military	Dependent wives	Dependent children Boys	Girls	Paupers and Servants
Alpes-Maritimes	62	285	31	1,361,500	43,919	18	5	23	20	.....	50	67	71	.....
Bouches-du-Rhône	265	869	117	4,414,800	37,733	22	4	94	41	15	162	177	212	25
Gard	115	414	50	1,086,500	21,730	7	.....	55	17	2	70	104	100	9
Hérault	60	177	16	315,000	1,687	7	14	12	13	10	26	39	30	10
Isère	6	15						6			2	4	3	
Rhône	58	184	7	34,000	8,457	4	1	48	.....	.....	31	48	41	4
Var	6	11	1	50,000	50,000	.....	.....	4	.....	.....	1	3	1	1
Vaucluse	222	654	113	1,680,300	14,869	19	8	63	24	4	128	133	148	14
Total	794	2,609	335	8,936,100	.....	77	32	305	115	31	470	575	606	63

the older settlements. Even there, however, poverty was far from unknown. A partial picture is afforded by the entries concerning family status and property in the consistorial census of 1809. The total possessions of some 794 families (2609 persons) was then assessed at 8,936,100 francs. Only 335 of them owned taxable property; the rest were too poor to be assessed. Among the latter were: 77 widows, 32 spinsters; 305 professionals and 115 non-professional heads of families; 63 paupers or hired servants; 470 women dependent entirely upon their husbands, and 1,181 children dependent upon their parents. Thirty-one men, mostly of the poorer class, were serving in the army. In Lyon there were only three families who possessed property sufficient to allow for taxation.

Of the large amount of wealth possessed before the Revolution by the Jews of Comtat, particularly those of Carpentras, nothing remained in the Department of Vaucluse. In 1786 one Jew of Carpentras had possessed a fortune of £100,000, another of £150,000, while a third had made a bequest of £792,000. Similarly, in 1789, a local Jew had left as much as £600,000, and a year later another assessed his wealth at £728,000,[34] while in 1794, there were still three Jews who ranked among the twenty wealthiest residents of the city. By 1812, however, there was no single Jew among the hundred highest taxpayers of the city.[35] When consistorial dues were paid in 1809, it was estimated that of 222 family groups in the department of Vaucluse, there were only 113 heads of families with a total wealth of 1,680,300 francs, an average of 14,869 francs per household.

Conditions were not quite so bad in the new Jewish settlements of Bouches-du-Rhône, Alpes-Maritimes, Gard and Hérault, since each of these, with the exception of the first-named, possessed a nucleus of Comtadin Jews who had emigrated before the Revolution. Yet even here, when exception is made of those few monied and propertied persons, poverty was widespread. Of 794 households in the regional consistory of Marseille, 355 heads of families had a total wealth of 8,926,000 francs, actually divided among only 304 families; that is to say, an average of 29,361 francs per family. More interesting than the gross figure, however, is that of the actual wealth possessed by each family. Such a picture is afforded by the tax returns of some 304 heads of families in 1809. The amounts registered range from 300 francs (four families) to 300,000

[34] Chobaut, H., op. cit., vol. ci (1937), 11.
[35] id., op. cit., 38.

francs (two families). Seventy-four families had between 300 and 5,000 francs each; fifty-three between 6,000 and 10,000; sixty-six between 12,000 and 25,000; forty-five between 25,000 and 50,000; thirty between 60,000 and 100,000; thirteen between 125,000 and 200,000, and three between 290,000 and 300,000 francs.

At first, taxpayers were divided into four categories, according to their incomes or holdings. Of 603 listed heads of families, 92 would normally have belonged to the first, or wealthiest group; 79 to the second group; 115 to the third, and 317 to the fourth. In point of fact, however, no more than 304 had it within their means to pay, and the taxes exacted from them amounted in all to 9,451 francs and 49 centimes. (These same individuals paid a total of 11,705 francs in civil, industrial and property taxes.)

It is interesting to observe that whereas at the outbreak of the Revolution and for some time afterwards a system of *progressive* taxation had operated in the Four Communities (*i.e.*, the wealthier the person, the more he paid), this later gave way to one of *regressive* taxation (*i.e.*, the wealthier the individual, the smaller the proportion of payment). The wealthy Jews had complained that besides taxes they were also obliged to give alms. It was for their benefit, therefore, that a proportionally regressive system of taxation was instituted. Five taxpayers, who possessed a joint total of 70,100 francs, paid between them 228 francs, 95 centimes, or fifty centimes for every hundred francs (0.5 percent). Another 121, having a total of 977,600 francs, paid 1,684.55 francs, or 1.75 per thousand (0.26-0.16 percent). Five others with a total wealth of 980,000 francs paid 551 francs and 25 centimes (from 0.60 to .05 percent). Unfortunately, however, we have no information as to the effect of this system on popular sentiment.

Equally indicative of the economic position at this time is the budget of the Carpentras community.[36] In 1865, for example, when approximately 250 Jews lived there, the total amounted to 3,178 francs, *i.e.*, an average of 3.9 francs per person. Forty-three families paid communal dues; three paid 200 francs each; two, 140 francs each; two, 120 francs; two others, 80 francs; six, 60 francs; three, 40 francs; seven, 30 francs; three, 20 francs; ten, 10 francs; and three paid five francs each (a total of 2,145

[36] According to documents now in the Yiddish Scientific Institute, New York.

francs). Thus, there was a constant deficit. From this budget the community appropriated 1,378 francs (approximately 21.50 fr. per week) for the relief of local paupers, and 200 francs for that of non-local mendicants. In 1884, poverty was so rife that out of a total 2,655 francs the community was obliged to allocate 600 for relief.

The situation was better in the younger settlements which had an element of Jewish émigrés from Comtat. If a contemporary report can be trusted, there were no paupers in Orange during the 'sixties. The local *Société des demoiselles hospitalières* occupied itself entirely with transient Jewish mendicants, buying ornaments for the synagogue out of funds which would otherwise have been spent in relieving the local poor.[37]

Family Status
(Table IV)

A revealing picture of Jewish family status in 1841 is provided by the official figures of the regional consistory (which now included the departments of Drôme and Loire).

The average number of children per family was 1.9 in Vaucluse; 1.7 in Rhône, and 1.4 in Bouches-du-Rhône. Prevalent conditions forced a break with the old Jewish tradition of large families, most of them being now limited to from one to three children. In Marseille there were three Jewish families each with eight children or more, and fifty-seven with only one child. In Lyon, there were fifty families, and in Carpentras fifteen, with one child each.

The picture did not change in later years. In 1892, of 116 Jewish families in Nîmes, 15 had but one child each; five had four children each; four had five children each, and only three had six children or more.

Besides parents and children, a goodly number of relatives lived with their immediate families. Thus, according to the figures for 1841, in Bouches-du-Rhône, 123 relatives resided with 77 Jewish families; in Gard ten relatives lived with ten families, and in Vaucluse, there were relatives in nine homes.

The number of individuals living alone was fairly large: 62 in Marseille (with 288 families), 31 in Lyon (175 families), and 11 in Montpellier (32 families).

[37] Mossé, B., *Progrès social et réligieux dans les communautés israélites du department de Vaucluse* (Avignon, (186..), p. 3.

TABLE IV

FAMILY STATUS OF JEWS IN THE CONSISTORY OF MARSEILLE, 1841

Department	Persons	Families	Children				Childless	Persons living alone	Heads of families	
			Boys	Girls	Sex Unknown	Total			Widowers	Widows
Bouches-du-Rhône	1,463	425	307	278	40	625	61	86	25	44
Drôme	39	9	14	3	.....	17	1	.....	.....	1
Gard	465	128*	98	120	.....	218	17	25	10	24
Hérault	131	48	25	33	.....	58	7	15	6	3
Isère	9	†	.....	.....	.....	.....	.....	.....	.....	.....
Loire	37	9	12	15	.....	17	.....	4	.....	.....
Rhône	621‡	175	168	136	.....	304	23	31	?	?
Var	35	10	.....	.....	14	14	.....	1	?	?
Vaucluse	865	206	209	194	.....	403	.....	29	16	36

* Data incomplete   † Information lacking   ‡ Excluding servants

Trades and Professions
(Table V)

Of the total Jewish population of 2,609 in 1809 we have information concerning only 641; and of a total of 3,954 in 1844 we have information concerning 1,304. For later years our data are likewise incomplete,

TABLE V

OCCUPATIONAL DISTRIBUTION OF JEWS IN THE CONSISTORY OF MARSEILLE, 1809-1902

	1809	1844	1866	1892	1902
	In the general population		Males over 25 years of age		
Industry and handicrafts	183	189	82	57	58
Trade	301	644	486	427	412
Office employees	7	103	94	73	104
Liberal professions	19	78	51	58	54
State officials	9	9	5	21	22
Military	31	10	5	5	7
Religious functionaries	14	21	17	14	14
Propriétaires	......	30	8	11	11
Rentiers	61	48	38	11	11
Brokers	1	56	38	56	55
Domestic and personal servants	......	......	19	19	16
	11	5	......	......	......
Agriculture	1	......	......	......	......
Unemployed	3	111	18	2	2
Total	641	1,304	861	754	766

except in regard to persons who had the right to vote in the consistorial elections of 1866 and 1892, *i.e.,* all males of twenty-five years or over. These, however, comprised the largest portion of economically active persons. Altogether, 896 individuals fell into this category (the area now excluding Lyon). For 1866 we have information concerning only some 861; while for 1892, out of a total of 761, we know the professional status of as many as 754. By 1902, the number of Jewish voters in the consistorial elections had declined sharply, despite an increase in the Jewish population; whereas in 1896, there were 833, and in 1900 as many as 929, two years later only 771 names were registered.

The category of "artisans and manual workers" was a catch-all for a wide diversity of operatives and laborers. In 1809, these included one metal worker, 21 tailors, 54 seamstresses and 10 apprentice seamstresses. The tailoring trade was thus the most highly represented; next came 2 laborers, 3 watchmakers, 4 chocolate makers, 15 twine weavers, 4 heavy laborers, 1 brewer and 1 cork-maker, besides divers manufacturers of tobacco products, etc., and one individual who described himself somewhat vaguely as "living by his work." As time passed, the number of those engaged in handicrafts and manual labor decreased, while the number of those occupied in trade and free professions increased, among them businessmen and employees. Similarly there was a decrease in the number of petty traders, whereas that of large-scale businessmen increased. Thus, as against 98 *colporteurs* in 1809, there were only 10 by the end of the century. Among the businessmen, horse-dealers, of whom there were 27 in 1844, played an important role. In 1809, only one broker lived on accumulated capital; but in 1844 there were already 56 such persons.

Religious and Civic Life

Immediately after the Emancipation, the religious and cultural life of the Four Communities began to decay, and in the newly-created neighboring settlements the situation was no better. The few poor Jews remaining in their old homes were at first strongly attached to their ancient customs and traditions. In the 'forties, there was a struggle in the Avignon community between the impoverished native Jews and the wealthy newcomers, the former demanding that services in the synagogue be conducted according to the traditional rite of the city, and the latter seeking to introduce a different one.[38] In administrative matters, the Four Communities suffered a similar decline. Decisions were now made in the new settlement at Marseille, where the head of the congregation was a rich émigré from Africa named Altaras.

In 1841, the constituents of the Marseille consistory were broken down into nine divisional centers located in the nine most important cities, and in turn grouping around themselves the Jewish communities of some forty-five small towns. The nine divisions were: (i) Marseille (three settlements with 1,042 Jews); (ii) Salon (five settlements with 356 Jews); (iii) Aix (eight settlements with 224 Jews); (iv) Avignon (seven settlements with 213 Jews); (v) Carpentras (three settlements with 325 Jews); (vi) Orange (seven settlements with 213 Jews); (vii) Nîmes (three settle-

---

[38] *Archives Israélites*, vol. i (1840), 291. For parallel situations elsewhere, cf. Roth, Cecil, *Venice* (Philadelphia 1930), p. 313-14; Bernstein, S., in *Horeb*, vol. v (1939), 43-122.

ments with 465 Jews); (viii) Montpellier (five settlements with 131 Jews); and (ix) Lyon (four settlements with 667 Jews). These divisions had between them nine rabbis, ten synagogues and ten cemeteries.

Until 1848, of all the Jews in the area, only 129 enjoyed full civic status. Of these, there were 60 in Bouches-du-Rhône, 21 in Rhône, and 18 each in Vaucluse and Gard. Only 136 enjoyed the right to vote in consistorial elections. After 1848, however, when the principle of universal suffrage was introduced also in the consistories, with franchise for all men of twenty-five years old and upward, the number of voters naturally increased. Nevertheless, by this time interest had waned. At the Montpellier elections of 1944, for instance, only 13 out of 39 persons registered their votes; while 40 years later no elections were held there at all. Similarly, only 25 persons voted at the Avignon elections of 1888.

Education

Especially serious was the plight of Jewish education. According to a survey made by the consistorial authorities in the 'sixties, Jewish children were receiving religious instruction in the following cities only: Marseille (three elementary schools with 155 children); Nîmes (two schools with 26 children; Nice (one school with 22 pupils); and Carpentras (one school with 26 children). Of the seven schools indicated, two were for boys (63 students); three for girls (94 pupils) and two were co-educational (72 children). In Aix, Orange and Avignon, modest religious courses were conducted by the local rabbi, or cantor. The exact number of all Jewish children receiving religious instruction at that time is unknown. For 1844, for example, there is information concerning the ages of only 2,816 children, of whom 245 were between five and fourteen, and 183 between fifteen and nineteen. Our figures on religious education, however, are for approximately twenty years after this date.

In other parts of France, with the exception of Alsace-Lorraine, conditions were not much better. In Paris, in 1860, only 892 boys and 683 girls received a Jewish education. There were no more than ten institutions for boys and nine for girls, although the Jewish population numbered approximately 251,000.[39]

[39] *La Verité Israélite* (1860), p. 155.

Cultural Life

With the material decline of the communities their cultural level also sank to almost abysmal depths.[39a] Typical was the situation in Avignon, where literary activity was confined, during the 'forties, to a few issues of Elissa Lisbonne's periodical, *La Loi Divine,* and for the following forty years found its only expression in Benjamin Mossé's *La Famille de Jacob* (1859-93) and in some twenty-odd devotional works by the same author. Nor did even these mediocre lucubrations reflect any general interests of the community as a whole; they were the productions of a single energetic individual whose inspiration appears to have been drawn less from the Muses than from a practical desire to augment his meagre stipend as local rabbi.

A similar situation obtained at Carpentras. During the 'forties the community still boasted a few educated Jews. Every Saturday afternoon, they would assemble for an hour's Bible-study at the home of the merchant, Elie Valabrègue.[40] These, however, were the pathetic remnant of a long and colorful past. In 1848, the local cantor, a certain Deitz (of Alsatian origin), felt compelled to issue a call for the "salvation" of the city's Jewish youth which was steadily drifting from the ancestral faith.[41]

In Cavaillon, there remained only the ancient synagogue, which was renovated in 1843. The building was opened, however, for the sole purpose of tending the "perpetual lamp." Even on holidays there was no *minyan*. The wealthy Jews, who were still wholeheartedly devoted to their tradition, had to hire a few of their coreligionists from the neighboring communities to make up the required quorum.[42]

Nor was it only within their own community that the cultural life of the Jews was at a low ebb. Even as late as the 'forties, the sub-prefect of Carpentras, Ladreit de la Chartière, barred his salon to them—an action which provoked a spirited protest from David Naquet, a member of the city council.[43] As time passed, however, this situation improved, particu-

---

[39a] On the earlier literary productions of Comtadin Jewry, see Roth, Cecil, "The Liturgies of Avignon and the Comtat Venaissin" in *Journal of Jewish Bibliography*, vol. i (1939), 99-105. Most of them, however, were published outside of the province.

[40] Mossé, B., in *Le Lien d'Israél*, vol. i (1858), 166.

[41] *Appel aux pères de familles israélites de France et de l'étranger* (Avignon 1848).

[42] *Le Lien d'Israél*, vol. i (1858), 167; *Archives Israélites*, vol. xiv (1854), 362.

[43] Ms. Carpentras, No. 16587.

larly in Avignon, which, from the outset of the Revolution, was closer then Carpentras to revolutionary Paris. In the 'sixties, Jews held seats in the municipal council and were represented in the Tribunal and in the management of the Caisse *d'Epargne* (savings bank) at Avignon, Carpentras and Lisle-sur-Sorgue; while in the first named city, Rabbi Benjamin Mossé was able to boast that "the foremost salons are now open to the *élite* of our coreligionists."[44]

In Aix, where on the eve of the Revolution there were, legally speaking, no Jews, there were in 1843 ten Jewish advocates and public prosecutors. Moreover, for some time this city, which had always professed to be the spiritual capital of Provence, also had a Jewish mayor. For Jewish circles this was the apogee of emancipation.

Before they themselves disappeared, the four older communities proved to be of help in the creation of new settlements in southeastern France; and from the latter emerged such truly significant personalities as Isaac Adolphe Crémieux (1796-1880), Gaston Crémieux (1836-71) — he was the head of the Marseille community in 1871—and the jurist Gustave Emanuel Bédarrides (1817-99). From those Jews who remained in the ancient settlement rose the eminent chemist and republican, Alfred Naquet (1834-1916), but his sole connection with Jewry was in his battle against reactionary forces during the Dreyfus Affair.

Disappearance of the Communities

By 1874, it was already apparent to the consistorial authorities that the Four Communities were beginning to die out.[45] At Carpentras, nothing remained of the old-time glory save the venerable fourteenth century synagogue, and an extraordinarily large cemetery—the latter an eloquent testimony to the fact that the heads of the community who bought the plot certainly anticipated that the community would continue for centuries. At Cavaillon there was likewise a synagogue, considered by Chobaut, the historian and archivist of Vaucluse, as the "jewel of

[44] *Progrès* . . . . . , p. 2.
[45] Consistoire Israélite de Marseille, *Etat des communautés de l'ancien Comtat* (Marseille 1874).

the city."[46]   (Both synagogues are now classed by the government as historical monuments.) [47]

During the past seventy years, decay has developed into dissolution. In 1919 only six men and two women prayed in the synagogue of Carpentras on the Day of Atonement. Later, it is true, the congregation was temporarily augmented by an influx of Polish-Jewish refugees, and a curious mixture of the old Comtadin rite and contemporary Ashkenazic usage ensued.[48] Today, however, no rite at all is used there.

In neighboring Cavaillon, by the end of the century, the community had dwindled to a mere seventeen persons. Four of these had Christian wives and their children were reared in the Christian faith.[49] Today, not even one professing Jew remains, the last of them, a certain Achille Jacob Astruc, who died at the age of seventy-nine, having been buried in 1925 in the small Jewish graveyard at the foot of a hill. The keys to the cemetery are at present in the possession of his son's foster-brother. The son himself lives in Aix-en-Provence. Together with his foster-brother he has transferred to Avignon the scrolls of the Law formerly in the synagogue. The latter has become a museum, the caretaker of which is a Christian woman; while an agreement reached between Astruc's son and the city council provides for the abolition of the Jewish cemetery and the transfer of the bodies there interred to a corner in the Christian graveyard.

Of the Jewish community in Lisle-sur-Sorgue nothing remains. Even its location is uncertain.[50]

In 1935 Chobaut estimated the number of Jews in Vaucluse at about three hundred. Of these, two hundred lived in Avignon, thirty-five in Carpentras, eight in Cavaillon and eight in Valreas. In Lisle-sur-Sorgue there were none.[51]

[46] *Avignon et le Comtat Venaissin* (Grenoble 1932), p. 181.

[47] Halphen, F. A., "Les synagogues du Comtat sont sauvés," in *Univers Israélite*, vol. lxxxv (1930), 841-45.

[48] *Univers Israélite*, vol. lxxxv (1929), 149. In 1927-29 a few Jewish immigrants from Poland settled on the land in this district; cf. Grinberg, H., "L'oeuvre agricole du Comité Central d'Assistance aux émigrants juifs" in the Colonie Scolaire's *Almanach Juif* for 1931, p. 41-44.

[49] The figures are those of the consistorial census.

[50] The Yiddish Scientific Institute possesses among its archives an interesting document of 1856 in which a Jew named David Abram makes representations to the prefect of police of Vaucluse concerning a plan to demolish the synagogue at Lisle. "Leave us our ruins," he pleads, "we have reason to be proud of them."

[51] *Revue des études juives*, vol. cii (1937), 39.

NOTES ON THE DEMOGRAPHY OF THE
SEPHARDIM IN FRANCE

MUCH has been written on the history of the Sephardim, their commercial activities, and other aspects of their life. However, very little is known about the demographic problems of the Sephardim during earlier periods, or even about the demography of contemporary Sephardim in many countries. The sources are scarce and not easily available. In this paper, we should like, as an example, to touch upon some demographic problems of Sephardim in one particular country — France.

The number of Sephardim in France was never larger than about 3,500. In 1752 only 327 Sephardic families (1,598 persons) lived in Bordeaux and about 1,100 in Saint-Esprit-lès-Bayonne. In 1806, 2,131 Jews lived in Bordeaux, of whom only 1,651 were Sephardim. In 1809 1,173 Jews lived in Saint-Esprit. Smaller Sephardic communities existed in Bidache, Dax, Peyrehorade, Paris and a few other places.[1]

In this study we should like to examine a few problems which are connected with the demography of the Sephardim in France: births, marriages, ages and deaths. It should be noted that the sources at our disposal are not always reliable. First of all, the Jews avoided giving absolutely reliable information when registering their état-civil. This was already observed by the historian A. Nicolaï in regard to the Jews and Protestants of Bordeaux.[2] The Bordeaux registries of burials of non-Catholics in 1737–1787 (introduced by the King's

The following abbreviations were used in the notes and appendixes: Ad — Departmental archives of Gironde; AmBa — City archives of Bayonne; AmBx — City archives of Bordeaux; Jerusalem — The Jewish Historical General Archives of Jerusalem; JTS — The Library of the Jewish Theological Seminary of America; GG — Registries of the État-civil. On the Jewish registries see Z. Szajkowski, "The Reform of the État-civil of the French Jews during the Revolution of 1789," The Jewish Quarterly Review, XLIX (1958), 63–75.

[1] Z. Szajkowski, "Population Problems of Marranos and Sephardim in France, from the 16th to the 20th Centuries," Proceedings of the American Academy for Jewish Research, XXVII (1958), 83–105.

[2] A. Nicolaï, La population de Bordeaux au XVIIIe siècle. 1700–1800 (Paris — Bordeaux, 1909), 7–8

Originally published in the Hebrew Union College Annual, vol. XXX (1959).

declaration of April 9, 1736 on such burials) contain many cases of
deceased Jews who were registered as *portugais*, or *juifs*. Many of
these were not recorded in the registry of deaths which was kept by
the Bordeaux *Nation* of the Sephardim.[3] Many Jews were not registered at all. Thus, on August 28, 1792 the births of four children of
Abraham Gomes Fonseque were registered; they were born in
Bordeaux between 1736 and 1790, but were not registered before.
In 1794 it was noted in a Bordeaux register that Hanna-Félicité, a
daughter of Jzaac Lange and Sara Torrès had never been registered.[4]
The Jewish registries of Saint-Esprit are incomplete. On October 5,
1801, Jacob Rodrigues stated in a petition to the judge Samuel
Nunes — a Jew himself — that he could not find any trace of his
birth in these registries. On July 17, 1831, the Mayor of Bayonne
stated in a note on the register of 1752 that the entries were faulty
and should be considered only as a "nomenclature of notes made
haphazardly."[5] In the later years, in 1865–1894, Mardochée Ernest
Naquet, Samuel Salzedo and Eugène Benjamin Léon compiled, from
these registries and from other sources, a list of births and deaths
of the Jews of Saint-Esprit.[6] But according to their list, only old
people died in the years prior to 1752 and from 1766 till the 1770's.
It seems that their register of births was compiled from entries in
the register of deaths.

Still, the available sources are of great value for students of
Sephardic demography.

What was the rate of births and deaths among the Sephardim and
how did this influence the increase or decrease of the Sephardic
population?

In 1739–1792 the Bordeaux *Nation* registered 1,694 births and
1,816 deaths. In sixteen of a forty-three years period (1741–1783)
the number of births among Christians of Bordeaux exceeded the
number of deaths, while the number of deaths among Jews in these
sixteen years exceeded the number of births. During six years the
contrary could be observed — proportionately more births among
Jews than among Christians and, during twenty-one years the process

---

[3] AmBx, GG 810 (1737–1750); GG 30 (1737–1787); GG 790. It is possible that
in some cases the *Nation* prohibited the burial of Jews in its cemetery. George
Cirot, *Recherches sur les Juifs Espagnols et Portugais à Bordeaux* (Bordeaux, 1908),
181.

[4] AmBx, GG 844 (Register of births in the Bordeaux *Nation*), Nos. 1880–83;
I E 3, No. 681.

[5] AmBa, GG, register of births in the *Nation* of Saint-Esprit.

[6] In possession of the Bayonne Synagogue.

was similar in births or deaths among both groups of the population. During seventeen years, the Jews registered more births than deaths, while the Christians registered more births than deaths during twenty-seven years. The Jews registered more deaths than births during twenty-five years, and the Christians registered more births than deaths during twenty-seven years. The Jews registered more deaths than births during twenty-five years and the Christians during sixteen years. Only throughout one year none of them had more deaths than births. (See Table I.)

But we must always keep in mind that our sources are not absolutely reliable. In a municipal registry of burial permits for non-Catholics of Bordeaux, we found 167 Jewish deaths between 1739 and 1750 which were not recorded in the register of the *Nation.*[7]

According to one source, there were, in the 1741–1783 period, twenty-seven years with more births than deaths among the Bordeaux Jews but, according to another source, there were, during the same period, twenty-four years with more deaths than births.[8]

According to one document the *Nation* of Bordeaux registered forty-four births, eleven marriages and fifty-eight deaths in 1784. During the same year the community of Avignonese Jews registered two births, no marriage, and one death. According to another document, the number of births among the Bordeaux Sephardim in 1786 was 56, deaths — 55, marriages — 9 and, among the Avignonese, there were 5 births, 5 deaths, and 2 marriages.[9] But the statistics of these two documents are different from the official registries of the *Nation.*

According to one source, 2,628 Jews were born in Saint-Esprit during the years 1709–1807 (see Table II). But we already noted that this list of births was largely based on information obtained from the registries of the deaths which recorded the age of the deceased. Thus we found names of Jews who were born outside of Saint-Esprit, but had died there, *e. g.* Moyse Ensheim (born in 1750 in Metz, deceased in 1839 in Bayonne). By comparing the two records of births and burials in Saint-Esprit for the period of 1780–1807, we noted 999 births and 419 burials. This is completely out of proportion to the more accurate data on the rate of births and mortality among the Jews of Bordeaux and in view of the decrease of the number of Sephardim.[10]

---

[7] AmBx, GG 810.   [8] Nicolaï, 202; Cirot, 83.

[9] *Journal de Guienne,* Apr. 1, 1785, 866; AdG, C 1312.

[10] According to the copies of the register of names of the Jews in Saint-Esprit, 1808–1810, Jerusalem.

It is worth while to compare data on births with the analysis of the register of names of 1220 Jews in Saint-Esprit (1808–1810). The author of this curious document included the data of birth of most of 1220 Jews. Thus we were able to obtain the number of 1,051 Jews who were born during the years 1728–1808 and still resided in Saint-Esprit in 1808–1810.[11] Many conclusions could be drawn from a comparison of the two statistics, but both of them are not sufficiently reliable to encourage such analysis.

A register of burials on the Jewish cemetery of Bayonne (Saint-Esprit became later part of Bayonne) contains the names of 2,622 persons deceased in the years 1780–1938. (See Table III.)

According to the already mentioned analysis of the names 843 Jews who still lived in Saint-Esprit on the beginning of 1808 had died during the years 1808–1883.[12] But according to the above mentioned record the number of burials in 1808–1883 was 1,351.[13] According to the already mentioned record of mortality compiled by Mardochée Ernest Naquet 1,527 Jews died in 1751–1795.[14] According to this document 486 died in 1780–1795. But according to the above mentioned record of burials only 319 died in 1780–1795. This only proves again the unreliability of the sources.

According to one source the number of births in the Sephardic community of Peyrehorade was 119 during the period 1793–1879 and the number of deaths 30. Of course, the low mortality could easily be explained by the emigration of the Peyrehorade Jews who died elsewhere after having left Peyrehorade.[15]

In the entire department of Gironde, there were 93 deaths for every 100 births and 3 births for every 100 inhabitants in the years 1806–1810. In 1861–1865, there were 92 deaths for every 100 births

[11] See Table VII.

[12] See Table VIII.

[13] See Table III. Another record of deaths (Jerusalem) brings the following data for Bayonne: 1891 — 20, 1892 — 21, 1893 — 15, 1894 — 16, 1895 — 20, 1896 — 12, 1897 — 10, 1898 — 11, 1899 — 9, 1900 — 16, 1901 — 10, 1902 — 9, 1903 — 12, 1904 — 17, 1905 — 20, 1906 — 25, 1907 — 7, 1908 — 2, 1909 — 13, 1910 — 7, 1911 — 11, 1912 — 10. Total — 293.

According to another register of mortality in Bayonne (Jerusalem) 195 died there in 1893–1912: 1893 — 13, 1894 — 15, 1895 — 10, 1896 — 11, 1897 — 13, 1898 — 12, 1899 — 4, 1900 — 15, 1901 — 7, 1902 — 8, 1903 — 8, 1904 — 12, 1905—4, 1906 — 9, 1907 — 5, 1908 — 8, 1909 — 11, 1910 — 13, 1911 — 9, 1912 — 8.

[14] See Table IX.

[15] In Peyrehorade were performed thirty-three circumcisions in the years 1725–1742, 1745, 1748, 1753–1754, 1756 and 1758. According to a list compiled (most probably) by the historian Henry Léon (Jerusalem). But it seems that the list is not complete.

and 2.3 births for every 100 inhabitants. In the arrondissement of Bordeaux, there were 80.2 deaths for every 100 births in 1813–1822. In the city of Bordeaux itself, there were 79.34 deaths for every 100 births in 1770–1780, 105.12 in 1801–1805, 88.41 in 1846–1850, 118.09 in 1866–1870. In 1864–1866, Bordeaux counted 3.61 births per 100 inhabitants and 21.8 deaths per 1000 inhabitants. In 1864–1866 Bordeaux, with a population of 194,241 (in 1866) had 4,964 births and 4,249 deaths.[16]

It seems then that the death rate was higher among the Sephardim than among non-Jews. But the rate of mortality was smaller among Ashkenazic and other non-Sephardic Jewish groups than among non-Jews, e. g. in Strasbourg.[17]

On Table IV we can compare the rate of births among the Sephardim and other Jewish groups in the middle of the 19th century. The time covered by this Table is too small to allow for definite conclusions for such a late period. But there is no doubt that, in an earlier period, the rate of mortality among the Sephardim was larger than among the other Jewish groups. In 1717–1808 the Jewish community of Metz registered 7,062 births, 1,427 marriages and 5,905 deaths, i. e. 1,157 more births than deaths.[18]

Between 1780 and 1789, the four Jewish communities of the papal province in Southeastern France (Avignon, Carpentras, Cavaillon and L'Isle-sur-Sorgue) registered 478 births, 86 marriages, and 497 deaths, i. e. 19 more deaths than births. In 1788 those four communities registered 29 births and 52 deaths.[19] This was, probably, a result of a constant emigration of the rich Jewish families from these four communities. The same could be said for the 19th century of which statistics for a larger period are available. In the Ashkenazic community of Dijon (where 413 Jews lived in 1846), 78 births, 20 marriages and only 39 deaths were registered in the ten-year period 1836–1845.[20]

[16] E. Féret, *Statistique générale . . . de la Gironde* (Bordeaux, 1889), I, 293, 304–05.
[17] E. Schnurmann, *La Population juive en Alsace* (Paris, 1936), 129–30.
[18] City archives of Metz; Departmental archives of Moselle.
[19] According to the Jewish registries in the City archives of Avignon, Carpentras, Cavaillon and L'Isle-sur-Sorgue, series GG.
[20] Census of the Jews in Dijon, 1846 (Jerusalem).
Following are, for comparison, a few data on the births in the Sephardic community of Amsterdam: 1737 — 112, 1738 — 103, 1739 — 123, 1740 — 103, 1741 — 95, 1742 — 95, 1743 — 92, 1744 — 92, 1745 — 95, 1746 — 101, 1747 — 82, 1760 — 85, 1761 — 62, 1762 — 78, 1763 — 77, 1764 — 74. But it seems that for many years not all births of girls were registered. Geboorte Register der Hollandsche Portugeesche Israelitische Gemeente te Amsterdam. Sept. 1, 1736 — 24 tamus 5571 in the City archives of Amsterdam, D. T. & B, No. 400.

The age composition of the Sephardim is one of the most phenom-
enal and curious facts in the subject of our study. Of course, the
incompleteness and unreliability of some of our sources should
always be kept in mind. Still, the percentage of old people is strikingly
large. In six registries of Bordeaux and Saint-Esprit covering the
years 1716–1810, the age of 4,521 Jews is mentioned. 2,721 of them
were between 51 and 81 years old or older: 497 between 51 and 60
years, 1,580 between 61 and 80 and 644 of 81 years or older. (See
Table V.) According to the already mentioned register of names,
653 of the 1,220 Jews of Saint-Esprit (1808–1810) were born before
1789, 205 in 1789–1799, 253 from 1800 on. (In 109 cases the dates of
birth were not noted.) At the period of registration, 168 of them
were younger than 6 years, 301 were between 6 and 20 years old,
261 between 21 and 40 years, 123 between 41 and 50 years, 104
between 51 and 60 years, 99 between 61 and 80 years and 3 were 81
years old or older. According to the census of June 15, 1812, eighty-
two of the 1,166 Jews in Saint-Esprit were older than 60 years; over
one hundred of the 706 Jews (according to a census of 1886) and
eighty-four of the 427 Jews (according to a census of 1921) were of
the same age.[21] In 1854 the Jewish population of Bordeaux comprised
2,411 persons (800 families). Of these, 215 (99 men and 116 women)
were between 61 and 80 years old and 30 (19 men and 11 women)
were older than 80. Out of 382 electors in the Bordeaux consistory
on July 30, 1849, 123 were of the age between 25 and 40, 60 between
41 and 50, 52 between 51 and 60, 47 between 61 and 80, 2 — 81
and older. The age of 98 was not noted. Out of 317 electors on June
1, 1858, 83 were between 25 and 40 years old, 71 between 41 and 50,
62 between 51 and 60, 83 between 61 and 80, 3 — 81 years or older.
The age of 15 electors was not noted.[22]

The percentage of older people among the general population
was much smaller. Out of 349,101 inhabitants in the department of
Gironde in 1872, only 9,520 were 80 years or older. Out of 215,140
inhabitants of Bordeaux in 1876, only 17,081 were of the age between
60 and 79, and 1,761 were of 80 years or older. The average age of
the Bordeaux inhabitants was only about 30 years, while the average
age for the entire population of France in 1860–1865 was 36½ years.[23]

Further studies could probably explain this phenomenon. It is
doubtful whether the economic situation had anything to do with

[21] According to the copies of the censuses between 1812 and 1921 (Jerusalem).
[22] Census of the Bordeaux Jews, 1854 (Jerusalem); Lists of consistorial electors
in the Gironde department, 1849 and 1858 (AdG, V).
[23] Féret, I, 289–301.

the longevity of the Sephardim. In fact, while analyzing some records of deaths, we noted deaths of a large number of aged paupers among the Sephardim.[24] The longevity of the Sephardim could also contradict some statements about the poor physical condition of the Jews which resulted in their rejection from military service. In 1843 such a statement was made by A. Gautier, Deputy Mayor of Bordeaux, and repeated by the Prefect of the Gironde department. The same applies to similar statements on the Jews of the former Papal province and the Ashkenazim. In fact, such statements were most probably excuses for rejecting Jews from military service because of purely anti-Jewish sentiments.[25]

Was this large number of older people among Sephardim only a statistical mirage, a result of a low rate of births? This may be exact only for some later periods. As noted below, the proportion of big families among the Sephardim was large.[25a]

How did the age composition of the Sephardim look in comparison with other Jewish groups? In 1809, 402 out of 1,617 Jews in the five cities of Marseilles, Nice, Lyon, Carpentras and Nîmes were between 41 and 80 years or older. 110 of them were 61 or older.[26] This is a large proportion of old people among these Jews who were mostly of Avignon and Comtadin origin. But, among the Ashkenazim, the percentage of older people was much smaller, although there were more older people among the Ashkenazim than among the non-Jews.[27] According to a census of sixty-nine Jewish communities in the Department of Moselle (including the main community of Metz),[28] 7,709 Jews lived there in 1846. The census shows the ages of 7,484 of them.

[24] The Jewish community of Bordeaux counted fifty-three deaths in 1866. According to a curious document of the Bordeaux consistory which classified the 53 cases according to 6 classes of consistorial taxes paid by the deceased, thirteen belonged to the 6th — lowest class, thirteen to the 5th, nine to the 4th, six to the 3rd, one to the 2nd and two to the 1st class. Nine deceased were *indigents* and did not pay taxes at all. All thirteen cases (out of the 53) of deaths of infants up to one year old were among the poor and the classes six to four. Does this prove a greater mortality among the poor Sephardim? (Jerusalem).

[25] Z. Szajkowski, "French Jews in the Armed Forces During the Revolution of 1789," *Proceedings of the American Academy for Jewish Research*, XXVI (1957), 6.

[25a] B. Saint-Jours noted the number of 1,785 Jews in Bordeaux in 1752 and 144 births from 1750 to 1754, or one birth per 50 persons ("La population de Bordeaux depuis le XIIᵉ siècle," *Revue historique de Bordeaux*, IV (1911), 402, according to Ad Gironde, C 1089).

[26] Census of Jews in the regional consistory of Marseille, 1809 (Jerusalem).

[27] Schnurmann, 129.

[28] Censuses of the Jews in the communities of the Moselle department, 1846 (JTS).

Of these 7,484 Jews, only 525 were between 61 and 80 old, and 83
were 81 or older. According to a census taken the same year in
the Department of Lower Rhine,[29] 4,012 Jews lived then in the six
communities of Strasbourg, Barswiller, Bouxwiller, Fegersheim, and
Hoënheim. Only 178 of them were between 61 and 80 years old, and
16 were 81 years or older. In the community of Dijon only 33 out of
413 Jews in 1846 were 60 years or older.[30]

It is worth while noting a few details concerning marriages among
the Sephardim, without yet drawing any conclusions. 178 marriages
were registered by the Bordeaux *Nation* from 1776 until October
1792.[31] According to one source, 131 marriages among the Sephardim
of Bayonne were registered during the period 1793 to June 30, 1812.
According to another source, 324 marriages were registered there
during the period 1812–1882. The number of marriages was never
higher than 14 a year (in 1873). We noted ten years with only one
marriage, fifteen years — with two marriages, fourteen
years — from three to five marriages, etc.[32]

Another striking phenomenon in the early period is the number
of large families among the Sephardim, especially in view of the
above mentioned statement made in 1846 by the Deputy Mayor of
Bordeaux that inbreeding among the Sephardim resulted in their
physical decline.

The proportion of big families among the Sephardim was rather
large, and certainly not smaller than among the other Jewish groups.
Of 36 families of wealthy *Portugais* (*i. e.* Jews) in Bordeaux, named
in a list of December 4, 1636, ten had seven or more children each.
In the 1740's, Moseh François Lopez de Paz and Louis Lopez de Paz
were each fathers of eleven children, and Abraham Lameyre of nine
children. In 1807, out of 375 Sephardic families of Bordeaux, 149
were composed of from five to more than ten persons each (14 families — ten or more persons each). Among the Avignonese Jews of
Bordeaux, sixteen out of twenty-seven families and, among the
Ashkenazim, thirty-three out of sixty-nine families were composed
of from five to more than ten persons. In 1809 one hundred and one
out of three hundred and twelve Sephardic families in Bayonne

---

[29] Censuses of Jews in the communities of the Lower Rhine department, 1846
(JTS).

[30] Census of Jews in Dijon, 1846 (Jerusalem).

[31] Number of Jewish marriages in Bordeaux: 1776 — 2, 1777 — 7, 1778 — 10,
1779 — 11, 1780 — 7, 1781 — 14, 1782 — 12, 1783 — 8, 1784 — 9, 1785 — 14, 1786 —
9, 1787 — 13, 1788 — 12, 1789 — 10, 1790 — 11, 1791 — 14, 1792 — 15 (Cirot, 183).

[32] Bayonne register of marriages (Jerusalem); E. C. M. (see Table VII).

and three out of eighteen families in Peyrehorade counted from five to ten or more children each. (See Table VI.).

In the middle of the 19th century, the number of large families decreased. According to a census of 1854 eight hundred Jewish families (2,411 persons) lived in Bordeaux. Only 464 of these families had children: 162 families had one child each, 136 — two children, 70 — three children, 41 — four children, 29 — five children, 14 — six children, 5 — seven children, 3 — eight children, 3 — nine children, and only one family had ten children. 336 couples were childless. Of course, a number of grown children had, most probably, already left Bordeaux at that time. Still, this census proves a tendency toward smaller families which was then more in line with the general trend in France. According to the census of 1872, the average number of persons per family in the department of Gironde was only 3.48 while, in France as a whole, the average number was 4.62. According to a census of 1911 the number of Jews in Bordeaux was then 1,640; 428 of them poor people. The remaining 1,212 Jews consisted of 426 families. 291 of them were of 1 or 2 persons each, 172 — from 3 to 5 persons, 13 — 6 or more persons each.[33]

Nor was the percentage of large families greater among the Ashkenazim. The Jewish community of Metz counted 505 families (3,075 persons) in 1708, 503 families (2,764 persons) in 1800, 456 families (2,186 persons) in 1806. In 1846, 172 Jewish families (875 persons) lived in the nine communities of the Moselle department, Bionville, Buding, Guinglange, Louvigny, Metzerwisse, Montigny-le-Metz, Montenach, Nelling and Servigny. 17 of them were composed of 1 person each, 17 — 2 persons, 21 — 3, 25 — 4, 23 — 5, 21 — 6, 12 — 7, 14 — 8, 12 — 9 and 10 families of 10 or more persons each.[34]

This paper should be considered not as a complete study with final conclusions, but only as notes to an important aspect of Jewish research.

[33] Censuses of Jews in Bordeaux, 1807, 1854, 1911, and in Saint-Esprit, 1809 (Jerusalem); Ad. Detcheverry, *Histoire des Israélites de Bordeaux* (Bordeaux, 1850), 59–62; Cirot, 182–83; Féret, I, 288.

[34] Censuses of Jews in the Moselle department, 1846 (JTS); S. Posener, "Les Juifs sous le Premier Empire," *REJ*, XCIV (1933), 163.

TABLE I

Births and Deaths in the Sephardic
Nation of Bordeaux, 1739–Oct. 1792*

Years	Births	Deaths	+or− among Christians	Years	Births	Deaths	+or− among Christians
1739	36	26	?	1766	13	43	+
1740	23	19	?	1767	27	24	+
1741	25	20	−	1768	16	31	+
1742	14	16	−	1769	19	24	+
1743	19	8	+	1770	32	28	+
1744	22	17	+	1771	27	27	−
1745	28	49	−	1772	21	37	−
1746	20	19	−	1773	18	38	+
1747	29	21	−	1774	15	31	+
1748	20	31	−	1775	20	42	+
1749	30	26	−	1776	50	31	+
1750	25	22	−	1777	32	36	+
1751	30	22	+	1778	47	32	+
1752	24	28	+	1779	36	52	−
1753	30	39	−	1780	37	44	+
1754	37	22	+	1781	36	49	+
1755	40	25	+	1782	35	52	−
1756	30	23	+	1783	46	49	+
1757	23	29	+	1784	45	66	?
1758	20	25	+	1785	60	46	?
1759	22	25	−	1786	57	55	?
1760	30	25	−	1787	51	34	?
1761	18	21	−	1788	56	47	?
1762	25	36	+	1789	45	41	?
1763	26	36	+	1790	61	64	?
1764	24	21	+	1791	53	70	?
1765	19	33	+	1792	50	39	?
				TOTAL:	1,694	1,816	

* Cirot, 183; Nicolaï, 201.

TABLE II

Births in the Sephardic *Nation* of
Saint-Esprit-lès-Bayonne

1709–1807*

1709— 4	1734 ⎫ 34	1759—40	1784—27
1710— 3	1735 ⎭	1760—42	1785—39
1711— 2	1736—11	1761—42	1786—38
1712— 3	1737—10	1762—38	1787—37
1713— 2	1738—15	1763—53	1788—23
1714— 3	1739—17	1764—40	1789—20
1715— 7	1740—14	1765—45	1790—25
1716— 5	1741—20	1766—24	1791—25
1717— 3	1742—13	1767—25	1792—30
1718— 9	1743—16	1768—33	1793—40
1719— 9	1744— 8	1769—42	1794—30
1720— 9	1745—16	1770—32	1795—32
1721—14	1746—16	1771—39	1796—44
1722— 8	1747—20	1772—42	1797—37
1723— 9	1748—30	1773—47	1798—40
1724— 4	1749—15	1774—36	1799—41
1725—13	1750—18	1775—38	1800—49
1726— 5	1751—13	1776—36	1801—42
1727— 7	1752—36	1777—31	1802—44
1728—11	1753—52	1778—28	1803—50
1729—19	1754—40	1779—39	1804—42
1730—20	1755—51	1780—40	1805—39
1731—17	1756—35	1781—24	1806—38
1732—20	1757—52	1782—36	1807—35
1733—15	1758—49	1783—32	
			TOTAL: 2,628

* According to the list compiled by Naquet, Salzedo and Léon.

TABLE III

A list of burials in the
Jewish Cemetery of Bayonne

1780–1938*

1780—22	1821—17	1862—18	1903—12
1781—23	1822—12	1863—17	1904—19
1782—30	1823—19	1864—22	1905—17
1783—20	1824—20	1865—18	1906—20
1784—16	1825—15	1866—21	1907—22
1785—10	1826—16	1867—13	1908—13
1786—15	1827—15	1868—27	1909—20
1787—15	1828—23	1869—14	1910—14
1788—31	1829—15	1870—21	1911—15
1789—21	1830—14	1871—25	1912—17
1790—15	1831—17	1872—30	1913—11
1791—15	1832—18	1873—18	1914—16
1792—12	1833—17	1874—17	1915—26
1793—26	1834—11	1875—20	1916—13
1794—22	1835—22	1876—31	1917—11
1795—26	1836—18	1877—11	1918—17
1796— 8	1837—25	1878—20	1919—17
1797— 3	1838—18	1879—15	1920—15
1798— 7	1839—14	1880—13	1921—10
1799— 4	1840—18	1881—19	1922—14
1800— 9	1841—16	1882—19	1923— 9
1801— 4	1842—15	1883—19	1924—19
1802— 8	1843—20	1884—10	1925—20
1803— 8	1844—10	1885—23	1926—22
1804—11	1845—18	1886—15	1927—19
1805—16	1846—21	1887—15	1928—16
1806—10	1847—18	1888—20	1929—14
1807—12	1848—17	1889—16	1930—12
1808—13	1849—18	1890—21	1931—12
1809—14	1850—21	1891—18	1932—14
1810—14	1851—16	1892—27	1933— 6
1811—22	1852—14	1893—15	1934—15
1812—20	1853— 8	1894—19	1935—15
1813—22	1854—19	1895—17	1936— 7
1814— 8	1855—31	1896—14	1937—11
1815— 7	1856—13	1897—16	1938— 8
1816—11	1857—15	1898—11	————
1817—12	1858—22	1899—12	TOTAL: 2,622
1818—13	1859—25	1900—21	
1819—16	1860—25	1901—13	
1820—23	1861—22	1902—11	

* In the possession of the Bayonne community.

TABLE IV

Births, Deaths and Marriages in Various Regional
Jewish Consistories of France, 1858–1861†

Regional Consistory	Years	Total Number of Jews	Births	Deaths at birth (not registered)	Deaths	Marriages
Bordeaux*........	1860	3,053	59	4	37	13
Bordeaux*........	1861	3,053	60	3	35	9
Bayonne*.........	1859	1,204	16	—	34	9
Bayonne*.........	1860	1,192	19	—	29	8
Marseilles**......	1859	3,550	67	2	41	17
Lyons***.........	1858	2,189	49	3	28	9
Strasbourg*......	1859	16,455	473	28	335	119
Colmar*..........	1860	1,031?	252	32	148	68
Metz*............	1859	7,253	140	9	86	30
Nancy*...........	1859	6,792	160	5	98	37
Paris****	1857–58	25,410	52[1]	96	787	253?

† According to statistical reports (Jerusalem).
* Sephardim.
* Ashkenazim.
** Mostly Comtadin Jews.
*** Mostly Ashkenazim.
**** A mixed community.
[1] Only in the communities outside of Paris.

TABLE V

Age of Sephardim in Five Registries of Bordeaux and Saint-Esprit-lès-Bayonne 18th Century*

Age	Source: Bordeaux Register of Deaths 1716-1722	Bordeaux Register of Deaths Jan. 7, 1739– Dec. 23, 1792	Bayonne Register of Deaths Jan. 11, 1788– Jan. 2, 1792	Restored Bayonne Register of Births	Ibidem Age at Death	Total
Until 5	19	482	13	272	10	796
6–20	5	158	1	86	17	267
21–40	5	213	7	141	61	427
41–50	5	120	10	111	64	310
51–60	5	205	11	180	96	497
61–80	7	464	49	651	409	1,580
81 or older	1	154	2	303	184	644
TOTAL:	47	1,796	93	1,744	841	4,521

* AmBx, GG 30, GG 845; Archives of the Bayonne Community.

TABLE VI

Number of Persons per Family in Bordeaux, Bayonne and Peyrehorade 1807–1809*

Number of Persons	Source: Bordeaux Census of 1807			Bayonne Census of 1809	Peyrehorade Census of 1809	Total Number of Families
	Sephardim	Avignonese	Ashkenazim			
1..................	45	2	3	77	8	135
2..................	59	2	11	70	3	145
3..................	53	2	10	51	3	119
4..................	69	5	12	33	1	120
5..................	40	5	6	41	—	92
6..................	37	5	8	20	1	71
7..................	32	2	8	20	1	63
8..................	18	2	6	13	1	40
9..................	8	—	1	5	—	14
10 or more..........	14	2	4	2	—	22
TOTAL NUMBER OF FAMILIES..........	375	27	69	332	18	821

* According to registries (Jerusalem).

TABLE VII

Births in the *Nation* of Saint-Esprit who
still resided there in 1808–1810*

1728— 3	1749— 6	1770—14	1791—11
1729— 7	1750— 7	1771—12	1792—17
1730— 1	1751— 8	1772—13	1793—22
1731— 5	1752— 7	1773—15	1794—16
1732— 8	1753— 4	1774—12	1795—18
1733— 4	1754— 7	1775—13	1796—29
1734— 6	1755—14	1776—16	1797—24
1735— 4	1756— 8	1777— 8	1798—28
1736— 7	1757—21	1778—11	1799—27
1737— 2	1758—12	1779—20	1800—30
1738— 4	1759—10	1780—13	1801—26
1739— 5	1760—13	1781— 6	1802—29
1740— 4	1761— 9	1782— 7	1803—29
1741— 3	1762—13	1783—17	1804—29
1742— 3	1763—17	1784—13	1805—27
1743— 8	1764—12	1785—21	1806—24
1744— 2	1765—11	1786—11	1807—23
1745— 8	1766—16	1787—15	1808—30
1746— 7	1767—11	1788— 9	
1747—10	1768—14	1789—11	TOTAL: 1,051
1748—15	1769—12	1790—17	

* According to a register of names (Jerusalem). According to another source, from January 1, 1793 till June 30, 1812, the Jewish community of Saint-Esprit registered 638 births, 477 deaths. E. C. M. [Coquebert de Montbret fils], *Notice sur l'état des israélites en France, en réponse à des questions proposées par un savant étranger* (Paris, 1821), 27.

TABLE VIII

Deaths in Saint-Esprit of Jews who had resided there in 1808*

1808— 6	1827—11	1846—12	1865— 7
1809— 8	1828—19	1847—12	1866— 7
1810—21	1829—11	1848—13	1867— 5
1811—21	1830— 9	1849—20	1868—11
1812—15	1831—15	1850—19	1869— 5
1813—19	1832—14	1851—11	1870— 5
1814— 7	1833—11	1852—11	1871—12
1815— 5	1834— 5	1853— 8	1872—10
1816—10	1835—17	1854—13	1873— 6
1817— 9	1836—14	1855— 5	1874— 7
1818—14	1837—20	1856— 9	1875— 5
1819—15	1838—12	1857— 8	1876—13
1820—18	1839— 8	1858—15	1877— 6
1821—14	1840—14	1859—10	1878— 6
1822—11	1841—15	1860—10	1879— 4
1823—15	1842— 9	1861— 9	1880— 9
1824—17	1843—17	1862— 8	1881— 6
1825—13	1844— 8	1863— 7	1882— 9
1826—13	1845—16	1864— 8	1883— 6

TOTAL: 1,351.

* See note to Table VII.

TABLE IX

Deaths in Saint-Esprit, 1751-1795*

1751—15	1763—27	1775—38	1787—19
1752—60	1764—36	1776—28	1788—34
1753—37	1765—38	1777—11	1789—31
1754—42	1766—60	1778—48	1790—21
1755—35	1767—25	1779—18	1791—23
1756—32	1768—26	1780—34	1792—14
1757—30	1769—31	1781—33	1793—38
1758—49	1770—41	1782—37	1794—62
1759—41	1771—55	1783—40	1795—32
1760—62	1772—40	1784—36	
1761—37	1773—65	1785—12	TOTAL: 1,527.
1762—39	1774—38	1786—20	

(1,662 together with an incomplete list until the end of the year VIII).

According to the record compiled by Mardechée Ernest Naquet.

THE ECONOMIC STATUS
OF THE JEWS
IN ALSACE, METZ
AND LORRAINE

(1648-1789)

V. - The Jewish Aspect of Credit and Usury

16. CREDIT IN NORTHEASTERN FRANCE

Usury existed not only in the Northeastern French provinces of Alsace and Metz and in Lorraine, but all over France, even where Jews were not allowed to reside.[172] In the 17th century, the Church's ban on granting loans on interest was still in force. Legally such loans were permitted only in the Northeastern provinces, but even the Parliaments of Grenoble, Toulouse, Bordeaux, Aix and other provinces tolerated loans on interest. The historian Marcel Marion wrote that France presented the picture of a state, where loans on interest were officially forbidden by the Church, but where the government openly practiced a similar policy of credit, the laws regulated such credit operations, the judiciary bodies recognized these regulations, and the Church itself granted loans. It should be noted, as the historian Jean Bouchary wrote, that prior to 1789 the number of Jewish financiers in France was very small, in spite of the important Jewish role in the economic life of the ports of Bordeaux, Nantes and Saint-Malo.[173]

---

[172] According to the historian G. d'Avenel, during the reign of Louis XII, all jewelers were pawnbrokers. The famous 13th century poems on usury, *Dolopathos* and *Credo de l'usurier*, did not mention Jews at all. In the poem *Patenoste de l'usurier* a Gentile usurer attacked a Jewish competitor. Provided they paid a percentage to the King, creditors were allowed to charge as much as 50 % interest. E. Boutaric, *La France sous Philippe le Bel* (P 1861) p. 224; T. Malzevin, Les Juifs dans le Sud-Ouest de la France. *Revue de l'Aunis, de la Saintonge et du Poitou*, vol. X (1869) p. 375; G. d'Avenel, La fortune mobilière dans l'histoire. *Revue des Deux Mondes*, vol. CXII (1892) p. 586; A. Méray, *La vie au temps des cours d'amour* (P 1876) p. 330-32; L. Say, *Dictionnaire des finances* (P - N 1894) vol. II, p. 1465; René Saulnier et Henri Van der Zée, *La Mort du Crédit. Image populaire*. Reprint from *Dawna Sztuka* (Lwow 1939); *Ordonnances royales sur le faict des usures depuis l'an mil trois cens onze cusques à huy* (P 1582) 70 p.; A. M. de Boislisle, *oc*, vol. I-III, index (usure, intérêt).
[173] R. T. Troplong, *Le droit civil expliqué...* Vol. XIV (P 1845) p. 280-81; M. Marion, *Dictionnaire des institutions de la France au XVIIe et XVIIIe siècles* (P 1923) p. 300. In 1714, the Bishop of Lyon prohibited sermons against usury. In February 1776, the Angoulême merchants Pierre and Jean-Louis Nouel paid 12-20 % of interest on loans. The Limoges Intendant A. R. J. Turgot wrote his famous memorandum in defense of usury at that time. E. Pages, *Dissertation sur le prêt à intérêt...* (Lyon 1819) p. ccvij; AN,K910; Turgot, *Théorie de l'intérêt de l'argent...* (P 1780); J. Bouchary, *Les Manieurs d'argent à Paris à la fin du XVIIIe siècle* (P 1939) p. 7.
The various facts on usury cited in this study do not concern usury as considered in the canons of the Church, i.e. the notion that any loan on interest was a sin, but — as defined by P. A. Merlin (*Répertoire universel et raisonné de jurisprudence* (Bruxelles 1825-28) vol. XXXV, p. 434) — higher than legal rates of interest charged by creditors. It is worth while to mention the opinion of the children of a Lorraine debtor who wrote in a 1786 factum (brief) against their father's creditor, the priest de Tonnoy of Saint-Dieuze, that the generosity of granting a loan without interest is not a very good business venture for the debtor, because under those circumstances the creditor can at any time demand repayment of the

Excerpts from the book published in 1954.

In Northeastern France, Jews were forced to make a living mostly by granting loans on interest. Jews were even allowed to charge higher rates of interest than Gentile creditors;[174] this was a compensation for the greater risk to which Jewish creditors were exposed and for the ban on Jews to take up any productive trades. But this higher rate of interest was also the justification for anti-Jewish propaganda and many anti-Jewish laws. Frequently, any wealthy Jew was smirched by Gentiles as a usurer, even if he was not at all engaged in credit operations. This was stated in 1780 by Munck, the bailiff of Guebwiller and by an author of a 1790 pamphlet.[175] The Jews of Alsace, Metz and Lorraine were not allowed to invest their money in agriculture, in real estate outside the ghettos, in construction of factories, etc.[176] But even under these circumstances the Jewish creditor fulfilled a useful economic function because Northeastern France, like France in general, suffered from a lack of credit, which shortage was the cause of the deficiency of agriculture and industry.[177] When a house was destroyed by fire in the early feudal times, the neighbors were forced to help the victim build a new house. If a neighbor refused to help, the family of the victim had the right to move into his house. But in the 18th century this custom was already an old forgotten tradition. The Abbot C. A. Hanauer wrote on Alsace: "Everybody took loans, the Kings, princes, bishops, priests, cities and villages, and the poorest peasant, too."[178] But it was not always so easy to find a creditor. Even Basel, whose bankers conducted a great part of the Alsatian credit operations, suffered from a lack of credit facilities.[179] The reign of Louis XVI was the period of

---

capital. *Précis pour les sieurs... Dieudonné... contre le Sieur de Tonnoy, Grand Doyen du Chapitre de Saint-Dieuze* (N 1786) p. 14. BmN6753.
   [174] In 1680 a Jew was allowed to take up residence in Landau under the condition that he would trade only with old clothing, cattle and money. Merlin, *oc*, vol. XVI, p. 238. A Metz ordinance of May 20, 1564, legalized the rate of 8 1/3 % interest on *rentes*, but an ordinance of Apr. 6, 1567, forced Jews to charge 21-22 % interest on loans. R. Clément, *La condition...* p. 174-184.
   [175] Ch. Hoffmann, *oc*, vol. IV, p. 445; *Les Juifs d'Alsace doivent-ils être admis au droit de citoyens actifs?* (S 1790) p. 27.
   [176] R. Anchel, *oc*, p. 168. During the Revolution of 1789, Jewish *Emigrés* who were merchants were granted permission to return to France. The Law granted such permission only to peasants and workers, but in some parts of France exceptions were made for Jews because prior to 1789 they were driven out of all honest professions. On March 8, 1796, the Councilmen of Haguenau declared on the case of the Jewish *Emigré* Raphaël Bernheim: "Considérant que Raphaël Bernheim étant de la secte juive à laquelle les lois anciennes interdisaient le droit de citoyen et d'exercer d'autre état que celui de marchand, négociant, fripier ou colporteur, on ne peut lui imputer de n'avoir pas été ce que les lois lui déffendaient d'être..." (AN,F7-5513). See note 136.
   [177] J. Loutchisky, *L'état des classes agricoles...* p. 62-66; [R. Lévylier,] *Notes et documents concernant la famille Cerfberr* (P 1902-06) vol. I, p. 1.
   [178] G. d'Avenel, *oc*, p. 596; C. A. Hanauer, *Etudes...* vol. I, p. 515.
   [179] The Alsatian anti-Jewish leader Hell attempted to obtain a loan of 230,000 pounds for the comtesse de Baignard from the Basel creditor Bourcard. On Nov. 2, 1782, Bourcard replied to Hell that the pockets of the Basel creditors were empty: "J'ai fait tout mon possible pour me procurer chez plusieurs personnes les facilités que je ne trouverai certainement pas chez un seul; mais inutilement; la disette des espèces en est la cause; vous ne sauriez, en effet, vous faire une idée de la rareté de l'argent; la

physiocracy, when the dignity and eminence of agriculture was discovered, but this did not ameliorate the peasant's condition. At that time the government attempted to induce the peasants to cultivate abandoned parcels of land, but Necker stated that the results of these efforts were particularly poor in Alsace owing to the lack of capital. Peasant-pawnshops granted to peasants seed on 5% interest, but even such pawnshops did not exist in Northeastern France. For a creditor, the peasant was a poor risk and consequently creditors frequently charged usurious rates of interest.[149] The Alsatian historian Goetzmann cited a memorandum of the Intendant d'Angervilliers (1716) who wrote that in difficult times, such as in times of war, etc., peasants could obtain loans from Jews in order to pay taxes, to buy cattle and seed. Of course, the Jews charged a high rate of interest, but in such emergency cases even usurious rates of interest were better than a complete ruin. Even the Alsatian anti-Jewish leader Hell wrote in 1779 that the peasants could obtain loans only from Jews.[150] This does not prove that only Jews practiced honest or usurious credit operations; we shall try to prove the contrary. But the Jewish creditor was the most easily accessible, the most willing to grant loans on conditions the peasant could meet. The Jewish creditor came himself to the village, or he could be reached easily through a mediator, the Jewish horse- or cattle-dealer, or the peddler. The Gentile creditor was more of a city-element; the peasant was forced to lose much of his valuable time in order to reach him, and, moreover, he was forced to incur expenses to do so. The peasant was trusted more by a Jewish than a Gentile creditor because the Jews came more often in close contact with the peasants and were familiar with their condition. But most important of all—the Jew was forced to grant loans because this was his main source of income, as he was shut off from all honest trades.

---

guerre d'aujourd'hui, qui ruine le commerce, semble avoir bouché tous les canaux pour le retrouver; les caisses sont vides... les termes des payements étant continuellement reculés de six mois jusqu'à dix-huit...” AdHR,E, Wendl.14.

[149] Henri Sée, *La vie économique et les classes sociales en France au XVIIIe siècle* (P 1924) p. 105; d'Avenel, *oc*, p. 595. L. F. de Beaufleury of Bordeaux, author of a history of the Bordeaux Jews, wrote in a study submitted to an Austrian contest on usury (1789) that the amount of interest was always fixed in conformity to the wealth of the debtor, especially the peasant-debtor, whose income from his land was lower than the interest paid by him for a loan. [L. F. de Beaufleury,] *Qu'est-ce que l'usure, et quels sont les moyens de l'arrêter sans recourir aux lois pénales* (sl [1791]) 53 p. BN,8F791. The author did not mention the role of Jews. In his history of the Bordeaux and Bayonne Jews Beaufleury stated that the priests were always the Jews' most dangerous ennemies: *Histoire de l'Etablissement des Juifs à Bordeaux et Bayonne* (P an 8) p. 148. On physiocracy see note 396.

[150] L. V. de Goetzmann, *oc*, vol. II, p. 317; Hoffmann, *oc*, vol. IV, p. 371; [Hell,] *Observations d'un Alsacien sur l'affaire présente des Juifs d'Alsace* (Francfort [Strasbourg] 1779) p. 41. According to the famous Metz attorney Roederer, poor Jewish creditors, specially widows, who possessed only 50, 60 or 80 *Louis* each, charged usurious rates of interest because they were forced to make a living by granting very small loans. The rich Jewish creditors were more honest and charged up to 12 % per annum (“Réflexions sur le projet d'un Mont de Piété à Metz”, AN,29AP99). For d'Angervillier's statement of 1716 see note 31 and Appendix II-2.

The lack of currency was one of the causes of the poor state of credit. Alsace suffered from a lack of coins in spite of the fact that coins were minted in many Alsatian cities.[142] Jews were not engaged in this fabrication of coins, but they played a very important part in the trade with precious metals and coins. As it was already related the various rates of currencies created a black-market trade of currencies (*billonnage*), which consisted in importing illegally coins from one province to another and in which Jews, too, were engaged, but surely not Jews alone.[143] Still, when a contraband in coins was discovered in 1703 in Metz, Jews were the first to be prosecuted, although the Jewish community proved that many Gentiles were smugglers. On Sept. 7, 1704, the Metz Intendant wrote that not only Jews, but Gentiles as well, Frenchmen and people of Lorraine, smuggled coins and that only the circulation of the same currency in all provinces could end this state of affairs. Because of this smuggling, Jewish merchants of Metz were not allowed to travel to Paris.[144] On many occasions Jews presented proposals on how to liquidate the crisis of currency. Thus, a Jew of Metz proposed to fabricate 10-sol coins from German marks, with a gain of 500,000 pounds for every 100,000 marks to be imported illegally by himself from Germany.[145]

17. NON-JEWISH USURERS IN ALSACE

According to the historian Abbot Xavier Mossmann, in the 14th century usury was not a strictly Jewish business in the Rhine provinces. The expulsion of Jews from Strasbourg (14th century) did not abolish usury there. In 1400, Strasbourg usurers paid a fine of 2,000 marks.[146] A Strasbourg decree of 1539 prohibited Gentiles to exchange or to buy loan-deeds from Jews. But Gentile creditors

[142] C. A. Hanauer, *oc,* vol. I, monnaies; Rod. Reuss, *oc,* vol. I, p. 687-97.

[143] An ordinance of Feb. 26, 1340, spoke of *plousours gens malicious* who illegally exported coins from Metz to France. The 1387, 1403, 1425 and 1480 treaties between Upper Alsace and neighboring provinces on the trade in precious metals forbade priests, Gentiles and Jews (*prêtre ou laïc, séculier ou régulier, chrétien ou juif*) to export gold or silver. Hanauer, *oc,* vol. I, p. 222; P. Mendel, *Les Atours de la ville de Metz* (M 1932) p. 319.

[144] The Jewish cattle-dealers Abraham Picard and Samuel Brisach were arrested in Belleville, near Pont-à-Mousson, and the coins which they attempted to smuggle from France into Lorraine were confiscated. Peddlers often bought up from peasants the rare coins, but according to an order of Sept. 1720, forbidding this practice, not only Jewish peddlers were involved. AcM,Lap59,112; E. Ginsburger, Les Juifs de Metz et le billonage *RJL,* vol. XIV, No. 156-159 (1938); Anchel, oc, p. 196, 203; "Qu'on voit journellement des personnes, et notamment des Juifs, aller dans les villages enlever le peu d'espèces d'argent qui s'y trouve": *ERPM. Du 26 Septembre* 1720 (M 1720). AdM980. A Gentile cheated a Jew by presenting himself as a messenger from a prospective buyer of coins. *Mémoire pour Moyse Alcan... de Nancy* (N 1718?) 4 p. BN,F111.

[145] Anchel, *oc,* p. 200-201; E. Ginsburger, *oc;* H. Baumont, *oc,* p. 406-10.

[146] X. Mossmann, *Etude sur l'histoire des Juifs à Colmar* (C-P 1866) p. 2; Hanauer, *oc.* vol. I, p. 528. On two 1583 and 1615 sentences against Gentile usurers in Alsace see: Otto Kosser, *Prozessakten aus dem Elsass...* (Berlin 1936) Nos. 268, 1362.

did not comply with the decree which was often repeated. On May 22, 1613, Leopold of Austria forbade Jews of the territory of the Strasbourg Episcopate to sell their mortgage-deeds to Christians. A Strasbourg ordinance of Jan. 15, 1700, mentioned Gentile usurers.'" A decree of 1728 forbade the signing of contracts with Jews and *Judengenossen*, i.e. Christian usurers.'" On Nov. 20, 1665, Strasbourg allowed Jews to trade on the market during two days rather than during one day, because Gentile merchants became arrogant and they had to be reminded to behave in a more Christian way (*plus chrétiennement*). A decree of 1526 on credit operations of the Bergheim Jews stated that real-estate could be mortgaged first in favor of seigniors, then in favor of Gentile creditors, while Jewish creditors were to be the last to use this right. The statute for the Haguenau Jews (1558) forbade using names of Gentile intermediaries for the acquisition of mortgages on the properties of their debtors.'"

The Alsatian historian Rod.E. Reuss wrote that Gentiles, too, practiced usury during the Thirty Years' War and the anti-Jewish minded Alsatian historian F. Chauffour wrote similarly concerning 16th century Alsace.'" The ordinance of Nov. 24, 1690, on the legal rate of interest in Alsace mentioned not only Jewish, but Christian usurers, as well (*non-seulement par les Juifs, mais par les Chrétiens*). A royal order on the liquidation of communal debts (Dec. 26, 1683) mentioned "abuse" committed by creditors in favor of seigniors and even in favor of the Court of Austria against the interest of the Alsatian communities.'"

In June 1714 a law was published against Christians who practiced "Judaism", i.e. usury (*chrétiens de cette province exerçaient le judaïsme envers leurs frères*) and ruined many people. The City of Colmar did persecute Jews (they were expelled from the city in 1337, 1348-49 and 1512); a statute of 1593 forbade Christians to trade with Jews. In 1719, on the occasion of renewing this statute, the city's *syndic* F.H.J. Chauffour declared that Christians, too, traded in a Jewish manner, i.e. practiced usury.'" In 1720, the

---

'" *Les Juifs d'Alsace...* (S 1790) p. 2; M. Ginsburger, *Histoire de la communauté israélite de Soultz* (S 1939) p. 15; "des contrats et conventions usuraires des chrétiens": M. Schwab, Documents... *REJ*, vol. XI (1885) p. 142-44.
'" A. Glaeser, *Gescichte der Juden in Strassburg...* (S 1894) p. 35, 72. Another source spoke of *chrétiens-juifs:* Ch. Hoffmann, *oc*, vol. I, p. 264. Later sources spoke of *beschnittenen und unbeschnittenen Wuchern; Israeliten oder unbeschnittenen Juden;* etc.: *Zuschrift an die Landleute im Elsass, über den Verkauf der National-Guter* (S 1790) p. 40; J., *Die Juden-Verfolgungen* (S 179-) p. 16; E. Schneider, *Ueber die Juden* (S 1793) p. 1 (see J. Sée, Idées d'Euloge Schneider sur les Juifs. *RA*, vol. XLII (1891) p. 131).
'" Elie Scheid, *Histoire des Juifs d'Alsace* (P 1887) p. 61-62; Ibid., *Histoire des Juifs de Haguenau... REJ*, vol. VI (1883) p. 237; M. Ginsburger, *Les Juifs à Ribeauvillé et à Bergheim* (S 1939) p. 80.
'" Reuss, *oc*, vol. II, p. 577; F. Chauffour, *Considérations sur les statuts de 1593* (Reprint) p. 362; Ch. Hoffmann, *oc*, vol. IV, p. 458.
'" de Boug, *oc*, vol. I, p. 187; N. de Corberon, *Essay...* p. 178-79. We do not know of any good study on the debts of the Alsatian communities. From a rapid analysis of sources, one has the impression that Jews were rarely creditors of such loans. No Jews were either creditors of the communal debts in the Metz province or in Lorraine.
'" de Boug, *oc*, vol. I, p. 437; Hoffmann, *oc*, vol. IV, p. 437; Merlin, *oc*, Juifs; AmC,C-V-6. A lawsuit between the *Collège de Strasbourg* and the

City of Wintzenheim requested the courts to force the *Reichsvogt* of Keysersberg to expel 24 of the 28 Jewish families in the city. On this occasion the famous Alsatian attorney Jean-François Bruges (1695-1766) demanded in his plea for the Jews proof that Jewish usurers ruined the city of Wintzenheim. Should all the usurers be expelled from Alsace, he maintained, then not only Jews, but "non-circumcized" (i.e. Gentile) usurers as well would have to be expelled, because they ruined people even more than Jews did."'

Usury against soldiers and officers was very frequently used as an anti-Jewish slogan. General Aubert-Dubayet wrote (1786) that by granting to soldiers loans on usurious rates the Jews ruined the army."' In fact, military men were even imprisoned for not paying their debts and in such cases they were forced to obtain new loans in order to repay the old ones."' But Gentiles, too, granted loans on usurious rates to soldiers and officers. A Strasbourg order of March 13, 1775, against selling on credit or granting usurious loans to officers, did not mention Jews at all. Later, the city published the royal decree of June 2, 1777, forbidding officers to buy on credit or to take loans without their superiors' permission. On May 3, 1784, Strasbourg forbade its residents—and "even Jews" (*même aux Juifs*) to buy from soldiers clothing, gold and other goods without written authorizations from their officers, because soldiers frequently sold stolen military property."'

According to a 1788 proposal of a pawnshop in Strasbourg, 7 and 8% was a normal rate of interest on loans. In 1780, a highly-placed Alsatian official spoke of Christian usurers. In 1789, the bailiff Clavé wrote that the peasant would be forced to take loans from "Jews and Christian-Jews" (*juifs ou chrétiens-juifs*), i.e. Gentile

---

heirs of Martin Lehmann (a non-Jew) involved a usurious loan of 1725 (AdHR,fonds Corberon-Bruges 27). In 1722 the Gentile merchant Jean Herr of Colmar granted a loan of 5,300 pounds to Bressler of Ricquewihr. From Nov. 1723 till Nov. 1732 he obtained from his debtor interest of 1,700 pounds (AmC,FF312). Jean Herr attacked the rights of the Jewish creditor Samuel Weill because an I.O.U. given to the Jew was signed by the debtor Bressler's wife while she was still a minor (Ibidem).

"' "...des gens qui, sans être circoncis, ruinent les sujets plus que ne le font les Juifs." Léon Hirsch, Un document alsacien du XVIII° siècle. *UI*, vol. XXXVIII (1882-83) p. 532-36; E. Scheid, *oc*, p. 158-62. The definitive text of Bruge's plea is to be found in AdHR,Corberon-Bruges24. See notes 305 and 306.

"' [Général Aubert-Dubayet,] *Le Cri du Citoyen contre les Juifs de Metz*, par un capitaine d'infanterie (Lausanne [Metz] 1786) p. 8-13. The pamphlet was prohibited by the Metz Parliament: *Arrêt de la Cour de Parlement de Metz, qui ordonne la suppression d'un libellé ayant pour titre: Le Cri du citoyen contre les Juifs de Metz ec. du 8 Juillet 1786* (M 1786) 3 p. The Jews replied by publishing the pamphlet: *Lettre du Sr. I.[saie] B.[er] B.[ing], juif de Metz...* (M 1787, 2nd edition-1805).

"' M° Lemaire, *Mémoire pour le sieur Jean Aubertin... contre le sieur Godchaux-Mayer Cahen... et Moyse-Salomon Emmericque, aussi Juif de Metz* (M 1790) 30 p. JTS.

"' *Règlement de police, qui fait défense... de prêter de l'argent et faire crédit aux officiers des Corps* [S 13 Mars 1775]. Placard. AmS,vol.R50-1; *Ordonnance du Roi, concernant les dettes des officiers. Du 2 Juin 1777* (S 1777) 3 p. AdBR,AS; *Ordonnance de la police qui fait défense d'acheter aucuns effects quelqconques des soldats* [S 3 Mai 1784]. Placard. AmS,vol. R50-77.

usurers.[197] Alsatian officials then again complained against Christian usurers who associated with Jews.[198]

Many usurers of Basel operated in Alsace. According to the historian A. Quinquerez, they ruined a large part of the Alsatian nobility. In the 18th century, Sundgau (Upper Alsace) residents, especially peasants, were still debtors of Basel creditors as a result of the events of January 1633, when the Swedish Army attacked and killed a large number of Sundgau peasants on the cemetery of Vézelois. From the peasants who were not killed they demanded large sums of money, which were granted as loans by Basel creditors. During the anti-Jewish riots in Alsace at the outbreak of the Revolution of 1789, a Paris newspaper wrote that Basel opened the gates for the Alsatian Jewish refugees because the Baselians subscribed to some of the Jewish principles of making a fortune, i.e. the practice of usury.[199]

18. NON-JEWISH USURERS IN METZ

The City of Metz always had a large number of usurers among its Gentile creditors, especially since for many centuries Jews were

---

[197] AN,C12-7,p.8; Hoffmann, oc, vol. I, p. 264, vol. IV, p. 459. Even A. Hertzog, a historian with anti-Jewish inclinations, wrote on non-Jewish usurers in the 18th century: Der Wucher im Elsass. Strassburger Post, No. 985 (1908).

[198] In a projected statute for Jews (September 1788) the Alsatian Intermediary Commission spoke of Gentile usurers, as well. The Alsatian chronicler Jean-Ulric Metzger spoke of les Juifs et leurs associés. AmS,AA2389; Hoffmann, oc, vol. I, p. 183, vol. IV, p. 460. Documents and pamphlets of the Revolutionary period frequently referred to Gentile usurers. The title of a 1792 pamphlet by Maria Salomea Schottin was Ueber Juden und Judengenossen im Niederrhein... (S). BuS101492. General P.-F. de Latour Foissac attacked in a 1790 anti-Jewish pamphlet Jewish and Christian usurers: Plaidoyer contre l'usure des Juifs des Evêchés de l'Alsace et de la Lorraine (sl 1790) p. 75. The author of a Strasbourg pamphlet (in 1790) wrote about Israeliten oder unbeschnittenen Juden. J., Die Juden-Verfolgungen, p. 16. The Alsatian Jews themselves stated in a petition to the National Assembly (Jan. 28, 1790) that more non-Jews than Jews were sentenced by the courts for usury: [Jacques Godard,] Pétition des Juifs... 28 Janvier 1790... (P 1790) p. 46. Alexandre and Bois, both members of the Club des Jacobins ou des Sans-culottes of Strasbourg declared at a meeting of May 10, 1794, that non-Jews were also usurers and sometimes Jews were only intermediaries for big usurers. On May 13 one member proposed to publish a broadside asking the people to deliver the usurers — Juifs ou chrétiens. F. Ch. Heitz, Les Sociétés politiques de Strasbourg pendant les années 1790 à 1795... (S 1863) p. 350. On May 31, 1794, two members of the Colmar Jacobins Club stated that Gentiles, too, practiced usury and that Jews were frequently only intermediaries for Gentile archi-usurers. P. Leuilliot, Les Jacobins de Colmar... (S 1923).

[199] A. Quinquerez, Notice sur les causes de l'appauvrissement graduel de plusieurs familles de la Haute Alsace... RA, vol. XIX (1868); Julien Feuvrier, Le Sundgau en 1785... RA, vol. XXXI (1902); Le Patriote François, No. XXII, Aug. 22, 1789, p. 4. During the fight for the occupation of Metz (1552-1648), the King borrowed money from Basel creditors. The City of Türckheim borrowed money from the Basel family Medinger and from the Basel Church heads. The Basel Prince Joseph of Roggenbach had an annual income of 60,000 pounds from Alsace, a part of it from interest on loans. Ca. 1718-20, J. J. Birr of Basel was the creditor of Scheppelin, Mayor of Colmar. G. Zeller, La Réunion... vol. I, p. 321; A. Scherlen, Histoire de la ville de Türckheim (1925) p. 158; G. Gautherot, La Révolution française dans l'ancien évêché de Bâle (P 1907) vol. I, p. 29; Mémoire pour les veuve et héritiers du feu Sieur Scheppelin... (C 172-) 8 p. BN,F3-15548.

not permitted to reside there."' A 1634 decree concerning the Jews
of Metz mentioned Jewish and Gentile creditors. The Abbot J.L.
Chaillot of the Metz Cathedral was a creditor of his debtor Géorgin
for 17,495 pounds. According to a 17th century document, Gentiles
were creditors not only of *rentes*, but of debts for loans granted on
simple I.O.U.s as well. The King's order of June 1669 abolishing
loans on I.O.U.s mentioned "even Jews" (*obligations... passées, même
par les Juifs*). The Metz bans on loans granted to minors (Dec. 11,
1717 and Jan. 26, 1754) mentioned "Jews and all other" creditors.
The Metz attorney C.L. Gabriel wrote (1784) that Gentiles, too, practiced usury."'

19. NON-JEWISH USURERS IN LORRAINE

Usury prevailed in Lorraine to an even higher degree than
in the neighboring provinces, because the Church's ban of credit
on interest was not so radical in Lorraine. This was probably
the reason for the lesser attacks on Lorraine Jews because of
usury."' According to the study which the Benedictine Dom Chais
of the Abbey of Saint-Avold submitted for the contest of the
Metz Academy on Jews, the legal rate of interest was in Lorraine

---

"' In the 13th century Gentile creditors of Metz charged 21.3 % of
interest, the creditors from Lombardy who operated in Metz (they were
also the Pope's financial agents) were legally permitted to charge twice
as much. When the Church refused religious burial to creditors who did
not repay the interest paid to them by their debtors, the *amans* (amanu-
enses) drew up wills for the creditors in terms which did not oblige them
to repay the interest, but forced the Church to grant religious interment.
This provoked a great number of conflicts between the Church and the
city-councilmen. Metz and the Metz province could not exist without credit.
Peasants frequently bought on credit merchandise at the Metz market and
they mortgaged their entire properties as security for very small loans.
J. Schneider, *La vie de Metz aux XIIIe et XIVe siècles* (N 1950) p. 250, 267-
72, 356; Ch. E. Dumont, *Justice criminelle des duchés de Lorraine et de
Bar...* (N 1848) vol. I, p. 266.
"' ACPM [23 Mai 1643] ..*cf* note 78; *Factum pour Mr. Jean Louis
Chaillot, prêtre, chanoine de la cathédrale de Metz...* [M 1718] 27 p. BmM,
ZZ173-1; "Non seulement les dit Juifs, mais même les citoiens de Metz
catholiques étoient dans l'usage de prêter leurs deniers, non seulement à
titre de constitution de rente, mais encore par obligations et billets à terme
stipulatifs d'intérêts:" BmM,ms170p.39; R. Clément, *oc* p. 174, 183, 189-190;
*ACPM qui défend aux Juifs et à toutes autres personnes, de prêter de l'ar-
gent aux enfants de famille, etc.* 4 Décembre 1717 (M 1717) Placard. JTS;
*ACPM qui ordonne que l'arrest du Règlement du 4 Décembre 1717 sera
exécuté... du 26 Janvier 1754...* [M 1754] 19 p. AdM,B986; C. L. Gabriel, *oc*,
vol. I, p. 48. The debtor Michel Servin's property was sold by the order
of the Metz Parliament for 44,400 pounds (Aug. 8, 1716); only three of his
23 creditors were Jews: *Louis par la Grâce de Dieu, Roi de France...* [Sen-
tence du 29 Septembre 1715, appel et sentence du Parlement de Metz du
8 Août 1716 contre Michel Servin] 13 p. JTS. In a similar case
of 1784, the debtor Jean Neisof of Malling had not only two Jewish creditors,
but many Gentile creditors as well, including high officials and the priest
of Malling. Only 4 of the 21 creditors of the peasant Nicolas Vigneron of
Lemesdroff were Jews. The priest Nicolas Thill of Téterchen was a creditor
of considerable holdings. AdM,J414,1115,1242.
"' M. Liber, *Les Juifs et la convocation des Etats Généraux* (1789).
REJ, vol. LXIII, p. 95.

indeterminate in the '80s of the 18th century."' Most of the many Lorraine ordinances and laws against usury did not even mention Jews."' Many Gentiles were sentenced there for practicing usury."' An ordinance of June 12, 1630, referred to a rate of 60% in the sale of wine and other products on credit. An order of Aug. 17, 1715, forbade Jews and Gentiles to grant loans to minors. Nancy ordinances of Nov. 2, 1754 and July 30, 1763 against selling to minors and soldiers alcoholic beverages on credit and an order of March 30, 1722, forbidding in Pont-à-Mousson the sale of liquor on credit to students without their parents' permission did not mention Jews at all."' At the end of the 17th century the debtor A. de Bouzey accused his Gentile creditors—including his own brother—of charging interest on interest of unpaid interest. Ca. 1715 the justice J.F. Léleal charged that the creditors François and Mathieu Fromentau were worse than the Jews."' Priests were frequently intermediaries between Gentile creditors and debtors."' Gentiles frequently took loans from Jewish creditors in order to speculate with the obtained

---

²⁰³ "en attendant que la loi ait prononcé sur la quotité de cet intérêt à prendre ou à percevoir pour une somme déterminée, le particulier, qui ne saisit pas l'esprit de la loi se persuade, que cent pour cent ne sera jamais qu'un intérêt, et non pas usure." BmM,ms1350,p.787. Some unreliable sources mention an ordinance of Apr. 1, 1535, fixing the legal rate of interst at 5 %. In 1301, the legal rate was 8.91 %; 6.44 % in 1557 and 4.66 % in 1751-75. P.D. de Rogéville, Dictionnaire historique des ordonnances et des Tribunaux de la Lorraine et du Barrois (N 1777) vol. II, p. 644; Ch. Guyot, Essai sur l'aisance relative du paysan lorrain à partir du XVᵉ siècle. Mémoires de l'Académie de Stanislas, 5ᵉ sér., vol. V (1888) p. 94-96.
²⁰⁴ E.g.: Charles III's ordinance of Feb. 12, 1581; the Lorraine and Barrois ordinances of Feb. 1582 (usurious sales of houses); Sept. 22, 1586, June 12, 1630 and May 6, 1631 (usury through the sales of rentes and crops); Apr. 2, 1597 (jurisdiction over usurers); Jan. 23, 1632 and May 31, 1666 (repeating the former ordinances); Nov. 25, 1667 (fixing the legal rate of interest on rentes and loans at 5 %); etc. (de Rogéville, oc, vol. II, p. 644-96).
²⁰⁵ E.g.: Jean Nicolas B. in 1709. The tavern-keeper Gueury Bagneux of Landremont granted loans à la petite semaine. His debtors complained and he was sentenced to 9 years of forced labor. Two Nancy usurers were sentenced in 1721. Jouhesmes, Etude sur la criminalité en Lorraine d'après les lettres de rémission (1473-1737). Annales de l'Est, vol. XV (1901) p. 383-85; RELéop, vol. II, p. 484-85.
²⁰⁶ Jules Liégois, Essai sur l'histoire de la législation de l'usure (P 1863) p. 106; RELéop. vol. II, p. 72-73, 549-51, vol. X, p. 247-48.
²⁰⁷ "il a non seulement tiré intérêt d'intérêt, il a encore tiré de l'intérêt de l'intérêt." Mémoire pour Antoine de Bouzey... [N 169-] 4 p.; Response pour Madame de Bouzey... [N 169-] 6 p. BmN6784-5. "les Fromentau, plus durs que n'est la Nation [juive] autrefois élue." Mémoire pour le sieur Jean-François Leleal... contre... les Fromentau... [N 171-] 14 p.; Réplique pour le sieur Jean François Leleal... [N 1720] 11 p. BmN7135-37. The bankrupt Count Duhan recognized debts owed by him for the amount of 4,310,802 pounds; only 68,000 were in favor of a Jew (Alcan of Nancy) and 57,300 pounds of the 162,071 pounds which he did not recognize were in favor of 6 Jews. There were no Jews among the creditors of the bankrupt Warin Bretteville of Nancy (1786-1793). Mémoire signifié pour Mᵉ George-Rémi Vernent... syndic établi, aux créanciers... du sieur Comte Duhan... (N 1722) 108 p. BmN7135;AN,DIII-158.
²⁰⁸ E.g.: Abbot Joly of Etang in 1749-51. The Nancy Abbot N. F. de Fressey was a creditor. In 1778 he vouched for three loans granted by another creditor to Mme. Cheneau. Mémoire pour le sr. Nicolas-François de Bressay... contre... Baudouin... [N 1781] 46 p.; Mémoire pour le sieur Claude-Nicolas Pierre... contre les héritiers bénéficiaires de M. l'abbé Joly... (N 1718) 19 p. BmN,ZZ172-2 and 7844-17.

capital, as, e.g. with stocks of the *Banque Royale.*[209] The Lorraine peasants were debtors not particularly in favor of Jewish creditors; most of their creditors were non-Jews. 60 out of 76 petty-peasants of Chaloy owed a sum total of 47,052 pounds to their creditors, all of them Gentiles, among them the merchants Bénard, Naudin and J.A. Guerre. Some peasants were forced to sell their properties. When the City of Sarlouis tried to expel the Jews (18th century) the latter stated in a pamphlet that the Sarlouis Christians practiced usury.[210]

Usury was so widespread in Lorraine that a bitter conflict arose at the end of the 17th-beginning 18th century between the Church which was then officially against usury and even against granting loans at a legal rate of interest on one side, and the laymen who favored credit operations.[211] Abbot J.J. Petit-Didier wrote in 1745 that even priests and Church institutions practiced usury. The legal rate of interest was not complied with.[212] In 1679, the Toul Bishop Jacques de Fieux (1675-1687) published his famous Pastoral Letter against usury. But people were afraid that this would ruin the credit and reacted sharply against de Fieux. One year later, in 1680, the Lorraine attorney François Guinet published a pamphlet against de Fieux's Letter, in which he supported the principle of usury. Guinet was shielded by the Lorraine government. J. de Fieux became alarmed and he withdrew the printed copies of his Letter (which are now great rarities), but in 1687, he forbade to receive the confession of usurers. After de Fieux' death, the Bishop de Bissy renewed the attack on usury. He tried to renew an old Lorraine decree forbidding usury. In 1703, he prohibited to read Guinet's pamphlet and he published a new edition of his predecessor's Letter of 1679, but his opponents published a new edition of Guinet's pamphlet. On Oct. 15, 1703, the Sovereign Court of Lorraine and Barrois took an official stand in the conflict and maintained that the Lorraine traditions had been unknown to de Fieux who had been educated at the Sorbonne, and that the attacks on usury by de Fieux' follower were directed against Lorraine's laws and economic interests. No Jews were ever mentioned in this conflict.[213] During a later period, the Revolution of 1789, many

[209] Brice Gome, who was for a time secretary to the Alsatian Intendant La Grange, contracted a similar loan of 150,000 pounds from the Jew Jacob Schaube [Schwabe]. He was almost ruined, but acquired four additional loans of 24,000 pounds. The priest Phister of Buettuviller inherited some money, so he obtained from Jews a loan of 21,095 pounds in order to speculate. *Factum pour Jacob Schaube... contre Mᵉ Brice Gome* [M 1722]; *Factum pour Mᵉ Pierre Phister, prêtre et curé de Buettuviller, contre Hirtz Salomon, Juif demeurant à Than...* (sl 1723) 26 p. BN,naf22705-232 and 2M3; BuS32881.
[210] AdMM,L2404; Jean Ollier, *oc*; Mᵉ Damours, *Mémoire pour les Maire, Syndics et Communauté des habitans de Sarlouis... contre les Juifs...* (sl nd) p. 2. BN,naf2206-89.
[211] Ch. E. Dumont, *oc*, vol. I, p. 266; "La pratique de prêts usuriers se généralisa." André Gain, *Cent ans d'épargne lorraine* (N 1937) p. XIV-XVIII.
[212] R. P. Jean-Joseph Petit-Didier, *Dissertation théologique sur les prêts par obligation stipulative usités en Lorraine et Barrois* (N 1745, 2nd edition-1748) preface; A. Gain, *oc*, p. XIV-XVIII.
[213] Jacques de Fieux, *Lettre pastorale... sur le prêt usuraire de l'argent...*

memorials of grievances (*cahiers des doléances*) of Lorraine complained against both Jewish and Gentile usurers."[4]

20. USURY THROUGH RENTES

Most of the historians agree that *rentes* were a way to grant loans on interest—a *moyens détournés*, as the historian P. Sagnac wrote. According to Alexis de Tocqueville, who was opposed to the parcellization of land, the prohibition of loans on interest had still retained the force of the law on the eve of 1789, and this helped in the process of pracellizing the land, as this law was conducive to the practice of *rentes*. Landlords unable to obtain loans parcellized their land by selling parts of their properties or by establishing *rentes*. The owners of *rentes* fought for their interests. A decree of 1720 reduced the interest on rentes in order to withdraw funds from the *rentes* for the benefit of John Law's projected bank. The debtors of *rentes* reacted sharply and forced the repeal of the decree in 1725. The Church did not prohibit the practice of interest through *rentes*."[5] But the protests against usury through *rentes* were so forceful that even Church leaders occasionally admitted that *rentes* were a usurious practice. In his famous declaration against usury, de Fieux defined as usury any interest paid in cash or in any other equivalent, i.e. products. The "Four Letters" of 1731 against usury are directed against *rentes*."[6] This did not restrain the Church from establishing *rentes*. The policy of the Church institutions was not to keep their capitals inactive (*ne point laisser de deniers oisifs*) but to obtain interest—as a group of creditors of the *Ordre du Refuge* of Nancy stated in 1782."[7]

(N 1679); 2nd edition: [de Fieux,] *De l'usure...* (Toul 1703). BmN85; Ibid., *Mandement...* (Toul 1687). BmN5030d; [François Guinet,] *Factum... sur la matière de l'usure...* (Ville-sur-Yllon [Strasbourg] 1680, 2nd edition-1703). BmN65; *Ordonnance de Monseigneur... Evêque comte de Toul...* (Toul 1703). BmN,85d; de Rogéville, *oc*, vol. II, p. 682-96; Abbé P.E. Guillaume, *Histoire du diocèse de Toul et de celui de Nancy* (N 1866-67) vol. III, p. 403-32; E. Martin, *Histoire des diocèses de Toul, de Nancy et de Saint-Dié* (N 1900) vol. II, p. 206. *Arrest de la Cour Souveraine... au sujet de l'ordonnance de... l'Evêque de Toul du 23 Septembre dernier* (N 1703) 16 p. BN,F23753(14); Lucien Parisot, L'Usure en Lorraine sous l'Ancien Régime. *Le Pays lorrain*, 1928, p. 359-65. In a letter of July 17, 1721, addressed to Léopold of Lorraine, the Bishop of Toul accused Lorraine officials of favoring usury. AffEtrang., Lorraine,vol.110,p.93-96.

[215] "usuriers juifs et chrétiens" (Lidrezing); "commerçants suspects de monopole [usure], particulièrement les Juifs" (Frémestroff); "plusieurs chrétiens qui sont juifs dans l'âme pour cet objet" (Hertzing); etc. M. Liber, *oc*, vol. LXIII, p. 90-94, 96; Charles Etienne, *oc*, vol. I, p. 252, 381, vol. II, p. 213; Fr. W. Hussong, *Cahiers de doléances... de Boulay et de Bouzonville* (M 1912) p. 148.

[215] Ph. Sagnac, *La Législation de la Révolution française* 1789-1804 (P 1898) p. 203; de Tocqueville, *L'Ancien régime et la Révolution* (P 1857) p. 380; Troplong, *oc*, vol. XIV, p. CXLVIII-CXLIX; Marion, *Dictionnaire...* p. 300.

[216] "Soit qu'on prenne de l'argent, ou quoi que ce soit qui vaille de l'argent," de Fieux, *oc*, p. 1. "usure, par rapport aux contrats de rentes rachetables des deux côtés," P. Mendel, *oc*.

[217] *Mémoire pour les créanciers de feu M⁴ Tourtel, contre les Dames du Refuge de Nancy* (N 1782) p. 5. BmN7573.

Already in 1501 an author of Dauphiné wrote about usury through "pensions" (rentes).[218] Rentes were very much responsible for the sad condition of the peasantry not only in the Northeastern provinces, but throughout France.[219] The Lorraine ordinances of Apr. 1, 1573; Apr. 11, 1582; Sept. 22, 1586; Apr. 2, 1597; June 12, 1630; May 6, 1631; Jan. 23, 1632; May 31, 1666 and Nov. 25, 1667, were directed not only against usurious rates of interest on loans, but also against usurious rentes.[220]

The conflict between the King and the Metz Parliament could best examplify the position of the creditors of rentes. Because of the wars, misery was extremely great in Metz and the province of Metz, Lorraine and Barrois, Toul and Verdun. Many debtors, unable to repay their debts, were ruined; peasants were forced to leave the villages. In his Declaration of July 7, 1643, the King reduced the rentes, but entire towns, Church institutions and individual creditors protested against the royal declaration, which the Metz Parliament refused to register. The debtors complained again against the excessive rentes-interest, and on March 9, 1644, the King commanded the Metz Parliament to register the Declaration of 1643. On Sept. 10, 1644, the King ordered the Intendant of Lorraine, de Ricey, to promulgate the Declaration against the will of the Metz Parliament, which at that time had jurisdiction over Lorraine, too. On Dec. 15, 1644, the Lorraine Intendant promulgated the royal Declaration. The Metz Parliament was forced to relinquish its fight and to register the Declaration (on Dec. 19, 1644) but not without introducing many modifications in favor of the creditors. The Parliament ordered the creditors and debtors to disregard the Lorraine Intendant's promulgation of the royal Declaration and on April 18, 1646, the King was forced to renew his Declaration of July 7, 1643.[221]

The Alsatian historian Xavier Mossmann criticized rentes on the same grounds as those he used against Jewish usurers. Peasants were forced to pay rentes not only in produce, but even in cash[222] and this forced peasants to obtain loans in order to pay rentes. In Northeastern France the peasant could frequently find a loan

[218] "Pension, a parler proprement,
C'est une usure paliée
...Certainement ce n'est que usure."
L. Delisle, Vers français sur une pratique usuraire abolie dans le Dauphiné en 1501. Extr. de la Bibliothèque de l'Ecole des Chartres, vol. LXVI (P 1905).
[219] Troplong, oc, vol. XIV, p. 336; Traité sur la nature des biens ruraux dans les deux départements du Rhin... (S 1802) p. 5; C. Oberreiner, oc, p. 141.
[220] par prest d'argent, achapt, de rente, de grains, vins et deniers... (1 avril 1535); usures palliées du nom de vente d'immeubles (11 avril 1582); usures palliées, sous ombre de constitution de rente (22 septembre 1586); usures en grains, vins et autres espèces qu'en deniers seulement... (5 avril 1597); usures pratiquées dans les ventes de grains et de vin (12 juin 1680); usures palliées, sous prétexte de vente de marchandises; rentes en argent et grains... (23 janvier 1632); Rentes et intérêts stipulés en espèces de grains et vins pour prêt de deniers (31 mai 1666); réduction des rentes et intérêts à cinq pour cent (25 nov. 1667). de Rogéville, oc, vol. II, p. 644 ss.
[221] Foissey, in: BmM,ms.920; R. Clément, oc, p. 176-78; J. L. C. Emmery de Grozyeulx, oc, vol. I, p. 616-22, vol. II, p. 64-66, 110-11, 128-36.
[222] X. Mossmann, oc, p. 11-19; M. J. Krug-Basse, L'Alsace avant 1789 (P-C 1876) p. 313, 318.

only from a Jew. Thus both the peasant and the Jew were caught in a vicious circle. The *rente* helped the peasant to "possess" his own parcel of land, to have the illusion of being independent. But rarely was the peasant in a position to pay the rente with the produce of "his" land and he was forced to become a Jew's debtor in turn. In many cases the Jewish creditors charged smaller rates of interest on loans granted by them to Gentile debtors than these debtors charged on land rented to peasants."[223]

No special laws prohibiting the establishment of land *rentes* in favor of Jews in Alsace, Metz or Lorraine were found. But there did exist many restrictions against Jews, not connected directly with *rentes,* but which created a jurisprudence in this respect, e.g.: the laws restricting the size of loans to be granted by Jews; the prohibition for Jewish creditors to obtain produce as security or as interest on loans; etc."[224] In their memorandum of 1717 the Alsatian Jews stated that the income from granting loans was restricted because in Alsace loans could be repaid mostly with produce, but Jews could not profit from such repayment. On Sept. 12, 1709, the Intendant of Metz, de Saint-Contest, wrote to the *Contrôleur général des finances* that Jews did not possess *rentes.*"[225] *Rentes* were the most advantageous and most secure way of gaining profits through money-lending, but this profitable field of credit operations was closed to Jews. The Letters patent of July 10, 1784, forbade Jews to accept from their debtors payment of interest in produce. In a memorandum of 1711 the Jews of Metz stated that they were not allowed to trade with *rentes.* (The Jews of Avignon and Comtat Venaissin were similarly not permitted to obtain *rentes.*)"[226]

---

[223] In the 17th century the Jew Alexandre Cahen granted a loan of 4,500 *écus* to the comte de Linange, who had to pay interest only for 2,400 *écus,* while the remainder was to be repaid within two years. As security for the debt, de Linange gave a *rente* which was established in 1536, when for a loan of 10,000 florins the duc Antoine of Lorraine established a *rente* of 1,500 florins, i.e. 15 %, in favor of de Linange's ancestors. A. Cahen charged much less than 15 % interest. Who was the usurer: the Jew Cahen or de Linange? A. Cahen, Le noble et le Juif prêteurs d'argent. Différence du taux de l'intérêt. *REJ,* vol. III (1881) p. 126.

[224] In 1497-1506, Jews were allowed to obtain only movable goods as security for loans in the seignoiry of Ribeaupierre. Orders of 1520 and 1530 prohibited to guarantee loans obtained from Jews with crops. Only old debts could be repaid to Jews with wine, at the highest market price. "Aucun Juif ne prêtera à un bourgeois, soit à sa sollicitation ou autrement sur un bien en fond ou sur sa maison ou vendange... Les Juifs ne prêteront à qui que ce soit autrement que sur des gages mobiliaires." AdHR,E699.

[225] *Mémoire pour les Juifs établis en Alsace,* [1717] 4 p.
"...ils [les Juifs de Metz] y portent toujours de l'argent, et, n'ayant ni charges, ni terres, ni maisons, ni rentes, il falloit nécessairement que tout leur argent roulât dans le commerce." Boislisle, *oc,* vol. III, p. 206. But Jews were, frequently, intermediaries in investing money in stocks for Gentile capitalists. In the 1720's, Nathan de Morhange of Metz took 20,000 pounds from Collart, attorney at the Paris Parliament, in order to establish for the latter a *rente* ("...il avoit assez de crédit pour faire placer ces effets en rente viagère". Arsenal,ms.10738).

[226] "D'ailleurs ils sont encore taxez comme aiséz pour acquérir des rentes, quoiqu'ils n'en ayent pas la faculté," AcM,Ce259; "La Constitution de pensions perpétuelles leur étant deffendue il leur est moins avantageux de prêter à jour quoique à un fond plus haut," a document of Carpentras. AIU, R43,No.96. Still, Jews were sometimes paid in produce, or

Proposals were made to improve the situation of the peasant-debtors by converting the debts owed to Jewish creditors into *rentes*,[227] but these projects were never realized. According to a 1790 pamphlet, the Gentile debtors were opposed to proposals of this nature.[228] In a memorandum of July 1789, addressed to the King, the Alsatian Jews pointed out that the project to convert the debts owed them into *rentes* was not workable, since the peasants owed to their Jewish creditors small sums. Jews would be unable to trade with *rentes* on such small sums, because they would not be accepted by bankers and merchants and because the expenses for selling them in distant cities (e.g. Paris) would be as great as the value of these small *rentes*. Only big capitalists could afford to convert their capital into *rentes*, but Jews were creditors of small loans.[229]

received *rentes* as security for loans granted by them. According to a decree of the Strasbourg Senate (Sept. 13, 1539), Jews acquired *rentes*, which they sold to Gentiles: "plusieurs Juifs, en trompant les pauvres gens... les induisent à des engagements usuriaires et ruineux, et qu'après leur avoir fait passer pour les dettes ainsi surprises, des constitutions de rentes et autres contrats, ils vendent et échangent les dits contrats à des chrétiens." Chauffour l'aîné, Chauffour le Jeune, Schirmer l'aîné et Mueg, *Consultation pour la ville de Strasbourg... concernant... Cerf Beer...* (S 1786) p 23. The Jew Jacob Zay of Metz paid rental for a loan of 100 pounds granted by the Gentile creditor Michel Gazier. In 1796, the Jew Marc Lazard Lévy bought this *rente* from Gazier (AcM,Pr158). According to a notarial act of 1752, the peasant-debtor Aubertin Ruzé was to deliver wine to his Jewish creditor Joseph Cahen of Daugny (AcM,Pr68). In 1757, a debtor of Leib Salomon of Ribeauvillé paid the interest in produce (AdHR, E1628). According to a lawsuit of 1769, Jean Herschberg was a debtor of David Weyl of Surbourg for the sum of 500 florins in capital plus interest in produce (ZS, a document dated March 30, 1769). In the 1770's the Jew Salomon Lyon was Nicolas Vebem's creditor for 1879 pounds and "une certaine quantité de bled et autres grains" (AN,29AP100,Roederer's brief).
[227] The Sovereign Council discussed such a proposal in February 1786. The anti-Jewish leader of Alsace, Hell, made such a proposal in 1789, in the *cahiers* of Haguenau-Wissembourg and in one of his anti-Jewish pamphlets. V.M.A. Holdt, *Journal du Palais du Conseil Souverain d'Alsace*, publié par A. Ingold (C 1903-7) Feb. 3, 1786; Hell, *Mon opinion sur les Juifs...* (P 25 Dec. 1789) p. 1; M. Liber, *oc*, vol. LXIII, p. 188-190.
[228] *Lettre d'un Alsacien sur les Juifs d'Alsace à M. Reubell...* (P 1790) p. 9-10.
[229] "Ce sont les capitalistes embarrassés de leurs richesses, qui placent à constitution, et pour avoir leur argent, il faut leur offrir à la fois de fortes valeurs et de grands avantages." AmS,AA2394.
On the other hand, the exclusion of Jews from the trade of land *rentes* was offentimes a blessing, because it made difficult to dispossess or to exile the Jews. In April 1702, de Saint-Contest, Intendant of Metz, declared himself against a proposed expulsoin of Jews from the Metz province, because the Jews possessed only cash and promissory notes and, if they would have taken away those possessions with them, the province would suffer from lack of money: "Je ne croy pas qu'il soit convenable quant à présent d'en chasser aucun [Juif], voicy mon raisonnement, ou il les faut chasser le bâton blanc à la main, ou leur permettre de recouvrer leurs effets. Dans le premier cas il y a de la dureté et même de l'impossibilité dans l'exécution, parce que tous leurs effets étant en argent ou en billets ils trouveront moyen d'en faire le recouvrement. Ainsy tout revient au second cas, qui certainement ruineroit le païs où l'argent est déjà très rare: mais je crois qu'il seroit d'une sage précaution d'empêcher qu'il ne s'y en établisse à l'avenir parce qu'il n'y en a déjà que trop." On Apr. 20, 1702, the Minister of War replied to de Saint-Contest: "j'en ay rendu compte au Roy qui ayant vu ce que vous me mandez à leur égard n'a pas jugé à propos d'en faire sortir aucun présentement, mais Sa Majesté m'a ordonné de vous faire sçavoir que Son intention est que vous ne sousfriés pas qu'il s'y en établisse d'avantage." (Guerre,A-1-1583,Nos.68,73). The Intendant of

21. JEWS AS INTERMEDIARIES FOR GENTILE CREDITORS

Very frequently Jews were only intermediaries between Gentile
creditors and Gentile debtors, because these Jews did not possess
any capital of their own, or they acted as "fronts" for Gentile
creditors who were afraid to engage openly in usurious business.
The famous Alsatian attorney, J.F. Bruges, called such a Jewish
intermediary the *maquignon de dettes*.[229] In 1634, the Metz Parliament forbade partnerships of Jewish and Gentile creditors.[231]

Very often Jews took loans from Gentile or Jewish creditors
in order to be able to grant loans in turn and make a living from it.
The Nancy Jewish creditor and horse-dealer, Lion Groutchou, wrote
about it in a factum of the beginning of the 18th century. In 1674,
Mayeur Schaube (Schvaub) of Metz wrote in a factum against the
widow Françoise Mangeot that he granted loans with money which
did not belong to him. Dom Chais of the Abbaye de St-Avold
wrote in his study on Jews for the contest of the Metz Academy
('80s of the 18th century) that Jews speculated with money obtained
from Gentile creditors.[232] Among the creditors of Alsatian Jewish
debtors were many Basel bankers. On Aug. 4, 1789, Pierre Ochs,

---

Alsace was afraid that, should the Jews be exiled from the Metz province,
they would have emigrated to Alsace (his letter to the War Ministry, 1728.
Guerre,A-1-2679,Nos.75-76,79).

[230] In his defense of a Jewish intermediary who received a commission
of 2,000 pounds as the brokerage fee of a loan of 20,000 pounds granted
by a Gentile creditor (AdHR,fonds Corberon-Bruges,34).

[231] R. Anchel, *oc*, p. 205. According to the documents of a law-suit
involving the Jew Mayeur Schvaub and the Gentile Daniel Nolibois of
Metz, a Jew practiced usury as a mediator for a Gentile (*Ibidem*, p. 206).

[232] "prêtent et empruntent des deniers." *Factum pour Lion Groutchou...
contre le sieur Claude François...* (N 172-) p. 2. BmN. "il y avait commerce
entre eux et Mayeur de prest d'Argent de Lettres de charge et semblables emprunts: et comme deffunt Bancelin étoit fort accommodé, il faisait de très
grandes avances, en sorte que Mayeur étoit toujours redevable de notables
sommes, ce qui ne sera pas difficile à croire, et ceux qui sçavent que le dit
Mayeur, quelque bonne mine qu'il fasse, ne trafique, et ne tient banque que
sur la Bourse d'autruy." *Inventaire de production... contre Mayer Schaube,
Juif...* (sl 1674]) p. 1. BN,naf22705-53. "une quantité considérable de citoyens particuliers, lesquels dépositaires de quelque argent pendant 6, 8, 10
ou 12 mois, sont assurés qu'en le prêtant aux Juifs pour le même temps,
ils en retireront la somme capitale et des rentes à proportion du temps;
ce qui cesseroit, le Juif ne pouvant plus prêter luy même." BmM,ms.1350,p.
793. In 1550, the Jew Haym of Rosenwiller was the creditor and the debtor,
too, of the Gentile Lienhart Wagner of Marlenheim: M. Ginsburger, Rosenviller. *Souvenir et science*, No. 1 (1930) p. 24. In 1715, Meyer Weill of
Ribeauvillé was a debtor of the Gentile creditor Jean Grollmond of Guémar for 400 Louis d'or vieux: *Plaise à Nosseigneurs du Conseil Souverain
d'Alsace, d'avoir pour recomandée en justice l'instance. D'entre Jean Grollmond... contre Meyer Weill, Juif...* (sl nd). BN,naf22705-148. Oury Lévy of
La Haute Youtz was a creditor, but also a debtor of three Jewish and eight
Gentile creditors: AdM,J1138. In 1757, the Gentile creditor G. J. Hoffman
of Haguenau asked his Jewish debtor Jacques Alexandre for payment of
two debts of 1743 (1700 pounds) and 1750 (595 pounds): AdBR.Gins.C224.
"Il [Sauvayre] avoit prêté de l'argent, sous un nom emprunté, à Cerf Lévy,
Juif" (1704): Boislisle, *oc*, vol. II, p. 180. In 1720, the Jewish banker Jacob
Worms of Metz borrowed 14,000 pounds from a Gentile: *Mémoire pour Jacob
Worms Banquier, Juif... contre Pierre Chartres Ecyer* (sl nd) 6 p.; *Addition
au Mémoire de Jacob Worms...* (sl nd) 4 p. AffEtrang.,Lorraine, vol. 109.
The merchandise displayed in 1736 by Moyse of Dimering (Lorraine) on
the market of Boackenom was confiscated at the demand of his Gentile
creditors (AN,E2901,p.261).

representative of Strasbourg in Basel, wrote that Jews speculated in Alsace with the capitals obtained from Basel creditors.[233]

This does not mean that the Jew who himself obtained a loan from a Gentile (or Jewish) creditor did it always in order to be able to grant loans to Gentile debtors in turn. He was frequently forced to obtain a loan in order to make a living by horse or cattle-trading, or to peddle, because he did not have any money of his own. Here is a striking example from the seigniory of Ajoye (now in the canton of Bern, Switzerland), where the living conditions were similar to those of Alsace: In 1777 the clerk of the seigniory made out an inventory of the possessions of the Jew Cerf Lévy, who was "tolerated" to reside in Miécour. His property consisted of: 6 horses in the value of 442-13-8 pounds, furniture, no cash whatever, but 20 debtors owed to the Jew debts for horses and cattle bought on credit—a sum total of 353-2- pounds. His entire property was evaluated at 795-15-8 pounds. At the same time the Jew was himself a debtor of 12 creditors for 848-8-9 pounds, all of them peasants from whom he bought horses and cattle on credit.[234]

Frequently laws were aimed at safeguarding the interests of Gentile creditors of Jewish debtors. On May 4, 1787, the bailiff of Ribeauvillé asked to allow Jews to keep open stores (boutiques) because Jewish peddlers and merchants without stores frequently went into bankruptcy and ruined their Gentile creditors.[235] In order to protect the Gentile creditors, the Sovereign Council ordered (on Jan. 21, 1701) that all Jewish marriage contracts drawn up by rabbis be deposited within 15 days in the notaries' offices, so that Jewish debtors could not keep secret from Gentile creditors information regarding their dowries and other financial marriage-settlements.[236] A prohibition of Sept. 27, 1719, to draw up inventories of or to seal properties of deceased Jews by rabbis aimed at the safeguarding of Gentile creditors' claims. Such inventories were to be drafted by royal notaries.[237]

[233] Rod. Reuss, L'Alsace pendant la Révolution française. RA, vol. LXX (1923) III, p. 302. The Bros. Félix and Lehman Leyser of Niederhagenthal were debtors for very large sums of the Basel bankers J. L. Isselin and J. C. de Michel: AdHR,IBE66.

[234] SBern,B216,f.281.

[235] "l'expérience nous a malheureusement que trop appris que le né-goce des Juifs soit marchands, soit colporteurs, finit presque toujours par des faillites ordinairement frauduleuses et ruineuses pour les créanciers." AdHR,E1629.

[236] "les Juifs établis en cette province, passoient des contracts de ma-riage par devant leurs Rabins, qu'ils prétendent porter hypothèque pour sûreté de la dot, et autres effects..., et ce au préjudice de tous autres créan-ciers du mary." Louis par la Grâce de Dieu... [Contracts de marriage des Juifs.] (C 11 Jan. 1701) Placard. JTS; Corberon, oc, p. 375-76. In 1787, the Jewish butcher Abraham Libman of Ribeauvillé refused, or was unable, to pay his debts. His wife then asked the bailiff to grant her a judicial separation of the property (séparation de biens). Of course, she only tried to save some of the family's property from being taken by the creditors. But such separations were then very common among both Gentiles and Jews (AdHR,IIIB700). According to Corberon (Recueil, vol. I, p. 375-76) and de Boug (oc, vol. I, p. 310) the above cited ordinance was of Jan. 21, 1701.

[237] "d'une conséquence dangereuse et injurieuse aux chrétiens, qui se trouveraient créanciers de ces sortes de successions." ERCSA. 27 Sept. 1717 (s! nd) 4 p. JTS. The same measure existed in Avignon and Comtat Ve-

168

Many Jews were only transferees (*cessionnaires*) who bought
the right to debts from Gentile creditors or were repaid for debts
owed by Gentiles with such rights to debts owed by Gentile debtors.[21]
In some parts of Alsace Jews were not allowed to become transferees
of debts owed to Gentiles. According to a document of Apr. 26,
1643, Jews of Dambach were not allowed to transfer to Gentile
creditors debts owed them. This was done also in cases where
Jews could not ask legally for payment of the debts. During the
famous bankruptcy of Samuel Lévy, Finance Minister of Lorraine,
several cases of Gentiles who allowed Jews to operate under their
names were mentioned. The famous Jewish banker Moyse Alcan
was one of these Jewish creditors who used the name of a Gentile
for his credit-operations.[22] Jewish army contractors were frequently

---

naissin: [F. R. Cottier,] *Dialogue sur le départ des Juifs de Carpentras*
[Carpentras 1789] p. 9. In 1765, rabbis were permitted to draw up some
inventories or to seal properties of deceased Jews in the seigniory of Ribeauvillé, who did not have any Gentile creditors: "Arrêt interprétatif de
celui du 27 Septembre 1719, qui permet aux Rabbins l'apposition de scellé
et sa confection d'Inventaire dans le cas où il n'y a pas de chrétien inté-
ressé [Ribeauvillé, 17 Octobre 1765]". AN,29AP3; de Boug, *oc*, vol. I, p. 537-
38, 545.
Frequently Jewish merchants came in conflict with Gentile creditors.
On Feb. 6, 1772, the Jews Jacques Wormser of Grussenheim and Abraham
Liebmann of Ribeauvillé bought land from Martin Weber who signed a
guarantee against claims of Weber's known creditors. Weber dit not reveal
to the Jews the names of all of his creditors. Weber's father vouched for
his son with his own property, but at the same time he made his holdings
secure by means of another guarantee in favor of a Gentile: *Mémoire pour
Jean-Henri Bürchoffer... contre Martin Weber... et encore Salomon Spirr,
Juif dudit Ribeauvillé...* (C 177-) 28 p. The officer Dujard bought an estate
for 15,562 pounds from the widow Fallois, whose former husband was a
Gentile's debtor for 86,144 pounds (Jews were not involved in this sale):
Mémoire pour les sieurs... Dujard... (N 1718) 44 p. BmN,ZZ173-2.
[228] "Moyses Hirtz, Juif de Wintzenheim disant que le nommé Michel
Dinthem, bourgeois dudit lieu, lui a fait cession avec subrogation... d'une
somme de 600 l. 60 de principal qui lui était dû en vertu de son contrat de
mariage par le nommé Antoine Dünther." AdHR,IBE70; "Nathan Braunschweig, Juif d'Horburg en qualité de cessionnaire du Sr. Philippe Rendel,
juriste de Colmar..." 1781 (Idem,IBE64); "Daniel Lévy, Juif de Moutzig, en
qualité de cessionnaire de Mannel Lévy, Juif de Balbrown et Meyer Netter,
Juif de Rosheim, en qualité de cessionnaire des héritiers de George Ritter,
vivant bourgeois de Dangolsheim" 1781. (Idem); "Saül Bernheim, Juif de
Zillisheim, en qualité de cessionnaire de Pierre Spar," 1781 (Idem); "Koshel
Marx Lévy, Juif de Wintzenheim... cessionnaire de Joseph Petit..." (Idem,
IBE72); "Hirtz Moyses, Juif de Wintzenheim en qualité de cessionnaire de
Mathias Gsell" (Idem); "Meyer Meyer, Juif de Dürmenach, en qualité de
cessionnaire de Joseph Baur, sergent seigneurial de Ferrette," 1785. (Idem,
IBE69).
[229] Th. Weiss, *Geschichte und rechtlichen Stellung der Juden im
Fürstbistum Strassburg...* (Bonn 1895) p. 150. Me Marcot, *Supplément pour
le Sieur Dominique Anthoine, contre Moyse Alcan, juif* (N 1718); Me Fournier, *Réponse pour Moyse Alcan...* (N 1719). BN,naf.22705,f.211et228; Chr.
Pfister, *oc*, vol. III, p. 316-17. Such operations are mentioned in the Sept.
13, 1539 decree of the Strasbourg Senate, cf. note 226 (factum of 1786),
p 23-24. Jacques Philippe Massias, *procureur fiscal* of the seigniory of
Hochlandsberg, sold in the 1760's to the Jew Sch. Bloch of Wintzenheim a
debt of 120 pounds against Jean Biechelin of Colmar. AmC,FF318. In 1743,
the comtesse Eléonore de Linange contracted a loan of 7,000 pounds from
the Strasbourg Gentile banker Ewald in order to repay an old debt to the
Jewish creditor Moyse Blien of Metz. Later she stated that Ewald lent
his name to Blien (*prête-nom*). In August 1745, her son, Frédéric Louis
de Linange, contracted from Blien a loan in order to repay to Ewald the
debt of 7,000 pounds, plus 7,583 pounds of interest, i.e., over 100 % for a
period of two years. On Jan. 29, 1762, the Metz Parliament ordered de

arrested because they lent their names to Gentile capitalists who went bankrupt." The *cahiers des doléances* of the districts of Belfort and Huningue (1789) requested the prohibition for Jews to become transferees of Gentile creditors. The same problem was discussed in pamphlets of the Revolutionary period." Oftentimes Jews vouched for Gentile debtors, but the position of a voucher was always very insecure, as he was often forced to pay the debts of the real debtor."

The existence of so many Jewish creditors caused many bankruptcies among Jews. In 1772-1775, there were in Metz 76 bankruptcies for the amount of 2,391,900 pounds. Among them were 16 Jews who went bankrupt for 623,700 pounds. But this was an exceptional period of a crisis in which many merchants were ruined. Prior to 1772, there were in Metz only 3-4 bankruptcies every year."

Linange to repay his debt to Blien. *Mémoire pour le comte de Lewenhaupt... contre Moyse Blien, Juif de Metz* (M 1762) and [*Requête au Roi par Adam, comte de Lewenhaupt, contre M. Blien*] (P 1771). BN,4F3-19452-3. In 1753, a Strasbourg Gentile was prosecuted because he had sold to a Jew the right to a debt of 8 florins. E. de Neyremand, *Petite Gazette des Tribunaux...* (C 1860) vol. III, p. 76-77.

²⁴⁰ Such, e.g., was the case of Mayer Lyon, Jacob Worms and Abraham Worms of Metz: L. Kahn, *Les Juifs de Paris au XVIIIᵉ siècle* (P 1894) p. 91-95.

²⁴¹ *Doléances générales des districts réunis de Belfort et Huningue* (Belfort 1789) p. 11. Rosman, an official of Mirécourt, proposed in 1790 to the Committee of Agriculture and Commerce of the National Assembly to establish in Champagne a colony for the Jews in order to fight usury. From his letter it is clear that the Jewish creditors "found money among non-Jews." ("Les personnes qui les soutiennent à prix d'argent sont complices de la manière qu'ils emploient pour s'en procurer"): F. Gerbeaux — Ch. Schmidt, *Procès-verbaux des comités d'agriculture et de commerce* (P 1906-37) vol. I, p. 702. The author of an anti-Jewish pamphlet (Strasbourg 1790) wrote: "...denn est ist allgemein bekannt, das überall, wo Juden sind, sie mehr mit Christengeld, als mit ihrem eigenen wuchern. Oft bedient sich der Christ, der zum wuchern geneigt ist, aber nicht dafür erkannt sein will, des Juden, un sein Geld über die gewöhnlichen Zinse anzulegen:" *Ueber die Vertreibung der Juden* (sl 1790) p. 8. Concerning Jewish creditors of Southern France who did not have their own money and were debtors of non-Jewish creditors, see: N. Roubin, La vie commerciale des Juifs comtadins en Languedoc au XVIIIᵉ siècle. *REJ*, vol. XXXV, p. 102-105. A very interesting case is to be found in a later period (1803). Marchand Aron of Phalsbourg (Moselle) signed a contract with the non-Jewish creditor Henriet. The Jew agreed to pay all expenses in attempting to recover 13,000 pounds from Henriet's debtors on condition that Henriet would pay him 1/3 of the recovered money: "Convention entre le Sr. Henriet et Marchand Aron de Phalsbourg par laquelle ce dernier s'oblige à faire à ses frais toutes démarches nécessaires pour le remboursement des sommes dues au sr Henriet, savoir par la maison neuve celle de sept mille livres et par le V. Despieds; celle de six mille huit cents livres, à charge par le Dr. Henriet de lui remettre le tiers des sommes qu'il pourra récupérer de ces sommes, le tiers des dites créances est de cinq mille deux cents francs. S. S. à Sarrebourg (Meurthe), le 6 Vend. (an 12). [29 Septembre 1803]" AdMM,Q,Actes sous seing privés,Nancy,vol.24,p.73.

²⁴² Such was the case of Abraham-Aaron Moch, a *caution solidaire* for the debtor Quessemme, who in January 1789 contracted a large loan from the Gentile creditor Eschenauer: *Précis dans la cause... entre Abraham-Aaron Moch... contre Catherine-Dorothée Eschenauer...* (S[1801]) BuS123086.

²⁴³ BmM,ms.4827-17. Bankruptcies were a frequent result of financial speculations. The Jewish Finance Minister of Lorraine, Samuel Lévy, who went into bankruptcy, stated that he became a victim of Jewish and Gentile usurers. The Lorraine Prince requested money and Lévy was forced to pay 100 % interest on loans. His creditors forced him even to accept jewelry at a very high price instead of cash. S. Lévy's bankruptcy ruined many of the richest Jewish merchants and bankers, among them

In cases of bankruptcies the law protected the claims of Gentile creditors against those of Jewish creditors.[?] In November 1712, the Intendant of Alsace proposed to force all the Jews of Alsace to pay the debts of Jewish bankrupts who left France.[?]-'

22. THE PROBLEM OF CREDIT IN THE MEMORIALS OF GRIEVANCES

The demands on credit in the memorials of grievances (cahiers des doléances) of 1789 are another proof of the importance of this problem in the period preceding the Revolution, not only in the provinces where Jews resided, but throughout the whole of France as well. Most of the grievances requested that loans on interest be legalized. This was, of course, indicative of the population's need of credit, but at the same time these grievances on credit were a disapproval of the Church's ban on loans on interest. Even priests requested to legalize such loans, because they wanted to derive income from their capitals—as the historian Roger Picard stated. The noblemen made the same demands because they wanted to obtain loans on a small legal rate of interest, while for commerce freedom of credit was a question of life or death. The requests to legalize loans were a part of the general demands to allow free production, for free movements in commerce and industry, etc.[?]

The cahiers of the districts of Huningue and Belfort demanded that Jews be prohibited from granting loans or to trade on credit, with the exception of trade operations on a large scale or in bank operations. Cahiers of Haguenau, Colmar and Metz requested to

Olry Alcan of Nancy and Ruben Schaube of Metz, the brother-in-law of S. Lévy. On S. Lévy's bankruptcy, cf. note 103, p. 47. The bankruptcy of the three brothers Moyses of Bouxwiller (1784) ruined 36 of their creditors (112,561 pounds), 12 of them were Jewish merchants: Précis... contre Abraham Hirsch Moyses, Juif de Bouxwiller [C 1786]. AmS,vol.948,No.24. Among the victims of the bankruptcy of the German Jewish banker Lion Weisweiller of Hamburg (600,000 pounds) were Alsatian Jews: Mémoire pour Aron Simon et Consors, Juifs de Landau, contre Lion Weisweiller, Juif détenu prisonnier... (sl nd) 15 p. BN.

[?] A Lorraine ordinance of March 3, 1738, prohibited Jewish creditors of a Jew who went bankrupt to obtain payment from the judicially liquidated property of the debtor, except in cases where the Jewish creditors were transferees of Gentiles ("les créanciers juifs ne seront pas admis, à moins qu'ils soient cessionnaires de catholiques"): Ch. E. Dumont, oc, p. 11. After the Bros. Collot went bankrupt for a million pounds, they moved to Nancy, where they did not reveal their past. One of their victims was the Jew Isaac Berr who bought from them a promissory note. Jacquemin, Pheyne et Grandjean, Mémoire à consulter pour le Sr. Jean-François Blaise, marchand à Nancy contre les héritiers d'Isaac-Berr, juif marchand en la même ville (N 1765) II p; Bordelux et autres, Mémoire à consulter pour la veuve et l'héritier d'Isaac Berr... au profit du Sr. Jean-François Blaise (N 1765) 17 p. BN,naf22706f.25,31.

[?]-' "lorsqu'il faudra sortir des règles ordinaires il me paroist qu'il conviendra pour le faire plus utilement d'établir une solidité sur tous les Juifs de cette Province pour le payement de tous les créanciers dudit Lyon. L'on prétend même, qu'il y a eucy des exemples à Metz d'une pareille contrainte contre tous les Juifs qui y sont établis" (Guerre,A-1-2394,No.126).

[?] Ph. Sagnac, oc, p. 204; R. Picard, Les Cahiers de 1789 et les classes ouvrières (P 1910) p. 144-48.

permit priests to grant loans, so poor people should not become debtors of Jews. As all three *cahiers* of Colmar made the same demand, they were probably the expression of a campaign designed to deprive the Jews of their credit operations for the benefit of priests. The *cahiers* of Longwy, Crigy, Cattenton and Walmestroff (bailiwick of Metz), Brounderdorf, Brühl, Boucheporn and Azoudange (Lorraine) demanded to legalize loans on interest, even on simple unlegalized I.O.U.s, so that the peasant should not become indebted to Jews. Gueberschwihr (Alsace) demanded to prohibit the circulation of Basel coins.[246]

Similar demands were voiced in other parts of France. A 1789 pamphlet on agriculture demanded a 4% legal rate of interest. In Avignon and Comtat Venaissin, where 2,000 Jews resided, *cahiers* demanded that Jews be limited to the same rate of interest as that allowed Gentile creditors. The Abbot Escoffier hoped to normalize credit through safeguarding the interest of the creditors, and the Avignon pamphleteer M. de Montvert complained about the lack of credit facilities. From the Department of Gard came a demand to repeal the Decree of June 1771 on mortgages, which did not safeguard sufficiently the creditors' interests. Verdun, where Jews were not allowed to reside, demanded to combat usury through legalizing credit on interest.[247] *Cahiers* from many Departments where Jews did not reside at all asked that usury be curbed, e.g., from Angoulême (Charente), the Department of Lot (there, the priest Rulié of Cahors published in 1780 a pamphlet on this problem), the Departments of Maine-et-Loire, Rhône, Marne, Ile-et-Vilaine, Haute-Saône, Cher, Loir-et-Cher, Aube, etc., etc.[248]

[246] *Doléances générales des districts réunis de Belfort et Huningue* (Belfort 1789) p. 11; *Archives parlementaires*, vol. III, p. 5, 8, 11, 419; *Cahier de l'Ordre de la Noblesse du baillage de Metz* (M 1789) p. 11; *Cahier de plaintes, doléances et remontrances du Tiers-Etat du baillage de Metz...* (M 1789) p. 4, 15; AdM,B4191; N. Dorvaux et Lesprand, *Cahiers de doléances des communautés en 1789* (M-Bar-le-Duc 1922) vol. II, p. 241, vol. III, p. 65, 365; Ch. Etienne, oc, vol. II, p. 46, 50, 153; *RA* (1908) p. 426.
[247] *La plus importante et la plus pressante affaire, ou la nécessité et les moyens de restaurer l'agriculture et le commerce* (sl 1789) p. 56-58. AN,ADIV17; *Articles de demandes, ou doléances arrêtés par MM. les Electeurs de Mallenort...* (sl [1790]) p. 8. Library of Avignon,ms.2987; L'Abbé Escoffier, *Réflexions...* (sl, Mars 1790) p. 5. Library of Avignon, ms. 2987; M. de Montvert, *De la restauration des campagnes* (Avignon 1789) p. 173-181 and *Supplément...* (P sd). BN,R44365 and 8Lb39-3078; E. Bligny-Bondurand, *Cahiers... de Nimes* (Nimes 1908) p. 46, 553; M. P. d'Arbois de Jubainville, Les cahiers de doléances de Verdun en 1789. *Mémoires de la Société de lettres... de Bar le Duc* (1908) p. 187.
[248] P. Boisonnade, *Cahiers de doléances de la sénéchaussée d'Angoulême et du siège royal de Cognac* (P 1907) p. 68, 74-75, 106, 510, 512; *Archives parlementaires*, vol. I, p. 613, 733, vol. II, p. 336, vol. III, p. 152, vol. V, p. 304, 371, 384, 727; E. le Parquier, *Cahiers... du Havre* (Epinal 1929) p. XVII, 92, 145, 202; Gustave Laurent, *Cahiers...* (Epernay 1906-11), vol. I, p. 863, vol. II, p. 777; J. J. Vernier, *Cahiers... de Troyes* (1910-11) vol. II, p. 65, 170, 740, vol. III, p. 171-72, 203; E. Bridery, *Cahiers... de Cotentin* (P 1907) vol. I, p. 722; J. Savina—D. Bernard, *Cahiers... de Quimper et de Concarneau* (Rennes 1927) p. 11, 61, 253, 273, 314; H. Sée—A. Lesort, *Cahiers... de Rennes* (1912) vol. II, p. 313, 409, vol. III, p. 129, 528, vol. IV, p. 276; M. Godard—I. Abensour, *Cahiers... d'Amont* (Auxerre 1927) vol. I, p. 333, vol. II, p. 547; Dr. E. Lesueur—A. Cauchie, *Cahiers... de Blois*, vol. I, p. 22, 117; G. Balencie, *Cahiers... de Bigorre* (Tarbes 1925) p. 121, 172, 431, 470; A. Chandillon, *Cahiers... de Bourges* (Bourges 1910) p. 282, 620, 696, 740; Ch. Poré, *Cahiers...*

Some demands concerning credit contained in the *cahiers* were directed against the interests of the peasant-debtor, e.g., the demand that loans be arranged only in the presence of notaries. It is well known that peasants disliked any publicity on loans. Such a demand was probably put forward at the request of the notaries in order to increase their income. M. Liber already proved that the demands in the *cahiers* concerning Jews were not always the expression of the free will of the people, but of the policy of priests, lawyers, notaries, judges, etc. who specialized in making anti-Jewish propaganda.[24] It is well known that because the peasants did not know how to write, many printed samples of *cahiers* were circulated. Two such samples from Lorraine did not mention the Jewish problem. In Alsace were circulated ready-printed *cahiers* to which only the name of the locality had to be affixed. Priests frequently told the peasants what demands they should put in the *cahiers*. The demands concerning Jews are similar in their wording in many *cahiers* of different localities, e.g., of Brouderdorf, Bühl, Mont-Didier and Neuf-Village (Lorraine). A pro-Jewish pamphlet of 1790 stated that the *cahiers'* demands against Jews were not made by the people of France, but by professional adversaries of the new regime. The Alsatian *Commission intermédiaire* itself printed a similar sample of *cahiers* (but the Jewish or credit problems are not mentioned in this sample; nor is there any mention of Jews in another Alsatian sample).[25] The Jewish Problem is laid down in a sample of a *cahier* of February 1789, published by the Alsatian anti-Jewish leader Hell. He proposed measures against usury and Jews; the annulment of all debts of over 20 pounds owed by peasants to Jewish and Christian creditors if these debts were not contracted

de Sens (Auxerre 1908) p. 818; J. Fournier, *Cahiers... de Marseille* (1908) p. 185-381; C. Bloch, *Cahiers... d'Orléans* (1906) vol. I, p. 333, vol. II, p. 144-45; P. Boissandre—L. Cathelineau, *Cahiers... de Civray* (Niort 1925) p. 9, 164, 367; F. Fourastié, *Cahiers... de Cahors* (1908) p. 17, 152, 164, 168, 271; [P. Rulié,] *Théorie de l'intérêt de l'argent...* (P 1780). BN,D53145; E. Champion, *La France d'après les cahiers de 1789* (P 1897) p 159, 181; E. Picard, *Les cahiers de 1789 au point de vue industriel et commercial* (P) p. 144-48; A. Le Moy, *Cahiers... d'Angers* (1915-16) vol. II, p. 684.
[24] M. Liber, *oc*.
[25] [J. S. N. Anthoine,] *Essai sur les Assemblées de communautés... la rédaction des Cahiers* (P 1789) 16 p. BN,Lb39-1395; P. Lesprand, *Quelques mots sur les cahiers... Jahrbuch der Gesellschaft für lothringische Geschichte und Altertumskunde*, vol. XVIII (1906) p. 167; L. Jérôme, *Les Elections et les cahiers du clergé lorrain* (P—N 1889) p. 18; Abbé D. Mathieu, *oc*, p. 433; R. Parrisot, *Histoire de Lorraine* (P 1924) vol. II, p. 11-12; Ch. L. Chassin, *Les cahiers des curés* (P 1882) p. 273-74; A. Onou, Les élections de 1789 et les cahiers du Tiers-Etat. *La Révolution française*, vol. LVI (1909) p. 524; [Delaure,] *Dénonciation... contre le Sieur Comte de Bussevent... d'Huningue, en Alsace* (P 1790) p. 2. AN,ADXVI62; Ch. Etienne, *oc*, vol. II, p. 46, 50, 263, 291. *Lettre d'un Alsacien sur les Juifs d'Alsace...* (P 1790) p. 9: "Mais par qui ont été rédigés ces cahiers? Par des gens de loi, approbateurs nés de tous les abus d'administrations, parce qu'ils en vivent; conspirateurs ardents contre les droits de l'homme, parce qu'il ne saurait y avoir que peu de procès, là où ces droits sont reconnus... Aussi la plupart des cahiers n'ont-ils exposé l'opinion publique que lorsqu'elle s'est trouvée d'accord avec les intérêts des gens de loi. Dans tout autre cas, ils l'ont masquée au lieu de la dévoiler"; *Avis adressé aux communautés de l'Alsace par la Commission intermédiaire provinciale* (sl, 25 Février 1789) 8 p. AN,Ball; *Instruction, ou si l'on veut, cahier de l'Assemblée du bailage de... 28 Février 1789* (sl nd) 32 p. City Library of Strasbourg, Affiches révolutionnaires.

with the written agreement of seven members of each debtor's family; the abolishment of the Jewish communities and the rabbinical courts; the restriction of marriages among Jews; etc.[251]

Demands were directed not only against usurers—Gentile and Jewish—but also against debtors who accepted loans on usurious rates of interest and in general, against debtors who accepted loans which they could not repay. The slogan to "moralize the credit" (moraliser le crédit), i.e., to force the peasant not to take any large loans, was strongly advocated in the 18th century, as it was later in the 19th century. Many proposals sought to improve the peasants' position by fixing the amount of money which they could borrow and the form of guarantee to be given; etc. In February 1786, the Sovereign Council discussed the size of loans which peasants could obtain. A Strasbourg memorandum of 1781 stated that peasants were being ruined because they borrowed money in order to buy land. The anti-Jewish leader Hell proposed that peasants should be required to obtain only small loans after securing their families' written approval. The same proposition was made in 1788, in a projected status for Jews, prepared by the Alsatian Intermediary Commission and in Hell's sample of a cahier.[252]

All this outcry for "moralizing" the peasant was mainly an expression of the opposition to the parcellization of land, to allow the peasant to buy land with borrowed money.[253] In this way the fight against Jews was frequently interlaced with the problem of ownership of land by the peasants, which was against the interests of the Church and the landlords.

---

[251] Le Roi ne voulant régner que sur des hommes libres... (sl Février 1789) 9 p. A sample of a cahier, by Hell. AN,Ba11. The Mayor of Strasbourg, de Dietrich, sent a copy of Hell's sample to the Ministry in Paris, but at the Ministry Hell's sample was strongly criticized because no samples of cahiers were to be circulated and because Hell's proposals were a result of scandals and intrigues: "Il serait peut-être bien intéressant de faire écrire promptement à M. Hell soit par le Ministre, soit par M. le comte de Puységur qu'il fera très bien de garder son projet en poche. Il ne vaut rien; c'est la sentence de 20 querelles et en tous ces doléances ne doivent point être suggérés." AN,Ba11,doc.19. Hell at that time favored autonomous rights for Alsace, which was not in accordance with the Government's views. Hell wrote the following on Jews in his sample of a cahier: "...Que la loi la plus nécessaire et celle que nous supplions Sa Majesté avec le plus d'instances de nous accorder, est celle de déclarer nulle toute obligation qu'un habitant de la classe du peuple aura contractée, à quel titre que ce puisse être, au profit de Chrétiens ou de Juifs, pour une somme au-dessus de 20 liv., sans qu'il ait été autorisé par délibération de sept de ses plus proches parents, faite sans frais devant la Municipalité de la demeure du débiteur, jointe au titre obligatoire, qui sera enregistré dans le mois au greffe de ladite Municipalité, aussi sous peine de nullité contre le créancier qui aura différé cet enregistrement plus longtemps. Que les Juifs contribuent à toutes les impositions comme nous, avec nous; qu'ils n'auront plus de rôles particuliers; qu'ils ne seront plus corps; qu'ils n'auront plus de syndics, ni agents, ni d'autres tribunaux [rabbiniques] que les nôtres; qu'ils ne pourront se marier que sur la permission des Etats provinciaux, permission qui sera gratuite et qui ne pourra être accordée que dans les cas qui seront exprimés par le règlement qui sera fait par lesdits Etats provinciaux."
[252] Holdt, oc, Feb. 4, 1786; AmS,AA2389 and 2393: Hell, Mon opinion sur les Juifs... (P 1789) p. 9-10; cf. note 251.
[253] "Tous les paysans achetaient; tous s'endettèrent et éprouvèrent plus ou moins les suites funestes de leur imprudence qui les avait jetés entre les mains perfides de l'usure." Hoffmann, oc, vol. I, p. 184.

23. THE IMPORTANCE OF JEWS IN CREDIT OPERATIONS

Almost all the classes of society had to borrow money from Jews, not only peasants, but seigniors, merchants, officers, etc.[254] While analyzing the inventories of Jewish inheritances, one finds that Jews were creditors of great numbers of small loans; they were like private bank institutions with a large number of customers. In 1714, a Metz Jew left to his heirs debts owed to him by 49 debtors; Salman Lagrange left a few hundred debts, and Lehman Hirtzel of Bouxwiller left to his heirs debts owed by 53 debtors.[255]

A series of conflicts between the Alsatian Jews and their peasant-debtors (known as the Case of the Counterfeit Receipts, *L'Affaire des Fausses Quittances* (see chapter VI), in 1777-1789 proved that a very large number of Alsatian peasants was in debt. According to one historian, only 2 out of 75 peasant families in Zellenberg were not indebted to Jews.[256] In connection with the falsified receipts, much was discussed on the causes forcing the peasant to make loans. On July 1786, the Jews wrote in a memorandum to the King that 2/3 of these debts were caused by the peasants' buying on credit parcels of land, houses, horses and cattle from Jews; only 1/3 of the debts were the result of cash-loans. Most peasants were debtors of small sums, 30—100 pounds, but rich debtors of large sums likewise tried to use falsified receipts. A Gentile memorandum of 1783 declared that only cash-loans could be usurious; debts resulting from sales on credit or ceded by Christian creditors to Jews were legal.[257] But no matter how wretched the peasants' situation was, the position of the Jews was not much better. The greatest part of the Jews' possessions consisted of unpaind loans granted by them to the debtors who bought falsified receipts. Most of the Jews were themselves debtors of Christian creditors who requested to be paid. This fact the Jews again brought out in a memorandum of July 1786. Much later, on March 7, 1792, the Jews wrote to the Legislative Committee of the National Assembly that the Case of Counterfeit Receipts, the expenses caused by the registration of the receipts, the lawsuits, and the inability to pay their own debts to Christian creditors forced them out of business and that in 1785 the wealth of all the Alsatian Jewish creditors (about 10 million pounds) was smaller than the wealth of 10 or 12 big Christian capitalists.[258]

---

[254] In the 16th century, the seignoir of Ribeaupierre exempted the Jews from paying protection money (*droits de protection*) for as long as he was to be the Jews' debtor (AdHR,E2481). The Nancy merchant François Baillot borrowed money from Olry Alcan in order to continue his trade. *Mémoire pour François Baillot... contre le sieur Mathieu Fromentau...* [N 17-] 11 p. BmN6630. Even de Rohan, Cardinal of Strasbourg, was a Jew's debtor, because he vouched for a loan of 5,000 pounds granted by Isaac Berr for the famous Lady de la Motte who did not repay the debt: *Mémoire pour... de Rohan... contre M. le Procureur Général...* (C 1786) p. 7. BmN,ZZ173-7.

[255] AcMetz,Jug.13,Pr.124; AdBR,Hypothèques,Saverne,vol.I.

[256] A. Goestermann, *oc*, vol. II, p. 83.

[257] AmS,AA2394.

[258] Ibidem and *Pétition de [Cent] soixante citoyens Français du Dé-*

According to one document, Krauss who was sent by the Sovereign Council to liquidate the falsified receipts, registered in 88 cities and villages of the Ferrette sub-delegation 2,085 debts in favor of Jewish creditors for the total of 335,612 pounds 10 sols 4 deniers.[259] Some debts amounted to 2,000 pounds each, others only to 20—30 pounds each, but on the average the debts were of a few hundred pounds each. The number of registered debts (2,085) does not signify that there were either that many debtors or creditors involved. In Atarschwiller (Attenschwiller), for example, Krauss registered 92 debts for the total of 13,408 pounds, but there were only 77 debtors, some owing a few debts, and the number of the Jewish creditors of these debts was only 22. The 2,085 debts were granted by only 226 Jewish creditors residing in 23 Jewish communities. The largest number of Jewish creditors resided in Dürmenach: 44 with 372 debts (according to the census of 1784, 73 Jewish families lived there). Let us try to use this register to determine the percentage of Jews engaged in money-lending. According to the census of 1784, 923 Jewish families lived in the 23 communities where the 226 creditors resided. It may certainly be assumed that the creditors also granted loans to debtors in other sub-delegations, even in Lorraine and other provinces. But we have to assume that most creditors of debtors residing outside of the Ferrette sub-delegation belonged to the same group of 226 and, thus, only about 1/4 of the Jewish families was engaged in the business of money-lending. The creditors seldom resided in the same localities as their debtors, but this can be explained by the small number of places where Jews were allowed to reside. Jewish creditors with 185 out of the 2,085 debts lived only in 9 of the 88 residences of the debtors. There were a few exceptions: Out of 122 registered debts for 21,969 pounds in Blotzheim, 100 debts were in favor of Jews residing there; all 22 debts for 3,430 pounds registered in Dürmenach were in favor of Dürmenach Jews; 35 out of the 51 Hegenheim debts for 8,068 pounds were granted by Hegenheim Jews; 12 out of the 17 Hagenthal-le-Bas debts for 4,688 pounds were granted by Hagenthal Jews.

A similar situation can be observed in the sub-delegation of Belfort, where—according ot one register—650 debts of 446 debtors were registered in 67 localities (the amount of the debts is noted only in 316 cases).[260] These 446 debts were granted by about 50 Jewish creditors who resided in 17 communities of the Belfort or other sub-delegations; according to the census of 1784, these 17 communities had a Jewish population of 613 families, showing that a small part of these families was engaged in money-lending. Debtors of some of these 50 creditors resided only in 5 of the 17

partement du Haut-Rhin classés par quelques malveillants, sous la dénomination de Juifs de la ci-devant Province d'Alsace, représentés par leurs fondés de pouvoir, les Citoyens Joseph Brouchvig, Emanuel Treysons et Daniel Cahen. Au Comité de Législation (Sl [1792) 12 p. AN,DIII214dr.ColmarNo.3300.
[259] AN,KK1240. See p. 128.
[260] AdHR,B,varia(H-I).

176

localities. Creditors of debts in the Ferrette sub-delegation lived in 14 of these 17 communities.

Usury would have been fought much easier if the practice of I.O.U.s (simple private agreements on loans, signed, but not sealed or witnessed) and of simple unwitnessed receipts given by creditors to debtors for repaid debts, would not have existed in Alsace. But, as already said, this problem was much discussed even before 1789. Simple I.O.U.s were very much in use, but in order to combat usury this practice was sometimes prohibited.

On Jan. 19, 1717, the Alsatian Sovereign Council forbade notaries to draw up or to renew obligatory notes other than by witnessing the paying of the full sum to the debtor. In a sentence of Jan. 22, 1725, the Council ordered that all documents in favor of Jewish creditors be drawn up by notaries or law-clerks in the presence of witnesses; simple I.O.U.s were prohibited; the old I.O.U.s had to be deposited with the notaries or in the law-courts. On March 24, 1733, the King published a declaration (registered on April 16, 1733, with the Sovereign Council) again prohibiting simple I.O.U.s, ordering the drawing up of loan and trade contracts in favor of Jews exclusively by notaries, etc. The Alsatian Jews protested. The Jews of Metz, too, protested and they presented to the King a memorandum written by the lawyer Godefroy in which they declared that the order of 1733 would force them to publish secret facts about their importing of horses, grain, gold, etc. for the King's armies and civil administrations; that even in private trade and loans, the merchants and debtors invariably avoided the divulgence of their secrets to the notaries; that peasant debtors would refuse to pay the notaries' fees; and that this practice would be detrimental to business and ruin the Jews economically. On Sept. 12, 1733, the King annulled his declaration of March 24, 1733. But on Feb. 19, 1735, in connection with a lawsuit between the Jew Fülckel of Ingolsheim and the Gentile Jean Valtin of Holtzheim, the Sovereign Council prohibited receipts given by Jews to their debtors and signed in Hebrew characters. The Council ordered that should a Jew be unable to sign a receipt other than in Hebrew, he must sign the document only in the presence of two witnesses and the receipt must be countersigned by a third person. If any remarks were added by the Jews in Hebrew on the receipts, they were to become null and void. On Oct. 24, 1767, the King recognized loans on simple I.O.U.s in favor of Jews in the areas administered by the Free City of Strasbourg, provided they be registered. On May 20, 1769, the Sovereign Council published a decree renewing almost all the articles of the King's declaration of March 24, 1733, ordering the registration in the law-courts of all simple I.O.U.s within three months. In Lorraine, too, a decree of Dec. 30, 1728, prohibited simple I.O.U.s on loans granted by Jews.[261]

[261] *ACSA portant défenses... de passer obligations au profit des Juifs, que sur deniers nombrés... Du 19 Janvier 1717* (C 1717) 8 p. AdBR,B598, *cf.* note 118, p. 52; *Déclaration du Roy, concernant les actes qui se passeront avec les Juifs... 24 Mars 1733* (C 1733) 8 p. AmC,AA174 and Corbe-

The order of the Metz Parliament of Sept. 6, 1670, that all contracts between Jews and Christians be written in French, was published after the Jews were accused of signing receipts in Yiddish. In 1706, the King ordered oll contracts drawn up by rabbis to be written in French. On Aug. 26, 1710, he ordered that Jewish commercial record-books be kept in French. On Feb. 19, 1739, and June 10, 1739, the same order was issued concerning the drawing up of promissory notes and contracts.[261]

But later events proved that the order of Feb. 19, 1735, was not carried out. Because of the expenses involved in drawing up of official documents, the number of loans guaranteed by simple I.O.U.s was always very large. This practice, naturally, was dangerous, but on the other hand it also offered many advantages. In some localities of France, where Jews did not reside (e.g., in Pas-de-Calais, in a later period) simple I.O.U.s were not recognized, and consequently it was impossible for peasants to contract any loans there. Many 1789 Memorials of Grievances of provinces other than Alsace, even where Jews did not reside, requested that the practice of loans on simple I.O.U.s be legalized, as was the case in Alsace and Germany.[263] For the same reason receipts given by Jewish creditors to their debtors were signed in Hebrew and not

---

ron, *Recueil...* p. 839-41. "C'est ce commerce toujours permis qui soutient leur établissement. En le détruisant, c'est leur ôter tout crédit, et les ruiner entièrement... Elles osent dire avec confiance, que jamais aucun Juif de Metz n'a été poursuivi en justice pour exaction et usure... Des prêts modiques faits à des laboureurs et Gens de la Campagne, leur donnent le moyen de payer la Taille et de cultiver leur Héritage. Sans quoy ils séroient souvent réduits à l'indigence." Me Godefroy, *Très humbles représentations de la communauté des Juifs de Metz sur la déclaration du Roi du 24 Mars 1733* (P 1733) 6 p. (BN,naf22705f,262); *Lettres patentes sur l'arrêt du Conseil d'Etat du Roy, qui suspend l'exécution de la Déclaration de sa Majesté du 24 Mars dernier...* 12 *Septembre* 1733 (C 1733) 8 p. AmC,AA174 and Corberon, *Recueil...* p. 848-49; *Arrest de règlement du Conseil Souverain d'Alsace, du 19 Février* 1735. *Au sujet des quittances et autres actes des Juifs et leurs débiteurs chrétiens* (C 1735) 8 p. JTS; *Extrait des registres du Conseil d'Etat du Roy* [24 Octobre 1767] (S 1767) 4 p. AmS,vol. 951-4; *ERCSA* [20 Mai 1769] (sl nd) 6 p. AdBR,C147; *Edit de son Altesse Royale, concernant les actes qui se passent avec les Juifs* [30 Décembre 1728] (Lunéville 1728) Placard. BN,ms.Lorr.470f.148; Corberon, *Recueil...*, vol. II, p. 839-40, 848-49; Guerre,A-1-2771,No.86.

[262] J. de Fombesque, *oc*, vol. II, No. 19 (1943) p. 69; Catalogue of the AcM, vol. I, p. 32; *Déclaration du Roy, qui enjoint aux Juifs établis en la ville de Metz faisant quelque commerce, d'avoir des registres en langue française... le 26 Aoust* 1710... (M 1710) 4 p. BN,F23619-860-61.

[263] *Le Pas-de-Calais au dix-neuvième siècle* (Arras 1900) vol. IV, p. 391; Ch. Etienne, *oc*, vol. II, p. 46, 50, 153; C. Bloch, *oc*, vol. I, p. 333, vol. II, p. 144-45; Boissandre—Cathelineau, *oc*, p. 9, 164, 367. According to a report of Sarre-Union dated Aug. 16, 1795, three different ways of granting loans existed before 1789 in Alsace: (1) For a fixed term (*à terme préfixe*); (2) To be repaid on the first term; (3) Granted on mortgaged properties, to be repaid not — as in the rest of France — on a fixed date, but on a date announced three months in advance by the creditor or the debtor. The first two types of loans were not made on the basis of legal documents, but only on the debtor's word or on a simple I.O.U. (AN,D-III-212). The 1684 Edict on I.O.U.s figured in de Corberon's collection, although the Edict was not registered with the Sovereign Council. *Edict... pour la reconnaissance des promesses ou billets sous seings privez... Décembre* 1684 (P 1685). BN,F23614(219); Corberon, *Recueil*, vol. I, p. 184-191. On the problem of I.O.U.s in the 19th century see: Z. Szajkowski, *Agricultural Credit...*, p. 59, 85-86.

legalized. This helped to falsify such receipts and to provoke the Case of Counterfeit Receipts.

It should be noted that simple I.O.U.s were not always a very good security for the Jewish creditors. Alsatian Jews lost much of their possessions because during the riots at the outbreak of the Revolution of 1789 peasants destroyed such notes.

Not Jews alone were creditors—honest creditors or usurers, but it is, probably, already too late to find out the percentage of Jews among all creditors. Still, a few documents may give us a hint on this problem. Such are, for example, the lists of creditors of *Emigrés* who left France during the Revolution. The lists were drawn up in order to repay the debts to the creditors with the money obtained from the sale of the *Emigrés'* properties. It must be noted that few of the important *Emigré* families were not indebted.[244] On the other hand, similar lists should be analyzed very critically, since many creditors did not request payment of the debts owed them by *Emigrés*. On a list of 819 such debts in the Lower Rhine were found only 58 debts owed to 28 Jewish creditors.[245] On another list of 221 creditors of liquidated corporations were found only 3 Jewish creditors.[246] Not one Jew appears among the 73 creditors of such a list in the Colmar district.[247] Only 6 Jews are listed among 240 creditors in the Department of Meurthe.[248] (There were also Jewish debtors of *Emigrés*.)[249]

24. THE CONDITIONS IN THE LAW-COURTS

Without the force of the Law, without the possibility of legal recourse against delinquent debtors, no individual would have lent money even to the most respectable debtor. In 1753 the Belfort attorney Claude Joseph Hengaud wrote, in a memorandum on the status of the courts of justice in Alsace, that lawsuits dragged on for many years, especially in cases where the creditor or debtor resided far from a judge's residence. Commerce and credit did not exist in such localities.[270] Very frequently the secondary, local judges were responsible for the sad situation of the peasant because they always attempted to profit by the peasant's conflicts with the law. As early as on Oct. 17, 1686, the King warned the Alsatian judges who in delivering sentences thought mostly of defending their own

---

[244] "Peu de familles considérables, surtout parmi celles qui étaient à la cour, étaient sans dettes." *Observations sur le projet de loi relatif à la restauration des biens invendus... d'Emigrés* (P 1814) p. 1. BN,Lb45-349.
[245] "Liquidation des dettes d'émigrés." AdBR,Q.
[246] "Répertoire des liquidations faites sur les corporations supprimées." AdBR,Q.
[247] AdHR,L483.
[248] AdMM,Q990.
[249] P. Hildenfinger, *Actes du district de Strasbourg relatifs aux Juifs, 1790-an II*. Extr. de la *REJ* (P 1911) p. 109, 117.
[270] "Dans les baillages où les audiences sont rares..., le commerce et le crédit sont entièrement bannis." Hoffmann, *oc*, vol. II, p. 274.

or the seigniors' interests.[271] Judges moved from village to village, were slow in rendering justice, and extorted money from the peasants. In many memoranda these judges, as well as attorneys, were pointed out as those responsible for the peasants' misery. Some historians made the Jewish creditors responsible for the emigration of the Alsatian peasants in 1785-86, yet the *Bureau intermédiaire* of Huningue stated that the judges and attorneys forced the peasants to emigrate. In 1750, the seigniorial cashier of Heitern stated that *procureurs* (judges nominated by seigniors to render justice in their seigniorities) sided with Jewish creditors against peasants. In 1785, M. de Rathsamhausen called the judges "vampires" (*vrai vampires... dont l'Alsace fourmille*). Even the anti-Jewish leader Hell wrote in 1789 that the judges and attorneys ruined the peasants by forcing them to provoke many lawsuits. He called for the organization of a credit system for the peasants so as to help them defend themselves against usurers, attorneys and other despots. People felt such a deadly hatred towards the dispensers of the law that in 1789 judges were not allowed to take part in drawing up the *Cahiers des doléances* (memorials of grievances). A *Cahier* of Avricourt (near Sarrebourg) stated that because of the high expenses involved, peasants frequently abandoned their right to seek justice. In an 18th century factum written in prison, the tavern-keeper Jacques Allemand of Guebwiller strongly attacked the judges.[272] In case the peasant lost a lawsuit and his property was to be sold by order of the court, he was again being ruined by the executors of justice in charge of the sale, the auctioneers (*huissiers, priseurs-jurés*) who appropriated a large part of the income from the sales. This was stated in many 1789 *cahiers*. In 1767 the Intendant of Alsace published a special order against such practices of the auctioneers.[273] It must also be stated that the mania of lawsuits greatly helped to corrupt judges and attorneys. The Lorraine historian A. Dedenon criticized the passion of the 18th century priests for everlasting lawsuits which consumed considerable time and caused a great deal of expense.[274] In such an atmosphere of bribery and perverted law, Jewish creditors were forced to seek justice in endless conflicts with their debtors.

25. LAWSUITS AGAINST JEWS BECAUSE OF USURY

The slogan "Fight against usury" was the legal justification for many anti-Jewish actions.[275] According to some historians

---

[271] "de juges qui ne dirigent les affaires qu'autant que l'interest du seigneur et leur bien particulier s'y trouvent." *Arrest du Conseil d'Estat du Roy. Pour retrancher les abus qui se commettent dans l'administration de la justice en Alsace... Du* 17 *Octobre* 1686 (C sd) 4 p. AdBR,C148g.
[272] AdHR,E1303 & coll. Wendl.13; BmM,ms.1350,p.796b; Hoffmann, *oc*, vol. II, p. 240-280; Ch. Etienne, *oc*, I, p. 46. "O pauvres villageois, que vous êtes à plaindre, les sous ministres de justice sont vos fléaux." *Requête d'atténuation pour Jacques Allemand...* (C [17-]) p. 2. BuS100440.
[273] Ch. Etienne, *oc*, vol. I, p. 46, 59, vol. III, p. 21, 44; AdBR,C147-76.
[274] A. Dedenon, *Histoire du Blamontois...* (N 1930) p. 96.
[275] "C'est cependant sous le prétexte affreux de l'usure que les Juifs

180

(E. Becourt and Vte. de Bussière), even the mass-annihilation of Jews in the 14th century was done not only because of religious hatred, but also in order not to have to repay to Jews the debts owed them. In Strasbourg the I.O.U.s signed by the Jews' debtors were burned at the same time as the more than 2,000 Jews themselves. But it is also possible that the debtors destroyed the I.O.U.s because they were afraid that the City of Strasbourg would force them to pay the debts for the City's treasury. Usury was also the legal excuse for the expulsion of Jews, e.g. from Sarlouis (Lorraine)."[6]

The Jewish creditor lived in an endless fear that Gentile debtors would refuse to repay the debts or to pay interest. He was always afraid of a new decree which would legalize the peasant's refusal to pay. Indeed, severe winters, heavy rains or bad crops always brought with them such decrees. Jews were then forced to engage the services of attorneys, send petitions and representatives to the Government, pay bribery-money and this entailed heavy expenses.

There were numerous lawsuits against Jews for practicing usury,[277] but such sentences should not be taken as proof that the practice of usury was prevalent among Jews. In the beginning of the 18th century the Jews of Metz wrote in a petition that the Gentile merchants were unable to prove their accusation that Jews were usurers. In 1733, they wrote in a petition to the King that not even one Metz Jew was sentenced for usury. The anti-Jewish minded historian and attorney of the Metz Parliament, C.L. Gabriel, cited only one case of sentencing a Jew, not for practicing usury, but for granting a loan to a minor. The Metz historian Roger Clément wrote that he could not find any case involving the sentencing a Metz Jew for usury. The same was stated by the Jewish historian R. Anchel.[278] Even if sentences against Jewish usurers could be unearthed, not only in Alsace, but even in Metz,[279] they were rare. There are to be found many more cases of sentencing Jews for fraud, forgeries, etc., even more sentences against Jewish thieves than against usurers.[280] But swind-

d'Alsace éprouvent continuellement des vexations de tout genre" ("Mémoire pour la Nation Juive..." [by Cerfberr], 1784. AN,F12-854B).
[276] E. Becourt, L'Abbaye, la ville et la famille d'Andlau au XIVe siècle. RA, vol. LXXII (1925) p. 247; Vte. de Bussière, Fragments des chroniques d'Alsace. Revue catholique d'Alsace, vol. III (1861) p. 267-68; Me Damours, Mémoire pour... Sarlouis... contre les Juifs... (sl nd) BN,naf22706 & AmS,AA 2381 (p. 27: "leurs usures et leurs autres rapines étoient les motifs que la ville faisoit valoir contre eux").
[277] In 1750, Isaac Abraham Cahen of Pontpierre was sentenced by the Sovereign Court of Lorraine and Barrois (AcM,Pr66). On Sept. 7, 1757, Joseph Salomon of Hellimer and Jacob Caen of Pont-Pierre (Lorraine) were sentenced to compensate their debtor Pierre Krantz. They appealed and the debtor later asked to force their heirs to pay the compensation (AdM,L532).
[278] AdM,E698; Me Godefroy, oc; R. Clément, oc, p. 191; C. L. Gabriel, oc, vol. I, p. 179.
[279] On June 12, 1709, Moyse May of Metz was sentenced to pay a fine of 50 pounds for practicing usury and to repay 100 pounds to his debtor: ER du bailliage, siège royal de Metz [M 1709] 3 p. BN,naf22705f.93.
[280] On March 29, 1771, Joseph Bloch of Cernay was sentenced for illegal commerce in pelts. On May 7, 1779, the Parliament of Metz sentenced Aaron

lers and thieves were not restricted to the Ghetto and the proportion of Jewish thieves was, surely, not greater than of thieves among non-Jews.[241] Jews themselves were frequently the first victims of Jewish swindlers.[242] Even the City of Strasbourg with its notorious tradition of anti-Jewish actions could not find many occasions to sentence Jews for usury. In 1772-1783, the city sentenced 14 Jews,

---

Abraham Gougenheim and Hayem Bernheim of Courcelles-Chaussy for their drawing up of an I.O.U. of their debtor François Mougin of Romilly for 60 pounds in such a manner that enough space was left for them to add later another 400 pounds. Because in another case the creditors used other than their own names, the Parliament ordered that court officials could not accept as valid any I.O.U.s or receipts from creditors drawn up not on their own names. On Dec. 1, 1762, the Metz Parliament punished Cerf Lévy of Vallières, who bought sheepskins, cut out the duty-stamps of the *Régie des cuirs* and hid the skins in the bed of a tavern-keeper whom he afterward denounced for having bought skins without official stamps. A Jew of Metz, with a Gentile, were engaged in the illegal forging of gold. The banker Jean Evrard Zetner earned some money in the Strasbourg jail by writing letters for arrested officers and Jews. *Catalogue des Alsatica de la bibliothèque de Oscar Berger-Levrault* (N 1886); *ACPM qui condamne Aaron Abrahm Gougenheim et Haeym Gougenheim, tous deux Juifs... pour crime de faux... du 7 Mai 1779* (M 1779) 8 p. JTS; *ACPM qui condamne Cerf Lévy, au carcan, à être battu, pour avoir caché dans la maison du nommé Jolivaldt, des peaux dont il avait enlevé la marque de la Régie... Du 1er Décembre 1762* (M sd) 4 p. JTS; *ACPM portant règlement concernant l'orfèvrerie... et qui condamne Lyon Moise, dit de Hambourg... pour contravention au statut et Atours du Corps, etc. Du 29 Juillet 1763* (M 1763) 12 p. AdM,B989; Rod. Reuss, Idylle norvégienne d'un jeune négociant Strasbourgeois. *RA*, vol. LX (1904). It would even be possible to cite a long list of sentences against Jewish thieves, as, e.g., the following sentences of Metz: *ACPM qui condamne Mayer Emmanuel, juif d'Amsterdam... pour crime de vol. Du 27 Août 17–; ACPM qui condamne François Thiéry, soldat... Ancel Lyon, juif... pour vol. Du 17 Oct. 1777* (M 1777); *ACPM qui condamne le nommé Henry Joanes... et renvoie Cerf-Isaïe Ullmann de l'accusation contre lui formée... Du 15 Février 1780* (M 1780); *ACPM qui confirme une sentence... par laquelle Isaac Samson, Juif de Mariendal, a été condamné... Du 29 Novembre 1780* (M 1780); *ACPM qui condamne Mayer Louis, Juif de la Vade... pour crime de vol. Du 14 Mars 1783* (M 1783); *ACPM qui condamne Lazard Hayem Cahen... pour crime de vol. Du 26 Août 1784* (M 1784); *ACPM qui condamne Moyse Lévi, Juif... pour crime de vol. Du 27 Mai 1785* (M 1785); *ACPM qui condamne Mathis Jacob et Sarah Joseph Mindelet, Juif et Juive étrangers... pour crime de vol et filouterie. Du 15 Juin 1785* (M 1785); *ACPM qui condamne le nommé Abraham Séligman, Juif roulant... pour crime de vol. Du 17 Mai 1786* (M 1786); *ACPM qui condamne les nommés Mayer Alkan, Abraham Israël et Isaac Israël... Du 27 Juillet 1786* (M 1786); *ACPM qui condamne le nommé Lyon Philippe, Juif étranger... pour crime de vol. Du 14 Mai 1787* (M 1787); *ACPM confirmatif d'une sentence... qui condamne le nommé Joseph Bloch, Juif... pour crime de vol. Du 27 Octobre 1788* (M 1788); *ACPM qui confirme une sentence... par laquelle les nommés Jacob Lévi et David Moyse, Juifs, ont été condamnés... pour crime de vol... Du 2 Décembre 1788* (M 1788); *ACPM qui condamne le nommé Lyon Renard, Juif... pour crime de vol. Du 17 Avril 1789* (M 1789); *ACPM qui condamne Joseph Bloch, Juif sans asyle... pour crime de vol... du 5 Octobre 1789* (M 1789). Placards, JTS and AdM,B2228-31. On Jewish terms in the language of Alsatian Gentile thieves see: Z. Szajkowski, The Action against Yiddish in France in the XVIIIth and XIXth centuries. *Jiwobleter*, vol. *XIV* (Wilno 1939) p. 49, 58.

[241] "...il serait difficile de raporter l'exemple d'aucun Juif justement condamné à des peines capitales: on ne trouve aucun individu de cette nation dans cette foule des malfaiteurs, que la vengeance publique retranche du sein de la société; ou s'il y a eu réellement quelques Juifs accusés et coupables de crimes, le nombre en est si petit, et les exemples ont été si rares, qu'il n'en peut résulter qu'une idée avantageuse en faveur de cette classe d'hommes en général." Mr. La Servolle, Avocat, *Requête au Roi, pour les Juifs de Sarrelouis* (P 1777) p. 13.

[242] "Moyse Schuabe étoit alors puissamment riche, mais Jacob son frère et le sistème l'ont tellement ruiné que tous les enfants ont répudié sa succession [pour ne pas payer ses dettes]." *Mémoire pour Elie Schuabe, Juif demandeur, contre Dame Barbe Renaut...* (M 1739) 7 p. BN,fol.F3-15560.

all of them for trading with stolen merchandise, not even one for usury."' Proportionately the number of sentenced Jewish usurers was not larger than the number of Gentile usurers similarly sentenced.

But the number of Jews appearing in lawsuits was proportionately larger. Of 162 lawsuits pleaded before the bailiff of Chalampe (Upper Alsace) between Nov. 27, 1771 and Dec. 30, 1783, 54 were of Jews against Gentiles. According to one source, the Alsatian anti-Jewish leader Hell, bailiff of Landser, rendered 7,000 sentences in a three-year period (in the '70s of the 18th century), 2,000 of them involving Jews."' These were almost always litigations resulting from business or credit operations, mostly judicial actions of Jewish creditors against their Gentile debtors, who refused to repay the debts for loans and commercial transactions, or demands of debtors to free them of their obligations toward Jewish creditors. Frequently such lawsuits involved demands of Gentile guilds to limit the rights of Jews in commerce. All these lawsuits could be taken as an indication of some cases of usury, but they also emphasize the vast number of debtors who picked quarrels with their Jewish creditors in order to avoid payment of debts.

Jews frequently demanded the reason for not sentencing Jewish usurers, if they really did exist. But the anti-Jewish elements maintained that Jewish usurers knew how to avoid the law. The truth is, however, that it was often possible to avoid—through bribery—severe sentences in cases involving, e.g., the commerce in coins, because in such cases the accusation had to prove that the accused was caught in the very act of breaking the law. Too many complicated legal documents and conflicting interests of the parties were involved in lawsuits resulting from usury to enable any usurer brought before the law-court to avoid punishment. Some lawsuits involving the practice of usury were even a result of well organized anti-Jewish campaigns, and in those cases any peasant who wanted to bring accusations of usury against his Jewish creditor could easily find financial, moral and juridical support.

In a memorandum of April 1781 the Alsatian Jews charged that judges assumed a right which was not a part of their jurisdiction, namely to seek out cases of usury and force debtors to bring their Jewish creditors to justice. According to the law, cases involving usury in Alsace were to be heard by a royal judge, yet such cases were also tried by various local judges, mostly ingorant individuals, as the Jews stated (*ignorants pour la plupart*). The Alsatian Jewish leader Cerfberr made the same statement in a memorandum of 1784."' The Alsatian officials did everything possible in order

---

[283] AmS,AA2393.
[284] AdHR,IE49 (2 vols.) & Wendl. 48/16, p. 44, 103. See note 389, p. 131.
[285] AN,H1641. "Cependant il est peu de justices seigneuriales dans la Province d'Alsace dont les officiers (ignorants pour la plus part et dont un seul gradué devient le maître de l'honneur et de la liberté d'un citoyen qu'il anéantit en le décrétant depris de corps) ne se soient permis des procédures aussi irrégulières que vexatoires" ("Mémoire par la Nation Juive..." [by Cerfberr], 1784. AN,F12-854B).

to fix convincing prosecutions against Jewish creditors. The manner of conducting the investigations and trials was fixed in advance, even by the Sovereign Council. In 1772-73, the officials of Hirsingen were engaged in looking for witnesses for a similar trial, while the Attorney-General of the Sovereign Council asked the bailiff of Landser, Hell, to take care of the affair and to find proof that the Jews practiced usury, because without such proof Jews could not be prosecuted.[216] In 1782, the Gentiles Joseph and Nicolas Ventz and Louis Carlé of Bergheim claimed that they and other creditors were ruined by the Jewish usurer Joseph Schuster of Ribeauvillé. But, being unable to prove it, they were afraid to start any legal proceedings because the Jew could request to classify the suit as a case to be judged under the royal jurisdiction and then use against them their own accusation on usury which could not be proved. On Feb. 16, 1782, the attorney Lang wrote to the Jew's three debtors that they should be more careful and not accuse openly their creditor of practicing usury. Of course, the Jew could be fined, but the debt would still have to be repaid if they would be unable to prove a clear case of usury. First of all, they were told, they must get the proof and witnesses.[217] Following is another case: The same Jew Joseph Schusta [Schuster] of Ribeauvillé was accused by many of his debtors of charging usurious rates of interest. According to one source, 72 out of the 75 families of Zallenberg were his debtors. The Chancellor's office of Ribeauvillé collected some accusations of the debtors in order to summon the Jew before the judge nominated by the seignior. In a brief of Dec. 24, 1769, three attorneys of the Sovereign Council gave their opinions on the best way of conducting the trial. The attorney Dupont advised to wait until the Jew would ask one of his debtors for payment of a debt, after which the latter was to bring against his creditor an accusation of usury. Then the Attorney-General on Fiscal Matters (*procureur fiscal*) would side with the debtor and the bailiff would order an investigation. Should the Jew appeal against a sentence of a local judge, the Sovereign Council would surely uphold the sentence of the lower court. But the matter was very complicated. The same attorney Dupont and his colleagues Queffeneme and Kieffer stated that usury was a public crime (*crime public*) and not only the debtor, but even officials could sue the usurer at law. In Schusta's case his debtors would be unable to sue him, because they would then be unable to act as witnesses in their own accusation. They could, however, appear as witnesses if the Jew were sued by the seigniory for general practice of usury (*usure générale*). In fact, this creditor was never brought to justice.[218] One of the

---

[216] AdHR,Wendl.48/16,p.49.

[217] "ils parviendront à faire punir le Juif, mais leurs dettes en ne seront pas pour cela acquittées, il faudra y faire honneur à moins qu'ils soyent à même de prouver par autres preuves, qu'ils ont été usurés... Si cependant les trois particuliers qui ont signé la plainte sont en état de prouver le fait personnel et propre de l'usure exercée contre eux, rien ne les empêche à donner eux mêmes leur requête de plainte au Conseil [Souverain]". AdHR, E1628.

[218] AdHR,E1628.

excuses for the Sovereign Council's order to the bailiffs for searching for documentary proof of Jewish usury was that ruined peasants would be unable to pay taxes.[289] Still, the Council was not always in a position to violate the law. On Nov. 20, 1771, the Jew Hirsch Samuel was sentenced by a Landau judge for usury. The investigation against him was conducted by the Attorney-General on Fiscal Matters and the Jew's debtor Otto Friederich Schwughard was the witness for the prosecution. The Jew appealed to the Sovereign Council which reversed (on Jan. 14, 1772) the sentence of the lower court and transferred the lawsuit to the jurisdiction of the bailiff of Lauterbourg and ordered that all judicial expenses be paid by the city of Landau.[290] On March 5, 1784, with reference to a similar case involving the Jewish creditor Salomon Wahl of Dürmenach, the Sovereign Council forbade the law-court to indict creditors on the basis of unchecked accusations.[291] A similar situation existed in the territory under the jurisdiction of the Metz Parliament. In the 1740's the Jew Cerf Moyse of Mittelbronn was sentenced for practicing usury against his debtor J.C. Moutier. The lawsuit was provoked by somebody other than the debtor, and the accusation could not be proved. In a sentence of Apr. 21, 1747, the Metz Parliament annulled the first sentence and ordered that the documents remain as a warning to the judges not to conduct such obscure investigations.[292] On May 17, 1747, and June 28, 1757, the Metz Parliament prohibited again organized unconvincing accusations against Jewish creditors. Such organized accusations were well prepared in advance, money was even raised to cover the expenses, peasant-debtors were told how to act in the law-court, etc.[293] The

---

[289] The Council gave such orders on March 14, 1757, in connection with a lawsuit between Joseph Weill of Wittolsheim and his debtor Louis Kebelin of Steinbach; on Feb. 4, 1745 in connection with a lawsuit between Lazare Brunsvick and his debotrs Dirnvell and others and also in the 1760's in connection with a lawsuit between the Gentile Clausman of Strasbourg and his debtor Hithsler. AdHR,C1284 and E1628.

[290] AdHR,IBE59.

[291] ERCSA. Du 5 Mars 1784 (C 1784) 3 p. BmC3784.

[292] "La cour fait défenses à tous ressort de recevoir d'aucun particulier des plaintes générales; aux fins de faire informer d'autres faits d'usure, que de ceux qui concernent personnellement les plaignans". ERPM, du vendredi 21 Avril 1747. Entre Cerf Moyse... (M 1747) 4 p. BN, F34494. Roederer was Cerf's attorney (AN,29AP3).

[293] "...les appels ont été portés à la Cour Luy ont appris les manœuvres qui se pratiquoient dans son ressort par les habitants de la campagne contre les Juifs dont ils avaient été secourus par des prêts d'argent. La Cour n'a vu qu'avec indignation, que sous prétexte de faire punir le crime d'usure dont on croyoit pouvoir se plaindre, l'on s'étoit porté à des crimes beaucoup plus graves, et plus énormes encore, en employant le complot, et la machination entre plusieurs paysans, pour concerter la perte des Juifs sur les quels on faisoit tomber l'accusation d'usure. Quelques uns des paysans se chargeoient du rôle de dénonciateurs, le reste étoit réservé à porter témoignages capables de faire réussir les dénonciations, et tous ensemble s'obligeoient à tout événement, à supporter les frais qu'entrainoient leurs tentatives. Un complot de cette nature, ayant été découvert par l'attention ordinaire de la Cour sur l'appel d'une instruction en cas d'usure, commencé au Baillage de Vic, en l'année 1740, la Cour s'y pourvut par un arrêt; et pour remédier avec efficacité à un abus aussy dangereux pour l'avenir, elle ordonna que les chambres seroient consultées. Une autre machination de cette espèce ayant occasionné en l'année 1747, il fût fait déffences à tous juges du ressort de recevoir d'aucuns particuliers, des plaintes générales aux fins de faire informer d'autres faits d'usure que de ceux qui concernent

same occured in Lorraine, where the Jews denounced a "peasants' conspiracy against the Jews". On Apr. 5, 1775, the Sovereign Court of Lorraine and Barrois prohibited such unconvincing accusations against Jews.[294]

All this does not prove that Jews did not at all practice usury, and to seek such proof is not the author's aim. Jews themselves denounced usurers.[295] But even honest Jewish creditors were often

---

personnellement les plaignans, et sur les réquisitions de la partie publique. Cet arrêt sembloit avoir mis fin à des voyes odieuses et punissables employées jusque là pour perdre ceux sur qui se réunissoit la malignité et la noirceur des complots. Mais comme l'on a pas pris dans les pays voisins du Ressort les mêmes précautions sur la matière dont il s'agit, que celles renfermées dans l'arrêt de la Cour du 17 May 1747, l'on y voit des particuliers se faire publiquement un titre lucratif de la licence qu'ils se donnent d'exciter des émotions pour rançonner ceux qu'ils alarment par des trames, et des machinations aussi répréhensibles, le fruit qu'ils en retirent a reproduit sous les yeux de la Cour la manœuvre que son arrêt a déjà condamné. Le 7 de ce mois il s'est présenté au substitut du procureur fiscal du Baillage de l'Evêché quatre particuliers de Bertring... qui luy ont dénoncé cinq Juifs comme coupables d'avoir commis dans le ressort de ce Baillage... des usures outrées, en percevant sur les billets des intérêts considérables, ils expriment que ce crime tend à ruiner la contrée... Cette dénonciation est sans doute une contravention bien formelle à l'arrêt du 17 May 1747; il est fait défences de recevoir des plaintes générales, l'on ne peut informer d'autres faits d'usure que de ceux qui concernent personnellement les plaignans, or icy les dénonciateurs ne désignent, et n'articulent aucuns faits positifs qui leurs soient personnels, ils se plaignent au nom de différents villages pour le ressort entier du Baillage de Vic. Ce n'est pas assez, ils semblent faire accuser ceux qu'ils dénoncent par toute la contrée elle même... En conséquence, la dénonciation générale, en cas d'usure, reçue le 7 du présent mois par le substitut du procureur fiscal de l'Evêché, être déclarée nulle, les informations d'informer, information et autres procédures faites en conséquence être cassées et annulées, sauf aux particuliers qui ont souscrit ladite dénonciation à se pourvoir s'ils se croyent fondés pour raison des faits d'usure qui pourroient les concerner personnellement... La Cour... ordonne que l'arrêt de Règlement de la Cour du 17 May 1747 sera exécuté suivant sa forme et teneur. En conséquence... fait défences aux officiers du Baillage de Vic de contrevenir dorénavant audit arrêt de Règlement à peine de demeurer responsables en leurs noms des dommages et intérêts des parties..." ("Extrait des Registres du Greffe du cy devant Parlement de Metz transféré à Nancy, du 28 juin 1757". AN,29AP3). Cf. Clément, oc, p. 191-92; Anchel, oc, p. 209.

[294] Ibidem and: Arrest de la Cour Souveraine de Lorraine et Barrois, qui condamne Jean-Balthazard Differdange, Huissier Royal à Thionville, et Antoine Godard, Marchand Tanneur à Kedange, en réparations et dommages-intérêts, pour avoir cherchés à nuire à l'état et à l'honneur de la Nation Juive, par des certificats mandiés, dans lesquels on a fait insérer que les Juifs ruinoient les Habitans de la Contrée par des usures énormes, et qu'ils refusoient la remise des titres acquittés. Du cinq Avril mil sept cent soixante-quinze (Nancy) Placard.

[295] Samuel Lévi — a pupil of Rabbi Meir Caremoli (Carmoly) — who on Nov. 16, 1700, was appointed Chef Rabbi of Upper Alsace by the King wrote in a petition against the communities which fought him that he tried to convince them not to take too high interest on loans. In 1717, the Alsatian Jews declared in a memorandum to the King's State Council that they would gladly expell usurers from the Jewish communities, such cases had already happened. In 1786, the Jewish community of Metz prepared a memorandum to the army officers asking them for the names of those Jewish creditors who granted loans to soldiers under legal age; in such cases the loans would be annulled. At the beginning of the 18th century the Jewish community of Metz posted announcements in the Synagogue denouncing those Jews who discredited the Jewish name by their dishonest activities and lawsuits. Carmoly, Histoire des Israélites en France. Revue Orientale, vol. II (1842) p. 242; de Boug, oc, vol. I, p. 360; Mémoire pour les Juifs établis en Alsace (sl [1717]); Is. Loeb, oc, p. 188; Isaïe-Ber-Bing, Mémoire particulier pour la communauté des Juifs établis à Metz [M 1790] p. 10; AcM,Ce57-58. On the

persecuted by their inscrupulous debtors as usurers. '''

Some decrees aimed against usurers resulted in aggravating the crisis of credit.'''

26. PSYCHOLOGICAL PROPAGANDA AGAINST JEWS IN THE LAW-COURTS

In lawsuits between Jews and Gentiles, especially between creditors and debtors, the latters took advantage of the traditional hatred against Jews.

The term *Jew* was used as frequently as possible. The word *Juif* (Jew) prefixed to a name in court or in everyday life was not parallel to the terms like "the peasant X," "the butcher Y," "the officer Z," "A of Colmar," "B of Huningue," etc., which gave the social status, profession, or place of residence of non-Jews. *Jew* in such cases did nothing to fix the profession or residence of the individual, but merely vented anti-Jewish malice, when for example Abraham Lévy was called "the Jew Abraham Lévy." Jews often protested against this discriminatory practice, which, as a matter of fact, was severely condemned even before 1789. In the '70s of the 18th century, M. Vatiaud of the Royal Agricultural Society of Laon wrote in his unpublished study submitted for the Metz Academy's contest on Jews (1785-1787) that in official docu-

---

19th century fight of Jews against usury see: Z. Szajkowski, *Agricultural Credit and Napoleon's anti-Jewish Decrees* (New York 1953) p. 94-103.
²⁹⁶ Decrees of 1706 and Aug. 26, 1710, ordered the Metz Jews to use only the French language and official paper for their bookkeeping. So many Jews were then sentenced for infringing against this order that special forms of sentences were printed (AcM,Col6. *Arrêt du Parlement de Metz, qui condamne les marchands et négociants juifs de la ville de Metz en l'amende, faute par eux d'avoir tenu leurs registres en papier timbré, et les oblige à en tenir à l'avenir. Du 22 juin* 1708 [M 1708]. Gentiles were not forced to use French for their bookkeeping. According to the Alsatian administration, too, Jews used Hebrew and Yiddish for dishonest activities. Much later, in 1793, the Council of Lower Rhine prohibited the use of Hebrew in the private or business correspondence between Jews. *Conseil général du Bas-Rhin. Défense de correspondre en langue hébraïque* (S 11 juin 1793) 4 p. (*Cf.* the catalogue of Berger-Levrault, vol. V, p. 9). See p. 98.
²⁹⁷ On Dec. 23, 1773, the Sovereign Council ordered that loan-contracts be drawn up and signed only in offices of notaries or other officials and in the presence of honorable men if the notaries were called outside their office. But peasants refused to accept loans in the presence of witnesses and in order to avoid such formalities, I.O.U.s and similar acts were dated in neighboring provinces. A decree of Jan. 7, 1783, prohibited this practice. *ERCSA. Du 23 Décembre* 1772 (C 1772) Placard. AmS,AA2381 & AdBR,C334; *ERCSA. Du 7 Janvier* 1783 (C 1783) 3 p. AN,K1142-55. The practice of drawing up documents in neighboring provinces existed also in cases not involving Jews: *Arrest du Conseil d'Estat du Roy, par lequel Sa Majesté défend à tous ses Sujets domiciliés dans les Généralités de Metz et Champagne limitrophes de la Lorraine, d'y aller ou envoyer leurs Procurations pour passer des Actes... Du 13 Décembre* 1740. *Extrait des Registres du Conseil d'Estat* (P 1741); *Arrest du Conseil d'Estat du Roy, par lequel Sa Majesté fait deffenses à tous ses sujets domiciliés en Franche-Comté, d'aller en Lorraine ou d'y envoyer leurs Procurations pour passer des Actes entr'eux... Du 26 Juin* 1742 (P 1743); *Déclaration du Roy qui fixe le Tribunal où doivent être discutez les Biens d'un Débiteur par lui possedez en même tems en France et en Lorraine. Donnée à Versailles le neuvième jour d'Avril* 1747 (P 1747). AN,AD-XVI-6A.

ments judges and other officials should be forbidden to qualify
Jews otherwise than by their names, professions and residence and
should not use the word "Jew".[¹]

The terme *Jew* was repeated 53 times in a 1782 factum of Jean
Rey against Leib Ulmann and 90 times in a factum of Joseph
Leymont and Giles Tressa against Aaron Simon.[²] In most cases
the term *Jew* went together with strongly worded anti-Jewish
slogans and appeals to the Catholic and anti-Jewish sentiments of
the judges.[³] In a factum of 1789, against Wolf Lévy, his debtor,
Baron de Haindel, asked his judges not to permit the property
which had belonged for many generations to his family to fall

---

[¹] "Les juges, officiers ou ecclésiastiques auront soin dans tous les
actes de leur ministère qui concerneront les Juifs, de ne leur point donner
cette qualification de Juifs, autant que faire se pourra, mais ils les dési-
gneront seulement sous les noms de leurs états, qualités ou professions, ou
s'ils n'en ont point, par ceux des pays d'où ils seraient, ou qu'ils habiteront,
en évitant de faire entendre la religion qu'ils professent." BmM,ms.1350,
p. 655-56. In the 19th century, Jews very frequently protested against using
the word Jew in legal cases. During the post-Napoleonic Restoration the
Judge Borely prohibited such practice in his court of Marseille (*AI*, vol.
LIII, 1892, p. 118). On Nov. 23, 1841 and in 1858, the Central Jewish Consistory protested against this practice in the courts (AN,F19-11031). The
attorney L. Aron Abraham, of Jewish origin, who tried to change his name,
wrote in a memorandum of the 1830's to the Minister of Justice: "Mon
nom m'est à charge parce que je dois vivre dans une petite ville de province... où, quoi qu'en disent les prôneurs de ce siècle des lumières, l'ignorance et les préjugés règnent encore... Mon nom [est un] obstacle à mon
avancement au barreau... Mon nom entrave ma faculté d'aller et de venir...
Mon nom s'oppose à mon mariage avec une femme chrétienne". *Mémoire
adressé à Son Excellence Monseigneur le Garde-des-Sceaux, par L. Aron
Abraham, licencié en droit, ...à l'appui d'une pétition en changement de
leur prétendu nom d'Aron Abraham en celui de Level...* (sl nd) 14 p. BN,Ln
27-671.
   Even a Jew's change of residence was used by his debtor as an excuse
to attack him: *Mémoire pour Pierre Delagrange... de Metz... contre le Sieur
Mayer Hadamar, Juifs, résidant à Metz, depuis Avril dernier, & ci-devant à
Paris* (M [1784] 8 p. BmM,TC-3-66.
[²] *Mémoire pour Joseph Leymont et Gilles Tressa... de Landau... contre
Aaron Simon, Juif... et encore contre Isaac Salomon, aussy Juif...* (sl nd)
35 p. AmS,vol.942; *Précis pour Jean Rey... contre Leib Ullmann, Juif de
Loumschwiller* (C [1782]) 44 p. BuS100669.
[³] "Sa chute présage celle de l'usure, si au contraire, il réussit, la ruine
du chrétien devient inséparable de son commerce avec le Juif"; "les vices
de son odieuse nation"; "le judaïsme par *le poids* de ses moyens a tâché
d'étouffer la procédure"; "son rabbin nous apprend qu'il suffit d'être Juif
pour prendre des intérêts outrés et user de surpris..."; "les malheureuses
victimes à secouer le joug judaïque;" *Mémoire pour Jacque Korum, Antoine
Hann et consorts de Bercheim... contre Abraham Sée, Juif de Berckheim...*
(Sl, [1744] 9 p.; *Supplément pour Jacque Korum... contre Abraham Sée* (Sl,
174-) 5 p.; *Défense d'Abraham Sée, Juif demeurant à Berkheim* (Sl, [174-])
13 p. BN,naf22705f.298,303,306;BmC5353. "L'appelant, toujours Juif..."; "Toute
autre qu'un Juif aurait donné les mains à une proposition si raisonnable";
"mauvaise foi du Juif"; "la sentence... ne peut être contestée que par un
Juif"; "cette nouvelle production de la chicane et du Rabinisme:" *Précis
pour Jean Rey... contre Leib Ullmann, Juif de Loumschwiller* (C [1782])
44 p. BuS,100669. "[Weill] ne triomphera pas de la justice, et de la simplicité
d'un Paysan:" Mathieu l'aîné et M. Coenin, procureur, *Plaise à Nosseigneurs
du Conseil Souverain d'Alsace d'avoir pour recommandée en justice l'instance. D'entre Jean Grollmond, Bourgeois de Guémar appelant de la sentence
rendue par le Baillis de Ribeauvillé le 21 May 1718 et demandeur en requête,
contre Meyer Weill, Juif demeurant audit Ribeauvillé...* (Sl nd) 39 p. BN,naf
22705f.148.
   Even in ordinances of the Sovereign Council the term *Jew* went together with anti-Jewish slogans, e.g.: "la ruse & la fraude judaïque... ces
monstres de la société civile", etc. in the ordinance of Jan. 19, 1717. Corberon, *Recueil*, vol. II, p. 601-602.

into the hands of a Jew."' Not only Gentile debtors, but even criminals used anti-Jewish slogans for their defense. Joseph Cahen of Metz sold cattle to butchers on credit. One of the latters, Jacques Durand, murdered the Jew and in his defense he stated that he was a victim of a Jewish conspiracy against the Catholics."' Debtors used anti-Jewish slogans even in cases where their creditors were Jews converted to Catholicism."'

The Jews protested against this kind of psychological warfare in the law-courts. Abraham Sée stated in a factum against his debtor that it was too easy to cry out for help against a Jew; some people thought, he wrote, that against Jews any action was lawful. In 1784 three Paris attorneys wrote in a factum for the Jewish merchant Hayem Worms of Lorraine that in the eyes of the common people the Jew was always the guilty one, because he was a Jew. The attorneys of the Metz Jew Joseph Gougenheim stated in a factum of 1783 that he was a Jew, but that he was nevertheless not less honest than Gentiles and even if he was a Jew, he would not give up his just rights granted to creditors by the law."'

---

[301] *Précis pour le Baron de Haindel...* (P 1789) 17 p.; *Mémoire pour Wolf Lévy, banquier à Strasbourg; contre le baron de Haindel...* (Sl nd) 81 p.; *Réponse pour le Baron de Haindel, au mémoire des Sieurs Lévi et consorts* (Sl nd) 94 p. BuS100524-26. In this lawsuit the debtor used a psychological argument which was very frequently used by debtors, namely that he himself did not take the loan, that the debt was only a part of his parents' inheritance and that he was made to suffer without cause ("le baron de Haindel oppose la substitution pour que les biens que ses ancêtres lui ont transmis ne soient pas employés à payer ce qu'il ne doit pas personnellement." "Que, le Conseil de Sa Majesté veuille un moment se peindre, d'un côté, les sept frères de Haindel, unis par le sang, par l'amitié, par l'honneur, et mus par les plus nobles sentiments... se dépouillant eux-mêmes des droits de la propriété pour établir sur un fondement durable la gloire de leur maison, pour soutenir leurs descendans au service de la patrie et mettre leurs biens et leurs noms à l'abri des révolutions, de la mort et du temps. De l'autre côté, les Juifs et les usuriers, rassemblés autour d'un malheureux jeune homme pour épier ses fautes ou ses faiblesses... pour vivre de ses erreurs").

[302] *Appelans à leurs secours les funestes préjugés introduits autrefois par l'ignorance ou par l'avarice contre la Nation Juive". "L'accusation... est l'ouvrage de la fureur dont les Juifs sont animés contre le nom & le sang des Chrétiens": Poutet, *Factum pour Esther Norden, veuve de Joseph Cahen, Juif, habitant de la ville de Metz, plaignante et appelante. Contre Jacques Durand, marchand boucher...* (M 1702) 11 p.; *Factum servant de défenses pour Jacques Durand... contre Esther Norden...* (M 1702) 17 p. BN,naf22705 f.62&68.

[303] E.g., Joseph Oudinot of Lorraine, a debtor of Paul Volsky of Varsovie, a "first servant of the Minister," who was of Jewish origin, *Mémoire pour le Sieur Joseph Oudinot... contre Paul Volsky, Juif converti de Varsovie* (N [1784]) 67 p. BN,naf22706f.126. Frequently converted Jews stated that they fell victims of the Jews, e.g., the converted Jew Jean Charles Schwabe, whose business went bankrupt, maintained in 1730 that he had been ruined by Jewish vengeance. [Jean Charles Schwabe,] *Au Roi et à' Nosseigneurs de Son Conseil* (sl 1730) 8 p. BN,fol.F3-15560.
This kind of psychological warfare was used even in lawsuits where both sides were Jews, e.g., in the 1730-36 conflict between the two brothers Isaac and Joseph Kahn of Obernheim who had a concession on salt. The attorney of one of them stated: "They are all Jews" — *ce sont tous des Juifs* (ZS). In 1747, the Jew Olry Alcan stated in a lawsuit with the Lorraine Rabbi Nehemiaz Raicher that the latter was an "usurious merchant" (*marchand usurier*): De Bourcier de Montureaux, *Précis pour Nahemiaz Racher, Rabbin des Juifs de Lorraine, demeurant à Metz* (N 1744) 5 p. BN,naf22705f. 290.

[304] *Défense d'Abraham Sée...* (sl [1744]) 5 p. BN,naf22705f.306. *Cf.:*

On March 31, 1732, the Sovereign Council of Alsace heard the
above-mentioned pleas of the City of Wintzenheim requesting
permission to limit the number of Jews to four families, and the
pleas of the Jews' attorneys Bruges and Wilhelm. The two attorneys
maintained that Wintzenheim used the argument of usury as
justification of their anti-Jewish action, and that usury became an
excuse for attacking Jews in the law-courts and an argument for
the creation of a public opinion frequently capable of killing the
truth. The case of a lone Jewish usurer is taken as proof of usurious
practices of the entire Jewish nation. But where are the proofs
of usurious practices of the Wintzenheim Jews? How many Jewish
usurers of Wintzenheim were brought to justice?" On another
occasion, during an appeal of the Jews to the Sovereign Council
against penalizing a Jew for baking bread on the eve of a Jewish
holiday, which happened to be on a Sunday, Bruges, one of the
best Alsatian attorneys, stated that in the courts anything could

Mémore pour Jacques Korum... contre Abraham Sée (sl [1744] 9 p. and
Supplément pour Jacques Korum... contre Abraham Sée (sl nd) 5 p. BN,naf
22705f.298 & 303. "Aux yeux d'une populace insensée, le Juif a toujours tort,
parce qu'il est Juif:" *Mémoire pour le sieur Hayem Worms, négociant juif...*
(P 1784) p. 1. BN,4F33106. "Il est né Juif, mais il ne cède pas pour cela aux
intimés du côté des sentiments:" Roederer et autres, *A la requête de Joseph
Gougenheim, Juif...* (M 1783) p. 87. BmM,TC2/40. The attorney of the well-
known Nancy banker Moyse Alcan wrote in a 1738 factum against the
Compagnie d'Aubonne that his opponents were too sure of themselves,
probably because Alcan was a Jew — "L'air d'assurance... a sans doute
prévenu, surtout contre un homme de sa race:" *Mémoire pour Moyse Alcan,
Juif, banquier à Nancy. Contre les Directeurs de la ci-devant Compagnie de
Commerce de Lorraine, dite d'Aubonne* (L 1738) 15 p. *Cf. Réponse des directeurs de la dernière Compagnie de Commerce de Lorraine, au Mémoire de
Moyse Alcan, Juif* (N sd) 9 p.; *Réponse de Moïse Alcan au second Mémoire
des Directeurs de la ci-devant Compagnie de Commerce, dite d'Aubonne* (N
1738) 5 p.; BN,naf22705f.273,289,294; Mᵉ Marcot, *Supplément pour le Sieur
Dominique Anthoine, intimé, contre Moyse Alcan, Juif appelant* (N 1718)
4 p.; Mᵉ Fournier, *Réponse pour Moyse Alcan, au Mémoire du Sieur Dominique Anthoine* (N 1719) 7 p.; BN,naf22705f.211 & 228. *Mémoire pour Moyse
Alcan, Juif, demeurant ci-devant en la ville de Nancy* (N 17-) 4 p. BN,naf
22705f.211,228,273,289,294 and FIII-290. "Il est absurde et odieux à un débiteur de vouloir caractériser d'une manière défavorable les motifs de son
créancier légitime, et de tenter d'éluder par une voye aussi lâche, une
obligation" (Roederer's brief for the Jewish creditor Jacob Emmeric, AN,
29AP100).
ᵃᵒ⁵ "Quand donc cette communauté de Wintzenheim vient exposer que
les Juifs du lieu dévorent les habitants chrétiens par leurs usures, et que
par cette raison, il faut réduire à quatre les familles juives de Wintzenheim, ce n'est qu'un moyen que l'imposture a fait inventer... Si il est un
lieu commun usé et rebattu dans le Barreau, c'est celuy de l'usure des
Juifs: on en surprend quelques-uns au fait et de là on conclut que tous sont
entichés de ce vice. C'est une étrange chose que l'opinion: au dire de Sopho-
cle, elle étouffe la vérité: *véritable potentior et opinio.* Mais où sont donc
ces preuves de cette usure qui vous dévore, demandeurs? Quels sont les
tribunaux qui ont ressenti de vos plaintes?... Combien de procès, le Conseil
a-t-il jugé entre des habitans et des Juifs de Witzenheim... Mais... Si l'on
chasse tous les Juifs à quatre près, vous laissez quatre usuriers... Les Juifs,
dites-vous, sont notoirement des créanciers impitoyables. Si vous les con-
naissez tels, rien ne vous oblige de contracter avec eux: empruntez plutôt
de ces chrétiens, qui, pour faire faire votre somme vous donneront de mauvais débiteurs ou vous feront prendre à haut prix des denrées dont vous
n'avez pas besoin, et qu'ils rachèteront de vous presque pour rien. Exter-
minez de la Province non seulement les gens qu'on accuse d'être usuriers,
mais encore une bonne partie de ceux qui placent à intérêt leur argent, et
qui sont en extérieur chrétien, ruinent les sujets plus que les Juifs." AdHR,
fonds Corberon-Bruges 24. *Cf.* note 193.

happen to a Jew, that he might even be forced to observe Catholic holidays which so many Catholics themselves did not observe."' Frequently Jews were insulted and even physically assaulted in the law-courts."'

27. THE ISSUE OF USURY AGAINST MINORS

One of the most popular slogans against Jewish creditors was that their debtors were frequently minors or irresponsible persons. This was also often pointed out in the law-courts by the families or attorneys of debtors not only of Jews, but also of Gentile creditors."' Usually the attorney started his plea with a sentimental description of his client's status while taking the loan, that he had then been a minor and should not be held responsible for the acts of his youth."' Some debtors or their attorneys stated that Jewish creditors changed the original dates on the I.O.U.s, so that they could not be fined for granting loans to minors."' Jews were arrested even for granting loans to adult sons of families."' Of course, honest families were frequently ruined because of loans that were taken by youthful debtors who liked to enjoy themselves."'

---

²⁰⁶ AdHR,fonds Corberon-Bruges 24. *Cf.* notes 193 and 305 and de Boug, *oc*, vol. I, p. 188 ("Ordonnance du Conseil pour faire observer par les Juifs les Dimanches et les Fêtes," Nov. 27, 1690), vol. II, p. 855. This did not prevent Bruges from attacking Jews in cases where he was attorney for Jews' opponents. On the other hand, anti-Jewish leaders were sometimes attorneys of Jews. The famous Reubell, who fought against the Jewish emancipation, was the Jews' attorney in a lawsuit between Jews and the *Grand Conseil* of the district of Bern. This was one of the causes of his antipathy towards Switzerland. *Lettre d'un alsacien, sur les Juifs d'Alsace...* (P 1790) p. 6; P. L. Hanet-Cléry, *Mémoires* (P 1825) vol. II, p. 19; J. Godechot, *Les Commissaires aux armées sous le Directoire* (P 1937) vol. II, p. 15-16.

²⁰⁷ Because of a similar assault on the Jew Olry Cahen of Metz, the Metz Parliament prohibited attacks upon Jews or other persons in the law-courts. *ACPM portant defenses à tous Laquais d'insulter dans l'enclos du Palais n'y ailleurs, aucuns Juifs n'y autres Plaideurs* [M 1763]. Placard. BmN320f.145.

²⁰⁸ A Lorraine debtor signed in March 1789 an I.O.U. for 8,000 pounds for a loan granted him by a Gentile. Later he refused to repay the debt. He maintained that he took the loan only in order to help an irresponsible minor-debtor pay his debts. *Précis pour Jean Pierre Goeury... contre Nicolas Bazile Prud'homme...* (N sd). BmN,ZZ19-7.

²⁰⁹ Such was, e.g. the plea of the attorney of Baron de Schauenbourg, seignior of Soutzbach, against Simon Lévy of Wintzenheim and Gentile creditors, too, in the 1760's: "Le Sr. Schauenburg étant mineur s'est livré avec l'inconsidération, qui était si pardonnable à cet âge, aux emprunts ruineux et usuraires, que lui proposaient les Juifs." *Précis de la cause d'entre le Sr. Baron de Schauenbourg...* [C 176-] p. 2. AmS,vol.944.

²¹⁰ *Ibidem.*

²¹¹ This happened to the creditor Isaac Lévy of Imling, who was a creditor of the Gentile Renault. The Jew's attorney stated in a 1758 factum that such an act of injustice never happened in the annals of justice: Mᵉ Jacquemin, avocat, *A Nosseigneurs, Nosseigneurs de la Cour Souveraine de Lorraine et Barrois, supplie humblement Isaac, habitant d'Imling... contre les Sieurs Renault...* (N 1758) 16 p.; *Premier interrogatoire du Sieur Renault fils, du 7 Juillet* 1757 (N 1758) 11 p. BN,naf22706f.22.

²¹² The youthful son of Le Tixerant of St.-Mihiel was sentenced to prison for failure to repay a debt of 8,000 pounds to his Jewish creditors Cayen and Wol of Nancy (1784-85): *Mémoire à consulter pour le Sr. Le Tixerant...* [N 1787] 84 p. BmN,ZZ172-1.

Usurers found easy victims among such young men. Still, debtors who refused to repay their debts often charged that their creditors tried to ruin minors. Following is an example: The Jews Aron Meyer of Moutzig and Meyer Blein of Metz sold, in 1747, their properties to the attorney François Joseph Schneider for 33,595 pounds. The attorney paid only a first installment of 7,970 pounds, which he took from his wife's dowry, but later he refused to pay the remainder of the sum or to return the properties. His argument was that because in the meantime his wife had died, his minor children had become—in accordance with his marriage contract—proprietors of one-half of his property, including the properties bought from the Jews, and that according to the law his children's property could not be taken away from them.[313] In fact, the courts frequently ordered even minors to repay their debts.[314] It is worth while to note that according to the Alsatian jurisprudence Jews at the age of 13 years were no longer minors and their signatures on commerce and credit documents were recognized as valid.[315] The Metz Parliament likewise rendered a similar decision on June 21, 1758, and even ruled that Jewish girls were no longer considered minors at the age of 12. Of course, this was contrary to the French jurisdiction, but the Parliament took into consideration not the laws of France, but the religious Jewish principles of the Metz Ghetto.[316]

28. JEWISH DEMANDS TO JUDGE CASES OF USURY IN ROYAL LAW-COURTS

Jews were frequently not permitted to bear witness in criminal or civil lawsuits. On July 9, 1721, the Alsatian Sovereign Council forbade Jews to bear witness in the lawsuit between the Protestant Pastor Golberi and Rabbi Hirtz Reinau of Soultz, and on Feb. 3 and 10, 1740, in the lawsuit of the Jew Gabriel Reinau of Guebwiller against Luc Streckheisen of Basel. On Dec. 14, 1690, the Metz Parliament also decided that a Jew could not bear witness for a Jew against a Gentile.[317] Even the Paris attorney Jacques Godard (who, during the Revolution, fought for Jewish emancipation)[318]

[313] Me Georges de Broussey et Me Thannberger, *Précis de la cause d'entre... enfans mineurs... de Me François Joseph Schneider... contre Aron Meyer, Juif de Moutzig* (Sl, 17-) 8 p. AmS,vol.943.
[314] On Feb. 4, 1695, the Sovereign Council sentenced a minor-debtor to repay his debt to Le Harel (a Gentile creditor), even if the debtor's property were to be sold by judicial order: N. de Corberon, *Essay...*
[315] Sentences of the Sovereign Council: in the lawsuit of Emanuel and Salomon Dreyfus of Blotzheim appealing against a sentence of the bailiff on Oct. 15, 1763; in the lawsuit between Simon Hussmann of Herrlisheim against Simon Cochet and Meyer Lévy of Wintzenheim, Dec. 23, 1756; in the lawsuit of J. J. Bursteim of Basel against Emmanuel and Salomon Dreyfus of Blotzheim, Feb. 13, 1764; in the lawsuit betewen the non-Jewish creditor Jean Rudler of Guebwiller and his Jewish debtor Moise Dreyfus of Hattstat, Feb. 18, 1704 (AdHR,E,coll.Wendl.48-16p.15; Corberon, *oc.*).
[316] A. Cahen, *Le Rabbinat de Metz...* Extr. de la *REJ*, p. 290.
[317] Corberon, *oc*; R. Clément, *oc*, p. 142-43.
[318] [Jacques Godard,] *Adresse présentée à l'Assemblée Nationale le 28*

192

declared in a 1787 brief that in criminal lawsuits Jews should not be allowed to bear witness against Christians."'

The practice of *More judaïco* (a special text for Jews' oaths in the law-courts) also existed in the Northeastern French provinces. (This practice was abolished as late as in the 1840's.)'" It is worth

Août 1789 par les Juifs résidant à Paris (P 1789); [Ibid,] *Pétition des Juifs... le 28 Janvier 1790...* (P 1790), édition allemande: *Unterthänige Vorstellung der in Frankreich unsässigen Juden...* (S 1790); Ibid, *Lettre des Juifs établis en France à M. le Président de l'Assemblée nationale* (P 1790); Ibid, *Discours prononcé le 28 Janvier 1790, en présentant à l'Assemblée générale de la Commune une députation des Juifs de Paris* (P 1790); Ibid, [Discours,] in: *Recueil de pièces relatives à l'admission des Juifs à l'état civil* (P 1790).

"" Jacques Godard, Consultation, p. 95-103 in: M. Ch. M. J. Dupaty, *Justification de sept hommes, condamnés par le Parlement de Metz en 1769, sur les seules dépositions de Juifs-plaignans...* (P 1787) 112+16 p. (4°), JTS, édition in 8°: BN,Ld184-276. *Cf.* J. Liblin, *Les sept martyrs de Lutzelbourg et les précurseurs de Schinderhannes, 1768-1786* (C 1864) 30 p. BuS101433. Dupaty's factum was written in connection with an appeal of the heirs of 7 Gentiles who were sentenced in 1769 by the Metz Parliament to be hanged for a robbery against Jews. The famous Metz attorney Roederer prepared a reply to Dupaty's factum ("Notes pour répondre à M. Dupaty", AN,29AP3). In the year XIII an appeal of the heirs was still pending (AN,BB16-467).

"" On the fight for and against the *More judaïco* in the 19th century see: A. Crémieux, *Plaidoyers sur cette question: le Juif français doit-il être soumis à prêter le serment More judaïco* (Nismes 1827) 32 p.; Ibid, *Second plaidoyer sur cette question...* (Nismes 1827) 40 p. BN,Ld184-212 & 12bis; Ibid, Plaidoyer devant le Tribunal de Saverne. Résistance d'un rabbin au Serment More judaïco. Audience du 31 Décembre 1838, in: *Persécution contre les Juifs. Extrait de l'observateur des Tribunaux, tome Ier, nouv. série de 1840* (Sl 1840) 72 p., p. 18-72. BmM,cart.32-33 ("Dans vos esprits, Messieurs, vivent encore ces tristes préjugés, dont le génie même de Napoléon ne fut pas exempt: les Juifs de 1839 sont pour vous les Juifs de 1539... Louis XVIII refusa de renouveler ce décret impie [du 17 Mars 1808]; mais la Restauration amenait après elle son inévitable cortège d'anciens préjugés. A peine donc si les Israélites peuvent compter en France vingt-cinq années d'émancipation. Eh bien! Je le dis hautement, Messieurs, ce qu'ils ont fait dans ce quart de siècle, c'est un miracle!", p. 60, 64.); Xavier Chauffour, *Mémoire adressée à Monsieur le Garde des Sceaux, Ministre de justice* (Mulhouse 1825) 8 p.; Ibid, *Observations sur le serment More judaïco déféré aux Juifs d'Alsace en matière civile, comme serment litis décisoire* (C 1844) 63+36 p. Litho. BN,Ld184-166 & 201; Guillet, *Le Juif français doit-il prêter serment More judaïco* (P 1827); S. Bloch, le Serment juif. *Régénération* vol. I-II (S 1836-7); *Serment dit More judaïco. Déclarations de Messieurs les Grands Rabbins des Consistoires Israélites de France* (P 1844) 16 p. AN,F19-11030; *Serment More judaïco, Extraits des Archives Israélites de France* (P 1844) 48 p. JTS; *Réponse du Consistoire Israélite de la circonscription de Colmar aux articles insérés dans les numéros des 8 et 12 ce mois du Courrier d'Alsace sur l'Abolition du serment More judaïco.* (C 22 Mars 1846) 3 p.; M. Hemerdinger, Le Serment More judaïco. *AI*, vol. V, p. 394, 490; Benoit-Lévy, Le Serment More judaïco. *UI*, vol. XXV, p. 716, 752, vol. XXVI, p. 169, 331; *La Gazette des Tribunaux* (1er Mars 1826, 3 Nov. 1827, 29 Oct. 1827, 22 Mai 1828); *Le Courrier des Tribunaux* (17 Juin 1827, 9 9 Fév. 1828, 11 Nov. 1829); *Recueil des arrêts de la Cour de Colmar*, vol. XXIII, p. 161; S. Posener, *Adolphe Crémieux* (P 1933) vol. I, p. 76-87; R. Anchel, *Napoléon et les Juifs* (P 1928) p. 559-568. On the practice of *More judaïco* in the German States see: Litteratur des Judenheides. *Zeitschrift für hebräische Bibliographie*, vol. I (1896-97) p. 17-22. In 1815, the courts of Upper Rhine requested that even Jewish women be bound by the *More judaïco* (ArchCC, 9. A letter from the Wintzenheim Consistory dated June 2, 1815). In 1809, the Court of appeals of Colmar based its decision of *More judaïco* on a German law of many centuries prior to 1789 (ArchCC, Copies of letters, vol. I, p. 140-41). Even the liberal newspaper *Courrier d'Alsace* protested in March 1846 against the decision of the Supreme Court of Appeals which abolished the practice of *More judaïco*. According to the historian A. Mathiez the *More judaïco* was not an act of intolerance toward Jews, but a part of the general fight against usury (*Annales historiques de la Révolution française*, vol. V (1928) p. 374). See also: Abr. Lévy, Le grand-rabbin

while to note that the Alsatian Sovereign Council's regulation of
June 10, 1739, on the *More judaïco* was published not as a purely
anti-Jewish order, but because of a conflict in connection with
a lawsuit of the Jewish creditor Lazare Brunschvick of Thann against
the widow of Jacques Rudler, Mayor of Willer. The Jew had to
take an oath and the widow requested that he do it before the
official Rabbi of Ribeauvillé who was appointed by royal Letters
patent. The Jew demanded that the widow pay the expenses
for bringing the Rabbi to the court. The Council then published
a regulation requiring the Jews to take oath in their manner and
language (*langue vulgaire*).[21] Later on the Letters patent of July 10,
1784, on Alsatian Jews fixed the *More judaïco* as forced upon Jews.
Nothing is known about any 18th century Jewish protests against
this custom. Curiously, the anti-Jewish City of Strasbourg disliked
this practice. In a letter of Oct. 18, 1769, de Meaupeou wrote to
the attorney de Boug that the *More judaïco* was not applied in the
law-courts under the jurisdiction of the City, but that recently
two Jewish witnesses had refused to take oath otherwise than
before the Rabbi, in accordance with the Sovereign Council's regulation of June 10, 1739. Should the *More judaïco* be applied in the
court, the expenses for bringing the Rabbi to the court would
aggravate the judicial budget. De Boug, one of the best jurists in
Alsace and author of a collection of decisions of the Council, replied
in a written brief on Oct. 30, 1769, that the use of the *More judaïco*
had already been regulated in 1739, but that in its contents this
oath was similar to any oath of Christians and should be taken
before a judge, as was the practice with Jews outside of Alsace.
The two Jews had no right to refuse taking oath before the judge.
According to de Boug the *More judaïco* was unknown in some lower
Alsatian courts and he himself saw Jews taking the oath before
the Council without a Rabbi; he knew only one case of practicing
the *More judaïco* before the Council, in a lawsuit against Aron
Bloch of Bischeim, who propagandized among the peasants inducing
them to emigrate, which was against the law. According to de
Boug, who was strongly anti-Jewish-minded, the *More judaïco* was
not a law in Alsace, but a custom.[22]

Isidor et le serment More judaïco. *UI*, vol. XXXXIV (1889) p. 373-74; L.
K.[ahn], Le Serment judaïque. *AI*, vol. XXXXVII (1892) p. 270-71. On a
More judaïco case in a Paris law-court in 1872 see: R., Le Serment More
judaïco à Paris. *AI*, vol. XXXIII (1872) p. 621-22.

[321] de Corberon, *oc.*; de Boug, *oc*, vol. II, p 208, 328. In 1739 the widow
and children of Jacques Rudler of Willer were sentenced to repay to Lazard
Brunschwick a 1731 loan of 1,539 pounds. As the Jew did not have any
cash-books, he had to take an oath before the Rabbi. The debtors asked
to bring the Royal Rabbi (appointed by Letters patent). The Jew agreed
if the debtors would pay the expenses. As the debtors did not reply, the
Sovereign Council ordered them on June 10, 1739 to repay the debt. *ERCSA*
[10 *Juin* 1739] 3 p. AmS,AA174; Corberon, *oc.*

[322] "Par la Loi Romaine que nous suivons dans [la] Province, les Juifs
sont tenus de se conformer à toutes les formalités judiciaires usitées dans les
Tribunaux de la justice. C'est donc à tort après cela que les deux Juifs assi-
gnés pour déposer comme témoins par devant les officiers de la Maréchaussée de Strasbourg, prétendant qu'ils refusent... être tenus de faire serment
entre les mains du juge qui reçoit leur déposition et que selon leurs obser-

Jews were not even permitted to reside in Colmar, the site of the Sovereign Council, which was the Alsatian supreme court. They could stay in Colmar only for very short visits."'

In a petition of December 1771, the Alsatian Jewish leaders demanded that the right to judge cases of usury be taken from the local judges and reserved only for royal law-courts functioning under the jurisdiction of the French laws. The Jews (with the aid of a brief written by H.P. Simon, who was since 1770 attorney at the Council) proved in accordance with Article 202 of the Ordinance of Blois of 1254, that usury was a criminal offense which could be punished by confiscation of property or deportation; that only royal judges could pass such severe sentences; that the privileges of local, seigniorial judges were mostly limited to watching over the safety of people's properties and over social welfare."' The Jews further stated that the Ordinances of 1311, 1312 and 1576 on fighting usury were drawn up as regulations for the royal judges only. In the same spirit were published the decisions of the Besançon Parliament of Nov. 17, 1751 and of the Paris Parliament of March 11, 1623 and March 18, 1625. The local, seigniorial judges of Alsace, they claimed, were people lacking in culture, without any spirit of justice, brutal and incapable of objectivity in the passing of sentences. The Jews stated that they approved of sentencing Jewish usurers, but that this should be done within the framework of the law

---

vations particulières, c'est à leur Rabbin à prendre ce serment, puisqu'en empire le contraire s'observe actuellement et qu'ils prêtent serment entre les mains des juges suivant la formule dont j'ai parlé [formule de 1538] et que je rapporte... je ne puis l'affirmer aussi positivement pour les matières criminelles, on m'assure au contraire qu'à cet égard l'usage est varié dans les justices subalternes et qu'il y a des juges que dans les procédures qu'ils instruisent à l'extraordinaire se servent du ministre des rabbins pour faire prêter aux Juifs et d'autres qui ne le font pas et donnent le serment eux-mêmes. Je me suis informé des officiers de la maréchaussée de cette ville [Colmar] quel était leur usage sur ce point et ils m'ont dit que le cas s'était présenté très souvent où des Juifs avaient été obligés de prêter serment par devant eux soit comme témoins, soit comme accusés, mais que jamais ils ne s'étaient servis du ministère d'un Rabbin à cet effet. A l'égard de l'usage du Conseil [Souverain] d'Alsace en matière criminelle, j'ai vu depuis 22 ans plusieurs Juifs impliqués comme accusés dans des procédures à l'extraordi- naire et être entendus à la Chambre, soit sur la sellette, soit derrière le Barreau suivant que le cas l'exigeait, plusieurs même ont été appliqués à la question; mais jamais, ils n'ont été assistés d'un rabbin pour prêter le ser- ment requis. M. le Président le leur donnait seul en observant simplement de leur faire mettre le chapeau parce que selon eux ils doivent être couverts quand ils parlent à Dieu et de les faire jurer dans les termes suivants[:] je jure et je promets par le Dieu tout-puissant qui a créé le ciel et la terre, sous peine de damnation de mon âme, de dire la vérité. Les officiers de la Maréchaussée de Colmar m'ont dit qu'ils en usaient de même" (ZS).

"'' A few Gentile innkeepers were allowed to keep Jewish servants for the Jews visiting Colmar, but in 1780 the Jewish servant David Lévi was ordered to leave the city. On Dec. 18, 1781, the Alsatian Jewish leaders Cerfberr and Isaac Meyer demanded that the city annul the order because many Jews must come to Colmar in order to plead before the Sovereign Council. The City Council allowed innkeepers to keep Jewish servants, but emphasized that this did not mean that the latter might reside in Colmar (AmC,AA176).

"'' The law-courts of the seigniorial cities were composed of a bailiff, a provost (prévot), four to eight advisers, an attorney-general on fiscal mat- ters, and a court clerk. They were all appointed by their seignior, who had the right to recall them.

and only by royal judges."" On Dec. 17, 1771, the Sovereign Council rejected the Jewish demand on the grounds that (1) the Jewish leaders were not the "guardians or the avengers" of the royal jurisdiction; (2) the Jewish petition was only a collection of unworkable maxims, since no local royal law-courts existed in Alsace, so that to deprive the seigniorial judges of the right to pass sentences on usurers would mean to reinforce the practice of usury; and (3) according to the Jews' demand, only the interested person (i.e. the debtor) could ask for justice, but according to the jurisprudence of the Alsatian Sovereign Council, the same right belonged to the administration (*partie publique*)."" In March 1781, the Jewish leader Cerfberr demanded again that cases of usury be tried only in royal law-courts."" The same demand was made in 1784 by de Mirbeck, in his memorandum against the Letters patent of July 10, 1784."" Not only Jews distrusted non-royal law-courts. In 1780,

---

²²⁵ " A Nos-Seigneurs du Conseil Souverain d'Alsace supplient humblement les préposés généraux des Juifs de la Province d'Alsace. Disant: que le crime d'usure intéresse essentiellement le public: sa vengeance doit donc appartenir aux seuls juges roiaux chargés de soin de veiller à la sûreté publique à l'exclusion des juges seigneuriaux dont les justices ne sont que de purs privilèges accordés aux seigneurs, plutôt pour la conservation de leurs domaines et droits que pour considération du bien public. Les justices seigneuriales ne sont exercées que par un Bailly, un Greffier, et un Procureur fiscal: en supposant aux Baillis de toute la province toutes les lumières naturelles et acquises, l'inexpérience, la malice et la crédulité de presque tous les procureurs fiscaux qui ne sont pas même gradués et qui ne sont ni reçus ni examinés au Conseil [Souverain] donnent lieu à des vexations et à des procédures extraordinaires contre la nation juive, sous prétexte d'usure, de sorte qu'il n'y en a pas un d'entre eux, quelque titre légitime dont il soit nanti, qui ne courre risque d'être appréhendé au corps sur la requête de plainte d'un débiteur authentiquement obligé. Ce qu'il y a même de plus frappant, c'est que dans les justices seigneuriales composées d'un seul juge, les accusés sont privés de la faveur que l'ordonnance leur accorde en voulant que les décrets passent à l'avis le plus doux; comment cela serait-il possible dans les juridictions où il n'y a qu'un sul juge, la liberté et le sort des citoyens dépendra donc d'un seul homme dans un royaume où les lois publiques ordonnent le contraire même, en matière d'instruction... L'article 202 de l'ordonnance de Blois fait défense d'exercer l'usure, sous peine pour la première fois d'amende honorable, bannissement et condamnation de grosses amendes et par la seconde confiscation de corps et de biens. Ces peines servent à faire connaître que le Roi réservait la connaissance de ce crime aux seuls juges royaux puisque les juges des seigneurs sont incompétents pour édicter la confiscation de corps et de biens contre un sujet du Roi. Les ordonnances de Philippe IV en 1311 et décembre 1312, de Louis XII en 1500 et Charles IX en 1567, de Henri III en 1576 concernant le crime d'usure, ne sont adressés qu'aux juges roiaux. Guenois, compilateur des Ordonnances de la Monarchie dit que par la pratique du Roiaume, la connaissance du crime d'usure est un cas roial... Les supplians n'entendent pas favoriser ni prêter appui aux Juifs qui auraient eu le malheur de s'abandonner à l'usure, ils déclarent qu'ils verraient leur punition avec plaisir pourvu qu'elle fut édictée par les juges roiaux et conformément aux règles tracées par l'Ordonnance criminelle au titre de plaintes, dénonciations. Signé: Simon, procureur des supplians " (ZS).
²²⁶ Holdt, QC., Dec. 17, 1771.
²²⁷ "Des ministres des Autels s'érigeant de leur chef où par des suggestions criminelles en Commissaires revêtus d'une autorité particulière se soient permis de rechercher avec autant de scandale que d'infidélité, des dépositions et plaintes d'usure pour ensuite les remettre à des procureurs fiscaux." AmStg,AA2383.
²²⁸ "L'usure étant un cas Royal, les Justices des seigneurs n'en devoient pas connoître; cependant il en est peu, dans la province d'Alsace, dont les officiers ne se soient permis les procédures criminelles et les décrets les plus rigoureux, contre les Juifs, sur toutes les accusations relatives à l'usure". AN,K1142.

non-Jewish official administrative circles prepared a project to create a royal law-court (*siège royal*) in the seigniory of Belfort (Upper Alsace). The authors of the project stated that Alsace was the province with the least number of royal law-courts."' There existed a lack in courts of the medium class. between the Sovereign Council and the seigniorial judges. Because of this state of affairs the Council was forced to occupy itself with minor suits and both parties of lawsuits were frequently ruined."'

29. LAWSUITS

It is worth while to analyze some lawsuits between Jews and Gentiles as they are one of the best sources on the condition of credit, commerce, etc.

Jews were accused of falsifying documents. The Gentiles Gropper, Belsch and Rendelsheim accused in the 1780's the Jews Jacques Lévy and Abraham Bernheim of Habsheim of falsifying I.O.U.s of the debtors Bauman of Riedisheim and T. Werner Berenzwiller; they maintained that the Jews had asked them to sign as witnesses, but the Jews stated that the three Gentiles were even unable to sign their names."' The Comte du Trevoux was a debtor for the sum of 86,000 pounds. In 1717, he decided to speculate with promissory notes which he took on loan from the Jewish banker Mayer de Coblents of Metz. He added on the notes a remark that they were already partly repaid, and in order to insure himself against any lawsuits he first brought the Jew to justice."' Very frequently debtors provoked lawsuits against their creditors just in order to postpone payment of the capitals of their debts or interest. In March 1778 Sébastien Diebolt of Schvindratzheim bought on credit cattle from the Jew Gotschel Löwel of Minwersheim. The debtor refused to pay and he provoked 7 lawsuits and appeals against his creditor, but the Sovereign Council sentenced him to repay the debt."'

"'" Royal law-courts existed only in Colmar (the Sovereign Council), in the bailiwicks of Haguenau, Wissembourg, Guermisheim and Landeck, in Brisach, Huningue, Ensisheim and Fort-Louis (AN,K1236. Florimond's notes).
"'" "Aucune province de France n'est plus dépourvue que l'Alsace de Tribunaux intermédiaires, entre la cour souveraine et les justices des seigneurs institués dans toutes les autres Provinces du Royaume, tant pour juger en dernier ressort ou par provisions des affaires médiocrement importantes, que pour remédier à la chicane des plaideurs, qui par le moyen d'appellation toujours difficile à anéantir, cherchent à éluder le paiement de ce qu'ils doivent légitimement; dispenser les sujets du Roi de quitter leurs foyers pour plaider sur des objets de peu de valeur... Le Conseil souverain d'Alsace... en est souvent distrait par les détails minutieux où il est forcé de descendre faute d'un pareil établissement dans la partie méridionale de cette province [Sundgau]. Toutes se portent indistinctement par appel des premiers juges devant ce Tribunal... les affaires majeures comme les minutieuses en souffrent et leur longueur obligeant les malheureux plaideurs à multiplier les voiages, achève de les écraser." AdHR,E2949.
"'" ZS.
"'" *Factum pour Mayer de Coblents, banquier juif de Metz, appelant Contre Mre André de Bressillac, comte de Trévoux* (M 17-) 10 p. BmN,ZZ 174/6.
"'" AdHR,IBE66. A lawsuit of Isaac Leib Sée of Bergheim and Israél Mayer of Scherwiller against their debtor Ch. M. Bussy, Attorney-General

The mania of lawsuits involved considerable expenses. If the debtors lost their suits—and in most cases the courts were forced to pass sentence against them—they had to pay not only the debts, but also the court expenses, pay their lawyers, the expenses of their creditors, etc."' On May 16, 1759, the Sovereign Council ordred the judges to pass sentences quickly because both parties suffered greatly from the long delays.'"

Frequently debtors disappeared and their creditors were forced to search for them. Of 25 Jews who resided without passports in Paris in 1721, eight came to search for their debtors or because of lawsuits.'" Creditors were forced to compromise and accept only parts of the debts. Meyer Weil of Ribeauvillé granted a loan of 20,543 pounds to the Prince Christian III de Deux Ponts. In 1739, the creditor requested the Sovereign Council to order his debtor to repay him the debt and interest, but many years later Mathias Weil, the creditor's heir, was forced to compromise and accept from the debtor's heir only 900 pounds.'" Well-known Jewish bankers were ruined because their debtors went into bankruptcy. This happened—among many others—to Gerson Jacob Goudchaux (1768-1818), the father of Michel Goudchaux, who became Minister of Finances in 1848.'" Sometimes a creditor was able through a lucky trick to obtain his money. The Comtesse du Barry refused to repay a debt of 60,000 pounds to Michel Oulif of Metz. In 1772, Oulif sold her a piece of jewelry for 6,000 pounds and without knowing it she signed an I.O.U. for 60,000 pounds, which she was forced to recognize as valid.'"

Many Jewish debtors, too, refused to honor their I.O.U.s. The

---

of St.-Hippolyte continued during the years 1773-1778 (Isaac Bloch, Une expulsion des Juifs en Alsace... *REJ*, vol. XXXI (1895) p. 87). The famous 18th century affair of the *Collier de la Reine* in which the Strasbourg Cardinal de Rohan was involved as a debtor of Cerfberr continued even during the 1860's (*AI*, vol. XXIV (1863) p. 775).

'"' In a lawsuit against his debtor Albrecht Helling of Cernay, the Jew Marx Guintzbourger of Brisack incurred one hundred different expenses (AdBR,IBE11d).

'" *ERCSA* [C16 Mai 1759] 3 p. AmS, vol. 951-121. Klinglin of Strasbourg took in 1749 a loan of 45,000 pounds from a Jew, but refused to repay the capital or interest because another of his creditors had already a juridical mortgage against him. Because of this the Jew himself could not pay his own debts. A lawsuit between the heirs of both parties went on during the Revolution (AdHR,E2757). Similar cases happened to Alexandre Séligmann (Cerfberr's son-in-law) who granted a loan of 20,000 pounds to a Catholic religious institution (AN,BB16-624), and in a lawsuit of Abraham Isaac Brisac against Goussard de Montigny (AdM,J1104). The same happened to the Gentile creditor Chabouille of Paris who was forced during the Revolution to abandon his business and search for his debtor. *Mémoire justificatif du citoyen Chabouille* (P an III). AN,AD-XL-59.

'"' L. Kahn, oc, p. 6-7, 14. Hayem Worms tried for many years to find his debtor: *Mémoire pour Hayem Worms...* (P 1784) 79 p. BN,4F'33106.

'"' AdHR,E899. J. F. Klinglin, the Royal praetor of Strasbourg, forced the Jew Raphael Lévy to grant him loans for a sum total of 80,000 pounds. Lévy, who was a well-known army contractor, was forced to accept in 1751 repayment of only 24,000 pounds. *Mémoire de M. Klinglin, prêteur royal de la ville de Strasbourg* (Grenoble 1753); I. Loeb, oc., p. 149-54.

'"' E. Carmoly, Galerie israélite française, Michel Goudchaux. *AI*, vol. XXIV (1863) p. 609.

'"' *Ibid.*, Michel Oulif et la comtesse du Barry. *AI*, vol. XXIII (1862) p. 111-12.

Jew Hirsch Heineman of Mülhausen in Thyringen granted a loan of 1,640 *carolinen* to Gerson Lévy of Metz. In 1789 the creditor wrote to the National Assembly that should the Assembly force his debtor to repay his debt, half of it would be donated for a patriotic institution."'

Jews frequently fell victims of the diversity in different jurisdictions. The Alsatian Jew Meyer Aaron Dreyfues granted a loan of 1,200 Louis to Marie Meyer Fechter of Basel, but later she agreed to repay only 1,170 pounds. Because she resided in Hegenheim (Alsace) the Jew took her to justice. The debtor then attacked the Jew before the Senate of Basel which obtained an Alsatian court's order to arrest the Jew on the basis of a Basel sentence (which was against the Alsatian Laws). The Jew appealed to the Sovereign Council which on Oct. 3, 1763, passed sentence in favor of the Jew, but in the meantime Dreyfues spent a long time in prison and incurred expenses, without any hope to regain his money."' Creditors could not regain their money because they lost the I.O.U.s."' Many debtors were themselves speculators, many were spendthrifts who never attempted to repay their debts."'

30. THE ATTITUDE TOWARD JEWS AND CREDIT

Usury was the main argument of anti-Jewish propaganda, especially on the eve of 1789, when the liberal circles could not be reached by anti-religious feelings against Jews. Two trends toward Jews could be observed in the public opinion of that time: According to one group, usury, laziness and dishonesty were a part of the Jews' nature and the Jewish religion. Another group stated that Jews

---

"' AN,D-XXIX-89.
"' *Mémoire pour Meyer Aaron Dreyfues... contre la veuve Fechter de Basle* [C 1763].
"' On March 30, 1699, Prince de Birckenfeld took from three Gentiles of Strasbourg a loan of 21,000 florins. They charged an usurious rate of interest because "money was rare" (*l'argent étoit rare*). The debtors' heirs refused to repay the debt and the creditors possessed only a copy of the original I.O.U. The same Prince left to his son a heritage which consisted of unpaid debts and the son was forced to obtain from the Jew Meyer Weil of Ribeauvillé a loan in order to repay these debts. In 1731, he took again 7,000 pounds from the Jew in order to cover the expenses of a voyage to Paris. Later he refused to repay the debts to Weil. AdHR, fonds Corberon-Bruges, vol.12,Nos.2,14.
"' The priest Jean-Pierre Phister of Buettuviller took in 1720 a large loan from Hirtz Salomon of Thann in order to buy 1/10 of the land of Fessenheim. *Factum pour Me. Pierre Phister, prêtre & curé de Buettuviller, contre Hirtz Salomon, Juif...* (sl 1723) 26 p. BN,naf22705f.243 & BuS32881. In 1780 Beatrice Krafft charged that her husband, who was a debtor of Marx Lévi of Wintzenheim, was a heavy spender (AmC,FF318). The Baron Charles Anselme de Warsberg was a spendthrift and refused to repay the debts to his creditors Isaac Mayer and Gottschalk. In the 1760's he had an annual income of 60,000 pounds, but he still was forced to sell in a short time a heritage in the value of 120,000 francs and to take loans totalling 300,000 francs (according to the rate of 1807). Fritsch et Georgel, avocats en la cour, *Le réveil trompeur de la Judée. Précis pour Charles Théodore et Alexandre de Warsberg, propriétaires résidans à Sarrebourg... contre Gotschalk et Isaac Mayer, Juifs, domiciliés à Mannheim* (Trèves 1807) 8 p. JTS.

were forced into dishonest professions by the many anti-Jewish laws and restrictions of the countries where they resided.

It was an almost universal belief that the Talmud allowed, and even ordered, to charge usurious rates of interest on loans granted to Gentiles. Nicolas de Corberon, First President of the Alsatian Sovereign Council in 1700, wrote so in his collection of Alsatian acts.[144] Turgot, the Minister of Finances of Louis XVI believed that Jews were allowed by their religion to engage in usury.[145] But soon more liberal voices began to defend the Jews. In 1780, the bailiff of Benfeld, Hoffmann, wrote that the anti-Jewish restrictions forced the Jew to engage in usury.[146] The Commission which prepared the Letters patent of July 10, 1784, and the famous Metz attorney P.L. Roederer, were of the same opinion.[147] In a 1784 Strasbourg

---

[144] de Corberon, Recueil..., p. 600-602. J. B. de Boyer Argens started his 1737 book Mémoires du Comte de Vaxere, ou le faux-Rabbin (Amsterdam 1749) with a letter to an imaginery Metz "Usurer and Rabbi." In the same spirit wrote the priest Ch. L. Richard in his anti-Jewish pamphlet Lettre du Rabbin de la Synagogue des Juifs de Metz, au Sieur Liefmann Calmer, propriétaire de la baronnie de Péquigny. 5 Août 1777 (sl nd) 10 p. BN,Fb 17810. [On Liefmann Calmer see: Un Juif seul contre tout le Parlement de Paris, in: Recueil de pièces intéressantes sur les deux questions célèbres, savoir, si un Juif converti au christianisme peut épouser une fille chrétienne... (P 1779);I. Loeb, Un baron juif français au 18ᵉ siècle, Liefmann Calmer. Annuaire des AI, vol. II (1885-86).] An 18th century Lorraine pamphlet presented the same idea in the form of a dialogue between Jews: Hattarat Nedarim, ou Absolution de promesses (sl nd) 8 p. BN,naf22706f.55.
[145] Turgot, Théorie de l'intérêt de l'argent... (P 1780) p. 3. On Feb. 12, 1751, the Marquis d'Argenson wrote that if the Protestants were fought against, they would be forced — the same as the Jews — to invest all their money in army contracting business and this would, of course, be useful to the Monarchy's finances. Arnaud Brette, La France au milieu du XVIIIᵉ siècle (1747-1757) d'après le journal du Marquis d'Argenson (P 1898) p. 125-26. During the Revolution as well as in the 19th century, many circles believed that Jews were permitted by their religion to engage in usury, e.g. in the Weltbote of Strasbourg (E. Mühlenbeck, Euloge Schneider (S-P 1896) p. 6); "L'usure... ce monstre paroit l'avoir choisi [le Juif] pour son argent" (A letter of the National Guard of Sarreguemines. AN,D-IV-XLIV d.1267); "leur Thalmud qui leur fait un devoir de tromper": Louis Poujol, Quelques observations concernant les Juifs... (P 1806) p. 51; "l'un de ses préceptes vous fait un mérite et presqu'un devoir de tromper un Chrétien": B..., avoué, Dialogue entre un avoué et un Juif de Metz, une brève dissertation sur le décret impérial du 17 mars 1808 (M 1808) p. 14; "Le Juif, imbu des maximes de son talmud, enhardi à l'usure et à la vexation par un faux zèle de religion: Quelques idées sur l'usure des Juifs dans les départements du Haut-Rhin et du Bas-Rhin, par un Sundgauien (P 1818) p. 39; Moreau, De l'incompatibilité entre le judaïsme et l'exercice des droits de cité (P 1819) p. 27, 80; de Lancastel, oc., p. 24-36; "la source du mal existait dans une habitude invétérée, dans leurs principes héréditaires et dans la fausse interprétation que des rabbins fanatiques avaient donnée au fameux passage du Deutéronome: Non fene rabis fratri tuo, sed alieno". Dagobert Fischer, Etude sur l'histoire des Juifs dans les terres de l'évêché de Strasbourg... (M 1867) p. 29 (reprint from Revue de l'Est); "L'usure est donc pour le fidèle du Talmud un acte de Sainteté": Gougenot de Mousseaux, Le Juif, le judaïsme et la judaïsation des peuples chrétiens (P 1869) p. 159, 180.
[146] "Nous ne leur laissons d'autre ressource que le prêt à usure, et les obligeons d'être usuriers sous peine de mourir de faim. Est-il étonnant qu'ils le soient?... je n'entends pas leur en faire un reproche, il ne peut tomber que sur ceux qui les ont mis dans la nécessité de cette profession malhonnête." Hoffmann, oc., vol. IV, p. 443-444.
[147] "Tous les moyens honnêtes de subsister leur sont interdits." R. Anchel, Les Lettres patentes du 10 Juillet 1784. Festschrift zu Simon Dubnows siebzigsten Geburtstag (Berlin 1930) p. 190; "ses vices ont été notre ouvrage." L. Kahn, Les Juifs de Paris pendant la Révolution (P 1898) p. 9.

manuscript, written in the form of a dialogue between a bailiff and an Alsatian named A-m-f, the latter stated that Jews could become honest men and anti-Jewish feelings could be destroyed by abolishing the anti-Jewish restrictions.[48]

But even the pro-Jewish circles sincerely believed that Jews were ruining the people. Very seldom was any attempt made to show how useful the Jewish creditor was to the country's economy. Even to the liberals the Jews were an uncivilized mass.[49] Some liberals voiced the opinion that by engaging in usury the Jews wanted to avenge themselves on the Gentiles for all the anti-Jewish persecutions.[50] Even H. Grégoire, the great fighter for the Jewish emancipation, believed on the eve of 1789 that Jews ruined the peasants and avenged themselves on the Gentiles. His proposals on the ways of fighting usury were based on his belief of "Jewish rapaciousness" (rapacité judaïque).[51]

In later periods, during the Revolution and the 19th century, too, liberal Gentiles stated that Jews were forced to engage in usury.[52] The Jews repated on many occasions that they were allowed

---

[48] "Fragments d'une conversation entre un Baillif d'Alsace et Mr. d'A-m-f de l'A-, touchant les Juifs d'Alsace." AmStg,AA2393 and AN,F12-854B.

[49] It is worth while to note the statement of the historian Paul Bettelin that the Alsatian Gentile population of the 18th century was not all cultured. *Le Général Marc-François-Jérôme, Baron Wolff...* (Ambilly-Annemasse 1943) p. 9.

[50] Such opinions were expressed by the Lorraine attorney P. L. Lacretelle in his above-mentioned plea of 1774 and by Jacques Godard in the above-mentioned brief of 1787.

[51] H. Grégoire, *Essai sur la régénération... des Juifs...* (M 1789) p. 71-80, 92-99. Even in 1806 the Jewish leader Berr-Isaac Berr was forced to reply to Gregoir's attacks on the Jewish religion. *Lettre du sieur Berr-Isaac Berr... à M. Grégoire, sénateur* (N 1806). The Nancy attorney Thiery held similar opinions — that Jews ruined the peasants, the youth, etc. *Dissertation...* (P 1788) p. 22-24. The historian Abraham Cahen noted that even the best defenders of Jews knew very little of the internal life of the Jewish communities, e.g., H. Grégoire believed that the prohibition of the Metz community to use powder was an anti-sanitary act, while actually the Jewish leaders intended to prohibit luxury. A. Cahen, *Règlements somptuaires de la communauté juive de Metz...* (Versailles 1881) p. 7-8.

[52] E. Seinguerlet, *Strasbourg pendant la Révolution* (P 1881) p. 65-66 (Euloge Schneider's statement of July 16, 1793); Charles du Bus, *Stanislas de Clermont-Tonnerre et l'échec de la Révolution monarchique* (P 1931) p. 213: "Des hommes qui ne possèdent que de l'argent, ne peuvent faire valoir que de l'argent, voilà le mal; qu'ils aient des terres et une patrie, et ils ne prêteront plus: voilà le remède"; M. Vieillard, *Dissertation sur la demande des Juifs de Paris...* (sl nd) p. 5-6; J. B. Sanchmau, *L'école des Peuples et des Rois, ou essai philosophique sur la Liberté, le pouvoir arbitraire, les Juifs et les Noirs* (P 1790) p. 82: "Nous leur arrachons presque tous les moyens de subsistance, et nous leur faisons le reproche d'user envers nous d'astuce et d'adresse"; *Revue des grandes journées parlementaires*, vol. I, p. 19, Prince C. V. de Broglie's statement of Dec. 24, 1789: "il faut convenir que les règlements mêmes en vertu desquels les Juifs sont tolérés en Alsace, ne leur présentant d'autre moyen de subsistance, d'autre genre d'industrie que le commerce de l'argent"; De Laissac, capitaine au Régiment de Limousin, *Lettre à M. le Chapellier, membre de l'Assemblée Nationale* [P 1790] p. 21: "Je conviendrai que n'ayant eu jusqu'ici d'autre ressource pour vivre que les métiers de fripier, d'usurier, d'espion &c, il leur étoit difficile d'être rigides observateurs de la probité"; Paul Leuilliot, *Les Jacobins de Colmar...* (S 1923) p. 339-40; [F. R. Cottier,] *Dialogue* (Carpentras 1789) p. 9: "[Le Juif:] Le mépris dont on nous accabloit, étouffait en nous le germe de la vertu... on aplanissait la route qui pouvoit nous conduire au crime"; "la morale des Juifs, elle ne peut être mauvaise, puisque Dieu la leur a enseignée, mais l'avilissement dans lequel nous tenons depuis treize siècles cette

to make a living only from granting loans; they were not permitted to engage in useful and honest occupations; that they were ruined by dishonest debtors, etc."'

---

nation malheureuse, n'a sans doute pas peu contribué à la dégrader..." (Statement of the Colmar *Bureau intermédiaire*, May 1790. AdHR,C1602); *Lettre d'un citoyen, aux Gardes-Citoyens de la Ville de Nancy, en réponse à la question: les Juifs doivent-ils être admis dans la Milice Nationale* (sl nd) p. 4: "l'existence précaire & équivoque que l'on a bien voulu accorder aux Juifs, les a forcés d'adopter pour mœurs, & de pratiquer pour commerce, la fraude, l'astuce & l'usure"; [Hell,] *Les Juifs d'Alsace doivent-ils être admis au droit de citoyen actifs. Lisez et jugez* (S 1790) p. 133; M... [de Foulaines,] *Harmonie des cultes...* (P 1808) p. 161: "Quoi qu'il soit doux de trouver à emprunter, il est dur d'être obligé de rendre. Le plaisir d'être secouru dans son besoin passe avec la satisfaction de ce besoin. Il est presque dans la nature des hommes et des choses que pour devenir odieux, il suffit de prêter même loyalement"; "...une population si longtemps habituée à ne pouvoir se fier à aucune chance de solidité et que les préjugés publics n'en retiennent que trop encore dans cette méfiance" (Report on usury in the arrondissement of Saverne, Aug. 27, 1820. AdBR,3M15); M. Auger, preface to: *Oeuvres de P. L. Lacretelle* (P 1823) vol. I, p. vj: "...cette nation, qu'à force d'oppression et de mépris, on avait réduite à chercher un refuge dans la fraude et une vengeance dans l'usure." "Il n'est personne qui n'éprouve un sentiment de répugnance à l'approche de l'un de ces êtres avilis, âpres au gain, impropres au travail, croupissant dans la misère la plus abjecte, au cœur desséché, à l'esprit vide de toutes grandes idées... c'est nous qui avons réduit cet homme à cet état de dégradation... c'est nous qui, en l'oppressant, en avons fait un ennemi" (*Le Glaneur du Haut-Rhin*, May 28, 1848).

[353] M. Chauveau, *Pétition de Messieurs les Juifs du Haut-Rhin à l'Assemblée Nationale* (P [179-]) p. 3: "Les vices des Juifs naissent de l'avilissement dans lequel vous les avez plongés; ils seront bons quand ils pourront trouver quelque avantage à l'être"; *Zuschrift der elsassischen Juden an die übrigen Einwohner des Elsasses* [S 1790]: "Ne nous forçait-on pas, en quelque sorte, à nous dédommager des privations qu'on nous imposoit, & à racheter les taxes arbitraires auxquelles nous étions condamnés?"; *Lettre du Sr. Lion Goudchaux, Juif de Nancy, à M. l'abbé Maury...* (sl 1790) p. 5, 11: "Vous parlez, Mr., de la fortune de quelques Juifs, vous ne dites rien de l'avilissement & de l'humiliation de tous... Ils (les Juifs d'Alsace) ne pourront pas être les fléaux des campagnes par l'usure, libres par la loi d'acquérir, de commercer, de travailler, de se livrer aux arts & à l'étude des sciences, ils ne seront pas restreints, pour subsister & faire subsister leur famille, à l'unique ressource de faire valoir leur argent. Ils seront soumis, pour la rédaction & l'exécution de leurs conventions, aux Lois & aux Statuts qui en prescriront la forme."

Signature on a Counterfeit Receipt (see also p. 17).

(Departmental Archives of Upper Rhine, IBE62.)

VI. - The Case of the Counterfeit Receipts in Alsace, 1777-1789

31. THE BACKGROUND OF THE CASE

Jewish history knows of many conflicts between Jewish creditors and their Gentile debtors. Yet the *Case of the Counterfeit Receipts in Alsace (L'Affaire des fausses quittances)* is unique in its character, its scope, and its repercussions. So great was the misery of the Alsatian peasants that when they were given a chance to avoid payment of their debts to Jewish creditors by illegal means, they readily seized the opportunity to do so. Thus, toward the end of 1777, began the unusual affair which endangered the economy of the entire French province, brought about the economic ruin of the Jews, threatened their very existence, and even influenced the struggle for the Jewish emancipation during the Revolution of 1789.

Towards the end of 1777, and particularly during 1778, Alsace was inundated by a mass of counterfeit receipts "signed" in Hebrew characters, purportedly by Jewish creditors (Alsatian Jews rarely signed documents in Latin characters). When the Jews requested the payment of debts owed them by Gentile debtors, they were presented with these falsified receipts for sums allegedly paid them in partial or full payment of the debts. It immediately became apparent that a well-organized group had persuaded the Gentile debtors, mostly the peasant-debtors, not to repay their debts. With the help of a few converted Jews, or of a Gentile who had learned to write the Hebrew alphabet, this group fabricated a mass of receipts, signed them in Hebrew with the names of the creditors, and sold these falsified documents to the debtors.[354] There had always been isolated cases of counterfeiting receipts on the part of debtors, of forcibly recovering I.O.U.s, or even of murdering creditors.[355] This time, however, the cases were far from isolated.

---

[354] See on p. 17 the reproduction of such a counterfeit receipt.
[355] In 1756, the Jew Abraham Lévy of Wittelsheim declared that a receipt dated Sept. 16, 1743, and presented to him by his debtor Jean George Rohrbach was falsified (AdHR,IBE54b). In 1702 the butcher Jacques Durand of Metz assassinated his Jewish creditor Joseph Cahen (see note 302). In 1767, a Gentile of Colmar was sentenced to die for killing his Jewish creditor: J. Sée, Hausbuch von Dominicus Schmutz. *Les Chroniques d'Alsace*, vol. I (C 1878); J. Liblin, Chronique du serrurier Dominique Schmutz de Colmar. *RA* vol. XXIV (1874) p. 260; Les Juifs d'Alsace au XVIIIᵉ siècle. *UI*, vol. XXXIV (1878) p. 200-202. Hyacinthe Renault, a lawyer of Blâmont, attacked his Jewish creditor Isaac Lévy of Imling and took away from him by force the I.O.U. *Consultation* [pour Isaac Lévy] (N 1758); *A Nosseigneurs... Isaac Lévy, Juif... contre le sieur Charles-Léopold Renault...* (N 1758); *Premier interrogatoire du Sieur Renault fils...* (N 1758); *Réplique pour les sieurs Reynault... contre Isaac Lévy...* (N 1758) BmN, 7844/6-12.

It was a mass movement to erase the debts by an illegal ruse."'

These were tragic times for the Alsatian Jewry. Right from the beginning the counterfeiting of the receipts was accompanied by wild acts of terror aimed against the Jews. Anti-Jewish riots occurred at the end of August 1778, and many Jews had to escape from their homes to save their lives."' On September 2, 1778, the abbot de Raze wrote to the Bishop of Basel that in Alsace (particularly around Than, Dürmenach, Hagenthal) preparations were made to assasinate all Jews at a time when they would be assembled in their synagogues. He wrote that in some localities Jews had already been "almost mortally" wounded, and that some Jewish houses had been destroyed."' A pamphlet published during the Revolution maintained that Hell, the bailiff of Landser, and his friends, were prepared to kill the Jews on the day of September 30, 1778 (when they would be assembled in the synagogues; in the year 1778, the Day of Atonement fell in the evening of September 30 and on October 1)."' A one-page leaflet entitled *Malédiction*, telling the story of the crucifixion of Jesus by the Jews and pointing out that Jews were permitted by their religion to deceive Christians, was distributed among the inhabitants of the province."' A book, *Observations d'un Alsacien* (written by Hell, as will be seen subsequently), full of anti-Jewish accusations and bringing the first account of the counterfeiting, largely helped to create the anti-Jewish atmosphere and to continuing the counterfeiteing activities."'

32. THE FIRST DECREE OF THE SOVEREIGN COUNCIL ON THE RECEIPTS, JULY 11, 1778

In 1790, the Jew Abraham Lambert of Metz wrote that the Jews lived in the 18th, not in the 9th century, and that they consequently could not be simply chased out so as to confiscate

---

"'' One document mentions the number of 127,000 counterfeit receipts in 1778. This is probably not an excessive number, if it is considered that when the Alsatian Sovereign Council started to close out the case, four or five thousands false receipts were registered by the debtors. *Lettre d'un Alsacien sur les Juifs d'Alsace à M. Reubell...* (P 1790) p. 16.

"'' J. Rochette, *Histoire des Juifs d'Alsace...* (P 1939) p. 120.

"'' SBern,B216f.381.

"'' See note 356, p. 15-16.

"'' *Malédiction* (sl nd) 1 p. (fol.) SBern,B216f.367. *Cf.* E. Scheid, *oc.*, p. 237. (See p. 140.)

"'' [Hell,] *Observations d'un Alsacien sur l'affaire présente des Juifs d'Alsace* (Francfort [Strasbourg] 1779) 136 p., second edition — Neuchâtel 1790. The anti-Jewish riots spread to the neighboring provinces. According to Zalkind Hourwitz, Gentile debtors attempted to set fire to the Metz ghetto in 1781. In Metz, an anti-Jewish pamphlet was likewise distributed, in 1786; but the Metz Parliament stopped its distribution. Z. Hourwitz, *Apologie des Juifs...* (M 1789) p. 18; Général Aubert-Dubayet, *oc. cf.* note 194. [A pamphlet with the same title was published in 1788 by M. de Foissac.] With respect to the attempt to set fire to the Metz ghetto it is worth while to note that since 1767 a company of Jewish firemen existed in the ghetto: L. Zéliqzon, *Deux documents relatifs aux Juifs de Metz sous l'Ancien régime. Cahiers lorrains*, 1934, p. 65-73.

the debts owed them."² Fortunately the Case of the Counterfeit Receipts occurred at a time when it was not possible to expel the Jews (although for a time it was decided to annul 80% of the debts). Not only did the King and his Alsatian administrators need the Jews owing to their role in the economic life of the province, but the affair had a distinct rebellious character, and it may have constituted a dangerous precedent for refusing to pay taxes and debts owed to non-Jewish creditors. In the borderline province of Alsace—the scene of many controversial interests and conflicts between various princes, seigniors, and cities; where the French Kingdom was constantly compelled to fight for its influence—in this province that belonged nominally to France only since 1648, the King's representatives had to act carefully and to enforce the laws. Otherwise the interests and the influence of the King of France could be placed in jeopardy. Because of this factor, the King and his judicial administration in Alsace, the Sovereign Council, were compelled to strive for legally liquidating the affair of the false receipts in some manner. Had this not been the state of affairs in Alsace, the Jews would have lost all their possessions at the very beginning of the Case.

The first official act of the Sovereign Council in this matter was a decree issued on July 11, 1778, which—according to the Alsatian jurist and historian N. de Neyremand—aimed to ruin the Jewish creditors."³ The decree ordered the debtors to register all falsified receipts in their possession. This measure was to have put an end to the use of the receipts and to the further falsification of such documents. But the travel expenses of the debtors—who had to come to town for the registration—as well as the registration fees (6 sols per receipt) were to be paid by the Jewish creditors. The decree also prohibited the Jews to grant future loans of more than 50 pounds on simple unregistered I.O.U.s (*quittances sous seing privé*), except in special cases. In the future, receipts issued to debtors by their Jewish creditors were to be signed and sealed in the presence of officials."⁴ This last point was to prevent the continued counterfeiting of receipts. In fact, debtors presented falsified receipts dated later than July 11, 1778.³⁶⁵

---

³⁶² Abraham Lambert, *Lettre à M. Reubell...* (M 1790) p. 6-7.
³⁶³ E. de Neyremand, Créances des Juifs. Procès des fausses quittances. *Petite Gazette d'Alsace*, vol. III (1861) p. 15.
³⁶⁴ ERCSA. Du 11 Juillet 1778 (C 1778) 7 p. BuS33227.
³⁶⁵ An example of a similar case follows: In a dispute over falsified receipts, Jacques Baldinger, a shoemaker of Grand-Huningue, maintained that even the signatures on a few receipts accepted by his Jewish creditor, Jacques Weil of Blotzheim, as genuine, were dissimilar. A Jew, he declared, was always prepared to falsify even his own signature in order to deceive a Christian. Weil replied with an argument frequently used by Jewish creditors: the receipts which he claimed were falsified dated later than July 11, 1778, the date when the Sovereign Council ordered Jewish creditors to sign receipts only in the presence of a law-clerk and two witnesses. To this Baldinger replied that the decree prohibited the unwitnessed signing of receipts by Jews, but did not forbid Gentiles to accept such receipts. The Jew had persuaded him, he said, that it would be foolish to spend money on legalizing a receipt, and that a simple unsealed receipt would be sufficient. The Jew replied that the decree applied to Gentiles as well and that they were forbidden to accept unwitnessed receipts. AdHR,IIIB1818.

33. THE KING'S LETTERS PATENT OF NOVEMBER 6, 1778

The Decree of July 11, 1778, caused considerable deterioration of the Jews' financial status.[366] As a result of the registration procedures the Jewish communities were forced to spend considerable sums of money, for which expenditures they contracted loans (as late as the '60s of the 19th century these debts were still being paid up). The debtors likewise had expenses, and from the existing documents it cannot be determined by whom these expenses of the debtors were born. There must have existed an organized group which financed, at least in part, the debtors' trials, otherwise most of the debotrs involved in the case would have suffered financial ruin.

Anti-Jewish circles maintained that the Decree of July 11, 1778, was issued at the Jews' instigation. They also strongly protested against another order, of May 17, 1779, which reduced the price of registering the receipts from 6 to 3 sols per receipt.[367]

In a petition to the King's State Council, the Jews protested against forcing them to pay all the administrative expenses of liquidating the Case. In order to save expenses, the Jews requested that all civil and criminal trials caused by the receipts be transmitted to the attention of but a single magistrate direction and one jurisprudence. The Jewish request was granted by the King's Letters patent of Nov. 6, 1778, which ordered the annulment of the procedure prescribed on July 11, 1778. The new Letters transmitted the entire affair to the First Chamber (*Première Chambre*) of the Alsatian Sovereign Council which became for this Case a sort of a Court of Accounts (*Cour des comptes*). The falsified receipts already registered were to be returned to the debtors, who were to destroy them or come to an understanding with their Jewish creditors. The Jewish creditors were to prove within 6 months that the loans granted by them were not paid by the debtors and within the same time the debtors were to prove the authenticity of the receipts in their possession. To the First Chamber was granted the right to appoint special commissioners, who were to listen to both parties, check the documents, and try to persuade the debtors to destroy the falsified receipts; grant the debtors sufficient time to repay the debts; and—if necessary—act with all the force of the law against those debtors continuing to make use of the falsified receipts to avoid payment of the debts.[368]

[366] Holdt, the author of a diary of the Council's activities, cited the sum of 6,000 pounds paid by the Jews for the registration by their debtors of but 2,400 receipts, as of January 7, 1784. Within a few months the law registrar of Ferrette registered 27,000 receipts, for which the Jews were required to pay all expenses (6 sols per receipt, i.e. more than 6,000 pounds). Holdt, oc., Jan. 7, 1784.

[367] In a memorandum of Dec. 4, 1779, the notaries and registars in the law-courts of Upper Alsace complained that the registration of the receipts demanded much time, and that owing to the Case of receipts, only a very few contracts were being drawn up by them and they consequently could hardly make a living. Holdt, oc., May 14, 1779.

[368] LPR, qui attribuent à la Première Chambre du Conseil Souverain d'Alsace la connaissance des inscriptions de faux & des contestations relatives aux créances des Juifs d'Alsace... Du 6 novembre 1778 (C 1778) 16 p.

In a letter accompanying the new Letters patents, the War Minister, prince de Montbarrey, in charge of Alsace, acquainted the Alsatian Council with the anxiety which the Case of falsified receipts caused in Paris. The Minister of Justice was so much disturbed that when the First President of the Alsatian Council visited Paris in November 1778, he asked him to return immediatly to Colmar (the Council's seat).[""]

34. CIVIL AND CRIMINAL LAW-PROCEDURES IN LIQUIDATING THE CASE

At first the deposition of the falsified receipts was carried out by the debtors in the form of ultimatums to the Jewish creditors. Here is an example from the Haguenau notarial office: In 1771, the Jew Benjamin granted a loan to Henri Mouches and Jean George Oberlin. In 1779, the debtors declared that a part of the loan was already paid by them and they proved it with a receipt that was not recognized by the Jew as genuine. So, through the notary and in a written petition the debtors requested the Jew to be present at a fixed hour in the notary's office where they would pay him the debt, deducting the part already paid (and not acknowledged by the Jew), or if so be the case, the Jew would repay them any overpayment they might have made.[""] In order not to lose his money the Jew had but one legal course: to refrain from going to the notary's office and to reply in writing to the debtor's request, then the conflict would come under the jurisdiction of the law-court. True, this automatically involved expenses, but it was

---

[p. 11-16: ERCSA. Du 12 Décembre 1778.] BmC5353.; Jourdan, Decrnoy et Isambert, *Recueil général des anciens lois françaises...* (P 1821-33) vol. **XXV** p. 448.

[369] E. de Neyremand, *Conseil Souverain d'Alsace. Créances des Juifs. Procès des fausses quittances* (C 1862) p. 20-22. BuS101319; Holdt, *oc.,* Nov. 24, 1778.

On Dec. 11, 1778, the Letters patent of November 6 were registered with the Council and on the following day, December 12, the Council published a decree regulating the liquidation of the Case. In Letters patent of April 7, 1779, the King published new detailed orders on this liquidation. In new Letters patent of May 27, 1780, the King repeated the transmission to the Council's First Chamber of all powers to liquidate the Case and granted the debtors a delay of two months to retract the falsified receipts or to face the law-courts as counterfeiters. In special instructions the Sovereign Council requested the bailiffs, provosts, *préposés,* and priests to announce everywhere the contents of the latest Letters patent and to tell the debtors that if they would refrain from using falsified receipts they would be granted a postponement of payments on the debts. Otherwise, if the debtors refused to obey the Letters, they would not be accorded any privileges (postponement of payments) and they would have to face the law: "ERCSA. Du 12 Décembre 1778" [See note 368]; *LPR, concernant les créances pour lesquelles les Juifs de la province d'Alsace seront dans le cas d'agir contre les débiteurs chrétiens de la classe du peuple. Du 7 avril 1779* (C 1779) 8 p.; *LPR, portant règlement pour l'instruction des affaires d'entre les Juifs d'Alsace & leurs débiteurs... Du 27 may 1780* (C 1780) 7 p.; Jourdan, *oc.,* vol. **XXVI,** p. 333; *Instructions pour les Baillis, prévôts et préposés* (C) 4 p.; *Avis aux sieurs Curés* (C) 4 p. AdBR,B598,C148h; AmS,AA2390; AmC, AA176.

[370] AdBR, Haguenauer Notariat, Schreibstübe Weber.

the only way out. Frequently, the Jewish creditors did not wait, but were the first to attack the debtors."[1]

Officially, the First Chamber of the Sovereign Council began busying itself with the receipts on Dec. 11, 1778, at its first session following the publication of the Letters of Nov. 6."[2] On Sept. 28, the Chamber nominated four commissioners who were sent to the three sub-delegations of Upper Alsace (approximately similar to the sub-prefectures of our days) in order to liquidate the receipts-case: Krauss was sent to the sub-delegation of Ferrette, Bruges to Belfort, and Michelet and Golbéry to Colmar. Their job was complicated and difficult, especially that of Krauss, whose sphere of activities included the region of Sundgau, the center of the entire affair. When Krauss arrived, on Oct. 16, 1780, to the Château of Blotzheim (near Huningue) where he established his office, he already found there 586 files of documents on the affair; till the end of his mission he analyzed 2,031 files (2,085 according to another source). Most of the debtors decided to abandon the falsified receipts and Krauss granted them long terms for repayment of their debts, often up to 15 annual terms."[3] He arrested persons for "cabaling," but, in general, his mission was successful. The other commissioners, too, accomplished their missions and received from the government bonuses."[4]

There were also conducted criminal investigations in connection with the receipts. An example had to be shown in order to discour-

---

[1] Here is an example: In 1779, Jean Jacques Kueny of Huningue refused to pay a debt of a loan granted him by the Jew Jaudel Ulmo of Sierentz, and presented a receipt. Ulmo declared that his signature on the receipt was falsified and was prepared to prove it by comparison with his signature on other receipts. The same debtor once had already been, before the Case, on trial for refusing to pay a debt. To this the debtor replied that the Jew was trying to use the Case in order to avoid recognition even of the good receipts signed by him. Should the signatures of a Jew on different good receipts be analyzed, no two of them would be similar, because to sign receipts the Jews used different kinds of inks and pens and the Jews were always nervous when they applied their signatures. Such was the reasoning used by many debtors (AdHR,IIIB1818). From the texts of the petitions (suppliques) and the replies (répliques) of the debtors, it is clearly seen that these documents were written for the peasants by professional lawyers, notaries and other persons, according to a circulated pattern. In a similar conflict between the Jew Meyer Rueff of Blotzheim and his debtor Jean Finsterbach of Cappellen, the creditor declared that had the debtor really paid his debt, he surely would have requested the return of his I.O.U. by the Jew. Rueff also used another frequent Jewish argument: He granted two loans to his debtor, one of 2,650 pounds on March 31, 1778, and a second of 324 pounds on April 9, 1778. Where did the debtor get so much money in such a short time without taking a third loan, to repay the two original loans? This was, indeed, unnatural (AdHR,IIIB1818).

[2] "Registre des séances de la Ière Chambre du Conseil d'Alsace tenues en exécution des Lettres patentes de Sa Majesté du Six Novembre 1778..." AdHR,B,varia.

[3] Here are a few examples: 15 annual payments for a debt of 216 pounds, 8 payments for 330 pounds, 12 for 1,060 pounds, 12 for 800 pounds, 4 for 147 pounds, 10 for 205 pounds, 6 for 480 pounds, 10 for 550 pounds, etc.

[4] Krauss received 2,000 pounds, while each of the other three received 1,000 pounds. de Neyremand, oc., p. 23-29, 39-40. Unfortunately, most of the archives of the four commissioners were destroyed in 1902. Still, a few documents were saved, and these present a valuable source for the study of Jewish credit operations. See p. 96.

age future falsifications. The first criminal suit was against a distributor of falsified receipts who was arrested in Mittelwirh after having been denounced by the peasants themselves. Usually, the First Chamber of the Council was the highest Alsatian judicial body for *civil* cases, but the Letters of Nov. 6, 1778, gave to the First Chamber the right to judge criminal cases as well, viz., those concerned with the receipts. The First Chamber sentenced the distributor of receipts to *carcan* with the inscription *Faussaire*, to be lashed, and sent away for life on the galleys; his assistant was sentenced to *carcan* with the inscription *Compagnon du faussaire* and to 20 years on the galleys.[375] The most important criminal trial in this Case, against a group of 32 persons involved in the counterfeiting and distributing of receipts, was concluded on June 25, 1779. Two of the 32 were Jews: the merchant Joseph Lévy of Leymen and Marx David of Zinswiller. Three of the accused, Lintzentritt of Rhimbachzel, Fr.-Joseph Fenderich, a pig-dealer of Hirtzenfelden, and the peasant Bernard Grosgueth of Waldighoffen, were sentenced to be hanged. Five accused were sentenced to the galleys for life; three accused were sentenced to 15 and 10 years on the galleys. In addition, they all had to stay on the *carcan* with the inscription *Distributeur des fausses quittances* in French and German and the initials *G.A.L.* were branded on their shoulders. The verdict was announced by large broadsides in French and German.[376] The sentence was severe, but not uncommon for the 18th century. Death or the galleys were common sentences for counterfeiting signatures.[377]

35. WHO PROVOKED THE CASE OF THE COUNTERFEIT RECEIPTS?

It was already mentioned that two Jews were accused of helping in counterfeiting receipts. Another few Jews who turned to Chris-

---

[375] de Neyremand, *oc.,* p. 34.
[376] One was sentenced to be exiled for 6 years from Alsace; three received light sentences: reprimands and 15 days in prison on bread and water. Of the rest, some were freed by the same verdict and some after a new investigation. According to the verdict the bodies of the three hanged men were to be left at the place of execution until they would disintegrate, but in view of the hot weather, the Council granted on July 6, 1779, permission for burial. *Arrêt du Conseil Souverain d'Alsace, qui condamne à mort les nommés Lintzentritt... pour avoir fabriqué & distribué das quittances fausses. ERCSA du 25 juin* 1779 (Colmar). Placard. BuS39228. Another edition of the same verdict: *ERCSA. Du 25 juin* 1779 (Colmar) 10 p. (4°), in the author's possession. E. de Neyremand (*oc*) cited a few lines of a different text of the verdict. It is not known whether he copied the text from a manuscript or from a third printed edition of the verdict. According to de Neyremand, the sentence was passed on June 25, 1781, but according to both printed editions, the sentence was passed on June 25, 1779. See p. 2.
[377] "Edit contre les faussaires", Mars 1680 (de Boug, *oc.,* vol. I, p. 82-83). In 1744, Jean Robert Koch and his accomplices were sent by the Metz Parliament on the galleys for counterfeiting a receipt: *Arrest de la Cour de Parlement, qui condamne Jean-Robert Koch... pour crime de faux, &c. Du 20 Juillet* 1744 (M 1744) 8 p. BN,naf.22709f.360.

tianity were involved.'" But it soon became apparent that not a few converted Jews, not even the men sentenced to die or to the galleys were responsible for provoking the Case. A more intelligent and important person was involved, and the name of this individual soon became known: *François-Joseph-Antoine Hell* (1731-1794), the bailiff of Landser (Upper Alsace). On Feb. 18, 1780, Hell was arrested and brought to the prison of the Strasbourg citadel. None of his friends was allowed to see him—as he wrote himself—and he was not permitted to receive any mail. His servant, who accompanied him to the prison, was not permitted to leave it. Hell refused to take any food except fresh eggs, he was afraid that the Jews might attempt to poison him. On Feb. 26, 1780, Hell was interrogated by the Intendant of Alsace himself.'"

A great number of falsified receipts was found in Hell's house.'" Was Hell only the initiator of the counterfeiting case, or did he himself falsify receipts? According to the results of the Intendant's investigation, Hell was suspected of both crimes; he himself stated that he learned Hebrew, but only out of curiosity for the language (he learned Greek and Latin, too).'" But the main accusation against Hell was his role as the anonymous author of the 1779 pamphlet on the receipts. Hell confessed to being the author of the pamphlet.'" He believed that this would free him from other responsibilities in the Case and that he would be acquitted. But when his authorship of the pamphlet became a serious reason for a trial against him, Hell denied the authorship. Hell's friends stated in a petition that he accused himself only out of magnanimity to the real author.'" At one point Hell became afraid. In a letter of June 3, 1780, he assured the prince de Montbarrey that, if he were only freed, he would never again concern himself with the Jewish question. He played the role of a martyr. In one of his many petitions he maintained that the "Jews and other oppressors of the people" were trying to ruin him; on March 17, 1781, he wrote again that "Jews and attorneys" looked forward to his ruin; much later he wrote about himself as of the victim of the "oppressors of the people." Hell tried to prove the existence of a Jewish plot against him. In 1780, he presented a list of 86 witnesses, who stated that the Jews requested them to murder

---

'" The Jews accused an apostate of Leymen of helping on the counterfeiting: some compromising documents were found in his house and he spent a year in prison. But he was freed and asked the Jews for 20,000 pounds compensation. On June 28, 1781, the Jews were sentenced to pay him 2,000 pounds (de Neyremand, Créances..., p. 180). In Alsace lived some converted Jews and any one of them was in a position to help in counterfeiting receipts.
'" AdHR,Wendl.48/16,p.62.
'" G. Hemerdinger, Le dénombrement des Israélites d'Alsace (1784). *REJ.* vol. XLII (1901) p. 253.
'" AdHR,Wendl48/16p.62. The Jews stated in a petition addressed to the King that in 1765 Hell wrote in Hebrew a letter to the Jewish leaders of a community proposing to defend them in a certain case for a fee of 400 Louis: "Mémoire sur l'état des Juifs en Alsace", in: Chr. W. Dohm, *Ueber die bürgerliche Verbesserung der Juden* (Berlin-Stettin 1781) p. 179-80.
'" AdHR,Wendl.48/16,p.55,62 (see note 361).
'" Ibidem, p. 248.

him, to give false testimony against him, etc."⁴ A well-organized campaign requested Heil's release."⁵ As a result of the pro-Hell campaigns the government did not put Hell on trial, but, as his presence in Alsace was dangerous, he was ordered on June 10, 1780, to leave Alsace for a forced residence in Valence (province of Dauphiné), where his wife's family resided. Hell spent three years in prison and exile."⁶

36. F.-J.-A. HELL—THE PORTRAIT OF AN ALSATIAN 18th CENTURY ANTI-SEMITIC LEADER

Very little was written in the Alsatian historiography on Hell and his various activities. An attempt will be made by this author to portray him on the basis of various printed and archival sources.

Hell came from a 15th century Frankfort family. He was born on June 11, 1731, in Hirsingue (Upper Alsace).³⁸⁷ At the start of the falsified receipts affair Hell was the bailiff of Landser, which belonged to the comtesse de Sénozan, Périgord, de Miramond and to de Veyne."⁸ As bailiff, Hell came frequently in contact with the Jews."⁹

---

³⁸⁴ Ibidem, 48/15, p. 234; 48/16, p. 88, 134; *De Hell en Haute Alsace* (sl nd) 14 p., p. 10 (AdHR,Wendl.47/15,p.173).
³⁸⁵ The author of an unsigned petition stated that Hell's only sin was his "great carelessness." Others called him a martyr in the fight for the peasants' interests. 45 Sundgau priests sent to the King a petition for Hell's release. Priests also sent petitions in his favor to high Church dignitaries. But the priests had to act carefully, especially since the Basel Bishop Frédéric requested on March 25, 1780, the Sundgau priests under his jurisdiction to preach justice toward the Jews and to tell the people that falsifying receipts was a sin. (Later, Hell wrote in his own draft of a petition for his release that the Jews paid the Bishop for a monitory letter against the peasants.) 92 Upper Alsace priests wrote in a petition addressed to their Bishop that Hell's pamphlet did not influence the people in any case, and that the Jews themselves were responsible for the counterfeiting because they gave an example by falsifying peasants' I.O.U.s. AdHR, Wendl.48/16p.43,64,75; SBern,B216f.385-86.
³⁸⁶ According to a document dated Jan. 19, 1786 (AdHR,Wendl.48/16, p.44). During Hell's exile, two of his portraits were printed in Alsace with the inscription "The friend and the love of his fellow-citizens." (*L'Ami et l'amour de ses concitoyens*), BmC, *cf. De Hell...*, p. 10, and a document on Hell's exile in AN,K1142. Most of the Alsatian historians presented Hell as a hero and martyr. One anonymous historian attempted to minimize Hell's punishment and to prove that he spent only a few days in prison and was never exiled, that his arrest and exile were merely Jewish boasts: X [Charles Hoffmann?], Le Bailli Hell et la Revue des Etudes Juives, *R.A*, vol. XXXI (1902). But the documents on which this study os based — including Hell's personal documents (in the collection of his notary, AdHR, collection Wendling) — prove that Hell spent three years in prison and exile.
³⁸⁷ *De Hell...*, see note 386. Hell's title of nobility "was renewed" on Dec. 7, 1784, by Joseph of Austria. Hell received his first education in Porrentruy, later in Pont-à-Mousson, and in 1749-1753, in Strasbourg. On Nov. 17, 1753, he was allowed to plead as attorney in the Sovereign Council. From 1755 until 1761, he was clerk-tabelion (*greffier tabellion*) of the Hirsingue bailiwick; in 1761 he became bailiff of Seppois; in later years he occupied the same post in other bailiwicks.
³⁸⁸ AdHR,Wendl.48/16,p.102-3.
³⁸⁹ According to a biographical note on Hell dated Jan. 19, 1786, Hell himself judget about 2,000 cases yearly. In a three year period he passed 7,000 sentences, 2,000 of them between Jews and Gentiles. According to

Hell himself was indebted to many creditors. He probably also had Jewish creditors, and if this was so, this fact greatly influenced his relationship to the Jews.'" Hell was greatly indebted not only because of his many financial speculations and his chase for riches, but also because of his squandering and his part in many obscure transactions."' He married the daughter of a rich Dauphiné man named Savoye only for her money. He warned his wife that he would divorce her if her father would refuse him money. On Feb. 17, 1787, Hell's father-in-law wrote in a letter to his daughter that Hell squandered about 40,000 pounds of the King's treasury. Hell asked his father-in-law to give him 30,000 pounds in order to repay the royal money before the embezzlement would be discovered, but Savoye did not have so much money, so Hell deserted his wife."'

Hell's entire personality was such that he was forced to become involved in conflicts with Jews. He believed that Jews were capable of committing all acts of evil."' Already in 1758, while being a simple clerk, Hell provoked trials against Jews in order to obtain bribes from them. When, as bailiff, he became the Landser judge, he presided at trials provoked against Jews by himself during an earlier period.'" His hatred of Jews was so notorious that he

---

another document written by Hell himself, 201 out of 5,331 sentences passed by him in a certain period were in favor of the Gentile sides against Jews, 591 in favor of Jews against Gentiles, 341 were preparatory sentences, etc. AdHR,Wendl,48/16,p.44,103. See p. 103.

'" On Feb. 14, 1775, a loan of 6,000 pounds was granted to him by the Basel creditor Ferdinand Cuentz. On March 21, 1787, the City of Basel granted him a 20,000 pounds loan. The debts owed by him were much larger than his possessions consisting of land valued at 9,800 pounds, buildings valued at 2,246 pounds, furniture, etc. (AdHR,L483). During the investigation of February 1780, Hell confessed taking loans and gifts from Jews. On March 3, 1780, Hell wrote to the Intendant of Alsace that even before being nominated to the post of bailiff he was a debtor to Jews. According to a document of 1790, Hell was involved in a trial with his Jewish creditor Blum Rueff (AN,K1142,No.53; AdHR,L48 and Wendl. 48/16, p. 72).

'"' After Hell's death a Strasbourg forage clerk (*commis aux fourrages*) named Du Bois gave the following account: in 1787 he was appointed as the principal guard of the forest of the valley of Saint-Amarin under Hell's supervision. Du Bois worked on this post for two years without ever receiving his salary, because Hell and a certain Breiman put his salary, as well as other incomes from the forest, in their own pockets. When Du Bois protested, Hell gave him an I.O.U. for the unpaid salary, but the money was never paid to him. About 1770, François Noblat, the sub-delegate of Belfort sent to the Alsace Intendant long accusations against Hell and the bailiff Clavé; that they speculated in the sales of communal forests, etc. Such speculations resulted in a 1767 trial involving the inhabitants of Carspach (bailiwick of Altkirch), who sent a representative to Paris with complaints against Hell. Hell was, probably, not worse than all the other bailiffs, who likewise looked for additional income. AdHR,L483; Ch. Hoffmann, vol. II, p. 247, 249-251.

'"' Hell's brother, an officer, was a well known squanderer; his family was forced to pay his debts. AdHR,Wendl.48/16,p.102-3.

'"' In 1783, Hell received a confidential report that a foreign Jew was trying to buy the land of Landser valued at 900,000 pounds. Jews were not allowed to possess land outside the ghettos and according to Hell's letter of Oct. 24, 1783, this prospective buyer was "an Avignon man who had the look of a Jew and of an usurer," and Hell wrote letters begging everybody to save the Landser land from falling into Jewish hands. AdHR,Wendl.48/14.

'"' In 1757 occurred the sudden death of the Gentile Ignace Ilch of Hirsingen; his will left his entire possessions to his widow, but the will

sometimes placed himself behind the scenes of anti-Jewish affairs in order not to compromise them by his open participation in them. In 1772-1773, the Sovereign Council prepared witnesses and other proof in Hirsingue in order to prepare an accusation and trial against the Jews as a collective group for practicing usury. The Council requested Hell to do the job, but Hell asked that somebody else be found, because his hatred of the Jews was too well known."'

Hell was interested in agriculture, botany, mechanics, physics, and other sciences; he was the author of many scientific memoranda and he corresponded with scientists. He studied the peasants' situation and even before the Case of receipts he proposed to conduct a survey of the peasants' debts and properties (because of the falsified receipts the first part of his project was carried out)."'' But, was Hell really a sincere friend of the peasants? Some documents prove the contrary. He was a partisan of the old, pre-1789 regime of the nobles and the Church. Let us take one example, his position in regard to the distribution of communal properties. In June 1788, the Alsatian Provincial Assembly (*Assemblée provin-*

---

was signed by him while lying unconscious on his death-bed. Ilch's family engaged the Jew Salomon Ulmann of Dürmenach, who was familiar with the laws, to attack the validity of the will. But Hell was deeply involved in this affair; he helped to falsify the will. Before this affair Ulmann had won two trials against Hell. Now, the bailiff Hell decided to take his revenge on Ulmann and he sentenced him to prison for life. The trial and the appeal lasted over 15 years. Ulmann published a factum that made a great impression. He requested to be judged by a magistrate other than Hell. More than ten years later Ulmann published another factum in which was related the following: The Gentile Joseph Stempfell assaulted some Jews as they were leaving the Dürmenach Synagogue, and the Jews defended themselves. Hell then decided to use the incident against the Jews, but in order to achieve it Stemfell had to have the looks of a very sick man, a victim of the Jews. A doctor gave him a medicine that was supposed to make him ill, but he died of it. Hell sentenced one Jew to be hanged and two others to the galleys: Bruis & Loiseau du Maulon, *Mémoire à consulter, et consultation pour Salomon Ulman* [P 1768] 18 p. BN,4F31760; *Salomon Ulmann, Juif de Dürmenach, contre la procédure extraordinairement instruite contre lui au bailliage d'Hirsingen* (C [177-]) 27 p. BN,4F 35695. Hell was, for a while, very much worried because of Ulmann's factums. He requested his friends to send him letters, so that he may use the information to draft a reply to the Jew, but the reply was never published (AdHR,Wendl.48/16, p. 14-42, 94, 133).
   '"' AdHR,Wendl.48/16,p.49. Hell bragged that he provoked the order forbading notaries to sign in Jewish houses I.O.U.s in favor of Jewish creditors. In 1766, Hell prepared an anti-Jewish pamphlet (Ibidem, p. 73 and 47/15 p. 243). Even before 1778 Hell instigated peasants not to pay their debts to Jewish creditors. In 1773, the Mayor of Seppois stated that Hell requested him to tell the peasants not to pay their debts, but Hell denied this and declared that the "Synagogue" paid the Mayor for making such a statement (Ibidem, 48/16 p. 48).
   '"' Much later, in 1790, he again proposed to defend the peasant against usury, but he was unable to propose any organization of agricultural credit; in fact, nobody was able to do it (AdHR,Wendl.46/1-7, 48/16, p. 78; Hell, *Vœu d'un agriculteur rhéno-françois* [P 1791] p. 9). Hell was a child of the 18th century France, where the physiocratic idea that agriculture is the most noble and useful profession was accepted by everybody. Beginning with the '50s many societies for the amelioration of agriculture (*sociétés d'agriculture*) were founded (de la Fournière, Les Comités d'agriculture de 1760 et de 1784. *Mémoires du Comité des sciences économiques et sociales* (1909) p. 94-121; Veulersee, *L'Expansion de la doctrine physiocratique de 1756 à 1770* (P 1911). The interest for agriculture arose in Alsace, too, but societies were founded there only after 1790 and Hell was dragged along with these ideas.

ciale) requested Hell to prepare a project for the distribution of communal properties. Hell fought against the equal distribution of these properties among all peasants; he proposed only a temporary distribution, because he claimed that the townsmen (*bourgeois*), too, should have, as a whole body, their rights to these properties. Hell's arguments were of such a nature: if poor people were allowed to buy their parts of these properties, they would be forced to take loans, and, being unable to repay the debts, the properties would be taken over by the creditors. Should the peasants receive communal properties free of charge, they would, in any case, be forced to abandon the land because of laziness. He proposed that *manants*—the poorest countrymen—should be excluded from receiving communal properties. Hell's ideas about peasantry can clearly be explained with his own words in one of his pamphlets published during the Revolution: "Peasants, you are now free and you can enjoy your freedom, provided that you do not harm anybody."[397]

Hell participated in many of the intrigues of the Upper Alsatian nobility against the Intendant of Alsace who defended the interests of the Kingdom.[398] Hell was never popular among the peasants. He had too high an opinion about himself; he liked many titles (at the Provincial Assembly he was called *docteur Confucius*). On July 21, 1789, peasants attacked his brother, who was a clerk at the Hirsingue bailiwick, because he wanted to hide the archives of the Huningue bailiwick and of the de Monjoie family; they tied and beat him up, and told him that he must pay for the sins of his brother who was brutal and unjust in passing sentences and in demanding taxes.[399] Still, when Hell returned from his exile in Dauphiné he was treated in Alsace like a hero and a victim of the

---

[397] Hoffmann, *oc.*, vol. I, p. 348-73; Hell, *Vœu...*, p. 2. During the Revolution of 1789, many riots occurred in Alsace because the *manants* requested their part of the communal properties (*biens communaux*). Similar riots occured also in Lorraine. Georges Bourgin, *Le partage des biens communaux...* (P 1907), p. 199-216; 572-79; Ph. Sagnac et P. Caron, *Les Comités des droits féodaux et de législation...* (P 1907) p. 574-78, 618-21; Henri Sée, *La Vie économique et les classes sociales en France au XVIIIe siècle* (P 1924) p. 72-75. Jews, too, requested during the Revolution their part of the communal properties: AdHR,L645; *Copie de la Pétition présentée par plusieurs Citoyens [Juifs] du Bas-Rhin, à la Convention Nationale* [avec: Extrait du registre des arrêtés du Comité de Législation du 11 Brumaire, an III] (C [an III]) 7 p. AmC,B63 ("nous sommes exclus du droit de partage des biens communaux"); P. Hildenfinger, Actes du district de Strasbourg relatifs aux Juifs. *REJ*, vol. LX (1910) p. 249-50. See note 29, p. 14-15.
[398] In 1767, he ordered a special tax to finance the nobles' fight against the Intendant's orders of 1742 and 1744, which aimed at stripping the nobles and the cities of their rule over the forests and at centralizing this power in the Intendant's hands. Hoffmann, *oc.*, vol. I, p. 648, vol. II, p. 250.
[399] *Ibid.* Les troubles de 1789 dans la Haute Alsace. *RA*, vol. LVIII (1907) p. 209-210. The peasants of the Landser bailiwick, where Hell was bailiff, were not happier than those of other parts of Alsace; their lot was even worse. The inhabitants of Hirsingen and other communities of the Landser seigniory were involved in lawsuits with the family of comte de Montjoie, seignior of Hirsingen, who refused to recognize the communal right of these inhabitants. In a memorandum of 1784, they complained that the seignior forced them into misery: *Mémoire pour les habitans & communautés de Hirsingen... contre... comte de Montjóye* (P 1784) 120 p. AdHR,IIE242.

Jews. He became an active member of the Provincial Assembly
and headed a special commission to prepare a project of a Statute
for the Alsatian Jews, which, in effect, aimed at worsening their
situation.[400] After the outbreak of the Revolution of 1789 Hell was
sent to the National Assembly as Deputy from Haguenau and
Wissembourg (Alsace); he became one of the principal opponents
of the Jewish Emancipation.[401] Hell was a fanatical monarchist;
he believed that justice was to be found only in the hands of the
King, who "is a God"—as he wrote in a letter to de Malesherbes—
and that those opposing the King's will must suffer both on earth
and in the other world.[402] Hell was arrested; it was not difficult
to prove his monarchist and anti-Republican activities. In 1794,
Hell died on the gillotine.[403]

37. THE LIQUIDATION OF THE RECEIPTS CASE BY THE ECONOMIC RUIN OF THE JEWISH CREDITORS

The King's transfer of the entire affair to the First Chamber
of the Sovereign Council was opposed by many Alsatian groups and
individuals. The fight of the free and independent City of Strasbourg for the maintenance of her privileges played an important
role in this case.[404] The Magistrates of Strasbourg protested against
the removal from under the city jurisdiction the cases involving
falsified receipts. A group of Parisian attorneys stated in a memorandum that the interests of Strasbourg would suffer as a result
of the King's decision. But it seemed certain that the King would
not yield to the request of Strasbourg. Strasbourg was interested
mainly in the aplication in cases of falsified receipts the special
Strasbourg Statute on Jews residing in the territory controlled by

---

[400] This subject will be treated in a separate study on the Jewish problem on the eve of the Revolution of 1789.
[401] Joseph Schwendt, who was himself a Deputy, wrote on Apr. 13, 1790,
that Hell prepared a pamphlet against the Jews, but after the Jewish leader
Cerfberr threatened to tell the entire story of Hell's anti-Jewish campaign,
Hell was afraid to publish the pamphlet. Schwendt himself was an
opponent of Jewish emancipation, but he disliked Hell. R. Reuss, L'Alsace
pendant la Révolution française. *RA*, vol. LXXIV (1927) p. 496-97. Hell did
publish a few anonymous pamphlets against Jews during the Revolution,
only one of these is signed with his initial, H.: H[ell], *Mon opinion sur les
Juifs...* (P 25 décembre 1789) 12 p. BN,Le29-408. In most catalogues a
certain Scarramuza is mentioned as the author of the book *Les Juifs d'Alsace doivent-ils être admis au droit de citoyens actifs? Lisez et jugez* ([S]
1790) 208 and 46 p. But according to the catalogue of Chauffour's famous
Alsatiana, the book was written by Hell: André Waltz, *Catalogue de la Bibliothèque Chauffour* (C 1889) p. 461. According to a note on the copy in
the Library of the Jewish Theological Seminary, New York, Hell was also
the publisher of the 1790 edition of *Requête des marchands et négocians de
Paris...* (P 1790).
[402] AN,W351dr.713-1,p.51,dr.713-2,p.19. During the Revolution Hell tried
to hide documents: *Extrait du registre des séances publiques... Haut-Rhin...
7 juin* 1793 (C 1793) 4 p. The Abbot Lellomé, Professor of the Colmar College, called Hell an *aristocrate* (AN,W351,dr.713,p.8).
[403] L. Delabrouse, Les Députés de l'Alsace à la Constituante (1789-1791).
Revue alsacienne, vol. XII (1888-89) p. 444-45.
[404] This subject will be treated in a separate study.

the city, which gave to judges the right to confiscate the debts, because according to this Statute Jews were not allowed to grant loans or sell on credit to Christians. This question was discussed at a special conference held by the Strasbourg Magistrates on Feb. 14, 1781, in Wasselonne."' The text of a speech by a jurist (his name is not mentioned) at this conference was fortunately located. His attitude toward Jews was very liberal, probably one of the most liberal speeches toward Jews before 1789. He pointed out that even in trials involving Jews justice must always reign. One had to be especially careful, he said, in cases involving the possibility of passing sentences in the spirit of the Strasbourg Statute on Jews, because the Statute was of a criminal rather than civil character. Jurists always disliked and distrusted passing sentences leading to the confiscation of property. According to the Roman tradition of jurisprudence, the judge in such cases was preferably to favor the accused. If Jewish creditors were not guilty of breaking the law, the courts should defend them against the debtors, who would otherwise easily refuse to repay their debts and threaten the Jews with the eventual confiscation of the debts by the courts. The anonymous jurist cited an example of a similar trial: a Christian paid a Jewish merchant for the purchased merchandise with a promissory note. This was—according to the jurist—a legal transaction, usurious rates were not involved, but the Jew was still brought to the law-court. Should cases of falsified receipts be judged in the spirit of confiscation, justice would surely suffer."'

On Jan. 9, 1779, the Jews declared in a memorandum (drawn up by three Colmar attorneys) that they would be ruined, because their debtors, using the falsified receipts, refused to pay the debts, while the Christian creditors forced their Jewish debtors to pay their debts, especially in cases of debts resulting from the purchase of horses, cattle, grain, land, etc. on credit by Jewish dealers. The decree on the liquidation of the falsified receipts refused to the Jews the right to request the law-courts to order their debtors to repay their debts, but Christian creditors were allowed to request the help of the law against their Jewish debtors."' In a later memorandum to the Council on the Letters patent of May 27, 1780, the Jews protested against granting too long terms to debtors. The Jews wrote about another dangerous practice: "The agents of the chicanery" (suppôts de la chicane), who attempted to increase the number of trials in order to augment their own profits (i.e., lawyers, notaries, etc.), tried to convince the debtors that the Letters patent of May 27, 1780, allowed all debtors of Jews (even those not holding falsified receipts) to request from the First Chamber alleviations in the payment of their debts. All the debtors had to do, it was claimed, was to make against their Jewish creditors general accusations of usury, which would insure them against any further trials at the creditors' requests. In any case such

---

⁴⁰⁵ AmS, Procès-verbaux de la Chambre des XIII, 1781, p. 36-38.
⁴⁰⁶ AmS,AA2390.
⁴⁰⁷ AdBR,C355,p.47.

accusations—debtors were told—would be forwarded to the Council's first Chamber, even if the creditors were in possession of legalized I.O.U.s. The Jews requested a special decree in the spirit of the Letters of May 27, 1780. These Letters—they wrote—were not granted in order to instigate new crimes, and as such the spirit of the Letters should be followed very strictly, i.e., only peasant-debtors who agreed to renounce their claims based on the falsified receipts were to be granted terms for the payment of the debts.[408] The Sovereign Council published an order in the spirit of the Jewish request. But lawyers were still persuading the debtors to make general accusations of usury against their debtors.[409]

It thus seemed that the Case would never end. The long terms granted to a great number of debtors were a sort of a premium of encouraging other falsifications—as the historian de Neyremand wrote.[410] Hell himself stated that the greatest number of receipts was falsified in the period between the publication of the first order calling for the registration of the receipts and the date set for the registration, because the counterfeiters assured the debtors that all registered receipts would be declared valid.[411] Even after the publication of the Letters of Sept. 28, 1780, many debtors bought falsified receipts bearing old dates. According to the Letters and the orders of the King and the Council, the debtors who refused to abandon the falsified receipts were to be punished. Something had to be done in order to put an end to the debtors' obstinacy and the criminal practices of their lawyers. And thus, on Dec. 28, 1780, the Council ruled that new falsified receipts would not be accepted as a basis for granting terms; and that the owners of such receipts would be punished.[412] This ruling was effective. First of all it permitted the Council to sentence only a small group of conterfeiters and distributors of receipts and prevented the mass-trials of thousands of debtors. Still, in 1784, the Jews complained that judges and lawyers forced debtors to bring accusations of usury against their Jewish creditors.[413] The courts were flooded with similar trials

[408] "Mémoire pour les Juifs d'Alsace, sur l'exécution des Lettres patentes du 27 mai 1780", in the author's possession.
[409] The Council declared that the practices of the lawyers often ruined peasant-debtors, who sent to Colmar their accusations against Jews. The Council could not accept these requests and accusations. The Council decided to dismiss all such cases forwarded to it by judges of lower courts and prohibit future trials of a similar nature. ERCSA. Du 28 Septembre 1779 (C 1779) Placard, BuS101339; ERCSA. Du 18 Août 1780 (C 1780) Placard and 4 p., AmS,AA230 and AmC,AA176; ERCSA. Du 28 Septembre 1780 (C 1780) Placard, BuS38979. Cf. Véron-Réville, Histoire de la Révolution française dans le département du Haut-Rhin 1789-1795 (C 1865) p. 10.
[410] de Neyremand, Conseil..., p. 29.
[411] AdHR,Wendl.48/16,p.76.
Hell wrote (Ibidem) that the best way to liquidate the Case was to provoke one lawsuit from a Jewish creditor against his debtor in possession of a falsified receipt. This would force all debtors to destroy the receipts in their possession. He boasted of having written to a judge that if it were up to him, he would have hanged one debtor and the entire Case would thus end. But this was only an opportunistic self-defense.
[412] ERCSA. Du 28 Décembre 1780 (C sd) Placard. AdBR,B598.
[413] Léon Halévy, Résumé de l'histoire des Juifs modernes (P 1828) p. 285-86.

Hell himself wrote in 1783 that if the Case were not liquidated very soon, the Jews with small properties would be unable to exist and the poor Jews would die from hunger, as they received from their debtors neither cash or products since 1781.[414] The historian Véron-Réville, who studied the archives on the Case before most of these files were destroyed, wrote in 1864 that many Jewish creditors were not richer than their debtors and that a great part of the debts had been drawn up in a perfectly legal manner. But the falsified receipts ruined the Jews because the decrees on the liquidation of the debts aimed to accomplish just this. A decree of Aug. 28, 1787, allowed Jewish creditors to request payment of debts, but this was done with so many guarantees for the debtors that it only helped to ruin the Jews[415] Because of a bad harvest, on Sept. 28, 1781, the Council permitted the judges to grant new 6-monthly terms in payment of the capitals for debts of debtors who lost 1/4 of their harvests; one-year terms to those who lost 1/2; while interest had to be paid. On Jan. 7, 1783, the Council forbade Jews to request payment of debts and granted another term of one year to the debtors. On Feb. 5, 1784, the Council extended the term for still another year.[416]

In Junuary 1785, the Jews proposed that debtors of 600 pounds or less repay their debts in two terms of three months each; while debtors of larger sums repay the debts in four terms of 6 months each. This proposal was rejected.[417] On Jan. 7, 1785, the Council ordered the Jews to present within 3 months a list of all debts owed them by peasants and artisans. Until then, Jews were not to grant any new loans or request payment of any old debts. The date was delayed and in January 1786 the Jews presented the list of debts for the total sum of about 11 million pounds in capital.[418] In the beginning of February 1786, the Council considered the following four proposals for the liquidation of the debts: (1) to control and compare the claims of the debtors and their creditors and to fix the sums to be paid by the debtors at once; (2) to grant terms to the debtors; (3) to annul the entire debts, or parts of the debts, and grant terms for the payment of the uncancelled parts (only the King could make such a decision); (4) to transform the debts into rentals (rentes). In November 1786, the King expressed the opinion that the Jewish creditors be allowed to request only 1/5 of their debts. This meant the dispossession of the Jews of 4/5 of their properties. On Jan. 10, 1787, the King's proposal was confirmed by the Council of Alsace, but in August of the same year this decision was the subject of many changes. The decision of January 10 was a very dangerous precedent; both the King and the Council

[414] AdHR,Wendl.48/16,p.79.
[415] Véron-Réville, Les Juifs d'Alsace sous l'ancien régime. Le Procès des fausses quittances. RA, vol. V (1864) p. 289-300.
[416] ERCSA. Du 28 Septembre 1781 (C 1781) 2 p. In the author's possession; ERCSA. Du 7 Janvier 1783 (C 1783) 3 p. BuS33228; ERCSA. Du 5 Février 1784 (Colmar) 3 p. (4º) and Placard. BuS33228; AmC,AA176. Holdt, oc., Feb. 5-6, 1784.
[417] Holdt, oc., Jan. 26 and 31, 1785.
[418] Ibidem, Jan. 14 and 31, Apr. 21, Aug. 18, 1785.

218

became afraid of the consequences of such an act. In August, 1787, the Council allowed Jewish creditors to request through the courts the payment of debts. But the Council granted the debtors two terms in payment of debts of 100 pounds or less (the second payment to be made on Saint-Martin's Day of 1788); four terms for debts of 100-600 pounds; 8 terms for debts of 600-1,000 pounds; and 10 yearly terms for debts of more than 1,000 pounds. This was, again, a hard economic blow for the Jewish money-lenders.[419]

The *Case of the Counterfeit Receipts* was never properly liquidated. At the outbreak of the 1789 Revolution the debts were not yet paid off, legally the debtors had still many terms for the payment of their debts. In a memorandum of 1790 the Jews asked not to use the Case of the Receipts against their struggle for citizenship, because they were prepared to respect the terms granted to the debtors. On Sept. 27, 1791, full citizenship was granted to the Jews, and in a Law dated the following day, Sept. 28, 1791, the National Assembly ordered the Alsatian Jews to present a list of debts owed them by peasant-debtors and directed that a way of paying these debts be worked out. Yet, this Law was never adhered to. The Jews refused to present the requested list and they were not forced to do so.[420]

The Case of the Counterfeit Receipts instigated a whole series of very important events in the history of the Jews in France, e.g.: the aggravation of the conflict between the Jewish leader Cerfberr and the City of Strasbourg;[421] the abolishment of the body-toll;[422] the publication of Dohm's book on the emancipation of Jews;[423] the Letters patent of July 10, 1784;[424] the census of Alsatian

---

[419] Ibidem, Feb. 3, Nov. 18, 1786, Jan. 10, Aug. 17, 1786; *ERCSA. Du* 28 Août 1787 (C 1787) 8 p. BuS101343.
The anti-Jewish historian Joseph Lémann wrote that even after the Council's order of Aug. 28, 1787, the counterfeiting continued: *La Prépondérance juive* (P 1889) p. 105. Other printed sources of the Case of the counterfeit receipts: *ERCSA. Du 7 janvier* 1783 (C 1783) 3 p. AN,K1142; Dr. Aug. Hertzog, Der Wucher auf dem elsässischen Lande. *Strassburger Post* (1908) N° 773; Dr. M. Ginsburger, Der Wucher im Elsass. *Ibidem* (1908) N° 854, 985 & 1012; Ibid, Der Unheber der falschen Quittungen. *Ibidem,* (1909) N° 431; Henri Labroue, Le Mécanisme de l'usure juive dans l'Est de la France au XVIIIᵉ siècle. *La Question juive en France et dans le monde,* vol. II, N° 9 (1943) p. 41-48.
[420] This will be treated in a study to be published in *Zion* (Jerusalem).
[421] See note 113.
[422] *Edit du Roi, portant exemption des Droits de péage corporels sur les Juifs. Du mois de Janvier* 1784. *Enregistré le* 17 *du même mois* (C 1784) 4 p.; French and German edition: *Koenigliches Edict welches die Juden von Leibzoll Gubühren befreyt.* 7 p.; edition of Metz: *Edit du Roi, portant exemption des droits de péage corporels sur les Juifs... Régistré en Parlement le 8 Mars* 1784 (M 1784) 3 p.; *Lettres patentes du Roi sur arrêt portant fixation de l'indemnité accordée à la ville de Strasbourg pour raison de la suppression des droits qu'elle percevait sur les Juifs sous la dénomination de péage corporel... le 25 Janvier* 1786 (M 1786) 4 p.; *Extrait des registres du Conseil d'Etat du Roi* [du 8 Septembre 1786] (S 1786) 3 p. AmS, AA2378-9 and vol.R39-12;JTS;BN,Ld184-21. This subject will be treated in a separate study.
[423] Christian Wilhelm von Dohn, *Ueber die bürgerliche Verbesserung der Juden* (Berlin-Stettin 1781); French edition: *De la Réforme politique des Juifs.* Traduit de l'allemand [par J. Bernoulli] (Dessau 1782).
[424] On the Letters patent of July 10, 1784, see: *Lettres patentes du Roi, portant Règlement concernant les Juifs d'Alsace. Du 10 Juillet* 1784. *Enre-*

Jews"[24] and the danger of expulsion for many Alsatian Jewish families;"[25] etc. But this is a subject for a separate study.

To summarize our study, we must come to the conclusion that on the eve of the 1789 Revolution the Jews of Alsace, Metz and Lorraine were persecuted by everybody, by the Gentile population, by the Catholic Church and even by the Protestants who were persecuted themselves; by the seigniors, local administrations and by the King and his military and civil administrators. These persecutions affected the political, economic. civil and religious life of the Jews. Sometimes, the Jews were tolerated because the French Monarchy needed the Jews' help for the armies; for the seigniors and some cities, too, the Jews were a source of income. The Jews were forced to accept this role of economic agents because they were forced to accept any means of making a living. Fhe French Monarchy did never possess any liberal feelings toward Jews, who were always regarded as enemies of the Church but, who had sometimes to be tolerated because the French Monarchy was unable to organize its armies without the help of the Jewish bankers and traders.

gistrées le 26 Août suivant (C 1784) 16 p.; German text in: *Privilegirte Strassburger Zeitung,* N° 76 (1784); R. Anchel, Les Lettres patentes du 10 Juillet 1784. Festschrift zu Simon Dubnows siebzigsten Geburtstag (Berlin 1930) p. 187-200, in: *REJ,* vol. XCIII (1932) p. 113-134 and in his book *Les Juifs en France* (P 1946) p. 213-33.
[425] See notes 46, 55 and: *ERCSA. Du premier Septembre* 1784 [Exécution des Lettres patentes du 10 Juillet 1784] (C 1784) 7 p. BuS33269.
[426] *ERCSA. Du 6 Mai* 1786 (C 1788) 4 p.; *ERCSA. Du 13 Décembre* 1788 (C 1788) 3 p. BuS101344 and AdBR,B598.

MALEDICTION.

Ii. eft une nation, qui toûjours en delire,
L'on fent deja d'avance ce que nous voulons dire.
C'eft le peuple Juif,
Qui toûjours fugitif,
Par une erreur groffiere
Aveugle, fans lumere,
Même fans Foy ni Loy,
Tuerent leur propre Roy.
Ce qui les rend malheureux,
Ils demandernt fur eux,
Et fur leur nation
La MALEDICTION.

INCSRIPTIO.

Sanguis ejus fuper nos) Fiat.   Jefus Nazarenus) Veritas.
Er fuper filios noftros.)   Rex Judeorum.)

JESUS

Qu'ay-je donc merité?
Je fuis la verité.

PILATE répond:

Quid eft Veritas?
C'eft une queftion, qui n'eft plus guere en vogue,
On l'ingnore abfolument dans notre Sinagogue.

MALEDICTION

Les Juifs d'aprefens, font de vrais gueux
Toûjours vagabons, ils n'ont ni feu ni lieux.
Fourberie, mauvaife foy, vices, qui leur font propres,
Il ne font plus dans le monde, que pour fervir d'opprobre.
Il en eft d'affez fous, de croire que c'eft un bien,
Pour honorer Moife, de tromper un Chretien.
Le fecond Evêque de RINCK, s'eft delors depêché,
De chaffer ces Frippons, de tout fon Evêché.

OBSERVATIONS

D'UN ALSACIEN

SUR L'AFFAIRE PRÉSENTE

DES JUIFS

D'ALSACE.

A FRANCFORT.

M. DCC. LXXIX.

Left: An Anti-Jewish Leaflet Distributed During the Case of Counterfeit Receipts. Right: Hell's Book on the Case, 1779 (see p. 124).

THE JEWISH STATUS IN EIGHTEENTH-CENTURY FRANCE AND THE "DROIT D'AUBAINE"

ONE of the most curious aspects of the legal status of the Jews in France prior to the Revolution of 1789 was the application of the *droit d'aubaine* (right of *aubaine*)[1] to them. Under this right the government took possession, in whole or in part, of the estate of a deceased alien. But were the Jews of France aliens or French *régnicoles* (natives)?

Although Charles VI banished the Jews on September 17, 1394, a few Jewish centers were formed in France in the course of ensuing decades. In 1550 Henri II permitted Spanish and Portuguese Jews to settle in Bordeaux and other places in the territory of the Bordeaux Parliament, but only as Portugais or "New Christians" (*nouveaux chrétiens*). In addition, there were the Jewish communities in the papal province of Avignon and the Comtat Venaissin. Very small groups of Jews also dwelled in other parts of France. On April 23, 1516, however, Louis XIII ordered them banished. His successor, Louis XIV, expelled them from the French colonies on September 30, 1683, while Louis XV on February 20, 1731 forbade the Jews throughout France to do business in localities where they were not permitted to live. Yet, at the same time three large centers of Ashkenazic Jews again sprang up in the northeastern provinces of France: in Metz and in the provinces of Alsace and Lorraine—all with the approval and even under the protection of the kings of France. The letters patent of 1550 in favor of the Sephardic Jews were renewed in 1574, 1656, and 1723, each time being limited to the territory of the Bordeaux Parliament. In the

---

[1] On the general aspect of the right of aubaine in France, see Pierre Lainé, *Étude sur la capacité successorale des étrangers en France* (Paris, 1900), pp. 1-32; Colette Danjou, *La Condition civile de l'étranger dans les trois derniers siècles de la Monarchie* (Paris, 1939), 159 pp.

Originally published in *Historia Judaica*, vol. XIX (1957).

letters patent of June, 1776, all mention of a limited area
was omitted, thus by implication allowing the Sephardic Jews
to settle anywhere in France. However, this authorization
was only theoretical, for all efforts to have these letters recognized by the Paris Parliament and in the colonies were in
vain.[2] It is important to note that the Chamber of Domain
(*Chambre de Domaine*), which was in charge of applying
the right of *aubaine*, played a very important part in the
fight against the recognition of the letters patent by the Paris
Parliament. Officials of the Chamber stated in many memoranda that the New Christians were Jews, dangerous to the
capital, and that they should be regarded as *aubains*.[3]

In the interior provinces of France the Jews were not
even considered foreigners; they were simply outlawed. Jews
from Bordeaux and Saint-Ésprit-lès-Bayonne were not tolerated in most of the French ports and other large cities.
Driven out of Bayonne, they had to settle in the suburb of
Saint-Ésprit. The Marranos were persecuted in Rouen and
in Nantes, and in August, 1729, Jews of Bordeaux were
driven out of La Rochelle. On June 22, 1724 and July 29,
1730, a few Bordeaux Jews were given permission to trade
one month in the year in the territory of the Dijon Parliament, but on February 20, 1731 the Council of State revoked the permission. In 1728 Jacob Carim of Bordeaux
settled in Poitiers, but in the 1740's he was ordered to leave
the city. On February 23, 1758 Sephardic Jews and Bordeaux
Jews of Avignon origin were forbidden to trade in Blaye.
In 1771 a Bordeaux Jew named Lopez was ordered out of
Marseille, the government stating as its reason that the privileges of the Sephardic Jews were limited to Bordeaux only.
In 1781 two Jews from Bordeaux were arrested in Orléans
and Rouen. In 1788 Abraham Garcia was not permitted
to settle in Pau. Bordeaux Jews were also driven out of

---

[2] BN [= Bibliothèque Nationale (Paris)], manuscripts of Joly de Fleury,
472; P. Hildenfinger, *Documents sur les juifs à Paris au XVIIIe siècle* (Paris,
1913), pp. 41-42. The letters patent were registered on February 12, 1788
by the Parliament of Aix-en-Provence; I. Bédarride, *Les Juifs en France, en
Italie et en Espagne* (Paris, 1859), pp. 372-73.

[3] BN, manuscripts of Joly de Fleury, 472.

Cognac, Rochefort and Saintes, and Jews of the papal province had great difficulty in trading in France.[4]

The Jews did not exist officially in Paris. They were tolerated there only as persons passing through the city.[5] In Lyon only Jews with patents or with individual letters patent granting them the rights of French natives were free to remain in the city without special permission; all other Jews had to carry certificates of good conduct issued by the syndics of their communities and to register in order to obtain passports. Still, they were not characterized there as foreigners.[6] Some Ashkenazic, Sephardic, Avignon, and Comtadin Jews obtained individual naturalization (*lettres de naturalité*) in order to secure recognition as *régnicoles* elsewhere in France and thus escape the application of the right of *aubaine*.[7] However, their number was small because the

---

[4] *Arrest de la Cour de Parlement de Tolo[u]se, portant que les juifs videront incessamment les villes de Nismes, de Montpelier, et autres du ressort de la Cour....* (Tolose, 1680), 7 pp.; *Arrêt de la Cour du Parlement, qui fait défenses aux juifs de s'établir à la Rochelle à perpétuité ou pour un temps. Du 22 août 1729* (Paris, 1729), 4 pp.; *Arrêt du Conseil d'Etat du Roi qui casse deux arrêts rendus au Parlement de Dijon . . . Du 20 février 1731* (Paris, 1731), 4 pp.; Camille Bloch, "Un Épisode de l'histoire commerciale des juifs en Languedoc (1738)," *REJ*, XXIV (1892), 272-80; P. Bonassieux, *Les Assemblées représentatives du commerce* (Paris, 1883), p. 451; Leon Brunschwicq, "Les Juifs de Nantes . . .," *REJ*, XVII (1888), 126-42; XIX (1889), 294; *idem*, "Les Juifs en Bretagne," *ibid.*, XXXXIX (1904), 113; Clement-Janin, *Notice sur la communauté juive de Dijon* (Dijon, 1879), pp. 65-66; Adolphe Crémieux, "Un Droit perçu sur les juifs étrangers venus en France au XVIIe siècle," *REJ*, XXXXIV (1902), 301; Salomon Kahn, "Les Juifs de Montpellier au XVIIIe siècle," *REJ*, XXXIII (1896), 285-93; E. B. Le Beuf, *Du commerce de Nantes.* (Nantes, 1857), pp. 37, 93; Cecil Roth, "Les Marranes à Rouen," *REJ*, LXXXVIII (1929), 113-55; N. Roubin, "La Vie commerciale des juifs comtadins en Languedoc au XVIIIe siècle," *REJ*, XXXIV (1897), 283; Henri Sée, "Note sur le commerce des juifs en Bretagne au XVIIIe siècle," *REJ*, LXXX (1925), 170-78; *ibid.*, "Les Marchands de Saintes et les juifs," *ibid.*, pp. 179-81; Jonas Weyl, "La Résidence des juifs à Marseille," *REJ*, XVII (1888), 99, 108; David Wolfson, "Le Bureau du commerce et les réclamations contre les juifs (1726-1746)," *REJ*, LXI (1910), 82-83, 92-97, 261-64.

[5] H. Monin, "Les Juifs de Paris à la fin de l'ancien régime," *REJ*, XXIII (1894), 85.

[6] Alfred Lévy, *Notice sur les israélites de Lyon* (Paris, 1894), p. 23.

[7] AN [=Archives Nationales], W 421, dr. 956-I, p. 190 (naturalization of Liefman Calmer). Hayem and Cerf Worms of Sarrelouis were naturalized in 1787 (AN, C 82-817-2). Z. Szajkowski, "The Jewish Problem in Alsace, Metz, and Lorraine on the Eve of the Revolution of 1789," *Jewish Quarterly Review*, XLIV (1954), 213 (naturalization of Cerfberr). *Lettres patentes du Roi qui accordent aux sieurs [Lion, Gerson, Eliézer] Homberg frères et*

official price or bribe exacted for such naturalization was very high. Thus, the historian Maurice Liber was correct in writing that the Jews "could not be compared to other Frenchmen, but they also could not be treated as real foreigners." In the opinion of the historian Robert Anchel, the Jews could not be Frenchmen because legally only Christians were Frenchmen. The Jews had an intermediate status,[8] but in their case the historical facts are often very complicated.

In the seventeenth century the jurisconsult Jean Bacquet considered the "New Christians" as *aubains*, but of a special privileged character, exempt from the right of *aubaine* and whose heirs were legally to be considered *régnicoles*. On the other hand, the jurist Lefèvre de la Planche, who, from 1693 to 1732, was the King's attorney in the Chamber of Domain in charge of the royal estates and thus in charge of the application of the right of *aubaine*, did not recognize the legal existence of the Jews in France. In his opinion their banish-

---

[*Joseph*] Lallemant, *négocians du Havre-de-Grâce, les droits de régnicoles et naturels françois, du mois de septembre 1775* (Paris, 1776). *Lettre du sieur Berr-Isaac Berr . . . juifs naturalisé en vertu de Lettres patentes du Roi . . .* (Paris, 1790), 20 pp. In 1736 six out of thirty-six Jewish family heads in Bordeaux were naturalized, five were born in France, and twenty-five arrived from Spain and Portugal; L. Cardozo de Béthencourt, "Le Trésor des juifs séphardim," *REJ*, XXV (1892), 96. Moise Dalpuget was naturalized in 1759; *Extrait des registres du Conseil d'Etat du 23 mai 1775* (Paris, n.d.); Moise Castro Solar of Saint-Êsprit-lès-Bayonne was naturalized in April, 1776 (AN, 0-1-236). The Jew Couen of Saint-Pierre (Martinique) was naturalized on October 3, 1765. A. Cahen, "Les Juifs dans les colonies françaises au XVIIIe siècle," *REJ*, V (1882), 80-81. Sara Allegry of Amsterdam was naturalized in 1772. La Servolle, *Au Roi et è nosseigneurs de son conseil* (n.p., n.d.), p. 12. A family named Bédarride was naturalized in 1730. Bédarride, *op. cit.*, p. 376. *Lettres patentes du Roi qui accordent aux sieurs Jacob de Perpignan, juif, négociant de Bordeaux, à sa femme, ses enfans et posterité les droits de régnicoles et naturels françois, données à Versailles au mois de mars 1776, enregistrées au Parlement de Bordeaux le 2 mai de la même année* (Paris, 1776). Israel de Valabrègue was naturalized in 1770 (AN, 0-1-234). Josué Gabriel de Pichaud, of Avignon origin, was naturalized in March, 1772 (AN, 0-1-235, f. 20). *Lettres patentes du Roi, portant naturalization du Sr. Jassuda David Crémieu, natif de la ville de Capentras . . .* (Aix, 1785), 10 pp. Ruben and Israél Moise of Lyon were naturalized in 1786 (BN, manuscripts of Joly de Fleury, 2494, f.155).

[8] M. Liber, "Les Juifs et la convocation des états généraux," *REJ*, LXIII (1912), 185; Robert Anchel, "Les Juifs à Paris au XVIIIe siècle," *Bulletin de la société de l'histoire de Paris et de l'Ile de France*, LIX (1932), 9-23.

ment from France by the declaration of April 23, 1615 was the only legal basis for considering their legal status. He did not even recognize the validity in the territory of the Paris Parliament of the letters patent of 1550 in favor of the "New Christian" refugees, or their later confirmation by letters of 1574, 1656, and 1723. La Planche's study was published posthumously by Paul Charles Lorry, who regarded the Jews' legal status from a more liberal point of view. He added a very strong pro-Jewish note to La Planche's legal attack upon Jews. The *procureur-général* of the Bordeaux Parliament wrote in 1758 that the Jews were not to be regarded as *aubains,* but as *régnicoles.*[9]

The government tried to assert its right of *aubaine* against the Jews, but in most cases it lost. These claims indicate, however, that there was a tendency in many instances to regard the Jews as foreigners and to disregard the privileges to which they were entitled.

In the 1720's to the 1730's the Jewish widow Gaspard Rodriguez Medine and her son Joseph won the right to inherit an estate left to them by a Christian attorney of the Bordeaux Parliament. In another case the Chamber of Domain ordered the confiscation of the estates left by Salomon Perpignan, who died in Paris in 1781, and of Abraham de Perpignan, who died in Lyon. In both instances the heirs proved that the deceased were members of the family of Jacob de Perpignan, who had been naturalized by letters patent of March, 1776, and the claims of the Chamber were rejected. Likewise rejected were the Chamber's claims to the estates of Phillips Heckser, who died in Paris on October 17, 1788, and Samuel Hirsch, who died in Paris in August, 1787. On May 3, 1783 the Chamber laid claim to the estate of Sara Mendes d'Acosta. But her husband, Charles Peixotto, who had been converted to Catholicism,

---

[9] *Les Oeuvres de Me Jean Bacquet* (Paris, 1688), p. 670; Lefèvre de la Planche, *Mémoires sur les matières domaniales ou traité du domaine* (Paris, 1765), II, 102-109; L.F.B. [Beaufleury], *Histoire de l'établissement des juifs à Bayonne* (Paris, 1799), p. 116; T. Malvezin, *Histoire des juifs à Bordeaux* (Bordeaux, 1875), pp. 228-29; Hildenfinger, *op. cit.,* pp. 35-38.

on August 20, 1783 vindicated the right of their two children to inherit her property.[10] Israel Bernard de Valabrègue, a well-known Parisian Jew of Comtadin origin, was a merchant and author, and interpreter at the Royal Library from 1749 on. In September, 1770, he obtained naturalization letter. Nevertheless, after his death on November 15, 1779 the Chamber of Domain, assuming that Valabrègue was an alien, ordered the confiscation of his property including a library of 1792 volumes. But on February 3, 1780 the Paris Parliament recognized the widow, Esther Salon Dalpuget, as the legal heiress and rejected the Crown's claim.[11]

Particularly illuminating is the case of Abraham Vidal, born in August, 1720, in Bordeaux to Joseph Haim bar Noah Vidal of Avignon origin, and Blanche Ravel, a Sephardic Jewess. In 1739 Vidal settled in Paris where he became a haberdasher and a respected member of the Jewish community; he was among the first founders of the *École gratuite de dessin*, a non-Jewish vocational school. Vidal was the uncle of Israél Baumarin (Bon Marino), who had converted to Catholicism in the 1750's in Britany and through the law courts had obtained custody of his two children from his wife, who had remained Jewish. When Vidal died in December, 1783, the syndic of the Sephardic Jews in Paris put his property under seal in order to protect the heirs. These were Vidal's daughter Miriam, who married Moyse Gard of Avignon, and Jean Charles-Marie (Joseph) Beaumarin and Marie-Gabriel-Beaumarin, children of the converted Israél. On December 23, 1783 the Chamber of Domain ordered the confiscation of the estate. Vidal's

10 Dulimon, Poitevin, *Mémoire pour Pierre Niaguès . . . contre Cathérine Lopez de Paz, veuve Gaspard-Rodriguez Medine, et Joseph Medine, son fils* (Paris, n.d.); idem, *Observations pour Pierre Niaguès* (Paris, 1735); Malvezin, *op. cit.*, p. 229; Hildenfinger, *op. cit.*, pp. 3, 42-43, 252-53, 266, 271; BN, manuscripts of Joly de Fleury, 472, f. 76; *Mémoire . . . Vidal* (see note 13), p. 25-26. On Perpignan, see note 7; on Sara Mendes Dacosta and on Peixotto, see AN, Z-i, f. 842, and Z. Szajkowski, "Marriages, Mixed Marriages and Conversions among French Jews during the Revolution of 1789," *Historia Judaica*, XIX (1957), 35-36.

11 AN, 0-1-234, f. 246 (Valabrèguès naturalization); Hildenfinger, *op. cit.*, pp. 34, 226-30; idem, *La Bibliothèque de Bernard Valabrègue* (Paris, 1911), 16 pp.

heirs appealed the decision. They hired the lawyer Martineau, who published a famous memorial on the subject, in which he recounted the fate of the Jewish people since the destruction of Jerusalem. The following are a few of the legal arguments presented by both parties:

(a)   Those who represented the Crown stated that the letters patent which renewed the privileges accorded by Henri II in 1550 were registered only with the Parliament of Bordeaux. Jews residing in the territories of other parliaments could, therefore, not claim the right of *régnicoles*. To this Martineau replied that after the death of Henri II the letters patent of 1550 did not lose their force. The later letters patent, which confirmed those of 1550, were merely collective naturalization letters (*lettres générales de naturalité*) for the entire *nation* of the Bordeaux Jews.

(b)   The Crown asserted that Vidal had not registered in Paris. To this Martineauu replied that the letters patent of 1776 did in fact require matriculation in the place of residence, but only for Jewish refugees newly arrived from Spain and Portugal, and not for those of French birth. In any case, on November 15, 1777, the Chief of Police had ordered the Paris syndic of the Bordeaux Jews to keep a register of the Sephardic Jews in the capital.[12] On November 28 of the same year Vidal was registered by the syndic. This, argued Martineau, should be recognized as a legal act of matriculation.

On February 18, 1784, the Parliament of Paris rejected the Crown's claim and the estate of Vidal went to his heirs.[13] The Chamber of Domain strongly protested against this decision. In a memorandum opposing the decision the Chamber

---

[12] *Copie d'une lettre . . . par M. Lenoir . . . au sieur Pereire . . . portant règlement pour les juifs portugais. Paris le 15 novembre 1777* [Paris 1778], 3 pp.

[13] Me Martineau, *Mémoire pour les héritiers d'Abraham Vidal, juif portugais, négociant à Paris; contre M. le procureur général* (Paris, 1784), 31 pp.; *Arrêt du Parlement de Paris portant qu'il n'y a pas lieu d'exercer le droit d'aubaine sur la succession d'Abraham Vidal* (Paris, 1784), 4 pp.; Béthencourt, *op. cit.*, XX (1890), 291-95; Hildenfinger, *op. cit.*, p. 266. On the Vidal family in Paris, see also L. Kahn, "Les Juifs de Paris de 1755 à 1759," *REJ*, XXXXIX (1904), 121-124.

stated that Vidal was not even a Portuguese Jew, but of Avignon origin. In any case, even the Portuguese Jews could not claim outside the territory of the Bordeaux Parliament the right to transfer their estates to their heirs.[14]

The right of *aubaine* was frequently asserted against Jews in the French colonies. On July 25, 1726, Abraham Gradis left Bordeaux for Martinique with the permission of the proper authorities. He died there in March, 1738. The King himself ordered the confiscation of his estate valued at over 70,000 livres. The colonial authorities wrote to the government on August 12, 1739 that although the Jews were not considered *aubains* in Bordeaux, they could be so regarded in the colonies on the basis of the *Code Noir* of March, 1685. However, on January 18, 1740, the government ordered the abandonment of the case because Gradis had been authorized to leave Bordeaux for the colonies. In March, 1751, Emanuel Cardoze of Bordeaux won his case against the colonial authorities who had ordered the confiscation of the estate left by his brother David. The Jew Campos of Saint-Ésprit-lès-Bayonne settled in San Domingo. After his death in 1757 the authorities tried to confiscate his estate. His children appealed to the Minister of the Naval Forces in charge of colonial administration, who requested the advice of the *procureur-général* of Bordeaux. On March 28, 1758, this magistrate replied that such confiscation contravened the decision of the Bordeaux Parliament which recognized the Jews as *régnicoles*. They could inherit property not only from Jews, but also from Christians, as had happened in the case of Medine. Campos' children obtained their father's estate. In February, 1758, the heirs of Moise Daguillard obtained permission to inherit his property in spite of the colonial administration's claim that he was to be considered an *aubain*. The same thing occurred in 1779 in the case of Benjamin Delbaille. Another Bordeaux Jew in the colonies, Depas, left his property to his daughter Esther,

---

[14] "Mémoire intéressant sur les successions des juifs de Paris," BN, manuscript of Joly de Fleury, 472.

who was married in Bordeaux to Jacob Gradis. In this case, too, the right of *aubaine* was claimed. But Gradis, in order to avoid a long and expensive lawsuit, obtained the estate as a gift from the authorities. In the case of another Bordeaux Jew named Tota, the *Conseil supérieur* of the colony in May, 1780, requested of his family proof that the deceased had been registered in Bordeaux.[15]

Of a very different and curious character was the case of the Faxardo family. Raphael Faxardo, the son of Dom Pedro Faxardo (born in 1623 in Toledo), was born in 1669 in Spain. In 1722 he settled in France with his wife Hyacinthe Magdeleine de Pinedo Gusman and their five children. There he remarried his wife according to Jewish law, and they assumed the Jewish names of Abraham Faxardo and Sara Pinedo. The children, too, were given Jewish names. In France four more children were born to Abraham and Sara. In 1735 the family settled in the French colonies, where most of its members converted to Catholicism. Jean, Abraham's oldest son, born in Spain in 1697, assumed the name of Isaac in France. When he died on June 15, 1767 at the Cap, the *Affiches américaines* announced the death of *"Faxardo, juif portugais."* His property was ordered confiscated on the basis of a double right of *aubaine*, because he was a Jew and a Portuguese. But his heirs proved that the deceased came from Spain, whose nationals were exempt from the right of *aubaine* in France, and that he was a Catholic. On May 21, 1768 the Court rejected the government's claim. Salomon, Abraham's youngest son, born in 1726 in France, immigrated to the colonies in 1747. On June 26, 1752, at Saint-Yag, he was converted to Catholicism and became known as Salomon-Pierre. He died on the Cap on September 29, 1773, and four years later, on October 30, 1777, the treasurer of the *aubaine* ordered the confiscation of his estate. The heirs protested. They did not argue that

[15] Moreau de Saint-Méry, *Loix et constitutions des colonies françoises de l'Amérique sous le Vent* . . . (Paris, 1784-90), IV, 66, 260, 293, V, 889; Beaufleury, *op. cit.*, pp. 115-19; Malvezin, *op. cit.*, pp. 220-29; A. Cahen, *op. cit.*, IV (1882), 133-39, 144-45, V (1882), 75, 91-92, 258-67.

Salomon-Pierre was a converted Jew, but only that he was a *régnicole*, born in France. The outcome of this case is not known.[16]

These frequent but isolated attempts of the French monarchy to declare certain deceased Jews to be *aubains* and to confiscate their estates aroused all French Jews to come to the defense of their prospective heirs, for they rightly saw in them a threat to the legal and economic status of all Jews in France. Thus Martineau, the lawyer of Abraham Vidal's heirs, stated that the conflict was important for the entire *nation* of the Sephardic Jews.[17] David Silveyra, the syndic of the Sephardim in Paris, wrote on April 2, 1784 to the *nation* in Bordeaux that Jews in the French colonies had submitted to baptism in order to avoid confiscation of their properties after their death.[18] The claim of the right of *aubaine* against Valabrègue's estate alarmed the Jews of the papal province of Avignon and the Comtat Venaissin. In a petition to the Assembly of the Comtat Venaissin the Jewish community of Carpentras stated in connection with the Valabrègue case that the Jews were not foreigners in France but *régnicoles*, that Jews would be afraid to travel in France for commercial purposes for fear of losing their properties in case of death, etc.[19] On March 12, 1780, the Ordinary Assembly of the Comtat Venaissin decided to write to the Cardinal Secretary of State and to the Nuncio of Paris in favor of the Jewish petition. On April 27, 1780, the General Assembly of the province took a similar decision.[20]

[16] Me Bourbon, *Mémoire pour le Sieur Alexandre Faxardo, neveu & légataire de Salomon Pierre Faxardo, appellant de sentence du juge du Cap du 27 mars 1779, aux fins d'arrêt & exploits des 19 & 21 juillet suivant: contre le receveur actuel de l'aubaine* . . . (Cap, 1780), 60 pp.

[17] "Mais la question que l'on nous force d'examiner est trop importante pour rien négliger. Elle n'intéresse pas seulement les héeritiers du sieur Vidal; elle intéresse toute la Nation juive portugaise"; *Mémoire pour les héritiers d'Abraham Vidal* . . . pp. 1-2.

[18] Silveyra's letter is in the library of the Jewish Theological Seminary, New York City.

[19] The full tert of the petition will be published elsewhere.

[20] Departmental archives of Vaucluse, E 12, C 43, ff. 20, 104.

Almost all attempts to apply the right of *aubaine* to Jews involved Sephardic Jews of France and the colonies or Jews of the papal province. Of the cases known to us, only Samuel Hirsch was, most probably, an Ashkenazic Jew.

The residents of Strasbourg and other free cities and Alsatian areas owned by foreign princes and other dignitaries were exempt from the right of *aubaine*. It would seem, then, that the right was not applied to Jews there either. The Alsatian historians L. V. Goetzman, Jules Krug-Basse, Charles Hoffmann, Rodolphe Reuss, and George Livet, the Metz historian Roger Clément, E. T. Bonvolat of Lorraine and many others, and the collections of local laws mention no such cases.[21] It may be possible to find, by long and painstaking research in the departmental archives, a few isolated cases in which the right of *aubaine* was applied to Jews of Alsace, Metz and its province, and Lorraine, but they would not permit the forming of any general conclusion. There were many other legal ways to take property away from the Jews. Nevertheless, on many occasions, though not involving claims to confiscate estates, the Ashkenazic Jews stated that they were not *aubains*, but French *régnicoles*.

In March, 1767, the King permitted certain foreigners to obtain *brevets* (patents), which gave them the right to engage in certain occupations and thus exempted them from

---

[21] L. V. de Götzmann, *Traité du droit commun des fiefs* . . . (Paris, 1768), 2 vols.; Jules Krug-Basse, *L'Alsace avant 1789* . . . (Paris, 1876); Charles Hoffman, *L'Alsace au dix-huitième siècle* . . . (Colmar, 1906-07), 4 vols.; Rodolphe Reuss, *L'Alsace au dix-septième siècle* (Paris, 1897-98), 2 vols.; Georges Livet, *L'Intendance d'Alsace sous Louis XIV*, 1648-1715 (Strasbourg, 1956), pp. 780-87: Jews; Roger Clément, *La Condition des juifs de Metz sous l'ancien régime* (Paris, 1903); E. T. Bonvalot, *Histoire du droit et des institutions de la Lorraine et des Trois-Evêchés* (Paris, 1895). The author wishes to express sincere thanks to the archivists Chr. Wilsdorf of Colmar, Gilbert Cohen of Metz, George Weill and Fucks of Strasbourg, and Et. Delcamb of Nancy who tried, though in vain, to find in the departmental archives cases in which the right of *aubaine* was applied to Jews. It is worth while to note a lawsuit between the Jew Judas Lévi of Metz and his debtor, Henri Millot of Burgaltroff, that concerned the right of *aubaine*: *Arrêt du Parlement de Metz sur l'inaliénabilité des fiefs contenu dans l'arrêt notable sur une question d'aubaine* (Colmar, 1783).

the right of *aubaine*. However, this edict did not apply to Jews. The lawyer Pierre-Louis Lacretelle the elder (1751-1824) pleaded, in 1775 before the Parliament of Nancy, in favor of two Jews of Metz who requested that they be granted *brevets* as merchants of Thionville. He stated that the Jews were not foreigners, but *régnicoles,* and that the right of *aubaine* was not applicable to them.[22] On the basis of this same edict of 1767 the four brothers Hayem, Cerf, Abraham, and Jacob Olry Worms, and Lyon Alexandre and Joseph Cahen of Sarrelouis obtained *brevets de maîtrise* in the city of Sarrelouis. Eight years later, however, the Christian merchants and butchers protested. They asserted that the Jews could not be considered *régnicoles,* that they were still aliens and that, in any event, only two Jews were allowed to reside in the city. The Jews contested this position. In a memorandum prepared for them by the lawyer La Servalle they stated that they could not be considered aliens because they were not regarded as *aubains* in the matter of inheritance.[23]

At the beginning of the Revolution the Jewish representatives of Alsace, Metz, and Lorraine stated in a memorandum submitted to the Minister of Finance and the government's real chief, Jacques Necker, that they were not foreigners but a *nation juive régnicole* and that the right of *aubaine* was not to be applied to them.[24]

The decree of April 30, 1790 (law of May 2, 1790) in favor of foreigners contained the clause: "without . . . prejudging anything regarding the problem of the Jews, which

---

[22] Pierre Louis Lacretelle the elder, "Plaidoyer pour Moise May, Godechaux et Abraham Lévy, juifs de Metz, contre l'Hotel de Ville de Thionville et le corps des marchands de cette ville," *Plaidoyers* (Bruxelles, 1775), pp. 15-16, reprinted in *Mémoire pour deux juifs de Metz contre l'Hotel de Ville et le corps des marchands de Thionville. Textes de 1777 et de* 1823 (Paris, 1928), pp. 219-20.

[23] M⁰ La Servolle, *Requête au Roi, pour les juifs de Sarrelouis* (Paris, 1777), p. 14. On this conflict, see also Mᵉ Dimours, *Mémoire pour les maire, syndics, & communauté des habitans de Sarelouis . . . contre les juifs . . .* (n.p., n.d.), 43 pp.

[24] Liber, *op. cit.,* LXIV (1912), 267.

was and remains postponed." This does not prove that the Jews were then considered foreigners. The paragraph had been added at the request of the Alsatian anti-Jewish Deputy Jean-François Rewbell (Reubell), who feared that the Jews would try to turn the decree to their own advantage for their emancipation. When Reubell stated on July 20, 1790 before the National Assembly that the Jews of Metz were foreigners, a voice replied: "This is not the truth."[25]

As late as March, 1790, after the Sephardic Jews had been granted (in January, 1790) full citizenship, the Chamber of Domain expressed its strong opposition to recognizing them as *régnicoles*.[26] According to Baruch Hagani, the law of May 2, 1790 setaside the discussion whether the Jews were *régnicoles* or aliens.[27] The right of *aubaine* was abolished altogether by a decree of August 6, 1790. Indeed, a decree of April 8, 1791 even permitted residents of foreign countries to inherit property in France. But the problem was still much discussed even later in connection with the Brancas tax and the liquidation of debts owed by the Jewish communities to Christian creditors.

From 1715 on the Jews of Metz were forced to pay a yearly tax of 20,000 livres to the Brancas family. This tax was abolished by the National Assembly on July 20, 1790. On this occasion the Jews of Metz argued, in a petition signed by Louis Wolff, with respect to a problem which was of great importance for the future of the Jewish communities. The Brancas family stated that the Jews of Metz were only tolerated foreigners and that the Brancas tax was to be considered similar to a *droit d'aubaine*. To this Wolff replied that the *droit d'aubaine* was well known in 1715, when the Brancas tax was originated, but, the Brancas tax was formulated only as a tolerance, protection, and residence charge. The Jews were not tolerated foreigners, but formed

[25]   A. E. Halphen, *Recueil des lois* . . . (Paris, 1851), p. 4; *Archives parlementaires*, XVII, 218.

[26]   Hildenfinger, *op. cit.*, p. 42, note 3.

[27]   B. Hagani, *Emancipation des juifs* (Paris, 1928), p. 188.

a well-organized body: "It is not as foreigners, but as constituents of a particular body [*corporation*] that the Jews obtained confirmation of their rights with every change in sovereign." In this respect they followed the practice of other Frenchmen, their fellow-citizens, forming corps or communities and obtaining confirmation of the rights of their already existing bodies. Jacques-François-Laurent de Visme [Devisme, 1749-1830], who, on July 20, 1790, reported to the National Assembly on the Jewish request, likewise argued against the claim of the Brancas family. He stated that the right of *aubaine* was only "a casual claim" resulting from the death of a foreigner and ending with the legal confiscation of his estate. The claim was not applied perpetually to the foreigner's descendants who, if born in France, became French natives (*régnicoles*). But here, the Brancas family had obtained a perpetual tax imposed upon Jews and their heirs. Moreover, the right of *aubaine* was a prerogative reserved to the King alone, and was not to be turned over to other persons.[28]

The Jewish communities had to pay such large amounts in taxes that they were forced to borrow money from Christians and thus became collective debtors to Christian creditors. During the Revolution the Jews demanded that the debts owed by them should be taken over by the government, as had been done with all debts of religious and other bodies that had been dissolved by the new regime. The Jews showed that prior to the Revolution they existed as autonomous communities, with their own constitutions and administrations. The Christian creditors, who fought the nationalization of the debts owed them by the Jewish communities, stated that the Jews were only tolerated foreigners, *aubains*. They argued that this could be established by the fact that after 1789 the local authorities ordered the Jews to continue the administration of their communal properties. In a reply

[28] Louis Wolff, *Mémoire pour les juifs de Metz* . . . (Paris, n.d.), pp. 6-7; J. F. L. de Visme, [Devisme], *Rapport fait* . . . *le 20 juillet 1790 sur le droit de protection levé sur les juifs* . . . (Paris, n.d.), pp. 5-9.

prepared on behalf of the Jews of Metz the lawyer Combines
stated that, prior to 1789, the Jews in France had the status
of a recognized body and that the order to continue the
administrative functions of the Jewish community was
forced upon them.[29] François-Balthazar Darracq (1750-
1808), in a strong attack against the Jews delivered on
March 7, 1799 at the Council of the Five Hundred (*Conseil
des Cinq Cents*), pressed the same arguments. This was part
of a well-organized effort to prove that the Jews—as foreigners—could not have been organized in communities
which were in the category of those dissolved by the new
regime. The Jews of Metz replied that they were not looked
upon as foreigners. Foreign Jews could not settle among
them; their possessions were not escheat to the Crown, because the right of *aubaine* was not applied to them. The
Council of Five Hundred appointed a commission to report
on the Jewish debts. On November 24, 1797, François-
Marie-Joseph Riou de Kersalaun (1765-1811) presented the
commission's conclusions in favor of nationalization of the
debts owed by the Jewish communities. He also rejected
the creditors' argument that prior to the Revolution the
Jews were considered foreigners.[30]

In conclusion it should be said that prior to the Revolution of 1789 the legal status of the Jews was not clearly
defined. This opened the way for many interpretations that
were prejudicial to the Jews, not only during the old regime,
but even during the Revolution. Thus, the debts owed by
the Jewish communities were not taken over by the government, partly as a result of the propaganda statement that
during the old regime the Jews were considered legally as
aliens.

[29]   The Library of the Jewish Theological Seminary, manuscript 01530-6.

[30]   Puyproux the elder, *Réponse aux juifs de Metz* . . . (Paris, n.d.), p. 2;
F. B. Darracq, *Opinion* . . . *dans l'affaire des juifs de Bordeaux* . . . (Paris,
an VII), p. 4 (" . . . les juifs ne furent en France que des *aubains*, des *étrangers*
vivant entre eux en *corps* de *nation*, de nation étrangère"); *Résumé pour les
juifs de Metz* (Paris, n.d.), p. 3; F. M. J. Riou [de Kersalaun], *Rapport* . . .
sur les pétitions des juifs de Metz et d'Avignon (Paris, an VI), p. 4.

RELATIONS AMONG SEPHARDIM, ASHKENAZIM AND AVIGNONESE JEWS IN FRANCE FROM THE 16TH TO THE 20TH CENTURIES

Prior to the Revolution of 1789 there were four centers of Jewish concentration in France: (1) Ashkenazic Jews in both parts of Alsace, in the city and province of Metz, and in Lorraine; (2) Sephardic Jews in southwestern France (Bordeaux, Saint-Esprit-lès-Bayonne, and in several smaller towns); (3) the four Jewish communities in the Papal possessions of Avignon and Comtat Venaissin; and (4) a mixed community in Paris. Isolated groups of Jews also lived in small numbers in Marseilles, Nimes, Montpellier and other cities. We wish to make it clear at the very outset that relations among these communities were hardly fraternal; on the contrary, they fought each other. This tragic chapter in the history of the Jews in France was not to end until the days of the First Empire, when Napoleon I convened the Sanhedrin and established the Central Jewish Consistory.

I. Sephardic Privileges

Some Jews in France managed to escape the expulsion decreed on September 17, 1394. The Jews of Bordeaux, which was then under English sovereignty, were not subject to the edict. On the return of the city to French rule in 1454, the resident Jews were seemingly permitted to remain. In 1474 Louis XI allowed the settlement of foreigners—Englishmen excepted—in Bordeaux. Following the expulsion from Spain in 1492, refugees from Spain and Portugal, arriving in small numbers, settled in Bordeaux and other towns of southern France. They were tolerated as "New Christians." As such, they were privileged in 1550 by the King of France to remain and engage in trade in Bordeaux and in the territory under the jurisdiction of the Bordeaux Parliament. These privileges were subsequently renewed. The Sephardim lived as Marranos, many of them going over to Christianity entirely,

Originally published in *YIVO Annual of Jewish Social Science,* vol. X (1955).

much as the French Marranos never returned to Judaism after the expulsion of 1394 and the later expulsion from Provence of 1487. These "New Christians"—the Sephardim from Spain and Portugal—were not affected by the expulsion of April 23, 1615.[1]

In attacking other Jews, the Sephardim put emphasis on their privileged status, claiming equality of rights with all Frenchmen. Hence, they felt, the other Jews were not their peers.[2]

Prior to 1789, historians and students of jurisprudence disagreed in their interpretation of the privileges accorded the Sephardim. Writing in 1765, de la Planche noted that Jews had not been permitted to dwell in France after the expulsion of 1615. He ignored the privileges accorded in 1550 and even those of 1723, despite the fact that the latter explicitly referred to the Sephardim as "Jews" and not as "New Christians." In this respect, his editor, the jurist Lorry, held a different opinion. In 1775 Denisart wrote that Jews had no legal right of residence; he made no exception for the Sephardim.[3] In the opinion of most modern historians, the Sephardim were granted privileges because they were a commercially important entrepreneurial element. Others maintain that there were no conditions attached to the privileges. The decree of January 28, 1790 bestowing full citizen-

---

[1] L. F. B. [Beaufleury], *Histoire de l'Etablissement des Juifs à Bordeaux et à Bayonne* . . . (Paris 1799) p. 1-15; Detcheverry, Ad., *Histoire des Israélites de Bordeaux* (Bordeaux 1850) p. 48-49; Malvezin, Théophile, *Histoire des Juifs à Bordeaux* (Bordeaux 1875) p. 88-91; Michel, Francisque, *Histoire du Commerce et de la Navigation à Bordeaux* (Bordeaux 1870) vol. ii, p. 415-416; Halphen, A. E., *Recueil des Lois . . . concernant les Israélites . . .* (Paris 1851) p. 166-167; Léon, Henry, *Histoire des Juifs de Bayonne* (Paris 1893) p. 16-17; Anchel, Robert, *Les Juifs en France* (Paris 1946) p. 125-146.

Archival sources in references will be designated by the following abbreviations: ArchAffEtr = Archives du Ministère des Affaires Etrangères (Paris); AdG = Archives départementales, Gironde (Bordeaux); AdVaucluse = Archives départementales Vaucluse (Avignon); AmAvignon = Archives municipales, Avignon; AmBx = Archives municipales, Bordeaux; Archives Gradis = Archives de la famille Gradis (Bordeaux); AN = Archives Nationales (Paris); BN = Bibliothèque Nationale (Paris); Calvet = Bibliothèque et Musée Calvet (Avignon); JTS = Jewish Theological Seminary (New York); JHS = Archives of the Jewish Historical Society of Israel.

[2] A number of historians have adopted this Sephardic thesis, employing it in their apologias for the old regime. Behold, they argue, the monarchy was good to Jews, or at least, to the worthy among them. This issue was discussed in 1938-39 by the rightist politician Henri de Kérillis and the anti-Semitic monarchist leader, Charles Maurras. See Carmona-Benveniste, Laurent, "Les Séphardins en France sous l'ancien Régime," *Revue Hébdomadaire*, vol. xlviii (1939) p. 469-488.

[3] Planche, Lefèvre de la, *Mémoires sur les matières domaniales ou Traité du domaine* (Paris 1765) vol. ii, p. 102-109; Denisart, J. B., *Collection de décisions nouvelles* (Paris 1775) vol. iii, p. 423; Hildenfinger, P., *Documents sur les Juifs à Paris au XVIIIe Siècle* . . . (Paris 1913) p. 35-36.

ship on the Sephardim and Avignonese (i.e., the Jews originally from Avignon) residing in Bordeaux, was so formulated that both groups continued to enjoy the privileges they had prior to 1789.[4]

Organized Jewish communities, however, were tolerated only in the centers of Ashkenazic Jews. Henry II, responsible for driving the Sephardic Jews out of Bayonne, granted privileges to the Jews of Metz. Some historians think that Sephardic Jews were tolerated because of the preoccupation of the Church with the persecution of Protestants. After the exile of 1615, the sole organized Jewish group to be tolerated was the Jewish community of Metz. The Sephardim were privileged not as Jews, but as "New Christians," Portuguese, Spaniards or simply as good "Catholics," as the General-Procurator of the Bordeaux Parliament referred to them in 1574, on the occasion of registering the privileges of 1550.[5]

None, however, harbored any illusions. It was well-known that they were Marranos, and they were subjected to Church persecution. A Marrano woman was burnt at the stake in 1619 in Saint-Jean-de-Luz for allegedly having insulted the Christian faith. The people perpetrated excesses of all sorts against the "New Christians." One Pinto, a Portuguese non-Jew, was robbed in a Bordeaux church in 1590 by a lawyer Duboys. He was threatened that, since he was undoubtedly a Jew, he would be torn to shreds and burned together with all the others of his nation in the city.[6] In a petition to the King in 1614, the frightened Sephardim declared that they were "most devout Christians

[4] Bethencourt, L. Cardozo de, *Ury ha Lévy* . . . (Amsterdam 1904) p. 12; Bail, *Etat des Juifs* . . . (Paris éd. 1823) p. 42; Lucien-Brun, Henry, "La Situation légale du Culte israélite en France," *Revue Catholique des Institutions et du Droit* (Lyon April 1902) p. 311; Lemoine, Albert, *Napoléon Ier et les Juifs* (Paris 1900) p. 12.

[5] Lamare, N. Nicolas de, *Traité de la Police* (Paris 1705) vol. i, p. 266; [de Guyot], *Répertoire . . . de jurisprudence* (Paris éd. 1784) ch. on "Juifs"; Hallez, Th., *Des Juifs en France* (Paris 1845) p. 68, 72; Alby, Ernest, *Des Persécutions contre les Juifs* (Paris 1840) p. 70; Bédarride, I., *Les Juifs en France, en Italie et en Espagne* (Paris 1859) p. 371-372; Cirot, George, II [= *Les Juifs de Bordeaux. Leur Situation Morale et Sociale de 1550 à la Révolution*] (Bordeaux 1920) vol. i, p. 2; Michel, Rolland Francisque, *Les Portugais en France, Les Français en Portugal* (Bordeaux 1882) p. 187. For an analysis of the concept "Marranos" in France see *idem, Histoire des races maudites de la France et de l'Espagne* (Paris 1847) vol. ii, p. 49-50.

[6] Cirot, III [= "Les Juifs de Bordeaux . . ." *Revue Historique de Bordeaux*] vol. xxix (1936) p. 209; Lancre, Pierre de, *L'Incredulité de Sortilège* . . . (Paris 1622) p. 472-477; Léon, p. 26-29; H. P. [P. Haguenauer], "Un Autodafé à Saint-Jean-de-Luz en 1619," *Annuaire des Archives Israélites* . . . 5663 (Paris 1902) p. 36-52; AmBx, FF 1 (affaire Belchior Fernandes Pinto vs. Duboys, 1590: "luy disant ql estoit juif et le feroit mestre en pièces et brusler ensemble les autres de sa nation qui estoint en cette ville").

and Catholics." Not until the beginning of the 18th century were they gradually able to profess Judaism openly. At great cost, they succeeded in obtaining the new privileges of 1723 in which, for the first time, they were referred to not as "New Christians" but as Jews. In a petition addressed to Minister Malesherbes in 1788, the Sephardim wrote that the King in granting privileges prior to 1723, had referred to them as "New Christians" rather than as Jews solely because he desired to protect them from the mob. In their subsequent collections of the printed documents containing the privileges, the Sephardim changed the words "New Christians" or "Portuguese" in the titles to "Jews." Notwithstanding their privileges, they continued to be persecuted for observing Judaism even after 1723. In 1734 the seven Bordeaux synagogues were closed, Jews were forbidden to employ Christian retainers, to maintain rabbis, or to keep their businesses closed on Saturday. In 1753 the Intendant demanded that new restrictions be imposed upon the Sephardim for adhering to Judaism. Not until 1789 were Jewish parents freed from providing for the maintenance of their baptized children. Prior to July 15, 1728 the Church even had the right to baptize Jewish children under the age of 12 without parental permission.[7]

In a certain sense, the lot of the Sephardim was worse than that of the Moors in France. The Moors too had the alternative of conversion or expulsion. They, however, had the possibility of moving to North Africa, whereas the Jews had no such escape. Those Moors who chose to remain—in number, about the same as the Jews—were oppressed no less than the Jews, but they did not have a similar power of collective endurance. It may be noted that Jews too did not always bear up under the ordeal. No more than a small minority of the Marranos who fled Spain and Portugal returned to Judaism. At the time of the privileges of 1723, when the Sephardim had begun to profess Judaism openly, there were less than 2,000 of them in France who did so. Similarly, in later years, Marranos in France did not

---

[7] AdG, C3383 (mémoire de l'Intendant, 1753); Malvezin, p. 121; Charleville, M., *Louis XIV et les Israélites* (Paris 1888) p. 9-10; Berman, L., *Histoire des Juifs de France* (Paris 1937) p. 242-244; Cirot, I [= *Recherches sur les Juifs Espagnols et Portugais à Bordeaux* (Bordeaux 1908)] p. 7, 40; *idem*, II, p. 10-11; Beaufleury, p. 9-10; Szajkowski, Z., *The Economic Status of the Jews in Alsace, Metz and Lorraine* (New York 1954) p. 27-28, note 70. In the title of the privileges of 1723, nothing is mentioned about Jews (see fn. 25). In the collections of privileges, however, the publisher Pereire altered the title to "Lettres Patentes . . . Pour les Juifs Portugais" (see fn. 44).

always take advantage of the opportunity to return to Judaism. Though the numbers of Sephardim in France more than doubled by the beginning of the 19th century, this was solely a function of the steady immigration in the course of the 18th century of new Marranos from Spain and, particularly, from Portugal.[8]

The greatest gain of the privileged Sephardim was the opportunity to engage in trade and to move freely, prerogatives denied the Ashkenazim. There were, incidentally, some strata of Christian society that had no freedom of movement or residence. This freedom of the Sephardim was not unlimited. The first set of privileges placed no restriction on it, but in 1656 and 1723, Sephardic settlement was limited to the territory under the jurisdiction of the Bordeaux Parliament. In very many cases, they were not tolerated elsewhere in France. In the other large ports of France through which the trade with the colonies passed, very small numbers of Jews lived as Marranos. Jews from Bordeaux were driven out of La Rochelle, Nantes, Poitiers, Rouen, Pau, Cognac, Rochefort and many other cities. In the majority of cases, indeed, the restrictions referred to the Avignonese Jews of Bordeaux, as can be seen by the characteristic names. All the Avignonese and Comtat Venaissin Jews were constantly subject to discrimination in their efforts to trade at fairs or otherwise in France. But in these cases the origin of these Jews made no difference. The fact that these Bordeaux merchants were originally from Avignon was not even mentioned; outside of Bordeaux they were considered Bordeaux Jews. Avignonese as well as Bordeaux Jews were equally undesirable elements. Not until the renewed privileges in June 1776, was all mention of a limited area omitted, therewith allowing the Sephardim to dwell anywhere in France.[9]

Though Sephardic Jews dwelt in Paris, as late as 1777 they were not able to acquire the right to own retail shops. Their efforts of 1776

---

[8] Michel, *Races* . . ., vol. ii, p. 71, 57, 88-89, 94-95. Of 755 circumcisions entered in the record-books of Bordeaux Sephardim during the 18th century, 617 were of newborn children and 138 of adults, among them old men, refugees recently arrived from Portugal and Spain. See Bethencourt, Cardozo de, "Le Trésor des Juifs Séphardim," *REJ*, vol. xxvi (1893) p. 254; AmBx, GG 70, f. 66-67. On the return of Marranos to Judaism in general, see Halkin, Abraham S., "A *Contra Christianos* by a Marrano," in *Mordecai M. Kaplan Jubilee Volume* (New York 1953) p. 399.

[9] Beaufleury, p. 109-110; Rochelle, E. la, *Jacob Rodrigues Pereire* . . . (Paris 1882) p. 122, 392; *Lettres-Patentes du Roi, confirmatives des privilèges dont les Juifs Portugais jouissent en France depuis 1550. Données à Versailles au Mois de Juin 1776*, (n.p., 1781) 4 p. (4°).

and 1783-85 to have the privileges of 1776 recognized by the Paris Parliament were all in vain.[10] Though the Sephardim were excluded from the expulsion of the Jews from the French colonies (April 23, 1615), they were barely tolerated there as Marranos. Professing Jews were not allowed to live there. Their requests that the privileges of 1776 be extended to the colonies were rejected. Hence, in their memorandum of 1778 to Malesherbes, they renewed the demand for the right to live as Jews in the colonies. The *syndic* (agent) of the Sephardim in Paris wrote to Bordeaux on April 2, 1784, that Jews in the French colonies had submitted to baptism in order to give their children the right of inheritance.[11] Otherwise, their possessions, as those of all foreigners—who had the status of *aubains*—escheated to the crown. There were also instances of attempts to deprive Sephardim of inheritances in France itself, as in the cases of Abraham Vidal and the widow Medine.[12] Vidal's case is particularly illuminating. Though a Bordeaux Jew, he was of Avignon descent, and not Sephardic. The *syndic* in Paris, therefore, refused to register him. The attempt of the regime to take possession of Vidal's estate upon his death, however, aroused all Sephardim to come to the defense of his heirs, for they saw in it a threat to them as well. In the *factums* (legal briefs) submitted by the attorney for the heirs, Vidal was referred to as a Sephardic Jew, on the presumption that only the rights of Avignonese and Ashkenazic Jews were limited. The Jews managed to win in all

---

[10] Kahn, L., *Les Juifs de Paris pendant la Révolution* (Paris 1898) p. 11; *idem, Les Institutions de Patronnage* (Paris 1885) p. 8; Hildenfinger, p. 41-42.

[11] AdG, C292; Beaufleury, p. 47, 115; Cahen, Ab., "Les Juifs de la Martinique au XVIIe siècle," *REJ*, vol. ii (1881), p. 93ff.; *idem*, "Les Juifs dans les colonies françaises au XVIIIe siècle," *REJ*, vol. iv (1882) p. 127-145; Hildenfinger, p. 41-42; Lettre de David Silveyra, 2 avril, 1784, JTS. There were two cases in which Jews in the colonies gained the right to have their children inherit their estate (Malvezin, p. 228-229). A similar lawsuit concerning inheritance involved the family of Alexander Faxardo, which had arrived in Bordeaux in 1722, there adopted Jewish names and remarried according to Jewish law. After 1735 the family lived in the colonies. See Bourlon, Me., *Mémoire pour le Sieur Alexandre Faxardo* ([A la Colonie du Cap] 1780) p. 44-45.

[12] Martineau, Me., *Mémoire pour les héritiers d'Abraham Vidal, juif portugais, négociant à Paris; contre M. le Procureur Général* (Paris 1784) 31 p.; Frouillebert, *Précis pour Me. Riffé de Caubray . . . contre Me. Jabineau de Morolles . . . défendeur en désaveau, et contre le sieur Vidal, juif de nation, intimé* (Paris 1786); *Arrêt du Parlement de Paris portant qu'il n'y a pas lieu d'exercer le droit d'aubaine sur la succession d'Abraham Vidal* (Paris 1784); Bethencourt, *REJ*, vol. xx (1890) p. 38-40; Hildenfinger, p. 30; JTS (Lettre de David Silveyra, see fn. 11); AdG, C3415; Dulimon, Poitevin, *Mémoire pour Pierre Niaguès . . . contre Cathérine Lopez de Paz, veuve Gaspard-Rodriguez Medine, et Joseph Medine, son fils* (Paris [1773]); *idem, Observations pour Pierre Niaguès* (Paris 1735); Malvezin, p. 229; Michel, *Histoire du Commerce . . .*, vol. ii, p. 433-434; Cirot, II, p. 8.

these trials concerning inheritance. The conflicts, however, proved that there was a tendency to apply a different set of legal standards from those applied to Frenchmen even in the case of the privileged Sephardic Jews. Jews were considered Frenchmen in Bordeaux—but only there.

Moreover, the Sephardim had not acquired their privileges gratis. They had to pay substantial sums for the privileges of 1550 and for each renewal, as in 1723, when they paid over 100,000 livres. Like the Ashkenazim and the Jews in Comtat Venaissin, they were compelled to pay huge taxes, to make forced loans, to present gifts, and the like.[13] Notwithstanding their privileges, the Sephardim suffered from all sorts of restrictions. Essentially, they were confined to trade, and barred from all other occupations, no less than the Ashkenazim. In his memoirs, the Bordeaux *parnas* (councillor) Salomon Lopes Dubec (1743-1837) relates that he studied arithmetic and banking methods, since only Christians were permitted to engage in crafts.[14] Medicine was closed to Jews. To be sure, one finds a very sizable number of Sephardic names among the doctors of Bordeaux as in all of southern France and even in Paris. These were, however, with few exceptions until the eve of 1789, Marranos or even faithful Christians. Jews engaging in medicine were punished.[15] Even in trade there were innumerable limitations imposed on Jews. They were, for example, excluded from the chamber of commerce. Christian firms constantly sought to restrict the rights of Jews. In the city of Bayonne, Jews were not allowed to engage in trade of any sort. The production of chocolate had been introduced there by Jews. Nonetheless, attempts were made to prohibit them from engaging in this enterprise.[16]

[13] Léon, p. 16, 114; Beaufleury, p. 37; Malvezin, p. 133-136; AmBx, II54 (papiers de Tresne, lettre a Fouquet, 30 Mai 1658); Beaufleury, p. 30-32, 58, 72-73; AmBx, 65D-III (Taxes, 1758); *Au Nom de Dieu* (see fn. 70); AmBx, BB, registre de la Jurade, 19 Sept. 1721.

[14] The memoirs are in JHS. On June 7, 1806, the Bordeaux *Société de Bienfaisance* announced that the children of the poor could thereafter be taught crafts, which had hitherto been forbidden. (*Société* minutes in JHS.) Isaac Lévy, the Rabbi of Bordeaux, made the same point in a sermon in 1892. See Lévy, Isaac, *Le Centenaire de 1792 au Temple israélite de Bordeaux. Discours . . . 22 Septembre 1892* (Bordeaux 1892) p. 6; cf., Léon, p. x (préface d'E. Ducéré).

[15] On June 7, 1765 and on February 26, 1783 the corporation of Bordeaux doctors took steps against Jewish doctors, AdG, C. reg. 1696, p. 44, 63.

[16] Léon, p. 153; Liber, M., "Les juifs et la convocation des Etats généraux," *REJ*, vol. lxi, p. 95-96; De Salviat, *La Jurisprudence du Parlement de Bordeaux* (Paris 1787) p. 335; Beaufleury, p. 63-64.

The decree of August 25, 1622, permitted the Marranos to remain in Bordeaux, but they were not allowed to engage in retail trade. A century later, some exceptions were made, but the restrictions as a whole had by no means been lifted. In 1738, the Bordeaux dealers in household goods sought to confiscate the merchandise of their Jewish competitors. A decade later, attempts were made to prevent the Jewish baker Jacob Rivière from dealing in pastries. The Sephardim felt that restrictions imposed upon one Jew endangered the existence of the entire community, and they assumed the costs of the baker's defense. There were, in general, manifold discriminations against Jews. Thus, for example, despite the fact that a Jew had financed the construction of the Bordeaux theatre, Jews were refused admittance.[17]

The Sephardim were subject to moral persecution just as much as the Ashkenazim. In legal trials, the Jewishness of the litigants was often stressed by their opponents. In the case of Salomon Rodrigue Brandam against a Christian, the latter declared that the worst of evils was to be expected from a Jew. In a second case, a debtor of Abraham Raphaël, a wealthy Ashkenazi of Bordeaux, tried to prevent the testimony of a Jewish witness on behalf of Raphaël, arguing that Jews would only stand up for each other.[18]

There is no reason to minimize the significance of the privileges accorded the Sephardim. The fundamental point is to refrain from seeking a consistent line in the policy of the crown and of the city of Bordeaux with regard to the Sephardim. Despite all the persecutions, for example, the Bordeaux Parliament, on August 14, 1719, liberated a Spanish-Jewish merchant, who had been arrested for having defaulted on a debt in Malaga, after he testified that his family had been wiped out by the Inquisition. By and large, the Sephardim were hardly any more privileged than were the Avignonese or Ashkenazic Jews. All pretense to such privileges was but an expression of their claim to superiority over other Jews.[19]

---

[17] *Sommaire, pour les Bayles de la Communauté des Maîtres Patisiers et Rotisseurs de Bordeaux contre le nommé Jacob Rivière, juif portugais* (Bordeaux [1749]) 17p.; *Addition . . . contre le nommé Jacob Rivière, juif* [Bordeaux 1749] 7p.; Duranteau, *A juger . . . pour Jacob Rivière . . .* [Bordeaux 1748] 7p.; *Sommaire responsif pour Jacob Rivière . . .* [Bordeaux 1749] 10 + 1 p.; *Inventaire Sommaire des Archives Hospitalières antérieurs à 1790. Bordeaux* (Paris 1885) vol. ii, B. J. 1738; Detcheverry, p. 68; *idem, Histoire des théâtres à Bordeaux* (Bordeaux 1860) p. 29; Beaufleury, p. 101-102; AmBx, Reg. de la Jurade, f. 290, 4 Juin 1749; Cirot, I, p. 14.

[18] According to legal briefs.

[19] [Lamothe,] *Coutumes du ressort du Parlement de Bordeaux* (Bordeaux 1768-

II. CONFLICTS AMONG SEPHARDIM, AVIGNONESE AND ASHKENAZIM

The Sephardim considered themselves to be the aristocracy of the Jewish people. One often meets the proud claim that their forefathers had come to Spain directly from Babylonia and that they were descendants of the tribe of Levi, whereas the Avignonese were of the tribe of Benjamin.[20] Every Sephardi maintained that he was a *kohen.* The case of Samuel Peixotto is of particular interest in this respect. On April 18, 1781, he underwent baptism in Spain. In a petition to the King of Spain for ennoblement, Peixotto wrote—after his baptism and assumption of a new name, Charles Paul Joseph—that he was a *kohen* and that he was "a descendant and the head of the House of Levi, renowned in the Bible and in political history." The King granted his request, titling him the "Head of the House of Levi." Thereafter, he thus signed his name. He did so even when acting as a witness at a baptismal ceremony on July 16, 1782. Representing himself as a *kohen* in the course of the French Revolution, he was persecuted as an aristocrat.[21] Gentiles tended to mock this would-be aristocracy of *kohanim.* During the elections to the Third Estate in 1789, the Bordeaux opponents of Jewish suffrage published an anti-

69) vol. ii, p. 86-89. Bordeaux and Bayonne Jews, like a number of wealthy Ashkenazim, made every effort to secure their positions by receiving individual privileges. See AN, O-1-236; Hildenfinger, p. 34 (lettres de naturalité pour Moise Castro de Bayonne, avril 1776); *Lettres patentes du Roi, qui accordent aux sieurs Jacob de Perpignan, Juif, négociant de Bordeaux, à sa femme, ses enfants et à posterité, les droits de Régnicoles et naturels Français. Données à Versailles au mois de Mars 1776* [Bordeaux n.d.] 7 p.

[20] See de Pinto's pamphlets, Guénée's Letters, the collections of Sephardic privileges, and Pereire's reply to the Parisian merchants (fns. 41, 42, 44-46, 49). Cf., Léon, p. 374; Malvezin, p. 180; Maupassant, Jean de, *Un grand armateur de Bordeaux. Abraham Gradis* (Bordeaux 1917) p. 2; Nicolaï, *La Population de Bordeaux au XVIIIe siècle 1700-1800* (Paris-Bordeaux 1909) p. 177; Michel, *Histoire du Commerce* . . . vol. ii, p. 435-442; La Rochelle, p. 121; Meijer, J., *Encyclopaedia Sefardica Neerlandica* (Amsterdam 5709) vol. i, p. 45.

[21] Peixotto's act of baptism is in the British Museum (ms. 21445, p. 153-154). On his aristocratism, see: AdGE, famille Peixotto (lettre de Peixotto à de Vignes, 21 Août 1784); AdG, G2628, f.172 (29 Mars 1786); AdG, L721 (Pétition de Peixotto, descendant d'Aaron, de la famille de Levin"); *Mémoire pour Me. François-Peixotto,* 4 Mars 1782); AmBx, BB (Registre de lettres des Jurats, 29 Juillet 1763, "prétention de Peixotto de jouir des droits de la noblesse"); AmBx, GG519 (No. 332, 16 Juillet 1782, "baptême de Marie Fouignet, parrain M. Charles Joseph *Jacques Thomas Marie de Saint-George* . . . sur l'appel fait par le sieur Peixotto, Juif de naissance* [Bordeaux 1789] p. 3, 17; *Mémoire responsif pour Dame Riqua Peixotto* . . . Bordeaux 1787) p. 19: Marionneau, Ch., *Victor Louis* (Bordeaux 1881) p. 470; fn. 1; *Petite Gironde,* 24 avril 1926; Malvezin, p. 269. There were clashes in Bordeaux in this matter as late as the 19th Century. On January 17, 1812, the Bordeaux Consistory wrote to Paris: "The Peixotto family has been accepted here as *kohanim* for 200 years" and because new arrivals also pretend to be *kohanim,* conflicts have arisen (Archives of the Central Consistory).

Jewish pamphlet in the guise of a sham protest of the *nobles Cohens*.[22]

In contrast to similar developments in a number of other countries, in the first grant of privileges to Sephardim there is no mention of the exclusion of other Jews from Bordeaux. (The number of Sephardim in Bordeaux was, in any case, not very great.)[23] It is also to be noted that originally, all grants of privileges and other official documents uniformly referred to Portuguese, i.e., the Marranos from Portugal, though Spanish Jews benefited no less than they. Spaniards are mentioned together with Portuguese for the first time in a Bordeaux ordinance of March 17, 1574, which forbade molesting them. But this was not done consistently until the second half of the 18th century. During the early period, there was no love lost between Portuguese and Spanish Jews.[24]

We have hitherto mentioned the Avignonese of Bordeaux a number of times. These were a group of Jewish merchants from the Papal possession in southeastern France who had quickly become known as *Avignonais* in French. Jewish merchants from the four communities of the Papal province, and particularly from Avignon,

[22] *Protestation en forme de lettres des nobles Cohens aux gentilshommes soi disant les Nobles de la Sénéchaussée de Bordeaux induement assemblés le 10 février 1789* (Bordeaux 1 Mai 1789) 8p. On the elections see Szajkowski, Z., "Mishlehotehem shel yehude bordo el vaadat Malesherbes (1788) vel haasefa haleumit (1790)," *Zion*, vol. xviii (1953) p. 41. A Sephardi, Martinez Paschalis, is reported to have founded a Freemason lodge "Cohanim." See Lémann, L'Abbé Joseph, *L'-Entrée des Israélites dans la Société française* . . . (Paris 1886) p. 351.

[23] According to various sources, there were some 500 Jews in Bordeaux in the 1720's (132 families in 1722). By 1753 there were 408 famiiles (1,778 people). Of these, 327 families (1,447 people) were Sephardim, and 81 (331 people) were Ashkenazim and Italian Jews (see Nicolaï, p. 179-180). Other sources give the number of Jews in 1752 as 1,557, of whom 1,447 were Sephardim. In a list of 222 non-Sephardim, 149 were Avignonese Jews and 73 from other countries, almost all of them Ashkenazim (Malvezin, p. 286; Cirot, I, p. 187-191). It must, however, be assumed that demographic data on Bordeaux and Bayonne Jews are uncertain. Nicolaï (p. 7) asserts that Jews and Protestants probably concealed their true numbers. This is another indication that the Sephardim, their privileges notwithstanding, were not altogether secure. Many facts can be marshalled in support of this thesis, e.g., according to the burial records of the Sephardim in Bordeaux (AmBx, GG 790) there were 1,943 deaths from January 7, 1739 to November 5, 1792. In a municipal registry of burial permits for non-Catholics (AmBx, GG 810), however, there are records of 167 Jewish deaths between 1739-1750 which do not appear in the Sephardic records.

[24] Léon, p. 18; Beaufleury, p. 10-11. It would be worthwhile to investigate this subject more thoroughly. Even a rapid glance at archival sources, however, reveals that Sephardim from Portugal, in the main, headed the Sephardic Kehillot. They were also more active economically and had better connections. On the restrictions upon Ashkenazim involved in the Sephardic privileges, see Shatzky, Jacob, "Sfardim in zamoshch," *Yivo Bleter*, vol. xxxv (1951) p. 108-113.

had sought, over the course of many years, to engage in trade in the French provinces, where Jews were forbidden to do so. For the most part, efforts were made to drive them out. Even the Sephardim, seeing in them potential competitors, hoped to be rid of them. Thus they effected the insertion of a provision in the renewal of privileges of June 1723, where the Portuguese were for the first time referred to as Jews, requiring new Jewish arrivals wishing to settle among the Portuguese to provide evidence of their place of origin. It would not be unreasonable to presume that it was with this in mind that the Sephardim sought to have the privileges renewed at that time.

The Sephardim accused the Avignonese, who were mostly drapers and silk merchants, of dealing in inferior goods, and the like. There was, indeed, truth in this charge, but the Avignonese were not to blame. It was the fault of the manufacturers and the result of the low business ethics characteristic of Bordeaux at the time. Nonetheless, the small group of Avignonese in Bordeaux became the scapegoat.[25] In due time, they organized their own Kehilla in Bordeaux, which negotiated with the Sephardic Kehilla. They maintained their own cemetery and were recognized as a collectivity by the city. The arrival and departure of Avignon Jews to and from Bordeaux, and similar matters, were vested in their hands.[26] Ultimately, however, the Sephardim won out, and on January 21, 1734 a decree was issued ordering Avignonese as well as Ashkenazic and Italian Jews to leave Bordeaux. This was but the first of a series of expulsions.[27]

At some cost, a number of Avignonese families obtained limited privileges (April 22, 1749, July 12, 1750, December 3, 1753). On December 1, 1759 six Avignonese families were granted rights which placed them almost on a legal par with the Sephardim. This was hardly to the liking of the latter, who once again began to intrigue against the Avignonese. Simultaneously, a conflict erupted within the

[25] Lettres Patentes du Roy, pour les Portugais des Généralitez de Bordeaux & d'Auch. Données à Meudon au mois de Juin 1723 (Bordeaux n.d.) 4p. (4°) & (Bayonne n.d.) 4p.; Wolfson, REJ, vol. lxi (1911) p. 274.

[26] Cirot, I. p. 71, 142; AdG, 3E, 448, minutes du notaire Boucherau, 23 Sept. 1728 (cimetière des Avignonais); AmBx, BB, registre de la Jurade, 1 oct. 1726, f.8. In the minutes of the Sephardic Kehilla of December 31, 1724 reference is made to a request from the Kehilla of Avignonese in Bordeaux (Cirot, II, p. 42).

[27] Extrait des Registres du Conseil d'Estat [21 janvier 1734] [Bordeaux 1734] placard; Au Roy et à Nosseigneurs de son Conseil [pétition de Joseph-Jacob d'-Alpuget et autres Avignonais] (Paris 1734) fol; Certificats que rapportent les Srs. Dalpuget ... (Paris 1734) 6p.; Beaufleury, p. 46-50, 68-71; Malvezin, p. 190-197; Schwab, M., Histoire des Israélites ... (Paris 1895) p. 289; Detcheverry, p. 74-78; Cirot, I, p. 63-66.

Sephardic Kehilla between the dominant wealthy *parnasim* and the middle-class group. As a consequence of this quarrel, which reached the ears of the Crown, the Sephardic Kehilla received a new series of *takanot* (statutes of a Kehilla), issued by the King on December 14, 1760.[28] Articles 10 and 11 of the *takanot* permitted the Sephardim to banish Jews from Bordeaux whom they considered undesirable. These articles were employed by the Sephardim against Avignonese, Ashkenazim and even against their own poor. Assisted by friends in Paris, they succeeded in prevailing upon Marshal Louis de Richelieu to issue a decree on September 17, 1761, expelling 152 Jews from Bordeaux: 6 Sephardim and the others Avignonese and Ashkenazim.[29] Thanks to the intrigues of the Sephardim, the aforementioned privileges granted to the six Avignonese families in 1759 did not go into effect in the form of *takanot*, until May 13, 1763 and were not approved until the following February. These *takanot* provided for the establishment of a Kehilla of Avignonese. This did not prevent the continuation by the Sephardim of incessant efforts at banishing other Jews as well as members of their own community, and on June 17, 1787, the municipal authorities once again granted them control over foreign Jews. In a memorandum to Malesherbes in 1788, they requested that no Jew be permitted to settle in a community without consent of three-quarters of that Kehilla. In the absence of an organized Jewish Kehilla, they proposed that new Jewish arrivals be required to present evidence of good conduct.[30]

Despite the fact that the privileges of 1759 referred to the Avignonese as "Jews or New Christians of Avignon," they were known as Jews and not as Marranos to a greater extent than the Sephardim.

One should not infer from the above that the Avignonese were morally superior to the Sephardim. The technique of self-defense by persecuting others was well-known to them. Thus the six wealthiest Avignonese families, recipients of the privileges, sought the power to banish from the city "vagabonds" and "other Avignonese Jews, mem-

---

[28] *Lettres-Patentes en faveur des Juifs ou Nouveau Chrétiens Avignonois, établis à Bordeaux* . . . May 1759 (Bordeaux n.d.) 4p. (4°); Beaufleury, p. 49, 51, 92-104; Cirot, I, p. 69-70; *Règlement de la Nation des Juifs de Bordeaux. Approuvé et autorisé par Sa Majesté* [14 décembre 1760, avec: Ordonnance du Roy, qui étend et confirme le règlement . . . le 13 mai 1763] (Bordeaux n.d.) 8p. & édition [1763] 12p. [avec: Extrait des registres du Conseil d'Etat, 22 Février 1763].

[29] See fn. 42.

[30] Beaufleury, p. 95-97; Cirot, I, p. 70-71; *Ordonnance de Messieurs les Maire* ...[17 juin 1787] (Bordeaux 1787) placard.

bers of the six families excepted." The Sephardim, however, jealous of
their prerogative of control over "foreign" Jews, successfully prevented
this power from passing into the hands of other "foreign" Jews.[31]

In their home province, in the four communities of the Papal possessions, the Avignon and Comtat Venaissin Jews likewise persecuted
"foreigners." On October 8, 1397, April 6, 1486, and June 15, 1493,
the city of Avignon granted their request to bar entry to "foreign,"
non-Comtat Venaissin Jews. In the *takanot* of the Avignon Kehilla of
1490 (Articles 47, 86, 91), of 1558 (Articles 26, 81), and of 1779
(Articles 25, 26) one finds rigid limitations upon "foreign" Jews.
They were forbidden to trade or to remain in the city longer than
eight days, were compelled to pay special taxes, and the like.[32] One
Jacob Vidal, compelled to flee his home in a nearby community during
a war, arrived in Avignon in 1589. In order to obtain permission to
settle there, he had to sign an agreement with the Avignon Kehilla not to compete with the local merchants for six years. On
October 24, 1764 at the request of the Kehilla, the Town Council
of Avignon forbade alien Jewish beggars from entering the city. This
was but a pretext to oust some Jews who were not beggars. In 1789,
the Kehilla ordered the expulsion of an Ashkenazic Jew, David Lévy,
and his wife Hannah.[33] In a similar fashion, the *takanot* of Cavaillon
and of L'Isle-sur-Sorgue of 1620 (Articles 15-18) and of Carpentras
of 1645 (Articles 76-79) imposed limitations upon the rights of
foreign Jews, though these were not limited by the non-Jewish authorities. In 1773 the Kehilla of L'Isle-sur-Sorgue drove out some 70
foreign Jews. In 1774 and 1775 the Kehilla of Carpentras petitioned
the municipality to prohibit the entry of Ashkenazic or other Jews.
The Kehilla appointed special municipal guards for this purpose.[34]
Although Sephardim did not settle in these four Kehillot to any
extent till after the Spanish Exile, a municipal instruction dated as early

[31] Beaufleury, p. 92-105; Detcheverry, p. 88-89; Malvezin, p. 210, 213-216;
Cirot, I, p. 70.

[32] AmAvignon, BB24, fol. 32, 8 oct. 1397; délibérations 1482-91, f.131, 1491-
98, f.44; de Maulde, M., *Les Juifs dans les Etats français du Saint-Siège au Moyen-
âge* (Paris 1886) p. 56, 117, 162; Loeb, Isidore, *Statuts des Juifs d'Avignon
(1779)* (Versailles 1881) p. 73-75.

[33] AdVaucluse, E, notaire de Beaulieu, 1589, No. 1260, f.233-235: Calvet, ms.
5228, f.170, ms. 5938, f.06641. Ashkenazim, however, served as rabbis in Avignon,
e.g., Moses Jacob Polague of Poland in 1734, and Jacob Espic of Prague in 1741.
See Calvet, ms. 5938, f.06634; AdVaucluse, E. Etienne Mégy, 1740-41, f.282.

[34] Mossé, Armand, *Histoire des Juifs d'Avignon et du Comtat Venaissin* (Paris
1934) p. 121, 132-133, 157, 175-183.

as June 15, 1493, prohibits the entry of foreign Jews into Avignon, lest more refugees from Spain arrive.[35]

Let us now briefly consider the behavior of the Ashkenazim in France. Among the Ashkenazim we find frequent records of conflicts between individuals and the Kehilla concerning rights of residence, which were not invariably inherited by one's children. Cases of hounding of "foreign" Jews, that is, Ashkenazim who had no such rights, were far from infrequent. Nevertheless, outsiders continued to live there, which could only be done with the aid of the Kehillot, thus establishing the fact that the Kehillot were not always opposed to them. Thanks to the intensive efforts of the Council of the Alsace Kehillot in 1784-1789, a decree to banish all Jews without rights of residence from Alsace was not carried out.[36]

Prevented from living within the limits of Bayonne itself, Jews settled in its suburb, Saint-Esprit. This Kehilla was larger, as well as culturally more advanced and more distinguished in the Jewish world, than its counterpart in Bordeaux. Until the 19th century, however, it was less wealthy than the latter and hence far less influential with the powers-that-were. Thus it was that the *parnasim* of the Bordeaux Kehilla took the lead in the later negotiations with the Malesherbes Commission, as well as in the delegation to the National Assembly at the start of the Revolution in Paris. This continued to be the case in the Sanhedrin convened by Napoleon I. The conflict of the Sephardim with non-Sephardim was milder in Bayonne than in Bordeaux,

[35] AmAvignon, reg. délib. 1491-98, f.44. The family of Joseph Hacohen, author of *Emek Habakha,* arrived in Avignon in 1496.

[36] Szajkowski, *Economic Status* . . ., p. 26-29, 49, 140; *idem,* "The Jewish Problem in Alsace, Metz, and Lorraine on the Eve of the Revolution of 1789," *Jewish Quarterly Review,* vol. xliv (1954) p. 225-226. It is possible that these "foreign" Jews were relatives of Alsatian Jews who did have rights of residence, and hence there prevailed some degree of solidarity among them. This is, however, no more than a supposition. In 1789 the *parnasim* of Nancy demanded that a Jew wishing to settle there be required to prove that he possessed 10,000 livres; for settlement in other cities of Lorraine, 6,000 livres; and 1,200 in villages (Liber, M., "Les Juifs et la Convocation des Etats Généraux," *REJ,* vol. lx [1913] p. 132). Despite all this, the attitudes of Jews toward "foreigners" and "vagabonds" were not of the worst. The non-Jewish contemporary world treated foreigners and the poor far more cruelly than did the Jews. Moreover, it doubtless did not have such well-organized institutions for the maintenance of the indigent as did the Sephardic or Ashkenazic Kehillot. The philo-Semite Abbé H. Grégoire did not take the hatred of Jews for Jews too seriously. He wrote that Ethiopian and English Jews were perhaps more similar to each other than were Frenchmen from Picardy and Provence (*Essai sur la Régénération* . . . [Metz 1789] p. 29). We have, however, become accustomed, in historical perspective, to expect Jewish communities to manifest more unity amongst different groups and classes than non-Jewish historians anticipate in the general society.

according to the historian Léon. Nonetheless, poor Ashkenazim could remain in the city no more than 24 hours, and Ashkenazim referred to the Sephardim as *jaroche de Bayonne*.[37] Yet we do find instances of marriages between Sephardim and Ashkenazim.[38] In the neighboring community of Peyrehorade, charity was divided into three categories: aid to the members of the Kehilla; to the "brothers" of Bordeaux and Bayonne, i.e., Sephardim; and finally, aid to the "friends" from Germany, i.e., Ashkenazim.[39] This division notwithstanding, we likewise find "mixed" marriages there.[40]

III. Voltaire's Attacks on the Jews and the Reply of the Sephardim

Jacob Rodrigues Pereire, the noted pioneer teacher of the deaf and dumb, played a leading role in the promulgation of the decrees against the Avignonese, Ashkenazim and other Jews in Bordeaux. He was the *syndic* of the Bordeaux and Bayonne Jews in Paris. David Lameyre, a *parnas* of Bordeaux and likewise an outstanding opponent of the Avignonese and Ashkenazim, was Pereire's brother-in-law. Pereire was aided by Isaac de Pinto of Amsterdam, who is said to have been from Bordeaux originally. It was Pereire who succeeded,

---

[37] Léon, p. 377; Lévi, Albert, *Les vestiges de l'Espagnol et du Portugais chez les Israélites de Bayonne* . . . (Bayonne 1933) p. 20.

[38] The following is a list, probably incomplete, of children and widows of such marriages, with dates of birth and death. Enclosed in parentheses are the first names of the fathers and full maiden names of the mothers of the children.

Rachel Louis Nounès (Benjamin & Sara Lévy) 1768-?; Ribca Lopes (veuve d'Isaac Lévy) 1707-1794; Rachel Lévy (veuve d'Isaac Rodrigue) 1691-1793; Lameyra Lévy Rebecca 1720-1788; Sara Dacosta (veuve d'Abraham Lévi) 1717-1790; Judith Gommès (Moïse & Esther Lévy) 1725-1806; Rachel Souza (Moïse & Judith Lévy) 1727-1794; Esther Lévy (Isaac & Rebeca Lopes) 1729-1794; David Lévy, Esther Lévy (Jacob & Ribca Lameyra) 1732-1807, 1739-1826; Jacob Lévy, Joseph Lévy, Salomon Lévy (Mardoché & Rachel Mendes) 1748-1810, 1751-1806, 1753-1757; Martinez Abraham Lévy, Gomez Jacob Lévy, Gomez Sara Lévy (David & Hana Olivera) -1753, 1755-1817, 1756-1840; Ribca Louis Nunes (Benjamin & Sara Lévy) 1757-1775; Rachel Lévy, Sara Lévy (David & Léva Gomès Cassera) 1758-?, 1759-?; Jacob Lévy (Abraham & Esther Lameyra) 1758-1760; Abraham Léon (Haïm & Sara Lévy Gomès) 1793-?.

The list is taken from the compilation of notes prepared in 1865-1881 by Mordecai Ernest Naquet and Samuel Salzedo. (The notes are deposited in the Bayonne Synagogue.) It is generally easy to distinguish between a Sephardi, Ashkenazi, Avignon and Comtat Venaissin Jew on the basis of name alone. On Franco-Jewish nomenclature, see Mendel, Pierre, "Les noms des Juifs français modernes," *REJ*, vol. cx (1949-50), p. 15-65.

[39] Léon, p. 377.

[40] Léon Lévy & Rachel Alvares (1782), Ginsburger, E., "Les Juifs de Peyrehorade," *REJ*, vol. civ (1938) p. 43.

at the very last moment, in getting Marshal Richelieu to order the
expulsion of the Avignonese from Bordeaux.[41]

The noted replies to Voltaire's attacks against the Jews were by no
means the result of a courageous stand against a Judophobe, but
were rather the product of the hostile relations between one group of
Jews and another. Voltaire's sharp criticism of Jews aroused the
Sephardim, because he had failed to distinguish between Sephardim
and Ashkenazim. Pereire requested his friend Isaac de Pinto to formu-
late a reply to Voltaire. In this reply, published in 1762, de Pinto
berated Voltaire for not having been aware of the difference between
the "good" Sephardim and the "bad" Ashkenazim. Sparing no detail,
he discussed the contempt in which the Ashkenazim were held by the
Sephardim. The differences between the two groups were not merely
in customs and rituals, but in moral standards. Sephardim were finer
and more honest. They had no criminals, usurers, or swindlers among
them. To whichever land they came, they brought only wealth and
prosperity. The low moral standards of the Ashkenazim resulted from
the persecutions which they suffered, whereas the Sephardim were
always privileged. They were descendants of Jews who had come
directly to Spain from Babylonia, and their noble nature was preserved
throughout the course of centuries. The two groups of Jews, he went
on to say, have always lived apart, without even commercial contact
between them. A Sephardic Jew despised each and every Ashkenazi.[42]
De Pinto's violent attack on the Ashkenazim aroused dissatisfaction
even among Christians. A London monthly of 1763 chided de Pinto
for besmirching the Ashkenazim. He replied with a pamphlet (in
1766) in which he reiterated his condemnation of the Ashkenazim.
In a pamphlet written by a Christian in reply to de Pinto (in 1768)
the author argued that even if the claimed distinctions between
Sephardim and Ashkenazim were true, de Pinto would have done
better to pass over them in silence.[43] The attacks against the Ashken-

---

[41] Pinto de, *Apologie* (see fn. 42) p. 3; Léon, p. 375-376; La Rochelle, p.
123-124, 385-386; Malvezin, p. 213-216; Wijler, J. S., *Isaac de Pinto, sa vie et ses
oeuvres* (Apeldoorn, n.d.) p. 43; Schwab, p. 291; Cirot, I, p. 68; Malvezin, p. 212;
Beaufleury, p. 81-83.

[42] [Isaac de Pinto] *Apologie pour la nation juive ou Réflexions critiques sur le
premier chapitre du VII tome des Oeuvres de Monsieur de Voltaire, au sujet des
Juifs* (Paris 1762) 48p. & (Amsterdam 1762) 40p.; Wijler, p. 26-27, 40, 43-51;
Léon, p. 374-375. De Pinto maintained friendly relations, however, with the Ency-
clopedist Diderot. See T. R. [Reinach], "Les Juifs dans l'opinion chrétienne aux
XVIIe et XVIIIe siècles: Peuchet et Diderot," *REJ*, vol. viii (1884) p. 143.

[43] *Monthly Review* (London) vol. xxviii (1763) p. 570; [de Pinto] *Réponse à*

azim were repeated in the introductions to the collections of privileges of Sephardim in France, published by the Bordeaux Kehilla in 1765 and 1777. The very language is almost identical with that in de Pinto's pamphlet. (The introductions were composed by Pereire.)[44] De Pinto's reply to Voltaire, including the scurrilous comments on the Ashkenazim, were reprinted in Abbé Antoine Guénée's noted collection of letters to Voltaire.[45] At about this time (1767) the Parisian merchants' corporation printed a *factum,* prepared by the lawyer Goulleau, opposing the right of Jews to live in Paris.[46] Goulleau did not spare the Sephardim. In an open letter dated September 4, 1767 Pereire accused him of transposing de Pinto's attacks on the Ashkenazim to attacks on the Sephardim.[47] Goulleau responded immediately that it would be most interesting to know what other Jews thought of the Sephardim. He concluded that, inasmuch as Jews themselves despised each other so greatly, it was hardly surprising that Christians were unable to tolerate Jews.[48] Pereire's reply to this was contained in a second letter, replete with new attacks on the Ashkenazim.[49]

For many years, a conflict concerning the Jewish cemetery raged between Parisian Sephardim and Ashkenazim. On March 7, 1780 the former received a permit for their own cemetery at La Villette.

---

deux critiques qui ont été faites de l'Apologie de la Nation juive . . . dans le Monthly Review . . . (The Hague 1766) 40p.; *Réflexions critiques sur l'Apologie pour la nation juive, par un Vénitien* (London 1768) 50p.; Wijler, p. 54-55.

[44] *Recueil de lettres patentes, et autres pièces, en faveur des Juifs portugais, contenant leurs Privilèges en France* (Paris 1765); *Privilèges, dont les Juifs portugais jouissent en France depuis 1550* (Paris 1777).

[45] [Guénée, Antoine], *Lettres de quelques Juifs portugais et allemands, à M. de Voltaire . . .,* (*Lisbonne* [Paris] 1769). Cf. Wright, Dudley, "Le prêtre qui réfuta Voltaire et son anti-judaïsme," *La Question d'Israël,* no. 71 (1939).

[46] Goulleau, Me., avocat, *Requête des marchands et négociants de Paris, contre l'admission des Juifs* (Paris 1767).

[47] 4p. (4°). BN, coll. Joly de Fleury 585, f. 282.

[48] 3 p. (4°), Archives Gradis: ". . . Il faudrait actuellement savoir ce que les autres Juifs pensent des Portugais. En attendant, on peut tirer une conséquence bien naturelle: S'il existe dans un petit nombre de Juifs un si grand mépris pour les autres, on ne doit pas être surpris de voir dans les Chrétiens quelqu' antipathie contre tous les Juifs. Une autre conséquence: Si une poignée de Juifs a cru pouvoir écrire librement la façon de penser sur les autres Juifs, il a dû paraître permis à des chrétiens d'exprimer leurs sentiments sur tous les Juifs en général. Le dédain des Portugais pour leurs frères, n'est établi que sur des conjectures de simples raisonnements. On ne trouve nulle part, ailleurs que dans la Préface du Recueil des Juifs Portugais, la distinction qu'ils font en leur faveur. La Déclaration de Louis XIII ne l'a pas adoptée: elle n'a excepté que les Juifs de Metz. . . . Si les Marchands ont témoigné quelques alarmes sur la prétention des Juifs, ils sont très-excusables, par la seule façon de penser des Juifs Portugais sur tous les autres Confrères."

[49] Pereire, [Jacob Rodrigue], *Seconde lettre circulaire en défense des Juifs portugais* (n.p. [1767]) 10p. (4°).

They were vexed by the fact that the Ashkenazim buried their dead there the following year. On February 8, 1782 the Parisian Ashkenazic *parnasim* Cerfberr and Goldschmit approached the Sephardic *parnasim* of Bordeaux with a request that the Ashkenazim be permitted to bury their dead in the Bordeaux cemetery. This request was refused on February 22, 1782. This compelled the Ashkenazim to maintain a cemetery of their own (in the suburb of Montrouge).[50]

During the 18th century there was no legal Kehilla in Paris. The Jews living there—a majority of whom were Ashkenazim—were merely tolerated. Since the Ashkenazim found it more difficult than the Sephardim to settle in Paris, they were accused by the latter of pretending to be Sephardim. The Sephardim effected an order by the Paris Police Commissioner that non-Sephardim in Paris were required to have passports, whereas certificates from their Kehilla sufficed for Sephardim.[51]

The Ashkenazim could not forgive the Sephardim their intrigues. Moses Mendelssohn's ire at de Pinto went deep.[52] There were dramatic flareups between Sephardic delegates from Bordeaux and Ashkenazic delegates to the National Assembly during the Revolution.[53] Beaufleury, the first historian of the Sephardic Jews of France, in 1799 sharply inveighed against differentiating between Sephardim and other Jews, and urged unity among all Jews.[54]

[50] When the Montrouge cemetery was closed down in 1809, a conflict once again broke out, for the Ashkenazim attempted to bury their dead at La Villette. See *Ordonnance qui autorise l'établissement d'un Cimetière particulier pour les Juifs Portugais à Paris*. Du 7 Mars 1780 ([Paris] 1780) 2p. (4°); La Rochelle, p. 445-455; Kahn, Léon, *Le Comité de bienfaisance* (Paris 1886) p. 98-120; Loeb, I., "Un Baron juif français au XVIIIe siècle," *Annuaire des Archives Israélites, 5646* (Paris 1885) p. 25; Hildenfinger, p. 16, 23-24; Mousset, Albert, *Un Cimetière juif portugais à Paris* (Lisbon 1939) p. 6-7; JTS (Lettres de Cerfberr et Goldschmit, 1782).

[51] Kahn, Léon, "Les Juifs de Paris de 1755 à 1759," *REJ*, vol. xlix (1904) p. 121-145; Szajkowski, *The Economic Status* . . . p. 43, fn. 96; *Copie d'une lettre . . . par M. Lenoir . . . au sieur Pereire . . . portant règlement pour les Juifs portugais. Paris le 15 novembre 1777* [Paris 1778] 3p. (4°); La Rochelle, p. 393-397; Detcheverry, p. 104-105; ArchAffEtr., Portugal 108, f. 129.

[52] Wijler, p. 55-56.

[53] Szajkowski, "Mishlehotehem . . ."

[54] Beaufleury, p. v, viii, 107-108. The historian Cirot (I, p. 68) maintains, without citing any evidence, that Beaufleury simply wished to settle accounts with the Sephardic *parnasim*, with whom his family had quarrelled. On Beaufleury, see Szajkowski, Z., "Louis Francia de Beaufleury, a yidisher fartreter-deputat beys der frantseyzisher revolutsye," *Davke* (Buenos Aires) no. 20 (1954) p. 241-248. In the course of time, the notion of the moral superiority of the Sephardim even came to be held by Ashkenazim, it being ascribed to the fact that the Sephardim had been less persecuted. Not only did Abraham Furtado, the Sephardic *parnas*, express this view; it was also voiced by the Polish Jew in France, Zalkind-Hourwitz, and

We have already noted the public reaction of Christians against de Pinto's attacks on Ashkenazim. During the Revolution, non-Jewish circles protested strongly against any policy of favoring Sephardim at the expense of other Jews.[55] The notion of the moral superiority of Sephardim, however, gradually spread. Some Christian historians of the 18th century and later exploited these inner Jewish conflicts to mock Jews or to demonstrate that Ashkenazim were really unworthy of civil rights, since they were morally inferior to other Jews.[56]

There were, nonetheless, instances of friendly relations between Sephardim and Avignonese. There were even marriages between the two groups, though almost invariably between Avignonese men and Sephardic women.[57] In 1787 a social club was founded in Bordeaux by 70 Sephardim jointly with a number of Avignonese.[58] There were even cases of marriage between Sephardim (mostly women) and Ashkenazim.[59] Such "mixed" marriages did not always find favor in

repeated in the 19th century by various rabbis, by Léon Halévy, Léon Kahn, and others. Moyse, Gabrielle, *Mémoire d'Abraham Furtado sur l'Etat des Juifs en France jusqu'à la Révolution* (Paris [1936]) p. 37; Zalkind-Hourwitz, *Apologie des Juifs* (Paris 1789) p. 34; Halévy, Léon, *Résumé de l'histoire des Juifs modernes* (Paris 1828) p. 247; Aron, Arnaud, *Lettre pastorale . . .* Strasbourg, 21 juillet 1834; Henri-Avigdor, F., *Quelques vérités à Monsieur Théophile Hallez . . .* (Paris 1845) p. 13, 76-79; Kahn, Léon, *Les Juifs à Paris depuis le VIe siècle* (Paris 1889) p. 52.

[55] *Journal de Paris*, no. 30, 30 janv. 1790; *Journal de la Correspondance de Nantes*, no. 28, 1790; Kahn, Léon, *Les Juifs de Paris pendant la Révolution* (Paris 1898) p. 66-68; Brunschvicq, L., "Les Juifs de Nantes . . .," *REJ*, vol. xix (1889) p. 300-301.

[56] [Marquis d'Argens] *Lettres juives . . .* (The Hague 1736) vol. i, p. 26, vol. iii, p. vij-iv; [Hell] *Les Juifs d'Alsace doivent-ils être admis au droits de citoyens actifs?* [Strasbourg 1790] p. 53; Moureau, *De l'incompatibilité entre le Judaïsme et l'exercise des droits de cité . . .* (Paris 1819) p. 12; Lancastel, Betting de, *Considération sur l'Etat des Juifs dans la société chrétienne et particulièrement en Alsace* (Strasbourg 1824) p. 2-3; Beugnot, Arthur, *Les Juifs d'Occident . . .* (Paris 1824) vol. i, p. 137, vol. ii, p. 39-80; Médelsheim, A. Cerfberr de, *Ce que sont les Juifs de France* (Paris-Strasbourg 1844) p. 18-19; 25; Leroux, Alfred, *Etude critique . . . sur le XVIIIe siècle à Bordeaux* (Bordeaux 1924) p. 59; Mathiez, A., in *Annales historiques de la Révolution française*, vol. v (1928) p. 379; Cirot, II, p. 49-50.

[57] The following are examples of such marriages during the 18th century: Jacob Waidll & Perpignan; Roget Junior, fils d'Aaron Roget & Abigaïl Solar; Roget Junior & Rébecca Lopes Dias: *Mémoire adressé a Son Excellence Monseigneur le Ministre Secrétaire d'Etat de L'Intérieur, par quelques Israélites de Bordeaux* (Bordeaux [1818]) p. 10, 17.

[58] AmBx, GG 30. One Mardoché Cordova signed the petition to permit formation of the club on behalf of the 70 members. Permission was granted on August 9, 1787. Meetings were held at the home of Moyze Mendes. One possibility is that the club was an attempt to form an organized opposition against the *parnasim*, for not one of the signers of the petition was a *parnas*.

[59] During the 18th century, Isaac Raphaël married Rose Rodrigue Pereyre; Salomon Joseph married a Sephardic woman; after having lived in Bordeaux for 14 years the Ashkenazi Mathieu married a Sephardic woman; Isaac Poreau after 12 years; Seref Haim after 8 years; Habraam Alcanan after 10 years (according to

the eyes of the Sephardim, and were not infrequently the source of sharp conflicts. One such case was that of Serf Pollac. Born in the hamlet of Polleville [?], near Colmar, he arrived in Bordeaux in 1771. There he married Judith Francia, a Sephardic woman who had been divorced by her first husband, Salomon Silva Salazar. The Sephardic *parnasim* ordered Pollac to leave Bordeaux. Since he refused to leave, the *parnasim* drove out the Jews who were the witnesses at the ceremony, and requested the authorities to expel Pollac from Bordeaux. In their memorandum, they reiterated the old arguments that Sephardim were always a superior element, loyal to King and country, in contrast to the terrible Ashkenazim. Serf Pollac replied with a memorandum in which he attacked the egotism of the Sephardim and the dictatorial character of their *parnasim*. He contrasted their behavior with relations in the small Kehilla of Marseilles, where Jews, Sephardim and Ashkenazim alike, lived in peace. He cited the fact that the Marseilles Jews acclaimed residence permission granted to Sabatto Constantini, who was not a Sephardi.[60] (The small Marseilles Kehilla did not come into being at once through a grant of privileges to a specific group. It consisted of tolerated individuals. It would seem that Marseilles Jews were only able to maintain themselves in the city thanks to their unity.) Replying to the charge of the Bordeaux *parnasim* that Alsatian Jews had no rights in other parts of France, Serf Pollac noted that the Sephardim, so inordinately proud of their privileges, did not even have the right to live or own shops in Bayonne, and were forced to live in the suburb of Saint-Esprit. It would seem that Pollac succeeded in remaining in Bordeaux.[61]

IV. SEPHARDIM, WEALTHY AND POOR

We have heretofore suggested that the underlying motive of the struggle of the Sephardim against the Avignonese and the Ashkenazim

---

documents of 1761 or 1762 in AmBx, GG 30; AdG, G 275). In a legal brief drawn up by Serf Pollac (see fn. 61) the names of Benjamin Abraham, the brothers Levi and Skaramel are mentioned as Ashkenazim who married Sephardic women. It should be noted that the Sephardic communities of the 18th century had a majority of women. In 1775 Serf Pollac, writing on this subject, held that marriages between Sephardim and Ashkenazim should therefore be encouraged. See *La partie de Serf Pollac* ... p. 7 (cf. fn. 61).

[60] A trial was later conducted against Constantini, though not in connection with his right of residence: Tributis, Roman, avocat, *A Nosseigneurs du Parlement* [Aix 1784] 56pp.

[61] Szajkowski, Z., "A konflikt tsvishn di parnosim fun di sfardishe yidn in bordo un an ashkenazishn yid (1774-75,)," *Davke*, no. 17 (1953) p. 325-330.

was the fear of commercial competition. Sephardic "aristocratism" only sharpened the conflict. The fact that the Sephardim were wealthier also played a certain role in these relationships. We have also noted that Sephardim—poor ones, for the most part—were among those expelled from Jewish communities. In January 1597, the Bordeaux *parnasim* succeeded in having the Parliament issue a decree banishing all Portuguese, i.e., Sephardic Jews, who had resided in Bordeaux less than ten years, from the city. The fear of competition from the newly-arrived Marranos was, undoubtedly, the basis of their action. The renewed exile of Jews from France of April 23, 1615 did not affect the Marranos of Bordeaux, but they took advantage of this occasion to see to it that no more Jews, even Sephardim, should be permitted to settle there, and that certain Jews, among them people who had lived there for 20 years, should be expelled.[62]

There were among the Sephardim, undoubtedly, a number of wealthy men. The Ashkenazim were, on the whole, considerably poorer. The Sephardim, playing an important role in the colonial and slave trades, were of great value to Bordeaux and the Crown. David Gradis is considered to have been one of the eleven most important inhabitants of 18th century Bordeaux. As a result of his activity, the value of exports to Canada rose from 2,365,266 livres in 1759 to 9,000,000 livres in 1763. It should be kept in mind that it was not only the Bordeaux Sephardim who were wealthier than the Ashkenazim; the entire city and province were wealthier than their counterparts throughout France. The growth of Bordeaux was allied to the growth of colonial trade, in which the Sephardim played an active role.[63] Participating in the economic growth of Bordeaux, the Sephardim followed the predominant pattern of surrounding life. The slave trade was a key factor in the rise to wealth of Bordeaux; Jews, too, were among the slave traders. At the time of the outbreak of the Revolution in 1789, there was a substantial movement for the emancipation of the slaves. Nonetheless, among those active in oppo[s]ing emancipation was David Gradis.[64] It should, however, also be

[62] Beaufleury, p. 16-17; Malvezin, p. 113-114; Léon, p. 19; Ginsburger, E., "Les Juifs de Peyrehorade," *REJ*, vol. civ (1938) p. 35; Schwab, p. 241.
[63] Kahn, L., *Les Juifs de Paris sous Louis XV* (Paris 1892) p. 47-48, 63; Courteault, Paul, "La Vie des foires bordelaises," *Revue historique de Bordeaux*, vol. xi (1918) p. 16; Detcheverry, p. 72; Leroux, p. 312; Bloch, Isidore, *Réflexions sur les Juifs* (Paris 1894) p. 111; Bloch, Maurice, *Les Juifs et la prosperité publique à travers l'histoire* (Paris 1899) p. 18.
[64] This question will be considered in a separate study by the author.

kept in mind that the Jewish horse and grain dealers of Alsace, Metz and Lorraine were no less valuable to the Crown than were the Sephardim. So indispensable was the Alsatian *shtadlan* Cerfberr to the Crown that the King allowed him to settle in Strasbourg against the wishes of this traditionally anti-Jewish and independent city.[65]

Historians have heretofore portrayed Bordeaux Sephardim as a community of generous, wealthy merchants. The Kehilla, from its very inception, was headed by a number of wealthy families, who succeeded in crushing all opposition.[66] There were, indeed, wealthy Jews in Bordeaux, but they were fewer in number than the poor and middle-class. Poor as well as rich arrived there from Spain and Portugal. From the protocol of a meeting of 52 Bordeaux Sephardim, gathered on June 24, 1764 to issue a protest against the *parnasim,* we learn that two-thirds of those who arrived in Bordeaux after the expulsion from Spain were impoverished. In the early period, the wealthy Jews were most charitable, even paying the taxes of the indigent Marranos. Later, however, the very small group of wealthy men dominating the Kehilla used its position to attempt to diminish its share of the tax burden. From other sources, too, we glean that poverty was rampant among the Marranos. According to a report of June 11, 1718, of 70 Sephardic families, only 40 had a source of income. In truth, one out of every two families depended upon charity throughout the 18th century.[67]

In 1735 the Sephardic Kehilla of Bordeaux decided that only the Sephardic poor were to receive charity. Actually, they too were not free of oppression. On November 20, 1648, 93 families, all poor Sephardim, were expelled from Bordeaux, Bayonne, Dax and Bidache. The wealthy families managed to avoid expulsion. On September 24, 1744 the Sephardic Kehilla agreed to drive out the Ashkenazic and Italian Jews, and to prohibit poor Sephardim from dealing in used goods. In 1753 a large number of Sephardim were once again ex-

---

[65] Szajkowski, *The Economic Status* . . . p. 152; *idem,* "The Jewish Problem . . .," p. 206-218.

[66] *Idem,* "Mishlehotehem" . . ., p. 37.

[67] Nicolaï, p. 182; AdG, E. notaire Rauzan père, 34, 24 juin 1764; ". . . la pauvreté leur ait fait relacher beaucoup de leurs cérémonies et religion," de Lancre, P., *L'incrédulité et mescréance du sortilège* . . . (Paris 1622); AdG, C1089; Malvezin, p. 172-173; Léon, p. 22, 26; Cirot, I, p. 32. On poverty among Sephardim in the 19th century, see Szajkowski, Z., *Poverty and Social Welfare among French Jews 1800-1880* (New York 1954) p. 53-55.

pelled.[68] Control of the passports of Jews lay in the hands of the Kehilla, and poor immigrant Marranos were compelled to leave Bordeaux.[69] On June 28, 1749 the Kehilla of Saint-Esprit managed to have a decree issued expelling *Juifs vagabonds.* At the same time, the number of "privileged" poor entitled to receive charity was limited to 100 families.[70]

In fighting against the Avignonese, as we have indicated, the Sephardim wished, first and foremost, to be rid of their competition in trade.[71] In the battle against their own poor, the *parnasim* argued that vagabondage had to be eliminated. This argument was even employed in editing Articles 10 and 11 of the Kehilla *takanot* of December 14, 1760 which gave the *parnasim* the right to expel vagabonds. This was, however, beyond any doubt, merely a pretext to achieve a broader aim: the power to expel anyone who endangered the privileged status of a group of rich merchants.[72]

V. The Sephardic "Nations"

One of the major achievements of the Ashkenazic Jews was the autonomous character of the Jewish Kehillot of Alsace, in the city and province of Metz, and in Lorraine. The organization of Kehillot and of the Kehilla Councils immeasurably aided the defense of the Jews against attacks of all kinds. Anti-Semites were by no means pleased by them. In 1784, the rights of the Alsatian Kehillot were restricted,

---

[68] Cirot, I, p. 36, 66; *REJ*, vol. xxv, p. 240-245; AdG, Registre des délibérations de la nation portugaise depuis [le] 11 Mai 1710, no. 110, 24 Sept. 1744.

[69] On November 29, 1713 five members of the family of Abraham Nunez left Bordeaux for London "à condition de ne plus revenir en France." (AdG, GB 45, fol. 2). In a legal brief against the Sephardic *parnasim,* Serf Pollac charged that they sold residence rights to new Jewish arrivals, assigning the money for the maintenance of Sephardic poor who had to be tolerated (see fn. 61).

[70] *Au nom de Dieu* [Règlement pour la Nation portugaise de Saint-Esprit, 21 décembre 1752] [n.p., 1753] 12p. art. 18; Beaufleury, p. 70-71; Léon, p. 62, 144.

[71] On August 3, 1787 Abraham Furtado wrote to Rodrigues, a representative of the Bordeaux Sephardim in Paris, that Gradis, who then happened to be in Paris, should concern himself with the petition against the Avignonese, since it would also be to the advantage of his business affairs (Archives Gradis, vol. x, no. 118b).

[72] Reinach, Théodore, *Histoire des Israélites* (Paris 1914) p. 279. Beaufleury, author of the first history of the Jews of Bordeaux and Bayonne (1799), wrote that it would have been preferable for the Sephardim to teach their poor crafts rather than drive them out (p. 82), but this was not done. It is by no means out of the question that their policy kept a good many poor Marranos from returning to Judaism and drove some, who had already openly professed their return, back to the Church. It might also be noted that Jews were not unique in this approach. Thus the Moors fleeing from Spain behaved similarly: in 1611 the wealthy Moors were permitted to settle in Bayonne, while the poor were driven out (Michel, *Races . . .,* vol. ii, p. 88-89).

258 Z. SZAJKOWSKI

and at the end of 1788 the anti-Semitic leaders of Alsace demanded that the Kehillot be disbanded entirely.[73] What was the situation of the Sephardic Kehillot?

Various Jewish sources refer to the Kehilla Kedosha of Bordeaux. The Bayonne Kehilla called itself K.K. Tfuzot Yisrael (according to some, Tfuzot Yehuda); the Kehilla of Bidache, Nve Shaanan (according to other sources, Beth El); the Kehilla of Peyrehorade, Beth El.[74] In official documents, the Sephardic Kehillot are called "Nations."[75] This is not to be taken as signifying "peoples," but rather as "corporations." The Kehillot of Ashkenazim and Comtat Venaissin Jews were likewise called "Nations." As yet, we are uncertain as to the origins of the Sephardic Kehillot. According to Beaufleury, the first syndic of the Sephardim of Bordeaux was elected on April 28, 1699. The Kehilla presumably existed at that time as a philanthropic society (Sedaca) and historians are in agreement that the Sedaca was the same as the "Nation."[76] In Bordeaux and in Saint-Esprit, however, there existed various societies, among them philanthropic societies, which were controlled by the Kehillot.[77] It is conceivable that the Kehilla was at

[73] Szajkowski, The Economic Status . . ., p. 24, fn. 52, p. 42, fn. 93; idem, "The Jewish Problem . . .," p. 223, 238.

[74] On the tombstone of Rabbi Joseph Falco one finds "beK.K. Bordeaux"; the words "Yakov Emanuel Rosh Mikehilatenu N.F.I." appear on a Bayonne tombstone of 1792. The expression "kehilla" referring to an organization of Bordeaux Jews is found even in 1841-42. See Mildola, Raphael and Elazar, Parshat haibur (Amsterdam 1734 ("K.K. Nefuzot Yisrael"); Bethencourt, REJ, vol. xxv, p. 236-237; Gross, H., Gallia Judaica (Paris 1897) p. 92, 114, 453; Léon, p. 215, 364; Carmoly, in Revue Orientale, vol. ii, p. 229; Kayserling, M., Die Juden in Navarra . . . (Berlin 1861) p. 150; Lévy, Emil, "Un document sur la Communauté de Peyrehorade (Landes) 1762-1812," Annuaire des Archives Israélites 5664 (Paris 1903) p. 50; Cirot, I, p. 132; Archives Israélites, vol. ii (1841) p. 253, vol. iii (1842) p. 3. In a document dated July 6, 1807 (in the writer's possession) the parnasim of Peyrehorade are referred to as the "Mrs composant le Kaal de Peyrehorade." Apropos of the Spanish tradition of calling Kehillot by such names as Israel, Judah, Jacob, and the like, it may be noted that the Gradis family named its ships Patriarche Jacob, Reine Esther, etc. See Extraits des Registres de Parlement [Affaire Gradis] [Bordeaux 1753] 7p.; Réponse pour Pierre Sorbé . . . (Bordeaux 1773) p. 6; Michel, Histoire du Commerce . . ., vol. ii, p. 425.

[75] One source refers to "nation" as the entire community, i.e., all Bordeaux Jews ("toute la nation juive connoît l'exposante"). See Raison d'appel, pour Sara Lameyra . . . Contre Louis Francia [Bordeaux 1762] p. 8.

[76] Beaufleury, p. 28-29; Cirot, I, p. 30-99; Léon, p. 139.

[77] The official minutes also refer to various types of societies: Tiferet Bahurim, to visit the sick; a yeshiva; a yeshiva Tiferet Shalom, founded by Joseph Dacosta; Gmilut Hasadim, founded by Rabbi Joseph Falco; Mishnat [Mishmeret?] Holim, a society with a membership of 100 (the society split in 1746, some members forming a new society, Bikur Holim); Ateret Zkenim, founded by the mohel Abram de Mezas. In the takanot of the Bayonne Kehilla similar societies are mentioned. In Peyrehorade there existed a philanthropic society and a yeshiva. See Bethencourt, in REJ, vol. xxvi, p. 250-251; Cirot, I, p. 80, 86, 89, 94, 96-99, 131; E. Lévy, p. 47.

first organized as a supposed philanthropic society, since the Sephardim could not as yet openly function as Jews. Long thereafter, subsequent to the grant of full citizenship on January 28, 1790 the "Nation" was disbanded and a philanthropic society assumed almost all its functions. We have here clear proof that the "Nation" was not only a philanthropic society but, to all intents and purposes a full-fledged Kehilla with all its manifold functions. The "Nation" not only collected taxes, distributed charity, supported a rabbi and ecclesiastical court, supervised kashrut, schools and the like, but also determined the national and municipal taxes to be paid by each individual Jew;[78] excommunicated a landlord for raising the rent of two widows;[79] and had jurisdiction over marriage.[80] In the memorandum to Malesherbes of 1788 the Sephardim of Bordeaux requested that the laws of inheritance according to Jewish law be maintained, as was the custom among the Ashkenazim.[81] During the Revolution, the Bordeaux Jews energetically affirmed that their "Nation" was never a Kehilla, but only a philanthropic society. This was, however, solely motivated by the desire to save the Jewish cemetery, which was sold as a confiscated national property. The property of a Kehilla was subject to confiscation, but not that of a philanthropic society.[82]

The Bordeaux Kehilla was, incidentally, founded long before 1699. There exists a notarial agreement dated 1629, between George Rodrigues and the "nation portugaise" of Bordeaux, in which the latter assumed all expenses arising out of Rodrigues' litigation with the Christian merchants of the city.[83]

The Sephardic Kehillot had *takanot* ratified by the King. In the

[78] In 1786 Moïse Gonzales requested the Kehilla to lower his taxes (AmBx, GG 30).

[79] Cirot, I, p. 80.

[80] The courts of Bordeaux ruled that Jews had the right to marry according to Jewish law instead of French civil law. On the conflicts concerning the divorce of the apostate Peixotto and the marriage of Abraham Robles, see fn. 21 and *A juger . . . pour Moyse Robles . . . contre Abraham Robles, son fils . . .* [Bordeaux 1743] 21 + 1p.; *A juger . . . pour Abraham Robles, Juif, du Faubourg Saint-Esprit . . . contre Moïse Robles, son Père* [Bordeaux 1743] 15p.; De Salviat, *La Jurisprudence du Parlement de Bordeaux* (Paris 1787) p. 23-30.

[81] Léon, p. 153.

[82] Beaufleury, p. 157-195; Szajkowski, Z., "Jewish Participation in the Sale of National Property during the French Revolution," *Jewish Social Studies,* vol. xiv (1952) p. 311. Avignon and Comtat Venaissin Jews, on the contrary, sought to prove that they had Kehillot as well as societies, precisely in order to have their debts to Christian creditors taken over by the government. The creditors argued that Jews had not had legal Kehillot. See Szajkowski, in *Davke,* no. 20, p. 241-248.

[83] AdG, E, minutes du notaire Lafite, 15 avril 1632, f. 257-258.

takanot of Saint-Esprit of 1752 (30 articles) reference is made to earlier *takanot* of 1666 and of 1703. There is little doubt that some Kehillot existed even earlier.[84] The Kehilla of Biarritz is reported in one source to have been founded in 1597.[85]

In its administrative relations with the Sephardim—as well as with the Avignonese—the non-Jewish world considered these bodies of Jews to be corporations of merchants. It was generally accepted that the term Jew—even when referring to a poor man—was synonymous with merchant. Nonetheless, Jews were persecuted on religious as well as on economic grounds. Prior to the time when the Sephardim began to live openly as Jews, and even subsequently, they were known as Portuguese and Spaniards, or as Spanish merchants. Portuguese was a synonym for Jew. Even Léon de Carcassonne, an Avignonese, was buried in 1720 as a Portuguese. We have already mentioned that the Avignonese were referred to in the privileges of 1753 as "Avignonese New Christians."[86] It was rather extraordinary that the Sephardim and Avignonese were considered as corporations, like the other 85 Bordeaux corporations of bakers, shoemakers, doctors, lawyers and the other 115 occupations which are mentioned in all the lists of the municipal corporations. Their two corporations were merely tolerated. Many of their rights were curtailed, though as corporations they were probably considered as commercial rather than mere religious bodies. When the decree in favor of Protestants of 1787 prohibited their organization in special corporations, Jews continued to be members of

[84] The following editions of the Bordeaux *takanot* are extant: *Ordonnance du Roy, qui étend et confirme le Règlement de la Nation portugaise de Bordeaux* [14 *décembre* 1760] . . . *Donné à Marly le 13 Mai 1763. De par le Roy* (n.p., n.d.) 4p. (4°); *Règlement de la Nation des Juifs portugais de Bordeaux, approuvé et autorisé par Sa Majesté* [13 Mai 1763] (Bordeaux n.d.) 4p. (4°); *Règlement . . .* [du 14 déc. 1760, avec: Ordonnance . . . du 13 Mai 1763] (Bordeaux n.d.) 8p.; édition 1763: *Règlement de la Nation des Juifs Portugais de Bordeaux, Approuvé et autorisé par Sa Majesté* [22 Février 1763] (n.p., n.d.) 12p. (4°). For the *takanot* of Saint-Esprit, see the following editions: *Copie de la lettre écrite par M. Amelot le 29 Mars 1741 à Mr. de Serilly* (n.p., n.d.) 12p. [recueil, avec Règlement pour la Nation Portugaise établie au Faubourg Saint-Esprit près Bayonne] [Bayonne 1754] 12p. (4°) & 8p. (4°); *Au Nom de Dieu* [Règlement, 1752] (n.p., n.d.) 4p.; cf., Degert, A., "Règlement des Juifs de Bayonne," *Revue Gascogne*, ns. XII (1912) p. 347. See fn. 44 for collections of Bordeaux privileges. There exists a later hectographed edition of the Saint-Esprit privileges: Ginsburger, Ernest, *Les Statuts Juridiques de la Communauté Israélite de Bayonne 1550-1941* (Paris 1941).

[85] Bethencourt, *REJ*, vol. xxv, p. 236.

[86] Things went so far in considering them as Portuguese and Spaniards that during the war with Spain, an order was issued in May 1625 to confiscate their property. Jurists did not speak of Jews, but of Portuguese, e.g., Bosquet. See Malvezin, p. 128; Cirot, I, p. 3, 111; Bosquet, *Dictionnaire raisonné des domaines et droits domaniaux* (2nd ed., Rouen 1763) vol. iii, p. 479.

the "Nations," which, as far as the municipal administration was concerned, were the equivalent of corporations. As such, these groups of Jews were permitted to vote in the elections to the Estates-General.[87]

It remains to be investigated whether the Ashkenazic Jews in Bordeaux had their own legal Kehilla. There is no record of an official grant of a privilege to establish an Ashkenazic "Nation" in Bordeaux, but there is little doubt that they were organized in a society, for they had their own synagogue and rabbi.[88]

VI. AFTER THE EMANCIPATION

In the course of the work of the Malesherbes Commission aimed at improving the lot of the Jews, and during the beginning of the Revolution, the major preoccupation of the Sephardic *parnasim* was with the prevention of the immediate grant of full citizenship to the Ashkenazim. This issue has been thoroughly investigated, and it would be superfluous to repeat the well-known details. It is a fact that the decree of January 28, 1790 bestowing citizenship upon the "privileged" Jews endangered the entire struggle for the emancipation of the Ashkenazic Jews. It took great courage and patience to overcome this danger, and in this struggle for citizenship of all the Jews of France the Sephardim had no share whatsoever. Relations between Sephardim and Avignonese had, however, by this time been improved to the point of amity. The Avignonese representative Salom also participated in the delegation of Bordeaux and Bayonne Jews to the National Assembly from December 1789 to February 1790. Sephardim and Avignonese worked jointly in the philanthropic society which replaced their dissolved Kehillot. The Sephardim and Avignonese from Bordeaux residing in Paris were members of one society and one synagogue. In Bordeaux itself, the two groups continued to maintain separate synagogues and cemeteries, though at the first assemblies of Bordeaux Jews after the Revolution (in 1803), Sephardim and Avig-

---

[87] AmBx, HH19 ("Noms des Bayles, Sindics, Gardes, jurés" [des Corporations] 1760-1791); AdG, C 313 (liste des corporations, 1785); Nicolaï, p. 184, 186, 190; Cirot, II, p. 15; *Liste des corporations par ordre alphabétique, et des noms de leurs députés, à l'Assemblée du Tiers-état de Bordeaux* (n.p., n.d.) placard, in JTS.

[88] See fn. 89. The Sephardim and Avignonese complied with the order, during the Revolution, for all religious groups to turn over their records of births, marriages and deaths to the municipality, but the Ashkenazim in Bordeaux did not do so. It would seem that they had not kept annals, for we consistently find cases of births, circumcisions and deaths of Ashkenazim in the registers of the other groups.

nonese sat together.[89] The number of Ashkenazim in the city had increased somewhat by then.[90]

During this period, new developments occurred. In the first post-Revolutionary attempts made to organize Kehillot in France (in 1805) it was difficult to achieve unity between Sephardim and Ashkenazim. On February 4, 1805 the government queried a number of Jewish leaders from Paris on their attitude toward reorganizing the religious Jewish administration.[91] Jewish community life in Bordeaux was at the time conducted by a philanthropic society (*Société de Bienfaisance*) which had been reorganized on June 29, 1803. At a meeting held on March 4, 1805 to consider the government inquiry of February 4th, the tendency of the Sephardim to dispense with the formation of official Kehillot and to restrict organization to philanthropic societies was manifested. On March 10, 1805 the *Société* protested against the supposed fact that the Commission to reorganize the Jewish religious administration was dominated by Ashkenazim, who were intent upon placing the Jews again "under the rabbinical yoke."[92] Essentially the fear of forming Kehillot derived from their realization that, under the Napoleonic regime, this would ultimately lead to a centralization of all Kehillot in France. Then Sephardim and Ashkenazim would be forced to cooperate. This was expressed in unmistakable terms by David Gradis at a meeting of the *Société* held on June 7, 1806. A week earlier, on May 30, 1806, Napoleon I had

[89] Ducaunnès-Duval, A., *Inventaire sommaire des archives municipales. Période révolutionnaire* (Bordeaux 1896) vol. i, p. 227; Kahn, *Les Juifs à Paris . . .*, p. 235-237. There were six synagogues in Bordeaux in the 18th century: the tiny Ashkenazic one of Rabbi Joseph Ephraïm of Berlin; the Avignonese synagogue Shaare Razon; and the four Sephardic ones, Ateret Zkenim of Cardozo, the Gradis synagogue, and two of philanthropic societies. In Year II of the Revolution, there were eight synagogues and eight rabbis. According to various documents, there were seven synagogues in Bordeaux in 1810 and 1811, including: three of Sephardim (Peixotto, Gradis, and Francia), one of Avignonese (led by Daniel Astruc), one of Ashkenazim (led by Alexander Cerf), and one called Lévy's Synagogue (led by A. Léon), which might also have been Ashkenazic. A larger synagogue was not opened until May 14, 1812. It burnt down on June 27, 1873 and was rebuilt in 1882. See AmBx, GG 794, no. 172; Cirot, I, p. 178; Leroux, A., *La Colonie Germanique de Bordeaux* (Bordeaux 1918) p. 231; Uhry, Isaac, *Monographie du Culte Israélite à Bordeaux* (Bordeaux 1892) p. 11.

[90] In 1806 there were 2,131 Jews in Bordeaux, of whom 1,651 were Sephardim, 336 Ashkenazim and 144 Avignonese (Malvezin, p. 286). In 1854 there were some 800 Jewish families in Bordeaux (2,411 people: 577 men, 656 women, 598 boys and 580 girls), of whom about 120 were Ashkenazic families. As regards Avignonese Jews, there were 16 families named Astruc alone (according to archives of the Departement).

[91] Anchel, R., *Napoléon et les Juifs* (Paris 1928), p. 56-61. He does not, however, mention anything about conflicts with the Sephardim.

[92] Minutes of the *Société* of March 4 and 10, 1805, in JHS.

issued the decree convening a Jewish Assembly, and the "danger" of the establishment of Kehillot in a centralized body had increased. Gradis came out most forcefully in favor of restricting organization to charity societies and for perpetuating the separation between Sephardim and Ashkenazim.[93] During the time of the Jewish Assembly, during the Sanhedrin period, and in the years in which Napoleon's anti-Jewish decrees were issued (1806-08) the Sephardim once again devoted all their energies to intrigues against the Ashkenazim.[94] They still attempted to salvage a Kehilla administration of Sephardim which would be distinct from that of the Ashkenazim.[95]

The conflicts between Sephardim and Ashkenazim did not cease even after Jewish Consistories (Kehillot) and a Central Consistory had finally come into being in March 1808 in France and in the occupied territories. The government was besieged with petitions by the Sephardim in Amsterdam, who constituted a minority of the Jewish population, requesting permission to organize a separate Sephardic Consistory.[96] At first, the Central Consistory of France had a majority of Ashkenazim.[97] Operating behind the scenes, Benjamin Rodrigues, a wealthy Bordeaux Jew residing in Paris, intrigued against the existence of an Ashkenazic majority. On January 3, 1810 he proposed that the Bordeaux Consistory support his anti-Ashkenazic drive. He wrote that, because of the Ashkenazic influence in the Central Consistory, Jews were being disregarded in official ceremonies.[98] On January 22,

---

[93] ". . . les Juifs de Bordeaux & de Bayonne penseraient dans ce qui leur est particulier n'avoir besoin pour toute nouvelle organisation qu'un simple règlement de police intérieure à peu près semblable à celui que les derniers Rois de France leur avaient accordé, afin de mieux pourvoir à l'entretien de leurs pauvres qui périraient plutôt que de mendier hors de chez eux & ce qu'ils n'ont pas moins à coeur afin de pouvoir les faire instruire à leurs frais dans tous les arts & métiers, depuis qu'ils ne sont plus rejetés par les corporations." (Gradis' speech, in the writer's possession.)

[94] Szajkowski, Zosa, *Agricultural Credit and Napoleon's anti-Jewish Decrees* (New York 1953) p. 96-98.

[95] Minutes of the session of the Bordeaux *Société*, August 20, 1806, in JHS.

[96] AN, F¹⁹1788. Since 1810 the Sephardim and Ashkenazim in Amsterdam had a concordat, in which it was agreed not to seek to recruit members from the other group (*Archives Israélites*, vol. xii, 1851, p. 286).

[97] Kahn, *Les Juifs à Paris* . . ., p. 195.

[98] ". . . Il étoit désirable que le Consistoire Central fût composé de Juifs Espagnols et Portugais, mais peut-être étoit-il déraisonnable de l'exiger puisque ces derniers forment à peine la douzième partie des Juifs de l'Empire. Quoiqu'il en soit les nominations ayant été faites, et des Juifs Allemands se trouvant à la tête de notre organisation Religieuse, nous pensons qu'il convient de se taire et de supporter sans murmure les désagréments qui pourront en survenir. La réclamation que vous indiquez entraîneroit le scandale d'une lutte entre les Allemands et nous. Ce scandale nous seroit infiniment plus nuisible que ce que nous avons à redouter . . . et

1810 and once again on April 29, 1811 Rodrigues renewed his proposal. This time the Bordeaux Consistory refrained from any official declarations against the Ashkenazim. It maintained this position on June 20, 1814 when Rodrigues raised the question again.[99] Rodrigues nonetheless took it upon himself to forward a request to the government to curtail the number of Ashkenazim in the Central Consistory. This action was censured by the Bordeaux Consistory.[100] When in 1817 Alphonse Theodore Cerfberr published a brochure opposing the demands to renew Napoleon's anti-Jewish decree of March 17, 1808, the Bordeaux Consistory wrote to him thanking him for the copy of the brochure he had sent them and for his action on behalf of the Jews of Alsace.[101] This step marked a fundamental change in the attitude of Sephardim to Ashkenazim. Henceforth, there were to be no official attempts to maintain the alienation between the two groups in France. This was one of the positive results of Napoleon's Sanhedrin. The Sephardim henceforth feared to attack other Jews, for they had no way of knowing whether restrictions imposed upon one group of Jews would not, in due time, be extended to all Jews in France.

During the time of the First Empire, a number of Ashkenazic Jews settled in Saint-Esprit, which was later to be incorporated into Bayonne. [102] Of the 363 Jewish families (1,173 people) there in 1809,

---

sommes nous bien sûrs ensuite que le gouvernement appréciera la différence énorme que nous cherché à établir sur quelques nuances de doctrine qui divisent deux branches de la même secte . . ." (From the reply of the Bordeaux Consistory to Rodrigues, dated January 14, 1810, in JHS.) On Jewish delegations to official receptions of Napoleon I, see Kahn, L., "Visites Officielles et Compliments d'Usage," *Annuaire des Archives Israélites,* vol. v (1888) p. 32-38.

[99] Letters from the Bordeaux Consistory to B. Rodrigues in Paris, dated February 12, 1810, May 9, 1811, and June 20, 1811, in JHS.

[100] ". . . J'ai convoqué mes collègues, et d'après la connaissance qu'ils en ont prise ainsi que de votre pétition au Ministre qui y étoit jointe, ils ont pensé comme moi que vos réfléxions toutes plausibles qu'elles paroissent n'en sont pas moins contraires aux vues adoptées par le Gouvernement depuis la révolution, de ne plus reconnaître ces anciennes désignations d'Allemands & de Portugais. Pourquoi prendre des Juifs Allemands cette mauvaise opinion, qu'ils choisiront toujours parmi eux les membres du Consistoire au préjudice des Juifs dits Portugais. Croyons plutôt que toutes les fois qu'ils pourront porter leur choix sur quelqu'un de ceux-ci ils se feront un devoir et l'honereront de l'avoir pour Collègue." (From a letter of the Bordeaux Consistory to B. Rodrigues in Paris, dated October 28, 1814, in JHS.)

[101] Cerfberr, A.-T., *Observations sur les voeux émis par les conseils généraux du Haut- et du Bas-Rhin relativement aux mesures à prendre contre les Juifs par suite du décret du 17 Mars 1808* (Paris 1817). The letter of thanks, dated December 1, 1817, is in JHS.

[102] Genevray, Pierre, "Les Juifs des Landes sous le premier Empire," *REJ,* vol. lxxiv (1922) p. 129.

18 were Ashkenazic.[103] As has been indicated, relations between Sephardim and Ashkenazim improved considerably. Thus, for example, we have the case of the maskil Moses Ensheim (born in Metz in 1750, died in Bayonne in 1839) who was appointed as tutor to the children of Joseph Furtado, a brother of Abraham Furtado. Joseph's eldest son married the daughter of the Parisian banker Fould, an Ashkenazi.[104] Of the 232 marriages of Bayonne Jews between 1859 and 1891, 52 were between Ashkenazim and Sephardim, most of them between Ashkenazic men and Sephardic women.[105] In 1863, a group of 30 Polish Jews in Bordeaux requested permission to establish their own synagogue.[106]

Only two of the matriculants of the Paris Rabbinical Seminary from 1830 to 1930 originated from Bordeaux: Elie Aristide Astruc (one of the founders of the Alliance Israélite Universelle), Rabbi of Bayonne and later Chief Rabbi of Belgium, and Edgar Sèche. Almost all of the rabbis in Bordeaux and Bayonne since 1830 were Ashkenazim, among them Samuel Marx, Rabbi of Bayonne in 1842-1887, and the historian Ernest Ginsburger, the last Rabbi of Bayonne, who fell at the hands of the Nazis.[107] Sephardim, Avignonese and Ashkenazim participated jointly in the various societies.[108]

---

[103] According to a census in the writer's possession.

[104] Morel, F., *Bayonne, vues historiques et descriptives* (Bayonne 1836) p. 411; Ducéré, Edouard, *Dictionnaire historique de Bayonne* (Bayonne 1911) vol. i, p. 457; Léon, p. 377-378; *Archives Israélites,* vol. xliv (1883) p. 175.

[105] According to a list of marriages compiled by the historian H. Léon (in the writer's possession). In addition to these 52 marriages, there were also "mixed" marriages between Sephardim and Avignonese Jews.

[106] AN. F¹⁹ 11029.

[107] Bauer, Jules, *L'Ecole Rabbinique de France 1830-1930* (Paris 1930) p. 184, 186-188; *Funerailles de M. Samuel Marx . . .* (Paris 1887) 23p.; Consistoire Central des Israélites de France et d'Algérie, *Mémorial. En Souvenir de nos Rabbins . . .* [Paris 1946] p. 18-19.

[108] In 1840, three of the seven members of the committee on the revision of the statutes of the Gmilut Hasadim in Bordeaux were non-Sephardim. In the elections of 1878, S. Wolf was elected to the Consistory. Five of the fifteen members of the philanthropic society in 1905 were Ashkenazim. Of the 500 members of the Consistory in the department of Gironde in 1928, 150 were Ashkenazim, about an equal number Avignonese, as well as some Jews from North Africa. Of the nine directors of the Bayonne society for the diffusion of handicrafts (1867), two were Ashkenazim and three Avignonese Jews. Albert Lévy served as president of the Bayonne Consistory in 1907, and Edmond Milhaud in 1930. Of the six members of the Parisian Sephardic synagogue, two were Ashkenazim and one a Comtat Venaissin Jew. See *Règlements de la Société de Bienfaisance de Guemilout-Hassadim* (Bordeaux [1840]) 26p.; *Rapport présenté par le Consistoire israélite de la Gironde . . .* [2 mai 1880] (Bordeaux n.d.) 7p.; *Société de bienfaisance israélite de Bordeaux* [appel] 1905; *Association cultuelle israélite de la Gironde . . . Assemblée générale du 29 Mars 1928 . . .* (Bordeaux); *Société protectrice de la jeuneuse israélite et des*

Of the 60 Bordeaux soldiers who lost their lives in World War I, 23 were Ashkenazim and a number of others Avignonese.[109] Nonetheless, there remained some degree of alienation of the Ashkenazim,[110] just as the latter looked with disdain on the Jewish immigrants from eastern Europe.[111]

During the German occupation of Bordeaux in 1940-44, 2,119 families (5,722 people) filled out questionnaires in a special Jewish census. Of these, 545 registered as non-Jewish. (The census included Jewish residents of pre-war Bordeaux as well as refugees from other parts of France.) There were 722 families who came from the interior of France, 153 from Alsace-Lorraine, and 112 from North Africa (70 from Algeria, 13 from French families in Tunis and Morocco, 21 Tunisians and Moroccans and 8 foreign families from Tunis and Morocco), and 316 naturalized French families. Only 542 families (1,198 people) came from Bordeaux and other parts of southwestern France. Most of the 316 naturalized families were originally from Poland. Between July 18, 1942 and February, 1944, 1,279 Jews were deported, among them 214 Sephardim of long-established families.[112]

---

arts et métiers de Bayonne. Séance publique du 26 avril . . . (Bayonne 1867) p. 23; *Consistoire israélite de Bayonne. Statuts . . . 1930* (Bayonne n.d.) 11p.; *Société civile du Temple israélite suivant le rite Espagnol Portugais . . . 30 Avril 1878* (Paris n.d.) 8p.

[109] *Nombre des coreligionnaires morts au Champ d'honneur ou des suites de la guerre ou disparus* [Bordeaux 1918] 1p.

[110] In a printed declaration dated July 27, 1923 a number of Bordeaux Jews charged that distinctions were being made among various groups of Jews in the Consistory: "Tu es juif mais tu n'es pas juif comme nous, tu es un juif inférieur, nous ne voulons pas que tu nous approches, l'association cultuelle est un cercle fermé, où nous ne pouvons accepter que nos partisans et amis."

[111] It is known to the writer that the Consistory of Nancy in 1920 placed a number of special benches in a corner of the synagogue for immigrants from Eastern Europe. Cf., the Strasbourg *La Tribune Juive,* January 5, 1934.

[112] According to documents in the possession of the Bordeaux Rabbi Joseph Cohen. During World War II a large group of refugees living in Bayonne attempted to make their way to Spain and Portugal (according to Hicem documents in the Archives of the Yiddish Scientific Institute). There are, however, no precise data on this.

It is noteworthy that in 1943 the Amsterdam Sephardim attempted to convince the Germans that Sephardim were descendants of the Latin rather than the Semitic race. This is, however, not to be interpreted as an attempt to set themselves off from the Ashkenazim, but rather as a means of deceiving the Germans and saving themselves. On this, see the following three studies. (The first is hectographed, the second is in manuscript. The second item also has a Dutch version.) Henriquez, Percy Cohen, *Die Herkunft der sogenannten portugiesischen Juden* (Amsterdam 1942) 34p.; de Froe, A., *Anthropologische Untersuchung der sogenannten portugiesischen Juden in den Niederlanden* (Amsterdam July-August, 1943) 102p.; Wallenstein, M., "The Marranos of Holland. A Memory of the Last War," *Jewish Chronicle,* August 17, 1951.

INTERNAL CONFLICTS WITHIN THE EIGHTEENTH
CENTURY SEPHARDIC COMMUNITIES
OF FRANCE

THE governmental structure of the eighteenth century Sephardic
community of Bordeaux — called Nation — was the outgrowth
of special historical circumstances at the turn of the preceding century.
Opposition to this structure provoked many internal conflicts.

Executive power in the Nation was in the hands of a syndic and
his deputies.[1] A body of elders (*anciens*) composed of all former syndics
also participated in the conduct of the Nation's affairs. The following
incident provides an example of the elder's role: On September 26,
1748, Jos. Rodriguez Pereire and son, and Raphaël Dacosta were fined
one hundred livres by the Nation for not observing the Sabbath.
However, three days later the rabbi and elders cancelled the fine.[2]
According to later sources, the elders appointed the staff of a "Bureau
of Reform or the Thirteen," to which complaints against excessive
taxation were addressed.[3] As a result of a decision of the Nation (on
April 21, 1716) not all taxpayers, but only the elders had the right to
vote in the election of the syndics and their deputies. Also, only the
elders were tax-assessors, i. e., they alone determined the amount of
taxes to be paid by each member of the Nation. On June 3, 1760,
however, the Nation decided that the syndic and his deputies should
be included in the number of assessors.[4]

In such a governmental structure there was a marked tendency
toward the exercise of dictatorial power on the part of the Nations'
leadership which was drawn from a small group of the richest families.
According to a petition of about 1764, it is clear that the elders were
members of nine families. Two elders were father and son, three were
brothers-in-law, etc.[5] These close family relationships were the basis of

---

[1] On the syndics see Z. Szajkowski, *Autonomy and Communal Jewish Debts
during the French Revolution of 1789* (New York, 1959), p. 4, note 11.

[2] Minutes of the Nation (in the Departmental Archives of Gironde, series I),
Nos. 166–67.

[3] City archives of Bordeaux, GG 30 (a complaint addressed by Moïse Gonzales,
ca. 1787).

[4] Minutes of the Nation, Nos. 11, 272.

[5] Departmental archives of Gironde, C 1090.

Originally published in the *Hebrew Union College Annual*, vol. XXXI
(1960).

constant conflicts between the leadership and the community, especially in the area of tax assessments.

Whenever people refused to pay taxes, the Nation's leaders first
tried coercion by "peaceful" means. Non-elders were invited to the
meetings at which taxes were assessed to create the impression that
the decisions reflected the popular will. The success of this policy was
limited. Thus, in 1730 all taxpayers were invited to a meeting, but
only a dozen non-electors in fact came. In 1734, when the number of
elders was reduced by death, six non-elders were requested to attend
tax-assessment meetings.[6] Since "peaceful" means of coercion could
not be relied upon, on April 12, 1730, the Nation's leadership used
stronger measures. On that date the Intendant published an ordinance
enjoining the Jews to pay taxes to their Nation.[7]

The dictatorial regime of the Nation was sharply attacked in the
1740's by the widow Mendes and her son, Joseph Mendes Darlac, both
of whom, from 1733 until 1742, refused to pay taxes. In a memorandum addressed to the King and his Council the Mendes family stated
that the six or seven "despotic rulers" of the Nation tried to ruin
everyone who displeased them.[8] In the 1750's many Sephardim protested against the tactics of their Nation's leaders in levying taxes and
refused to pay them. This refusal was regarded as evidence of "disorders" by the syndics, who presented for approval to the King new
by-laws to reinforce the syndic's authority. The by-laws were approved
on December 14, 1760.[9] According to Louis Francia de Beaufleury,
author of the first history of the Jews in Bordeaux and Saint-Esprit-
lès-Bayonne (published in 1799), the new by-laws aroused much discontent among the Sephardim. The text of the by-laws was obscure
and hence favorable to arbitrary rules by the syndic and the elders.[10]
Despite the new by-laws many Sephardim refused to pay taxes. The
Nation's leaders then turned to the King once more for a new set of
by-laws, dated May 13, 1763, which again strengthened the hand of
the syndics.[11]

On June 24, 1764, fifty-two taxpayers assembled in the house of

<hr/>

[6] Minutes of the Nation, No. 48; G. Cirot, *Recherches sur les Juifs Espagnols et
Portugais à Bordeaux* (Bordeaux, 1908), pp. 47–48.

[7] Cirot, *op. cit.*, (*supra*, n. 6), p. 51.   [8] *Ibid.*, pp. 52–53.

[9] *Règlement de la Nation des Juifs de Bordeaux, approuvé et autorisé par Sa
Majesté* (n.p., n.d.), pp. 1–4. The by-laws of Dec. 14, 1760, were also published
separately with the same title (n.p., n.d.), 4 pp.

[10] L.F.B. [Louis-Francia de Beaufleury], *Histoire de l'établissement des Juifs à
Bordeaux et à Bayonne depuis 1550* (Paris, an 8), p. 85. On Beaufleury see Z. Szajkowski, *op. cit.*, (*supra* 1), p. 62.

[11] See note 9, pp. 5–9. The by-laws of May 13, 1763, were also published separately: *Ordonnance du Roy . . .* (n.p., n.d.), 4 pp.

the above mentioned Joseph Mendes Darlac to protest against the leadership of the Bordeaux Nation.[12] Thanks to the practice of the Sephardim of registering with notaries all private, commercial, and social events of importance, the detailed minutes of the meeting, together with the names of those present, were preserved.[13]

According to the minutes of the meeting, the Sephardic Nation of Bordeaux had its origin at the end of the 17th century and not an earlier period. The minutes thus confirm the theory that almost all first-generations of Marranos who arrived from Spain and Portugal were lost to the then existing Jewish communities. Those Marranos who remained Jewish arrived at a later period. No link existed between the Nations of these two groups.[14]

The minutes of the assembly present a rare contemporary explanation for the autocratic character of the regime of the Nation. Many Marrano families who came to France at the end of the 17th century — according to the minutes — were poor, all their possessions having been plundered by the Inquisition. The rich among the Marranos extended help to their poor brethren, even to the extent of paying taxes for them. This circumstance was highly influential in determining the organization of the government of the Nation. A small group of wealthy Jews who helped the poor and paid taxes for them was gladly recognized as the Nation's legal representatives. Now this form of government of the Nation was perpetuated even though in later years the economic status of the Marranos had improved and taxes were paid by a large number of families. Still, a small number of the richest families continued to direct the affairs of the Nation and to levy taxes in an arbitrary fashion. The fifty-two Sephardim present at the meeting represented — according to the minutes — the majority of the Nation's taxpayers.[15] They agreed to oppose the despotic tendencies of the Nation's leadership. They elected a committee composed of Abraham Lopes, Moise Azevedo, Jacob Azevedo, Abraham Gabriel de Castro, Louis Francia, and Raphaël Julian[16] to fight for a more just administra-

[12] Th. Malvezin wrote incorrectly about fifty-four present at the assembly: *Histoire des Juifs à Bordeaux* (Bordeaux, 1875), p. 217.

[13] Departmental archives of Gironde. E. Rauzan's notarial minutes, file 34. June 24, 1764. See the Appendix.

[14] Z. Szajkowski, "Population Problems of Marranos and Sephardim in France, from the 16th to the 20th Centuries," *Proceedings of the American Academy for Jewish Research*, XXVII (1958), pp. 83–105.

[15] According to the Intendant's report of Sept. 8, 1764, these fifty-two Sephardim had paid one third of the Nation's taxes. The total number of taxpayers was then 171. Cirot, *op. cit.*, (*supra*, n. 6), p. 56.

[16] According to all other sources the assembly elected a committee of six, including Joseph Mendes d'Arlac in whose house the assembly was held. See note 9, p. 12, and Beaufleury, *op. cit.*, (*supra*, n. 10), p. 88.

tion of the Nation, if necessary by means of civil suits in courts-of-law. Two days later, on June 26, 1764, the committee presented the grievances at a meeting of the Nation's leaders who requested a delay of eight days before giving their decision.[17] On July 3, 1764, the committee again petitioned the syndic and his deputies to act on the taxpayers grievances.[18] The syndic summarily dismissed the petition. The committee then offered the syndic the following ultimatum: Unless the latter called a meeting within three days at which the taxpayers would be given the opportunity to present a plan for a new administration, the opposition to the leadership would be brought to the attention of the legal authorities.[19]

According to the historian, Louis Francia de Beaufleury, the meeting of taxpayers on June 24, 1764, directed the committee of six to discuss their grievances not with the syndics and his deputies, but with the elders, whose number was then twenty.[20]

The syndic (the elders, according to Beaufleury) complained to the King that the dissidents who attended the meeting of 1764 were trying to replace a "real and legitimately constituted body" by a "phantom." The opposition, too, addressed many petitions to the French authorities requesting a more democratic leadership for the Nation. Their main argument was that the elders were a group of relatives belonging to only nine wealthy families. Thus, the Nation was ruled not by duly elected representatives, but by a hereditary group of "arrogant aristocrats," which was contrary to the traditional spirit of the Jews and to their legal status in France. The opposition demanded that the title elder (*ancien*) should be applicable not only to former syndics, but to all taxpayers of the Nation. However, in a subsequent petition the committee of six requested the following immediate remedy: four representatives duly elected by all taxpayers should join the "so-called" elders at their meetings on taxation. These four representatives should be elected for the period of one year only, thus ending the unhealthy system of appointing elders for life. In still another petition the opposition demanded permission to elect not four, but six representatives.[21]

The elders of the Nation tried to discredit the fifty-two dissident taxpayers in the eyes of the authorities. They stated that four of the

[17] See note 13. No mention of this fact was made in the minutes of the Nation's meeting on June 26, 1764. (Minutes of the Nation, No. 324.)

[18] See note 13. No mention is made in the Nation's minutes about a meeting of July 3, 1764.

[19] See note 13.

[20] Beaufleury, *op. cit.*, (*supra*, n. 10), p. 88. For a list of the elders see Malvezin, *op. cit.*, (*supra*, n. 12), pp. 218–19.

[21] Departmental archives of Gironde, C 1090.

elders "elected" in 1725-1764 were reliable shipowners, five were bankers and twelve were accredited merchants, while most of the dissidents were small merchants — some were even peddlers. The elders sent to the authorities observations on the reputation of the fifty-two. They recalled that Louis Francia, who was a son of Antoine Francia, was sentenced to death in 1753 with his two other sons, Abraham and Jacob, and a few Christians, for their role in arranging the fraudulent loss of two ships with fictitiously insured merchandise. Mendes was accused of being the widow of Delvaille [Delbaille], sentenced for the same crime.[22] Arson Brandon was accused of the crime of arson; Joseph Silva, David Estenede, Jacob Molimer and others having declared themselves bankrupt; Isaac Gaspard Henriques was accused of stealing 8,000 livres from his aunt; Noües Lopes of being the son of a converted Jew who was later sentenced to death. Others were accused of belonging to the lower social class of peddlers and one of them, Jacob Lopes Pereyre of being married to a domestic. Many others were noted as newly arrived in the city, and as paying low taxes, etc.[23]

On February 22, 1766, the King quashed the action of the opposition of June 24, 1764, and forbade the committee of six, under the penalty of one thousand livres each, to hold similar meetings. The King also ordered the Jews to respect the by-laws of 1760 and 1763.[24]

However, in new by-laws of February 22, 1766, the King took into consideration the opposition's protests; the new by-laws provided that two representatives chosen from taxpayers other than the elders should attend all meetings, at which tax matters would be discussed.[25] Beaufleury wrote that this change reconciled everyone. The syndic's rights in matters of taxation were restricted, the dissidents gained two legal representatives and, thereafter, peace prevailed among the Sephardim of Bordeaux.[26] The two non-elders, however, were to be appointed by the elders themselves, not by the taxpayers. As already noted, the role

[22] *Mémoire pour les sieurs Bernard Lichandre, Bernard Laserre, & autres négocians de la ville de Bayonne, assureurs de Pieurre Dulorier & d'Abraham Francia* . . . [Bordeaux, 1751], 26 pp.; *Mémoire pour les assureurs . . . Contre . . . Abraham et Jacob Francia père et enfans* . . . [Bordeaux, 1751], 8 pp.; *Seconde mémoire pour les assureurs* . . . [Bordeaux, 1752?], 25 pp.; *Arrest de la Cour de Parlement. Qui condamne Pierre Dulorier, négociant de Bordeaux, Delbaille, Salzedo, Antoine Francia, père, Abraham Jacob Francia, . . . être pendus, pour crime d'avoir comploté la perte & abandon des deux navires . . . Du 3 août 1753* (Bordeaux, [1753]), 4 pp.

[23] Departmental archives of Gironde, C 1090; Malvezin, *op. cit.*, (*supra*, n. 12), p. 219; Cirot, *op. cit.*, pp. 56–57.

[24] See note 8; Beaufleury, *op. cit.*, (*supra*, n. 10), p. 88.

[25] According to one source this decision was taken earlier, on April 26, 1765. Departmental archives of Gironde C 1090 (note on a petition of the opponents).

[26] Beaufleury, *op. cit.*, (*supra*, n. 10), p. 91.

of the elders also was disputed. The dissidents urged that the elders be chosen from the oldest living heads of the families, or from the oldest residents. The syndics, on the other hand, wanted to retain the existing composition of the body of the elders which was limited to former syndics and deputies.[27] In these matters, as in so many others, the leaders of the Nation were once again victorious. However, some of the assessors chosen from the group of non-elders were participants in the 1764 meeting of the dissidents, e. g., David Mendes the elder (in 1766), Daniel Telles Dacosta (in 1767), David Lopes (in 1769), David Raphaël (in 1783).[28]

The new by-laws of 1760 were directed solely against those who refused to pay taxes for the support of paupers. Another object of the various by-laws and ordinances was to restrict unlimited immigration of Jews to Bordeaux. The Nation was given the necessary authority to order the expulsion of foreign Jews and even of the poor Sephardim.[29]

Even earlier, by his ordinance of April 12, 1730, the Intendant — at the elders' request — not only enjoined the Jews to pay their taxes, but also enacted severe measures against "vagabond" Jews.[30] On this occasion the authorities of the city of Bordeaux, who registered the by-laws of 1760 and 1763, in effect extended official recognition to the Nation's existence as a legal body.[31]

The by-laws of 1764 did not completely resolve the internal conflicts within the Sephardic Nation of Bordeaux. Evidence to that fact is found in the juridical briefs published in 1775, in connection with a dispute between the Nation and the Ashkenazic Jew Serf Polac who had settled in Bordeaux in 1771. There he married Judith Francia, a Sephardic woman who had been divorced by her first husband, Salomon Silva Salazar. The Sephardic Nation ordered Polac to leave

[27] Malvezin, op. cit., (supra, n. 12), p. 218.

[28] A list of such appointments in 1776–1785 was noted in the minutes of the Nation (after No. 447, May 11, 1777).

[29] Beaufleury, op. cit., (supra, n. 10), p. 82; Ad. Detcheverry, Histoire des Israélites de Bordeaux (Bordeaux, 1850), p. 80. See also Z. Szajkowski, "Relations among Sephardim, Ashkenazim and Avignonese Jews in France from the 16th to the 20th Centuries." Yivo Annual of Jewish Social Science, X (1955), 184–87.

[30] A Monsieur Boucher, Intendant en Guienne [Bordeaux, 1730], 2 pp. [The Nation's request together with the Intendant's order of April 12, 1730.]

For other orders against "foreign" Jews see: Extrait des registres du Conseil d'Etat (Bordeaux, 1734), broadside [Jan. 21, 1734]; De par le Roy . . . (Bordeaux, n.d.), broadside [August 10, 1735]; Extrait des registres du Conseil d'Etat (Bordeaux, n.d.), broadside [Sept. 9, 1737]; De par le Roy . . . (Bordeaux, 1740), broadside [Feb. 28, 1740]; De par le Roy . . . (Bordeaux, n.d.), broadside [June 6, 1751]; Ordonnance de Messieurs les Maire . . . (Bordeaux, 17 juin 1787), broadside.

[31] George Cirot, Les Juifs de Bordeaux . . . (Bordeaux, 1920), p. 13.

Bordeaux. Since he refused, the community leaders requested the Bordeaux authorities to expel him. Each of the parties published briefs challenging the other's position. Serf Polac attacked the dictatorial tendencies of the syndic David Lameyra, going so far as to accuse him of unscrupulously availing himself of the choicest cuts of *kasher* meat.[32] The Nation's brief praised Lameyra,[33] and called attention to the kinship of Judith Francia with Louis Francia, who had participated in the fight of the 1760's against the Nation's leadership.[34] (It is possible that for commercial reasons a strong animosity existed between the Francia family and the family of Lameyra, which numbered the most influential syndics of the Nation among its members.[35])

About 1787 Moïe Gonzales complained against the high taxes imposed upon him by the Nation, while the Lameyra family, whose capacity to pay could be judged from the superb house they had built, was subject to low taxation.[36] In 1787 a social club was founded in Bordeaux by seventy Sephardim jointly with a number of Avignonese Jews who had settled in Bordeaux. The petition to permit the establishment of the club was signed by Mardochée Cordova and the

[32] "Homme injuste & méchant! faites valoir tant qu'il vous plaira, vos prétendus soins pour l'assermissement de la Synagogue; perpétuez-vous dans le Syndicat, contre la disposition des Réglemens; maintenez-vous dans le maniement de la Caisse formée pour la subsistance des Pauvres; ne faites participer à ce secours que ceux que vous voulez bien distinguer parmi ces malheureux; écartez des émplois & des assemblées tous ceux qui auroient l'adresse de balancer votre autorité ou le courage de vous contredire; rendez vous l'arbitre des taxes; présidez, puisque vous en êtes si jaloux, à la distribution des chairs de la boucherie; ne nous faites délivrer, en payant, que les morceaux que vous n'aurez pas jugé dignes de votre bouche; exercez en un mot, sur vos frères, le despotisme le plus révoltant & le plus odieux; mais cessez au moins d'attenter à leur bonheur & à la liberté de leur personne!" *Mémoire pour le Sieur Serf Polac* . . . (Bordeaux, 1775), pp. 1–2.

[33] "David Lameyra, . . . ce citoyen zélé, ce Négociant honnête, ce père des pauvres, ce frère, cet ami, ce bienfaiteur de tous ses frères, ce défenseur des droits de la Nation." *Réponse pour David Decosta, David Lameyra . . . Contre le nommé Serf-Polac* . . . (Bordeaux, n.d.), p. 2.

[34] "Louis [d'Antonio] Francia excita alors une révolte d'une partie de la Nation contre ces mêmes Réglemens, ce qui donna lieu à une instance qui fur jugée au Conseil, par Arrêt contradictoire du 22 Février 1766, faisant parti du recueil de ses Réglemens, par lequel il fut fait défenses de récidiver sous peine de 1000 liv. d'amende." *Ibid., (supra*, n. 33), p. 5. On this conflict see also: Z. Szajkowski, "A Conflict between the Syndics of the Sephardic Jews in Bordeaux and an Ashkenazic Jew (1774–75)." *Davke*, No. 17 (1953), 325–30 (in Yiddish).

[35] On such a conflict see: *Raisons d'appel, pour Sara Lameyra, veuve de Jacob Fernandes, négociant à Bordeax, appellante d'une sentence rendue au Sénéchal de Guienne le 14 août 1762. Contre Louis Francia, aussi négociant de la même ville* . . . [Signé: Bouquier, avocat.] [Bordeax, 1762?], 20 pp. fol.

[36] City archives of Bordeaux, GG 30.

club's meetings were held at the home of Moyze Mendes. It is possible that the club represented another attempt to form an organized opposition to the syndics of the Nation, for not one of the club's members was a syndic.[37]

In Saint-Esprit-lès-Bayonne also, the structure of the government of the Nation was the cause of many conflicts. On March 29, 1741, the Secretary of State, Amelot, wrote to the Intendant, de Sérilly, of the necessity to combat the abuses in the Nation's administration, which were attributed to the arbitrary and excessive powers of the syndics and to the procedures of electing them. As a result, the King ordered that in the future the syndics should be elected by assemblies composed of three syndics, four deputies, and six assistants chosen from among the former syndics. These thirteen notables were to elect annually three syndics, a cashier, and four assistants to direct the Nation's affairs.[38] It seems that this electoral provision did not settle matters, because on June 28, 1749, the King ordered that all disputes should be referred to the authority of the Intendant.[39] On December 21, 1752, the Nation presented its statutes to the Intendant for his approval, which he granted on January 6, 1753. The statutes accepted the King's electoral provisions for thirteen electors who would annually choose three syndics, six notables, four assistants, and a cashier. The syndics were to be chosen only from among the former assistants or cashiers. One of the three syndics, and one of the six notables, had to be chosen from among former notables. The effect of this rule was to insure that the thirteen electors would always include four members of the outgoing administration.[40] In fact, the administrative system of the Nation in Saint-Esprit-lès-Bayonne was not less wicked and anti-democratic than in the Nation of Bordeaux. (It should be noted, incidentally, that in earlier periods the Nation of Saint-Esprit attempted to force its authority upon the smaller communities of Saint-Jean-de-Luz, Bidache, Peyrehorade, and Biaritz. There were inter-communal clashes.[41]) Dissidence in Saint-Esprit did not end after the publication of the statutes of 1752. This was, most probably, the reason for the

[37] *Ibid.*

[38] *Copie de la lettre écrite par Mr. Amelot le 29. mars 1741. à Mr. de Serilly* (n.p., n.d.), 1 p.; Henry Léon, *Histoire des Juifs de Bayonne* (Paris, 1893), pp. 139–40.

[39] H. Léon, *op. cit.*, (*supra*, n. 38), p. 140.

[40] *Au nom de Dieu* (n.p., n.d.), 4 pp., and another edition of 12 pp. Reprinted in H. Léon, *op. cit.*, (*supra*, n. 38), pp. 141–51, and A. Dégat, "Règlement des Juifs de Bayonne." *Revue Gascogne*, XII (1912), 347 ff.

[41] Henri Gross, *Gallia Judaica* (Paris, 1897), pp. 92–93.

Nation's decision of March 17, 1776, to close a few of the private synagogues in Saint-Esprit.[42]

In Saint-Esprit also expulsion of "undesired" Jews in 1749 was undertaken at the request of the Nation itself, by authority of the above mentioned King's ordinance of June 28, 1749.[43]

The delegation to discuss the Jewish problem with the commission to study the status of the French Jews, headed by de Malesherbes, was appointed by the elders of the Bordeaux Nation.[44] Only the events leading to the Revolution of 1789 changed the undemocratic system of elections in the Bordeaux Nation. Probably all taxpayers, even widows of deceased taxpayers, participated in the elections of March 1, 1789, to choose Jewish deputies to the Assembly of the Third Estate.[45] The election of deputies by the elders alone would have been illegal. It seems that the delegation to the National Assembly was also elected by all taxpayers.[46] After the Sephardic Jews were granted full citizenship on January 28, 1790, the elders themselves decided to dissolve the Nation and that the community would remain organized only as a philanthropic society.[47] In later years, however, all taxpayers participated in the meetings of this society which took over most of the religious and social functions of the former Nation.[48]

The conflicts in the Sephardic communities, and similar discontent in the communities of the Ashkenazic Jews and of the Jews in the papal province of Avignon and Comtat Venaissin, induced the Jewish leaders, after the Revolution, to adopt democratic procedures for governing the Jewish communities. As late as 1836, S. Mayer-Dalmbert, a member of the central consistory, opposed the use of the term syndics as a designation for communal Jewish leaders, reflecting the tradition of distrust by Jews of their syndics prior to the Revolution of 1789.[49]

---

[42] Departmental archives of Gironde, C 1090.

[43] H. Léon, op. cit., (supra, n. 38), p. 140.

[44] Z. Szajkowski, "The Diaries of the Delegations of the Bordeaux Jews to the Malesherbes Commission (1788) and the National Assembly (1790)." Zion, XVIII (1953), 50, in Hebrew (" . . . l'assemblée des anciens . . . nomma pour Députés deux de ses membres").

[45] Idem, "The Sephardic Jews of France during the Revolution of 1789." Proceedings of the American Academy for Jewish Research, XXIV (1955), 156–57.

[46] Idem, "The Diaries . . . " (supra, n. 44), 65. See also the petition of the Bordeaux Jews: Adresse à l'Assemblée Nationale (Paris, 1789 [1790]), 8 pp.

[47] Z. Szajkowski, "The Diaries . . . " (supra, n. 44), 43, n. 33.

[48] Idem, Autonomy . . . (supra, n. 1), pp. 132–34.

[49] Ibid., p. 164.

APPENDIX

Minutes of the meeting of fifty-two taxpayers
of the Bordeaux Nation, June 24, 1764.[50]

Par devant les Conseillers du Roy notaires à Bordeaux soussignés,
sont comparus les cy après nommés, savoir
1. Joseph Mendes Darlac; 2. Aaron Rodrigues; 3. David Mendes
père et fils; 4. Abraham Lopes; 5. David Lopes; 6. Daniel Telles
Dacosta; 7. Abraham Rodrigues Nunes; 8. La demoiselle veuve de
sieur Antoine Francia; 9. Raphael Jullian; 10. Jacob Lopes Pereyra;
11. Moise Azevedo; 12. Charles Joseph Lopes Pereira . . . agissant
pour la d^lle sa mère; 13. Izaac Victoria; 14. Jacob Azevedo; 15.
David Nones; 16. La demoiselle veuve Mendes; 17. Louis Francia;
18. Abraham Rodrigues Alvarez; 19. Dias Pereira; 20. Pereira
Dubec; 21. David Raphaël; 22. Jacob Bargues; 23. Joseph d'Is.
Penamacor; 24. Aaron Lopes Cordova; 25. Moise Mendes; 26.
Aaron Pereira Brandon; 27. Joseph Gabriel de Silva; 28. Daniel
Rodrigues Lima; 29. Abraham Mendes Cardoze; 30. La demoiselle
veuve Gaspard Henriques; 31. Moise Mezes; 32. Jacob Mendes;
33. Daniel Carrasco; 34. Izaac Mezes; 35. Rodrigues Henriques;
36. Daniel Lopes Chaves; 37. Anthoine Cardoze; 38. Nones Lopes;
39. Abraham Fonseca; 40. Abraham Henriques; 41. Abraham Gabriel de Castro; 42. Abraham Rodrigues Henriques; 43. David
Esteves; 44. La demoiselle veuve Sasportes; 45. David Rodrigues
Henriques; 46. Jacob Molina; 47. Rodrigues Henriques jeune;
48. Manuel Pereira Soires; 49. Izaac Cardoso, agissant pour la
dem.^lle Ve Cardoso sa mère; 50. Izaac de Gaspard Henriques;
51. Moise Telles Dacosta; 52. David Molina fils.[51]

Ces dits Sieurs surnommés composant la majeure partie de la
nation Portugaise établie à Bordeaux et contribuant chacun à leur
égard au payement des charges et jmpositions de lad. nation, tous
assemblés dans la maison du Sieur Joseph Mendes Darlac, l'un d'eux
rue du Cahernan, pour aviser aux moyens de remedier aux abus qui se
sont glissés dans l'administration des affaires et dans la repartition
des charges et jmpositions communes à la nation.
Dans laquelle assemblée a été dit observé et representé que vers la

---

[50] See note 13. The document is reprinted without changes in the original spelling.
[51] The addresses of the fifty-two taxpayers are omitted.

fin du siècle dernier, différentes familles juives poursuivies en Portugal et en Espagne par l'Inquisition, depouillées de leurs biens par ce tribunal et craignant pour leur vie, furent forcées de chercher ailleurs d'autres azilles, qu'un grand nombre de ces infortunés se retirerent en France ou Louis Quatorze leur accorda sa protection dont ils ont jouy et qu'ils y jouissent encore de celle de son successeur Louis Quinze le Bien aimé. Que c'est là a peu pres l'origine de l'établissement en corps dans la ditte ville de Bordeaux de la nation des juifs portugais, que lors de l'établissement les deux tiers des malheureux qui vinrent jcy, etans reduits à la plus extreme judigence, eurent recourus à leurs frères qui avoient encore quelques facultés et qui ces derniers se preterent d'autant plus vollontiers a secourir leurs compatriotes, qu'ils venaient en partie d'essuyer les mêmes disgraces, que les chefs des familles aizées dans les corps de la nation se taxerent vollontairement pour procurer à leurs frères leur necessaire, qu'ils se chargerent de la representer et porterent la générosité jusqu'a payer eux seuls tous les jmpots au nom de tous les Juifs domicilliés composant la nation, dont partie par leur misere étoient alors hors d'état de contribuer a lad. jmposition. Qu'en suivant cette ancienne forme un petit nombre de contribuables de la nation sous le nom de pretendus chefs, se sont atribués sans aucun droit la faculté de mettre les autres a contribution en les chargeant d'impositions par des repartitions arbitraires qu'ils font à leur gré, qu'il était naturel que dans l'origine de l'établissement de la nation dans Bordeaux, elle laissat à certains d'entr'eux qui avoient des facultés d'honneur de la representer et le droit de repartir les jmpositions dont jls suportoient tous les poids et qui se cotisoient dailleurs pour fournir aux besoins des pauvres, mais que ce plan daministration qui était alors très sage et que la nation avoit jnteret de soutenir au lieu de la contester, parceque les Deliberations prises par ceux qui administrtoient ne portoient aucun prejudice aux autres membres de la nation qui ny assitoient pas, puisquils ne suportoient rien dans les charges des jmpositions, est depuis devenu abusif et tres nuisibles a un grand nombre des membres de la nation, parce que cette nation setant augmentée d'une quantité de familles portugaises et espagnolles qui se sont aussi retirées a Bordeaux et qui ayant des facultés honnêtes pouvant soulager et soulagent en effet ceux qui suportoient autrefois toutes les charges et jmpositions, en contribuant au payement d'jcelles, qu'jl y a même plusieurs des anciennes familles qui etoient autrefois dans l'jndigence et ausquelles le travail l'jndustrie et l'economie ont aussi procuré des facultés qui les mettent pareillement en etat de suporter et qui suportent en effet a present leur portion des jmpositions et de la taxe des pauvres de la nations, ce qui leur donne sans difficulté le droit de veiller à ce que la repartition s'en fasse avec justice et equité et de s'oposer a celle qui se fait par lesd. pretendus chef arbitrairement et a leur faintaisie. Que se sont ceux qui concourent aujourd'huy au payement des jmpositions et a l'entretien des pauvres et qui representent jncontestablement la nation puisqu'ils replacent les anciennes familles qui secourirent si genereusement leurs freres dans l'origine de l'établissement de laditte nation, que ce nombre est considerable, que cependant quelques membres se sont attribués en seul vn pouvoir aristocratique d'autant plus dur qu'ils l'exercent tyraniquement sur leurs egaux et qui au lieu d'imiter les anciens qui aidoient la nation de leurs conseils et de leurs biens, abusent d'vne autorité vsurpée en repartissant a leur gré de leurs passions les jmpositions de même que des pensions et des presens qu'ils font a qui bon leur semble, et enfin d'autres depenses qu'ils font suporter a tous les contribuables qu'ils accablent de contrainter les plus rigoureuses en faisant proceder par saisie et vente de leur meubles en vertu d'vn arret du conseil obtenu sur requeste au nom de la nation dont lesdits pretendus chefs se servent en particulier pour molester jmpunement les autres lorsquils font quelque jncistence pour le payement des taxes aussy mal entendues qu'jnjustes quil plait en particulier d'jmposer et repartir comme jls trouvent a propos. Quil resulte de tout ce dessus que lors que les peres des comparans vinrent setablir à Bordeaux, les familles aisés, c'est a dire les contribuables au payement des charges et jmpositions representoient la nation et quelle doit etre representée aujourdhuy par les familles qui existent et qui concourent a present au payement desd. charges et jmpositions, ou par des membres choisis et nommées par tous ceux qui composent lad. nation a la pluralité des suffrages. Quil est par consequent de l'jnteret des comparans qui font la majeure parti des contribuables de soposer au pouvoir arbitraire de quelques persones de la nation ont deja que trop etably et de prendre un party efficace pour conserver les droits du corps de la nation en faissant cesser les abus quelle a tollerés jusques icy et qui ne peuvent prendre fin qu'autant que tous les contribuables rassemblés et éclarés sur leurs vrays jnterets fixeront par eux mêmes ou par la voye de leurs députés vne forme d'administration plus convenable a l'jnteret de chaque particulier et plus honnorable pour le corps en general que celle qui c'est pratiqué cy devant.

Sur toutes lesquelles observations et representations il convient d'statuer dans la presente assemblée ce qu'il est a propos de faire.

La matière mis en deliberation jl a été vnaniment deliberé et arreté par tous les comparans apres mure reflection, de nommer comme

jls nomment par ces presentes pour representer tous lesdits sieurs
Abraham Lopes, Moise Avezedo, Jacob Avezedo, Abraham Gabriel
de Castro, Louis Francia et Raphael Julian, en consequence les autres
susnommés leur donnent pouvoir de travailler pour la nation avec
les plus competens et les plus eclairés de ceux qui la composent, a
l'établissement d'vn plan d'administration juste, equitable et convenable aux jnterets du corps en general et des membres en particula,
de se rendre a cet effet a la premiere et subsequentes assemblées qui
seront tenues par les pretendus chefs de la nation,[52] de les requerir
d'en faire a suposer qu'ils effectent de ne pas convoquer p.ʳ eviter
l'execution de cette deliberation, de proposer dans lesd. assemblées
les moyens qu'ils jugeront les plus propres de parvenir de concert
et a l'amiable s'il est possible a se fixer sur un nouveau plan d'administration qui devra etre etably et les plus faciles et les plus salutaires
a son execution, de donner leurs suffrages dans les deliberations qui
seront prises ausd. assemblées, de soposer au nom de la nation a ce
que l'ancien plan d'administration soit suivy et a ce quil soit fait pas
une taxe et repartition arbitraire par les pretendus chefs qui sont
dans l'vsage d'en faire de faire toutes protestations au cas quil fut
passé outre, de se pouvoir même au besoin sera a suposer que les
pretendus chefs de la nation refusent lassistence et le suffrage desd.
sieurs representans[53] dans les assemblées, afin de si faire admettre et
de faire executer ce qui y sera deliberé a la pluralité des voyes de
faire a raison de ce tous actes necessaires, d'jntenter et poursuivre
contre qui jl appartiendra tous proces et jnstances, playder, appeller,
obtenir tous jugemens les faire executer, et enfin de faire dans l'jnteret
de la nation generalement tout ce que lesdits sieurs representans
aviseront, promettant les comparans d'approver et avoir pour agréable
tout ce qui feront lesdits sieurs representans, et de leur rembourser
a leur premiere requisition leur contingente portion de tous les fraix
et debours que lesdits sieurs leurs representans seront obligés de faire
pour l'execution de la presente deliberation.

De quoi a eté requis et octroyé acte.

Fait et deliberé dans la maison dudit sieur Joseph Mendes Darlac
le vingt quatre Juin mil sept cens soixante quatre et ont lesdits sieurs
comparans signé.[54]

Le   [55] Juillet 1764 sont comparus devant les conseillers

---

[52] The words "d'y proposer et arreter les" were crossed out.

[53] The word "syndics" was crossed out.

[54] The names of the fifty-two signers, being the same as those in the beginning
of the minutes, are omitted.

[55] The exact date is missing.

du Roy notaires à Bordeaux soussignes, les sieurs abraham Lopes, Moise azevedo, Jacob azevedo, abraham Gabriel de Castro, Louis Francia et Raphael Jullian . . . lesquels ont dit que pour eviter la voye des actes . . . jls auraient verballement remis le 26 Juin dernier aux pretendus chefs de la nation portugaise dans l'assemblée par eux tenue le dit jour, vne expedition de laditte deliberation . . . ces messieurs demanderent alors aux comparans vn delay de huitaine quils requirent de leur accorder pour examiner et reflectir la deliberation a eux remise . . . a l'expiration dudit delay les trois du present mois a l'assemblée qui fut de nouveau tenue par lesd. sieurs, les comparans les auroient priés vne seconde fois de se conformer a lad° deliberation, mais . . . jls sy sont refusés . . . Lesd. sieurs comparans se trouvent obligés de leur denoncer . . . par ces presentes lad. deliberation et la personne du sieur Edouard Brandon[56] leur syndic . . . Lesd. S^{rs} comparans requierent et sommes lesd. Pretendus chefs de convoquer sous trois jours pour tout delay vne assemblée ou les comparans seront appellés et admis et donneront leur suffrage a l'effet de travailler . . . au nouveau plan d'administration . . . a defaut de quoy les comparans . . . se pourvoiront par les voyes de droit . . . A Bordeaux en l'étude de Rauzans et ont lesd. sieurs comparans signé.

[56] Edouard Brandon was later reelected as syndic on April 19, 1770, and March 22, 1782. City archives of Bordeaux, HH 19.

THE JEWISH COMMUNITY OF MARSEILLES
AT THE END OF THE EIGHTEENTH CENTURY

The history of the Jews in the large Jewish communities of France prior to the emancipation during the Revolution of 1789 is well known. The history of many small communities, however, is completely unknown though they were often located in large commercial centers. One of these is the Jewish community in Marseilles; its story, based mainly on hitherto unknown pamphlets and archival documents, is told on the following pages.

After their expulsion from France in the fourteenth century (and their later expulsion from Provence) Jews were permitted by law to reside in the three centers of Ashkenazic Jewry, the northeastern provinces of Alsace, Metz, and Lorraine; in the Sephardic communities in the southwest of France; in the papal province of Avignon and Comtat Venaissin, a center of Comtadin Jews; and in Paris, where a mixed Jewish community was tolerated. Elsewhere, too, small Jewish communities sprang up and were tolerated as in Lyons, where in 1781 the authorities appointed a syndic of the Jewish community in order to have ready control over the small number of Jews there[1].

After their expulsion from Provence, Jews tried on many occasions to settle in Marseilles, and a group of them did live there in the seventeenth century[2]. However, they were accepted on sufferance and could hardly be considered legal residents. An Edict of May, 1682, ordering them to leave Marseilles was renewed on July 19, 1683, September 14, 1683, and November 15, 1690[3]. During the eighteenth century

---

1. Alfred Lévy, *Notice sur les Israélites de Lyon* (Paris, 1894), p. 22-24.

2. Ad. Crémieux, « Un Établissement juif à Marseille au xviie siècle, » *REJ*, LV (1908), 119-45 ; LVI (1908), 99-123.

3. *De par le Roy. Comte de Provence* (Marseille, [2 mai 1682]), broadside (« ... ordonne [aux Juifs] de sortir incessament... même de son Royaume, pour aller où bon leur semblera ») ; *De par le Roy...* (Marseille, [19 janvier 1683]), broadside (order to respect the edict of May 2, 1682) ; *Thomas Alexandre Morant ... Intendant ... en Provence* (n. p., [14 septembre 1683]), broadside (order to respect the edicts of May 2, 1682, and July 19, 1683) ; *De par le Roy ...* (n. p., [15 novembre 1690]), broadside (order to respect the edict of 1682).

Originally published in *Revue des Etudes Juives–Historia Judaica*, vol. CXXI (1962).

the Parliament of Provence published similar ordinances against Jews who tried to establish residence or to trade in that city[1]. Yet, in the 1760's we find a small, but well-organized Jewish community in that city. About 1768 they opened a modest synagogue on the rue de Rome, and the notarial act on the sale of a parcel of land on chemin du Rouet for a Jewish cemetery is dated December 5, 1783[2]. These two important events in the life of a Jewish community took place in spite of the fact that by law Jews were forbidden to live in Marseilles. On March 27, 1776, the Parliament again prohibited Jews from trading in that harbor city on days other than legal market days[3]. Similarly, Jews were forbidden to trade or to reside in other cities under the jurisdiction of the Provence Parliament[4] and of neighboring Parliaments[5].

1. *Extrait d'arrest* de *Nos seigneurs de la Cour de Parlement de ce pays de Provence, rendu sur la requête des srs. syndics des marchands, drapiers, merciers, toiliers, dantelliers, jouailliers et quinquailliers de la ville de Marseille contre les Juifs, portant défense aux dits Juifs de hanter, fréquenter et de demeurer à Marseille sous les peines portées par les ordonnances et par ledit arrêt ; avec injonction auxdits Juifs de vuider la ville dans 3 jours, comptables de la publication du susdir arrêt* (Aix, 12 juin 1758), broadside ; *Arrest de la Cour de Parlement de Provence, qui fait défenses à Salomon Roger & frères, Moyse de Roquemarline & autres Juifs, de venir dans la ville d'Aix & son terroir, même dans les Villes & lieux de la Province. Du 7 février 1760* (Aix, 1760), broadside.

2. *Mémoire* (see n. 2, p. 374), p. 3 ; A. Latil, « Assistance publique. Culte israélite à Marseille, « *Répertoire des travaux de la Société de Statistique de Marseille*, XXX (1867), 127-28 ; Jacob Molina, in *Anuuaire israélite pour l'année 5648 de la création du monde...* (Marseille, 5647), p. 32. See also *Histoire du commerce de Marseille*, publiée par la Chambre de Commerce de Marseille, sous la direction de Gaston Rambert (Marseille, 1954), III, 29-31 ; IV, 537-38. The author of one of the studies in this *Histoire* (III, 29) made the following remark on Jewish debtors : « Ceux-ci [les Juifs] sont aussi bien prêteurs qu'emprunteurs (chose assez inattendue !). »

3. *Arrêt du Parlement de Provence défendant aux Juifs de hanter, ni d'y faire aucun commerce, excepté en temps de foire* (n. p., [2 mars 1776]), broadside.

4. In 1768, the Christian merchants of Aix-en-Provence prevented Daniel Beaucaire from settling in the city. *Consultation pour les sieurs Syndics du Corps des Marchands de cette ville d'Aix, demandeurs en opposition aux fins prises dans la Requête du 11 décembre dernier. Contre Daniel Beaucaire, Juif de nation, défenseur* (Aix, 1768), 50 pp. fol. See also *Arrest du Parlement de Provence qui enjoint aux Juifs établis à Apt, Forcalquier, Pertuis, Manosque, la Tour d'Aigues, Riants, Cadenet, Cucuron, Rogues & Saint-Mitre, & qui y vendent des marchandises, d'en sortir... du 11 septembre 1775* (Aix, 1775), 3 pp. 4° ; *Arrest du Parlement de Provence, qui enjoint aux Juifs établis dans les villes d'Arles, Tarascon, St. Remy, & autres Villes & lieux de la Viguerie de Tarascon, d'en sortir dans la huitaine... du 11 décembre 1775* (Aix, 1776), 6 pp. (issued at the request of the Christian merchants of Arles, Tarascon, St.-Remy, Eyragues, Château-Renard, Maillane, Gravezon, Barbentanne, Noves, Cabannes, St.-Andliol, Mollegés, Eygaliers, Mouriés, Mauxannes, and other places).

5. In 1685, the Jews of Toulouse were sentenced to death ; see Z. Szajkowski,

In June 1776, King Louis XVI renewed the old privileges (which was registered on March 8, 1777, by the Bordeaux Parliament) that had been granted since 1550 to the Marranos who had arrived from Spain and Portugal and who since 1723 had lived openly as Sephardic Jews[1]. In the previous privileges—including the letters patent of 1723— the right of residence for the Sephardim was limited to the territory within the jurisdiction of the Bordeaux Parliament. Thus, even the privileged Sephardic Jews could not move freely. They were driven from many large commercial centers, such as Dijon, Poitiers, Orléans, Pau, Cognac, Rochefort, Saintes, and others. A memorandum submitted as late as 1788 by the Sephardic Jews to the Minister, Ch. G. L. de Malesherbes, contained a plea for the right of residence in the whole of France[2] and in the French colonies[3]. The restriction of residence to the territory of the Bordeaux Parliament was omitted from the 1776 renewal of privileges, and this fact was used by other communities, which tried to gain legal status by registering the letters patent of 1776 with the Parliaments of the provinces in which they were settled. It was in this way that the Jewish community of Marseilles obtained legal status, though not until many years later and in the face of numerous difficulties. On February 12, 1788, the

« An Auto-da-Fé against the Jews of Toulouse in 1685 », *Jewish Quarterly Review*, XLIX (1959), 278-81 ; also *Arrest de la Cour de Parlement... du 15 novembre 1717. Qui ordonne aux Juifs de sortir du ressort de la Cour*. Grenoble, 1717), 4 pp. Jews were not allowed to import merchandise from Lisbon by ship to Salés: *Advertissement pour Capitaine Claude Fougasse de la Ciotat...* (n. p., [1670 ?]), 8 pp. ...(« donne ordre expressement de ne laisser charger aucune marchandise aux Juifs pour porter audit Salez »).

1. *Lettres patentes du Roi, confirmatives des privilèges dont les Juifs Portugais jouissent en France depuis 1550. Données à Versailles, au mois de juin 1776,* *enregistrées au parlement de Bordeaux le 8 mars 1777* ([Bordeaux ?], n. d.), 4 pp., was registered also by the Paris Parliament: *Lettres patentes... enregistrées au Parlement de Paris le 22 décembre de la même année...* ([Paris], n. d.), broadside.

2. Henry Léon, *Histoire des Juifs de Bayonne* (Paris, 1893), p. 153; Z. Szajkowski, « The Jewish Status in Eighteenth-Century France and the « Droit d'Aubaine », *Historia Judaica*, XIX (1957), 147-49; Z. Szajkowski, « The Demographic Aspects of Jewish Emancipation in France during the French Revolution », *Historia Judaica*, XXI (1959), 8.

3. It seems that the letters patent of 1776 were not applied in favor of Sephardic Jews in the French colonies. However, Moreau de Saint-Méry noted: « Les dispositions de ces Lettres-Patentes ont été adoptées par le Conseil du Cap, en faveur des Juifs »; *Lois et constitutions des colonies françaises d'Amérique sous le Vent* (Paris, 1784-90), V, 715-16. Ab. Cahen, « Les Juifs dans les colonies françaises au xviiie siècle, » *REJ*, IV (1882), 127-236 ; V (1882), 68-92, 258-72.

letters patent of 1776 were registered by the Parliament of Provence in whose territory the city of Marseilles was located[1]. According to one source the Jews of Marseilles paid the sum of 6,000 livres to have these letters patent registered, thereby securing for themselves the right of residence not only in Marseilles but in all of Provence[2]. To achieve their purpose the Jews of Marseilles had to declare themselves a community of Sephardim, for the letters patent of 1776 were granted to Sephardim only. But this was only a legal subterfuge for in reality the Jewish community of Marseilles at that time was composed of Jews of varied origin and only a few were Sephardim.

Shortly before the outbreak of the Revolution, on May 6, 1789, an assembly of the Marseilles Jewish community adopted by-laws which the Parliament of Provence legalized on June 20, 1789. These by-laws granted to the leaders of the Jewish community, called syndics, complete control over the right of residence in the city[3]. Among the syndics were not only Sephardim, but also Comtadin Jews (Beaucaire, Puget), and the actual leader of the community was Daniel de Beaucaire, known as Rigaud, who came to Marseilles from Comtat, the neighboring papal province[4]. There is no doubt that

---

1. Archives départementales des Bouches-du-Rhône. Dépôt d'Aix, fonds du Parlement de Provence. B 3465, fol. 29; « Les Lettres-patentes de l'année 1776, qui lui accordèrent cette faveur sous le dernier règne, admirent dans l'État des Juifs Espagnols et Portugais; et l'on sait que sous cette dénomination étaient compris tous ceux réputés régnicoles en France. Aussi les Juifs Avignonais ont-ils joui du même privilège, qui fut ensuite concédé aux Juifs Provençaux par d'autres Lettres-patentes, enregistrées au ci-devant Parlement de Provence le 12 février 1788 » (*Mémoire*, pp. 2-3) ; Les Bouches-du-Rhône. *Encyclopédie départementale*. X (Paris-Marseille, 1923), 698.

2. « ... la somme exorbitante de 6000 liv., dont ce certificateur trouva moyen de ne pas rendre compte, en prétextant qu'elle lui avait servi à payer les lettres-patentes de 1788, données en faveur des Juifs Provençaux, tandis qu'elles ne lui ont rien couté » (*Réponse*, p. 14, see below, n. 2, p. 374).

3. See Appendix I.

4. Daniel de Beaucaire's name was noted in connection with conflitcs of a commercial character. See, *e.g.*, the briefs: *De par le Roi. Jugement de la jurisdiction consulaire de la ville d'Arles* [*du 22 février 1764*] *qui condamne solidairement Moyse & Daniel Beaucaire...* (Lyon, 1764), broadside ; *Mémoire pour Claude Jouve, ménager de la ville d'Arles ... contre Moise et Daniel de Beaucaire, négocians Juifs de la carrière de L'Isle ...* (Aix, 1766) ; *Réponse pour Claude Jouve ... contre Moyse et Daniel Beaucaire ...* (n. p., 1766), 28 pp.; *Mémoire servant de réponse. Pour Moise & Daniel de Beaucaire ...* (Aix, 1766), 19 pp.; *Mémoire instructif pour le sieur Pierre Clément Roussel de la ville d'Apt ... contre Moyse & Jacob de Beaucaire, frères & d'autre Beaucaire dit le Rigaud, Juifs de la ville de L'Isle, defenseurs.* [Signés : Gasqui, avocat; Chambaud,

these by-laws drew on the texts of the by-laws of the Sephardic communities in Bordeaux and Saint-Esprit-lès-Bayonne; many articles were copied almost verbatim, among them those on the election of the syndics, on taxes, and on regulations concerning «foreign» Jews[1]. The by-laws of the Marseilles community speak also of possible meetings with the syndics of other Jewish communities of Provence in a sort of council of the Jewish communities of Provence. Thus, it is highly probable that small Jewish communities also existed in other cities of Provence. There is, however, no evidence that such a meeting of representatives of these communities ever took place.

Many sources establish that the Jewish community of Marseilles was composed of Jews of different origins. Serf Pollac, a Jew from Alsace, who lived in Bordeaux and whom the «Sephardic Nation» tried to expel from the city, in a pamphlet of 1775 against this Nation offered evidence that in other cities Sephardic and non-Sephardic Jews were living in peace, and he cited Marseilles[2], where, for example, Sabatto Constantini, of non-Sephardic Jewish origin, was permitted to live[3]. Constantini was later to play a role in a conflict within the community of Marseilles. Coming from

procureur.] (n. p., 1769), 20 pp.; *Précis pour le sieur Pierre Clement Roussel ... servant de réponse au dernier Mémoire imprimé de Moyse de Beaucaire, Daniel de Beaucaire, dit Rigaud & Jacob de Beaucaire, Juifs de la Ville de L'Isle.* [Signé : Gasqui, avocat.] (n. p., [1770]), 27 pp. In 1768, a violent anti-Jewish brief was also published by the Christian merchants of Aix in connection with Beaucaire's demand that he be accepted into their guild. *Consullation pour les sieurs Syndics au Corps des marchands de cette Ville d'Aix, demandeurs en opposition aux fins prises dans la Requête du 11 décembre dernier. Contre Daniel Beaucaire, Juif de nation, défendeur.* [Signés: Arnulhy; Arnoulhy fils.] (Aix, 1768), 50 pp.

1. See below, n. 2 on p. 372.

2. « On scait que dans cette ville [Marseille], les Juifs, Portugais & non-Portugais, se regardant *tous* comme frères; qu'ils ne forment qu'un corps, qu'ils n'ont qu'un même esprit, parce qu'ils ont une même Religion, les mêmes mœurs, une même origine. » *La Partie de Serf Pollac, marchand Juif français* (Bordeaux, 1775), p. 9.

3. « C'est sur les mêmes principes que le Parlement d'Aix vient de maintenir le sieur Sabathon Constantiny, Juif non-Portugais, mais honnête home, dans la liberté de résider & de commercer à Marseille » (*ibid.*, p. 9); « On trouve dans les principales villes de France des Juifs non originaires d'Espagne ou de Portugal, établis dans ces différentes villes depuis plusieurs générations, & dont le Gouvernement autorise la résidence, parce qu'ils ne sont ni moins fidèles au Roi que les Juifs Portugais, ni moins réglés dans leurs mœurs & dans leur conduite. Tels sont les Juifs établis à Marseille, à Lyon »; *Mémoire pour le sieur Serf Pollac* (Bordeaux, 1775), p. 9-10.

Canea, he lived for a while in Trieste, and later settled with his family in Marseilles. Accused of passing counterfeit money, he published a brief to the effect that he was being persecuted because he belonged to the Jewish faith. «We no longer live in a time of intolerance and fanaticism,» he wrote[1].

Not all the Jews of Marseilles were satisfied with their community by-laws of 1789. (The by-laws of the Jews of Bordeaux and Saint-Esprit-lès-Bayonne also provoked sharp conflicts[2].) In 1792 a group of Jews in Marseilles stated in a pamphlet that the by-laws had been drawn up by a few «ambitious members who wanted to control the community»[3]. Most probably at that time, on the eve of the Revolution, a cleavage existed in the community.

In September, 1790, a meeting of the Jewish community of Marseilles pronounced itself a *Sephardic* community, having once again come legally into existence on the basis of the decree of January, 1790, granting full citizenship to the Sephardim[4]. However, in contrast to the practice of the Sephardic communities, which decided to dissolve as a result of Jewish emancipation, the community of Marseilles continued to exist officially as a corporation of Sephardim, that is, as a regular Jewish community[5], although this was in direct

1. « Le suppliant est Juif! *hinc prima mali labes* ... le crime dont ont a cru le suppliant capable parce qu'il est Juif, a-t-on eu souvent l'occasion de l'imputer aux hommes de cette religion?... « La place de Marseille, qui est ouverte aux étrangers de toute Nation, de toute religion, invités à venir y commercer & à s'y fixer même sous la protection, du Roi, ne sera-t-elle fermée qu'aux étrangers qui sont nés dans la religion Juive ?... Nous ne sommes plus dans le temps d'intolérance & de fanatisme. » *A Nosseigneurs du Parlement supplie humblement sieur Sabatto Costantini, Juif, originaire de Cannée, négociant ci-devant résident à Trieste, actuellement résidant en la ville de Marseille.* [Signé: Roman Tributirs, avocat.] (Aix, 1784), pp. 52-55.

2. Z. Szajkowski, « Internal Conflicts within the Eighteenth Century Sephardic Communities of France », *Hebrew Union College Annual*, XXXI (1960), 167-80.

3. ...« étaient l'ouvrage de l'ambition de quelques membres qui voulaient primer dans la Communauté, et qu'elles ont donné lieu à une foule d'abus » (*Mémoire*, p. 3).

4. « Les Juifs Espagnols et Portugais, établis à Marseille, en vertu de leurs Lettres-patentes confirmées par un Décret de l'Assemblée Nationale, sanctionné par le roi... » (*Réponses ...*, pp. 36-37). The Decree of January, 1790, was also published in Aix-en-Provence : *Lettres-Patentes du Roi, sur un Décret de l'Assemblée Nationale, portant que les Juifs, connus en France sous le nom de Juifs Portugais, Espagnoles et Avignonois, y jouiront des droits de Citoyen Actif. Données a Paris, au mois de janvier 1790, Transcrites sur les registres des Cours Supérieures* (Aix, 1790).

5. « Nous soussignés, nous étant assemblés suivant l'usage établi dans notre Corps de Juifs Espagnols et Portugais » (*Réponses ...*, p. 3).

conflict with the general rules on the dissolution of corporations of the old regime. It is strange, indeed, that an entire community composed for the most part of Jews of non-Sephardic origin, should have taken for itself the benefits of the decree on the emancipation of Sephardic Jews, while all the Ashkenazic Jews of France had to wait for the decree of September 27, 1791, to obtain full emancipation[1]. Even the Jews of the neighboring papal province of Avignon and Comtat Venaissin, annexed by France on September 14, 1791, did not claim earlier the privileges granted by the decree of January, 1790, to the Sephardim[2].

At the end of 1790 a sharp conflict broke out in the Jewish community of Marseilles. A group of syndics and other members of the community, under the leadership of Daniel de Beaucaire (Rigaud), Sabaton Constantini, Léon Constantini, d'Armon (Darmon), Foy, Puget (Salomon Silva Puget), Coste, Samaria (Samaria Salon), Salom, Silva, Mirandes (Franco de Miranda), Pax, Broude (Chay Darmon Samuel Bruda), and Emanuel Foa, decided to establish a separate community. They removed five Torah scrolls from the synagogue, took religious books and other articles, and opened their own small synagogue in a private house[3]. The majority of the community, however, under the leadership of Israél Vidal, Salomon Cohen, and Hobadya Cohen, remained loyal to the old community[4]. Both groups were composed of Sephardim, Comtadin Jews, and Jews from the Arab countries. Israél Vidal, who came from the papal province of Comtat Venaissin, became the leader of one group. For his services as an army purveyor in 1757-1758 the King of France granted him naturalization and exempted him from wearing

---

1. It is worth noting the individual case of a Jew from Avignon who tried in October, 1790, to settle in Toulouse on the basis of this decree. Ad. Crémieux, « Pour contribuer à l'histoire de l'accession des Juifs à la qualité de citoyen français, » *REJ*, XCV (1933), 44-53.

2. Z. Szajkowski, « The Comtadin Jews and the Annexation of the Papal Province by France, 1789-1791, » *Jewish Quarterly Review*, XLVI (1955), 187.

3, According to one source a synagogue was opened in 1790 on rue Moise. Latil, *op. cit.*, p. 128.

4. A few of these names are noted in the notarial act on the Jewish cemetery: d'Armon [Mardoché Chay Darmon], Sabaton Constantini de Canéa, Pax [Samuel Hai de Paz], Broude [Samuel Brudo], Silva [Salomon de Silvay] (Molina, *op. cit.*). Only a few of these names figure in the Jewish census of Marseilles of 1809: Esther Rigaud Beaucaire, Sabaton Constantini, Paz, Samuel Brude (General Historical Jewish Archives or Israel [Jerusalem]).

the yellow hat[1]. The opposition group was headed by another Comtadin Jew, the abovementioned Beaucaire.

The opposition tried to expel Vidal and his friends from the synagogue, there were several scandals, the municipal authorities had to intervene, and the conflict was brought to the courts. Both groups issued pamphlets setting forth their respective cases. Although they probably caused much harm to the community, they are the only known source for its history at the end of the eighteenth century[2]. On November 17, 1791, the controversy was taken up by the conciliation office (Bureau de Conciliation) of Marseilles in the presence of representatives of both Jewish parties, but no amicable settlement was reached[3]. The Vidal group accused the other side of attempting to put the leadership of the community in the hands of a faction of wealthy Jews; of trying to preserve communal traditions of the old regime, contrary to the spirit of new republican ideas; of establishing a separate community of Sephardim, «a nation within a

---

1. *Réponses...*, p. 27 ; *Lettres patentes du Roi pour le sieur Vidal l'aîné, natif d'Avignon* (n. p., n. d.), 13 pp. (contains also « Brevet du Roi qui dispense le sieur Vidal l'aîné, de porter le Chapeau jaune »). See also P. Charpenne, *Histoire des réunions demporaires d'Avignon et du Comtat Venaissin à la France*, II (Paris, 1886), 449. On the yellow hat in the papal province, see also Latil, *op. cit.*, pp. 132-33 ; Jules Bauer, « Le Chapeau jaune chez les Juifs Comtadins, » *REJ*, XXXVI (1898), 36-64. Vidal's name has also been noted in connection with a commercial conflict. See the following document: *Arrêt du Parlement de Paris rendu en faveur du Sr. Israel de Valabregue dit Vidal Frères d'Avignon. Contre les Srs. Teite père & fils... négocians de Lyon* (n. p., n. d.), broadside.

2. *Mémoire pour les Sieurs Israel Vidal aîné, Salomon d'Abraham Cohen, Hobadya Cohen, tant pour eux, que comme représentant la pluralité des Juifs résidans dans cette ville de Marseille. Contre les Sieurs Beaucaire, dit Rigaud, Sabaton Constantini, Léon Constantini, d'Armon, Foy, Pugel, Coste, Samaria Salom, Silva, Miraude, Pax et Broude.* [Signés: Israel Vidal aîné, et Consorts, Leclerc fils, Homme de Loi, Audibert, Avoué.] (Marseille, 1792), 37 pp. ; *Réponses à de nouvelles objections. Pour les Sieurs Vidal et Consorts.* [Signés: Israel Vidal aîné, et Consorts, Leclerc fils, Homme de Loi. Audibert.] (Marseille, 1792), 38 pp. According to the second pamphlet, the other party, too, had published a pamphlet.

3. *Mémoire...*, p. 6. Many other facts on the life of the Marseilles community are noted in these pamphlets: the existence of the societies Gemiloth Hasadim and Bikour Holim, and of Talmud-Torah in 1792; foreign paupers were granted only the sum of 6 sols; the cantor's name was Penso; Vidal was appointed special collector of a patriotic tax among Jews: « Une députation du sieur Vidal, l'année dernière, auprès du Club de cette Ville, pour y présenter, au nom de sa nation, à l'occasion de la prise des Forts, une somme d'argent pour la répartition de laquelle il avait été nommé taxateur » (*Réponses...*, p. 33). On collectors in other communities see Z. Szajkowsli, *Autonomy and Communal Jewish Debts during the French Revolution of 1789* (New York, 1959), p. 27.

nation»—all this in violation of the spirit of the decree of September 27, 1791, on the Jewish emancipation[1].

On February 23, 1792, the civil court of the Marseilles district handed down a decision in the matter. Daniel Beaucaire and his followers, who described themselves as «Spanish and Portuguese Jewish merchants,» had asked that the synagogue be turned over to them, but their petition was denied[2].

All these facts add up to something of considerably greater significance than a collection of interesting information about a small Jewish community in France at the end of the eighteenth century. No doubt, to a certain extent Jews were tolerated at that time because they were living «in the age of mercantilism,» as one historian has written[3]. But the usefulness of Jews in the mercantile scheme of things was rarely appreciated by local authorities. More often than not, Jews were able to exist only by virtue of the protection offered them by the King, for whom their usefulness was sometimes more important than local anti-Jewish feelings[4]. For exam-

---

1. « Les dominans, au nombre de douze, y ont voulu conserver des préséances que répronne l'égalité des droits entre les hommes. » « Un petit nombre de dissidens a voulu se séparer du corps de la nation, » « On a voulu conserver dans l'école des distinctions et des préséances que les nouvelles lois de l'État ont sagement proscrites dans les Temples du Seigneur. » « Nos objets religieux violés, nos cérémonies troublées, nos assemblées dispersées, le scandale opéré dans la Synagogue, répandu dans toute la Ville, provoquant l'autorité municipale; et cela dans un tems où une révolution bienfaisante assure en France à tous les Cultes leur libre exercice, et où quelques Juifs turbulans semblent avoir voulu faire répentir la nation de cette tolérance sublime, que veut-on de plus scandalieux! » (*Mémoire ...* pp. 1-2, 5, 37). « Qui dans un tems où la révolution égalise et nivelle tout, parlent de places distinguées pour eux dans le Temple, de certificats, de droit d'entrée, et de l'ancien régime des Corps. » « Le tribunal doit donc frapper sur cette coserie hébraïque qui, née de l'ancien régime, voudrait lui survivre » (*Réponses...*, p. 38).

2. Archives départementales des Bouches-du-Rhône, Série L, liasse 3259. Tribunal du district de Marseille, Jugements civils, 23 février 1792. See also Appendix II.

3. Marcus Arkin, « West European Jewry in the Age of Mercantilism, » *Historia Judaica,* XXII (1960), 85-104.

4. See, e. g., *Arrest du Conseil d'Estat du Roy, portant évocation au Roy & à Son Conseil de toutes les contestations nées & à naître, entre les marchands des Villes & Communautés du Royaume, & les Juifs; au sujet de l'exposition des marchandises & du commerce que lesdits Juifs prétendent être en droit de faire dans les foires. Du 26 décembre 1751* (Aix, 1752), broadside (« Sa Majesté voulant autoriser la liberté desdits foires, en permettant à toutes les marchands sans distinction de les fréquenter... »); *Extrait des registres du Conseil d'État* (n. p., [13 mai 1760]), 4 pp. (in connection with the Edict of Feb. 7, 1760): « L'intention de Sa Majesté n'a jamais été de leur ôter cette faculté qui est de droit accordée

ple in the seventeenth century, Jews participated in a sub-
stancial way in clearing swamp land around Arles, and in
controlling the Durance river in the beginning of the eighteenth century[1]. Yet even then they were not allowed to
reside in the area. Also, the King's protection was given
only on rare occasions[2]. Moreover, whatever service the
Jews rendered in commerce did not entitle them to the right
of residence or to exist as a Jewish community recognized by
law. Only a long legal battle combined with large bribes
for high officials and even for the King was finally effective
in securing for the Jews the right to settle anywhere in France.
And even where such rights were achieved, the authorities
permitted the Jewish communities, not «for the fulfillment
of many needs (religious, educational, social, legal, economic,
and others)»[3] of the Jews, but rather in order to have easy
control over them, particularly for the purpose of tax collection[4]. The history of the small Jewish communities in

à tous les Humains sans distinction ... si les Turcs, les Arabes & toutes les autres
Nationes étrangers qui n'exercent pas la Religion Romaine ont la pleine liberté
d'aller à Marseille ... ne doit-on pas être surpris de ce que le Parlement de
Provence ait rendu des Arrêts si contraires à l'intérêt de l'État, contre les
Supplians .... »

1. Latil, op. cit., pp. 124.

2. On September 25, 1709, the Parliament of Provence enacted an ordinance
permitting a few Jewish merchants (Arctous Ravel, Joseph Hain de Lasia,
Joseph Dalpuget, Samuel de Bezieux, Mourdacay de Lasia) to travel to Paris
and other cities. On February 15, 1710, the King annulled this ordinance.
Extrait des registres du Conseil d'État (n. p., [15 février 1710]), broadside. On
February 29, 1716, the King annulled the ordinances of Dec. 2, 1695, April 5,
1698, February 18, 1705, March 1, 1706, July 6, 1708, and February 15, 1713,
passed by the Parliament permitting Abraham de Carcassonne and Israël
and Nathan Astruc of Avignon to sell their merchandise in Toulouse, Montpellier, and other cities. Arrest du Conseil d'État du Roy, du vingt-neuvième
février 1716. Qui ordonne aux Juifs de vuider incessament de la Province de
Languedoc (n. p., n. d.), 4 pp. On February 20, 1731, the King annulled ordinances of June 22, 1724, and July 29, 1730, permitting Joseph Raphaël de Lazia
and other Jews of Bordeaux to trade in the territory of the Dijon Parliament.
Arrest du Conseil d'Estat du Roy. Du 20 février 1731. Qui casse deux Arrêts
rendus au Parlement de Dijon ... (Paris, 1731), 4 pp. The text of this Arrest
was reprinted in Paris as late as 1784.

3. Bernard D. Weinryb, in Historia Judaica, XXII (1960), 81.

4. Weinryb, loc. cit., calls an opinion of this kind « the line of Jewish Marxist
[!] historiographny ». This author has misinterpreted a well-known and
accepted thesis as a Marxist theory.

France, such as those of Lyons and Marseilles, is a striking example of this governmental policy[1].

APPENDIX I

Statutes of the Jewish Community of Marseilles, 1789.

(Archives départementales des Bouches-du-Rhône. Dépôt d'Aix. Fonds du Parlement de Provence. Registre B 3466, fols. 345-357. 1799).

Délibération du corps de la nation des Juifs de la ville de Marseille du 6 mai 1789, arrêt du 20 juin suiv[ant].

Au nom de Dieu, ainsi Soit. Nous soussignés, représentants le corps de la nation des juifs de cette ville, nous étant assemblés dans la sale où nous faisons nos prières, avons de commun accord, deleliberé ce qui suit :

Primo : La manutention de la police interièure de la nature des affaires communes et des impositions, tant locales que générales, sera conficé à une assemblée composée du syndic de la nation établie pour le ressort de la Cour par l'arrêt d'enregistrements des privilèges de la dite nation ou de celui qui lui succèdera dans la dite charge, d'un syndic local et un trésorier, et en outre de dix sept membres de la nation. Il y aura encore un Secrétaire pour tenir les Registres et Ecritures de la nation.

2º Le syndic local et trésorier demeureront pendant un an en exercice ; après lequel terme, ils seront remplacés par d'autres tirés par sort de ceux qui formeront l'assemblée de la nation, sans qu'ils puissent être élus de nouveau à la même place qu'après un intervalle de trois années. Les parens jusques au degré de cousin germain, inclusivement, ne pourront être ensemble syndic local et trésorier.

3º Il sera tenu chaque année deux assemblées, une dans le mois d'avril et l'autre au mois de septembre, en moins que

---

1. *Cf.* J. B. Depping, *Correspondance administrative sous le règne de Louis XIV* ..., III (Paris, 1852), 29, a letter from Colbert to the Intendant of Provence on the Jews of Marseilles: « Vous devez bien prendre garde que la jalousie du commerce portera toujours les marchands a estre d'avis de les chasser; mais il faut vous élever au-dessus de ces mouvements d'interests particuliers. »

quelque cas en requière des extraordinaires ; on décidera dans lesdits assemblées des affaires de la nation et dans celle du mois de septembre seront élus le syndic local et trésorier, lorsque l'exercice de ceux actuellement en charge devra finir. Le Secrétaire restera en office pour tout le temp qu'il sera agréé de la pluralité des composants de l'assemblée.

4º Tous ceux qui seront élus aux dits charges seront tenus de les accepter et d'en remplir les fonctions, à peine de septante deux livres qui seront versées dans les caisses des dépenses locales.

5º Le syndic général nommé pour le Ressort de la Cour et celuy qui luy succèdera aura la première place dans les assemblées où il faira les propositions, sur lesquelles il devra être deliberé à pluralité des voix, par balote secrète, après s'être concesté toutesfois sur les objets à proposer avec le syndic local et trésorier, de même qu'il sera permés à chacun de l'Assemblée à proposer pour être delibéré comme-cy-dessus.

6º Il sera tenu, chaque trois années, une assemblée, dans laquelle on tirera par sort cinq taxateurs, lesquels procéderont à la cottisation de tous les contribuables aux charges locales pour les necessités des pauvres et autres. Lesdits contribuables seront cottisés en proportion de leurs revenus ou des profits qu'ils retirent de leur commerce ou industrie. Il sera deliberé, dans la même assemblée sur la prerogature, diminuture ou augmentation de l'imposition d'un par mille actuellement établie sur les affaires que ceux de la nation residente à Marseille fairont pour le compte des juifs étrangers.

7º Ladite imposition sera acquittée non seulement par les membres de la nation duement autorisés à jouir des privilèges, mais encore par tous les juifs étrangers exceçant par tolerance leur industrie dans la ville de Marseille ; lesquels seront également soumis aux cotisations, comme participans, pendant leur résidence passagère aux avantages qui forment l'objets des charges locales.

8º Tous ceux qui seront redevables à la caisse commune, sorti de leurs cotisations, offres volontaires ou autrement seront tenus à les payer entre les mains du trésorier huit jours après l'avertissement qui leur en aura été donné, à peine d'y être contraint par saisie ; pour raisons de quoy, le syndic et trésorier s'adresseront à M. le Lieutenant civil pour en obtenir la permission, laquelle sera accordée sur la simple exhibition du rôle et imposition autorisée par l'assemblée, de même que sur les comptes extraits du registre, et certifiés par le syndic local et trésorier de ce qu'ils pourront devoir.

9º Le trésorier sera tenu de faire payer tous ceux qui seront cotisés et de faire toutes les diligences necessaires pour les y contraindre. Il rendra son compte toutes les années en sortant de sa charge à l'assemblée de la nation et sera tenu d'en payer le reliquat à son successeur, et dans le contracie il sera remboursé par prompte cotisation.

10° Tous ceux qui voudront se faire immatriculer seront tenus de payer au syndic général du ressort, lors de l'expédition du certificat préalable à l'immatriculé, un droit d'entrée qui sera suivant leurs facultés du recépiendaire, ce qui sera laissé au jugement de l'assemblée de la nation qui sera, à cet effet, convoquée. Le produit des droits d'entrée, dont le dit syndic rendra compte, à chaque fin d'année, sera versé dans la caisse commune.

11° Il sera fait par le syndic particulier et trésorier un état de tous les vagabonds, gens sans aveu et autres se disant de la nation, dont la conduite est irregulière et reprochable, même de ceux qui étant de la nation ne se seront pas fait inmatriculer aux formes établies, et se seront par loi même rendus suspects ; ledit état sera représenté à une assemblée de la nation, et ceux qui soient jugés par ladite assemblée à la pluralité, au moins dans ce cas, de trois quarts de voix, ne devoir pas rester dans la ville, seront avertis d'en sortir par le syndic du ressort, et s'ils ne l'ont fait trois jours après, ledit syndic s'adressera à M. le Lieutenant civil pour y faire contraindre.

12° Les assemblées de la nation seront convoquées par billets signés du secretaire de la nation par l'ordre verbal des syndics dont l'àvertissement devra être fait la veille à chacun des membres desdites assemblées. On ne pourra y deliberer qu'au nombre de sept au moins, et si l'assemblée ne peut se tenir faute du nombre de deliberans suffisant, ou qui auront manqué de s'y rendre sans cause legitime payeront la somme de vingt quatre livres à la caisse, lesquels seront employés, comme les autres deniers de la recette, à l'acquittement des charges locales. L'assemblée de la nation prononcera sur la validité des excuses qui pourront être proposés.

13° Il pourra être appellé des membres de la nation établie dans les autres principales villes de la province aux assemblées ou seront traitées les affaires de la nation concernant le maintien de ses privilèges et autres urgences.

14° Pour conserver l'unanimité dans l'ordre du Rit des prières on adoptera, comme l'ont fait des autres corps des espagnols et portugais des autres provinces de france, celui de Livourne, sans qu'on puisse s'en écarter.

15° Les syndics et trésorier, chacun en droit soy et pour a

qui depend de sa decharge, s'adresseront à M. le lieutenant civil pour obtenir les contraintes necessaires à l'exécution des deliberations de l'assemblée de la nation et du présent règlement lequel sera transcrit dans les registres des deliberations imprimé et affiché partout où besoin sera.

Deliberé à Marseille le six may mille sept cent quatre vingt neuf.

Signés, Daniel de Beaucaire... Salomon de Silva, Moyse Puget... etc.

Pour extract, signé Daniel de Beaucaire dit Rigaud, syndic.
Il y a arrêt du 20 juin 1789.

APPENDIX II

Court Decision in the Jewish Community Conflict of Marseilles
    (Archives départementales des Bouches-du-Rhône. L 3259)

23 Février 1792.

En la cause du sieur Daniel de Beaucaire dit Rigaud, Sabaton Constantini, Chay Darmon Samuel Bruda, Isaac Abraham Costa, Léon Constantini. Samuel Vita Paz, Franco de Miranda, Salomon Silva Puget, Emanuel Foa, et Samaria Salon négocians juifs espagnols et portugais résidans en cette ville, demandeurs en requête du 23 novembre dernier, requierent à présent être dit qu'il sera poursuivi au fonds et principal ainsi qu'il apartient, et cependant que les requerans seront reintegrés en la jouissance de leur synagogue, et de tous les effets qu'elle renferme, permis à cet effet, de faire ouvrir les portes et changer les serrures par le premier serrurier requis, en présence d'un officier ministériel porteur de la commission qui en dressera procès verbal, et de suite qu'inhibitions et défenses seront faites aux adversaires de s'y introduire, de troubler et inquieter les requerans dans leur jouissance, et les cérémonies de leur culte, à peine de dix mille livres d'amende, et d'en être informé de votre autorité, en cas de contravention, et que la sentence qui interviendra sera exécutée nonobstant, et sans préjudice de l'apel, et les adversaires condamnés aux dépens, d'une part,

Contre

sieurs Israel Vidal, Salomon Abraham Cohen, et Obrada Cohen, négocians juifs, défendeurs d'autre.

M.L.C.D.R.

Seytre assisté de maître Lavabre
homme de loi
Audibert assisté de maître Leclerc
homme de loi.

Plusieurs juifs attachés à la synagogue de cette ville en sont sortis à la suite de dissentions intérieures dont la police s'est occupée : ils en ont emporté des effets précieux dont ils se disent propriétaires.

Requête de leurs parts en maintenue définitive dans la synagogue avec droits d'exclusion et d'admission, et en inhibitions et défense au sieur Vidal et consorts de s'y introduire et demandé au reintégrandre provisoire avec les mêmes defenses contre ledit sieur Vidal et consorts.

Actes du sieur Vidal et consorts portant invitation de rentrer dans le temple, ils concluent à ce que sur le fonds il soit poursuivi ainsi qu'il s'appartient et au deboutement des fins provisoires du sieur Rigaud et consorts.

Pendant le cours des plaidoiries sur ces fins provisoires le défenseur du sieur Rigaud et consorts a demandé acte au Tribunal de l'interpellation qu'il faisoit au sieur Vidal et consorts de communiquer ses quittances sur lesquelles ceux-ci se fondoient pour établir la contribution commune aux frais de la sinagogue cette communication n'étoit consentie par ceux-ci qu'à condition que le sieur Rigaud et consorts remetroient les registres de la sinagogue avec paraphement.

Un autre acte encore a été demandé par le défenseur du sieur Rigaud et consorts au sujet des certaines inculpations faites à lui Rigaud concernant ces certificats d'entrée et l'emploi de leur produits.

Sur quoi considérant en point de faits que le sieur Rigaud et consorts n'ont point produit de titre personnel de propriété ; que l'on induit au contraire de plusieurs circonstances que la sinagogue dont il s'agit n'est point une église particulière et privée, mais un lieu de prière commun à tous les Juifs de Marseille ; qui si l'acte de souscription pour la location de cette église n'est que sur un petit nombre de têtes, il est neamoins convenu que ces individus n'en supportent pas le poids ; qu'une partie des frais réligieux est établie sur des offrandes communes ou mieux encore par une taxe imposée sur la nation entière ; qu'il en résulte un état d'association de communion religieuse de propriété indivise.

Considérant en droit que l'action en réintegrande qui apartient au propriétaire expulsé doit reposer sur un titre ; que celle qui appartient au communiste s'éteint, lorsqu'on lui propose de rentrer en jouissance de la chose commune,

Considérant enfin sur la forme de procéder que l'état des quittances et registres réclamés dans les actes respectifs en supposant qu'ils existent et puissent influer sur la question, ne doivent point arrêter la marche rapide d'une réintégrande.

que cette question ainsi que l'inculpation faite au sieur

Rigaud, au sujet des certificats d'entrée retombent au fonds et reviendront avec les nouveaux développements de la cause, ouï le Commissaire du Roi

Nous Pierre Barthelemy Grosson, Gabriel Antoine Richard, Antoine Paul Joseph Courmes et Lazare Vincent Esquier présidents de la seconde chambre juges et juge suppleants du Tribunal du district de Marseille, au bénéfice de l'offre faite par le sieur Vidal et consorts à la charge par eux de l'exécuter, sans nous arrêter à la demande en reintegrande du sieur Rigaud et consorts dont nous les avons demis et débouté, avons mis sur icelle ledit sieur Vidal et consorts hors d'instance et de procès avec depens, ordonnons en outre que sur le surplus des fins du procès il sera poursuivi au fonds et principal ainsi que s'appartient. Fait en jugement à Marseille le vingt trois février mil sept cent quatre vingt douze.

(Signé) GROSSON.

THE JEWISH PROBLEM IN ALSACE, METZ, AND LORRAINE ON THE EVE OF THE REVOLUTION OF 1789

IN the approximately fifteen-year period preceding the French Revolution of 1789, a number of events occurred that ought to be considered the forerunners of the emancipation of the Jews of France. Among these were the conflict between Cerfberr and the authorities of the City of Strasbourg; the Letters Patents of January and July 10, 1784; the contest on the Jewish problem sponsored by the Metz Academy in 1786–1787; etc. During this period many liberal voices advocated — in pamphlets, books, articles in periodicals, and memoranda — the improvement of the Jews' status. These years are regarded by some historians as having prepared the Jewish emancipation, i. e. not only as having given rise to liberal sentiments toward Jews, but also as having laid the groundwork for the act of emancipation itself.

Much has already been written concerning some of these

ABBREVIATIONS:

AdBR = Archives départementales du Bas Rhin (Strasbourg).
AdHR = Archives départmentales du Haut Rhin (Colmar).
AdM = Archives départementales de la Moselle (Metz).
AmColmar = Archives municipales, Colmar.
AmStrasbourg = Archives municipales, Strasbourg.
AN = Archives Nationales (Paris).
BmMetz = Municipal Library of Metz.
BN = National Library (Bibliothèque Nationale), Paris.
BuStg = University Library of Strasbourg.
JTS = Library of the Jewish Theological Seminary, N. Y.

Originally published in *The Jewish Quarterly Review,* vol. **XLIV** (1954).

events. Many other important details, however, have not been sufficiently explored, and these happenings have not been considered as part of the history of events in Northeastern France. The historians have failed to investigate the manner in which the Jewish problem was taken up by the Provincial Assemblies (*Assemblées provinciales*) created on June 22, 1787, which played an important part in the events leading to the Revolution. These local administrative bodies were permeated with pre-revolutionary ideas and nothing could be done without their consent in favor of the Jews before the actual outbreak of the Revolution. Yet it appears that the old anti-Jewish sentiments prevailed in these Provincial Assemblies as well as in other local and central government agencies. The new liberal feelings toward the Jews failed to penetrate the Provincial Assemblies, whose views were traditionally anti-Semitic. For this reason despite the liberal sentiments in France, nothing might have been done to better the Jews' status, and had the Revolution of 1789 not come, Jewish Emancipation might not have been realized till a much later date.

I. The Conflict between the Jewish Leader Cerfberr and the City of Strasbourg

The conflict between the City of Strasbourg, in Alsace, and Cerfberr (Cerf Berr, 1730–1793), one of the Alsatian Jewish leaders, should be considered the first of these pre-Revolutionary events. This conflict greatly contributed to the struggle for the emancipation of the Alsatian Jews. Cerfberr succeeded in defeating the Magistrates of Strasbourg, and this was possible only because the King's administration was in great need of the services of the Jewish contractors, who supplied the armies with horses, food, etc.

Strasbourg had an old tradition of anti-Jewish laws. In 1349 approximately 2000 Jews were burned there alive. In 1369 five Jews were temporarily allowed to reside in the city, but in 1388 the Jews were definitely expelled,[1] and since that date the city had published numerous decrees against the Jews living under its jurisdiction. Oficially, the practice of usury by the Jews was invariably given as the excuse for these decrees. In April, 1781, the city declared in a memorandum submitted to the King's praetor that the anti-Jewish laws were not a result of a special Strasbourg policy toward the Jews, but that they were an outgrowth of the need to defend the interests of the Christians against the Jewish usurers. The same excuse was cited in 1781 in a memorandum on the special toll imposed on Jewish merchants entering the city, and again in 1787, in a *mémoire* of the city against Cerfberr.[2] This in spite of the fact that very few Jews were sentenced for usury in Strasbourg. The truth was that the city magistrates still believed that in the 14th century the Jews poisoned the wells of the city: In June, 1785, it was declared during a discussion on a *mémoire* against Cerfberr that the Jews had been accused, "perhaps wrongly" (*peut-être à tort*), of poisoning the city wells in the 14th century.[3] This traditional anti-Semitism came to the surface in a number of economic and political conflicts.

On March 16, 1530, Strasbourg prohibited all Christians dwelling in the city and in the Strasbourg area from contracting loans from Jewish creditors. But the decree was apparently not enforced, since on September 13, 1539, the

[1] Isidore Loeb, Les Juifs à Strasbourg depuis 1349 jusqu'à la Révolution. *Annuaire de la Revue des Etudes Juives*, vol. II (1883).

[2] AmStrasbourg, AA2374, 2392; Mᵉ Damours, *Mémoire pour les Préteurs, Consuls & Magistrats de la ville de Strasbourg: contre le Sieur Cerf-Berr, Juif* (Strasbourg, 1787). 13 pp. (4°), p. 13.

[3] AmStrasbourg, AA2382.

same prohibition was repeated. On April 19, 1570, the city ordered all Christian debtors to pay their debts to Jewish creditors within one year's time, and not to contract any new loans from Jews. Jews were not allowed to trade or make contracts with Christians. On October 10, 1570, Maximilian II granted the City of Strasbourg a privileged diploma (renewed in 1582 and 1621) prohibiting "usurious" contracts between Christians and Jews;— any loans granted by Jews could be interpreted as "usurious." Similar regulations were published by the Strasbourg Senate on January 24, 1616, October 12, 1661, August 24, 1668, and in 1728. An order of 1579 prohibited Jewish trading in the city markets without a special permit.[4] But the most important of all these anti-Jewish regulations was the Statute of October 12, 1661, which recapitulated all previous anti-Jewish rulings. This Statute also prohibited all trade and contracts between Jews and Christians, except for cash transactions dealing with horses and cattle. Trading in horses and cattle on credit terms was prohibited. The assets in money and merchandise of those violating this law were subject to confiscation. But the provisions of this Statute were likewise not always adhered to, and there were even cases of judges ordering Christian debtors to repay loans granted them by Jewish creditors. The Statute of 1661 was almost forgotten until the year 1753, when the Jew Schmoulin Weyl of Westhoffen purchased a debt of 80 florins granted by the Strasbourg Christian creditor Jean-George Mendoche to a Christian debtor. The debtor

---

[4] Chauffour l'aîné, Chauffour le jeune, Schirmer l'aîné et Mueg, *Consultation pour MM. les Préteurs, Consuls et Magistrats de la Ville de Strasbourg, concernant les Lettres-patentes du mois de Mars 1775 dont le Sr. Cerf Berr, juif, demande l'enregistrement & l'exécution dans lad. ville* [Strasbourg, 1786]. 63 pp. (4°), pp. 17–20, 22–25, 31–35, 37–44; J.-D. Schoepflin, *Alsatia illustrata . . .* (Colmar, 1751), vol. II, p. 369.

refused payment on the loan to his new creditor, the Jew. On June 19, 1753, the bailiff of Dorlisheim, recalling the Statute of 1661, ordered the debt confiscated and fined the Jew the sum of 100 florins. The Jew appealed to the Sovereign Council (*Conseil Souverain* — Parliament) of Alsace. On March 20, 1754, the Council rendered the sentence of the bailiff of Dorlisheim null and void, and thus forbade subsequent sentences based upon the Strasbourg Statute of 1661. The City of Strasbourg immediately appealed this decision to the King's Council (*Conseil d'Etat*). This was a very serious matter for Strasbourg — a free and independent city with a record of fighting for her privileges on many occasions. In this particular case Strasbourg was sensitive about the danger of losing the right to her own statute concerning the Jews; and, in addition, the city magistrates were certainly adverse to the process of the Sovereign Council of Alsace — which was the juridical administrative body of the French Monarchy — interfering in internal Strasbourg affairs. The Council, on the other hand, was concerned with the much wider interests of the French Monarchy, and was prepared to utilize even a conflict regarding Jews to curb the independent and excessively proud city of this troubled province. Yet on June 18, 1757, the King's Council sided with the City of Strasbourg. Their reasons for this were that Jews were allowed by their religion to charge usurious rates on loans; that for a like cause the Sovereign Council of Alsace had also issued a number of regulations against the Jews; and that consequently the annulment by the Alsace Council of the Statute of 1661 was not at all comprehensible.[5]

---

[5] *Arrest du Conseil d'Etat du Roy, qui confirme par provision le Statut du Magistrat de la ville de Strasbourg de 1661 portant defenses à ses Bourgeois, Manans & justiciables de contracter avec les Juifs. Du 18. juin 1757. Extrait des registres du Conseil d'Etat du Roy* (Strasbourg, [1757]). 8 pp. (fol.) AmStrasbourg, AA2388.

On similar occasions Strasbourg alone was united and consistent in her anti-Jewish policy. The Sovereign Council and the King himself invariably acted according to the interests of the moment. In this particular case the King supported the argument of Strasbourg, but in the later conflict between the city and the Jew Cerfberr the King refused to side with the city while, on the other hand, the Sovereign Council did so.

On October 24, 1767, the King's Council again was called upon to decide on the Statute of 1661. Some anti-Jewish regulations were upheld (Jews were not permitted to keep stores openly). But Jewish merchants were allowed to grant loans to Christian merchants (i. e. to sell on credit) at non-usurious rates; all debts in favor of Jewish creditors contracted prior to June 18, 1757, and legalized by notaries were recognized as valid; debts contracted by I.O.U.'s (i. e. by simple private contracts, signed but not sealed or witnessed) could be legalized by simple registration; Jewish merchants were allowed to trade in jewelry; butchers were allowed to buy cattle on credit from Jewish merchants, but only in times of war, etc.[6] This was a Jewish victory, but Strasbourg merely waited for a chance to fight back. On November 27, 1771, on the occasion of equalizing the Lyon money exchange rates with the Paris rates (August 1771), Strasbourg again prohibited the trading in jewelry by Jews without a special permit. A hand-written note on the poster announcing this ruling permitted the guild of Christian goldsmiths to make searches in private houses. In a petition to the Prince de Montbarrey, Minister of War, the Jews complained that this regulation was only an excuse to confiscate all gold and jewelry belonging to Jews.

---

[6] *Extrait des registres du Conseil d'Etat du Roy* [*24 Octobre 1767*] (Strasbourg, 1767). 4 pp. (fol.) AmStrasbourg, vol. 951, No. 4 & AA2381.

At that time but a single Jewish family was legally permitted to reside in Strasbourg itself, and because of the number of robberies, the Jews residing in the neighboring villages made it a practice to keep their gold and jewelry in the home of the Strasbourg Jew. The Jews requested that the King issue Letters Patent based on the decision of his Council of October 24, 1767. But the results of this request are unknown — no such Letters are to be found in the records.[7]

In 1785, a similar conflict occurred between Strasbourg and the Sovereign Council of Alsace. The Christian J. M. Raoul of Nordheim was a debtor of the Jew Jacob Raphaël of Odratheim for the sum of 116 pounds. The debt was not the result of a loan, but rather of a business transaction involving the sale of a parcel of land by Raphaël to the Christian, partly on credit. The papers were drawn up and legalized by the Royal Notary of Haguenau. Still the City of Strasbourg confiscated the debt. This was a small sum, but Arm. G. F. Xav. Loyson, Advocate General of the Sovereign Council since 1759, wrote on January 15, 1786, that a matter of principles was involved and that the amount of money involved was of no importance. The Sovereign Council annulled the confiscation of the debt, and the conflict was also referred to the King's Council. In this case however Strasbourg was not very certain of her legal position, since the debt was the result of a legal transaction in land. Still, Strasbourg feared even the smallest breach in the Statute on Jews.[8]

Thus Jews were not allowed in the city, but only to enter its area for business purposes, accompanied by city

[7] *Arrest de la Cour des monnaies, qui fait défenses à tous juifs ... de vendre, acheter, troquer ou débiter aucuns ouvrages, bijoux, vaisselles ou marchandises d'or & d'argent sans y être autorisés ... Du 27 Nov. 1771* (Strasbourg, [1771]). Affiche. AmStrasbourg, AA2381.

[8] AmStrasbourg, VCG–D56.

sergeants. A Jew was rarely permitted to stay within the city limits overnight. In 1743, the Jewish military contractor Moise Blin and his partners were allowed by the military commandant of Alsace, the Marquis d'Argenson, to reside temporarily in Strasbourg because the army needed his services.[9] Such was the atmosphere of animosity toward Jews when the conflict between the City of Strasbourg and the Alsatian Jewish leader Cerfberr erupted.[10]

Cerfberr was a large-scale contractor for the King's armies and, until 1786, also a banker.[11] He resided with his family in Bischheim, a village in the vicinity of Strasbourg, but

[9] "Comme ce commerce est d'une nécessité indispensable au service de Sa Majesté dans les circonstances présentes." AmStrasbourg, AA2372 (a letter of the marquis d'Argenson, May 15, 1743).

In 1780–1785, Strasbourg rejected the petitions of the Jews Jacob Weyl of Worblingen and Isaac Lehmann of Bischheim to be allowed openly to keep stores in the city during market-days. Jews were forced to send their merchandise to the Strasbourg markets through the custom-office and finally to check their wares with the custom-office. This cost the Jews a great deal of money (AmStrasbourg, AA2391– 2392). Only through bribery and similar tricks a Jew was sometimes allowed to stay overnight in the city. Still, in 1778, a Jewish student was registered at the Strasbourg University. S. Charléty, Strasbourg au XVIIIe siècle. Mélanges offerts a M. Nicholas Jorga (Paris, 1933), p. 814.

[10] The facts already known are to be found in the following studies: Abbé Joseph Lémann, L'Entrée des Israélites dans la Société française . . . (Paris, 1886), pp. 90–140; [Hell,] Les juifs d'Alsace . . . (1790), pp. 14–33; I. Loeb, op. cit., pp. 154–160; Die Juden im Elsass vor und während der Schreckensherrschaft. Blaetter für jüdische Geschichte und Litteratur (Mainz), vol. I (1900), pp. 2–3, 11; [M. Lévylier,] Notes et documents concernant la famille Cerfberr. 3 vols. (Paris, 1902–1906).

[11] The following event shows how important Cerfberr's contracting business was for the army: On May 31, 1776, the comte de Saint-Germain abolished the old system of contracting exclusively by private individuals and created in each regiment administrative supply councils. Alsace and Lorraine were included in this new system, but still the Army appointed Cerfberr as contractor in these two provinces, in the Trois Evêchés and the Franche-Comté. Mémoire justificatif pour le Sieur Cerf Berr . . . (Metz, 1783). 79 pp. (4°), pp. 2–5. JTS. According to a printed announcement dated Dec. 20, 1786, 3 pp. (4°). JTS., Cerfberr ceded his banking business to his sons and sons-in-law.

because of the robberies occurring there and because the
army needed his services, the King's representatives in
Alsace forced Strasbourg to grant him permission for temporary residence in the city. Cerfberr was determined to
remain in the city permanently, and he secretly purchased
a house within the city limits. In March 1775 the King
expressed his thanks to Cerfberr for his services to the
army by presenting him with Letters Patent granting him
the rights enjoyed by other citizens but refused to Jews,
including the right to purchase and possess real-estate
property.[12] These Letters were recognized and registered
without any difficulty by the Parliaments of Paris and
Nancy and by the Sovereign Council of Alsace (April 5,
1775), and Cerfberr could thus legally take up residence
in any city. But when he attempted to legalize his own
residence, that of his family, and that of his employees
(a total of 35 men and 35 women)[13] in Strasbourg, the
city refused to recognize the King's Letters. This was
the beginning of a bitter conflict. At first it appeared that
the Jew would have to yield to the mighty and privileged

[12] Such "naturalization letters" ("Lettres de naturalité") were usually
granted to foreigners and Cerfberr was not the first Jew to receive them.
In 1769, such Letters were obtained by Dutch and Avignon Jews;
and in Sept. 1775 — by a whole Jewish family that took up residence in
Le Havre (AN, K1142). The privileges granted to Cerfberr made an
impression even beyond the borders of France. *Karlsruher Zeitung*,
June 12, 1786, p. 323.

[13] According to documents dated 1773–1775, Cerfberr had 119
members of his family, servants, and employees in his contracting
business. 63 of them resided in and near Bischheim, 23 in other parts
of Alsace, 16 in Lorraine, 5 in Metz, 9 in other parts of the Metz province (Trois Evêchés), and 3 in the Comté de Bourgogne. In 1775,
Cerfberr requested that he and his employees should be exempted from
paying the special toll imposed on Jews (*péage corporel*). According to
statistics of Strasbourg this would comprise 152 Jews who paid 4,419
pounds yearly (AmStrasbourg, AA 2376–2377). According to the
1784 census of Alsatian Jews, the four families of Cerfberr and his
children numbered 68 persons.

city. The Strasbourg magistrates had many important friends in the central administrative bodies in Paris, in the Sovereign Council, and in the smaller local administrations, among the attorneys, judges, and others,[14] all of whom were prepared to aid the City of Strasbourg in fighting the arrogance of a Jew. But it was also clearly apparent that the King was in great need of the Jew's services for his armies. Cerfberr was so certain of his position that he warned the King of his intention to cease furnishing the armies with provisions, should Strasbourg stop him, his family, and his employees from establishing residence in the city.[15] In a *mémoire* of 1781 Strasbourg wrote that a great power like France could not get along without Jewish contractors because she did not yet learn from the King of Prussia the secret art of feeding the armies in times of war by war, i. e. by forcibly acquiring the necessary provisions from the conquered territories. The anti-Jewish Decree of 1700 (?) was annulled for the same reason.[16]

[14] A similar conflict arose in Colmar, where Jews were not allowed to reside. In 1698, the Magistrate of Colmar learned that the Jewish army-contractor Alexandre Doterlé of Brisac was going to request the King for permission to reside in Colmar. Dietermann (1656–1729), the Colmar royal praetor was then in Paris, and the city of Colmar asked him to oppose the Jew's request. But the Magistrates of Colmar soon became convinced that in a conflict of such a nature they would lose; so they decided to limit their fight to restricting the Jew's right of residence to him personally, but not to any other Jews. "Le Magistrat ... voyant qu'il ne pourroit pas parer ce coup ny se dispenser de la réception du dit juif sans attirer l'indignation des puissances, dont il estoit appuyé, ne songea plus qu'à rendre la permission à luy accordée, personnelle et à l'exclusion de tous autres juifs, qui voudroient profiter de cet exemple." AmColmar, AA 174.

[15] AmStrasbourg, AA 2377.

[16] "Réflexions détachées, touchant la tolérance des juifs en Alsace ... Un Etat militaire comme la France, qui est dans le cas de porter ses armes en Allemagne, et qui n'a pas encore appris du Roi de Prusse le secret de nourrir la guerre par la guerre, cet Etat ne peut se passer des juifs pour l'approvisionnement de ses troupes." AmStrasbourg, AA 2362.

Did Cerfberr seek to better his own and his family's position only, or did he aim at much more important goals, i. e., was he attempting to establish a precedent for all the Jews of Alsace? Cerberr's adversaries thought that the latter was the case. In March 1785, Damours, the Paris attorney acting for the City of Strasbourg, wrote that Cerfberr with his obstinate decision to establish residence in Strasbourg, sought a "revolution" favoring the Jews of France.[17] In any case, this conflict was a challenge not only to the City of Strasbourg, but to the anti-Jewish elements in general.

Cerfberr and his household lived on a temporary permit in Strasbourg while the juridical and the political struggle to oust them continued. In 1786 the city sent to the King a *mémoire* on the conflict, compiled by some of the best Alsatian lawyers (F. H. J. Chauffour Sr., Chauffour Jr., J. L. Schirmer Sr., Mueg). This was a verbose brief of 63 pages which included the texts of a great number of anti-Jewish laws, beginning with the Statute of 1322. According to this memorandum, Jews had always constituted a dangerous element in France, while Strasbourg had always enjoyed her special privileges in establishing a policy towards the Jews; this was a result of the King's own desire to defend the inhabitants of Strasbourg against the Jews and their usury. The magistrates did not object to the granting of privileges to Cerfberr, but maintained that this ought to be done in other parts of France rather than in Strasbourg.[18] In 1787 Cerfberr replied in a *mémoire* written by the attorney Fenouillot du Closey.[19] In the

[17] "On ne peut douter que ces premières démarches n'ayant caché d'autres vues et que la nation juive espère de là une révolution favorable dans sa manière d'exister dans les provinces du royaume où elle est admise." AmStrasbourg, AA 2382.

[18] See note 4.

[19] M⁰ Fenouillot du Closey, *Resumé pour le Sieur Cerf-Berr . . .*

same year, 1787, Strasbourg published another *mémoire*, written by the Paris attorney Damours, who reiterated the thesis of the Alsatian lawyers, but did so in a much stronger and condensed form, eliminating the long preface and the texts of the laws cited in the first *mémoire*. Damours' main argument was that it was improper to upset the constitution and the independence of Strasbourg to please an obdurate Jew.[20]

Apparently the two *mémoires* of Strasbourg did not exert any great influence upon the King or his ministers. Strasbourg was advised by her friends not to attempt to force a showdown at this time, but rather to await future events and a change of personnel in the government. On June 9, 1786, the Alsatian attorney Chouffour Sr. likewise advised Strasbourg to await another occasion, when the city would be in a better position to retaliate and request that the King recognize the 1661 Statute. Cerfberr was mortal, he wrote, and so were his mighty protectors.[21] Similar counsel was given on September 6, 1787, by de Crolbois of Paris, who wrote that a change in the composition of the War Ministry in charge of the Province of Alsace would be favorable to Strasbourg.[22] Damours, who

contre les *Préteurs, Consuls & Magistrats de la ville de Strasbourg* (Sl, 1787). 4 pp. (4°). AN, K1142.

[20] See note 2.

[21] "En gagnant du tems, on gagne tout ce qui dépend du changement des hommes, et de leurs opinions, je suis très persuadé, que vos conseils et agens à Paris, et à Versailles trouveront des voyes pour vous procurer l'indécision, jusqu'à ce que des circonstances plus favorables, vous mettent dans le cas de solliciter vous-mêmes un arrêt qui perpétue légalement l'exécution de vos statuts concernant les juifs. Cerf Beer est mortel, il peut d'un moment à l'autre devenir inutile, ses Protecteurs sont sujets aus mêmes vicissitudes de l'humanité que luy et si l'un ou les autres disparaissent, je doute très fort que personne autre prenne beaucoup de part à l'extension, même à l'exécution des lettres patentes." AmStrasbourg, AA 2385.

[22] "Nous pensons que le changement dans le ministère ne pourra être qu'avantageux à notre cause, et qu'il faut prendre les devants

led the fight against Cerfberr in Paris, placed the responsibility for the situation on the inefficient manner in which the struggle had been conducted. On December 29, 1789, shortly before his death, Damours wrote that he knew well the provincial character of Strasbourg, where one liked long *mémoires* and trials. The ministers in Paris, he wrote, did not, however, relish voluminous documents nor did they have the time to read them. Talent did not constitute in setting forth all matters, but rather in selecting only the important.[23] In this respect Cerfberr acted with much more understanding of the situation than his enemies: his *mémoire* was short and convincing.

For a while Strasbourg found a powerful ally in the pre-revolutionary Provincial Assembly of Alsace (created on June 22, 1787), which supported her argument against Cerfberr. According to a memorandum prepared by one of the attorneys of the Assembly, it appears that it acted in this spirit mainly because the seigniors — whose influence in the Assembly was great — feared similar conflicts with the Jews residing in their holdings throughout Alsace.[24] In a memorandum favoring Strasbourg, the Inter-

avec le Ministre futur, en le prévenant par notre mémoire." *Idem*, AA 2388.

[23] "Le talent ici n'est pas de tout dire, mais de ne dire que l'essentiel. Ces détails que les parties croient tous importants, noient les véritables moiens et les font perdre de vue." *Idem*, AA 2389.

[24] "la contestation . . . intéresse non seulement la Capitale, mais encore plusieurs villes d'Alsace et le plus grand nombre des seigneurs de cette province dont les vues ont absolument écarté les juifs de leurs terres et les autres ont exercé à leur gré le droit de les admettre ou de les exclure. Ces Seigneurs dont le droit sur les juifs est fondé, comme celui de la ville de Strasbourg sur des titres positifs, ne peuvent rester spectateurs indifférents d'un procès dont l'événement seroit un préjugé dans leur propre cause et après le jugement duquel leur silence dans le moment présent pourroit leur être opposé. Il en est de même des villes d'Alsace qui, à l'instar de Strasbourg ont toujours repoussé la nation juive de leurs murs. Et comme l'Assemblée provinciale d'Alsace représentée par la Commission intermédiaire doit veiller avec soin à

mediary Commission (*Commission intermédiaire*) of Alsace based its resolution on the fact that Strasbourg was a Free City. But this was not a very ingenious argument, since the tendency to centralize the administration of the province to further the interests of the kingdom as a whole was prevalent at this time. (The Commission itself protested against allowing Strasbourg to send deputies directly to the *Etats Généraux*.[25]) Yet, in any case, Paris did not favor Strasbourg's argument. On January 10, 1789, du Closey, Cerfberr's attorney, again advised the City of Strasbourg to wait.[26] Six months later the Revolution broke out. Even then Strasbourg asked the National Assembly to respect the old city statutes regarding the Jews and to oust them from the city.[27] In a Strasbourg memorandum of April 1790, it was mentioned that the lawsuit between Cerfberr and the city was still going on (*encore pendant*).[28] Yet the suit was never pleaded. On September 27, 1791, the Alsatian Jews were granted full citizenship rights. Only then did the conflict between Strasbourg and Cerfberr end.

la conservation des droits et des privilèges de la Province ... elle croit devoir exposer à Sa Majesté les obstacles légitimes qui s'opposent à l'effet des prétentions du Sr. Cerfberr." AN, K 1142.

F. de Dietrich, was the Commission's representative in Paris, see: Gabriel G.-Ramon, *Frédéric de Dietrich* (Nancy-Paris, 1919), pp. 12–13. According to a letter of Jan. 15, 1788, written by Dietrich, the Commission requested the Minister comte de Brienne to intervene in the conflict in favor of Strasbourg. AmStrasbourg, AA2389; AN, O¹ 610; AdBR, C752, p. 33.

[25] AN, BA–11.

[26] AmStrasbourg, AA2389. Does this mean that Cerfberr's attorney Closey played a double-faced game, or that Cerfberr himself was then interested in gaining time, because of his activities in favor of the Alsatian Jews during the last months prior to July 1789?

[27] *Réimpression de l'ancient Moniteur*, vol. IV, p. 170.

[28] *Très-humble et très respectueuse adresse que présente à l'Assemblée nationale la commune tout entière de la ville de Strasbourg* (Paris, avril 1790). (8°); (2nd edition — Strasbourg, 14 pp. (4°), German edition — 11 pp. (4°).

II. The Abolition of the Body Toll (*Péage corporel*) Imposed Upon Jews, January 1784

As a result of a long series of conflicts between Jewish creditors and their Christian debtors (since 1778), anti-Jewish feelings grew considerably. This circumstance, however, also helped to arouse the Jews' own realization of the importance of organized Jewish defensive action. Cerfberr then sent a *mémoire* to the Council of State on the condition of the Alsatian Jews. This event marked the beginning of his connection with the German writer Chr. W. von Dohm, whose book on the condition of the Jews (1781) greatly influenced the struggle for the Jewish emancipation. Cerfberr asked the German-Jewish philosopher M. Mendelssohn to help him in his efforts to defend the Alsatian Jews and was directed by him to Dohm. It was in response to Cerfberr's request that Dohm started work on his book. At first it was his intention to prepare material on the condition of the Alsatian Jews only, but he finally expanded his writings to include a description of the condition of the Jews in general, to which he added Cerfberr's *mémoire* on Alsace. As a result the conflicts between the Alsatian Jewish creditors and their Jewish debtors influenced the position of the Jews throughout Europe. Cerfberr published Dohm's book in a French translation by J. Bernoulli Dessau, and he attempted to sumggle it into France.[29]

---

[29] Mémoire sur l'état des Juifs en Alsace, in Chr. Wilh. Dohm, *Ueber die bürgerliche Verbesserung der Juden* (Berlin-Stettin, 1781), pp. 155–200 and in the French edition: *De la réforme politique des Juifs* (Dessau, 1782); M. Ginsburger, *Cerf Berr et son temps* (Strasbourg, 1936), p. 7; M. S[chwab], Un écrit français par Dohm et Mendelssohn. *Archives Israélites*, vol. XXVII (1866), pp. 641–643; Prof. H. Graetz, *History of the Jews* (Philadelphia, 1895), vol. V, pp. 351–57; Willy Cohn, Christian von Dohm, *Historia Judaica*, vol. XIII (1951), pp. 101–108. On the conflict between the Jewish creditors and their Gentile debtors (called "The Case of the Counterfeit Receipts") see:

At the time of the official census of Alsatian Jews in 1780, some local administrators brought up the question of permitting the Jews to earn their livelihood by following honest trades hitherto closed to them. All these proposals, however, were contingent upon the granting of more freedoms to the Jews, while in reality more restrictions upon them were requested instead.[30] In the wake of the conflicts between the creditors and their debtors in Alsace, the government sought the views of the Alsatian administrations regarding the Jewish problem in the province and as to possible ways to improve their status. The Jews, on the other hand, likewise wrote a number of *mémoires*, and the government appointed a special commission charged with the preparation of regulations concerning the Alsatian Jews. On August 27, 1783, this commission presented its findings to the government. The first result of the report was the King's Edict of January 1784 abolishing the special body toll (*péage corporel*) hitherto imposed upon the Alsatian Jews. On January 17, 1784, the Edict was registered with the Alsatian Sovereign Council; on March 4, 1784, with the Nancy Parliament; and on March 8, 1784, with the Parliament of Metz (where this special toll had been abolished at the end of the 17th century).[31]

The issuance of the Edict evoked a short but violent struggle. The City of Strasbourg categorically contended against the abolishment of the special toll on Jews. This

Z. Szajkowski, *The Economic Status of the Jews in Alsace, Metz and Lorraine* (New York, to be published in 1954).

[30] AdBR, C336.

[31] *Edit du Roi, portant exemption des Droits de péage corporels sur les Juifs, Du mois de janvier 1784. Enregistré le 17 du même mois* (Colmar, [1784]). 4 pp. (4°). German edition: *Koenigliches Edict welches die Juden von Leibzoll Gubrühren befreyt.* 7 pp. (4°). Metz edition — 3 pp. (4°). AmStrasbourg, AA2378–79 & Bibliothèque nationale Ld¹⁸³ 21; I. Loeb, *op. cit.*, pp. 167–175; *Recueil des Edits* ... (Nancy, 1733–1786), vol. XV, pp. 417–418; Jourdan et autres, *Recueil général des anciennes lois* ... (Paris, 1821–33), vol. XXVII, p. 360.

toll had been a source of revenue to the city since every Jew arriving there for business reasons was required to pay it. Jews spent approximately 100,000 man-days in the city of Strasbourg every year. In 1780, 27,626 Jews entered the city through the three gates of Blanches, Saverene, and Pierre. In January – July 1781 20,610 Jews entered these three gates and the other two, Porte des Juifs and Wickhaussel. From October 1783 to January 1784, the revenue derived from the special toll amounted to 3680 pounds.[32] Hence Strasbourg opposed the abolition of the toll. Considerable discussion ensued, much was written on the condition of the Jews, and the government apparently did not feel morally justified in maintaining this special body toll, a "humiliation to humanity," as the Edict itself declared.[33] Strasbourg had to yield and post the Edict, but not without protesting. On February 8, 1784, Strasbourg's King's Praetor, Conrad-Alexandre Gérard wrote to General Finance Comptroller de Calonne that the Edict had caused much discontent. Some people had expected that the Edict would be announced together with another regulation compensating the City of Strasbourg for the losses due to the abolishment of the toll. On January 25, 1786, the King indeed compensated Strasbourg by granting

[32] AN, K 1142; AmStrasbourg, AA 2374–75, 2382.
[33] "Une imposition que semble avilir l'humanité." The Strasbourg cardinal de Rohan (1734–1803) advocated stringent yet "honorable" regulations for the Jews. He proposed to replace the special body-toll for yearly dues, less "humiliating," but still effective (AmStrasbourg, AA 2362, 2376). He frequently came in contact with Jews. On Dec. 24, 1788, the King permitted him to return to France (F. Funck-Brentano, "L'Affaire du Collier;" *Revue d'Alsace*, vol. XXXI (1902), p. 215). On Feb. 12, 1798, when passing through Mutzig on his way back to Strasbourg, the Mutzig Jews, too, organized in the house of Daniel Lévy a party in honor of the cardinal, "drinking wine and beer till dawn." In the Synagogue Jews chanted a special ode in his honor. *Rélation exacte de la rejouissance publique que la ville de Moutzig a faite au retour de son Altesse . . . de Rohan* (Sl, nd) 4 pp.; O. Meyer, *La Régence épiscopale de Saverne* (Strasbourg, 1935), p. 94.

the city an annual rent of 2400 pounds, i. e. about one-half
the revenue from the special toll. But Strasbourg still
protested and requested a more substantial compensation.
In the meantime the King ordered the city to refund
Cerfberr 1800 pounds which he had paid as a yearly
advance on the toll for himself, his family, and his employees. Even after January 1784, the Jews entering the
city by way of the bridge over the Rhine were required to
pay a bridge toll amounting to double the sum exacted
from non-Jews. On September 8, 1786, a special order of
the King (renewed on December 3, 1786, by the intendant
de la Galaziére) forbade this practice.[34] But Strasbourg
still refused to yield. The Edict of January 1784 was a
financial blow to the city and the seigniors. Even just
prior to the Revolution of 1789, Strasbourg published a
memorandum requesting obedience to some old Strasbourg
privileges, including the privilege to "protect" Jews — for
a special toll, of course. The memorandum declared that
"many noblemen of moderate means as well as their
families would be ruined and would lose ¾ of their possessions if the Jews were exempted from paying the special
toll on Jews and if the duty services were likewise abolished
without compensation."[35]

[34] AmStrasbourg, AA 2378; *Lettres-patentes du Roi, sur arrêt portant
fixation de l'indemnité accordée à la ville de Strasbourg pour raison de la
suppression des droits qu'elle percevoit sur les Juifs sous la dénomination
de péage corporel ... le 25 Janvier 1786* (Metz, [1786]). 4 pp. (4°);
Extrait des registres du Conseil d'Etat du Roi [du 8 Septembre 1786]
(Strasbourg, [1786]). 3 pp. (4°).

[35] "Plusieurs gentilshommes peu riches seroient ruinés et perdroient
les trois quarts de leur fortune, si d'un côté les juifs à la faveur d'une
loi générale pouvoient se libérer de la redevance de protection, et que
d'un autre les corvées pussent être abolies sans rachat." *Mémoire
de droit public sur la ville de Strasbourg et l'Alsace en général* (Strasbourg, 1789), p. 21. German edition: *Abhandlung des Staatsricht der
Stadt Strassbourg* ... AmStrasbourg, vol. R40–37&37a.
According to an Alsatian Jewish tradition, the Jews decided to
petition for the abolition of the toll because of a conflict between two

III. The Letters Patent of July 10, 1784

The work of the King's commission appointed to study the Jewish question resulted in the publication of the Letters Patent of July 10, 1784 — a veritable statute for the Alsatian Jews.[36]

The Letters comprised 25 articles. According to these, Jews without legally assigned residences were to leave Alsace within three months' time; foreign Jews were forbidden to reside in Alsace; Jews were allowed to own factories and cultivate the land, but not to employ Christian farm laborers; Jews were not allowed to purchase houses, except for their own use; the rights of the rabbis in charge of the juridical administration of the Jewish communities were restricted; Jews were required to request permission to marry; contracts between Jews and Christians had to be legalized in the presence of two officials, except contracts with bankers; interest on loans was to be paid by Christian debtors to Jewish creditors in cash, never in products; the *More judaïco* was introduced in law-courts; Jewish women were not to enjoy the benefits of the law on separate maintenance of property in cases where Christian creditors might suffer thereby.

In a memorandum by the attorney M. de Mirbeck, a masterpiece in the use of juridical and economic arguments,

---

Jewish candidates for the office of collector of this toll. I. Loeb, *op. cit.*, pp. 173–175. On such conflicts see: AmStrasbourg, AA 2374.

[36] *Lettres patentes du Roi, portant Règlement concernant les Juifs. Du 10 Juillet 1784. Enregistrées le 26 Août suivant* (Colmar). 16 pp. (4°); in German: Offener königlicher Brief betreffend die Juden Verordnung im Elsass, vom 10 Juli 1784. *Priviligirte Strassburger Zeitung*, No. 76 (1784). JTS & BuStg 33269, 101300; Robert Anchel, "Les Lettres patentes du 10 Juillet 1784." *Festschrift zu Simon Dubnows siebzigsten Geburtstag* (Berlin, 1930), pp. 187–200 (French text in: *Revue des Etudes Juives*, vol. XCIII (1932), pp. 113–134); Ph. Sagnac, "Les Juifs et la Révolution française," *Revue d'histoire moderne et contemporaine*, vol. I (1899), pp. 18–21; Abbé J. Lémann, *op. cit.*

the Jews strongly protested against these Letters. The memorandum asserted that since Alsace had become a French province the status of the Jews had steadily worsened, and that many privileges enjoyed by them were now being abolished by the new Letters. Jews were still restricted to reside in small cities and villages, far from the large commercial centers; the order making it mandatory for a Jew to request permission to marry was new and inhuman, unknown even in the *Judenordnung* of May 22, 1613.[37] Prior to July 1784 jurisprudence on Jews of the Alsatian Sovereign Council allowed them to purchase real estate property, provided that the property be sold in the course of one year and that Christian buyers be favored. Article X of the new Letters forbade Jewish real estate transactions. According to the memorandum, this was harmful not only to the Jews, but to the Christians as well, since the new Letters practically abolished free competition in the real-estate field and thus enabled Christian traders to force high prices upon prospective buyers. In addition, Article XIV prohibiting simple I.O.U.'s would be costly to Christian debtors of small sums, because of the high rates charged by the notaries.[38]

The Letters aimed at reducing the number of Jews in Alsace in the name of "justice and humanity." Most of

---

[37] AN, K 1142, No. 45 & H 1641; R. Anchel, *op. cit.*, pp. 193–198; Rod. Reuss, *L'Alsace au 17ᵉ siècle* (Paris, 1897–98), vol. II, p. 579.

On June 29, 1786, the three famous Alsatian Attorneys Chauffour Sr, Chauffour Jr, and Hahn declared that seigniors had no right to prohibit Jewish marriages. AdHR, E 280 & 1629; Charles Hoffmann, *L'Alsace au 18ᵉ siècle* (Colmar 1906–07), vol. IV, p. 350.

[38] R. Anchel, *op. cit.*, pp. 192, 198. In fact, it is hard to draw a clear line between the friends and foes of the Jews in this commission. The anti-Jewish point-of-view was advocated by the Intendant of Alsace de la Galazière, who was the representative of the usually pro-Jewish-minded King's administration in Alsace. F. N. de Spon, the First President of the Sovereign Council since 1776 showed strong pro-Jewish sentiments.

the chroniclers and historians, however, considered the Letters of July 10, 1784, not as an act of pre-emancipation, but as part of an anti-Jewish development.[39] The anti-Semitic historian Henri Prado-Gaillard justly wrote (in 1942) that Louis XVI by his letters of July 10, sought to compensate the angry people of Alsace for the pro-Jewish Edict of January 1784 abolishing the special toll on Jews. The French-Jewish historian Robert Anchel wrote (in 1930) that Louis XVI was much praised for his actions favorable to the Jews, but that in reality the King's Letters were timid and conservative, and accomplished very little in favor of the Jews. Without the Revolution of 1789, the Jews would have had to wait a long time before they were granted citizenship.[40]

On the basis of these Letters, a census of the Jews "tolerated" in Alsace was conducted at the end of 1784 in order to legalize the number of Jews in each community.[41] Many Jews were driven out.[42] Where Jews were not permitted

[39] On Dec. 24, 1789, the Alsatian anti-Jewish leader himself declared in the National Assembly that the Letters of July 10, 1784, caused the Jews to shed many tears (*Revue des grandes journées parlementaires*, vol. I, p. 16). Even the converted Jew Lémann revolted against the prohibition of Jewish marriages (Lémann, *op. cit.*, p. 66). The historian Ferdinand Dreyfus (of Jewish origin) wrote that the Letters worsened the Jewish status (*Misères sociales*... (Paris, 1901), p. 217). The Jewish historian Raphael Mahler rightly did not include the Letters in his selection of documents on Jewish Emancipation (*Jewish Emancipation. A Selection of Documents*, New York, 1941).

[40] Henri Prado-Gaillard, *La Condition des Juifs dans l'ancienne France* (Paris, 1942), p. 103; R. Anchel, *op. cit.*, p. 200.

[41] *Dénombrement général des Juifs qui sont tolérés en la province d'Alsace*... (Colmar, 1785). 386 pp. (fol.); *Supplément au dénombrement*... (Colmar, 1785). 2 pp. (fol.); *Récapitulation du dénombrement général des Juifs*... 1 p. (fol.); Gabriel Hemerdinger, "La population israélite en Alsace. Recensement de 1784...," *L'Univers Israélite*, vol. LVIII–I (1902–03); *Ibid.*, "Le Dénombrement des Israélites d'Alsace (1784)," *Revue des Etudes Juives*, vol. XLII (1901), pp. 253–264.

[42] AdHR, E 1070.

to reside, even short visits by them were prohibited.[43] The article on marriages in the Letters was likewise strictly enforced. As late as in June 1789 the King was granting official permits to marry to Alsatian Jews.[44]

On August 26, 1784, the Letters Patent of July 10 were recognized and registed by the Sovereign Council of Alsace. On September 1 of the same year, the Council published regulations on the enforcement of the Letters. On May 6, 1786, the Council decided that all Jews who had not been reported in the census of 1784 would have to leave Alsace in the course of one month to be designated by the Council. The order ousting the Jews was published in December 1788, and they protested its delayed publication and the intent to expel them during the cold winter, when they might perish before being able to find new places of residence. Therefore on December 13, 1788, the Council decided that the order of expulsion was to be enforced during the month of May 1789. But this was somehow delayed, and the Revolution broke out before the expulsion order was actually carried out.[45]

The Letters of July 1784 even failed to settle the con-

---

[43] Colmar allowed only short visits of Jews for business or for trials at the Sovereign Council. On Nov. 20, 1784, Colmar forbade Jews to have in the city permanent storage-rooms for their merchandise. Only specially-appointed inkeepers were allowed to receive Jewish guests for the limited duration of only 8 days. The Jews protested in a memorandum. Colmar — they wrote — is important for them as a trade center; the Christians of Colmar themselves will suffer because of the Order of Nov. 20, 1784. AmColmar, AA 176; *De par . . . la ville de Colmar. Du 20 novembre 1784* (Colmar). Affiche.

[44] AN, H-1.

[45] *Extrait des registres du Conseil Souverain d'Alsace. Du premier Septembre 1784* (Colmar). 7 pp. (4°). BuStg 33269; — *Du 8 janvier 1785* (Colmar). 6 pp. (4°). BuStg 33229; — *Du 6 Mai 1786* (Colmar, 1786). 4 pp. (4°). AdBR, B 598; — *Du 13 décembre 1788* (Colmar). 3 pp. (4°). BuStg 101344; V. M. A. Holdt, *Journal du Palais du Conseil Souverain d'Alsace*, publié par A. Ingold (Colmar, 1903–07), vol. II, Dec 13, 1788.

flict between the Jewish creditors and their Christian debtors. On September 2, 1784, the Sovereign Council informed the Marechal de Ségur that the July Letters did nothing to regulate the debts, that the peasants-debtors would be forced to emigrate, and that the Jews themselves suffered from such a situation.[46] Meanwhile Louis XVI and his ministers continued to concern themselves with the Jewish problem. C. G. de Malesherbes was in charge of a special commission and was appointed to study the Jewish question in the whole of France.[47]

The French-Jewish historian Léon Kahn summarizes the policy of Louis XVI toward the Jews as follows: "There could be no question of granting them the full rights enjoyed by other citizens. The Jews did not dare to request that much, Malesherbes and the King did not wish to grant them that much. Later, the Church pretended that in the Act of Emancipation of the Jews the Revolution of 1789 only carried out the initiative and acted upon the proposal of the Church. This was a willful mispresentation . . . Louis XVI gave the Jews a . . . mask of liberty. . . . The Revolution was more generous and displayed considerably more justice."[48] Yet historians and Jewish leaders have not always properly presented the policy of Louis XVI and his regime towards the Jews in this manner.[49] Gradu-

---

[46] AdHR, C2, vol. 2.

[47] L. Kahn, *Les Juifs de Paris pendant la Révolution* (Paris, 1898), pp. 8–10. Malesherbes' Commission aimed at improving the Jews' status, but nothing is known on the attitude of Louis XVI toward the Commission's project. The only important document on the Commission is the diary of the delegation of Bordeaux Jews to the Commission (1788) which was found by this author: ז. שייקובסקי, משלחותיהם של יהודי בורדו אל ועדת מאלזרב (1788) ואל האסיפה הלאומיט (1790). תעודות חדשות לתולדות האמנציפציה של יהודי צרפת. ציון, שנה י"ח, ספרים א–ד (ירושלים, תשי"ג), ד' 31–79.

[48] *Ibid.*, p. 11.

[49] After the publication of the Jan. 1784 Edict, N. H. Wessely wrote in the *Meassef* in honor of Louis XVI. Much later, in 1841, the Metz

ally a legend was created that Louis XVI started the emancipation of the Jews. A story was told how the King had seen a Jewish burial in the vicinity of Versailles and now, moved by pity, he had ordered his minister to improve the Jews' status.[50] This legend may well date from the post-Napoleonic Restoration years when the Jews, too, had to praise the Bourbon family and to relate the virtues of the "martyr" Louis XVI and "his" emancipation of the Jews.[51] This was, in part, a Jewish reaction to Napolen's anti-Jewish Decrees of May 30, 1806 and March 17, 1808.[52]

Jew Moyse Alcan published the following sonnet in honor of Louis XVI:

> "Louis, tu brilles plus que l'or du diadême,
> ... Vers les fils de Jacob tu tends aussi les bras;
> Ton âme s'indignait de ces impurs rachats . . . ."

M. Alcan, *Noéma, poésies* (Metz-Nancy, 1841), pp. 123–124.

[50] Ben Lévi, "Le Cimetière de Versailles, nouvelle," *Archives Israélites*, vol. I (1840), pp. 607–611.

[51] On April 22, 1814, at a reception by the brother of Louis XVIII, Jacob Lazard declared in the name of the delegation of the Central Jewish Consistory that the Jews should be grateful to Louis XVI for their Emancipation. On June 25, 1814, Joseph Raphaël Cohen of the Marseille Jewish Consistory called the execution of Louis XVI "a juridical assassination." On Jan. 21, 1815, the Chief Rabbi A. de Cologna bewailed the memory of the "good King" and Marie Antoinette. In 1820, D. Drach, director of the Paris Jewish school (who later turned to Christianity) wrote that Louis XVI made a "wonderful gift to the Jews." In a Synagogue-ceremony of Oct. 12, 1824, Louis XVI was called the "Monarque législateur." *Le Moniteur*, April 25, 1814, p. 454; "Les Juifs royalistes sous la Restauration. *La Révolution française*, vol. LXXXVI (1928), pp. 248–49; AN, F¹⁹ 11031; A. de Cologna, *Discours religieux prononcé le 21 Janvier 1815* . . . [Paris, 1815] 9 pp.; M. D. Drach, *Ode hébraïque sur la naissance de son Altesse Royale Mᵍʳ le Duc de Bordeaux . . . présenté . . . 23 octobre 1820* (Paris, 1820). 11 pp.; *Service funèbre pour sa Majesté Louis XVI . . . à la synagogue consistoriale de Strasbourg, le 12 Octobre 1824* (Strasbourg, 1824). 12 pp.

[52] In 1818, in a petition against Napoleon's anti-Jewish Decrees, the Central Consistory wrote that the Jews first saw the light of Emancipation under the reign of Louis XVI. *Requête adressée au Roi par le Consistoire Central des Israélites, contre la prorogation du Décret du 17 Mars 1808* . . . (Paris, 1818), p. 3.

Later, however, the Jews praised the memory of Napoleon I as opposed to the anti-Semitism of the reactionary circles.[53] Much later even the memory of Louis XVI was praised by Jews.[54]

IV. PRO-JEWISH SENTIMENTS IN METZ

The details of the contest on the Jewish problem sponsored by the Metz Academy are already known. This contest and the published pro-Jewish studies of the Abbé

[53] The cases of Michel Berr, the son of the Lorraine Jewish leader Berr-Isaac Berr, and the Comtadin Jewish poet J.-M. Mossé, prove only that all this ode-singing was a product of the new regime. During the Hundred Days Michel Berr praised Napoleon I, but in 1818, he called Louis XVI "the religious and philosophical King," who inaugurated Jewish Emancipation. (During the Revolution, his father himself refused to remove a royal sign from his house until forced by the Mayor of Nancy to do so.) In 1824, M. Berr declared himself a partisan of a constitutionnel monarchy; in 1837 he again proposed to organize a special guard for the protection of the King and the "national, constitutionnel monarchy." J. M. Mossé wrote odes in honor of Napoleon I, his family, his victories, and his patronage of writers. But when a new regime entered, he attacked Napoleon's memory and praised the memory of Louis XVI as "the beautiful, perhaps the greatest period known in the course of centuries." Albert Troux, *La Vie politique dans le département de la Meurthe d'août 1792 à octobre 1795* (Nancy, 1936), vol. I, p. 62; M[ichel] B[err], *Observations sur l'Acte additionnel aux constitutions de l'Empire* ... (1815), p. 2; *Ibid., Lettre sur les premières livraisons de l'Israélite Français* ... (Paris, 1818), p. 13; *Ibid., Un mot* ..., p. 5; *Ibid., Au Rédacteur de l'Indépendant de la Moselle. Sur le dernier attentat à la vie du Roi* ... (Nancy, 1837); J. M. Mossé, *La France consolée. Ode sur la naissance de S. M. le Roi de Rome* (Paris, 1811); *Ibid., Ode aux insurgés d'Espagne* (Paris, 1810); *Ibid., Ode sur la guerre présente* (Paris, 1809); *Ibid., Poésies* (Paris, 1809); *Ibid., Chronique de Paris* ... (Paris, 1812); *Ibid., Le Cri du Peuple français* (Paris, 1814).

[54] In 1840, M. Th. Milhaud spoke in the Aix Synagogue about the "most unfortunate Louis XVI" (*Discours prononcé ... le 22 septembre 1840* (Aix, 1840), p. 7). In 1888, Rabbi M. Charléville wrote in the same sense (*Louis XVI et les Israélites*. Extrait des *Archives Israélites* (Paris, 1888), p. 8), and so did Rabbi Benjamin Mossé in a collection of Rabbinical sermons published on the occasion of the 100th anniversary of the Revolution (*La Révolution française et le Rabbinat français* (Avignon, 1890), p. 280). See the discussion in· Laurent Carmona-

H. Grégoire, the attorney Thiery, and the Polish Jew
Zalkind Hourwitz, contributed measurably to aid the
struggle for Jewish emancipation.[55] It should be noted,
however, that this contest was the result of local pro-Jewish
sentiments. It would be impossible, for instance, to discern
in this case any influence of the Encyclopaedists or of
neighboring Alsace. The attorney of the Metz Parliament
Pierre-Louis Roederer, who initiated the contest, was a
local notable; and the Encyclopaedists, who, with the
exception of Montesquieu, were strongly anti-Jewish, surely
could not have influenced him in a pro-Jewish sense.[56] The
studies of Grégoire, Thiéry, and even of the Jew Hourwitz
himself[57] have been judged in general from a purely literary
point of view, but their proposals for the improvement of
the Jews' status were not the most liberal or pro-Jewish.
The Parisian Abbé La Louze proposed in his (unpublished)
study submitted to the contest that "the Jews be accepted
among the citizens" (*les admettre au nombre des citoyens*);
in his unpublished study M. Vatiaud of Laon proposed
full citizenship for the Jews.[58] Grégoire, Thiéry, and
Hourwitz did not go that far in their proposals.

Benveniste, "Les Séphardins en France sous l'ancien régime,"
Revue hebdomadaire (25 Mars 1939), pp. 469–470.

[55] A. Cahen, "L'Emancipation des Juifs devant la Société royale des
sciences et arts de Metz et M. Roederer." *Revue des Etudes Juives*,
vol. I (1880).

[56] The antisemitism of the Encyclopaedists should in a way be understood as an opposition to the Catholic Church, just as the attacks by
some Marxist Socialists (G. Tridon, E. Picard, Albert Regnard, and
others) upon the Jews as the moral fathers of the Church. Z. Szajkowski, *Anti-Semitism in the French Labor Movement. From the Fourierist
Movement until the Closing of the Dreyfus Case, 1845–1906* (New York,
1948, in Yiddish).

[57] H. Grégoire, *Essai sur la régénération physique, morale et politique
des Juifs* ... (Metz, 1789); Thiéry, *Dissertation sur cette question:
Est-il des moyens de rendre les Juifs plus heureux et plus utiles en France?*
(Paris, 1788); Zalkind Hourwitz, *Apologie des Juifs* ... (Metz, 1789).

[58] BmMetz, ms. 1350.

There exists some proof that after the publication by Louis XVI of his Edict in favor of non-Catholics (Protestants),[59] the Metz Parliament undertook to study the Jewish problem. According to a memorandum on the subject,[60] the Parliament discussed the question of whether the Jews would likewise enjoy the rights granted the Protestants by the Edict, or whether Jews would still not be allowed to earn an honest living. According to this document, the Parliament inquired in Paris regarding this matter. But some members of the Parliament showed interest in the status of the Jews only because they feared that in the event the Jews were allowed to share in the benefits of the new Edict, Metz would become "a second Jerusalem." It is possible that this discussion was the cause of the delay in the registration of the Edict with the Parliament (March 10, 1788).[61] The unknown author of the memorandum requested that the rights newly granted the Protestants also be given to the Jews.[62] On the other

[59] *Edit du Roi concernant ceux que ne font pas profession de la Religion Catholique. Donné à Versailles au mois de Novembre 1787* (Paris, 1788). 16 pp. AdM, A.

[60] BmMetz, ms. 1108–25–II. 12 pp.

[61] AdM, B 100, f. 276.

[62] "Les juifs de Metz participeront — ils aux avantages que le droit naturel assure à tous les hommes et dont l'édit de 9bre 1787 leur permet de jouir désormais en France, on bien seront-ils sous le joug des prohibitions que leur ôtent presque tous les moyens honnêtes de soutenir leur existence? C'est la question que le Parlement de Metz a cru devoir faire au gouvernement avant d'enregistrer l'édit des non-catholiques. Le parlement a trop de lumières pour n'être pas convaincu que la rigueur avec laquelle les juifs sont traités, les empêche d'être aussi utiles qu'ils pouvaient le devenir sous un régime plus doux. Le Parlement est trop sage de souhaiter que les juifs soient réduits à l'alternative cruelle de mériter une partie des reproches qu'on leur fait, ou de se résigner à mourir de faim, il applaudirait à supplier [?] à la loi qui donnerait aux juifs tout ce que l'humanité et la saine politique réclament en leur faveur; pourvu que cette loi ne leur laissât pas la facilité de l'entendre d'une manière alarmante pour les chrétiens. C'est la crainte de voir leurs possessions envahies par les juifs, et Metz

hand, the memorandum may have been merely a proposal
and the action of but a single man (the existing copy is

devenir dans peu de temps une nouvelle Jérusalem, qui, seule, a dicté
les observations du Parlement sur l'édit de 9bre et qui a fait penser
à quelques magistrats que l'intention du roy n'avoit pas été de com-
prendre les juifs de Metz. Qu'il leur soit permis de voir que la justice
et la bienfaisance du roi s'étendent sur eux comme sur toutes les nations
de la terre, dont aucune n'est exclue du bénéfice de l'édit; et que ce
grand acte, qui place le nom de Louis XVI au premier rang parmi
ceux des législateurs de l'humanité, ne cèdera point à la possiblité
d'inconvénients, qu'il est aisé de prévenir par les précautions les plus
simples ... C'est un très grand malheur pour les juifs de Metz et pour
la ville elle-même qu'on n'aît pas pensé dans le temps [à l'époque des
lettres patentes de 1632] à rendre l'usure inexcusable, on avait eu le
droit de la poursuivre et de la proscrire, cette habitude seroit aujourd'hui
déracinée. Les juifs profitant de la liberté de se livrer au commerce, et
portant dans cette profession la sobriété et l'économie qui leur sont
propres, la ville de Metz eût reconquis par eux les avantages que sa
position tend à lui assurer et dont il est avéré qu'elle ne profite pas.
On commettra la même faute toutes les fois qu'on envisagera que le
moment présent et qu'on aura [été] plus touché des clameurs de l'envie,
qui cherche à éloigner la concurence, qu'animé du désir de mettre les
homes en valeur, en excitant parmi eux une émulation utile à la
société. L'état des juifs est, comme on le voit, très avantageux du
côté de la religion, et très déplorable relativement à tout le reste. Ils
ont une synagogue ouverte, ils forment une communauté reconnue,
mais ils sont accablés de charges pécuniaires, privés de la culture de la
terre, exclus cles arts, réduits à l' impossibilité de faire le commerce en
gros, et infiniment gênés dans celui des détails, en égard aux objets
qu'il peut embrasser et à la manière de l'exercer ... Faisons enfin des
lois qu'on puisse observer, s'est dit le législateur, frappé des maux
qu'entraîne nécessairement la violation de celles de la nature. Loin
de vouloir ni l'autoriser, ni même la souffrir, Louis XVI a déclaré
solennellement qu'il n'était pas en son pouvoir de refuser à des hommes
l'usage du droit naturel; les deux mots du préambule de l'édit de
Novembre 1787 en développent tout le système et ne permettent pas
de se méprendre sur l'application qu'il faut en faire aux juifs comme aux
mahométans, comme aux calvinistes et à tous ceux qui ne professent
pas la Religion dominante ... Pourquoi l'action du droit naturel
que le roi ne veut plus arrêter, seroit-elle encore suspendue relativement aux juifs de Metz? ils ont d'anciennes concessions. Est-ce un
motif pour que leur condition devienne plus mauvaise?" BmMetz,
ms. 1108–25–II.

It is very possible that Roederer himself, who organized the contest
of the Metz Academy on Jews, was the author of this memorandum on
Protestants and Jews. In fact, another version of the memorandum is

unsigned, and no discussions on the Jews mentioned are in the Parliamentary records). In the same period the Metz Parliament acted with such intolerance toward the Jews in connection with their expulsion from the seigniory of Bourscheidt and its three component villages (Bourscheidt, Saint-Jean, and Coustzerode), which were incorporated into the Kingdom in 1661. Jews had lived in these villages for many generations. They had been allowed to maintain a synagogue, and they had paid their share of the special taxes imposed upon the Metz Jews. In 1780 the seignior of Burscheidt began ousting the Jews from his seigniory; on January 7, 1788, the Metz Parliament rejected a Jewish appeal. The Jews then declared in a memorandum that, strangely, this decision was taken by the Parliament at the time of prevailing liberal sentiments professing a concern for the improvement of the Jews' lot; that the decision was contrary to the principles of French jurisprudence;

to be found in Roederer's private family archives (AN, 29 AP3). Robert Anchel mistook this document as a memorandum written by a Jew (*Les Juifs de France* (Paris, 1946), p. 233), which is impossible because of some very strongly worded anti-Jewish sentences. The Edict of November 1787 on Protestants greatly influenced the attitude towards Jews in Southwestern France (Z. Szajkowski, *op. cit.*, see note 47), in Nîmes and Avignon et Comtat Venaissin (P. Angeras, *L'Edit de 1787 et son application dans la sénéchaussée de Nîmes* (Nîmes, 1925), pp. 161–178; H. Chobaut, "Les Juifs d'Avignon et du Comtat et la Révolution française," *Revue des Etudes juives*, vol. CI (1937), pp. 38–40). Later, in 1787, the anonymous author of a pamphlet in favor of Protestants wrote that the status of Jews was better than of Protestants:

"Je sais que votre sort pourrait etre plus doux
"Et que même les Juifs sont mieux traitéz que vous;
"Les temples qu'on leur laisse élever en grand nombre,
"De leur Sion au moins leur retracent quelque ombre."

Essai sur la tolérance des non-Catholiques en France. Poème adressé à MM. les Députés des Trois Ordres ([Bordeaux?,] 1789), p. 12. It is worth while to mention a much later pamphlet in defense of Protestants and Jews: B. D . . . t, *La Boîte à perrette des Protestants et des Israëlites* [Paris, 1815], 8 p. (BN, Ld [176] 753.)

and that the seignior of Burscheidt fought the Jews because he was jealous of the protection accorded them by the King himself.[63]

V. The Jewish Problem in the Alsatian Provincial Assembly

The Jewish problem in the Provincial Assembly of Alsace,[64] evoked unanimous and open anti-Jewish reactions. F. Hell, C. W. de Broglie, J. A. Pflieger, and E. F. J. Schwendt, who together with J. B. Rewbell later led the fight against the Act of Jewish Emancipation in the National Assembly, were all members of the Provincial Assembly of Alsace. The Alsatian Intermediary Commission (*Commission Intermédiaire*) appointed a special committee to prepare a proposal of a new statute for the Alsatian Jews, and F. Hell became president of this committee. Hell was the man responsible for the conflict between the Jewish creditors and their Christian debtors (he organized the counterfeiting of receipts), and for this he had been expelled from Alsace for a time. But he again played an important part in Alsatian politics on the eve of the Revolution. Hell expressed his ideas on the Jews in his sample of Memorials of Grievances (*cahiers de doléances*). The influence of these Memorials on the Revolution was very great; many of them were concerned with the Jewish problem.[65] Although these Memorials were supposed to have mirrored the freely-expressed opinions

[63] BmMetz, ms. 1108–25.

[64] On the Alsatian Assembly see: Charles Hoffmann, *La Haute Alsace devant l'administration provinciale. I. L'Administration provinciale.* Extr. de la *Revue catholique d'Alsace* (Rixheim, 1886); *II. Les villes impériales en 1789* (Colmar, 1886).

[65] M. Liber, "Les Juifs et la convocation des Etats Généraux (1789)." *Revue des Etudes Juives*, vol. LXIII, pp. 185–210, LXIV, pp. 89–108, 244–277 (1912).

of the people, many individuals and groups attempted to influence their contents by publishing sample proposals and even entire texts of grievances to be included in the *cahiers*.[66] The Alsatian Intermediary Commission as well as other groups published similar samples, but no mention was made in them of the Jewish problem.[67] Hell, in his sample dated February 1789 (hitherto unmentioned by the historians), did propose the text of grievances on the Jews.[68] His proposals regarding the Jews are similar to

[66] Two such patterns of Lorraine did not mention the Jewish problem. [J.-S.-N. Anthoine,] *Essai sur les Assemblées . . . la rédaction des Cahiers* (Paris, 1789). 16 pp. BN, Lb[39] 1395; P. Lesprand, "Quelques mots sur les cahiers de doléances des communes en 1789," *Jahr-Buch der Gesel-schaft für lothringische Geschichte und Altertumskunde*, vol. XVIII (Metz, 1906), p. 167; L. Jêrome, *Les Elections et les cahiers du clergé lorrain* (Paris-Nancy, 1899), p. 18.

[67] *Avis adressé aux communautés de l'Alsace* par la Commission inter-médiaire provinciale (Sl, [25 février 1789]). 8 pp. (8°). AN, BA-11; *Instructions, ou si l'on veut, cahier de l'Assemblée du bailliage de . . . 28. Février 1789* (Sl, nd). 32 pp. Bibliothèque municipale de Strasbourg.

[68] "Comme tout ce qui émane de l'autorité royale prouve combien vivement le Roi est animé du désir des no maux [?], *La chicane et l'usure*: lui dire franchement, que s'il ne nous met pas à couvert de ces deux fléaux, sa Majesté n'aura rien fait pour nous & supplier le Roi d'ordon-ner que par des juges ou jurisconsultes que la province choisira, il sera fait un règlement qui nous assure ce bonheur par une très grande réforme dans l'administration de la justice & par des précautions qui rendent l'usure impossible & qui forcent de malheureux étrangers [Juifs], admis parmi nous à devenir laborieux, utiles & honnêtes & qui les mettent à même de se soutenir sans bassesse & de participer à la félicité publique que le Roi destine à tous ses sujets. Que la loi la plus nécessaire & celle que nous supplions Sa Majesté avec le plus d'instances de nous accorder, est celle de déclarer nulle toute obliga-tion qu'un habitant de la classe du peuple aura contractée, à quelque titre que ce puisse être, au profit des chrétiens ou juifs, pour une somme au-dessus de 20 liv. sans qu'il aît été autorisé par délibération de sept de ses plus proches parens, faite sans frais devant la Municipalité de la demeure du débiteur, jointe au titre obligatoire qui sera enregistré dans le mois au greffe de la dite Municipalité, aussi sous peine de nullité contre le créancier qui aura différé cet enregistrement plus longtemps. Que les juifs contribueront à toutes les impositions comme nous; qu'ils n'auront plus de rôles particuliers; qu'ils ne feront plus corps; qu'ils n'auront plus de syndics, ni agens, ni d'autres tribunaux

the proposals of the committee on the Jewish problem headed by Hell himself. At the end of September 1788, the committee presented its report as well as a letter of explanation to the Third Bureau (*Bureau du Bien Public*) of the Intermediary Comimssion.

The report is a mixture of some pity for the Jews and at the same time of disgust for them: "All our chronicles are full of [anti-Jewish] persecutions ... Happy are the kingdoms that had never had Jews amongst them! But shall we be so brutal as to expel them after having received them? Do they not have the right to request the protection of the laws, the very same laws which had permitted them to settle amongst us? Let us only limit their harmful activities ...", etc.[69] On September 20, 1788, the Inter-

que les nôtres; qu'ils ne pourront se marier que sur la permission des Etats Provinciaux, permission qui sera gratuite & qui ne pourra être accordée que dans les cas qui seront exprimés par le règlement qui sera fait par les dits Etats provinciaux." [Hell, Plan d'un cahier (Sl Fév. 1789.] 9 pp. (4°). AN, BA–11. Hell's pattern was strongly attacked by the Minister of War as a document without any value, as a result of intrigues. The Minister wrote that, in general, such pattern should not be published. This attack on Hell had to do with his tendency to obtain more provincial autonomy for Alsace. AN, Ba–11, doc. 19.

[69] "Messieurs, il n'y a, à la fois, pas d'objet plus triste et plus intéressant dans nos délibérations, que l'Etat des juifs. Cette nation proscrite et errante, forcée de vivre parmi les hommes dont elle se sépare par sa religion, par ses lois, sa langue, ses meurs et ses usages, a toujours été l'objet de notre mépris, elle semble porter sur son front sa sentence inéffaçable de réprobation, toutes nos annales sont remplies des persécutions, des injustices, des cruautés qu'on leur a fait essuyer; de siècle en siècle et dans tous les Etats, on[ne] leur a supposé avoir commis des crimes, que pour en faire une boucherie cruelle pour diminuer leur population qui s'augmentait trop, et inquiétait les Etats. Cependant, elle existe encore, et elle est répandue partout. Corrompue dans ses principes, dans son genre de vie, infâme par ses usures, et son industrie, on ne peut la connaître sans désirer d'en être éloigné. Heureux les Etats qu'n'ont jamais eu de juifs dans leur sein! mais sera-t-on assez cruel pour les chasser, après les avoir reçus? n'ont-ils pas le droit de réclamer des lois sous la foi desquelles ils se sont établis parmi nous? bornons-nous à mettre des obstacles aux maux de tout genre qu'ils nous causent. C'est l'objet des différents règlements du Roi; mais

mediary Commission inquired concerning the opinions of
the local administrations on the various projects, including
the report on the Jews.[70]

The proposal asserted that no organized groups with
autonomous offices and laws — such as the Jewish Community Councils should be tolerated;[71] the Jews were earning a living only by charging usurious rates on loans; they
were not yet prepared to undertake agricultural work
because they were victims of their numerous religious
holidays;[72] etc. According to the proposal, Jews were to

ils ont sçu jusqu'à présent les éluder, c'est pourquoi, Messieurs, les
sindics Provinciaux nous communiquent leurs sages réflexions auxquelles le Bureau du bien public ajoute quelques observations ... Si
quelque chose est capable d'opérer une révolution à leur égard, c'est
le règlement tel que Messieurs les sindics provinciaux les proposent;
par ces moyens on leur rendra utiles et ils pourront devenir meilleurs.
Si contre notre attente, ce dernier Règlement ne devait pas avoir les
effets qu'on peut et doit en espérer, on serait tenté de croire que les
violences qu'ils ont ci-devant essuyées de la part de nos pères, sont des
maux qu'ils s'attireront encore et que nos descendants se verront
obligés de les chasser ou de les détruire." AdBR, C 670.

[70] We could not locate the original of the project among the archives
of the Intermediary Commission in both Departmental Archives of
Alsace. But copies of the project were sent to local authorities and we
found one such copy in the City Archives of Strasbourg (AA 2389).
This copy of the project ("Projet de Règlement sur les Juifs d'Alsace")
was sent together with a letter dated Sept. 25, 1788, and signed by Hell.

[71] On the Jewish aspect of autonomous groups and national unity
during the Revolution see: Kurt Stillschweig, "Die Judenemanzipation
im Licht des französischen Nationsbegriffs." *Monatschrift für Geschichte
und Wissenschaft des Judentums*, vol. LXXXI (1937), pp. 457–478.

It is worth while to mention a Carpentras proposal of 1789 that Jews
should be treated as individual members of the Jewish community
and not as a separate sect. An exception should be made only for
religious problems: "Les Membres de cette Congrégation [juive], à
l'exception de ce qui regarde la religion, ne seront réputés que comme
individus, & non comme formant une société." *Préliminaire d'un
projet d'arrangement* [de la communauté juive de Carpentras] [Car-
pentras, 1789,] p. 1.

[72] In 1781, Strasbourg opposed any law allowing Jews to become
peasants because they would force the Christian peasants to sell their
lands and to work for the Jews (AmStrasbourg, AA 2393). Christian
peasants, too, lost much valuable time because of religious holidays

be afforded the opportunity of plying some productive and honest trades. It was the purpose of this proposal to make certain that the Letters Patent of July 10, 1784, would be enforced, while some articles of these Letters were even to be strengthened by new anti-Jewish regulations; the Jews were to be allowed to form only 1/10 or 1/8 of the total population of the cities and villages where they were permitted to reside; where the number of Jews exceeded these fractions, marriages were to be prohibited until the number of Jews decreased to the prescribed 1/10 or 1/8; the Jewish Sabbath was to be observed on Sunday; the autonomous Jewish Community Councils were to be abolished; any trade on credit between Jews and Christians was to be prohibited; etc. The proposal noted that Jews would not be permitted to join the trade guilds, but that in the villages they would still be able to work in various home trades without belonging to the appropriate guilds. The Third Bureau made a few new proposals (fines imposed on poor Jews were to be paid by the Jewish Community Councils and Jews under 25 years of age were not to be granted permission to marry). The proposal considered the advisability of granting to the King alone the right to expel Jews, thus making them more secure and inducing them to take up agricultural work. The Third Bureau however, remarked that the peasants would undoubtedly assail the Jews attempting to work in the fields.[73]

This proposal foresaw strong anti-Jewish regulations until then unknown in the jurisprudence of Alsace. Had the projected laws been accepted and enforced, the Alsatian

(J. B. Ravold, *L'Ancien régime dans le canton de Gerbéwiller, et la Révolution* (Lunéville, 1881), p. 26). As late as on June 1, 1810, Beving, the Prefect of Rhin-et-Moselle warned that peasants were sacrificing the interest of the agriculture in favor of an exaggerated piety, that they deserted the fields and went away to look for miracles. AN, F⁷ 8068.

[73] AdBR, C 670.

Jews would have found their position truly precarious. They would have been driven forcibly to become the poorest class of Alsatian inhabitants, deprived of any and all social, political, and religious rights. With the abolition of the Jewish Community Councils, the Jews would not have been in a position even to appeal to the King.

The Intermediary Commission of Lorraine likewise discussed the Jewish problem. On October 25, 1788, the Commission of Sarreguemines requested that the Letters of July 10, 1784, be applied in Lorraine, and that, in particular, the number of Jews in the province be restricted. On October 21, 1788, the Commission of Thionville similarly requested anti-Jewish measures.[74]

It is worthwhile to analyze the financial policy of the Intermediary Commission of Alsace toward the Jews. At first the Commission enforced the old regulations. In instructions dated August 30, 1788, the Commission ordered the collection of the special "protection toll" imposed upon Jews.[75] According to the 1744 order of the Intendant de Vanolles (renewed by the Council of State on March 4, 1747), the amount of communal taxes (*charges au soulagement de communautés*) paid by the Jews was to have been proportioned according to the special duty paid by each Jew to the King (*capitation*). For every 20 sols *capitation*, 25 sols were to be paid for community taxes in peacetime and 50 sols were to be paid in times of war, i. e. if a Jew paid, say, 3 pounds *capitation* to the King, he was required to pay 3 pounds 15 sols in community taxes in peacetime and 7 pounds 10 sols in wartime. But the same order of de Vanolles compensated the Jews by exempting them from paying other special duties (housing of soldiers,

<hr>

[74] AdM, C 897, 899.

[75] *Administration provinciale d'Alsace. Instruction* [30 août 1788] (Sl, nd). 4 pp. (fol.) BuStg.

service duties, etc.)[76] Yet the Intermediary Commission ordered the Jews to pay an additional tax of 6363 pounds 9 sols for road repairs. On July 18, 1788, the Jews appealed to the King, explaining that their economic situation was poor, most of their possessions consisting of debts owed them by peasants who refused to repay them. On July 27, 1788, the Jewish appeal was transmitted from Paris to the Alsace Intermediary Commission. Here it was considered by a committee presided over by Schwendt (who later fought the Act of Jewish Emancipation). On August 28, 1788, the Commission informed Paris that not only the Jews, but intellectuals and other merchants as well protested against the service duty imposed on them. Indeed, it would be difficult to consider this particular case as an expression of a special anti-Jewish policy. The King's Council rejected the Jewish plea. On October 14, 1788, the Jews appealed once again.[77]

[76] *Extrait des registres du Conseil d'Etat du Roi. Du 4 Mars 1747* (Sl, nd). Affiche. AN, C 12–9, p. 2.

[77] AdBR, C 686. After the outbreak of the Revolution the Alsatian Jews requested that they be freed from paying 25,000 pounds of various taxes for 1789 because many Jews had been ruined during the pogroms of 1789. The Finance-Minister J. Necker was in favor of granting the Jewish request (AdBR, C 752, pp. 149–150, 172). In 1791, Jews protested against paying taxes because they had already paid a tax especially imposed before the Revolution on Jews. On June 11, 1791, the *Directoire* of the Lower Rhine ordered them to pay only the balance (*Délibération du Directoire du Département du Bas-Rhin. Du Samedi onzième du mois de juin 1791* (Sl, nd). 4 pp. (4°). BN, LK⁴ 731, I, 15). This meant that in paying taxes Jews were on a par with all other citizens. However, already earlier the Intermediary Commission tried to include the Jews in the general tax-system. The Commission decided that Jews should not pay separately the 7,582 pounds of the tax *vingtième d'industrie*, but that they should be inscribed together with all other citizens on the supplementary lists for this tax. The Council of State decided however, that this tax should be paid by the Jews according to the old rule, i. e. separately as a group, because the supplementary lists would comprise only the tax *vingtième* on real-estate and not industry. Accordingly, on June 1, 1790, the Intermediary Commission ordered that, except for this tax the Jews should

The Jews certainly knew of the new anti-Jewish proposal
of the Intermediary Commission and of the anti-Jewish
grievances in the *cahiers*. On April 15, 1789, Cerfberr
wrote about it in a memorandum to the Minister of War,
P. de Puységur. In this document Cerfberr asked permission to assemble Jewish representatives of Alsace, Metz,
and Lorraine to discuss the Jewish question and to send
one or a few deputies to the *Etats-Généraux* to plead for
the rights of the Jews. Such a permit was granted to him
in May of 1789.[78] We know very little about this Jewish
assembly itself, except about the *cahier* prepared by the
Jews. In another memorandum Cerfberr wrote that the
Jews should be in a position to aid considerably in securing
the future of France, particularly through trade with the
North.[79]

be included in the general tax-system. *Extrait du Procès-verbal des
Séances de la Commission intermédiaire provinciale d'Alsace, du premier
Juin 1790* (Sl, nd). 3 pp. (4°). BuStg.

After the Emancipation, on Nov. 2, 1792, the *Directoire* of Lower
Rhine published an order that practically aimed at abolishing the
financial system of the Jewish Communities: except for the special
Jewish tax to cover the debts of the former Jewish Communities, no
Jew was to be forced to pay any special tax for the Jewish Community,
the Rabbi, etc. *Délibération du Directoire du Département du Bas-
Rhin du 2 Novembre 1792* ... (Strasbourg, sd).

[78] "Les juifs sollicitent un arrêt du Conseil qui leur ordonne de nommer des députés pour venir discuter conjointement avec moi les intérêts
de la Nation juive et prier un ou plusieurs députés aux Etats-Généraux
de défendre les droits qui sont ceux de l'humanité opprimée." AN,
B–A, 11.

The Sephardic Jews of Paris, too, asked permission to assemble and
send their *cahier*: Ch.-L. Chassin, *Les Elections et les cahier de Paris
en 1789* (Paris, 1888), pp. 151–152.

[79] "Voici d'ailleurs quels sont ses droits pour paraître aux Etats
Généraux. I°) La Nation juive des trois provinces comprend environ
5.000 familles: cette classe d'hommes dont on ne s'est point occupé,
dans les convocations baillagères, est assez considérable pour ne pas
se voir oubliée. 2°) Les juifs qui la forment, sont régnicoles français,
sujets du Roi, établis en France depuis longtems sous la protection de
l'autorité souveraine qui leur a conservé leurs rites et leur juridiction
particulière ... 3°) La différence de religion ne peut être un motif

The Jews complained that they were not permitted to take part in local assemblies. On March 6, 1789, Rolland, Police Chief of Etain (Lorraine) inquired in a report to Paris whether Jews were to be permitted to participate in the assemblies. The reply from Paris was strictly in the negative.[80]

pour exclure de l'assemblée des sujets du roy soumis aux charges publiques; puisque la contribution dont toutes les classes de citoyens sont tenus, n'a rien de commun avec leur dogme. 4°) La loi nouvelle infiniment sage, concernant les non-catholiques, bénéficie à toutes les sectes étrangères à la catholicité: et a pour principal object, en leur assurant un état en France, de les faire concourir à la prospérité du royaume. 5°) La nation juive est en position de rendre des services considérables à l'état; c'est elle qui le plus souvent chargée de la fourniture des armées et de celle de l'intérieur du Royaume, s'est portée toujours avec un zèle infatigable à seconder les vues du Gouvernement ... Si cette nation industérieuse parvient à faire entendre sa voix aux Etats généraux, elle fera ses efforts pour contribuer au bien public et étendre, surtout vers le Nord, les rapports de commerce de la France. Enfin, pour tâcher de concilier toutes les convenances et ne point blesser les préjugés, la Nation juive demande à être représentée par un ou plusieurs des Députés aux Etats généraux choisis par elle: elle donnera à ces représentants les autorisations nécessaires pour qu'ils puissent au nom de tous les juifs regnicoles, concourir à la prospérité générale de l'Etat." "Mémoire pour la nation Juive régnicole établie dans les Généralités de Metz, d'Alsace et de Lorraine." AN, B-A-I, 11, 52.

[80] "Nous avons sept à huit juifs nés en France, âgés, domiciliés ici, et payant impositions. Ont-ils droit d'assister aux assemblées en vertu de l'art. 25 [du règlement du 24 Janvier 1789]? Il semble que non; parce que leur puissance est subordonnée aux lois qui ne les tolèrent en cette province que comme étrangers; qu'ils ont un rôle d'imposition particulier entre eux pour toute la province, et ne sont pas compris dans le rôle de nos impositions; qu'on ne les regarde pas comme bourgeois, qu'ils ne participent ni aux bénéfices, ni aux charges, et ne paraissent jamais aux assemblées de ville. Cependant, on nous objecte que, quoiqu'ils n'eussent jamais payé d'industrie, la Chambre des Comptes les a, l'année dernière et la présente, compris dans la liste des corps sujets à cette imposition et qu'ils paient. Cette circonstance peut-elle faire décider en leur faveur?" [Réponse de Paris]: "Je pense, comme vous, que les juifs ne doivent pas être convoqués, ni conséquemment admis aux assemblées." AN, B-A-I, 19.

It should be noted that the Sephardic and Avignon Jews of Bordeaux and Saint-Esprit-lès-Bayonne (Southwestern France) were permitted

Until the very last days preceding the outbreak of the Revolution, the Jews were an oppressed, barely tolerated group. All liberal voices favoring the Jews did not achieve any practical improvement in their status. It took a far more important event to accomplish this — the Revolution of 1789.

to participate in the assemblies. But this happened after a strong fight between the Jews and the local anti-Jewish elements. In this case Paris declared that the Jews should be granted the right to hold their own assemblies and send their delegates to the general assemblies of electors. AN, Ba 22, 80 B III–146, C24, C-II–3; Archives départementales de la Gironde, Procès-verbeaux de la Nation Juive, 1788–89; *Protestantion, en forme de lettre des nobles cohens, aux gentilshommes soi-disant les Nobles de la Sénéchaussée de Bordeaux, induement assemblés le 10 Février 1789* (Bordeaux, 1 mars 1789), 8 p.; T. Malvezin, *Histoire des Juifs à Bordeaux* (Bordeaux, 1875), pp. 254–55; Michel Lhéritier, *La Révolution à Bordeaux*, vol. I (Paris, 1942), p. 213; *Cahier général des remontrances, plaintes et demandes du Tiers Etat de la sénéchausée d'Albret au siège de Tartas, réduit* . . . (Sl, nd).

THE DISCUSSION AND STRUGGLE OVER JEWISH EMANCIPATION IN ALSACE IN THE EARLY YEARS OF THE FRENCH REVOLUTION

ANY statement that during the French Revolution the Jews of Paris, the Sephardic Jews of the Southwest, or the Comtadin Jews of the former Papal provinces were persecuted just because they were Jews, could be strongly and easily opposed and dismissed. But there is no doubt that in many instances Jews were persecuted as such in both parts of Alsace, in Metz, and in Lorraine; they were persecuted even by the revolutionary elements. Thousands of cases of mistreatment of Jews can be cited from archival and published sources. Here are some of them:

The Alsatian Jews complained that they were not given the opportunity to share in the distribution of communal property (*biens communaux*).[1] At the request of the departmental *Directoire* the city of Huningue (Lower Rhine) collected from eighty communities petitions against the emancipation of the Jews.[2] In Issenheim armed patrols entered Jewish houses and extinguished the lights, thus forcing the Jews to go to bed early. In Bollviller the Jews were not allowed to leave their houses at night; the roofs and windows of Jewish houses were broken; Jews were arbitrarily arrested and fined by the Mayor. On April 29, 1790, at the request of the Alsatian Jewish leader Marx Berr, the Alsatian *Commission intermédiaire* ordered the Bollwiller Mayor to stop persecuting Jews.[3] The Lower Rhine *Direc-*

---

[1] Z. Szajkowski, "Jewish Participation in the Sale of National Property during the French Revolution," *Jewish Social Studies*, XIV (1952), 311-12.

[2] City Archives of Strasbourg II-80; R. Anchel, *Napoléon et les Juifs* (Paris, 1928), p. 11.

[3] Veron-Réville, *Histoire de la Révolution française dans le département du Haut-Rhin* (Colmar, 1865), p. 45; AdHR[=Archives départmentales, Haut-Rhin], C 1597.

Originally published in *Historia Judaica*, vol. XVII (1955).

toire attacked the Mayor of Bischeim for assigning exclusively to Jewish houses soldiers who had been sent to prevent a pogrom in the town.[4] On April 23, 1790, the Christians of Bergheim petitioned the National Assembly against the emancipation of the Jews, requesting that they be deported to commercial centers to live among their Sephardic coreligionists.[5] On May 8, 1790, the city of Molsheim stated that the Jews wrote their petition for emancipation "in a moment of folly."[6] The author of a Nancy pamphlet against the acceptance of Jews by the National Guard wrote that to defend Jews was to prostitute a writer's talent.[7]

A large number of Strasbourg people petitioned the King to refuse to sign the Law of September 27, 1791 granting citizenship to the Jews.[8] One Alsatian counter-Revolutionary pamphleteer wrote in 1792: "The Jews replace the bourgeois."[9] During the elections in Lixheim (Meurthe) on Novembre 25, 1792, Jews were chased out of the church where the election was held because they refused to act against their religious convictions and did not uncover their heads.[10] In a petition dated April 13, 1793, demanding the expulsion of the Jews, the Colmar

---

[4] *Avis . . . Délibération du Directoire du département du Bas-Rhin. Du lundi 21 mai 1792* (Strasbourg, 1792). 4 pp. (4°). Suzanne Salomon Cerf of Metz rented her house to Abraham Gringuelot until July 3, 1793. Then, against her will and without any formalities, city officials rented the house to six families. Their contention was that she was Jewish and wanted to rent the house only to Jews. On September 23, 1795, the *Directoire* expelled the six illegal tenants. *Extrait des registres des délibérations du départment de la Moselle . . . du 1 vendémiaire, l'an 4 . . .* (Metz, 1795), placard.

[5] AN[=Archives Nationales, Paris], DIX-IV-LVI (1638).

[6] *Ibid.*

[7] *Lettre d'un citoyen, aux gardes-citoyens de la ville de Nancy, en réponse à la question: Les Juifs doivent—ils être admis dans la Milice Nationale?* (no place and no date given), 6 pp., p. 1 (Nancy Library, 702013-6).

[8] AN, BB-16-622.

[9] *Je vous dirai vos vérités* (no pl., no date), p. 28.

[10] A. Troux, *La Vie politique dans le département de la Meurthe d'août 1792 à Octobre 1795*, I (Nancy, 1936), 138-39. In Lixheim (Lorraine) anti-Jewish feeling was so violent that Jewish creditors were afraid to collect the debts owed to them by Christians, and because of this they were granted a delay in paying their tax. J. Godechot, "Les Juifs de Nancy de 1789 à 1795," *REJ*[=*Revue des Etudes Juives*], LXXXVI (1928), 8.

District accused the Jews of discrediting the *assignats* (paper-money) and stated that the Jewish leader Cerfberr prepared warehouses full of food for the invading armies from Germany and that "offers were made by Jews to the Pope adverse to our liberty," etc.[11] In the eyes of the brand new Alsatian revolutionaries the Jews were a lazy people, because they observed the Sabbath. During a wheat crisis, when the peasants were short of help for the harvest, the Strasbourg District decided to send to help them "especially those of Moses' religion, who live in laziness."[12]

Jews were forced to pay higher taxes and to make larger revolutionary contributions than Christians. In some areas, "patriotic" contributions were imposed only on Jews, and frequently they refused to pay because they did not have enough money.[13] On the other hand, the same thing happened after the Terror, e.g., in 1796 in Jungholtz, Bollwiller, Soultz, and Rimbach. In Rimbach on October 21, 1796, thirty-two Jews proved that even poor Jews were taxed for large sums. This compelled the authorities to assess the richest Christian family three-quarters of the total local taxes.[14] On September 4 and 25, 1790, the city of Strasbourg restricted the rights of Jewish peddlers and ordered gatherings of Jews in the market to be dispersed.[15] In August, 1793, the City Council brutally scattered Jewish merchants found on the *Poële des pelletiers*. Eighteen Jews protested against such ruthlessness, which could only reinforce anti-Jewish feelings, but their protest was rejected. The Mayor arrested twenty-three Jews and held them in

---

[11] ". . . des offres faites par les Juifs au Pape contre notre liberté." AdHR, L645.

[12] Henry Brunschwig, *Les Subsistances à Strasbourg pendant les premières années de la Révolution française* (Strasbourg, 1932), pp. 90-91.

[13] Z. Szajkowski, *Poverty and Social Welfare among French Jews* (1800-1880) (New York, 1954), pp. 6-7.

[14] M. Ginsburger, *Histoire de la communauté israélite de Soultz* (Strasbourg, 1939), pp. 40-41.

[15] *Proclamation de par les Maire et officiers municipaux de la ville de Strasbourg* [4 septembre 1790]. *Placard; Proclamation de par les Maire et officiers municipaux*, Strasbourg, 25 septembre 1790. Placard; *Réimpression de l'ancien Moniteur*, VI, 83.

prison for 65 days. Two of them, Abraham Schwartz of Westhoffen and Samuel Weyl of Westhausen, later asked for compensation of 800 and 700 pounds respectively.[16]

The Jews continuously protested against the persecution and made strong demands for protection.[17] On April 16, 1790, the National Assembly ordered that the Alsatian Jews be protected. On April 9, 1790, the Alsatian Jewish leader Marx Berr [Cerfberr], a son of Cerfberr de Medélsheim, called on the Strasbourg Mayor for help. On November 1, 1794, the National Assembly again discussed and granted an Alsatian Jewish request for protection.[18] At the end of 1794 the Jews of Lower Rhine stated in a petition to the National Assembly that enemies of the Republic in their department were treated much better than Jews; they declared that taxes were more equitably distributed in countries where slavery was practiced than in Alsace; that Jews were still being chased out of Strasbourg, and so forth. The petition concluded with these words: "Long live the National Convention, which should establish the empire on a basis of liberty and equality."[19]

Essentially, the Christian population and even the Jacobins desired to maintain the anti-Jewish restrictions, of the pre-Revolutionary days, especially the prohibition against the Jews taking up free residence. The Nancy Bishop, A.L.H. de la Fare, well known for his fight against Jewish emancipation, stated in 1790 that the Jews did not

[16] AdBR[=Archives départementales du Bas-Rhin], L-I-1222; AdHR, L123.

[17] Individual Jews protested against the delay in granting citizenship to the Jews, e.g., the Worms brothers of Lorraine, who, as early as 1787, were granted all rights as a reward for their services to the army. AN, C82-817/12(43).

[18] Réimpression de l'ancien Moniteur, IV, 133; R. Reuss, L'Alsace pendant la Révolution, II (Paris, 1894), 25-26; Opinion de M. le Comte Stanislas de Clermont-Tonnerre, relativement aux persécutions qui menacent les Juifs (no date, no place), 4 pp.; Extrait du registre des arrêtés du Comité Législation. Séance du 11 brumaire, l'an troisième . . . (Strasbourg, 1795), 2 pp.; M. et E. Ginsburger, "Contribution à l'histoire des Juifs d'Alsace pendant la Terreur," REJ, XLVII (1903), 297-98.

[19] Copie de la pétition par plusieurs citoyens du Bas-Rhin, à la Convention Nationale (avec: Extrait du registre des arrêtés du Comité de Législation lu 1 novembre 1794) (Colmar, 1794), 7 pp. (Colmar Library B63).

monopolize any trades that were against the people's interests. The main reproach made against Jews was their settlement all over the province, their purchases of houses and land, and their new privileges which had not been granted to them by the old regime.[20] Out of forty-three cases of anti-Jewish actions in the Lower Rhine in 1790-1794, cited by the historian Rod. Reuss, twenty-two were against Jews who desired to take up new residences, trades, etc.[21] In 1790, a Jew of Wintzenheim received protection from the army against the bourgeois who wanted to expel him from the city. Thionville requested the expulsion of the Jew Mayer Levy.[22] On September 25, 1790, the district of Sarreguemines proposed to the Metz district action to maintain the old anti-Jewish restrictions.[23] The Jewish market-merchants Marix Wolf and Mathias Caen, in their petition to the Agricultural Committee of the National Assembly of December 10, 1790, complained that for the past year they had been forced to pay 15 sols per day for limited permission to sell their merchandise in Besançon. Because they sold it at a cheaper price than the local Christian merchants, the latter obtained an order forbidding their trade altogether.[24]

On July 20, 1790 the National Assembly abolished the protection and residence tax imposed on Jews,[25] thus giving them the right of free residence. Yet at the end of September, 1789, Colmar tried to expel the Jews. On the other hand,

---

[20] [A. L. H. de la Fare], *Opinion de M. l'Evêque de Nancy, député de Lorraine, sur l'admissibilité des Juifs à la plenitude de l'état civil, et des droits le citoyens actifs* (Paris, 1790), p. 12.

[21] R. Reuss, "L'Antisémitisme dans le Bas-Rhin pendant la Révolution," *REJ*, LXVIII (1914), 247.

[22] J. Liblin, "Chronique du serrurier Dominique Schmutz de Colmar," *Revue d'Alsace*, XXIV (1874), 389-90; N. Dorvaux et P. Lespraud, "Cahiers de doléances . . . de Thionville èn 1789," *Annuaire de la Société d'histoire et d'archéologie*, XXXI (1922), 555.

[23] Archives départementales de la Moselle, L532.

[24] Ch. Schmidt et F. Gerbaux, *Procès-verbaux des comités d'agriculture et de commerce . . .*, I (Paris, 1896), 703.

[25] *Lettres patentes de Roi, sur de Décret de l'Assemblée Nationale, du 20 juillet dernier* [1790], *portant suppression des droits d'habitation, de protection, de tolérance et de redevances semblables sur les Juifs. Données à Saint-Cloud le 7 août 1790. Transcrites en Parlement, le 21 du même mois* (Metz, 1790), 3 pp.

a Christian innkeeper, Jacques Gretschar, stated then that he would kill anybody trying to expel his Jewish lodgers. On April 25, 1791, Colmar protested even against the Jews' taking up residence in the city's suburbs.[26] On September 21, 1790, the Strasbourg district declared that the city of Bischeim had no legal right to bar Jews. On December 7, the district reproached the city of Mutzig for demanding a residence tax from a Jew. But on December 11 the same district stated that since the National Assembly had not yet come to any decision on the status of the Jews, the city of Lingolsheim had the right to refuse to permit new Jews to establish themselves there.[27]

Strasbourg petitioned the National Assembly to expel Cerfberr and other Jews who had moved in before 1789 against the city's will.[28] On February 1, 1793, a Jew paid to the city of Soultz 66 pounds in silver as a residence tax. No Jew was allowed to stay overnight in Rouffach. In Mutzig and Langensoultzbach Jews were asked to pay special residence taxes. In Gottershausen Jews had to pay a special toll to pass through the village with a funeral procession. In Bouxwiller they still paid a special tax for the ritual slaughtering of cattle. In Bollwiller, Jews continued to pay a special tax for the poor Christians.[29] The Jacobin Clubs

---

[26] City Archives of Colmar, B63; *Très-humble et très-respectueuse Adresse à l'Assemblée Nationale, exprimant le voeu de la commune de Colmar* [le 25 avril 1790], (Colmar, 1790), 4 pp. Even at the beginning of the First Empire Jews were not allowed to reside in Colmar itself, but only in the neighboring villages of Wintzenheim and Hofbourg. Edmond Compagnac, "D'une rive à l'autre du Rhin en 1793," *Annales. révolutionnaires*, XI (1919), 554.

[27] AdBR, L-1-825, L-6-85; AdHR, L645.

[28] *Très-humble et très-respectueuse adresse que présente à l'Assemblée Nationale la Commune toute entière de la ville de Strasbourg* [Strasbourg, 1790], 14 pp. (4°) and (Paris, 1790), 20 pp. (8°). German edition: *Unterthänigste-gehorsamste Vorstellung* . . . (Strassburg, no date), 11 pp.

[29] G. Durwell, "Histoire de la ville d'Alsace et de ses environs," *Revue d'Alsace*, L (1899), 154; AdHR, L645; Reuss, *REJ*, LXVIII, 246-64; R. Anchel, *Napoléon et les Juifs* (Paris, 1928), p. 12. In 1790, Isaac Israël and Joseph Moïse of La Beuvery (near Etanges) protested against the levying of special taxes for the Church's lighting, for the Christian teacher and the priest, de Monthalon. The tax was probably paid, because in 1791 there were repeated protests from the Jews. Archives of the Metz Jewish Community, Gal 29-30-31.

of Colmar, Nancy, and Toul in 1793 requested that the
Jews be expelled, and the Nancy Club petitioned the Paris
Clubs to expel the Jews from France altogether.[30]

It should be noted that the persecutions were not
directed against Jews only, but also against non-Catholic
Christians and new residents.[31] The same is true with regard
to the economic protectionism directed against the Jews.
The brewers of Landau (Lower-Rhin) had a concession for
brewing beer; in March, 1791 they demanded compensation if they should lose their profits as a result of the law
on patents.[32] But the persecution of non-Catholic Christians and foreigners was not so well organized nor was it
carried out on as large a scale as the anti-Jewish persecution,
in which all sections of the population and all political
parties took part. It should be pointed out that, although
the Alsatian Protestants were often attacked themselves,
they nevertheless participated in the well-organized campaigns of the Catholics and even of the lay Jacobins against
the Jews.

Even most of the sincere revolutionary leaders in Alsace
and the neighboring regions were anti-Jewish, among them
Jean-Baptiste Reubell (Rewbell, 1748-1810), deputy from
Colmar and Sélestat to the National Assembly, who became
one of the leading anti-Jewish figures. A man of great
influence, energetic, and cultured, he regarded as lawful
any means that furthered his purpose and availed himself
of every legal trick to carry through his ideas. According
to Rewbell, even Robespierre himself was too timid; he,

[30] Paul Leuillot, *Les Jacobins de Colmar* (Strasbourg, 1923), pp. 67-68;
R. Pariso, *Histoire de Lorraine*, III (Paris, 1924), 240; Dr. J. F. E. Robinet,
Le mouvement religieux à Paris pendant la Révolution, I (Paris, 1896), 330.
[31] The Colmar and Seléstat Catholic clergy called for the renewal of
the 1624 restrictions against Lutherans and Calvinists and the destruction of
their churches. The people of Bassing (near Nancy) requested the expulsion
of the Anabaptists. The people of Uberkinger, Dienze, Grening, and Insming
(Lorraine) submitted petitions not only against Jews, but against Anabaptists,
too. *Archives parlementaires*, III, 5; M. J. Krug-Basse, *L'Alsace avant 1789*
(Paris-Colmar, 1876), p. 228; Charles Etienne, *Cahiers de bailliages des Généralités de Metz et de Nancy . . .*, I (Nancy, 1912), 685; II, 31-32, 119, 180,
234.
[32] Schmidt et Gerbaux, *op. cit.*, II, 121.

surely, was the strongest personality in the *Directoire*.[33] Rewbell, a lawyer and the son of a notary, grew up in the Alsatian atmosphere, where every Jew was looked upon as a usurer. He appeared before Alsatian courts in cases involving Jews and Christians. Although the Alsatian Jewish pamphleteer Michel Berr wrote on Rewbell's anti-Jewish *déclamations interessés*, we know that Rewbell disliked Switzerland because he lost a lawsuit in which he defended Jews against the *Grand Conseil* of the Berne canton.[34]

One historian has noted two phases in Rewbell's anti-Jewish activities: the one prior to July 14, 1789, and the other since the outbreak of the Revolution.[35] It seems that at the beginning of the Revolution Rewbell favored the Jews. On August 15, 1789, he wrote from Versailles to the Colmar *Commission intermédiare* that the anti-Jewish laws did not help to improve their morale, and he expressed the hope that the new laws would better the Jews' status and make of them honest working people.[36] It seems, then, that only later, and under the influence of the other Alsatian deputies, did Rewbell join the anti-Jewish circle. He had ample vigor to fight his Alsatian colleagues on many issues,[37] but not on the Jewish problem. But when the Jews were granted full citizenship on September 27, 1791, he fully respected the law and during the Terror he tried to combat the special restrictions with which a Commissioner of the *Comité de Salut Public* threatened the Alsatian Jews.[38]

[33] A. Mathiez, *Le Directoire de 11 brumaire an IV au 18 fructidor an V*, publié par Jacques Godechot (Paris, 1934), pp. 43-45.

[34] *Lettre d'un Alsacien, sur les Juifs d'Alsace, à M. Reubell* . . . (Paris, 1790), p. 6; Michel Berr, *Euloge d'Abraham Furtado* (Paris, 1917), p. 13; P.-L. Hanet-Cléry, *Mémoires*, II (Paris, 1825), 19; Jacques Godechot, *Les Commissaires aux armées sous le Directoire*, II (Paris, 1937), 15-16.

[35] Jean Braun, "La Révolution de 1848 et la Seconde République dans le Haut-Rhin," *Le Département du Haut-Rhin commémore trois siècles de vie française* (Colmar, 1948), p. 105.

[36] AdHR, C1603; *Revue d'Alsace* (1862), p. 531.

[37] On the different attitudes towards Protestants of Rewbell and the Deputy Abbot Eymar de Wachrétien, see: *Dire et opinion de M. l'Abbé d'Eymar, député d'Alsace sur l'adresse de M. les Protestants* . . . (no place, no date), pp. 3-8.

[38] Félix Schaedelin, "Reubell," *La vie en Alsace* (1928), p. 233.

According to the historian Albert Troux even thoroughgoing *Montagnards* expressed the blind hatred of the common people (*petit peuple*) toward the Jews. For some Jacobins their anti-Jewish propaganda was a means to defend themselves against accusations of being too moderate revolutionaries. This was the explanation of Rapinat's (Rewbell's brother-in-law) anti-Jewish attitude given by the historian Jacques Godechot.[39] The same thing happened with Rewbell. When he was accused, in April-June, 1791, of speculating with nationalized properties, his hatred of the Jews helped him to regain popularity among the people of Haut-Rhin.[40] But his popularity and influence gradually waned. L. M. M. Carnot charged him with helping speculators; Rewbell and his family were accused of financial speculations and of seeking the friendship of aristocrats. He was then forced to be cautious in order not to discredit himself in Paris by imprudent acts, and he stopped his attacks against the Jews.[41]

It took much courage for an Alsatian Jacobin to defend Jews. He would make many enemies and jeopardize his career. This happened to the deputy public prosecutor of Strasbourg François-Laurent Xavier Levrault (1762-1821), who signed a pro-Jewish report prepared by the Strasbourg Friends of the Constitution (*Société des Amis de la Constitution*). On February 7, 1790, this Society decided to accept Jewish members and to censure P. F. de Latour-Fossaic's anti-

---

[39] Troux, *op. cit.*, II, 101; Godechot, *Les Commissaires*, II, 71.

[40] Raymond Guyot, *Documents biographiques sur J. F. Reubell, 1747-1807* (Tours, 1911), p. 16.

[41] *Ibid.*, p. 172; A. Mathiez, "Les Malles de Reubell," in *Annales révolutionnaires*, IX (1917), 541-43; X (1918), 246-47; XV (1923), 414; *ibid., Le Directoire* (Paris 1934), p. 44; L. Bour, *La Grande Révolution dans l'arrondissement de Sarrebourg sous le Directoire et le Consulat, 1795-1802* (Metz, 1936), p. 12; F. Normand, "Jean-François Reubell," *Les Contemporains*, No. 940 (Paris, 1910), p. 7: *Testament de Rewbell* (Colmar, 1799), 21 pp.; Etienne François Housset, *Rapport . . .* (Paris, an VII), 26 pp.; *Observation de Reubell . . . sur le rapport fait par Housset* (no place given, 1799), 3 pp.; Georges Mauguin, "La Carrière militaire d'un ami de Moreau; Le Général Jean-Jacques Reubell," *Revue des études napoléoniennes*, XL (1940), 219.

Jewish pamphlet.[42] On February 20, 1790, Marx Berr [Cerf-berr] was officially enrolled as a member. The Society voted to publish Berr's speech together with the Society's statement that this was the first public manifestation in Alsace against anti-Jewish feelings, and to nominate a special commission of five members to study the problem of Alsatian Jewry.[43] On February 27, 1790, R.-F.-P. Brunck, one of the Society's founders, reported, in the name of the Commission, in favor of granting full citizenship to the Jews. The report stated that the rich landowners and the officials were against emancipation of the Jews because they were afraid of losing a source of income; the priest circulated the counter-Revolutionary statement that the Jews would buy the nationalized properties and enslave the peasants; many Christian artisans were afraid of Jewish competition. But the report declared that the Jews would become an economically useful element. "How many villages do not have any shoemaker? Should a Jew take up this trade, he would sell his shoes much cheaper to the peasants than the Christian shoemakers of the cities. . . . If we made peasants and handicraftsmen of the Jews, they would expand the industry and commerce of our province."[44] The same meeting of the Society voted that a request be made to the City to discontinue the blowing of the Shofar, a tradition of pre-Revolutionary days, a sign to Jews not

[42] P. F. de Latour-Foissac, *Plaidoyer . . . contre les Juifs . . .* ([Strasbourg], 1790), ii+109 pp.

[43] F. C. Heitz, *Les Sociétés politiques de Strasbourg pendant les années 1790 à 1795* (Strasbourg, 1863), pp. v, 13.

[44] The same idea—that emancipated Jews would enrich France—was repeated in many other pamphlets: La Baronne de Vasse, Anglaise, *Mémoires à L'Assemblée Nationale, pour demontrer aux français, les raisons qui doivent déterminer à admettre les Juifs indistinctement aux droits de citoyens* (Paris, 1790), 9 pp.; *Recueil de pièces relatives à l'admission des Juifs à l'état civil* (Paris, 1790), p. 25 (Discours de l'Abbé Bertolio); *Adresse de l'Assemblée des représentants de la Commune de Paris, à l'Assemblée Nationale, sur l'admission des Juifs à l'état civil . . .* (Paris, 1790), p. 11; [Israel Bernard de Valabregue], *Schreiben eines Lords . . . Zur Verteidigung der Juden* (Breslau, 1804), pp. 60-61.

authorized to stay in Strasbourg, that they should leave the city.[45]

Brunck's report drew furious attacks—verbal and written—from the anti-Jewish elements.[46] Since Levrault, as secretary of the Society, had signed the pro-Jewish report, the anti-Jewish elements attacked him strongly. The Strasbourg Second Section stated that he was a "bad citizen," and demands were made that the Society be disbanded. Levrault sued his attackers. However, on April 3, 1790, the General Council of Strasbourg called a special meeting for April 7 to discuss the pro-Jewish report, and it seems that Levrault became frightened. In a letter published on April 7, 1790, he stated that he signed the pro-Jewish report, not because of any personal pro-Jewish sentiments, but in his capacity as secretary of the Society. He stressed the fact that he had not prepared the report and had never pleaded before the National Assembly in favor of the Jews, and he declared himself ready to execute any order of the General Council concerning this problem. The Council voted to petition the National Assembly against the emancipation of the Jews, and on April 8 the City Council published

[45] F. L. X. Levrault, *Rapport de l'Assemblée de la Société des Amis de la Constitution, le 27 février 1790, sur la question de l'etat civil des Juifs d'Alsace* (Strasbourg, 1790), 32 pp. Another edition of the same report was signed by the President and two secretaries of the Society: [R. E. P. Brunck], *Rapport lu à l'assemblée de la Société des Amis de la Constitution de Strasbourg, le 27 fevrier 1790, sur la question de l'état civil des Juifs d'Alsace* [Signé: Barbier de Tinan, président; Genthon, Levrault, secrétaires] (Strasbourg, 1790), 31 pp. German edition: *Bericht welcher in der Gesselschaft der Freunde der Konstition über die Frage vorgelesen wurde: Konnen die Juden in Elsasse des Burgerrechts teilhaftig werden?* (Strasbourg, 1790), 38 pp.; *Observations sur la possibilité et l'utilité de l'admission des Juifs en Alsace aux droits de citoyens adressées à un Membre de la Société des Amis de la Constitution à Strasbourg, par un ami de l'homme* (Strasbourg, 1790), 20 pp.; *Réflexions sur la Société des Amis de la Constitution* (Question des Juifs) (Strasbourg, 1790), 4 pp.; Heitz, *op. cit.*, pp. 17-18. On Brunck see: E. Barth, *Notes biographiques sur les hommes de la Révolution à Strasbourg* (Mulhouse, 1877), pp. 20-22.

[46] Foissac, *Observations sur un écrit en faveur des Juifs de l'Alsace, présenté au Comité des Amis de la Constitution de Strasbourg, le 27 février dernier* [Phalsbourg, 1er avril 1790] (Strasbourg, 1790), 20 pp.; Ginzrot, *Antwort über eine Schrift betitelt: Bericht welcher in der Gesellschaft der Freunde der Konstition über die Frage vorgelesen wurde . . .* (no place given, 1790), 15 pp.

the text of its request to the Deputy E. F. J. Schwendt and to the National Assembly to fight Jewish emancipation.

During a discussion on the Jewish problem in the City Council on April 10, 1790, a fight broke out between the anti-Jewish elements and Levrault and his friends. The discussion of April 10 makes it clear that this conflict was not confined to the Jewish problem alone. The fight against Jews was a pretext for a general attack on the revolutionary principles of the Society of Friends of the Constitution. A move even got under way to exclude Levrault from the City Council because of his "memberhip in this dangerous Society" (*Mitglied einer gefährlichen Gesellschaft*). The next day, April 11, Levrault's friend published a pamphlet which stated that this "dangerous Society"—the Friends of the Constitution—was a lawful association and that Levrault had the right to sign the pro-Jewish report because on February 27 he had not yet officially taken over his office on the City Council. The pamphlet maintained that Levrault had the right to express his private opinion on the Jewish problem, and that the attacks against him were directed against the personal liberty of every citizen. In fact, the title of the pamphlet was a statement in itself: "Citizens of Strasbourg, look out for your liberty."[47]

The political clubs did not always represent the large

[47] *Reproche fait à M. Levrault d'avoir signé, comme secrétaire de la Société des Amis de la Constitution, le rapport sur l'état civil des Juifs* (Strasbourg, mars 1790), 2 pp.; *Assemblée de la Comune. Extrait dés registres du Conseil Général de la Commune de la ville de Strasbourg. Du 3 avril 1790* (Strasbourg, 1790), placard; Levrault, *Lettre écrite par le Substitut du Procureur de la Commune de Strasbourg, à M. Poirot . . . 7 avril 1790* (Strasbourg, 1790), 1 p. (fol.); *Bürger zu Strasbourg, gebt acht auf euere Freyheit* (Strasbourg, 11 avril 1790), 4 pp.; *Trés humble adresse présentée à l'Assemblée Nationale par la commune . . . de Strasbourg . . .* (Strasbourg, avril, 1790), 14 pp. German edition: *Unterthänigste Vorstellung der Gemeinde von Strassburg . . .* (no place no date), 11 pp. *Lettre écrite à M. Schwendt, deputé à L'Assemblée Nationale, par MM. les Maire et officiers municipaux de la ville de Strasbourg, le 8 avril 1790* (no place, no date), 1 p. (fol.); Heitz, *op. cit.*, p. 30; Barth, *op. cit.*, pp. 97-99; Anchel, *op. cit.*, p. 11; P. Hildenfinger, "L'Adresse de la commune de Strasbourg à l'Assemblée Nationale contre les Juifs (avril 1790)," *REJ*, LVIII (1909), 112-128.

masses.[48] Still, they were always a revolutionary force, especially in Alsace. The discussion on Jews only aggravated the general political struggle there. The reactionary elements failed in their nationwide move of February-May, 1791 to hamper the activities of the clubs. The Jacobin clubs came out of this struggle stronger everywhere in France except in Alsace, where the *Amis de la Constitution* of Colmar, Thann, Cernay, and other places were forced to disband.[49]

There was not a single Alsatian revolutionary leader capable of stopping the organized attacks upon Jews. Even the Strasbourg Mayor Frédéric de Dietrich joined in these attacks and signed the anti-Jewish petitions sent to the National Assembly. The historian Gabriel G. Ramon notes one main fault in Dietrich's career—the help he gave to the anti-Jewish elements. The hatred against Jews was so strong among the Alsatian Catholics and Protestants that nobody made an effort to understand the Jewish problem and, of course, nobody admitted *"mea culpa."*[50] Dietrich

[48] F. V. A. Aulard, *Histoire politique de la Révolution française* (Paris, 1901), p. 94.

[49] L. de Cardenal, *La Province pendant la Révolution. Histoire des Clubs Jacobins 1789-1795* (Paris, 1929), p. 25.

[50] Gabriel G. Ramon, *Frederic de Dietrich* . . . (Nancy, 1919), p. 116. On October 28, 1790, the Paris Jewish leader David D. Silveyra obtained a document from the Constitutional Committee which stated that all those Jews who had obtained letters patent prior to the Revolution could now benefit from the Law of January 28, 1790, granting citizenship to the Sephardic Jews: *Decision du Comité de Constitution. Requise par David D. Sylveyra, Syndic Agent des Juifs français patentes* (Paris, 1790), 1 p. Sylveyra sent a printed copy of this statement to the Alsatian Jewish leader Cerfberr, who showed it to Dietrich, "who was among his friends"—as he wrote—and the Mayor requested that a copy be sent officially to his office. It seems that Cerfberr wanted to use this statement in his controversy with the city about the right of residence for himself and his family. AN, D-IV-LVI (1638). On Cerfberr's conflict with Strasbourg see: Z. Szajkowski, "The Jewish Problem in Alsace, Metz, and Lorraine on the Eve of the Revolution of 1789," *Jewish Quarterly Review*, XLIV (1954), 206-21. It is worth while to mention a pamphlet of February 11, 1790 (the day Levrault's friends published their pamphlet, cf. note 47) addressed to Jews, Protestants, and Catholics, in favor of the Mayor Dietrich: "Croyez vous qu'il [Dietrich] fera des injustices à sa patrie, aux Catholiques, aux Calvinistes, aux Juifs?" *A la Garnison de Strasbourg*, par un Strasbourgeois qui a voyagé vingt-quatre ans (Strasbourg, ce 11 février 1790), 3 pp.

was a *nouveau riche* aristocrat (his father was made a baron
in 1761). The historian A. Mathiez declared that he never
was a democrat. He liked to live in luxury, and in the
revolutionary clubs he detested men from the lower classes
who wanted to compete with the wealthy people. His
revolutionary career was full of intrigues against the unity
of the Republic.[51] Alsace was a strong counter-Revolutionary center, teeming with reactionary plots against the
Republic,[52] and the anti-Jewish propaganda was one of the
many devices used by the reactionary forces to combat the
Revolution. On September 18, 1792, the officials of the
Haguenau district sent a special commissioner to Strasbourg
with a request for help in preventing an anti-Jewish pogrom,
which was being prepared by twelve cities and villages.
On October 3, 1792 they protested against the silence of
the Strasbourg officials in this matter. They declared that
the main criticism against the Jews was that without their
money there would have been no Revolution, and the
counter-Revolutionary priests would not have been deported. If the anti-Jewish pogrom were not prevented, it
could very well be the signal for civil war.[53]

In spite of well-organized anti-Jewish propaganda and
persecution the Jews found many sincere friends not only
in Paris, where only one out of sixty districts opposed
Jewish emancipation,[54] not only among the Paris Commissioners and other leaders connected with the provinces,[55]

[51] Dietrich escaped to Switzerland, but fearful that his property would
be confiscated and hoping for the defeat of the Robespierreists, he returned.
The Strasbourg Jacobins were afraid to take him before a court in Strasbourg,
where he could be freed; on a petition to transfer his case to a different court
is to be found the signature of a Jew, Simon Mayer. Dietrich was tried in
Besançon; he was deported and, during the Terror, he was sentenced to death
in Paris. Mathiez, "Un complice de Lafayette, Fréderic Schneider d'après les
documents inédits," *Annales révolutionnaires*, XII (1920), 389-408, 471-499.

[52] E. Vingtrinier, *La Contre-révolution*, I (Paris, 1924-25), 254-64,
357-61; II, 155-56.

[53] AdBR, L-I-825.

[54] Sigismond Lacroix, "Ce qu'on pensait des Juifs à Paris en 1790," *La
Révolution française*, XXX (1898), 97-117.

[55] On April 6, 1792, Lafayette wrote to Metz officials on the Jewish
problem: "Les soldats de la Constitution doivent savoir que la liberté religieuse

but also among local Alsatians.[56] The Alsatian Jews found a great friend in Jean George (Eulogius) Schneider, who was born on December 20, 1756 in Wipfeld, a small village of Franconia. For a time he was a Franciscan monk. Later he became professor of Hebrew at Augsburg, and this period of his life probably influenced his later attitude in favor of the Jews. In June, 1791, Schneider arrived in Strasbourg. Breaking away from the Church, he married an Alsatian woman. A very talented man, Schneider soon became an extremist Jacobin orator and leader, even more extremist than A. L. L. de Saint-Just himself, who was Robespierre's representative in Strasbourg, and was appointed public prosecutor of the Revolutionary Tribunal of the Lower Rhine department.[57]

Unlike the other Alsatian Jacobins, Schneider was not an anti-Semite. When Marx Berr [Cerfberr], the son of the Alsatian Jewish leader Cerfberr de Medelsheim, paid for the uniform of a soldier volunteer, Schneider celebrated this act in a song.[58]

---

est un de ses principes les plus sacrés" (City Archives of Metz, 3 P2). André Foussedore, Commissioner in Alsace, published a proclamation against the anti-Jewish persecution: *Foussedoire, Représentant du peuple dans les départements des Haut- et Bas-Rhin* (Colmar, [an III]), 4 pp. French and German.

[56] In 1790, an anonymous Strasbourg pamphlet stated that the granting of full rights to Protestants and Jews would bring back to France all the wealth which despotism and intolerance had compelled them to export: *A la Garnison de Strasbourg,* par un Strasbourgeois qui a voyagé vingt-quatre ans (Strasbourg, 11 février 1790), 3 pp. The Société des Amis de la Constitution of Epinal (Vosges) warned the peasants against despotism, which divided men according to their religion, Christians and Jews, and thus isolated them from each other: *Adresse de la Société des Amis de la Constitution à ses frères les habitants des campagnes* (Epinal, 1792), pp. 2-3 . Among the candidates for the Jury of the Colmar district in 1794 were three Jews: *Liste des citoyens domiciliés dans l'étendue du District de Colmar . . . de Jurés d'accusation et de jugement dans le cours du troisième trimestre de la troisième anneé* (Colmar, no date), 4 pp. On the other hand, not one Jew was on the Metz jury, cf, e.g., *Liste des quatre-vingt quatre citoyens, à raison d'un par mille âmes . . . pour remplir les fonctions de jurés . . .* [5 juin 1794], 6 pp.

[57] Charles Nadier, *Oeuvres complètes,* VIII (Paris, 1833), 48-49.

[58] "Eine That, wie deine That,
        Ist der Franken-Freiheit wert!"
in *Argos,* No. 9 (July 9, 1793). In one case, 9 out of 69 persons donating clothing and helping the families of volunteers were Jews: *Dons patriotiques pour l'equipement du bataillon des volontaires de Strasbourg et pour les*

Jews and peasants—but mostly Jews—were at that time
violently attacked as food speculators.[59] The Lower Rhine
even accused the Jews of developing among the peasants
a love of money.[60] The food crisis was no worse in Alsace
than in other parts of the country; for a while the situation
was even better there. But, as all over France, many Alsatians, too, were accused of being speculators. Cities organized punitive expeditions against villages for not delivering
enough supplies.[61]

Mention should be made of the role of the Jewish army
purveyors. They were always of great importance to the
government, but they also were much disliked, especially
by the peasants, who were not always happy to sell their
products, particularly if they were paid with *assignats*.[62]
A Strasbourg pamphleteer wrote in 1790 that the Jew is
the one who takes over "the often distasteful occupation
of a contractor for the government."[63] They were also hated
as speculators by the revolutionaries[64] and by the admin-

*secours à fournir aux femmes et enfants des citoyens qui sont voués à la
défense de la Patrie aux frontières* [Strasbourg, aout 1792], pp. 11-12. Later,
in July, 1793, Schneider wrote that Marx Berr acted in such a patriotic
manner at a time when the majority of the "uncircumcized" were fighting
against the Jacobins. J. Sée, "Quelques idées d'Euloge Schneider sur les Juifs,"
Revue d'Alsace, XLI (1891), 134.

[59] *Allgemeine Zeitung für alle Stande*, March 18, May 12, Aug. 2, 1793;
"Die Juden legten die Hand auf alle Landesprodukte, die sie erfassen konnten";
A. Gestermann, *Geschichte der elsässischer Bauern- und Landwirtschaft*, II
(Colmar, 1939), p. 95.

[60] Reuss, *op. cit.*, p. 255.

[61] In 1793, Guebwiller sent such an armed expedition against the peasants
of Gundolsheim. On November 12, 1795, 800 horses were requisitioned from
the peasants of Moselle. Brunschwig, *op. cit.*, p. 110; R. Foller, "Le massacre
de Gundolsheim," *Revue d'Alsace*, LXXXIII (1936), 339-60; [André Ulrich],
Recueil des pièces servant à l'histoire de la Révolution à Strasbourg [=Livre
bleu], (Strasbourg, 1795), 29-30; René Paquet, *Bibliographie analytique de
l'histoire de Metz pendant la Révolution* (Paris, 1921), p. 1290.

[62] Reuss, *op. cit.*, p. 267.

[63] "Er ist es, welcher Lieferungen, Zahlungen und so andren eben nicht
immer beliebtes Geschäft für Regierungen übernimmt." J.. *Die Juden-Verfolgungen* (Strasbourg, [1790]), p. 15.

[64] The *Montagnard* Joseph-François Wulliez declared in 1793 that because of the failure to buy provisions at the legal *maximum* price, the profits
would now go to speculators, especially Jews. Troux, *op. cit.*, II, 66.

istration, which in the end had to pay for the supplies.[65] This was a vicious circle during the Revolution. The number of Jewish financiers was small,[66] but the tradition of the economic usefulness of the Jews, the idea that the Jews could accomplish great things in this field, still persisted. In 1795 Paris was threatened with famine, and the people in a public demonstration at the Convention on May 20, 1795 asked for bread. At the time the walls of Paris were covered with posters dated June 8, 1795 and signed by the citizen Seigneur of the Section de la Butte-des-Moulins, who proposed that the Jews (the *nation juive*) be asked to import to Paris wheat from abroad, because only they with their commercial connections could do it.[67] As a matter of fact, in some instances the Jewish merchants saved the people from starvation. During the bread crisis in Strasbourg (August, 1789-March, 1790), a Jewish secret agent of the wheat-commission of Mayence helped to import wheat from Germany to Strasbourg.[68] In 1789 Berr-Isaac Berr made a loan of 6,000 livres to Nancy for the purchase of sacks, and Cerfberr de Medelsheim saved Lorraine from starvation by importing wheat from Germany.[69] In the year III (1794-95), the district of Metz commissioned the Jew Zacharias-Cerf to import wheat to the extent of 1,500,000 livres.[70]

Here mention also should be made of the well-known attacks against Jews by Charles-François Dumouriez, com-

[65] According to the historian Jacques Godechot the request of Jewish creditors, in 1789-1790, to be paid for their deliveries to the administration aroused anti-Jewish feelings among the officials in Lorraine, who could not pay them. Godechot, *op. cit.*, pp. 9-10.

[66] Only 8 out of 150 financiers listed by the historian E. Soreau were Jews and they did not play an important role. Edmond Soreau, "Les hommes de finance pendant la Révolution, *Revue des études historiques*, CI (1934), 315-18.

[67] Etienne Charavay, "Un appel à la nation juive pour se charger de l'approvisionnement de Paris," *La Révolution française*, XXIV (1893), 62-68.

[68] Brunschwig, *op. cit.*, p. 30.

[69] Godechot, *op. cit.*, pp. 15-16; Charles Poisson, *Les Fournisseurs aux armées sous la Révolution française. Le Directoire des Achats* . . . (Paris, 1932), pp. 119-120.

[70] Paquet, *op. cit.*, p. 1323.

manding general of the Army of the North. These attacks
were aimed not against Jews directly, but against the *Directoire des Achats* (Purchasing Directory), created on November 4, 1792 by the three Ministries of Defense, and
headed by the Protestant banker Jacques Biederman, of
Swiss origin, Professor J.-A.-J. Cousin, and the Strasbourg
Jew Marx [Cerf=] Berr (1758-1817). Dumouriez struck
at the entire Directory, but particulaly it's Jewish purchasing agents, Marx Berr and the brothers Lipmann (1760-
1827) and Théodore Cerfberr (1766-1832). It has already
been noted that army contractors were frequently criticized, but at that time the Directory's leaders also fell
victims to the conflict between the Minister of War, J.-N.
Pache, and the Minister of Interior, J. B. D. Roland. Pache
was pushed into the Ministry by his Girondist friends, but
when he later went over to the Montagnards, Roland took
away from the Directory the right to supply his Ministry.
Dumouriez was a known friend of the Girondists and this
strengthened his assaults on the Directory. This agency had
been created in a moment of grave financial crisis, drought,
speculation, and political conflict. Bankers were active in
both factions of the Revolution. Biederman was a friend
of both the Girondists and the Dantonists, and he was not
impartial. But the Jews in the Directory—all of them were
Ashkenazic Jews—did not participate in these factional
conflicts. Marx Berr was undoubtedly a very ambitious
banker, but his activities were restricted to the contracting
business. On February 12, 1793, the Directory was suspended, but Marx Berr probably continued his activities
for the naval forces.[71]

71 Bidermann et Marx-Berr, *Réponses . . . aux questions du Comité de la
Guerre* . . . (no place, no date), 103 pp. et tableaux; *Observations pour le
citoyen Baruch Cerf-Berr . . . en réponse au Général Custines* (no place, no
date), 30 pp.; *Observations pour le citoyen Lippmann Cerf-Berr . . .* (Paris,
no date), 19 pp.; Poisson, *op. cit.*, pp. 8, 14, 30, 117-18, 119, 129, 141, 204-08,
219, 222-23, 235-46; Camille Wolf, "Cerf-Berr et Coustine," *L'Univers israélite*,
LIII, (1898), 705-07; [Levylier], *Notes et documents concernant la famille
Cerfberr*, II (Paris, 1905), pp. 6-135. Laurent, Representative of the People,
ordered the execution of all Jewish peddlers who followed the French army

Schneider, too, criticized Jews, but not being ideologically an anti-Semite, he could observe and judge the situation with an open mind. He vehemently assailed the peasants for hiding their products and for speculating. In his periodical, *Argos,* of July 15, 1793, he strongly censured the attacks upon Jews. Usury, speculation, and other evil phenomena should be destroyed, he wrote, but all those responsible for these misfortunes should be attacked, and not the Jews alone, because any charge directed especially against Jews would be contrary to the spirit of Liberty and Equality. The peasants, even more than the Jews, are responsible for discrediting the *assignats* (paper-money). "It has been proved," he wrote, "that one could be a Jew and at the same time a good citizen. The Jewish religion does not make anybody lazy or a speculator." If, prior to the Revolution, Jews made a living out of dishonest and "unproductive" occupations, than the anti-Jewish laws and restrictions were responsible for this state of affairs. "Law and reason recognize only the man, the citizen, and not the baptized or the circumcized. In our Temples we are religious, but in the market and in the popular assemblies we are citizens." Schneider repeated his defense of the Jews in the Strasbourg Jacobins' Club on July 16, 1793, and for this he was called a man who had sold himself to the Jews. In a special supplement to his *Argos* he published a paper by Abraham Lambert, a Jew of Mannheim, who took up residence in Alsace and became a known patriot.[72]

in Belgium: Emile Ouverleaux, "Notes et documents sur les Juifs de Belgique, sous l'ancien régime," *REJ,* IX (1884), 283.

[72] E. Schneider, in *Argos,* July 3, 1792, June 16, and July 15, 1793; *Über die Juden,* supplement to the *Argos,* III (July, 1793), after p. 56. 8 pp.; Julien Sée (see note 58); Dr. M. Ginsburger, *Ein Urteil über die Juden* (no place, no date), 1 p. (fol.) reprint; F. C. Heitz, *Notes sur la vie et les écrits d'Euloge Schneider* (Strasbourg, 1862), pp. 76-77; Campagnac, *op. cit.,* pp. 553-54. On Schneider see also: E. Mühlenbeck, *Euloge Schneider,* 1793 (Strasbourg-Paris, 1896); C. W. Faber, *Eulogius Schneider* (Mulhouse, 1886), 52 pp.; R. Jaquel, "Eulogius Schneider et l'historiographie allemande," *Annales historiques de la Révolution française,* VIII, 399-417; IX, 1-27, 103-15; X, 61-73; XII, 218-48; I. Ehrhard, *Schneider, sein Leben* (Strasbourg, 1894), 223 pp.; J. Grass, "E. Schneider auf der Guillotine," *Cahiers d'archéologie et d'histoire d'Alsace,* III, 1108-12.

H. Grégoire and others were the great protectors of the Jews in Paris, but Schneider, the Jacobin of German origin, became the defender of the Jews in Alsace. Their philo-Semitism had different origins: Grégoire was driven to the defense of the Jews by various philosophical influences, Schneider by his practical revolutionary ideas on the economic problems of the Revolution. Schneider was much swayed by the ideas of Christian Wilhelm von Dohm and Anacharsis Cloots that the anti-Jewish laws and not the Jews' nature of religion was responsible for all the evils connected with the Jewish problem.[73] In a way, all three of them argued as economists, and they were all influenced by the pro-Jewish sentiments then prevailing in Germany.

Schneider's intervention greatly helped the Jews of Alsace. The Revolutionary Tribunal was established in Strasbourg by Saint-Just, who arrived together with Lazare Hoche in November, 1793 to save Alsace for the Republic by terror.[74] With another man than Schneider as the public prosecutor, the Jews would have suffered far more than they did. For a time, his word was law in Strasbourg. In November, 1793 an imaginary war of words and propaganda took place between the Cathedral of Freiburg in Breisgau, on the left bank of the Rhine River, and the Cathedral of Strasbourg. From Germany came the ironic remark that the Protestants and the Jews had probably already given up their religions. Schneider replied that not only Protestants and Jews, but everybody was converted to the new Religion of Reason and the Fatherland (*Culte de la Raison et de la Patrie*).[75] It was probably under Schneider's influence that the Strasbourg Mayor, P. F. Monet, on November 19, 1793 called upon Jews, Calvinists, Lutherans, and Catholics to

---

[73] C. W. Dohm, *Ueber die bürgerliche Verbesserung der Juden.* (Berlin, 1781); French edition: *De la réforme politique des Juifs* (Dessau, 1782); Anacharsis Cloots, *Lettres sur les Juifs* . . . (Berlin, 1789), 90 pp.; L. Kessler, "Anacharsis Cloots and his 'Lettres sur les Juifs,'" *The Jews in France,* II (New York, 1942), 75-92 (in Yiddish).

[74] Bonnal de Ganges, *Les Représentants du peuple en mission près les armées 1791-1797* (Paris, 1898), pp. 300-75.

[75] Campagnac, *op. cit.,* pp. 485-87.

unite, to forget hatred and fanaticism, and the like.[76] This could not have happened during the previous administration of Mayor Dietrich.

Schneider himself fell victim to the terror and the struggle among the revolutionary leaders. On order of Saint-Just and P. F. J. Lebas he was arrested in November, 1793, and on April 10, 1794 he was guillotined in Paris.

On May 3, 10, and 13, 1794, the Strasbourg *Club des Jacobins ou des sans cullotes* again discussed the Jewish problem. Most members were then unfriendly toward the Jews, who were accused of being usurers, and some even demanded their expulsion. Others, however, stated that Christians, too, were usurers, and the Club passed a resolution proposed by Bois and Lazare Zay, a Jew, to combat all usurers, and not Jews alone. A similar resolution was passed on May 3, 1794 by the Strasbourg *Société populaire.*[77] This was a resolution in the spirit of E. Schneider. But in any case, the officials did not care very much for resolutions in Schneider's spirit. On May 11, 1794, the prosecutor of the Lower Rhine Criminal Court called on the patriots to combat the speculators, especially the Jews. On July 29, 1794, the National Agent (*Agent national*) of the Strasbourg district warned the city councils to watch out for Jewish usurers.[78] A similar warning, directed especially against Jews, was given on June 12, 1794 by the proesecutor of the Upper Rhine Criminal Court at Yves.[79] The *Société*

[76] "Prosélytes de Moïse, de Calvin, de Luther et de Rome, tendez-vous tous une main fraternelle; trop souvent le fanatisme arma vos bras pour vous entre détruire; oubliez vos haines dans les épanchements de l'amitié, dans les doux sentiments de la nature, dans les touchantes maximes de la morale." P. F. Monet, le Maire de Strasbourg, *Au Peuple* [Strasbourg, 29 brumaire, an 2]. Placard (Jewish Theological Seminary, New York, N. Y.). The appeal was published on the eve of a demonstration in favor of the new revolutionary religion (*fête de la Raison*): R. Reuss, *La Constitution civile du clergé et la crise religieuse en Alsace 1790-1795*, II (Strasbourg, 1922), 230-237.

[77] Heitz, *op. cit.*, pp. 346-50; Lazare Zay, "Judenschaft," *Strassburgische Zeitung* (1794), p. 253; Mühlenbeck, *op. cit.*, p. 7.

[78] F. Neuman, *Invitation de l'accusateur public près le tribunal du département du Bas-Rhin, à ses frères les sans-culottes* (Strasbourg, May 11, 1794), placard; Mühlenbeck, *op. cit.*, p. 7.

[79] *L'Accusateur public près le tribunal criminel du département du Haut-*

des Amis de la Constitution of Thann rejected the proposition
of the Colmar Society calling for the expulsion of the Jews,
but it did decide to keep them under observation.[80]

In conclusion it should be stated that, with rare exceptions, even the majority of revolutionaries in Alsace and
neighboring departments were strongly anti-Jewish. Jewish
emancipation was obtained and safeguarded against their will.

Rhin, à tous les bons patriotes du même département (Colmar, June 12, 1794),
placard.

[80] Henry Poulet, "L'Esprit public à Thann pendant la Révolution," *Revue
historique de la Révolution française*, XV (1923), 367-68.

THE REFORM OF THE *ÉTAT-CIVIL* OF THE FRENCH JEWS DURING THE REVOLUTION OF 1789

THE Edict of August 1, 1539, which was confirmed by subsequent royal ordinances, introduced in France the *état-civil* — the official registration of births, marriages and deaths — to be carried out by the Catholic clergy. Protestants and Jews were excluded from the authoritative *état-civil*; they had their own registries kept respectively by Pastors and Rabbis.[1] The official registration of the birth, marriage or death constituted a recognition of the legal status of a person, in many cases even of his family. Thus, the problem of the *état-civil* of non-Catholics became a major issue in the fight for the emancipation of the Protestants and the preparation of the Edict of November 1787 in their favor.

Chrétien-Guillaume Lamoignon de Malesherbes, who — on the eve of the Revolution — headed the so-called Malesherbes Commission for the study of the status of the Jews, favored the inclusion of the Jews in a general law regulating the *état-civil*.[2] This would have promoted Jewish emancipation, but Malesherbes' idea was not carried out. The Jews of Nîmes, however, tried to use the Edict of November 1787 in their own behalf. They registered between March 19 and December 18, 1788, Jewish births, marriages and deaths in the registry newly opened for Protestants for this purpose; although the same births and marriages were already noted on the special registry of the Jewish community of Nîmes or in the registries of the communities of Avignon, Carpentras, Cavaillon and L'Isle-sur-Sorgue in the neighboring papal province of Avignon and the Comtat Venaissin from where most of the Jews of Nîmes originated. Their example was followed by the Jews of Remoulins, Aix, Saint-Esprit and other neighboring localities, where small groups of Jews from the papal province had settled on the eve of

[1] Dalloz, *Répertoire de Législation*. Vº Acte de *l'état-civil*, section I, 10.

[2] [Ch. G. Lamoignon de Malesherbes,] *Second mémoire sur le mariage des Protestans*, Londres, 1787, pp. 68–70.

Originally published in *The Jewish Quarterly Review*, vol. **XLIX** (1958).

the Revolution.[3] Jews were registered together with Protestants in other parts of France, too. But this was done only in an administrative manner, without taking position on the problem of Jewish emancipation.[3a] But all this did not change the status of the Jews, and the Edict of November 1787 was not applied in their favor. They continued to live as a merely tolerated group.

From the very beginning of the Revolution many voices demanded the secularization of the *état-civil* in order to check the power of the Catholic Church and unite the various religious groups in the Republic. Thus, on May 20, 1790, the Society of the Friends of the Constitution of Epinal (in the Vosges) published a pamphlet against the practice of an *état-civil* divided according to the religious groups, which only helped the old despotic regime to separate and isolate these groups. "Is it not true — the pamphlet demanded — that all Frenchmen are born and are Citizens before being Christians [Catholics], before being Protestants, before being Jews? Only through the abolition of the distinctions of acts which establish the right of citizenship, by introducing a uniform *état-civil*, real liberty and equality could prevail."[4] It took over three years before the Revolution deprived the Catholic Clergy of control over France's *état-civil*. A law of September 20, 1792, secular-

---

[3] P. Angeras, *L'Edit de 1787 et son application dans la sénéchaussée de Nîmes*, Nîmes, 1929, pp. 168–72.

[3a] Thus, e. g., David Meyer, a Jewish child of 9 months, and Israël Cerf of Nîmes (who died in 1790 at the age of 31) were registered on the *état-civil* of non-Catholics in Versailles (City archives of Versailles, GG).

[4] "N'est-il pas vrai que tous les Français naissent & sont Citoyens avant d'etre Chrétiens, avant d'être Protestans, avant d'être Juifs: le baptême ni la circomcision ni autres cérémonies religieuses ne donnent pas la légitimité, ils donnent seulement la qualite de Chrétien, de Juif &c . . . Dans lordre précédent & actuel des choses, nul Citoyen ne peut prouver son existence civile par un acte uniforme: le catholique représente des actes faits par les Prêtres; le Juif rapporte des certificats de ses rabbins, ou de ses parens, . . . Par-tout la confusion de l'acte civil avec l'acte religieux présente des varietés contraires à l'ordre social; par-tout ces actes sont des brevets de haine réciproque entre les différentes sectes. Le despotisme était si bien parvenu à diviser les hommes, à les isoler les uns des autres . . . Il est donc tems de prendre autant des moyens de reprocher les hommes que l'on en a pris de les éloigner les uns des autres . . . comment laisseroit-on subsister des distinctions dans la forme des actes qui établissent les droits du Citoyen?": *Adresse de la Société des Amis de la Constitution à ses frères les habitans des campagnes. Epinal, le 20 Mai 1790*, Epinal, nd., pp. 2–4.

ized the *état-civil*. All existing registries of births, marriages, and deaths had to be turned over to the local civil authorities and from now on the *état-civil* of all religious groups was to be recorded in the same registries to be opened for this purpose. This was, indeed, a new and major step toward the abolition of the major role played in the history of France by the Catholic Church and toward a more complete emancipation of the religious minorities, the Protestants and the Jews. On August 12, 1793, the National Convention was forced to decree penalties upon priests opposing the law on the secularization of the *état-civil*. In fact, as late as 1804, some circles still hoped that the registries of the *état-civil* would be returned to the priests.[5]

As we shall see, many Jews, especially those of Alsace and the neighboring provinces, had no confidence in the law of September and avoided registering the birth of their children. Of course, such an attitude was not confined to Jews. Christians, too, acted in this way not only during the Revolution, but even in the later years of the First Empire.[6] There were many reasons for such a negative attitude: the traditional distrust of new laws, the fear that children might be drafted into military service, etc. Still, the fact remains that the law on the secularization of the *état-civil*, which indirectly was another important step toward the emancipation of religious minorities was not understood or accepted immediately nor with ardor by all of those who were to profit from it by becoming full citizens.

How did the law of September 20, 1792, affect the various Jewish communities?

The Jewish Community of Metz possessed a register of deaths which had been started in 1564.[7] But for some reason, the Jews of Metz since May 1717 kept registries in French, of which the following were turned over to the authorities at the end of October 1792: (1) A register of the period May 30, 1717—December 31, 1750. (2) A register covering the period January 1, 1752—December 28, 1779. (3) A register of the period 1779—October 27, 1792; in these three registries the births, marriages, and deaths were noted. (4) A register of 53 births and 8 marriages in 1789. (5) A register of 57 deaths in 1789. (6) A register of 61 births and 11 marriages in 1790. (7) A register of 47 deaths in

[5] E. d'Hauterive, *La police secrète du Premier Empire*, Paris, *1908*, Vol. I, p. 220.

[6] Robert Anchel, *Napoléon et les Juifs*, Paris, 1928, pp. 437–39.

[7] L. Cardozo de Béthencourt, "Le Trésor des Juifs séphardim." *REJ*, XXVI, 1893, p. 245.

1790. (8) A register of 46 births and 9 marriages in 1791. (9) A register of 106 deaths in 1791. (10) A register of 50 births and 6 marriages in 1792 (till October 27). (11) A register of 34 deaths in 1792 (till October 27).[8] Altogether in these eleven registries are recorded for the period of May 1717—October 27, 1792, 7,198 births, 1,159 marriages and 5,074 deaths. No such registries were, probably, delivered during the Revolution by the Jews of other communities in the Moselle department.[9]

It seems that the Jews of Metz did not willingly register their children. An ordinance of September 13, 1793, forced them to declare the number of their children and servants.[10]

As a result of the Letters Patent of July 10, 1784, concerning the Jews of Alsace, a census of the Jews was conducted in the entire province at the end of 1784.[11] In a few cases this census brought then about the introduction of registries for the *état-civil* of the Jews.

The departmental archives of the Upper Rhine have sixteen Jewish registries which were deposited with the local authorities during the Revolution. The following of these registries were used also during the first years of the Revolution for the registration of the *état-civil* of the Jews: (1) Biesheim — only circumcisions, 1709–1791. (2) Bollwiller — births, marriages and deaths, 1784–1791. (3) Froeningen — births, marriages and deaths, 1786–1789. (4) Hattstatt — only births, 1715–1791. (5) Hirsingue — births, 1784–1790, deaths, 1784–1789 (and

---

[8] Departmental Archives de Moselle, E 11115–17. The city archives of Metz have two registries of 1792, which are original copies of those in the Departmental archives. These registries were mentioned in 1848 by the *Archives israélites* (vol. IX, pp. 162–63,) but they do not figure in T. Richard's study "Kirchenbucher als Geschichtsquelle." *Annuaire de la SHAL*, vol. XX, 1910, pp. 587–625. According to R. Anchel the judge of the Metz district legalized in 1792, two separate registries for the Jews' *état-civil* (*op. cit.*, p. 437). But this happened before September 20, 1792.

[9] J. N. Christiany, *Archives départementales de la Moselle. Répertoire numérique de la Série E*, Metz, 1927. Only the Metz registries E 11115–17 are mentioned in this inventory.

[10] "Arrêt du Conseil général de la commune de Metz du 13 Sept. 1793, pour obliger les Juifs à faire la déclaration de nombre d'enfants et des domestiques de leurs familles" (City Library of Metz, ms. 919, f. 248).

[11] Z. Szajkowski, "The Jewish Problem in Alsace, Metz and Lorraine on the Eve of the Revolution of 1789," *Jewish Quarterly Review*, vol. XLIV, 1954, p. 223, note 36.

marriages only for 1785). (6) Jungholtz — births, marriages and deaths, 1725–1792. (7) Luemschwiller — only births and deaths, 1784–1790. (8) Oberdorf — births, 1784–1790, deaths, 1785–1790 (and marriages for 1785–1788). (9) Seppois-le-bas — births, 1785–1790, marriages, 1785–1789, deaths, 1785–1790. (10) Wettolsheim — only marriages, 1719–1793. (11) Zillisheim — births and deaths, 1789 (and births, marriages and deaths for 1784–1788). From (12) Riedwihr, (13) Rimbach, (14) Steinbrunn-le-Haut, (15) Uffholtz and (16) Watt-willer remain only registries from-prior to the Revolution (1784–1788). With a few exceptions and unlike such Jewish registries in other French provinces, most of these registries of Alsace were never kept by Jews, but by the civil authorities who kept track of the number of the Jews. Some of these registries come from notarial sources. Of the few registries kept by the Jews themselves it is worthy to note the one of Bieschheim with 212 entries of circumcision; of these 209 were copied from a Hebrew *pinkas* dating back to 1669. After the register was deposited with the authorities in 1792, three new entries of circumcisions in 1780, 1790 and September 14, 1790, were added.[12]

To our knowledge, the departmental archives of Lower Rhine have only one Jewish register of the Revolutionary period — the register of Mutzig which was introduced in connection with the census of 1784 and maintained until January 1790.[13] Some cities, e. g. Haguenau (Lower Rhine), continued during the Revolution to keep not a regular legalized register for the Jewish *état-civil*, but a list containing the same information.[14]

[12] Departmental Archives of Upper Rhine, 5 E 56 (200), 66 (177), 174 (20), 204 (192), 223 (19–21), 246 (1), 291 (20–21), 350 (6–8), 409 (84), 412 (164), 460 (22–24), 482 (21), 507 (17–20), 535 (17–18), 541 (188), 561 (19–23). Cf. Emile Herzog, *Archives départementales du Haut-Rhin. Répertoire méthodique de la Série V. E. Etat Civil*, Colmar, 1937, p. IX.
[13] Departmental archives of lower Rhine, 3 E 313. Compare with: Lucien Metzger, Pierre d'Herbecourt et Louis Monnier, *Archives départementales du Bas-Rhin. Répertoire numerique du Fonds de l'Etat civil*, Strasbourg, 1936; *Archives départementales du Bas-Rhin. Etat des registres paroissiaux des communes de l'arrondissement de Sélestat deposés aux Archives départementales du Haut-Rhin*, Strasbourg, 1938.
[14] City archives of Haguenau, 66/68/54. Of other registries in the Lower Rhine it is worth while to note the introduction to the registry of Itterswiller (1769–1778): „דז וואז איך האב דאניין גישריבן האב איך ניט פון מיר זעלבשטין גטאהן נייארט דז האב איך אן בפאלין בקומין מן כהרר העֶרך מעטלנסצה מן בישא ואנט פרנס אין עלואס פר אלי קינדר דרייען צי שרייבן כ"ד הקן

In November, 1792, the City Council of Strasbourg asked the Jewish leader Cerf Berr [Cerfberr] of Médelsheim to deposit the Jewish registries of births, marriages and deaths. But Cerfberr stated that to his knowledge no such registries existed in the archives of the Alsatian Council of Jewish Communities. In fact, at the Council's assembly in 1788 he requested that a register of deaths be introduced.[15] In the year II, Strasbourg ordered the Jews to comply with the regulations on the *état-civil*. It happened sometimes that revolutionary laws were used by local authorities, especially in the traditionally anti-Jewish departments of Alsace, for anti-Jewish propaganda and persecution. Thus, e. g. on June 27, 1794, the District of Strasbourg strongly attacked the Jews because they secretly buried a Jew in the Jewish cemetery of Rossenviller — which was then forbidden — and ordered the rabbis to surrender all registries of births, marriages and deaths. On July 24, 1794, the Strasbourg municipality discussed the bigotry of the Jews who refuse to register their children in accordance with the law of 1792.[16]

There were no registries of the Jewish *état-civil* in Nancy or in other Jewish communities of the Meurthe department. Only registries of

צבי הירש בר ברוך ז"ל איטרשוילר" (Departmental archives of Lower Rhine, 3 E 226.)

It is also worth while to note that in Sarreunion (Lower Rhine) a Jew named "Nathan Joseph, agent de la commune de Saarunion" registered the births, marriages and deaths (according to a document of year VIII, in the author's possession).

[15] "Le Commissaire aux fonctions municipales a communiqué à la municipalité provisoire la réponse du citoyen Cerf Berr à la demande qu'il lui a adressée de faire déposer au Greffe de la Municipalité les registres de naissances, mariages et décès de la religion judaïque, lad. reponse du 21 de ce mois portant: "que led. citoyen Cerf Berr ne peut satisfaire à la demande, que depuis 1788 qu'il a quitté la Province il a laissé toutes les affaires civiles et politiques en d'autres mains pour ce qui concerne ces sortes d'objets, qu'il veut dire cependant qu'il n'a jamais été fait de registre à l'égard des circoncisions, que les parens seuls en tenaient note ainsi que pour les mariages dont il y avoit un contrat entre les parties contractantes; que dans une assemblée générale tenue à Oberhenheim en 1788 lors de sa retraite il a recommendé spécialement que l'on tient registre mortuaire; que depuis son sejour ici qui n'est que momentané il ne s'est mêlé en rien de ces mêmes objets; qu'à lad. assemblée de 1788 il a laisse tous les papiers au Citoyen Wittersheim de Mutzig qui a été nommé pour suivre tous objets." City archives of Strasbourg, minutes of the city council, vol. 3, p. 1095, Nov. 24, 1792.

[16] *Déliberation du Directoire du District de Strasbourg, du 9 Messidor,*

circumcisions were known there. In fact, the local authorities did not immediately grasp the spirit of the law of September 20, 1792. Thus, on October 20, 1792, the municipality of Nancy decided to ask the Convention that Jews be allowed to register their *état-civil*.[17]

In Bordeaux, Saint-Esprit-lès-Bayonne and other centers where Marranos refugees from Spain and Portugal settled as New Christians, their births, marriages and deaths figured — at first — in the Catholic parochial registries. But, after they were permitted to live openly as Jews, they introduced their own registries. According to one source, the last marriage registered by a Sephardic Jew of Bordeaux in a Catholic parish was of August 9, 1753. Although rabbis performed marriage ceremonies and delivered *cartes nuptiales* even earlier, the *Nation* of the Sephardic Jews started its register of marriages only on December 26, 1775; this meant that during a period of over twenty years the marriages of the Sephardic Jews of Bordeaux were not registered, except in notarial acts.[18]

On January 28, 1790, Sephardic and Avignonese Jews of Bordeaux and Saint-Esprit-lès-Bayonne were granted full citizenship. They dissolved their *Nations* and organized, instead, *Sociétés de Bienfaisance*. But they still continued to register their births, marriages, and deaths in their own registries. The Jews of Saint-Esprit played an important role in the local revolutionary events; they formed the majority in the Jacobin Club and in the municipality during the Terror. Still, prior to September 20, 1792, the Sepharic Jews continued to register their births, marriages and deaths in their own registries of the Jewish communities.[19]

l'an second . . ., [Strasbourg, 1794.] 7 pp.; R. Anchel, *op. cit.*, pp. 438–39.

[17] "Inventaires des registres contenant les actes civils des communes du département de la Meurthe, déposes en ses Archives en Exécution de la Loi du 20 Septembre, 1792." (Departmental archives of Meurthe-et-Moselle, L 241–42); A. Troux, *La vie politique dans le département de la Meurthe d'août 1792 à octobre 1795*, Nancy, 1936, vol. I, pp. 87; R. Anchel, *op. cit.*, p. 437.

[18] Georges Cirot, *Recherches sur les Juifs Espagnols et Portugais à Bordeaux*, Bordeaux, 1908, pp. 163–65.

[19] Only the inscription at the beginning of each year changed. Instead of naming the *syndicat* (i. e. the syndics of the *Nation*), the registries contained now the names of the Society's leaders. Thus, we find the following inscription of April 1790 in the Bordeaux Jewish register of births: "De l'administration de Bienfaisance de MM. Carvallo, D^d Avezado, J^e Mezes de Salom, administrateurs, et de Mr.

On November 5, 1792, the Mayor of Bordeaux ordered to deposit by the following November 12 all registries of the *état-civil*, and demanded that in the future, citizens of all religions (*de quelque culte que ils soient*) should use the new *état-civil* in the offices of the city.[20] The following Jewish registries were then deposited:[21] (1) A register of births in the Sephardic *Nation*, from December 22, 1738, to December 27, 1792; this register was started by decision of the *Nation* of December 7, 1738. (2) A register of marriages in the Sephardic *Nation* from December 24, 1775, till December 17, 1792; this register was established by the *Nation's* decision of December 19, 1775. (3) A register of deaths in the Sephardic *Nation* from January 7, 1739, to December 23, 1792; this register was started by the *Nation's* decision of December 7, 1738. (4) A Sephardic register of 746 circumcisions, which was kept from February 28, 1706, to February 16, 1742, by Jacob de Mezes and was continued by his son Abraham de Mezes (known also as Alexandre Mezes) from August 9, 1742 to January 26, 1775. (5) A Sephardic register of 267 circumcisions, by Abraham de Silva; the inscriptions in the first part of the register are not in chronological order, and were probably copied from an earlier register; the earliest entry is of November 19, 1730; the second part is kept chronologically and dates from 1764 to August 13, 1793. (6) A Sephardic register of 169 circumcisions, which was kept by Himanuel Jacob de Mezes from June 9, 1750, to July 29, 1784. (7) A Sephardic register of 207 circumcisions, which was kept by Abraham Bargues from August 10, 1773, to May 1, 1793. (8) A Sephardic register of 20 circumcisions which was kept by Abraham de Aron Mendes from December 2, 1774, to February 20, 1793. (9) A Sephardic register of 95 circumcisions, which was kept by Izaac de Abraham Mezes from January 14, 1779, to December 1, 1791. (10) A register of births in the *Nation* of the Avignonese Jews, deposited in 1792, but without entries since the end of 1788. (11) A register of the Avignonese Jews of Bordeaux in which Elie Astruc recorded 38

Raba aîné Trésorier de la ditte administration" (City archives of Bordeaux, GG 789, fol. 73).

[20] City archives of Bordeaux, E. 1.

[21] This was noted already in a pamphlet of the Revolutionary period: "lorsque les nouvelles lois sur *l'état civil*, ont été mises à l'exécution, les syndics de Portugais remirent plusieurs registres qui constatoient l'exercice de ces mêmes fonctions, relativement aux naissances, mariages et décès": Despiau et Pujol, *Mémoire pour les Citoyens Despiau et Pujol, de Bordeaux*, Bordeaux, nd., p. 29.

circumcisions from June 9, 1785, to November 26, 1793. The registries of births, marriages, and deaths were deposited on November 12, 1792, but the authorities continued to use them until the end of December 1792 for the entries of the Jewish *état-civil*. The registries of circumcisions were still used and deposited much later, some of them in November 1793.[22]

The following Jewish registries were deposited on March 20, 1793, at the municipality of Saint-Esprit-lès-Bayonne: (1) A register of circumcisions, which was kept by Jacob Silva from November 24, 1717, till 1766. (2) A register of circumcisions kept by Samuel Jonas Atias from 1725 till 1766. (3) A register of births, marriages and deaths, from 1752 till the eve of the Revolution. (4) A register of deaths, from January 11, 1788, till January 2, 1792.[23]

All four communities of the papal province of Avignon and Comtat Venaissin deposited their registries during the Revolution.

In 1738 the Bishop of Carpentras, Malachie d'Inguimbert, ordered the Jewish Community to keep a register of all Jewish births, marriages and deaths. These registries (ספר היחס and הזכרת נשמות) also contained entries on the *état-civil* since 1736; these entries were probably copied from an earlier register. These two registries were kept regularly by the community's religious teacher and scribe Elijah Crémieux until his death in 1773. They were later continued by others, but only in Hebrew. In 1763 the son of the scribe was forcibly baptized and many Jews fled to French territory, to Nice, and other places. The papal authorities feared that the Jewish emigration might ruin the local commerce, and in 1763, Pope Clement XIII ordered the four Jewish communities of the province to keep special registries in French and

[22] City archives of Bordeaux, GG; Béthencourt, *op. cit.*, *REJ*, vol. XXVI, 1893, pp. 249–51; Cirot, *op. cit.*, pp. 23–24. In the recent years an index was added to the *état-civil*, which comprises — for the Jewish registries — of the period 1706–1792 — 3,569 births, 178 marriages and 1,907 deaths. On April 17, 1786, the Sephardic *Nation* compiled a list of all graves on its cemetery (Cirot, *op. cit.*, p. 29). If such a list existed, then it was lost. It should be noted that the register of the minutes of the Sephardic *Nation* remained in the archives of the Jewish community until about 1910.

[23] City archives of Bayonne, GG. According to a notarial act of Bordeaux, a Jew named Alexandre possessed in 1767 a register of circumcisions, which were performed in Saint-Esprit by "Moise Carrion alias Sanssen" (Departmental archives of Gironde, E, Minutes de Rauzan, Feb. 12, 1767).

Hebrew for the recording of births, circumcisions, marriages, and deaths, in order better to keep track of the number of Jews and their movements.[24]

The new Carpentras register was used for the first time for the recording of a death case on June 3, 1763; the last death was entered on Aug. 6, 1792. The first birth — on July 17, 1763, and the last on August 17, 1792. The first marriage — on August 20, 1763, and the last — on May 27, 1792. In 1789–1792, 109 births, 16 marriages and 86 deaths were listed. On December 7, 1792, the register was taken over by the city officials, who entered three Jewish births (the last one on December 20, 1792) and five deaths (the last one on December 30, 1792). On November 27, 1792, the City-Council of Carpentras asked the rabbi to announce in the Synagogue that the citizen Domere, member of the Council, will keep the registries of the état-civil. This was announced on the same day by the town-crier Marsan in the streets of Carpentras, including those inhabited by the Jews.[26]

According to article XIX of the rules of the Avignon Jewish Community the rabbi had to keep a register of the entire Jewish population. The register of 1763 was started on June 1, was closed in November 1792, and was deposited at the municipality together with an earlier Hebrew register.[26]

In Cavaillon the register was started on June 1, 1763, by *pinhas Lion Poliacre Rabin des hommes*. The first birth was registered on June 29, 1763 and the last one on December 20, 1792; the first marriage on October 7, 1763 and the last one on October 4, 1791; the first death-case — on August 1, 1763, and the last one on November 22, 1792. In the years 1789–1792, were registered 31 births, 7 marriages and 40 deaths. On November 23, 1793, the register was turned over to the City-Council, which continued to use the same register for the inscription of three Jewish births from January 26, 1793, to October 1793.[27]

On November 29, 1792, the Mayor of L'Isle-sur-Sorgue came to the synagogue and asked for the Jewish état-civil registries. Only one

[24] Z. Szajkowski, "18th Century Pinkasim from Carpentras," *Yivo-Bleter*, vol. XXI (1943), 351–353 (in Yiddish).

[25] City Archives of Carpentras, GG 47 and Rev. 25.

[26] Isidore Loeb, "Statuts des Juifs d'Avignon (1779)." *Annuaire de la Société des Etudes Juives*, vol. I, 1881, p. 234; Departmental archives of Vaucluse, GG; Ph. Prévot, *A travers la carrière des Juifs d'Avignon*, Avignon, 5701, pp. 7–9.

[27] City archives of Cavaillon, GG 27.

register, also started in 1763, was found and it was declared closed by the Mayor. In 1789–1792, 16 births, 4 marriages and 22 deaths were registered.[28]

The register of the Jewish état-civil in Nîmes, which contains 58 births, 13 circumcisions, 15 marriages, and 47 deaths was started on July 11, 1778. The last entry was a birth on September 27, 1792. On the following October 26, the register was closed by the Mayor Scipion Lagarde. Of 224 names mentioned in the Nîmes register, forty bear the family name allemand, which shows that they were of Ashkenazic origin.[29]

In Dijon (Côte-d'Or), where a group of Alsatian Jews settled during the Revolution, the departmental Directoire introduced in 1792 the single register for all religious groups. But there, probably, arose some difficulties, because in the year VII the Directoire asked the Ministry of the Interior for instructions as to how to establish the état-civil of foreigners who settled in the department, particularly "persons practising the Jewish religion."[30]

We do not know of any registries of the état-civil of the Jews in Paris for that period. If such registries did exist and they were deposited with the authorities in 1792, they must have been destroyed together with all registries in 1871. In Paris Jewish deaths were notified to the police in accordance with the ordinance of 1736, which was then a step toward the laicization of the état-civil.[31]

Of course, many circumcisers kept registries of circumcisions even during the Revolution, but the registries did not always belong to the community and were not deposited with the civil authorities in 1792.[32]

How reliable are all these Jewish registries from the demographic point-of-view?

[28] City archives of L'Isle-sur-Sorgue, GG 23.

[29] Departmental archives of Gard, UU 161. The following inscription appears at the beginning of the register: "Le present Registre Pour savoir a couché les Enfants qui naîtrons et les sepultures & et les mariages aussy des Juif han^t en cette ville de Nimes Commencé le 11 Juillet 1778."

[30] Departmental archives of Côte-d'Or, L 492.

[31] P. Hildenfinger, Documents sur les Juifs à Paris au XVIIIᵉ siècle. Actes d'inhumation et scellés, Paris, 1913. VIII, 290 pp.

[32] E. g.: M. Lambert, "Liste des circoncis opérés par le mohel Isaac Schweich (1775–1801)." REJ, vol. LII, 1906, p. 282 ss; Moise Schwab, "Manuscrits hébreux de la Bibliothèque municipale du Havre." Ibidem, vol. LXVIII, 1914, pp. 265 ss. (Circumcisions by Mayer Weill).

Many Jews were not registered at all. Thus in 1794 it was noted in a Bordeaux register that Hanna-Félicité, a daughter of Isaac Lange and Sara Torrès, was never registered.[33] According to the death records of Bordeaux Jews there were 1,943 deaths from January 7, 1739, to November 5, 1792. In a municipal register of burial permits for non-Catholics were found 167 Jewish deaths between 1739–1750 which do not appear in the Jewish records.[34] According to the historian A. Nicolaï there were in the Sephardic community of Bordeaux in 1741–1783 during twenty seven years more births than deaths and during sixteen years more deaths than births. But according to the historian G. Cirot there were during the same period 24 years with more deaths than births.[35] The Jewish registries of Saint-Esprit-lès-Bayonne are incomplete. Already on July 17, 1821, the Mayor of Bayonne stated in a note on the register of 1752 that the entries were faulty and should be considered only as a "nomenclature" of notes made hazardously." On October 5, 1801, Jacob Rodrigues stated in a petition to the Judge Samuel Nunes — a Jew himself — that he could not find any trace of his birth in these registries.[36] In the later years (1865–1895) Mardochée Ernest Naquet, Samuel Sazedo and Eugène Benjamin Léon compiled from these registries and similar sources a list of births and deaths of the Jews of Saint Esprit.[37] But according to their list, only old people died in the years prior to 1752 and from 1766 till the 1770's. It seems then that the register of births was made in a later period from the entries in the register of deaths. The same thing could be said about many other Jewish registries. Many Jews were, probably, often afraid to figure in such registries, and this is also true for the Protestants, who kept their records in Bordeaux secretly.[38] According to the four registries of the former papal provinces there occurred in 1780–89, 478 births and 487 deaths in the four communities, but according to a Carpentras *pinkas* the Jewish population had had an excess of births over deaths in preceding generations, except when a plague prevailed. It is likely that in order to avoid payment of taxes and because of other difficulties the Jews often failed to enter births in the official registries. Still, these registries contain very valuable demographic material.

[33] City archives of Bordeaux, I E 3, No. 681.   [34] *Ibidem*, GG8 10.
[35] A. Nicolaï, *La population de Bordeaux au XVIIIe siècle (1700–1800)*, Paris-Bordeaux, 1909, p. 183; G. Cirot, *op. cit.*, p. 83.
[36] City archives of Bayonne, GG.
[37] In the archives of the Bayonne synagogue.
[38] Nicolaï, *op. cit.*, pp. 7, 183.

In conclusion it should be said that the law of September 20, 1792 which regularized the *état-civil*, was an important administrative measure toward the total emancipation of the French Jews.

PROTESTANTS AND JEWS OF FRANCE IN
FIGHT FOR EMANCIPATION, 1789–1791

According to some sources, the Edict of November 1787 decreed in favor of the French non-Catholics (Protestants) is supposed to be considered as one of the forerunners of the emancipation of the Jews. In the present study we shall try to analyze the sources and the common interests of these two religious minorities: the Protestants and the Jews.

During the preparation of the Edict and subsequent to its issue a large number of pamphlets was published in favor of the Protestants or against them[1] and on this occasion some pamphleteers also expressed their opinions on the Jewish problem. Perhaps the most important of such opinions was voiced in 1787 by Chrétien-Guillaume Lamoignon de Malesherbes himself in a pamphlet on the legal status of marriage among Protestants. His role in the preparation of the Edict of November 1787 is well known. Later he headed the so-called Malesherbes Commission which, on the eve of the Revolution of 1789, prepared the groundwork for a new status in favor of the Jews.[2] Malesherbes collected a great number of notes on Jews, and, according to his early biographers, wrote a study on Jews which, unfortunately, is lost.[3] This loss makes de Malesherbes' opinion of 1787 on Jews

---

[1] Arnaud Lods, *Centenaire de l'Edit du 17 Novembre 1789. Les partisans et les adversaires de l'Edit de tolérance. Etude bibliographique et juridique 1750–1789*, Paris, nd.

[2] ז. שייקובסקי, .משלחותיהם של יהודי ברדו אל ועדת מאלזרב (1788) ואל האסיפה הלאומית
62–31 ,צ י ו ן, י"ח, תשי"ג."(1790).

[3] *Catalogue des livres de la Bibliothèque de feu Chrétien-Guillaume Lamoignon-Malesherbes . . .*, Paris 1797. (p. 10: ". . . il avoit recueilli beaucoup de matériaux concernant les Juifs dont on trouve les manuscrits dans sa Bibliothèque"; "No. 5059. Recueil des pièces manuscrites, concernant les Juifs, ramassées par M. de Malesherbes, pour faire un travail sur cet object, comme il en avoit fait un sur les Protestans; dans un carton in-fol."); Jean-Baptiste Dubois,

Originally published in *Proceedings of the American Academy for Jewish Research,* vol. XXV (1956).

even more valuable. According to Malesherbes, the Jews were more favored than the Protestants in the matter of the legal registration of births, marriages and deaths. He was in favor of the inclusion of the Jews in a general law regulating the *état civil* which, surely, would have favored the Jewish emancipation.[4] He even expressed a desire to reduce the hatred against the Jewish people by wanting to see Christians contented in detesting only the Jewish religion. Malesherbes' main reason for adopting a more favorable attitude towards the Jews was his conviction that such a change would contribute greatly toward the conversion of the Jews.[5] In fact, Malesherbes was then one of those

Notice historique sur Chrétien-Guillaume Lamoignon-Malesherbes, 2nd ed., Paris, nd. (p. 32: "j'indiquerai un travail immense qu'il a fait sur les Juifs, et qui est resté manuscrit. Je ne connois aucun ouvrage sur cette matière, qui renferme des recherches aussi multipliées et aussi curieuses.") This is not mentioned in Dubois' first edition of 1788 and the third edition of 1805. Malesherbes' manuscript on Jews was not mentioned by M. Guillard in his: *Vie ou éloge historique de M. de Malesherbes*, Paris, 1805. The Comte de Baissy-d'Angelas mentioned Malesherbes' manuscript in his *Essai sur la vie, les écrits et les opinions de M. de Malesherbes . . .*, Paris, 1819, II, 52–53.

[4] [de Malesherbes,] *Second mémoire sur le mariage des Protestans*, Londres 1787. (p. 70: "il y a des Provinces où ils ont des lois qui leur sont propres. Leurs Rabbis ou Rabbins sont non-seulement des Officiers publics, dont le certificat constate leur état, mais des Juges que le Roi nomme dans quelques lieux . . . que sont tellement reconnus que les Cours supérieurs reçoivent l'appel de leurs sentences . . . il n'est pas inutile d'observer qu'à cet egard ils sont mieux traités que les Chrétiens Protestans ne le sont en present en France"; pp. 68, 73: "il sera aisé d'y inscrire aussi les décès des autres Hérétiques & Schismatiques, des Juifs . . . il suffit de ne point nommer spécialement dans la loi, les sujets du Roi de la R. P. R. . . . Par ce moyen, les Calvinistes & tous ceux dont je viens de parler, se trouveront compris dans l'énonciation générale, sans que le Roi ait à statuer particulièrement sur les Lutheriens, les Anabaptistes, les Juifs & c.")

[5] "Il serait bein à desirer que l'horreur pour la nation juive s'affoiblit chez les Chrétiens, & qu'on se contentât de détester leur religion: 1°. Parce que la tache indélible d'être d'une famille originairement juive est un grand obstacle a leur conversions, rien n'étant plus fait pour redoubler leur attachment à leur Religion que de savoir que s'ils la quittent, ils seront en horreur à toute leur nation & éternellement méprisés parmi les Chrétiens: 2°. Parce que trouvant exclus presque par-tout de la plupart des professions, ils sont obligés de se livrer à l'agiotage et à l'usure: 3°. Parce que n'ayant nulle part l'appui des loix communes à tous les citoyens, ils sont dans la nécessité absolue

pro-Jews who favored the emancipation of the Jews as a means
toward their conversion to Christianity. It is known that a
similar opinion was expressed by the great fighter for Jewish
emancipation, Abbot Henry Grégoire.[6]

Did the Edict of November 1787 really apply to the Jews?
The text of a number of articles in the Edict could easily be so
interpreted. Article 1, for instance, speaks of non-Catholics,
without mentioning the Protestants.[7] As we shall see the Jews
of Nîmes did actually ask for certain rights on the basis of this
article. According to P. Angeras, author of a study on the
application of the Edict in the Seneschalship of Nîmes, its
article 25, which deals with the registering of the births of new-
born children whose parents did not recognize baptism, applied
as well to Jews.[8] The attorney Louis-Francia Beaufleury, author

de suivre les loix qui leur sont propres, d'avoir des juges et des tribunaux de
leur nation. Il en resulte que la plupart des particuliers juifs étant fort malheureux, la nation juive est un corps puissant, & qui fait souvent de la puissance un abus treš-préjudiciable à la société, car tout corps a de la puissance;
j'en ai vu de cruels effets, j'en ai vu aussi de très-cruels de la haine acharnée
de quelques Chrétiens contre les Juifs. Si on vouloit s'occuper de cette nation,
on pourroit lui appliquer une grande partie des principes établis dans ces
deux Mémoires; car si pendant la durée de l'Edit de Nantes, les P. R. étoient
en France *Imperium in Imperio*, les Juifs sont dans l'univers entier *Imperium
in Imperiis*. Il n'est pas dans le pouvoir des Souverains de détruire en peu
de temps cette horreur pour la nation Juive que est sûrement portée trop loin.
Mais je crois que l'Edit qui, sans les nommer, leur permettra de procéder
dans leurs actes & de paroitre dans les Tribunaux, sans y perdre la qualification
de leur Religion, pourra contribuer a en rapprocher quelques-uns du Chris-
tianism": *Ibidem*, 71. Reprinted by de Boissy-d'Angelas in his *Essai ...*,
183–84.

[6] M. Ginsburger, "Zwei unveroeffentlichte Briefe des Abbé Grégoire."
Festschrift zu Simon Dubnows siebzigstem Geburtstag, Berlin, 1930, 201–206.

[7] "à ceux de nos sujets qui professant une autre religion que la religion
catholique."

[8] "La naissance des enfants de nos sujets non catholiques ... sera con-
statée ... soit par l'acte de leur baptême ..., si ce n'est que l'enfant fût de
père et de mère d'une secte qui ne reconnait pas la nécessité du baptême,
auquel cas, ceux qui le présentaient déclareront la naissance de l'enfant, la
secte dans laquelle il est né et justifieront que le père et la mère ont été mariés
sous la forme prescrite par le présent edit"; P. Angeras, *l'Edit de 1787 et son
application dans la sénéchanssée de Nîmes*, Nîmes, 1925, 177–78.

of a history of the Jews in Bordeaux and Bayonne (1799) stated that article 37 of the Edict, which spoke of "other subjects" than Lutherans, applied to Jews, because they were the only other religious minority legally residing in France.[9]

 ⌡ The Jews of Nîmes, where a large part of the population was Protestant made an attempt to use the Edict in their favor. On the basis of article 1, Izaac Monteil took up a request already brought forth in 1784, asking that Jews be accepted in the guild of tailors. The guild's syndics tried to obtain the opinion of the Intendant of Languedoc, Ballainvilliers, who, in turn, consulted his Nîmes Sub-Delegate, Pheline. According to Pheline, who advised his superior to take the opinion of the Minister in Paris, this was a "delicate affair." But Ballainvilliers was advised by Paris that the Edict did not apply to Jews. A similar demand by the Jews of Nîmes was repeated by the syndics of the guild of the dealers in linen. But, as they were not sure about the spirit of the Edict concerning Jews, the syndics advised the Intendant to reject the Jewish demand without discussing the character of the Edict. The Jews could be told that they were foreigners, who could not benefit from article 1. Of course, the Jews were more than just tolerated foreigners, so the Intendant again asked for the advice of the Government and on April 13, 1788, he was advised that the Edict did not abolish the restrictions against Jews who, therefore, could not benefit from the Edict without the King's opinion in connection with his plans

---

[9] "N'entendons, au surplus, déroger, par le présent édit, aux concessions faites aux luthériens établis en Alsace, non plus qu'à celles faites à ceux des autres sujets auxquels l'exercice d'une religion différente de la religion catholique, a pu être permis dans quelques provinces, à l'égard desquelle les règlemens continueront d'être exécutés." [Article 37.] Il est bien évident que l'on a entendu parler des Juifs, puisqu'il n'y avoit que leur secte et celle de luthériens qui fussent etablies alors en France par l'autorité publique, et qu'on a voulu leur conserver leurs privilèges pour eux été d'avoir des cimetières particulières": L. F. Beaufleury, *Mémoire à consulter et consultation* [par: Francia-Beaufleury, Ferey, Cambacérès, Dobonnieres], *pour les citoyens Français, professant le culte Judaïque à Bordeaux, connus sous le nom de Juifs Portugais et Avignonais,* np, an 7, 171–72; Reprinted in: L. F. B. Beaufleury, *Histoire de l'établissement des Juifs à Bordeaux et à Bayonne, depuis 1550,* Paris, an 8, 169–70.

concerning Jews. But the Jews did not give up their fight. On April 25, 1788, Mardochée Carcasonne of Nîmes requested the Intendant and the Government that the articles of the Edict mentioning non-Catholics without any specification of Protestants should be applied to the Jews. He wrote that the Jews of the neighboring papal province of Avignon and Comtat Venaissin would then emigrate to France and create prosperity in the province of Languedoc. His request was not granted.[10]

But it seems that, in spite of the Government's negative reply, the local authorities were not sure if it would be legal to exclude the Jews from the benefits of the Edict. Thus, they registered Jewish births, marriages and deaths in the registry now opened to Protestants for this purpose. The Jews of Nîmes, as well as those of Avignon, Carpentras, Cavaillon and L'Isle-sur-Sorgue in the neighboring papal province from where the Jews of Nîmes originally came, had their own registries kept by the Rabbis.[11] It is known that the registries problem of a legal *état-civil* was a major issue in the preparation of the Edict because the official registration of the birth, marriage or death of a non-Catholic constituted a recognition of his legal status. The Jews of Nîmes knew this and between March 19 and December 31, 1788 they registered their births, marriages and deaths in the office of the Judge, and many signed their names in Hebrew characters. Births and marriages of Jews which took place prior to 1787 — some in 1775 — and were already entered in the Jewish registries of the papal Province or of Nîmes, were now again registered by them in the French territory, in registries reserved for Protestants of Nîmes, Remoulins, Aix, Saint-Esprit, etc. Surely, the judges who kept the registries knew of the Government's advice of April 13, 1788. Still, eight months later the Jews requesting to be entered were inscribed by the judge of Nîmes in a registry reserved for Protestants and thus established a legal status for them. Jews were registered together with Protestants in other

[10] Alphonse Jobez, *La France sous Louis XVI*, Paris 1893, III, 326; D. Kahn, *Notice sur les Israélites de Nîmes (1672–1808)*, Nîmes, 1901, 14–18; N. Roubin, "La vie commerciale des Juifs Comtadins en Languedoc au XVIII-e siècle." *REJ*, XXXIV, 1897, 279; P. Angeras, *op. cit.*, 164–68.

[11] These registries will be the subject of special study.

parts of France, too, but this was done only in an administrative manner, without taking position on the problem of Jewish emancipation. Thus, e. g., two Jews were registered on the *état-civil* of non-Catholics in Versailles.[12]

After the publication of the Edict, the Metz Parliament, according to some documents, undertook to study the Jewish problem. According to an unpublished memorandum by Pierre-Louis Roederer, who initiated the contest of the Metz Academy on Jews in 1786–1787, the Metz Parliament inquired in Paris about this matter. Roederer himself requested that the rights granted to Protestants also be given to the Jews.[13] It is known that many provincial Parliaments were delayed in the registration of the Edict and it is possible that the discussion on Jews was the cause of such a delay in Metz, where the Edict was registered with the Parliament only on March 10, 1788.[14] Later, in 1789, the Metz Deputy, Abbot François-Martin Thiébaut who fought against Jewish emancipation in the National Assembly wrote that, in 1787, the Jews of Metz tried to use the Edict in order to force their entry into the guilds, to own real-estate property. In order to appease the protesting Catholics, the City officials of Metz were compelled to state that the Edict favored only Christians.[15]

It is possible that the discussions on the Jewish aspect of the Edict were one of the reasons for the establishment of the

[12] Archives departementales du Gard, UU 106 (Registry of Protestants); Angeras, *op. cit.*, 168–72; city archives of Versailles, GG.

[13] City Library of Metz, ms. 1100–25–II; Archives nationales, 29 AP3; Z. Szajkowski, "The Jewish Problem in Alsace, Metz, and Lorraine on the Eve of the Revolution of 1789." *Jewish Quarterly Review*, XLIV, 1954, 231–33.

[14] Roger Chastanier, *L'Etat civil des Protestants 1550–1792*, Nîmes, 1922, 213; *Edit du roi, concernant ceux qui ne font pas profession de la religion Catholique . . . Novembre 1787. Registré en Parlament le 10 Mars 1788*, Metz, 1788.

[15] "a peine l'édit de 1787 fut enregistré au Parlament de Metz, que les Juifs dirent, ce qu'ils répètent dans leur mémoire, pag. 22, qu'ils pouvoient être *affiliés au corps d'artisans*, acheter des maisons, & c. aussi-tôt ce n'est plus, de la part de la bourgeoisie, que craintes, qu'inquiétudes, que murmures, jusqu'à ce que le Magistrat repond que l'édit ne concerne point les non-baptisés": F.-M. Thiébaut, *No. ou Récit IV, et suite du compte rendu à ses comettans . . . Sa Discussion de la demande des Juifs, d'avoir désormais droit de cité indéfini*, Metz, 1789, 14–15.

Malesherbes Commission set up to prepare a status for the Jews. Thus, it is worth while to note the opinion of the Bordeaux chronicler Pierre Bernardau, a talented man with a very vicious tongue, who wrote that the Sephardic Jews in 1788 sent their delegation to the Malesherbes Commission in Paris because they were afraid that the Edict of November 1787 would limit the privileges accorded to the Sephardic Jews.[16]

The Edict of November 1787 was referred to in many Christian and Jewish chronicles, newspapers and pamphlets in connection with the Jewish problem on the eve of 1789 and during the Revolution. The well-known Zalkind Hourwitz writes that, on the basis of the Edict of 1787, many Jews bought masterships and that Paris Jews stated their religion in registrations at the Office of properties (*Bureau des Domaines*).[17] An attorney and author of a *factum* for the Carpentras Jewish debtors of Christian creditors related in the year VII, that, on the eve of the Revolution, the Comtadin Jews, thanks to the Edict, were able to take up legal residence in France.[18] Earlier, on June 21, 1789 the First Consul of Carpentras repeated the statement that the Edict was an attraction for the Comtadin Jews to emigrate to France.[19] The author of a pamphlet on the emigration of Comtadin Jews, published in Carpentras during the Revolution, wrote that the

[16] "Lundi XXI [avril 1788]. Les Juifs établis à Bordeaux craignant que l'Edict concernant les non-Catholiques ne portassent atteinte aux privilèges qu'on leur avait accordé durant le dernier Règne, ont députè en Cour les sieurs Furtado et Lopes du Bec, pour savoir à cette occasion l'intention du Gouvernment, et mettre tout en oeuvre pour maintenir leur état-civil, dont la nouvelle loi peut restreindre beaucoup la liberté" (Tablettes de Bernardau, ms. 713-1 of the Bordeaux City Library, April 1788, p. 206)." M. Furtado Juif portugais que sa Nation avait députè vers le Ministère pour traiter des intérêts des Iraélites qui semblaient compromis dans l'Edit de Versailles concernant les non-Catholiques est de retour de sa mission qu'il a remplie au gré des intéressés. Ses Frères lui ont temoigné la plus grande reconnaissance pour la manière heureuse avec laquelle il avait négotié en Cour" (*Ibidem*, Aug. 7, 1788, p. 277).

[17] Z. Hourwitz, *Apologie des Juifs*, Paris, 1789, 87.

[18] *Mémoire pour le Citoyen Jassé-Haïm Crémieu* . . . [signe: Chamaud], Aix, an VII, 19.

[19] H. Chobaut, "Les Juifs d'Avignon et du Comtat Venaissin." *REJ*, CII (1937), 5–6.

Edict of 1787 gave all civil rights to the Jews.[20] On September 9,
1789 *Le Courrier français* asked the Abbot Henri Grégoire why
he was fighting for the Jews, since the latter were already given
civil rights by the Edict of 1787.[21] We have mentioned the Abbot
Thiébaut's statement on the effects of the Edict in Metz. Unfortunately the above reports were only misrepresentations of
the official interpretation of the 1787 Edict. A more sober Jewish
pamphleteer, Isaie-Berr Bing of Metz, wrote that the Edict was
beneficial to everyone except the Jew.[22]

There were a few legal holes favoring a pro-Jewish interpretation of the Edict, but the events of Nîmes and Metz prove that
the anti-Jewish elements saw to it that Jews should not benefit
from the Edict. The Decree of the National Assembly of December 28, 1789, which completed the emancipation of the Protestants[23] — "without intending to prejudge relative to Jews on
whose status the Assembly intends to pronounce itself" —
definitely sanctioned the official interpretation that the Edict of
1787 was not applicable to Jews.

Still, the legend that the 1787 Edict affected the status of the
Jews continued to exist even in the later, post-Revolutionary
years. In the 1820s the Lorraine Jewish leader, Berr-Isaac Berr
in a request to the Nancy Consistory to do honor to the memory
of Malesherbes, wrote that he obtained the Edict of 1787 in
favor of the Jews.[24] E. Coquebert-Monbret, author of a report

---

[20] *L'Enfant du patriotisme* [by J. J. Raphaël, or Cottier Julian], Carpentras,
1789, 5–6.

[21] *Le Courier français*, Sept. 9, 1789; L. Kahn, *Les Juifs de Paris pendant la
Révolution*, Paris, 1898, 21.

[22] Isaïe-Berr Bing, *Mémoire particulier pour la communauté des Juifs établis
à Metz*, [Metz, 1789], 22.

[23] A. E. Halphen, *Recueil des Lois . . . concernant les Israélites . . .*, Paris,
1851, 183–94.

[24] ". . . d'exprimer notre reconaissance pour la mémoire du vertueux Mr.
de Malesherbes, reconnaissance qui était sans doute partagé par tous les
Israélites du Nord de la France pour qui il fit briller le premier l'aurore de la
liberté civile en obtenant en leur faveur l'édit des non-Catholiques et l'autori-
sation de nommer des députés pour apporter aux pieds du Trône leurs veux
et doléances." (In the archives of the Historical Society of Israel.) On August
19, 1819, the Nancy Consistory decided to mark the memory of Malesherbes,

on the French Jews, wrote in 1821, that the Edict contained also some dispositions in favor of the Jews[25] and the Jewish historian J. Bédarrides wrote that the Edict "was the forerunner of the complete emancipation of the Jews."[26] Perhaps the first acceptable thesis on the value of the Edict for the Jewish emancipation was given in 1909 by Théodore Reinach who wrote, that since citizenship was no more dependent on the adherence to the Catholic faith there was no more reason to ignore the Jews.[27] The Edict in favor of the Protestants was the first major victory in a fight for the emancipation of a religious minority, and this paved the way for the later emancipation of the Jews, too.

It would be hard to find a common rule for all French Protestants in their attitude towards Jews. We do not know of any active anti-Jewish movement among Bordeaux Protestants during the Revolution; but, in Alsace, the Protestants joined their enemies, the Catholics, in a common fight against Jewish emancipation. Both, Jews and Protestants, were persecuted in Bordeaux, but being busy with the persecution of the Protestants the Catholic Church sometimes neglected its anti-Jewish policy. In some respects the situation of the Protestants there — but not in Alsace and neighboring provinces — was even worse than that of the Jews. Until 1751 the Bordeaux Protestants had to bury their dead like animals and only in 1780 they were officially allowed to have a cemetery of their own. In 1757, the Bordeaux Protestants complained that as Christians they had to suffer, but that the Jews who had crucified Christ were tolerated. In 1787 an anonymous Protestant pamphleteer again complained that the status of Jews was better than that of Protestants. It is true, in the eyes of the Catholic Church the Sephardic Jews

the "Ministre fidèle, ami incomparable de l'auguste et infortuné Louis XVI." (*Ibidem*).

[25] E. C.[oquebert-] M.[onbret], *Notice sur l'état des Israélites en France . . .*, Paris, 1821, 43.

[26] I. Bédarrides, *Les Juifs en France, en Italie et en Espagne . . .*, Paris, 1859, 391.

[27] Théodore Reinach, *Les Juifs et la Révolution française. Resumé de la Conférence faite à l'Université Populaire Juive de Paris le 16 Mai 1909*, Vincennes, 1909, 3.

were less dangerous than the Protestants. The activities of these Jews were directed mainly toward the acquisition of economic riches and, therefore, they were useful for the monarchy and the city of Bordeaux. Intellectually they were less active than the Protestants who, although richer than the Jews, through their religion, Freemasonry and other media were able to help prepare the new ideas of 1789 in this Southwestern part of the country.[28] During the Revolution the Protestants of Bordeaux showed more initiative and courage as a religious minority than the Jews. They took the initiative to send the Bordeaux militia against the anti-Revolutionary Catholics of Montauban. Of course, Bordeaux was greatly interested in safeguarding its economic position and from the Montauban region came a large part of wheat exported by Bordeaux to the colonies. Still, this was not the only reason for such a punitive action. The Bordeaux Protestants maintained liaison with their Montauban coreligionists who were partisans of the Revolution and they were eager to help them.[29] But the Bordeaux Jews never even tried to help their coreligionists in other communities.[30]

[28] In 1698, there were about 3,000 Protestants in Bordeaux, and over 1,700 Jews in 1753: A. Nicolaï, *La Population de Bordeaux au XVIIIe siècle, 1700–1800*, Paris-Bordeaux, 1909, 184; G. Cirot, *Recherches sur les Juifs Espagnols et Portugais à Bordeaux*, Bordeaux, 1908, 137; A. Leroux, *Les Religionnaires de Bordeaux de 1685 à 1802*, Bordeaux, 1920, 81; *Idem, Etude critique, sur le XVIIIe siècle à Bordeaux*, Bordeaux, 1921, 61; *Essai sur la tolérance des non-Catholiques en France. Poème adressée à M. M. les Députés des Trois Ordres*, Bordeaux, 1789, 12.

[29] L'héritier, *La Liberté, 1789*, Paris, 1947, 310; R. M. Brace, *Bordeaux and the Gironde 1789–1798*, New York, 1947, 2, 98–121; P. Marion, "Etat des classes rurales au XVIIIe siècle dans la généralité de Bordeaux." *Revue des études historiques*, LXVIII, 1902, 455.

[30] On the attitude of the Sephardic Jews to other Jewish groups see: Z. Szajkowski, "Relations among Sephardim, Ashkenazim and Avignonese Jews in France from the 16th to the 20th Centuries." *Yivo-Bleter*, XXXIX, 1955, 70–103. The anti-Jewish minded historian E. Labadie wrote that both, Protestants and Jews, continued during the Revolution their religious practices, but they persecuted the Catholics: *La Presse bordelaise pendant la Révolution*, Bordeaux, 1910, 57. It is worthy of note that the editors of a Bordeaux Protest of 1791 against the anti-Pope pamphlet *Rélation véritable . . . du grand voyage du Pape au Paradis* mentioned Protestant and Jewish signa-

In spite of the Treaty of Westphalia (1648) the rights of the Alsatian Protestants were often restricted. The antagonism between Alsatian and neighboring Catholics and Protestants was amplified during the Revolution. The Catholics lost everything, their influence and power, while among Protestants the new regime was accepted as a logical consequence of the religious reform started by them.[31] Of course, Protestants and Jews were not as dangerous to the Revolution as the mighty Catholic Church. Both were the target of Catholic attacks.[32] Very often the Catholic anti-Revolutionary actions expressed themselves in a combined attack on both, Jews and Protestants.[33] In the region of Nantes, the Marquis de Juigné made propaganda against both religious minorities.[34] A counter-Revolutionary pamphleteer denounced Protestants, Jews and atheists as "the sole creators of the Revolution."[35]

Jewish pamphleteers wrote about the Catholic hatred of the Protestants, and the Jacobins asked that the "good relations" existing in certain localities between Catholics and Protestants should serve as a pattern for the adoption of a friendly attitude toward Jews.[36] But this did not prevent the persecuted Protestants from attacking another persecuted religious minority. On

tories to their protest: *Dénonciation d'un article scandaleux & impie, inséré dans le Journal de Bordeaux . . . No. 79*, Bordeaux, 1791. 15 p.

[31] Charles Hoffman, *L'Alsace au XVIIIᵉ siècle*, Colmar, 1906, I, 187–94; *Dénonciation. On veut donc encore nous désunir*, np., nd. 1 p.; Emile Dard, *Hérault de Séchelles*, Paris, 1907, 136–37; Hubert Thomas, *Le Tribunal Criminel de la Meurthe sous la Révolution 1792–1799*, Nancy, 1937, 483; L. Bourguignon, *Bischwiller depuis 100 ans*, Bischwiler, 1875, 143.

[32] In the year VI the Paris police wrote that Jews and Protestants *ne sont pas dangereux*: A. Aulard, *Paris pendant la réaction thérmidorienne et sous le Directoire*, Paris, 1898–99, IV, 730.

[33] L. Kahn, *op. cit.*, 48–49.

[34] Letter of May 24, 1790, to the *Comité des recherches*, Archives Nationales, D–XXIX bis 6 (81/15).

[35] *Les intrus juges au tribunal de la religion*, par l'auteur du Catéchisme nouveau et raisonné. Seconde edition, Paris 1792, 6.

[36] Zalkind-Hourwitz, *op. cit.*, 69; *Pétition des Juifs établis en France, adressée à l'Assemblée nationale, le 28 janvier 1790 . . .*, Paris, 1790, 33; Abraham Lambert, *Lettre à M. Reubell . . .* np, 1790, 3; *Rapport de l'Assemblée de la Société des Amis de la Constitution, le 27 fevrier 1790 . . .*, Strasbourg, 1790, 14.

May 29, 1791, shortly before the emancipation of the French
Jews, the Alsatian Protestant Pastor Jean-Laurent Blessig
(1745–1816) wrote to Abbot Henri Grégoire on the difference in
culture between the noble Sephardic Jews and the "mongrel"
Alsatian Jews. According to him the latter should not be given
full citizenship at once by the National Assembly.[37] The official
attitude of the Alsatian Protestants towards Jewish emancipation could best be illustrated by the activities of the well-known
Alsatian Protestant leader, Professor Christian-Guillaume Koch
(1737–1813), who was also Deputy from Alsace. In the National
Assembly Koch, together with the anti-Jewish Alsatian Deputy
E.-J.-F. Schwendt was active in fighting Jewish emancipation.
Koch's ideas about Jews were clearly expressed in an unpub-
lished memorandum of June 1790, in which he repeated the anti-
Jewish accusation of his momentarily Catholic friends.[38]

In his memorandum Koch reiterated one of the major arguments against Jewish emancipation, namely, that the Jews
would continue to exist as a separate Jewish nation. Over a
year later, after the Jews had been granted full citizenship

[37] "Il y a à peu près un an que nos assemblées primaires ont énoncé sur leur
compte un voeu très fortement prononcé, qui dans une adresse particulière
a été mis sous les yeux de l'Assemblée nationale. J'ai essayé de calmer alors
un peu les agitations de ma section; mais quoi'on m'ait toujours écarté avec
bonté, quique j'aie présenté le côté défavorable aux Juifs avec autant d'impar-
tialité que les motifs qui limitent en leur faveur, j'ai vu que je ferais très
bien de descendre de la tribune pour éviter d'en être rappelé avec trop d'éner-
gie. Ma profession de loi au sujet des Juifs était alors et elle est constamment
le même: il faut bien distinguer les Juifs Hollandais, les Juifs de nos ports
d'avec les Juifs allemands qui ont inondé notre province; ceux-ci, sont à
peine des metis, des quarterons, quand les autres seraient des grands blancs,
des blancs nobles et titrés . . . Il est infiniment à desirer que l'Assemblée
nationale veuille placer incessamment les Juifs au parvis et ne leur fermer
encore l'entrée du temple que pour leur donner le temps de s'y préparer digne-
ment:" "Lettres de Blessig à Gregoire." *Revue d'Alsace* XI, 1910, 479–80.
On Blessig see: Ed. Dollfus, *Biographien berühmter Elsässer*, Mülhausen, 1873,
158–72.

[38] "Réflexions sur les Juifs, redigés par M. Koch au mois de Juin 1790."
Archives du Chapitre de St.-Thomas (Strasbourg), No. 148-b 77–6 (II–2),
see the Appendix. On Koch see: J. G. Schweighaeuser, *Vie de Christ. Guil.
Koch*, Strasbourg, nd. 78 pp.

(on September 27, 1791), the National Assembly voted an amendment proposed by the Alsatian Deputy prince Victor Broglie, that the Jews should renounce their privilege of maintaining separate communities. In letters addressed to the Mayor of Strasbourg dated October 28 and 29, 1791, Schwendt and Koch interpreted this amendment as a victory over the Jews who would cease to exist as a *corps de nation* (national body).[39] In Koch's position on the Jewish problem the fact is interesting that he himself played a major part in the fight against the abolition of separate Protestant communities and the privileges accorded them prior to 1789. Thanks to Koch and his oratorical and legal ingenuity, and some arrangements with the Catholics and promises made to them, the Protestant Chapter of Saint-Thomas of Strasbourg was not nationalized and sold as Church property. Declared private property belonging to the Protestant University, the Chapter, to this day, benefits from pre-Revolutionary annuities and other prerogatives. The Deputy Pierre André of Lower Rhine stated in February 1799, that the Protestants who suffered from religious intolerance should not fight for the maintenance of privileges whose destruction could only help to bring about social happiness.[40] It is worth while to note that the Jewish community of Bordeaux tried a similar scheme, but on a much more limited scale involving only the Jewish cemetery, without trying to save privileges of an open counter-Revolutionary character. They fought against the nationalization of the Jewish cemetery, which was bought before the Revolution in the names of a few Jewish individuals. When the cemetery was confiscated and put on auction the Jews attempted to have some

[39] *Extrait de deux lettres de MM. Schwendt et Koch, Députés à l'Assemblé Nationale, à M. Dietrich Maire de Strasbourg, datées de Paris 28 et 29 Septen 1791*, Strasbourg, 1791. 4 pp.

[40] R. Reuss, *Les églises protestantes d'Alsace pendant la Révolution 1789–1802*, Paris, 1906, 27–28, 31–33; Jean Richerateau, *Le rôle politique du Professeur Koch*, Strasbourg, 1936, 33–77; *Opinion de Frédéric Herman, Député par le département du Bas-Rhin, sur le project de résolution concernant les biens ... protestans. Séance du 9 ventôse an 7*, Paris, an 7. 26 pp.; *Opinion d'André (du Bas Rhin), sur le projet de résolution tendant à supprimer les établissemens protestans, et à nationaliser les biens qui en dépendent. Séance du ventôse au 7*, np., an 7, 22.

Jews buy back the cemetery in their own names. But when this failed the Jews demanded that the transaction be declared null and void, because the cemetery was not an official communal property, but only a philanthropic undertaking. The departmental administration acceded to the Jewish demand, but this conflict stirred up anti-Jewish feelings and became the subject of many polemics between anti-Jewish and Jewish pamphleteers.[41]

One reason for the anti-Jewish attitude of the Protestants was the lack of stability in the Protestant attitude toward the Revolution itself, which had given them full freedom. In many provinces the Protestants were, of course, the best partisans of the new regime. Still, the French Protestants — as the historian Dr. J. F. E. Robinet notes — did not as a body and on a national scale endorse the Revolution, its principles, its fight against the anti-Revolutionary Church, etc. The Protestant dislike of the Revolution can easily be traced in histories dealing with the Protestants' situation during the Revolution. Alsatian Protestant leaders were suspected as aristocrats and traitors by the Strasbourg Jacobins and Prof. Koch spent eleven months in prison during the Terror.[42]

Later, in post-Revolutionary years, Protestants and Jews often fought together against the Catholic reaction. In 1804, the author of a *factum* warned that an anti-Jewish policy would bring about the emigration of Jews in the same way as the repeal of the Edict of Nantes by Louis XIV had driven Protestant capitalists, merchants and artists out of France.[43] In 1806, the

---

[41] *Mémoire* . . . [cf. note 9]; *Réponse à un Mémoire imprimé sous le nom des Citoyens français, professant le culte judaïque à Bordeaux*, np., nd.; *Rapport fait par Prévot, sur une petition des citoyens Pujol et Despiau, habitans de la commune de Bordeaux, soumissionnaires de biens appartenans aux Juifs établis en cette commune. Séance du 21 germinal an 7*, Paris, an 7. 7 pp.; *Opinion de F. B. Darracq dans l'affaire des Juifs de Bordeaux. Seance du 18 floreal au VII.* Paris, an VII; Beaufleury, *Histoire* . . ., 157–95; Z. Szajkowski, "Jewish Participation in the Sale of National Property During the French Revolution." *Jewish Social Studies*, XIV, 1952, 311.

[42] Dr. J. F. E. Robinet, *Le Mouvement religieux à Paris pendant la Révolution*, Paris, 1896, I, 306, 311, 314; R. Reuss, *op. cit.*, 119–20.

[43] *Mémoire et consultation sur pourvoi en grâce pour Baer Abraham* . . ., Paris, [1804,] 53.

author of a pamphlet written against Napoleon's anti-Jewish policy warned that the persecution of the Jews would be followed by an anti-Jewish policy.[44] In 1815 a pamphleteer defended the common interests of Protestants and Jews.[45]

APPENDIX

PROF. KOCH'S MEMORANDUM AGAINST JEWS

Réfiexions sur les Juifs, rédigés par M. Koch au mois de juin 1790.

La loi de Moïse fait des Juifs une nation distincte de toutes les nations de la terre; elle prend les plus grandes precautions pour qu'ils ne puissent jamais être mélés ni confondus avec d'autres nations . . .

Cette loi n'embrasse pas seulement les opinions religieuses, elle s'etende également sur le civil qui est si intimement allié à la religion même par l'identité de l'auteur de l'une et de l'autre loi qu'on ne saurait les séparer ni attribuer à l'une plus d'autorité qu'à l'autre . . .

En admettant donc les Juifs comme sectateurs de la loi Moïse, dans un état quelconque, on ne peut les admettre que comme une nation ou, si l'on aime même comme une corporation distincte qui non seulement communiquera pas avec la nation qui les reçoit quant à ce qui touche le culte et les opinions religieuses mais encore ce qui est relatif à l'exercice des droits civils.

[44] Masson, avocat, *Sur les Juifs*, Paris, mai 1806. 3 pp.

[45] B. D . . . t, *La Boîte à perette des Protestants et des Israëlites*, Paris, 1815, 8 pp. In Nîmes the animosity between Catholics and Protestants prevailed in the 1830s and even later: S. Posener, "La Révolution de Juillet et le département du Gard." *Mercure de France*, 1930, 607–36. On the anti-Protestant attitude of the Alsatian Catholic leaders in the 19th century see the pamphlet *L'Alsace . . .*, Clermont-Ferrand, 1874, by the Alsatian Jewish leader Julien Sée and the bibliography on the same subject in his diary *Guerre de 1870 . . .*, Paris, 1884.

Les Juifs ne se marieront jamais avec les Chrétiens; ils n'habiteront, ils ne mangeront pas avec eux; ils conserveront leur jurisprudence particulière.

Il en resultera nécessairement une masse de privilèges en leur faveur, dont voici les principaux:

1. Celui de ne pouvoir être astreints à aucuns travaux publics ni privés les jours de Sabbat et pendant les autres fêtes que leur sont prescrites par leur loi. Ces fêtes d'ailleurs n'étant pas coincidentes avec celles des Chrétiens troubleront nécessairement l'ordre de la société, si les Juifs participaient à quelques fonctions publiques dans l'état.

2. Celui de ne se marier qu'entre eux seuls, de conserver leur race pur et sans le moindre mélange et de concentrer par consequent aussi leurs biens dans leurs familles.

3. Celui d'avoir leurs habitations, leur logements et même leurs auberges à part.

4. Celui d'avoir les boucheries particulières.

5. Celui d'être jugés d'après leur loi civile et d'avoir leurs Rabbins pour interprêtes de cette loi et pour premiers juges.

Il leur est impossible de renoncer à aucun des ces privilèges sans renier leur loi, sans cesser d'être Juifs.

Une renonciation quelconque faite par quelques individus de la nation à l'un ou l'autre de ces privilèges ne diront absolument rien; il faudroit de toute nécessité que leurs Rabbins et tous les chefs de famille y adhérassent formallement; et encore ne craint-on pas d'avancer qu'une pareille renonciation générale ou partielle, ne serait jamais sincère de leur part, qu'ils la désavouereioient intérieurement et qu'elle leur vaudroit plutôt le mépris que d'approbation de tous les gens de bien.

Comme il leur donc est impossible de renoncer aux droits et privilèges qui en font et qui en feront toujours une nation distincte, il est également impossible que la nation qui les reçoit dans son sein puisse leur communiquer indifférement tous les avantages tandis qu'ils ne communiqueroient que très imparfaitement avec elle ceux qu'ils pourroient eux mêmes répandre sur la société si on les considéroit comme simple hommes et non comme Juifs et comme privilégies.

Leur accorder sans aucune restriction, sans examen préalable de leur facultés . . . tous les droits de la cité Françoise, ce feroit attirer de Juifs étrangers chez nous, se seroit blesser essentiellement les droits des autres citoyens, se seroit faciliter les moyens aux Juifs de faire des conquêtes légales sur les Chrétiens qui bientôt ne pourroient plus soutenir leur conquerence et seroient obligés de leur céder en tout et partout la place.

Cependant si les privilèges exclusifs des Juifs sont, généralement parlant, destructifs de la société, celui de leur union conjugale exclusive avec des conjoints de leur race seroit dejà plus que suffisant pour empêcher qu'ils ne puissent jamais devenir nos frères, ni nos concitoyens, attendu que pendant qu'ils emprétéroient continuellement, de mille manières, sur nous, à la faveur de leur privilèges, nous ne pourrions jamais recouvrir, pas même par la réciprocité du bien conjugal, ce qu'ils auroient acquis ou gagné sur nous . . .

RELIGIOUS PROPAGANDA AGAINST JEWS DURING
THE FRENCH REVOLUTION OF 1789

"The emancipation of the Jews was an anti-Catholic act,"
the Alsatian Jewish physician Michel Lévy (1809–1872) wrote
in 1836.[1] Indeed, if anti-Jewish propaganda during the French
Revolution of 1789 is accepted at face value, such a conclusion
must follow.

At the National Assembly the spokesmen of the Catholic
Church, of whom Abbot Jean-Sifrein Maury was the most
vehement, fought bitterly against granting citizenship to the
Jews. Maury's role as a Catholic leader is not taken too seriously
by modern historians. Maury, who before 1789 had no status
in aristocratic circles, is characterized as an extrovert who loved
the limelight, and dreamed of becoming France's greatest orator.
He seized the issue of emancipation to make speeches against
the Jews. However, his superficial arguments were extremely
useful to the reactionary elements that sought to prove the
danger to Christian life inherent in the emancipation of the
Jews.[2] The more serious arguments against Jewish emancipation
were presented by officially recognized leaders of the Church,
e. g., A.-L.-H. de la Fare, bishop of Nancy.[3]

In addition to the official position against Jewish emancipation
that it adopted at the National Assembly, the Catholic Church
conducted a well organized popular campaign aiming not only to

---

[1] Michel Lévy, *Coup d'oeil historique sur l'état des Israélites en France et
particulièrement en Alsace* (Strasbourg, 1836), p. 27 ("L'émancipation des
Israélites est un fait anti-catholique").

[2] A. Aulard, *Les orateurs de la Révolution. L'Assemblée Constituante* (Paris,
1905), pp. 213–64.

[3] C. Constantin, *L'Evêche du département de la Meurthe de 1791 à 1802*
(Nancy, 1935), pp. 40–74.

Originally published in *Proceedings of the American Academy for Jewish
Research*, vol. XXVIII (1959).

raise anti-Jewish feelings and thus force the legislative authorities to abandon the proposal of Jewish emancipation, but also to help to provoke an uprising against the new regime. *La Rocambole*, published by the anti-Jacobin David Sabalut, encouraged the counter-revolutionary elements by telling them that only Protestants, Jews and brigands supported the Revolution, that a victorious counter-revolution would banish all Jews and Protestants.[4]

The Catholic enemies of the Jews viewed their opposition to Jewish emancipation in the context of their struggle for the survival of the Church.[5] The Jews were held responsible for the new regime's decrees directed against the Catholic Church. A "coalition in many communities which tries to mislead the citizens by insinuating that the Jews solicited the decree against the priests," was referred to by the mayor of Barr (Lower Rhine) in a report dated September 1792, to the Departmental *Directoire*. In fact, these communes became the scene of disorders.[6]

The canard that the new regime favored Jews and Protestants while discriminating against Catholics became popular. *L'Ami du Roi*, published by Abbot T.-M. Royou and Galart de Montjoie, charged that the National Assembly promoted the interests only of Jews and Protestants. *Les Sabats jacobites*, published by F. Marchant, reported that churches were closed while religious establishments of Protestants and Jews were not disturbed.[7] The same argument was repeated by *Le Mercure Universel* (published by A. Tournon) and *Le Journal de Louis XVI*.[8] The *Journal de la Cour* (edited by G.-M.-A. Brune and

[4] *La Rocambole ou Journal des honnêtes gens*, No. 3, Jan. 8, 1792; *Le Réviseur universel et impartial*, No. 69, June 10, 1792.

[5] P. Boutin, *Le Cardinal de la Fare* (Fontenau-le-Comte, 1922), pp. 7–8.

[6] R. Reuss, "L'antisémitisme dans le Bas-Rhin pendant la Révolution." *REJ*, LXVIII (1914), 259.

[7] *L'Ami du Roi*, No. 226, Jan. 21, 1791; *Les Sabats jacobites*, No. XVII, 1791.

[8] *Le Mercure universel* XXXIV, No. 100, Dec. 5, 1793 ("la liberté qu'ont le juif et le protestant de se réunir en société particulière et de célébrer leur culte comme ils le jugent convenable"); Prospectus of *Le Journal de Louis*

Gautier de Syonnet) compared the Catholic religion to a deserted
and persecuted legitimate wife, while favors were heaped on
the religions of the Protestants and Jews like beloved mistresses.[9]
The authors of popular pamphlets described how Jews took
under their protection all enemies of the Church. For example,
in a pamphlet directed against the Alsatian republican, Jean-F.
Froesamlé, François-Louis Rumpler, the Alsatian anti-Jewish
pamphleteer, told this fantastic story: Froesamlé died suddenly
in a café and Christians refused to bury him; but the Jews, in
gratitude for Froesamlé's fight against the Church, interred him
in the Jewish cemetery and prayed at the synagogue for his
soul.[10]

Christians were warned that Jewish usurers would compel
them to forsake Christianity.[11] According to one newspaper,
should the existing state of affairs continue, all Christians would
be forced within thirty years to undergo circumcision. The
editor of another newspaper lamented: "It is necessary to
judaize in order to be a citizen . . . Only together with the Jews
may you pray to Jesus."[12] J.-M.-A. Servan, author of a popular
anti-Jewish pamphlet jested that the Count H.-G.-R. de
Mirabeau was ready to accept "Moses' magnificent laws."[13]

XVI, and L. Kahn, *Les Juifs de Paris pendant la Révolution* (Paris, 1898),
p. 48 ("Tes rois, peuple, refusent aux ministres de la religion de l'Etat la
tolérance, le repos accordé aux juifs, aux luthériens, aux calvinistes . . .").

[9] *Journal de la Cour et de la Ville*, No. 24, Feb. 11, 1791 ("la religion catholique a été repoussée, depouillée, persécutée; c'est la femme! la religion
protestante, la juive est combl.'e de faveurs: on fait tout pour elle . . . c'est
la maîtresse").

[10] F.-L. Rumpler, *Prösamle angezeigt dem Zuchtpolizei-Gerichte . . .* (Strasburg, 1801), pp. 31–32.

[11] This argument was used by the Deputy Hell in the introduction to a
new edition of a pamphlet published first in 1769: *Requête des marchands et
négociants de Paris, contre l'admission des Juifs* (Paris, 1790), pp. 22–23.

[12] *Journal de la Cour*, No. 36, Jan. 16, 1791 ("Il faut judaïser pour être
citoyens"); No. 34, Apr. 3, 1791 ("Qui peut nous assurer, que nous ne serons
pas forcés de nous faire tous circoncire avant trente ans . . .?"); *La Rocambole
des journaux*, No. 31, Oct. 9, 1791 ("Ce n'est qu'avec les Juifs qu'il faut prier
Jézus"); L. Kahn, *op. cit.*, pp. 54–56.

[13] J.-M.-A. Servan, *Evénements remarquables et intéressant . . .* (n. p., 1790),
p. 12; (". . . les juifs sont nos pères, & nous enfans dénaturés, nous délibérons

Partisans of Jewish emancipation such as Ch.-M. de Talleyrand-Périgord (bishop of Autun), Abbot Henri-Baptiste Grégoire, were ridiculed as dishonest deputies who were bribed by the Jews, or as circumcised, hidden Jews, or as rabbis who planned to convert the National Assembly in a synagogue.[14]

To curb the anti-revolutionary activities of the Catholic Church, the new regime decided in April 1790 that bishops and priests should be elected by all citizens possessing the right to vote, i. e., theoretically including not only Catholics, but also Protestants, Jews and even atheists.[15] This became the excuse for anti-Protestant, anti-Jewish and anti-revolutionary propaganda. The *Directoire* of Lower Rhine warned in a petition of December 31, 1790 that should Jews be granted full citizenship, they would participate in the election of priests and bishops.[16] The Nancy bishop and Deputy La Fare, who fought against Jewish emancipation, stated that his diocesans wrote to him: Should we lose you, a Jew will take your place and become our bishop.[17] The same warning was given by the bishop of

si nous les admettrons à nous proposer des loix ... Venez donc, Izachar; venez Zabulon, venez Iscariot, venez Aaron, & vous Juda, venez, accourez, mêtez-vous enfin à vos enfans, qui déjà ouvrent leurs bras à vos magnifiques loix mosaïques!").

[14] L. Kahn, *op. cit.*, pp. 57–59, 61–62.

[15] Js. Foesser, *Meistratzheim*, (Strasbourg, 1939), p. 190 ("Nach dieser Civilverfassung solte "das Volk" den Bischof wählen, auch Juden und Protestanten waren Wähler"); Louis Villat, *Le Révolution et l'Empire* (Paris, 1940), 106 ("... de toutes les innovations, la plus dangereuse était celle qui remettait au seul corps électoral le soin de choisir les évêques et les curés: non seulement les catholiques, mais les adeptes d'autres religions et les libres-penseurs, ennemis de l'Eglise, étaient chargés de lui procurer ses ministres...").

[16] Charles Hoffmann, *L'Alsace au dix-huitième siècle* (Colmar, 1907), IV, 526 ("Le danger d'assimiler les Juifs aux autres citoyens serait bien plus grand encore, s'ils devaient concourir comme eux, au choix des ministres de l'Eglise. Jamais le peuple ne se familiariserait avec l'idée que le souffrage d'un Juif, par précepte et par fanatisme ennemi; d'une croyance destructive de la sienne, dût être reçu pour lui désigner un pasteur ou un évêque").

[17] Joseph Denais-Darnays, *Les Juifs en France avant et depuis la Révolution. Comment ils ont conquis l'égalité* (Paris, 1901), p. 35 ("si nous venions à vous perdre, nous verrions un Juif devenir notre évêque tant ils sont habiles à s'emparer de tout").

Speier.[18] One newspaper noted that Jews were appointed to various administrative posts and that soon they would be elected to bishoprics.[19]

This propaganda was essentially directed against the constitutional clergy who favored the new regime. Abbot Jacob Couturier taunted the National Assembly that the constitutional bishops should be consecrated "in the synagogues of the Jews."[20] J.-B.-J. Gobel, who was elected in March 1791 to the bishopric of Paris, was attacked as being of Jewish origin.[21]

During the election of François-Antoine Brendel as constitutional bishop for Alsace, Catholic circles published a pamphlet (*Cerf-Behr aux trois rois*) in which Brendel, whose physical resemblance to a Jew was noted, was described as a Jewish candidate. The Alsatian supporters of the new regime replied by publishing a pamphlet *Contre-Révolution*.[22] In order to discredit the election of Brendel Catholics cast five votes for the Alsatian Jewish leader Cerfberr of Médelsheim. During the election of the constitutional bishop for Saint-Flour the electoral authorities counted four votes for a Jew, eight for

[18] *Feierliche Erklärung des Herrn Fürst- Bischof zu Speier gegen die von der sogenannten National-Versammlung in Frankreich beschlossene bürgerliche Verfassung der Geistlichkeit* . . . (n. p., 16 März 1791), p. 9 ("Soll von einem Haufen weltlicher Wahlmänner abhängen, unter welche nicht nur Protestanten sondern sogar auch Juden, ohne Unterschied, als sogenannte Aktiv = Bürger zugelassen werden").

[19] *Journal de la Cour et de la Ville*, No. 5, March 5, 1792: "Il paraît, qu'en plusieurs endroits on place des juifs dans tous les corps administratifs; il faut espérer qu'avant peu nous les verrons élire aux évêchés."

[20] *Mercure universel*, March 2, 1791; *Journal de la Noblesse*, No. XI, March 1, 1791; *Annales de Mercier*, No. DXVI, March 2, 1791; *Journal général de France*, No. 61, March 2, 1791; L. Kahn, *op. cit.*, p. 54.

[21] Dr. J.-F. E. Robinet, *Le mouvement religieux à Paris pendant la Révolution* (Paris, 1898), II, 435.

[22] *Cerf-Behr aux Trois Rois* (n. p., 1791), 10 pp. ("La couleur de ses cheveux, la coupe de son visage, sa saleté et ses goûts le font paraître juif"). The pamphlet was also published in German. See also F.-C. Heitz, *La Contre-Révolution en Alsace de 1789 à 1793* (Strasbourg, 1865), pp. 144–49; R. Reuss, *La Cathédrale de Strasbourg pendant la Révolution* (Paris, 1888), p. 172–73; Idem, *La Constitution civile du clergé et la crise religieuse en Alsace* . . . (Strasbourg, 1922), I, 160.

Count de Mirabeau and twenty for a notorious thief.[23] Another warning against the participation of Jews in religious life of Catholics came from the pen of an anti-revolutionary pamphleteer in 1793.[24] While some Protestants did, in fact, participate in the election of Catholic bishops[25] there is no proof that any Jews similarly exercised their constitutional right.

Churches and synagogues should not be permitted on the same streets, because Jews and Moslems would attack the churches, a Calais newspaper warned. Another newspaper, published by Abbot L.-A. de Fontenai predicted that Protestants and Jews would organize a carnage in the churches of the majority, i. e., Catholic Church.[26] A more insidious campaign was conducted in connection with the confiscation of Church properties and their sale as national property (*biens nationaux*). The argument was advanced that Jews would buy up the churches and desecrate the holy places. Thus, the Society of the Jacobins of Strasbourg reported that clerical propaganda against the Revolution harped on the story that the Jews would buy up Church property and become the rulers of Alsace. Of course, this propaganda against the Jews was equally hostile

[23] E. Seinguerlet, *Strasbourg pendant la Révolution* (Paris, 1881), p. 63, 83; Heitz, *op. cit.*, pp. 144–49; *Le Journal de la Cour*, No. 16, March 12, 1791; *Bulletin et Journal des Journaux*, No. 40, Aug. 4, 1791; L. Kahn, *op. cit.*, pp. 55–56.

[24] *Kurze Widerlegung einer sogenannten Einladung zur Wiedervereinigung, Die Hr. [Th.] Anton Deresen, Konstitutionspriester zu Strassburg an die katolischen Bürger dieser Stadt ergehen lassen* ([Strassburg,] 1793), p. 4 ("Sehet, ihr könnet nicht nur geschworene Priester, sondern auch protestantische Minister, sogar Rabiner bei eueren Leichbegängnissen haben, auch Lutherische Kirchen, auch die Sinagogen der Juden, die Moscheen der Türken, die Tempel der Heiden stehen eauch zu euerem Gebrauche offen . . ."). In his pamphlet *Einladung zur Wiervereinigung an die katolischen Bürger Strassburgs* . . . (n. p., 1793), 16 pp., Deresen did not mention the Jews.

[25] *Adresse d'un Ministre Protestant à ses concitoyens Protestans électeurs du département du Bas-Rhin* [Strasbourg, 1791.] 4 pp. The author called the Protestants to help elect a catholic priest "éclairé, vertueux, patriote."

[26] *Le Postillon par Calais*, Apr. 16, 1791; *Journal général*, No. 3, Feb. 3, 1791 ("le carnage dans les temples de l'Eglise dominante"); L. Kahn, *op. cit.*, p. 179.

to the economic policies of the Revolution and was meant to persuade Catholics not to buy national property.[27]

The *Gazette de Paris* warned that although "the arrogant Protestant and the insolent Jew," by buying nationalized Church property would ruin the priests, they would starve rather than beg for bread from Protestants and Jews. The *Journal de la Cour* announced that churches would be separated into three sections, with the *calvaire* reserved for the synagogue; that Jews had, in fact, tried to buy a church and transform it into a synagogue. The *Courrier français* recounted a similar story about the Saint-Antoine church in Paris. According to the *Rôdeur français*, edited by G.-T.M. Villenave, Jews visited the bishop of Autun in order to pay him for church properties.[28]

Variations of the same theme were voiced in the National Assembly by anti-Jewish deputies, *e. g.*, Abbot F.-M. Thiébault, deputy from Metz who warned that nationalized church property would be taken over by the Jews and the clergy would be forced to engage in usury. J.-A. Pflieger, the anti-Jewish deputy from Altkirch, wrote that the Jews were being considered as possible buyers of national property. Maury attacked the Jews for demanding equal rights in the purchase of national property. Abbot Peyretta of Corsica warned that church property would be sold in order to repay national debts owed to Jews and merchants.[29] A large number of Alsatian and other local counter-revolutionary pamphlets used the same anti-Jewish theme in order to discredit the sale of national property: the government would use church properties to repay debts owed to the Jewish

[27] *De l'état civil des Juifs en Alsace. Rapport lu à l'assemblée de la Société des amis de la constitution de Strasbourg, le 27 février 1790* . . . ([Strasbourg,] 1790), pp. 5–6.

[28] *Gazette de Paris*, March 26, 1790; *Le Journal de la Cour*, No. 24, Jan. 24, 1791, No. 6, May 6, 1791; *Le Courrier français*, No. 108, Apr. 17, 1790; *Le Rôdeur français*, No. 39, 1790; L. Kahn, *op. cit.*, p. 60.

[29] [F.-M. Thiébaut,] *Considérations catholico-politiques sur les immeubles du clergé* (Metz, [1789]), pp. 24, 27; E. Muhlenbeck, "Il y a cent ans!" *Revue d'Alsace*, XLIV (1893), 438; *Opinion de M. l'abbé Maury . . . sur la propriété des biens ecclésiastiques* . . . (Paris, 1789), p. 13; Jean Jaurès, *Histoire Socialiste, I. La Constituante* (Paris, 1901), p. 450; R. Reuss, *Histoire de l'Alsace* (Paris 1912), p. 230.

leader Cerfberr; the Jews would use the large sums owed to them by peasants to buy up land belonging to the Church and thus force peasants to work for them;[30] Churches would be converted into synagogues, mosques and Protestant temples; Protestantism and Judaism would prevail.[31] One counter-revolutionary pamphleteer, supposedly a woman, claimed that she actually had seen many former churches serving as clubs, Protestant religious establishments and synagogues.[32]

Even the Jacobin deputy of Alsace, J.-J. Reubell, who defended the economic policies of the Revolution, but opposed Jewish emancipation, stated in the National Assembly on January 28, 1790 that counter-revolutionary elements would use the Jews' citizenship for their slogan that Jews and speculators would acquire the nationalized properties.[33] Some supporters of the new regime who were not necessarily anti-Jewish minded referred to purchase of churches by Jews. *L'Observateur* of Gabriel Feydel, who used to attack all religious groups, wrote that Jews would replace Christians in the churches and the clergy would forsake doubtful virginity for conjugal bonds. He, Feydel, reported that a group of Jewish capitalists had offered 800,000 livres for the property of the Chartreux in Paris.[34] According

[30] *Avis aux Alsaciens*, (Strasbourg, 1790), pp. 12, 26; *Je vous dirai vos vérités* (n. p., 1790), pp. 19, 21, 82; Heitz, *op. cit.*, pp. 14–17.

[31] *L'Assemblée nationale ou Courrier français*, No. 128, May 1791 ("On propose de convertir nos temples en synagogues, en mosquées, en temples de Luthériens et d'anabaptistes"); *Journal de la Cour et de la Ville*, No. 43, Feb. 12, 1791 ("Vous voulez placer le calvinisme, le judaïsme, le luthérianisme sur le trône").

[32] *Historie de la conversion d'une Dame parisienne. Ecrite par elle-même.* Seconde édition (Paris, 1792), p. 6 ("Je voyais plusieurs de nos églises converties en clubs politiques, en temples des protestans, en synagogues de juifs").

[33] "L'Alsace est inondée de libellistes dont les ennemis publics se servent pour chercher à soulever les peuples, et aprés vos décrets, ils leur diront qu'il existe une confédération des juifs et des agioteurs pour s'emparer de toutes les propriétés:" *Revue des grandes journées parlementaires*, I (1897), 45.

[34] "Les descendants d'Aaron, de Moyse, d'Elie, de tous les Patriarches de la Palestine, vont s'emparer successivement des retraites tranquilles et riantes des disciples de saint Bruno, de saint Benoît, du Séraphique saint

to a letter published in *La Gazette Universelle* and supposedly written by a Jew, the city of Paris expressed its desire to sell to Jews a church which would be converted into a synagogue.[35] Most probably this letter was written not by a Jew but by the editors themselves who tried in such a way to encourage the sale of nationalized properties.

In any event Jews were not engaged in buying national property on a large scale. In a much later period some churches were transformed into synagogues. In most of these cases Jews did not even know the religious origin of the buildings bought by them for use as synagogues.[36]

The vehement Catholic propaganda against the Jews had a double objective: to oppose the emancipation of the Jews and, at the same time, to discredit the new regime and to help counter-revolutionary elements. Many supporters of the new regime, *e. g.*, some Jacobins of Strasbourg, clearly saw the Church's design and therefore openly advocated the emancipation of the Jews.[37] However, many sincere supporters of the new regime, *e.* g., Reubell who was a sincere Jacobin, were prevented by their traditional hatred of the Jews from seeing the anti-revolutionary tendency in the fight against Jewish emancipa-

François, du convertisseur et rôtisseur saint Dominique et autres saints de parecil acabit; ou vous voyez des moines incirconcis, vous verrez incessamment des usuriers déprépucés; où se faisait le trafic des indulgences et des messes, on vendra désormais du brocart et des galons; la Bible y supplantera les quatre évangélistes; une virginité douteuse y sera remplacée par les douceurs du lieu conjugal, qui, pour l'ordinaire, est infiniment plus chaste et surtout beaucoup moins sterile. En deux mots, une société de capitalistes juifs a offert 800,000 livres de l'emplacement des Chartreux de Paris, d'où l'on peut conclure qu'il vaut bien le double:" *L'Observateur*, No. 89, Feb. 27, 1790; L. Kahn, *op. cit.*, p. 50; P. Sgnac, "Les Juifs et Napoléon," *Revue d'Histoire moderne et contemporaine* I, (1900), 230–31.

[35] "La ville de Paris désire que nous achetions une église pour la convertir en maison de prières pour notre nation. Je voudrai que cela se fit:" *La Gazette universelle*, No. 299, Oct. 26, 1791; L. Kahn, *op. cit.*, p. 126.

[36] Z. Szajkowski, "Jewish Participation in the Sale of National Property during the French Revolution." *Jewish Social Studies*, XIV (1952), 291–316; Idem, "Synagogues during the French Revolution of 1789–1800." *Ibid.*, XX (1958), 226–27.

[37] See note 27.

tion.[38] A justice of the peace of Lorraine, while attacking Grégoire's attachment to the Church, derided him for acting like a Jew.[39] On July 12, 1790 J.-M. de la Rue, a priest of Huningue, spoke against Jewish emancipation at the *Club des amis de la Constitution* in Paris.[40]

It is ironic that a few reactionary elements at times disclaimed responsibility for the persecution of the Jews. The aristocratic emigré press took up their defence because in many places the Jews were robbed by the revolutionary regime.[41]

The Jews also had many sincere friends among Catholics and noblemen, including Abbot Grégoire, Abbot A.-R.-C. Bertolio, Abbot Claude Fauchet, Abbot F.-V. Mulot. Among the members of the *Société de philosophie chrétienne*, which engaged in Christian apologetics, were sincere friends of the Jews, e. g., Grégoire himself, the Hebraist Rivière of the College de France, and Abbot Antoine Guénée, author of the *Lettres*, published in 1769 in reply to Voltaire's anti-Jewish attacks.[42] However, these Catholics supported the new regime and openly opposed the counter-revolutionary activities conducted by the Catholic Church. The official circles of the Catholic Church remained anti-Jewish. God will punish those responsible for the emancipation of the Jews, became a popular by word.[43] Anti-Jewish behavior was a part of daily life. In 1792 the

[38] Z. Szajkowski, *Autonomy and Communal Jewish Debts during the French Revolution of 1789* (New York, 1959), pp. 11–13.

[39] H. Baumont, *La Société populaire de Lunéville, 1793–1795* (Nancy, 1889), p. 26 ("Grégoire d'Embermenil a fait le j . . . f . . ." [juif]).

[40] Hoffmann, *op. cit.*, IV, 516.

[41] E. de Mirecourt, *Avant, pendant et après la Terreur. Echos des gazettes françaises indépendantes, publiées à l'étranger de 1788 à 1794* (Paris, 1865), II, 265.

[42] A. Gazier, *Etudes sur l'histoire religieuse de la Révolution française* (Paris, 1887), pp. 284–85.

[43] Mme Elisabeth, sister of Louis XVI wrote: "L'Assemblée a mis hier le comble à toutes ses sottises et ses irreligions en donnant aux juifs le droit d'être admis à tous les emplois. Je ne puis te rendre combien je suis en colère de ce décret. Mais Dieu a ses jours de vengeance, et s'il souffre longtemps le mal, il ne punit pas avec moins de force." (*L'Univers israélite*, XXV (1864), 823).

priests of Châtel-sur-Moselle rejected an invitation by Grégoire Nirel, Commandant of the local National Guard, to attend an official ceremony. "Would you" — they asked — "also invite the Jew Gaudechaux?"[44]

The Church spread both anti-Jewish and anti-Protestant propaganda. Yet the Protestants often helped the enemies of the Jews in their opposition to Jewish emancipation.[45]

Anti-Jewish propaganda as a means of discrediting the regime is a policy that can be identified in later periods, *e g.*, during the Revolution of 1830. In 1832, when Bergheim and other Alsatian localities became the scene of anti-Jewish riots, the local administration charged the priests with responsibility, and the sub-prefect of Sélestat reported to his superiors that the riots were to be the signal for a general attack upon the July Revolution.[46] The Catholic Church and all other adversaries of the republican regime favored the *partie légitimiste*. In Alsace the Protestants and Jews were then the chief supporters of the republican regime. Catholics spread the rumor that their Church was in danger and the traditional hatred against Jews and Protestants became the basis for organizing riots and disorders.[47]

Michel Lévy's statement of 1836 was correct. The Jewish emancipation in France came in spite of the efforts of the Catholic Church.

---

[44] Abbé C. Olivier, *Châtel-sur-Moselle pendant la Révolution* (Citeaux, 1896), p. 121.

[45] Z. Szajkowski, "Protestants and Jews of France in Fight for Emancipation, 1789–1791." *Proceedings of the American Academy for Jewish Research*, XXV (1956), 119–21.

[46] Departmental archives of Lower Rhine, 3 M 49.

[47] *Courrier du Bas-Rhin*, Feb. 17, 1843.

THE ATTITUDE OF FRENCH JACOBINS
TOWARD JEWISH RELIGION

FRATERNIZATION of all religious groups was a slogan often used after the outbreak of the French Revolution in 1789, and many revolutionary leaders were very serious about it. The Jewish emancipation was not the result of a political plot, but of a sincere desire to put an end to the restrictions imposed upon the Jews.

On October 27, 1791, the Deputy Raymond de Carbonnières spoke at the Legislative Assembly on the fraternity of the faiths, and he proposed that the Government cover the budgets for the religious activities of all faiths, including the Jews.[1] (This was realized only in 1831.) The Minister of Justice, in his circular of January 10, 1792, declared to the tribunals that the law does not make any distinction between Jews, Christians, or others. Not the opinions, but the actions of everyone should be taken into consideration.[2] Later, on November 27, 1793, during the Terror, the Representative to the Army of the Western Pyrénées called on the army to keep alive hatred only against the Spanish enemies and to express feelings of friendship and fraternity to all Frenchmen, Catholics, Jews, Protestants, and Moslems, provided that they would defend France's unity.[3]

---

[1] *Moniteur* (réimpression), (1791), 255; R. Reuss, *La Constitution civile du clergé et la crise religieuse en Alsace* (1790-1795) (Strasbourg, 1922), I, 336-37.

[2] *Lettre de M. Dupont, Ministre de la justice, à tous les tribunaux sur la liberté des cultes religieux* . . . du 10 janvier 1792 (Bordeaux, n.d.), p. 5: "Elle [la loi] ne distingue pas entre le Juif & le chrétien, le Protestant & le Catholique, le conformiste et le dissident. Elle ne juge pas les opinions et les personnes, mais les actions."

[3] [B.J.B.] *Monestier, répresentant du peuple près l'armée des Pyrénées occidentales . . . à ses frères d'armes* . . . (Pau, n.d.), 3 pp. ["Amitié, fraternité à tous les Français, catholiques, juifs, protestants, musulmans, pourvu qu'ils aiment et qu'ils défendent l'unité. . . ."]

Originally published in *Historia Judaica*, vol. XVIII (1956).

Fraternization of all faiths was not always mere empty talk. In the traditionally anti-Jewish province of Alsace the Fête de la Constitution of 1791 was observed together by Christians and Jews in the churches and synagogues of Bischheim and Bischwiller. In Bischheim one hundred Christians and Jews assembled at a banquet in the house of a rich Jew.[4] Of course, Jews were requested to give up something of their traditional life. An Alsatian pamphleteer of 1790 asked that an end be put to the legend of the Jews' guilt for the crucifixion of Christ and of God's condemnation of the Jews to eternal damnation. But at the same time he appealed to the rabbis to purge the Jewish religion of a multitude of superstitions and ceremonies incompatible with the new state of the nation.[5] In June, 1791 a member of the *Société populaire* of Saverne stated that there could be no equality as long as superstition reigned among the Jews.[6]

Basically, the Jacobins considered the Jewish religion dangerous as all other "old" religions, and the founders and followers of these religions were described as dangerous charlatans and enemies of the human race.[7] Anacharsis Cloots,

---

[4] *Geschichte der gegenwertiger Zeit*, II, Oct. 26, 1791; *Les Annales patriotiques littéraires de la France*, V, July 26, 1791; *L'Auditeur national*, I, Oct. 29, 1791; Reuss, *op. cit.*, I, 336-37.

[5] *Observations sur la possibilité et l'utilité de l'admission des juifs en Alsace aux droits de citoyen* . . . (Strasbourg, 1790), pp.14-17.

[6] Dagobert Fischer, *La Société populaire de Saverne pendant les années 1791 à 1794* (Mulhouse, 1869), p. 15.

[7] "Tous les religionnaires ont été et sont encore les ennemis nés de l'humanité, des charlatans, des empiriques, *Moyse* chez les *Egyptiens*, *Jésus* chez les *Juifs*." Sébastien Lacroix, *La Religion nouvelle* . . . (Marseille, an II), p. 3 [a speech at the general assembly of the "Sociétés populaires du Midi"]. —"C'est ainsi que les Mahomet, les Luther, les Calvin se sont entés sur Jésus, lequel s'étoit ci-devant enté sur Moyse." *Discours prononcé par Balthassard Faure dans l'église ci-devant cathédrale la Commune de Nancy*, . . . 20 *brumaire, an second* . . . (Nancy, n.d.), p. 5.—". . . J'ai parlé des prêtres en général, tels que le papiste, le disciple de Luther et de Calvin, le Rabin. . . le Moufti . . . tous, sans exception, n'ont en vue que de soigner leur intérêts." *Discours sur le fanatisme et la célébration des fêtes décadaires, prononcé au temple dédié à l'Être surprême*, par un Membre de la Société Républicaine de Bruyères (Bruyères, n.d.), p. 11.—"Ouvrez l'histoire des Juifs, voyez Moise leur dictant des loix que Dieux lui même avoient confiées, sur le Mont Sinai." *Discours prononcé à la Société populaire de Charolles* . . . *le 21 brumaire de l'an deux* . . . (Macon, n.d.), p. 7.—"Le catholique, le juif, le protestant, qu'une différence d'opinion et de culte divisait depuis tant de siècles, heureusement réunis, ne reconnaissent plus d'autre divinité que la liberté, la nature, la

author of *Lettres sur les Juifs* (1782), who was always friendly towards Jews and defended them from a revolu-tionary-cosmopolitan point of view, showed his contempt for religion by drawing a comparison between the "dreams of Moses and Christ" and the accomplishments of the Con-vention.[8] Manuel, procurator of Paris, attacked all religions, the priests and rabbis.[9] Still, to some Jacobins, including the pro-Jewish minded Alsatian Jacobin of German origin, Eulogius Schneider, Christianity was at first a revolt against a degenerated Judaism.[10] One Alsatian revolutionary called upon Jews not only to forget about the Messiah, because they now lived in a state of equality and liberty, but he also ex-pressed his hope that some day they would accept Christ's teaching.[11] To many Jacobin pamphleteers the Jewish re-ligion was the source of many evils in Christian life. Thus, e.g., Sunday rest was only a logical result of the Jewish Sab-bath and should be replaced by the more Revolutionary *Décadi*.[12] Here the influence of the Encyclopaedists, who hated the Jewish religion as a source of Christianity, may

raison." *La Gazette française*, No. 688, 28 brumaire an II.—"Le Dieu farouche d'Israél, l' implacable Jehova, le Dieu équivoque des chrétiens . . . vont donc courber leurs têtes superbes devant la seule divinité des hommes libres, la Raison de tous les temps. . . ." *Le Batave*, II, No. 286, Nov. 28, 1793.

8 *Anacharsis à Paris ou Lettre de Jean-Baptiste Cloots, à un Prince d'Allemagne* (Paris, 1790), p. 24. On Cloot's attitude towards Jews see L. Kessler, "Anacharsis Cloots and His "Lettres sur les Juifs," *The Jews in France* (New York, 1942), II, 75-92.

9 *Le Courrier français*, No. 131, May 10, 1792; L. Kahn, *Les Juifs de Paris pendant la Révolution* (Paris, 1898), p. 183.

10 "Jesus hatte den grossen Plan entworfen, dass sinnliche, sklavische, durch Aberglauben und Priesterlist verdorbene Judentum zu zerstören, und auf dessen Trümmern eine geistige, freie, aufgeklärte Religion zu gründen." Eulogius Schneider, *Das Bild des guten Volkslehrers* . . . (Strasbourg [1792]), p. 2.— "Duldet jede Religion, aber duldet keine Pharisäerreligion." Dr. Thaddaus Anton Dereser, *Über religiöse und politische Toleranz* . . . (Strasbourg [1792]), pp. 18-19.

11 *Johann Friedrich Riechter in der Gesellschaft der Jacobiner an seine Mitbürger. Strassburg den 14 October 1792 . . . Erste und zweite Rede* (n.p., n.d), p. 39.

12 "Die Sabbats-Feyer ist ein jüdisches Gesetz, an welches die Christen so wenig gebunden sind, als an die blutigen Opfer." Matthias Engel, *Meine Meinung über die Verlegung der Sonntags-Feyer auf den Dekadi* [Strasbourg, 1794], p. 10. For a Jacobin analysis of the Jewish Sabbath see J. J. Käm-merer, *Die Religion der Jugend und der Vernunft über die Feier der Dekaden* (Strasbourg, 1793), pp. 14-20.

clearly be seen. Biblical and other historical Jewish subjects, which were very popular among Christian scholars and in the dramatic literature prior to 1789, were neglected during the Revolution. Biblical heroes were replaced by Greek and Roman legendary figures, which could more easily be adapted to the revolutionary slogans.[13]

But the anti-religious propaganda had its positive effects, too. Hatred of Jews and other non-Catholics was no longer an official policy. B. Faure, the leader during the period of the Terror in Nancy, stated on November 10, 1793: "There are no longer in the Republic Jews, nor Protestants, nor Anabaptists, nor Catholics; there are only French republicans."[14] Dechristianization was the first major factor paving the way for full freedom of religious minorities, including the Jews.[15] The Catholics ceased to be the dominant element in France's life; they became merely the largest of many religious groups. At the inauguration of the Temple of Reason in Epinal on January 29, 1794 the Jacobin Christophe Denis stated: "I am not asking you today to abjure the Catholic faith which you worshipped yesterday, but I must warn you that this religion cannot claim any domination, that this religion is not the public religion any more than the religion of the Jews, of the Moslems, the Anabaptists, or others. . . . I am asking you citizens to consider the fact that of every hundred people on this earth, only one at most practises your faith; the others profess religions established by Moses, Confucius, Brama, Mohammed, Luther, Calvin, etc."[16]

As a result of the break with the Catholic Church, the religious freedom of the Jews was sometimes protected by non-Jews. Thus, e.g., at the beginning of the Revolution

[13] Biblical subjects came back already during the First Empire, but only later did they again enjoy popularity on a large scale.

[14] *Discours prononcé par Balthazard Faure . . . 20 brumaire an second . . .* (Nancy, an II), 7 pp.; G. Floquet, "Le Culte de la Raison . . . à Nancy pendant la Révolution," *Revue de l'Est*, XIV (1900), 541.

[15] R. Anchel, *Napoléon et les juifs* (Paris, 1927), p. 572.

[16] J. K., "L'Inauguration à Epinal du Temple de la Raison le 10 pluviôse an II," *La Révolution dans les Vosges*, XVI (1927), 92, 94. On Chr. Denis (1742-1813), a notary who later became secretary of the Vosges departement, see A. Philippe, *ibid.*, III (1924-25), 244-51.

Paris protested against the participation of the National Guard in Catholic processions because Jewish guards could not to be forced to take part. The *Société populaire* of Nice protested—in the name of freedom of commerce—against prohibiting Jews to open their stores on Sundays.[17]

According to the historian Robert Anchel, the Terror gave the persecutions of the Jews an anti-religious color. However, the opinion of the historian A. Aulard that the condemning of Jews during the Terror was not an act of anti-Semitism, but rather punishment for counter-revolutionary activity seems to be more acceptable.[18] So are the conclusions of the well-known Alsatian historian Rodolphe Reuss, that the anti-religious laws were directed mainly against the Catholic Church because of its anti-revolutionary attitude; "the brutal violences of the iconoclastic Jacobins were directed against Jews only in the form of ricochets."[19] The Jews could not be as dangerous to the Revolution as the Church was. Although the idea of having separate Jewish communities was repugnant to the Revolution,[20] there was no need for drastic action against Jews as a group. Robespierre himself was one of the first to demand citizenship for the Jews.[21] Already prior to the Terror the Friends of the Constitution stated that Jews and Protestants more readily respected the new order than the Catholics did. In 1791, François de Neufchâteau, in a discussion on the civic oath to be taken by Catholic priests, stated to the Legislative Committee: "No other faith presents this system of resistance to the law. The Protestants, the Jews, have different religious

[17] Kahn, *op. cit.*, p. 183; Joseph Combet, *La Révolution à Nice* (Paris, 1912), p. 58.
[18] Anchel, *op. cit.*, p. 14; A. Aulard, in *La Révolution française*, LXXXI (1928), 272.
[19] Reuss, "Quelques documents nouveaux sur l'antisémitisme dans le Bas-Rhin de 1794 à 1799," *REJ*, LIX (1910), 269; *idem, Notes sur l'instruction primaire en Alsace pendant la Révolution* (Paris-Nancy, 1910), pp. 50-51.
[20] Kurt Stillschweig, "Die Judenemanzipation im Licht des französischen Nationsbegriffs," *Monatsschrift für Geschichte und Wissenschaft des Judentums*, LXXXI (1937), 457-78.
[21] A. Mathiez, "Robespierre et l'émancipation des juifs," *AHRF* [*Annales historiques de la Révolution française*], VIII (1931), 261-62, and "Robespierre et Grégoire sous la Constituante," *ibid.*, 261.

maxims than ours; but they are submissive to the law, they respect all established authorities."[22]

The Jacobins were not ideological atheists, as has already been proven by the historian Albert Mathiez in his discussion with Aulard. The Jacobins did not fight religion as a principle, but only the Catholic Church for its association with the counter-revolution. Because of the Church's position dechristianization of the population meant for the Jacobins saving the Revolution. Robespierre was not an atheist; he attacked those enemies of the country who fought the Revolution with the help of the "dagger of fanatism and the venom of atheism." The Girondists, too, were not atheists, i.e., non-believers in God as a matter of principle. Already on June 8, 1791, the Directoire of the department of the Gironde warned against "those men without religion . . . who identify the Clergy with the sacred law of religion and faith."[23] In Marseille, Moignet warned that the Monarchy wanted to make a come-back through atheism. The revolutionary song writer Aristide Valcourt urged that the Church be renounced, but that the Creator be respected and he shunned atheism. The Jacobin Claude Liégerot of Epinal declared in a speech of August 7, 1794: "God exists; this truth is known by all ages and peoples: let us worship him and adore his greatness and his goodness; but mean cere-

22   *Le Mercure universel,* II, Apr. 21, 1791; *L'Auditeur national,* I, No. 60, Nov. 30, 1791; Kahn, *op. cit.,* pp. 182-83.

23   Pierre Flottes, "Le Club des Jacobins de Bordeaux et de la monarchie constituonnelle," *La Révolution française,* LXIX (1916), 337-62; Mathiez, *Robespierre et le Culte de l'Être Suprême* (Le Puy, n.d.), 32 pp.; *idem, Robespierre et la déchristianisation* (Le Puy, n.d.), 63 pp.; G. Lenôtre, *Le Mysticisme révolutionnaire. Robespierre et la "Mère de Dieu"* (Paris, n.d.), 335 pp.; Mathiez, "Le Robespierre de M. Lenôtre," *AHRF,* IV (1927), 97-110; G. Kerl, *Robespierres Kirchenpolitik* (Leipzig, n.d.), 67 pp.; A. Richard, *Le Gouvernement révolutionnaire dans les Basses-Pyrénées* (Paris, 1927), pp. 153-160; G. Lefebure, "Le Culte de la raison et l'athéisme," *AHRF,* IV (1927), 593-94; Mathiez, *La Révolution et l'eglise* (Paris, 1910), p. 144; *idem, Contributions à l'histoire religieuse de la Révolution* (Paris, 1907); Aulard, *Le Culte de la raison et le culte de l'Être Suprême* (Paris, 1892); Edith Bernardin, *Les idées religieuses de Mme. Rolland* (Paris, 1933); *Discours de Maximilien Robespierre .. . 20 prairial, an second* (Bordeaux, 1794), p. 5; G. Rouanet, "La Religiosité des Girondins," *AHRF,* V (1928), 108-109; Aulard, *Études et leçons sur la Révolution française* (5e serie, Paris, 1907), pp. 203-303; *Adresse du Directoire du Département de la Gironde . . . 8 juin 1791* (n.p., n.d.), 10 pp. (City archives of Bordeaux, BI).

monies should not disgrace our veneration for him."[24]   This
was also the policy of the Jewish Jacobins of Saint-Esprit-
lès-Bayonne who, in a proclamation of May 31, 1794, on the
Festival of the *Etre Suprême,* cautioned against the aristocracy and godlessness.[25]

Did the Jacobins persecute the Jews because of their
religion?   According to the majority of Jewish historians,
a Jew named Jean de Mendes was guillotined in Bordeaux for
having stated that he could not accept the Constitution because of his religious principles.[26]   But the same Mendes
(known later as Blondin) had been converted to Christianity
in 1776 and, upon his conversion, received a yearly pension
of 150 livres from the King of France.   On July 20, 1794,
he was sentenced to death. In most official documents Mendes
figures as a converted Jew (*ex Juif*).[27]   Of course, Bordeaux
Jews, too, suffered from the Terror but not to the extent of
having to pay with their lives.   On July 19, 1794, a 34-year-
old Jewish peddler, Jassé Carcassonne, was guillotined in
Nîmes (department of Gard). According to some historians,
Carcassonne, and other Jewish victims (the Cantor Mardochée Mayrargues and David Crémieux), were executed
because of their refusal to recognize the new revolutionary
religion of Reason.[28]   Before the Revolution, only thirty-

---

[24] Moignet, *Discours prononcé dans la fête célebrée en l'honneur de
l'Être-Suprême de Marseille, le 20 prairial* (Marseille, an II), p. 4; Aristide
Valcourt, "Strophes sur l'Être Suprême," in *Recueil d'hymnes républicaines . . .*
(Paris, an II), p. 99; Claude Liégerot, *Discours prononcé au Temple de
l'Eternel, au Clerjus le 20 thermidor, l'an II . . .* (Epinal, n.d.), 6 pp.; *La
Révolution dans les Vosges,* VII (1913), 53.

[25] E. Ginsburger, *Le Comité de surveillance de Jean-Jacques Rousseau,
Saint-Esprit-lès-Bayonne* (Paris, 1934), p. 32.

[26] T. Malvezin, *Histoire des juifs à Bordeaux* (Bordeaux, 1879), p. 27;
H. Léon, *Histoire des juifs de Bayonne* (Paris, 1893), p. 163; Léon Berman,
Histoire des juifs en France des origines à nos jours (Paris, 1937), pp. 637-68;
Salo W. Baron, *A Social and Religious History of the Jews* (New York, 1937),
II, 227; A. Tcherikower, "The Jewish Struggle for Rights during the French
Revolution," *The Jews in France* (New York, 1942), II, 55 (in Yiddish).

[27] Departmental archives of Gironde, C 84 and 1093, L 57, p. 127; city
archives of Bordeaux, fonds R. Brouillard, Inventaire de la serie L, V, 59a;
A. Vivie, "Dictionnaire des arrestations," VI, 573, and documents, XV, 36;
Journal du Club National, March 22, 1794; A. Vivie, *La Terreur à Bordeaux*
(Bordeaux, 1877), p. 386; printed sentence of July 20, 1794. Broadside.

[28] Joseph Milner, *Jews in France* (Paris, 1953), p. 72 (in Yiddish).

seven Jewish families lived in Nîmes; during the Revolution
many Jews from the neighboring Papal territory of Avignon
and Comtat Venaissin emigrated there. Nîmes became a
center of bloody riots, most of them growing out of the
conflicts between the Catholics and the large number of
Protestant inhabitants. The small Jewish community suffered, too. The Cantor, Mardochée Mayragues, was forced
to bow before the altar of the new religion. When, on
December 8, 1793, a Jewish delegation was received by the
city council, a Jewish representative made a patriotic speech
and offered 930 livres and a basket of gold (probably from
the synagogue ornaments). But Mayrargues and Crémieux
did not suffer physically and Carcassonne was not guillotined
because of his religious principles. Nîmes was for a time
governed by a federalist city council, of which Carcassonne
was a member, and as a result of his federalist activities he
was guillotined together with other Nîmes federalists.[29] In
fact, we do not know of any Jew anywhere in France who
during the Terror lost his life because of his religion.

The question arises whether the attitude towards Jews
should be discussed chronologically according to the various
political periods of the Revolution. In this case, too, the
conclusion should be negative for some regions. Where
anti-Jewish feelings existed during the old regime and at the
beginning of the Revoltuion, it also became the policy of the
local Jacobins during the Terror and was later continued
during the Thermidor.[30] Some Jacobins disliked Jews as a

---

[29] City archives of Nîmes, Club populaire, December 8, 1793; S. Kahn,
Notice sur les Israélites de Nîmes (Nîmes, 1901), pp. 9, 18-19, 29; F. Rouvière,
Histoire de la Révolution française dans le département du Gard (Nîmes, 1889),
IV, 327-34, 459; *Jugement rendu par le Tribunal révolutionaire etabli à Nîmes,
qui condamne les nommés . . . Jassé Carcassonne . . . membre de la municipalité
à l'époque du fédéralisme . . . à la peine de mort . . . du 1er thermidor an
second . . .* (Nîmes, 1794). Broadside; F. A. Aulard, in *Révolution française*,
XIII (1887), p. 380. On the bloody conflicts between Protestants and Catholics
in Nîmes see *Victoire remportée par les patriotes de la ville de Nismes sur les
soi-diseurs Catholiques . . .* (Paris, n.d.); *Anniversaire du massacre des catholiques
de Nismes, le 13 juin 1790*, and many other contemporary pamphlets.

[30] On November 21, 1793, Robespierre proclaimed the end of the official
anti-religious persecution and freedom of religious practices. Still, the fight
against religion continued till the end of the Terror, and even later, during the
Thermidor. As late as December, 1798, the Jews of Hochfelden were denounced

group of merchants, but on the other hand, Thermidor rulers were ideological adversaries of the Jews. The historian Jacques Godechot divided the history of the Jews in Nancy during the Revolution into three periods: (1) the time prior to the Terror, (2) the time of the Terror, and (3) the Thermidor. But such a division can be accepted only with the understanding that it represents no more than a reflection of the city's general events. If Jews suffered during the Terror more than before or afterward, then it was due solely to the fact that this was a time of violence in which everybody suffered more. Since Nancy was known as an aristocratic city, everyone there including the Jews suffered during the Terror. However, when the Nancy dictator, B. Faure, demanded of the Jews that they forget their Messiah, this should not be understood as an anti-Jewish act. The next day the Nancy Rabbi, Jacob Schweisch, resigned from his office. Of course, he was forced to do so, but as a result the Jew Salomon Lévy was appointed member of the city council.[31]

In the Revolution the Jews had many foes in various regions, among the Jacobins of Alsace and neighboring departments and among the counter-revolutionaries. They also had many friends among the partisans of the Revolution; without them the Jews would never have been granted citizenship. Persecution of the Jewish religion by Jacobins should not be understood as an ideological struggle for the abolition of the Jewish faith, or as action of an anti-Jewish character, as some historians maintain. Jews who desired to perform their religious rites and follow their religious traditions—to observe the Sabbath, to wear Sabbath garments, to have separate Jewish cemeteries, and the like—were victims of the general drive against those who were regarded as being

for practicing their religion. Reuss, "Quelques documents . . ." pp. 273-74. On other similar facts see Kahn, *op. cit.*, pp. 312 *et seq.*

[31]   J. Godechot, "Les Juifs à Nancy de 1789 à 1795," *REJ*, LXXXVI (1928), 23, 25-27; *idem*, "Le Comité de surveillance révolutionnaire de Nancy," *La Révolution française*, LXXX (1927), 249, 254; B. Faure, *Discours . . . 20 brumaire an second*, 7 pp.; A. Troux, *La Vie politique dans le département de la Meurthe d'aout 1792 à octobre 1795* (Nancy, 1936), II, 225-27; Floquet, "Le Culte de la raison et de l'Être Suprême et les fêtes civiques à Nancy pendant la Révolution," *Annales de l'Est*, XIV (1900), 544.

opposed to the Revolution.[32] The Colmar Jacobins protested
against the Jews' not working on the Sabbath.[33] In Nancy,
Tomblaine, Sarrebourg, Metting, and Lixheim (Lorraine)
anti-Jewish feeling arose over the Sabbath observance, but
no anti-Jewish acts were then noted there.[34] The people of
Bordeaux protested against permitting a separate Jewish
cemetery.[35] Even in Saint-Esprit-lès-Bayonne (where the
Jacobin Club was composed mostly of Jews) Jews were forbidden to wear Sabbath garments or to light Sabbath candles.[36] In order to wreck anti-Republican sentiments and
fanaticism, Strasbourg Jews were forbidden, on June 27,
1794, the use of the Jewish cemetery at Rosenviller. The
same order forced the Jews to state their means of livelihood,
which could be taken as motivated by anti-Jewish feelings.[37]
During the Terror the District of Strasbourg took severe
measures against the Jews for the practice of their faith.
Simon, the agent of the District, spied on the Jews and reported to Mayor Monet that he did not see any Jews at the
Temple de Génie, probably because "they are more attached
to their Talmud than to the Constitution of the Republic."[38]
The famous Strasbourg Jacobin leader and friend of Jews,
Eulogious Schneider, praised the attitude of some Protestant
pastors who declared themselves partisans of the new religion
and enemies of all priests, rabbis, and preachers.[39]

The drive against religion was often exaggerated by
local Jacobins and commissioners sent from Paris, but this

[32] These subjects will be treated in separate studies.
[33] P. Leuillot, Les Jacobins de Colmar . . . (Strasbourg, 1923), p. 271.
[34] Godechot, op. cit., p. 834; Troux, op. cit., II, 639-40.
[35] G. Ducaunnes-Duval, Ville de Bordeaux. Inventaire sommaire des
archives municipales. Période révolutionnaire (Bordeaux, 1929), IV, 291.
[36] Guerre aux tyrans. Paix ou peuples, les représentants du peuple près
des Pyrénées occidentales 5 juillet, 1794 (Bayonne, n.d.). Broadside; Albert
Darricau, Scènes de la Terreur à Bayonne . . . (Bayonne, 1903), p. 149; Ed.
Ducéré, Dictionnaire historique de Bayonne, (Bayonne, 1911), I, 459.
[37] Délibération du Directoire du district de Strasbourg. Du 9 messidor,
l'an second . . . (Strasbourg, 1794), 7 pp.; L'Agent national du district de
Strasbourg à ses concitoyens (Strasbourg, June 26, 1794), 7 pp.
[38] R. Reuss, Séligmann Alexandre ou les tribulations d'un israélite strasbourgeois pendant la Terreur (Strasbourg, 1880), pp. 26-27.
[39] E. Schneider, Le Saint décadi, 20 novembre 1793 (n.p., n.d.), 5 pp.;
Argos, oder der Mann mit Hundert Augen, III, 489; F. C. Heitz, Notes sur la
vie et les écrits d'Euloge Schneider (Strasbourg, 1862), p. 109.

was done against the will of Robespierre and his close friends. Of course, in some cases of excessive suppression of religion, local administrators demonstrated their anti-Jewish feelings. Nevertheless, their acts could rarely be called open anti-Jewish demonstrations, because not Jews alone were persecuted. On November 22, 1793, February 1, 1794, and June 1, 1794, the city of Strasbourg forbade Jews to pray in their synagogues, but the same order forbade all other gatherings, both Jewish and Christian, except those of the new revolutionary religion and revolutionary clubs.[40]   The closing of the Lunéville synagogue[41] was, most probably, not an anti-Jewish act but part of a general campaign against religious fanaticism.   Rabbis were forced to take an oath of allegiance to the Republic, but this occurred even in the post-Terror period,[42] and the same oath was forced upon Catholic priests and Protestant ministers.   The Deputies N. Hentz and J.M.C.A. Goujon ordered the arrest not of rabbis alone, but also of Catholic priests and Protestant pastors.[43]   Seven Alsatian cantors and ritual slaughterers of Diebolsheim, Muettersholz, and other communities were arrested and held four weeks in the prisons of Sélestat, Colmar, and Besançon. But they were not arrested because they were Jews; they were apprehended together with sixteen Catholic priests and ten Protestant ministers as a result of the destruction by counter-revolutionaries of the Tree of Liberty in Hirsingue.

Of course, anti-Jewish feeling was always strong in Alsace. Yet when, at the end of 1793, the Convention's commissioner in Alsace, M. A. Baudot, called for *régénération guillotinière* against the Jews, he probably meant to fight religious Jewish fanaticism and not Jews as such.[44]   In fact,

40   *Délibération du Directoire de Strasbourg du 13 pluviôse l'an second* . . . (Strasbourg, an II).   Broadside; *Agent national du district aux Communes,* Strasbourg, June 25, 1794 (n.p., n.d.), 2 pp.; Reuss, *Les Eglises protestantes pendant la Révolution* (Paris, 1906), p. 148.

41   Edouard Gérardin, *Histoire de Lorraine* (Paris, 1925), p. 79.

42   "Etat des Rabbins qui ont prêté le serment de haine à la royauté et à l'anarchie, et la fidélité pour le maintien de la Constitution de l'an trois et de la République" [Cernay, 1797].   Departmental archives of the Upper Rhine, L 645.

43   F. Schaedelin, *Un Jacobin: Joseph Bruat* (Colmar, 1932), p. 213.

44   On these arrests see Johann Karl Gerold, *Bilder aus der Schreckenszeit.*

every religious leader was suspect.[45] Ornaments of churches
were confiscated and so were ornaments of synagogues.[46] At
the revolutionary parades in honor of the new Religion of
Reason all old religions were ridiculed. At such a parade in
Bordeaux on December 10, 1793, four rabbis, many priests,
judges, and others represented the old regime. A midget
named Richefort was dressed like the Pope, and a giant Jew
named Mardochée Cordova kept leaping over the midget's
head.[47] At the first such festival of the new religion in
Strasbourg rabbis holding torn copies of the Talmud paraded
beside Catholic priests and Protestant pastors. It is probable
that they were not really rabbis but only Jacobins in rabbinical garments. On the other hand, it was in preparation
for this event that Mayor P. F. Monet, on November 19,
1793, called upon Jews, Calvinists, Lutherans, and Catholics
to unite, to forget hatred and fanaticism. After the festival,
however, the Jacobins complained that not one rabbi or minister had as yet renounced his superstitious practices.[48] Thus,
Jewish participation in demonstrations of the revolutionary
religion became a part of the decorative program of such
festivals even in places where Jews did not reside. According

Erlebnisse eines deportirten elsässischen Geistlichen (Strasbourg, 1883), pp.
13-15; Abbé C. A. F.[rayhier], *Histoire du clergé catholique d'Alsace* . . .
(Colmar, 1876), pp. 338-43; A. Waltz, *Sigmund Billings kleine Chronik der
Stadt Colmar* (Colmar, 1891), p. 316; F. L. Rumpler, *Quelques pièces fugitives*
(n.p., n.d.), pp. 6-7; Dereser, *Rechenschaft über mein Betragen vor und in
der Revolution* [Strasbourg, 1795], p. 12; Reuss, *Les Églises protestantes* . . . ,
pp. 188-192; E. Becourt, "Années de jeunesse de Jean-Louis Stoltz," *Revue
d'Alsace*, LXXII (1925), 231-32; André Ulrich, *Recueil des pièces servant à
l'histoire de la Révolution à Strasbourg*[-*Livre Bleu*] (Strasbourg, 1795), I, 100;
II, 127; J. Foesser, *Meistratzheim* (Strasbourg, 1939), p. 227.
[45] "Verdächtig wer irgend ein Kirchenamt bekleidet hatte als Sakristan,
Organist usw. bei Christen und Juden"; Foesser, *op. cit.*, p. 209.
[46] This subject will be treated in a special study.
[47] Vivie, *op. cit.*, II, 134; *Fête de la raison* (Bordeaux, 1793),8 pp.;
Histoire des théâtres de Bordeaux (Bordeaux, 1860); Dr. Jean Barraud, *Vieux
papiers bordelais* (Paris, 1910), pp. 103-106; P. Bernardau, *Annales* . . .
(Bordeaux, 1803), pp. 290-291; Vivie, "Inauguration de la désée de la raison
à Bordeaux," *La semaine religieuse du diocese d'Angoulême*, Sept. 10, 1865.
[48] [Pierre François] Monet, le Maire de Strasbourg, *Au Peuple*, Strasbourg,
29 *brumaire*, an II (no place, no year given). Broadside; *Description de la fête
de la raison, célébrée pour la première fois à Strasbourg, le jour de la troisième
décade de brumaire de l'an II* . . . (Strasbourg, n.d.), 16 pp.; Reuss, *La Constitution civile* . . . , pp. 230-237; Z. Szajkowski, "The Discussion and Struggle
over Jewish Emancipation . . .", *Historia Judaica*, XVII (1955), 140-141.

to a report by the Deputy Joseph Marie Lequinio (1755-
1813) on his revolutionary mission in Rochefort, Jews there
and in St.Jean-d'Angély renounced their religion during
festivals of the new faith.   But no mention of such acts
could be found in the archives of the cities or departments,
or in regional historical studies on this period.   It is possible
that Lequinio, who called himself "citoyen du globe" and
demanded the destruction of the three religions of the Catholics, Protestants, and Jews, found for the celebrations fig-
urants who dressed as rabbis.[49]   Again, this does not prove
that there were no anti-Jewish acts, but those that occurred
were the result of local feelings and not evidence of anti-
Jewish feelings on the part of the French Republic at the
federal level.

How did the Jacobins' attitude towards the Jewish faith
influence the religious life of the Jews?   This will be the
subject of a larger special study, but a few characteristic
facts should be mentioned in conclusion.

On December 10, 1793, the Jew Alexandre Lambert
delivered a speech against the Jewish religion in the Temple
de la Vérité of Saint-Jean-d'Angély.[50]   On March 8, 1794,
a Jew of Montaigne Seignanx (in the Landes) invited the
Paris Representative, B.J.B. Monestier, to attend his wedding
to a gentile woman, this wedding being a symbol of "equality
and brotherhood."[51]   In Saint-Esprit, Peyrehorade, and
other places where Jews were forbidden to observe the Sab-

---

49 ". . . nous avions trois religions à detruire, la catholique, la protestante
et la juive, et par conséquant, autant intérêts différents à ménager et à combattre.
. . . A. Rochefort, à Saint-Jean-d'Angély, etc. les Juifs ont, aussi publiquement
que les autres, abjuré les mensonges de leurs prêtres et dévoué leurs livres
d'impostures au feu des bûchers patriotiques qui portoient dans les airs les
flammes epuratrices de la raison." [J. M.] Lequinio, *Guerre de la Vandée et des
chouans* (Paris [1794]), pp. 168-69. On Lequinio's mission see Ch. L. Chassin,
"La mission de Lequinio . . .", *Révolution française*, XXVIII, 119-140; Aulard,
"Lequinio et la déchristianisation," *ibid*, XXXI, 295-99. According to L. Kahn,
op. cit., p. 187, the Jews of Rochefort did manifest their disinterest in their
past religious attachments. On Saint-Jean d'Angély see note 50.
50 Alexandre Lambert, *Discours de morale, prononcé le 2 décadi,* 20
*frimaire l'an 2e de la république une et indivisible, au Temple de la Vérité, ci-
devant, l'église des bénédictins, à Angély-Boutonne, ci-devant Saint-Jean
d'Angély, fait par le citoyen Alexandre Lambert fils, juif et élevé dans les
préjugés du culte judaïque* (Rochefort, n.d), 23 pp.
51 Richard, *op. cit.*, p. 185.

bath or to engage in other religious practices, they often refused to obey such orders. There is a story about a revolutionary meeting in Saint-Esprit, during which Jews applauded a speaker who criticized the Christians, and the latter applauded a speaker who criticized the Jews.[52]   In Peyrehorade a Jew was named as one of twelve preachers for the Religion of Reason.   But the Jews there refused to bring to the revolutionary club their Torah scrolls and religious ornaments because the Catholics had refused to give up their crosses and religious pictures.   Nevertheless, with the exception of a speculator, not one Jew in the district was arrested or fined during the Terror.[53]   Rabbi Nounès of Saint-Esprit was taken into custody because he chose to close the synagogue rather than preach revolutionary ideas.   While Nounès was in prison, two other synagogues were closed by the Jacobins.   Perhaps this should establish the existence of a religious revolutionary faction among the Saint-Esprit Jews. The historian H. A. Taine noted the existence of such factions among Christians in various parts of France.   According to some sources, Rabbi Abraham Andrade, a leading Jacobin of Saint-Espirit, hid scrolls of the Torah.[54]   On the other hand, leaders of Jewish communities may have felt that they should officially accept the new regime in order to save not only their own lives but also their entire communities. Thus, for example, the Jewish Jacobin leader of Saint-Esprit-lès-Bayonne, Louis Gomez aîné, stated in a petition of April 29, 1795 against his arrest that he accepted his role during the Terror for fear of being persecuted, but thanks to him and his colleagues the guillotine was very active in the department, but not in Saint-Esprit itself.[55]

In summing up, it should be said that the Jews were not persecuted because they were Jews, and the anti-religious campaigns were not directed mainly against the Jewish religion as such. Where Jews suffered, it was because of general anti-religious acts.

[52]   Ducéré, op. cit., I, 459.
[53]   E. Ginsburger, "Les Juifs de Peyrehorade," REJ, CIV (1938), 50-51.
[54]   Ginsburger, Le Comité de surveillance . . . , p. 96; Darricau, op. cit., p. 150; Léon, op. cit., pp. 162-63.
[55]   Archives Nationales (Paris), D-III-99 (dr. 1, p. 21-27).

Gli Ebrei nei club dei Giacobini durante la rivoluzione francese del 1789

I Giacobini, che formarono l'estrema fazione rivoluzionaria, ebbero una importantissima parte nella Rivoluzione francese del 1789. Attraverso i loro numerosi club, i Giacobini esercitarono non solo una grande influenza sull'opinione pubblica, ma in molti casi sorvegliarono e diressero l'attività delle amministrazioni federali e locali. Le loro opinioni e le loro decisioni ebbero spesso forza di legge. È quindi importante analizzare la partecipazione degli Ebrei nei club dei Giacobini e l'atteggiamento di questi club nei riguardi degli Ebrei.

È necessario prima di tutto rilevare il fatto che un gran numero di club giacobini sostenevano apertamente una politica anti-ebraica. Questo atteggiamento non era ispirato da una qualsiasi politica anti-ebraica che venisse dagl'istituti governativi centrali di Parigi. Era invece il risultato di tradizioni anti-ebraiche. Ma i rappresentanti federali mandati da Parigi ai centri civili o militari della provincia erano spesso soggetti all'influsso dei sentimenti antisemiti tradizionali locali. Così Marcantonio Baudot, rappresentante dell'esercito del Reno e Mosella, scriveva al suo amico Carlo Duval, deputato e direttore del *Journal des Hommes Libres* che nell'Alsazia, a Bordeaux, a Bayonne e in tutti gli altri luoghi gli Ebrei erano nemici della Repubblica. Egli proponeva di iniziare fra gli Ebrei « un'educazione coll'aiuto della ghigliottina ». Il 3 novembre 1793 l'Amministrazione del Basso Reno fu assunta dai Giacobini che venivano per lo più dall'interno della Francia. Il 4 aprile 1794 questa nuova amministrazione scriveva al Comitato di salute pubblica di Parigi che gli Ebrei erano causa di distruzione e di morte. Il 3 maggio successivo la stessa Amministrazione inviava a Parigi un altro memoriale anti-ebraico ed il 17 giugno attaccava fortemente gli Ebrei in una circolare trasmessa ai distretti. Il 27 giugno 1794 proponeva al rappresentante di Parigi N. Hentz di mettere in prigione tutti gli Ebrei sino alla fine della guerra e poi di evacuarli dalle provincie di

Originally published in *La Rassegna Mensile di Israel*, vol. XXIV (1958).

confine e di togliere agli Ebrei i figliuoli per dar loro « un'educazione nazionale » ecc. (1).

Tutto ciò indusse molti club giacobini a rifiutare l'ammissione agli Ebrei. Tuttavia — come vedremo — gli Ebrei appartenevano a diversi club. D'altro canto molti Ebrei, specialmente a Bordeaux, si astenevano dall'estrema attività giacobina e sostenevano i club più moderati. L'ebreo polacco Zalkind Hurwitz, che combattè in Francia per l'emancipazione degli Ebrei, attaccò Marat come « il profeta dell'assassinio e della anarchia ». Michel Berr, figlio del capo ebreo lorenese Isaac Berr, scriveva nel 1801 che gli Ebrei non partecipavano al movimento terrorista per quanto quelle azioni avrebbero potuto esser giustificate dalle persecuzioni anti-ebraiche dell'antico regime (2).

Molti club giacobini d'Alsazia e dei dipartimenti vicini erano apertamente anti-ebraici. Il 16 luglio 1793 il Consiglio municipale di Strasburgo discusse una protesta degli Ebrei di quella città che erano attaccati dappertutto, perfino nei club giacobini (3).

Il 14 luglio e il 17 agosto 1793 il club giacobino di Colmar chiese l'espulsione degli Ebrei « da tutta la Repubblica » e tentò di ottenere per questo l'aiuto degli altri club. Nel settembre 1793 il club giacobino di Nancy tentò di ottenere l'aiuto di quello di Toul e d'altri club nella lotta per il bando degli Ebrei. Ma alcuni club, anche quelli dei dipartimenti dell'Alsazia tradizionalmente anti-ebraici, non essendo così estremi nel loro atteggiamento verso gli Ebrei, protestarono contro la propaganda anti-ebraica condotta da alcuni giacobini. Così i club di Ribeauvillé e Tham si rifiutarono di unirsi all'azione antiebraica praticata dai giacobini di Colmar. I club di Parigi protestarono energicamente contro la decisione presa dai giacobini di Nancy. Lo stesso fece il club di Saint-Esprit-lès-Bayonne, composto in gran parte di membri ebrei (4).

(1) ANDREAS ULRICH, Recueil des pièces authentiques servant à l'histoire de la Révolution à Strasbourg [Libro blu] (Strasburgo, [1795], II, 127 ; DR. J. F. E. ROBINET, Le mouvement religieux à Paris pendant la Révolution (Paris, 1898), I, 330 ; ROD. REUSS, Documents nouveaux sur l'antisémitisme dans le Bas-Rhin de 1794 à 1799. REJ, LIX (1910), 253-56.

(2) La Chronique de Paris, n. 330 (19 novembre 1792) ; MICHEL BERR, Appel à la justice des Nations et des Rois (Strasburgo, 1801), pag. 17.

(3) Archivi municipali di Strasburgo, minute del Corps municipal, vol. 4, pagine 753-54.

(4) PAUL LEUILLIOT, Les Jacobins de Colmar... (Strasburgo, 1923), pagg. 48, 67-68, 75, 258, 271 ; ROBERT PARISOT, Histoire de Lorraine (Paris, 1924), III, 240 ; ALBERT DENIS, Le Club des Jacobins de Toul (Paris-Nancy, 1895), pag. 41 ; HENRY POULET, L'Esprit public à Thann pendant la Révolutioh, « Revue historique de la

Al principio della Rivoluzione erano pochi gli Ebrei che partecipavano attivamente al club di Strasburgo. Il più influente fra loro era Max Berr (Cerfberr), figlio del leader ebreo Alsaziano Cerfberr di Médelsheim. Durante il Terrore, alla fine del 1794, solo l'ebreo Lazard [Lazare] Zay rimase nella *Société populaire*. Zay era venuto da Metz nel 1791 e un anno più tardi era stato nominato maestro in una scuola pubblica. Zay aveva energicamente ribattuto nel club e nei giornali agli attacchi contro gli Ebrei. Il giacobino ebreo Wolf Lévi era fra i firmatari d'una petizione del 25 aprile 1793 contro i Girondini. Ma durante il Terrore, un ricco ebreo che nell'ottobre del 1793 era stato costretto a pagare un contributo di 15.000 lire, figurava in una lista di giacobini di Strasburgo il 25 ottobre 1794. Marx Wolf figurava in un elenco di giacobini di Strasburgo il 30 marzo 1793 ma era considerato da tutti come un pazzo (5).

Alcuni ebrei erano pure membri dei club giacobini nelle piccole città dell'Alsazia. I fornitori dell'esercito Salomone Lippmann e Abraham Lévi appartenevano al club di Saverne, dove gli Ebrei erano spesso criticati. Questi due ebrei erano probabilmente giacobini sinceri, perchè erano fra i ventidue membri che vi rimasero dopo la purga durante il Terrore. Il rabbino Abraham Kellermeister divenne impiegato municipale e — secondo la testimonianza del nipote Alexandre Weill — era amico dei capi terroristi Robespierre e Saint-Just. Meyer Lévi apparteneva al club di Hagnenau (6).

Révolution française », XV (1923), 367-68 ; R., *Second établissement des Israélites à Paris*, « Archives israélites », II (1841), 502 ; ROBINET, *op. cit.*, I, 330 ; F. A. AULARD, *La société des Jacobins . . . de Paris* (Paris, 1895), V, 479 ; « Journal des Débats et de la correspondence de la Société des Jacobins », nn. 524 (1793), 524 ; ERNEST GINSBURGER, *Le Comité de surveillance de Jean-Jacques Rousseau* (Paris, 1934), pag. 96 ; IDEM, *Le Comité de surveillance de J. J. Rousseau et les sans-culottes de Nancy*, REJ, LXXXXVIII (1934), 91-93.

(5) E. MÜHLENBECK, *Il y a cent ans*, « Revue d'Alsace », XLIV (1893), 439 ; *Liste des membres composans la Société populaire de Strasbourg . . . 25 vendemiaire, l'an trois* [15 novembre 1794] pag. 31 ; F. CH. HEITZ, *Les sociétés politiques de Strasbourg* (Strasbourg, 1863), pagg. 346-50 ; E. BARTH, *Notes biographiques sur les hommes de la Révolution à Strasbourg et les environs* (Strasbourg, 1885), pag. 174 ; LAZARE ZAY, *Judenschaft*, « Strassburgische Zeitung » (1794), pag. 253 ; MARX WOLF (nato nel 1774) era nel 1789 studente dell'Università di Strasburgo. Nel febbraio del 1792 gli furono pagate 50 lire per aver denunziato un contro-rivoluzionario. Presentò a quel club uno studio : « *Traité sur la morale de la République* ». Nell'ottobre 1794 figurava ancora come membro (BARTH, *op. cit.*). Vale la pena di notare che il libellista antisemita F. L. Rumpler scrisse dell'ebreo Joseph Lehman e di suo cognato che erano « famosi clubiti » : *Prosamlé denoncé* (Strasb. anno IX), pag. 32.

(6) DAGOBERT FISCHER, *La société populaire de Saverne*. « Revue d'Alsace », serie 3ª, V, 33 ; ROBERT SCHNERB, *Les Jacobins de Saverne*, ib., LXXVII (1930) ; ALEX.

A Metz, il medico Jacob Berr era l'unico ebreo giacobino dopo la purga durante il Terrore. Berr combattè l'idea di conservare le Comunità ebraiche autonome. Fu il primo ebreo francese che sposò una cristiana durante la Rivoluzione senza cessare di essere ebreo. Secondo una fonte un terrorista e spia ebreo provocò l'arresto di Terquem, padre di quell'Olry Terquem che nel XIX secolo fu uno dei leaders ebrei. Al principio della Rivoluzione un gruppo di Ebrei apparteneva al club giacobino di Nancy, ma tutto fa credere che non fossero giacobini convinti. Durante il Terrore furono esclusi dal club. Fra loro c'erano i due ricchi capi delle Comunità Berr-Isaac Berr e Cerf Berr che vennero esclusi il 27 luglio 1793. L'11 agosto 1794 il club giacobino di Toul accoglieva un ebreo (*israélite*) chiamato Léon quale suo membro (7).

Molti Ebrei di Parigi appartenevano ai vari club, e alcuni club erano diretti da segretari ebrei. Così Hazan era segretario del *Comitato Centrale di Sorveglianza* e Azur della *Société populaire des Amis de l'Egalité*. Con tutto ciò si constatavano anche a Parigi sentimenti anti-ebraici. Una delle sezioni parigine si espresse contro l'emancipazione degli Ebrei (8).

Secondo qualche storico le opinioni filo-ebraiche venivano dalle provincie francesi con scarsa popolazione ebraica. Lì era facile ai capi rivoluzionari difendere i principî umanitari dall'aspetto astratto. Ma ciò non poteva avvenire in Alsazia colla sua numerosa popolazione ebraica (9). Sarebbe facile confutare questa teoria come non corrispondente ai fatti storici. Solo poche famiglie ebree vivevano nei dipartimenti orientali della Francia. Ma in una petizione alla Convenzione nazionale, il Club giacobino di Saint-Vincent-la-Montagne attaccò vigorosamente gli ebrei,

---

WEILL, *Ma jeunesse* (Paris, 1888), pag. 23 ; P. HILDENFINGER, *Actes du district de Strasbourg relatifs aux Juifs* (1790), REJ, LXI (1911), pag. 109.

(7) E. CARMOLY, *Hist. des médecins juifs anciens et modernes* (Bruxelles, 1884), pag. 204 ; LEON BULTINGAIRE, *Le Club des Jacobins de Metz* (Paris-Metz, 1906), pag. 101 ; CHR. PFISTER, *Hist. de Nancy* (Paris 1902-09), III, 327 ; ABR. CAHEN, *Le Rabbinat de Metz pendant la période française*, REJ, XIII (1886), 112 ; *Noms des individus exclus de la Société populaire de Nancy ... 27 juillet 1793 ...* [Nancy, 1793], manifesto ; A. DENIS, *op. cit.*, pag. 130.

(8) LÉON KAHN, *Les Juifs de Paris pendant la Révolution* (Paris, 1898), pagg. 112-150 ; SIGISMUND LACROIX, *Actes de la Commune de Paris pendant la Révolution* (Paris, 1921), I-VII, 1123 ; IDEM, *Ce qu'on pensait des Juifs à Paris en 1790*, « Revue politique et littéraire », XXXV (1898), 417-24. Il 28 dicembre 1793 i giacobini di Parigi ritirarono la tessera di socio ad un giacobino ebreo di Strasburgo che era venuto a Parigi per protestare contro un'imposta rivoluzionaria di 20.000 lire. AULARD, *op. cit.*, V, 584-85.

(9) ROD. REUSS, *Séligmann Alexandre ...* (Strasburgo, 1880), pag. 7.

per la maggior parte merciai ambulanti, come speculatori della peggiore specie. Ciò nonostante l'ebreo Michel Samuel era membro attivo dello stesso club e agente di Robespierre. Un altro ebreo, Jacob Brandin, era membro del tribunale rivoluzionario di Brest (10).

Molti Ebrei delle quattro Comunità dell'antica provincia papale di Avignon e del Comtat Venaissin erano impegnati in attività giacobine. Ma lo spirito giacobino degli Ebrei non era il medesimo in tutte le Comunità. Era questo il risultato della guerra fra Avignone, che lottava per l'annessione alla Francia e gli avversari dell'annessione nel resto della provincia. I giacobini ebrei di Avignone erano stati per lo più attivi prima del Terrore. Probabilmente per effetto di questi sentimenti moderati ebraici, l'ebreo Benjamin Monteux fu nominato al principio del Termidoro membro del Consiglio municipale dal rappresentante di Parigi. Gli Ebrei di Carpentras non parteciparono ad alcuna attività giacobina nel primo periodo della Rivoluzione, molto probabilmente a causa dei sentimenti fortemente anti-ebraici e anti-rivoluzionari predominanti in quella città. Ma nel febbraio 1793 gli Ebrei si mostravano già attivi nel club degli *Amis de la liberté et de l'égalité*. I giacobini ebrei di Carpentras svolsero notevole attività anche durante il Terrore e per conseguenza non occuparono nessuna carica ufficiale prima del 1798. Nell'Isle-sur-Sorgue, Menachem Cavaillon fu impegnato in attività terroristiche. Durante il Terrore Cavaillon ebbe un sindaco ebreo, Lange Cohen, ma sembra che fosse tanto liberale da salvare molti beni della Chiesa dalla distruzione (11).

(10) L. BRUNSCHVICQ, *Les Juifs de Nantes et du Pays nantais*. REJ, XIX (1898), 300-302 ; IDEM, *Les Juifs de Bretagne au XVIIIe siècle*, ib., XXXIII (1896), 102-103.

(11) Z. SZAJKOWSKI, *The Comtadin Jews and the Annexation of the Papal Province by France, 1789-1791*. « The Jewish Quarterly Review » XLVI (1955), 192-95 ; Archivi municipali di Carpentras, Revolution, P. 14 § 46, fol. 79 (*Conseil général*, 19 febbraio 1793). In settembre 1793 l'ebreo Milliaud apparteneva al Comitato di sorveglianza. Egli firmò pure un proclama del 6 maggio 1794 e nel giugno di quello stesso anno fu fatto presidente del suo club ; *ibidem*, 46 fol. 139 ; Manoscritto 4215 della libreria Calvet di Avignon, ottobre 1793 ; *Proclamation, le Comité de Surveillance de la section de la Fraternité de la commune de Carpentras aux citoyens de son arrondissement* (17 floreal anno 11). Gli Ebrei di Carpentras, Abraham Lévy, Mardochée, Haim Monteux, Isaac Valabrègue, Abraham De Digne, Mayse Millau[d] anziano, firmarono una petizione contro l'arresto di quattro giacobini di Carpentras che avevano criticato gli aristocratici. Stando ad un documento del 28 maggio 1794, Jossué Lunel apparteneva alla *Société populaire*. I nomi degli Ebrei Couen, Aaron Hain, Abraham, Sabatai Crémieux, Cay Carcassonne Isaac, Jacob Lyon, Baxe Manuel, Joseph Samuel, Abraham Deigne, Rubon Crémieu, Samuel Lyon, Samuel Naquet, e David Crémieux figuravano fra i 130 firmatari d'una petizione dell'agosto

Nel vicino Orange, Moïse Millaud era presidente del Comitato di sorveglianza durante il Terrore. A Nîmes Jassé Carcassonne fu ghigliottinato per la sua azione federalista, mentre Samuel Roque Martine fu arrestato durante il Termidoro a Carpentras per supposta attività terrorista a Nîmes (12).

A Bordeaux gli Ebrei appartenevano alla maggior parte delle 28 *Sezioni* durante tutti i periodi della Rivoluzione, al principio del nuovo regime, durante l'amministrazione girondina, durante il Terrore, e poi anche durante la reazione del Termidoro. Il capo ebreo Abraham Furtado aveva collaborato al libello sui club (13). Pochi Ebrei si trovavano anche fra gli estremi giacobini rivoluzionari, ma di regola il maggior numero degli Ebrei di Bordeaux membri dei club avevano tendenze politiche moderate. Era questo il resultato della speciale condizione economica degli Ebrei di Bordeaux, fra i quali c'erano molti poveri, ma c'erano anche molte famiglie ricchissime. Era di moda fra loro l'esser membri di un club, che serviva anche come una specie di salvacondotto. A Bordeaux la massa degli operai e della gente povera non controllava i club e pochi in quelle classi ne erano membri.

David Azevedo ed altri Ebrei appartenevano al *Club du Café national* che diventò più tardi il *Club national*. Fondato il 6 novembre 1789, era uno dei primi club di Francia e il primo di Bordeaux. Durante l'amministrazione dei girondini il club fu chiuso per le sue tendenze Maratiste, ma fu riaperto il 4 agosto 1793 ed esercitò un'azione importante durante il

---

1794 contro l'arresto di sei giacobini : *Les Sans-culottes de Carpentras à leurs frères d'Avignon* (18 ventoso, anno II), 16 pagg. ; Archivi municipali di Carpentras, Rev. 46, fol. 212 ; *Les citoyens soussignés, membres épurés de la Société de Carpentras, au citoyen Maignet, représentant du peuple . . .* (Carpentras, 15 termidoro, anno II); H. Chobaut, *Les Juifs d'Avignon et du Comtat et la Révolution française*, REJ, CII (1938), 27, 29 ; M. J. de Joannis, *Le Fédéralisme et la Terreur à l'Isle-sur-Sorgue* (Avignon, 1884), pagg. 250, 252, 301 ; *Archives Israélites*, IX (1848), 452-53.

(12) Libreria Calvet, ms. 5938 (00648). L'ebreo Benjamin fu denunziato dallo stesso club d'Oranges, V. De Baumefort, *Episodes de la Terreur, Tribunal révolutionnaire* (Avignon, 1875), pag. 134 ; *Jugement rendu par le tribunal révolutionnaire établi à Nîmes, qui condamne . . . Jassé Carrassonne . . . membre de la municipalité à l'époque du fédéralisme . . . à la peine de mort . . . Du Ier Thermidor au second* (Nîmes) ; manifesto. Archivi comunali di Carpentras, Rev. 47, (26 giugno 1795).

(13) *Acquitaine littéraire* di Pierre Bernadau. Libreria civica di Bordeaux, ms. 713-1, vol. III, pag. 350 ; vol. IV, pag. 140. Il 7 novembre 1789, Furtado ed altri abbandonavano il monarchico *Musée* e fondavano un nuovo club letterario : *Lettre aux Commissaires du Musée* [Bordeaux, 1789], 4 pagine ; Henri Chauvot, *Le Barreau de Bordeaux* (Paris, 1856), pag. 118 ; Michel L'Héritier, *La Liberté 1789* (Paris, 1947), pag. 50.

Terrore. Durante la reazione del Termidoro, il girondino e *leader* ebreo Salomon Lopes Dubec diventò membro attivo del club e tenne discorsi molto moderati. Così il 2 gennaio 1795 attaccò alcuni anonimi informatori. Colla medesima tendenza, Azevedo affermava il 14 gennaio 1795 al club : « Noi stiamo tentando di smascherare le canaglie, non già la massa dei patrioti traviati » (14).

Alcuni ricchi e influenti Ebrei di Bordeaux (Abraham Furtado, David Gradis, Lopes Dubec, Pereire, David Azevedo, Joseph Lopes Dias) appartenevano pure alla *Société des Amis de la Constitution* fondata il 16 aprile 1790 da un gruppo di membri moderati del *Club national*. Questo nuovo club era avverso alla politica estrema dei Club di Parigi e diventò centro d'attività girondina(15). Preti, elementi vari contro-rivoluzionari e aristocratici e gli Ebrei Jacob Gradis, Louis Gomes e David Athier appartenevano al reazionario *Club monarchique*. Un Ebreo di nome Azevedo era presidente della *Sezione 18* (Club del « 10 agosto »), che il 6 maggio 1793 affermava che tutto il male veniva da Parigi. Un altro Ebreo di nome Noé era uno dei segretari dell'attivissimo club della gioventù di Bordeaux (16).

Durante l'amministrazione girondina di Bordeaux molti club attaccarono apertamente il governo federale di Parigi, ciò che provocò una purga dei club durante il Terrore. Nove Ebrei, fra cui cinque ricchi fratelli Rabà, furono esclusi dalla *section Michel Montaigne*. Ma, dopo il Terrore, uno dei cinque fratelli fu riammesso. Due Ebrei, Azevedo e Aaron Salcedo, del club « 10 agosto », furono nominati il 22 gennaio 1795 membri della Commissione per purgare i 28 club di elementi terroristi (17).

(14) RENÉE DUBOS, *Une Société populaire bordelaise. Les Surveillants de la Constitution*. « Revue historique de Bordeaux », XXV (1932), 99-100. ERRNEST LABADIE, *Les Billets de confiance ... 1791-1793* (Paris, 1914), pagg. 13, 34, 39 ; *Journal du Club national de Bordeaux*, n. 1 (18 messidoro anno II), n. 93 (24 nevoso, anno III), n. 99 (6 piovoso, anno III).

(15) *Archivi dipartimentali della Gironda*, L. 2108, II, L. 17 ; A. VIVIE, *Histoire de la Terreur à Bordeaux* (Bordeaux, 1877), I, 29 ; LABADIE, *op. cit.*, pag. 69 ; L'HÉRITIER, *op. cit.*, pagg. 254-55 ; P. BECAMPS, *La Révolution à Bordeaux* ; LACOMBE (Bordeaux, 1953), pag. 57. L'11 maggio 1792 un ebreo, certo Cordoba, denunziava una donna perchè aveva ricevuto la visita d'un prete. *Archivi dipartimentali della Gironda*, L. 2109.

(16) *Archivi dipartimentali della Gironda*, II, L. 57, pag. 127 ; 11 L. 9 ; *Des travaux des sections permanentes dans le moment actuel ...* [Bordaux 1793]. L'Ebreo Manassé Azevedo l'anziano operava nella Sezione del « 10 agosto » ; *Adresse de la société populaire de la jeunesse bordelaise à ses concitoyens* (Bordeaux, 3 settembre 1793) ; manifesto.

(17) *Tableau des membres de la section Michel Montaigne, n. VIII, qui ont été*

Ma anche a Bordeaux, nonostante la vasta partecipazione degli Ebrei ai club, molti di essi attaccarono apertamente gli Ebrei. Nel 1793 la *Société des Amis de la Liberté et de l'Egalité* votò una risoluzione contro la « speculazione degli Ebrei ». Il 27 aprile 1793 i Club *Brutus* e *de la Loi* (sezioni 7 e 9) attaccavano gli Ebrei di Saint-Esprit-lès-Bayonne che avevano abbandonato Bordeaux a causa della guerra sulla frontiera spagnuola. Ma il gran numero di Cristiani che avevano pure abbandonato Bayonne e dintorni non erano stati criticati. In una riunione del 15 giugno 1793 un membro del club degli uomini liberi (Sezione 23) affermò che gli Ebrei erano speculatori per quanto fossero i più favoriti dalla Rivoluzione. Dall'altro canto un altro membro sosteneva nel già ricordato Club degli amici della libertà e dell'eguaglianza che « secondo Voltaire gli Ebrei si potevano trovare dovunque ci fosse denaro. Certo Voltaire intendeva lodare l'operosità e l'intraprendenza di quei cittadini [ebrei]. Oggi noi possiamo affermare che dovunque c'è ladrocinio si possono trovare capitalisti e speculatori ». Può darsi benissimo che, allo scopo di combattere i sentimenti anti-ebraici che regnavano in alcuni club di Bordeaux, l'ebreo Pereyre scriveva già (6 ottobre 1792) allo stesso club : « Gli Ebrei amerebbero sacrificare i loro averi e le loro vite per la Repubblica » (18).

Vale la pena di notare che il 29 marzo 1793 David Dalpuget, un ebreo di Bordeaux residente a Parigi, si congratulava col *Club national* per il

---

épurés par son Comité nommé à cet effet (Bordeaux, 1793), manifesto. (Aaron Fereyra, Francia Beaufleury, Loppes Pereyra, Rabà junior, Fs. Henriques, Rabà ainé, Rabà medico, Rabà Aaron, Rabà Salomon, Rabà Condurno) ; *Archivi municipali di Bordeaux*, I, 59, pag. 68 ; *Archivi dipartimentali della Gironda*, L. 2153 ; *Arrêté du Représentant du Peuple Bordas* . . . 3 piovoso, anno III . . . (Bordeaux), 8 pagine. In vari periodi Fonseca nipote, J. Rodrigues e Lopes Dubec furono segretari della *Section Bon accord* (n. 19). Carvallo era membro del suo Comitato. J. Rodrigues era pure uno dei dirigenti della *Section de la Convention* (n. 20). Uno dei Rabà apparteneva agli Amici della Libertà (Sez. n. 21). *Archivi dipartimentali della Gironda*, 11 L. 10, 12, L. 2134 ; *Adresse de la Section du Bon-Accord, n. 19, aux Gardes nationales de Bordeaux* . . . (Bordeaux), 4 pagg. ; *Réclamation du citoyen Carvallo fils, négociant de Bordeaux* (Bordeaux, 1793), manifesto ; *Les Sections de Bordeaux à tous les corps administratifs et à tous les citoyens de la Republique*, (Bordeaux, 1793), 4 pagg. ; *Adresse de la Section de la Convention* . . . *concernant les riches* (Bordeaux, brumaio, anno II), manifesto.

(18) *Archivi dipartimentali della Gironda*, L. 2106, 2134, 2138 ; *Archivi municipali di Bordeaux*, I, 65, n. 46 ; G. Ducannès-Duval, *Ville de Bordeaux. Inventaire sommaire des archives municipals. Période révolutionnaire* (Bordeaux, 1929), IV, 341 ; *La Section de l'Egalité* [n. 4] *aux agioteurs*, manifesto ; *Discours sur les causes de l'agiotage* . . . *lu à la société des Amis de la Liberté et de l'Egalité de Bordeaux, le 20 septembre 1792* (Bordeaux), pag. 13.

suo atteggiamento giacobino e anti-federalista (19). Durante la reazione del Termidoro il cronista di Bordeaux Pierre Bernadau notava che la plebe aveva assalito un terrorista ebreo (20).

Presenta uno speciale ed importantissimo interesse la storia singolare del club giacobino di Saint-Esprit-lès Bayonne (durante il terrore il nome di questo sobborgo di Bayonne fu mutato in quello di Jean-Jacques Rousseau). Quel club era composto per lo più di Ebrei e dirigeva il consiglio comunale. (Siccome agli Ebrei era proibito di risiedere a Bayonne essi abitavano a Saint-Esprit). Di fatto era una specie di club giacobino ebraico (21). Ma questo esula dal nostro argomento che riguarda soltanto l'atteggiamento dei club giacobini nei confronti degli Ebrei.

Gli Ebrei appartenevano ad altri club della Francia sud-occidentale. A Labastide gli Ebrei Dandrade [D'Andrade] e Rodrigues appartenevano al *Club de la Société Républicaine*. Il Club di Bidache aveva pochi Ebrei fra i suoi membri. Un Ebreo di Saint-Esprit di nome Castro divenne membro del Comitato di Sorveglianza di Dax. Durante il Terrore Marcquefoi di Saint-Esprit fu membro del Consiglio municipale di Bayonne. Il 17 ottobre 1793 i giacobini di Saint-Esprit accettavano 11 giacobini quali membri corrispondenti — tutti ebrei — che lavoravano a Saint-Jean-de-Luz (22).

In conclusione si può dire che molti giacobini non potevano liberarsi dalle loro tradizioni anti-ebraiche, nonostante i principi giacobini di eguaglianza universale. Si sa che il giacobino che combatteva contro le pratiche e le tradizioni della religione ebraica non era — salvo alcune eccezioni locali — ispirato da sentimenti anti-ebraici (23). La tradizione anti-ebraica era così forte che si manifestava in molte altre occasioni quali la partecipazione ebraica ai club giacobini.

(19) Z. SZAJKOWSKI, *The Sephardic Jews of France during the Revolution of 1789*, « Procedings of the American Academy for Jewish Research » XXIV (1955), 162-63.

(20) La Cronaca di Bernadau, 15 settembre 1795 (vedi nota 13). Samuel Jacob presentava al suo club un busto di Marat. Il 15 giugno 1794 fu arrestato. *Archivi municipali di Bordeaux*, VIVIE, vol. 17, pagg. 26-28. Nel 1791 « l'ebreo di Bordeaux Helasisa « fu espulso dal suo club giacobino di Parigi per sentimenti non patriotici ». *Archivi nazionali*, F 7-3688 (3) ; TUETEY, *Répertoire de l'histoire de Paris pendant la Révolution française* (Paris, 1910), IX-2, 422.

(21) GINSBURGER, *op. cit.*, pagg. 78, 86.

(22) ABBÉ P. HARISTOY, *Les Paroisses du pays pendant la période révolutionnaire* (Pau, 1895), I, pagg. 360-61 ; GINSBURGER, *op. cit.*, pag. 78.

(23) Z. SZAJKOWSKI, *The attitude of French Jacobins toward Jewish Religion*, « Historia judaica », XVIII (1956), 107-120.

FRENCH JEWRY DURING THE
THERMIDORIAN REACTION

O N the ninth day of Thermidor in the year II of the
French Revolution (July 27, 1794), Maximilian Marie
Isidore Robespierre and his friends were arrested. This
marked the beginning of the end of the "Terror" that had
lasted since July, 1793. The dissolution of the National
Convention on October 26, 1795, brought with it the begin-
ning of the *Directoire,* and Napoleon's *coup d'état* on
November 9, 1799, ushered in the era of the *Consulat.*

The account of anti-Jewish persecutions during the
period of the Terror was told by chroniclers and later accepted as fact by historians. Legends were even circulated
of how Jews were miraculously saved from the Terror.
Hanna Jacques Brunschwig-Padagay, daughter of Joel
Padagay of Dornach (Upper Rhine), related that her father
was warned to escape to Mulhouse because the Terrorists
would arrest him. While leaving the house an old man came
along, asked for food and blessed him. When Joel came
back during the Thermidor, he found the key in the keyhole and everything inside the house in perfect order. The
old man was none other than Elijah the Prophet, who had
kept the house clean.[1]

What was the status of the Jews during the Thermidorian reaction which followed the tragic era of the Terror?

According to the historians Rodolphe Reuss and Robert
Anchel the end of the Terror did not eradicate anti-Jewish
feelings and acts. On the contrary, it seems that during
the Thermidorian reaction anti-Jewish feeling survived not
only in the local administrations, but also in some departmental and federal agencies. At the beginning of the

---

[1] S. Mock, "Sur l'origine de la communauté israélite de Mulhouse,"
Univers israélite, LII-2 (1897), 491-494, 526-530.

Originally published in *Historia Judaica*, vol. XX (1958).

Thermidor the Jews in Alsace suffered less, but a little later, at the beginning of 1796, anti-Jewish attitudes there were reinforced when more radical elements with Jacobin tendencies again took over the Alsatian administration.[2] The Alsatian Jewish teacher and scribe, Jessel Lehman, recorded in his diary at that time that the Jews were living in fear of being banished from France.[3]

It is only natural that a Jewish historian should apply to the period of the Thermidorian reaction the assumption that reactionary victories encouraged anti-Jewish persecutions. But let us first examine the facts and see whether a similar situation prevailed during the period of the French Revolution which followed the Terror.

Jacobin violence against Jews and Judaism was a part of the drive against the Church in general. In some provincial centers, where a strong anti-Jewish feeling prevailed, Jews were singled out for persecution. During the Thermidorian reaction the fight against religion was relaxed. In the beginning of the period the Alsatian religious teacher Jessel Lehman noted in his diary: "On the Sabbath people again went to the synagogues and they [the Christians] went to church on Sunday, but they still did it with fear in their hearts, because this was not yet really permitted. . . . The men of the Revolution [*revolucje lajt*] were recalled because they were too strict with people and they even shed much blood. This [terrorist leader Eulogius] Schneider of Strasbourg who was arrested by the men of the Revolution was publicly guillotined."[4] In Bordeaux representatives of synagogues and individual Jews requested that the religious articles confiscated during the Terror be returned to them.[5]

It is the author's conviction that the fight against Judaism, the nationalization of synagogues, cemeteries, and other communal Jewish properties during the period of the

---

[2] R. Reuss, "Quelques documents nouveaux sur l'antisémitisme dans le Bas-Rhin de 1794 à 1799," *REJ*, LIX (1910), 252, 263; R. Anchel, *Napoléon et les juifs* (Paris, 1928), p. 25.

[3] Lehman's diary, manuscript in the Alsatian museum of Strasbourg, p. 29 A.

[4] *Ibid.*, p. 28.

[5] Departmental archives of Gironde, L 2177, 2203, 2214, Q 881.

Terror should not be regarded as acts of anti-Jewish policy, for these measures were not directed against Jews alone. However, it should be noted that the drive against religious practices—including Jewish religious practices—did not stop completely after the arrest of Robespierre and his friends.

In 1796 Pierre Charles Louis Baudin, deputy of the Ardennes, stated that a citizen could remain a Jew or a Moslem on the condition that he reject the religious observances and dogmas of Moses and Mohammed, because in a theocracy religion is closely tied in with the existing social order. In 1797 the deputy Albert Augustin Antoine Joseph Duhot attacked, at the Council of Five Hundred, the observance of the Sabbath by Jews and of Sunday by Christians. But again Jews were not singled out by him.[6] After the Terror synagogues and Jewish cemeteries were also nationalized and sold. In Metz the synagogue was put up for sale in 1795, but as a result of legal technicalities the sale was annulled in 1796.[7] After the publication of the law of May 30, 1795, granting religious freedom, the Jews of Carpentras requested that their synagogue be returned to them. However, as late as 1800 the synagogue was only rented to them. The Jewish cemetery of Avignon was nationalized and sold on August 4, 1797, to the Christian Etienne Bonnet for the sum of 1,188 livres.[8] In December, 1797, the Jews of Saverne protested against an order to destroy the monuments in the Jewish cemetery. In vain did they point out that even during the Terror this was not done.[9] Earlier, on November 28, 1794, Alexandre Halphen and Aaron Piquard of Metz were fined for carrying out Jewish religious burials.[10]

[6] [Pierre Charles Louis] Baudin, *Du maintien de la liberté des opinions religieuses* . . . (Paris, an IV), p. 7; *Le Journal de France,* Nos. 749-750, November 24-25, 1797.

[7] Departmental archives of Moselle, V, 166.

[8] City archives of Carpentras, Revolution 42, September 10, 1794, and May 15, 1800; H. Chobaut, "Les Juifs d'Avignon du Comtat et la révolution française," *REJ,* CII (1938), 33-35.

[9] D. Fischer, *Geschichte der Stadt Zabern* (Zabern, 1874), p. 125; Reuss, *op. cit.,* p. 270; Elie Scheid, *Histoire des juifs d'Alsace* (Paris, 1887), p. 277.

[10] *Extrait des jugements de la police municipale de la Commune de Metz: du 8 frimaire an III* [28 *Novembre* 1794] [Metz, 1794], broadside.

In contrast, the Jews of Sierck were permitted in 1795 to use their cemetery.[11] In Nice five Jews were sentenced in October, 1798, for building tabernacles for the Succoth holidays.[12]

In handling financial and other economic affairs of the Revolution, the Jacobins, who in their fight against religious practices rarely singled out Jews, were more influenced by traditional anti-Jewish feelings. This found expression in various forms of chicanery against individual Jews, who were forced to pay high taxes and fines. During the Thermidor, Jews demanded the annullment of fines imposed upon them during the Terror. Most of them did it without proclaiming their hatred for the defeated Robespierre.[13] An exception was a pamphlet published during the Thermidor by the rich merchant Séligmann Alexandre of Strasbourg, a son-in-law of the Alsatian Jewish leader, Cerfberr of Médelsheim. He sought not only justice, but also revenge against the Robespierre regime.[14] Generally speaking, during the Thermidor the Jews suffered less than during the Terror from the revolutionary economic policies. However, this should not be regarded as a change in the attitude toward Jews. With the end of the Terror the general situation in the country changed, and Jews, too, profited from it. Nevertheless, in many cases they were even then forced to pay extremely high taxes and were often singled out for discriminatory treatment.

On October 4, 1794, Léopold Samuel and Marx Samuel of Niederhagenthal (Upper Rhine) were taxed 4,500 livres each; they had to pay almost the entire taxes of the city.[15]

---

[11] Departmental archives of Moselle, Sierck 13.

[12] *Liberté, égalité, fraternité. Extrait du registre des jugements du Tribunal Correctionel de l'Arrondissement de Nice . . . du 8 brumaire an VII.* [Nice, 1798], broadside.

[13] The deputy Philippe Charles Aimé Goupilleau reported in favor of Charles Peixotto's demand to cancel his fine of 1,200,000 livres. *Rapport fait par Goupilleau sur la pétition du citoyen Charles Peixotto . . . du 24 vendémiaire an 7* (n.p., n.d.), 7 pp.

[14] Séligmann Alexandre, *Dénonciation à mes concitoyens . . .* (Strasbourg, an III), 38 pp.; R. Reuss, *Séligmann Alexandre . . .* (Strasbourg, 1880), 44 pp.

[15] Departmental archives of Upper Rhine, L 700.

426 FRENCH JEWRY DURING THE THERMIDOR

On December 10, 1795, thirteen Jews figured prominently on a list of the fifty-eight richest people of Strasbourg, who had to grant a forced loan; five of the twenty-two families who were required to pay the highest taxes were Jews.[16] Two Jewish families resided in Diedenhoffen prior to 1789 and fourteen new families settled there during the first five years of the Revolution. In 1795 they were all, even the poor, forced to pay the compulsory tax. The Jews protested and won their case, with the exception of the wealthy Abraham. On October 21, 1796, Elie Lévy and thirty-one other Jews of Rimbach (Upper Rhine) stated in a petition that none of them was wealthy and that some were even paupers; but the city council nevertheless taxed them for large sums, while wealthy Christians were exempted from paying taxes. As a result of the Jews' complaint, however, one Christian family, which owned three-fourths of the property in the village, had to pay a similar percentage of tax. On February 24, 1796, Gabriel Bloch of Soultz (Upper Rhine) was asked to pay a tax of 11,000 livres; he proved that his entire possessions were worth only 4,400 livres and was reclassified among those taxable in the sixth category. Similar petitions were submitted by other Jews of Soultz, Bollwiler and Jungholtz. In the year VII (1799) the Jewish brothers Samuel were at the top of the 439 richest taxpayers (from 46 to 75,000 francs), but they refused to pay more than 5,200 francs.[17]

As they were earlier, so during the Thermidor, Jews were accused of speculating. On the other hand, a Jewish employee at the Ministry of the General Police in Lyon was the author of a song ridiculing speculation, aristocrats, and false democrats.[18] In 1795, when Paris was threatened with famine, the walls of the capital were covered with posters dated June 8, 1795, and signed by the citizen Pierre Seigneur

[16] Reuss (*supra*, n. 2), pp. 263-264.

[17] A. J. Kohn, *Zur Geschichte der Juden in Diedenhoffen.* (Diedenhoffen, 1913), p. 32; M. Gunsburger, *Histoire de la communauté israélite de Soultz* (Strasbourg, 1939), pp. 40-41; F. L'Huilier, *Recherches sur l'Alsace napoléonienne* (Strasbourg, 1947), p. 12.

[18] Léon Kahn, *Les Juifs de Paris pendant la révolution* (Paris, 1898), p. 306.

of the *Section de la Butte-des-Moulins,* proposing that the *nation juive* be asked to import wheat from abroad, because only Jews with their business connections could do it.[19]

While, during the Terror, Jews served as councilmen and in other official capacities, they fell into disgrace during the new regime. A few Parisian Jews who were active during the Terror were arrested during the Thermidor.[20] According to the historian René Cuzacq Jewish Jacobins, who directed the affairs of Saint-Esprit-lès-Bayonne during the Terror, did not persecute Christians, and Christians did not persecute Jewish Jacobins there during the Thermidor. However, this was not so. Jewish Jacobins were persecuted there, and a Jew could not become a councilman. From the end of the Terror until 1838 no Jew could be mayor of Saint-Esprit, and in 1838 ten out of fifteen councilmen resigned because the Jew David Rodrigues was elected mayor.[21] The same happened in Bordeaux. There, in the beginning of the Thermidor, no important official functions were entrusted to Jews. The new rulers of the Thermidor considered it more advantageous not to have Jewish officials, though no Jew was among the important terrorist leaders of Bordeaux.[22] In the same city a few influential Jews were active in the Federalist movement of the Girondists. This, however, did not protect them from being singled out later in attacks against terrorists; for instance, in the lists of terrorists Jews were pointed out by notation of their religious affiliation.[23] In Carpentras, where some Jews were active

[19] Etienne Charavay, "Un Appel á la nation juive pour se charger de l'approvisionment de Paris," *Révolution française,* XXIV (1893), 62-68.

[20] Kahn, *op. cit.,* pp. 299-304.

[21] René Cuzacq, Introduction to E. Ginsburger, *Le Comité de surveillance de Jean-Jacques Rousseau, Saint-Esprit-lès-Bayonne* (Paris, 1934), p. 4; Henry Léon, *Histoir de juifs de Bayonne* (Paris, 1893), p. 170; Peillic, *Le Vieux Saint-Esprit* (Bayonne, 1938), p. 15.

[22] Z. Szajkowski, "The Sephardic Jews of France during the Revolution of 1789," *Proceedings of the American Academy for Jewish Research,* XXIV (1955), 157.

[23] *Liste alphabétique des hommes de sang . . . à Bordeaux* (A Raison [Bordeaux], edition of 1802), pp. 2-3, 8, 11, 19, 21, 22: "Azevedo cadet; Astruc Fayan, juif section 9"; "Azévédo cadet, dit le Tauré, juif. Aaron (Di Soria), juif. Astruc Fayan, juif. Brandon, ex-juif. Dias frères, juifs. Furtado, juif, membre de la commission des neutres requisitors.

428 FRENCH JEWRY DURING THE THERMIDOR

during the Terror, no Jews became members of the local administration before 1798. In Cavaillon Jewish Jacobins, including Lange Cohen, who was mayor of the city, were removed from office by the Paris representative Phillippe Charles Aimé Goupilleau. It is doubtful, however, that Goupilleau's act was of an anti-Jewish character, for on October 29, 1794, the same Goupilleau appointed Benjamin Monteaux, a rich Jew, as councilman of Avignon, most probably because of the absence there of active Jews during the Terror. Moreover, in a report asking that a fine of 1,200,000 livres imposed on Charles Peixotto during the Terror be rescinded, the same Goupilleau spoke of Jews in friendly terms.[24] In Nice, it was not until March 27, 1794, that Jews were appointed to the local administration of pure patriots, but no Jews were among the active terrorists there. Yet they were excluded from the administration appointed during the Thermidor by the Paris Representative, Pierre Etienne Befroy de Beauvoir. Only as late as March 24, 1801, and May 28, 1804, were Jews again appointed to administrative functions.[25] It must be emphasized, however, that the Thermidorian policy of dismissing terrorists from public office was not directed against Jews alone, though as always happened in cases involving minorities, entire communities were often held responsible for the acts of individual Jews who took part in political movements.

On November 19, 1797, Léon Aaron Worms was elected councilman of Landau. The liberal historian, Rodolphe Reuss, called this "a rare, if not unique, case for the period."[26] The case was, indeed, rare but not unique.[27]

Mendes, juif. Olivera, juif. Petit frères, juifs." A similar list of September, 1815 singled out many Jews of Bordeaux who had favored Napoleon I during the Hundred Days: *Esprit de 93, des descendants de Bonaparte et des hommes sans caractères* . . . (Bordeaux, September, 1815). On these lists, called *Livres rouges*, see A. Vivie, *La Terreur à Bordeaux*, II (Bordeaux, 1877), 469-474.

[24] Chobaux, *REJ.*, CII (1938), 27-29; Z. Szajkowski, "The Comtadin Jews and the Annexation of the Papal Province by France, 1789-1791," *Jewish Quarterly Review*, XLVI (1955), 192-193. On Peixotto's fine see *supra*, n. 13.

[25] Victor Emanuel, *Les Juifs à Nice*, 1460-1860 (Nice, 1905), pp. 46-48.

[26] Rodolphe Reuss, *La Grande Fuite de décembre 1793 et la situation politique et religieuse du Bas Rhin de 1794 à 1799* (Strasbourg, 1924), p. 157.

[27] In the year III Hayem Worms was councilman of Sarre-Libre

At the same time, it should be remembered that this was a rare event for the traditionally anti-Jewish Alsatian province during all regimes, and the Thermidorian reaction should not be singled out.

(In 1845, more than fifty years after Jewish emancipation in France, the number of Jewish officials and officially respected professions of Jews was still relatively small: only one member of a departmental general council, two members of the Institute, eighty-one members of city councils, five mayors, nine judges, two deputy-attorneys, one consul, four huissiers, three notaries, one chief of a minister's office, two deputies, one police commissioner, seven lawyers, twenty-two physicians. There were also nine hundred and eighteen Jewish *notables*, who had the right to vote.[28])

The most striking and the most frequently cited fact of anti-Jewish persecution during the Thermidorian reaction was the order given on November 1, 1794, by the Legislative Committee to the Alsatian authorities that they should protect the Jews. However, a more careful study of the available sources reveals that this order was the result of a petition submitted by the Jews of the Department of Lower Rhine in June or in the first days of July, 1794 — a few weeks before the end of the Terror. The Jews complained that they were being persecuted, that they were still not allowed to visit the city of Strasbourg on certain days, the use of communal properties was refused to them, they were forced to pay higher taxes than Christians, etc. The petition was received by the authorities of Lower Rhine and in Paris on or about July 13, 1794. As a result the Paris representative in Alsace, André Foussedoire, warned on August 19, 1794, against persecuting the Jews. Subsequently, on November 1, which was already in the period of the Thermidor, the Legislative Committee ordered protection for the Jews. In

(Moselle). Joseph Lang was a councilman of Dortmarsheim. He was arrested in July 28, 1794, and liberated on the following August 16, 1794. In 1794, two Jews were councilmen of Niederrodern. L. Koch, "Die Juden in Niederrodern," *Strassburger israelitische Wochenschrift*, VII (1910), No. 14, 3. Tische (Hirschel) was mayor of Danendorf. "Sterbende Gemeinden: Danendorf," *Tribune juive*, May 25, 1934, p. 411.

[28] *Archives israélites*, VI (1845), 831-836.

other words, the action of the Legislative Committee grew
out of local anti-Jewish feelings which prevailed during the
Terror. The historian, Raphael Mahler, states, on the basis
of this fact, that in Alsace a slogan was adopted for "a
reinforced offensive against the Jews." This is much exaggerated, even if we take into account the anti-Jewish tradition of the Alsatian province.[29]

Anti-Jewish propaganda, where it did exist, was mostly
a part of the general anti-revolutionary propaganda. In
December, 1798, the municipal agent of Dambach was denounced for a statement made by him in a tavern to the
effect that religion was being persecuted because a few Jews
were in the government. He also warned against buying
nationalized properties, and he predicted the outbreak of a
revolt and an invasion. Curiously enough, a Jew was then
a member of the city council, and the agent mentioned his
name among the opponents of the regime.[30]

Some adverse policies of previous revolutionary periods
were continued during the Thermidor, e.g., the refusal to
nationalize the debt owed by former Jewish communities
to Christian creditors. Prior to the Revolution the Jewish
communities were forced to borrow money, mainly in order
to be able to pay taxes. During the Revolution the Jews
demanded that these debts be assumed by the government,
as had been done with the debts owed by all other corporate
bodies that had been dissolved by the new regime. This
demand was rejected, an act in which the Council of Five
Hundred concurred. The Council likewise refused to act

[29] Departmental archives of Lower Rhine, IL 825, 1222, 2L 43, L 1584;
[André] Foussedoire, représentant du peuple dans les départments des Haut-
et Bas-Rhin (Colmar, [1794]), 4 pp.; Extrait du registre des arrêtés du Comité
de Législation. Séance du 11 brumaire, l'an troisième [1 Novembre 1794] de la
république française une et indivisible (Strasbourg, [1704]), 4 pp. The Jewish
petition was printed in Copie de la pétition par plusieurs citoyens du Bas-Rhin,
á la Convention Nationale (Colmar, [1794]), 7 pp., together with the decision
of November 1, 1794; Raphael Mahler, History of the Jewish People, I (New
York, 1957), 272 (in Yiddish).

[30] Reuss (supra, n. 2), p. 274; idem, La Grande Fuite (s. note 26), pp.
207-208. In the canton of Ribeauvillé, Catholic priests who were persecuted
but refused to emigrate found hiding-places among the Jews during the
Directoire. Robert Faller, "Le Canton de Ribeauvillé et la politique religieuse
du Directoire," Revue d'Alsace, LXXIX (1932), 342.

on reports in favor of the Jewish demand presented by specially appointed commissions. On the other hand, the Thermidorian regime followed the policy of the previous regimes in the case of the debts owed by Alsatian peasants to Jews. The decree of September 28, 1791, ordered the Alsatian Jews to present a list of debts owed to them. This the Jews refused to do. In the end, this list of debts was never presented.[31]

Among the emigrés who left France were some Jews. Most of them did not favor the old regime, but they took the anti-revolutionary line to escape the revolutionary events. The Thermidor did not whitewash the emigrés. The law of January 11, 1795, permitted the return of those emigrés who, at the time of their departure from France, had been earning their living by working with their hands, i.e., peasants, workers, artisans, etc. The Terror had not singled out Jews in the fight against the emigrés and neither did the new regime in enforcing the policy on emigrés. On the contrary, in some locations a very liberal policy enabled Jewish emigrés to benefit from the law of 1795 by a declaration that traditionally Jewish occupations of peddlers, traders in second-hand goods, horses, and cattle, were useful to the local population and that, as a result of anti-Jewish restrictions during the old regime, Jews were forced to make a living in such way.[32]

Of course, there were many public anti-Jewish attacks. The aristocratic newspaper *Le Babillard* proposed the levy of a special tax on Jews because they all possessed well-lined purses. Other newspapers protested, and the Jew Zalkind Hourvitz wrote that he himself knew many hundreds of Jews whose wallets contained no more than their safety identifications as loyal citizens.[33] From the Convention's

---

[31] The debts owed by the Jewish communities will be the subject of a special study. On the law of September 28, 1791, see Z. Szajkowski, "The Law of September 28, 1791, on Jewish Creditors in France," *Zion*, XIX (1954), 163-170 (in Hebrew).

[32] Z. Szajkowski, "Jewish Emigrés during the French Revolution," *Jewish Social Studies*, XVI (1954), 319-334.

[33] *Amis des lois*, October 25, 1797; *Journal de Paris*, No. 36 (brumaire,

rostrum the left-wing *montagnards* were on a few occasions accused of being Jews.[34] But the statement of the historian Raphael Mahler that "the propaganda against the remains of Robespierre's party took on in some newspapers an air of anti-Semitic propaganda" and that "whoever dared to say a good word about the previous regime was called a Jew,"[35] is greatly exaggerated. One of the strongest attacks against Jews from the rostrum of a legislative body during the Revolution was delivered on May 7, 1799, by the deputy François Balthazar Darracq at the Council of Five Hundred. His tirade was directed against the Jews of Bordeaux, who refused to permit their cemetery to become nationalized property. However, his speech could hardly be taken as an expression of the feelings of the Council of Five Hunderd. In fact, the Council refused to follow him, and the cemetery was given back to the Jews. On an earlier occasion Darracq was censured for his anti-Jewish remarks.[36]

In conclusion, it may be said that it would be very difficult to point out special anti-Jewish restrictions or other kinds of persecution that resulted from the general political developments during the Thermidorian reaction. There were many cases of anti-Jewish propaganda, even of the plundering of Jewish property,[37] but these instances did not take place on the order or under the influence of federal or departmental authorities.

Jewish emancipation in France was already well established. Of course, it was not yet accepted by the entire Christian population. A story was told about a Jew who visited a deputy. Still accustomed to the good old days of fraternization, he acted in a familiar manner toward him. This the deputy took as an insult.[38]

an VI); Kahn (*supra*, n. 18), p. 139; A. Aulard, *Paris pendant la réaction Thermidorienne et sous le Directoire*, IV (Paris, 1902), 412.

[34]   Kahn (*supra*, n. 18), pp. 295-296.

[35]   Mahler, *op. cit.*, I, 271.

[36]   Z. Szajkowski, "Jewish Autonomy Debated and Attacked during the French Revolution," *Historia Judaica*, XX (1958), 43-44; *Journal de France*, Nos. 751-752 (November, 1797), 607.

[37]   On March 21, 1798, the synagogue of Pfastatt was plundered; M. Ginsburger, *Aus dem Revolutionskriege* (Breslau, 1916), p. 4.

[38]   A. Aulard, *Paris sous le Consulat*, I (Paris, 1903), 81.

The Thermidorian period may perhaps be characterized as a period of struggle by the Jews to retain the rights secured by them in the first years of the Revolution. But the entire French nation was engaged in a similar struggle. Be that as it may, the Thermidorian period—or the previous Terroristic periods—did not produce measures directed against Jews as a specific group. The Terror dealt even-handedly with the Jews as a group, and the same can be said of the Thermidor and the Directoire, and even of the Consulat. The historian Simon Dubnow was correct in writing that "during the ten years between the *Directoire* and Napoleon's Empire nothing important happened in the life of the French Jews."[39] Even Napoleon's anti-Jewish policy came in a later period, in 1806. Surely his appeal of 1799 to the Jews, in which he promised to restore Jerusalem to them, was in direct contrast to his later attitude toward Jews in 1806 and 1808.

[39] Simon Dubnow, *World History of the Jewish People*, VIII (New York, 1954), 123 (in Yiddish).

THE SEPHARDIC JEWS OF FRANCE DURING
THE REVOLUTION OF 1789

On the eve of the Revolution of 1789 the Sephardic Jews of France were concentrated in Bordeaux, Saint-Esprit-lès-Bayonne and a few other small communities of Southwestern France. The most influential community was that of Bordeaux. So far, the historians of the Sephardic Jews followed the tendency of the general Bordeaux historiography, which painted an idyllic picture of 18th Century Bordeaux: a rich Jewish Community, where the Jews, who were useful to French commerce with the colonies obtained ideal privileges. But in reality the life of the Jews in Southwestern France was not so idyllic. In the 18th century Bordeaux enriched itself thanks to its commerce with the colonies, and especially to its traffic with slaves between Africa and the colonies, which was authorized by the ordinances of 1716 and 1717. But only a very small percentage of the about 100,000 Bordeaux inhabitants on the eve of 1789 lived richly. Most of the Bordeaux population were poor working people who lived in misery.[1] The life of the Jews, too, was not always

The following abbreviations of sources are being used in the notes:

AdG = Departmental archives of Gironde (Bordeaux)
AdLandes = Departmental archives of Landes (Mont-de-Marsan)
AdVaucluse = Departmental archives of Vaucluse (Avignon)
AmBa = City archives of Bayonne
AmBx = City archives of Bordeaux
AmNîmes = City archives of Nîmes
AN = National Archives (Paris)
BmBx = City library of Bordeaux
BN = National Library (Paris);
JTS = Jewish Theological Seminary (New York, N. Y.).

[1] Pierre Bécamps, *La Révolution à Bordeaux (1789–1794). J.-B.-M. Lacombe, Président de la Commission militaire*, Bordeaux, 1953, 21–40.

Originally published in *Proceedings of the American Academy for Jewish Research,* vol. XXIV (1955).

cheerful. For the privileges obtained from the Kings of France the Jews were forced to pay large sums of money and even then they were forbidden to make a living by learning honest professions. The percentage of rich Jews was small, and most of the others lived poorly. The same can be said of the Jews of Saint-Esprit, a suburb of Bayonne where they were not tolerated.[2]

The Sephardim participated, much more than the Ashkenazic Jews, in the events of the Revolution, on the local scene and even in Paris. Most of the latter stood aside of the revolutionary adventures. In those departments where their communities were located (in the former Provinces of Alsace, Metz and the Metz Province, and Lorraine) a very active anti-Semitism prevailed during the entire Revolution among all parts of the Gentile population, the revolutionary Jacobins and the counter-Revolutionary circles of the Catholic Church. Jews were very seldom allowed to occupy public offices. In Bordeaux the situation was different. After a short protest against granting full citizenship to the Jews passed over,[3] they were accepted there as equal to all the other inhabitants.

In studying the history of Jews in Southwestern France during the Revolution, one should first of all try to find out if they participated in the Federalist movement. Surely, this movement represents one of the most important and most complicated aspects of France's revolutionary historiography.

At the very first sessions of the National Convention sharp conflicts arose between the extreme left wing of the Jacobins (which was helped by the popular clubs and was known as the

---

[2] ז. שייקובסקי, „משלחותיהם של יהודי בורדו אל ועדת מאלורב (1788) ואל האסיפה הלאומית (1790)". ציון (ירושלים), שנה י"ח, 31–47.

[3] *Le Moniteur*, Feb. 11, 1790; *La Gazette de Paris*, Feb. 10 & 12, 1790; L. Kahn, *Les Juifs à Paris pendant la Révolution*, Paris, 1898, 80–82; A. Vivie, *La Terreur à Bordeaux*, Bordeaux, 1877, I, 27; M. Lhéritier, *Liberté (1789–1790). Bordeaux et la Révolution française*, Paris 1947, 69; *Idem, Les débuts de la Révolution à Bordeaux....*, Bordeaux, 1919, 82. On the other hand many Gentiles were in favor of the Jews. One pamphleteer stated that they should not only be granted citizenship, but should also be accepted as equal, free citizens: M. Gergerez fils, *Adresse aux défenseurs de l'humanité, sur le Décret rendu par l'Assemblée Nationale, en faveur des Juifs,* [Bordeaux,] 1790. 8 pp.

Montagnards) and the moderate wing known as the *Girondins*, because its best leaders came from the department of Gironde (of which Bordeaux was the departmental capital). The Girondist movement requested various departments for help to fight France's capital, Paris, which was the main center of the *Montagnards*, and this provoked the liquidation of the Girondist wing at the Convention. One of the main arguments used against the Girondists was the latter's federalist propaganda, their favoring not the one and undivided Republic with a strong central revolutionary government in Paris, but a sort of federative Republic. In fact, the Girondists caused a stubborn struggle against Paris and they endangered France's unity. Nevertheless, the question whether the Girondists — not those of the departments, but their Paris leaders — really desired a federative Republic and wanted to divide France's unity, or desired only to use the departments against their Paris opponents — all this remains unanswered. According to the great historian of the French Revolution, A. Mathiez, Girondism was not a doctrine. Up to May 31, 1793, this movement was only a part of the anti-Paris fight, and beginning August 1, it became a desire for vengeance.

We have already noted that the history of Girondism is extremely complicated, and so is also the Jewish participation in the activities of this faction. One should not imagine that Girondism was principally a counter-Revolutionary movement. It preached some very liberal ideas, and many of its leaders were left minded. If the Church helped this movement, it was only in order to use it against the Revolution.[4]

Bordeaux and other provincial centers gladly accepted the federalist ideas of the Girondists. The Bordeaux city leaders,

[4] Dom H. Leclercq, *Feuillants et Girondins*, Paris, 1940, 207–08; Bernard Combes de Patris, *L'Esprit financier des Girondins*, Paris, 1909, 24–25, 48–51, 156; Henri Calvet, "Subsistances et Fédéralisme," *AHRF* [=*Annales historiques de la Révolution française*], VIII, 1931, 229–38; A. Mathiez, *La vie chère et le mouvement social sous la Terreur*, Paris, 1927, 190; Hedwig Hintze, *Staatseinheit und Federalismus im alten Frankreich und in der Revolution*, Stuttgart, 1928, 623 pp.; A. Mathiez, in *AHRF*, VII, 1930, 576–86; Léon Dubreuil, *L'idée régionaliste sous la Révolution*, Besançon, 1919.

who represented the interest of the rich merchants, desired even more federalism than their representatives in Paris. In Bordeaux, as in many other places, the desire for an economic federalism was followed by a strong desire for political federalism and provoked the action to starve out Paris. On June 10, 1793, the departmental Council (*Conseil départemental*) of Gironde nominated the Popular Commission of Public Safety of the Gironde (*Commission populaire de Salut public de la Gironde*), which contacted other departments in order to create an army to march upon Paris. There is no doubt that this Popular Commission committed acts of open treason against Paris and the fatherland. In the first place, the creation of such a Commission was an adventure, because Bordeaux could expect a sharp reaction from Paris, where the anti-Girondist wing of Robespierre and his friends was already in power. In fact, on August 6, 1793, the Convention ordered the arrest of all members of the Bordeaux Popular Commission and the confiscation of their properties.[5]

Two important leaders of the Bordeaux Jewish community, Abraham Furtado and Salomon Lopes Dubec, were members of the Popular Commission. Later, during the Terror, they declared that they belonged to the Commission not because of any anti-Paris principles, but because of their being city officials: Furtado having been then a Commissionary of the General Council of the Bordeaux county and Lopes Dubec a judge of the Court of Commerce.[6] But this was not a very clever excuse; many other officials did not belong to the Commission.

[5] P. Bernardau, *Histoire de Bordeaux, depuis l'année 1675 jusqu'au 1836*, Bordeaux, 1837, 204–08; Vivie, I, 232–43; E. Labadie, *La Presse bordelaise pendant la Révolution*, Bordeaux, 1910, 115, 117.

[6] *Commission populaire de Salut Public du département de la Gironde*, Bordeaux, June 9, 1793, 4 pp. & placard. Jews could be found in many offices of the Popular Commission: in the Commission of supplying food (created on Aug. 1, 1793), and even in the departmental army (*Force départementale*) which projected a march against Paris. The following Jews were members in the 3rd *Grenadiers* batallion of the *Légion du Sud* in the departmental force: Dacosta jeune, Julian jr., Cordova, David Casserace [?], Molina, Jean Lévi, Abraham Mendes, David Lopes Gonsales, Rodrigues, Delvaille, Jacob Pereire

Was the participation of the two important Jewish leaders in the Popular Commission characteristic of the sentiments of a large part of the Bordeaux Jews? Probably in the same proportion as the Popular Commission was an expression of the desires of the Bordeaux people. Of the economically active Bordeaux inhabitants only 1,300 were merchants, lawyers, etc. — i. e. rich people, who would have been interested in a Federalist victory. There were 1,500 employees, 3,000 servants, 300 occupied in various liberal professions, 4,000 artisans, and 29,000 workers. Still, the small minority of rich merchants influenced the city in favor of the Federalist movement, and the mass of poor inhabitants was politically passive. Even from the Sections (Popular Clubs) the working people were absent and so these Sections quickly went over to the Girondists. Twenty eight Sections were active in Bordeaux and very often they controlled events. Without this "poor bourgeoisie" of the Sections (as Jean Jaurès called them) and without the control of the Representatives sent from Paris, Bordeaux would have had during the entire Revolution a city administration of politically moderate rich merchants. But at the time when the Popular Commission was created the voice of the poor people was absent from the Sections. In a way the Popular Commission was not the expression of the desires of the entire city. It was only a result of the people's passive attitude.[7]

(AdG, L1138). In a statement of Aug. 22, 1793, in favor of Rodrigues Alvares of the 2nd company, 7th battalion of this Legion we find the following signatures of Jews: A. Cardoze fils, A. Lopes fils, Peixotto jeune, Peynado jeune, Salomon Athias, Caspar Trigfus, Astruc jeune, Totta, Moïze Lopes fils, and a Hebrew signature אשר פטארש (AdG, L2193). It is worth noting that according to one source the Jews desired to form in 1792 their own *compagnie franche* (a letter of Oct. 9, 1792, to the *Club des Amis de la Liberté*, AdG, L2155).

[7] Bécamps, 106–09; C. Jullian, *Histoire de Bordeaux*, Bordeaux, 1895, 67; Jean Jaurès, *Histoire socialiste de la Révolution française*, Paris, 1922, I, 413. In all periods of the Revolution Jews were active in many of the Bordeaux Sections. Furtado was the author of a pamphlet on the Sections (*De l'utilité des clubs*). We could not find this pamphlet, cf. Tablettes de Bernardau, vol. 4, p. 140, May 25, 1806.) (BmBx).

II

Abraham Furtado, a leading figure among the French Jews of the Emancipation period, was the best known active Jewish Girondist.[8] His role as a member of the Bordeaux Jewish delegation to the Malesherbes Commission in 1788 and at the Napoleon I's Jewish Assembly and Sanhedrin in 1806–1807, are well known.[9] But his role in the non-Jewish political activities

[8] Furtado was the oldest son of Elie Furtado Ferro and Hana Feiga, who left Lisbon after the earthquake of 1755. First they went to London, where Abraham was born; from there they emigrated to Saint-Esprit-lès-Bayonne. Abraham established himself in Bordeaux where he married Sarah Rodrigues-Alvarès (notarial act of May 8, 1775. AdG, not. Rauzan). His mother-in-law died from the wounds inflicted by the Lisbon inquisition. His wife bore him two daughters, Emilie and Clémentine, and died a young woman. Short notices on A. Furtado could be found in all works on modern Jewish history and Jewish and French encyclopaedias. All these notices were based on two early biographies: Michel Berr, *Eloge de M. Abraham Furtado . . .*, Paris, 1817, 34 pp., and another edition of 47 pp.; extracts were reprinted in *La Régénération — Die Wiedergeburt*, Strasbourg, 1837; J. Rodrigues, *Discours . . .* [Feb. 23, 1817], Paris, 1817. Other sources on Furtado: A. de Cologna, *Discours . . . en l'honneur de Furtado*, Paris, 1817; *Abraham Furtado*, [Amsterdam, 1841], reprinted in *Archives israélites*, II, 361–68; H. Léon, *Histoire des Juifs de Bayonne*, Paris, 1898, chapt. XIX; C. V., in *Courrier de la Gironde*, Feb. 4, 1873; E. Féret, *Statistique générale . . . de la Gironde*, Bordeaux, 1889, III, 260; Gabrielle Moyse, "Abraham Furtado. Notice biographique." *Foi et réveil*, I, 1913–14, 376–79 (Furtado's autobiographic letter of Oct. 2, 1784); P. Bernardau, *Histoire de Bordeaux*, 361; L. L. [Lamothe], *Notes pour servir à la biographie des hommes utiles de Bordeaux*, Paris, 1863, 28; Pascal Thémanlys, "Un écrivain et un sociologue: Abraham Furtado." *Les Cahiers de l'Alliance israélite universelle*, no. 89, 1955, 3–9. As we shall see, A. Furtado's brother, Joseph, was an active Jacobin of Saint-Esprit. Another member of his family, Jacob Furtado, emigrated to New York (AdG, L1246). For a list of lithographed portraits of Furtado see: G. Duplessis et G. Riat, *Catalogue de la collection des portraits . . .*, Paris, 1899, IV, 121.

[9] Z. Szajkowski, pp. 32–33; *Idem, Agricultural Credit and Napoleon's anti-Jewish Decrees*, New York, 1953, 97–98. The following are Furtado's writings of this period: *Exhortation aux Israélites de France et du Royaume d'Italie*, Paris, sd 4 pp.; *Mémoire sur les projets de décrets au Conseil d'Etat, concernant les Israélites*, [Paris, 1808], 16 pp.; *Rapport au Grand Sanhédrin. En lui proposant les trois premières décisions doctrinales*, [Paris, 1807], 16 pp.; *Réclamation des Juifs portugais . . .*, [Paris, June 1807]; Furtado's reply to de Bonald, in

during the Revolution is almost unknown. A diary written by Furtado while he was hiding during the Terror provides us a detailed picture of the sentiments of this and other Jewish Girondists during the Terror.[10] It is thus important to analyze this curious document. Let us begin with the course of Furtado's life during the Terror.

When the Bordeaux Girondist administration ended and the Terror began, Furtado wanted to give himself up to the new authorities in order to clear himself. But a friend proved to him that he would have to face men in whose eyes "justice is nothing," so he decided to hide, and he began to search for a hiding-place. The first few days he still spent his daytime at home and the nights with his friend Robles, or in the house of Solar.[11] But after a search in his house and even in those of his neighbors (on

Mercure, Feb. 8, 1806; _Discours de M. les Commissaires de S. M. Impériale et Royale_ . . ., Paris, 1806 [with Furtado's reply]; _Réponse. Détail officiel de l'assemblée des Juifs_ . . . A. Furtado, _Discours prononcé à cette assemblée par MM. les commissaires de S. M. Impériale et royale_, Paris, [1806]. Furtado translated from Italian into French Abraham de Cologna's _Discorso_ . . . _Discours prononcé à la grande synagogue de Paris, à l'occasion de l'ouverture du grand Sanhédrin_ . . ., Paris, 1807, 23 pp.

[10] Furtado's diary was originally in the possession of the banker, writer and bibliophile Euryate (Félix) Solar (1811–1870), a grandson of A. Furtado: Féret, III, 587; Henri Lauzac, _Galérie historique_ . . . _Félix Solar_ . . . ., Paris, 1861, 5. But the diary was not mentioned in the catalogues of Solar's library: Brouillier et Desbois, _Catalogue de la Bibliothèque de M. Félix Solar_, Paris, 1860, 516 pp. and Paris, 1861, 60 pp. In 1889, the Bordeaux historian and bibliophile, Ernest Labadie, bought the diary from the former Solar collection: Labadie, p. 116; _Catalogue de la Bibliothèque de feu M. Ernest Labadie_, Bordeaux, 1918, 3 ("Abraham Furtado, Mémoires d'un patriote proscrit, in 8° de 179 pp., bas zac., dos orné, Rel. anc."). Labadie's library was sold out and we were unable to locate the original diary. In 1943, the City library of Bordeaux purchased from the bibliophile Féret a copy of the diary, made by E. Labadie from the original in his possession (now Ms. 1946 of the Bordeaux Library). Some details on the history of the diary were noted by Labadie in his copy, but it seems that some original notes in the copy were written not by Furtado, but by Labadie.

[11] According to Labadie's note. Furtado noted only the initial R. Robles was a common name among Sephardim. Moïse de Robles was a scholar of the Bayonne community: Henri Gross, _Gallia Judaica_, Paris, 1897, 93. The name of Solar is noted only with an initial.

September 24, 1793), Furtado was forced to hide completely. Beginning September 27, 1793, he found a sanctuary in a small secret room in the house of two sisters named Solar.[12] With the help of a knife he bored a small hole through which he was able to observe the life on the street; to watch revolutionary processions of prostitutes and "pitiable citizens" — as he wrote; to see soldiers conducting people to the guillotine. According to various confused rumors circulating in Bordeaux, Furtado had escaped to Holland, or to Italy, or he hid somewhere in Bayonne. For a while Furtado still hoped to find sympathy among the Terrorists. But the Terror was so strong in the city, that he soon gave up all hopes, specially after his "colleague and friend" Saige, a former Bordeaux mayor during the federalist administration, was guillotined. As a few bankers and merchants belonged to the Solar family, Furtado was afraid that his hiding-place would be raided. "It was a crime to be rich" — Furtado noted in his diary and he was afraid that the Solars could be arrested "on the basis of general precaution" which violated — according to Furtado — all social legislation. According to Furtado, Robespierre's party tried to incite the poor against the rich by promising to the poor *sans-culottes* that they will get the aristocrats' properties. Furtado tried to free himself with the help of bribery, he spent a few days with his cousins and even in his own house. But when one of his cousins was arrested only because his name, too, was Furtado, Abraham Furtado thought of committing suicide if being arrested. For a week he hid again in the house of the Solar family, but at the end of September 1793 he was forced to seek sanctuary in the house of a poor relative, where he remained 135 days. His friend, Robles, often came to see him, bringing with him news from the city, mostly dreadful

[12] On the street Sainte-Thérèse, according to Labadie, 116. The name of the sisters is noted only with an initial. According to Michel Berr (p. 15) Furtado was saved during the Terror by the mother of a woman N. R. On the copy of the BN (18) appears Berr's note giving her full name as Nancy Rodrigue. According to the same Berr (14) Furtado escaped abroad, which was not true. According to C. V. [Vivie] Furtado was saved by his maid (*Courrier de la Gironde*, Feb. 4, 1873).

news, as the execution of Constantin Péry. Furtado noted then: "I was his friend."[13]

A Bordeaux councilman and a suppliant — Deputy to the Convention in September 1792, Emmermeth, — intervened in favor of Furtado with the Paris Representative of the Convention, Ysabeau, who gave him a hopeful promise. Alexandre Deleyre obtained from the Paris representative Beaudot a recommendation in favor of Furtado.[14] The latter was then already eight months in hiding, now he spent fifteen days in the house of his friend, Robles, in order to devote himself to the effort of freeing himself. Furtado tried to get from his Section a testimonial of civicism (*certificat du civisme*), but his Section was afraid to do it. At the end, Furtado legalized himself with the administration and he was even named a member of the government committee for negotiations with neutral countries.

Let us, for a while, leave the chronological order of the events described in Furtado's diary in order to analyze the earlier events, which helped Furtado to free himself during the Terror. In all his pleadings addressed to the Terror administration, Furtado stated that he became a member of the Popular Commission not because of any federalist opinions, but because of his status as a city official. He was drafted as a member of this unfortunate Commission which was founded without his help.

---

[13] Constantin Péry (1754 — guillotined on Dec. 6, 1793), a son of the Bordeaux lawyer and writer, Gabriel Péry (Féret, III, 496). Furtado, probably, knew him from the *Musée* circle and the *Société de la Jeunesse bordelaise*, where both were active members.

[14] On Emmermeth [Emmerth in the diary] see: Dr. Robinet, *Le Mouvement religieux à Paris pendant la Révolution*, Paris, 1896, I, 739. Alexandre Deleyre (1726–1797), a former pupil of the Jesuits, became a close friend of the Encyclopedists; he was the author of the article on fanaticism in the Encyclopedia. As a deputy from Gironde to the Convention he voted for the death of Louis XVI. He was a Girondist, but he managed to save his life (Vivie, I, 201). Furtado was an old friend of Deleyre. Mr. Alain d'Anglade of the AdG possesses a series of letters from Deleyre's daughter Caroline and from Furtado to Marauld l'aîné of Metge, near Clérac. According to this correspondence Furtado was much interested in helping his friend's daughter in her financial difficulties.

As member, he fought the idea of a departmental anti-Paris army, he never wrote anything in favor of the Commission.[15] On August 3, 1793, the National Convention dissolved the Bordeaux Popular Commission and ordered on August 6, to arrest its members. Ysabeau and Baudot were sent by the Convention to Bordeaux to carry out the decisions of August 3 and 6. On August 18, 1793, the Convention's Representatives received a hostile welcome from the Bordeaux population. Furtado stated in his diary and his letters that he was the only councilman who openly demanded to respect the two Paris Representatives. The latter left for La Réole, to organize a military force against Bordeaux, where they arrived again on October 16, 1793.[16] During the Terror this action of Furtado was recalled to the Representatives' minds and helped him to regain the status of a free man.

But soon Furtado again went into hiding. This happened during the arrival of a new Paris Representative, M.-A. Jullien, who reinforced the Terror. Together with his friend, Solar, Furtado departed for Aiguillon and from there to Granges (Lot-et-Garonne), where Solar possessed a small property.[17]

---

[15] On July 30, 1793, Furtado wrote to a friend in Paris that he was against the Popular Commission's policy: AdG, 11L47; cf. Richard Munthe Brace, *Bordeaux and the Gironde 1789–1798*, New York, 1947, 209. Furtado repeated the same idea in his diary.

[16] On the events of Oct. 16, 1793, see: M. A. Baudot et C. Alex. Yzabeau, *Rapport de ce qui s'est passé à Bordeaux à l'arrivée et pendant le séjour des Réprésentants du Peuple . . .*, Bordeaux, sd, 15 pp. and another report of 13 pp. Furtado's defense of the Representatives was not mentioned in these reports. In a letter of Oct. 24, 1793, Furtado gave details on his role during the events (AdG, 11L47). According to the diary, Ysabeau stated to Furtado's friend, Martheilhe: "Nous n'avons trouvé à la municipalité qu'un seul homme qui ait voulu prendre notre défense; c'est Furtado . . ."

[17] There Félix Solar was born, the oldest of the five children of Emilie Furtado and Aimé Solar. All the descendants of Félix Solar were converted to Christianity. In the 1930's Gabrielle Moyse, a granddaughter of Emilie's youngest child, Amélie Solar, was still active in Jewish life. She married Armand Lipmann, a son of the Metz Rabbi. According to her, Furtado hid during the Terror in Castelmoron (Lot-et-Garonne) where he wrote his memories and thoughts, published by her: "Les pensées inédites de Furtado,"

From there they left for Barsac, where they stayed in the house of Furtado's friend, Laborde.[18] The latter's son went to Bordeaux for information. In the meantime Furtado was advised by Robles through a special messenger, a young cousin of Furtado's, that he should not return to Bordeaux. He retired to Bayonne; on the way he had occasion to observe the guillotine in action in Dax and Pau. In Bayonne Furtado did not hide; he spent there five weeks in his own property. A few days after his return to Bordeaux Lacombe was arrested: this was the end of the Terror.

While hiding, Furtado tried to forget the events by reading books. At first he tried to translate Appian's fragments on the civil-wars of the Romans, but this, too, reminded him of the actual events, so he read the works of Buffon, La Fontaine, Corneille, J.-J. Rousseau, Montesquieu, La Bruyère, La Rochefoucauld, the memories of the Maréchal de Villars, a biography of Paolo Giovio, etc. While reading *Don Quixote* he found peace of mind and was even able to laugh. He read Dante in order to find out if the poet's fantasy could dscribe something similar to the events in France — and he found many similarities. Furtado noted in his diary: "I build an intellectual world according to my fantasy, peopling it according to my will." In his imagination he lived a few weeks among the nomadic tribes of Arabia or among the patriarchal Jews described by Fleury. He began to write a book on the love of Jacob and Rachel.

Furtado frankly noted in his diary his social and political conceptions, although he was rather cautious. He stated that the departmental administration of Gironde imprudently accepted to play a leading role in the Girondist movement. It would be hard to say whether in Furtado's eyes this was a tactical mistake, or he tried to be careful even in his diary. He correctly noted

La Revue littéraire juive, VI, 1931, 456–69. In his *pensées* Furtado repeated many ideas found in his diary, e. g. his distrust of the common people.

[18] Probably Jean-Joseph de Laborde (1724–1794), or Jean-Benjamin de Laborde (1734–1794). The first was a banker and founder of the *Caisse d'escompte*; the second was a banker, musician and writer. Both were guillotined.

that in Bordeaux the Revolution came in an orderly manner, without bloodshed. His statement that for a time the city lived quietly in a stormy country was also correct. According to Furtado, Bordeaux committeed its first mistake by electing to the Legislative Assembly and to the Convention deputies of "mediocre value, some of them even of bad choices." They were not without some talent, but they did not possess enough maturity, prudence and severe probity, that should be demanded from legislators. As soon as they came into office, intrigues, jealousy and rivalry appeared. It seems that Furtado did not believe in the existence of a Girondist party, but he believed, that in spite of some mistakes committed by the Girondist leaders, they defended justice and fought political crimes. In his eyes the founding of the Bordeaux Popular Commission, to which he himself belonged, was an "imprudent and precipitated" act; the elements who fought against the dissolution of the Commission were called by him "imprudents." The Commission did not seek to tear the Republic to pieces, but on the contrary, to avoid such an act. But he recognized the fact that Bordeaux representatives tried to incite other departments, too, against Paris and this could, probably, lead to the founding of departmental Republics and a civil-war. He laid much blame on the Bordeaux common people, who acted hastily against the Paris Representatives Baudot and Ysabeau. Of course, later everyone regretted this. "Such is the crowd."— Furtado noted —"The tumultuous and precipitated deliberations inevitably bring fruitless regret, as the crime brings remorse into the soul of the guilty." Furtado did not feel any respect toward the crowd. He wrote that the same people who helped the Girondists later applauded the Terrorists. The crowd always follows the victor and hates the vanquished. Of the *sans-culottes* he wrote that they were called the "*popoluce*, the difference between them and the people being the same as between an honest artisan or a hard-working peasant and a stupid, lazy and drunken beggar."[19]

---

[19] Furtado's distrust of the common people was also shown in his demand of June 1790 that electors should not be paid, so that the richest, i. e. the most

There is not a sign in Furtado's diary of understanding the Terror period, which followed Girondism. He believed that Robespierre's men tried to starve Bordeaux; that the new city administration was a "mob of brigands." In his eyes Robespierre was the personification of evil and his Bordeaux followers were murderers, thieves, prostitutes, etc. He also believed that Lacombe, president of the Military Commission to try federalists and other enemies of the Revolution, was determined to shoot all Bordeaux merchants during a mass-execution at the *Champs de Mars*.[20]

Furtado's diary is full of historical comparisons. Later, after the Terror, he wrote in a note to his diary:[21] France could be compared to a wreck, the passengers lost everything and are to be pitied. In great political revolutions one can find not only moments of high moral instincts, but also of low impulses. This depends on the value of the public morale and, especially, of the nation's leaders. Only by the degree of the happiness brought to the masses one can judge if a revolution was a good event. For a while Furtado showed a fatalist mood: All revolutions, events and discoveries — as he noted — which brought only unhappiness are like unpredictable storms, like a sickness. The great number of educated people who were stronger and cleverer than the laws, were responsible for France's mistakes; they destroyed the Monarchy. The idea that a Republic could exist only in a limited territory comes from the mistake of confusing the conception of a republic with democracy, which are two very different systems. In a democracy the people govern themselves; in a republic the people rule through their agents. Because of this a democracy could exist only in a small territory, but a republic could embrace an entire country. Perhaps France could produce a synthesis of these two ideal regimes. These ideas

cultural peasants would be elected: *Journal de Bordeaux et du département de la Gironde*, No. 51, June 16, 1790, 343–44.

[20] Up to 1953 all Bordeaux historians violently attacked and dishonored Lacombe. The first to write a good and objective study was Bécamps, who was himself attacked for this (see note 1).

[21] "Quelques réflexions sur le passé et sur les effets dans l'avenir."

noted in Furtado's diary were not original; they were old and often used by the federalist theorists. He also believed that instruction was good only for citizens of a free country. In an absolutist regime instruction would only show people their miseries and make them unhappy. He preferred France, with its mistakes, to a despotic regime, but he would have rather had an evolutionary course of events. He did not advocate a return to the old regime. On the contrary, he wrote that if Plato, Aristotle, Xenophon, Hobbes and Haller, who advocated that a limited monarchy could bring more happiness than a popular government could observe France's constitution of the year III (1794–1795), they would have changed their political ideas. But of course, France was paying dearly for the benefits of the new regime.

The Jewish aspect of the events was noted only once in Furtado's diary: the people saw men and women of all classes and positions being guillotined, except a Jew. Jews were only arrested or fined, but this did not satisfy the crowd. Furtado satirically noted that this happened in a period, when the differences of religions were abolished and religion itself was a subject of revolutionary buffoonery. Of course, if he had been arrested, the crowd's demand for a Jewish victim would have been satisfied. Did Furtado only imagine this, or did the people really request a *Jewish* victim? As we shall see, many Jews were arrested and could have been sentenced to death, still not one was guillotined during the Terror.[22]

Let us summarize his ideas noted in his diary: He was a strong opponent of Robespierre's wing. Of course, he was a Girondist, but to him this movement was more a struggle against the Paris leaders of the Revolution than a political party.[23] Later Furtado wrote that during the Revolution he did not belong to any political party, he was only full of love of his country and of

[22] Furtado's Jewish origin was mentioned in a petition in his favor: "C'est un bon israélite d'origine et de caractère dans le sens que la Bible donne à ce mot. Il s'est montré dès la révolution constant et fidèle Patriote, ami d'une liberté qui relévoit et surtout sa nation persécutée et flétrie depuis dix huit siècles" (AdG, IIL47, undated or signed).

[23] Compare with Mathiez in *AHRF*, VII, 1930, 576–86.

justice; he was not broken by the hatred and did not seek any favors; he preferred to remain in his obscure position than to pay with his virtue. But he recognized that the Bordeaux Girondists made mistakes and that the federalists could become dangerous to the Republic's unity. Still, he always found some excuse for them: their sincerity in their beliefs. As a man he showed himself as an aristocrat who hated the common people. He was a man of a rich, privileged class and was proud of it. But with all his mistakes he remained, in his own way, a sincere republican. Girondism was a fraction of the Revolution, its interests were not always those of the old regime. Already on November 7, 1789, Furtado and his friend Vergniaud, who later became a Girondist leader, left the monarchist inclined Bordeaux *Musée* and they founded a new literary circle.[24]

It is of interest to compare the ideas noted in Furtado's diary with his later writings.[25] As a result of the Terror he became

[24] *Lettres aux Commissaires du Musée*, [signé:] Vergniaud, Ducos fils, Boyer Fonfrède aîné, Furtado, ss, nd, 4 pp.; Henri Chauvot, *Le Barreau de Bordeaux*, Paris, 1856, 118; Lhéritier, *Liberté*, 50.

[25] According to various sources Furtado left manuscripts of two major works: 1 vol. of *Pensées et réflections morales et politiques* and 4 vols. of *Harmonie et la nature des pouvoirs et des institutions politiques*. According to another source Furtado left a manuscript *Essai sur les dissensions civiles*, which was, probably, the same one as the 4 vol. manuscript. The first manuscript was used by G. Moyse for the publication of Furtado's *Pensées*: M. Berr, 30; Féret, III, 260; AmBx, Ms. 712, vol. 8, 5 (Laboudée's notes). In 1873, C. V. [Vivie] published an analysis of Furtado's 4 vol manuscript: C. V., "Variétés," *Courrier de la Gironde*, Feb. 4, 1873; followed by "Extrait du manuscrit de M. Furtado (Mort en 1817). Essai sur les Dissensions civiles et les Révolutions." By good-luck we located a 31 pp. pamphlet with a similar title: *Considérations sur les dissensions civiles et les révolutions*, sl, sd, 8°. According to the copy in the JTS the pamphlet was written "par Abraham Furtado," and there could be no doubt about Furtado's authorship. The pamphlet contains only an "introduction" and was published as such to his unpublished 4 vol. manuscript. The pamphlet contains the following motto: "Omne regnum in seipsum divisum desolabitur. S. Luc." According to one source *Essai sur les Dissensions civiles* was an unfinished manuscript: Pascal Thémanlys, "L'Oeuvre connue & l'oeuvre inconnue d'Abraham Furtado," *Le Judaïsme Séphardi*, I, No. 5, 1932. In addition to the works by Furtado already mentioned, the following writings should be noted: "Versos d'Aabram Furtado,"

more sentimental. Writing with much nostalgia of the old regime, he often regretted the Monarchy, much more than he had showed in his diary. He stated that the Monarchy disappeared because people made Louis XVI personally responsible for all the abuses of his administration. It was a mistake and madness to try to ameliorate the situation through changing the entire social regime, this was a "fatal design." A democracy could not correct the mistakes of the Monarchy. The Monarchy lost its case because since the end of the feudal regime the social revolutions were not followed by enough political changes. The Revolution of 1789 was the result of an open struggle between the possessors of titles and the owners of money. The men's love of freedom could easily become an exaggerated and dangerous passion. Man is born with a good nature; only the men who have not been touched by modern civilization are of pure morals. Since man came advanced in civilization, he has become victim of a conflict within himself: the will to live together with other people and the opposite desire. Furtado tried to play the role of a moralizer. He urged people to respect authority, fight abuses, act carefully, with justice, disinterestedness, and order. Should men fail to reach such a voluntary state, only one thing could save them: absolute domination by one man.

III

Did some rich Bordeaux Jews follow the Girondists because this movement was linked to their financial interests? The Girondist leaders were friends of the big financiers and when the Girondists were defeated, bankers tried to discredit the Republic's finances. The Paris banker Haller tried to buy up in Southern France gold for paper-money with the help of a few Jewish speculators. But in spite of a large number of great

Ha-Lapid, No. 61, pp. 2–3 (reprinted from *Le Judaïsme Sépharadi*); Furtado's review of *Essai sur la décomposition de la pensée*, by C***, [Bordeaux, 1803,] in *L'Indicatuer*, Dec. 6, 1804, p. 3; *Mémoire d'Abraham Furtado sur l'état des Juifs en France jusqu'à la Révolution*, publié par Gabriella Moyse, Paris, sd, 47 pp. (reprinted from *Revue littéraire juive*, vol. IV, Nos. 1–3, 1930.)

Jewish merchants, the number of big Jewish bankers was very small. The Swiss bankers were then the most active in France. Almost no Jews were associated with the various plans of founding banks, lotteries and various funds.[26] In 1790, eight of the eleven Bordeaux money-changers were still Jews,[27] but the economic role of the Bordeaux Jews decreased largely since 1789. The Gradis family and other Jewish owners of plantations and other properties in the French colonies suffered much from the Negro uprisings there. Some Jews were asked to pay large revolutionary contributions, although they were not forced to pay more than non-Jews, as happened in Alsace. It should be noted that few Bordeaux Jews assailed the Revolution's financial policies. But on the other hand all this happened at the beginning of the Revolution, prior to the onset and the defeat of Girondism, when some still had faith in the Revolution, and others hoped to be able to carry on their commerce. All this changed much during the Terror.[28]

In Bordeaux, Girondism based itself largely on the big wine-merchants and shipowners.[29] But no Jews there were engaged in the Girondist movement because of their being Jews. In this case it should be noted that the Jews, as a minority, did not follow the Gentile majority, as can be seen by the fact that the Jews of Saint-Esprit (during the Revolution the name was changed to Jean-Jacques Rousseau) actively fought Girondism. At the beginning the Jews, who made up the majority of the about 6,000 inhabitants of Saint Esprit, were not very active in the city administration, although they participated in the activities of the Popular Society. When the Paris Representatives J.-B. Monestier and Jacques Pinet created on October 11, 1793, the Saint-Esprit Surveillance Committee (*Comité de surveillance*),

[26] Jean Bouchary, *Les Manieurs d'argent à Paris à la fin du XVIIIᵉ siècle*, Paris, 1939–1943, I, 7, 9, III, 140; *Ibid., Les Compagnies financières à Paris à la fin du XVIIIe siécle*, Paris, 1940–1941, 2 vols.

[27] E. Labadie, *Les billets de confiance émis par les Caisses patriotiques du département de la Gironde 1791–1793*, Paris, 1914, 15.

[28] This subject will be treated in a separate study.

[29] A. Richard, *Le Gouvernement révolutionnaire dans les Basses-Pyrénées*, Paris, 1927, 25.

Jews became the leaders of this important body, which also controlled an entire small county and functioned till March 16, 1794.[30] The fanatic Catholic Basque region of the Lower Pyrénées, near the Gironde department, was a strong counter-Revolutionary center. According to the historian Antoine Richard the Revolution had to be imported there. Bayonne became a sanctuary for counter-Revolutionary refugees from Paris. Although there was no open federalist revolt in this region, the federalist sentiments were very strong there. Only two isolated revolutionary and anti-federalist strongholds existed in the entire department of the Landes: Mont-de-Marsan and Saint-Esprit with its "Jewish" Surveillance Committee. In 1793 the Paris Representatives reported that because of the Bayonne counter-Revolutionary sentiments the city's important citadel was unreliable; one could depend only on the inhabitants of Saint-Esprit, but their number was too small to be used in a military operation on a large scale. On September 15, 1793, Saint-Esprit vowed to combat "the moderatism, which kills freedom," and on November 12, 1793, it congratulated the Paris Representative, Ysabeau, for its fight against "the flame of federalism." A Jew from Saint-Esprit, Castro, became a member of the Surveillance Committee in Dax and another Jew, Marcquefoy, was a councilman of Bayonne during the Terror. In fact, the small Jewish town of Saint-Esprit served as an important revolutionary and anti-federalist center of the Lower Pyrenees.[31] Why did the Saint-Esprit Jews refuse to follow the Girondist activities of some of their Bordeaux co-religionists? Even if they were poorer than those of Bordeaux, there were

[30] Ernest Ginsburger, *Le Comité de surveillance de Jean-Jacques Rouseau, Saint-Esprit-lès-Bayonne*, Paris, 1934, 338 pp.
[31] A. Richard, 188; *Idem*, in *AHRF*, VII, 1930, 25; Ginsburger, 82, 98–100, 116, 125, 338; J. Légé, *Les Diocèses d'Aire et Dax*, Air-sur-l'Adour, 1875, 12; H. Labroue, *Le Conventionnel Pinet d'après ses mémoires inédits*, Paris, 1907, 48–51; [J. B. Bailac,] *Nouvelle chronique de la ville de Bayonne*, Bayonne, 1827, 288–89; AdLandes, G351 & 12L30; Louis-Samson Batbedat, *Rapport . . . des Landes . . . 13 octobre 1793*, Bordeaux, sd, 46 pp.; *La Municipalité de Bayonne, aux Citoyens* [18 Messidor an II], sl, nd. Placard; René Cuzacq, "Le Comité révolutionnaire de Bayonne," *Société des Sciences . . . de Bayonne*, III, 1929, 21–22.

still among them many rich merchants. Abraham Furtado's brother, Joseph, a member of the Saint-Esprit Surveillance Committee, possessed 180,000 livres. According to a survey of February 10, 1794, the richest Jews of Saint-Esprit possessed 7,500,000 livres and the richest Gentiles 1,290,000. This situation could be explained by many assumptions: The Jews, emancipated by the Revolution, were a majority of the inhabitants and as a group they had to act carefully and not to get mixed up in political adventures. Perhaps they were on the side of Paris because the majority of non-Jews in their region, those who always persecuted them, were adversaries of the Revolution's capital. Ever since the outbreak of the Revolution a group of poor Jews in Saint-Esprit, unlike Bordeaux, was active in the revolutionary clubs. Some Jews had even at an earlier period been influenced by liberal ideas. Joseph Rodrigues Bernal (called "the American"), the most influential Jacobin leader in the community, was impressed by the War of Independence of the United States, where he lived for many years.[32] It should also be noted that Jews were among the first active Jacobins in the neighboring communities of Saint-Jean-de-Luz, Bidache, and Labastide.[33]

Although the Paris Representatives knew very well of the attachment of the Saint-Esprit Jews to the Revolution, not even one Jew was appointed to an important office on a departmental level. As we shall see, the Jews observed all orders of the Representatives, but they never became extreme terrorists. The guillotine was not brought to Saint-Esprit or to any other community under the jurisdiction of the "Jewish" Jacobins, and this probably displeased the Paris Representatives. According to the historian René Cuzacq, St.-Esprit was a center of political agitation, but without any social idea, while in other small places the class-struggle prevailed. In this respect the Jews, who had just become full citizens, were less revolutionary than their Gentile neighbors. It may be they were careful, or opportunistic; according to Cuzacq they wanted to appear as

[32] Léon, 162, 167–68.
[33] Ginsburger, 78, 86; Léon, 165.

revolutionaries, but "at little cost" (à peu de frais).[34] On the other hand, most Jewish officials were dismissed after the Terror.

The degree of Jewish participation in the factional struggles defined the administration's attitude toward Jews. At the beginning of the Revolution Jews held many administrative functions in Bordeaux, but-they were moderate; and later some Jews became active Girondists, because of this they were dismissed from almost all offices during the Terror. With the defeat of Girondism, the Bordeaux and departmental administrations were taken over by the ultra-republican sans-cullotes, sailors, printers, butchers, locksmiths, etc. But only a few Jews occupied minor offices.

Throughout the Terror some Jews were active in the Bordeaux clubs, there were even some Jewish terrorists. But, with the exception of David Azévédo, there were no Jews among the leaders. Even Azévédo was nominated as a member of the Military Commission at the very end of this period, in a tragic moment for the Terror itself, when the terrorist leader Lacombe was to be tried. Azévédo was a peddler and as such, i. e. as a poor Jew, he could rise to an important function only during the Terror. The leadership of the Jewish community always consisted of the richest Jewish families, and at the beginning of the Revolution only rich Jews occupied even non-Jewish offices. Among the Bordeaux Jews the strong class-differentiation predominated the social life during the Revolution much more than among Gentiles, and more than among the Bayonne (i. e. Saint-Esprit) Jews. This prevented poor Jews from becoming active even in general city affairs. The following is one case: Many poor non-Jews, workers, signed the petition of Aug. 13, 1790, to keep the library of the Bordeaux Academy open in late hours, as a convenience for working people; but all seventeen Jews who signed the petition came from rich families.[35] On the eve of the Revolution, probably not all Jews, but only those of rich families

---

[34] René Cuzacq, introduction to Ginsburger, VI, VIII.

[35] G. Ducaunnès-Duval, Ville de Bordeaux. Inventaire sommaire des Archives municipales. Période révolutionnaire 1789 — an VIII, Bordeaux, 1929, vol. IV, pp. 528–31.

took part in the elections of March 1, 1789, to send Jewish deputies to the assembly of the Third Estate.[36]

We have already noted that during the Thermidor, Jewish revolutionaries of Saint-Esprit were dismissed from office; some were even forced to hide.[37] In a way, the same happened in Bordeaux. Of course, at the end of the Terror Jews were no longer held in prison there,[38] but no important official functions were at once entrusted to Jews. The new rulers of the Thermidor, too, felt much better without Jewish officials;[39] it took a few years before this situation changed. The Thermidor should then be characterized as a period of struggle for retaining the rights obtained by Jews in the first years of the Revolution. But this is a subject for a separate study.

IV

The Jewish community leader Salomon Lopes-Dubec, member of the Popular Commission, hid during the Terror and saved his head. On October 16, 1793, his mother's house was searched, and

[36] When a rich Jew died, his widow had the right to vote as the head of the house, but it seems that she could vote only through a man. We found such notarial powers of vote for the elections of March 1, 1789: a procuration given by Rebeka Peixotto, widow of the banker Izaac Alexandre, to Daniel Lévi; of Rachel Rodrigues, widow of the banker Izaac Rodrigues, to Jacob Salzedo; of Sara Pas, widow of Lopes Depas, to Abraham Mendes; of Rachel Alexandre, widow of Isaac Mercade, to David Lévy (AdG, E, minutes du notaire Dugarry, March 1, 1789, ff. 53–56).

[37] Léon, 170.

[38] AmBx, doc. Vivie, vol. 20, p. 280.

[39] There were no Jews in the Commission named on March 7, 1795, to investigate speculations during the Terror, in the Bordeaux administration and among the judges named on March 7 and June 19, 1795, etc.: Tablettes de Bernardau, vol. 7, 60; *Arrêté des Représentants du Peuple, en mission dans le département du Bec-d'Ambres, du 17 ventôse de la troisième Année Républicaine*, sl, nd, placard; AmBx, documents Vivie, vol. 20, pp. 37–40 (placard), 537–43. But the Jews Azévédo and Aaron Salcedo of the Section No. 18 were named on Jan. 22, 1795, to the Commission to investigate the high taxes during the Terror: *Arrêté du Représentant du Peuple Bordas, du 3 Pluviôse, an 3e*, Bordeaux, sd, 8 pp. In November 1798 the Police investigated the case of the agitator Salvador: AmBx, 179, no. 21.

a month later his own house; his silverware was sealed and his
bookkeeping taken away. On Nov. 29, 1793, his 17 years old
son, Samuel [Tridi], was arrested as a hostage and he spent six
months in prison. On May 7, 1794, Mrs. Lopes-Dubec was told
by the prison-authorities that her son would be set free if the
father would deliver himself. In a petition sent to his Section
(No. 19, *Bon Accord*), Salomon Lopes-Dubec stated that by
ill-luck he belonged to the Popular Commission because of his
official position as a judge of the Court of Commerce, but that
he never accepted the ideas of this "disastrous establishment"
and worked against it. At a meeting of Oct. 16, 1793, some
members of the Section defended Lopes-Dubec; however, he got
from his Section not a specific certificate of civicism, but only
an extract from the minutes of the discussion, which was in his
favor. This extract was printed and signed by the leaders of the
Section, all of them Jews.[40] Lopes-Dubec's life was saved. But
we do know now that this man, who held many official functions
during the Revolution, did not trust the new regime. According
to his memoirs he and his son speculated in paper-money. In
November 1793, before being drafted into the army, his son hid
Spanish gold-coins to the sum of 8,000 pounds, which the father
secretly sold in April 1794.[41]

We are not trying to say in this study that only the Terror
could save the Revolution and that the tragic dissensions were
unavoidable. But, while writing on victims of the Terror, we
should like to note that during that tragic period of 1793–1794,
less people were executed than during the few days at the end of
May 1871, when the Commune of Paris was defeated by Adolphe
Thiers.

On August 23, 1794, 1,492 persons were in the Bordeaux
prisons. During the Terror there (Oct. 23, 1793 — July 31, 1794)

---

[40] AdG, L1132, 2193; AmBx, dictionnaire des arrest., vol. 6; *Extrait des
registres de la Section du Bon-Accord, No. 19. Séance au 25 du premier mois de
la deuxième année* ... [Signé: Azévédo, president; Bonfin fils, secrétaire;
Fonseca neveu, secrétaire], [Bordeaux, Octobre 1793,] 2 pp. JTS. For a
short time Lopes-Dubec was secretary of this Section (AdG, 11L10).

[41] Lopes Dubec's autobiography, in the archives of the Jewish Historical
Society, Jerusalem.

314 persons were guillotined, 129 received prison-terms, 55 were fined, the rest were released.[42] Of course, this was undoubtedly a large number of victims, particularly when considering that the city numbered then only about 100,000 inhabitants. On the other hand, the very active part taken by the city in Girondism should be taken into consideration. But we are concerned particularly with the number of Jews among the victims of the Terror. Most of the 314 victims were of a non-Jewish sphere: 43 noblemen, 18 military men, 24 priests, 15 nuns, 50 lawyers and judges, 39 workers, etc. Only thirty of them were merchants, and because of the large number of Jews among the richest Bordeaux merchants, one could expect to find some Jews among the guillotined people. We have already noted that, according to Furtado's diary, the people demanded that a Jew, too, should be executed. But, after a very careful search of all existing sources we have concluded that not one Jew was guillotined in Bordeaux. According to almost all Jewish historians a Jew named Jean de Mendès was killed because he was a Jew. But, as we shall prove in a separate study, Mendès was not a Jew.

According to the Bordeaux historian, Ernest Labadie, who was a vigorous adversary of the Revolution and also a well-known anti-Semite, the Bordeaux Jews were loyal to the old, pre-1789, regime, but in the meantime they — and the Protestants, too — served the Revolution. They did it carefully, with reserve, or out of fear. During the Girondist administration of Bordeaux these ambitious merchants remained hidden behind the scene of political struggle; they exposed other people and those fell victims to the Terror. E. Labadie exaggerated in his statements on Jews and Protestants. But this does not minimize the fact that Jews were not guillotined, that the few Jewish victims of the Terror in Bordeaux were fined or imprisoned.[43]

---

[42] AmBx, fonds Brouillard, XXV. According to Bécamps, 141, the real Terror continued in Bordeaux only until Feb. 11, 1794, and 85 persons perished during that period.

[43] Labadie, 16, 46, 137. It should be noted that the Gradis, Raba and other very rich Jewish families did not suffer physically during the Terror. The fines imposed upon Jews during the Terror will be treated by the author in a separate study.

It would also be hard to prove that anybody was even arrested or fined there because he was a Jew. The counter-Revolutionary historian, Abbot O'Reilly wrote, that in a sentence against Isaac Perreyre the fact of his being a Jew was specified. But the word *Jew* was actually never used. According to the text of the sentence Perreyre belonged to the class of greedy people (*cupides*), which O'Reilly interpreted as *Jew*. Charges of being greedy or egotistic were brought against many people, Gentiles and Jews and the entire class of rich merchants was marked as egotist. Pereyre was released. During the trial he stated that as a Jew he blessed the Revolution that gave him citizenship.[44] Other Jewish prisoners, too, made the same statement. Some declared that by buying nationalized property they proved their confidence in the Revolution. Many stated that they were arrested because of a general order to take all possible precautions. The family of the jailed Astruc Sr. wrote in a petition for his liberation, that he endured the fate of all merchants.[45] Some fell as victims of their moderatism, because they were not active anti-Girondists. According to a special order the accused were to be questioned on their attitude towards federalism and on whether they fought the Patriotic Commission. Jews, too, were asked the same questions and people were sentenced not only for helping the Commission, but also for not fighting it actively.[46]

As a result of Robespierre's arrest in Paris, the Bordeaux leader of the Terror, Lacombe, was arrested. On August 13,

[44] *Jugement . . . qui ordonne qu'Isaac Pereyre, agent de change, sera sur le champ mis en liberté, Du 13 Nivôse, l'an second . . .*,Bordeaux, sd, placard (BN); O'Reilly, *Histoire de Bordeaux*, Paris, 1863, part 2, I, 119; *Journal du Club National de Bordeaux*, Dec. 22, 1793.

[45] AdG, 11L39, 57 (p. 46), 58 (p. 14).

[46] *Arrêté du Réprésentant du Peuple Garnier . . .* [July 10, 1794], Bordeaux, sd, placard. The brothers Raba stated that they were forced by the Popular Commission to pay a contribution, but the Military Commission judged that they should have refused to pay. Aaron Lopes stated that because of ill-health he could not fight the Popular Commission, but he did not contribute to forming the departmental army. Still, for his "neutral position" and moderatism he was fined by the Military Commission 50,000 livres. *Jugement . . . qui condamne les Frères Raba . . .*, Bordeaux, sd. Placard; *Jugement qui condamne Aaron Lopes . . . Du 23 Ventôse, l'an deuxième*, Bordeaux, sd. Placard (BN).

1794, the Paris Representative named a new Military Commission of eight people for the purpose of judging its former president. The new judges had to be reliable men, and anti-Girondists, but certain to sentence Lacombe. One of them was the already named Jewish peddler, David Azévédo, who was active in revolutionary clubs and in the departmental Surveillance Committee. At the beginning of July 1794, just after Lacombe's arrest, he was named by the Paris Representative, Ysabeau, as a first deputy to the city-council. Azévédo's younger brother, known as Le Tauré (the Heifer) was an agent of Lacombe. On Aug. 15, 1794, Lacombe was guillotined.[47]

<h1 style="text-align:center">V</h1>

The relation of Jews to Girondism leads us to some events in Paris itself. We will try to indicate a few of these events, although they demand a separate detailed study.

First of all an account follows of the very complicated history of Jacob Pereyra. He was born in Saint-Esprit (ca. 1742) and became a tobacco-manufacturer in Bordeaux. In 1790 he came to Paris, where he became a leading figure among the Jacobins. He helped to discover the treason of General Dumouriez; he assisted in directing France's propaganda in England; and with the help of Dutch Jews he tried to discredit the Bank of England. He was a close friend of the universalist Anacharsis Cloots and the group of Hébertists. Together with them Pereyra dreamed of a world-revolution and together with them he fell victim to the bloody interior intrigues that corroded the Revolution. On March 24, 1794, they were collectively sentenced to die and they were together guilltoned.[48] Surely, Pereyra was not a federalist;

[47] *Arrêté du Réprésentant du Peuple . . . Du 26 Thermidor, an 2*, Bordeaux, sd, placard; Dr. Jean Barraud, *Vieux papiers bordelais. Etudes sur Bordeaux sous la Terreur*, Paris, 1910, 19; Labadie, 132; *Journal du Club National de Bordeaux*, July 6, 1794; Bécamps, 216, 308, 340, 342, [*Livre Rouge =*] *Liste par ordre alphabétique des Hommes de sang . . . à Bordeaux*, [Paris, 1815], II. A Jew, Ravel, was one of the people who arrested Lacombe: Bécamps, 297.

[48] AN, W78, 339 (617), F⁷4742, 4774 (67); L. Kahn, 236–47; Tuetey, *Répertoire de l'histoire de Paris pendant la Révolution française*, X, 569, 581,

on the contrary, he actively fought Girondism. We know very little of Pereyra's attitude toward Judaism, but on one very curious occasion he did mention Jews. This happened in a case in which François Désfieux, a Bordeaux wine-merchant and famous Jacobin, was involved. Désfieux related in one of his pamphlets that he forced Bordeaux to accept the Decree of Jan. 28, 1790, granting citizenship to the Sephardic and Avignon Jews. Apparently, Désfieux and his friend, Pereyra, later criticized the Bordeaux Jews for not being good Jacobins and for not assisting Désfieux in his fight against Girondism. At the beginning of April 1793, the Paris Jacobins sent a special messenger to Bordeaux with the news of General Dumouriez's treason, because they feared to send such message by ordinary mail. In a letter dated Apr. 6, 1793, sent by Pereyra to his sister in Bordeaux by the same messenger, he wrote on the "ingratitude of Israel [i. e. the Jews] toward Désfieux."[49] In the same letter Pereyra wrote on a victory of the revolutionary elements in the *Club National* of Bordeaux. (On March 29, 1793, another Bordeaux Jew (of Avignonese origin) who resided in Paris, David Dalpuget, complimented the same Club and denounced one man as a federalist.)[50]

796, XI, 126, 860; *Réimpression du Moniteur*, XVI, 15–18, 76, XVII, 170, 509, 688, XVIII, 2, XIX, 82, XX, 17, 40; A. Mathiez, "Une lettre de Pereyra," *AHRF*, VIII, 1931, 444. In 1768 Pereyra was forced to escape to England because of an affair with the daughter of a Bordeaux Jewish banker: Paul d'Estrée, *La vieillesse de Richelieu*, Paris, 1921, 223–25.

[49] Tuetey, IX, 178, X, 570–73, 709, XI, nos. 73, 209, 214, 221, 226, 230, 234, 2448, 2554; A. Schmidt, *Tableau de la Révolution française*, Leipzig, 1867, I, 242; *Désfieux, détenu dans la prison de Sainte Pélagie, à ses concitoyens*, sl, nd, 12 pp. (2–3: "j'y fis respecter les décrets au sujet des Juifs"); *Désfieux, à Monsieur Laure*, sl, nd, 2; *Convention Nationale. Pièces contenus dans l'envoi des Corps administratifs du Département de la Gironde, dont l'impression a été ordonnée par décret de la Convention, du 18 avril* . . ., sl, nd, 22 pp. (16: "Paris, le 6 avril 1793, l'an II de la Républiq[ue] franç[aise]. Chère Soeur, C'est du centre du patriotisme, les vrais Jacobins de Paris, que je t'écris, t'embrasse & te prie de donner une bonne bouteille de vin au courrier patriotique que nous envoyons aux bonnes sociétés, non aux récolets, mais au club national fondateur du club, avec le brave Désieux [Désfieux], malgré l'ingratitude d'Israël à son égard . . . [signé:] Pereyra.")

[50] "Le jour est donc arrivé ou les vrais Républiquains du Club National l'emporte, qude jouissance pour moy de lire dans la lettre des Représentans

The brothers Emmanuel and Junius Frey of Frankist origin were well known anti-federalists. According to most modern historians, e. g. A. Mathiez, they were Austrian spies. But this is still to be proved by documents and not by anti-Jewish hatred of some modern historians. Junius published two anti-Girondist pamphlets. Their sister, Léopoldine, married the well-known anti-Girondist, François Chabot. Both brothers and their brother-in-law were guillotined.[51] We have already remarked that Pereyra was one of the first to denounce the treason of General Ch.-F.-P.-J. Dumouriez, who was also a well-known anti-Semite.

We should like to make a comparison between the political sentiments of the Sephardic Jews and the Ashkenazic Jews of France. The latter could hardly become involved in any federalist movement. Unlike the Bordeaux Jews, who were helped by many of their Gentile neighbors in demanding full citizenship, the Jews of Alsace, Metz and Lorraine were granted citizenship (on Sept. 27, 1791) against the will of the Gentile population and officials. In Alsace the federalist sentiments were revealed in an open treason of the Republic and a pact with enemy armies for the defeat of the Republic. But one should not imagine that the Ashkenazic Jews accepted, or realized the importance of the Revolution, more than their Sephardic coreligionists. Many cases of loyalty to the old regime could be found even among Ashkenazim. Very few Sephardic Jews escaped abroad, but the number of such Jewish Emigrés from both parts of Alsace and neighboring departments was very large. During the Thermidor some Bordeaux Jews demanded annulment of the fines imposed upon them during the Terror, but they did this without shouting

---

du Peuple que nous sommes installé à la ci devand intandence sur les debris de la Ristocratie expirante ... [signe:] David Dalpuget (AdG, 11L.24). Perhaps he is the same David Semac Dalpuget, who resided in 1787 in Paris, see: P. Hildenfinger, *Documents sur les Juifs à Paris au XVIIIe siècle*, Paris, 1913, 269.

[51] L. Kahn, 248–66; *Idem*, "La femme de Chabot," *Annuaire des Archives Israélites pour l'an 5654*, Paris, 1893; [J. Frey,] *Philosophie sociale*, Paris, 1793, 236 pp.; [*Idem*,] *Les aventures du Père Nicaise, ou l'Anti-fédéraliste*, Paris, 1793, 72 pp.; 2nd edition — 71 pp.; Tuetey, XI, 208–22, 233, 239; Madeleine Albert, *Le Fédéralisme dans la Haute-Garonne*, Paris, 1931, 52–53.

hatefully against the defeated regime. Such an offensive pamphlet against the Terror as the one published by the Alsatian Jew, Séligmann Alexandre, the son-in-law of Cerfberr, was not published by any Bordeaux Jew.[52]

Besides Gironde other departments, too, became centers of federalist activities. In Nîmes (department of Gard) a Jewish federalist leader was guillotined. Nîmes was for a time directed by a federalist city-council of which the 39 years old Jewish peddler of Carpentras origin, Jassé Carcassonne, was a member. On July 19, 1794, he was guillotined together with other Nîmes federalists "for trying to weaken, and even to destroy the national authority . . . [and for] being federalists."[53] Probably a few other Jews, too, shared Carcassonne's lot.[54] But the fact itself that a Comtadin Jew could become a federalist leader of Nîmes was extraordinary and unnatural, because the lot of the Comtadin Jews depended upon the fate of a centralized France. Or, perhaps this Carcassonne case could serve as an example of how carefully the history of the federalist movement should be studied.

[52] Alexandre Séligmann, *Dénonciation à mes concitoyens, des vexations que m'ont fait éprouver les fidèles suppôts du traître Robespierre lors du système de terreur . . .*, Strasbourg, an III, 38 pp.; R. Reuss, *Séligmann Alexandre, ou les Tribulations d'un Israélite strasbourgeois pendant la Terreur*, Strasbourg, 1880, 44 pp.

[53] AmNîmes, Club populaire, 18 frim. an II; F. Rouvière, *Histoire de la Révolution française dans le département du Gard*, Nîmes, 1889, IV, 327–34, 459; *Jugement rendu par le Tribunal révolutionnaire établi à Nismes, qui condamne les nommés . . . Jassé Carcassonne . . . membre de la municipalité à l'époque du fédéralisme . . . à la peine de mort . . . Du 1er Thermidor an second . . .*, Nismes, sd, placard (JTS).

[54] On July 8, 1793, the merchant Azarias Vidal was guillotined in Lyon. Antonin Portallier, *Tableau général des victimes & martyrs de la Révolution en Lyonnais . . .*, St.-Etienne, 1911, p. 462; A. Lévy, "Notice sur les Israélites de Lyon," *L'Univers israélite*, XXXXVIII, 1893, 398. In Orange was denounced the Jew Benjamin, but another Jew, Moïse Milliaud, was then chairman of the Surveillance Committee of the *Section de la Fraternité*. Isaïe Cavaillon was forced to renounce his rabbinate: AdVaucluse, L.5 (district d'Orange, 19 Ventôse an II); Calvet, Ms. 5938 (00648); V. de Baumefort, *Episodes de la Terreur. Tribunal révolutionnaire d'Orange*, Avignon, 1875, 134.

THE COMTADIN JEWS AND THE ANNEXATION OF THE PAPAL PROVINCE BY FRANCE, 1789–1791

IN 1348, Avignon and Comtat Venaissin were sold by Queen Jeanne of France to Pope Clement VI. With the outbreak of the Revolution in 1789 the return of this province to France was strongly demanded. In a way, this was a break with the old treaty system of European powers, a transition to the concept of respecting the natural right of peoples. But while Avignon being a commercial and industrial center immediately demanded to become again a part of France, the agricultural areas of Comtat Venaissin wanted to remain a Papal province. This led to a civil war between Avignon and Comtat Venaissin (July 1790); and only as late as Sept. 14, 1791, the Papal province was reunited with France.[1]

The first impressive request for the annexation of the Papal province by France was made in 1789 by the deputy from Aix-en-Provence, Charles François Bouche (1737–1795). His printed demand contained a project of a status for Jews in which Bouche requested that they should be placed under the protection of the National Assembly, but that nothing should be mentioned about their religion or citizenship (*ne rien dire ni sur leur culte ni sur le titre*

---

[1] A. Mathiez, *Rome et le clergé français sous la Constituante*, Paris, 1911; Karl Metz, *Die Annexionsgedanke in der verfassunggebenden Nationalversammlung Frankreichs vom 1789. L'Affaire d'Avignon*, Giessen, 1928, 83 pp.

Originally published in *The Jewish Quarterly Review*, vol. **XLVI** (1955).

de citoyens). On this occasion, he repeated some old imputations on Jewish usury, disloyalty to the country, etc. In November 1789, Bouches' proposition of annexation was rejected by the National Assembly. At the end of January 1790, after the Sephardic Jews and Avignon Jews of Bordeaux had been granted citizenship (on January 28) Bouche demanded the same right for the Jews of the Papal province. The adversaries of his project had already attacked it strongly, but once the Jewish problem was brought up they discussed it, but were careful not to commit a blunder by attacking the Jews. The well-known anti-semite, Abbot Maury, did not mention the Jewish problem in his anonymous replies to Bouche; the author of another anti-Bouche pamphlet was even more liberal in his attitude toward the Jews than Bouche himself. He denied that they were usurers and demanded citizenship for them. The Jewish problem became a major argument in the bloody dispute between the partisans and foes of annexation. Ultimately the Comtadin Jews became citizens, but not with the assistance of the local adversaries of a reunion with France. They owed their citizenship to the support of members of the Paris mission and the local pro-French patriots.[2]

Bouche's raising the Jewish question in connection with

---

[2] Charles François Bouche, *De la Restitution du Comté Venaissin, des villes et Etat d'Avignon*, Paris, 1789, 40 pp. 2e édition — 46 pp.; [Abbé Maury,] *Des droits du Pape sur le Comté Venaissin . . .*, Genève [Carpentras], 1790; [Ibid,] *Opinions sur la souveraineté d'Avignon . . .*, Paris, 1792; [Joseph François Benoit de la Paillone,] *Réponse d'un Comtadin, à la brochure . . . par M. Bouche . . .*, sl, nd, pp. 13–15. Two other Carpentras pamphlets were in favor of Jews; *L'Hermite du Luberon au solitaire du Mont-Ventoux, salut et repos*, sl, nd, 7 pp.; *Avis plus que pressant*, sl, nd, p. 7. On Bouche see: Abbé Carriol, *Les Deputés Bas-Alpins de la période révolutionnaire*, Forcalquier, 1935, pp. 35–40; C. F. H. Barjavel, *Dictionnaire historique . . . de Vaucluse*, Carpentras, 1841, vol. I, pp. 266–67.

THE COMTADIN JEWS—SZAJKOWSKI

his demand for annexation was not accidental.[3] The Jews

his demand for annexation was not accidental.[3] The Jews
represented about 10% of the population in the four
cities of Avignon, Carpentras, Cavaillon, and L'Isle-sur-
Sorgue. They paid high taxes but had no rights whatever.
The Jewish problem had been acute for a long time.
Because of the persecutions against Jews prior to the
Revolution and the bloody conflicts in Avignon and Comtat
Venaissin in 1789–1793, a large number of Jews, especially
the rich Jews, emigrated to France. Public opinion among
the non-Jewish population, because of fears of losing capital
and commerce as a consequence of the Jewish emigration,
was favorably to an improvement of the Status of Jews.[4]
The Avignon partisans of annexation, continuously reminded the public of the Jews' suffering during the Vatican

[3] According to one historian Bouche's proposal on Jews was only
a *"sort of hors-d'oeuvre"* to the main problem: H. Chobaut, "Le premier
épisode de L'Affaire d'Avignon. La motion Bouche à L'Assemblée
Nationale (12–21 Nov. 1789)." *Mémoires de l'Institut Historique de
Provence*, vol. II, 1925, p. 24.

[4] *L'Enfant du Patriotisme*, [Carpentras, 1789], 13 pp. (by J. J. C. V.
Raphaël, or Cottier Julian, a pro-Jewish pamphlet); *Dialogue* [Car-
pentras, 1789], 15 pp. (by F. R. CH. J. Cottier, an anti-Jewish pamphlet);
Demandes et doléances de la ville de L'Isle, sl, nd, p. 10 (art. XXVI,
a pro-Jewish demand in connection with the Jewish emigration);
Departmental Archives of Bouches-du-Rhône, L.1991 (statement by
Barbeau on the Jewish emigration, July 11, 1793); AM Avignon
[=Archives municipales d'Avignon], I–II–40; H. Chobaut, "Les Juifs
d'Avignon et du Comtat et la Révolution Française" *REJ* [=*Revue
des Etudes Juives*], vol. CI, p. 40; A. Mossé, *Histoire des Juifs d'Avignon
et du Comtat Venaissin*, Paris, 1934, pp. 247–48; Z. Szajkowski, "The
Decline and Fall of Provençal Jewry." *Jewish Social Studies*, vol. VI,
1944, pp. 37–40.

It should be noted, that unlike most of the Alsatian and neighboring
historians, and also some Bordeaux historians (Labadie and others),
the counter-Revolutionary historians of the former Papal province
were not anti-Jewish, e. g.: M. J. de Joannis, *Le Fédéralisme et la Terreur
à l'Isle... 1793–1794*, Avignon, 1884, p. 88; J. F. André, *Histoire
de la Révolution avignonaise*, Paris, 1884, 2 vols.; Charles Soulier,
Histoire de la Révolution d'Avignon et du Comté-Venaissin, Paris-Avignon,
1845, 2 vols.

regime. They probably forgot that in the pre-1789 France the Jews suffered too, and that they were banned from most French provinces — as the historian P. Charpenne indicates. As we shall see, these French patriots of Avignon were not too eager to grant full citizenship to the Jews of their own city. Not all partisans of annexation were friendly towards Jews. The Avignon annexationist and Terrorist leader, Agricol Moureau (1766–1842) was the author of an anti-Jewish pamphlet, which he published in 1819.[5]

The Comtadin Jews supported the movement for a reunion with France. Out of the 1,061 signatures of the Avignon petition for re-union of June 12, 1790, 36 were those of Jews, including that of the Rabbi.[6]

Both factions used the Jewish problem for purposes of their own. Many pamphlets for example described imaginary stories of rebellion movements in behalf of Paris or against it. The author of one such pamphlet told of a revolt against the Papal administration, prepared for Sept.

[5] *Manifeste de la ville et Etat d'Avignon, publié par ses députés . . .* sl, nd, p. 15; [Randon,] *Rapport et conclusions . . . sur l'application de l'Armistice . . .*, Paris, 1792, p. 15; P. Vaillandet, "Correspondance des Députés d'Avignon près l'Assemblée nationale (1790–1791)." *Annales d'Avignon et du Comtat Venaissin*, vol. XX, 1939, p. 140; P. Charpenne, *Histoire des réunions temporaires d'Avignon et du Comtat Venaissin à la France*, Paris, 1886, vol. II, pp. 401, 467–68; [Agricol] Moureau, *De l'Incompatibilité entre le Judaïsme et l'exercise des droits de cité . . .*, Paris, 1819. On Moureau see: J. C. A. V. Ramuel, *L'Homme rouge, ou Agricol-Moureau . . .*, Paris, 1818; Pierre Lauris [Michel Jouve], *Avignon révolutionnaire*, Cavaillon, 1907, pp. 55–57; Barjavel, vol. II, pp. 204–05. On the other hand, Avignon revolutionairies attacked the Pope for sheltering Jewish bankrupts: Vaillandet, p. 140; *Manifeste . . .*, p. 18. On these bankruptcies see: Vatican archives of Comtat Venaissin, Nos. 130–04 and a collection of factums of 1782–1784, in the Avignon Calvet Museum.

[6] *Observations pour les Juifs d'Avignon, à la Convention nationale,* [signe:] Aaron Ravel, Aaron Vidal, Milhaud, sl, an III, p. 8; Chobaut, vol. CI, pp. 47–48. The Avignon petition was signed by the Jews at an assembly held in a Church: *Arrêté de la Municipalité* [2 déc. 1791], Avignon, sd. (Calvet, atlas 315–72).

15, 1789, by the Jews of Avignon. According to his account the Avignon rabbi assembled representatives of the four Jewish communities and spoke to them of "the freedom that our [Jewish] Nation would enjoy under French administration." Should France refuse to accept the Papal province as a gift, then the Jews would emigrate to Germany. The Jews bought arms, prepared the details of the revolt, but their plans were discovered prematurely. "All Christians of Comtat" attacked Avignon, arrested the Jews, beheaded five rabbis, and ten of the richest Jews. This fantastic tale was immediately denied in the Papal province and in Paris.[7] On the other hand, the Avignon revolutionary and annexationist, Sabin Tournal, published in his newspaper another account. Because the Jews did not trust the anti-Paris Assembly of Comtat, they gave only a small loan to this administration, and because the Papal representative could not obtain any loan from the Jews he renewed anti-Jewish restrictions. The Carpentras rabbi then assembled the Jews and comforted them by saying: The Babylonian exile lasted seventy years, but the Comtat Assembly will not exist even seventy days. This Comtat Assembly was anti-annexionist and, on a few occasions, Tournal told his readers that the rabbi's prophecy would soon come true. But a Carpentras newspaper wrote that the demand of annexation was made by foreigners, Jews and other ambitious scoundrels. Apparently

---

[7] Martin, ex-consul de la ville d'Avignon, *La Révolte des Juifs à Avignon, ou le noir complot le Vice-légat suivi de ce qui s'est passé dans cette ville, le 15 de septembre, écrit par un notable bourgeois de la ville,* sl, 1789, 8 pp.; *CA* [=Courrier d'Avignon], Oct. 24, 1790, p. 1038, Dec. 16, 1790, p. 1222, Dec. 22, 1790, p. 1242. A fantastic Carpentras story of an attack against Paris did not mention Jews: *Plan de l'attaque que l'on devait exécuter dans la nuit du 14 au 15 juillet...1789 contre la ville de Paris,* [Carpentras, 1789], 4 pp., Carpentras Library, Tissot, vol. 34.

everybody in Avignon and Comtat Venaissin thought of the Jews as partisans of annexation. The Avignon Terrorist Agricol Moureau wrote in 1819 in his anti-Jewish pamphlet that it was natural for the Jews to take such a pro-French position, because they had suffered very much during the Papal regime. According to H. Chobaut and other historians, Jews took such a position because of their commercial interests in France and because they wanted citizenship in accordance with the Law of January 28, 1790.[8]

Evidently, the Comtadin Jews wanted to benefit from this Law, which granted citizenship to the Sephardic Jews, to the Bordeaux Jews of Avignon origin and, according to various interpretation probably also to some Comtadin Jews residing in other Southern towns of the Rhône-Valley. In Nîmes pro-Jewish sentiments were expressed already in connection with the Law of November 1787 pertaining to the Protestants. An Avignon Jew based his demand for the right to reside in Toulon on the Law of Jan. 28, 1790. On Jan. 29, 1790, the deputy Bouche demanded that the Law passed the previous day should apply to Comtadin Jews. But his proposition was not discussed by the National Assembly, and he probably tried only to renew on this occasion his proposition for the annexation of the Papal province.[9] The Comtadin Jews could not benefit from the Law of Jan. 28, because

---

[8] *CA*, Oct. 24, Dec. 16 and 22, 1790, pp. 1038, 1222, 1242; Moureau, p. 35; Chobaut, p. 48; K. Metz, p. 12.

[9] The Law of Jan. 28, 1790, was published in Aix (Marseille Library, fonds de Provence); P. Angeras, *L'Edit de 1787 et son application dans la sénéchaussée de Nîmes*, Nîmes, 1925, pp. 161–78; *Le point du jour*, No. 200, Jan. 30, 1790, p. 223 (Bouché's proposal), Chobaut, p. 24; Ad. Crémieux, "Pour contribuer à l'histoire de l'accession de Juifs à la qualité de Citoyens français." *REJ*, vol. XCV, 1933, p. 49.

the territory had become a part of France only on September 14, 1791.

No local decree, order or regulation could be found indicating that the Jews from the Papal province, now the Department of Vaucluse, could benefit in any way from the Law of January 28, 1790. On Sept. 27, 1791, nine days after the annexation, the Ashkenazic Jews of France were granted full citizenship, but the Comtadin Jews were not mentioned on this occasion. The opinion of the historian A. Mossé that the Comtadin Jews became citizens only after and as a result of the Law of September 27 is not acceptable.[10] The Avignon Jews were granted all civil rights on June 10 and 11, 1791, and those of Comtat Venaissin on July 20, 1791, i. e. shortly before the Papal province became a part of France. But there is no doubt that the Jews were then looking toward France for a secure future.[11] In fact, the Jews became citizens only because the high pressure exerted by the pro-French elements.

In May 1790, the Avignon Jews demanded permission to wear the national cockade and black hats instead of the special yellow hats which were then forced upon them, and to have the practice of being nightly locked up the Jewish Ghetto abolished. On May 26, 1790, the Avignon Corporations requested that the Jews' demand should be granted. But the City Council took no action and let the matter drag on. Tournal published a letter from a French traveler who praised the Avignon revolutionaries,

---

[10] Mossé, pp. 242–45.

[11] "Le voeu de réunion à l'Empire Français émis par le peuple Venaissin étant accueilli, les associations, les carrières des Juifs seront détruites, ils cesseront d'être corps": *Copie de la Supplique présentée par les Administrateurs de la Carrière des Juifs de la Commune de Carpentras, à MM. les Maires et Officiers Municipaux* [17 Juillet, 1791], Carpentras, sd, 6 pp. (Calvet 2523–113).

but he criticized them for not having as yet abolished the yellow hats for Jews. When the Mayor of the neighboring city of Orange, Rodolphe d'Aymard, arrived with his national guard to restore order in Avignon (June 11–13, 1790), a Jewish delegation renewed the request for the abolition of the yellow hats. R. d'Aymar replied that in accordance with the Declaration of Human Rights which was then already adopted by Avignon, Jews should get the benefits of all rights. In spite of this the Jews became full citizens only a year later. It appears that even in revolutionary Avignon there was an anti-Jewish faction. According to one source, the Jews paid 18,000 pounds for the permission to wear black hats and to keep the gate of the ghetto open at night.[12] In Comtat Venaissin the abolition of the yellow hat was much more difficult to achieve. In fact, Avignon annexionists stated that the Jews were still persecuted in Carpentras, and that counter-Revolutionary emigrés from Avignon agitated against the Jews. The partisans of the old regime were shocked by many signs of fraternization between Jews and Gentiles. In April 1790, Jews and Gentiles danced together at an Avignon festival, with Jews wearing black hats and Gentiles parading in yellow hats. In September 1790, a Carpentras

---

[12] *Journal patriotique sur la Révolution d'Avignon et du Comté Venaissin*, April 25, May 27, 1790; AMAvignon, DI, ff. 25, 30–32; Abbé S. Bonnel, *M. Rodolphe d'Aymard, Maire, et la Garde nationale d'Orange à Avignon les 11, 12, et 13 Juin 1790*, Avignon, 1883, pp. 26–28; Chobaut, vol. CI, p. 51; Calvet, ms, 5938–00755 (Olivier Rouret's letter to his father on the 18,000 pounds paid by Jews). It should be noted that one Avignon corporation demanded that Jews should pay a certain sum for granting them citizenship (Chobaut, vol. CI, p. 44). On the yellow hat see: Jules Bauer, "Le chapeau jaune chez les Juifs comtadins." *REJ*, vol. XXXVI, pp. 53 ss.; In 1778, Israel Valabrègue (called Vidal) demanded permission to wear a black hat in the papal province; on March 12, 1771, he obtained such a permission for France from Louis XV. Vaucluse Archives, E4 (43); Gironde Archives, C3662.

newspaper published a story about a city-councilman, who dined with his wife in a Jewish home. "They spoke there mainly of the equality of men, the French Revolution and equality between Jews and Christians, between swindlers and honest men." The same newspaper reported that at a ceremony in an Avignon Church Christians and Jews were seated side by side. Anonymous authors of pamphlets mocked at giving citizenship to Jews, at a Carpentras guard major who was supposed to be of Jewish origin, etc.[13]

The Jewish problem was discussed several times at the Assembly of Representatives (*Assemblée représentative*) of Comtat Venaissin, which was against annexation and anti-Jewish. But, unlike the Avignon Jews, their Carpentras coreligionists were afraid to make official demands. Others made such demands in their behalf on June 17, 1790. The Assembly decided not to grant citizenship to Jews.[14] But the Avignon annexionists used this decision as a weapon against their adversaries. On one occasion, the Assembly invited representatives from neighboring French departments; among them was Julien Trélis, a Protestant representative from Nîmes, who on October 28, 1790 had asked the Assembly to abolish the yellow hats. This request was granted, but a proposition to grant full citizenship to Jews was postponed. Isle-sur-Sorgue and Cavaillon immediately

[13] Chobaut, vol. CII, p. 14; CA, Nov. 6, 1790; P. Charpenne, *Histoire de la Révolution dans Avignon et le Comtat et leur réunion définitive à la France*, Paris-Avignon, 1892, pp. 58, 421; *NACV* [=Nouvelles Annales du Comtat Venaissin], No, 22, 29, Sept. 21, Oct. 12, 1790; *Ran-Tan-Plan, ou les loisirs d'un Tambour de la Milice citoyenne*, sl, 1790, p. 13.

[14] In his speech of June 9, 1790, before the Assembly, the Carpentras Jewish representative, Mossé Monteil, did not make any demand, even not on the yellow hat. Carpentras Library, Tissot, vol. 36, ms. 1761, p. 44; J. F. André, vol. I, pp. 116–118; *APCV* [=Annales patriotiques du Comté Venaissin], June 10 et 21, 1790; *NACV*, July 27, 1790; Chobaut, vol. CII, p. 13.

carried out the decision of abolishing the yellow hats, but
in Carpentras, crowds attacked not only Jews, but even
those Representatives who had voted for the proposition
of J. Trélis. The Jews feared being attacked and demanded
that the practice of the yellow hats be reestablished, but
J. E. B. Duprat, a Jacobin leader of Avignon, called on
the Jacobins of Aix-en-Provence to defend the Carpentras
Jews. When the departmental authorities of Marseille
were informed of these developments, they asked Comtat
Venaissin to respect its own decision in abolishing the
yellow hat. Carpentras was forced to prove that the
Assembly would be able to respect this decision and was
not a counter-Revolutionary center. Thus, the struggle
for abolishing the yellow hat became a part of the conflict
between the partisans and adversaries of annexation. On
November 10, 1790, the city council of Carpentras confirmed the Assembly's decision of October 28. On November 14 a Te Deum was sung in the Carpentras Cathedral
in honor of the unity of all citizens; this was done against
the Bishop's will. But the Jews were again attacked in
the streets of Carpentras. According to the Avignon
Jacobin Tournal, the Te Deum was only a manoeuvre
and during this ceremony the Jews were locked up in
the ghetto. As Avignon was then getting ready to resume
the war against Carpentras, the Assembly swiftly declared
itself for France and invited French mediators to come to
Comtat. When the latter arrived it became necessary to
prove that Comtat Venaissin was not at all reactionary.
On Jan. 25, 1791, the Jews were forbidden to wear yellow
hats and the Gentiles were warned not to attack Jews.
On July 20, 1791, Carpentras gave the Jews full citizenship
and the right to vote.[15]

[15] Chobaut, vol. CII, pp. 15–17, 19, 21; *APCV*, Oct. 30, Nov. 16,

According to one source a Jew armed with a rifle and
wearing his yellow hat was a member of a revolutionary
patrol during the counter Revolutionary Avignon uprising
of June 10, 1790. J. E. B. Duprat, president of the Avignon
Jacobins, stated that Jews were the first to defend the
city against the counter-Revolutionists. The Jew Menassès
took part in the massacre of October 16–17, 1791, when
the Avignon revolutionaries killed about 70 of their adversaries. On July 7, 1793, the federalist army of Marseille
occupied Avignon and among the anti-federalists killed by
them was the 44 year old Jewish horse-dealer Michel
Cohen.[16]

During the Terror, Jews were active in the popular
clubs.[17] Manassé jr. was appointed to the departmental

1790, Jan. 29, 1791; *NACV*, Nov. 2, 1790; Ch. Soullier, vol. I p. 41;
*Extrait du Procès-verbal de L'Assemblée Réprésentative du Comté Venaissin,
du 28 Octobre 1790*, Carpentras, sd, placard; *Proclamation*, [Carpentras,
Jan. 25, 1791] placard; *Journal administrative de la ville de Carpentras*,
Jan. 24, 1791; Charpenne, vol. I, pp. 419, 421–26; *CA*, Nov. 5, 18,
1790, Jan. 29, 1791. One of the Paris mediators, Abbot François-
Valentin Mulot (1749–1804) was known as a friend of Jews: *Recueil
de pièces relatives à l'admission des Juifs à l'état civil*, Paris, 1790,
pp. 9, 18. In Carpentras he forced the local authorities to return to
his parents the young Jassuda Michal Mossé, who prior to the Revolu-
tion was forcibly converted to Christianity: *Compte rendu par M.
l'Abbé Mulot, à l'Assemblée nationale, comme commissaire du Roi à
Avignon le 19 Novembre 1791*, sl, nd, p. 41. On the Mossé case and
other conversions in the papal province see: Chobaut, vol. CI, pp.27–28;
E. Carmoly, in *Archives israélites*, 1862, pp. 461–66; Léopold Stein,
Der Knabenraub von Carpentras, Berlin, 1863 and Prag, 1897; Z.
Szajkowski, "The Conversion of Zemah Carmi in Carpentras." *Yivo
Bleter*, vol. XXIV, pp. 123–30 (In Yiddish); J. Bauer, "Les conversions
juives dans le Comtat Venaissin." *REJ*, vol. L, 1905, pp. 90–111;
C. Roth, "Une mission des communautés du Comtat Venaissin à
Rome." *REJ*, vol. LXXXIV, 1927, p. 1.

[16] Chobaut, vol. CI, p. 47, vol. CII, p. 29; J. E. B. Duprat, *Discours
sur la Révolution . . . le 19 Décembre 1791 . . .*, Marseille, 1792, p. 51;
Soulier, vol. II, p. 530; de Joannis, p. 53. On Aug. 28, 1793, Sarah
Cohen demanded the body of her brother (Calvet, ms. 2820, f. 305).

[17] In October, 1793, Moïse Milhaud was a member of the Surveillance

Court of Commerce.[18] But this did not prevent the departmental administration from publishing a proclamation
against speculation in 1793, attacking especially the Jews.
Later, during the Thermidor, Jewish Jacobins of Carpentras
were persecuted and no Jews could become members of
the administration before 1798.[19] In Isle-sur-Sorgue, which
was a federalist center, Menahem Cavaillon became a
member of the Surveillance Committee, during the Terror.
He even endorsed a charge against the priest Nourrit.[20]
On July 27, 1794, Lange Cohen was nominated by the
Paris Representative, Maignet, as Mayor of Cavaillon.
According to some sources he was a middle-of-the-road
revolutionary and even saved property of the Church. But
during the Thermidor, Jewish Jacobins, including Cohen,
were removed from office, by the Paris Representative
Goupilleau. In 1792, a Jew became a member of the
Jacobin city-council of Avignon, but during the Terror
itself Jews were not active there. Perhaps for this reason
the same Goupilleau, on October 29, 1794, appointed a
rich Jew, Benjamin Monteux, as a councilman of Avignon,

Committee of the Carpentras Club *Fraternité*. Ten Jews were among
the 64 Carpentras Club members who signed a petition of March,
8, 1794, protesting the arrest of members who criticized aristocrats.
On Aug, 2, 1794, nine Jews signed a similar petition of the *Société
populaire*: Calvet, ms, 4215; *Les sans culottes de Carpentras, à leurs
frères d'Avignon. 18 Ventôse, l'an second*, sl, nd, 16 pp. (Calvet,
ms, 2544–10). *Les Citoyens soussignés, membres épurés de la Société
populaire de Carpentras, au Citoyen Maignet* . . . [15 Thermidor an 2],
Carpentras, sd, 4 pp. (Carpentraś Library).

[18] Maignet, *Proclamation concernant l'épuration des autorités constitués
du département de Vaucluse* . . ., Avignon, an II.

[19] *Proclamation de l'Administration du département de Vaucluse,
relative à l'Agiotage*, Avignon, 3 Sept. 1793, 3 pp. (Tissot, ms, 1763,
p. 493, and placard, Jewish Theological Seminary, N. Y.); André,
vol. I, pp. 235–36; Chobaut, vol. CII, p. 27.

[20] De Joannis, p. 252. According to one source, the aristocrats of
L'Isle attacked the Jews. *Les Annales de la République française*,
August, 10, 1793.

which indicates that he was not anti-Jewish minded.[21]
During the Avignon disorders of March 14, 1797, the Jew
Eleazard Carcassonne was arrested together with many
other revolutionaries for his participation in breaking up
a counter-Revolutionary uprising.[22]

[21] Chobaut, vol. CII, pp. 28–29; *Archives israélites*, vol. IX, 1848,
pp. 452–63. Goupilleau reported in favor of Charles Peixotto's demand
to withdraw his fine of 1,200,000 pounds: *Rapport fait par Goupilleau
sur la pétition du citoyen Charles Peixotto . . . du 24 vendémiaire an 7*,
sl, nd, 6 pp.

[22] *Quelques réflexions sur une proclamation . . . de Vaucluse, du 11
Thermidor . . .*, Valence, sd, 7 pp.; *Acte d'accusation*, sl, nd, 78 pp.;
Les Républicains avignonnais . . . Au peuple français, pour la 2e fois,
Valence, sd, 24 pp.; *Les Républicains avignonnais . . . au Peuple français*,
Valence, sd, 24 pp.; *Observations sur le dernier massacre d'Avignon*,
sl, nd, 32 pp.; E. J. F. Mottet, *Acte d'accusation*, sl, nd, 77 pp.;
Rapport . . ., sl, nd, 44 pp.; *Procès-verbaux . . . . . les journées des 24
et 30 pluviôse dernier*, Avignon, sd, 57 pp.; *L'Administration . . . à
leurs administrés*, Avignon, sd, 4 pp.; *Corps législatif. Conseil des Cinq-
Cents. Opinion de Martind sur l'affaire des prisonniers avignonnais . . .*,
Paris, an VI, 8 pp.

It should be noted that the Paris Representative to the former
Papal province during the Terror was not an atheist: E. Ch. Maignet,
*Discours prononcé à la Société populaire d'Avignon . . . . 10 Floréal,
[1794]*, Avignon, sd, p. 7; Ibid, *Discours . . . . Marseille, le 20 Prairial*,
Marseille, an II, p. 4.

JEWISH PARTICIPATION IN THE SALE OF NATIONAL PROPERTY DURING THE FRENCH REVOLUTION*

The Problem of National Property

National Property (*biens nationaux*) is the term used for property confiscated by the revolutionary government on the basis of the decree of November 2, 1789. Church property was described as of primary origin (*première origine*), while that of emigrés and convicted counter-revolutionaries was known as property of secondary origin (*seconde origine*). While much has been written about the situation of the Jews during that period, the emphasis has been on the struggle for emancipation rather than on economics. Thus far no accurate study on national property has been made for Alsace in general. It is quite possible that the delay in the publication of studies in this field may have been due to the reluctance on the part of some prominent Alsatians and residents of other localities to reveal the fact that their ancestors had bought national property.[1] Moreover, there are difficulties in ascertaining the religion of the purchasers merely by their names.[2] Nevertheless, French historical literature is replete with state-

---

* The following abbreviations are used in the notes: ACC - Archives of the Central Jewish Consistory (Paris); ADBR - Departmental Archives of Lower Rhine; ADHR - Departmental Archives of Upper Rhine; ADL - Departmental Archives of Landes; ADM - Departmental Archives of Moselle; ADMM - Departmental Archives of Meurthe-et-Moselle; AMM - City Archives of Metz; AN - National Archives, Paris; *AR - Annales revolutionaires*; BMC - City Library of Colmar; BMN - City Library of Nancy; BN - National Library, Paris; BUS - University Library, Strasbourg; *JCV - Journal de la cour et de la ville; RA - Revue d'Alsace; REJ - Revue des études juives;* and *RF - La Révolution francaise.* The footnotes include the names of the collections where the rarer publications are housed and their identification numbers.

1 When the first study of this kind in France (Légay's three volumes on the Department of Sarthe) was published in 1885, the descendants of the buyers bought up all the copies. Loutchisky, J., *Quelques remarques sur la vente des biens nationaux* (Paris 1913) p. 12.

2 Unlike the administrative documents of Alsace and other departments, which almost always identified Jews as such, those pertaining to the purchases of national property rarely did. Family names like Weill, Lévy, Wurmser, Olry and Lehman, even when preceded by first names like Jacob or Abraham, do not constitute absolute indication of Jewishness.

Originally published in *Jewish Social Studies*, vol. XIV (1952).

ments that the Jews were greatly involved in the purchase of national property and speculation with it. For instance, the antisemitic historian J. B. H. R. Capefigue wrote that as soon as Jews were permitted to enter Paris, they immediately engaged in usury and speculation in *assignats* (paper money). Even the objective pro-Jewish historian Rodolphe Reuss wrote that Jews speculated in confiscated church property and *assignats* and that they shipped money out of the country. He failed to prove this; he merely repeated what others had written before him.[3]

The present study is based on a sampling of the available material dealing mainly with northeastern France, where the majority of the French Jews lived at the revolution's outbreak. It cannot undertake to solve all the historical problems of the period. In some cases, the author had to be content merely with stating the problem, leaving its solution to future studies.[4]

In Alsace, Moselle and Lorraine, the Church and the counter-revolutionaries were opposed to the nationalization of church and emigré property more so than elsewhere in France.[5] The clergy resented the abrogation of the feudal privileges.[6] The purchasers of national property were so terrorized that the administration of Lower-Rhine (Bas-Rhin) had to issue a warning to those hindering the sales. The Strasbourg district was unable to effect the first sale in a village until December 17, 1790. This occasion was considered so important that the *Société des Amis de la Constitution* gave a dinner in honor of the purchaser, who was then presented with a musket for self-defense in case of attack. In the year VII a plot was uncovered to murder all Protestants, Jews and purchasers. Threats against

---

[3] Capefigue, J. B. H. R., *Histoire des grandes opérations financières* . . . vol. ii (Paris 1855) p. 24; Reuss, Rod., "Quelques documents nouveaux sur l'antisémitisme dans le Bas-Rhin de 1794 à 1799." *REJ*, vol. lix (1910) 250.

[4] George Avenel wrote that nothing in history is as complicated as the history of national property in France of the revolution. *Lundis révolutionnaires, 1871 - 1874* (Paris 1875) p. 29. It is the present author's belief that his basic conclusions are valid for the entire area of the relation of the Jews to the sale of national properties.

[5] *Cf.* d'Eymar, Abbé, *Discours sur la propriété des biens ecclesiastiques* (Paris 1789). BN-Le 29-2042; *Opinion de M. l'abbé Maury* . . . *sur le clergé d'Alsace* . . . 17 *octobre* 1790 (Paris 1790). BN-Le 29-1025.

[6] *Cf.* Sagnac, Ph., *La Législation civile de la Révolution française* (Paris 1898) p. 92; *Motifs de l'opinion et de l'amendement proposé par M. Schwendt* . . . *sur le droits féodaux en Alsace* (Paris 1789). BN-Le 29-1055; *Réflexions* . . . *destruction de la féodalité* . . . *d'Alsace* (s.l. [1789]) p. 10. BN-Lb 39-2134; [de la Fare, A.L.H.] *Considérations temporels du clergé*, par M. l'Evêque de Nancy (Paris 1789). BN-Lb 39-2176; *Idem, Opinion et réclamation* . . . *sur le projet de décret portant invasion générale et absolue des biens & fonds patrimoniaux des Eglises* . . . (Paris 1791). BN-Le 29-573.

prospective buyers were common.[7] On the other hand, a pamphleteer in Metz urged that capitalists be forced to buy national property.[8]

Speculation with such properties was not a specifically Jewish problem, nor was it limited to Alsace. However, frequently historians are apt to forget this, and report only on its practice by Jews. Nationalized property was bought at highly inflated prices.[9] Resales of property were frequent.[10] According to almost all historians, peasant buyers had to resort to borrowing from usurers.[11] There is ample proof of rampant speculation and of the rise of a new class of wealthy persons in its consequence. In a report dated August 10, 1800, Laumond, prefect of Lower-Rhine, wrote that the departmental administration was for many years in the hands of individuals who were only interested in their own enrichment. Raimond Blanié, a son of a peasant and a new-comer to Alsace, became a millionaire as a result of such speculation. Even General F. Kellerman (whose report was very influential in the preparation of the anti-Jewish Decrees of

7 The Vosges priest C. E. Feys refused to hear the confession of the wife of a purchaser. As late as 1797, a Besançon buyer received a threatening letter. Purchasers were also terrorized in other parts of France. *Proclamation du conseil général du département du Bas-Rhin* (Strasbourg, 16 Decembre 1790) Affiche. BUS, vol. 4-213; Reuss, R., *La Cathédrale de Strasbourg pendant la révolution* (Paris 1888) p. 83-84; Marion, Marcel, *La vente des biens nationaux . . . avec étude spéciale . . . de la Gironde et du Cher* (Paris 1908) p. 93; *L'Administration centrale du département du Bas-Rhin, et le commissaire du directoire exécutif près elle, à leurs concitoyens, le 29 messidor de l'an VII* [Strasbourg]. ADBR-LI 762; Véron-Réville, *Histoire de la révolution française dans le département du Haut-Rhin, 1789-1795* (Colmar 1865) p. 51-52; *Hans Bessergemeynt an den Hannss Wohlgemeynt* [Strasbourg 1791] p. 4. BUS 105626; M[athiez,] A., "Menaces à un acquéreur de biens d'église," *AR*, vol. xii (1920) 245-46; Aulard, A., *L'Etat de la France en l'an VIII et en l'an IX . . .* (Paris 1897) p. 133; Documents in AN-DXXXIX 12-96.

8 *Moyen à employer pour faire obtenir aux assignats la confiance accordé à l'argent* (Metz [1790]) p. 4-5, BN-Lb 39-4086.

9 Between January 1791 and March 1792, when the value of the *assignats* had not as yet greatly depreciated, property in the Vosges (near Alsace) valued at Fr.617,489 was sold for Fr.956,895. Even higher prices were paid following the depreciation of paper money. A. Claude thinks that the sale of national property proves that the peasantry was not poor, but included many real *coqs de village*, who possessed hidden money. He was the only historian of this part of France to hold this point of view. Schwab, Léon, *Documents relatifs à la vente des biens nationaux. Departement des Vosges.* 2 vol., (Epinal 1911-13) ; Claude, André, *L'Administration du district de Neufchâteau-Mouzon Meuse* (Clamecy 1933) p. 138; Vilminot, "Au sujet de la misere materielle du paysan à la fin de l'ancien régime," *La Révolution dans les Vosges,* vol. xxiii (1934) 56-64.

10 In Lower-Rhine, the sale of such property up to October 31, 1791, brought in Fr.4,214,301, far above its actual value. Fesquet tells, without mentioning Jews, that speculators in Alsatian Protestant sections paid almost twice as much as did those in the Catholic sections, where the population hesitated to buy. Property was sold and resold, often changing hands five or six times in ten years. According to F. Ponteil, pious Catholics engaged in speculation. Fesquet, J. L., *Voyage de Paris à Strasbourg . . .* (s.l. [1802].) p. 35-36; Ponteil, F., *La Situation économique du Bas-Rhin au lendemain de la révolution . . .* (Strasbourg 1928) p. 58.

11 Even before 1789, exorbitant prices for land led peasants into indebtedness. Competition for the purchase of national property was keen among the peasants and they had to pay higher prices than city buyers. Some organized themselves in groups in order to buy the

Napoleon I in 1806 and 1808) was a big buyer. The Alsatian Jacobin and antisemite Joseph Bruat bought a nationalized monastery and died the possessor of huge estates. Saint-Just purchased considerable property in Oise. One of the biggest deals took place in the Department of Lot. It began in Strasbourg, and not one Jew was involved in it. In all of France, particularly where no Jews resided, speculators were often organized in syndicates, some without capital of their own. In the district of Laon (Aisne), where not a single Jew resided, only 629 of the 1,269 sales made between 1791 and 1793, were made to individuals, the rest going to such organized groups.[12]

Anti-Jewish Propaganda

The enemies of the Jews described their war against Jewish emancipation as a struggle for the existence of the Catholic Church.[13] The Catholic-royalist campaigns against nationalization of property afforded them ample opportunities. Its principal argument was that the nationalization of church property would increase the government's expenditures, because it would now be required to support the Church and the church-assisted poor. The argument was also brought out that Jews, Protestants and foreigners would buy up the churches and other nationalized property. The effort was thus made to frighten Catholics into thinking that Jews and

property at a cheaper price. The abbot L. Rumpler tells that when he tried to buy land he was nearly killed by peasants. Hoffmann, Charles, *L'Alsace au dix-huitième siècle*, vol. i (Colmar 1906) p. 184; Rumpler, L., *A Mes amis de tous les cultes* [Strasbourg 1791]. BN-Ln 27-18135; Heitz, F. C., *Les Sociétés politiques de Strasbourg . . .* (Strasbourg 1865) p. 156-57.

[12] G. F. Teutsch, a Protestant banker, bought property valued at approximately ten million francs. The Metz judge A. S. Lambert issued a pamphlet stressing that he sold property not because of his expectation of a counter-revolution, but because of his fear of inability to pay his debts. On March 4, 1799, the dramatist Ch. F. F. de Quigey, Metz agent of the Ministry of the Interior, recommended that the departmental treasurer Thirion be removed, because since his appointment he became a large property owner and a banker, operating with the aid of his government staff. AN, F20-244 (Letter of Laumond), and FIC III, Moselle (Cart I, Thirion); Matter, *Mémoire . . . Blanié* (Strasbourg 1822) p. 3-4. BUS 32723; Reuss, R., *Souvenirs alsatiques . . .* (Strasbourg 1897) p. 79-80; Vermale, F., "Kellerman acquéreur des biens . . ." *AR*, vol. v (1912) 249, 263, 265; D[ommanget], M., "Saint-Just acquéreur . . ." *AR*, vol. xiv (1922) 424-25; Caillet, R., "Spéculateurs et biens nationaux." *RF*, vol. lxxxiii (1930) 194-202; *Quelques observations données par G. F. Teutsch . . .* (Colmar 1827) p. 2. BN-4F 3-30931; Lambert, *Pétition . . .* (Metz an XI) p. 1. AN-BB 16-501; Paquet, R., *Bibliographie analytique de l'histoire de Metz pendant la révolution* (Paris 1926) p. 1298-99; Loutchisky, *op. cit.,* p. 62-75; Mathiez, A., *Le Directoire* (Paris 1939) p. 129. The same situation existed in the occupied Rhine territories, where usurious rates of interest were paid on loans made in this connection. In fact, the administrator of national property requested that sales be suspended for a few years, so that prices would return to normal and the local people would be able to buy the property. Sagnac, Ph., *Le Rhin français pendant la révolution et l'empire* (Paris 1917) p. 260-61.

[13] Boutin, P., *Le Cardinal de la Fare* (Fontenay-le-Comte 1922) p. 7-8.

Protestants would desecrate the holy places. This was in line with Catholic propaganda, which claimed that the revolution favored Jews and perse-cuted Catholics.[14] Such arguments were particularly effective in Alsace, Moselle and Lorraine, where most Jews lived, and where the Church was very strong.

The threat was frequently expressed that the properties of the peasants would eventually be expropriated by the Jews. Such predictions also emphasized that the Jews would be the eventual owners of church property and that they would enslave the peasants. Such propaganda was used to persuade the peasants not to buy national property[15] and often also served as a weapon in the struggle against Jewish emancipation.[16] The pamphlet-eers stressed the threat to the French and Catholic way of life and the

[14] *Gazette de Paris*, March 29, 1790; *JCV*, vol. v, no. 28 (1791) 217-18; *L'Ami des lois*, no. 1437 (17 Thermidor an VII); Reuss, R., *La Grande fuite de décembre 1793* . . . (Stras-bourg 1934) p. 258-63; Marion, *op. cit.*, p. 92-93. Pflieger, the anti-Jewish deputy from Altkirch, wrote that Jews were being considered as possible buyers of national property, but not one Jew had as much as planted a garden. Abbot Maury severely criticized the Swiss and Dutch bankers for not saving the church from expropriation by coming to the rescue of French finances. He attacked the Jews for demanding equal rights in the purchase of property in order to "confiscate" church property. Abbot Peyretta of Corsica warned that church property would be sold to pay debts owed by the government to Jews and merchants. Muhlenbeck, E., "Il y a cent ans!" *RA*, vol. xliv (1893) 438; *Opinion de M. l'abbé Maury* . . . *sur la propriété des biens ecclésiastiques* . . . (Paris 1789) p. 13. BN-Le 29-260; Jaurès, Jean, *Histoire socialiste*, vol. i. *La Constituante* (Paris 1901) p. 450; Reuss, R., *Histoire d'Alsace* (Paris 1912) p. 230.

[15] An Alsatian deputy warned of the peasants' impoverishment due to the purchase by Jews of the church lands on which they were working. F. M. Thiébaut, a Metz priest warned that nationalization of church property which would be taken over by the Jews, will force the clergy to engage in usury. The author of *Warnung an die Elsasser*, a popular antisemitic pamphlet, predicted that church property would fall into the hands of people from Geneva, Basel, Holland, Parisian usurers and the Jews. Alsatians would then have only one alterna-tive, that of emigration and the Jews would force Christians to become Jews. He also accused the Jews of bribing the deputies by sending them Jewish women. *Le Patriote français*, no. 457 (November 8, 1790); *Le Moniteur*, vol. ii (1790) 534-36, 1206-07; [Thiébaut, Abbé F. M.] *Considérations catholico-politiques sur les immeubles du clergé* (Metz) [1789] p. 24, 27. BN-Lb 39-8003; *Warnung an die Elsasser* [Strasbourg May 1790]. French edition: *Avis aux alsaciens*. BUS 105600, 106929; Heitz, C. F., *La Contre-révolution en Alsace de 1789 à 1793* (Strasbourg 1865) p. 14-17. Another counter-revolutionary pamphlet warned that the Jews would use the 12,000,000 francs owed to them to buy up church lands and force the peasants to work them. He warned the peasants not to buy national property, because they would have to borrow money from Jews, who would eventually take over the land for debts. Christians who bought such properties were termed baptized Jews (*Juifs baptisés*). *Je vous dirai vos vérités* (1792) p. 19, 21, 82. BUS and BMC.

[16] The bailiff of Flachslanden, in a counter-revolutionary brochure, warned that if Jews would be permitted to become citizens, the poor German Jews would flood Alsace, and would control land property in a few years, leaving the then impoverished Alsatians either to emi-grate or to become enslaved to this *horde étrangère*. *Compte rendu par le bailli de Flachs-landen* . . . *Protestation contre les décrets de l'assemblée prétendue nationale* . . . (s.l. 1790) p. 10. AN-AD XVI 61 no. 388.

danger of an influx of foreign Jews who would eventually own most of the property.[17]

This was carefully prepared propaganda. A report by the *Société des Amis de la Constitution* of Strasbourg told that the priests frightened the people with the rumor that foreigners and Parisians would buy up all the property, raise rents, and take their profits out of Alsace, thus impoverishing the province, already suffering from money shortage. The report also stated that since Jewish emancipation began to be discussed, clerical propaganda concentrated on the Jews, with the line that they would buy up church property and become the rulers of Alsace. This was characterized in the report as terroristic propaganda, because in truth if the government would have counted only on Jewish buyers, little property would have been sold.[18]

All kinds of fantastic items appeared in the press. For instance, a news item told that a *société de capitalistes juifs* offered Fr. 800,000 for the Chartreux church in Paris in order to substitute the Old Testament for the New one. Similarly, the news appeared that the Jews of Paris wanted to buy the Saint-Antoine church and turn it into a synagogue. A Parisian Jew was reported to have said that the city wanted Jews to buy a church and convert it into a synagogue. A newspaper reported that many Portuguese Jews came to Paris to buy national property. Another paper opined that soon there would not be even one church left to sell to the "brave tribe of Polish Jews" (*braves gens des Juifs polonais*), who in their enthusiasm for the French revolution, left the banks of the Vistula to settle on the banks of the Loire. Feydel's *Observateur* wrote that the parish of the du Marais quarter of Paris sold religious objects from its church to a Jew named Alexandre for 10,000 pounds. When Jews protested against this accusation, Feydel replied that no religious objects were sold, and that in any case the sellers and not the buyers were to blame. The Jews, however, investigated the incident. It turned out that the church silver was offered for sale to the

17 For instance, an antisemitic pamphlet stated that the Jews had already bought up half of Paris, and forced their Christian debtors to forsake Christianity and engage in usury (*Judaiser*) with them. *Requête des marchands et négociants de Paris, contre l'admission des Juifs* [Paris 1790] p. 22-23. The first edition was published in 1769. According to a hand written note on the copy in the Library of the Jewish Theological Seminary (N. Y.) the 1790 edition was published by Hell.

18 [Brunck] *De l'Etat civil des Juifs en Alsace. Rapport lu à l'assemblée de la société des amis de la constitution de Strasbourg, le 27 fevrier 1790 . . .* ([Strasbourg] 1790) p. 5-6.

Jew Abraham Hesse, who refused to buy it. Whereupon, honest Feydel published the true story.[19]

Those opposed to the revolution utilized antisemitic propaganda also to discredit other revolutionary acts, as, for instance, the election of constitutional bishops. During the elections in Strasbourg (F. A. Brendel was elected) a pamphlet charged that the Jewish leader Cerf-Beer [Berr] wanted to be a candidate. A similar printed canard was attributed to a rabbi of Rappoltsweiler. Later, a pamphlet published in 1792, stated that Cerf Beer would be elected Brendel's successor. In another election for a bishop, Catholics cast five votes for Cerf-Beer. The bishop of Nancy declared that in the election of Saint-Flour eight votes had been cast for Mirabeau, four for a Jew, and 20 for a convicted thief.[20]

In various parts of France Jews suffered from considerable chicanery in connection with the sales of national property. The district of Colmar prohibited purchases by Jews. The Alsatian Jews complained in 1789 that they were being excluded from all professions and were not permitted to own land. Four years later, the opponents of Jewish emancipation in Upper-Rhine (Haut-Rhin) wrote that the Jews still had the nerve to complain that they were not permitted to purchase national property. In August 1794, Foussédoire, the Paris representative in Strasbourg, forwarded a petition on behalf of the Jews, listing persecutions against them, including

19 *L'Observateur de Feydel,* February 27, 1790; *Le Courrier Français,* April 17, June 17, 1790; *La Gazette universelle,* October 26, 1791; *Annales de la republique française* (15 Brumaire an IV); *JCV,* May 6, 1791; *Gazette de Paris,* March 26, 1790; *Le Rodeur français,* no. 39 (1791); *L'Observateur,* October 15, 17, 20, 1789; Kahn, L., *Les Juifs à Paris pendant la révolution* (Paris 1898) p. 114-16.

20 *Cerf Behr aux trois rois* (1790). Germain edition: *Hirtz Bahr an die drei Koeniglein zu Strassburg* (1790). BUS; Heitz, *La Contre-révolution* . . . p. 144-49; Seinguerlet, E., *Strasbourg pendant la révolution* (Paris 1881) p. 63; Reuss, R., *La Constitution civile du clergé et la crise religieuse en Alsace,* 1790-1795 vol. i, (Strasbourg 1922) p. 150, 160; "Je commence à croire, que Cerf Behr pourroit bien finir par être le successeur de Brendel." *Je vous dirai vos vérités* [1792] p. 83; *Bulletin et journal des journaux* (August 4, 1791); *JCV* (March 12,1791); [Seybold, David Christoph,] *Erfleuliche Nachricht für die Juden von einem bald zu erwartenden Hohen priester oder Brief des Rabbiners zu Rapoltsweiler an den Rabbiner zu Metz. Aus dem Jüdischteuschen Original treulich übersetzt* (1790). BUS 106820; Reprinted in Ginsburger, M. "Aus der Zeit des Terrorismus in Elsass." *Blaetter für Jüdische Geschichte und Litteratur,* vol. iii (1902) no. 12.

In 1791, a petition from the district of Colmar expressed the fear that Jews would participate in the election of priests and bishops. This idea was constantly repeated in the Catholic press, in counter-revolutionary pamphlets and even in a poem. ADHR-L645; *JCV,* 14 juin 1791; *Déclaration des droits de l'homme. Arcticle XI* . . . (1791). Cf. Heitz, *op. cit.,* p. 137-38.

their exclusion from the purchase of national property. Foussédoire repeated the same grievances in a warning against the persecution of Jews.[21]

Jews were attacked by reactionaries for wanting to buy national property and threatened by revolutionaries with deportation for not buying it. One officer suggested that well-to-do Jews be forced to buy such property. Attempts were made to coerce peasants into buying church property by the threat that otherwise it would be taken over by strangers and the debt-ridden peasantry would become subservient to the Jews.[22]

Jewish Attitudes

Jews did not participate in the theoretical discussions on nationalization. An exceptional case was the attack by the Polish Jew Zalkind Hourwitz on Abbot Maury and his friends in defense of nationalization of church property, termed by the Jew "the people's" (*nos biens*).[23] Much later, during the restoration, when it became fashionable for the erstwhile purchasers to hide the origin of their fortunes and to accentuate their counter-revolutionary activity, the Cerf-Beer family followed suit, despite the fact that Cerf-Beer was one of the few Jews to buy national property in the Strasbourg district.[24]

It stands to reason that Jews should have been active purchasers of national property, as this was their first legal opportunity to own land and houses.[25] This had been expected of them, particularly since they were viewed as rich, and therefore their failure to buy much property evoked considerable disappointment. They were sharply criticized for this failure by attorney Moreau, who remarked ironically that Jews probably did not

---

[21] *Opinion d'un membre du departement du Haut-Rhin, sur les individus Juifs . . .* [Colmar 1793] p. 10. BUS 101458; *Foussédoire, représantant du peuple dans le départements des Haut-et-Bas-Rhin.* (2 p.). AN-BB 30-102; Ginsburger, M. and E., "Contributions à l'histoire des Juifs d'Alsace pendant la terreur." *REJ*, vol. xxxxvii (1903) 295-97.

[22] *Annales de Mercier*, October 16, 1793; Kahn, *op. cit.*, p. 49; AN, AR 1361 (118); Hildenfinger, P., "Actes . . ." *REJ*, vol. lx (1910) 253; *Ein Brief von Hanuss Wohlgemeht, Derselbe bietet seinen Mitbrüdern, die das Feld bauen, seinen briderlichen Gruss an* [Strasbourg 1790] p. 15. BUS 6837.

[23] *Le Courrier de Paris dans les 83 departements*, January 10, 1790, p. 151-53.

[24] Lévylier, M., *Notes et documents concernant la famille Cerfberr*, vol. ii (Paris 1905) p. 121-23; Solms-Roedelheim, *Die National-güter-Verkäufe im Distrikt Strassburg 1791-1811* (Strassburg 1904) p. 89.

[25] In fact, the specialist M. Marion writes that a rush of Jewish purchasers had been expected. "Du role des Juifs dans la vente des biens nationaux dans la Gironde," *Actes de l'académie nationale des sciences, belles-lettres et arts de Bordeaux*, 3e série, vol. lxx (1908) 5.

want to own property outside of Jerusalem.[26] There is an accusation on record that Jews preferred speculation to land ownership,[27] as well as a proposal that no Jew be allowed to live in France, unless he purchased at least 10,000 pounds worth of property.[28]

It is difficult to treat objectively the problem of sales of national property. It must be remembered that in the eyes of adherents of the revolution, the purchase of such property (not for speculation, of course) was viewed as an act of revolutionary courage and patriotism.[29] In view of the impact of the revolution on Jewish emancipation, it is interesting to note that the number of Jews who bought national property was very small and that they purchased it mainly for purely business purposes, primarily for resale. Unlike Protestants in Alsace who became large land owners overnight, Jews failed to take such advantage.

Some Jews showed little confidence in the ownership of national property. The decision of the revolutionary government to pay the debts of the emigrés whose property was nationalized was made known through countless placards. "Lawyers" and bankers even undertook to collect these debts for the emigrés' creditors.[30] Some creditors, including Jews, demanded the payment of these debts.[31] However, not even a majority of the Jewish creditors made such demands of the government. Proof thereof is furnished from the perusal of the proportion of Jews among the creditors

[26] *De l'Incompatibilité entre le judaisme et l'exercice des droits de cité* . . . (Paris 1819) p. 72.

[27] This was raised by Woirot, Strasbourg sergeant at arms of the National Guard. *Der Weltbote* (Strasbourg) March 18, 1793.

[28] This was proposed by Charles François Bouche in *De la Restitution du Comté Vensaissin* . . . (Paris 1789) p. 38-39.

[29] Michelet wrote that in the atmosphere of hate and intrigue against the buyers of nationalized property, the very act of purchasing such property served as a means of recognition among the friends of the revolution, and bound their fortunes to its success. *Histoire de la révolution*, vol. iii (Paris 1898) p. 227. On August 9, 1801, Laumond, the Prefect of Lower-Rhine, wrote that when he needed honest persons for the administration, he sought them from among the buyers of national property. AN, F20-244.

[30] *Troisième proclamation* (Strasbourg, 15 avril 1793). BUS 39881, V, no. 380; *Déliberation de l'administration centrale du département du Bas-Rhin, du 21 Fructidor an VII.* BN-LK 4-731-II, no. 130; AMM-12-16; [Lemaire, François], *Annonce aux créanciers d'emigrés* . . . [Paris 179—]. BN-Lb 41-4991.

[31] In the year IV, a few Jewish creditors of the emigré Louis Joseph Klinglin of Essert asked that their debt of 45,000 pounds be paid. Séligman Alexandre (Cerf-Beer's son-in-law) demanded payment of the 73,000 pounds owed him by the Abbaye de Schwarzach. Mayer Aaron of Strasbourg demanded 30,000 pounds owed him by the emigré Bodeck. A list of creditors whose debts were paid included the names of Isaac Dreyfus (an intermediary for Isaac May of Strasbourg in a debt of Fr. 22,880) and of Isaac Netter, both Jews of Haguenau. Jacob Israél of Moselle was the creditor of the emigré Henry Choppar, who owned an iron works in partnership with a non-emigré. When his partner sold the iron works, Israél began

who had made such demands. Of 819 debts in a list of creditors who
demanded the payment of debts owed by emigrés from the department of
Lower-Rhine, 58 were owed to Jews. Three Jews are listed in another
list consisting of 221 creditors demanding payment of debts loaned to
religious and private corporations, dissolved by the revolution.[32] No Jews
are included in a Colmar list of 73 creditors. Only six Jews appear in a
list for the year X of 240 debts in the department of Meurthe, while another
list for the district of Blâmont in the year III includes no Jews.[33] The low
proportion of Jews in these lists may be interpreted by some persons as indicating that the number of Jewish creditors was small. This assumption,
however, is still to be proven.

In 1814, when the restored monarchy levied a tax of a billion francs
for the purpose of compensating the returned emigrés for their confiscated
property, creditors appeared who had not cared to collect their debts during
the revolution. One pamphlet stated that the returned emigrés would be
in a sorry state indeed if some thought was not given to the debts. The
Jewish question was also slightly involved. The emigré Comte Ferrand,
an ardent monarchist and author of the law of December 15, 1814, which
dealt with the return of the non-nationalized emigré property, expressed
the fear that restored property would come into the possession of Jews,
should Jewish creditors demand the repayment of debts owed them by
returned emigrés. In his campaign for a declaration of a moratorium on
debt payments he engaged in propaganda against the Jewish creditors.[34]
His fears were, of course, groundless. Nevertheless, a number of Jewish
creditors who had been patient during the revolution, demanded payment

to ask for his money. As late as 1810, the Jew Moyse Romain of Phalsbourg was engaged
in a law suit to collect a debt owed him by an emigré, for which he had asked payment at the
beginning of the revolution. ADHR-L 482, vol. ii; AN, BB 16-500, 504; Hildenfinger, *op. cit.*,
no. 127, 169, 190; Ginsburger, M., "Arrêtés . . . " *REJ*, vol. lxxv (1922) 67-68.

[32] *Liquidation des dettes d'emigrés* and *Répértoire des liquidations faites sur le corporations
supprimées.* ADBR-Q.

The antisemitic tendencies in the historiography of Alsace-Lorraine are illustrated in
André Gain's remarks about the first list (the second list was unknown to him), to wit, that
whenever the principal of the debt is encumbered with interest, the creditor happens to be a
Jew. To cite, "Presque chaque fois que l'on rencontre des créances grossies d'intérêts, on
constate quelles émanent des Aaron, des Levy ou des Séligmann de Strasbourg." *La Restauration et les biens des emigrés . . . 1814-1832,* vol. ii (Nancy 1928) p. 265. However, the list
contains only one general sum, without specifying the amount of interest, in all these cases.

[33] ADHR-L 483; ADMM-Q 990, 1036-1037.

[34] *Observations sur le projet de la loi relatif à la restitution des biens invendus . . .* (Paris
[1819] p. 2, 4. BN-Lb 45-349; Gain, *op. cit.,* vol. i, p. 152-53.

now. Among them was the Gradis family of Bordeaux, which demanded payments from 29 debtors.[35]

There are several possible explanations for this delay in efforts to collect outstanding debts during the revolution. First, there was little confidence in the *assignats*.[36] While *assignats* could be used to purchase national properties, some creditors feared that the emigrés would some day return and reclaim them. It is necessary to note that there were many Jewish emigrés and that their property was also confiscated.[37] Another reason for the relatively few purchases by Jews can be found in their impoverishment during the revolution when many rich Jews lost their entire fortunes.[38] Some Jews who bought such property could not afford to pay for it in cash.[39]

It would stand to reason that the Sephardim in Southern France should have been heavy purchasers, having always evinced as they did the desire to own buildings and land.[40] M. Marion and H. Léon correctly state that for some wealthy Jews of St.-Esprit and Bordeaux, the purchase of national property would be a means of liquidating their paper money fortunes. During the revolution many people in Bordeaux tried to get rich quickly by buying as much property as they could for *assignats*. Peasants bought or rented national property, and instead of tilling the soil destroyed and looted the buildings and sold the livestock with no thought for tomor-

35 Gain, *op. cit.*, vol. ii, p. 277.

36 Article 68 of the decree of April 20, 1795, on the payment of emigré debts specified that debts of 1,000 to 2,000 pounds could be paid in *assignats*. *La Monnaie et le papier-monnaie* (Paris 1912) p. 357.

37 The Jewish emigrés Salomon Wolf, Hirtzel Wolf, Isaac Dreyfuss, Gumbel (Abraham) Lévy, and Abraham Mayer were among the emigrés of Lower-Rhine, who received compensation for their nationalized property. *Etats détaillés des liquidations faites par la commission d'indemnité, à l'époque de la loi du 27 avril 1825 . . . IIIe partie, département du Bas-Rhin* (Paris 1828). BN-Lf 158-40. In Moselle the Jew Mayer Lévy received such a compensation. Gain, *op. cit.*, vol. ii, p. 136.

38 Among those were the Schwabe family of Metz and Rabbi Abraham-Isaac Lunteschutz of Romansweiller. Wogue, L., *Eloge funèbre . . .* (Metz 1837) p. 9; *Archives israélites*, vol. xxiii (1862) 157-59.

39 After the Napoleonic Decree of May 30, 1806, Joseph Hertz of Sarreguemines complained that without the payments of the debts owed him by Christians, he would be unable to pay for the national property he had bought. AN-BB 16-502 (Letter of February 8, 1807).

40 For instance, under Louis XIII Sephardic Jews offered 12,000,000 pounds for an agreement calling for the transformation by them of the Durance river into a canal to the Rhone, under a grant of land on both sides of the river with permission of religious autonomy. This project was mentioned by a member of the National Assembly as late as 1789. In 1760, under Louis XV, they offered to pay 80,000,000 pounds for a part of Landes near Bordeaux and to build a fortified town there. In 1791, the Sephardic Jews of Amsterdam (the Jews of Bordeaux were probably consulted) offered 25,000,000 pounds for land along the coast of Arcachon and the territory between Bayonne and Bordeaux, so that Jews could develop it.

row.[41]   Unlike in Alsace, Jews were not threatened in southwestern France. On the contrary, when Jews were tried by revolutionary tribunals, their defense emphasized that as Jews, they were necessarily devotees of the revolution.[42]   Directly, and through middlemen, Charles Peixotto and his famliy bought 33 nationalized estates for 835,980 pounds.   This purchase stood him later in good stead.   The same happened with Aaron Lopes.[43] To return to the problem of purchases, as we shall see, Bordeaux Jews failed to buy much national property.   The attitude of the Jews to the sales was a hesitant one, like their general attitude towards the revolution.   They showed little desire to join in the terror or the civil war, although they were willing to shed their blood for the defense of the country.[44]   Victims of persecutions, they were far from ready to persecute others.   And for some Jews the sale of national property held implications of terror and injustice.

According to M. Marion, Bordeaux Jews bought national property at the beginning of the revolution, when such investments seemed secure and when speculation was at a minimum.   Between 1796 and 1798, at the height of the speculation, the number of Jewish buyers decreased.   Most of the property bought by Jews was of primary origin, namely, church property. Very rarely, did a Bordeaux Jew buy property of secondary origin, that is,

They were to pay immediately 5,000,000 pounds, but the Bishop of Arras put an end to the project. Bouche, *op. cit.,* p. 35; d'Hauterive, E., *La Police secrète du premier empire,* vol. iii (Paris 1908) p. 152.

Interestingly, in 1790, the city of Strasbourg asked that a territory for a "new Jerusalem" be given to the Jews, so that they could leave Alsace and never come back. *Très-humble adresse ... présenté ... par la commune de Strasbourg ...* [Strasbourg, April 1790] p. 10. German edition: *Unterthänigste Vorstellung ...*

41 Marion, *"Du rôle ...,"* (*Cf.* note 25), p. 6; Léon, Henry, *Histoire des Juifs de Bayonne* (Paris 1893) p. 161-62; Caudrillier, G., "Bordeaux sous le directoire." *RF,* vol. lxx (1917) 26-40.

42 *Jugement .. qui condamne Samuel Astruc ...* (Bordeaux an II); *Jugement ... qui ordonne que Isaac Pereyre, agent de change, sera sur le champ mis en liberté* (Bordeaux an II). BN-Lb 41-1201, no. 46-87.

43 The Peixotto family sold later some of this property.   Peixotto was later fined 1,200,000 pounds by a revolutionary tribunal.   The fine would have been greater, had he not defended himself by pointing out that he bought national property.   Aaron Lopes, who was fined 50,000 pounds, also cited in his defense his purchases of national property and the confidence in the revolution that it implied.   Marion, M.; Benzacar, J.; and Caudrillier, *Documents relatifs à la vente des biens nationaux* (Bordeaux 1911-12) Index (Ch. Peixotto); *Jugement ... qui condamne Charles Peixotto à une amende de 1,200,000 livres ...* (Bordeaux an II); BN-Lb 41-1201, no. 17; Detchevery, A., *Histoire des israélites de Bordeaux* (Bordeaux 1850) p. 101; Peixotto was probably a converted Jew. *Cf.* Marion, *"La Vente .."* p. 55; *Jugement ... qui condamne Aaron Lopes ... à une amende de 50,000 livres ...* (Bordeaux an II). BN-Lb 41-1201, no. 184 bis.

44 Thus, in 1801, Michael Berr wrote that although it was to be expected that Jews should participate in the terror against the old regime, they failed to do so.   They were willing to shed blood in the country's defense but unwilling to take part in the civil war.   Berr, M., *Appel à la justice des nations ...* (Strasbourg 1801) p. 46.

property confiscated from emigrés and convicted persons.[45]   In Alsace, Jews usually bought more property of secondary origin.   It can therefore be concluded that the Catholic propaganda against the purchase of church property was a factor in Alsace, whereas the Jews of Bordeaux did not want to act counter to the interests of individual emigrés.

In the first half of the nineteenth century Alsatian Jews played an important role in real property transactions.   To a large measure, they had made it possible for peasants to own their own land and for city dwellers to buy their own dwellings.   At the beginning of the century, some of the land and buildings that were being bought and sold were still national or communal property and their purchase involved considerable financial risks, as the fear of the emigrés' return was generally prevalent.   Later, during the restoration, Prussian tactics in troubling the purchasers served to frighten the peasants in Moselle.   Accordingly, officials were forced to give proper assurances to the people.[46]   It therefore required considerable courage to risk such transactions, which were particularly hazardous in Alsace, where the position of the Jews was so delicate.   In 1820, when Lippmann Lippmann, a rich Jew of Nancy, paid approximately Fr. 100,000 for a farm, originally a national property, his partner Lazare Lévy refused to participate in the transaction, because of the political and financial risk involved.[47]

Jews as Agents

In the buying of national property, we must differentiate between speculators and intermediaries or agents.   To act as an intermediary or agent was normal and legal.[48]

---

[45] Marion, "Du rôle . . . , (Cf. note 25), p. 7.

[46] Thus, the Prefect of Lower-Rhine, assured the mayors in a printed letter, dated January 28, 1820, that the rumors about the reinstatement of feudal privileges and the nullification of the property sales were fantastic.   He wrote that it was the government's aim to make these sales as secure as possible.   On the eve of the revolution of 1830, the reactionaries tried to exert pressure on the peasants of Moselle, by making threats against those who had bought national property.   A. de Puymaigre, Prefect of Moselle (and later of Upper-Rhine) achieved popularity by publishing in 1820 an article in which he reassured the buyers of national property.   Gain, op. cit., vol. i, p. 5; Vidal de la Blache, P., La France de l'Est (Paris 1917) p. 93; ADBR-3M 19; Contamine, H., "La Revolution de 1830 à Metz." Revue d'histoire moderne, vol. vi (1931) 116; de Puymaigre, Comte A., Souvenirs . . . (Paris 1884) p. 213.

[47] Lippmann wrote later that such a transaction was indeed risky in 1820 because of the general fears of the strength of the reactionary party which was organizing the original owners of national property.   Volland and Xardel, Mémoire pour M. Lippmann . . . contre les créanciers du sieur Catoire de Bioncourt (Nancy 1837) p. 7.   BMN 6841.

[48] Agents were governed by law of June 3, 1793, which permitted the purchase of property for other parties (un ami ou command).   The names of such purchasers could be submitted during the six months following the purchase.   Bouloiseau proved that groups of such agents

In Alsace and neighboring departments, Catholics who hesitated to buy national property openly, often bought it through Jewish agents. Abbé L. Rumpler of Lower-Rhine stated that he, himself, bought such property in 1792 through his Jewish partner. On August 28, 1797, Samuel Séligmann of Wittersheim bought ten pieces of property for a Gentile.[49] There are also examples of transactions[50] involving the purchase of national property by Jews in partnership with Christians for commercial purposes only.

Jewish Buyers of National Property in Alsace

According to most historians, Alsatian Jews bought national property for speculation in order to resell it to the peasants. F. L'Huillier even called Jewish buyers "Jewish money-lenders who acquired national property" (*prêteurs Juifs acquéreurs de domaines nationaux*). However, not one document pertaining to national property in the departmental archives (series Q) contains such a description of Jewish buyers.[51]

There is no detailed study of national property in Lower-Rhine, where the pertinent archives are not as yet properly organized.[52] For the time being, only published studies and a few selected lists can be utilized. An analysis of selected documents indicates that there was a considerable number of Jewish buyers in Lower-Rhine, but that they were not the very first among the purchasers. Obviously Jews began buying after the first rush. It also becomes clear that historians exaggerated to a considerable extent the role of Jews in speculation with national property.[53] There is

or intermediaries were well established in the district of Rouen (Seine-Inférieur), where, incidentally, very few Jews lived. There, 67 percent of all the sales were handled by agents Bouloiseau, M., *Le Séquestre et la vente des biens des émigrés dans le district de Rouen* (Paris 1937) p. 235-36.

[49] Hildenfinger, *op. cit.*, no. 71.

[50] Samuel Mayer of Mutzig was one of several Jewish parties of Jewish and Gentile partnerships which bought national property in January 1792. Similar transactions are on record for Ribeauvillé (Upper-Rhine). Mayer Sée, a Jew, bought property with P. L. Kress, who later became the municipal agent. *Ibid.*, no. 186; Faller, Robert, *La Situation économique du canton de Ribeauvillé à l'époque du directoire* (Strasbourg 1932) p. 86-88.

[51] L'Huillier, Fernand, *Recherches sur l'Alsace napoléonienne* (Strasbourg 1947) p. 17.

[52] Series Q of the departmental archives in Lower-Rhine was not classified in 1951. To study one aspect of a subject such as national property, the scholar must have access to materials on all aspects. For example, in order to study the subject of Jewish buyers, it is first necessary to have a complete list of all the purchasers. This would require a lifetime of intensive research for the coverage of Alsace alone.

[53] In the district of Strasbourg, 271 church and secular estates were sold between 1791 and 1811; fifty-six percent of the buyers were city-dwellers. Solms-Roedelheim was able to

THE SALE OF NATIONAL PROPERTY

absolutely no indication that the number of Jewish buyers in the district of Strasbourg was large. A printed list covering 1,926,405 pounds worth of property sold in the Haguenau (Lower-Rhine) district between March and December 1791, does not contain even one definitely Jewish name. A list for this district with names of buyers of 268,891 pounds worth of property, January to June 1791, includes one identified Jew (*Meyer Weyl, Juif de Haguenau*). A printed list of transactions for January to December 1792, in the amount of 857,813 pounds, includes names of six Jews who bought 17 pieces of property for 42,000 pounds, some of it former church property. Another list for the same district, covering 150 buyers, dated February 27, 1810, contains three names of Jews.[54]

On the basis of research covering the period 1789-1803 (years VIII to XII), F. L'Huillier tried to prove that Alsatian Jews were very active speculators in national property. An analysis of the sources reveals that, through bids and auctions, 109 sales were made to Jews, but there were only 24 to 25 Jewish buyers, mostly of small parcels from one to three hectares. Of those, only sixteen had peasants as debtors. Christian buyers were the real speculators. There were only two large Jewish buyers. Cerf Jacob bought 10 parcels (a total of 21 hectares) for Fr. 13,308. Martz Lévi bought seven parcels (21 hectares) for Fr. 13,308.[55] These purchases could not compare with those made by the six biggest Christian speculators of Alsace.[56] The Christian G. F. Teutsch alone paid Fr. 1,869,020 for some of his purchases. After 1805, the number of Jewish buyers increased, as did the scope of their purchases. The number of Jewish buyers increased from 24-25 to 33-34, and sales rose to 425 hectares costing approximately Fr. 600,000. The largest number of transactions by a single Jew was 14, a total

find only a few Jews among them. His study was not too carefully made and there were probably a few more Jews. *Solms-Roedelheim, op. cit.*; Hildenfinger, *op. cit.*, p. 253. In one document we found the names of seven Jewish buyers. Six other names may be Jewish. *Registre des acquéreurs . . .* [480 auctions, December 27, 1790 - September 29, 1794]. ADBR-Q. In another document we found 23 Jewish buyers, and a few Jews who bought together with Gentiles. *Registre des contrats de vente expediés dans la forme de la loi du 28 ventose IV. Ibid.*

54 ADRR-Q.

55 At thirty auctions, where more than 400 hectares of land were sold for Fr. 4,002,525 in Lower-Rhine, Jews bought 27 hectares for Fr. 32,000. Of forty-nine bids on 900 hectares amounting to Fr. 1,203,508, Jews only bid on 90 hectares for approximately Fr. 80,000. *Cf.* note 58.

56 The Christians, G. F. Teutsch, Ch. Knoderer, L. Rausch, L. Bottemer, F. Rosat and J. P. Knoblach, formed the *Bande noire*. *Cf.* note 58.

of 102 hectares for Fr. 161,260.[57] In contrast to this, G. F. Teutsch alone bought more than all the Jews together. Jews also participated in the purchase of 600 hectares of communal property after April 1813. The Jew Théodore Cerf carried out 25 transactions and bought 60 hectares of land and a building. However, Teutsch engaged in 66 transactions and bought 250 hectares of land and buildings.[58]

Nowhere is there a detailed study of national property for the Upper-Rhine. Here and there a Jewish name can be found among the buyers.[59] There was not one Jew among the buyers in Ricquewihr between 1794 and 1797 (194,293 pounds). There were, however, a few Jewish buyers in Ribeauvillé. The greatest number of speculators came from Colmar, where at the beginning of the revolution, Jews were not even permitted to reside. F. L'Huillier also writes that there were only about a dozen Jewish buyers in Upper-Rhine. Only one Jew bought a large property costing Fr. 46,155.[60] Our conclusion is that Jews bought national property in Alsace, but not to any great extent, and that their speculation with this property has been greatly exaggerated by chroniclers and historians.

Purchases in the Department of Moselle

One would assume that in the department of Moselle, with its large Jewish community of Metz, Jews were large purchasers of national property, particularly since they were not permitted to buy buildings outside the Metz ghetto before the revolution, and almost a third of all the property sold in Metz consisted of buildings. Jews were even urged to buy national property. Here, too, it was proposed that they be forced to buy it.[61] There were Jews in Moselle who did buy national property.[62] The extent

[57] Other numbers of purchases by Jews are as follows: Two concluded transactions each (11 and 26 hectares); three from 4 to 6 transactions each; and the remainder from 1 to 3 transactions, often involving less than one hectare. *Cf.* note 58.

[58] L'Huillier, *op. cit.,* p. 473-79.

[59] Definitive conclusions on Jewish participation will have to wait for the publication of a detailed study. To complicate matters, Series Q for Upper-Rhine of the departmental archives seems to be far from complete.

[60] Zeyer, F., "La vente des biens nationaux à Ricquewihr." *Societe d'archéologie de Ricquewihr,* no. xiv (1930) 13-87; Faller, R., "La situation économique de Ricquewihr . . . 1795-1799." *Ibid.,* no. xviii (1939) 14, 49; Ginsburger, M., "Arrêtés . . . ," L'Huillier, *op. cit.,* p. 479.

[61] L. S. Mercier's newspaper printed a correspondence from Metz, proposing that Jews be forced to shave off their beards, dissolve their community organizations, pay off the communal debts owed to Christian creditors, and be deported, if after six months, they would be unable to prove that they had bought national property. Marion, *op. cit.,* vol. ii, p. 546; *Annales partriotiques et littéraires* (October 16, 1793) 1346.

[62] On June 21, 1806, the prefect of Moselle wrote to the Minister of the Interior that Joseph Hertz of Sarreguemines, a candidate for the Paris Sanhedrin, had an excellent reputation

of such purchases will never be known because of the destruction of the series Q of the departmental archives during World War II before their examination by historians. According to other sources which are very limited in scope, the Jews of Moselle bought very little national property. There were only a few Jewish purchasers in the district of Briey.[63] A. Gain, whose writings are often unfriendly to Jews, states that Jewish creditors collected their debts, but failed to utilize the mortgages on properties of emigrés held by them to purchase national property. Many Jewish creditors were impoverished, and the small creditors did not have sufficient resources to buy.[64] Not a single Jew was listed in a printed list of buyers from the Metz district from December 15, 1790 to May 31, 1791.[65]

Purchases in the Departments of Meuse, Vosges, Meurthe and in Other Localities

There were several rich Jews in the department of Meurthe. Here, Jews were active in the real estate business, but not to the same extent as in Alsace. There is on record the name of only one important Jewish real estate dealer during the early years of the revolution. He was Jacob Brisac of Lunéville.[66] The number of Jews in this business increased in Lorraine during the revolution's later years. It seems that Jews were not very active in the purchase of national property.[67]

A good inventory exists of dossiers of sales, which includes the names of the buyers.[68] However, caution must be exercised in the identification

because he had made his huge fortune from speculation in national property. On July 21, 1796, the Jewish community of Metz submitted a bid for national property adjacent to the Jewish cemetery. ADM, V 149; Archives of the Metz Consistory (soumission no. 2302).

[63] Here 274 inhabitants bought 434 parcels of land; most of the buyers were peasants, but at the end of the year IV, city-dwellers also began to buy. Among them were the Jews, Samuel Cahen and Cerf Worms. At the sale of 1813, one Christian bought ten percent of the property sold. Contamine, *op. cit.*, vol. i, p. 124-25.

[64] Gain, *op. cit.*, vol. ii, p. 265.

[65] This list is composed of the names of 375 buyers who bought property originally valued at 1,620,168 pounds, for 3,150,235 pounds. *Département de la Moselle. District de Metz. Vente des biens nationaux depuis le* 15 *decembre* 1790, *jusqu'au* 31 *mai* 1791 (Metz s.d.). BN-Lb 41-5198; Paquet, *op. cit.*, p. 1264-1276.

[66] *Table alphabétique des vendeurs* . . . ADMM-Q.

[67] In the district of Toul, speculation in national property was especially heavy, but the historian of the sale of national property of primary origin for this district, failed to mention the role of the Jews. Ollier, Jean, *La Vente des biens nationaux de première origine dans le district de Toul* (Nancy 1949) (manuscript). ADMM 5861. There is no general study of the sale of national property for this department.

[68] *Inventaire de la serie Q,* vol. xii-xvii (manuscript). ADMM.

of their religion from their names.[69]   Among the buyers of national property
of primary origin in the department of Meurthe (April 20, 1791-September
5, 1795), less than ten were Jews.[70]

In the district of Nancy, there were only two purchases by a Jew,
namely by Beer Isaac Beer [Berr] in 1794.[71]   On the other hand, there were
some Jewish buyers in the district of Sarrebourg.[72]   In the six other districts, there does not seem to have been even one Jewish buyer.   Jewish
participation was greater in the third sale of property in this department
(June 4, 1796 to January 29, 1800) with 30 out of almost 3,000 sales.[73]   In
the last period (from January 1800 to the 1860's), in which there were
1,474 purchases, there were only a few Jewish participants.[74]

There were several Alsatian Jews living in Rouen (Seine-Inférieure),
but there was not even one Jew among the buyers of national property in
this city.[75]   During the revolution, a few Alsatian Jewish families which
settled in Dijon (Côte D'Or) bought national property.[76]   Of the 901 buyers of national property in the districts of Remiremont and Epinal (Vosges)
two were Jews.[77]   According to a confirmation issued by the city, the Lipp-

---

[69] The names in the inventory must be compared with the original transaction documents in
series Q, because a name which sounds characteristically Jewish is not always that of a Jew.
For example, the speculators Picard were the Christians Dominique and Louis Ferdinand
Picard. Lang is the Christian Mathias Lang. Antoine Fromenthal, a heavy speculator, was
a Christian; Victoire Olry, one of the most active speculators, was a Christian.

[70] Among the Jewish buyers were Cerf Beer [Berr], with two purchases (March 12, 1793)
and Raphaël (October 8, 1794). The buyers of property of secondary origin in the district of
Blâmont, include Isaie Spire with two purchases and Wolff (possibly a Jew), with one purchase. Altogether, there were 334 sales of property of secondary origin in the district. See
note 68.

[71] Cf. Godechot, J., "Les Juifs à Nancy de 1789 à 1795." REJ, vol. lxxxvii (1929) 34.

[72] Elias Solomon made 20 purchases (between 1794 and 1798). Israel Lévy made nine purchases, and Jacob, possibly a Jew, made 20 purchases. Cf. note 68.

[73] The name of the Jew Isaie Spire appears in connection with 29 transactions (including two
in partnership with the Christian Claudel) ; that of Raphaël Abraham in three; of Lazard
and Israël Lévy in three; of Louis Isaac Beer in two; and of Kahn, in one transaction. There
were also a few transactions involving the name Brisac, which probably referred to Jacob
Brisac of Lunéville. Cf. note 68.

[74] The following Jews participated: Spire - six transactions, Lippmann and Son in seven,
various Lévys in fifteen, and Lion in one transaction. Cf. note 68.

[75] Bouloiseau, op. cit.

[76] In a petition to the Minister of the Interior, submitted in 1810, in which they asked to be
exempted from the decree of March 17, 1808, the Jews of Dijon wrote that the Sanhedrin
delegate David Blum, who had settled there in 1790, owned national property. His father,
Samuel Blum, had his entire fortune tied up in it. Salomon Israél, a soldier who had been
wounded in battle, "showed his loyalty to France by buying national property." The Jews
Abraham Cahen, Hubert Aaron and Leman Lévy did the same. The document is in the
possession of the Library of the Jewish Theological Seminary of America.

[77] AN-BB 16-912 (B. Lévy); Schwab, op. cit.

mann brothers, Mayer, Oulry, and Lippmann, bought national property in Verdun (Meuse).[78] Julien Rovère wrote that in the occupied territory on the left bank of the Rhine, many Jews had an interest in companies which would buy large estates and sell them to peasants in small parcels. F. Bodmann, a well-known economist of the first Empire, wrote that few Jews bought national property in the department of Mont-Tonnerre, but that Gentile buyers were able to borrow money from Jewish money-lenders. Jews, he wrote, received the hatred, but others got the profits.[79]

Purchases in Southern France

According to all indications, the Sephardic Jews of southwestern France, should have bought much national property. Yet they failed to do so. Some 51 Jews of Bordeaux bought 93 buildings and 60 parcels of land suitable for building, for Fr. 5,500,000. The original value of these properties was Fr.2,000,000. Almost all of them were of primary origin and almost all were concentrated in the neighborhood of Bouhaut and Cahernan Streets, the voluntary ghetto before 1789. Most of these properties were bought from the Carmes, who used to rent them to Jews. Only two or three purchases were made in other neighborhoods, none for speculation or cultivation. At that time, it was considered a sign of opulence to buy a piece of land near town. Since, in the whole department of Gironde, there were 900 buyers, 570 of whom were from Bordeaux, it must be concluded that the Jews of Bordeaux bought national property with great hesitation because they lacked confidence in the whole business. Of course, not all the Jews were rich enough to buy national property. Of 400 Jewish families in Bordeaux in 1806, only 200 owned the houses in which they lived. In any case, there can be no question of speculation with national property by Bordeaux Jews. It is interesting to note that the millionaire family Gradis was not among the buyers.[80]

Interesting are the actions of the Jews of St.-Esprit, where the Jews were in the majority and where the Jacobin Club consisted almost entirely of them. Situated across the river from Bayonne, this town was a great commercial center and had considerable capital available. The revolution, the *assignats* and other factors ruined trade and credit; the townspeople

[78] *Certificats delivrés, par les autorités militaires et civiles, à messieurs Lippmann (frères)* . . . (Verdun [1808]). AN-F 19-11009.
[79] Rovère, J., *La Rive gauche du Rhin de 1792 à 1814* (Paris 1919) p. 186; Bodmann, F., *Annuaire statistique du Mont-Tonnere pour l'an 1809* (Mayence 1810) p. 124.
[80] Marion, "Du rôle . . . ," (*Cf*. note 25) p. 7-19; *Idem, La vente* . . . p. 55-65; T. Malzevin, *Histoire des Juifs à Bordeaux* (Bordeaux 1875) p. 285.

hoarded gold, silver, and other precious articles, and tried to make their fortunes secure by buying national property. Jews, too, engaged in purchases, but not more than the Gentiles. In that town, where there were many rich Jews, quite a number of Jewish speculators were arrested, together with many Gentile ones. In 1812, the mayor of St.-Esprit wrote that the Jews deserved their equality because they had become land owners; by this he probably meant that they had bought national property.[81]

In other parts of southern France, purchases by Jews were minimal. In the department of Vaucluse, where 2,000 Jews lived before the revolution in the four communities of Avignon, Carpentras, Cavaillon and Isle-sur-Sorgue, there was only one Jewish buyer, namely, Precieuse Beaucaire of Isle-sur-Sorgue, who bought property for 42,432 pounds.[82] Most rich Jews left the department and settled in neighboring ones, but here, too, there were only some five Jewish buyers in comparison with the total number of 2,725 buyers of buildings alone.[83] In the department of Rhone, where Jews had already settled in Lyon, there was not one Jew among the buyers.[84] There were only 11 Jews among the buyers in the department of Bouches-du-Rhone.[85] Jews in Nice were active participants in revolutionary activity, although they were not exactly welcomed with open arms. Victor Emanuel wrote that they dealt in national property.[86]

Effects of Nationalization on Jewish Communal Property

It is necessary to touch briefly on the effect of the nationalization of Church property on Jewish communal property. Jewish community

---

[81] The rich Jew, Benjamin Louis Nounez, whose fortune during the revolution, was estimated at 1,200,000 pounds, had to exchange all his money for *assignats*. To stabilize his finances he purchased a nationalized estate on the banks of the river Adour. The famous Chateau Maurac was sold as national property to a Spaniard, who sold it to the Jew Margfoy, from whom Napoleon I purchased it in 1808. ADL V6; Ginsburger, Ernest, *Le Comité de surveillance de Jean-Jacques Rousseau* . . . (Paris 1936); Léon, H., *op. cit.*, p. 169, 419-20.

[82] Chobaut, "Les Juifs d'Avignon et du Comtat et la révolution française, *REJ*, vol. cii (1938) 35-36.

[83] Jean Jaurès could find only one Jewish buyer in the department of Gard, namely, Crémieux, who bought 150,000 pounds worth of property of primary origin. Actually, there were four other Jewish buyers (Jessé Carcassonne, David and Jacob Carcassonne, Moyse Vidal). Jaurès, *op. cit.*, p. 506; Rouviere, François, *L'Aliénation des biens nationaux dans le Gard* (Nimes 1900) p. 19, 133, 501, 649.

[84] Charléty, Sébastien, *Département du Rhône. Document relatifs à la vente des biens nationaux* (Lyon 1906).

[85] Moise Alphandéry, Michael Bédarrides, Michel Bédarrides, Abraham Carcassonne, Bénedict Carcassonne, Jacob Carcassonne, Hananel-David Crémieux, Moise-Hanael Crémieu, Salomon-Haim Crémieu, Jasse-Haim Crémieu, Mardoché Crémieu. Cf. Moulin, Paul, *Documents relatifs à la vente des biens nationaux* (Marseille 1911) 4 vols.

[86] Emanuel, Victor, *Les Juifs de Nice*, 1400-1860 (Nice 1905) p. 48.

property was undoubtedly expropriated, and there is much proof of this.[87] However, for various reasons, expropriation of Jewish property was not as consistent — not to say as brutal — as was that of church property. The Jewish communities did not own as much property as the church, their properties were not as valuable nor did they present any danger to the state. Wherever they could, Jews secretly, and often openly, fought against the nationalization of their communities' properties. In Metz, the Jews attempted to prevent the nationalization of the synagogue.[88] In Bordeaux, the Jews fought stubbornly against the nationalization of their community's property, especially of the cemetery, which belonged to the community's philanthropic society. This case was used as an argument against the government's acceptance of responsibility for the payment of Jewish communal debts which were never taken over by it.[89]

A brief treatment of communal property (*biens communaux*) is in order. There were protests against the sharing by Jews of such properties.[90] In Ribeauvillé, the Jews did benefit from the distribution of communal

[87] Most Jewish communities were in debt to Christian creditors, from whom they had to borrow before 1789 in order to cover their communal expenses. During the revolution, Jews demanded that these debts be taken over by the government, and one of the reasons given was that Jewish communal property had been nationalized. In 1797, a committee of the Council of Five-Hundred reported favorably on the Jewish demands. *Rapport fait par Chappuis, au nous d'une commission composée des représentans du peuple Grégoire, Laurençot (du Jura), Saladin & Chappuis. Séance du 16. germinal [an V]* (Paris an V). *Rapport fait par Saladin . . . sur les pétitions des Juifs de Metz & d'Avignon. Séance du 7 Fructidor an V* (Paris an V). 15 p.; *Rapport fait par Riou sur les pétitions des Juifs de Metz & d'Avignon, au nom d'une commission spéciale. Séance du 4 frimaire an VI* (Paris an VI).

[88] Cahen, A., *Le Rabbinat de Metz.* Reprint from *REJ*, vol. vii-xiv, p. 78.

[89] The cemetery land was bought in the names of a few Jewish individuals. When the administration of the department of Girone confiscated the property and sought to sell it, the Jews protested. The community's attempt to have some Jews buy back the property in their own names failed. It was bought by Gentiles. The Jews then demanded that the transaction be declared null and void, because the cemetery was not officially communal property and was a philanthropic undertaking. The administration of Girone acceded to the Jewish demands, but the conflicts with the buyers and enemies of the Jews could not be avoided. The matter was even taken up in Paris. *Mémoire à consulter et consultation pour les citoyens français, professant le culte judaïque à Bordeaux, connus sous le nom de Juifs portugais et avignonais* (s.l. [an VII]). *Despiau et Pujol, Réponse à un mémoire imprimé sous le nom des citoyens français, professant le culte judaïque à Bordeaux.* (I did not see this pamphlet); *Rapport fait par prévot sur une petition des citoyens Pujol & Despiau, sou-missionnaires de biens appartenans aux Juifs établis en cette commune. Séance du 21 germinal an VII* (Paris an VII); *Opinion de [F.B.] Darracq dans l'affaire des Juifs de Bordeaux. Séance du 18 floreal an VII* (Paris an VII); de B[eaufleury], L. F., *Histoire de l'établissement des Juifs à Bordeaux et à Bayonne depuis 1550* (Paris 1799) p. 157-95.

[90] On April 15, 1790, Duc de la Rochefoucault stated that people in Alsace were so sure that Jews would be granted citizenship, that they were already being assigned shares in communal property to be given immediately after the promulgation of the decree. However, three of the communes where he said such action had been taken, protested. They argued that they could not do it because they did not want Jews to live among them. *Observation intéressante, relative a la demande du droit de citoyens actifs, faite au nom des Juifs d'Alsace* (s.l. [1790]). 2 p.

property,[91] but such instances were rare in Alsace. In the year III, Jews from Lower-Rhine complained that they were not given the opportunity to share in the parcelization of communal property. They also complained that taxes were more equitably distributed in countries where slavery was practiced than in Alsace, because the Jews were taxed there out of all proportion to their wealth and numbers.[92] There was even greater discrimination against the poorest peasants (*manants*) in connection with the distribution of communal property. Here Alsace's reactionary character became evident. Jews were especially singled out for persecution because the weak and defenseless were the natural objects thereof. In the distribution of communal property, the administration of Upper-Rhine wanted to maintain the principle of dividing the inhabitants into *bourgeois* and *manants*. The directoire of Lower-Rhine ordered the communes to distribute communal property without regard to the recipients' previous status. However, after the issuance of the decree of June 10, 1793, which ordered distribution according to the inhabitants' needs, very few Alsatian communes made any effort to carry out its provisions. The same was true for neighboring departments.[93]

Land Parcelization through Commercial Transactions in National Property

Very few Jews bought national property for farming purposes. It was difficult for Jews who had never legally been permitted to own real property outside of the ghetto and who had been prevented from engaging in farming and labor to become farmers and workers overnight, particularly during such chaotic times.[94] Most Jewish buyers purchased national property for resale or trade.

Jews played an important role in the parcelization of land in northeastern France. Here they made it practicable for masses of peasants to become landowners by offering parcels on credit or lending funds for

---

[91] Faller, *op. cit.*, p. 93.

[92] AN-BB 30-102.

[93] J. L. Fesquet, who traveled in that area, wrote that he saw neglected farmland on one side of a bridge over the Moselle and cultivated land on the other side. He was told that the tilled land was distributed communal property, while the untilled land was communal property which had not been distributed and could, therefore, only be used for pasture. Véron-Réville, *La Révolution* . . . p. 21; *Les Administrateurs du directoire du département du Bas-Rhin, aux communes de leur arrondissement*, 25 Prairial, an II. 4 p. BN-Lk 4-731, I, 65; Ortlieb, Jean Michel, *Plan et instructions fondées sur l'expérience* . . . (Strasbourg 1789) p. 35-36. BN-S 15971; F[esquet]. *op. cit.*, p. 22-23.

[94] The degree of "productivization" of French Jewry cannot be judged by the proportion of peasants and workers among them. The idea that a productive occupation was synonymous

the purchase of not only national properties but also of land acquired from other sources which they bought and sold to a much larger extent. This aspect is, however, also beyond the limits of the present study.

It is almost impossible to determine how much of the land bought and sold was originally national property. Resales, frequently in small parcels, played an important role in the parcelization. It will probably never be possible to establish the extent of Jewish participation in this process.[95]

It is also impossible to ascertain in this study whether peasants in Alsace and neighboring departments owned the land they tilled before 1789, or whether they acquired it later by purchases of national and other property.[96] The present author's conclusions are that in Alsace and in neighboring departments most peasants became land owners after 1789. One of the greatest achievements of the revolution was the creation of a class of free and independent peasants, which assured the permanent cessation of the nobility's control of agricultural land and made impossible the seizure of power by that class. This way the restoration had no alternative but to permit the continuation of the new system of land ownership.[97]

However, the revolution because of its great need of money only divided the land by giving everyone an opportunity to buy confiscated property. Even the peasants had to buy some of the feudal land rights (*rentes rachetables*). No organized credit existed and that is why in most

with labor or farming was foreign to France. A Jewish peddler, who was fortunate enough to become a rich and successful merchant, became productive, according to the concept of his times. Sometimes, he would even be awarded a medal by the government. This, however, is a subject for a separate study.

[95] George Pariset stated that the history of the resales will never be written because of the complexity of the research involved. It is made more complicated by the use of assumed names (*prête-noms*) in the transactions. Pariset, G., *Etudes d'histoire révolutionnaire et contemporaire* (Paris 1929) p. 94-95.

[96] One school of historians seeks to prove that most peasants owned even before 1789 the land which they worked and that the chief beneficiaries of the sale of national property were the city-dwellers. We must, however, keep in mind that any discussion of the consequences of the sale of national property is greatly influenced by the subjective attitude of the historian to the revolution. Concerning the objective historians (J. Loutchisky and others), their attitude depends on the documents selected, and on the department and period studied by them. This matter will be considered more fully in a separate study to deal with Alsace.

[97] This conclusion is not likely to meet with the approval of a considerable number of Alsatian historians. However, even a reactionary like Abbé Charles Hoffmann does not deny that a large number of Alsatian peasants did not own even a small piece of land before the revolution. As L. de Lavergne points out, nobody wanted to be an agricultural laborer after 1789, everyone preferring to be his own master. In the neighborhood of Bischwiller, not only permanently settled peasants, but even servants, recent newcomers, bought land during the

cases the peasant had to apply for loans to private money-lenders or usurers. In Alsace and the neighboring departments, a large percentage of the money-lenders who helped the peasants to become land-owners were Jews.

In countless documents and chronicles, Jews were accused of selling small parcels of land and of breaking up large estates and of holding peasants in indebtedness.[98] Jews did not deny it. On June 28, 1810, and on August 19, 1814, the Jewish Central Consistory wrote to the Minister of the Interior, that it is well known to every Frenchman that before the revolution, the Alsatian peasants had no property; and that they bought land during the revolution and borrowed the money to pay for it from Jews. These debts could have been repaid with 1/15 of the newly purchased property, but instead of repaying them, the peasants began making demands on the Jewish creditors.[99] The same information is mentioned by

revolution. J. L. Fesquet states that during the *assignats'* heyday, the income from harvests of two to four years afforded a peasant enough to pay for land bought. In 1805 the prefect of Upper-Rhine wrote that during the revolution the peasants bought up expropriated church lands which they had previously rented from the church. On the eve of the Hundred Days (*Cent Jours*), Comte de Kergarion wrote that the peasants favored the revolution because it gave them an opportunity to become landowners. The same statement was made by a deputy for Lower-Rhine on October 8, 1807, and by the prefect of Upper-Rhine in 1818. The author of a history of public notaries in Alsace-Lorraine, calls these peasants who bought land during the revolution *cultivateurs-propriétaires* (farmers-owners). Because of the sale of national and communal property, the number of landowners in 1789 (year IX) was increased by 13,743 in Moselle, and by 7,242 in Meurthe, while the number of farmhand day laborers decreased from 18,221 to 10,997 in Moselle, and from 20,836 to 16,437 in Meurthe. L. Schwab called this true "democratization of land." This was also the case in other parts of the country, *e.g.,* Bouches-du-Rhône. In Vaucluse, the peasants were no less anxious to own land than in Alsace. Hoffmann, *op. cit.,* vol. i, p. 181; de Lavergne, Léonce, *Economie rurale de la France* (Paris 1860) p. 168; Bourguignon, Eugène, *Bischwiller depuis cent ans* (Bischwiller 1875) p. 163; Fesquet, *op. cit.,* p. 35; ADHR-M 42-1; Leuilliot, Paul, "L'Opposition libérale en Alsace à la fin de la restauration." *Deux siécles d'Alsace française* (Paris 1948) p. 292; AN-F 19-11011 (*Mémoire du 8 octobre 1807 sur les créances des Juifs*); Leuilliot, P., "L'Alsace en 1815." *RA,* vol. lxxv (1928) 549-50; Bernard, E., *La Réforme du notariat en Alsace-Lorraine* (Henin-Lietard 1907) p. 123; Hottenger, G., *La Lorraine économique au lendemain de la révolution d'après les mémoires statistiques des préfets de l'an IX* (Nancy 1924) p. 43; Schwab, *Documents, op. cit.,* vol. i, p. vi, p. vi, xli-xlii, lxxxi; Masson, P., *Le Bouches-du-Rhône, Encyclopédie départementale,* 2e partie, vol. vii (1928) p. 2-32; Lefebure, George, *Questions agraires au temps de la terreur* (Strasbourg 1932).

[98] A memorandum of the Conseil Général of Lower-Rhine, in the year X, contains such a statement. In the same year, the prefect of Lower-Rhine wrote that because of this, peasants are in debt to Jews; the commissioners, appointed by Napoleon I to prepare a report on the Jews, made the same statement in March 1807; on October 8, 1807, the same statement was repeated by Metz, deputy for Lower-Rhine; and in 1810, by the prefect of Lower-Rhine. L'Huillier, *op. cit.,* p. 520-21; ADBR-3MS; AN-AF IV, 300, dr. 2150; Fauchille, Paul, *La Question juive en France sous le premier empire* (Paris 1884) p. 8-9; Lemoine, A., *Napoleon et les Juifs* (Paris 1900) p. 38; AN-F 19-11011; Anchel, R., *Napoléon et les Juifs* (Paris 1928) p. 121-22; Lambla, J. B., "L'Esprit public dans le Bas-Rhin sous la première restauration." *L'Alsace française,* vol. ii (March 1922) 190.

[99] ACC, 45, minutes; Halphen, A. E., *Recueil des lois ... concernant les Israélites ...* (Paris 1851) p. 325; Anchel, R., "Contribution levée en 1813-1814 sur les Juifs du Haut-Rhin." *REJ,* vol. lxxxii (1926) 500.

many historians, both with pro-and anti-Jewish points of view.[100] Not all of them, however, describe the Jewish role in parcelization as a positive development.

The revolution's principle of a free economy (except for the interference of the war) was also applied to agriculture. It did not lead to a concentration of large estates; on the contrary, it lead to an opportunity for everyone to become one's own master. The church, the wealthy classes, and, in later years, the administration and the intellectuals, with rare exception, opposed the parcelization of land and frowned on the rise of a new class of small land-holders. Like the bourgeois theoreticians, Charles Fourier was opposed to land parcelization. However his opposition was based on his collectivist position.[101]

It should be remembered that the families of emigrés, priests, and reactionaries were opposed to the sale of national property. To the charge that Jews were involved in the sales of national property was added the accusation that through their dealings in land and through making loans to peasants, Jews helped to parcelize the land.[102] This was viewed as detrimental to agriculture. The writings of the Alsatian historian Abbé Charles Hoffmann (1855-1905) are very characteristic of this kind of thinking. One of his main accusations against the Jews was that before 1789, and primarily afterwards, the Jews helped to parcelize the land, by dealing in national property.[103]

The Jewish historian M. Liber tried to deny the anti-Jewish accusations of speculation in national property by accepting a position advocated

100 Szyster, Boruch, *La Révolution française et les Juifs* (Toulouse 1929) p. 129; Spaer, E., *Le Juifs de Fance et l'égalité des droits civiques* . . . (Paris 1933) p. 53-54; Baumont, H., *Historie de Lunéville* (Lunéville 1900) p. 468; Lefebure, *op. cit.,* p. 9; Hoffmann, *op. cit.,* vol. i, p. 183.

101 Leroy-Beaulieu, P., *Essai sur la répartition des richesses* . . . (Paris 1881) p. 163; Fourier, Charles, *Traité de l'association,* vol. i (Paris 1822) p. 9-10; *Idem, Théorie de l'unité universelle,* vol. ii (Paris 1841-45) p. 11-12; Silbering, F., *Dictionnaire de sociologie phalanstérienne* (Paris 1911) p. 11-12, 286.

102 Among historians, chroniclers and politicians, there was a synthesis of the attitudes of devotion to the old feudal regime, opposition to the nationalization of property, the parcelization of the land and traditional antisemitism. It resulted in the conclusion that Jews were a danger to the Alsatian peasantry, because Jews helped peasants to become owners of small parcels of land.

103 His history, however, has the good point of not even attempting to be objective. He has but one aim; to utilize the background of the 18th century in order to combat the achievements of the revolution, the nationalization of church property, parcelization of land, etc. In order to achieve this aim, he seeks first of all to prove three things, namely, that conditions were better before 1789, that the relationship between the church and the peasantry was ideal, and that Jews were responsible for all the bad acts of the revolution. Antisemitism

by some historians; to wit, that the new city bourgeoisie gained conrol of almost all the national property and created a new bourgeois nobility. Liber concluded that the new nobility carried on the propaganda that Jews had enslaved the peasants. [104]   However, it had never been definitely established that peasants did not benefit from the sale of national property.

Instead of accepting the point of view of the chroniclers and historians who see the parcelization of land as the beginning of a bad agricultural system, let us try to consider the condition and psychology of the peasants. They were not very much concerned with the future of agriculture as a whole. For them parcelization was a blessing, because it permitted them to realize a dream: to become their own masters. Individualism in agriculture was a strong French movement which began even before 1789.[105]   This movement was not detrimental to France, certainly not to its republican freedom. Wherever Jews helped to create individualism in agriculture, they were a blessing for the peasantry, even if the peasant had to pay usurious rates of interest on loans, because there was no organized system of agricultural credit.

is a carefully thought out means of introducing his historical opposition to an independent peasantry, and to the confiscation of church property during the revolution. Hoffmann, op. cit., vol. i, p. 85.

[104] Liber, M., "Napoléon et les Juifs . . . " REJ, vol. lxxii (1921) 12.

[105] Bloch, Marc, "La Lutte pour l'individualisme dans la France du XVIIIe siècle." Annales d'histoire économique et sociale (1930).

OCCUPATIONAL PROBLEMS OF
JEWISH EMANCIPATION
IN FRANCE, 1789-1800

I

RESTRICTIONS DURING THE OLD REGIME

THE nature of Jewish occupations was cited as a major
argument both in favor of and against Jewish emancipation in the course of the great debate on that issue after
the outbreak of the French Revolution in 1789.

During the old regime Jews were permitted to engage
only in certain occupations, namely, money lending, horse
and cattle trading, selected branches of commerce, peddling,
and similar activities. No Jews were admitted into either
industry or agriculture. And even in those economic activities which were normally open to them, the Jews had to
struggle bitterly in order to maintain their positions. The
right, sometimes granted, to engage exclusively in business
activities was often an empty one. Most Ashkenazic Jews
of Alsace and neighboring provinces enjoyed such a right in
localities where almost no business opportunities existed.[1]

Even the economic pursuits of the privileged Sephardim
were restricted to the field of commerce. The Jewish leader
of Bordeaux, Salomon Lopes Dubec (1743-1837), recorded
this fact in his autobiographical notes.[2] The Jews of Saint-

---

[1] S. Posener, "The Immediate Economic and Social Effects of the Emancipation of the Jews in France," *Jewish Social Studies*, I (1939), 271, 281; Z.
Szajkowski, *The Economic Status of the Jews in Alsace, Metz and Lorraine
1648-1789* (New York, 1954), p. 25.

[2] "On me fit apprendre à lire le français et l'hébreu; à écrire, l'arithmétique et les opérations de changes: c'était alors la seule instruction qu'on
donnait aux enfants israélites qui, se trouvant exclus par les lois du royaume
de toutes les professions, même des arts et métiers, pour l'exercice desquels il
fallait être de la religion catholique, n'étaient uniquement destinés qu'au
commerce" (in the General Historical Archives of Israel, Jerusalem).

Originally published in *Historia Judaica*, vol. XXI (1959).

Esprit-lès-Bayonne introduced the manufacture of chocolate
in France, but in the 1760's the Christians tried to take this
business away from them.[3]   In Bordeaux and Saint-Esprit
Jews were prohibited from keeping open shops or selling
merchandise at retail.   Every year lawsuits were provoked
by this prohibition, as in 1631-1632, when Christian merchants and the city council of Bordeaux brought an action
against George Roderigues, whose defense was financed by
the *nation* of the Marranos of the same city.[4] The first
scheduled election to the Chamber of Commerce of Bordeaux, on May 10, 1787, was canceled because a Jew, David
Gradis, received one vote.[5]

II

DISCUSSIONS ON JEWISH PRODUCTIVITY
DURING THE FIGHT FOR EMANCIPATION

During the fight for Jewish emancipation its adversaries argued that the Jews were unworthy of French citizenship because they were engaged exclusively in unproductive
and dishonest economic pursuits.   The champions of Jewish
emancipation replied that the many anti-Jewish restrictions
of the old regime were responsible for this.   The lawyer
Pierre-Louis Lacretelle stated even earlier, in 1775, that the
Jew, "by force of oppression and contempt, was reduced to
seek refuge in fraud and to revenge himself by the practice
of usury."[6] Adolphe Thiéry, recipient of a prize awarded

---

[3] H. Léon, *Histoire des juifs de Bayonne* (Paris, 1893), pp. 69-76.
[4] Archives départmentales de la Gironde. E. Lafité's notarial minutes,
1631, fol. 703, and 1632, fol. 257-58; Léon, *op. cit.*, p. 77. A few rare
exceptions were made in later years. Thus, on Oct. 31, 1759, Vidal Lange
obtained permission to have a shop for silk and cloth (city archives of Bordeaux,
HH16). But in general the prohibition was in force until the outbreak of
the Revolution.
[5] Departmental archives of Gironde, C 4258. Much later Rabbi Isaac
Lévy stated in a sermon that Jews "were enclosed in the circle of one single
occupation," *Le Centenaire 1792 au temple israélite de Bordeaux. Discours . . .
22 septembre 1892* (Bordeaux, 1892), p. 6. See also E. Ducéré's introduction
to Léon, *op. cit.*, p. x ("Le Commerce, qui était seul permis aux juifs").
[6] *Oeuvres de P. L. Lacretelle*, I (Paris, 1823), vj.

by the Academy of Metz for his essay on Jews, wrote: "We are the ones who should be accused of the crimes unjustly blamed on Jews . . . we should lay the responsibility on the barbarous conduct of our fathers."[7] Abbé Henri-Baptist Grégoire wrote in his essay, also awarded a prize by the same Academy: "The Jews' offences, their misfortune, accuse our conduct toward them. Nations, lament and confess that this is your work! The Jews presented the results, but you laid down the basis for them: who are the more responsible?"[8] In the course of the discussion on Jews held on December 23, 1789, at the National Assembly, Stanislaus de Clermont-Tonnerre made the following statement: "Men who have only money can be only as good as money is; there lies the evil. If they had land and a fatherland they would not lend money anymore; there is the remedy."[9] During the same discussion Robespierre remarked that the Jews would become honest only when the restrictions imposed on them were abolished.[10] Similar expressions of opinion were made on February 4, 1790, in a resolution of the Saint-Joseph district of Paris in favor of Jewish emancipation[11] and in a report on the same subject submitted by Vion.[12] "Humiliation and slavery extinguished all emulation and skill among the Jews. Slaves in chains lose everything," wrote Abbé A.-

[7] A. Thiéry, *Dissertation sur cette question: Est-il des moyens de rendre les juifs plus heureux et utiles en France?* (Paris, 1788), p. 29.

[8] Henri Grégoire, *Essai sur la régénération . . . des juifs.* (Paris, 1789), pp. 32, 44.

[9] *Opinion de M. le Comte Stanislas de Clermont-Tonnere, député de Paris; le 23 décembre 1789* (Paris, n.d.), p. 12; Charles du Bus, *Stanislas Clermont-Tonnere . . .* (Paris, 1931), p. 213.

[10] "Après les avoir exclus de tous les honneurs, même des droits à l'estime publique, nous ne leur avons laissé que les objets de spéculation lucrative. . . . Les vices des juifs naissent de l'avilissement dans lequel vous les avez plongés; ils seront bons quand ils pourront trouver quelque avantage à l'être," *Revue des grandes journées parlementaires*, I (1897), 12-13.

[11] "C'est aux Loix en général qu'il faut imputer les vices des hommes beaucoup plus qu'à la Nature qui les destina aux impressions qu'on veut leur donner," *Addresse de l'Assemblée des Représentants de la Commune de Paris . . .* (Paris, 1790), p. 10.

[12] "Si nous en accuson les juifs, n'oublions pas que les vices et l'ignorance des uns et des autres sont l'ouvrage des Peuples que leur ont donné l'asyle; que l'avilissement de tous est le fruit des institutions qui les ont environnés. . . . Le comble de l'injustice est donc de reprocher aux Juifs le crime que nous les forçons de commetre," *Rapport fait par M. Vion . . .* (Paris, 1790), p. 15.

A. Lamourette, author of a pro-Jewish pamphlet published
in 1790. Another pamphleteer, J.-B. Sanchamau, wrote:
"We extorted from them all means of subsistence and re-
proach them for acting towards us cunningly and cleverly."
So also wrote the pro-Jewish pamphleteers Valois and
Vieillard.[13]

These arguments greatly influenced the struggle for
Jewish emancipation. But despite their highly humanitarian
character, they show that even the best friends of the Jews
did not really know much about Jewish life. Most of them
spoke of usury practiced by Jews as a sort of "revenge."
Jewish trades were presented not only as unproductive, but
also as dishonest, criminal. A Jewish character in a pamphlet
on Jewish emigration from Carpentras said that anti-Jewish
restrictions killed honesty among the Jews and forced them
into criminal pursuits.[14]

Even leaders of the fight against Jewish emancipation
recognized the fact that the anti-Jewish restrictions of the
old regime had forced the Jews to engage in unproductive
trades. Statements to this effect were made on August 5,
1789, by Jean-François Reubell;[15] on December 24, 1789, by
C.-V. de Broglie and the Nancy Bishop A.-N.-L. de La
Fare.[16] And they were echoed by anti-Jewish pamphleteers.[17]

[13] Abbé L. . . . [A.-A. Lamourette], *Observations sur l'état civil des
juifs* . . . (n.p., 1790), pp. 8-9; J.-B. Sanchamau, *L'Ecole des peuples et des
rois* . . . (Paris, 1790), p. 82; M. Valois, *Apologie de l'opinion de M. Ranxin*
. . . [Nancy, 1790], p. 2; P. Vieillard, *Dissertation sur la demande des juifs
de Paris* . . . [Paris, 1791], pp. 5-6.
[14] [Cottier-Julian], *Dialogue* [Carpentras, 1789], p. 9: "le mépris dont
on nous accabloit, étouffoit en nous le germe de la vertu . . . on applanissoit
la route qui pouvoit nous conduire au crime."
[15] "Lettre du député à l'Assemblée nationale Reubell, à la commission
intermédiaire du district de Colmar," *Revue d'Alsace*, XIII (1862), 530-31.
[16] "Il faut convenir que les règlements mêmes en vertu desquels les juifs
sont tolérés en Alsace, ne leur présentent d'autre moyen de subsistance, d'autre
genre d'industrie que le commerce de l'argent," *Revue des grandes journées
parlementaires*, I (1897), 19; "Les juifs établis en France ont, je l'avoue, des
griefs légitimes, dont ils peuvent demander, et ont droit d'attendre le redresse-
ment. S'il le falloit, j'en ferois moi-même la dênonciation à cette l'assemblée,"
Opinion de M. l'Evêque de Nancy . . . (Paris, 1790), p. 4.
[17] "Je conviendrai que n'ayant eu jusqu'ici d'autre ressource pour vivre
que les métiers de fripier, d'usurier, d'espion, &c., il leur étoit difficile d'être
rigides observateurs de la probité," De Laissac, Capitaine au Régiment de
Limosin, *Lettre a M. le Chapellier, membre de l'Assemblée nationale* [Paris,

The resolution against Jewish emancipation adopted in May, 1790, by the *bureau intermédiaire* of the Colmar district contained a self-incriminating statement on the Christian contribution to the degradation of the Jews.[18] The same feeling of guilt can be found in a draft of a report made by the Jacobins of Colmar.[19]

The Jews, in defending themselves, also made the point that the anti-Jewish restrictions left unproductive activities as their only means of survival. Zalkind Hourwitz, the Polish Jew who fought for emancipation in France, advanced the argument that even the commercial rights of the Jews were of limited value since they were not permitted to keep stores open to the general public.[20] Statements on the responsibility of the regime for the unhealthy occupational status of the Jews were made in 1789 by I. Berr Bing, author of a memorandum on the Jews of Metz, and by the Jews of Lunéville and Sarreguemines;[21] in the Jewish petition addressed on January 28, 1790, to the National Assembly; in a pamphlet by the Jews addressed to the Alsatian people; in a pamphlet addressed by Lion Goudchaux of Nancy to the anti-Jewish leader, Abbé J.-S. Maury; in a pamphlet published by Berr-Isaac Berr of Nancy and in a petition addressed to the National Assembly by the Jews of Upper Rhine.[22] The same argument was used by Jews and Christians in pamphlets of the post-emancipation period.[23]

1790], p. 21. The same idea may be found in a pamphlet issued in Nancy against accepting Jews in the National Guard: "L'existence précaire et équivoque que l'on a bien voulu accorder aux juifs, les a forcés d'adopter pour moeurs & de pratiquer pour commerce, la fraude, l'astuce & l'usure," *Lettre d'un citoyen, aux gardes-citoyens de la ville de Nancy, en réponse à la question: les juifs doivent-ils être admis dans la Milice Nationale?* (n.p., n.d.), p. 4.

18   "L'avilinement dans lequed nous tenons depuis treize siècles cette nation malheureuse, n'a sans doute pas peu contribué à la dégrader" (Departmental archives of Upper Rhine, C 1602).

19   Paul Leuilliot, *Les Jacobins de Colmar* . . . (Strasbourg, 1923), pp. 339-40.

20   Z. Hourwitz, *Apologie* . . . (Paris, 1789), p. 17.

21   I. Ber-Bing, *Mémoire particulier* . . . (n.p., 1789), p. 3; *Mémoire pour les juifs de Lunéville et de Sarreguemines* (n.p., [1789]), p. 3.

22   *Petition des juifs* . . . *adressée à l'Assemblée nationale le 28 janvier 1790* (Paris, 1790), pp. 42-43; *Adresse des juifs alsaciens au peuple d'Alsace* (n.p., 1790), p. 2; *Lettre du Sr. Lion Goudchaux, juif de Nancy, à M. l'abbé Maury* . . . (Nancy, 1790), pp. 5, 11; *Instruction salutaire* . . . *par* . . .

III

DISCUSSION ON USURY

Usury became a major subject of discussion in the debate on Jewish emancipation.

On October 3, 1789, the National Assembly legalized loans at interest which, prior to the Revolution, were lawful only in certain parts of the country, although the practice of usury was widespread. In Moselle the legal rate of interest rose from 4 per cent in 1789 to 8 per cent in 1801. Nevertheless, in the mind of the public all Jews were usurers.[24] True, some people did take up the defense of Jews, e.g., Benoît de la Pailhonne, a counter-revolutionary leader of the papal province Comtat Venaissin, who in 1789 denied that Jews were usurers.[25] Also, a revolutionary pamphleteer of 1789 called upon Jews and Christians to combat usury: "As we are all equal . . . equal in possessions, equal in wealth, equal in humanitarian feelings, equal in charity. We are equal, then! No more creditors, no more debtors. . . . The most useful job for Jews and Christians would be to give us a more progressive state of fortune. . . ."[26] In most cases, however, Jews were attacked as usurers, as unable to become a productive element, e.g., in a large number of *cahiers des doléances*;[27] by pamphleteers;[28] in complaints addressed to the Commission of agriculture and trade;[29] and otherwise. In a resolution of June 30, 1794, the Jacobins

Hartwig Wessely, 2e edition (Paris, 1790), pp. 31-33 (published by B. Isaac Berr); *Pétition de messieurs les juifs du Haut-Rhin à l'Assemblée nationale* (Paris, 1792), p. 3.
[23] *Société fondée à Metz, pour l'encouragement des arts et métiers parmi les israélites* (Metz, le 15 juin 1829), 3 pp.; *Consistoire israélite. Circonscription de Colmar* [Colmar, 1850], p. 3; *Le Glaneur du Haut-Rhin*, May 28, 1848.
[24] R. Parisot, *Histoire de Lorraine*, III (Paris, 1924), 25, 185.
[25] H. Chobaut, "Les Juifs d'Avignon et du Comtat et la Révolution française," *REJ.*, CI (1937), 30.
[26] *Le Meuilleur des amen à l'usage des juifs et des chrétiens* (n.p., [1789]), 7 pp.
[27] Szajkowski, *op. cit.*, pp. 91-94.
[28] *Les Juifs d'Alsace doivent-ils être admis au droit de citoyens* (n.p., 1790), p. 133; Johann Stephan Albert, *Fränkischer Republikaner, zu Colmar erwählter Richter* . . . (n.p., n.d.), p. 13.
[29] F. Gerbaux et Ch. Schmidt, *Procès-verbaux des comités d'agriculture et de commerce de la constituante*, I (Paris, 1906), 327, 701.

of Colmar expressed their belief that the Talmud authorized the practice of usury by Jews against Christians. Earlier the same opinion was expressed by S. de Clermont-Tonnerre, who was a sincere friend of the Jews.[30]

The Jews replied, not only by recalling the effects of anti-Jewish restrictions, but also by pointing out the number of Christian usurers. The existence of Christian usurers was acknowledged by the anti-Jewish lineup, e.g., in many *cahiers*. On August 4, 1789, Pierre Ochs, representative of Strasbourg in Basel, wrote that Jews speculated in Alsace as intermediaries for creditors of Basel. Documents and pamphlets of the revolutionary period frequently referred to *Judengenossen, unbeschnittenen Juden*, etc., i.e., Christian usurers. "Usurers are to be found not only in synagogues," wrote the anti-Jewish pamphleteer P.-F. de Latour Foissac. Similar statements were made by a pamphleteer of 1790; at the meetings of the Jacobins in Strasbourg on May 3 and 10, 1794; and at a meeting of the Jacobins in Colmar on May 31, 1794.[31]

The discussion on the role of Jews as usurers was somewhat artificial, without any practical understanding of the real evil of usury during the revolutionary period, for which Jews were not at all responsible. Of 1,704 mortgages in the aggregate sum of 7,091,549.00 francs registered in the Strasbourg office of mortgages between November 4, 1798, and April 5, 1799, only 210 in the sum of 215,548.66 francs were held by Jewish mortgagees against Christian mortgagors. Of 741 mortgages in the sum of 1,164,034.06 francs registered in the Saverne office between May 22 and June 14, 1799, only 121 for 89,554.81 francs were in favor of Jews against Christians. Of 787 mortgages of the value of

[30] Leuilliot, *op. cit.*, p. 257; Ch. du Bus, *Stanislas de Clermont-Tonnerre* . . . (Paris, 1931), p. 213.
[31] [Jacques Godard], *Pétition des juifs . . . le 28 janvier 1790 . . .* (Paris, 1790), p. 39; Szajkowski, *op. cit.*, p. 83; R. Reuss, "L'Alsace pendant la Révolution française," *Revue d'Alsace*, LXX (1923), III, 302; *Die Judenverfolgungen* (Strassburg, 1790), p. 16; Maria Salomea Schottin, *Ueber die Juden und Judengenossen* (Strassburg, an XI), p. 7; P. F. Latour-Foissac, *Plaidoyer contre l'usure des juifs . . .* (n.p., [1790]), p. 75; *Ueber die Vertreibung der Juden* (n.p., 1790), p. 8; F. Ch. Heitz, *Les Sociétés politiques de Strasbourg . . .* (Strasbourg, 1863), pp. 347-49; Leuilliot, *op. cit.*, p. 257.

2,244,126.46 francs registered in the Metz office between
June 3 and June 18, 1799, only 46 of the value of 87,838
francs were held by Jews against Christians. Of 312 mortgages of the value of 890,431.09 francs registered in the
Nancy office between March 13 and March 27, 1799, only
7 of the value of 24,442.20 francs were in favor of Jews
against Christians.[32]

Even the anti-Jewish minded Alsatian historian Fernand
L'Huillier wrote that until the year X for the Lower Rhine
and the year XI for the Upper Rhine Jews were not particularly incriminated in public discussions on usury. According to him, the introduction of an anti-Jewish trend was
the result and expression of general discontent.[33]

However, the evil was done, and the injection of the
question of usury into the discussion on Jewish emancipation
prolonged the fight.

It should be noted that even among serious chroniclers
and historians very few understood this problem. Thus,
A.-T. Desquiron, who attacked Napoleon I's anti-Jewish
decrees of 1806 and 1808, wrote in 1808 that while France
was being torn apart by struggles, the Jewish nation practiced usury. Felix Ponteil wrote in a similar vein in 1927,
as did a large number of other modern historians. According
to Jacques Godechot the Jews of Nancy started to practice
usury after 1795.[34]

IV

THE ATTITUDE OF THE GOVERNMENT
AND OF LOCAL AUTHORITIES

There were some attempts to make Jews "productive"
by force. The district of Strasbourg ordered the requisition

---

[32] Z. Szajkowski, *Agricultural Credit and Napoleon's Anti-Jewish Decrees*
(New York, 1953), Table I.

[33] F. L'Huillier, *Recherches sur l'Alsace napoléonienne* (Strasbourg,
1947), p. 520.

[34] A.-T. Desquiron, *Considérations sur l'existence civile et politique des
israélites* (Mayence, 1808), p. 46; Félix Ponteil, *La Situation économique du
Bas-Rhin au lendemain de la Révolution française* (Strasbourg, 1927), pp.
93, 140; Jacques Godechot, "Les Juifs de Nancy de 1789 à 1795," *REJ.*,
LXXXVII (1929), 35.

of all citizens, "especially those of Moses' faith, who live in idleness," to help the peasants in the fields. The peasants, however, demanded help from the National Guard instead of the Jews, who were not familiar with this kind of work.[35] On September 4, 1790, the city council of Strasbourg restricted the activities of Jewish peddlers.[36] On December 10, 1790, two Jewish peddlers, Marix Wolf and Mathias Caen, complained in a petition addressed to the Committee of agriculture and commerce that they were forbidden to trade in Besançon where Christian merchants were afraid of honest competition by Jewish peddlers. On November 21, 1790, a former royal adviser of Lunéville named Rosman proposed to this committee that 800,000 acres be set aside in order to form an agricultural colony of Jews. Thus, he wrote, the Jews would become peasants and the French nation would be freed from usury.[37]

Some references by local administrators to the occupational status of the Jews were mixed with strongly worded anti-Jewish sentiments. Thus, the proclamation against speculation, published on September 9, 1793, by the departmental administration of Vaucluse, singled out the Jews. They were called on to show proof of being worthy of the emancipation granted them by the new regime and to give up usury. If they wanted wealth, they could gain it by honest means, such as buying national property.[38]

Unofficial anti-Jewish acts also hampered Jewish economic activities. The Jews of Carpentras were afraid to engage in new occupations.[39] In Alsace and neighboring departments there were protests against allotting communal properties (*biens communaux*) to the Jews, who thereupon

---

[35] Henry Brunschwig, *Les Subsistances à Strasbourg pendant les premières années de la Révolution française* (Strasbourg, 1932), pp. 90-91; R. Werner, *L'Approvisionnement en pain de la population du Bas-Rhin . . . 1789-1797* (Strasbourg, 1951), pp. 223, 379.

[36] *Proclamation de par les maire et officiers municipaux* (Strasbourg, 25 septembre 1790), broadside.

[37] Gerbaux et Schmidt, *op. cit.*, I, 702-03.

[38] *Proclamation de l'administration du département de Vaucluse relative à l'agiotage* (Avignon, 1793), 3 pp.; J. F. André, *Histoire de la Révolution avignoise*, I (Paris, 1844), 116-18.

[39] Chobaut, *REJ.*, CI (1937), 36-37.

complained that they were not given the opportunity to share in the parceling out of such property.[40]

However, these were expressions of local anti-Jewish feelings, which were not taken too seriously by the central authorities. The liberal attitude of national and even of some local leaders of the new regime toward the occupational status of the Jew can best be illustrated by their treatment of Jewish emigrés, who left France in the wave of largely anti-revolutionary emigration. The law of January 11, 1795, permitted the return of those emigrés who, at the time of their departure from France, had manual occupations: peasants, workers, artisans, etc. But since agriculture and all other productive pursuits were closed to Jews during the old regime, how could a Jewish emigré prove that he made a living by working with his hands? In many cases the authorities decided that Jewish emigrés who were peddlers, merchants, and the like should benefit from the law because during the old regime they were forced to make a living at dishonest occupations. In other cases the authorities declared that Jewish peddlers and traders in second-hand goods, horses and cattle were useful to the local population. Some Jewish emigrés stated that they were so poor that they could rightly be called hard-working people.[41]

The effect on Jewish productivity of the observance of the Sabbath and other Jewish holidays was another argument advanced against granting Jewish emancipation. The statement of a pamphleteer, made in 1790, that because of their religion Jews would be able to work only six months a year, was repeated in the National Assembly by A.-N.-L. de La Fare, bishop of Nancy.[42]

[40] Z. Szajkowski, "Jewish Participation in the Sale of National Property during the French Revolution," *Jewish Social Studies*, XIV (1952), 311-12.

[41] Z. Szajkowski, "Jewish Emigrés during the French Revolution," *Jewish Social Studies*, XVI (1954), 319-34.

[42] *Les Juifs d'Alsace* . . . , p. 118; the argument was again repeated in 1801: J. L. F[esquet], du Gard, *Voyage de Paris à Strasbourg* . . . (n.p., 1801), p. 77. See also Z. Szajkowski, "French Jews in the Armed Forces during the Revolution of 1789," *Proceedings of the American Academy for Jewish Research*, XXVI (1957), 142-43; Z. Szajkowski, "Jewish Religious Observance during the French Revolution of 1789," *Yivo Bleter*, XLI (1957-58), 193-94 (in Yiddish).

V

AGRICULTURE

In their fight for emancipation the Jews contended that by granting them citizenship France would attract Jews from abroad, who would enrich the nation's economy. The same argument was made by the Deputy Charles-François Bouche; by an English woman, author of a pro-Jewish pamphlet; by Abbé A.-R.-C. Bertolio at a meeting of the Paris council on January 30, 1790; and in a resolution adopted by the same council on February 24, 1790.[43] All these referred to Jewish capital and skill in trade, not limiting the role of Jews solely to manual labor.

It is true that, upon the abolition of the old regime, many Jews failed to seize the opportunity to escape out of their old occupations. This slow Jewish response to the possibility of shifting to productive activities can best be seen in the limited Jewish acquisition of national property (*biens nationaux*), such as church and other properties confiscated and sold by the revolutionary government. It stands to reason that Jews should have been active purchasers of national property, as this was their first legal opportunity to own land and houses outside the former ghettos. However, unlike the Protestants, who became large landowners, the number of Jews who bought national property was very small and they purchased it primarily for resale. Needless to say, there were many reasons for the Jews' reaction. The Catholic Church spread the word that the Jews would desecrate former churches. Many Jewish creditors were often afraid to ask for payment from the nationalized properties of emigrés of debts owed to them. At the same time it should be remembered that the purchase of national property was viewed as an act of revolutionary patriotism. With

---

[43] *Pétition des juifs . . . le 28 janvier 1790* (Paris, 1790), pp. 23, 28-30; Ch. F. Bouche, *De la restitution du Comté Venaissin . . .* (Paris, 1789), p. 38; La Baronne de Vasse, Angloise, *Mémoire . . .* (Paris, 1790), pp. 2-3, 7; *Recueil de pièces relatives à l'admission des juifs à l'état civil* (Paris, 1790), p. 25; *Adresse de l'Assemblée des représentants de la Commune de Paris, sur l'admission des juifs à l'état-civil . . .* (Paris, 1790), p. 11.

few exceptions the Jews distrusted this aspect of the Revolution's economic policies. They could not quickly comprehend the significance of the changes in their economic potential made possible by the Revolution. Thus, they lost a unique opportunity to change to agricultural occupations.[44]

Indirectly, Jewish creditors and Jews who bought national property for resale made it possible for many peasants to realize their dreams of becoming owners of their own land. In 1792 a counter-revolutionary pamphleteer complained against Jews and Christians who divided and sold land in small parcels.[45] But this Jewish participation in the process of cutting up large pieces of land remained in the sphere of commerce and not of so-called "productive" activities.

Everyone advised the Jews to take up agriculture. This was the subject of one of the very few contemporary lithographs on Jews.[46] Sébastien Bottin, a Jacobin, economist and secretary general of the Lower Rhine department, wrote in 1798 that only when the Jews took up agriculture, "the most noble art," would they become "entirely citizens." During the revolutionary period Jewish landowners were exceptional. One of them, Hirtzelboch of Diegolsheim, was much praised by Bottin.[47]

[44] Szajkowski, *Jewish Social Studies*, XIV (1952), 291-312.

[45] *Ibid.*, pp. 312-16; Szajkowski, *The Economic Status* . . . , pp. 54-57; Szajkowski, *Agricultural Credit* . . . , pp. 60-63; *Je vous dirai vos vérités!* (n.p., 1792), p. 19.

It is worth while to note that in 1777 the Alsatian Jewish leader Cerfberr of Médelsheim wanted to convert 3,000 acres of the *Forêt Sainte* to arable land. He offered to pay 400,000 livres plus 8 livres annually per acre. G. Huffel, *La Forêt Sainte de Haguenau en Alsace* (Nancy-Paris-Strasbourg, 1920), pp. 85-86.

[46] In *Les Juifs d'Alsace.* . . .

[47] S. Botin, *Annuaire politique et économique du département du Bas-Rhin* (Strasbourg, an VIII), p. 74; A. Benoit, "Les Israélites en Alsace sous le Directoire et sous le Consulat," *La Revue nouvelle d'Alsace-Lorraine et du Rhin*, VIII, No. 11 (1889), 401-03.

VI

POVERTY AND LACK OF TIME, TWO REASONS FOR THE SLOW PROCESS OF OCCUPATIONAL SHIFTING

It was impossible, even by the revolutionary standards of 1789, to change overnight the occupational status of a minority long kept down by economic restrictions. This was recognized even on the eve of the Revolution: in a report of August 25, 1788, by the Metz Academy of Science; by Abbé La Louze, who sent to the Academy an essay on the Jews; in Abbé Grégoire's essay presented to the same Academy, and in his later *Motion* at the National Assembly in favor of Jews; by the Jews themselves;[48] and even by the author of a widely disseminated book against Jewish emancipation.[49]

In 1818 the Central Jewish Consistory, in a petition against the renewal of Napoleon I's anti-Jewish decree of March 17, 1808, stated: "The government of 1806, unaccustomed to awaiting developments, but acknowledging force alone, was indignant that fourteen years of living through the storm of the Revolution were not sufficient to eradicate completely from a large portion of the population the traces of centuries-long humiliation and enslavement." In 1829 the founders of the Metz Society to stimulate vocational training among Jewish youth stated: "It is not in the nature of things that mores established over centuries can be uprooted within just a few years." The same view was expressed by the nineteenth century Alsatian *maskil*, Gerson Lévy.[50]

[48] *Prix proposés, en 1788, par la Société Royale des Sciences et des Arts de Metz pour le concours de 1789 et 1790* [Metz, 1788], p. 3; *Affiches des Evêchés et Lorraine*, No. 35, 1788; Ab. Cahen, "L'Emancipation des juifs devant la Société Royale des Sciences et des Arts de Metz et M. Roederer," *REJ.*, I (1880), 103; City Library of Metz, manuscript 1350, fol. 684 b; Grégoire, *Essai . . .*, p. 189; Grégoire, *Motion en faveur des juifs . . .* (Paris, 1790), p. 30; *Adresse des juifs alsaciens au peuple d'Alsace* (n.p., 1790), pp. 4-5; Berr-Isaac Ber, *Lettre à M. Grégoire . . .* (Paris, 1806), pp. 15-16.

[49] *Les Juifs d'Alsace . . .* , p. 43.

[50] *Requête adressée au roi par le Consistoire Central des Israélites, contre la prorogation du décret du 17 mars 1808 . . .* (Paris, 1818), p. 4; *Société fondée à Metz, pour l'encouragement des arts et métiers parmi les israélites*

A sympathetic position was taken by the historian P. Sagnac, who maintained that the Jews tried to rediscover and restore their noble professional traditions. However, some historians, in commenting on the occupational status of the Jews during the revolutionary period, were more severe in their judgments than the revolutionary politicians and pamphleteers. Typical of this group was the historian Rodolphe Reuss, who, while in general very favorably disposed towards Jews, stated that in respect of their choice of occupations, only a small number of them justified the good will of the legislature. Most Jews were unable to take up useful professions, although this was not their fault. Consequently, they flocked into the field of speculation.[51]

Although emancipation widened the range of economic pursuits open to Jews, this great benefit was in part offset by unfavorable developments affecting economic activities in general. Most Jews continued to live in misery.[52] In spite of the much publicized role of Jewish merchants, there were almost no Jews among the big financiers of the revolutionary period.[53] The Revolution did not enrich the Jews.[54] On the contrary, Jews as well as Frenchmen were often ruined by the economic policies of the Revolution. For in-

(Metz, 15 juin 1829), 3 pp.; Gerson Lévy, *Du paupérisme chez les juifs* . . . (Paris, 1854), pp. 45-46: "Nous concevons cependant qu'ils ne devaient pas passer brusquement aux extrêmes; qu'on ne pouvait leur dire: fermez aujourd'hui vos boutiques, renoncez au colportage et au brocantage, et venez demain labourer la plaine avec nous. Le bienfait des droits civiles est tombé sur les juifs comme une bombe; rien n'était disposé pour les préparer à ce grand acte d'émancipation; ils savaient bien répondre à l'appel de la loi, verser leur sang dans les champs de bataille, mais sans organisation dans l'intérieur de leur communion, sans autorité religieuse, sans écoles, sans aucune institution à la hauteur des circonstances, ils ne pouvaient devenir tout d'un coup des hommes nouveaux, renoncer spontanément à leurs habitudes, à leurs moeurs, à leur caractère, fruits de l'ancienne oppression." See also I. Bédarride, *Les Juifs en France, en Italie et en Espagne* (Paris, 1859), pp. 399-400.

[51] Ph. Sagnac, *Les Juifs et Napoléon 1806-1808* (Paris, 1902), p. 4; Rod. Reuss, "Quelques documents nouveaux sur l'antisémitisme dans le Bas-Rhin de 1794 à 1799," *REJ.*, LIX (1910), 250.

[52] Posener, *Jewish Social Studies*, I (1939), 304-07.

[53] Jean Bouchary, *Les manieurs d'argent à Paris à la fin du XVIIIe siècle*, I (Paris, 1939), 7; also Jean Bouchary, *Les Compagnies financières à Paris à la fin du XVIIIe siècle* (Paris, 1940-41), 2 vols.

[54] Paul Bettelin, *Le Général Marc-François Jérôme Baron Woiff* (n.p., [1941]), p. 9: "la Révolution ne les enrichit pas."

stance, during the Terror the widow of Moïze Mendes asked for a reduction in her taxes because her husband had been ruined by the law of maximum.[55] It is incorrect, however, to assume that the period of the Terror exclusively led to the economic downfall of wealthy people. David Crémieux of Nîmes, father of the nineteenth century Jewish leader Adolphe Crémieux and a supporter of the new regime, was imprisoned at the beginning of the Thermidorian reaction. When released from prison he found his business had been ruined and went into bankruptcy.[56]

Some Jewish emigrés, who were peddlers and wanted to benefit from the amnesty in favor of productive emigrés, stated—as has already been noted—that although they were peddlers, they were very poor and could hardly make a living, so that they could be called hard working people.[57] In his memoirs Gabriel Schrameck, who was born in Isenheim (Upper Rhine), in 1795 told of the miseries of a poor Alsatian Jewish family. His father and older brother were peddlers, who came home only for the Sabbath; his two sisters were servants. At the age of nine he was a peddler himself, and at eleven employed other children. He was considered a "rich" man at eighteen because he owned merchandise of the value of 400 francs. His career was late in starting because his father was ashamed to take him on his peddling trips, so poorly clothed was the child. However, in his memoirs Schrameck refers to his "work," "working," "workers" (*Arbeit, arbeiten, Arbeiter*), and not to peddlers and peddling. He had to find a way to get clothing and food, and peddling was not an unproductive or disreputable occupation to him. The Alsatian author of a pamphlet on Jews published in 1790 related that most Jews possessed only between 80 and 200 livres each.[58]

Even poverty served as an argument against Jewish emancipation. Another Alsatian pamphleteer wrote in

---

[55] City archives of Bordeaux, G 6, No. 89.

[56] S. Posener, *Adolphe Crémieux*, I (Paris, 1933), 5-6.

[57] Szajkowski, *Jewish Social Studies*, XVI (1954), 332.

[58] *Erlebnisse von Gabriel Schrameck* . . . (Barr, 1907), pp. 5-15; *Ueber die Vertreibung der Juden* (n.p., 1790), pp. 6-7.

1790 that, since half of the Alsatian Jews were paupers,
citizenship would be useless and even disastrous to them,
unless the French nation, in the name of justice and humanity, helped them improve their economic condition.[59]

VII

Some Facts on Shifting Occupations

Emancipation led some Jews to become active in industrial enterprises, quickening a development that had been
restricted earlier but had not been unknown. Before the
Revolution David Silveyra, agent of the Sephardim in Paris,
was a builder of bridges.[60] In 1787 Lipmann and Théodore
Cerfberr of Nancy operated a cloth factory in Pont-Saint-
Vincent, where between thirty and forty children were
employed. At the beginning of the Revolution they were
operating another factory in Tomblaine.[61] Berr-Isaac Berr
of Nancy owned a tobacco factory.[62] Shortly before 1800
a Jew named Worms and a Christian named Thomas jointly
began to import coal from the Saar to the Moselle region,
which they transported by barges over the Moselle river
instead of by the more expensive overland routes. This was
a great pioneering contribution to the industrialization of
the entire region.[63] In 1794 Samuel Ah was engaged in the
manufacture of oil in Haguenau.[64] At the beginning of
the Revolution Hayemson Créhange opened a cloth factory
in Sedan.[65] In Strasbourg Cerf Lanzenberg manufactured

[59] *Observations sur la possibilité et l'utilité de l'admission des juifs . . .*
(Strasbourg, février, 1790), p. 11.
[60] Archives départementales, Landes, BB 31 and C 112-114; *Project du
sieur Silveyra . . .* (n.p., n.d.), 12 pp.; L. Kahn, *Les Juifs de Paris pendant la
Révolution* (Paris, 1899), pp. 133-34.
[61] P. Boyé, *La Lorraine industrielle sous le règne nominal de Stanislas*
(Nancy, 1900), p. 60; Jacques Godechet, "Les Juifs de Nancy de 1789 à 1795,"
REJ., LXXXVI (1928), 4.
[62] Departmental archives of Meurthe-et-Moselle, L 104, pp. 103, 106
(Berr's petition of Dec. 21, 1791, on taxes).
[63] Albert Eiselé, *Le Charbon mosellan, ètude historique & économique*
(Paris, 1936), pp. 73-74.
[64] Elie Sched, "Histoire des juifs de Haguenau," REJ., X (1885), 230.
[65] *Archives israélites*, V (1844), 754.

leather; Hauch Oppenheim had a shirt factory run with advanced techniques; the city was also known for the soap factory of a Jew named Weill and his partners.[66] The Sephardic Jews of the revolutionary period included not only well-to-do merchants and poor peddlers, but also industrial workers.[67]

While the main focus of this essay is on the revolutionary period of 1789-1800—the occupational distribution in later periods was different—it is helpful in judging the situation in the earlier period to compare it with the classification of occupations of Jews during the first Empire. There is no doubt that a change occurred, and it was most probably the result of a trend that started during the revolutionary period.

"At last the French Jews are men, several of them are already useful citizens," Michel Berr wrote in 1801. Five years later his father, the Jewish leader of Lorraine, Berr-Isaac Berr, stated: "We already have among us tailors, joiners, tinsmiths, and other workers and artisans."[68] This was no exaggeration. According to the census of 1784 there were then in Alsace 19,707 Jews, of whom 942 were servants and 1,286 officially recognized paupers. According to a report made to Napoleon I by the Minister of Interior on December 21, 1808, Alsatian Jews employed Christian workers in their cloth factories. In 1809, twenty-eight Jews worked in the munitions factory in Mutzig. Thirty-one Jewish family-heads were classified as manufacturers, thirty-seven as tailors, thirty-six as shoemakers, and fifty-nine were peasants.[69] In 1808 seventy-five Jews were classi-

---

[66] *Ibid.*, XVI (1855), 506-07.

[67] On a Bordeaux list dated Dec. 4, 1792, are noted the knitter Rachel Machade, the tobacco worker Samuel Coitiguo, etc. City archives of Bordeaux, G 9.

[68] Michel Berr, *Appel à la justice des nations* . . . (Strasbourg, 1861), p. 15.

[69] G. Hemerdinger, "Le Dénombrement des israélites en Alsace," *REJ.*, XLII (1901), 264; Paul Fauchille, *La Question juive en France sous le Premier Empire* (Paris, 1884), p. 73; "Etat nominatif des israélites, qui ont établi, et qui exploitent des manufactures . . . Département du Bas-Rhin, 1809" (a document in the author's possession).

fied as workers employed by manufacturers.[70] In Nancy there were two Jewish manufacturers in 1793 and ten in 1808, fifteen day laborers in 1793 and forty-seven in 1808, one artisan in 1793 and nine in 1808.[71] In 1809, 47.9 per cent of the 2,908 Jews in Paris were small merchants or peddlers and 26.8 per cent were artisans.[72] Abraham Gabay, a Sephardic Jew of Paris, had a factory in which he employed two hundred workers.[73] In 1808 there were nineteen Jewish peasants in the department of Bouches-du-Rhône.[74] According to a report of June 23, 1810, France had 250 Jewish manufacturers, and 2,360 Jews were in schools or were employed in "useful professions."[75]

These first steps toward a shift in occupations took place in spite of many difficulties. Even in the post-emancipation period Jews were often prevented from engaging in certain occupations. To cite just a few cases: In 1806, according to Berr-Isaac Berr, Jewish children were refused employment in factories. In 1825 the Alsatian Jew Prosper Wittersheim made the same statement and added that peasants terrorized Jews who wanted to take up agriculture. As late as 1853 the vocational school of Toulon requested certificates of baptism from its pupils.[76] In 1806 the Catholic Church authorities tried to prevent the brothers Lippmann of Nancy from buying the crystal factory of Baccarat

[70]   Archives nationales (Paris), F 19-11009.
[71]   Posener, *Jewish Social Studies*, I (1939), 299.
[72]   L. Kahn, *Les Professions manuelles et les institutions de patronage* (Paris, 1885), pp. 65-67.
[73]   According to the inscription on the monument on his grave at the cemetery Père Lachaise in Paris: "Ici repose / le corps de Abraham Gabay / décéde le 16 aoust 1812[?] à l'àge de 45 / en son domicile propriétaire / d'une manufacture des bazins / Il emporte avec lui les regrets / de son épouse et de ses amis / et de plus de 200 ouvriers / et ouvrières / qui ont suivi le convoi / et [qui ont] versés des larmes / [sur sa] châse."
[74]   Departmental archives of Bouches-du-Rhône, 112 VI.
[75]   A.-E. Halphen, *Receuil des lois . . . concernant les israélites . . .* (Paris, 1851), pp. 307-328; Posener, *Jewish Social Studies*, I (1939), 271-326.
[76]   Berr-Isaac Berr, *Lettre . . . à M. Grégoire* (Nancy, 1806), p. 15; Prosper Wittersheim, *Mémoire sur les moyens de hater la régénération des israélites de l'Alsace* (Metz, 1825), p. 11; *Ville de Toulon. Académie départementale du Val. Ecole professionelle de Toulon* (n.p., 15 décembre 1853), 4 pp.; I. Uhry, *Recueil des lois . . . concernant les israélites depuis 1850* (Bordeaux, 1878), p. 10.

(Meuse), although but for the Lippmanns' purchase the factory would have closed and the local population would have starved or had to emigrate. Sephardic Jews of Saint-Esprit-lès-Bayonne were afraid to trade in Bayonne, where Jews officially were not permitted to reside prior to 1789 and were unwelcome even much later.[77]

VIII

Occupational Diversification

Already during the old regime Jewish leaders tried to counter accusations of Jewish unproductivity by giving vocational training to the youth among the poor. But then, the vocational education of poor children was an old tradition in the Jewish communities. In 1770 and 1771 the Jewish community of Cavaillon (in the Papal province of Avignon and Comtat Venaissin) signed a contract with a Christian seamstress to teach her trade during a period of thirty-four months to the children Regine de Bedarrides and Esther de Lunel, nine and ten years old, respectively, on condition that they would not be forced to work on the Sabbath.[78] On the eve of the Revolution, however, and especially after emancipation, vocational training became a subject of public debate. During the old regime it was useless to give Jewish children vocational training in occupations that were closed to Jews, but on June 7, 1806, the Philanthropic Society of the Bordeaux Jews maintained that poor Jewish children could at least be taught arts and manual trades, for Jews were no longer excluded from these economic opportunities.[79] On December 4, 1830, the Alsatian Deputy Pierre André stated that before the Revolu-

[77] S. Posener, "Lippmann Lippmann de Baccarat. Fragment de l'histoire économique des juifs de France," *Festschrift zu Simon Dubnows siebzigstem Geburtstag* (Berlin, 1930), pp. 207-14; Léon (*supra*, n. 3), p. 394.

[78] Departmental archives of Vaucluses, Guis' notarial minutes, No. 300, fol. 244 (Apr. 26, 1770), and 661 (June 18, 1771).

[79] Minutes of the Society, in the Archives of the General Historical Archives, Jerusalem.

tion Jews had not been allowed to open vocational schools.[80] At the same time, however, some sources have it that before the Revolution the Alsatian Jewish leader Cerfberr of Médelsheim and Berr-Isaac Berr of Nancy founded agricultural colonies in order to mitigate the charge that Jews were not productive. Very little is known about these two projects; according to an anti-Jewish pamphleteer in 1790, Berr wanted only to exploit "his Jewish slaves or workers."[81] In 1789 the Jews of Metz promised to establish vocational schools for "poor children." After the Ashkenazic Jews were granted full citizenship, Berr-Isaac Berr called upon them to open *ateliers de charité*, where poor children and "all those who were not destined for higher purposes" would be taught useful crafts.[82] This plan no doubt reflected the belief that physical labor was the lot of the children of the poor. It is apparent that the first organized attempts to achieve mass improvement in the nature of Jewish occupations were concentrated on the children of needy Jews and thus had a philanthropic aspect. The same development may be observed in the nineteenth century.[83]

The diversification of Jewish occupations—not only those of Jewish children, but of adults as well—was often influenced by anti-Jewish restrictions, e.g., the fight against Jewish peddlers in Bordeaux. There the Christian merchants complained of the competition by Jewish peddlers, and in 1738 the Parliament of Bordeaux ordered the confiscation of merchandise in the possession of these *petits marchands juifs*.[84] The *nation* of the Sephardic Jews, fearful of the "bad name" brought upon Jews by peddlers, in 1744 contrived the expulsion of foreign Jews and ordered Sephardic Jewish merchants dealing in second-hand clothing to give

[80]   *Moniteur*, Dec. 6, 1830; Halphen, *op. cit.*, pp. 406-07.
[81]   M. Ginsburger, *Cerf Berr et son temps* (Strasbourg, 1936), p. 7; Chr. Pfister, *Histoire de Nancy*, III (Paris-Nancy, 1908), 327; *Antwort über eine Schrift betitelt: Können die Juden im Elsass des Bürgerrechtes theilhaftig werden?* (n.p., 1790), p. 10: "Seine jüdischen Knechte oder Arbeiter."
[82]   Ber-Bing, *Mémoire particulier* . . . , p. 23; D. Tama, *Organisation civile et religieuse des israélites* . . . (Paris, 1808), p. 34.
[83]   This will be the subject of a separate study.
[84]   *Inventaire sommaire des Archives Hospitalières à 1790,* II (Bordeaux-Paris, 1885), II, B 5.

up their trade on pain of being forced to do so by the authorities.[85] The opposition of the Sephardim to "foreign" Jews was also motivated largely by fear of competition. Thus, on August 3, 1787, Abraham Furtado wrote to David Gradis that the fight against the Avignonese Jews who had settled in Bordeaux was important for the house of Gradis.[86] The wealthy leaders of the Sephardic *nation* of Bordeaux were afraid of the "evil" that had manifested itself among their poor and sought to prevent the "infection,"[87] by religious education during the old regime and also by vocational training after the emancipation. The above noted statement on vocational education for children made on June 7, 1806, by the Jews of Bordeaux referred to "poor children" exclusively.[88]

IX

CONCLUSIONS

After 1791, according to the Alsatian economist Henry Laufenburger, the Jews had their "economic revenge" (*revanche économique*): they survived the revolutionary storm and with their *internationalisme économique* adapted themselves to the new regime, surpassing the Christians in trade. Christian energies were spread over many industries, while Jewish energies were concentrated in trade. This was Werner

---

[85] ". . . et, quand aux portugais quy sont dans l'usage de vendre ou acheter des vieux [h]abits, il leura sera defendeu [défendu] de continuer ce commerce et, s'ils veulent y presister [persister], on demandera eg[a]lement la protection de Monseigneur l'Intendant pour les y forcer" (Minutes of the *nation*, in the Departmental archives of Gironde, I, fol. 110, No. 110, Sept. 20, 1744).

[86] Archives of the Gradis family in Bordeaux, vol. 10, No. 118 bis: "Les intérêts de la nation qui sont également ceux de cette maison."

[87] "Car, Messieurs, nous ne devons point nous dissimuler que . . . c'est dans le bas étage de la Nation que le mal s'est le plus manifesté de nos jours; mais c'est avec une telle force, & ses progrès en sont si rapides, qu'ils ne laissent envisager pour nous l'avenir que desastre & qu infamie. C'est alors que nous voudrions arrêter la contagion, & qu'il n'en sera plus. C'est alors que notre autorité & nos représentation seront meprisées, & que là ou nous aurions besoin des remèdes les plus violents, nous n'aurons que de vains paliatifs à employer" (an undated document written by Gradis before 1789, *ibid.*, vol. 10, No. 117).

[88] See *supra*, n.79.

Sombart's view, which Laufenburger repeated without supporting factual data drawn from the lives of the Alsatian
Jews.[89] If one can speak of a specific economic character
of the Jewish population in Alsace at that period, one can
do so only in a negative sense, for as a minority the Jews
continued to suffer from the restrictions imposed on them
by the old regime. During the Revolution the Jews of
Alsace and the neighboring departments continued to engage
in occupations that cannot be rated as economically valuable
or indispensable. Even in the world of commerce they
continued to be mostly go-betweens, peddlers, etc.[90]

Of course, statements about "productive" or "unproductive" occupations are provocative. Was the merchant
Raphaël Lopes, who in 1817 saved the city of Bordeaux
from famine[91]—as did many other Jews in many places before him—an "unproductive" element? Also, Jews who had
no choice but to engage in peddling were not alone in this
"unproductive" field of activity. In Metz Jews were not
even mentioned in connection with the opposition to peddlers during the eighteenth century.[92] In many places
peddlers were the only merchants. According to a list of
the year VII there were seventeen licensed merchants in the
district of Hirsingue. All of them were peddlers, and sixteen
of them were Jews.[93] Because the Jewish peddlers helped
to democratize local commerce and to introduce free competition, they were disliked and persecuted by Christian
merchants.[94] Even among the "unproductive" peddlers, Jews
formed the more "productive" element. Thus, of the 124
places allotted in August, 1800, at the market of Metz

[89]   Henry Laufenburger, *Cours d'économie Alsacienne. I. Les Bases matérielles, morales et juridiques* (Paris, 1930), pp. 111-14, 215.
[90]   Anché Neher, *"La Bourgeoisie alsacienne. Etudes d'histoire sociale*
(Strasbourg-Paris, 1954), pp. 435-36.
[91]   A. Detcheverry, *Histoire des israélites de Bordeaux* (Bordeaux, 1850),
p. 103. For similar cases see Szajkowski, *The Economic Status . . . *, p. 50.
[92]   *Arrêt du Parlement en faveur du corps des marchands de Metz, contre
les colporteurs de balles. 26 février 1738* (Metz, 1740); *Consultation pour les
syndics . . . des marchands . . . contre Antoine Tissot et George Guérin,
colporteurs sans domicile . . .* (Metz, 1781). See also *Dialogue concernant le
colportage . . .* (Metz, 1783), pp. 8-40.
[93]   Departmental archives of Upper Rhine, L 101.
[94]   Szajkowski, *The Economic Status . . . *, pp. 62-63.

twenty-three were operated by twelve Jews. But they did not operate any of the twenty-one cabarets and similar places in the market.[95]

In the course of the debate on emancipation the Jews had to listen to the views of the physiocrats among the Christians and the *maskilim* among the Jews on the "productivity" or "unproductivity" of certain occupations. They could not have imagined the change of opinion that was to come almost 150 years later. For the period when Jews were legally able to change their occupations judgment cannot be rendered on the basis of a census of Jewish workers, employers, or merchants, i.e., on the percentage of Jews who were proletarian. Such judgment would ask of Jews more than of others. At the time when Jews were permitted to enter "productive" occupations, many of them were too old to give up money lending, peddling, horse trading, etc., to which they had previously been restricted. In the country at large widespread industrialization had not yet begun. Productivity was no longer conceived as inherent only in the status of a worker. The trend away from the life of a poor agrarian laborer in favor of ownership of a piece of land, away from the village and to the city, toward entering into business for oneself, away from the life of a poor worker in favor of ownership of a small factory, or a store, had already started.[96]

Most Jews happened to live in centers that were slow in becoming industrialized. Metz was still known for its famous army center, and industry in Moselle did not start until seventy years later. Strasbourg was more a trade than an industrial center. This applies to Alsace in general, with the exception of Mulhouse and a few smaller places,[97] mostly where Protestants pioneered in local industries. In Nancy the number of Jewish manufacturers rose from two in 1793 to ten in 1808, the number of artisans from one to nine, of

[95] City archives of Metz, F 4.
[96] Z. Szajkowski, *Poverty and Social Welfare among French Jews* 1800-1880 (New York, 1954), pp. 73-74.
[97] H. Contamine, *Metz et la Moselle de* 1814 *à* 1870, II (Nancy, 1932), 34-36; Brunschwig, *Les Subsistances à Strasbourg* . . . , p. 7.

workers from fifteen to forty-seven, of teachers from four to eleven. However, the number of peddlers also rose rapidly: from seven in 1793 to twenty-three in 1808, and the number of *rentiers, i.e.,* men of independent means, from seven to twenty-five. But Nancy was not a center to spur occupational shifts; on the eve of the Revolution of 1848, seven thousand men, half of the economically active population, were engaged in the liberal professions.[98] The Sephardic Jews of Saint-Esprit-lès-Bayonne continued to engage in commerce. But the entire department of Landes was without any industry.[99]

This article is a response by a student of the French Revolution to a statement made by the Marxist Jewish historian Dr. Raphael Mahler, that the French Revolution did absolutely nothing to industrialize the Jews or to make them take up agriculture so that they might achieve economic equality with the rest of the population.[100] He did not elaborate how this could have been done. Did he expect the Revolution of 1789 to force a change in the occupational status of the Jews, such as occurred during the Russian Revolution of 1917? Love of manual work during the Revolution of 1789 was not based on such methods. In fact, Mahler's statement shows only that he tried to apply a twentieth-century yardstick to eighteenth-century events. The French Revolution was liberal in its attitude toward the occupational status of the Jews, and once they were emancipated, it was up to them to maintain or change their occupational status. Additional opportunities were given to them, such as the right to buy national property, of which they did not avail themselves. Surely any force applied in this case by the revolutionary regime would have been rightly denounced as an exceptional policy directed exclusively against the Jews.

[98]   Posener, *Jewish Social Studies,* I (1939), 299; Pierre Braun, "Le Département de la Moselle à la fin de la Monarchie de Juillet," *La Révolution de 1848,* XV, No. 82 (1920), 146.

[99]   Pierre Genevray, "Les Juifs des Landes sous le Premier Empire," *Comité des travaux historiques et scientifiques. Bulletin de la section de géographie,* XXXVII (1922), 133.

[100]   Raphael Mahler, *History of the Jewish People, Modern Times,* I (New York, 1957), 67 (Yiddish edition).

The Jewish Aspect of Levying Taxes during
The French Revolution of 1789

THE financial policies of the French Revolution of 1789 present one of the most essential, yet complicated chapters in the history of the period. It is therefore important to examine the Jewish aspect of the levying of the revolutionary taxes, and especially to consider whether Jews were singled out in the drive to save the Republic's finances through high taxation and fines.

From the beginning of the Revolution Jewish communities made voluntary gifts for various revolutionary causes. In Lunéville (Meurthe) the Jews proposed at the very beginning of the Revolution, on August 3, 1789, to collect a patriotic tax. On February 15, 1790 Marx Berr, Syndic of the Council of the Alsatian Jewish communities, presented buckles and other silver articles collected among the Jews of Bischheim, Türchheim, Wintzenheim, and other communities to the National Guard of Strasbourg. The Jews of Soultz organized a collection to help the parents of poor soldiers.[1] Individual Jews, too, contributed large sums. On May 3, 1791 the city of Carpentras obtained from Abraham Crémieux and Jaccassuye a loan of 1,600 *livres* for aid to the poor[2]. In 1792 Solomon Moyse Lévy, Louis-Isaac Berr and Lippman Cerfberr of Nancy presented gifts for the poor and working women of the local tobacco factory.[3] The names of D. Lopes Dias, David Azevedo, Abraham Mendes, Fonseque (junior) and other Jews appeared on the list of subscribers to the patriotic loan of 30 million *livres* in Bordeaux. During the

---

[1] *Nouveau mémoire pour les Juifs de Lunéville et de Sarguemines . . .* (sine loco, 1790), pp. 5–6; *Suite de l'Etat des boucles et autres effets en argent, remis au Bureau du Comité de la Garde Nationale Strasbourgeoise, pour don patriotique offert à la Nation* (15 *février* 1790) (sine loco et anno), Broadside ; M. GINSBURGER, *Histoire de la communauté israélite de Soultz* (Strasbourg, 1939), p. 40. On voluntary contributions by Strasbourg Jews see also LÉON KAHN, *Les Juifs de Paris pendant la Révolution* (Paris, 1898), pp. 155–56, 160–61. In Marseilles the syndic of the Jewish community, Israél Vidal, was appointed in 1791 as collector of a patriotic tax among the Jews: "Une députation du Sieur Vidal, l'année dernière, auprès du Club de cette Ville, pour y présenter, au nom de sa nation, à l'occasion de la prise des Forts, une somme d'argent pour la répartition de laquelle il avait été nommé taxateur". *Reponses a des nouvelles objections. Pour les Sieurs Vidal et Consorts* (Marseille, 1792), p. 33.
[2] City Archives of Carpentras, CC 178.
[3] City Archives of Nancy, minutes, vol. 6, p. 124 (Apr. 5, 1792), vol. 8, p. 221 (May 8, 1792), vol 9, p. 18 (Nov. 10, 1792); CHR. PFISTER, *Histoire de Nancy* (Paris, 1909), III, 333; J. GODECHOT, *Les Juifs et la contribution volontaire sous la Révolution, Revue Juive de Lorraine,* i (1926), 71–74.

Originally published in *The Journal of Jewish Studies,* vol. XI (1960).

famine at the end of 1792 Bordeaux Jews donated large sums—the Gradis and Raba families 20,000 *livres* each.[4] But these gifts were not always voluntary. Thus, the Jews of Nice donated large sums to buy wheat for the army from a Spanish ship. But the population was warned that those who would not donate would be prosecuted.[5]

Soon—especially during the Terror—the patriotic gifts were replaced by forced revolutionary taxation. The Revolution looked for money and in many cases it became urgent to find victims who possessed the badly needed cash. Bankers, merchants, persons suspected of speculation and various counter-revolutionary acts and wealthy people in general were taxed, fined and arrested. Jews were often found among them. J. B. O. Garnerin, the Committee of Public Safety's agent for the Upper Rhine, sent to Paris on July 26, 1794 lists of suspects, wealthy peasants, merchants, and Jews.[6]

But were the Jews in fact the victims of economic attack precisely in virtue of their being Jews?

According to the historian A. Aulard, Jews who were sentenced during the Terror fell victims not as a result of any anti-Jewish feelings, but because they either were—or were suspected of being—counter-revolutionaries. But according to Baruch Szyster, the author of a thesis on Jews during the Revolution, the Terror merely revived the traditional anti-Jewish persecution, adding to it grievances of an economic character.[7] In fact, it seems that Jews did often fall victims to revolutionary financial policies. The Decree of September 27, 1791 granted to the Ashkenazic Jews full civil rights but they were still the object of detestation by the people and the local administrations. Hence they suffered from the rancour of the local anti-Jewish administrations and the drastic economic and other exigencies of the Revolution. This was true not only in matters of taxation. In April 1792 the city council of Bischheim (Lower Rhine) billeted soldiers exclusively on the Jews.[8] But it

---

[4] *Noms de Messieurs les souscripteurs de Bordeaux, pour l'emprunt de trente millions* . . . (Bordeaux, no date); TH. MALVEZIN, *Histoire de Juifs à Bordeaux* (Bordeaux, 1875), p. 272. On voluntary gifts by the Jews of Paris see KAHN, *op. cit.*, pp. 152–59.

[5] JOSEPH COMBET, *La Révolution à Nice* (Paris, 1912), p. 67.

[6] ANDRÉ BOIDIN, *La contribution patriotique* (Nancy, 1909), p. 303; MARCEL MARION, *Histoire financière de la France depuis 1715* (Paris, 1921), III, 199, 201; P. LEUILLIOT, *Les Jacobins de Colmar* (Strasbourg, 1923), p. 311.

[7] A. AULARD, in *La Révolution française*, LXXXI (1928), p. 272; BORUCH SZYSTER, *La Révolution française et les Juifs* . . . (Toulouse, 1929), p. 126.

[8] P. HILDENFINGER, *Actes du district de Strasbourg relatifs aux Juifs* (1790), *REJ*, LX (1910), pp. 248–49.

should be remembered that the Jews' troubles were not the result of any anti-Jewish feelings in the federal, central economic agencies of the Government, although representatives sent from Paris were sometimes influenced by the local anti-Jewish feelings. Thus, according to one source, one such a representative named Milhaud stated in a report to the Paris Jacobins that "many very rich and very tough Jews" were among the counter-revolutionaries of Strasbourg. Pierre Philip, a Jacobin of Bordeaux origin who directed the Terror in Nancy, wrote that, at his arrival, Nancy was an aristocratic centre of "the former nobility, a multitude of Jews, rich merchants, priests and monks".[9] In the Strasbourg *Société populaire* the Jews were attacked on May 3, 10 and 13, 1794 as speculators and usurers. The Society had adopted a resolution against usurers in general, Christian and Jews, but Joseph Antoine Mainoni, the national agent for the Strasbourg district, warned the municipalities to be wary of the Jews especially, and ordered the Jews to show proof of income. This was an open invitation to economic persecution directed against the Jews.[10] When it became necessary to make an example in the fight against speculation, the Alsatian authorities chose as their victims two Jews. Simon Dreyfus was sentenced on November 16, 1793 to six years in chains; but on January 18, 1795, the Convention revoked the sentence as unjust. Samuel Chazen of Niedernai was also sentenced to six years, the severest sentence in such cases.[11] This rigorous procedure against Jews occurred also when fines were imposed. Raphaël Bloch of Wentzenheimb (Upper Rhine) was fined 25,000 *livres* for selling leather above the maximum price. In a petition to the Legislative Committee he showed that according to the law of September 29, 1793, he ought to have been fined 1,386 *livres*, i.e. but twice the price of the confiscated leather; that he was not wealthy, and had been forced to borrow from friends in order to avoid imprisonment. The Legislative Committee quashed

[9] VICTOR DE ST. GENIS, *Une conspiration royaliste à Strasbourg en* 1792 (Paris, 1880), pp. 427–28; H. POULET, *Le sans-culotte Philip, président de la Société populaire de Nancy* (1793–1794), *Annales de l'Est*, series 2, ii (1906), p. 265.

[10] *L'Agent national du district de Strasbourg aux communes de l'arrondissement* (Strasbourg, 11 Thermidor an II); LAZARE ZAY, "Judenschaft", *Strassburgische Zeitung* (1794), p. 253; F. CH. HEITZ, *Less Sociétés politiques de Strasbourg* . . . (Strasbourg, 1863), pp. 346–50; E. MÜHLENBECK, *Euloge Schneider*, 1793 (Strasbourg-Paris, 1896), p. 7.

[11] Archives Nationales, D III 213 (dr. 1, pp. 70–71); *Une affaire Dreyfus en l'an III*, *Archives israélites*, LXIX (1904), p. 172; R. WERNER, *L'approvisionement en pain de la population du Bas-Rhin pendant la Révolution* (Strasbourg, 1951), p. 344.

the fine.[12] In some areas where anti-Jewish feeling prevailed even during the Revolution heavy patriotic taxes were imposed mainly on Jews. Frequently Jews refused to pay because they did not possess sufficient money. Because of this many Jews of Issenheim (Upper Rhine) were imprisoned until a court of law freed them.[13] The brothers Hayem and Cerf Worms of Sarrelouis were forced to pay one sixth of the city's entire patriotic tax.[14] A rumour spread in Alsace that the terrorist leader Eulogius Schneider had decided to force the Jews to pay a levy of one and a half million *livres*. This was not true. Schneider was one of the rare Alsatian Jacobins who were friendly towards the Jews, and he did not single them out in his terrorist activities. The rumour did, however, inspire others to persecute Jews.[15] Wealthy Jews, and Jews who were suspected of being wealthy, were heavily taxed and attacked by the Jacobins. The Paris Representative Milhaud reported on November 21, 1793 from Alsace about a Jew who was forced to pay 200,000 *livres*. He refused to pay and was sentenced to kneel for two hours on the scaffold of the guillotine. It was only after being laid down under the guillotine for the second time that the Jews paid the fine. A Jewish Jacobin from Strasbourg who came to Paris in order to solicit for the repeal of a heavy fine was requested by the Paris Jacobins on December 28, 1793 to hand over his membership card and his name was forwarded to the Committee of Public Safety.[16]

The tobacco and cloth manufacturer Alexandre Séligmann, a son-in-law of Cerfberr, was taxed 200,000 *livres* during the Terror. He spent two months in prison, a part of his property was confiscated, and his partner Abraham Auerbach was also arrested. During the Thermidorian Reaction Séligmann published a sharp pamphlet against the *régime* of the Terror during which, he stated, he had lost 635,413 *livres* and he declared that the fact of his being

---

[12] Archives Nationales, D–III–215; *Pétition. Le Citoyen Raphaël Bloch, habitant de la commune de Ventzenheimb, district de Colmar, département du Haut Rhin, au Comité de Législation* (Colmar, an 2), 4 pp.

[13] VÉRON RÉVILLE, *Histoire de la Révolution dans le département du Haut-Rhin* (Colmar, 1865), p. 45; F. B. BALZWEILER, *Histoire de la ville & du bailliage de Soultz, Revue d'Alsace*, XLVI (1898), p. 293.

[14] Archives Nationales, C 82 (817–2).

[15] R. REUSS, *Séligmann Alexandre* . . . (Strasbourg, 1880), p. 27. On Schneider's attitude toward Jews see Z. SZAJKOWSKI, *The Discussion and Struggle over Emancipation* . . . , *Historia Judaica*, xvii (1955), pp. 139–40.

[16] F. A. AULARD, *La Sociéte des Jacobins* . . . *de Paris* (Paris, 1895), V, 526, pp. 584–85. The religious teacher and scribe Jessel Lehman noted in 1793 in his diary (written in a ciphered Yiddish) that large sums had already been taken away from Strasbourg Jews. The diary is in the Alsatian Museum of Strasbourg, see p. 25b.

a Jew had prejudiced the persecution against him.[17] Marx Berr, another member of the Cerfberr family, who had been a Jacobin until the purge during the Terror, was taxed 25,000 *livres* on October 31, 1793. He appealed, and on the following November 15, the tax was reduced to 10,000 *livres*. But during the Thermidorian Reaction he was again required to pay 600,000 *livres*. The request of another Cerfberr, Baruch Baerr, to reduce his taxes was rejected because "he never showed any proofs of patriotism". Loew Lévi was ordered on December 3, 1793 to pay his part of a 20,000 *livres* compulsory tax within 24 hours.[18] Among the 193 richest people of Strasbourg, who were forced by the Representatives A. L. L. de Saint-Just and P. F. J. Lebas to pay a compulsory tax of nine million *livres*, the sum of 1,405,000 *livres* was contributed by 31 Jews, including 300,000 *livres* to be paid by the head of the Cerfberr family.[19]

On the other hand the case of Abraham Alcan is worth mentioning. Alcan was a merchant of Nancy, who settled in Paris during the Revolution and later in Strasbourg. On the list of the forced tax of October 31, 1793 he is recorded as paying 15,000 *livres*. But he also managed to get himself accepted into the Strasbourg Jacobin Club, and appears on the list of its members of October 25, 1794.[20]

About four hundred Jewish families lived in Metz (Moselle). One hundred and ninety of them were listed in the "voluntary" tax which began to be drafted on December 1, 1789 and 329 in a printed list of tax-payers in the ghetto. According to one source, the Surveillance Committee on September 9, 1793 requested that the Jewish community of Metz pay a tax of 20,000 francs. Only three Jews were among the 100 persons listed as the richest inhabitants of

[17] Séligmann Alexandre, *Dénonciation à mes concitoyens des vexations que m'ont fait éprouver les fidèles suppôts du traître Robespierre* . . . (Strasbourg, an III), 38 pp.; Reuss, *op. cit.* Séligmann was a deputy to the Assembly called in 1806 by Napoleon I. He was then called by the Alsatian authorities a victim of the Revolution. Departmental archives of Lower Rhine, M 192; *Souvenir et Science*, V, No. 5 (1934), p. 4.

[18] A. ULRICH, *Recueil de pièces* . . . (= *Livre Bleu*) (Strasbourg (1795)), I, 18, 36; F. L'HUILLER, *Recherches sur l'Alsace napoléonienne* (Strasbourg, 1947), p. 12; Departmental archives of Lower Rhine, 1 L 1204 (Marx Baer's petition of October 27, 1797).

[19] Another list of October 31, 1793, comprising 315 wealthy citizens of Strasbourg who had to pay 6,824,113 *livres* included 23 Jews with 330,200 *livres*. It should be noted that all the Jewish names were grouped together. J. G. TREUTEL, *Tyranie exercée à Strasbourg par Saint-Just et Lebas* (Versailles, no date), p. 19; *Livre bleu*, I, 213; *Arrêté des Représentants du Peuple* (Strasbourg, no date), Broadside.

[20] ETIENNE BARTH, *Notes biographiques sur les hommes de la Révolution à Strasbourg et les environs* (Strasbourg, 1885), p. 174.

Metz, but in general the Jews paid a much larger proportion of the compulsory taxes. One hundred Jews had to pay their proportion of such a tax of 408,340 *livres* in coined money, excluding *assignats*, in the year IV (1793–1794). In the second section of Metz (which included the ghetto) 89 Jews had to pay 18,700 *livres* in coined money and 1,287,000 in *assignats*.[21] It should be noted that in Metz, too, Jews were singled out in the fight against speculation and forestalling.[22] In Nancy (Meurthe), economic chicanery against the Jews was a distinct part of Jacobin policy during the Terror. The Jewish community, though numerically small, was forced to present one-twelfth of all the shirts, and one-tenth of all the shoes which were required for the army from the entire city. On November 11, 1793 a compulsory tax of 5,026,000 *livres* was imposed upon the opulent citizens of Nancy. Twelve Jews were to pay two thirds of the entire sum, and 214 Christians the remaining third, Cerf Berr was forced to pay 200,000 *livres*, Lippman Cerf-Berr. Mayer-Max and Berr-Isaac Berr 300,000 *livres* each, Théodore (the son of Cerf-Berr) and Mayer-Max the younger 50,000 *livres* each, and six other Jews from 6,000 to 20,000 *livres* each. Berr-Isaac Berr, Lippman and Théodore Cerf-Berr were unable to pay such large sums and preferred to be arrested. Nobody in Nancy made a secret of the fact that rich Jews were singled out. Thus the terrorist leader of Nancy, Pierre Philip, wrote in a pamphlet of "rich Jews and speculators taxed with considerable sums".[23]

A Jew of Paris named Moses was requested on May 15, 1793 by

[21] City archives of Metz, 2G2; *Contribution patriotique. Liste de toutes les personnes domiciliées et résidantes sur la paroisse Saint-Ferroy, de la ville de Metz* (Metz. (1789)), Broadside. Reprinted by R. PAQUET, *Bibliographie analytique de l'histoire de Metz pendant la Révolution* (Paris, 1926), I, pp. 55–58; A. CAHEN, *Le Rabbinat de Metz . . . , REJ* XIII (1886), p. 111; R. ANCHEL, *Napoléon et les Juifs* (Paris, 1928), p. 24; *Liste des cent Citoyens les plus imposés de la commune de Metz* (13 janvier 1794) (*sine loco et anno*), Broadside (Jacob Cahen, Cerf Goudechaux fils, Cerf Zacharias).
[22] *Police. De par le maire et les officiers municipaux de la ville de Metz. Sentence concernant les amidonniers, boulangers, marchands de farine, juifs et autres* (Metz, October 9, 1790), Broadside. It should be noted that a Jew, Jacob-Godchaux-Beer, was one of the four commissioners nominated on July 26, 1794, to combat forestalling and speculation: *Extrait de registre des délibérations du Conseil général de la commune de Metz. Du 8 Thermidor an II* (Metz (1794)), Broadside; PAQUET, *op cit.*, I, p. 497.
[23] ALBERT TROUX, *La vie politique dans le département de la Meurthe d'Août 1792 à Octobre 1795* (Nancy, 1936), II, pp. 101–02; *Arrêté des Représentants du Peuple envoyés extraordinairement près l'armée du Rhin, relatif à la levée de cinq millions imposés sur les riches de la commune de Nancy. Du 21 Brumaire an socond* (Nancy, an 2), 8 pp. JACQUES GODECHOT, *Les Juifs à Nancy de 1789 à 1795, REJ* LXXXI (1928), pp. 27–30; P. PHILIP, *Exposé succint des événements contre-révolutionnaires . . .* (Nancy, n.d.), p. 33.

the revolutionary Committee of the *faubourg* Montmartre to pay 500 *livres* in the form of a loan for the army. When he refused to pay Moses was accused of anti-revolutionary acts.[24]

Of special interest are the forced taxes and fines imposed upon the Jews of Bordeaux. The Ashkenazic Jews were not as rich as their Sephardic co-religionists, whose taste for wealth and magnificence exposed them to many disturbances and persecutions in times of war and revolution. The historian Ad. Detchevery noted correctly that the prosperity of the Bordeaux Jews was like a talisman which always brought catastrophy to them.[25] From October 30, 1793 until July 10, 1794 90 wealthy persons of Bordeaux were fined 6,940,300 *livres* by the Military Tribunal. Among them were the following seven Jews, who were fined 775,000 *livres*: Moyse Lange (*l*.80,000), Moyse Marc-Foi (*l*.50,000), Samuel Astruc (*l*.30,000), the five brothers Raba (*l*.500,000), Jean Perpignan (*l*.50,000), Jean David (*l*.15,000), Raphael Lopes (*l*.50,000). To this may be added a fine of 1,200,000 *livres* imposed upon Charles Peixotto who, though a convert, continued to be considered as a Jew by outsiders.[26]

But it should be noted that, unlike the compulsory taxes and fines imposed upon Jews in the Alsatian and neighbouring departments, the fines imposed upon the Jews of Bordeaux were not inspired by anti-Jewish feelings. This is another proof that economic persecution of Jews was a result of local feelings, and not of any policy directed by the Government. All the very rich Jews of Bordeaux, even those who participated in the Girondist movement, got off with fines during the Terror and not one was sentenced to death. David Gradis and his family, one of the richest men of Bordeaux, did not suffer much during the Terror. His office was sealed by the authorities and he was put under house arrest guarded by four *sans-culottes*. But his life and fortune were spared.[27]

Among those who got off with fines were the five Jewish brothers Raba who were fined 500,000 *livres* on September 30, 1793. This was a huge sum, but the Rabas were among the richest men in

[24] L. KAHN, *op. cit.*, pp. 221–22.

[25] AD. DETECHEVERRY, *Histoire des Israelites de Bordeaux* (Bordeaux, 1850), p. 72.

[26] *Examen critique ou Réfutation de l'Histoire de Bordeaux . . . par l'Ermite de Floirac* (Bordeaux, 1838), pp. 126–132; A. VIVIE, *Histoire de la Terreur à Bordeaux* (Bordeaux, 1877), II, pp. 343–401; TH. MALVEZIN, *Histoire des Juifs à Bordeaux* (Bordeaux, 1875), pp. 266–71.

[27] Departmental archives of Gironde, L 1957, p. 2193; City archives of Bordeaux, "Dictionnaire des arrestations", by VIVIE, vol. 4.

Bordeaux and the price was not too high for saving their five heads. In a notice published in a commercial newspaper the Rabas promised to pay 50,000 *livres* to anyone able to prove that the accusation of speculation made against them was justified. At the same time they tried to bribe the terrorist rulers. They gave a dinner-party in their famous house in Talence for 40 important revolutionaries of the department, including the terrorist leader, J.-B.-M. Lacombe. This provoked a storm of protests; in time of hunger the Rabas' guests were served the best food. On July 16, 1794 the five brothers stated that the dinner was merely a patriotic gathering of *sans-culottes* in honour of the Republic's victories; the guests chanted "revolutionary hymns" in a spirit of "republican gaiety", and the fare was frugal. Two weeks later, on the night of July 31/August 1, 1794, with the defeat of Robespierre in Paris, Lacombe himself was arrested, and that was the end of the Terror in Bordeaux. It also saved the Rabas from the probable vengeance of the Terrorists, concerned to save those of their colleagues who had banqueted with millionaires. It should be noted that the Rabas were not the only people to give such dinner-parties; Bardineau, Robrahn, and other non-Jews did the same. But the case of the Rabas' dinner-party has been much used by historians in order to discredit Lacombe. These historians overlook the fact that it also disgraced the Rabas, from whom Lacombe refused to accept a bribe of 200,000 *livres*.[28] Certainly in

---

[28] City archives of Bordeaux, 65 D 10 & vol. 7, pp. 444 of A. VIVIE's "Dictionnaire"; Departmental archives of Gironde, L. 29, 1935, 1957, 11 L. 54; *Journal de Commerce* (Bordeaux), June 21, 1793; pp. 698–99; A. VIVIE, *op. cit.*, II; 290–94; R. BROUILLARD, *Des impositions extraordinaires sur le revenu pendant la Révolution* . . . (Bordeaux, 1916), pp. 201–03; P. BÉCAMPS, *La Révolution à Bordeaux* . . . (Bordeaux, 1953), pp. 220–21, 321; E. LABADIE, *La presse bordelaise* . . . (Bordeaux, 1910), p. 136; MAURICE FERREUS, *Histoire de Talence* (Bordeaux, 1926), pp. 69–83; *Idem*, *Le Serment des Allées Damour*, roman, *Petite Gironde*, May 9, 1936, Aug. 17, 1937, Apr. 10, 1938. On the Raba house in Talence see : (PIERRE) BERNADAU, *Promenade à Talence, ou Description de la maison de campagne de MM. Raba frères* . . . (Bordeaux, 1803), 14 pp. (According to Bernadau's "Tablettes" the publication of this pamphlet was financed by the Raba family, see City Library of Bordeaux, manuscript 713–1, vol. 8, p. 41, Oct. 14, 1803); *Bulletin Polygmathique* (Bordeaux, 1808), p. 240; *Le Guide ou Conducteur de l'étranger à Bordeaux* (Bordeaux 1827), pp. 428–31; MESTE VERDIÉ, *Oeuvres gasconnes* (Bordeaux, 1921), p. 106 (reprint from the first edition of 1817); MERLET (J. F. LOUIS), *Talence, La France*, Sept. 22, 1937). Many Jews possessed summer houses in Talence, which is located four kilometres from Bordeaux and was called "Chantilly of Bordeaux". Abraham Gradis, who died on July 17, 1780, left a house there of the value of 64,150 *livres* (Departmental archives of Gironde, C, D384–II f. 99). But in 1874 there were no more Jews there: E. FÉRET, *Statistique* . . . *de la Gironde* (Bordeaux, 1889), II, pp. 191–94.

During Thermidor the Raba brothers demanded the return to them of the fine paid during the Terror (Archives nationales, D–III–99, 3, p. 81).

return for large sums of money the Military Commission of Bordeaux reopened sealed houses and offices and even released prisoners, both Jews and non-Jews.[29] These were not, however, cases of bribery, although cases of bribery probably did exist. Every revolutionary period produces people who are determined to bribe, but historians have too often forgotten to find out whether these bribes were accepted by the revolutionaries.[30] Similarly, these practices of securing release for money could not be said to be anti-Jewishly inclined, even though such practices in Alsace have been deemed by historians to be anti-Jewish acts. The Jewish revolutionaries of Saint-Esprit-lès-Bayonne, where the Jacobin Club was composed mostly of Jews, used the same method to secure money badly needed for the Revolution. In that place merchants also were arrested for being "egotistic", and released only after making gifts of large sums to the Republic. Shall we then condemn the Jewish revolutionaries of Saint-Esprit as anti-Jewish?[31] Saint-Esprit had many rich Jewish merchants. According to a list of May 10, 1794 drawn up for the purpose of levying a tax of 40,000 livres, 78 families possessed 9,490,000 livres, among whom the largest proportion—8,790,000 livres—belonged to rich Jews. Seventy-three families possessed 8,790,000 livres (l.400,000 or more each), and 34 possessed from l.10,000 to l.400,000 each. Many people were forced to make "voluntary" gifts of large sums for various patriotic purposes beyond the official tax imposed on the entire population. Thus Benjamin Ls. Nounes, the richest Jew of Saint-Esprit, gave a gift of 150,000 livres in May 1794 for the construction of a frigate.[32] This economic policy pursued by Jewish Jacobins in Saint-Esprit was in line with the policy applied everywhere else, and rich Jews could not have been excepted from the general rule.

[29] City archives of Bordeaux, Minutes copied by VIVIE, Aug. 15, 1794.

[30] According to testimony given at the trial of Lacombe, the latter accepted 32,000 livres for a promise to liberate Isaac Pereyre, and Lacombe's wife accepted a gold ring. But this could not be accepted unreservedly as a fact: see the printed sentences against Lacombe and his wife; Journal de Club National de Bordeaux (30 Thermidor, an 2), p. 14; BÉCAMPS, op. cit., pp. 280–83.

[31] ALBERT DARRICAU, Scènes de la Terreur à Bayonne et aux environs, 1793–1794 (Bayonne-Biarritz, 1903), p. 149; E. GINSBURGER, Le Comité de surveillance de Jean-Jacques Rouseau, Saint-Esprit-lès-Bayonne (Paris, 1936), pp. 117, 120, 123, 158, 164, 183, 220, 245, 271.

[32] Proclamation du citoyen Monestier . . . sur l'établissement d'un carême civique. Tarbes, ce 22 floreal an 2 (16 mai 1794) (sine loco et anno), 22 pp; H. LÉON, Histoire des Juifs de Bayonne (Paris, 1893), pp. 167–69; GINSBURGER, op. cit., pp. 37–38, 118, 164–66, 180–81.

In the port of La Rochelle Salomon Rouget paid in 1791 500 *livres* —a quarter of his income—towards the compulsory patriotic levy and 1,300 *livres* for the compulsory loan of 1793.[33] Jews were also singled out in the economic policies of the former papal province of Avignon and Comtat Venaissin, which became a part of France on September 14, 1791. Thus, Jews especially were attacked in a proclamation against speculation.[34] (But similar attacks occurred there also during the Thermidorian reaction.[35]) In the occupied city of Carouge, Moyse Treyfulz had to pay 10,000 *livres* as· a compulsory tax; he protested, and the authorities acknowledged that the sum should be reduced.[36]

Many Jews protested against the heavy taxation. The Alsatian Jews complained not only individually, but also as a collective group. As a result of such a protest the Paris Representative André Foussedoire complained to the Government against anti-Jewish chicaneries and the daily accusations raised against them of speculation and every other possible crime. The Jews stated in a petition that they were victims of despotism and tyranny: "the enemies of the Republic are better treated in the Lower Rhine than we are; in slave countries taxes are raised with less inhumanity than the arbitrary and exorbitant taxes required from us". The Jews concluded their petition with the following words: "Long live the National Convention! may it establish an empire on the basis of liberty and equality". As a result of this protest the Legislative Committee ordered the Alsatian authorities in November, 1794 to afford protection to the Jews.[37]

It was only after the Terror was over that the Jews were able to make such protests against chicanery. There is no doubt that many Jews arrested during the Terror were saved by the Thermidorian reaction which followed the Terror. But the Thermidor also saved the lives of non-Jews, and this had nothing particularly to do with

[33] *Revue de Saintonge et d'Aunis*, xxviii (1908), p. 25.
[34] *Proclamation de l'administration du département de Vaucluse, relative à l'agiotage* (Avignon, 1793), 3 pp.; J. F. ANDRÉ, *Histoire de la Révolution avignonaise* (Paris, 1844), I, pp. 235–36.
[35] An Avignon petition of February 1795 requested strong measures against Jewish speculation in gold which was used by Avignon to purchase wheat from Genoa: City archives, Rev. D 55, no. 62.
[36] E. GINSBURGER, *Histoire des Juifs de Carouge* . . . , *REJ*, LXXVI (1923), pp. 152–53.
[37] *Foussedoire, Représentant du Peuple dans les Départemens des Haut-et-Bas-Rhin* (Colmar (1794)), 4 pp.; *Extrait du registre des arrêtés du Comité de Législation. Séance du 11 Brumaire, l'an troisième* . . . (Strasbourg, 1795), 2 pp.

JEWISH ASPECT OF LEVYING TAXES IN FRENCH REVOLUTION 535

Jews. Nevertheless, the end of the Terror did not completely eliminate anti-Jewish feeling and activity.[38] On the contrary, it seems that during the Thermidorian reaction and later anti-Jewish feelings prevailed in federal governmental agencies also. In Alsace the Jews suffered at the beginning of Thermidor, but anti-Jewish acts were reinforced there a little later, at the beginning of 1796, when more radical elements with a Jacobin tendency again took over the Alsatian administration.[39] The Jewish teacher and scribe Jessel Lehman then noted that the Alsatian Jews feared that they would be banished from France.[40]

Economically, the Jews suffered less during the new *régime*. But this should not be regarded as a change in the attitude towards Jews. The general situation in the country changed with the end of the Terror and Jews, too, profited from it. Still, in many cases even during Thermidor Jews were forced to pay extremely large taxes. The aristocratic newspaper *Le Babillard* proposed to levy a special tax upon Jews, because they all possessed well-lined purses. But other newspapers protested and the Jew Zalkind Hourwitz wrote that he himself knew many hundreds of Jews whose portfolios contained safety identifications only.[41] On October 4, 1794 the two Jews Léopold Samuel and Marx Samuel of Niederhagenthal (Upper Rhine) were taxed 4,500 *livres* each; they had to pay almost the whole tax of the entire city.[42] On December 10, 1795 13 Jews figured out a list of the 58 rich people of Strasbourg who had to grant a forced loan; five of the 22 wealthiest families to pay the largest sums were Jewish.[43] Two Jewish families resided in Dredenhoffen prior to 1789 and 14 families settled there during the first five years of the Revolution. In 1795 they were all, even the poor, forced to pay the compulsory tax. The Jews protested and won their case, with the exception of the wealthy Abraham.[44] On October 21, 1796 Elie and 31 other Jews of Rimbach (Upper Rhine) wrote in

[38] "La fin de la Terreur n'apporta aux Juifs ni la sécurité, ni la tranquilité absolues": R. ANCHEL, *op. cit.*, p. 25; "l'antipathie contre les concitoyens du culte mosaïque subsista chez les autorités thermidoriennes comme chez leurs prédécesseurs jacobins": R. REUSS, *Documents* . . . , *REJ*, LIX (1910), p. 252.
[39] REUSS, *op. cit.*, p. 263.
[40] Lehman's diary, p. 29 A (see note 16).
[41] *Amis des Lois*, Oct. 25, 1797; *Le Journal de Paris*, No. 36 (Brumaire, an VI); KAHN, *op. cit.*, p. 139; A. AULARD, *Paris pendant la réaction thermidorienne et sous le Directoire* (Paris, 1902), IV, p. 412.
[42] Departmental archives of Upper Rhine, L 700.
[43] REUSS, *op. cit.*, p. 263–64.
[44] A. J. KOHN, *Zur Geschichte der Juden in Diedenhoffen* (Diedenhoffen, 1913), p. 32; M. GINSBURGER, *op. cit.*, pp. 40–41.

a petition that none of them was wealthy and that some were even paupers, but the City Council nonetheless taxed them with large sums while exempting wealthy Christians from paying taxes at all. As a result of their complaint one Christian family, which possessed three quarters of the properties in the village, had to pay a similar percentage of tax. On February 24, 1796 Gabriel Bloch of Soultz (Upper Rhine) was asked to pay a tax of 11,000 *livres*; he proved that his entire possessions were worth only *l.*4,400 and he was reclassified among those taxable under the sixth category. Similar petitions were sent by other Jews of Soultz, Bollwiler and Tungholtz.

*   *   *   *

Financial problems often shed light upon other important facts about the Jewish life during the Revolution. It is worth noting a few of these.

In a petition of November 23, 1790, almost one year before the emancipation of the Ashkenazic Jews, the family of Cerfberr demanded of the city council of Strasbourg to be granted all civil rights, including that of paying the patriotic taxes as well as regular city taxes. A petition signed by Marx Berr, Baruch Berr, Samuel Séligmann Alexandre, Marx Alexandre, Mayer Lazare and Wolf Lévi of the Cerfberr family recalled the King's Letters patent of March 1775 which granted to the family the right of residence in Strasbourg and requested that they be given all civil rights granted on January 28, 1790 to the Sephardic Jews and to those possessing such Letters Patent. On December 20, 1790, and later again on September 20, 1791, the Cerfberr request was rejected.[45] In some cases taxes were used as an excuse for anti-Jewish persecution. The Jews of Wentzenheimb (Upper Rhine) complained that they were not permitted to take the oath of allegiance to the Republic and thus become full citizens, because they owed 505 *livres* in arrears of taxes.[46] In some cases inspectors of taxes used tax registers of the Jewish communities in order to determine the amount to be paid by Jews. On December 17, 1792 the City Council of Metz rejected

---

[45] City archives of Strasbourg, minutes of the *Corps municipal*, vol. 2, pp. 89–91, 161–62, 760; R. REUSS, *L'Alsace pendant la Révolution française* (Paris, 1894), II, pp. 85–86. According to ADOLPHE SEYBOTH (*Das Alte Strasbourg* (Strassburg, n.d., p. 173) Cerfberr refused to pay taxes before being granted full citizenship. I have not been able to find any archival source to prove this.

[46] AN, D–III–215.

a protest of Nathan Terquem against high taxes because the Jewish community had appraised his revenue at over 4,000 *livres*.[47]

In conclusion, it should be said that anti-Jewish feelings prevailed even during the Revolution, and that symptoms of this can be observed in the Revolution's financial policies. The Jacobins, who in their fight against religious practices did not single out Jews,[48] were in their handling of the financial and other economic affairs of the Revolution, more influenced by traditional anti-Jewish feelings. But even these symptoms of anti-Jewish feeling in financial policy found their expression in *chicaneries* practised against Jews, but not in open financial measures directed openly and exclusively against Jews as a community. There was no official revolutionary levy against Jews as a collective body.[49] In this respect the Revolution was even more liberal than the later *régimes* at the beginning of the 19th century, when Jews of the Alsatian departments were singled out as a collective body and forced to pay heavier taxes than were Christians.[50]

[47] City archives of Metz, minutes, vol. 9, fol. 329.

[48] Z. SAZJKOWSKI, *The Attitude of French Jacobins Toward Jewish Religion*, *Historia Judaica*, xviii (1956), pp. 107–120.

[49] The statement by some historians (J. HERMANN, in *L'Univers Israélite*, XXXIX (1884), pp. 255–57 and R. ANCHEL, *op. cit.*, p. 24), that the Cerfberr family had to pay such a levy is not correct.

[50] Z. SZAJKOWSKI, *Poverty and Social Welfare Among French Jews* (New York, 1954), p. 15.

JEWISH EMIGRÉS DURING THE FRENCH REVOLUTION*

The fate of the emigrés who left France during the Revolution and of the anti-revolutionary elements who were deported or sentenced is one of the important subjects in the historiography of the French Revolution. Their exact number is unknown. All those who left without permission were listed as counter-revolutionary emigrants, and they were arrested if they came back without permission. Their property was confiscated and sold as national property (*biens nationaux*).[1] Their families were either assigned restricted residences, fined, or declared as emigrants and their goods seized. The law permitted only certain categories to return later to France. According to some sources, about 30,000 Alsatians emigrated from Lower Rhine alone. Up to 1825, only 1,507 of them had received indemnities for their confiscated properties.

There is no doubt that special laws were necessary and justified in regard to emigrants who were enemies of the new regime. Unfortunately, among those who were listed as emigrants or who were deported or sentenced there were also people who were not adversaries of the Revolution, but rather victims of various unhappy circumstances, plots or laws. Many had never left the country.[2]

There were Jews among these people. Some openly favored the old regime. For example, on September 2, 1792, the Lorraine Jewish leader Berr-Isaac Berr and his father signed the petition of the *aristocrates* of Nancy against the destruction of the monument of Louis XV on the city's Place Royale.[3] On July 23, 1794, a Jewish spy, Léopold Bernheim of

---

*The following abbreviations are used in the notes: AD—Archives départementales; AN—Archives nationales (Paris); *REJ—Revue des études juives.*

1 Szajkowski, Z., "Jewish Participation in the Sale of National Property during the French Revolution," in JEWISH SOCIAL STUDIES, vol. xiv (1952) 291-316.

2 Ragon, Marcel, *La Législation sur les émigrés, 1789-1825* (Paris 1904); Marion, Marcel, *Quelques exemples de l'application des lois sur l'émigration. Récits du temps de la Terreur,* Extrait de la *Revue historique* (Paris 1911) p. 3; Reuss, Rodolphe, *La Grande fuite de Décembre 1793 et la situation politique et religieuse du Bas-Rhin de 1794 à 1799* (Strasbourg 1924); Gain, André, "Liste des émigrés, déportés et condamnés pour cause révolutionnaire du département de la Moselle (1791-1800)," in *Annuaire de la Société d'histoire et d'archéologie de la Lorraine,* vol. xxxiv (1925) 335-36.

3 Godechot, Jacques, "Les Juifs à Nancy de 1789 à 1795," in *REJ,* vol. lxxxvi (1928) 16.

Originally published in *Jewish Social Studies,* vol. XVI (1954).

Kembs, was sentenced to death.[4] Israël Rheus was a purveyor for the
army of Condé.[5] During the Terror, one, Goudchaux of Nancy, though
himself a suspect, did not hesitate to hide in his house the priest Joseph
Charlot.[6] Olry Terquem took the risk of transporting emigrants' jewelry
abroad.[7]

However, the number of Jews involved in major offenses against
the Revolution was very small. To understand the place of the Jews in
the emigré problem, we must appreciate how much the problem of the
emigrants was part of the general struggle between partisans and adversaries of the new regime. By and large, the Jews were neither the
only suspect group nor the one most under suspicion. In Alsace, where
the greatest number of French Jews lived, most Catholics favored the
old regime, while the minority groups, the Protestants and the Jews,
approved of the Revolution.[8] The Alsatian deputies in 1789 were, with
the exception of Jean-François Reubell, supporters of the old regime;
some later emigrated and served the enemy, others were guillotined.[9]
The partisans of the new regime were very few in number in this border
province, and they would have perished without the support of the
commissioners sent from Paris. Even the commissioners themselves
faced attacks against their lives from the local population.[10] The
Directoire of Lower Rhine was forced to withdraw troops from the front
line in order to combat the counter-revolutionary elements in Alsace.[11]
On August 22, 1792, when the National Assembly suspended the Strasbourg Municipality, a leaflet calling for help from the Austrians and
Prussians was distributed in the city.[12] Members of the association
Les Amis de la Constitution of Metz were so afraid of the anti-revolutionary elements that they received their mail at a private address.[13]

4 Mühlenbeck, E., *Euloge Schneider* (Strasbourg 1896) p. 414; *Strassburgische Zeitung* (October 18, 1795).

5 AD of Lower Rhine, M-III-1 (report of June 11, 1806).

6 Pfister, Chr., *Histoire de Nancy*, vol. ii (Paris 1909) p. 334.

7 Salomon, H., and Bamberger, E., "Un Alsacien et une famille lorraine au XIX siécle," in *Études et documents divers*, vol. vii (Paris 1922) p. 228.

8 Robinet, Dr., "Hérault de Sechelles, sa première mission en Alsace," in *La Révolution fran-çaise*, vol. xxii (1892) 457, 459.

9 Delabrouse, Lucien, "*Les Députés de l'Alsace à la Constituante* 1789-1791," in *Revue al-sacienne*, vol. xii (1888-89) 441-46.

10 *Rélation exacte du 4 Février 1791, de ce qui s'est passé à Colmar, à l'arrivée de MM. les Com-missaires du roi prés les départments du Rhin*, (s.l., s.d.) 3 p.; Dumas, Mathieu, *Souvenirs de 1770 à 1838*, vol. i (Paris 1839) p. 484.

11 AN, D-XXIX, 12-94 (report of May 25, 1791).

12 "Wir wollen unsern Mair und unsere Munizipalität lebehalten, und ender als diese zu ver-lieren, wollen wir lieber die Oestreicher und Preussen zu Hilfe rufen." AN, F. I-C. III Bas-Rhin, 13.

13 City Archives of Colmar, B. 34.

On November 24, 1893, J. A. Lacoste, the commissioner of Alsace, wrote to Paris that one quarter of the Alsatian population should be guillotined; that only those Alsatians who actively fought for the Revolution should remain; and that the others should be exiled and their properties confiscated.[14]　A Strasbourg revolutionary club discussed the advisability of deporting Alsatians to the French interior.[15]　Even some revolutionary elements had not altogether forgotten the old regime; the 1791 minutes of the Colmar *Friends of Liberty* began with the words: "In nomine redemptoris nostri Jesu-Christi † amen." Only later the words were added: "Au nom de la République une et indivisible."[16]

In such an atmosphere, aggravated by the traditional anti-Jewish hatred, Jews could not escape criticism, suspicion and persecution.　On one occasion, for example, 42 Jews were arrested in Strasbourg without an official order.[17]

According to the modern Alsatian historian, Rodolphe Reuss, many Jews, particularly merchants, became emigrants' agents.[18]　Although accounts of such activity by Jews were often much exaggerated, one may well believe that some Jewish merchants, especially peddlers, played this role unwittingly.　The General Council of the Lower Rhine stated on June 27, 1794, that emigrants obtained information on France's projects through Hebrew (probably Yiddish) letters of Jews.　Despite all the good done to them by the Revolution, the Council charged, the Jews wanted to bring about a counter-revolution with all its destruction and death.[19]　On June 11, 1793, the same General Council prohibited Jews from sending abroad letters written in Hebrew.[20]　Jews were not the only suspects, for, on July 29, the Council prohibited all correspondence with foreign lands.[21]

Just how confused the picture sometimes was is revealed in the careers of the Alsatian Jewish leader, Cerfberr of Médelsheim, and his

14 Aulard, F. A., *Recueil des actes du Comité de salut public*, vol. viii (Paris 1895) p. 683.

15 *Weltbote* (Strasbourg) (December 9, 1793).

16 Véron-Réville, *Histoire de la Révolution française dans le département du Haut Rhin* (Paris n.d.) p. 37.

17 [Ulrich, André], *Recueil des pièces servant à l'histoire de la Révolution à Strasbourg* [*Livre bleu*], vol. i (Strasbourg 1795) p. 69.

18 Reuss, *op. cit.*, p. 273; *idem.*, "Quelques documents nouveaux. . . .," in *REJ*, vol. lix (1910) 250-51.

19 AD of Lower Rhine, L-I-825.

20 Conseil Général, Bas-Rhin. *Défense de correspondre en langue hébraïque* (Strasbourg, June 11, 1793) 4 p. Cf. *Catalogue des Alsatica de la bibliothèque de Oscar Berger-Levrault*, vol. v (Nancy 1886) p. 9.

21 *Délibération du Conseil général du départment du Bas-Rhin du 29 Juillet 1793.* (Placard).

son, Marx Berr [Cerfberr]. Soon after the monarchy was restored after Napoleon's death, Marx Berr tried to obtain a decoration. At that time he wrote that in 1793 his family had saved the lives of two hundred royalist emigrants. This statement was probably an exaggeration, but it is certain that Cerfberr did rescue some aristocrats. He saved the life of Maréchal de Ségur, for example, by permitting the latter to go abroad disguised as one of his drivers. General A. P. de Custine, who was guillotined on July 28, 1793, declared four months earlier that Cerfberr, then director of the military purchasing agency of the Rhine Army, was an enemy of the Republic.[22]

But between 1789 and 1792 Marx Berr had openly manifested his sympathy for the Revolution, and he was the first Jew to be accepted in the National Guard of Strasbourg. His royalist statement after the Restoration was probably the consequence, at least in part, of his family's conflict with Napoleon over the latter's refusal to pay debts owing for deliveries made to the army by the Berr family. And Baruch Cerfberr himself, under the revolutionary regime, sued the editor of the *Rheinische Zeitung* for writing that he and his *"Helden aus der Brigade Baruch"* had not taken the oath of allegiance to the Republic and were continuing to dream of a king. The court sentenced the editor to pay a fine and to apologize to Cerfberr.[23]

Some members of Cerfberr's family were listed as emigrants, but they, too, expressed their sympathy for the Revolution. According to the law, the possessions of some categories of foreigners residing in France were to be confiscated, and there were very few such curious instances involving Jews, including that of Cerfberr's daughters, Jeanette and Eve. They were married to bankers: Eve to David Spire of Frankfort in 1786, Jeanette to David Salomon of Hanover in 1791. After Cerfberr's death, they were each to receive 1/48th of his heritage, which, according to the law, was to be confiscated for the benefit of the Revolution. In protesting the confiscation, Eve wrote that, even while residing

22 [Levylier, R.], *Notes et documents concernant la famille Cerfberr*, vol. ii (Paris 1906) p. 133-36; Poisson, Ch., *Les fournisseurs aux armées sous la Révolution française* (Paris 1932) p. 118, 120, 284-85; *Observations pour le citoyen Baruch Cerf-Berr, régisseur des achats des subsistances militaires de l'armée du Rhin, en réponse au general Custine* (Paris n.d.); Wolf, C., "Cerf-Berr et Custine," in *Univers israélite*, vol. liii (1898) 705.

23 *Justice de Paix du troisième arrondissement de la Commune de Strasbourg. Séance publique. L'an quatre . . . . entre le citoyen Baruch Cerf-Berr . . . . contre le Citoyen Cotta* (Strasbourg an IV) 7p. This alleged Jewish love for the *ancien régime* also found expression in anti-Jewish jokes. A newspaper told the story of a Jew who said in broken French that Louis XVI was the Jews' Messiah: "Louis XVI pou Roi de tout son quir père de son Piple, & protectir des pauvres opprimes, voilà notre vrai Messie." *Journal général de la Cour et de la Ville*, no. 33 (February 2, 1790) 263. In Prague, where a certain number of French emigrants found refuge, there appeared in 1793 a Judaeo-German translation of a counter-revolutionary brochure on the death of Louis XVI. It is possible that this booklet was edited by a Jewish emigrant, but it could also be that the printer, Ignace Elsenvanger, prepared it himself Cf. Shatzky, Jacob, "A Yiddish Weekly in the Times of the French Revolution," in *Yivo Bleter*, vol. ii (1931) 71-72.

abroad among slaves, her heart was full of love for France and the
glorious Revolution; that only her duties as a mother prevented her from
returning to her birthplace to enjoy the precious gains of the fall of
despotism.[24]

Although there were not a few Jewish emigrants, the number of
Jews involved in major crimes against the new regime was very small.
Of 3,956 emigrants, deportees and sentenced people in the Moselle
department in 1791-1800, only 31 or 32 were Jews. Two of these were
sentenced to death for speculation with *assignats* (paper money): the
70 year old Moyse David of Uckange and Joseph Jacob of Pirmasens.[25]

In the department of Meurthe there were 1,544 emigrants and deportees, 507 of them from the city of Nancy. A few Jews were included.[26]
In August, 1793, during the Terror, thirteen Jews were imprisoned in
Nancy, among them Godechaux (the son-in-law of Berr-Isaac Berr) and
Mayer Marx, who were arrested for dealing in silverware. Among the
sixty suspected people who were listed by the fourth section of the
Comité de Surveillance was the Jew Salomon Isaac. Of 679 people tried
in 1792-99 in the department, only seven were Jews; four were tried as
thieves and two for illegal dealings in money. Not one Jew figured
among those sentenced for "major" crimes against the Revolution, although one Lorraine Jew, Isaac Samuel, was sentenced to death in 1798
as a thief.[27]

On October 6, 1793, the City Council of Nancy discontinued granting
passports to Jews. This was a heavy economic blow. Of the 4,000 passports issued earlier by Nancy, in the months of July-September 1794,
no less than 200 had been given to Jews to travel to distant cities of
France and even abroad.[28] The passport situation must be considered
as part of the history of Terror which prevailed in Nancy from March

---

24 "La France m'a vit naître. Je n'avais pas dix-huit ans lorsqu'en 1786 je fut unie avec Daniel
Spirr, Banquier à Francfort; depuis j'ai constament habité cette commune, mais en m'éloignant
de ma patrie bien avant notre glorieuse révolution je m'en trouvais rapprochée par un amour
pour elle, toujours au milieu des esclaves je conservai le coeur français, et certes si des liens
serrés par la tendresse maternelle ne m'avaient retenue, on m'auroit vu voler pour partager
avec mes concitoyens ces precieux avantags qu'ils puisoient dans la chute du despotisme." AN,
F7 - 5513.

25 Gain, *op. cit.*, nos. 2, 526-27, 536, 835 (death), 1103, 1434-35, 1783 (death), 1862-64, 2234, 2236,
2265-66, 2479, 2480-84, 2594-97, 2695,2714, 3095, 3365, 3599 (a Jew?), 3750.

26 Troux, A., *La Vie politique dans le département de la Meurthe d'Août 1792 à Octobre 1795*,
vol. ii (Nancy 1936) p. 900-01; Worms, Léon, "Liste des émigrés (1791-1800)," in *La Revue
juive de Lorraine*, vol. ix (1933).

27 Troux, *op. cit.*, vol. ii., p. 44, 105-06; *idem, La Révolution en Lorraine*, vol. ii (Nancy 1931)
p. 105-06; Godechot, *op. cit.*, p. 18-19; Thomas, Hubert, *Le Tribunal criminel de la Meurthe sous
la Révolution, 1792-1799* (Nancy 1937) p. 340 (no. 168), 346 (no. 189), 377 (no. 304), 475 (no.
677), 499 (no. 3), 547, 549 (nos. 235, 243).

28 Troux, *op. cit.*, vol. ii, p. 102; Godechot, *op. cit.*, p. 32-33.

1793 to August 1794. Nancy was considered an aristocratic center of anti-revolutionary feelings.[29] The events in the city fell into three distinct periods: before the Terror, during the Terror, and after the Terror.[30] This distinction applied to Jews and non-Jews alike; there is no proof whatsoever that during the Terror Jews as such suffered more than non-Jews.

The leader of the Terror in Nancy, August Mauger, who was responsible for the order of October 1793 forbidding the grant of passports to Jews, was an immoral person. He used to investigate prisoners while he was drunk and in the company of prostitutes. In such a state, he sentenced his victims, or let them go if they paid a bribe. He forced the Jews Louis Isaac Berr and Lévy to pay him a few thousand pounds.[31] Another leader of the Terror in Nancy, Phillip, strongly attacked the "coalition" between Jewish speculators like Cerfberr and the aristocrats.[32] But such statements and actions were primarily the consequence of the accident that the Nancy Jacobins chose unscrupulous characters for their leaders. The Jews of Nancy therefore suffered more than in other communities, but non-Jews were also victimized. On the other hand, a few unwise acts of Cerfberr helped to increase anti-Jewish feelings.

The situation changed for the better in the course of the Terror. On November 17, 1793, the General Council of Meurthe authorized the granting of passports to Jews. In a speech delivered on November 10, the Nancy dictator Faure appealed to the Jews to give up their waiting for the Messiah and to recognize the French people as the Messiah who would free the entire world.[33] On November 18, Faure again appealed to the Jews to give up their religion. The next day Rabbi Jacob Schweich [Schweisch] of Nancy resigned and the Jews gave up the gold and silver of the synagogue. Jews became members of the *Société populaire;* Salomon Moyse Lévy was even elected to the City Council during the Terror. These revolutionary manifestations helped the Jews

29 Aulard, A., *Recueil des actes du Comité de salut public,* vol. 1 (Paris 1889) p. 284; Godechot, J., "Le Comité de surveillance révolutionnaire de Nancy," in *La Révolution française,* vol. lxxx (1927) 249, 254.

30 Godechot, *op. cit.,* p. 1-35.

31 Troux, *op. cit.,* vol. ii, p. 102, 106.

32 Philip, *Exposé succint des événements contre-révolutionnaires, arrivés à Nancy pendant le le jour de la seconde décade, 20 brumaire, an second de la République française* . . . . (Nancy, n.d.) p. 28, 77.

33 Faure, *Discours prononcé* . . . . *dans l'église ci-devant cathédrale de la commune de Nancy, le jour de la seconde décade, 20 brumaire, an second de la République française* . . . . (Nancy, an II) 7 p.

to escape strong measures against them as a community and to survive the Terror.[34]

Only eight Jews are to be found among the 2,895 officially listed as emigrants or sentenced counter-revolutionaries in Upper Rhine. Not one Jew was sentenced to death there,[35] although anti-Jewish feelings were always very strong in this part of Alsace. The actual number of Jewish emigrants was not very small, but it never reached that of the neighboring Lower Rhine. This could be explained by the fact that the Terror was much stronger in Lower Rhine. Many Jewish emigrants instinctively followed the non-Jewish exiles, especially the peasants. But in Upper Rhine the anti-Jewish sentiments among the peasants were always stronger than in other sections of Alsace. It should be noted that in 1789 anti-Jewish riots had taken place almost exclusively in Upper Rhine. Many Jews fled to Basel at that time, and some never returned to Alsace.

Names of 226 Jews appear on the printed lists of emigrants from Lower Rhine.[36] One must be very cautious in accepting these lists for non-Jews as well as for Jews. Some names appear on several lists; others are of people who had never left the country. Significantly, even in Lower Rhine only one Jew, the Spy Léopold Bernheim, was among the 40 odd victims of the Revolutionary Tribunal.

Despite the well-organized propaganda against the Jews on charges of economic speculation, it is noteworthy that not one Jew was sentenced to death in Lower Rhine for an economic crime against the Revolution, and only very few such cases are to be found in the whole of France; two in Moselle, one in Nîmes (Jassé Carcassonne) one in Lyon (Azaria Vidal), one in Paris (Antoine Louis Isaac Calmer).[37] However, when the cases of the guillotined Jews are scrutinized more closely, it can be shown that some at least fell victim not because of their Jewish origin or because of economic sabotage, but for their participation in political opposition. Thus, Jassé Carcassonne of Nîmes was accused of economic sabotage, according to some historians, but in

---

34 Godechot, *op. cit.*, p. 23, 25, 27; Troux, *op. cit.*, vol. ii, p. 225-27; Floquet, G., "Le Culte de la Raison et de l'Etre suprême etles fêtes civiques à Nancy pendant la Révolution,' in *Annales de l'Est*, vol. xiv (1900) 544.

35 Anselme Bloch, Meyer Bloch, Aaron Lévy, David Lévy, Meyer Lévy, Moïse Lévy, Samuel Lévy, Jacob Lippman. *Cf.* Schaedelin, Félix, *L'Emigration révolutionnaire du Haut-Rhin* (3 vols.) (Colmar 1937-46) vol. ii, nos. 220, 222; vol. iii, nos. 1248-1332, 1456.

36 *Cf.* Appendix.

37 Mühlenbeck, *op. cit.*, p. 414; Kahn, S., "Le Juifs a Nîmes, au XVIIe et au XVIIIe siècle," in *REJ*, vol. lxvii (1914) 243; Lévy, A., "Notice sur les israélites de Lyon," in *Univers israélite*, vol. xxxviii (1893) 398; AN, W. 351, dr. 956, III No. 125.

reality he paid with his life for having been a member of the municipality during the period of the federalist movement.[38]

Not one Jew is to be found among the 1,705 people who were imprisoned or deported, or who emigrated from the department of Meuse and whose properties were confiscated.[39]

In the later years of the Revolution, emigrants' families openly blamed the Terror for the emigration. Wolf Isaac of Neuwiller (Lower Rhine) stated that his son left France "at this deplorable time, when terror replaced order and justice." The father of Jacques Aron, Meyer Aron, and Salomon Lévi, of Ingwiller (Lower Rhine), who left France in November 1793, wrote that his children were "tempted by the imprudence of their youth and by the Terror."[40] A petition by his father requesting amnesty for Isaac Seligmann Strasburger explained that the latter left for Strasbourg on October 13, 1793, when Wissembourg, his place of residence was invaded by the enemy. He stated:

There he was a witness of the horrors committed by the Revolutionary Tribunal; he saw how blood was shed by the axe of the guillotine. These terrible scenes made him leave Strasbourg and he looked for a way to reach Wissembourg while the enemy was still there. When the enemy was driven out, he remembered the terror of the Revolutionary Tribunal in Strasbourg and was afraid that Wissembourg, too, would become a site of such a Tribunal and that he himself would then fall a victim; and on December 24, 1793, he left his community and the Republic and followed the enemy who was driven out of the country.[41]

Some Jews were listed as emigrants although they had never left the country.[42] Alexandre and Séligmann Lyon-Cahen of Blisbrück (Moselle) were listed "by mistake and ill-will," said their father in a petition to have their names striken from the list. It was *after* their names had been listed as emigrants that they were forced to leave the country to avoid persecution.[43] The Alsatian Jew, Anselme Israël, was arrested for enlisting in a "German Legion," but he proved that the order to arrest him also spoke of his father who had died in Ribeauvillé thir-

38 *Pièces et documents officiels pour servir à l'histoire de la Terreur a Nîmes* . . . . (Nîmes 1867) p. 41. Rouviére, M., *Histoire de la Révolution française dans le départment du Gard,* vol. iv (Nîmes 1889) p. 327-34, 459; *Jugement rendu par le Tribunal révolutionnaire établi à Nismes qui condamne . . . Jassé Carassonne . . . à la peine de mort . . . du 1er Thermidor an second* (Nimes n. d.) placard.

39 Dubois, Jean, "Liste des émigrés, des prétres, deportés et condamnés pour cause révolutionnaire du département de la Meuse," in *Mémoires de la Sociée des lettres, sciences et arts de Bar-le-Duc,* 4 ser., vol. viii (1910) 3-193.

40 AN, F7-5563 (4), 5539.

41 AN, F7-5557 and BB-I-94 pl.3.

42 Benestruc Bédarrides of Aix-en-Provence; Jacob Raphaël Carcassonne (fils) of Avignon. AN, F7-4908, 4915.

43 AN, F7-5369.

teen years prior to the Revolution. Consequently, the court ordered his release.[44]

Others were placed in the category of emigrants after their return to France. This happened, among many others, to Isaac David of Wissembourg, employed since 1791 by the army contractor Löw Lévy. In that capacity he spent much of his time abroad, and when he came back he was declared an emigrant.[45] Some people fell victim to mistakes of officials. In November, 1798, Joseph Lévi was prosecuted as an emigrant merchant, although he declared that he was only a "supposed emigrant" and that he "made a living as a real day-laborer." On December 26, 1800, the Prefect of Lower Rhine stated that despite all the prosecutions against Lévi, he was never listed officially as an emigrant.[46] The "emigrant" Emmanuel Isché, a butcher of Niederhochstadt (Lower Rhine) was pardoned after proving that he had never left France. He had merely moved to another Alsatian community, Trimbach, because his house had been destroyed by the invading army.[47]

The cattle-trader Moyse Nathan Coshel of Haguenau proved that he left France with his wife and seven children when the invading army asked him to pay a special war-tax within twenty-four hours or face removal as a hostage.[48] The father of the Jewish writer Alexandre Weill escaped to Germany because he feared the invading army. He spent ten years abroad. His grandfather, the richest Jew of the invaded village Schirein, died because he hid all night in the river.[49] The "emigrants" Raphaël Jacques Lévi of Ingwiller and Cain Weil of Haguenau had been arrested as French spies and taken by force to Germany. Lévi subsequently proved that he left the I.O.U.'s of his debtors in Alsace, hidden in a pillow as evidence that he did not want to leave France.[50] Séligman Raphaël of Landau (Lower Rhine) left his native city for a business trip; on his way back the enemy did not allow him to return. After the enemy left, he did come back and he was then arrested as an emigrant. The *Directoire* of Lower Rhine favored his release.[51]

Many more Jews fell victims — as did so many non-Jews — to the invading armies. The following are a few examples: The peddlers Jacob (called Lévi), Isaac Jacob, Moyse Jacob Lévi and Goetsch Netter

---

44 AN, W246 (4).

45 AN, F7-5517.

46 AN, F7-5539.

47 AN, F7-5533.

48 AN, F7-5517.

49 Weill, Alexandre, *Ma jeunesse* (Paris 1888) p. 22, 24.

50 AN, F7-5539, 5563 (1).

51 AN, F7-5557.

of Ingwiller—all emigrants—were pardoned in the year VIII (1799-1800) by the Prefect because it was proved that they were forcibly taken away by the retreating enemy army. The same happened to the Jewish butcher Leyser Weil of Haguenau and to Aron Gradwohl and Jonas Wolff Reichshoffer of Bouxwiller.[52]

The Jewish butchers Lipman Picquart and Mayer Lévy of Waldwisse (Moselle) were employed by the French army, following it into Germany; they were listed as emigrants.[53]

Since many Jews traded with foreign countries, some found themselves on the lists of emigrants, especially horse-dealers who always imported horses from abroad. Article 5 of the Law of January 11, 1795, on the amnesty for emigrants, foresaw this necessity for merchants to travel abroad, and Jews, too, benefitted from it. This happened, among many others, to the Jewish horse-dealers Samuel Feiselt, Loevel Feist, Séligmann Raphaël Lévy, Moises Lévy, Sholem Abraham Lévy, Salomon Lévy, and Aaron Meyer of Ingwiller.[54] The Jewish merchant Abraham-Isaac Berr of Metz left France in July 1790, in connection with his trade; he came back in the year III (1794-1795), listed as an emigrant.[55] In some cases merchants were declared emigrants because they stayed abroad longer than the time permitted by their passports. On March 27, 1793, Jacob Lévi of Nice was granted a passport for Italy for forty days. He did not return in time. At first he was taken off temporarily the emigrants' list, but later he was again declared an emigrant.[56] People who went to Basel on business for one or a few days found their names among the emigrants because they did not have regular passports. This happened, among many others, to David Lévy of Blotzheim and to Mayer Lévi. The latter declared that it was well known that the French border guards let people go to Basel without passports; they merely asked for a gratuity—3 to 4 sols from poor people and 9 to 12 sols from the rich.[57]

Some Jews and non-Jews left France in order to avoid being drafted into the army.[58] On March 6, 1793, the General Council of Lower Rhine

---

52 AN, F7-5534, 5563 (1, 4).

53 Gain, *op. cit.*, nos. 225, 2479. It is worth noting the order of the Commissioner in the French Army in Belgium, Claude Hilaire Laurent, Deputy of Lower Rhine, that any Jew following the army be shot within 24 hours. Lt. Cl. Veling, "Quelques représentants de l'Alsace à la Convention," in *L'Alsace française,* vol. x (1925) 319; Overleaux, Emile, "Notes et documents sur les Juifs de Belgique sous l'ancien régime," in *REJ*, vol. ix (1894) 283.

54 AN, BI-84 pl. 4.

55 Gain, *op. cit.*, no. 3750.

56 AN, F7-4863 and BBI-89 pl. 5.

57 AN, F7-5570 and BBI-89 pl. 5.

58 The emigrants, Salomon Lévi, Aron Ber, Loevel (Schimmel's son), Baruch Caïn, Isaac Jacob Jeckel, and Moïse Lévi of Ingwiller (Lower Rhine) were suspected of evading military service and were not pardoned. AN, F7-5539, "'tous ces jeunes gens sans état montrent une persévérance opinâtre dans le crime, en se refusant de prendre les armes pour la défense'").

accused certain Jews who requested passports of having tried to evade military service.[59] The parents of two such emigrants, Salomon Ergem and Olry Oulif of Metz, had to pay a fine.[60] Some Jewish youths probably left France only in order to study or they chose a German Jewish community as the place in which to learn some profession, without any desire to escape from the Revolution. Thus, the father of the emigrant Jonas Aaron of Phalsbourg declared that his son had gone to study in a yeshiva in Germany.[61] It was easily proved that some youths had left France prior to 1789. Knandel Noë, the widow of Gerson Lévi of Bischwiller, wrote that when her husband died "she was left with five children as her only riches." In 1787 she sent her oldest son to Kaiserwert to learn trading, but during the Revolution he was declared an emigrant. She asked the authorities not to confiscate her property and to allow her son to return to France.[62] The son of Louis Goudchaux of Nancy was listed as an emigrant because he left in May 1791 to study medicine in Germany. His father wrote in a petition to the National Convention that the laws did not permit a Jew to study medicine in France, and he was therefore forced to send him abroad. In fact, the son decided to return to France, but on his way back home he learned his name was listed among the emigrants. He, therefore, waited in Switzerland for a pardon, which was granted to him.[63] On the other hand, it is hard to believe that Mayer May of Metz, who sent all his five sons to the yeshiva of Frankfort during the Revolution, was not trying to save them from military service.[64]

Many people were imprisoned or listed as emigrants because their enemies denounced them as such to the authorities. This happened to Jews, too. In the year IV (1795-1796) the peddler Mayer Lévy of Hagenthal-les-Bas was sentenced to one year in prison; his own brother denounced him as a man of too much debauchery (*libertinage*).[65] Elie Salomon Terquem, the father of the Jewish leader Olry Terquem (Tsarphati), was denounced as an adversary of the new regime by a Jewish Jacobin who wanted to obtain his property. Terquem escaped to Germany—he was sentenced to death and his property was confiscated —but later he was pardoned, came back to France, and regained his

---

59 AD of Lower Rhine, L-I-497.

60 *Etat formé en exécution de la Loi du 12 Septembre des pères et mères dont les fils sont absents* . . . . (Metz n. d.).

61 This also happened to Nathan Joseph Gougenheim and Isaïe Nordon of Metz. *Cf.* Troux, *op. cit.,* vol. i, p. 215; Gain, *op. cit.,* nos. 1434-35, 2695.

62 AN, F7-5539.

63 *Ibid.,* D-III-158; Troux, *op. cit.,* vol. ii, p. 481; Godechot, *op. cit.,* p. 33, 34.

64 Gain, *op. cit.,* p. 403 and no. 2480.

65 Schaedelin, *op. cit.,* vol. iii, p. 24, no. 1430.

property.[66]   Undoubtedly some Jews were listed as emigrants by anti-Jewish elements.   Seven of the thirty-one Jewish emigrants of Moselle came from Waldwisse, where anti-Jewish feelings were strong.   On October 29, 1793, the administration of Moselle ordered special searches in Jewish houses.   The brothers Alexandre and Séligmann Cahan of Sarreguemines were both denounced by the same person as emigrants; when their names appeared on the emigrants' lists they were still in France.[67]

Among the emigrants were many adventurers who went abroad in order to avoid payment of their debts, etc. Among them, too, could be found a few Jews.   In 1787, Abraham Isaac Beer of Metz went into bankruptcy; in July, 1790, he left France, but in July, 1793, he asked for permission to return.   The local authorities stated that such permission should be granted to him because some of his debtors could profit from his presence in France.[68]

In many cases emigrants took with them their entire families.   The butcher Abraham Isaac of Oberlauterbach (Lower Rhine) left France on December 23, 1793, together with his wife and children.   They returned on February 2, 1795, and were pardoned.   The entire family of the Comtadin Jew Abraham Vitta Mayse, his wife Ester Crémieu, and their children, emigrated.[69]

The law of Nivose 22, year III (January 11, 1795), permitted the return of those emigrants who, at the moment of their departure from France, had made a living by working with their own hands, *i.e.*, peasants, workers, artisans, etc.   This posed a very special problem for the Jewish emigrants.   Prior to the Revolution, the Jews, especially in Alsace, Metz and the Metz province, Lorraine, and Paris, were forced to earn their living by lending money to Gentiles, by peddling, trading in horses and cattle, and dealing in old clothes.   Agriculture and all other "productive" activities were closed to them.   Emigrants who were not merchants were easily pardoned, for example, Jacob Samuel of Bouzeiller, a *maître d'écriture* (scribe), the mattress-maker Lazare Jacob of Ingwiller, the soap-maker Jacques Isaac of Weitersweiller, and the servant (*domestique juif*) Isaïas Séligmann of Haguenau.[70]   But how could all Jewish emigrants prove that they made a living by working?

66 Cahen, Abraham, *Le Rabbinat de Metz pendant la période française* (Paris 1886) p. 77; Paquet, R., *Bibliographie analytique de l'histoire de Metz pendant la Révolution* (Paris 1926) p. 611, 872; Gain, *op. cit.*, no. 3365.

67 Gain, *op. cit.*, p. 202 and nos. 225, 526-27, 2479, 2594-97; Troux, *op. cit.*, vol. ii, p. 102.

68 AN, F7-5367.

69 AN, F7-5533 and *676.

70 AN, F7-5333-34.

Jewish emigrants began to seek proof of their "productive" occupations. Hertzel Wolff of Mommenheim, who was listed as a merchant, stated that he had bought a parcel of land on May 15, 1789. But this did not prove that he tilled it, and his name remained on the lists of emigrants.[71] Some were able to convince the authorities that even if their professions were not productive, they still did work with their hands. Moise Lévi of Ingwiller, a cattle dealer, spent some time in a Strasbourg prison when he came back to France. Lévi stated that he was only an employee of the cattle dealer, Hertzel, on a yearly salary, that he cleaned the stables, chopped wood and took care of the proprietor's garden. One witness stated that he saw Lévi while the latter was working for Hertzel.[72]

Many instances can be cited where Jewish emigrants could not benefit from the amnesty of January 11, 1795, because their professions, prior to the day of emigration, were not "productive."[73] The butcher Meyer Lévi of Brumath (Lower Rhine) went away in September or October 1793, and returned on March 18, 1795. He was refused a pardon although he once had been captain of a company of the National Guard in his canton, and despite his proof that he himself butchered the cattle, *i.e.,* that he did work with his hands. The emigrant Samuel Jonas of Haguenau, a dealer in old clothes, was granted a pardon, but he was ordered to prove that he "positively was a peddler living from his daily work."[74]

In some cases the authorities decided that Jewish emigrants who were peddlers, merchants, etc., should still benefit from the law of January 11, 1795, because, before their emancipation by the Revolution, Jews were forced to make a living from "dishonest" professions, were not permitted to till the land, etc. Such statements were made by the Councillors of Haguenau on February 23, 1796, in the case of the emigrant Raphaël Bernheim, a peddler; on March 8 and 15, 1796, in the cases of Jacques Lévi and Hirtzel Lévi, cattle dealers, the peddler Samuel Jacques Lévi and his wife Kaile, and in many other cases.[75]

In still other cases, the authorities found a way to enable Jewish merchants to benefit from the law by declaring that occupations of peddlers, traders in old goods, horses and cattle, were useful to the local

---

71 AN,F7-5563 (4).

72 AN, F7-5539.

73 Isaac and Joseph Samuel Séligmann; Raphaël Schiele Lévi of Ingwiller; Susset Lévi and Séligmann Aron of Bouxweiller; Emmanuel Isaac of Billigheim; Séligmann Isaac and Joseph Samuel of Weiteweiller; and many others. AN, BB-1 94 pl. 3; F7-5539, 5557, 5533.

74 AN, F7-5539, 5534.

75 AN, F7-5513, 5539.

population. The cattle dealer Moyse-Weyel of Haguenau left France in order to avoid arrest by the invading enemy for refusing to pay a war tax, and he was listed among the emigrants. A certificate delivered by the Councillors of Haguenau stated that he had learned from his father the butcher's trade, that for a time he had tilled a parcel of land, and that he helped the inhabitants by selling them grain in a time of dearth at a legal price (maximum).[76] Some emigrants stated that, although they were peddlers or merchants, they were poor and could hardly make a living; that they had to wander from village to village and peddle a few pieces of old clothing; that they were so poor that they could be called hard-working people, etc. In many cases, these arguments were repeated by the local administrators in reports sent to higher authorities, and the emigrants benefited from the amnesty, *e.g.,* Joseph Isaac and his wife of Haguenau, Elie Simon Lévi of Ingwiller, Cerf Lehmann and Abraham Jacob of Bouxwiller, Foestal Moyse Weill and his wife, Séligmann Strasburger Isaac of Wissembourgh, Jonas Wolff and his wife Dreitel of Neuwiller.[77]

It should be noted that very few of the Jewish emigrants of Alsace, Metz and Lorraine were rich. Cerf Lehmann of Bouxwiller was declared an emigrant because he was suspected of being a rich man. But when it was proved that he was only a poor peddler, he was pardoned.[78] The author of an official report concerning the emigrant Samuel Jacques Lévi and his wife Kaile of Haguenau, peddlers, stated that a Jewish peddler should not be listed as a merchant. "Lévi's profession was as painful as that of any other laborer," especially because the laws prior to 1789 forced him to make a living in such a way.[79]

On the other hand, some of the Jews who left France were very rich, as, for example, Isaac Berr de Turique, of Berr-Isaac Berr's family, who was pardoned in the year VII (1798-1799).[80]

However this liberal attitude towards Jewish emigrants that enabled peddlers, horse and cattle dealers, and others to benefit from the law of January 11, 1795, prevailed in only a few localities, largely in the district of Haguenau. It is possible that some officials there were really liberal. On the other hand, it should not be surprising if documents will still be discovered proving that even there Jews obtained such benefits for large sums of money.

76 AN, F7-5563 (1).

77 AN, F7-5516, 5533-34, 5539, 5557, 5563 (1, 4).

78 Reuss, *op. cit.*, p. 84.

79 AN, F7-5539.

80 AN, F7-*116-I, p. 723.

Any immigrant who was not able to take his possessions abroad with him—and very few could do this—was ruined economically, because emigrants' properties were confiscated and sold as national property.[81] The amnesty later granted to emigrants also meant restoration of the confiscated properties or of revenue if the properties had been sold. The emigrant Hertzel Bloch of Mertzweiller (Lower Rhine), a 64-year old butcher, was pardoned and received the income from the part of his property that had been confiscated and sold.[82] But this was not brought about without conflicts. The rich Jew Jacob Trèves emigrated from Nice, which was occupied in September 1792 by the Republican troops. His house was confiscated and sold. Trèves was later pardoned and he returned to Nice, but the new owner refused to return the house. It is worth noting that in Nice a Jew was a member of the Commission which decided who were to be deported as counter-revolutionaries.[83] There were even some Jewish emigrants who returned to France during the post-Napoleonic Restoration and demanded indemnity for their confiscated properties, but this is a subject for a special study.

The history of the Sephardic Jews in Southwestern France during the Revolution will be treated in a separate study. But, it should be noted that very few Jews were among the counter-revolutionary emigrés from that region. There were no Jews among the Bordeaux emigrés in the crucial period of June 6, 1792-May 18, 1794.[84] In the years of the Revolution every rich man was suspected and it was inevitable that some rich Jews, too, should be victims. However, no case of special persecution against Bordeaux Jews as such has been recorded.

Many Sephardic Jews left France, but they did it legally. During the Revolution legal emigration abroad was not prohibited. However, departure from France was often regarded as an unpatriotic act and many legal emigrants were suspected of trying to escape army service or of evading various revolutionary laws. We noted names of many Jews who left for the French colonies[85] and various European countries. Most Sephardic Jews who had spent many years in the French colonies went back to Bordeaux during the uprisings at the beginning of the Revolution. There they soon requested passports to leave France

81 On confiscated properties of some Jewish emigrants see Hildenfinger, P., "Actes du district de Strasbourg relatifs . . . ." in *REJ*, vol lxi (1911) p. 115-17, nos. 155, 161-62, 164-65.

82 AN, F7-5513.

83 Emmanuel, Victor, *Les Juifs à Nice 1400-1860* (Nice 1905) p. 46-47. Some Jews are to be found even among those who were deported as counter-revolutionary elements, among them Rabbi Jacob Gougenheim and his wife, of Haguenau (Lower Rhine). *Cf.* Reuss, *op. cit.*, p. 186.

84 *Cf.* Constrasty, J., *Le Clergé française exilé en Espagne* (Toulouse 1910) p. 392; O'Reilly, Abbé P., *Histoire de Bordeaux*, vol. i, part 2 (Paris 1863) p. 165-203.

85 Among them was J. Furtado of Saint-Esprit-lès-Bayonne, a brother of Abraham Furtado.

again.[86] Of course, Bordeaux Jews were criticized for leaving the country, even legally. But such reproofs were also made by the Jewish Jacobins of Saint-Esprit-lès-Bayonne.[87]

It is clear, therefore, that many Jews did not favor the Revolution and even opposed it, despite their gain of citizenship and equality.

APPENDIX

NAMES OF JEWS APPEARING ON THE LISTS OF EMIGRES FROM LOWER RHINE.

Bloch Heimann, Block Mennel (négociants, Hoehnheim); Herzel Hendélé (Hoehnheim); Isaac Abraham, sa femme, 2 fils, 1 fille (Haguenau); Aron Moses (Bouxweiller); Aron Séligmann (ibid.); Fromel, fils du rabbin (ibid.) Abraham Gugenheim, sa femme, 1 fils, 2 filles (Haguenau); Gugenheim, rabbin, sa femme, 3 fils, 2 filles (ibid.); Samuel Gugenheim, sa femme, 1 fils (ibid.); Jacob Abraham (Bouxweiller); Jacob Isaac (Neuweiller), Isaac Wolf, sa femme, 1 fils (Neuweiller); Calmen Israël (Haguenau); Salomon Koschel (Schweighausen); Hirtzel Lehmann (Bouxweiller); Elias Lévy, Josue Lévy, Judel Lévy, Leyser Lévy (ibid.); Hirtzel Lévy, sa femme (Haguenau) Samuel-Jacob Lévy, sa femme, 1 fils, (ibid.); Schlumen Lévy (Neuweiller); Wolff Lévy (ibid.); Fromel Meyer (Herlisheim); Moyses Meyer, sa femme, 1 fils, 1 fille (Neuweiller); Fromel Meyer, sa femme, 3 enfants (Offendorf); Wolff Moch (Haguenau); Nathan Moyses, sa femme, 4 fils 2 filles (ibid.); Baruch Baër Netter (Bouxweiller); Safel, juif (Herlisheim); Salomon, juif (Haguenau); Meyer Weyl (Bouxweiller); Cain Weyl, 3 fils, 1 fille (Haguenau); Goetschel Weyl, sa femme (ibid.); Leyser Weyl (ibid.); Mauschen Weyl (ibid.); Nochem Weyl (ibid.); Nathan Weyl (Herlisheim); Nathan, Jonas, Leibel Weyl (Schirhoffen); Hertzel Wolff, sa femme et ses enfants (Momenheim); Isaac Dreyfus, juif, et Riele sa femme (Wissembourg); Nathan Dreyfus (ibid.); Frommel Dreyfus fils (ibid.); Möises Dreyfus (ibid.); Jones Dreyfus (ibid.); Frommel Dreyfus fille (ibid.); Gressel Dreyfus (ibid.); Eisic Dreyfus, garçon juif (ibid.); Loëb Dreyfus, juif (ibid.); Nathan Dreyfus, juif (ibid.); Nathan Dreyfus garçon (ibid.); Hertzel Jacob, marchand (Niederrödern); Leibel Lazar, garçon juif (Reichshoffen); Jacques Lazar, garçon juif (Birlenbach); Lévi Zoll, boucher (Nierderrödern) Benjamin Lévi, sa femme, née Blumel (ibid.); Lévi Kaufmann, boucher (ibid.); Bela Lévi (ibid.); Lévi Gutel (ibid.); Itzig Löwi, juif (Reichshoffen); Fromel Machen, juif, Dina sa femme, Gertel et Elie, enfants (Wissembourg); Macholen (ibid.); Meyer Moïses, juif, Regal, sa femme, David et Roesel, enfants (ibid.); Loebel Schlummen, juif, Kinelé, sa femme, Madelé, Sorle, Dolf, enfants (ibid.); Riedseltz Séligmann, marchand juif, Delse, sa femme (Reichshoffen); Vitoire Weil, juif, sa femme, Behle & Jean, enfants (Wissembourg); Honel Wolff, juif, Kiehle, sa femme, Sorle, Loebel et Ixbora, enfants (ibid.); Elie Wolff, juif, Bleimel, sa femme, Zipfel, Loebel, Schiehl, Moïses, Marthie, Woelfel, enfants (ibid.); Hirsch Meyer, négociant (Ebersheim); Fromel Lévi, négociant (Hochfelden); Samuel Lévi (ibid.); Cerf Baehr, déserteur du régiment de Salm-Salm; Samuel Daniel (Herxheim); Samuel David, mercier (Gunstett); David Loeb, marchand (Niederbronn); Isaac Loeb, sa femme Jachert et leurs cinq enfants (Ingenheim); Emmanuel Isché, juif (Niederhochstadt); Samuel Lévi, garçon juif (Hersheim); Moses Liebmann, juif (Niederhochstadt); Jacques Machul, juif, sa femme, leurs huit enfants (ibid.); Lazare Machul, juif, sa femme, leur enfant (ibid.); Baruch Raphaël, juif (Gumbrechtshoff); Abraham Salomon, juif (Essingen); Samson, juif (Mertzweiler); Schihlen, juif (ibid.); Salomon Lévi, juif (Kaltzenhausen); Royses Loeb, juif (Oberlauterbach); Abraham Schlumen, juif (Offendorf); Abraham, sa femme Mangelé et leurs quatre enfants (ibid.); Samuel Isaac, juif, mendiant (Wingersheim); Isaac-Raphaël Lévy, fils, juif réquisitionnaire (Ingwiller); Lipmann Lévy fils, juif, nég. (ibid.); Mayer Löwel, juif, mendiant (Mühlhaussen); Fromel Meyer, juif (Herrlisheim); (Fromel Meyer, sa femme avec deux enfants (ibid.); Wolff Lipmann (Bergzabern); Isaac Raphaël, juif (Pleisweiler); Aaron Baer, réquisitionnaire (Ingwiller); Baruch Feiber, juif (Klingenmünster); Goetschel Fohlen, juif marchand (Reichshoffen); Frommel, avec sa femme et quatre enfants, juif (Herrlisheim); Leib Koppel et sa famme, juif (ibid.); Raphaël-Schillen Lévi, juif réquisitionnaire (Ingwiller); Salom-Raphaël Lévi (ibid.); Schlumel, veuf, juif (Herrlisheim); Meyer Weyl (Printzheim); David Weyl (Bouxweiller); Zacharie Wolf, juif, marchand, sa femme et sa fille (Herrlisheim); Ruben Wolf, juif marchand, et so fille (ibid.); Lévi Chusel, garçon juif (Soulz); Loebel Dreyfuss, juif (Redseltz); Nathan Dreyfuss, juif (ibid.); Mayer Dreyfuss, fils de Salom (Gunstett); Liebman Susskind, garçon juif (Soulz). Source: printed lists of emigrants of Lower Rhine, AD of Lower Rhine, series Q.

---

86 This will be treated in a separate study.

87 Cf. Ducaunnes-Duval, A., Inventaire sommaire des archives municipales, Période révolutionnaire . . . , vol. ii (Bordeaux n. d.) p. 337; Ginsburger, Ernest, Le Comité de surveillance de Jean-Jacques-Rousseau, Saint-Esprit-lès-Bayonne . . . . (Paris 1934) p. 180.

FRENCH JEWS IN THE ARMED FORCES
DURING THE REVOLUTION OF 1789

Were there Jews in the armed forces of the French Republic during the Revolution of 1789? How many of them served in the army and how many in the National guard? What was their attitude to army life and how did the Christian population look upon them? It was, perhaps, only natural for the Jews of France not to be too enthusiastic about being drafted in the army. Their distrust in the army was traditional and natural. As a matter of fact the Christian population did not even accept them everywhere among the defenders of the Republic. The great liberal Alsatian historian, Rodolphe Reuss (1841–1924), wrote that no more than a "moderate enthusiasm" was to be expected from the Jews — "these outlaws of the civilization of the old regime."[1]

There is no doubt that Jews avoided service in the army, some were even among the deserters and for this they were branded as émigrés.[2] But this was not an essentially Jewish fact. Evasion of service and desertions were a common occurrence. In the department of Meurthe it was officially announced in 1792 that nobody could be drafted against his own free will. Napoleon I stated in 1804 that only 64,000 out of 90,000 young men to be drafted presented themselves to the draft boards and of those, 14,000 later deserted. The traditional attachment of

The following abbreviations of sources are being used in the notes: *AI* — *Archives israélites*; AN — Archives nationales (Paris); Ca — City archives of; Da — Departmental archives of; *JSS* — *Jewish Social Studies*; *RA* — *Revue d'Alsace*; *REJ* — *Revue des études juives*; *SIW* — *Strassburger Israelitische Wochenschrift*; *SS* — *Souvenir et Science*; UI — L'Uunivers israélite.

[1] R. Reuss, "Documents nouveaux sur l'antisémitisme dans le Bas-Rhin," *REJ*, LIX (1910), 251.

[2] Z. Szajkowski, "Jewish Émigrés during the French Revolution," *JSS*, XVI (1954), 319–34.

Originally published in *Proceedings of the American Academy for Jewish Research,* vol. XXVI (1957).

the Alsatians to the army — so glorified by many historians — was only a legend. In the border departments 80% of the conscripts deserted. Parents registered newly born boys as girls; people attacked city halls and destroyed registries of births. Thus, the registries of 1785 in Tarbes (H^{tes} Pyrénées) were destroyed in 1804. Jews did not participate in such organized acts against serving in the army. Still, the historian P. Fauchille wrote that these acts were a result of the "bad example" shown by Jews.[3]

On the other hand, the National guard refused in many places to accept Jews.

In Strasbourg (Lower Rhine) the Jewish leader and Jacobin Marx [Max] Berr [Cerfberr] was accepted in the National guard in spite of a strong opposition. On March 2, 1790, the Society of Friends of the Constitution sent its thanks to Captain M. Weber of the guard for accepting Berr.[4] The National guard of Nancy (Meurthe) refused to accept Jews and this caused a public discussion and the publication of a series of pamphlets, defending and condemning Jews. Some of them were written in connection with the actors, who were also refused admittance to the guard.[5] Jewish volunteers were also turned down by the

[3] *Extrait du registre des procès-verbaux des séances du Conseil permanent du département de la Meurthe, déclarant qu'on ne peut contraindre les citoyens à partir pour l'armée* (Nancy, 1792), 10 pp.; Pierre Braun, "Une Commune du pays messin pendant la Révolution [Téterchen]," *Le Pays lorrain*, (1905), 165–73; F. L'Huiller, *Recherches sur l'Alsace napoléonienne* (Strasbourg, 1947), 4–11, 188; J. B. Lambla, *Das Unter-Elsass in den Jahren 1814–1818* (Strassburg, 1913), 191; *Correspondence de Napoléon Ier* (Paris, 1859–69), X, 28; H. Taine, *Origines de la France contemporaine. Régime moderne* (Paris, 1901), I, 137–39; E. d'Hauterive, *La Police Secrète du Premier Empire* (Paris, 1908), II, 120; S. Posener, "The Immediate Economic and Social Effects of the Emancipation of the Jews in France," *JSS*, I (1939), 318–19; P. Fauchille, *La question juive en France sous le Premier Empire* (Paris, 1884), 12–13.

[4] F. C. Heitz, *Les Sociétés politiques de Strasbourg pendant les années 1790 à 1795* (Strasbourg, 1865), 18.

[5] *Lettre d'un citoyen aux Gardes-Citoyens de la ville de Nancy, en réponse à la question: Les Juifs doivent-ils être admis dans la Milice Nationale?* [Nancy, 1790], 6 pp.; M. C. [Charles-Nicolas Sigisbert] Sonnini de Manoncour, *De l'admission des Juifs à l'Etat civil. Adresse à mes compatriotes*, par un citoyen du Nord de la France (Nancy, 1790), 16 pp.; [Jacob Berr,] *Réflexions sur la*

guards of Wintzenheim (Upper Rhine) and by many other localities of Alsace and neighboring departments.[6] When the Representatives of Paris organized the National guard in Saint-Esprit-lès-Bayonne (Landes) they found there enough volunteers to form nine companies. But there were so many brawls between the Christians and Jews that the City Council decided in November 1790 to organize two separate companies composed of Jews only. The departmental *Directoire* of Landes annulled this decision as contrary to the spirit of the Constitution.[7] The priest of the church Saint-Eloi in Bordeaux (Gironde) protested against the presence of Jews who came there on August 6, 1789, to register in the National guard.[8]

On the other hand, some City Councils found a good excuse to exempt Christians from service — they drafted mostly Jews,

Lettre d'un Citoyen aux Gardes Citoyens de la ville de Nancy, en réponse à la question les juifs doivent-ils être admis dans la Garde Nationale? (Nancy, 1790); Valois, *Apologie de l'opinion de M. [J. J.] Ranxin sur cette question: Les Juifs doivent-ils être admis dans la milice nationale?* par M. Valois, garde-citoyen de la compagnie de Nicolas le jeune (Metz, 1790), 3 pp.; *Idem, Appel aux Gardes citoyens sur la Lettre anonyme à eux adressée* [Nancy, 1790], 7 pp.; *Lettre de M*** Garde Citoyen à M**** [Nancy, 1790]; *Ma façon de penser sur l'inadmission des comédiens à la garde citoyenne de la ville de Nancy* [Nancy, 1790], 6 pp.; *Adresse de remerciament, de la part des Comédiens de la ville de Nancy, à l'auteur enrocé, borgne et bossu de l'écrit intitulé: Ma façon de penser sur l'admission des Comédiens dans la Garde-citoyenne de cette ville* [Nancy, 1790], 7 pp.

[6] A. Lévy, "Notice sur les Israélites du Duché de Lorraine," *UI*, XL (1885), 288; A. Cahen, "Le rabbinat de Metz pendant la période française", *REJ*, XIII (1886), 7; Capitaine Chognard, "Etude sur les Gardes Nationales et sur les levées de troupes dans le Département du Haut-Rhin pendant la Révolution," *Bulletin de la Société Belfortaine d'émulation*, no. 35 (Belfort, 1919), 39.

[7] *Revue d'Histoire*, (Nov. 1910), 203; Ch. Juncar, "Le Blocus de Bayonne en 1814," *Société des Sciences . . . de Bayonne. Bulletin trimestriel*, no. 1, (1911), 25.

[8] M. Lhéritier, *Les débuts de la Révolution à Bordeaux d'après les Tablettes manuscrites de Pierre Bernardau* (Paris, 1919), 82. As late as on May 8, 1831, the Bordeaux chronicler Pierre Bernardau noted in connection with an incident between a soldier and a Jew that the Jews would probably be forced to form their own National guard because they were not accepted in the general National guard. City Library of Bordeaux, manuscript 713–1, vol. 6, p. 655.

although they comprised a striking minority of the population. In 1793 the department of Meurthe had to draft 2,957 soldiers, and in some places of the department mostly Jews were drafted. Seven out of eighteen draftees in Schalbach were Jews; Phalsbourg, which had to send draftees, chose Jews only. The same anti-Jewish policy with a patriotic sense prevailed in many Alsatian communities.[9]

Members of the National guard and soldiers of the regular army often attacked Jews. In December 1790, the Jews of Ingwiller were molested, principally by guards. In Metz and Nancy soldiers prevented Jews from praying in the synagogues. It is worth relating an incident recorded on June 19, 1793, by the Christian secretary of the village of Dossenheim (Lower Rhine) pertaining to the Jew Scheilen Lévi. A group of National guards, among them Captain Lutz of the 5th battalion of the Lower Rhine, accused Lévi of shouting in Neuveiller "Long live the King." Lévi testified that the National guards made fun of him, forced him to call out certain slogans and under tension he may have used also the anti-Republican slogan. He was beaten by the guards who wanted to hang him. On his way back home, while attending to his wounds, he was again caught and beaten by the guards who brought him to Dossenheim. They drank a lot and warned Lévi that, unless he pays them 250 livres, they would take him away. The Jewish community collected the requested sum and the City Council decided to protest to the district against the guards' behavior.[10]

Orthodox Jewish recruits tried often to find ways to enable them to observe religious precepts and traditions while in the army. The scribe and religious teacher Jessel Lehmann of Ribeauvillé (Upper Rhine) wrote that when the order of September 13, 1793, to draft all men between 25 and 45 was announced, the Jews were afraid this will force them to desecrate the Sab-

[9] Albert Troux, *La Vie politique dans le département de la Meurthe d'Août 1792 à Octobre 1936* (Nancy, 1936), I, 265–266; R. Reuss, *op. cit.*, 251.

[10] R. Reuss, "L'Antisémitisme dans le Bas-Rhin pendant la Révolution," *REJ*, LXVIII (1914), 250–51; Ca Metz, 3P2; Jean-Julien [Barbé] *La Fayette à Metz* (Metz, 1920), 29; Ca Nancy, minutes, vol. 6, p. 7. E. Wolf, *Chronik . . . Dossenheim* (Strassburg, n. d.), 109–111.

bath. Many Jews participated in the French battles against the Germans and Austrians. But Lehmanns' description shows no patriotic manifestations on the part of the Jews, just fear of not being able to observe the Sabbath. They felt relieved when the battles were over.[11] Jews of many communities tried to gain exemption from duty on Sabbath.[12] In 1790 the Jews of Saint-Esprit-lès-Bayonne were permitted to ask Christian National guards to substitute for them on Jewish holidays.[13] On April 22, 1791, the city of Avignon (Vaucluse) decided that the Jews would have to serve on Passover. In 1792 the Jews of Metz requested to be exempt from duty in the National guard on Sabbath. On November 7 and December 3, 1792, the civil authorities rejected similar requests by the Jews of Haguenau and Niederroedern (Lower Rhine).[14]

The choosing of a military career was in fashion among the rich Jews. There were many officers in the family of the Alsatian Jewish leader Cerfberr of Médelsheim. One of them was Marc-François-Jérôme Baron Wolf (1776–1848), a son of Minette Cerfberr and Lévy Wolff, who volunteered in 1794 at the age of 17, converted to Christianity and during the First Empire became the first general of Jewish origin. Simon Mayer, the son of Mayer Lazare Dalmbert and Rosette Cerfberr volunteered in 1794 and became an officer in 1796.[15] (Much later in 1843,

[11] Dr. M. Ginsburger, *Aus der Zeit der Revolutionskriege* (Breslau, 1916), 12 pp.

[12] In 1761 the Jews of Bordeaux obtained permission to be exempt from duty in the milice on Sabbath. But on May 14, 1773, the two visitors from Palestine, Yom Tob Algazy and Jacob Le Beth, permitted them to serve on Sabbath. This was done probably because of the hunger and the fear of possible attacks against the Jews. The taxes had to be paid the next day, on May 15, 1773, which was a Saturday, and the Jews feared to be attacked then. Minutes of the Bordeaux *Nation* (Da Gironde), I, pp. 104–05, no. 412; P. Bernardau, *Histoire de Bordeaux depuis 1675 jusqu'à 1836...* (Bordeaux, 1837–38), 169–70; A. Detcheverry, *Histoire des Israélites de Bordeaux* (Bordeaux, 1850), 88.

[13] Ch. Juncar, *op. cit.*, 25.

[14] Da Vaucluse, L-1-80, f. 114; Ab. Cahen, *op. cit.* 107; N. Netter, *Vingt siècles d'histoire d'une communauté juive...* (Paris, 1938), 197–99; R. Reuss, *op. cit.*, 260.

[15] Paul Bettelin, Le Général Marc-François-Jérôme Baron Wolf, (n. p., [1942]); General J. Dennery, "Les trois frères Dalmbert," *UI — Pour le*

the Mayor of Lunéville, M. Guerard, wrote that military service is unpopular among the poor Jews, but there are military men in the wealthy families, as this happens also among the higher Christian classes.)[16]

It should be noted that many Jewish conscripts were rejected from military service because of poor health, a result of long persecutions, privations and poverty. 229 out of 391 Jewish conscripts of Lower Rhine were rejected in 1807 and 65 out of 72 in the Department of Moselle.[17]

Jews, with their knowledge of the German language and family contacts with Germany were often in a position to supply the French with valuable information about enemy positions. In fact, some Jews served as French spies. The 62 years old Jewish dealer in second-hand goods and engraver Joseph Godchaux of Thionville was a spy for the French general Félix de Wimpffen (1744–1814), who defended Thionville in 1792. Godchaux also employed his son-in-law Abraham Lazare for spying. In the beginning of 1793 Wimpffen was accused by Godchaux of being a traitor to his country. Godchaux related how the general sent him with treasonable messages to the émigré army. The Jewish element, too, came into this affair. Godchaux

Foyer, pour l'Ecole, LXIX (1914), 6; "Ibrahim-Manzour-Effendi," SIW, X, no. 19 (1913), 33; Le Général Francfort, "Les Trois frères Cerfberr [Edouard Cerfberr, Alphonse-Théodore Cerfberr, Max-Théodore Cerfberr] (Quelques souvenirs)," Carnet de la Sabretache, 2e série, XI (1912), 353–70.

[16] Maurice Aron, "Quelques documents historiques concernant la communaute de Lunéville," Annuaire des AI, 5667 (Paris, 1906) 50–51. Most soldiers came back to civilian life without any means of livelihood. In 1860 the Prefect of Lower Rhine reported that 19 out of 47 former Jewish soldiers, who served until 1815, live in poverty. M. Ginsburger, "Au service de la France," SS, I (1930) 10–17.

[17] Ad. Seyboth, Strasbourg, historique et pittoresque depuis son origine jusqu'en 1870 (Strasbourg, 1894), 201; D'Hauterive, op. cit., III, no. 753. The same situation was noted in 1808 in the department of Vaucluse (Maxime Pazzis, Mémoire statistique sur le département de Vaucluse (Carpentras, 1808), 46–47; in 1821 [by Coquebert de Montbret] in his Notice sur l'état des israélites en France; in Dr. Jean Champouillion's Recueil de mémoires de médicine . . ., de chirurgie et de pharmacie militaires, 3e série, XXXIII (Paris, 1872); by the Mayor of Bordeaux, A. Gautier, in 1843, Da Gironde, V13; A. Charles, La Révolution de 1848 et la Seconde République à Bordeaux (Bordeaux, 1945), 82.

related how he cried because the fate of Thionville was in his hands and how he prayed to God for counsel. Being a Jew he could not betray France, "such an honest nation, which gave even to the Hebrew people the same equality and liberty as to the other citizens; that since the destruction of the Temple, the Jewish people remained the least of all nations and there is no such intelligent nation as the French." The Jew did not deliver Wimpffen's treacherous message, but instead he gave to the émigrés false information and Thionville was saved. Wimpffen defended himself and counter-attacked the "Jewish spy." But the impression remained that Wimpffen did have relations with the émigrés.[18] On the other hand some Jews did serve as spies for the émigrés.[19] Israël Rehms of Strasbourg — willingly or unwillingly — was a purveyor of the émigré army of Condé.[20] On March 6, 1792, the wine-merchant L. Caule denounced Cerfberr for sending from Paris a Certain Drumelle as emissary to the émigrés in Geneva. We do know now that Cerfberr did help émigrés.[21] But only one Jew, Léopold Bernheim of Kembs, was found guilty of espionage and was sentenced to death on September 9, 1795.[22]

II.

In spite of all this a large number of the almost 40,000 French Jews at the time of the Revolution of 1789 served in the armed forces. Let us now find this out in a regional order.

According to one source over one hundred of the 500 Jews of Paris enlisted in the National Guard.[23] But this seems to be a

---

[18] AN, AF–II 281 (2347); *Pétition adressée à la Convention nationale par Joseph Godchaux* [Paris, nd.], 8 pp.; Paul Heckmann, *Félix de Wimpffen et le siège de Thionville* (Paris, 1926), 112–17.

[19] R. Reuss, *La Grande fuite de Décembre 1793 et la situation politique et religieuse du Bas Rhin de 1794 à 1799* (Strasbourg, 1924), 173.

[20] "Les Députés à l'Assemblée de 1806," *SS*, V, no. 5 (1934), 4.

[21] A. Tuetey, *Répertoire général des sources manuscrites de l'histoire de Paris pendant la Révolution française* (Paris, 1900), VI, 26.

[22] *Strassburgische Zeitung*, Oct. 18, 1795; Reuss, "Documents . . .," 260.

[23] J. Godard, *Discours prononcé le 28 janvier 1790 . . .* (Paris, 1790), 5. See also *Adresse de l'Assemblée des Représentants de la Commune de Paris à*

gross exaggeration. Fifty one Jewish volunteers served in the first battalion of the Altkirch (Upper Rhine) district. Thirty or forty of the prisoners taken by the enemy after the attack on Fort Louis (Lower Rhine), all of them volunteers of the Lower Rhine, were Jews.[24] There were pathetic examples of readiness to serve France. Rabbi Aaron Worms of Metz shaved his long beard in order to be able to keep his pike in the National guard. According to some sources the first French Jew to become an army officer during the Revolution was Enchel Nordon of Metz, who volunterred in 1789 at the age of 33.[25]

In Bordeaux (Gironde) many Jews served in the armed forces of the Revolution.[26] According to one source the Jews of Bordeaux tried to form in October 1792 their own company of National guards.[27] Many Jews participated in the armed forces

l'Assemblée Nationale (Paris, 1790), 5. For details on Jews of Paris in the armed forces see L. Kahn, Les Juifs de Paris pendant la Révolution (Paris, 1898), 162–171.

[24] Dr. M. Ginsburger, "Elsässische Juden als Soldaten," Jahrbuch der Gesellschaft für die Geschichte der Israeliten in Elsass-Lothringen, I (Gebweiller, 1917), 29; R. Reuss, op. cit., 2.

[25] Gerson Lévy, "Nécrologie de M. A. Worms . . .," La Régénération, I, (1836), 226. His two sons were killed in action. M. Ginsburger, "Der erste jüdische Hauptmann," SIW, VI, no. 37 (1909); Dr. Max Grünwald, Die Feldzüge Napoleons . . . (Wien-Leipzig, 1913), 10; Arthur Chuquet, La légion germanique, 1792–1793 (Paris, 1904), vi, vii, 42, 325.
Cerf maître juif was among the fusiliers of Metz, who were sent to Saverne L. Klipffel, "La garde nationale de Metz à Saverne, 1793," RA, LXXV 1928), 117.

[26] Lopes Dubec was substitute to the commissioner in the regiment of St.-Eloy: Règlement pour l'armée patriotique bordelaise (Bordeaux, 1790), 81. A monument on the Jewish cemetery of Bordeaux tells the story of Daniel Iffla, who fought in 1791: "Au vénérable Daniel Iffla, administrateur du temple de Bordeaux décédé à l'âge de 92 ans le 12 septembre 1864 soldat de 1791 volontaire de la Gironde. Il combatti [sic] à la prise de Toulon et fut fait lieutenant sur le champ de bataille." G. Cirot, Recherches sur les Juifs Espagnols et Portugais à Bordeaux (Bordeaux, 1908), 152. On February 27, 1793, the wounded soldier Lazare juif demanded relief (Departmental archives of Gironde, L 2150). Jacob Vayl, an Ashkenazic Jew of Bordeaux, was in October 1793 in the National Guard. F. Dreyfus, Misères sociales et études historiques (Paris, 1901), 245.

[27] Da Gironde, L 2155 (Letter of Oct. 9, 1792 to the Club des Amis de la Liberté).

of the Girondist movement of Bordeaux — a movement designed to combat the federal government of Paris.[28]

The testimonies on the participation of the Jews of the former papal province of Avignon and Comtat Venaissin are conflicting. According to J. E. B. Duprat, president of the Jacobins of Avignon, the Jews were the first to defend the city against the counter-Revolutionists during the uprising of June 10, 1790. But the Avignon annexationist and Terrorist leader, Agricol Moureau, wrote in an anti-Jewish pamphlet, which he published in 1819, that only two Jews were in the three Avignon battalions formed in 1792. A German traveller wrote during the Terror that the Jews of Avignon must serve in the army. But on June 22, 1793, a member of the *Société Républicaine* of Avignon complained that the Jews under arms were not doing their duty. The society then decided to disarm the Jews.[29] The names of

---

[28] The Jews Dacosta jeune, Julian Cordova, David Casserace [?], Molina, Jean Lévi, Abraham Mendes, David Lopes Gonsales, Rodrigues and Jossiou served in the 3rd *Grenadiers* battalion of the Southern legion in the departmental force. Delvaille and Jacob Pereire were in the 3rd company of the same battalion (Da Gironde, L 1138). Among many others the following Jews signed a certificate on favor of Rodrigues Alvares, a Jew of the 2nd Company in the 7th battalion of the Southern Legion: A. Cardoze fils, Peixotto jeune, Peynado jeune, Salomon Athias, Caspar Trigfus, Astruc jeune, Totta, ... פ אשר, Moïze Lopes fils (Da Gironde, L 2193). The following Jews signed a petition of the same battalion: Th. Rodrigues fils aîné, Peixotto jeune, David Nougues, Jean-Baptiste Silva, Mendes, Petit, M. Mendes, D. Lopes-Dubec, Mendes jeune, D. Pimensel [Pimentel], Raphaël père, Raphaël fils, J. Francia jeune, Rodrigues, Mansanto fils, Elie Alvarin, Daniel Vaz, Mendes-Tequa, Pimentel: *La Compagnie du septième bataillon de la Legion du Sud, à leurs concitoyens* (Bordeaux, [1793]), 8 pp.

[29] J. E. B. Duprat, *Discours sur la Révolution ... le 19 Décembre 1791 ...* (Marseille, 1792), 51; [Agricol] Moureau, *De l'incompatibilité entre le Judaïsme et l'exercice des droits de cité ...*, (Paris, 1819), pp. 34–35; Wilhelm Bauer, *Un allemand en France sous la Terreur. Souvenirs de Frédéric-Christian Laukhard ... 1792–1794* (Paris, 1915), 288 (... "on les oblige à faire leur service militaire comme les chrétiens"); Ca Avignon, I 47: "Séance du 22 Juin 1793 l'an 2eme. de la République Française, de la Société Républicaine d'Avignon. Sur la pétition faite par un membre que les juifs dans toutes les occasions ne faisoient pas leur devoir, la société délibere que petition sera faite à la municipalité pour proceder au désarmement des juifs, pour armer les vrais républicuns avignonois en s'en rapportant à qui de droit. A Avignon

nineteen Jews appear on a list of Carpentras volunteers of July 28, 1792; eighteen Jews appear on another Carpentras list of 228 volunteers of March 16, 1793; eight on a list of October 3, 1793; and nine on a list of October 5, 1793. But eight Jewish volunteers deserted and their parents were called for an investigation.[30] In 1791 the Jews of L'Isle-sur-Sorgue paid 1,200 livres in order to be exempt from service; this happened shortly before the annexation of the former papal province by France.[31] It was natural for the Jews of this former papal province to evade service in military units directed against France. In the beginning of the Revolution the province was the victim of civil wars between partisans and adversaries of annexation by France. Those Jews who could manage emigrated to France.

In Nîmes (Gard) where the Jewish community was composed mostly of Comtadin Jews, four Jews volunteered during the Revolution.[32] In Montpellier (Hérault) the small Jewish community counted a dozen soldiers.[33] 46 Jewish families (230 persons) lived in Nice at the time when the city was occupied by France in September 1792. Their number reached 65 families (295 persons) in 1808. From the year X (1801–1802) to 1808, 24 Jews of Nice served in the army.[34]

---

le 22 Juin 1793 l'an 2me. de la République Française. Quinche prdt. Pasca secretare Waton Secre. La Municipalité voulant faire droit à la péttition des amis de la liberté, le citoyen Jelin chef de légion faira executer la pettion mentione cydessus. Avignon ce 22e Juin 1793 l'an second de la Répb. fse., Cartoux maire."

[30] Ca Carpentras, uncatalogued documents of the Revolutionary period, including a register *Déserteurs juifs*. A counter-Revolutionary pamphleteer ridiculed, in 1790, the leader of the Carpentras milice, supposedly of Jewish origin. [Grasson,] *Ran-Tan-Plan, ou les loisirs d'un tambour de la milice de C . . . tras* (n. p., [1790]), 13 ("*Ran-Tan-Plan:* . . . Mr. le Gros-Major, dont l'origine se perdroit dans la unit du temps, si les Rabins n'en avoient pas conservé précieusement l'histoire").

[3] Ca L'Isle-sur-Sorgue, minutes, 1–80, fol. 197, May 18, 1791.

[32] S. Kahn, *Notice sur les Israélites de Nîmes* (Nîmes, 1901), 29.

[33] Salomon Kahn, "Les Juifs de Montpellier au XVIIIe siècle," *REJ*, XXXIII (1896), 294.

[34] V. Emanuel, *Les Juifs de Nice, 1400–1806* (Nice, 1905), 48.

III

Aside from direct participation in the National guard and the army, the Jews were helpful to the armed forces of the Republic in many other ways.

On May 5, 1792, a group of young Metz Jews presented the sum of 51 livres in coins and 74 livres in *assignats* (paper-money) for war expenses. In many communities Jews worked on the fortifications. On August 26, 1792, the Jews of Metz offered their services for the work on the ramparts.[35]

As was then customary, wealthy Jews paid volunteers to serve for them in the Revolutionary army.[36] It was easy for wealthy people to play the role of heroes of a musical comedy. Marx Berr became the "adopted" son of the 77 years old woman Rehm. He financially rendered support to his "mother" in order to enable her real son to volunteer for the defence of France.[37]

The replacing of recruits by substitutes was very popular until it was abolished by law in 1872. Private agencies for providing substitutes benefited from adventurous elements, but particularly from poor youths, who were eager to take the place of a wealthy recruit. Such dealings bring to our mind the trade of slaves and was regarded odious. But such offices were legalized by the government. Of course, Jews were no exception and

[35] Ca Metz, minutes of the City Council, vol. 9, ff. 63, 75, Aug. 29, 1792.

[36] On a Strasbourg list of Apr. 12, 1792, eight such names are listed: Marx Beer [Berr], Meyer Lazare, Jos. Lehmann and Lippmann, Salomon and Michel Lévy, Cerf Léo Séligmann, Alexandre Samuel Séligmann. On the same list Moyse Isaac figures with a gift of 200 livres for a volunteer, Abraham Isaac — 3 livres, and Moyse Isaac — 100 livres yearly for the duration of the war. *Dons patriotiques pour l'équipement du Bataillon des Volontaires de Strasbourg* . . . [Strasbourg, Apr. 12. 1792], 14 pp.

[37] *Précis du procès-verbal du Conseil général de la commune de Strasbourg du 26 Juillet 1792* . . . (n. p., n. d.) p. 7: "Mr. Marx Behr [Berr] s'est fait adopter par la mère de M. Rehm, âgée de 77 ans: son fils a dit, si l'on avait soin de ma mère, je défendrais ma Patrie. Je suis votre frère, a dit M. Marx Behr, présentez-moi à votre mère, je remplirai envers elle les devoirs de fils: & si elle a le malheur de vous perdre, elle aura un second fils, qui la secourra avec le même zèle que vous."

often Jewish recruits, too, looked for Christian substitutes.[38] On the other hand Jewish recruits were often substituted by Jews, or even Christian recruits by Jews.[39] Jews were also found among the owners of agencies which provided substitutes and they, too, were highly disliked.[40] In 1793 the scribe Jessel Lehmann noted in his diary written in a ciphered Yiddish that: "on Shabbat Hagadol [the Sabbath preceeding Passover] the sermon was delivered before the evening service because the youths were forced to go to the communal assembly. Eight were drafted into the guard. On the 7th day of Passover they were forced to get into uniforms. Thus, the holiday was marred." Finally, they were replaced by eight Christians.[41] But Schmulen Isac of Ingwiller recruited soldiers for the Revolutionary army.[42]

[38] For a contract of Nov. 27, 1803, between the recruit Abraham Lévy of Bliesbrucken (Moselle) and his Christian substitute Joseph Hollender see *SIW*, IX, no. 22 (1912), 11. The Jews of Blotzheim collected in 1846 enough money to pay a substitute for the son of a poor Jew who lived from his son's earnings. *La Pure Vérité* (1846), 20.

[39] This was noted in 1808 by Abraham Furtado in his pamphlet *Mémoire sur les projets des décrets présentés au Conseil d'Etat, concernant les Israélites* [Paris, 1808], p. 4. On May 31, 1799, Samuel Lopes Raimont of Bayonne became a substitute for the Christian recruit Ant. Lafargue. On June 2, 1799, the Jewish recruit Isaac Castro of Bayonne hired the Jewish substitute Abraham Moraes (City archives of Bordeaux, H 9, f. 37–39, nos. 32, 54). In 1809 the two brothers Lazard of Phalsbourg voluntarily served for two Christians (Report of the Nancy consistory, in the author's possession).

[40] In March 1845 the Prefect of Upper Rhine refused to accept the name of Abraham Mayer on a list of consistorial notables because of his trade with substitutes (Da, V 91). On a few conflicts in the 1830's–1840's between such traders, among them Jews, see Simon Lévy, *Mémoire pour le Sieur Simon Lévy ... contre le Sieur Mayer Godchaux* [Paris, 183-], 34 pp.; *Note pour MM. Lévi frères contre MM. Delassalle et compagnie* [Sèvres, 1848], 16 pp. It is worth while to mention two later pamphlets by Jewish authors on this subject: J. Aron fils, *Quelques réflexions ... concernant le remplacement* (Lille, [1847]); Simon Lévy, *Quelques réflexions ... sur le recrutement ...* (Lille, [1854]).

[41] In the Alsatian Museum of Strasbourg.

[42] In 1802, his son-in-law, Aron Cain demanded payment of 300 livres which the authorities owed to Schmulen: Willy Guggenbuhl, *Ingwiller* (Saverne, 1951), 196.

IV

Information on Jewish participation in the armed forces during the First Empire could provide us also with some data on the Revolutionary period.[43]

In 1810, 294 Jews of Alsace served in the army. On October 21, 1808, the Prefect of Moselle reported that since 1799, 137 Jews of the Moselle department served in the army, among them 41 soldiers, three officers and three surgeons, of Metz. He noted that a lack of desire to serve exists among Jews, and this was the result of a refusal by officers to accept Jews. According to another report 236 Jewish recruits and 13 volunteers of Metz served in the years VII (1798–1799)–1809 in the army. There were 55 Jewish soldiers among 3,289 Jews in the department of Meurthe and four in the department of Meuse. The class of 1810 and two special mobilizations in the department of Meurthe supplied 2,286 soldiers out of a total population of 365,808, *i. e.* one soldier for every 118 inhabitants. The proportion of the Jews, on the other hand, was one to 67. In 1798–1810, 52 Jews of the department of Vaucluse served in the army; six of them were volunteers. There were 58 Jewish families in Lyon in 1810, ten Lyon Jews served in the army. In Dijon 25 out of 231 Jews served in the army, in Nîmes — 23 out of 371, in Montpellier — 11 out of 105.[44]

According to a report of the Central Consistory of June 23, 1810, 797 Jews served in 1808 in the army, including the occupied countries. According to another report of the Central Consistory there were 36,663 Jews in 45 French departments, 462 of them

---

[43] During the First Empire Jewish communities called upon Jews to become soldiers. Such appeals were made in 1807 by the Jewish Community in Metz, in 1809 by the Central Consistory, by Italian Consistories on September 5, 1809. by rabbi L. Calbourg of Creveld on May 7, 1810, by the Consistory of Mainz on Apr. 18, 1811, etc. AN, F¹⁹ 1841; d'Hauterive, *op. cit.*, III, 282; Z. Szajkowski, "Judaica Napoleonica," *Studies in Bibliography and Booklore*, II (1956), nos. 288, 304.

[44] Archives of the Central Consistory, minutes, June 23, 1810 (Alsace); AN, F¹⁹, 11010; City archives of Metz, 1 F 11; Report of the Nancy Consistory, 1809 (in the author's possession).

serving in the army. But their number was probably higher. According to historian Charles-Joseph Bail 630 of 48,850 Jews in 1810 served in the army.[45]

V

It would be worth while to mention the role of the Jewish army provisionaries. They were always of great importance to the government but they were also much disliked.

On many occasions Jewish purveyors saved entire cities and provinces from starvation. During the dearth of 1714, Jewish merchants coming to Paris were free from paying duties. The army purveyors Hayem and Cerf Worms were granted in July 1787 citizenship because in 1770 and 1771 they saved the North-Eastern provinces from famine. During the winter of 1788–1789 Lipmann Cerf Berr granted to the city of Nancy a loan of 50,000 livres in order to buy wheat and he also promised to buy wheat for the city himself. As the wheat did not arrive in time the people accused Cerf Berr of hiding it for speculation and attacked his store houses. The city and provincial authorities

[45] Dr. M. Grünwald, op. cit., 13; A. E. Halphen, Recueil des lois . . . concernant les israélites (Paris, 1851), 327; Ch. J. Bail, Des Juifs au dix-neuvième siècle . . . (Paris, 1816), 106, 110.

It is worth while to bring some data on Jewish participation in the French army in the later period. Marx Cerfberr was the first Jewish colonel and Edouard Cerfberr the first Jewish general who remained a Jew: AI, XXXV (1874), 207–12. Only after the Revolution of 1830 it was easy for Jews to become officers. There were 69 Jews among 8,260 officers in 1867, although only one of every 360 Frenchmen was a Jew: Sylvain May, in Moniteur de la Meurthe, July 27, 1867. For a complete list of Jewish officers in 1859 see AI, XX, (1859), 351–55, 458–61. According to a survey made in 1882 by the historian Isidore Loeb, there were then in the French army 5 Jewish generals, 5 colonels, 9 lieutenant-colonels, 23 chiefs of battalions, 90 captains, 89 lieutenants, and 104 second lieutenants. L. Kahn, Les professions manuelles . . . (Paris, 1885) p. 19. See also: J. Bielinki, "Les Engagements des Juifs dans les Armées de la République," Le Volontaire juif, nos. 1–6 (1930), nos. 1–2 (1931); Maurice Bloch, "Les vertus militaires des Juifs," REJ, XXXIV (1897), xxix–xxx.; L. Lévy Bing, AI, XXVIII (1867), 743–47, 779–85; François Jacquet, Recherches historiques sur l'esprit militaire et l'éducation chez les Hébreux (n. p., 1867).

took him under their protection. On January 19, 1789, the people of Boulay attacked a convoy of 78 sacks of wheat which were on the way to Cerf Berr's store house. Berr Isaac Berr granted then a loan of 6,000 livres to buy sacks for wheat. During the bread crisis in Strasbourg (August 1789–March 1790), a Jewish secret agent of the wheat-commission of Mayence helped to import wheat from Germany to Strasbourg.[46] In 1790 the Jews of Metz submitted a petition to the National Assembly in which they stated that on many occasions the Jews saved the population of Metz from starvation and advanced enough money to pay the soldiers their solde.[46]

Jewish army purveyors were accused of causing all evils. The Terrorist leader of Nancy, B. Philip, strongly attacked the rich Jews and purveyors.[47] On October 8, 1793, the *Directoire* of the Sarrebourg (Meurthe) district demanded the *Comité Central des subsistances* of Strasbourg that Jews should not be allowed to provide provisions for the army.[48] The *Montagnard*, Joseph François Wulliez, too, stated in 1793 that because of the failure to buy provisions at the legal *maximum* price, the profits would now go to speculatos, especially Jews.[49] Jews were accused of exporting cattle and wheat abroad and reimporting it later again to France. J. B. O. Garnerin, commissionner at

[46] Paul M. Viollet, *Droit privé et sources. L'Histoire du Droit français* (Paris, 1896), 359; R. Anchel, "Comment on écrit l'histoire," *Samedi*, no. 16 (Apr. 18, 1936), 2; *AI*, XLV (1884), 30–31; *Le Moniteur*, Dec. 23, 1789; C. Constantin, *L'Evêché du département de la Meurthe de 1791 à 1802* (Nancy, n. d.), I, 46; Ca Nancy, minutes, vol. 1, p. 105, Oct. 8, 1789; *Arrêt de la Cour de Parlement, qui ordonne . . . à l'occasion de l'émeute populaire arrivé à Boulay, le 19 Janvier 1789. Du 27 Janvier 1789* (Metz 1789), 4 pp.; Alfred Lévy, *Notice sur les Israélites du Duché de Lorraine* (Paris, 1885), 18; Cardinal F. D. Mathieu, *L'Ancien régime dans la province de Lorraine et Barois* (Paris, 1878), 401; J. Godechot, "Les Juifs de Nancy de 1789 à 1795," *REJ*, LXXXVII, (1926), 15–16; Henry Brunschwig, *Les subsistances à Strasbourg pendant les premières années de la Révolution française* (Strasbourg, 1932), 76; *Mémoire pour la communauté des Juifs établis en la ville de Metz. Contre les prétentions de Monsieur le Duc de Brancas* (n. p., n. d.), 2.

[47] B. Philip, *Exposé succint des événemens contre-révolutionaires, arrivés à Nancy . . .* (Nancy, 1794), 28.

[48] Da Meurthe and Moselle, L 2132.　　　　[49] A. Troux, *op. cit.*, II, 66.

the Army of the Rhine and Moselle, reported from Alsace to the Committee of Public Safety that the "Jews and priests" discredit the nation. Jews were suspected of being purveyors for German princes in occupied territories who had to provide provisions for the French armies.[50] The Jewish army purveyor Baruch Cerfberr was accused of employing recruits who evaded service (*beschnittene Erstklaessler*).[51] Revolutionary pamphleteers accused the Jews of serving the army not as soldiers, but as purveyors.[52] When civil servants were forbidden on June 22, 1799, to be army purveyors, a newspaper wrote that this decision was favorable only to Jews.[53]

This was a vicious circle. During the Revolution the number of Jewish financiers was small. Only 8 of 150 important financiers during the Revolution, as listed by the historian Edmond Soreau, were Jews (Calmer, the brothers Frey, Pereire, Peixotto, Azévédo and Lange). These Jews were not the most important financiers and some of these eight (Frey, Peixotto) could hardly be called Jews.[54] But the tradition of the Jews' economic use-fulness, the idea that the Jews could accomplish great things in this field still persisted. In 1795, Paris was threatened by famine and the people in a public demonstration at the Convention,

[50] Ad. Gasser, "Histoire d'une petite ville de la Haute-Alsace, Soultz & son ancien bailliage," *RA*, XLVI (1895), 491; F. V. A. Aulard, *Recueil des actes du Comité de Salut public* (Paris, 1889–1933), XIV, 569; R. Werner, *L'approvisionnement en pain de la population du Bas-Rhin et de l'armée du Rhin pendant la Révolution, 1789–1797* (Strasbourg, 1951), 226–67, 565. C. H. Laurent, Representative of the People, ordered to execute all Jewish peddlers who would follow the French army in Belgium: Emile Ouverleaux, "Notes et documents sur les Juifs de Belgique sous l'ancien régime," *REJ*, IX (1884), 283.

[51] *Geheime Geschichte der Regierung des Landes zwischen Rhein und Mosel*, (n. p., 1795), 55; R. Reuss, "*Documents . . .*," 265.

[52] Moureau, *op. cit.*, 35.

[53] *Amis des Lois*, June 26, 1799; F. Aulard, *Paris pendant la réaction thermidorienne et sous le Directoire* (Paris, 1902), V, 588–89.

[54] E. Soreau, "Les hommes de finance pendant la Révolution," *Revue des études historiques*, CI (1934), 315–38. Jews were often only sub-dealers of Christian purveyors. Such was during the Revolution the case of Mathias Lazare and his partners (AN, BB16 625).

on May 20, 1795 asked for bread. The walls of Paris were then covered by a poster dated June 8, 1795, and signed by the citizen Seigneur of the *Section de la Butte-des-Moulins*, who proposed to ask the Jews (the *nation juive*) to import to Paris wheat from abroad, because only the Jews with their commercial connections could do it.[55] A Strasbourg pamphleteer wrote in 1790, that the Jew is the one who takes over "the often disliked occupation of a contractor for the government."[56] They were disliked as speculators by the revolutionaries and by the administration, which in the end had to pay for the supplies. According to the historian, Jacques Godechot, the request of Jewish creditors that they be paid for their deliveries to the administration caused in 1789–1790, anti-Jewish feelings among the officials in Lorraine, who could not pay them.[57] These Jewish army purveyors were hated by the peasants who were not always too happy to sell their products, especially if they were paid with *assignats*. In Alsace and neighboring provinces the supplying the army was mostly of intermittent character and the local commerce did not profit from it. Only dealing in horses was of a local interest and in this case the local population distrusted the purveyors who personified the army. Jewish purveyors were often able to get horses and food for the army only with the help of tricks of their trade. In January 1794, the butchers of Altkirch complained that livestock is very high because peasants prefer to sell their cattle to the Jewish army purveyors who pay in species instead of *assignats*. But the National agent of the district of Strasbourg warned in a circular of July 1794 against

[55] E. Charavary, "Un appel à la nation juive pour se charger de l'approvisionnement de Paris," *La Révolution française*, XXIV (1893), 62–68.

[56] "Er ist es, welcher Lieferungen, Zahlungen und so manchen eben nicht immer beliebtes Geschäfft für Regierungen übernimmt." J., *Die Juden-Verfolgungen* (Strassburg, [1790]), 15.

[57] Godechot, *op. cit.*, 9–10. In the year VI (1797–98) the purveyor Isaac May of Strasbourg and his partners demanded from the Government payment of a debt of 464,474 francs for wheat (AN, BB[16] 625). Napoleon I refused to pay the debts owed by the Government to the Cerfberr family: *Memoirs of Comtant, First Valet de Chambre of the Emperor* ... (New York, 1895), III, 125–128.

the "given Jewish citizens" (*citoyens nommés Juifs*) who operated with false requisitions and pay with assignats.[58]

Of course, many purveyors were speculators, who quickly enriched themselves. One company of which the Jew Vitta Cohen was the lessor of funds, subleased its contracts and pocketed a huge profit without having to perform any duty.[59] Among the arrested purveyors who operated on a large scale were Jacob Benjamin, who had a contract for over 500,000 livres for the army of Briançon; Olry Hayem Worms, suspected in bribing an official of the Ministry of War. The purveyors Meyer, Wolf, Lévy, Lazard and Isaac Netter were arrested in Mirecourt and kept in prison for a long time for profiteering.[60]

[58] R. Reuss, *op. cit.*, 267; L'Huillier, *op. cit.*, 392; R. Paquet, *Bibliographie analytique de l'histoire de Metz pendant la Révolution* (Paris, 1926), II, 1290; R. Werner, "Altkirch pendant la Terreur," *RA*, LXXXI (1934), 232; Ca Strasbourg, minutes of the *Corps municipal*, vol. 5, July 3, 1794.

[59] George Pariset, *Etudes d'histoire révolutionnaire et contemporaine* (Paris, 1929), 101. Chayen Netter and the Christian Philippe Knobloch were sentenced by the Military Court of Strasbourg for selling 409 stolen shirts (AN, D[III] 213, dr. 1). On Jews among the buyers of stolen army horses see Js. Foesser, *Meistratzheim* (Strassburg, 1939), 263. The Jewish purveyors Moyse Cahen of Biesheim and Joseph Hemerdinger and Hirtz Weil of Grussenheim were sentenced as a result of a law-suit by three other Jews: Baruch Picquart and Benjamin Bloch of Herlisheim and Marx Dreyfuess of Hattstatt. AN, D[III] 214. On October 1795, the General Council of Metz cancelled contracts with Marx and Alcan and accused Zacharias Hertz and his partners of speculation. *Arrêtés du Conseil général de la Commune de Metz* ... (Metz, an IV), 19, 22.

[60] *La Femme de Jacob Benjamin à la Convention nationale* (n. p., n. d.), 32 pp.; L. Kahn, *op. cit.* 197–198; Arthur [Maxime] Chuquet, Les Guerres de la Révolution (Troisième série). *Hoche et la lutte pour l'Alsace, 1793–1794* (Paris, 1893), 45. During the Terror Meyer Dreyfuss was allowed to leave the prison of Strasbourg in the company of an orderly in order to continue his purveyance of dried vegetables for the army. Some Jewish purveyors were among those persecuted for irregularities. The National Agent of Nancy accused Jacob Allemand and Salomon Fribourg of not giving the correct weight of meat sold to the army hospital of Nancy. On April 18, 1794, both stated they are "real Republicans." [André Ulrich,] *Recueil des pièces servant à l'histoire de la Révolution à Strasbourg* [— Livre Bleu] (Strasbourg, 1795), I, 48–49, 67; AN, W 30 (1792). Moïse Hertzel of Schwindratzheim was among the accused of a swindle against the army. Werner, *op. cit.*, p. 590.

But again, not only Jews were speculators. Purveyors were often victims of peculiar situations. Simon Dreyfus of Osthoffen (Lower Rhine) was ordered by the army to surrender the two cows, which he bought from the wife of François Khiel for 132 livres, because Khiel was an émigré. But the army ordered him to buy the cows and then sentenced him to six years in prison for buying the same cows twice.[61]

Still Jewish purveyors often gained the confidence and respect of the administration and the Christian population. Meyer Lévy, keeper of the forage warehouse of Thionville, was elected during the Revolution to the City Council, a rare event in considering the attitude toward Jews in this part of France. During the *blocus* of Thionville he demanded his partners to sell to the army meat at a lower price. In Obernai, officials complained that the supply of meat was not good because the Jews did not come to the cattle fair.[62]

VI

Politically, the most important factor of the Jewish aspect in the army purveyance was the Jewish participation in the purchasing Directory (*Directoire des Achats*), which was created on November 4, 1792, by the three Ministries of defence and was headed by the Protestant banker Jacques Biderman, of Swiss origin, Prof. J.-A.-J. Cousin and the Strasbourg Jew Marx Berr [Cerfberr] (1758–1817). The Directory was violently attacked, among others by Charles-François Dumouriez, commanding general of the Northern Army. The Directory's leaders were victims not only of the traditional distrust to army contractors, but also of the conflicts between the Minister of War, J.-N. Pache, and the minister of Interior, J. B. D. Roland.

---

[61] AN, D^{III} 211, dr. 30. Isaac Berh of Forbach was sentenced to prison for speculation with two sacks of tallow. From prison he wrote that he is being victimized by the "aristocracy and injustice." *Ibid.*, D^{III} 174.

[62] *Service funèbre célébré à la synagogue de Thionville, le 15 mars 1820 en l'honneur de feu Mr. Mayer Lévy* . . . (Metz, [1820]), 20 pp.; Werner, *op. cit.* 446.

Pache was pushed to the Ministry by his Girondist friends, but when he later went over to the *Montagnards*, Roland took away from the Directory the right to supply his Ministry. Dumouriez was known as a friend of the Girondists and this reinforced his attacks against the Directory. This agency was created in a moment of crucial financial crises, drought, speculations, and political conflicts. Bankers were active in both factions of the Revolution. Biederman was a friend of both, the Girondists and the Dantonists, and was not impartial. But the Jews in the Directory — all of them Ashkenazic — did not participate in these factional conflicts. Marx Berr was, undoubtedly, a very ambitious banker, but his activities were restricted to contracting-business and not to politics. On February 12, 1793, the Directory was suspended, but Marx Berr, probably, continued his transactions with the naval forces. It should be noted that Marx Berr did not appoint only Jews as the Directory's agents. Only two of ten agents for the Rhine Army in Lower Rhine were Jews (Baruch Cerfberr and Cahen).[63]

Lippman Cerfberr was commissioned by the Directory to purvey the armies of the Center, Meurthe, Moselle and the Vosges. Even before being able to begin his work, he was sent to Belgium to save the disorganized quartermasters of the army of General Dumouriez. But the general attacked openly the Jewish representative of the Directory. Lippman Cerfberr replied "on my honour as a Jew" (*sur ma foi de Juif*) that he tried to serve his country well. Later the *Comité de Guerre* stated that not Biderman and Marx Berr but Dumouriez was responsible for the Northern Army's lack of provisions. Dumouriez later abandoned his country and escaped abroad.

The brothers Baruch and Théodore Cerfberr who had to purvey the Army of the Rhine were strongly attacked by General A. P. Custines. Baruch Cerfberr in turn accused the General of sabotage. In fact, on March 12, 1793, a special commission composed of Merlin, Hausman and the Alsatian anti-Jewish leader

---

[63] Charles Poissoin, *Les fournisseurs aux armées sous la Révolution française. Le Directoire des Achats (1792–1793). J. Biedermann, Cousin, Marx Berr* (Paris, 1932), pp. 8, 14, 30, 117–18, 119, 129, 141, 204–08, 219, 222–23, 235–36.

Reubell cleared the names of the two Jewish brothers and in August 1793, the General was sentenced to death for treason.[64]

Olry Hayem Worms was a purveyor of shoes and socks for the army of Maréchal Luckner. He signed a contract for 1,490,333 livres and he had already started to buy merchandise when the Ministry of War accepted a bid of Worms' competitors who accepted 100,000 livres less. In 1791, Worms appealed to the National Assembly.[65] On August 5, 1795 the Committee of Public Safety accepted a proposition by the Jewish purveyors Abraham Alcan, Mayer Marx fils and Cerf Zacharias to supply 300,000 sacks of wheat and 2,500 sacks of dried vegetables for the army of Rhine-and-Moselle. In 1795 Wittersheim, who was purveyor of wheat for the army magazin of Saverne, proposed to the Committee of Public Safety to supply the army for 27 million food at a 2% commission. His proposition was not accepted only because of the large sums in such a commission which, by itself, was not usurious. He still advanced 450,000 livres for purchasing food in the occupied territories.[66] But it

[64] *Observations pour le citoyen Baruch Cerfberr* . . . (n. p., n. d.), 30 pp.; Camille Wolf, "Cerf-Berr et Coustine," *UI*, LIII, (1898), 705–07; [M. Lévylier,] *Notes et documents concernant la famille Cerfberr* (Paris, 1905), II, 6–135.

[65] *Olry Hayem Worms, à l'Assemblée nationale* (n. p., 23 mai, 1791), 8 pp· The Representative Nion ordered the local authorities to protect the purveyors Simon Cerf of Saverne and his son. In Sarralbe Moyse Cahen was during the Revolution manager of the stud, of which Cerf Berr was for many years tenant. On July 9, 1795, the Jew Isaac May was appointed by the Representative Dentzel as purveyor for Landau, Wissenbourg and Germersheim, because the previous Christian purveyor Savanier became an émigré. Robert Schnerb, "La Terreur à Saverne," *RA*, LXXX (1933), 516. In the Saverne magazines were also active the station-master Salomon Lippmann and the purveyors Libermann Israël and Salomon Lévy. *Ibid.*, 516–520; Arthur Benoit, "Sarralbe pendant les années 1792 et 1793," *Ibid.*, XLIII (1892), 87; Werner, *op. cit.*, 352.

[66] Aulard, *op. cit.*, XXIV, p. 534; Werner, *op. cit.*, 535. In some operations Zacharias and Alcan were partners of the Christian purveyor Charles Durbac of Soisy (Da Moselle, J, fonds Finot 505); In Saverne the Jew Samuel Meyer was Wittersheim's agent. Werner, *op. cit.*, 536. Salomon Lévy and Simons Cerf and son of Saverne were commissioned to buy in the departments of Vosges and Meurthe food for the army of the Rhine. Werner, *op. cit.*, 382.

should be noted that purveyors often had to fight too. In 1796 Marx Cerfberr armed his 120 employees and for 15 days helped to keep order in Antwerp, while most of the French garrison was out of the city.[67]

Jews were often appointed as members of important civil and military commissions for purveyance and commerce. Thus, e. g., David Moïse was a member of the supplies committee created in July 1793 in Nice. David Azévédo, Raba junior, Rodrigue fils and Lopes Dubec were among the fifty members of the Bordeaux commission to collect funds for buying wheat abroad.[68] A few Bordeaux Jews, including Abraham Furtado, who were sentenced during the Terror, were liberated and demanded to serve as members of the commission on commerce and of the commissions dealing with neutral countries.[69]

A study on this subject is hampered by the apologetic attitude taken by authors of studies on Jews in the armed forces of other countries and of a few studies on the same problem in France. They all come to the same apologetic conclusions: Jews were always ready to die for their respective countries and they fought in great numbers. The author of this study desires to take a different position.

In conclusion it should be stated that in spite of their traditional distrust of the army the Jews as a whole participated in the armed forces of the French Revolution. The army purveyors were of a very great value to the Revolutionary armies. On the other hand, the Christian population often disliked the idea of having to protect the Republic together with the Jews. In many places they refused to accept the Jews in the National guard.

---

[67] Lévylier, *op. cit.*, II, 133; M. Ginsburger, "Au service de la France," *SS*, no. I, (1930), 10.

[68] Joseph Combet, *La Révolution à Nice, 1792–1800* (Paris, 1912), 57; *Arrêté du Conseil général du département de la Gironde, concernant les subsistances, du trente septembre 1792* . . . [Bordeaux, 1792.] Broadside.

[69] Information furnished to the author by the Bordeaux historian Pierre Bécamps.

JEWISH AUTONOMY DEBATED AND ATTACKED DURING THE FRENCH REVOLUTION

I

ON the eve of the Revolution of 1789 the Jews and Christians of France were not less socially separated from each other than in the Middle Ages.[1] Disliked and persecuted as they were, the Jews nevertheless were often able to defend themselves in an organized manner through their autonomous communities. These communities, largely agencies for collecting taxes and performing other duties for the government and local officials, were carefully controlled by the authorities, and the scope of their self-rule never afforded the Jews a great many legal rights. But without the communities the Jews would have been defenseless. It may be safely assumed that this was one of the reasons why they demanded in the beginning of the Revolution that their communal bodies be preserved. Uncertain about their future, they wanted to maintain a collective organization which could speak up in their name and defend them.

The Christian advocates of Jewish emancipation demanded—even before the outbreak of the Revolution—not only a better understanding of the Jewish problem by Christians, but also a partial or complete abolition of the autonomous Jewish communities as a condition for Jewish emancipation. Chrétien Guillaume Lamoignon de Malesherbes, who headed the so-called Mallsherbes Commission for the preparation of a new status advantageous to the Jews, looked

---

[1] Robert Anchel, "Sur l'histoire des Juifs en France," *Cahiers juifs*, XIX (1936), 33.

Originally published in *Historia Judaica*, vol. XIX (1957).

with much disfavor upon the Jewish communities. Pierre Louis Roederer of the Metz Academy, wrote in a draft of a study on the Jews for the Academy about the necessity to break up the Jewish communities. On the other hand, the Nancy lawyer A. Thiéry maintained in his *Dissertation,* which was honored by the Metz Academy, that the Jews should continue to retain their communities and chiefs for some time. According to the historian Maurice Liber, Thiéry's position was influenced by the Jewish leader Berr-Isaac Berr, who was then opposed to the dissolution of the autonomous Jewish communities. The abbot Henry Grégoire, whose study also received a prize by the same Academy, favored abrogation of the autonomous rights of the Jewish communities in all non-religious matters. He demanded prohibition of the use of autonomous Jewish law in matters of marriage, inheritance, the performance of notarial functions by rabbis, and in other functions practiced contrary to French civil law. Grégoire maintained that the Jews should be assimilated to the other inhabitants in all civil matters. They should be allowed to congregate only for religious affairs, and this, too, should be done under the supervision of French officials. Zalkind Hourwitz, a Polish Jew who fought for Jewish emancipation in France, was the author of the *Apologie,* a third study awarded a prize by the Metz Academy. He went even further and demanded that the rabbis and syndics of the Jewish communities be forbidden to control the life of Jews outside the synagogue. Indeed, Hourwitz went so far as to advocate the abolition of the functions of rabbis altogether. On September 20, 1789, he warned the Committee of Reports of the National Assembly against the "devotees of my nation, the rabbinical inquisition," and the "sewer" of the Jewish community.[2]

---

[2] Z. Szajkowski, "Protestants and Jews of France in Fight for Emancipation, 1789-1791," *Proceedings of the American Academy for Jewish Research*, XXV (1956), 119-121; A. Cahen, "L'Emancipation des juifs devant la Société Royale des Sciences et Arts de Metz et M. Roederer," *REJ*, I (1880), 101; Adolphe Thiéry, *Dissertation sur cette question: Est-il des moyens de rendre*

With the outbreak of the Revolution, the discussion on the abolition of the autonomous Jewish communities became even more lively. Many *cahiers des doléances* (memorials of grievances) demanded that they be done away with. On December 23, 1789, Stanislas de Clérmont-Tonnèrre, in the National Assembly, made his famous statement that "all should be refused the Jews as a nation, but everything should be granted to them as individuals." The corporate body (*corporation*) of the Jews, he argued, should be abolished; their judges (*i.e., rabbis*) should be dismissed; they should not form any separate political body within the French nation. In Paris only the *Section* of Mathurins voted on February 20, 1790 against granting citizenship to the Jews. Their main argument was that, being organized as a separate nation, the Jews could not remain loyal to the French nation. All other Paris sections decided in favor of the Jews but insisted on abolishing the separate Jewish communities. In February, 1790 the *Section* of Saint-Germain-l'Auxerrois resolved to demand of the Jews "a formal renunciation of their laws and particular judges." The resolution of June 30, 1790 adopted by Paris in favor of the Jews contained the same demand to put an end to "the particular nation within the nation."[3]

The opponents of Jewish emancipation used this discussion as an argument against the Jews in general. The abbot Jean-Sifrein Maury stated on December 23, 1789, in the

---

les juifs plus heureux et plus utiles en France? (Paris, 1788), pp. 98-100; M. Liber, "Les Juifs et la convocation des États Généreaux," *REJ*, LXIV (1912), 105; Henri Grégoire, *Essai sur la régénération physique, morale et politique des juifs* (Paris, 1789), pp. 151-161; Zalkind-Hourwitz, *Apologie des juifs* (Paris, 1789), pp. 38-39; Anchel, "Un Juif polonais en France: Zalkind Hourwitz," *L'Univers israélite*, XCII, No. 38 (1937).

[3] Liber, *REJ*, LXIII, 188; *Opinion de M. le comte de Clérmont-Tonnèrre, député de Paris, le 23 décembre 1789* ([Paris], n.d.), p. 13; *Extrait du procès-verbal du district des Mathurins: du vingt février mill sept cent quatre-vingt-dix* [Paris, 1790], 4 pp.; *Rapport fait par M. Vion . . . sur les diverses adresses & pétitions des juifs de Paris* (Paris [Mars, 1790]), p. 23; *Adresse de l'assemblée des représentants de la Commune de Paris . . .* ([Paris], 1790), p. 12; Sigismond Lacroix, "Ce qu'on pensait des juifs à Paris en 1790," *Revue politique et littéraire*, XXXV (1898), 412-24; *idem, Actes de la Commune de Paris pendant la révolution* (Paris, 1898), III, 638; IV, 201-02; VII, 551-60.

National Assembly, that the Jews formed not only a religious sect, but a separate nation with its own laws. In these
conditions, to grant citizenship to the Jews would be exactly
the same as granting French citizenship to Englishmen and
Danes without asking them to cease being Englishmen and
Danes. The next day the Alsatian anti-Jewish leader
François-Joseph de Hell renewed a project to abolish all
autonomous rights of the Jewish communities, which had
been debated in 1788 by the Alsatian Intermediary Commission. The Alsatian Deputy, Jean-François Reubell, wrote
on January 5, 1790: "What do you think of people who
demand to become Frenchmen, but still wish to preserve
Jewish administrators, Jewish judges, Jewish notaries . . .
their particular laws on heritage, marriage, tutelage, majority, etc.?" Another Alsatian Deputy, Charles de Broglie,
asserted that the Jews' existence as a nation within a nation
was dangerous and anti-social.[4]

Nor were the Jews themselves all of the same opinion
on this matter. In their petition of August 26, 1789, the
Jews of Paris renounced the privilege of having their own
particular chiefs. But their brethren of Alsace, Metz, and
Lorraine demanded, in a petition addressed on August 31,
1789 to the National Assembly, permission to retain their
synagogues, rabbis, and syndics in the same manner as before.
Only after the discussion of December 23 and 24, 1789 in
the National Assembly, during which the separation of the
Jews was strongly attacked, did all Jews—in their new
petition of January 28, 1790—give up their request to maintain their independent communities. For a time the Jewish
leader of Lorraine, Berr-Isaac Berr, refused to renounce
autonomy of the communities in exchange for all civil rights.

[4] Maury, in *Gazette nationale ou moniteur universel*, Dec. 23, 1789;
Opinion de M. le Prince de Broglie . . . (n.p., n.d.), p. 4; *Archives parlementaires*, X (1877), 756-57; *Revue des grandes journées parlementaires*, I, 16;
Charles Hoffmann, *L'Alsace au dix-huitième siècle* . . . , IV (Colmar, 1906-07),
517-18; Szajkowski, "The Jewish Problem in Alsace, Metz and Lorraine on the
Eve of the Revolution of 1789," *Jewish Quarterly Review*, XLIV (1954),
235-37.

This provoked a strong attack by Jacob Berr, a Jewish physician of Nancy, who advocated the complete abolition of autonomous Jewish communities. In a pamphlet he maintained that Berr-Isaac Berr wished to keep the Jews in a state of estrangement from non-Jews and to perpetuate their isolation. Jacob Berr held the "despotic regime" of the Jewish community responsible for many evils and criticized Berr-Isaac Berr for his "dangerous" request that the autonomous Jewish communities be maintained. But after the Ashkenazic Jews had been granted full citizenship, on September 27, 1791, Berr-Isaac Berr published a *Letter* to his coreligionists in which he called upon them to abandon the spirit of a distinct community. Jews, he wrote, should remain organized as a group only for religious matters; in civil and political spheres they should remain individuals and act as such.[5]

However, the decision was not left to the Jews. Citizenship was granted to them only on condition that they renounce under oath all particular privileges. This was clearly laid down in the text on the emancipation of the Ashkenazic Jews proposed by the Alsatian anti-Jewish deputies and adopted by the National Assembly. On the following October 8, 1791, the anti-Jewish deputy Etienne-François

[5] [Jacques Godard,] *Adresse présentée à l'assemblée nationale le 26 août 1789 par les juifs résidans à Paris* (Paris, 1789), pp. 6-7; *Adresse présentée à l'assemblée nationale, le 31 août 1789* . . . [Paris, 1789], p. 13; Jacques Godard, *Pétition des juifs* . . . *adressée à l'assemblée nationale, le 28 janvier 1790* (Paris, 1790), p. 95; Berr-Isaac Berr, *Lettre à Monseigneur l'Evêque de Nancy* . . . (Paris, 1790), pp. 17-19; *Lettre du Sr. Jacob Berr* . . . (n.p., 1790), 10 pp.; Berr-Isaac Berr, *Lettre d'un citoyen, membre de la ci-devant communauté des juifs de Lorraine, à ses confrères* . . . (Nancy, 1791), pp. 8-10. On Dec. 23, 1789 Adrien Duquesnoy, deputy from Bar-le-Duc, noted in his diary concerning the National Assembly's discussion about Jews: "Mr. Duport avait d'ailleurs fait un raisonnement fort puissant à ceux qui assurent que les juifs ne consentiront jamais à se soumettre à nos lois: Vous avez exigé un serment; si les juifs le prêtent, ils sont dans le même cas que les autres citoyens français. Ce raisonnement ne frappait personne, parceque rien ne frappe ceux que des préjugés religieux aveuglent ou égarent." Robert de Crévecoeur, *Journal d'Adrien Duquesnoy, député du tiers état de Bar-le-Duc* . . . , II (Paris, 1894), 204.

Schwendt wrote to the city council of Strasbourg that the
National Assembly regarded the Jews, not as a *corporation*
which could no longer exist, but as individuals practicing
their particular religion. The Jews had ceased to exist as a
nation. This was a revengeful statement by a leader of the
anti-Jewish opposition in the National Assembly, intended
to pacify the defeated Alsatian fighters against Jewish emancipation.[6] Some modern Jewish historians have argued that
by giving up their autonomous Jewish communities the Jews
paid too high a price for their emancipation, that this was
the beginning of complete renunciation of Jewish life. It
is doubtful, however, whether the Jews could have retained
the pre-revolutionary status of their communities, even if
they had resigned themselves to live without civil rights. In
the long run the status of non-citizens for the Jews would
have been incompatible with the ideology of the new regime.
Clérmont-Tonnèrre, who fought for Jewish emancipation,
stated in the National Assembly on December 23, 1789 that,
should the Jews refuse to dissolve their communities and
become citizens, they should be banished. The same attitude
was taken on the next day by Count Honoré-Gabriel de
Mirabeau.[7]

The Jewish emancipation in France was a result of the
revolutionary nationalist principles, *Prinzipienreiterei,* to
use Max Nordau's term. There was only one way out for
the Revolution: to integrate the Jews within the French
people. This attitude sprang not only from humanitarian

---

[6] "Aux individus juifs, qui prêteront le serment civique, qui sera regardé
comme une renonciation à tous privilèges et exceptions introduits précédement
en leur faveur" (Decree of September 27, 1791); R. Reuss, *L'Alsace pendant
la révolution française,* II (Paris, 1894), 247-48. According to Berr-Isaac
Berr (*Lettre d'un citoyen,* p. 10), this proposition by the Alsatian deputies was
rejected, but this is not exactly so.

[7] E. Tcherikover, in *Oifn Scheidweg,* II (1939), 12-13 (in Yiddish);
Clérmont-Tonnèrre, *op. cit.,* p. 13; *Gazette nationale ou moniteur universel,*
December 25, 1789 (Mirabeu: "Eh, messieurs, serait-ce parce que les juifs ne
voudraient pas être citoyens, que vous ne les déclareriez pas citoyens? Dans
un gouvernement comme celui que vous élevez, il faut que tous les hommes
soient hommes; il faut bannir de votre sein ceux que ne le sont pas, ou qui
refuseraient de le devenir").

feelings toward the persecuted Jews, but also from an urgent desire to amalgamate all segments of France's population. The revolutionary leaders looked upon the Jews as persecuted human beings, but they hardly gave consideration to the religious problem or to internal Jewish conflicts. Of course, it was difficult, indeed almost impossible, for the Jews suddenly and completely to abandon their millenia-old traditions and principles. On the other hand, there was nothing particularly anti-Jewish in the attitude of the revolutionary leaders against separate Jewish communities. The historian Graetz noted correctly that the Revolution emancipated the Jews without asking them to renounce even one iota of their religion.[8]

It should be mentioned that the Jews were not the only religious group trying to preserve their particular privileges of the pre-revolutionary period. The Protestants of Alsace, too, were organized in autonomous bodies, and this fact was mentioned in 1779 by the author of a pamphlet on the legality of Jewish law with regard to divorces in France.[9] During the Revolution it was difficult to accept the idea of being a Frenchman in the spirit of the new regime and to remain a Christian in the spirit of the old regime. Yet the Alsatian

---

[8]   Heinrich Graetz, *Geschichte der Juden,* XI (Leipzig, 1911), 221. Cf. Max Nordau, *Zionistische Schriften* (Berlin, 1923), pp. 45-46; Baruch Hagani, *L'Emancipation des juifs* (Paris, 1928), pp. 153, 187-90; Louis Ménard, *Les Questions sociales dans l'antiquité* (Paris, 1898), p. 15; Mainfroi Maignal, *La Loi de 1791 et la condition des juifs en France* (Paris, 1903), pp. 21, 177; P. Sagnac, "Les Juifs et Napoleon," *Revue d'histoire moderne et contemporaine,* II 1901), 461; Kurt Stillschweig, "Die Judenmanzipation im Licht des französischen Nationsbegriffs," *Monatsschrift für Geschichte und Wissenschaft des Judentums,* LXXXI (1937), 457-78.

[9]   "Les luthériens d'Alsace ne sont pas moins autorisés dans le royaume que les juifs; ils y sont reçus, comme les juifs, avec leurs usages et les lois de leur religion; ils y ont de plus que les Juifs un Tribunal de leurs Frères, chargé de juger leurs contestations, et de régler leurs droits, suivant les principes reçus parmi eux"; *Réplique pour la Dame Peixotto: Contre le Sieur Peixotto, son mari* (n.p., 1779), p. 29; Szajkowski, *Proceedings of the American Academy for Jewish Research,* XXV, 119-135. For a bibliography on the struggle of Alsatian Protestants against the nationalization of their properties, see Frédéric-Charles Heitz, *Les sociétés politiques de Strasbourg pendant les années* 1790 à 1795 (Strasbourg, 1865), pp. 61-62; André Waltz, *Catalogue de la Bibliothèque Chauffour* (Colmar, 1889), 454-57.

Protestants retained many of their old privileges. Thus, thanks to some legal hair-splitting and arrangements with the Catholics, the Protestant Chapter of Saint Thomas of Strasbourg was not nationalized. The deputy Pierre André of Lower Rhine stated in February, 1799 that the Protestants who suffered from religious intolerance should be the first to give up privileges whose destruction could only help to bring about social happiness. But Professor Christian-Giullaume Koch, the Alsatian Protestant leader and deputy who directed the Protestant fight against the abolition of their privileges, opposed Jewish emancipation because the Jews would continue to exist as a separate Jewish nation. The insistence of the National Assembly that the Jews surrender their former privileges was interpreted by Koch and Schwendt as a victory over the Jews, who would cease to exist as a *corps de nation* (national body).[10]

It is clear from the controversy on the abolition of the autonomous Jewish communities that the Jews were organized in legal corporate associations (*corporations*),[11] with their *syndics* and with statutes pertaining to almost all phases of collective and individual Jewish life.[12]

---

[10] The term *corporation* for the Jewish community was used in many documents of various periods: *Prix proposés, en 1788, par la Société Royale de Metz* (Metz, 1788), p. 2, and *Affiches des Evêchés et Lorraine*, No. XXXV, 1788 ("Les Juifs forment, presque par-tout où ils sont établis, des corporations autorisées"). The same term was used by the Central Consistory in a document of May, 1809, *Le Consistoire Central des israélites, à messieurs les membres du consistoire départemental* . . . [Paris, mai, 1809], p. 3: "Qu'il y a loin de votre organisation actuelle à celle qui réglait ces corporations anciennes." In some sources Jewish autonomy was called *police particulière*; see Stillschweig, *op. cit.*, p. 458.

[12] In legal and other French documents the leaders of the Jewish communities (*parnassim* in Hebrew) were called *syndics*, a term that pointed up the communities' functions as *corporations*. On the term *syndic*, see A. Chéruel, *Dictionnaire historique des institutions* . . . II (Paris, 1884), 1193. The syndic's function was called *syndicat*, a term employed even in the nineteenth century by the Jews of Bordeaux and Bayonne. According to the minutes of the Nancy Consistory (May 11, 1817), the syndic's functions ceased to exist after the founding of the consistories in 1808: "Que ses fonctions de syndic ayant cessé par l'effet du décret du 17 mars 1808." Berr-Isaac Berr wrote then: "Comme il n'existe plus ni communauté ni syndic des juifs"; *minutes* in the Archives of the Historical Society of Israel, Jerusalem.

II

In connection with another controversy, namely, that over the debts of the Jewish communities, the Jews had to establish that during the old regime they were organized as *corporations*. In this they were contradicted by their adversaries.

Prior to the Revolution the Jewish communities were forced to borrow money from Christians in order to pay high taxes and thus became collective debtors to Christian creditors. During the Revolution the Jewish communities demanded that these debts be assumed by the government, as was done with all debts owed by religious and other bodies that had been dissolved by the new regime.

In a petition addressed to the National Convention, Aaron Ravel, Aaron Vidal, and Milhaud stated in behalf of the Avignon Jews, that they had been organized as a *corporation* which had been dissolved by the Revolution and whose properties had been nationalized. They even criticized violently the very existence of these *corporations* "which cut up the State into an infinitude of parties. The *corporation* formed a multitude of separate small nations in the midst of the nation itself. Each of these *corporations* had different and often opposite interests. . . . All these revolting divisions must disappear in the light of the torch of Philosophy. . . ." The petitioners stated that the Jews had been an organized *corporation* which was forced to make loans guaranteed by mortgages on the communal Jewish properties. But the Jews were unable to repay the debts because they no longer existed as a *corporation* and because of the nationalization of the mortgaged communal properties. Would the government, they asked, dare to refuse the nationalization of their debts? "Will the Jews again be treated as before, *i.e.*, as citizens only in matters of paying taxes, but as foreigners in matters of rights? . . . No! French legislation will not be thus insulted. A contradiction that would disgrace our laws shall not be tolerated. . . . When a system is fundamentally just, then it is necessary to accept the consequences. . . . It is not possible to have abolished the *corporations* and yet to admit the existence of one of them. The National Convention cannot recognize the Jews. There are no more Jews in France. There are no more Catholics, Protestants, Jews, sectarians of any kind, there are only Frenchmen."

It seems that the doubts as to whether the Jews indeed had been organized before the Revolution as *corporations* under the law, constituted the main reason for not nationalizing their debts. Consequently, the Jews of Avignon published a second petition to the National Convention, in which they again tried to prove that during the old regime even the French occupation forces in the former papal province dealt with the Jews in tax and other matters, not as individuals, but as members of a *corporation*. This was repeated in a report that A. J. B. Chappuis submitted on April 5, 1797 to the Council of Five Hundred. He advocated the nationalization of the debts, recalling that when in 1768 France had occupied the papal province, the Jews petitioned the Parliament of Provence to register and thus to recognize as valid all previous privileges and statutes accorded them by the papal authorities. This the Parliament did on April 11, 1771.[13]

However, the Christian creditors, who feared the nationalization of the debts, thought differently. Dominique Chambaud, a creditor of the Carpentaras Jews, stated in a memorandum against Jassé-Haïn Crémieu, the son of one of the Jewish guarantors of the loans obtained by the Carpentras community, that the Jews never formed a legal body but existed only as a "tolerated tribe" (*peuplade toléré*). To this Cremieu replied, in a brief prepared by the lawyer

---

[13] *Observations pour les juifs d'Avignon à la convention nationale* [Signé: Aaron Ravel, Aaron Widal, Milhaud.] [Paris, 1794], 10 pp.; *Nouvelles observations pour les juifs d'Avignon* [Signé: Aaron Ravel, Aaron Vidal, Milhaud.] [Paris, 1794], 15 pp.; *Rapport fait par* [A.-J.-B.] *Chappuis, au nom d'une commission . . . séance du 16 Germinal* [5 avril 1797] (Paris, 1797), pp. 3, 5.

Chansaud, that the Jews of Carpentras formed a "real political community," with their own communal constitution. Even the manner in which the loans were made demonstrated that the Jews were organized in special bodies. Thus, loans were ratified by general assemblies of their community and approved by the papal authorities. When, after their emancipation, the Jews lost their communities, they also ceased to be debtors. Chansaud compared the situation of the Jews to the status of the members of the Marseille Parliament, who ceased to be debtors of the Parliament's creditors after the Parliament had been dissolved in 1771. The Christian creditor replied in a brief prepared by the lawyer Granet, that the Jews enjoyed a "legal existence, *i.e.*, a permission to exist, but not a political existence."[14] Yet, on March 5, 1799, the Civil Tribunal of the Vaucluse department (the former papal province) stated that the former Jewish community did exist as a *corps de communauté*. The same statement was made much earlier (on April 30, 1795) by the civil authorities of Avignon, and repeated again on August 2, 1799.[15]

The Jews of Metz, who also demanded nationalization of debts owed by them, put forward the same argument. In a petition addressed to the National Assembly they stated that their community was of a "political character." They formed "an unparalleled corporation, a state, a particular government in France." They had not only a synagogue, but also rabbinical judges, who were recognized by the Parliament and French jurisprudence. They had their own legislation on heritage and other civil matters. They paid

---

14 *Mémoire pour le citoyen Jassé-Haïn Crémieu . . . contre le citoyen Dominique Chambaud . . .* [Signé: Chansaud] (Aix, an VII), pp. 2, 4-5, 27; *Précis pour les citoyens Dominique Chambaud . . . contre le citoyen Jassé-Haïn Crémieu . . .* [Signé: Granet] (Aix, an VII), pp. 11, 19, 38.

15 *Mémoire pour . . . Crémieu,* p. 12. On April 30, 1795 the district of Avignon sent to the City Council a copy of a decision (of April 8, 1795) by the Legislative Committee ordering suspension of all suits by Christian creditors against the Jews of Avignon because the debts had been "contracted by them as a *corporation*"; Municipal Archives of Avignon, D 56, No. 26.

general taxes not as individuals but as an autonomous collective body. The Jewish community of Metz had authority over the provincial communities. This Jewish state of Metz was dissolved by the same revolutionary spirit which dissolved all other *corporations*.

Many officials openly affirmed the justness of the Jews' argument. The deputy Jacques-François de Visme stated in his report of July 20, 1790 to the National Assembly on the abolition of the Brancas tax which the Jews of Metz were forced to pay, that they formed a "particular *corporation*." On August 18, 1791 the district of Metz, in an order on Jewish taxes, spoke not of Jews as individuals, but of the *communauté des Juifs*. A member of the Council of Five Hundred, Chappuis, also defended very strongly the thesis of the Metz Jews.[16]

The Christian creditors, on the other hand, stated that the Jews were only tolerated foreigners, *aubains,* and thus had no legal right to be organized in *corporations*. This point-of view was strongly opposed by Jews and non-Jews alike, who showed that prior to the Revolution the Jews were not considerded as *aubains*.[17]

There was no unanimity on the problem under discussion among the Jews themselves, and a conflict involving the Jewish community of Bordeaux became a subject of propaganda against the nationalization of the debts owed by the Jewish communities.

[16] Library of the Jewish Theological Seminary, New York, manuscript 01530-1; *Pétition à la convention nationale, pour les ci-devant syndics et élus de la ci-devant communauté des juifs de Metz* [Signé: Mayer Cahen Goudchaux] (n.p., [1792]), pp. 1-7; *Loi qui renvoie au directoire du district de Metz les contestations nées et à naître du rôle de contribution fait par les juifs de Metz, donné à Paris, le 27 mai 1791* (n.p., n.d.) 4 pp.; together with the decision of the Moselle department, August 18, 1791; Chappuis, *op. cit.,* p. 3-5; [J.-F.L.] de Visme, *Rapport fait au comité des domaines, le 20 juillet 1790, sur de droit de protection levé sur les juifs* . . . [Paris, 1790], p. 8.

[17] Szajkowski, "The Jewish Status in Eighteenth Century France and the 'Droit d'aubaine,' *Historia Judaica,* XIX (1957), 147-161.

III

In September, 1791 the city of Bordeaux decided to abolish all separate religious cemeteries and to replace them with one large national cemetery. The Jewish cemetery was then confiscated and sold in 1796 as nationalized property to two Christians, Pierre Despiau and Augustin Pujol. In petitions of May 12 and June 8, 1796 the Jews demanded that the departmental authorities of Gironde annul the sale, which the authorities did on June 29, 1796. The decision was later approved by the Ministry of Finances.

This was the beginning of a very sharp conflict between the Jews of Bordeaux and the two buyers of the cemetery. Both parties put forward strongly worded and legally based arguments; both published pamphlets on the conflict. The Jewish point of view was defended by the lawyers Louis-Francia Beaufleury, the first author of a history of the Jews in Bordeaux and Bayonne, published in 1799; François-Placide Ferey, J.-J.-R. de Cambacérès, Minister of Justice in the year VII, and A.-J.-B. Debonnières. A representative of the Bordeaux Jews, Fonseca, was even sent to Paris. The defense of Despiau and Pujol was taken up by the lawyer and deputy François-Balthazar Darracq (1749-1817), who on this occasion attacked the Jews in general at the Council of the Five Hundred. This was the strongest attack of that period against Jews. Despiau and Pujol stated that no exception should or could be made in favor of the Jews, who, prior to the Revolution had been organized as a *nation,* and thus their properties should be nationalized, as was done with all other corporate bodies abolished by the new regime. The Jews replied that they had never been organized as such a body (*corporation*), but only as a philanthropic society, which owned the cemetery. Officially the cemetery was, in fact, always owned by such a society, but under the strict control of the *Nation.* Thus, on April 26, 1750 Alexander the elder was appointed by the *Nation* as treasurer of the cemetery. On March 22, 1761 the *Nation* granted from the cemetery's funds a loan to David Lameyra for one year at an interest of five percent. On April 17, 1786 the *Nation* decided to prepare a register of all graves and provided that this register should remain with the Burial Society *Guemilut Hasidim* for safekeeping.[18]

The statement of the Bordeaux Jews that they had not been organized before 1789 as a *corporate* body was historically not correct; they did form a well-organized body known as the *Nation*.[19] Their argument was strongly attacked by their adversaries, who sought to nationalize the cemetery. At the same time, this argument was used as a weapon in the hands of those who fought the idea of nationalizing the debts of the former Jewish communities of the papal province and of Metz. It demonstrated, they said, that the Jews were never organized as *corporations* and thus could not request the nationalization of debts owed by them.[20]

IV

Of a very different character were the debts owed by the Alsatian Jewish communities. There, Jewish leaders, in-

[18] Minutes of the Bordeaux *Nation* in the departmental archives of Gironde, series I, Nos. 177, 282, fol. 41, 68, 139.

[19] Szajkowski, "Relations among Sephardim, Ashkenazim and Avignonese Jews in France from the 16th to the 20th Centuries," *Yivo Annual of Jewish Social Science*, X (1955), 187-191. Charles-Maurice Duc de Tayllerand-Perigord's statement of January 28, 1790, that the Jews of Bordeaux had no special laws, magistrates, or particular officials, was not accurate; *Revue des grandes journées parlementaires*, I (1897), 94. The text of the decision of February 18, 1790 to dissolve the Bordeaux *Nation* proves that the Sephardic Jews considered themselves as a *corporation*: "Les Juifs de Bordeaux ne pouvant plus être considérés comme Corps de Nation, l'assemblée des Anciens qui les représentoient s'est occupé immédiatement de la formation d'une Association de Bienfaisance"; Minutes, February 18, 1790 (see *supra*, note 18).

[20] *Mémoire pour les citoyens Pierre Despiau et Augustin Pujol de Bordeaux* (Bordeaux, n.d.), 32 pp.; *Mémoire à consulter et consultation, pour les citoyens français, professant le culte judaïque à Bordeaux* . . . [Signé: [Louis-] Francia Beaufleury, Ferey [J.-J.-R. de] Combacérès, [A.-J.-B.] Debonnières, [29 November 1798] (n.p., an VII), 7, 47 pp.; Despiau et Pujol, *Réponse à un Mémoire sous le nom des citoyens français, professant le culte judaïque à Bordeaux* [Paris, an VII; *Rapport fait par* [M.-F.] *Prévot, sur une pétition des citoyens Pujol et Despiau* . . . (Paris, an 7), 7 pp.; *Opinion de* [F.-B.] *Darracq dans l'affaire des juifs de Bordeaux* . . . (Paris, an 7), 31 pp.; L.F.B. [Louis-Francia Beaufleury], *Histoire de l'établissement des juifs à Bordeaux et à Bayonne* . . . (Paris, 1799), pp. 161-95.

cluding Cerfberr of Médelsheim, were the main creditors. According to Forbin des Issarts, the deputy of the Vaucluse department, who spoke out in favor of the Christian creditors of the former papal province, the government rejected a demand by the Alsatian Jews for the nationalization of the debts. However, if we are not mistaken, there never was any demand for nationalization of the debts owed by the Alsatian Jewish communities. This was due, perhaps, to the desire of Alsatian Jews to allow nothing to interfere with their struggle for emancipation and with their opposition to the decree of September 28, 1791 which had stopped the regular repayment of debts owed by peasants to them. Or, perhaps, Cerfberr, to whom the largest debt was owed, feared the nationalization of the debts. Much later the Alsatian Jewish consistories advocated, not the nationalization of the debts, but the rejection of the creditors' claims on the ground that the Council of Alsatian Jewish communities (the *Nation juive*), which had borrowed the money, had ceased to exist during the Revolution. This thesis was sustained in a brief submitted on November 11, 1834 by the three lawyers, Martin, L. Liechtenberger, and Michaux-Bellaire, and supported by the lawyer Rauter. A similar position was taken in 1851 by the lawyer Paul Fabre.[21]

Many more proofs that the Jews were in fact organized as *corporations* are known to us today, e.g., the contemporary statutes of the Jewish communities. But the proofs put forward by the Jews during the Revolution were sufficient in themselves to confirm that they did in fact form corporate associations. In the end, however, the Jews lost the struggle. Many motives shaped the government's policy against taking over the debts owed by the Jewish communities. The Jews were compelled to repay these debts, and in order to do this

---

[21] *Rapport de M. le marquis Joseph-Charles de Forbin des Issarts* . . . [Paris, 1821], p. 4; *Consultation pour les israélites habitant le départment du Bas-Rhin contre les porteurs des créances de l'ancienne nation juive d'Alsace* [Signé: Martin, L. Lichtenberger, Michaux-Bellaire, Rauter] (Strasbourg, 1835), 20 pp.; Fabre's brief, in the author's possession.

they were forced to retain some form of community organization to collect taxes and discharge other obligations. Thus,
while the French Revolution emancipated the Jews on condition that the autonomous communities would be dissolved,
it nevertheless continued the old patttern by forcing the Jews
to maintain communities for the purpose of paying taxes.

Autonomy and Communal Jewish Debts During the French Revolution of 1789

CONTENTS

593

ABBREVIATIONS OF SOURCES USED IN
THE NOTES AND THE APPENDIXES

AACV	— *Annales d'Avignon et du Comtat Venaissin.*
Ad BdR	— Departmental archives of Bouches-du-Rhône, Marseille.
Ad BR	— Departmental archives of Lower Rhine, Strasbourg.
Ad Gironde	— Departmental archives of Gironde, Bordeaux.
Ad Hérault	— Departmental archives of Hérault, Montpellier.
Ad HR	— Departmental archives of Upper Rhine, Colmar.
Ad Moselle	— Departmental archives of Moselle, Metz.
Ad Vaucluse	— Departmental archives of Vaucluse, Avignon.
AHRF	— *Annales historiques de la Révolution française.*
AI	— *Les Archives israélites.*
AIU	— Library of the Alliance Israélite Universelle, Paris.
Am Ales	— City archives of Ales.
Am Altkirch	— City Archives of Altkirch.
Am Avignon	— City archives of Avignon.
Am Bx	— City archives of Bordeaux.
Am Carpentras	— City archives of Carpentras.
Am Cavaillon	— City archives of Cavaillon.
Am L'Isle	— City archives of L'Isle-sur-Sorgue.
Am Metz	— City archives of Metz.
Am Stg	— City archives of Strasbourg.
AN	— Archives Nationales, Paris.
AnAI	— *Annuaire des Archives israélites.*
AP	— *Les Archives parlementaires.*
AR	— *Annales révolutionnaires.*
Arsenal	— The Arsenal Library, Paris.
ASEJ	— *Annuaire de la Société des Etudes Juives.*

Barjavel	— C.-F.-H. Barjavel, *Dictionnaire historique, biographique et bibliographique du département de Vaucluse* (Carpentras, 1841). 2 vols.
Bibliography	— Bibliography on the debts of the Jewish communities in France, see pp. 139–57.
BJGL	— *Blätter für jüdische Geschichte und Literatur.*
Bm Bx	— Municipal Library of Bordeaux.
Bm Carpentras	— Municipal Library of Carpentras.
Bm Metz	— Municipal Library of Metz.
Boug	— De Boug, *Ordonnances d'Alsace* . . . (Colmar, 1775). 2 vols.
BSHP	— *Bulletin de la Société de l'Histoire de Paris et de l'Ile de France.*
BuStg	— The National and University Library of Strasbourg.
Calvet	— The Calvet Library of Avignon.
Chauffour	— André Waltz, *Catalogue de la Bibliothèque Chauffour* (Colmar, 1889).
CJ	— *Cahiers Juifs.*
Columbia	— The Libraries of Columbia University, New York, N. Y.
Documents	— A collection of "Documents on the Jewish Communities in France during the Revolution of 1789," in the Library of the Hebrew Union College, Cincinnati (Ohio).
EcSt	— Z. Szajkowski, *The Economic Status of the Jews in Alsace, Metz and Lorraine 1648–1789* (New York, 1954). 152 pp.
Emancipation	— Z. Szajkowski, "The Emancipation of Jews During the French Revolution. A Bibliography . . . 1789–1800." *SBB*, III–IV (1958–59).
GNMU	— *Gazette nationale ou Moniteur universel.*
Guerre	— Archives of the War Ministry, Château de Vincennes (Seine).
Halphen	— A.-E. Halphen, *Recueil des lois* . . . *concernant les Israélites* . . . (Paris, 1851).
Hildenfinger	— P. Hildenfinger, *Documents sur les Juifs à Paris au XVIIIe siècle* (Paris, 1913).
HJ	— *Historia Judaica.*

HUC	— Library of the Hebrew Union College-Jewish Institute of Religion, Cincinnati, Ohio.
Jerusalem	— The Jewish Historical General Archives, Jerusalem.
JFrance	— *The Jews in France.* Edited by E. Tcherikower (New York, 1942). 2 vols. (In Yiddish.)
JQR	— *The Jewish Quarterly Review.*
JSS	— *Jewish Social Studies.*
JTS	— Library of the Jewish Theological Seminary, New York, N. Y.
Kuscinski	— A. Kuscinski, *Dictionnaire des Conventionnels* (Paris, 1918).
Landmann	— Salomon Landmann, Catalogue des Archives Consistoriales Israélites de Metz. 1934. 2 vols. [Manuscript.]
Lévylier	— [Roger Lévylier,] *Notes et documents concernant la famille Cerfberr* (Paris, 1902–06). 3 vols.
Liber	— Maurice Liber, "Les Juifs et la convocation des Etats Généraux. 1789." *REJ*, LX–LXVI (1912–13).
MGWJ	*Monatsschrift für die Geschichte und Wissenschaft des Judentums.*
Napoleonica	— Z. Szajkowski, "Judaica-Napoleonica. A Bibliography ... 1801–1815." *SBB*, II (1956), 107–152, 524 Nos.
Nation	— "Registre et Répertoire des délibérations de la Nation Juive Portugaise de Bordeaux, commencé en Mai 1790 et terminé en Février 1790" (in Ad Gironde).
NBG	— Firmin-Didot Frères, *Nouvelle Biographie Générale* (Paris, 1852–66). 46 vols.
Pacquet	— René Pacquet, *Bibliographie analytique de l'histoire de Metz pendant la Révolution 1789–1800* (Paris, 1926). 2 vols.
PAJR	— *Proceedings of the American Academy for Jewish Research.*

QJFM	— *La Question Juive en France et dans le monde.*
Robert	— A. Robert, E. Bourloton, G. Cougny, *Dictionnaire des parlementaires français* (Paris, 1891).
SBB	— *Studies in Bibliography and Booklore.*
Sitzmann	— Fr.-J.-E. Sitzmann, *Dictionnaire de biographie des hommes célèbres de l'Alsace . . .* (Rixheim, 1909–1910). 2 vols.
SS	*Souvenir et Science.*
SIW	— *Strassburger israelitische Wochenschrift.*
RA	— *Revue d'Alsace.*
RdGJP	— *Revue des grandes journées parlementaires.*
Rég.	— *La Régénération — Die Wiedergeburt* (Strasbourg).
REJ	— *Revue des Etudes Juives.*
RF	— *La Révolution française.*
RHBG	— *Revue historique de Bordeaux et du département de la Gironde.*
RHMC	— *Revue d'histoire moderne et contemporaine.*
RJL	— *Revue juive de Lorraine.*
RO	— *Revue Orientale.*
UI	— *L'Univers israélite.*
YAJSS	— *Yivo Annual of Jewish Social Science.*
ZS	— In the author's possession.

Excerpts of documents are quoted in the notes without changes in the original spelling.

For a complete list of printed sources see the index on pp. 177–82.

For the detailed description of pamphlets and printed documents on the Jews during the Revolution see "Emancipation," and for those under the First Empire see "Napoleonica."

I. THE JEWISH COMMUNITIES IN FRANCE ON THE EVE OF THE REVOLUTION OF 1789

Prior to the Revolution of 1789 there were four main centers of Jewish population in France:

(1) Three sub-centers of Ashkenazic Jews in both parts of Alsace (with 182 communities according to the census of 1784); in the city of Metz and the Trois-Evêchés (about 50 communities); and in Lorraine (52 communities according to the privileges of 1753).

(2) Sephardic Jews in southwestern France (Bordeaux, Saint-Esprit-lès-Bayonne, Dax, Peyrehorade, and in several smaller towns).

(3) The four Jewish communities of Avignon, Carpentras, Cavaillon and L'Isle-sur-Sorgue in the papal possession of Avignon and Comtat Venaissin.

(4) A mixed community of Ashkenazic, Sephardic, Avignonese and Comtadin Jews in Paris. Small Jewish communities also existed in Marseilles, Nîmes, Montpellier, Lyons, Fontainebleau, Versailles and other cities.[1]

Until the expulsion of the 14th century the Jews of various French provinces were organized in a single body.[2] The situation was quite different, however, at the outbreak of the Revolution in 1789. Jewish groups in the various centers were not united by any organizational ties, nor even by a feeling of solidarity, of

---

[1] For a general picture of the number of Jews in France see Z. Szajkowski, "The Growth of the Jewish Population in France." *JSS*, VIII (1946), 179–92, 297–318; Idem, "The Demographic Aspects of Jewish Emancipation in France during the French Revolution." *HJ*, XXI (1959), 7–36; Idem, "Population Problems of Marranos and Sephardim in France, From the 16th to the 20th Centuries." *PAAJR*, XXVII (1958), 83–105.

[2] Simon Schwarzfuchs, *Etudes sur l'origine et le développement du rabbinat au moyen âge* (Paris, 1957). 79 pp.

Originally published in 1959.

sharing persecution because of their common origin. On the contrary, they were antagonistic.[3] Only one exceptional case of cooperation occurred when the Sephardic and Ashkenazic Jews of Paris signed a joint petition of August 26, 1790 demanding full citizenship.[4] This tragic chapter in the history of the Jews in France was not to end until the days of the First Empire, when Napoleon I convened the Sanhedrin and established the central Jewish consistory.[5]

The Jewish communities of Alsace were organized in a council (called *Nation Juive*) that dealt with financial and other matters. The council met annually in Obernai, where its by-laws were adopted on June 28, 1763. The last session prior to the Revolution took place there on November 10, 1788. The Jews of Lower Alsace were also organized separately in a council of the Lower Alsatian communities.[6]

As we shall see a strong union existed between the Jews of

[3] Z. Szajkowski, "Relations among Sephardim, Ashkenazim and Avignonese Jews in France from the 16th to the 20th Centuries." *YAJSS*, X (1955), 165–96.

[4] [Jacques Godard,] *Adresse présentée à l'Assemblée Nationale le 26 Août 1789, par les Juifs résidant à Paris* ([Paris], 1789). 9 pp.; Léon Kahn, *Les Juifs de Paris pendant la Révolution* (Paris, 1898), p. 18; Liber, LXVI, 176; E. Tcherikower, "The French Revolution and the Jews." *JFrance*, II, 145–46.

[5] Szajkowski, "Relations . . .," 192–94.

[6] See De Boug, contains much information on Jewish autonomy; M. Ginsburger, *Die rechtliche Stellung der elsässischen Rabbiner unter französischer Herrschaft* (Zürich, 1907), reprint; Idem, "Elie Schwab, rabbin de Haguenau (1721–1747)." *REJ*, XLIV (1902), 104–21, 260–82, XLV (1902), 255–84 (on the conflicts in Jewish communities of Alsace); Idem, *Histoire de la communauté israélite de Bischheim au Saum* (Strasbourg, 1937), pp. 18–28 (on the syndics of Alsatian communities); Idem, "Mutzig." *SS*, IV, No. 5 (1933), 9 (Mutzig was the residence of the general Alsatian syndic); Idem, "Rechte und Pflichten eines Judenvorstehers in der Grafschaft Rappolsheim." *BJGL*, IV (1903), 67 ff.; Idem, "Samuel Sanvil Weil, Rabbin de la Haute et Basse Alsace (1711–1753)." *REJ*, XCV–VI (1933), 54–75, 179–98; Idem, "Une élection rabbinique au XVIIIe siècle." *UI*, LVIII (1902), 625; Idem, "Un emprunt . . ." (see Bibliography, No. 147); I. Loeb, "Les Juifs de Strasbourg de 1349 à la Révolution." *ASEJ*, II (1883), 139–98; Rodophe Reuss, *L'Alsace au dix-septième siècle* (Paris, 1898), II, 590–91 (on the functions of rabbis); Elie Scheid, *Histoire des Juifs d'Alsace* (Paris, 1887). 424 pp.; Julien Weill, "Contribution à l'histoire des communautés alsaciens au XVIIIe siècle." *REJ*, LXXXI (1925), 169–80.

Metz and the smaller communities of the Metz province.[7] The Jews of the entire Lorraine province were legally recognized as only one community — Nancy — directed by three syndics and one rabbi. Even before the Revolution the smaller Jewish communities of Lorraine tried to break away from the community of Nancy. In 1788 the Jews of Lunéville were denied the right to elect their own rabbi. During the Revolution the Jews of Lunéville and Sarreguemines petitioned the National Assembly for their own rabbis and syndics, claiming that the Nancy syndics "multiplied expenses and did not even deign to consult . . . the Jews of Lunéville and Sarreguemines."[8]

There was some cooperation among the three groups of Ashkenazic Jews. We do know, e. g., that in 1787 Cerfberr, the Paris agent of the Alsatian Jews, and Moïse Weill, the agent of the Metz Jews, combined their efforts in behalf of the Ashkenazic Jews.[9] In 1789 the Ashkenazic Jews of all three provinces held a joint assembly which drew up its memorial of grievances (*cahier des doléances*).[10] However, these united actions were limited to the Ashkenazic Jews.

[7] On the autonomy of the Metz community see Abraham Cahen, *Le Rabbinat de Metz pendant la période française (1567–1871)*. Extrait de la *REJ* (Paris, 1886). 91 pp. Contains much information on the rabbis' functions; Roger Clément, *La condition des Juifs de Metz sous l'ancien régime* (Paris, 1903). 296 pp.; J. de Fombesque, "Les Juifs de Metz." *QJFM*, II, No. 9 (1943); N. Netter, *Vingt siècles d'histoire d'une communauté. Metz et son grand passé* (Paris, 1938). 536 pp. See also Appendix II.

[8] *Mémoire pour les Juifs de Lunéville et de Sarreguemines. A Nosseigneurs de l'Assemblée Nationale. 3 Août 1789* (n. p., [1789]). 8 pp.; *Nouveau mémoire pour les Juifs de Lunéville et de Sarreguemines; présenté à l'Assemblée Nationale, le 26 Février 1790* ([Paris,] 1790). 8 pp.; Alfred Lévy, *Notice sur les Israélites du Duché de Lorraine* (Paris, 1885), pp. 25–26; H. Baumont, *Histoire de Lunéville* (Paris, 1900), p. 211; Chr. Pfister, *Histoire de Nancy* (Paris-Nancy, 1908), III, 324; [A. Benoît,] *Lunéville et ses environs. V. Les élections aux Etats généraux de Lunéville* (Lunéville, [1879]), 105–111.

[9] Landmann, Ce 106. The councils of Jewish communities, or even individual large Jewish communities, maintained their agents (*syndics*) in Paris to seek privileges from the government. In 1790 Moïse Weil paid large sums to high officials in Paris for some favors obtained for the Jews of Metz (Landmann, Ce 98–101, 113, 117). Mayer Hadamar (or Hademar) was also mentioned as the Paris agent of the Metz community. P. Hildenfinger, index, p. 280. See also Appendix III.

[10] On this assembly see AN, BA–11 (Alsace), dr. 7, and BA–52, Metz I,

There was, most probably, no common council of the Sephardic Jewish communities in France, although the Paris agent of the *Nation* of Bordeaux, Jacob Rodrigues Pereire (1715–1780), was also the agent of the *Nation* of Saint-Esprit-lès-Bayonne.[11] In 1788 the Jews of Bordeaux and Saint-Esprit jointly sent a delegation to the so-called Malesherbes commission, in charge of determining a new status for the Jews, and in 1789 to the National Assembly.[12]

p. 9; H.-B. Grégoire, *Motion en faveur des Juifs* . . . (Paris, 1789), p. v; Berr-Isaac Berr, *Lettre* . . . *à Monseigneur l'évêque de Nancy* . . . (Paris, 1790), pp. 3–5; Lévylier, I, pp. 32–33; Liber, LXIV, 265–74, LXV, 97–133, LXVI, 161–62; Jacques Godechot, "Comment les Juifs de Lorraine élurent leurs députés en 1789." *REJ*, LXXXI (1925), 48–54.

[11] On Pereire see Ernest La Rochelle, *Jacob Rodrigues Pereire* (Paris, 1882). 576 pp. After Pereire's death David Silveyra became the Paris agent of the Bordeaux *Nation*. In 1785 the *Nation* dismissed him, but he regained his position and held it until the Sephardic Jews were granted full citizenship on Jan. 28, 1790 (Nation, fol. 137, No. 536). Benjamin Mendez and Aaron Hananel Vidal were mentioned as *syndics* in Paris of the Sephardic Jews (Hildenfinger, 148–49, 201, 221, 230, 232, 235), but most probably were visiting *syndics* of the Bordeaux *Nation*. (In earlier years the community of Saint-Esprit attempted to force its authority upon the smaller communities of Saint-Jean-de-Luz, Bidache, Peyrehorade, and Biarritz. As a result there were many conflicts. Henri Gross, *Gallia Judaica* (Paris, 1897), pp. 92–93.) Saint-Esprit was incorporated into Bayonne in 1857. In one document Pereire was called "syndic de la nation portugaise des Juifs de [Saint-Esprit-lès-] Bayonne." Ad Gironde, C 2896.

It is worth while to note the description of the Bordeaux chronicler, Pierre Bernardau, of the role of a Jewish *syndic*: "Raba junior est nommé syndic de la Nation juive, à la place du bel-esprit Furtado. Celui qui est revêtu de cet emploi a inspection sur ses commettans et est comme médiateur de leurs diférens" (Bm Bordeaux, ms. 713–1, vol. 1, p. 201, Apr. 11, 1788). Silveyra was a bridge builder. *Projet du sieur Silveyra pour l'établissement d'un pont sur la rivière de Garonne* (n. p., n. d.). 12 pp.; L. Kahn, *Les Juifs de Paris pendant la Révolution* (Paris, 1899), 133–34.

[12] Z. Szajkowski, "The Diaries of the Delegates of the Bordeaux Jews to the Malesherbes Commission (1788) and the National Assembly (1790)." *Zion*, XVIII (1953), 31–79 (in Hebrew).

On the autonomy of the Sephardic *Nations* see L. F. B. [Louis-Francia de Beufleury], *Histoire de l'établissement des Juifs à Bordeaux et à Bayonne, depuis 1550* (Paris, an 8 [1799]). 198 pp.; L. Cardozo de Béthencourt, "Le trésor des Juifs Sephardim." *REJ*, XX (1890), 287–300, XXV (1892), 97–110, 235–45, XXVI (1893), 240–56; G.-E.-A. Cirot, *Recherches sur les Juifs Espagnols et Portugais à Bordeaux* (Bordeaux, 1908). 198 pp.; Idem, "Les Juifs de

The Jews of Carpentras, Cavaillon, L'Isle-sur-Sorgue, and a few smaller communities (Caromb-Montel, Châteauneuf, Entraygues, Maulaucène, Mazan, Mornas, Noirmoiron, Pernes, Thor, Vaison) in the papal province of Comtat Venaissin were organized in a council of communities, or rather in a single community. Thus, the by-laws of 1490, January 5, 1605, March 24, 1620, January 5, 1665, and of 1733, were common for all these communities of Comtat Venaissin. In many documents they are mentioned as forming one community.[13] (The same documents also often refer to the Jews of these communities as "travelling-Jews" (*juifs forains*), because they were mostly itinerant merchants and peddlers.[14]) It seems, however, that the

Bordeaux, leur situation morale et sociale de 1554 à la Révolution. XIV. Appendice. Ce que désiraient les Juifs à la veille de la Révolution." *RHBG*, XXII (1939), 60–66; Idem, "Notes sur les "Juifs Portugais" de Bordeaux." *Miscelâna de Estudas en Honra D. Carolina Michaëls de Vasconcellos* (Coimbra, 1933), pp. 158–72; Ad. Detcheverry, *Histoire des Israélites de Bordeaux* (Bordeaux, 1850). 116 pp.; H. Léon, *Histoire des Juifs de Bayonne* (Paris, 1893). 436 pp.; T. Malvezin, *Histoire des Juifs à Bordeaux* (Bordeaux, 1875). 375 pp.; Z. Szajkowski, "Relations . . .," 187–91 ("The Sephardic Nations").

[13] Ad Vaucluse, annex of Carpentras, 8, fol. 212–16 (Jan. 1, 1665); H. Chobaut, "Les Juifs d'Avignon et du Comtat et la Révolution française." *REJ*, CI (1937), 7 ("communauté des Juifs de Carpentras et de tout le Comté de Venise," 1616); Armand Mossé, *Histoire des Juifs d'Avignon et du Comtat Venaissin* (Paris, 1934), pp. 121, 128–31, 138.

[14] *Ibid.* In a printed document of 1820 we read the following about these itinerant Jews: "Tous les Juifs de la Carrière, tant habitans que forains . . . Ces Juifs forains se rendaient presque tous dans leur Carrière respective, aux approches de Pâques, pour y manger l'agneau pascal, et fin septembre, pour célébrer la fête des Tabernacles" (*Observations*, pp. 3–5, see Bibliography, No. 104). The term *forains* was also applied to Jews who had settled in other communities: "l'arrangement qui fut pris vers le commencement de la révolution entre les juifs *forains* de la communauté et ceux de Carpentras" (Columbia, X 893C–C22, vol. 2). For a bibliography on the legal and economic status of the itinerant Jews from Comtat in France see Z. Szajkowski, "The Jewish Status in the Eighteenth-Century France and the "Droit d'Aubaine." *HJ*, XIX (1957), 149, note 4.

On the autonomy of the Jewish communities in the papal province see P. Charpenne, *Histoire des réunions temporaires d'Avignon et du Comtat Venaissin à la France* (Paris, 1886), II, 402–49; H. Chobaut, *op. cit.*, *REJ*, CI (1937), 5–52, CII (1937), 3–39; Isidore Loeb, "Statuts des Juifs d'Avignon." *ASEJ*, I (1881), 165–75; M. de Maulde, *Les Juifs dans les Etats français du Saint-Siège au moyen-âge* (Paris, 1886); Armand Mossé, *op. cit.*; P. Pansier, "Les

Jews of Avignon did not belong to the council of the other communities in the papal province.

In Lyons the Jews formed an unofficial community of about fifteen families, with their own small cemetery. In 1781 the head of the police, acting on instructions from Paris, appointed Elie Rouget of Avignon as the Jewish syndic, with the object of keeping a check, through him, on the movement of the Jews. This appointment, however, impelled the Jews to organize a community.[15] Well organized communities existed also in Nîmes, Montpellier, Marseilles and a few smaller places.[16]

On the eve of the Revolution of 1789 the Jews were socially segregated from the Christians of France no less than they were in the Middle Ages.[17] The Jews were disliked and persecuted. Still, they were often able to defend themselves in an organized manner through their autonomous communities. Of course, the Jewish communities were carefully controlled by the authorities and the scope of their autonomy never afforded the Jews more than limited legal rights. The Jewish communities were largely agencies for collecting taxes and performing other administrative duties for the government and local authorities. The historian, S. Posener, noted that:

". . . these offices of "agents" and "syndics" were really created for fiscal and administrative purposes, in order to help the central and local authorities maintain surveillance of the Jewish population, particularly in Paris, and in order to levy taxes. If an "agent of the Portuguese Jewish nation," such as Pereire, as a "syndic" of the Jews of Alsace, such as Cerf-Berr [Cerfberr] or that of the Jews of Lorraine, such as Berr-Isaac Berr, interceded with the government in behalf of the Jews in economic or political matters, they did so invariably, not in their capacity of agent or syndic but by virtue of their personal position as important purveyors of the army, or as great importers of wheat

oeuvres de charité juive à Avignon du XIVe au XVIIIe siècle." *AACV*, X (1924), 71–133.

[15] Alfred Lévy, *Notice sur les Israélites de Lyon* (Paris, 1894), pp. 20–24; Elaine Dreyfus et Lise Marx, *Autour des Juifs de Lyon . . .* (Lyon, 1958), pp. 131–34.

[16] S. Kahn, *Notice sur les Israélites de Nîmes* (Nîmes, 1901). 48 pp.

[17] R. Anchel, "Sur l'histoire des Juifs en France." *CJ*, No. 19, (1936), 33.

and fodder, or thanks to their connections in Paris and at the court."[18]

But without the communities and their syndics the Jews would have been defenseless. It may be safely assumed that this was one of the reasons why the Jews demanded at the beginning of the Revolution that the existence of their communities be assured. Uncertain about their future the Jews wanted to maintain a collective body which could speak in their name and defend them.

[18] S. Posener, "The Social Life of the Jewish Communities in France in the 18th Century." *JSS*, VII (1945), 203.

II. ATTACKS UPON JEWISH AUTONOMY DURING THE REVOLUTION*

Even before the outbreak of the Revolution the Christian advocates of Jewish emancipation urged not only a better understanding of Jews by Christians, but also a partial or complete abolition of the autonomous Jewish communities as a condition for Jewish emancipation. Ch.-G. Lamoignon de Malesherbes (1721–1794), who headed the so-called Malesherbes commission, looked with disfavor upon the Jewish communities.[19] In a draft of a study of the Jews which he undertook for the Metz Academy, Pierre-Louis Roederer (1754–1835) proposed the dissolution of the Jewish communities.[20] On the other hand, the Nancy lawyer, A. Thiéry, who was the recipient of a prize awarded by the Metz Academy for his *Dissertation*, suggested in this essay that for some time the Jews should continue to retain their communities and chiefs. According to the historian, Maurice Liber, Thiéry's position was influenced by the Jewish leader Berr-Isaac Berr, who was then opposed to the dissolution of the autonomous Jewish communities.[21] The well known fighter for

* This chapter is based mainly on the author's study "Jewish Autonomy Debated and Attacked During the French Revolution." *HJ*, XX (1958), 31–46.

[19] Z. Szajkowski, "Protestants and Jews of France in Fight for Emancipation, 1789–1791." *PAJR*, XXV (1956), 119–21.

[20] A. Cahen, "L'Emancipation des Juifs devant la Société Royale des Sciences et Arts de Metz et M. Roederer." *REJ*, I (1880), 101. During the Thermidor, while attacking the government's policy on credit, Roederer made a cutting anti-Jewish remark about a *sanhédrin d'usuriers juifs*. For this he was strongly criticized by J. Rodrigues, who later became secretary of the Jewish consistory. *Journal de Paris*, No. 95, Dec. 25, 1796; L. Kahn, *op. cit.*, pp. 8–9.

[21] [Adolphe] Thiéry, *Dissertation sur cette question: Est-il des moyens de rendre les Juifs plus heureux et plus utiles en France?* (Paris, 1788), pp. 98–100; Liber, LXIV, 105. About Thiéry we were able to find only a few details in: Justin Lamoureux, *Mémoire pour servir à l'histoire littéraire du département de la Meurthe, ou Tableau statistique* (Nancy, 1803).

Jewish emancipation, abbot Henri-Baptist Grégoire (1750–1831), whose study was also awarded a prize by the Metz Academy, favored the abrogation of the autonomy of the Jewish communities in all civil matters. He advocated abolition of autonomous Jewish law in matters affecting marriage and inheritance, and in the performance of notarial and other functions by rabbis in disregard of French civil laws. Grégoire maintained that the Jews should be indistinguishable from other inhabitants in all civil matters. They should be allowed to assemble only for religious affairs, provided there was supervision by French officials.[22] Zalkind Hourwitz (1740?–1810?), a Polish Jew who fought for Jewish emancipation in France, and the author of *Apologie*, a third study awarded a prize by the Metz Academy, went even further: he proposed that outside the synagogue the rabbis and syndics of the Jewish communities be forbidden to control the life of Jews. Indeed, Hourwitz advocated stripping rabbis of their functions altogether. On September, 20, 1789 he warned the Committee of Reports of the National Assembly against the "devotees of my nation," "the rabbinical inquisition" and the "sewer" of the Jewish community.[23]

The Alsatian Intermediary Commission (*Commission intermédiaire*) appointed a special committee to prepare a draft of a new statute for the Alsatian Jews. In its report, which was presented to the third bureau (*Bureau du Bien Public*) at the end of September 1788, the committee, presided over by the Alsatian anti-Jewish leader François-Joseph-Antoine Hell (1731–1794), advocated the abolition of all Jewish communities.[24]

[22] Henri Grégoire, *Essai sur la régénération . . . des Juifs* (Paris, 1789), pp. 151–61. There is no complete study on Grégoire's fight for Jewish emancipation. See: P. Grunebaum-Ballin, *L'abbé Grégoire et les Juifs* (Paris, n. d.). 22 pp.

[23] Zalkind Hourwitz, *Apologie des Juifs* (Paris, 1789), pp. 38–39; Robert Anchel, "Un Juif polonais en France. Zalkind Hourwitz." *UI*, XCII, No. 38 (1937). On Hourwitz see L. Kahn, *op. cit.*, pp. 130–50.

[24] "L'intérêt de l'Etat et le bien public, même celui des juifs en particuliers, exigent, et l'Edit du mois du novembre dernier décide, que les juifs ne pourront plus avoir de Syndics ni agens, ni poursuivre aucune affaire au nom collectif, sauf aux particuliers à agir en justice, en leur propre nom, dans la même forme que les chrétiens; qu'ils n'auront plus d'autre préposé que celui de la sinagogue, qui continuera à être nommé par le Seigneur du lieu. Qu'il

With the outbreak of the Revolution the discussion of the future of the autonomous Jewish communities became even livelier. Many *cahiers des doléances* (memorials of grievances) demanded that they be done away with.[25] On December 23, 1789 Stanislas de Clermont-Tonnerre (1757–1792) made his famous statement in the National Assembly that "all should be refused the Jews as a nation, but everything should be granted to them as individuals." The corporate body (*corporation*) of the Jews, he argued, should be abolished, their judges (*i. e.*, rabbis) should be dismissed, and they should not form any separate political body within the French nation.[26] In Paris only the district (*section*) of Mathurins voted on February 20, 1790

soit fait défense aux juifs de s'assembler, excepté ceux demeurants dans le même endroit, pour l'élection de leur chantre, ou pour régler leurs contestations qui pourroient troubler l'ordre et la tranquilité dans la sinagogue; pour le quel effet le préposé de la sinagogue aura le droit de prononcer contre ceux qui refuseroient de lui obéir, des amendes qui ne pourront excéder le —, desquelles prononciations ledit préposé fournira l'Etat dans la huitaine, au Procureur fiscal du lieu de la demeure, pour les faire condamner au payement par le Juge ordinaire des lieux; qu'il leur soit pareillement fait défenses de faire aucuns rôles et de lever aucuns deniers sur eux-mêmes; qu'il sera cependant permis aux juifs de chaque endroit, de faire des états particuliers entre eux de leurs contributions, pour le soulagement des pauvres et le payement de leurs chantres, de maitres d'école, dans lesquels chaque individu se cotisera soi-même, avec défenses aux Rabins et aux Juifs des autres endroits de s'en mêler" (Am Stg, AA 2589); Z. Szajkowski, "The Jewish Problem in Alsace, Metz, and Lorraine on the Eve of the Revolution of 1789." *JQR*, XLIV (1954), 234–43 ("The Jewish Problem in the Alsatian Provincial Assembly"). On Hell's anti-Jewish activities see *EcSt*, pp. 123–40 ("The Case of the Counterfeit Receipts in Alsace, 1777–1789").

[25] Liber LXIII, 188.

[26] *Opinion de M. le Comte Stanislas de Clermont-Tonnerre, député de Paris, le 23 Décembre 1789* ([Paris], n. d.), p. 13. There is no proof whatsoever for the statement of the Marxist Jewish historian, Dr. Raphael Mahler, that Tonnere's slogan was directed exclusively against Jewish autonomy. *History of the Jewish People* (New York, 1957), I, 73 (in Yiddish). There is no detailed study on Clermont-Tonnerre's fight for Jewish emancipation. He was often attacked by anti-revolutionary elements as a friend of Jews, e. g. by a pamphleteer who wrote: "Puisq'il faut, je le vois, que l'innocent périsse,/Appelons, dit-il, parmi nous, / Les Juifs et les bourreaux jaloux / De faire cet office." / *Actes des Apôtres*, version seconde, No. 31 (1791), 15; Ch. Du Bus, *Stanislas de Clermont-Tonnerre et l'échec de la Révolution monarchique* (Paris, n. d.), p. 220.

against granting citizenship to the Jews. The main argument was that, since they were organized as a separate nation, the Jews could not remain loyal to the French nation. All other Parisian districts decided in favor of the Jews, but insisted on the abolition of the separate Jewish communities. In February 1790 the district of Saint-Germain-l'Auxerrois resolved to demand of the Jews "a formal renunciation of their laws and particular judges." The resolution adopted on June 30, 1790 by Paris as a whole in favor of the Jews contained the same demand for them to abandon "the particular nation within the nation."[27]

The opponents of Jewish emancipation used this discussion as an argument against the Jews in general. Abbot Jean-Sifrein Maury (1746–1817) stated on December 23, 1789 in the National Assembly that the Jews formed not only a religious sect, but a separate nation with its own laws. In these conditions to grant citizenship to the Jews would be exactly the same as granting French citizenship to Englishmen and Danes without asking them to renounce their English or Danish loyalties. The next day Hell renewed the proposal, which had been debated in 1788 by the Alsatian Intermediary Commission, to abolish all autonomous rights of the Jewish communities. The Alsatian deputy, Jean-François Reubell (1747–1807), wrote on January 5, 1790: "What do you think of people who seek to become Frenchmen, but still wish to retain Jewish administrators, Jewish judges, Jewish notaries . . . their particular laws on inheritance, marriage, tutelage, majority, etc.?" Another Alsatian deputy, C.-W. de Broglie (1756–1794), asserted that the Jews' existence as a nation within a nation was dangerous and anti-social.[28]

[27] *Extrait du procès-verbal du district des Mathurins. 20 Février 1790* [Paris, 1790.] 4 pp.; *Rapport fait par M Vion . . . sur les diverses adresses & pétitions des Juifs de Paris* (Paris, 1790), p. 23; "Extrait du procès-verbal des délibérations . . . du district des Carmélites . . . du 29 Janvier 1790," in Jacques Godard's *Recueil de pièces relatives à l'admission des Juifs à l'état civil (28–30 Janvier 1790)* (Paris, 1790); *Adresse de l'assemblée des Représentants de la Commune de Paris à l'Assemblée Nationale sur l'admission des Juifs à l'état civil . . .* ([Paris,] 1790), p. 12; Sigismond Lacroix, "Ce qu'on pensait des Juifs à Paris en 1790." *Revue politique et littéraire*, XXXV (1898), 412–24; Idem, *Actes de la commune de Paris pendant la révolution* (Paris, 1898), III, 638, IV, 201–02; VII, 551–60.
[28] Maury, in *GNMU*, Dec. 23, 1789; *Opinion de M. le Prince de Broglie . . .*

Nor were the Jews themselves all of the same opinion on this matter.

([Paris,] n. d.), p. 4; *RdGJP*, I (1897), 16; Charles Hoffmann, *L'Alsace au dix-huitième siècle* (Colmar, 1906–07), IV, 517–18.

There is no study on Reubell's attitude toward Jews. During the old regime he (or his brother) was the lawyer for the family of the Jewish martyr Hirtzel Lévy (Isidore Loeb, "Hirtzel Lévy." *ASEJ*, I (1881), 154–55). An Alsatian pamphleteer wrote in 1790 that Reubell's anti-Jewish sentiments were a consequence of his participation in lawsuits involving Jews: "étant chargé en Alsace, depuis plusieurs anneés, des affaires des juifs, il étoit assez naturel que vous pensiez réellement sur leur compte ce que d'autres feignent d'en penser: car, dans quelque religion que ce puisse être, il est peu de cliens réputés honnêtes aux yeux de leur avocat." *Lettre d'un alsacien, sur les juifs d'Alsace, à M. Ruebell, Député de cette Province, à l'Assemblée nationale* (Paris, 1790), p. 6. Michel Berr wrote in 1817 on Reubell's "déclamations intéressées:" *Eloge de M. Abraham Furtado* (Paris, 1817), p. 13. On the other hand Reubell disliked Switzerland because he lost a lawsuit in which he defended Jews against the authorities of the Berne canton. P.-L. Hanet-Cléry, *Mémoires* (Paris, 1825), II, 19; Jacques Godechot, *Les Commissaires aux armées sous le Directoire* (Paris, 1937), II, 15–16. On Aug. 5, 1789 Reubell wrote a letter in favor of the Jews to the Intermediary Commission of the Colmar district: "Il n'y a pas jusqu'à la nation juive que ne mérite quelque compasion. Je sais combien elle étoit haissable, mais ce sont des hommes et l'on ne peut se dissimuler que la manière dont leur existence étoit réglée par le gouvernement n'a pas peu contribué à leurs vices à jamais odieux, mais comme nous espérons que nos nouvelles lois les rendront honnêtes gens et laborieux, prêchez, Messieurs, la pitié pour ces misérables créatures et vous aurez rempli le plus beau des devoirs." "Lettre du député à l'Assemblée nationale Reubell, à la commission intermédiaire du district de Colmar." *RA*, XIII (1862), 530–31. Reubell was, perhaps, friendly toward Jews at the beginning of the Revolution, but he was later influenced by the traditional anti-Jewish elements of Alsace. The historian, Jean Braun, noted two phases in Reubell's attitude toward Jews: the one prior to July 14, 1789 and the other after the outbreak of the Revolution. "La Révolution de 1848 et la Seconde République dans le Haut-Rhin." *Le Département du Haut-Rhin commémore trois siècles de vie française* (Colmar, 1848), 105. While visiting Bordeaux Reubell's son stayed in the house of the Rabas, a wealthy Jewish family. The Bordeaux chronicler, Pierre Bernardau, noted a rumor, which was not factual, that Reubell was of Jewish origin (Tablettes de Pierre de Bernardau, Feb. 19, 1796. Bm Bx, 713–1). All this suggests the need for more detailed studies before reaching conclusions on various aspects of Jewish history during the French Revolution, e. g., the attitude of some Jacobins toward Jews. Reubell was a great revolutionary leader, energetic, cultured; there is no doubt that he was a sincere Jacobin, in spite of grave accusations of speculation directed against him. (On this see *Testament de Rewbell* (Colmar, 1799). 21 pp.; Etienne-François Housset,

On the eve of the Revolution the Sephardic Jews of Bordeaux tried to retain many autonomous privileges,[29] which they gave up only after being granted full citizenship on January 28, 1790. The projected by-laws for the Jewish community of Carpentras (published in 1790 or 1791), anticipated that, aside from religious problems, the members of the community "would be known only as individuals, and not as forming a society." Jews could even refuse to belong to the community, but they must sign a statement to that effect.[30]

At first the Ashkenazic Jews did not dare to request full citizenship. The very first pamphlet published by the Jews of Metz after the outbreak of the Revolution demanded only the right to live, to work and to be accepted in the professional *corporations*. No mention was made of citizenship, for Jewish emancipation was then not yet an accepted idea.[31]

The Sephardic Jews were not granted full citizenship unani-

Rapport . . . (Paris, an VII). 26 pp.; *Observations de Reubell . . . sur le rapport fait par Housset* (n. p., 1790). 3 pp.; R. Guyot, *Documents biographiques sur J.-F. Reubell, 1747–1807* (Tours, 1911), p. 172; "Reubell et Bonaparte (1802)." *Nouvelle Revue rétrospective*, XX (1904), 374–75; A. Mathiez, "Les malles de Reubell." *AR*, IX (1917), 541–43, X (1918), 246–47, XV (1923), 414; Idem, *Le Directoire* (Paris, 1934), p. 44; L. Bour, *La Grande Révolution dans l'arrondissement de Sarrebourg sous le Directoire et le Consulat, 1795–1802* (Metz, 1936), p. 12; F. Normand, "Jean-François Reubell." *Les Contemporains*, No. 940 (1910), 7; Georges Mauguin, "La Carrière militaire d'un ami de Moreau; Le Général Jean-Jacques Reubell." *Revue des études napoléoniennes*, XL (1940), 219.) The Jewish historian, Raphael Mahler, oversimplified the entire problem of the anti-Jewish attitude of the Jacobin Reubell by stating that the latter deserted the Jacobins and enriched himself by speculation. (*op. cit.*, I, 66). In spite of the large number of studies on this subject the accusations have not been proven. Such accusations were also used against Jews because some accused Jacobins (e. g. Reubell himself and his brother-in-law J.-J. Rapinat) regained then some popularity by their anti-Jewish propaganda. Guyot, *op. cit.*, p. 16; Jacques Godechot, *op. cit.*, II, 71.

[29] H. Léon, *op. cit.*, pp. 153–54; G. Cirot, "Les Juifs de Bordeaux . . .," XXII (1939), 60–66.

[30] *Préliminaire d'un projet d'arrangement* (n. p., n. d.). 8 pp.

[31] Isaac-Ber [Berr] Bing, *Mémoire particulier pour la Communauté des Juifs établis à Metz* (n. p., [1789]). 30 pp. Abbot Grégoire warned a friend, to whom he presented a copy of his *Essai*, that "it would not be prudent to let young persons read the book." André Spire, "L'Abbé Grégoire . . ." *NL*, Sept. 21, 1935.

612

mously. There was a strong anti-Jewish opposition in Bordeaux and Saint-Esprit-lès-Bayonne.[32] At the National Assembly some right wing deputies proposed to continue to register the Sephardic Jews as *New Christians* (*nouveaux chrétiens*), a title which was abandoned as early as 1723.[33]

In their petition of August 26, 1789 the Jews of Paris renounced the privilege of having their own particular chiefs.[34] But their brethren of Alsace, Metz and Lorraine, in a petition addressed on August 31, 1789 to the National Assembly, sought permission to retain their synagogues, rabbis and syndics in the same manner as before.[35] However, in this petition they did not request full citizenship. Later the Jewish leader of Lorraine, Berr-Isaac Berr, wrote that the Jews did not dare to demand full citizenship then, since not even all Frenchmen possessed it. They desired only to cease being slaves.[36]

[32] *Le Moniteur*, Feb. 11, 1790; *La Gazette de Paris*, Feb. 10, 11, 1790; L. Kahn, *op. cit.*, pp. 80–82; A. Vivie, *La Terreur à Bordeaux* (Bordeaux, 1877), I, 27; M. Lhéritier, *Les débuts de la Révolution à Bordeaux* (Bordeaux, 1919), p. 82; Idem, *Liberté (1789–1790). Bordeaux et la Révolution française* (Paris, 1919), p. 69.

[33] Robert de Crévecoeur, *Journal d'Adrien Duquesnoy, député du Tiers Etat de Bar-le-Duc* . . . (Paris, 1894), II, 224–30. In the Letters patent of 1723 the Marranos were referred to for the first time not as "New Christians" but as Jews. See Szajkowski, "Relations . . .," 168.

[34] [Jacques Godard,] *Adresse . . . 26 Août 1789* . . ., pp. 6–7 ("nous renonçons . . . au privilège que nous avoit été accordé d'avoir des chefs particuliers tirés de notre sein, nommés par le gouvernement"). There is no study of Jacques Godard (1762–1791), or of his fight for Jewish emancipation. For some general information on him, see his correspondence with the Dijon lawyer Jean Cortot, 1786–1789: A. Huguenin, *La Cour plenière et les édits de 1788* (Dijon, 1905). 89 pp. In 1787 Godard stated in a brief that in criminal lawsuits Jews should not be allowed to bear witness against Christians. Jacques Godard, "Consultation." *Justification de sept hommes, condamnés par le Parlement de Metz en 1769, sur les seules dépositions de Juifs-plaignans* . . . (Paris, 1787), pp. 95–103, by M.-Ch.-M.-J. Dupaty. On this affair see J. Liblin, *Les sept martyrs de Loutzelbourg et les précurseurs de Schinderhannes, 1768–1786* (Colmar, 1864), 30 pp.; *EcSt.*, pp. 112–13.

[35] *Adresse présentée à l'Assemblée Nationale, le 31 Août 1789, par les Députés réunis des Juifs, établis à Metz, dans les Trois Evêchés, en Alsace & en Lorraine* (n. p., [1789]), p. 13 ("Que nous serons maintenus dans le libre exercice de nos loix, rites & usages, que nous conserverons nos *Synagogues*, nos *Rabbins* & nos *Syndics*, de la même manière que le tout existe aujourd'hui").

[36] Berr-Isaac Berr, *Lettre* . . ., p. 4; Liber, LXV, 133.

Only after the discussions of December 23 and 24, 1789 at the National Assembly, during which the autonomy of the Jews was strongly attacked,[37] did the Jews — in their new petition of January 28, 1790 — give up their request to maintain their independent communities.[38] For a time Berr-Isaac Berr still refused to renounce autonomy of the communities in exchange for civil rights.[39] This provoked a strong attack by Berr-Isaac Berr's nephew, Jacob Berr, a Jewish physician of Nancy, who advocated the complete abolition of the Jewish communities. In a pamphlet he maintained that Berr-Isaac Berr wished to keep the Jews in a state of estrangement from non-Jews and to perpetuate their isolation. Jacob Berr accused the "despotic regime" of the Jewish community of being responsible for many evils and criticized Berr-Isaac Berr for his "dangerous" request that the autonomous Jewish communities be maintained.[40]

But after the Ashkenazic Jews had been granted full citizenship on September 27, 1791 Berr-Isaac Berr published a *Letter* to his coreligionists in which he called upon them to abandon their involvement in a distinct community. Jews, he wrote,

[37] On Dec. 23, 1789 Adrien Duquesnoy, deputy from Bar-le-Duc, noted in his diary in connection with the discussion at the National Assembly on the question of Jewish emancipation: "Mr. Duport avait d'ailleurs fait un raisonnement fort puissant à ceux qui assurent que les juifs ne consentiront jamais à se soumettre à nos lois: Vous avez exigé un serment: si les juifs le prêtent, ils sont dans le même cas que les autres citoyens français. Ce raisonnement ne frappait personne, parce que rien ne frappe ceux que des préjugés religieux aveuglent ou égarent." On the following day, Dec. 24, he noted: "On n'a pas cru devoir prononcer sur l'état des juifs, et je crois cette réserve prudente, parce que, comme l'a observé le président Beaumetz, on ne savait pas si les juifs veulent eux-mêmes un état civil et s'ils désirent d'être citoyens français . . ." Crévecoeur, *op. cit.*, II, 204, 208.

[38] [Jacques Godard,] *Petition des Juifs établis en France . . . le 28 janvier 1790* . . . (Paris, 1790), p. 95 ("Il faut que les Juifs aient leurs loix religieuses, il faut qu'ils aient des règlemens intérieurs relatifs à l'exécution de ces loix. Mais dans tout ce qui concerne l'ordre civil, évitez toute distinction entr'eux & les Chrétiens").

[39] Berr-Isaac Berr, *Lettre* . . ., pp. 17–19.

[40] *Lettre du Sr Jacob Berr, Juif, maître en chirurgie à Nancy, à Monseigneur l'Evêque de Nancy* . . . (n. p., 1790), 10 pp. On Jacob Berr see E. Carmoly, *Histoire des médecins juifs, anciens et modernes* (Bruxelles, 1844), p. 204; Idem, *RO*, II (1842), 92; Chr. Pfister, *op. cit.*, III, 327.

should remain organized as a group only for religious matters; in civil and political spheres they should act as individuals.[41]

However, the decision was not left to the Jews. Citizenship was granted to them only on condition that they renounce under oath all particular privileges. This was clearly laid down in the text of the decree on emancipation of the Ashkenazic Jews as proposed by the Alsatian anti-Jewish deputies and adopted by the National Assembly. On the following October 8, 1791 the anti-Jewish deputy, Etienne-François-Joseph Schwendt (1748–1820), wrote to the city council of Strasbourg that the National Assembly regarded the Jews not as men forming a *corporation* which no longer had the right to exist, but as individuals practicing their particular religion; the Jews had ceased to exist as a nation. This was a vindictive statement, intended to pacify the defeated Alsatian opponents of Jewish emancipation.[42]

In the eyes of the generation of Jews which was emancipated by the Revolution the new regime was just and beneficent to them. Olry Terquem (Tsarphati, 1782–1862), the 19th century leader of the proponents of a reform of Jewish religious practices, in 1843 called the new regime *notre sainte révolution.* According to most impartial historians, thanks to the revolutionary attitude toward the Jewish problem Jews developed strong French patriotic feelings. The historian, H. Graetz, aptly remarked that "the

[41] [Berr-Isaac Berr,] *Lettre d'un citoyen, à ses confrères* . . . (Nancy, 1791), pp. 8–10.

[42] "aux individus Juifs qui prêteront le serment civique, qui sera regardé comme une renonciation à tous privilèges et exceptions introduits précédement en leur faveur" (Decree of September 27, 1791, which became law on the following November 13). According to Berr-Isaac Berr (*Lettre d'un citoyen* . . ., p. 10), this proposition by the Alsatian deputies was rejected, which is not correct. R. Reuss, *L'Alsace pendant la Révolution* (Paris, 1894), II, 247–48. On the anti-Jewish attitude of Strasbourg see P. Hildenfinger, "L'Adresse de la commune de Strasbourg à l'Assemblée Nationale contre les Juifs (Avril 1790)." *REJ*, LVIII (1909), 112–28; Z. Szajkowski, "The Jewish Problem in Alsace, Metz, and Lorraine on the Eve of the Revolution of 1789." *JQR*, XLIV (1954), 206–18; Idem, "The Discussion and Struggle over Jewish Emancipation in Alsace in the early Years of the French Revolution." *HJ*, XVII (1955), 130–34.

French Revolution was a judgment sent to erase the sins of a
thousand years in one day."[43]

Some modern Jewish historians have argued that in giving up
their autonomous communities the Jews paid too high a price
for their emancipation; that this was the beginning of complete
renunciation of Jewish life.[44] It is, however, doubtful whether the
Jews could have retained the pre-revolutionary status of their
communities, even if they had resigned themselves to doing
without civil rights. In the long run a status of non-citizens for
the Jews would have been incompatible with the ideology and

[43] "Lorsque notre sainte révolution éclata:" Z. [Terquem], in *AI*, IV (1843),
726. On Terquem see note 212. "Politiquement les Juifs alsaciens se sont
toujours montrés patriotes. Ils n'oublient pas qu'ils doivent leur émancipation
à la Révolution française:" Frédéric Hoffet, *Psychanalyse de l'Alsace* (Paris,
1951), p. 82; "Je ne me suis jamais caché . . . d'apartenir à une race qui à dû
à la Révolution française la liberté et l'égalité humaines, et qui ne devrait
jamais l'oublier": André Blumel, *Léon Blum, juif et sioniste* (Paris, 1952),
p. 9; "La reconnaissance qu'il [mon père] lui portait parce qu'elle avait
émancipé sa race, donné aux juifs les libertés civiles et politiques:" J. Benda,
Jeunesse d'un clerc (Paris, 1936), p. 42. See also: Pierre Aubrey, *Milieux
juifs de la France contemporaine* (Paris, 1957), pp. 195–96, 363, 366: "Les
bourgeois juifs . . . ne sont pas toujours réactionnaires. Etre réactionnaire les
ramènerait en effet en deça de la Révolution de 1789, c'est-à-dire les conduirait
à combattre leur propre émancipation"; H. Graetz, *Popular History of the
Jews* (New York, 1919), V, 373.

There were some exceptions. Gerson Lévy (1784–1864), another proponent
of a reform of Jewish religious practices, in noting the memoirs of a Jewish
peddler, attacked the "cannibals" who sentenced Marie Antoinette. The
Jewish philosopher, Adolphe Franck (1809–1893), advocated love for the old
regime. G. Ben Lévy, "Mémoires d'un colporteur juif." *AI*, vol. III, 1842,
pp. 461–62. (On Gerson Lévy see M. Thiel, *Notice biographique sur M. Gerson-
Lévy* . . . (Metz, 1865). 16 pp.; *Notice sur la vie de M. Gerson-Lévy* . . . (Metz,
1865). 40 pp.) *Distributions des prix aux éléves des écoles consistoriales de Paris*
(30 Août 1883). *Discours de M. Adolphe Franck* . . . (Paris, n. d.), p. 5.
Franck was well known for his dislike of all revolutionary regimes, including
the Revolution of 1848, and of later socialistic ideas: Adolphe Franck, *Le
communisme jugé par l'histoire* (Paris, 1848). 71 pp. (2ᵉ édition, Paris, 1849).
98 pp.; Idem, *La vraie et la fausse égalité* (Paris, 1867). 52 pp.; Idem, *Le Capital*
(Paris, 1872). 23 pp. Z. Szajkowski, "The Jews and the Parisian Commune
of 1871." *JFrance*, II, 151; Idem, *The Parisian Commune and the Jews* [Tel-
Aviv, 1956], p. 49 (in Hebrew).

[44] E. Tcherikower, in *Oifn Scheidweg*, II (1939), 12–13 (in Yiddish).

the very existence of the new regime. Clermont-Tonnerre, who fought for Jewish emancipation in the National Assembly, stated on December 23, 1789 that, should the Jews refuse to dissolve their communities and become citizens, they should be banished. The same attitude was taken on the next day by Count H.-G.-R. de Mirabeau.[45]

Jewish emancipation in France was a consequence of the revolutionary rationalist principles, *Prinzipienreiterei*, to use Max Nordau's term. There was no alternative for the Revolution but to integrate the Jews with the French people. This attitude sprang not only from humanitarian feelings toward the Jews, but also from an urgent need to amalgamate all segments of France's population. The revolutionary leaders who looked upon the Jews as persecuted human beings[46] were repelled by the

---

[45] Clermont-Tonnere, *op. cit.*, p. 13; *GNMU*, Dec. 25, 1789 (Mirabeau: "Eh, messieurs, serait-ce parce que les Juifs ne voudraient pas être citoyens, que vous ne les déclareriez pas citoyens? Dans un gouvernement comme celui que vous élevez, il faut que tous les hommes soient hommes; il faut bannir de votre sein ceux que ne le sont pas, ou qui refuseraient de le devenir"). Mirabeau was, of course, a great friend of the Jews and his influence on the early fight for Jewish emancipation can not be denied. But during the Revolution he used the discussion on the emancipation of the Jews to arouse popular prejudice in order to compromise the Revolution and to reinforce the position of the monarchy. On Mirabeau's attitude toward Jews see *RdGJP*, I, 21; Louis Farges, *La question juive il y a cent ans* (Paris, 1886), p. 6; B. A. [Ben-Ami], "Mirabeau et les Juifs." *UI- Pour le Foyer, pour l'Ecole*, LXVIII (1913), 203–05; Hanns Reissner, "Mirabeaus Judenpolitik." *Der Morgen*, VIII (1932), 122–30; P. Lang, "Mirabeau et Grégoire." *RJL*, II, 248–54; Ferdinand-Dreyfus, *Misères sociales et études historiques* (Paris, 1901), pp. 223–24; Baruch Hagani, *L'Emancipation des Juifs* (Paris, 1928), pp. 177, 202–03. Mirabeau was often attacked by anti-Jewish elements, e. g. in Joseph-Michel-Antoine Servan's parody *Evénements remarquables et intéressants, à l'occasion des décrets de l'auguste Assemblée nationale, concernant l'éligibilité de MM. les comédiens, le bourreau et les Juifs* (n. p., 1790). 37 pp. A Jew of Avignon named Moïse published a pamphlet against Mirabeau: *Requête du sieur Moïse, Juif d'Avignon . . .* (according to *Courrier d'Avignon*, No. 87, Apr. 12, 1790, 148).

[46] Max Nordau, *Zionistische Schriften* (Berlin, 1923), pp. 45–46. (On Max Nordau's attitude toward the French Revolution see Meir Ben-Horin, *Max Nordau. Philosopher of Human Solidarity* (New York, 1956), pp. 115, 124, 147, 156, 168, 186, 227, 230, 235, 243;) Baruch Hagani, *op. cit.*, pp. 153, 187–

idea of excluding them alone from the family of liberated peoples. The religion of the Jews was viewed as their private concern. The deputy, Joseph-Marie Lequinio (1755–1813), who called himself *citoyen du globe*, clearly expressed this opinion in his *Adresse* of 1791 in which he concluded as follows: "The first principle of patriotism is to love one's fellow-citizens of whatever religion they may be . . . Undertake to live in peace with priests who accepted the Constitution and with those who did not, with the Jews, with the Turks."[47] Adrien Duport (1758–1798), the deputy, in proposing the vote on the grant of citizenship to the Jews on September 27, 1791, stated that the Jews should not remain the only nation of the world to be excluded from the enjoyment of civil rights.[48] Even earlier, Mirabeau's *Courrier de Provence* propounded the view that in church men are Catholics and in synagogues Jews, but in all civil matters patriots are of the same religion.[49]

This spirit of the times was evident not only in the declarations of influential officials, but also in the views of the populace.

190; Louis Ménard, *Les Questions sociales dans l'antiquité* (Paris, 1898), p. 15; Mainfroy Maignial, *La Loi de 1791 et la condition des Juifs en France* (Paris, 1903), p. 21, 177; P. Sagnac, "Les Juifs et Napoléon." *RHMC*, II (1901), 461; Kurt Stillschweig, "Die Judenemanzipation im Licht des französischen Nationsbegriffs." *MGWJ*, LXXXI (1937), 457–78.

[47] [Joseph-Marie] Lequinio, *Adresse populaire aux habitans des campagnes* (Nismes, 1791), pp. 10–11, 16. On Lequinio see: A. Aulard, "Lequinio et la dechristianisation." *RF*, XXXI, 295–99; P. Gaudet de Lestard, *Un Terroriste adversaire de la peine de mort* (La Rochelle, n. d.). 38 pp.

[48] The text of Duport's resolution of Sept. 27, 1791 was incorrectly reported in the *Moniteur*. The correct text is to be found in *Journal logographique de l'Assemblée Nationale*, XXXIV, 36: "Je demande que l'on révoque le décret d'aujournement, que l'on déclare que, relativement aux Juifs, comme à tous les peuples du monde, en remplissant les conditions prescrites par les constitutions, ils puissent devenir des citoyens actifs; je demande qu'il n'y ait pas, parmi toutes les nations du monde, les juifs seuls d'exceptés pour la jouissance de ce droit, tandis que musulmans y sont admis, tandis que les païens, les Chinois y sont admis."

[49] *Le Courrier de Provence*, IV, Dec. 23–24, 1789: Qu'importe la diversité du culte? C'est à la messe qu'on est catholique, c'est au prêche qu'on est protestant, c'est à la synagogue qu'on est juif. Mais dans le monde, devant les tribunaux, dans les différantes fonctions sociales, les patriotes sont tous de la même religion."

Playing cards were called after the three main religions.[50] Marie-Joseph Chenier, author of a popular song on July 14, 1789 wrote:

"Dieu du peuple et des rois, des cités, des campagnes,
De Luther, de Calvin, des enfants d'Israël."[51]

Even the partisans of restricting religious freedom did not single out Jews.[52]

However, the revolutionary leaders hardly gave consideration to the religious problem, and even less to internal Jewish conflicts. The best of the Jews' friends were absolutely ignorant of internal Jewish matters, as Zalkind Hourwitz noted in his *Apologie*. Grégoire ridiculed the strict sumptuary by-laws of the Jewish communities,[53] without understanding the great value of these by-laws against luxury for Jewish self-preservation.

Of course, it was difficult, indeed almost impossible, for the Jews suddenly and completely to abandon their millennia-old

---

[50] *Nouvelles cartes à jouer de la République Française* (Bordeaux, n. d.). 4 pp. ("Dame de *Coeur*" became "Liberté de Coeur, ou des Cultes . . . Le Thalmud, Le Coran, l'Evangile simbole de trois plus célèbres religions, sont réunis par elle").

[51] Louis Damade, *Histoire chantée de la Première République 1789 à 1799* (Paris, 1892), p. 68.

[52] In 1796 Pierre-Charles-Louis Baudin (1748–1799), deputy of the Ardennes, stated that a citizen could be a Jew or a Moslem provided he rejected the religious observances and dogmas of Mohammed. His reason was that religion was indivisible from the social system in a theocracy: *Du maintien de la liberté des opinions religieuses et des cultes, et du système de déportation générale, ou Nouvelles observations sur la résolution du 17 floréal de l'an 4, relative aux prêtres assermentés* . . . (Paris, an IV). On Baudin see A. Hannedouche, *Les illustrations ardennaises* (Sedan, n. d.), pp. 15–19.

[53] Zalkind Hourwitz, *Apologie* . . . (Paris, 1789), p. 9 ("vue l'ignorance absolue de la plupart des savans mêmes, sur l'article du Judaïsme);" Abraham Cahen, *Règlements somptuaires de la communauté juive de Metz à la fin du XVIIᵉ siècle. 1696–1697*. Extrait de l'*ASEJ* (Versailles, 1881), pp. 7–8; For other sumptuary laws of the Jewish communities in France see: כרוז הנכרו בשתי בתי כנסיות פה קהלתינו מיץ יע"א ביום השלישי כ"ח אדר תקל"ט לפ"ק למען ידעו כל איש ואשה בחור ובתולה איך יתנהגו בתכשיטיהם ובמלבושיהם לכל ילכדו ח"ו. ([Metz,] 1779). 1 p. fol.; Cecil Roth, "Sumptuary Laws of the Community of Carpentras." *JQR*, XVIII (1927–28), 357–83; Isidore Loeb, "Les juifs à Strasbourg . . .," 192–98, Alsatian Sumptuary laws of 1774 or 1777, reprinted in: *JFrance*, II, 312–14. For sumptuary laws of Saint-Esprit (1729) see H. Léon, *op. cit.*, p. 387.

traditions and principles. On the other hand, there was nothing particularly anti-Jewish in the attitude of the revolutionary leaders against separate Jewish communities. As Graetz remarked, the Revolution emancipated the Jews without asking them to renounce even one iota of their religion.[54] Jews were persecuted, some were even guillotined, but not because they were Jews.[55]

The Protestants of Alsace, too, were organized in autonomous bodies, and this fact was mentioned in 1779 by the author of a pamphlet on the legality in France of Jewish law with regard to divorce.[56] A group of seven Christian creditors of the Carpentras Jews argued in the year VII that unlike the Jews the Protestants never insisted that prior to the Revolution they were organized as a separate body.[57] But this was not exact. In fact, the Jews were not the only religious minority group trying to preserve their particular privileges of the pre-revolutionary period. During the Revolution it was difficult to accept the idea of being a Frenchman in the spirit of the new regime and Christian in the spirit of the old regime. Yet, the Alsatian Protestants retained many of their old privileges. Thus, thanks to some legal hairsplitting and arrangements with the Catholics, the Protestant Chapter of Saint-Thomas of Strasbourg was not nationalized. The deputy Pierre André (1767–1848) of Lower Rhine stated in February 1799 that the Protestants who suffered from religious intolerance during the old regime should be the first to give up privileges the destruction of which could only add to social welfare. But Professor Christian-Guillaume Koch (1737–1813), the Alsatian Protestant leader and deputy who directed the Protestant fight against the abolition of their privileges, opposed Jewish emancipation on the ground that the Jews would con-

[54] Heinrich Graetz, *Geschichte der Juden*, XI (Leipzig, 1911), 221.

[55] Z. Szajkowski, "The Attitude of French Jacobins Toward Jewish Religion." *HJ*, XVIII (1956), 111–19; Idem, "Jewish Religious Observance during the French Revolution of 1789." *S. Niger Memorial Volume* (New York, 1958), pp. 193–216 (in Yiddish); Idem, "French Jewry during the Thermidorian Reaction." *HJ*, XX (1958), 98.

[56] *Réplique pour la Dame Peixotto. Contre le Sieur Peixotto, son mari* (n. p., 1779), p. 29.

[57] *Mémoire pour . . . Chambaud*, p. 23 (see Bibliography, No. 89).

tinue to exist as a separate nation. The insistence of the National Assembly that the Jews surrender their former privileges was interpreted by Koch and Schwendt as a victory over the Jews, who would cease to exist as a *corps de nation* (national body).[58]

[58] "Réflexions sur les Juifs, redigés par M. Koch au mois de Juin 1790." Archives du Chapitre de St.-Thomas, 148–b, 77–6, II–2 (Am Stg); On Koch see J. G. Schweighaeuser, *Vie de Christ. Guil. Koch* (Strasbourg, n. d.). 78 pp. See also *Opinion de Frédéric Herman, Député par le département du Bas-Rhin, sur le projet de résolution concernant les biens . . . protestans. Séance du 9 ventôse an 7* (Paris, an 7). 26 pp.; *Opinion d'André (du Bas Rhin), sur le projet de résolution tendant à supprimer les établissemens protestans, et à nationaliser les biens qui en dépendent. Séance du ventôse an 7* (n. p., an 7). 22 pp.; R. Reuss, *Les églises protestantes d'Alsace pendant la Révolution 1789–1802* (Paris, 1906), pp. 27–28, 31–33; Jean Richerateau, *Le rôle politique du Professeur Koch* (Strasbourg, 1936), pp. 33–77; Z. Szajkowski, "Protestants and Jews . . .," 119–35. For a bibliography of contemporary pamphlets concerning the fight of the Alsatian Protestants against the nationalization of their Church properties see *Chauffour*, pp. 454–57; Charles Heitz, *Les Sociétés politiques de Strasbourg pendant les années 1790 à 1795* (Strasbourg, 1865), pp. 61–62.

On Dec. 6, 1797 Riou warned the Council of the Five Hundred that the refusal to nationalize the Jewish debts, because they were persecuted during the old regime, could serve as a precedent against Protestants: "En droit il est certain que quoique les Juifs ne fussent pas admis au fonctions publiques, quoiqu'ils ne fussent pas citoyens français, ils étaient habitants et domiciliés en France, et si aujourd'hui on fait une arme contre eux de l'oppresssion sous laquelle ils vivaient, on pourrait également tourner cette arme contre les protestants français" (Halphen, p. 336).

III. COMMUNAL JEWISH ACTIVITIES
DURING THE REVOLUTION

In the first years of the Revolution the Jewish communities continued to elect their syndics, and to act in every other aspect of communal Jewish life exactly as they did during the old regime.[59] But of course, the new regime had some influence even in the Jewish communities. Thus, a new spirit prevailed at the Avignon elections of October 2, 1790. Rabbi Elie Vitte Spire [Espire] stated in a sermon at the synagogue that the *baillons* (syndics) should no longer be elected to represent existing social classes, because this was against the new principle of equality. In protest against this new conception the community's treasurer, Moïse Petit, resigned and Aron Rouget was elected in his place.[60] (Note that an anti-Jewish pamphleteer of 1790, who was against the immediate grant of full civil rights even to all classes of the Christian population, demanded that equality should exist among the Jews. The motive for this demand was not so much love of justice for the poor Jews, as dislike of the function of the syndics.[61])

In many places the revolutionary authorities tried to restrict activities of the Jewish communities even at the beginning of the Revolution. On September 29, 1790, the *Directoire* of Upper

[59] R. Anchel, *Napoléon et les Juifs* (Paris, 1927), p. 9.

[60] "... sans s'asservir comme par le passé à des distinctions de mains, vue que l'égalité qu'on vient de consacrer et d'établir parmi les hommes ne comporte pas aujourdhuy une nuance qui souvent tient le merite enchaîné" (Ad Vaucluse, notarial minutes of Gaudibert, fol. 1094, Oct. 2, 1790). On the elections in the Jewish communities of the papal province on the eve and in the beginning of the Revolution see H. Chobaut, *op. cit.*, CI, 19–20, CII, 3–5, 11.

[61] *Sur les Juifs en France* (n. p., 1790), p. 15: "Qu'entr'eux ils seront tous égaux en rang, même dans leurs assemblées privées ou religieuses; qu'il n'y aura aucune distinction, ni de prééminence, ni de faveur graciable; qu'il n'y aura de membres distingués parmi eux, que les préposés de leur Nation leur seront donnés par le pouvoir territorial: ce pour le service religieux & les écoles d'instructions, sur la présentation de la communauté qui formera un scrutin: ceux pour la police, au choix de l'autorité territoriale."

Rhine prohibited the excommunication of Wolf Netter of Wintzenheim. The Jews of Bolwiller, who were dissatisfied with
their syndic, sought permission to elect another in accordance
with the spirit of the Letters patent of July 10, 1784. On January 14 and February 22, 1791 the departmental *Directoire* discussed and refused the request.[62]

But this was not a consistent policy. On March 12, 1791 the
departmental *Directoire* of Upper Rhine permitted the Jews of
Wintzenheim to elect three syndics.[63] The special Jewish *état-
civil* (registries of births, marriages and deaths) was recorded by
Jewish community officials even after the Jewish emancipation.
Only when the law of September 20, 1792 secularized the *état-civil*
were the Jews, too, ordered to turn over to the civil authorities
all existing registries and from then on the *état-civil* of all religious
groups was recorded in the same registries by the civil authorities. But some Jewish communities continued for a short time
to register their *état-civil* in the old Jewish registries: Wettolsheim (Upper Rhine) in 1793; some registries of Bordeaux until
September and November 1793; of Cavaillon — until November
1793; etc.[64]

In simple police matters the authorities prefered to act through
the communal Jewish leaders.[65] The local and even the central
government authorities acted as if they preferred to continue
to deal with the Jews not as individuals but as collective Jewish
bodies, especially in matters of taxation. In fact, in this respect
at the beginning of the Revolution the Jews were considered to

[62] M. Ginsburger, "Arrêtés du Directoire du département du Haut-Rhin
relatifs aux Juifs (1790)." *REJ*, LXXV (1922), 47, 52–53.

[63] *Ibid.*, 56–57.

[64] Z. Szajkowski, "The Reform of the *Etat-Civil* of the French Jews During
the Revolution of 1789." *JQR*, XLIX (1958), 63–74.

[65] On June 29, 1790 the civil authorities of Avignon ordered the *bailons*
(syndics) of the Jewish community to put a stop to the noise in the ghetto
that was disturbing the rest of the *nation Juive*, especially sick persons. This
order was issued at the request of Isaac Allegri, whose wife was in child-bed
(Am Avignon, D–II–7). The same thing happened in later periods. Thus the
Jewish community of Metz was charged with the duty of providing quarters
in the former ghetto for soldiers stationed in the city: Am Metz, H–2–102;
Extrait des minutes de la Mairie de Metz. Du 23 Fructidor de l'an 13 (Metz,
n. d.). Broadside.

be autonomous bodies.[66] In September 1789, even in Bordeaux, the much privileged Sephardic Jews paid their taxes through their *Nation* (9,406 livres 13 sols 3 deniers in *capitation* taxes, which was collected by the *Nation* from one hundred and sixty families.)[67] The Alsatian Jews requested that they be freed from paying collectively various taxes for 1789 amounting to 25,000 livres, because many Jews had been ruined during the anti-Jewish riots of that year.[68] The finance Minister, J. Necker, was in favor of granting the Jewish request. In 1791, the Jews again protested against paying taxes because they had already paid a tax before the Revolution especially imposed on Jews. On June 11, 1791 the *Directoire* of Lower Rhine ordered them to pay only the balance. This meant that in paying taxes Jews were on a par with all other citizens. However, even earlier the Intermediary Commission had ruled that Jews should not pay separately the 7,582 livres tax *vingtième d'industrie*, but that they should be inscribed together with all other citizens on the supplementary lists for this tax. The Council of State decided, however, that this tax should be paid by the Jews according to the old rule, *i. e.* separately as a group, because the supplementary lists would comprise only the tax *vingtième* on real estate and not industry. Accordingly, on June 1, 1790 the Intermediary Commission ordered that, except for this tax, the Jews should be included in the general tax system.[69] In 1790 the Jews of Metz still paid their taxes not as individuals but as a collective body.[70]

---

[66] In 1813–1814 the Jews of Upper Rhine were forced to pay a special tax. R. Anchel, "Contribution levée en 1813–1814 sur les Juifs du Haut-Rhin." *REJ*, XCIII (1932), 113–34. In 1815 the Jews of Altkirch (Upper Rhine) were forced to deliver to the army 200 shirts, 100 matrasses, 200 sheets, 100 pillow cases, 2 wooden bath tubs, food and 40,000 francs in cash (Am Altkirch, Juifs).

[67] Am Bx, CC 1098.

[68] On the anti-Jewish riots of Alsace see Z. Szajkowski, "Anti-Jewish Riots during the Revolutions of 1789, 1830 and 1848." *Zion*, XX (1955), 82–102 (in Hebrew).

[69] Ad BR, C752, pp. 149–50, 172; *Extrait du Procès-verbal des séances de la Commission intermédiaire provinciale d'Alsace, du premier Juin 1790* (n. p., n. d.). 3 pp.; *Délibération du Directoire du Département du Bas-Rhin. Du Samedi onzième Juin 1791* (n. p., n. d.). 4 pp.

[70] Landmann, Ce 291–93.

As late as August 18, 1791 the district of Metz referred in an account of taxes to be paid by Jews not to Jews in particular but to the *communauté des Juifs.*[71]

In many instances the local authorities approved special taxation of Jews by the Jewish communities according to the pre-revolutionary system. The local authorities often forced the Jewish communities to pay back salaries to their rabbis and other employees. On December 18, 1791 the *Directoire* of Lower Rhine ordered the former *Nation* of the Alsatian Jewish communities to pay back salaries totaling one thousand livres to its secretary and translator, Simon Halle.[72] In August 1790 Abraham Hirsch demanded payment of 72 livres for expenses incurred during his stay in Strasbourg in connection with the assembly that drafted a *cahier des doléances* on behalf of the Alsatian Jews. One month later Marx Berr [Cerfberr] sought permission to levy a tax on all Jews to cover the expenses of this assembly. On September 1, 1790 the *Directoire* of Upper Rhine granted the demand of Hirsch David of Rosheim, treasurer of the council of Alsatian communities, to force Lazare Meyer and Goschel Bloch of Dürmenach and Wintzenheim to pay the arrears in taxes for 1788 and 1789. On March 3, 1791 the *Directoire* of Lower Rhine permitted the Jews of Hattstatt to levy a tax for support of paupers.[73]

This state of affairs continued even after the Ashkenazic Jews were granted full citizenship and their communities were officially dissolved.

The syndics Salomon Benjamin, Schillé Baruch and Isaac of Bouxwiller complained to the departmental authorities that many communities were very much behind in paying their rabbis' salaries. The Revolution had abolished *eo impso* their functions and thus they had no right, without special permission from the departmental authorities, to levy taxes. Such permission was granted to them.[74] On May 29, 1792 a tax to cover the salary of the rabbi of Mutzig was still obligatory. But it should be remembered that the law of September 4, 1792 requiring non-Catholics to defray the expenses of their religious activities, was

See Bibliography, No. 20.   [72] Ad BR, 1 L 825.

[73] Hildenfinger, "Actes du district de Strasbourg relatifs aux Juifs (1790)." *REJ*, LX (1910), 238–39; Ginsburger, "Arrêtés . . .," 45, 55–56.

[74] Julien Weil, "Contribution . . .," LXXI (1925), 176.

still in force. The Revolution did not abolish the financial restrictions imposed upon religious minorities.[75]

It seems that even "voluntary" revolutionary gifts, which were more often nothing less than confiscations of gold, silver, copper and other valuables, in some places were taken from Jews not as individuals but as organized Jewish communities.[76] Only on November 2, 1792 did the *Directoire* of Lower Rhine publish an order that practically aimed at abolishing the financial system of the Jewish communities: except for a special Jewish tax to cover the debts of the former Jewish communities no Jew was to be forced to pay any special tax for the Jewish community.[77] In Alsace the official and general liquidation of the Jewish communities came later, and most probably as a result of the regime of the Terror. On July 1, 1793 the *Directoire* of Upper Rhine announced the general liquidation of the "Jewish Nation." The decision was announced again on the following

---

[75] It was not until August 6, 1831 that the government agreed to consider rabbis as government employees and to pay their salaries. Halphen, pp. 93–94.

[76] On Feb. 15, 1790 Marx Berr [Cerfberr], "general syndic of the Jewish Nation," presented a patriotic gift in the name of the Wintzenheim Jews. *Suite de l'Etat des boucles et autres effets en argent, remis au bureau du Comité de la Garde Nationale Strasbourgeoise pour don patriotique offert à la Nation* (n. p., n. d.). Broadside. In the district of Altkirch there existed a special register of such patriotic gifts with the names of Jewish communities and individual Jews. Following are a few of the patriotic "gifts" noted in this register: "La commune Juive de Hirsingen Don 150 livres [de cuivre] . . . La commune juive de Seppois-le-Bas 1 main [en argent] servant d'index, 1 lustre de cuivre . . . Zillisheim. Les Juifs 4–17 [de cuivre,] 4–87 [d'étain,] — 09 [de plomb]" (Documents, Alsace, No. 8, fol. 23–34).

[77] *Délibération du Directoire du Département du Bas-Rhin. Du 2 Novembre 1792* (Strasbourg, n. d.). 4 pp.; R. Reuss, "L'antisémitisme dans le Bas-Rhin pendant la Révolution." *REJ*, LXVIII (1914), 260; Hildenfinger, *op. cit.*, 19. (". . . la liquidation des anciens intérêts qui les lioient, a nécessité la continuation d'un régime qui ne peut plus subsister sous la règne de la liberté & de l'égalité, & lorsque tous les citoyens de la république ne doivent plus connoître de loix que celles qui leur sont communes à tous; considérant en outre, que les loix assurent aux individus de la religion de Moïse la faculté de choisir à leur gré les ministres de leur culte . . . Le Directoire . . . a arrêté: qu'à compter du 1er Novembre courant, aucuns individus de la religion de Moïse ne pourront être contraints au payement d'aucunes sommes destinées à acquitter le traitement dû à des soi-disans préposés, caissiers, rabbins ou autres qui exerceroient une jurisdiction particulière, à la charge néamoins par eux de payer comme du passé les sommes arriérées . . .")

August 16, A similar announcement was made by the *Directoire* of Lower Rhine.[78]

The financial system of the Jewish communities was officially and in fact destroyed by the law of September 29, 1795 which abrogated obligatory taxes for religious activities,[79] but this law was not aimed exclusively against Jews.

In most Jewish communities many religious and social activities continued during the Revolution, often even during the Terror. Synagogues, cemeteries, philanthropic societies, slaughtering according to Jewish law, officials including rabbis and cantors were maintained and payment was required for their upkeep or services. In many places the communal organizations were continued through the bodies which were formed for the liquidation of the debts owed to Christian creditors by the former communities. In order to pay for protection, residence permits, and the heavy taxes imposed on them, the Jewish communities of France and the papal province of Avignon and Comtat Venaissin which were in existence before 1789, had to borrow large sums. The communities of Metz, Avignon, Carpentras and L'Isle-sur-Sorgue were in debt to Christian creditors, and the Jewish communities of Alsace to Jewish creditors. The revolutionary regime refused to take over these debts and thus forced the Jews to remain organized in order to collect taxes. As a result the French Revolution, which emancipated the Jews on condition that the separate Jewish communities would be dissolved, made it necessary for the Jews to maintain communities for the purpose of discharging pre-revolutionary debts.

[78] Ginsburger, "Arrêtés . . .," 65.

The Jewish community of Nice hired, in October 1797, night watchers over Jewish stores. Their salaries were paid with money from the philanthropic society. J. Bauer, "L'Université israélite de Nice de 1785 à 1803." *REJ*, LXIII (1912), 274. In many instances Jewish community councils continued to exist as "former" communities. Thus, e. g., a financial document of Nancy for the years 1794–1800 is titled "Extrait du Registre des recettes et dépenses de la ci devant Communauté d'Israélites de Nancy, écrit en caractère[s] hébraïque[s], par Mr Mayer Marx père" (Documents, Metz, No. 121, fol. 703).

[79] In the year XIII Rabbi David Sintzheim dunned the Jewish communities for the arrears of his salary. Because of the law of 1795 the court could not decide what action it should take on this matter. Anchel, *Napoléon . . .*, pp. 44–45.

IV. THE ORIGIN OF THE DEBTS OWED BY
THE JEWISH COMMUNITY OF METZ

The King and the local authorities assessed the Jews of Metz a maximum in taxes. Prior to the Revolution the Jews constituted only one eighteenth of the general population of Metz, but they paid one sixth of the *capitation* tax. In 1757–1766 the non-privileged bourgeois of Metz paid the city 221,727 livres and the Jews paid 55,248 livres. In 1789 they constituted only one twentieth of the general population of Metz, but they paid 9,648 of 57,736 livres in city taxes. In addition they were forced to pay annuities and bribes to a large number of civil and Church institutions and officials. Even the palms of the Ministers in Paris were greased. Moïse Weill of Bischheim, who was the Paris agent of the Jewish community of Metz, on the eve of the Revolution lavished thousands of livres in yearly gifts on various Ministers. On many occasions he presented geese to Ministers, including Necker, the famous Minister of Finance. All this was a heavy burden on the budget of the Jewish community. During the seventy-seven years covered by the periods 1605–1610, 1650–1660, 1700–1735, 1765–1780 and 1785–1789 the budgets of the Jewish Community of Metz aggregated 427,783 livres, of which only 138,651 livres was spent for the community itself and the rest on gifts for government and city dignitaries, the Brancas tax (beginning 1715, which is discussed below) and annuities to pay off debts owed by the community. In 1785–1790 its average annual expenses amounted to 108,479 livres 10 s. whereas average income was only 69,086 livres 11 s. 6 d. In 1790 it planned an annual expense budget of 108,479 livres 10 s. and anticipated only 39,392 livres 18 s. 6 d. in revenues. Among the expenses were 36,744 livres it was assessed in various taxes and 47,735 livres 10 s. in annuities it paid to Christian creditors of the community. This was also a burden on each Jew individually. In 1785–1789 each of about four hundred and ten Jewish families of Metz paid over 360 livres in Jewish community taxes in addition to various city and government taxes. According to a yearly list of city taxes paid by the community until

1790 (54,495 livres yearly) only four families paid 1,000 livres
or more each, ten — from 500 to 999 livres, ninety — from 100
to 499 livres and the rest, less than 100 livres each.[80]

The case of the Brancas tax was particularly striking in the
history of taxes paid by the Jewish communities. Charles-
François de la Baume de Blanc, the marquis de la Vallière, was
a nephew of a famous duchess who was a mistress of the King.
The marquis, too, decided to profit from the duchess' affair, so
in 1714 he requested the privilege of imposing an annual tax of
40 livres upon each Jew of Metz. The Jews sent many petitions
and Vallière's request was refused. But on Dec. 31, 1715 Louis
de Brancas, duc de Villars was granted such a privilege by
Philip of Orléans, the Regent, with the help, of course, of his
mistress, the beautiful wife of an officer, Fontaines (Countess
Marie-Louise-Charlotte de Pelard de Givry), and a mistress of
the Regent also. All the petitions of the Jews and bribes they
paid were unsuccessful. By Letters patent of July 1718 the
existing annual tax of 40 livres per Jew was changed to an annual
tax of 20,000 livres imposed upon the Jewish community of Metz.
Also, the Jews were forced to pay 70,000 livres for the preceding
three years and various expenses. Altogether, the community
spent 100,000 livres in vainly opposing the new tax. Voltaire
who, it is well known, disliked Jews, wrote on the occasion of
the publication of Mme de Fontaines' novel *La Comtesse de Savoye*
[Paris, 1726]:

> Adieu; malgré mes épilogues,
> Puissiez-vous pourtant, tous les ans,
> Me lire deux ou trois romans
> Et taxer quatre synagogues.

Brancas received 75 per cent of the tax and Madame de Fontaines 25 per cent. In 1745 the tax was renewed for another
thirty years, the proceeds this time assigned only to the Brancas
family. As early as 1750, however, the Brancas family obtained

---

[80] Am Metz, 1 G 4 (taxes paid by Jews); Landmann, Ce 98–115 (Weill's
letters to Goudchaux Lévy-Spire, syndic of the Metz community); Louis
Wolf, *Mémoirs*; Gerson-Lévy, *Extinction*; Olry Terquem, *Souvenirs*; N.
Netter, *Die Schuldennot* (see Bibliography, Nos. 12, 139–40, 143); A. Cahen,
"Budget de la communauté juive de Metz." *Mémoires de la Société d'archéologie
lorraine*, series 3, III (1875); R. Clément, *op. cit.*, pp. 118–19; *EcSt*, pp. 71–72.

a further renewal of the tax until 1805. In a period of seventy-five years the Jews paid the Brancas family 1,875,000 livres. Only during the Revolution did the Jews of Metz feel it was safe to denounce the Brancas family for living in idleness on Jewish misery. In a petition to the National Assembly dated August 31, 1789 the Jews included a demand for the abolition of the Brancas tax. But the National Assembly did not act at once and the Jewish demand was renewed the next year in a special petition which argued that the Brancas tax would force rich Jews to emigrate and the Kingdom would thus suffer financially. The petition was debated by the National Assembly on July 20, 1790. M.-M.-I. Robespierre stated that the Brancas tax was illegal.[81] Charles-François Bouche (1737–1795), author of a study of the Jews of Avignon and the Comtat Venaissin, described it as a gift from the King to his corrupted courtesans. Among those who fought the abolition of the Brancas tax were abbot François-Martin Thiébault (1749–1795), deputy from Metz to the National Assembly and the Alsatian deputy Jean-François Reubell, both adversaries of Jewish emancipation. The report to the National Assembly on the Jewish petition was presented by Jacques-François-Laurent Devisme (1749–1830), a lawyer and deputy from Laon, where no Jews resided.[82] Devisme was active on many commissions of the National Assembly and helped draft decrees on important financial matters. In his report Devisme approved the abolition of the Brancas tax without compensating the Brancas family for the loss. He stated that this tax did not represent a purchase from the King, but was "a real act of generosity, a clear pecuniary favor." Still, Devisme proposed that Brancas be granted a small annuity, not to replace the tax, nor as a compensation, but as a pension for a general in the army who participated in eleven campaigns, was seventy-seven years old and sick. On July 20, 1790 the National Assembly abolished the Brancas tax. This act was much publicized and

---

[81] On Robespierre's friendly attitude toward Jews see: Ludwig Schosz, "Robespierre und die Juden." *SIW*, IX (1912), No. 28, 10, No. 29, 10–11; A. Mathiez, "Robespierre et l'émancipation des Juifs." *AHRF*, VIII (1931), 261–62; Idem, "Robespierre et Grégoire sous la Constituante." *Ibid.*, 261. On Bouche's project see Z. Szajkowski, "The Comtadin Jews and the Annexation of the Papal Province by France, 1789–1791." *JQR*, XLVI (1955), 181–82.

[82] On Devisme see Robert, II, 382.

hailed throughout France as an important step toward national self-respect and Jewish emancipation.[83]

As noted, the heavy taxes imposed on the Jewish community of Metz forced it to borrow immense sums from Christian creditors, including priests. From November 4, 1748 until May 3, 1789 it borrowed from Christian creditors on ninety occasions the grand sum of 526,336 livres.[84] These debts were converted into life-annuities (*rentes viagères*) in the amount of 42,172 livres 10 d. to be paid yearly. The largest sum — 21,000 livres — was borrowed on November 17, 1781. From 1760 to 1770 the community of Metz paid for new annuities totalling 6,955 livres; from 1771 to 1780 — 8,996 livres; from 1781 to 1785 — 5,880 livres.[85] As we shall see, it owed to its Christian creditors almost 500,000 livres for unpaid annuities at the outbreak of the Revolution.[86]

[83] AN, D–III–174; Bibliography, Nos. 1–3, 12–18; Voltaire, *Oeuvres*, édition of Garnier (Paris, 1777–85), X, 215; *Adresse . . . le 31 Août 1789 . . .*, pp. 5–7; [Godard,] *Pétition . . . le 28 Janvier 1790 . . .*, p. 101; F.-M. Thiébault, *No. ou Récit IV . . .* (Metz, 1789), p. 11 (on Thiébault see H. Thibout, "Un émigré messin." *Cahiers lorrains* (1932), 57–60); *RdGJP*, I (1897), 55–58; *AP*, XVII (1884), 215–19; *Moniteur universel* (réimpression), V, 186, VI, 185; *Mercure de France*, Jan. 16, 1790, 135 ("Réclamation," by Brancas); *Journal de Bordeaux et du département de la Gironde*, No. 73 (July 24, 1790), 504 ("Croiroit-on qu'on continnoit, dans ce siècle de philosophie, à percevoir une taxe sur les Juifs, à cause de leur religion"). The Decree of July 20, 1790 was registered in August 1790 by the Toulouse parliament (Ad Hérault, B 1877); Netter, pp. 17–21 (see Bibliography, No. 143).

[84] Large sums were borrowed on earlier dates: 1,570 livres from the brothers Houselle in 1698; 20,000 livres from Charles Colbert in 1713, etc. (Landmann, R 1–2).

[85] AN, D–III–174, dr. Metz; JTS, No. 01565. Terquem, p. 9 (see Bibliography, No. 140). According to another inventory of May 8, 1794, the Jews had borrowed during the same period only 415,237 livres on 79 occasions, for which they paid annuities of 41,897 livres 10 s. (Documents, Metz, No. 10, fol. 49–52). Among the Christian creditors of Metz were the priests Joseph Saintignon, Jean-Pierre Vendel, Guillaume de la Neve, François-Dominique du Ballé, Claude-Nicolas Edme (called Fidry), Louis Woirhaye (according to an inventory of Apr. 18, 1792. Documents, Metz, No. 1, fol. 1–2).

[86] According to an inventory of May 8, 1794, the Jewish community also owed 15,999 livres 11 s. 8 d. to ten Jewish creditors, mostly sums for minors left by deceased Jews in the care of the community (Documents Metz, No. 38).

On the value of the livre *tournois*, which was used in Metz, see Natalis de Wailly, "Mémoire sur les variations de la livre tournois." *Mémoires de l'Académie des inscriptions et belles lettres*, XX-2 (1857), 177–427. A livre was valued at 20 sols and each sol at 12 deniers.

V. THE ORIGIN OF THE DEBTS OWED BY
THE JEWISH COMMUNITIES IN THE
PAPAL PROVINCE OF AVIGNON
AND COMTAT VENAISSIN

The four Jewish communities of the papal province of Avignon and Comtat Venaissin borrowed large sums from Christian creditors in order to pay high taxes imposed upon them. These Jews were taxed on many pretexts: for permission to wear beards, to marry, to bear children, to bury their dead, to protect their ghettos during Christian holidays. In addition they paid general taxes and bribes to Church dignitaries and their servants, *corporations*, city officials. In Carpentras, for example, the *évêque des fous* and the *abbé de la jeunesse*, who presided at local celebrations and enjoyed the traditional right to shave the beards of the Jews by force, collected sums from them for not exercising it. Similarly, Christian children who, on the day of Innocents had the right to create a breach of the peace in front of the synagogue, exacted a fee for keeping the peace. In Avignon the Jews were forced to sweep the *Place du Palais* on the eve of Corpus Christi. On June 28, 1771 the Jews were exempted from this humiliating duty in return for paying the *Chapitre de Notre Dame* 300 livres and other gifts yearly. The anonymous author of the pamphlet *L'Hermite de Luberon*, published in Comtat during the Revolution, told how Jews arrested during the old regime in Cavaillon were confronted with two alternative conditions: either to pay a large sum or to desecrate the Sabbath. They chose to pay. The same situation was described during the Revolution by the anonymous author of another Comtadin pamphlet (*Avis plus que pressant*). As late as December 28, 1789 the Jews of Avignon paid 36 livres as a compulsory Christmas gift to the city; on October 12, 1790 — 288 livres to the *Chartreuse de Villeneuve*.

According to one document the Jewish community of Carpentras borrowed 110,000 livres from Christian creditors from 1767 until 1786. But according to another, during this period the community borrowed a total of over 283,000 livres on eighty occasions. In 1747, during the French occupation of the papal province, the three Jewish communities of Comtat Venaissin were compelled to lend the occupation forces a sum of 50,000

631

livres, 23,000 livres of which they had to borrow from the provincial administration. In 1779 the Carpentras community had expenses of 38,358 livres, including 24,664 for annuities to Christian creditors. In 1780 all four communities of the papal province had an annual income of 43,300 livres, but their outlay on pensions and annuities to their Christian creditors was far greater. On the eve of the Revolution the debt of the four communities, exclusive of unpaid annuities, amounted to about 800,000 livres.[87]

The Christian creditors of the Jewish community of Avignon were organized in a *Corps de Messieurs les créanciers* which often influenced the activities of the Jewish community. Thus, they determined the amount of communal taxes to be paid by the Jews. On May 24, 1673 the Christian creditors of Carpentras granted the Jewish community a delay of five years in repaying its debts on condition that the Jews impose a sufficiently large tax to cover current expenses.[88]

There was frequent conflict between the Jewish communities and their Christian creditors. As a result of such a conflict a sale of the properties of the Jews of Avignon was ordered in 1662. On October 21 of that year the *Auditeur Général de la Légation* of Avignon classified the Christian creditors in categories according to the priority of their mortgages, and the sums to be repaid to them. But the idea of selling the properties was abandoned, because of the heavy expenses which such a sale would have involved and because it would have ruined not only the entire Jewish community but also the revenue obtained by the city from the Jews' commercial activities. It was then arranged that the Jews would pay yearly annuities of 2,700 livres to be distributed among their Christian creditors. This arrangement was approved on September 12, 1735 by the papal author-

---

[87] Ad Vaucluse, G 447, fol. 346, 353 (contract between the Jews of Avignon and the *Chapitre de N. D.*, June 28, 1771 and Oct. 22, 1772); Calvet, ms. 2104, Nos. 688, 787; Columbia, 893C–C22, vols. 5, 7; *Observations*, p. 3; *Impôts et budget*, p. 5 (see Bibliography, Nos. 104, 106); P. Charpenne, *op. cit.*, II 457, 540–41; *Avis plus que pressant* (n. p., n. d.), p. 7; *L'Hermite du Luberon au Solitaire du Mont-Ventoux. Salut et repos* (n. p., n. d.), p. 2; J. Bauer, "Les troupes du maréchal de Belle-Isle et les Juifs du Comtat-Venaissin (1746–1758)." *REJ*, XXVII (1893), 263–68; Chobaut, *op. cit.*, CI, 24.

[88] Calvet, ms. 2103 (the *Corp*'s minutes, 1735–66); AIU, R 43, p. 49 (delay of May 24, 1673).

ities of Avignon and on September 22, 1736 by an assembly of the Avignon Jews. The 2,700 livres were paid yearly to the treasurer of the *Corps* of creditors, whose salary of one hundred livres was also the responsibility of the Jews. The arrangement was changed, first by a notarial act of August 8, 1748 which reduced the treasurers salary to sixty livres; second, in 1766 by the Jews who decided to pay the annuities directly to their creditors without an intermediary. This step provoked a chain of lawsuits, but from 1766 until 1791 the Jews paid the annuities directly to their creditors or through the judicial authorities. In the meantime the Jews of Avignon borrowed new sums and the annuities to the new creditors, which totalled about 1,300 livres, were paid in the same manner.[89]

The Jewish community of Avignon paid a total of 7,232 livres in annuities to Christian creditors from 1755 to July 20, 1789. As late as August 16, 1789 the community decided to borrow again, this time a sum of 12,000 livres.[90]

As a result of the dissolution and nationalization by the revolutionary regime of properties of religious and other corporate bodies which were creditors of the Jewish communities, the government and various municipal agencies acquired their assets. Thus, the Jewish community of Avignon became a debtor of the government in the sum of 11,367 livres 1 s. 4 d. incurred between 1791 and 1806 for unpaid annuities to twenty-two dissolved Catholic institutions. During the Revolution the community of Carpentras paid the government annuities for six pensions owed to former Catholic bodies. In 1816 the Carpentras commission, appointed to liquidate the debts, tried to settle the debt of 18,131.94 francs in sums borrowed and 15,298.80 francs for unpaid annuities owed to the government. The commission asked the King to cancel this debt, but the request was rejected and on April 27, 1824 the government accepted the sum of 20,000 francs. Of the 129,515.88 francs owed in 1818 by the

[89] Documents, Comtat, No. 21, fol. 71–72. Earlier, on Aug. 29, 1569, the community of Avignon appointed Lion Alfandri to discuss with the Christian creditors a proposed sale of the synagogue and other communal Jewish properties as a way of repaying its debts (Ad Vaucluse, notarial minutes of Vincenti, 1350, fol. 575).

[90] Calvet, ms. 2104, fol. 122–25; Ad Vaucluse, Gaudibert's notarial minutes, 1789, fol. 1040.

former Jewish community of L'Isle-sur-Sorgue, which represented fifteen loans, three had to be paid to the government and the city, including one loan of 34,103.70 francs.[91]

Did the Jewish community of Cavaillon owe any debts? The above mentioned loan of over 23,000 livres was granted in 1747 by the authorities of Comtat Venaissin to the communities of Carpentras, L'Isle and Cavaillon.[92] On July 30, 1765 the latter community borrowed 1,200 livres for various synagogical expenses and on September 25, 1775 another 6,000 livres for the reconstruction of its synagogue.[93] A source of 1823 refers to "debts of the Cavaillon community."[94] But we know very little of these debts and no mention of them was ever made in the official documents on the discharge of the debts owed by the three other communities of the former papal province. It is, thus, possible that most of the debts were settled by the community of Cavaillon before the emancipation.

[91] Documents, Comtat, No. 21, fol. 72; *Observations* (see Bibliography, No. 104), p. 17 ("Leurs créanciers, qui sont au nombre de plusieurs centaines parmi lesquels est le Gouvernement, qui représente les Corps supprimés"); Columbia, X893C–C22, vols. 1, 6, 9, 10 ("Reçu des Juifs de la Commune de Carpentras la somme de deux mille cinquante deux livres pour quatre annuités des six differentes pensions . . . qu'ils servaient aux ci-devant Religieuses de Ste. Claire d'Avignon. A Avignon le 2 Germinal 4me Rép. [Signé:] Le Reçeveur de l'Enregistrement et du Domaine National"); Chobaut, *op. cit.*, CII, 35.

[92] Columbia, X893C–C22, vol. 5 (Nos. 11, 12), vol. 7 (list of creditors).

[93] Ad Vaucluse, Poncet's notarial minutes, July 30, 1765; Guis' notarial minutes, 327, fol. 652. See also Calvet, ms. 2160, fol. 26 ("Graduation de Messieurs les créanciers des carrières de L'Isle et Cavaillon").

[94] "Quant aux contribuables des lieux voisins, il n'y a que MM Cremy frères de Marignanne [Marignane] qui consentiront à payer, si vous leur garantissez le remboursement en cas qu'on vienne à les rechercher pour les dettes de la C^té de Cavaillon." A letter from Aix to Carpentras, Jan. 23, 1823, signed by J. [Jacob] Lisbonne, Rabbi Mardochée Crémieu[x] jr. and Th. Milhaud (JTS, No. 01529).

Following are a few examples from Avignon and Carpentras that illustrate the value of the livre in the papal province: On February 14, 1737 the Christian Pierre Fructus sold to Mordacay Petit of Avignon a razed house (*entièrement démolie*) for 800 French livres. On Aug. 14, 1752 the Jewish community of Avignon paid 300 livres to Monteux and Joseph Semat Pichot for a yard (*cour, escour vannade*) to be used for the construction of a hospice for foreign paupers. According to a contract of 1747 the *sagarein (shohet)* Ain Lévi was paid a yearly salary of 300 livres. In the 1790's, the annual salary of rabbi Elie Ispir of Carpentras was 860 livres. Ph. Prévot, *A travers la carrière des Juifs d'Avignon* (Avignon, 5702), I, 10, 32, 37, II, 9.

VI. THE FIGHT FOR THE NATIONALIZATION OF THE DEBTS OWED BY THE COMMUNITY OF METZ

At the very beginning of the Revolution, while still fighting for emancipation the Jewish community of Metz promised to repay the debts owed to Christian creditors. A *Mémoire* of the community (1789), which has the character of a *cahier des doléances*, argued against an immediate dissolution of the Jewish community, because among other things, the repayment of its debts would be endangered. Later, when the Jews of Metz requested their nationalization the Christian creditors reminded them of their earlier promises to repay them. To this allegation the report of a special commission appointed by the Council of the Five Hundred (*Conseil des Cinq Cents*) replied that in the early days of the Revolution, when the Jews were still organized legally as autonomous communities, they could not have acted otherwise. At that time even the debts owed by non-Jewish corporate bodies had not yet been nationalized, and the Jews had no legal basis for requesting such action in relation to their own debts.[95]

By a law of May 20, 1791 the National Assembly referred all conflicts over the debts to the administration of the Metz district.[96] But four months later, on September 27, 1791, the Ashkenazic Jews were granted full citizenship and the autonomous Jewish communities were therefore dissolved. Nationalization of the debts owed by a dissolved corporate association then became a possible legal solution of the problem.

At first the Jews of Metz did not consider asking the government to nationalize their debts and repay their Christian creditors from public funds. In their petition to the National Convention they merely showed that the assets of the Jewish community (evaluated at 917,559 livres 7 s. 11 d.), were larger than the

---

[95] Isaac-Berr Bing, *op. cit.*, pp. 26–27; Déprille, p. 4 and Riou, p. 4 (see Bibliography, Nos. 28, 34).

[96] Decree of May 20, 1791 (see Bibliography, Nos. 19–21).

636

liabilities (365,000 livres). However, in the assets were included not only the synagogue and other communal real estate of the value of about 70,000 livres, but also unpaid taxes owed by local Jews and the provincial communities. The petition requested the Government to repay the debts from a fund to be set up from the proceeds of the sale of communal Jewish property and from the taxes to be collected from the Jews over a period of ten years. The basis for the request was that only penalties imposed in the name of the Republic for failure of Jews to pay taxes for the liquidation of the debts would be effective. Otherwise, the Jews would be forced to maintain their own syndics and tax collectors — and in effect recreate the dissolved Jewish communities. As a result unhealthy relations would develop between the Jews of Metz and those of the smaller communities and would perpetuate a spirit — or even fanatical and superstitious ideas — contrary to that of the new regime.

As we shall see in the following section, unlike the Jews of Metz, their coreligionists of Avignon, directly upon the dissolution of their community, called upon the Government to assume and repay the debts.[97] It was not until much later that such a request was also made by the Jews of Metz.[98]

[97] "Mais ce seroit rétablir une Corporation supprimée, renouer des relations continuelles entre les ci-devant juifs de Metz et ceux du plat pais; ces relations pouroient réveiller dans beaucoup de têtes l'esprit de corps si contraire à l'égalité, à la liberté; peut-être même des idées fanatiques et superstitieuses, et faire manquer, dans un coin de la France et pour un objet modique le but sacré de la révolution et de la loi salutaire qui a assimilé les juifs aux autres citoyens." "Pétition à la Convention N^{ale} pour les ci-devant Sindics et Elûs de la Ci-devant Communauté des Juifs de Metz" (JTS, 01530–1); *Petition*, pp. 17–19 (see Bibliography, No. 23); *Observations*, pp. 4–10 (see Bibliography, No. 85); Landmann (Co–5) mentioned a "Projet d'un état de l'actif de la ci-devant communauté, présenté à la Convention Nationale."

[98] Michel Wolf and Goudchaux Mayer Cahen were sent on missions to Paris to seek the nationalization of the debts. On July 1, 1792 Wolf was paid 85 francs for travel expenses and Cahen was paid 600 francs on Jan. 18 and 1,200 francs on Nov. 1, 1797 ("Bordereau des sommes payées par les ci-devant administrateurs de la Communauté des Juifs de Metz pour dépenses diverses à la charge de la dite Communauté." Documents, Metz No. 38, fol. 211). Goudchaux Mayer Cahen was the father of Jacob Aronssohn, who became a physician at the end of 1790. Carmoly, *Histoire des médecins . . .*, pp. 202–203.

How to avoid demands by creditors before nationalization of the debts was achieved, became a crucial problem.

Three Metz lawyers stated in a brief dated November 27, 1791 that since the debts were incurred as a result of the Brancas tax,[99] and with dissolution of the Jewish communities, the Jews could not be held responsible to the Christian creditors. The lawyers held that the Jews were individually in the same position as the inhabitants of Metz were in regard to debts contracted by the city of Metz. In order to avoid lawsuits by the creditors, while the question of the nationalization of the debts was pending, they advised the Jewish syndics to discontinue all their activities and to transfer the community's funds to the departmental authorities. The latter, they suggested, should prepare an inventory of the Jewish community's properties.[100]

[99] The Jews also argued on moral grounds for the nationalization of the debts, claiming that they were forced to borrow money as a result of various anti-Jewish restrictions (*Petition*, pp. 1–7, see Bibliography, No. 23).

[100] "Le Conseil soussigné qui a vue le décret [du 27 septembre 1791], non encore officielement connu, concernant les Juifs . . . estime qu'il n'est pas douteux que le premier et infaillible effet de la publication du décret, sera de dissoudre le régime actuel des Juifs de Metz, qui ont subsisté jusqu'à présent en corps de communauté, ayant une administration particulière, tant pour le spirituel que pour le temporel . . . Il sera prudent, par exemple de sitôt l'affiche et la publication du décret qui déclare les Juifs citoyens actifs [. . .], que les sindics et administrateurs cessent toutes fonctions actives et passives, en cette qualité. Qu'ils en préviennent sans délais M. le Procureur Général Sindic du département, auquel ils offriront les clefs de la caisse commune, en l'invitant par une pétition particulière, de requerir du Directoire la nomination d'un ou plusieurs commissaires, à l'effet d'arrêter leurs registres, et de faire l'inventaire des biens de la communauté . . ." Déliberé à Metz, le.27.9bre 1791" (Documents, Metz No. 7, fol. 37–38).

The brief was signed by the lawyers, Jean-Baptiste Juzan de la Tour, Baudesson and François Aubertin. Juzan de la Tour was a lawyer of the Metz Parliament from 1758 on, a member of the Patriotic Committee in 1789 and a judge of the criminal tribunal in 1792. Baudesson the elder was a judge of the civil tribunal during the Revolution. Aubertin was a lawyer of the Metz parliament from 1760 on. Emmanuel Michel, *Biographie du Parlement de Metz* (Metz, 1853); Paquet, I, 21, 36, 111, 303, 443, II, 1484.

Among the lawyers who were later consulted by the Jews of Metz were the famous Claude-François Chauveau-Lagarde (1765–1841) and Jean-Jacques-Régis de Cambacérès, who wrote two pamphlets in favor of the Jews' demand for the nationalization of the debts (see Bibliography, Nos. 29, 31). Chauveau-

The decree of September 27, 1791 granting citizenship to the Ashkenazic Jews was published in Metz on Sunday, December 15, 1791.[101] In accordance with the lawyers' advice the Jewish syndics sealed their office[102] and on the next day, December 16, requested the departmental *Directoire* to take over all the assets of the Jewish community and to appoint commissioners to draw up an inventory of communal Jewish properties.[103] Joseph Gougenheim and Goudchaux Mayer Cahen addressed a petition to the *Directoire* in the name of the former syndics of the Jewish community. They stated that the most natural consequence of the decree of September 27 was to abolish the "political body" (*Corps politique*) and the autonomous "administrative system" which the Jews had formed.

In general the Christian creditors of the Metz Jews did not favor assumption of the latter's debts by the government, although on one occasion they did so.[104] To begin with, the creditors had little faith that the government would repay them and later they were alarmed by the prospect of being repaid in *assignats* (paper money).

It seems also that at first the local civil authorities of Metz

Lagarde was appointed by the revolutionary courts-of-laws to defend Francisco-Antonio-Gabriel Miranda, Marie-Antoinette, Charlotte Corday and Mme. Elisabeth. During the Terror he was himself arrested. E. Pascallet, *Notice biographique sur M. Claude-François Chauveau-Lagarde* (n. p., n. d.). 29 pp.; Doublet de Boisthibault, *Chauveau-Lagarde* (Chartres, 1841). 8 pp.; Vital Pillore, *Eloge de M. Chauveau-Lagarde* (Toulouse, 1854). 29 pp.; L. Aimé-Martin, *Quelques esquisses de la vie judiciare de M. Chauveau-Lagarde*. Extrait de *Journal des Débats* (Paris, 1841). For other pamphlets by J.-F. Chauveau-Lagarde on Jews see Emancipation, Nos. 198, 200; Napoleonica, No. 425.

[101] "dimanche dernier, le décret qui les déclare citoyens actifs ... a été rendu public par la voie de l'impression et de l'affiche" (in the Jewish memorandum of Dec. 16, 1791. Paquet, II, 1087). We did not find any Metz edition of the decree of Sept. 27, 1791. See Emancipation, Nos. 180–81.

[102] "... la chambre sindicale qu'ils ont fermée à l'instant de la publication du décret qui a mis les Juifs au rang des Citoyens" (from the departmental *Directoire*'s decision of Feb. 7, 1792. Documents, Metz, No. 52, fol. 520–39).

[103] Netter, 126–27 (see Bibliography, No. 143). The inventory of communal properties was drawn up by the notary Conflans from March 22 through December 12, 1792 (*Compte*, p. 4, see Bibliography, No. 39).

[104] *Précis* (see Bibliography, No. 28); Paquet, II, 1415.

unofficially favored the nationalization of the debts. On January 11, 1792 the general council of the Metz district stated that only by eliminating the council of Jewish communities would it be possible to improve the Jews' morals, and their usurious practices and defeat the rabbis' superstitious influence. Should the government not assume the debts, the Jewish community of Metz and its organic ties with the other communities of the province would continue, in spite of the law abolishing these communities.[105] The departmental *Directoire* acted as if it had already been decided to treat the debts as national debts. But on January 4, 1792 the city council took a stand against nationalization, because the creditors would no longer have anyone to dun for payment. The city officials manoeuvred to postpone the decision until the National Assembly could rule on the question. They also insisted that the former syndics of the Jewish community should be forced to remain in office and be authorized to collect taxes and to repay debts, and that no Jew should be allowed to move to another community before paying one eighth of his fortune as his contribution toward paying off the debts. A formal request was made to the *Directoire* to prevent a premature dissolution of the Jewish community (*à empêcher cette société de se dissolve prématurement*). On January 14, the *Directoire* of the Metz district approved the city council's resolution of January 4 and on February 7, 1792 the departmental *Directoire* authorized the continuation of the special tax imposed by the Jewish community for repayment of debts.[106]

The Jews did not give up. They asked the *Société populaire* of Metz to help them gain nationalization of the debts and protested against being forced to continue the financial activities of

[105] AN, D–III–174.

[106] "Et jusqu'a ce que l'Assemblée Nationale ait prononcé, d'enjoindre aux cy devant sindics de continuer leur gestion par recette et dépense ... D'ordonner, en autre, que les mêmes ci devant sindics seront tenûs de s'opposer, de tout leur pouvoir, et à peine d'une responsabilité personnelle à ce qu'aucun juif n'abandonne son domicile en cette ville, en transportant son mobilier, qu'il n'ait satisfait aux obligations qui lui étoient imposées par la cy devant communauté, c'est, à dire qu'il n'ait remis à la caisse le huitième de sa fortune pour l'acquit de sa portion contingente dans la dette commune." See also Paquet, II, 1087–88.

their dissolved community.[107] But the local law-court ordered them to elect five syndics, who should direct the liquidation of the debts. The Jews were then forced to appoint (in January 1792) a commission for the purpose of levying taxes and repaying the debts.[108] The "citizens of the former Jewish community of Metz" (*Les citoyens composant la cy devant communauté des juifs de Metz*) were called by a town crier to assemble on April 26, 1792. To the presidium of the meeting were elected: Mayer Godchaux as president, Joseph Lévi as secretary, Marchand Mayence, Mayeur Hayem Bingue and Moyse Gompertz. At the first meeting, with ninety-seven voters present, only two Jews won election as syndics: Marchand Mayence obtained fifty-one votes and Louis-Isaac Cain forty-nine. It was then necessary to call another meeting on April 27 at which Louis [-Moyse] Gompertz was elected, winning thirty-three votes of the fifty-six cast. As the second meeting also could not complete the election of the syndics, a third meeting was called on April 28 at which Aron-Marx Lévy and Mayeur-Louis Schaube [Schwabe] were elected.[109]

[107] "A la difference de toutes les autres Corporations la Ci-devant Communauté des Juifs de Metz, quoique formellement supprimée par les loix comme Corporation a cependant été obligé de conserver la gestion de ses propriétés foncières et mobilaires, avec toutes les charges dont elles sont grevées. Cette distinction n'aurait certainement pas eu lieu sous le régime de l'égalité, si elle eut été bien connu des Législateurs .... La ci-devant Communauté est prête d'abandonner tout son actif, la Nation doit le prendre pour son compte, ainsi que son passif. Qu'on ne crye pas qu'il existe une grande disporportion entre l'un et l'autre, au contraire le premier offre des grandes ressources, et le second ne consiste qu'en rentes viagères dont les titulaires sont pour la plupart très vieux, mais ces ressources deviendroient nulles si elles restoient entre les mains qui faute de lieu et d'assemblée n'ont plus ni le droit ni les facultés de les faire valoir" (Undated petition by the Jews of Metz to the *Société populaire*, JTS, No. 01565). It is possible that the petition was written by a Jewish Jacobin. On Jews in the Jacobin Club of Metz see L. Bultinghaire, *Le Club des Jacobins de Metz* (Paris, 1906), p. 101; Z. Szajkowski, "Gli Ebrei nei club dei Giacobini durante la rivoluzione francese del 1789." *La Rassegna Mensile di Israel*, XXIV, No. 7 (1958), 299. The Jews stated that because of their emancipation they had lost all "common means" to pay their debts, *i. e.*, the right to levy taxes (*Resumé*, pp. 1, 6–7, see Bibliography, No. 31).

[108] AN, D–III–174.

[109] Minutes of the elections, Apr. 26–27, 1792 (Documents, Metz, No. 5, fol. 23–28).

VII. THE FIGHT FOR THE NATIONALIZATION OF THE DEBTS OWED BY THE COMMUNITIES OF THE FORMER PAPAL PROVINCE

Reference was made earlier to the request of the Jews of the former papal province for the nationalization of the debts owed by their former communities, although during the Revolution they continued for a while to pay annuities to creditors.[110]

On the whole, the Jews, far from favoring, openly opposed the nationalization of their communal properties in order to repay the debts, although on one occasion, in a petition to the Convention for the nationalization of their debts, the Jews of Avignon declared themselves ready to give up their synagogue inasmuch as God does not reside in temples.[111] Still, most communal properties of the four communities in the former papal province were nationalized. This fact was constantly cited by the Jews as an argument in favor of the government's assumption of their debts.

On April 18, 1795 the Legislative Committee (*Comité de Législation*) of the National Convention ordered all judicial

---

[110] Calvet, 2104, No. 880 (124 livres paid on Feb. 29, 1792 by the community of Avignon to a creditor). The community of Carpentras paid annuities during the entire revolutionary period, e. g. 20,167 livres to four creditors from Jan. 19 to Feb. 1, 1792 (Columbia, X893C–C322, vols. 4, 8, 10).

[111] Calvet, 4340, fol. 67. The Avignon Jews petitioned the Prefect in 1817 that they "ont vu envahir par la nation tous les biens de la Communauté de leurs pères ... Et qu'on ne vous dise pas, Mr. le préfet, qu'en ce moment nous possédont un de nos anciens temples. Le local ou nous pratiquons nos cérémonies religieuses est une propriété nationale. On nous a permis de la consacrer à notre culte, mais elle ne nous appartient pas ... section des contributions foncières, section dite de l'Egalité, lettre No. 795, justifient ce fait important" ... (Documents, Comtat, No. 1, fol. 2). The Jewish cemetery of Avignon was sold on March 24, 1796 for the sum of 1,188 francs (Documents, Comtat, No. 6, fol. 36, No. 7, fol. 38). In 1817 the seven Jewish families who remained in L'Isle-sur-Sorgue wrote to the authorities: "la révolution, les excès populaires, les ordres des autorités départementales ont envahi, dissipé, on détruit ces trésors, ces temples, cette Communauté" (AN, F–19–1847). According to an inventory of 1816 the revolutionary regime confiscated from the Carpentras synagogues objects valued at 44,465 livres (Columbia, X893C–C22, vol. 1).

procedures over the debts to stop temporarily until the Convention would come to a decision on this matter. In spite of this order the widow of Pierre-Louis Chalertan of Lyons, one of the creditors, requested 10,000 livres from the Avignon Jews for unpaid annuities. In rejecting the plaintiff's request, on April 28, 1795 the tribunal of the district of Avignon was guided by the spirit of the decision of the Legislative Committee.[112]

The question of the Avignon debts was again debated on March 12, 1799 by the second section of the *Tribunal civil* of the Vaucluse department (the former papal province). The substitute to the government's commissioner stated in a memorandum submitted to the tribunal that the Jews were never organized as a corporate body and that their communal properties were nationalized by mistake. The Jews were represented by F.-R.-Ch.-J. Cottier who requested the tribunal to delay a decision until the legislative authorities would rule on nationalizing the Jews' debts. The judge stated that while the Jews did form a *corps de communauté*, which was approved by the government of the old regime and whose communal properties were nationalized by the Revolution, the merit of the Jews' demand for the nationalization of the debts had still to be considered by the legislative authorities. In the meantime the judicial authorities could not anticipate a future decision by the legislative authorities. The judges then ordered the Jews to pay only annuities for non-transferable principal of the debts. The request for payment of annuities for transferable principal was rejected with the proviso that the ruling could be appealed after the legislative authorities would reach a decision.[113]

[112] *Extrait* . . . Apr. 8, 1795 (see Bibliography, No. 87); Documents, Comtat, No. 4, fol. 22–31.

[113] Documents, Comtat, No. 3, fol. 6–21. François-Régis-Charles-Joseph Cottier was a lawyer and highly placed official of Comtat. On July 21, 1790 he became one of the eight members of the provisional superior tribunal. In the year VI he was a judge of the civil tribunal of Carpentras and in the years VII–VIII its president. Cottier was the author of many historical studies, including *Notice historique sur la ville de Carpentras* (Carpentras, 1827), 172 pp., in which he wrote favorably about the Jews. See Barjavel, I, 409–413. Cottier was the author of *Dialogue* [Carpentras, 1789], a 15 pp. pamphlet on the emigration of the Jews from Carpentras. Another pamphlet on the same subject, *L'Enfant du patriotisme* [Carpentras, 1789], 13 pp., by Cottier-Julian, was much more favorably inclined toward Jews. See also note 312.

VIII. THE ATTITUDE OF THE GOVERNMENT TOWARD THE JEWS' DEMANDS FOR THE NATIONALIZATION OF THE DEBTS

In October 1790 the National Assembly dissolved the *corporations*, including religious communities;[114] their debts were assumed by the Government by the decrees of June 14 and July 30, 1791 and by the law of August 15, 1793. At that time the debts owed by the Catholic Church were estimated to be 140 million livres by Necker, the Finance Minister, and 130 million livres by Marquis A.-P. de Montesquiou-Fezensac. According to the latter estimate institutions had accumulated 45 million livres of the Catholic debt, individuals 85 million livres. The clergy claimed that the debt had been incurred because of huge sums paid by the Church to the government. Later Jews, like the Catholics, also argued that their debts were incurred in order to pay huge sums in taxes and bribes.[115]

It seemed then only a matter of time until the government would accept the demand of the dissolved Jewish communities that their debts be nationalized. But the eventuality was not so simple. At first the legislative, judicial and executive authorities were unwilling to speak out openly for or against the nationalization of the debts owed by the Jews and all decisions taken on this matter were of a temporary character.

Discussions concerning the debts in the first years of the Revolution had no effect on the outcome of the Jewish fight for emancipation. The civil authorities of Carpentras stated on October 14, 1791 that the Jews could not be refused full citizenship for not paying their debts, since they had not been declared bankrupt. The Jews as a body were no longer organized for political ends, but to fulfill civil obligations (*i. e.*, to repay the debts).[116]

---

[114] On the abolition of the *corporations* during the Revolution see Fr. Olivier-Martin, *L'organisation corporative de la France d'ancien régime* (Paris, 1938), pp. 541–57.

[115] A. Denys-Buirette, *Les questions religieuses dans les cahiers de 1789* (Paris, 1919), pp. 108–125.

[116] Am Carpentras, Rév. 45, p. 191, 199.

The prospects for nationalization of the debts were, however, injured by the fact that emancipation and dissolution of the Jewish communities did not take place until September 27, 1791.

No special law was enacted regarding the dissolution of the Jewish communities and the nationalization of their properties. The decree of September 27, 1791 on Jewish emancipation applied to a particular case. Of course, the decrees of June 14 and July 30, 1791 and the law of August 15, 1793 on the dissolution of all corporate bodies made no reference to Jewish communities. When their creditors seized on this point the Jews of Metz replied that the general law of 1793 on the dissolution of corporate bodies applied also to the Jewish communities, even though they were not mentioned by name. They also noted that the Republic could not tolerate the continued existence of Jewish communities in view of the general law of 1793.[117]

Nevertheless, on December 6, 1797 the Council of the Five Hundred decided that the Jewish communities were not included in the dissolution order of the laws on communities and other corporate bodies. The Council also decided that the laws on communities and the sale of the properties of these dissolved associations were not applicable to the dissolved Jewish communities.[118] As late as on March 30, 1801 this argument of the creditors was the basis for the rejection by the Moselle prefecture of a petition by Samuel Hayem Worms, Lyon Worms and other Jews against the special tax to repay the debts of the Jews. The prefecture ruled that the decree of September 27, 1791, which abolished the Jewish communities, had no retroactive effect with respect to nationalization of their debts.[119] As late as in the

---

[117] *Consultation*, p. 4 and *Résumé*, p. 4 (see Bibliography, Nos. 29, 31).

[118] Valabrègue, p. 7 (see Bibliography, No. 146).

[119] ". . . les décrets du 14 Juin et 30 Juillet 1791, d'après lesquels toutes Corporations ont été abolies, n'offrent dans leurs dispositions, rien de relatif aux Juifs; que la raison de ce silence est facile à concevoir, à expliquer; c'est que les Juifs ne formoient pas à proprement parler, une communauté d'habitans français; mais qu'ils étoient une classe d'hommes, une étrangère dans l'état où ils étoient tolérés, sans qu'ils puissent espèrer au droit de cité que depuis la Révolution, ils ont sollicités et dont, après plusieurs ajournement succesifs, il leur a été permis de jouir par la loi du 27 7bre 1791, à condition qu'ils préteroient le serment civique; d'où sort la conséquence que, jusqu'à cette époque, ils n'avoient participé en rien, aux avantages de la Révolution, et que

1820's the Vaucluse deputy, Forbin des Issarts, repeated the same argument.[120]

Most syndics of the Jewish communities underwrote the loans granted by Christian creditors. They naturally desired to be relieved of personal responsibility for the debts and, accordingly, perhaps, they did not always wait for the nationalization of the debts. On the other hand they were up against a wall of prejudices, a well organized campaign conducted by the creditors and a mass of complicated legal factors. The Jews of Metz stated that their creditors would profit from the nationalization of the debts inasmuch as the Jewish co-signers could not be held judicially responsible.[121] This was hardly the case. According to the creditors the guarantors were personally responsible,[122] and they warned that if the Jewish communities should refuse to discharge the debts the courts would enforce payment by the underwriters or their heirs. The syndics and their heirs protested against such action by the creditors, but there was little reason to expect that the debtors' cause would prevail after long and expensive lawsuits. In fact, occasionally the courts did order the co-signers to repay the debts. The only hope for the syndics then remained not in the expensive and doubtful outcome of the lawsuits, but in a general decision on the governmental level in favor of nationalization of the debts.

This was the policy not alone of the leadership of the Jewish communities but also of the government itself, although for different reasons. In a report submitted in 1807 to Napoleon I,

les réformes par elle introduits, leur avoient été étrangères; que c'est donc uniquement des expressions de cette dernière Loi, qu'il convient de partir, pour bien déterminer les effets que la Révolution a du produire à leurs égards et les changements qu'elle a du apporter à leur état" (Documents, Metz, No. 44, fol. 261).

[120] "La communauté fut dissoute, mais les engagemens vis-à-vis des tiers ne purent l'être, la loi aurait eu un effet rétroactif impossible ou à supposer." Forbin des Issarts, p. 5 (see Bibliography, No. 107).

[121] *Résumé*, pp. 8–9 (see Bibliography, No. 31).

[122] [François-Balthazar] Darracq, *Opinion de Darracq dans l'affaire des Juifs de Bordeaux, Séance du 18 Floréal an 7* [7 Mai 1799] (Paris, an 7), p. 20 ("des sommes empruntées, non pas tant par la *nation juive* mais par quelques *Juifs* individuellement, & avec OBLIGATION PERSONNELLE"). On Darracq see G. Cabannes, *Galerie des Landais* (n. p., n. d.) I, 103–04; NBG, XIII (1855), 130–31.

the government recognized that the debts owed by the Jews of the Italian States were a result of anti-Jewish restrictions during the old regime. Still, the Jews were forced to repay and the authorities favored the settling the debts by a decree rather than through judicial channels. The Jewish communities were officially dissolved and a court would have been unable to appoint a commission for the purpose of collecting taxes for the liquidation of the debts.[123]

In the former papal province the policy of the Christian creditors was from the beginning to sue first the individual Jewish guarantors and then their heirs. This procedure was, most probably, adopted as a result of Jewish emigration from the province during the course of which most rich guarantors left their communities. A group of seven creditors of the Jewish community of Carpentras sued Jassé-Haïn Crémieu, son of the rich former syndic Jassuda-David Crémieu, who was the guarantor for many loans contracted by the former Jewish community. Crémieu was naturalized as a French citizen and settled in 1785 in Arles. In the year VII his son argued that the naturalization released his father and heirs from any individual responsibility to the creditors of the Jewish community of Carpentras. This argument was so weak that Jassé-Haïn Crémieu was ready to turn over to the seven creditors six houses valued before 1789 at 40,000 livres which he owned in the Carpentras ghetto.[124] Anyway, as long as the former leaders of the Jewish community or their heirs were held individually responsible by the courts of the revolutionary regime for the community's debts, their effort to liquidate the debts through special taxes was morally correct.

[123] AN, F–19–1847.

[124] *Mémoire pour . . . Crémieu*, pp. 5, 15, 30 (see Bibliography No. 89). On the eve of the Revolution J.-D. Crémieu signed himself "négociant juif de Carpentras, citoyen de la ville d'Arles" (Ad Vaucluse, Martin's notarial minutes, 1789, No. 1305, fol. 47). In 1790 Crémieu appraised his own property at 329,693 livres (*ibid.*, 1790, No. 1310, fol. 146). For Crémieu's act of naturalization as a French citizen see *Lettres patentes du Roi, portant naturalisation du Sr. Jassuda David Crémieu, natif de la ville de Carpentras . . . Négociant Juif en la ville d'Arles, de sa femme & de leur descendans naturels & légitimes, qui leur permettent de demeurer dans le Royaume, d'y vivre & trafiquer . . . à la charge par ledit Jassuda David Crémieu de donner, suivant ses offres, une somme de 3000 liv . . . .* (Aix, 1785). 10 pp. (Calvet).

IX. THE ABSENCE OF JEWISH CREDITORS

The historian, S. Posener, characterized the loans granted by Christians to Jewish communities as "business relations with the surrounding non-Jewish world, thus performing a valuable social function in the national economy."[125] Of course, Christian institutions and individuals with large capital sums were eager to find Jewish borrowers. Not only Jewish communities, but even individual Jews borrowed money from Christians in exchange for pensions and annuities.[126] But these financial relations between Christian creditors and Jewish communities boded ill for the latter. The Jewish communities borrowed the money because they had no other choice.

This raises another problem. Why did the Jewish communities borrow money from Christians and not from Jews?[127] Jassuda-David Crémieu, to whom reference has been made, helped obtain loans for the Jewish community of Carpentras from Christians, but he himself was a very rich man. According to a notarial act of April 15, 1790 he placed a value of 398,224 livres upon his possessions (two houses in Carpentras valued at 5,000 livres; two houses in Avignon — 3,000 livres; a property in Arles — 34,000 livres; furniture and other house items — 300 livres; the rest in cash and promissory notes).[128] Individual Jews did borrow from Jewish money lenders. A large percentage of lawsuits at the commercial tribunal of Strasbourg involved Jewish creditors and their Jewish debtors,[129] and the same situation prevailed in other provinces. As we shall see, the Sephardic *Nation* of Bordeaux did borrow money from Jewish creditors,

[125] S. Posener, "The Social Life . . .," 210.
[126] Chobaut, *op. cit.*, CI, 15.
[127] Chobaut writes of the debts owed by the communities of the papal province: *le plus souvent aux chrétiens* (*op. cit.*, CI, 23), without naming even one Jewish creditor.
[128] Ad Vaucluse, E. Martin's notarial minutes, No. 3110, fol. 146, Apr. 15, 1790.
[129] Ad Lower Rhine, 122–L–1–8.

647

but as a result of special circumstances. Otherwise Jews borrowed from Christians.

One of the reasons that the Jewish communities borrowd only from Christian creditors was that loans from Christians were available for very long periods and could be transformed into *rentes* (annuities). Most Jewish creditors were themselves debtors[130] and thus could not lend for long periods large sums which did not belong to them.

Although *rentes* were the most profitable and secure way of money-lending, this field of credit operation was closed to most Jews in France. No special laws existed prohibiting *rentes* as a form of money-lending by Jews in Alsace, Metz, or Lorraine. But there did exist many restrictions not connected directly with *rentes*, which in effect achieved that end, e. g. the laws restricting the size of loans that Jews could grant, the prohibition against produce as security or as interest on loans granted by Jews, etc. In a memorandum of 1717 the Alsatian Jews stated that their income from granting loans was restricted because in Alsace loans were repaid mostly with produce and Jews could not profit from this form of repayment. On September 12, 1709 the Intendant of Metz, de Saint-Contest, wrote to the *Contrôleur général de finances* that Jews did not hold *rentes*. In a memorandum of 1711 the Jews of Metz stated that they were not allowed to trade in *rentes*. The Jews of Avignon and Comtat Venaissin were also not permitted to trade in *rentes*.[131] But there were no

---

[130] *EcSt*, pp. 87–91 (Jews as intermediaries for Christian creditors).

[131] In 1497–1506, Jews were allowed only chattels as security for loans in the seigniory of Ribeaupierre. Orders of 1520 and 1530 prohibited the use of crops as guarantee for loans obtained from Jews. Only old debts could be repaid to Jews with wine, at the highest market price. "Aucun Juif ne prêtera à un bourgeois, soit à sa sollicitation ou autrement sur un bien en fond ou sur la maison ou vendange ... Les Juifs ne prêteront à qui que ce soit autrement que sur des gages mobiliaires" (Ad HR, E699). *Mémoire pour les Juifs établis en Alsace* (n. p., [1717]), p. 4. "... Ils [les Juifs de Metz] y portent toujours de l'argent, et n'ayant ni charges, ni terres, ni maisons, ni rentes, il falloit nécessairement que tout leur argent roulât dans le commerce." A. M. Boislisle, P. de Brotonne, *Correspondance des contrôleurs généraux des finances avec des intendants des Provinces* (Paris, 1897), III, 206. But Jews were frequently intermediaries in investing money in stocks for Christian capitalists. In the 1720's Nathan de Morhange of Metz was given 20,000 livres by Collart, an attorney at the Paris Parliament, in order to establish

such restrictions on the Sephardic Jews of Bordeaux and Saint-Esprit.[131a]

In a memorandum of July 1789 addressed to the King, the Alsatian Jews pointed out that a project to convert the debts owed them into *rentes* was not workable, since the peasants owed Jewish creditors small sums. Jews would be unable to trade *rentes* in such small sums because they would not be accepted by bankers and merchants and because the expense of selling them in distant cities would be as great as the entire value of these small *rentes*. Only big capitalists could afford to convert their capital into *rentes*, but Jews made only small loans.[132] On the other hand the exclusion of the Jews from the trade in *rentes* was in other respects a blessing, because it lessened the possibility of dispossession or exile of the Jews. In April 1702 de Saint-Contest, intendant of Metz, declared himself against a proposed expulsion of Jews from the province of Metz, because the Jews possessed only cash and promissory notes and, if they should leave with these assets, the province would suffer from lack of cash.[133]

a *rente* for the latter (". . . il avoit assez de crédit pour faire placer ces effets en rente viagère." Arsenal, 10738). "D'ailleurs ils sont encore taxez comme aiséz pour acquerir des rentes, quoiqu'ils n'en ayent pas la faculté." (Landmann, Ce 259); "La Constitution de pensions perpétuelles leur étant deffendue il leur est moins avantageux de prêter à jour quoique à un fond plus haut" (a document of Carpentras, AIU, R43, No. 96). During the year 1785, Jewish merchants and creditors of Carpentras granted seven hundred sixty-one loans to Christian creditors. Almost all of these loans consisted of small sums, which in most cases had resulted from credit sales by the Jewish merchants (Ad Vaucluse, E 46). Of 446 debts owed to Jews in the district (*subdélégation*) of Belfort (Alsace), only 9 were of 1,000 livres or more each; 96 debts were of less than 100 livres each. (According to a register of 1780, compiled in connection with the Affair of counterfeit receipts. Ad HR, varia).

[131a] Abraham Furtado, e. g., was the recepient of a yearly *rente* of 210 livres (Am Bx. Revolutionary period, P 8).

[132] "Ce sont les capitalistes embarrassés de leurs richesses, qui placent à constitution, et pour avoir leur argent, il faut leur offrir à la fois de fortes valeurs et de grands avantages" (Am Stg, AA2394).

[133] Guerre, A-1-1583, Nos. 68, 73, 2679, Nos. 75–76, 79; *EcSt*, pp. 83–87. The statement made by the historian, Raphael Mahler, that Jewish creditors received interest in products (*op. cit.*, I, 168) is completely contrary to the facts. See also the author's review of R. Mahler's book, in *Yivo Bleter*, XLI (1957–58), 348–55 (in Yiddish).

Contemporary opinion did not always attribute the debts to the heavy taxes during the old regime. On April 7, 1799 the anti-Jewish minded deputy to the Council of the Five Hundred, J.-F. Darracq, stated that the Jewish communities of Metz and Avignon had borrowed the money for business purposes.[134] In 1801 the author of a Metz memorandum also stated that the Jewish community had borrowed the money for business speculation.[135] On March 29, 1819 the Minister of the Interior reported incorrectly to the King that the Jewish community of Metz had borrowed the money during the old regime for religious purposes.[136] In 1820 the creditors of the Comtadin Jews stated that the former Jewish communities had borrowed money in order to purchase houses.[137] The same explanation of the debts was presented in a prefectural report at the beginning of the 19th century.[138]

[134] ". . . les fonds qui leur avoient été prêtes avoient servi non-seulement à payer leurs *taxes communes d'hospitalité*, mais encore à réaliser leurs spéculations particulières, à étandre leur commerce, à centupler leurs riches mobilières . . ." (Darracq, *op. cit.*, pp. 15, 17).

[135] ". . . la contribution Villars n'a été que le prétexte et le·manteau qui couvrait la bourse commune, le monde de piété, établi pour l'avantage de toute la Corporation . . . il peut donc déjà passer pour certain que la dette ne résulte ni de la contribution Villars, ni de étrennes aux puissants de Metz, mais uniquement d'emprunts faits pour alimenter le fond commun qui faisoit la ressource de tous le chefs de familles de la Corporation, et à l'aide du quel elle augmentoit son agiotage . . . Le mont de piété prétoit à ceux de la Nation juive domiciliés dans la Généralité, pour soutenir le commerce de l'emprunteur, ou pour faire face à des engagements actuels qui excédoient ses moïens. . . . Enfin le mont de piété donnait encore l'avantage d'établir les enfans de famille par le mariage" ("Mon opinion développe et discutée sur la prétention des jeunes gens juifs contre les anciens," an unsigned memorandum of March 30, 1801. Documents, Metz, No. 6, fol. 31–36).

[136] "elle avait emprunté le capital pour le service de son culte" (AN, F-19-1848).

[137] "Pour l'achat des maisons, pour la construction de leur Temple, pour les frais de leur Culte . . ." (*Observations*, p. 3, see Bibliography, No. 104).

[138] Documents, Comtat, No. 21, fol. 69. The Jews did borrow large sums for the reconstruction of synagogues. The Carpentras community borrowed 12,000 livres for this purpose on June 20, 1741, May 16, 1742 and Apr. 30, 1743. Similarly, on Sept. 25, 1771 the Cavaillon community borrowed for this purpose 6,000 livres (Ad Vaucluse, annex of Carpentras, reg. prov. 23, fol. 145, 227, 327 and Guis' notarial minutes, 327, fol. 652).

It is true that in Poland the elders of the Jewish communities borrowed from Christian creditors at about a 7 per cent interest rate and lent the money to Jewish business men at a much higher rate. There was a similar development in Rome.[139] But there is no proof whatever that borrowing for business purposes was the source of the debts of the Jewish communities in France.

[139] Salo W. Baron, *The Jewish Community* (Philadelphia, 1942), III, 191–92. On the debts owed by the Jewish communities of Poland and the German States see Baron, *op. cit.*; Judyta Freylich, "The Problem of Liquidating the Debts of the Community of Kazimierz after the Third Partition (1795–1809)." *Miesięcznik żydowski*, III–1 (1933), 467–78 (in Polish); I. Galant, "The Indebtedness of the Jewish Communities in the Seventeenth Century." *Evreiskaya Starina*, VI (1913), 129–32 (in Russian); Dr. J. Landsberger, "Schulden der Judenschaft in Polen." *Jahrbuch der Jüdisch-Literarischen Gesellschaft*, VI (1909), 252–79; Manfred Laubert, "Die Schuldenregulierung der jüdischen Korporationen in der Provinz Posen." *MGWJ*, LXVII (1924), 321–31; David Kaufmann, "Die Schuldennot der Gemeinde Posen während des Rabbinates R. Isak b. Abrahams (1668–1685)." *MGWJ*, XXXIX (1895), 38–46, 91–96; S. Rothschild, *Die Abgaben und die Schulden Last der Wormser jüdischen Gemeinde 1563–1854* (Worms, 1925); Dr. J. Schipper, "The Financial Collapse of the Central and Provincial Autonomy of Jews in the Old Poland (1650–1764)." *Ekonomishe Schriftn*, II (Wilno, 1932), 1–19 (in Yiddish).

X. THE REPORTS PRESENTED TO THE COUNCIL OF THE FIVE HUNDRED

Many influential personalities favored the nationalization of the debts owed by the Jewish communities.

The Council of the Five Hundred appointed a special commission to report on the requests of the Jews of Avignon and of Metz for the nationalization of their debts. The commission was composed of Henri-Baptiste Grégoire (1750–1831); Jacques-Henri Laurenceot (1763–1833); Haycinthe-Adrien-Joseph Chapuy [Chappuis] (1764–1817), and Jean-Baptiste-Michel Saladin (1752–1812).[140] But the commission did not meet regularly and its report, which was in favor of the Jews, was never presented to the Council. The Council then appointed a second commission composed of Grégoire, Chappuis, Saladin, Pierre-Florent Louvet (1757–1818) and Joseph-François Baron de Beyts (1763–1832).[141] On August 24, 1797 Saladin presented to the Council the report of the commission. It held that the laws

[140] Grégoire was the well known fighter for Jewish emancipation. Laurenceot was a lawyer, a moderate in politics. While on a mission to the Cher department he helped the Catholics reinforce their position. Chappuis, born in Carpentras, was a former abbot who favored the new regime and became a Carpentras official. He probably knew the situation of the Jews from his experience in Carpentras. Saladin, a lawyer and adversary of the clergy, voted for the death sentence for Louis XVI, but was later in contact with counter-revolutionary elements. Kuscinski, II, 371, 553–54; Robert, II, 48; Th. Lemas, "Les représentants du peuple Cherrier et Laurenceot en mission dans le Cher après le 9 Thermidor." *RF*, XXIV (1893), 272–83, 289–303. At the beginning of the Revolution it did not occur to Grégoire that the debts of the Jewish communities could be liquidated by having the government take them over. In 1789 he wrote that the Jews who emigrated from Metz would have to contribute funds for the repayment of the community's debts. However, the Jews themselves had not yet conceived the plan of liquidating the debts through nationalization. H.-B. Grégoire, *Motion en faveur des Juifs . . .* (Paris, 1789), pp. 33–34.

[141] Louvet was a Paris lawyer and moderate politician. During the Thermidor he defended persecuted republicans. In the Council of the Five Hundred he often reported on taxes and other financial matters. Beyts was a deputy from Belgium. In the Council he spoke out against the Terror in Alsace, but he also favored the exclusion of noblemen from administrative offices. Kuscinski, II, 419; Robert, I, 312.

on the dissolution of *corporations* and nationalization of their properties and debts applied also to the Jewish communities. To act otherwise would be unconstitutional inasmuch as the Jews could reorganize themselves in *corporations*. It would also be impracticable because of the impossibility of returning to the Jews those units of their communal property which had been nationalized and sold. The Republic — the report stated — "elevated the Jews to the status of French citizens, she cannot now degrade them." But the Council did not act on Saladin's report. A third commission to report on the debts, which was appointed by the Council of the Five Hundred, was composed of Grégoire, Laurenceot, Saladin and Chappuis. On April 5, 1797 Chappuis presented a report to the Council urging the nationalization of the debts. Chappuis elaborated the point that if the Jews would be forced to levy taxes to repay their debts they would have to reconstitute their former separate communities. Again the Council did not act and the commission's report was tabled. Later the Council appointed a fourth commission composed of Beyts, Chappuis, Louvet, Grégoire and François-Marie-Joseph Riou de Kersalaun (1765–1811), a lawyer of Brest.[142] On November 24, 1797 Riou reported that the commission rejected the arguments of the Christian creditors and favored the nationalization of the debts owed by the Jews of Metz and Avignon. Riou stated that the existence of the debts gave the impression that the political life of these emancipated Jews was impermanent. As the law of 1793 did not except the former Jewish communities, there was no reason for the government not to assume their debts. Otherwise the unity of the Republic would be broken, the constitution violated; there would exist a class of citizens, with religious ties who would be united even more closely by political ties. They would have communal debts, tax-collectors, agents, communal properties, they would therefore form anew a real *corporation*. The report therefore supported nationalization of the debts.[143]

In the end the debts were not taken over by the government and this created a confused situation. The refusal to nationalize

---

[142] On Riou, see P.-J. Levot, *Biographie bretonne* (Vannes, 1852–57), II, 714–16.

[143] Reports of Chappuis, Saladin and Riou (see Bibliography, Nos. 32–34).

the debts owed by the Jewish communities was the result of a short-sighted policy. It is also possible that this policy expressed a well organized opposition to Jewish emancipation. A memorandum of the Jewish community of Metz complained that people of the old regime were appointed to settle the question of the debts.[144]

Economic reasons also influenced the decision not to nationalize the debts. The Christian creditors supported the view that since the sum owed to them by the Jews was much larger than the value of the communal Jewish properties,[145] assuming the debts would involve the French nation in the loss of a large sum. To this the Jews of Metz replied that it would be insulting for "a miserable calculation of finances" to deter the government from nationalizing these debts. Chappuis also stated in his report to the Council of the Five Hundred that the law on the nationalization of the debts of the dissolved *corporations* was not based on financial considerations; it was not a fiscal edict. The law reflected a more important consideration — the union of all Frenchmen in a social order with liberty. But the powerful Committee of Finances thought otherwise, namely, that the nationalization of these debts would be ruinous to the Republic's finances. The Committee decided that it would be better to discontinue the nationalization of communal Jewish properties and to let the Jews themselves liquidate the debts they owed.[146]

[144] "Des gens de l'ancien régime ont été chargés des intérêts réciproques des parties, ils ont fait des volumes d'écritures" (JTS, 01565).

[145] The same situation prevailed in other countries. "The problem of liquidating their debts offered a formidable obstacle to Jewish emancipation . . . by 1800, the indebtedness of the community of Worms was six times larger than the comulative value of all communal property" (Baron, *op. cit.*, II, 274).

[146] "Quoi! vous vous êtes chaigés, sans examen, de payer les dettes des pénitens de toutes les couleurs, dont la plupart n'avoient pour hypothèques que des collectes éventuelles, & vous refuseriez d'acquitter celles dont le gage est entre vos mains! La loi qui a prononcé la suppression des communautés n'auroit donc eu pour base qu'un intérêt pécuniaire? Ce n'étoit donc qu'un édit bursal? Ah! craignons de nous arrêter sur une pareille idée; ne dégradons pas les vues élevées qui ont dicté cette loi. Non, ce ne fut point une étroite opération de finances. Des intérêts d'une bien plus haute importance, la réunion des Français en un seul faisceau & l'affermissement de la liberté, voilà son objet:" *Résumé*, pp. 2, 5; Chappuis, pp. 8–9 (see Bibliography, Nos. 31–32); AN, D–III–174.

XI. DISCUSSION ON JEWISH AUTONOMY DURING THE OLD REGIME*

The controversy over the abolition of the autonomous Jewish communities made clear that the Jews were organized in legal corporate associations (*corporations*),[147] governed by their own syndics[148] and by statutes pertaining to almost all phases of collective and individual Jewish life. Yet, in order to win the

* This chapter is based mainly on the author's study "Jewish Autonomy Debated and Attacked During the French Revolution." *HJ*, XX (1958), 31–46.

[147] The term *corporation* for the Jewish community was used in many documents of various periods: *Prix proposés, en 1788, par la Société Royale de Metz* (Metz, 1788), p. 2, and *Affiches des Evêchés et Lorraine*, No. 35, 1788 ("Les Juifs forment, presque par-tout où ils sont établis, des corporations autorisées"). The same term was used by the central consistory in a document of May 1809: *Le Consistoire Central des Israélites, à Messieurs les Membres du Consistoire départemental* . . . [Paris, Mai 1809,] p. 3 ("Qu'il y a loin de votre organisation actuelle à celle qui réglait ces corporations anciennes"). In some sources Jewish autonomy was called *police particulière* (Stillschweig, *op. cit.*, 458).

[148] In legal and other French documents the leaders of the Jewish communities (*parnassim* in Hebrew) were called *syndics*, thus employing a term which emphasized the communities' functions as *corporations*. On the term *syndic*, see A. Chéruel, *Dictionnaire historique des institutions* . . . (Paris, 1884), II, 1193. In Alsace the *parnassim* or *schetadlanim* of the *Nation* were called mostly *préposés géneraux* and *préposés particuliers* (local). After 1784 they were also called *syndics généraux*. Isidore Loeb, "Les Juifs à Strasbourg . . .," 178. In Bordeaux the Hebrew expressions *gabaym* or *parnassim* were often applied to the syndics and the period during which the *gabay*'s functions, the *syndicat*, were exercised was referred to as *gabayat*. Cirot, *Recherches* . . ., pp. 59, 131. *Parnas*, in its abbreviated form P[s], is found on the grave of Abr. Allourquerque, founder of the *Bikur Holim* in Bordeaux. Cirot mistakingly copied P[r] (*Ibid.*, p. 135). The term *syndicat*, referring to the syndic's activities, was employed even in the 19th century by the Jews of Bordeaux and Bayonne. According to the minutes of the Nancy consistory (May 11, 1817) the syndic's functions ceased after the founding of the consistories in 1808: "que ses fonctions de syndic ayant cessé par l'effet du décret du 17 Mars 1808." Berr-Isaac Berr then wrote: "Come il n'existe plus ni communauté ni syndic des Juifs" (Minutes of the Nancy consistory, Jerusalem, 300/5). See Appendix VII.

nationalization of the debts owed by the dissolved Jewish communities the Jews had to disprove the contention of their Christian creditors and other adversaries that during the old regime they had not existed as *corporations*.

In the petition addressed to the National Convention, Aaron Ravel, Aaron Vidal and Milhaud stated in behalf of the Avignon Jews that they had been organized as a *corporation* which was dissolved by the Revolution and the properties of which were nationalized. They violently criticized the very existence of *corporations* "which cut up the State into an infinity of parties. The *corporations* formed a multitude of separate small nations in the midst of the nation itself. Each of these *corporations* had different and often opposing interests . . . All these undesirable divisions must disappear in the light of the torch of Philosophy . . ." The petitioners stated that the former *corporation* of the Jews was forced to borrow and mortgage communal Jewish properties. Since they no longer existed as a *corporation* and their mortgaged communal properties had been nationalized, would the government, they asked, dare to refuse to nationalize their debts? "Will the Jews again be treated as before, *i. e.*, as citizens only when taxes were due, but foreigners when they claimed their rights? . . . No! This would be an insult to French law. A contradiction which would disgrace our laws shall not be tolerated . . . When a system is fundamentally just, then it is necessary to accept the consequences . . . It is not possible to abolish the *corporations* and yet to continue the existence of one of them. The National Convention cannot recognize the Jews. There are no more Jews in France. There are no more Catholics, Protestants, Anabaptists, Jews, Sectarians of any kind, there are only Frenchmen." The doubts concerning the evidence that before the Revolution the Jews indeed had been organized as *corporations* under the law, constituted the main reason for not nationalizing their debts. Consequently, the Jews of Avignon prepared a second petition to the National Convention, in which they again tried to prove that during the old regime even French occupation forces in the former papal province dealt with the Jews in reference to tax and other matters, not as individuals, but as members of a *corporation*. This argument was later repeated in the report that A.-J.-B. Chappuis submitted on

April 5, 1797 to the Council of the Five Hundred, advocating the nationalization of the debts. He recalled that when in 1768 France had occupied the papal province, the Jews petitioned the parliament of Provence to register and thus recognize as valid all previous privileges accorded them and existing statutes approved by the papal authorities.[149]

The counter-argument that the Jews had never formed any legal body, but existed only as a "tolerated tribe" (*peuplade toléré*) was presented by Domonique Chambaud, a creditor of the Carpentras Jews, in a memorandum against Jasse-Haïn Crémieu, son of one of the Jewish guarantors of the loans obtained by the Carpentras community. To this Crémieu replied in a brief prepared by the lawyer Chansaud that the Jews of Carpentras formed a "real political community," with their own communal constitution. Even the manner in which the loans were made demonstrated that the Jews were organized in special bodies. Thus, loans were ratified by general assemblies of their community and approved by the papal authorities.[150] When their autonomous communities were abolished upon their emancipation, the Jews also ceased to be debtors. Chansaud compared the situation of the Jews to that of the members of the Marseilles parliament, whose indebtedness to the parliament's creditors ceased after that body was dissolved in 1771. The Christian creditor replied in a brief prepared by the lawyer Granet, that the Jews enjoyed a "legal existence," *i. e.*, permission to exist, but no political existence.[151] Yet, on March 5, 1799 the civil tribunal of the Vaucluse department (the former papal province) acknowledged that the former Jewish community did exist as a *corps de communauté*. The same statement was made earlier

[149] Petition of the Avignon Jews, and Chappuis' *Rapport*, pp. 3, 5 (see Bibliography, Nos. 32, 85–86). On Jan. 17, 1793 the Jewish paupers of Avignon demanded financial help from the city council since, as a result of the Revolution, the Jewish *corporation* (community) had been dissolved (*l'assemblée nationale ayant aboli leur corporation*) and rich Jews had left for other communities (Chobaut, *op. cit.*, CII, 28).

[150] According to a document of 1718 the Jews could not decide on taxes without the presence at their assemblies of the *recteur* or his representative (Ad Vaucluse, annex of Carpentras, register 28, "Livre d'audience de la Rectorie," 1718, fol. 286.)

[151] *Mémoire*, p. 12 (see Bibliography, No. 89).

658

by the civil authorities of Avignon, and repeated again on August 2, 1799.[152]

The Jews of Metz, who also demanded nationalization of their debts, put forward the same argument. In a petition addressed to the National Assembly they stated that their community was "political in character." They formed "a unique *corporation*, a state, a particular administrative subdivision in France." They had not only a synagogue, but also rabbinical judges, who were recognized by the parliament and French jurisprudence. They had their own legislation on inheritance and other civil matters. They paid general taxes not as individuals, but as an autonomous collective body. The Jewish community of Metz had authority over the provincial communities. This Jewish state of Metz was dissolved by the same revolutionary action which dissolved all other *corporations*.[153]

Many officials openly affirmed the justness of the Jews' argument. The deputy J.-F.-L. de Visme stated in his report of July 20, 1790 to the National Assembly on the abolition of the Brancas tax that the Jews formed a "particular *corporation*." On August 18, 1791 the district of Metz, in an order on taxes, referred to Jews not as individuals, but as the *communauté des Juifs*. Mention has been made above of the support the Jews received from A.-J.-B. Chappuis, member of the Council of the Five Hundred.[154]

Many more proofs that the Jews were in fact organized as *corporations* are known to us today, e. g., the contemporary statutes of the Jewish communities.[155] But the proofs put forward by the Jews during the Revolution were sufficient in themselves to confirm that they did in fact form corporate associations. In the end, however, the Jews lost the argument.

[152] *Ibid.*; Am Avignon, D 56, No. 26; Documents, Comtat, No. 10, fol. 44, Aug. 2, 1799 ("Certifie et atteste que les citoyens proffessant la religion juive qui habitoient dans cette commune avant la réunion à la France formoient depuis un tems immémorial & sans interruption une communauté distincte & separée des catholiques . . .").
[153] JTS, 01530–1; *Pétition*, pp. 1–7 (see Bibliography, No. 23).
[154] Reports by Devisme, p. 8, Chappuis, pp. 3–5 and the law of May 20, 1791 (see Bibliography, Nos. 13, 20, 32).
[155] See Appendix II.

XII. THE LACK OF UNITY AMONG THE JEWS

Among the Jews themselves there was no unity on the nationalization of their debts. The Jews of Avignon stated in their
petition that their case was completely different from that of the
Metz Jews.[156] The fact that both petitions were discussed together
by the Council of the Five Hundred was not the result of a joint
Jewish appeal. Even much later, in the 1820's, a strong tone of
Jewish disunity was evident in a memorandum of the Jews of
Carpentras and L'Isle-sur-Sorgue on the liquidation of their
debts. They stated then that the decision not to nationalize was
probably correct in regard to the debts of the Jews of Metz, but
not in regard to those of the Comtadin Jews.[157]

A conflict involving the Jewish community of Bordeaux provided propaganda against the nationalization of the debts owed
by the Jewish communities in general.

In September 1791 the city of Bordeaux decided to abolish all
separate religious cemeteries and to replace them with one large
national cemetery. This was a chapter in the general drive of
the Revolution to centralize and reinforce secular influence in the
new regime. Many Jewish cemeteries were confiscated and sold
— not as an anti-Jewish act, because the policy was not directed
against Jews alone, and Jewish cemeteries were never singled
out.[158]

---

[156] *Observations*, pp. 1–2 (see Bibliography, No. 85).

[157] "Car le motif qui fit prévaloir la question prélable au Conseil des 500
[le 16 Frimaire an 6 — Dec. 6, 1797] fut que les juifs étaient autrefois étrangers
à la France, que leurs communautés n'étaient pas reconnus, que le gouvernement ne pouvait donc considérer leurs dettes que comme des dettes privées
et que par conséquent les lois sur les dettes des corporations ne pouvaient
leur être appliqués. Or, ce motif, peut-être plausible pour les juifs de Metz,
est absolument dénué de fondement à l'égard des communautés juives de
Comtat..." (JTS, 01529. Petition of the Jews of Carpentras and L'Isle).
Compare with the *Mémoire* of 1818, pp. 24–25 (see Bibliography, No. 103).

[158] Z. Szajkowski, "Jewish Cemeteries during the French Revolution of
1789." *Horeb*, XII (1958), 165–78 (in Hebrew).

This was the background for the confiscation and sale of the Jewish cemetery of Bordeaux to two Christians, Pierre Despiau and Augustin Pujol. In petitions of May 12 and June 8, 1796 the Jews demanded annulment of the sale by the departmental authorities of Gironde. The authorities did so on June 29, 1796 and the decision was later approved by the Ministry of Finance.

As a result of these events a sharp clash developed between the Jews of Bordeaux and the two buyers of the cemetery. Both parties put forward strongly worded arguments and each claimed to be legally in the right; both published pamphlets on the conflict. The Jewish point of view was defended by the lawyers Louis-Francia de Beaufleury, the author of the first history of the Jews in Bordeaux and Bayonne, published in 1799; François-Placide-Nicolas Ferey; J.-J.-R. de Cambacérès; Minister of Justice in the year VII; and Alexandre-Jules-Benoît Debonnières.[159] A representative of the Bordeaux Jews was even sent to Paris. The defense of Despiau and Pujol was assumed by the lawyer and deputy François-Balthazar Darracq (1749–1817), who in this connection attacked the Jews in general at the Council of the Five Hundred. This was the strongest attack of that period against Jews.[160] Despiau and Pujol stated that no exception to nationalization of communal property should or could be made in favor of the Jews, who, prior to the Revolution had been organized as a *Nation*.[160a] This was done to the properties

[159] On Beaufleury see Z. Szajkowski, "Louis-Francia de Beaufleury, a Jewish Substitute-Deputy during the French Revolution." *Davke*, No. 20 (1954), 241–48 (in Yiddish). On Ferey (1735–1807) see *NBG*, XVII, 424–25. On Debonnières see Brunetière aîné, *Eloges du premier Consul Bonaparte et du jurisconsulte de Bonnière . . .* (Paris, [1709]). 4 pp. There are many sources on Cambacérès.

Beaufleury was the son of the Bordeaux banker Louis-David Francia de Beauflury. In 1766 he married a girl named Veniere, most probably a Christian (Ad Gironde, E, Familles, Francia. Testament of Francia's mother, Rebecca-Marie, March 20, 1786). According to one source (Bm Bx, ms. 713–1, vol. 46, p. 231, P. Bernardau's chronicle) Beaufleury died in 1817 at the age of 65 in Carbonblanc (Gironde), but no trace of his death could be found in the local registries of the *état-civil*. In the same chronicle of Bernardau (vol. 7, p. 503, Jan. 26, 1800) Beaufleury was described as a converted Jew (*ex-juif*).

[160] Darracq, *op. cit.*, pp. 11–13, 15, 17–18, 23.

[160a] "Les Juifs Portugais établis à Bordeaux en 1550 . . . avoient en outre

of all other corporate bodies abolished by the new regime. The Jews replied that they had never been organized as such a body (*corporation*), but only as a philanthropic society, which owned the cemetery. Officially the cemetery was, in fact, always owned by such a society, but under the strict control of the *Nation*. Thus, on April 26, 1750 Alexander the elder, was appointed by the *Nation* as treasurer of the cemetery. On March 22, 1761, using the cemetery's funds, the *Nation* granted a loan for one year to David Lameyra at an interest rate of five per cent. On April 17, 1786 the *Nation* decided to prepare a register of all graves and to leave it for safekeeping with the burial society, *Guemilut Hasidim*.[161] The statement of the Bordeaux Jews that before 1789 they had not been organized as a *corporation* was attacked by those who sought to nationalize the cemetery. At the same time their statement was seized by those who fought the idea of nationalizing the debts of the former Jewish communities of the papal province and Metz. It demonstrated, they said, that the Jews were never organized as *corporations*, and thus could not request nationalization of the debts they owed.[162]

des statuts ou règlemens particuliers, pour l'ordre intérieur de leur réunion ... On trouve dans la rédaction de ces statuts tout ce qui sert à reconnoître une corporation .... Il n'est aucun autre statut de toutes les corporations sup-primées, qui ne présente les mêmes résultats ... Qui pourra, à la vue de cette pièce, douter un instant de l'existence d'une corporation composé des Juifs Portugais? ... Il n'y avoit guères de différence dans le régime de la corpora-tion Avignonaise, comparée avec celle des Portugais ... Les Lettres-patentes qui leur firent accordées au mois de mai 1759 ... contiennent les bases du même régime que celui des Portugais" (*Mémoire pour les citoyens Despiau et Pujos de Bordeaux*). See also the Statutes of the *Nation* of the Avignonese Jews in Bordeaux: *Lettres-patentes en faveur des Juifs ou Nouveau-Chrétiens Avignonois établis à Bordeaux* (Bordeaux, n. d.). 4 pp.

[161] Nation, Nos. 177, 282, 545, fol. 41, 68, 139.

[162] *Extrait de l'Arrêté de l'Administration départementale de la Gironde, du 11 Messidor, an IV ... [29 Juin 1796]* (n. p., n. d.). 4 pp.; *Mémoire pour les citoyens [Pierre] Despiau et [Augustin] Pujos [Pujol], de Bordeaux* (Bordeaux, n. d.). 32 pp.; *Mémoire à consulter et consultation, pour les citoyens Français, professant le culte Judaïque à Bordeaux, connus sous le nom de Juifs Portugais et Avignonais* (n. p., n. d.). 47 pp. Dated Nov. 29, 1798. Reprinted in Louis-Francia de Beaufleury, *op. cit.*, pp. 161–95; Despiau et Pujol, *Réponse à un Mémoire imprimé sous le nom des Citoyens français, professant le culte judaïque*

The Jewish statement that before 1789 they had not been organized as a corporate body was historically incorrect. There is abundant proof that they did form a well organized body, known as a *Nation*.

Various Jewish sources refer to the *Kehila Kodosha* of Bordeaux. The *Nation* of Saint-Esprit-lès-Bayonne called itself *Kehila Kodosha Tfuzot Yisrael* (also *Tfuzot Yehuda*); the *Nation* of Bidache — *Nve Shaanan* (also *Beth El*); the *Nation* of Peyrehorade — *Beth El*.[163] According to the historian Beaufleury, the first syndic of the Sephardim of Bordeaux, then known officially as New Christians, was elected on April 28, 1699. But the Bordeaux *Nation* was founded long before 1699. There exists a notarial agreement dated 1629, between George Rodrigues and the *nation portugaise* of Bordeaux, in which the latter assumed all expenses arising out of Rodrigues' litigation affecting the Christian merchants of the city.[164] The *Nation* not only collected taxes, distributed charity, supported a rabbi and ecclesiastical court, supervised *kashrut*, schools and the like, but also determined the national and municipal taxes to be paid by each individual Jew;[165] excommunicated a landlord for raising the rent

à Bordeaux (n. p., n. d.); [Marc-Florent] Prévot, *Rapport fait par Prévot, sur une pétition des citoyens Pujol & Despiau, habitans de la commune de Bordeaux, sousmissionaires des biens appartenans aux Juifs établis en cette commune. Séance du 21 Germinal an 7* [10 Avril 1799] (Paris, an 7). 7 pp.; [François-Balthazar] Darracq, *op. cit.*; Z. Szajkowski, "Jewish Autonomy Debated and Attacked During the French Revolution." *HJ*, XX (1958), 43–44.

[163] On the tombstone of Rabbi Joseph Falco one finds "beK.K. Bordeaux." The words "Yakov Emanuel Rosh Mikehilatenu N. F. I." appear on a Bayonne tombstone of 1792. The expression *kehilla* referring to an organization of Bordeaux Jews is found even in 1841–42. See also Raphael and Elazar Mildola, *Parshat haibur* (Amsterdam, 1734): "K.K. Nefuzot Yisrael"; Béthencourt, *op. cit.*, XXV (1892), 236–37; H. Gross, *op. cit.*, pp. 92, 114, 453; H. Léon, *op. cit.*, pp. 215, 364; *RO*, II (1842), 229; M. Kayserling, *Die Juden in Navarra* . . . (Berlin, 1861), p. 150; Emil Lévy, "Un document sur la communauté de Peyrehorade (Landes), 1762–1812." *AnAI 5664* (Paris, 1903), 50; G. Cirot, *op. cit.*, p. 132; *AI*, II (1841), 253, III (1842), 3. In a document dated July 6, 1807 the *parnassin* of Peyrehorade are referred to as the "Mrs composant le Kaal de Peyrehorade" (ZS).

[164] Ad Gironde, E, Lafite's notarial minutes, Apr. 15, 1632, fol. 257–58.

[165] In 1786 Moïse Gonzales asked the *Nation* to lower his taxes (Am Bordeaux, GG 30).

of two widows;[166] and had jurisdiction over marriages and divorces. A Jew of Bordeaux was not even allowed to lodge a complaint in court against another Jew without the *Nation*'s permission. On October 8, 1777 the *Nation* discussed the case of such a complaint against Moïse Silva lodged with the police by Lopes the elder, without the *Nation*'s approval.[167]

In its administrative relations with the Sephardim — as well as with the Avignonese Jews of Bordeaux — the non-Jewish world considered these bodies of Jews to be *corporations* of merchants. It was generally accepted that the term *Jew* — even when referring to a poor man — was synonymous with *merchant*. The Sephardim and Avignonese were considered *corporations*, like the other 85 Bordeaux *corporations* of bakers, shoemakers, doctors, lawyers and the other 115 occupations which are mentioned in all the lists of the Bordeaux *corporations*.[168]

In the memorandum of 1788 to Malesherbes the Sephardim of Bordeaux requested that the laws of inheritance according to Jewish law, as was the custom among the Ashkenazim, be maintained.[169] After the Sephardic Jews were granted full citizenship, on February 18, 1790 they disbanded the *Nation* and a philanthropic society assumed almost all its functions. Obviously the *Nation* was a *corporation* with all its manifold functions. The text of the decision to dissolve the *Nation* is another proof.[170]

---

[166] Cirot, *Recherches* . . ., p. 80.

[167] Nation, No. 453.

[168] Am Bx, HH19 and Ad Gironde, C 313 (lists of *corporations*, 1760–1791, 1785); A. Nicolaï, *La population de Bordeaux au XVIIIe siècle* (Paris-Bordeaux, 1909), pp. 184, 186, 190; G. Cirot, *Les Juifs de Bordeaux. Leur situation morale et sociale de 1550 à la Révolution* (Bordeaux, 1920), p. 15; *Liste des corporations par ordre alphabétique, et des noms de leurs députés, à l'Assemblée du Tiers-Etat de Bordeaux* (n. p., n. d.). Broadside.

"En un mot, ils formaient une espèce de communauté sous la surveillance du gouvernment." *L'Indicateur* (Bordeaux), July 31, 1804, 2–4.

[169] Henry Léon, *op. cit.*, pp. 153–54.

[170] "Les Juifs de Bordeaux ne pouvant plus être considérés comme Corps de Nation, l'assemblée des Anciens qui les représentaient s'est aussitôt dissoute, et on s'est occupé immédiatement de la formation d'une Association de Bienfaisance" (Nation, Feb. 18, 1790). Ch.-M. duc de Tayllerand-Périgord's statement of Jan. 28, 1790 that the Jews of Bordeaux had no special laws, magistrates or particular officials (*RdGJP*, I (1897), 94) was not exact.

(Even after their emancipation in January 1790 the Sephardic Jews continued to use the expression *Nation*.[171])

[171] In 1791 David Mendes France bequeathed a few hundred livres to the "poor of the *Nation*" (*pauvres de la Nation*, Am Bx, GG 14, p. 81). In 1792 Izaac Pindes figures as the "Seigneur [saigneur] des Boeufs de la Nation Juive" of Bordeaux (AmBx, CC 1098). On June 13, 1794 a document certifying good conduct (*bonne vie*) was signed by the "sindic et adjoints de la nation portugaise à Bordeaux" (Ad Gironde, G 2462). On the monument of Jacob Emmanuel, who died on March 17, 1792, his position as "chief of our community" of Saint-Esprit is noted (H. Léon, *op. cit.*, p. 215; Moïse Schwab, "Rapport sur les inscriptions hébraïques de la France." *Nouvelles Archives des Missions Scientifiques et Littéraires*, XII — 3 (1905), 378). In May 1792 Gabriel de Jacob Gomez was "administrateur des pauvres Juifs français du bourg Saint-Esprit-lès-Bayonne" (E. Ducéré, *Histoire topographique et anecdotique des rues de Bayonne* (Bayonne, 1887), II, 76.) The 1797 rules of the Jewish commaunty of Peyrehorade referred not only to a society, but also to a community — *Kal*: "Règlement fait entre nous, Israélites du Kal de Peyrehorade le 22 Germinal, 5e année Rne ..." Emile Lévy, *op. cit.*, 44–58.

XIII.   THE JEWISH STATUS AND THE
*DROIT D'AUBAINE**

One of the most curious aspects of the legal status of Jews in France prior to the Revolution of 1789 was the application to them of the right of *aubaine (droit d'aubaine)*.[172] Under this right the government took possession, in whole or in part, of the estate of a deceased alien. But were the Jews of France aliens or French *régnicoles* (natives)? Various historians had presented their views. Maurice Liber wrote that the Jews "could not be compared to other Frenchmen, but they could also not be treated as real foreigners." In the opinion of Robert Anchel the Jews could not be Frenchmen, because legally only Christians were Frenchmen. The Jews had an intermediate status. Roger Clément pointed out that as *sujets du Roi* the Jews of Metz, insofar as the public rights were concerned (*dans le droit public*), did not enjoy any of the rights of the existing social Christian groups, such as the *serfs, aubains, bourgeois*, etc. They were an entity in themselves, a separate group, "the Jews of Metz" (*les Juifs de Metz*) who were protected by a series of royal ordinances which, however, were so unprecise that they always left a wide field for anti-Jewish chicanery.[173]

The government tried, but, on the whole, unsuccessfully to assert its right of *aubains* in the case of the Jews. These claims indicate that there was a tendency to regard the Jews as foreigners and to disregard the privileges to which they were entitled. The right of *aubaine* was frequently asserted in the case of Jews in the French colonies and of Sephardic Jews of

---

* This chapter is based mainly on the author's study "The Jewish Status in the Eighteenth-Century France and the *Droit d'Aubaine*." *HJ*, XIX (1957), 147–61.

[172] For a detailed study on this subject, see Z. Szajkowski, "The Jewish Status . . ." *HJ*, XIX (1957), 147–161.

[173] Liber, LXIII, 185; R. Anchel, "Les Juifs à Paris au XVIIIᵉ siècle." *BSHP*, LIX (1932), 9–23; R. Clément, *op. cit.*, p. 40.

France. These frequent but isolated attempts of the French
monarchy to declare certain deceased Jews to be *aubains* and
to confiscate their estates aroused all French Jews, for they
rightly viewed these cases as a threat to their economic and legal
status.[174] The residents of Strasbourg and other free cities and
of Alsatian areas owned by foreign princes and other dignitaries
were exempted from the right of *aubaine*. It would seem that
the exemption applied also to Jews there. The Alsatian historians, L.-V. Goetzmann, Jules Krug-Basse, Charles Hoffmann,
Rodolphe Reuss and George Livet, Roger Clément of Metz,
E.-T. Bonvolat of Lorraine and many others, and the collections of local laws mention no cases involving Jews.[175] It may
be possible, by long and painstaking research in the national and
departmental archives, to find a few isolated cases in which the
right of *aubaine* was applied to Jews of Alsace, Metz and its
province, and Lorraine. But no general conclusion could be
based on such hypothetical cases. There were many other legal
ways beside the right of *aubaine* to take property away from the

[174] According to a contract of March 28, 1359 between Anan Lévy of Valvéas
in the papal province and the seignior of Grignon, the latter was to receive
one-third of a Jew's estate (Calvet, 5938). In this connection, note a conflict
between David Naquet and Elies Perpignan over an estate left in 1784 to
Naquet by Abraham Perpignan who had obtained naturalization letters. Elies
Perpignan stated that since Naquet was a Jew of Comtat Venaissin, he was in
fact an *aubain* and as such could not inherit any property in France. *Mémoire
responsif, pour le sieur David Naquet, Juif, natif de Carpentras, & habitant à
Bordeaux, contre le sieur Elies Perpignan, aussi Juif & habitant à Bordeaux.*
[Signé: Me. de Cazelet.] (Bordeaux, 1787). 28 pp.

[175] L.-V. de Götzmann, *Traité du droit commun des fiefs . . .* (Paris, 1876);
Charles Hoffmann, *op. cit.*, 4 vols.; R. Reuss, *L'Alsace au dix-septième siècle*
(Paris, 1897–98). 2 vols.; Georges Livet, *L'Intendance d'Alsace sous Louis XIV,
1648–1715* (Strasbourg, 1956), pp. 780–87; R. Clément, *op. cit.*; E.-T. Bonvalot,
Histoire du droit et des institutions de la Lorraine et des Trois Evêchés (Paris,
1895); De Boug; N. de Corberon, *Essay de recueil d'arrêts notables du Conseil
Souverain d'Alsace* (Colmar, 1738). 2 vols.; J.-L. C. Emmery de Crozyenl,
Recueil des édits . . . au Parlement de Metz (Metz, 1774–1788). 5 vols.; *Recueil
des Edits . . . du règne de Léopold Ier . . .* (Nancy, 1783–86). 15 vols. The right
of *aubaine* was applied in the case of a Jew from Hamburg who died in France
on March 22, 1789. In reference thereto J.-B. Poinsignon, administrator of
the King's domain, stated on Nov. 26, 1789: *les juifs sont incapables d'aucuns
effets civils en France* (Hildenfinger, 272).

Jews. Nevertheless, on many occasions, though not in connection with claims to confiscate their estates, the Ashkenazic Jews stated that they were not *aubains*, but French *régnicoles*.

In March 1767 the King permitted certain foreigners to obtain *brevets* (patents), which gave them the right to engage in certain occupations and exempted them from the right of *aubaine*. However, this edict did not apply to Jews. The lawyer Pierre-Louis Lacretelle the elder (1751–1824) pleaded in 1775, before the parliament of Nancy, in favor of two Jews of Metz who requested that they be granted *brevets* as merchants of Thionville. He stated that the Jews were not foreigners, but *régnicoles*, and that the right of *aubaine* was not applicable to them.[176] On the basis of this same edict of 1767 the four brothers Hayem, Cerf, Abraham and Jacob Olry Worms, and Lyon Alexandre and Joseph Cahen of Sarrelouis obtained *brevets de maîtrise* in the city of Sarrelouis. Eight years later, however, the Christian merchants and butchers protested that the Jews could not be considered *régnicoles*, that they were still aliens and that, in any event, only two Jews were allowed to reside in the city. The Jews contested this position. In a memorandum prepared for them by the lawyer La Servalle they stated that they could not be considered aliens because they were not regarded as *aubains* in the matter of inheritance.[177]

At the beginning of the Revolution the Jewish representatives of Alsace, Metz and Lorraine stated in a memorandum submitted to the Minister of Finance and the government's real chief, Jacques Necker, that they were not foreigners, but a *nation juive régnicole* and that the right of *aubaine* was not applicable to them. The decree of April 30, 1790 (law of May 2, 1790) in

[176] Pierre-Louis Lacretelle, "Plaidoyer pour Moïse May, Godechaux et Abraham Lévy, juifs de Metz, contre l'Hôtel de Ville de Thionville et le corps des marchands de cette ville." *Plaidoyers* (Bruxelles, 1775), reprinted in 1823 and by André Spire in 1928. See also André Spire, "Pierre Louis Lacretelle." *Menorah*, II, Jan. 1923. Lacretelle's brief was reprinted in *RJL*, VI (1930), 37–44 ("Les Juifs sous l'ancien régime. Un intéressant document lorrain").

[177] Me. La Servolle, *Requête au Roi, pour les Juifs de Sarrelouis* (Paris, 1777), p. 14. On this conflict see also Me. Dimours, *Mémoire pour les maire, syndics, & communauté des habitans de Sarrelouis . . . contre les Juifs* (n. p., n. d.). 43 pp.

favor of foreigners contained the clause: "without ... prejudging anything regarding the problem of the Jews, which was and remains postponed." This does not prove that the Jews were then considered foreigners. The paragraph was added at the request of the Alsatian anti-Jewish deputy, Jean-François Rewbell (Reubell), who feared that the Jews would try to turn the decree to their own advantage in their fight for emancipation. When on July 20, 1790 Reubell stated before the National Assembly that the Jews of Metz were foreigners, a voice replied: "This is not the truth." As late as March 1790, two months after the Sephardic Jews had been granted full citizenship, the Chamber of domain expressed its strong opposition to recognizing these Jews as *régnicoles*. According to Baruch Hagani, the law of May 2, 1790 bypassed the issue of the Jews' status as *régnicoles* or aliens. The right of *aubaine* was abolished altogether by a decree of August 6, 1790. Indeed, a decree of April 8, 1791 even permitted residents of foreign countries to inherit properties in France. But the problem still arose even later in connection with the Brancas tax which, as noted above, was abolished by the National Assembly on July 20, 1790, over the opposition of the Brancas family and some deputies. They stated that the Jews of Metz were only tolerated foreigners and that the Brancas tax was to be considered similar to a *droit d'aubaine*. On this occasion the Jews of Metz argued, in a petition signed by Louis Wolff, that the *droit d'aubaine* was well known in 1715, when the Brancas tax originated, but the Brancas tax was formulated only as a tolerance, protection, and residence charge. The Jews were not tolerated foreigners, but formed a well-organized body: "it is not as foreigners but as constituents of a particular body [*corporation*] that the Jews obtained confirmation of their rights with every change in sovereign." In this respect they followed the practice of other Frenchmen, their fellow-citizens, forming corps or communities who confirmed the righs of their existing *corporations*. J.-F.-L. de Visme, who on July 20, 1790 reported to the National Assembly on the Jewish request, likewise argued against the claim of the Brancas family. He stated that the right of *aubaine* was only "a casual claim" resulting from the death of a foreigner and ending with the legal confiscation of his estate. The claim was not applied perpetually to the foreigner's

descendants who, if born in France, became French natives
(*régnicoles*). But in this instance the Brancas family had obtained a perpetual tax imposed upon Jews and their heirs.
Moreover, the right of *aubaine* was a prerogative reserved to the
King alone, and was not to be turned over to other persons.[178]

In arguing against the Jews' request for nationalization of the
debts owed by their former *corporations*, the Christian creditors
also claimed that during the old regime the Jews were only
tolerated foreigners, *aubains* with no legal right to be organized
in *corporations*.[179]

The creditors cited as proof the fact that after 1789 the local
authorities ordered the Jews to continue the administration of
their communal properties. In a reply prepared on behalf of
Jews the lawyer Combines stated that, prior to 1789, the Jews
in France had the status of a recognized body and that the order
to continue the administrative functions of the Jewish community was forced upon them.[180] François-Balthazar Darracq,
in a strong attack on the Jews delivered on March 7, 1799 at
the Council of the Five Hundred, pressed the same arguments
offered by the creditors.[181] This was part of a well-organized
effort to prove that the Jews — as foreigners — could not have
been organized in communities which were in the category of
those dissolved by the new regime. There were rebuttals by
Jews and by many non-Jews.

The Jews of Metz stated that they were not looked upon as
foreigners. Foreign Jews could not settle among them; their
possessions were not escheated to the Crown, because the right
of *aubaine* was not applied to them. In his report presented on

---

[178] Liber, LXIV, 267; Halphen, 4; AI, XVII (1856), 218; Hildenfinger,
op. cit., p. 42; B. Hagani, *op. cit.*, p. 188; L. Wolff, pp. 6–7 and Devisme's
Rapport, pp. 5–9 (see Bibliography, Nos. 12–13).

[179] Puyproux, p. 2 (see Bibliography, No. 30).

[180] JTS, 01530–6.

[181] Darracq, *op. cit.*, p. 4. See also Halphen, pp. 335–36 (statements by
Darracq, Gay de Vernon and Riou).
". . . il est évident que n'étant pas alors Français, ils ne peuvent être compris dans les décrets qui ont déclare dettes nationales les dettes des corporations
de France; ce serait donner un effet rétroactif aux lois . . ." (Léonard-Honoré
Gay de Vernon (1748–1822) at the Council of the Five Hundred, Dec. 6, 1797.
Halphen, p. 335.)

670

November 24, 1797 to the Council of the Five Hundred Riou also rejected the creditors' argument that prior to the Revolution the Jews were considered foreigners.[182]

The arguments advanced by the Jews and their friends were not generally convincing. The decision on the nationalization of the debts was influenced by the outcome of the debate on the right of *aubaine*. Thus, the fact that prior to the Revolution of 1789 the legal status of the Jews was not clearly defined opened the way for many interpretations which were prejudicial to the Jews not only during the old regime, but also during the Revolution. The debts owed by the Jewish communities were not taken over by the government, partly as a result of the propaganda that during the old regime the Jews were legally aliens and that as such they could not have been organized as *corporations*.

[182] Riou, p. 4 (see Bibliography, No. 34).

XIV. THE COMMUNAL ACTIVITIES OF THE COMMISSIONS TO LIQUIDATE THE DEBTS

We noted earlier that in order to collect taxes for the liquidation of the debts the Jews were forced to maintain the existence of their former communities. The creditors then argued that the Jews had no right to request the nationalization of their debts because they still existed as separate bodies, collected taxes, etc. The Jews of Metz replied that such taxes were no longer collected by syndics of a separate Jewish community for communal expenses, but by administrators, newly appointed by the local authorities, for the sole purpose of repaying the debts.[183]

The newly formed bodies for the liquidation of the debts were not designated as *communities, nations,* or *carrières,* but as *commissions* to liquidate the debts. However, the functions of these commissions were much broader than their names indicated. They not only had to levy taxes, prosecute tax delinquents, and pay the debts. These commissions also were in charge of all communal Jewish properties and activities, and conducted many religious and social activities of the dissolved *corporations.*

From March 20, 1792 to December 25, 1795 the Metz commission to liquidate the debts made 408 payments to the creditors in the sum of 163,487 livres 5 s. 3 d. in *assignats,* 12,455 livres in drafts and 4,657 livres 5 s. in cash.[184] From August 26, 1792 to

---

[183] *Consultation,* pp. 4–5 (see Bibliography, No. 29).

[184] Documents, Metz, No. 38, fol. 152–57.
Following are a few expenses contracted by the same commission in 1791 — year V: "pour le racommodage des fennettre de lopitalle des etranger . . .; pour avoir defait les Tabelot sur les portes des cimetières . . ., pour avoir nétoiet la boucheris et plas . . .; dans la Maison du cidevant hopital des Pauvres pour les vitres . . .; pour rétablissement de la Cour de la Boucherie . . .; pour avoir travaile dans la sinagot . . .; pour une vitre neuve des vitres du bain . . .; pour avoir racomodé le balancier . . .; pour la pompier . . ., pour main d'euvre de dans la cour de la sinagogue . . .; des pavées retablis par Nicolas Bertrand au devant et au derrière de differente maisons appartenant à la communauté des juifs . . .; pour des ouvrages faits en couverture au dessus

December 25, 1796 the same commission paid out salaries to employees of the Jewish community and compensation for other communal expenses in ninety-four payments totaling 7,236 livres 2 s. 3 d. in assignats and 853 livres in cash. Among the employees were: the three rabbis, Olry Cahen, Mayeur and Louis May; the five cantors, Seligmann Caën, Lion and Emmanuel Bing, Naheme and Salomon Zay; the *sergent* Joseph Olry Cahen; the *portier* Moyse Zay; the Christian *gardien* and *crieur* Birié, who announced the coming of Sabbath; the Christian *allumeur* Dominique, who was employed by the Jews as a lamp-lighter on Saturday. The commission took care of the synagogue and ritual slaughtering, the hospices for native and foreign Jewish paupers, the communal bath etc.[185]

Until the Jewish communities were organized into consistories by Napoleon I's decree of March 7, 1808 discipline in the Jewish communities was not the same as during the old regime.[186] The consistories took over all the religious and social functions of the Jewish communities. The commissions to liquidate the debts continued to exist for that sole purpose, although the Metz commission on many occasions was in conflict with the local, central and Paris consistories on jurisdictional questions.[187]

du citoien Rabi. Ouvrages au cimetière; entretien de la boucherie; ouvrages à la sinagogue; reparations à l'hop[it]al; entretien de la sinagogue; construction de places; hôpital des pauvres; ouvrages à la boucherie; réparation du cours d'eau devant la boucherie" (Documents, Metz, No. 38, fol. 167–68, 179–80, 209, 225–26, No. 48, fol. 323–466).

[185] *Ibid.*, fol. 208–09.
[186] AN, F–19–11014; Anchel, *op. cit.*, pp. 45–46, 48.
[187] Documents, Metz, Nos. 25–27, fol. 107–13.

XV. THE CONFLICT BETWEEN THE JEWISH COMMUNITY OF METZ AND THE PROVINCIAL COMMUNITIES

The royal Letters patent of July 9, 1718, which renewed all previous privileges granted the Jews of Metz, provided that the Jews of the *Généralité* (the province outside of the city itself) were to contribute to the sums paid by the Jews of Metz for protection. Accordingly the Jews of Metz asked the intendant, Jean-François de Creil, to force the Jews in these communities to pay part of the various taxes imposed upon the Metz Jews. On February 7, 1724 de Creil granted the request and ordered that all Jews refusing to pay the tax within eight days should be expelled. Permission to tax the provincial Jews was renewed periodically by the incumbent intendants (on December 11, 1742, January 17, 1748, December 27, 1752, August 2, 1759, February 2, 1763, January 31, 1768, November 9, 1772, February 10, 1777).[188] This provision led to an internal struggle between the Jews of Metz and those of other communities within the province.

There is no doubt that the Jews of Metz sought to burden the smaller Jewish communities with the payment of part of the taxes, for which perhaps only they themselves were liable, e. g., in the official documents establishing the Brancas tax only the Jews of Metz were mentioned. But there is another aspect of the question, which we shall now explore and which suggests that the Jewish community of Metz showed a great deal of statesmanship in insisting that the Jews of the province share its tax burden. One must not forget that Metz had been at one time a German imperial free city, and that in the 13th century the city freed itself from the rule of the Bishop so that Metz and the *Pays Messin* were entirely separated from the rest of the province (the *Terres de l'Evêché*). Despite later changes owing to France's acquisition of the province, this unity of Metz and

[188] Landmann, Ce 380; Bibliography, Nos. 4–5, 7–11.

the *Pays Messin* remained. However, the royal privileges accorded to Jews were confined to residents of the city of Metz proper. The Jews of the other communities in the province enjoyed no legal status but were merely tolerated by the royal or local authorities. The local seigneurs had no authority to sell the Jews rights of residence and, if they sometimes extended permission to Jews to live in given localities, they also could withdraw it at will.[189] Sometimes the Jews managed — by paying a bribe — to stay an imminent expulsion, or even to receive permission to dwell in another village. But money in sufficient amounts was not always available, and in many cases the Jews attempted to stay an expulsion by taking refuge in the law. The Jewish community of Metz, for this reason, cited the intendant's order requiring all Jews within the province to pay taxes as proof that they did enjoy rights of residence. They claimed that each Jew paying taxes automatically enjoyed these rights. Thus, payments by the Jews in the smaller communities became a kind of unofficial *droit de manance*.[190] This advantage did not

[189] ". . . les Juifs de la campagne n'ont qu'un titre indirect de tolérance dans les Lettres patentes du 9 Juillet 1718 et seulement en ce qu'elles les ont assujettis à contribuer à la redevance de 20,000 livres imposée sur les Juifs de Metz" ("Copie d'une lettre écrite par M. le Marquis de Paulmy [Marc-Pierre d'Argenson, Ministre de la Guerre] à M. de Caumartin, Versailles, le 15 Février 1755." AN, 29AP3).

[190] C.-L. Gabriel, *Observations détachées sur les coutumes et usages anciens et modernes du ressort du Parlement de Metz* (Metz, 1784), I, 39; R. Clément, *op. cit.*, pp. 3–4, 108; *EcSt*, pp. 35–38. Landmann, Gal. 11 ("Requête des Juifs de Metz, adressée à l'Intendant de Creil, demandant que les Juifs habitant le pays messin, qui sont compris dans le rôle de la taxe de Brancas ne soient plus menacés d'expulsion par les seigneurs, mais qu'ils soient maintenus sous l'autorité de l'intendant"); Terquem, p. 15 (see Bibliography, No. 140). The Jews of Metz itself were often forced to obey the strict letter of the law which accorded them privileges of residence. In 1704 the civil authorities of Metz complained that the number of Jews exceeded expectations. The Jewish community then appointed a special commission to designate the Jews who should leave Metz (Landmann, Ce 23). On Dec. 21, 1782 the parliament of Metz held up a sentence pronounced by the syndics of the community upon one of its members for giving refuge to a foreign Jew (Bm Metz, ms. 919, fol. 152).

In 1786 the Jewish syndics of Lorraine lodged a complaint with the authorities against foreign Jews who had taken up residence in the province. As a result of this complaint the parliament ordered, on July 4, 1786, to compile a

reconcile the Jews of the provincial communities to the burden of contributing to the taxes imposed upon the community of Metz.

In the papal province the taxpayers of smaller communities gained a corresponding advantage. When the Jews were expelled from Orange in 1732, they were accepted by three Comtadin communities to which they had paid taxes.[191]

The conflict between the community of Metz and the provincial communities may be reviewed in terms of the debts owed by Metz. The first debt, which resulted from the fight against the introduction of the Brancas tax, amounted to 70,000 livres, of which the provincial communities were assessed one third (23,333 livres 6 s. 8 d.). Together with interest for unpaid taxes these provincial communities were expected to pay an annual tax of 8,666 livres 13 s. 8 d. from 1718 until 1742. As they paid only 1,800 livres, their debt over these twenty-four years amounted to 164,785 livres 17 d. In 1742 the share of taxes for

census of all Jews, especially mentioning those who did not belong to the 180 Jewish families authorized to live in Lorraine by the Letters patent of Jan. 29, 1753 (*Extrait des registres du parlement. Du 4 juillet 1786* (Nancy, n. d.). 3 pp.). In 1789 the syndics of Lorraine requested that only Jews possessing not less than 10,000 livres should be permitted to settle in Nancy; those possessing 3,000 livres should be permitted to settle in smaller communities and those possessing only 1,200 livres in the smallest communities (Liber, LXV, 132). These facts, and many more, cited by De Boug and other sources, compelled the author to revise his earlier conclusion that among the Ashkenazim the attitude toward "foreign" Jews was friendlier than among Sephardim (Szajkowski, "Relations . . .," 178). The same should be said about the Jews of the papal province. In the beginning of July 1789 the Jewish community of Avignon refused to grant permission for the marriage of Anna (called Manon) with David Lévi, an Ashkenazic Jew known as Malbourouth. The community leaders were afraid that their permission for the marriage could be interpreted as a residence right for the "foreign" Jew. The couple was forced to cross the border and get married in France. (Ad Vaucluse. Gaudibert's notarial acts, fol. 863, July 6, 1789. This is, probably, the same case mentioned by Armand Lunel in "La solidarité juive." *Revue juive de Genève*, IV, No. 31 (1935), 35.) It should be noted that in Brussels the Jewish community leader, Hertogh Samuel, requested in 1791 that the authorities should renew a decree forcing foreign Jews to be registered by him. He claimed that foreign Jews were responsible for many thefts (Izak Prins, "Une curiosité historique." *Revue juive de Belgique*, No. 2 (1945), 22–25).

[191] Columbia, X893C–C 22, vol. 2.

the provincial communities was increased to 11,235 livres 6 s. 8 d. annually. On this new basis the provincial communities over a period of seventeen years from 1742 to 1758 owed 91,765 livres 6 s. 8 d. in unpaid taxes and during the period 1758–1789 an additional 97,659 livres 10 d. in unpaid taxes and another 60,000 livres for various expenses. In aggregate the provincial communities owed the sum of 437,544 livres, which was paid by the Jewish community of Metz from loans obtained from Christian creditors.[192]

Upon the outbreak of the Revolution the Jews of Phalsbourg refused to pay taxes to the community of Metz and they were soon followed by other Jewish communities. The opposition of the provincial communities was strengthened by a series of events, including the National Assembly's declaration of November 29, 1789 forbidding officials to accept gifts,[193] and the abolition on July 20, 1790 of the Brancas tax.

On September 1, 1789 the syndics of the Jewish community of Metz asked the authorities to approve a roll of taxes to be paid in four annual installments. On December 24, 1789 the intendant, Jean de Pont, ordered the Jews of Phalsbourg to pay their taxes in accordance with a request of the Metz Jews and on July 1, 1790 rejected an appeal by the former. On November 4, 1790 the Metz community put up for sale the property of the Phalsbourg syndic, Alexandre Aron, who had refused to pay the taxes levied upon the province. A ruling that the sale of Aron's property should be postponed was made on February 25, 1791 by the district of Sarrebourg.[194] Nathan [-Louis] Cahen of Louvigny, collector of taxes for the communities of Louvigny, Chaptel and Poinerieulx stated in a pamphlet published in 1792 that the only desire of "the former potentates and viceroys of the synagogue" of Metz was to drive the Jews of the smaller communities into misery. The provincial Jews were not members of the Metz community, but only its slaves. Metz always lured the richest Jews of the small communities to its midst and thus itself paid as little in taxes as possible. The provincial Jews did

[192] AN, D–III–174, dr. Metz; JTS, 01565.
[193] M. Aron, *Liquidation*, p. 11 (see Bibliography, No. 141).
[194] *Ibid*. pp. 8–12.

not participate in the election of syndics and were not consulted on the assessment of taxes to be paid. In their decision on the finances the Jewish syndics of Metz ignored their brethren of the province; only when taxes were paid were the latter honored with the title of citizens.[195]

The petition to force the provincial Jews to pay taxes was sent by the Jewish syndics of Metz not only to the local authorities but also to the National Assembly. They most probably did so because of the new partition of France into departments. Many communities of the former Metz province became a part of the neighboring Meurthe department of which Nancy was the departmental capital. Only through a federal decision in the form of a decree by the National Assembly could the Jews of Metz hope to avoid complicated and expensive lawsuits in courts of various departments.[196]

To the arguments formulated by Nathan Cahen in the name of the smaller communities the Jews of Metz replied with a long list of legal and moral proofs of the lawfulness of the taxes imposed upon the Jews of the province. They presented the minutes of a council held on January 6, 1772 by the syndics of the Jewish community of Metz and the tax collectors of the provincial communities which approved the taxes and the loans made by the former.[197] They showed that the tax assessment was fixed as a result of each Jew's own evaluation of his property. They also noted that the allegation of the smaller communities that they did not participate in determining the tax assessments was not new. During a conflict of 1779 between the Jewish community of Louvigny and the communities of Phalsbourg, Mittlebronn, Imling and Bourscheid, the Jews of Louvigny complained in a printed memorandum addressed to the King, that the other four communities were invited to attend a meeting of all the communities, but had refused to come.[198]

[195] *A Messieurs*, pp. 1–2, 5, 8 (see Bibliography, No. 25). In 1785 nineteen Jewish families of Louvigny paid their taxes. Ten paid 4 or 8 livres each, six — 13 or 15 livres, one — 39 livres 12 s. and one — 69 livres 12 s. Nathan Louis Cahen paid the largest tax — 132 livres (JTS, 01528). See Appendix VI.

[196] Documents, Metz, No. 3, fol. 7.

[197] *Ibid*. fol. 8, 10.

[198] "A Messieurs Messieurs du Directoire du Département de la Moselle,"

The local authorities of the Metz district and the Moselle department ruled in favor of the Jews of Metz. In their opinion the Jews of the former province of Metz were legally a part of the Jewish community of Metz. Only as members of the Metz community did they enjoy during the old regime the privileges and tolerance granted officially to the Jews of Metz alone.[199] The smaller communities attacked this opinion and the decision based on it. They stated that this was not a conflict over public taxes, but a dispute at law upon which no administrative body, but only judges could rule.[200] But on June 23, 1795, August 21, 1799, January 2, 1801 and again in February 1801 the Jews of Metz were supported by orders from the departmental Moselle authorities that the other communities should pay their share of the taxes. In 1801 these communities appealed to the State Council (*Conseil d'Etat*), which was then composed of many liberals familiar with the situation of the Jews. However, the Council rejected the communities' petition and asked the prefect of Moselle to appoint a commission which should assess the share of each tax payer.[201]

memorandum by the Jews of Metz, [1792] (JTS, 01528). We could not find the printed memorandum of 1779.

[199] AN, F-19-1846; *Extrait*, p. 6 (see Bibliography, No. 27): "avant la révolution cette communauté [juive de Metz] achetoit pour ces membres la tolérance du gouvernement, et la protection des chefs de la province, qu'il est certain que les Juifs de la généralité ont joui comme ceux de Metz de tous les avantages de cette tolérance et de cette protection."

[200] "Ils disent que le directoire du district n'étoit pas compétant pour prononcer parcequil ne s'agissoit pas d'impositions publiques, mais seulement d'un objet litigieux et qui étoit de la compétance des juges ordinaires ..." (Documents, Metz, No. 5, fol. 7-8).

[201] Aron, *Liquidation*, pp. 19-21 (see Bibliography, No. 141).

XVI. THE CONFLICT BETWEEN THE JEWS OF METZ AND NANCY

Before the Revolution many Jews of Nancy and other communities not within the jurisdiction of the Metz parliament paid taxes to the community of Metz. Among such taxpayers were Jews who had moved from Metz to other communities, and also some, who for various reasons, desired membership in their local communities as well as in the community of Metz.[202] The explanation for the dual membership of Lorraine Jews is to be found in the Letters patent of January 26, 1753 and April 22, 1762 which did not, however, authorize a Jewish cemetery in Lorraine. Hence the Jews there were forced to bury their dead in the cemeteries of Metz or of other communities outside Lorraine. For example, on January 6, 1791, the Jewish leader of Lorraine, Berr-Isaac Berr, wrote to the Jewish community of Metz, that he had paid it 75 livres annually for the privilege of being buried in its cemetery.[203]

---

[202] For some reason the Cerfberr family desired to maintain its membership in the Metz community. In 1770 Cerfberr de Médelsheim paid taxes to the community of Metz (Landmann, Ce 390). A decree of May 13, 1805 ordered the name of Marx Cerfberr stricken from the roster of the Metz Jews. Much later his son, Max-Théodore Cerfberr, appealed against this decree, but on December 29, 1847 the civil tribunal of the Seine department approved it (*Le Droit*, Dec. 30, 1847).

[203] AN, D–III–174, F–19–1849–I. On the Jewish cemeteries of Nancy and Lunéville see Ch. Pfister, *op. cit.*, III, 326; René Wiener, *L'Ancien cimetière juif de Nancy* (Nancy, 1912). 4 pp.; Idem, "Les cimetières israélites de Nancy." *RJL*, 1927, 198–205. Compare with a much earlier responsum: "A city which has a cemetery may compel the villages which bring their dead to that cemetery to come under the jurisdiction of its court:" Louis Finkelstein, *Jewish Self-Government in the Middle Ages* (New York, 1924), p. 198. See also note 204.

Berr-Isaac Berr's father, Isaac Berr (or Behr) settled in Nancy between 1721 and 1733. His name was not mentioned among the 78 Jewish families permitted to settle in Lorraine on Apr. 12, 1721. He was first mentioned in a later list of 1733. On January 29, 1753 Berr, Simon Alcan and Michel Godechaux were appointed by Stanislas Leckzinski [Leszczyński] as the Jewish

The Jewish communities of Lorraine did not have any large collective debts of their own to pay after 1789,[204] but some Jews of Lorraine, including Berr-Isaac Berr himself, were requested by the Jewish community of Metz to pay a part of the taxes levied to liquidate the Metz debts. Berr and the other Lorraine Jews refused to pay and appealed to the National Assembly. Berr, however, was related to a Jewish family of Metz, having married Cathérine Karch, a daughter of the Jewish banker, Michel Goudechaux, the son of Lion Halter (called Goudechaux). In 1791 the Jewish community of Metz presented to the govern-

syndics for Lorraine. Isaac Berr died in 1755. E. Carmoly, "Berr[-Isaac Berr] de Turique." *Biographie des Israélites de France* (Frankfurt-sur-le-Mein, 1868), pp. 54–62. On Isaac Berr see also Me. Mirbeck, *Mémoire pour Mayer-Isaac Berr, juif, banquier à Nancy* (Nancy, n. d.), p. 4; *Mémoire à consulter pour le Sr. Jean-François Blaise, marchand à Nancy, contre les héritiers d'Isaac-Berr, Juif marchand de la même ville.* [Signés: Jacquemin, Pheyne, Grandjean] (Nancy, 1765). 11 pp.; *Mémoire à consulter pour la veuve & héritiers d'Isaac Berr . . . sur l'appel qu'ils ont interjetté d'une sentence . . . au profit du Sr. Jean-François Blaise.* [Signé: Bordelux] (Nancy, 1765). 17 pp. On Berr-Isaac Berr see also Isaïe Berr de Turique, *Discours prononcé aux funérailles de M. Berr de Turique, prononcé le 16 novembre 1828, par un petit fils* (n. p., n. d.); Z. Szajkowski, in *Davke*, No. 24, (1955), 238–48 (the last years of B.-I. Berr's life).

[204] The Jewish community of Nancy had to borrow money for the construction of the synagogue at which services were first held in 1790. J. Godechot, "Les Juifs de Nancy de 1789 à 1795." *REJ*, LXXXVII (1929), 6. "En 1787, en ma qualité de Syndic général des Juifs de la Lorraine, et particulièrement de Nancy, j'ai obtenu du Roi des lettres Patentes, pour l'acquisition d'un cimetière, et la construction d'une nouvelle Synagogue. Défunt Mr. Mayer Marx, père, également Syndic particulier des mêmes Communautés, étant animé, comme moi, de sentiments religieux et de bienfaisance, nous avons convoqués tous les Israëlites, demeurant alors à Nancy, et obtenu, par des actes authentiques, leur procuration pour faire des emprunts, au nom de la Communauté entière, comme nous le pourrions le mieux, soit en rentes viagères, constitution ou autres . . ." (Berr-Isaac Berr's letter of Apr. 13, 1820. Jerusalem, 300/5). "Extraits des livres des délibérations de la Communauté israélite de Nancy." *RJL*, IV, No. 36 (1928), 113C ("19 décembre 1830. Le Consistoire de Nancy fait connaître au Consistoire central qu'il n'a aucune dette").

In 1769 the Jews of Lorraine paid a tax of 14,300 Lorraine livres (11,371 French livres). In all probabilities, the community of Lorraine was not forced to borrow in order to pay this tax. L. Vanson, "Imposition sur les Juifs en Lorraine dans l'ancien régime." *RJL*, IX (1933), 197–207, 230–41.

ment copies of documents proving that Berr belonged to the Metz community. In 1752 his father obtained the King's Letters patent permitting him to reside in Metz; this right was confirmed in an ordinance of August 10, 1752 signed by the intendant J.-F. de Creil. (In addition to Berr five other Jews of Nancy obtained such individual Letters patent.) Berr replied that he was only a "subscriber" to the Metz community, and not a direct member.[205] At first it seemed that the position of the Nancy Jews was unassailable since they resided outside the Moselle department of which Metz was the capital. But by a decree of May 20, 1791 the National Assembly referred all conflicts over the Metz debts to the jurisdiction of the Metz administration. As a result the Jews of Nancy had to pay their share of the tax for the liquidation of the debts, although they protested the decree of May 20. Nevertheless, on August 18, 1791 the Metz district granted the Jewish community of Metz the right to enforce payment of taxes by all subsidiary communities. An ordinance of October 3, 1811, signed by Napoleon I, enjoined Berr-Isaac Berr to pay his part of the tax to liquidate the debts.[206]

[205] AN, F–19–1849; Documents, Metz No. 2, fol. 3–4. P.-L. Lacretelle was one of the lawyers who signed a brief in favor of Berr and the other Jews of Nancy against the community of Metz (AN, D–III–174). On Lacretelle's friendly attitude toward Jews during the old regime see note 176.

[206] AN, F–19–1849; Halphen, 8; Aron, p. 13 (see Bibliography, No. 141). In the year IX Berr-Isaac Berr had to pay 460 francs and in the year X, 210 francs (AN, F–19–1849–I).

XVII. THE "YOUNG JEWS" OF METZ

The debts provoked a conflict between the rich and the poor, and the old and the new generations in the community of Metz.[207] After the outbreak of the Revolution the "young Jews" (*jeunes juifs*) — those who were newly married or newly settled in Metz — refused to pay the tax to liquidate the debts because in the past they had not paid for protection. According to a brief dated February 17, 1801, prepared by three lawyers of Metz (Rondeville, Jean-Philippe Lambert and Mirion), who were asked for advice by Terquem, Samuel Hayem, Michel Abram and other "young Jews," prior to the Revolution only a limited number of Jews was tolerated. For this reason the "young Jews" who were married after 1789 and became French citizens in 1791 should not pay any debts incurred in the past to buy protection.[208] The number of such "young Jews" was large enough to create a serious crisis in the community. Two hundred and seventy-four marriages were registered among the Jews of Metz from 1792 until the end of August 1809.[209] According to a register of Floréal in the year II (April-May 1794) the debt-tax had to be paid by 590 old settled families and 45 young couples married after 1789, including 35 from Metz and 10 from other communities: in these cases the brides were Metz girls.

Implicit in this refusal to pay the tax, there was a more serious conflict between the two generations, the older generation of orthodox Jews and the young generation of partisans of a reform

[207] The Jewish community of Metz was divided even geographically, each of three social classes residing in its own district: Tsarphati [Olry Terquem], *Neuvième Lettre d'un Israélite français* ... (Paris, 1837), p. 33.

[208] AN, F–19–1846; Documents, Metz, No. 6. Mathieu de Rondeville, a lawyer of the Metz parliament from 1768 on and a deputy to the National Assembly, or his son, Charles-François, a lawyer of the parliament from 1786 on. Lambert was a lawyer of the parliament from 1763 on (Michel; *op. cit.*; Paquet, I, 4–5, 11, 12, 18, 36, 64, 110, II, 1484). We could not establish the identity of the lawyer Mirion, who is not mentioned by Michel or others. (A lawyer named Mirgon is mentioned in a manuscript list of Metz lawyers, Ad Moselle, B.)

[209] Am Metz, 1–F–11; JTS, 01565.

of Jewish religious practices.[210] A report concluded that the "young Jews" were born debtors and thus were forced to share in the repayment of the debts. The report incidentally argued that the Jews would always remain a separate body.[211]

Olry Terquem, one of the members of the young group who later became influential among the reform Jews in France published his famous twenty-seven *Lettres Tsarphatiques* (1821–1846), directed against the orthodox Jews.[212]

According to one source an opposition movement of the "young Jews" in the community of Avignon also developed.[213]

---

[210] A prefectural report of March 30, 1801 commented on this conflict: "La scission commenca entre les Juifs de campagne et ceux de Metz, comme elle existait déjà entre les villages qui s'étaient coalisés pour faire la loi aux villes. Elle s'étendit ensuite entre les anciens et les jeunes juifs. Les moteurs de ces discordes étoient de certains hommes qui croient au fanatisme contre quoionque tenoit à une religion. Beaucoup parmi les enfans de Moyse ont resisté aux efforts de ces sectaires fanatiques eux même: mais les jeunes gens voulant faire écho, *se sont mis au pas* en frondant les anciens. De la deux opinions opposés ont formé deux partis parmi eux" ("Mon opinion développée et discutée sur la prétention des jeunes gens Juifs contre les anciens." Documents, Metz, No. 6, fol. 31–36). The deputy and Paris representative to the Moselle department, François-René-Augustin Mallarmé (1755–1836), reported on the orthodox Jew, Joseph Gougenheim, who was arrested during the Terror: "il s'était opposé à ce que les Juifs ne demanderent pas plutôt de jouir des droits de citoyens actifs; que c'est un homme dangereux et fanatique" (Paquet, 640, 759, 932, 1090, 1093). Mallarmé was not anti-Jewish. Among the local officials appointed by him were a few Jews (*Ibid.*, II, 1370). On Mallarmé see H. Poulet, *La vie de F.-R.-A. Mallarmé . . .* (Nancy, n. d.). 62 pp. According to one source Cerfberr (of Nancy), too, had a similar attitude: "Cerf Berr en 89, était dans le mécontents, machinait contre notre émancipation." [Tsarpati,] "Michel Berr." *AI*, IV (1843), 725–26.

[211] "Mon opinion . . .," see note 210.

[212] On Terquem, his fight for the reform of religious Jewish practices and his other activities see Isidore Loeb, *Biographie d'Albert Cohn* (Paris, 1878), pp. 154–57; E. Prouhet, *Notice sur la vie et les travaux d'Olry Terquem . . .* (Paris, 1862). 11 pp.; Isidore Cahen, in *AI*, XXIII (1862), 313; Hip. Lévy, in *AI*, XLVIII (1887), 222; M. de Bressolles, *Discours prononcé sur la tombe de M. Olry Terquem . . . le 8 mai 1862* (Paris, n. d.). See also note 43.

[213] "Il y avait eu . . . des réclamations de la part des Juifs forains et des jeunes Juifs" (*Observations*, p. 15, see Bibliography, No. 104).
On an "insurection" by tax payers in the seventeenth century Avignon community see Jules Bauer, "Un commencement d'insurection au quartier Juif d'Avignon au XVIIᵉ siècle." *REJ*, XXXVIII (1899), 123–36.

XVIII. THE SALE OF COMMUNAL PROPERTIES IN METZ

In order to repay their debts the Jews of Metz favored the sale of all communal properties except for the synagogue, according to a petition dated December 22, 1791. In another petition dated September 1, 1794 they reviewed the course of events starting with the decree granting citizenship to the Jews, the abolition of their communities, and the decision that all properties of these communities were to become public.[214] Some communal properties of the Metz Jews were, in fact, confiscated and sold as national property.[215] But most of the communal property escaped nationalization. The Jewish cemeteries of Metz were destroyed for national military defense purposes but not as nationalized property, as happened in other places. The authorities were even willing to compensate the Jews of Metz for the loss of these cemeteries.[216]

In the year IV the civil authorities of Metz nationalized the main synagogue and put it up for sale. The Jews protested. In a petition to the departmental *Directoire* they stated that the confiscation and sale of the synagogue, which was a place of prayer, would contravene the spirit of the laws guaranteeing

---

[214] AN, F–19–1846, 1848.

[215] AN, D–III–174; *Résumé*, pp. 11–12 (see Bibliography, No. 31). Z. Szajkowski, "Synagogues During the French Revolution." *JSS*, XX (1958), 221. In 1704 Abraham Schwab and his wife Agathe bequeathed to the Jewish community of Metz a house and 6,000 livres in annuities for the establishment of a *yeshiva*. According to one source the capital left by Schwab was confiscated in 1793. It is improbable that this confiscation occurred. Jules Bauer, *l'Ecole rabbinique de France, 1830–1930* (Paris [1939]), pp. 32–33. Schwab's will was published in the *AI*, V (1844), p. 388.

[216] See note 158.

freedom of religion. They also argued that since all the other communal properties of their dissolved corporation and the debts it owed Christian creditors had not yet been nationalized, the civil authorities were wrong to have nationalized the synagogue. They claimed further that the synagogue should be regarded as property mortgaged to the Christian creditors of the Jews. On April 23, 1796 the *Directoire* decided not to sell the synagogue while the status of the Jewish community and the debts were uncertain. This decision was later approved by the Ministry of Finance which was in charge of the sale of nationalized properties.[217] The synagogue was given back to the community and reconditioned by the syndics who were elected at the assembly of the Metz Jews on September 3, 1796.[218]

The Christian creditors used for their own interest the fact that the communal Jewish properties of Metz were not nationalized, although on one occasion they asserted that one communal Jewish house situated on 27 *rue de l'Arsenal* was nationalized and sold to the Jew, Jacob Samuel. In fact, however, the house was not the property of the Jewish community: it belonged to a school founded by the terms of Lyon Ditz' will of 1755, but it is possible that the school was a communal Jewish institution. Puyproux the elder stated in the name of the Christian creditors that the furniture of the synagogue was not nationalized but plundered.[219] · Incidentally, the Jews of Metz did not oppose nationalization of their communal properties on the ground cited by the Jews of Bordeaux and Saint-Esprit-lès-Bayonne against the nationalization of their cemeteries, namely that these properties belonged not to the communities, but to philanthropic societies.

Was the synagogue of Metz — the main synagogue — sold together with other communal properties in order to repay the community's debts? No documentary proof was found, although

[217] Ad Moselle, V 166.
[218] AN, F–19–11014; Anchel, *op. cit.*, p. 27.
[219] *Encore un mot*, pp. 1–2 (see Bibliography, No. 35). A Jew named Lion Ditze lived in Metz during the Revolution. Ditz was also a Christian name (see Paquet, I, 57, II, index, p. 36. See also note 221).

it is of course possible that one of the many synagogues was closed and the building then sold.[220]

According to an inventory of the year II (1793–1794) the Jewish community of Metz was the owner of twenty two houses or apartments, which were used as synagogues, for various other communal purposes, or rented to private families.[221] According

[220] There were five synagogues in Metz in 1793: (1) the old synagogue; (2) various houses of prayer for women, (3) the new synagogue; (4) the synagogue of Nathan Terquem; (5) the synagogue of Abraham Schwabe (Am Metz, P–3–1, an inventory of Jan. 4–5, 1794). (According to one source there were two synagogues in 1779. See note 53.)

[221] (1) The Great Synagogue and two joint synagogues for women; (2) a house in the courtyard of the synagogue, formerly inhabited by the rabbi; (3) another synagogue, together with a synagogue for women in the same courtyard (two floors above the second synagogue were used by the collectors of taxes; the cellars of the great synagogue belonged to Louis Olry and others); (4) a four story house next to the womens' great synagogue; (5) one sixth of the house of the heirs of Lyon and Alexandre Etting; (6) one half of the house of the heirs of Cerf and Alexandre Halphen; (7) one sixth of the house of Lyon Trenel; (8) one half of the house of Lazard Lambert; (9) a house situated between the properties of Nathan Terquem and Marc Terquem's heirs; (10) one half of the house of the heirs of Moyses Worms; (11) a house situated between the Jewish butchery and Anchel Lévy's house; (12) One half of Gompers Lévy's house; (13) a house serving as the Jewish hospital; (14) one quarter of Ely Cahen's house; (15) a house occupied by the cantor; (16) the house of Lion Ditze; (17) a great hall serving as the butchery, with four apartments above the hall; (18) one sixth of the house of Nathan Grodval's heirs; (19) two parts of Grodval's house; (20) a part of Lyon Picard's house; (21) one half of Jacob Treve's house; (22) a part of Jacob May's house (JTS, 01565).

In 1750, 161 of the 3,272 houses in the city of Metz were in the ghetto. Up to 1767 the number of houses in the ghetto was unchanged but the total number of houses in Metz declined to 3,157 in 1766 and 2,871 in 1767 (Am Metz, 3P3). On June 26, 1797 the "former" Jewish community of Metz paid 155 livres in land-taxes for the houses belonging to the community (Documents, Metz, No. 48). In 1793 the main synagogue of Metz served as a warehouse where the authorities deposited 19,640 pounds of copper and other valuable articles confiscated from the Jews (Documents, Metz, No. 49, fol. 465–87, No. 50, fol. 480–517).

On the 19th century synagogues of Metz see *Rapport au Conseil Municipal de Metz sur la demande d'un secours faite par le Consistoire de cette ville pour aider à la réédification de la Synagogue. 13 Février 1845* (Metz, n. d.). 23 pp.; Szajkowski, *Poverty . . .*, p. 26. On the poor housing conditions among Jews of Metz in the 19th century see O. Terquem, *Quelques réflexions à propos d'une*

to another source the Jewish community of Metz also owned 6,000 pounds of copper.[222] Still, the debts owed by the Jews of Metz exceeded the value of all their communal properties.

The departmental *Directoire*'s decision of June 23, 1795 ordered the sale of communal Jewish properties before an attempt had been made to liquidate the debts from the proceeds of a special tax. But the sale was deferred and officially authorized only on August 9, 1798.[223] On August 26 the departmental authorities of Moselle ordered the sale of the chattels of the former Jewish community of Metz and the proceeds to be paid to the creditors. At the request of the creditors' syndic, Jacques-François Adam,[224] this property was sold by the *huissier*, J.-Louis Adam,[225] on January 6, 7 and 8, 1799 at an auction which was announced by broadsides and town-criers and which took place in the office of the community, 16 *rue de l'Arsenal*. Adam was assisted at the auction by the Jews, Nathan-Lazare Cahen and C[erf] Morhange, who acted as crier. All together 138 articles were sold for the sum of 8,479.45 francs.[226] It seems that, except for the furniture, most of the items sold were religious objects. It is also possible that the most valuable communal properties were bought by

lettre (Metz, [1845]). 6 pp.; *UI*, I (1845), 124; Szajkowski, *Poverty* . . ., pp. 26–27.

[222] AN, D–III–174.

[223] AN, F–19–1846; Documents, Metz, No. 43, fol. 259–60; *Compte*, p. 5 (see Bibliography, No. 39).

[224] J.-F. Adam, syndic of the Christian creditors of Metz, died on May 7, 1801 (Am Metz, 3–P–16).

[225] Louis Adam fils was appointed on Aug. 24, 1791 by the district of Metz as the official *huissier* of the commission to liquidate the debts. *Loi*, p. 3 (see Bibliography, No. 20).

[226] Following are some of the 138 articles together with the names of buyers and prices: "Onze vases en cuivre . . ., une fontaine et son basin en étain . . ., deux grandes registres reliés en parchemin . . ., le Talmud en dix huit volumes adjugé à Jsaye Morhange à soixante un francs, seize volumes hebraïques adjugés à Lion Morhange a cinq francs dix centimes, un ornement pour la table de moyse au velour bleu ciel brodé en or et dentelle de main adjugé au C[itoyen] Samuel Cahen à Soix[te] neuf francs cinq[te] centimes, six bras et mapot de fer adjugé à Lion Grodeval à deux francs soixante, deux petites armoires . . ., dix veieilles chaises . . ., deux chandeliers de cuivre . . ." (Documents, Metz, No. 66, fol. 262–71, minutes of the auction).

Jews for the community. Thus the building of the refuge and the hospital for Jewish paupers was sold on June 15, 1799, to a group of rich Jews who collected enough money to pay 2,250 francs. Later they turned it over to the community.[227]

[227] "Notice sur l'origine, les ressources, le personnel et les besoins de l'Hospice israëlite de Metz," a 19th century document, ZS: "En 1793, la communauté fut suspendu, tous les services suspendus et les administrations dispersées. L'Hospice continuait néamoins à functionner d'une manière sans doute très irregulière . . . En l'an 7 de la République sur la requête des créanciers de l'ancienne communauté, un arrête de l'administration centrale du département ordonnait la vente forcée de tous les immeubles ayant appartenu à la dite communauté. Le bâtiment de l'Hospice reconnu être la propriété de la communauté fut compris dans la licitation et le 27 Prairial an 7 [June 15, 1799] une adjudication publique eut lieu devant Monsieur Purnoy, notaire à Metz. Pour conserver cet établissement à la communauté, plusieurs israélites aîsés se cotiserent et six d'entr'eux qui formaient alors l'administration achèterent avec le produit de cette collecte la dite maison au prix de 2250 francs pour être consacrée de nouveau a recevoir des infirmes et des malades pauvres."

XIX. THE LIQUIDATION OF THE METZ DEBTS

The financial activities of the commission to liquidate the debts were conducted through special agents appointed by the local authorities.[228] Through them the Christian creditors controlled many Jewish activities, e. g., the lease of houses belonging to the community, of synagogue seats. On May 7 and 15, 1796 houses belonging to the community and synagogue seats were rented publicly. The rent of sixty-eight seats for men and women in the main synagogue, and sixty-one seats for men and fifty-two for women in the smaller synagogue situated in the yard of the main synagogue produced 1,244 livres 10 s.[229] A sale of communal Jewish properties which was started on April 25, 1798 by the notary Claude Purnot, who was put in charge of the sale, ended in 1799. Among the items sold were seventeen Tablets of the Ten Commandments.[230] The auction of 138 articles (on January 6–8, 1799) produced the sum of 7,981.65 francs.[231] Sales of houses and chattels in 254 lots produced in the year VIII (September 1799 — August 1800) the sum of 43,111.99 francs. All the buyers were Jews.[232]

On February 21, 1800 the Jews were in arrears to fifty-three creditors to whom they owed 82,306.44 francs, and according to an inventory of May 30, 1802 they owed 29,571.50 francs to fifty-four creditors.[233]

[228] On Jan. 19, 1801 Pierre Boucherat was appointed treasurer of the Metz commission to liquidate the debts (Am Metz, 3P16).

[229] *Ibid.*, 3–P–4.

[230] According to Purnot's report of Apr. 25, 1799: "Vente de biens appartenant à la ci-devant association connue sous la dénomination de la ci-devant communauté des Juifs de Metz, reçus par le citoyen Purnot, notaire à Metz." 76 pp. (*Ibid.*, P–3–2). Purnot (? — 1845) was a Metz notary of Toul origin. In 1795 he became president of the departmental *Directoire* and on Oct. 20, 1795 a civil judge (Paquet, I, 32).

[231] Documents, Metz, No. 46, fol. 262–71.

[232] Documents, Metz, No. 38, fol. 190–95.

[233] *Ibid.*, No. 20, fol. 92–93.

690

In case of death the heirs of a creditor to whom the Jewish community paid interest were generally able to claim only the unpaid interest due at the time of death, but in many cases the capital as well. Thus, the age of the creditors was an important factor in the liquidation of the debts. The interest due to Jeanne Godfrin of Metz, for example, amounted to 320 livres a year. After her death on March 14, 1804 her heirs were paid only 153 livres 6 s. for unpaid interest covering five months and twenty-three days from the last payment until her death. The heirs of Anne Lajeunesse, who died on March 9, 1804, were paid only 149 livres of the yearly sum due of 320 livres. On a list of payments made December 21, 1800 to fifty-four creditors it was noted that fourteen of them had died and that thirteen were supposed dead. According to a 1810 list of twenty-nine creditors nine of them were between 62–70 years old, nineteen between 71–80 years old and one was 92 years old.[234]

The commission to liquidate the Metz debts reported an income of 282,747 livres 6 s. 4 d. in *assignats* (paper money), 34,816 livres 8 s. 6 d. in drafts and 6,638 livres 5 s. 2 d. in cash, and expenses of 282,547 livres 4 s. 5 d., 28,928 livres 10 s., 9,494 livres 3 s. 7 d. respectively, in a financial report presented on September 2, 1802. Upon the dissolution of the former community the commission found in the treasury only 1,330 livres in *assignats* and 267 livres 5 s. in cash. The rent of the communal houses produced an income of 10,015 livres 4 s. 9 d. in *assignats*, 20,937 livres in drafts and 3,761 livres 10 s. 5 d. in cash. Arrears for unpaid taxes produced 230,809 livres 6 s. 10 d. in *assignats* and 1,248 livres 8 s. 6 d. in drafts. The commission also received 16,236 livres 16 s. 6 d. from communal trusts. The sale of communal properties, silver, chattels, real estate and new loans produced the sum of 24,355 livres 18 s. 3 d. in *assignats*, 9,481 livres in drafts and 2,609 livres 9 s. 9 d. in cash. Another 3,150 livres in drafts were acquired by the exchange of *assignats* for drafts. The main expenses consisted of 163,487 livres 5 s. 3 d. in *assignats*, 12,455 livres 5 s. 3 d. in drafts and 4,657 livres 5 s. in cash paid to the creditors. Maintenance of the communal properties (not including 7,236 livres 2 s. 3 d. in *assignats* and

[234] *Ibid.*, Nos. 44, 47, 74.

583 livres in cash spent on the synagogue) cost 10,159 livres 5 d. in *assignats*, 16,048 livres 10 s. in drafts and 898 livres 9 s. 7 d. in cash.[235]

In 1828 the Jews of Metz were said to owe the sum of 120,000 francs in unpaid interest. On April 19, 1855 they still owed, together with interest, 100,056.54 francs. Of this amount 48,270.20 francs was paid to fifteen creditors or their heirs who won this sum in the 1850's as the outcome of various lawsuits.[236]

The expenses of the commission and court expenses incurred in creditors' lawsuits increased the taxes for the liquidation of the debts. The commission's budget amounted to 18,527 francs in 1819, of which, 3,488.90 was for payment of interest to fourteen creditors, the remainder for legal fees, etc. In 1853, 48,321 francs was collected to pay off debts, of which only 26,328 was used for a partial payment on a debt, the remainder for administrative expenses, including court expenses. The tribunal of Metz ordered payment of a debt of about 10,000 francs to the heirs of one creditor, but the expenses incurred in this lawsuit amounted to 20,000 francs.[237]

The taxes for the liquidation of the debts were collected by the regular collectors of governmental taxes, who were paid by the commission for extra work involved.[238]

Of the roll of taxes of 1843 only 18,776 of the 21,721 francs assessed was collected and only 48,200.50 francs of the 50,618.42 francs assessed of the 1853 roll. All together only 66,976.50 francs were collected between 1843 and 1855.[239]

[235] *Compte* (see Bibliography, No. 39).

[236] Documents, Metz, No. 20, fol. 92–93; *Analyse* and Report of 1843, p. 8 (see Bibliography, Nos. 50, 58).

[237] AN, F–19–848; Reports of 1843, p. 5, and 1855 (see Bibliography Nos. 58, 75).

[238] The collectors of Metz taxes were paid 3 per cent of the proceeds, according to the circular of July 30, 1843 (see Bibliography No. 60).

[239] Report of Sept. 3, 1855 (see Bibliography, No. 75).

XX. THE CONFLICT BETWEEN THE COMMUNITY OF METZ AND JEWS OF PARIS AND OTHER COMMUNITIES

No group of inhabitants of France other than the Jews was forced by the Revolution to maintain communal ties by reason of a tax. The Jews took exception in a long series of lawsuits. Cerf-Jacob Godchaux and Abraham Borlweilers of Metz, Samuel Hayem Worms of Sarrelibre and other Jews stated in a petition of August 23, 1801 that forcing them to pay the debt-tax because they were formerly members of a legally dissolved community would be "one of the gravest blunders."[240] But many Jews who were forced to pay the tax were not even former members of the dissolved community. The Alsatian Jewish leader, Auguste Ratisbonne (1771–1830), was born abroad. Still, he had to pay a yearly Metz tax of 60 francs because he married Adelaïde Cerfberr, a daughter of Marx Cerfberr, whose wife, Esther Boas, was a daughter of Simon Boas of Metz origin.[241] In the 1840's ten Jewish families of Bordeaux were required to pay the Metz tax, among them David Marx (1807–1864), an Ashkenazic Jew who became chief-rabbi of Bordeaux;[242] four Sephardic families of Bordeaux (Salzédo, Lopes-Dubec, Furtado and Nunes); and five Ashkenazic Jews of Bordeaux. Salzédo was related to a family of Nancy which, in turn, was related to a family of Metz. His appeal against the tax was rejected on April 12, 1845 by the State Council, the country's highest judicial body.[243]

In 1821 a Jew of Nancy challenged the legality of the Metz tax before the tribunal of Nancy. But on June 27, 1822 the prefect of Moselle raised the question of a conflict of jurisdiction in this matter. A royal ordinance of February 19, 1823 upheld the prefect who ordered the sale of the Jew's furniture in order

[240] AN, F–19–1846.

[241] Documents, Metz, No. 40, fol. 253–54. On Ratisbonne see "Biographie — Auguste Ratisbonne." *La Rég.*, I (1836), 93–96. See also note 303.

[242] On Rabbi Marx see Elie-Aristide Astruc, *Oraison funèbre du vénérable David Marx, grand rabbin de Bordeaux, Extrait des AI* (Paris, 1864). 14 pp.

[243] Documents, Metz, No. 114, fol. 672–73.

to cover his unpaid tax.²⁴⁴ A Metz newspaper, which displayed the motto *Liberte! 1789–1830*, noted in 1845 that it would have been advisable for the government to pay off the old debts owed by the Jewish communities. But, since the revolutionary authorities of 1789 had decided otherwise, this decision must stand.²⁴⁵ In fact, all appeals to judicial and other authorities against the liquidation of the debts through special taxes were lost.

In 1816 a royal ordinance required all descendants of the Jews of the former papal province to pay the special tax for the liquidation of the debts. Only the direct heirs of the former members of the former Jewish communities — *i. e.* all those who received an *inheritance* — were liable for communal debts, in the view of the well known republican lawyer and Jewish leader Adolphe Crémieux (1796–1886), which was stated in a letter to the Alsatian Jewish deputy Max-Théodore Cerfberr (1792–1872), dated September 15, 1843. Since not only the heirs, but all descendants of these Jews were forced to pay the debts, to Crémieux this seemed an "incredible abuse."²⁴⁶ This point was made again on April 30, 1851 by the Metz commission to liquidate the debts which recalled that in accordance with the Government's decision of December 26, 1801, not only the heirs, but all descendants had to pay the debts.²⁴⁷ On the other hand Forbin des Issarts, a deputy of the Vaucluse department, pointed out in 1821 that the decisions of the legislative and judicial authorities on the debts were taken on the basis of the pre-revolutionary usages of the Jewish communities which recognized

²⁴⁴ *Mémoire* (see Bibliography, No. 65). On December 9, 1844 before the civil tribunal of Sarreguemines, Moyse Cahen, Mayer Oppenheimer, Isaac Banheim, David Hirsch and Rose Lazard (the widow of Marx Kremer), all of Frauenberg, challenged the legality of the tax for 1842 for the liquidation of the Metz debts. *Ibid.*

²⁴⁵ *Courrier de la Moselle*, June 30, 1845.

²⁴⁶ Documents, Alsace, No. 3, fol. 5–6. Crémieux became a member of the central consistory in 1831 and its president in 1843. Cerfberr became a member of the central consistory in 1836 and its president in 1848. See Léon Kahn, *Les Juifs de Paris depuis le VIᵉ siècle* (Paris, 1889), pp. 195–96. On Crémieux's activities in the consistory see S. Posener, *Adolphe Crémieux* (Paris, 1933), I, 150–97. On Cerfberr see Isidore Cahen, in *AI*, XXXV, 207; Robert, II, 7. He was the son of Thédore Cerfberr (1766–1832) and Julie (Jeanette) Mayer Max of Nancy. He married Eliza Ratisbonne (1813–1853), daughter of Auguste Ratisbonne.

²⁴⁷ Documents, Metz, No. 25, fol. 107–108.

the responsibility not only of the heirs, but of all descendants.[248] This could not be denied.[249]

Only emigration abroad delivered a Jew and his descendants from the financial ties to the dissolved Jewish community of his ancestors. Even conversion to Catholicism did not free a Jew from paying his part of the debts. Thus, on the tax rosters of Metz for the years 1842 and 1853 were listed the names of the nun Cecile Terquem, the countess de Breteuil, the countess Girardin (daughter of the countess Lefèvre de la Chavière), countess de Grouchy, Varinot of Toul, the widow Paquin Dudin, D'Angély and others.[250] (The Carpentras commission for the liquidation of the debts had decided on June 11, 1816 that converted Jews should pay the tax.[251])

Many Jews of Paris were forced to pay the tax for the liquidation of the debts of the Metz Jews because they were related to Jews of Metz origin, e. g., the Jewish leader Adolphe Crémieux himself, because his wife Amélia Silny was of Metz origin.[252] In the 1840's Adolphe Crémieux, Edmond Halphen, Cahen, the notary Emile Fould and Alphonse Cerfberr, all of them well known Jewish leaders of Paris, distributed a printed statement for which they solicited the signature of those opposed to payment of the tax for the liquidation of the Metz debts and willing to support the fight for its annulment. They also appealed for funds amounting to one third of the tax in order to cover the

[248] "Il y a été procédé selon les anciens usages établis par les juifs eux-mêmes dans leur intérêt" (Forbin des Issarts, p. 6, see Bibliography, No. 107).

[249] "une des bases du pacte social qui a présidé à la formation de nos communautés religieuses, est l'engagement pour la postérité" (Minutes of the Carpentras commission, Feb. 16, 1817. Columbia, X893C–C22, vol. 2).

[250] See Bibliography, Nos. 57, 72; Henri Contamine, *Metz et la Moselle de 1814 à 1870* (Nancy, 1932), II, 359.

[251] "un membre a demandé si on y comprenait les descendans ou représentans, de quelque religion qu'ils soient, d'individus qui ont fait partie de l'ancienne communauté, soit que ces représentans aient eux-mêmes ou leurs aïeux changé de religion. La commission considérant que la question n'offrait pas même une difficulté raisonable, qu'il suffisait de consulter le texte de l'ordonnance Royale et qu'enfin un changement de religion ne peut jamais affranchir des obligations civiles, a décidé unanimement l'affirmative" (Columbia, X893C–C22, vol. 1, fol. 4–6).

[252] They were married in 1824. *UI*, XXXV (1879–80), 363; S. Posener, *op. cit.*, I, 66–67.

expenses of the fight.[253] In a letter addressed on October 31, 1843 to the commission to liquidate the debts of Metz, they predicted that no administration or court of law in 1843 would approve the execution of the law of 1791 on the debts. They also stated that the law of the revolutionary period anticipated the sale of the communal Jewish properties in order to repay the debts, although this was never done. Should the commission continue to consider them as debtors and force them to pay the tax, in turn they threatened to invoke the law and force the sale of these communal properties.[254] To this the commission replied in a letter dated November 22, 1843, that the synagogue of Metz and the religious articles had been sold, but it was still necessary to levy another tax of 37,784.75 francs. Only the cemetery and the home for aged people, which did not then belong to the community, had not been sold.[255] In March 1845 a Paris Jew named Dreyfuss obtained a writ against the tax-collector who had ordered the sale of his property for not paying the Metz tax. This was a pre-arranged test case. On July 9, 1845 the tribunal of the Seine department annuled the sale and imposed a fine on the tax-collector to cover expenses incurred. But the prefect of the Seine department appealed and Dreyfuss lost his case.[256] On December 29, 1847 the arguments of Crémieux and his friends were rejected by the civil tribunal of the Seine department. At the same time the tribunal denied the claim made by the Jewish leader, Olry Worms de Romilly, that he was not liable for the tax because his father had been naturalized by Louis XVI's Letters patent of July 1787.[257]

[253] Documents, Metz, No. 109, fol. 663. In 1832 Alphonse Cerfberr became a member of the central consistory. L. Kahn, *op. cit.*, p. 95.

[254] Documents, Metz, No. 22, fol. 98–99; Report of Jan. 3, 1844, see Bibliography, No. 63.

[255] Documents, Metz, No. 23, fol. 100; Report of Jan. 3, 1844, see Bibliography, No. 63.

[256] Documents, Metz, No. 111, fol. 666; Circular of 1846, see Bibliography, No. 67.

[257] *Le Droit*, Dec. 30, 1847. The banker Worms de Romilly became a member of the central consistory in 1825 and its president in 1826 (L. Kahn, *op. cit.*, p. 195). In 1849 after the death of Worms de Romilly, the editor of *Les Archives Israélites* disparaged him because he had left very little money for Jewish charity. R. [S. Cahen], in *AI*, X (1849), 422–23. On his father's naturalization in 1787 see AN, C–82–817–2.

XXI. THE LIQUIDATION OF THE DEBTS OF THE FORMER PAPAL PROVINCE

The Jews of the former papal province were ordered to repay the debts by a decree of Napoleon I, dated October 7, 1807. The prefect of Vaucluse was instructed to appoint two commissions of five members each for the liquidation of the debts of Avignon and of L'Isle-sur-Sorgue. These commissions were appointed on April 9, 1808. An order by Napoleon could hardly be opposed and the Jews had to obey.[258] Still, this was one of the rare instances when the Jews refused to carry out blindly orders reflecting the First Empire's policy toward Jews. Each appointee to the commission for the liquidation of the Avignon debts withdrew. Another commission was then appointed on May 16, 1809. It reported the debt as 240,402.74 francs (113,872.75 francs for capital borrowed, 124,919.99 francs for interest and 1,500 francs for expenses of the commission). It was decided that this sum would be repaid in ten yearly installments of 24,040.27 francs each. In 1817 the prefect appointed the Christian Valayer to supervise the liquidation of the Avignon debts.[259]

The debt of the Carpentras community was set at a larger sum. On July 26, 1808 the prefect appointed a commission of the

---

[258] "On ne savait alors que commander une servile obéisance. On voulait une liquidation parce que on a ordonnait une liquidation" (a petition addressed in 1817 by the Jews of Avignon to the prefect of Vaucluse. Documents, Comtat, No. 1, fol. 2).

On July 6, 1820 the liberal deputy, Benjamin Constant, discussed the founding of the Jewish consistories during the First Empire in the following words: "L'organisation des communautés israélites a été faite dans un temps où l'on organisait à peu près a coup de sabre" (Halphen, p. 340).

[259] Calvet, 2104; Bordeaux pamphlet of 1818 (see Bibliography, No. 103); Documents, Comtat, No. 20, fol. 63–68. Valayer was probably Placide-Bruno Vallayer, in 1811–1814 priest of the Paris parish St.-Germain-l'Auxerrois and later bishop of Verdun. He was a friend of the famous abbot Jean-Siffrein Maury, who fought against the emancipation of the Jews. Barjavel, II, 467.

three Christian jurists of Avignon, Pinatelli, Campan and Mallosse, to report on the liquidation of the Carpentras debts.[260]
They were active from April 24, 1809 to April 28, 1810 and
according to their report, the former Jewish community of
Carpentras owed 301,166.68 francs (182,710.16 for the face of the
loan and 118,456.52 in unpaid interest accumulated since 1790).
But because of the political crisis and the change of regime almost
nothing was done to liquidate the Carpentras debts. It was not
until April 2, 1816 that a royal ordinance again directed the
liquidation of these debts. The prefect of Vaucluse called an
assembly of the Carpentras Jews, presided over by the sub-
prefect, at which a commission of nine members, including two
Jews of Carpentras origin who had settled in Aix and Nîmes,
was appointed to supervise the liquidation of the debts.[261]

During the four years from 1816 through 1819 Jews of Carpentras origin had to pay 170,752.32 francs in taxes for the
liquidation of the debts. As in the meantime creditors who had
previously neglected to request payment presented their demands, on May 2, 1816 the prefect appointed a new commission
composed of the Christians Sagnier, Jules Texte and Giraudy.
On March 23, 1819 the commission fixed at 94,199.24 francs
the debts owed this new group of creditors, and on October 28,
1819 the prefect approved the commission's report. The Jews
protested strongly and addressed a petition to the Chamber of
Deputies. On July 6, 1820 the Chamber refused to order the
liquidation of these debts through the regular administrative
channels and expressed a wish to see the matter settled in the
courts of law. An ordinance of August 31, 1820 confirmed the
position of the Chamber of Deputies. Finally a settlement was
made the terms of which provided that in order to avoid long
and expensive lawsuits the Jews of Carpentras would pay only
one half of the unpaid debts to the creditors on the original list

[260] Antoine-Privat Campan was chief secretary of the Vaucluse department.
Paulin Mallosse was a priest and author of many studies on local archeology
(Barjavel, I, 535, II, 139–40). We could not find any information about
Pinatelli.

[261] *Avis* of Apr. 29, 1817; Memorandum of 1821; Circular of Feb. 1822;
Valabrègue, pp. 8–12 (see Bibliography, Nos. 101, 106, 108, 146); Columbia,
X893C–C22 (Ordinance of Apr. 2, 1816 and minutes of the meeting).

and only the face of the loan but not the interest to the newly registered creditors. This involved a sum of 116,078.90 francs. All together the Jews of Carpentras paid 286,831.22 francs from 1816 until September 1825.[262]

In 1816 the Jews of Carpentras origin were taxed at the rate of 6.87½ francs per 1,000 francs of wealth; in 1817 — 6.50 francs; in 1818 — 6 francs; in 1819 — 5.50 francs; in 1822 — 2%. In evaluating each Jew's wealth the commission counted his holdings of real-estate, furniture, metals, merchandise, debts owed to him, jewelry, dishes, income from interest exceeding over 500 francs, and the wife's dowry, even if she was not of Carpentras origin. Only linen and uncertain debts owed to Jews were not included.[263]

The decree of October 7, 1807 on the liquidation of the Avignon debts also provided for the debts of L'Isle-sur-Sorgue. These debts amounted to the sum of 129,515.88 francs in 1818 payable to fifteen creditors or to their heirs. Of this sum only 65,137.17 francs represented sums borrowed and 64,378.71 accrued interest until the end of 1817. In accordance with the ordinance of December 24, 1817 the community had to repay one tenth of the sum in 1818, plus current interest, in total a sum of 20,857.25 francs. Including expenses incurred by the commission, the sum was 23,875.44 francs.[264]

The Jews of the former papal province protested increasingly against the order requiring them to repay the debts. In a petition addressed in 1817 to the prefect they called the policy of the revolutionary regime toward the debts owed by them *un des caprices de la révolution,* and in 1819 again asked the government to take over their debts. In the same year, the former Avignon revolutionary leader, Agricol Moureau, stated in his anti-Jewish pamphlet that the communal properties of the Avignon Jews were confiscated during the Revolution and that the Government made a mistake in its policy of forcing the

[262] *Ibid.*

[263] *Ibid.*

[264] Three debts were owed to the charity office of L'Isle (2,121.65 francs), two debts to the *Régie des domaines* (11,537.62 francs), and to the *Trésor public* (34,103.70 francs). Documents, Comtat, No. 18, fol. 59.

Jews to repay their debts themselves.[265] The Jews' protests were rebuked by the deputy, Joseph-Charles-Louis-Henri marquis de Forbin des Issarts (1755–1851), a man with strong anti-revolutionary and anti-Jewish sentiments.[266] In the end the Jews of the former papal province, like those of Metz, lost their fight.

[265] Memorandum of 1821 (see Bibliography, No. 106); Agricol Moureau, *De l'incompatibilité entre le judaïsme et l'exercice des droits de cité* . . . (Paris, 1819), pp. 83–85 ("Le gouvernement commit une *erreur de fait* relativement aux Juifs d'Avignon . . . le gouvernement d'alors aurait dû savoir que la nation s'était antérieurement emparée des biens *meubles* et *immeubles* de cette communauté [d'Avignon], et qu'elle en avait disposé"). On Moureau see Z. Szajkowski, "The Comtadin Jews and the Annexation of the Papal Province by France, 1789–1791." *JQR*, XLVI (1955), 184.

[266] Issarts (see Bibliography, No. 107). During the Revolution Issarts emigrated to Spain and served in the Spanish army's campaigns against France. He came back to France in 1815 and was elected in 1815 as a deputy from the Vaucluse department. A. Robert, III, 25.

On the liquidation of the debts in the former papal province, see also Ad Vaucluse, 7–Q–72–73; Am Avignon, 2894, 2896, 2899, 3304, 3306, 3309, 3399, 3498–99; Columbia, X893C–C22, vols. 1–10.

XXII. THE ALSATIAN DEBTS

The debts owed by the Alsatian Jewish communities were somewhat different in character from the debts owed by others. Even so, their origin can be traced to anti-Jewish restrictions and the poor financial condition of the Alsatian communities before 1789. In those difficult times the economic status of Jews was calamitous: they had to borrow in order to defend their meager privileges and also to maintain *yeshivoth*, rabbis and charitable societies.

The budget of the council of Alsatian Jewish communities (known as the *Nation Juive*) amounted to 32,617 livres 10 s. 9 d. over the period November 1781 — September 1787. Aside from the amount devoted to the upkeep of the *yeshivoth*, the largest sum, 16,868 livres, was allocated to travel expenses, the preparation of memoranda and fees for consultations, most probably in connection with the affair of counterfeited receipts, when Christian debtors presented to their Jewish creditors false receipts for debts which had supposititiously already been paid off. This incident almost brought financial ruin to the Alsatian Jews and provoked the Letters patent of July 10, 1784.[267] In 1775 the council borrowed 24,000 livres and on January 6, 1778 authorized its leader Cerfberr of Médelsheim to look for a Parisian creditor who would grant it a loan of 40–50,000 livres to be converted into annuities. In 1784 the council borrowed 100,000 livres and in 1787 — 7,652 livres. From November 1789 until April 1791 the council's treasurer, Aron Mayer, paid to eight creditors — all of them Christians — 20,645 livres 15 s. 3 d., mostly interest on the debts.[268]

---

[267] Szajkowski, *EcSt*, pp. 123–40 ("The Case of the Counterfeit Receipts in Alsace, 1779–1789").

[268] Tecomp (who granted a loan of 20,000 livres), Chubel (10,000 livres), Zollicoffer (10,000 livres), Chapui (6,000 livres), Dartin (30,000 livres), Fried (12,000 livres), Striebeck (18,000 livres), De Salomon (6,000 livres): "Compte général des Sieurs Arrom Mayer demeurant à Moutzig & Lehman Netter de

During the Revolution the Alsatian Jews maintained their communal ties in order to repay the debts. For a time even the council of Jewish communities continued in existence. On December 30, 1789 the office of the Intermediary Commission of Strasbourg granted a request by Aron Mayer, general syndic of the Jews in the territory of the episcopate of Strasbourg, to assemble the syndics of the Jewish communities in the bishopric. A fine of one hundred livres was to be imposed on those syndics who would not attend the meeting which was arranged in Mutzig on April 20, 1790. The following Jewish syndics were present: Simon Herz of Saverne, Abraham Gabriel Bloch and Mayer Szmul of Soultz, David Scholem of Soultzmatt, David Emanuel of Markolsheim, Abraham Lévy of Dambach, Michel David of Epfig (who represented also Jacques Lévy of Markolsheim), Samuel Wittersheim and Samuel Loeb of Strasbourg. The syndics decided to levy a tax of 6,900 livres for the budget covering the period April 18, 1788 — October 28, 1789. Samuel Wittersheim was appointed the council's chief syndic and Samuel Mayer treasurer.[269] But according to a statement of July 1,

Rosheim en qualité des Preposés généraux des Juifs de la Province cy devant Alsace de l'année 1781 à celui de 1791 . . ." Document dated May 25, 1792 (Documents, Alsace, No. 9, fol. 35–38); M. Ginsburger (see Bibliography, No. 147). The Council's income came mostly from estates left for the Council's institutions: "reçu pour amente des héritiers de Moyse Bloch de Win[t]zenheim — 7,000 . . . Des héritiers de Marx Plotzheim — 8,400 . . . Des héritiers Mayer de Plotzheim — 720 . . . Des héritiers de Benef de Romansweiler — 360 . . . Des héritiers des frères Drayfusse de Moutzig — 2,700 . . . des héritiers de Jacob d'Ingweiller — 1152 . . . pour imposition d'Arron Wolf de Zillerheim [?] et son père par accommodement — 1,800 . . . des héritiers d'Alexandre Bloch de Wintz[en]heim — 1,320 . . ." In total 9,971 livres were spent on the *Yeshivoth* ("donné au Sr. Lazard Arron pour entretien des Collèges"). Documents, Alsace, No. 9, fol. 35–38.

On the value of the Alsatian livre see A. Hanauer, *Etudes économiques sur l'Alsace ancienne et moderne* (Paris-Strasbourg, 1876), I: "Les monnaies"; Roger Dufraisse, "Problèmes monétaires du XVIIIe siècle, particulièrement en Basse-Alsace." *RA*, XCV–II (1956), 194–219. There were two sorts of livres in Alsace: the livre of Strasbourg (from 1726 on) and the livre *tournois* (or French, called also Alsatian), worth 1/4 of the Strasbourg livre.

[269] Among the proposed expenses were: 2,250 livres for administrative expenses of the council; 216 livres 11 s. 3 d. for expenses to convene the next two meetings of the council; an annuity of 700 livres 16 s. 6 d. to be paid to the council's former leader, Aron Meyer; 300 livres "Klaper-Geld"; 300 livres

1805 signed by the treasurer, no taxes were collected and no payments were made during those years.[270]

The creditors (and later their heirs) began to demand the repayment of the principal and interest of the debts owed them by the council of Alsatian Jewish communities. The matter was taken to courts and brought to the attention of the legislators. On August 23, 1791 and April 30, 1792 the *Directoires* of both Rhine departments appointed François-Antoine Rémy, a former bailiff of Reichshoffen, and François-Hypolite Collombel comissioners in charge of the liquidation of the debts owed by the Jewish communities.[271] On July 1, 1793, after having received their report, the *Directoire* of Lower Rhine fixed the total debt of the Jewish communities of Alsace at 84,960 livres 19 s. 6 d. The immediately payable debt was only 40,568 livres, but since payment was out of the question, the additional sum was added to cover interest until a future date when the debt would be fully discharged. In order to afford the Jews an opportunity to repay the debts, they were authorized to levy a tax of 95,000 livres on all Jews who had lived in both Alsatian departments at the end of 1790. The tax was to be prorated on the basis of the amount of government taxes each Jew paid in 1791. On July 1, 1793 the *Directoire* of Lower Rhine appointed Samuel Séligmann Wittersheim of Haguenau, Isaac Samuel of Westhoffen, Daniel Lévy of Strasbourg and Raphael Lévy of Ingwiller members of a special commission to liquidate the debts and the Christian François-Mathieu Hombourg of the commercial court of Strasbourg the commission's treasurer.[272]

to the rabbi of Mutzig; 100 livres to the rabbi of the episcopate [?], etc. (According to the minutes of the meeting. Documents, Alsace, No. 14, fol. 52–57, No. 67, fol. 224–25).

[270] Documents, Alsace, No. 15, fol. 58 ("par suite de la Révolution . . . j'ai été mis dans l'impossibilité d'en faire aucune recouvrement des fonds par les contribuables habitant les Terres de l'Evêché, et par conséquence aucun payment n'a été fait par mes mains")."

[271] *Ibid.*, No. 12, fol. 47, No. 13, fol. 49.

[272] The commission paid 3,000 francs for services rendered by twenty-two employees and for other office expenses, incurred by the Alsatian tax offices in drawing up the list of Jewish tax payers during the year X (Sept. 23, 1801 — Sept. 22, 1802). *Ibid.*, No. 23, fol. 70. Another S. Wittersheim was one of the richest Jews of Metz: "l'un des plus riches et des plus honnêtes négocians de

For nine years no tax was imposed, probably owing to the troubled revolutionary period. Finally, on November 10, 1803 Napoleon I confirmed the *Directoire's* decision of 1793 relating to the Jews' debts. Instead of 1791, however, the year X (1801-1802) was substituted as the base for the special tax to be paid by the Jews for the liquidation of the debts.[273]

In 1793, shortly before his death, Cerfberr of Médelsheim (1730–1793)[274] became the principal creditor of the Alsatian Jewish communities. According to some historians the Cerfberr family paid fines imposed during the Terror upon the Jews. The family thus became a creditor for debts known as the "Cerfberr debts" or "Herz-Gelder."[275] However, there was no collective

la ville de Metz." *Service funèbre, célébré à la synagogue de Thionville, le 15 Mars 1820, en l'honneur de feu Mr. Mayer Lévy* . . . (Metz, [1820]), p. 13.

[273] Bibliography, No. 114.

[274] Cerfberr, or Cerf Berr was the eldest son of Berr de Médelsheim (1670–1762). He left four sons: (1) Mardoché Nathanaël (1758–1817), known mostly as Marx [or Max] Berr, known also as Cerfberr; (2) Lipmann (alias Hippolyte) Cerfberr (1760–1827); (3) Baruch Cerfberr (1762–1824); (4) Théodore Cerfberr (1766–1832). According to the Alsatian census of 1784 (see note 1); three vols. of Lévylier's *Notes* . . .; M. Ginsburger, *Une fondation de Cerf Berr* (Paris, 1923), p. 4.

[275] "Nous supposons que ces fameux *Herz-Gelder* proviennent d'une contribution frappée sur les Juifs de la Basse-Alsace pendant la Terreur et acquittée par la famille Cerfberer ou Hertz-Baer de Bischheim, à charge de s'en faire rembourser par les communautés" (J. Hermann, in *UI*, XXXIX (1884), 255–57); "Séligman Alexandre, arrêté du 30 mai 1794 jusqu'après le 9 Thermidor eut à payer des sommes considérables, tant pour son propre compte que pour celui des communautés du pays" (Anchel, *op. cit.*, p. 24). On the arrest of Alexandre during the Terror see his pamphlet *Dénonciation à mes concitoyens* . . . (Strasbourg, an III). 38 pp. and R. Reuss' study *Séligmann Alexandre, ou les Tribulations d'un Israélite strasbourgeois pendant la Terreur* (Strasbourg, 1880). 44 pp. Another incorrect statement was made by the historian, Raphael Mahler, who claimed that the Jews of Alsace borrowed money from Cerfberr in order to pay a large sum to the city of Strasbourg, since the King's abolition at that time of the per capita toll paid by Jews, reduced the city's revenues (*op. cit.*, I, 179). On the abolition of the body toll see *Lettres-patentes du Roi, sur arrêt portant fixation de l'indemnité accordée à la ville de Strasbourg pour raison de la suppression des droits qu'elle percevoit sur les Juifs sous la dénomination de péage corporel* . . . *le 25 Janvier 1786* (Metz, [1786]). 4 pp.; Z. Szajkowski, "The Jewish Problem in Alsace . . .," 219–22.

fine imposed upon Jews. The source of the Cerfberr debt was much more prosaic.

In 1793 Cerfberr paid 130,000 livres in *assignats* to the principal creditors of the Council of Jewish communities. Was this an honest act?

Many people tried to safeguard the real value of their possessions by making quick investments and paying off debts with *assignats*.[276] Those who held *assignats*, which were shrinking in purchasing power, tried to get rid of them by exchange for any conceivable asset of fixed value. One of the results of the increase in the currency which the revolutionary government printed freely was the race of debtors to repay in *assignats* debts which they had incurred in hard money. In the first years of the Revolution many peasants enjoyed increased incomes, part of which they used to repay their debts with paper money.[277] A Colmar chronicler complained in 1790 that some swindlers (*Betrüger*) repay their debts in *assignats*. A German traveller noted in the same year that in Strasbourg it was impossible to obtain credit even on the best mortgaged securities because creditors feared repayment in *assignats*. A counter-revolutionary parody written in the form of a prayer ironically thanked its author for making *assignats* out of old rags. The repayment of debts with paper-money was also mentioned in an anti-Republican pamphlet of 1792 and in a parody directed against Cerfberr.[278] Offi-

[276] According to a diary written by the religious teacher Jessel Lehman of Ribeauvillé, *assignats* were called כתבים by Jews (in the Alsatian Museum of Strasbourg, 1795, p. 29a). Among the Jewish creditors who were repaid with *assignats* was Rabbi Mardochée Crémieu of Aix-en-Provence (previously of Carpentras): P. Millaud, "Notice biographique du rabbin Mardochée Crémieu d'Aix." *AI*, III, (1842), 12. In 1790 rabbi Crémieu bought the rights of a Christian creditor and thus became a creditor of the Jewish community of Carpentras. In 1816 he accepted token repayment of the debt owed him. *Ibid.*, 14.

[277] Marcel Marion, *Histoire financière de la France depuis 1715* (Paris, 1921), III; Ph. Sagnac, "Les Juifs et Napoléon." *RHMC*, II–III (1901–02), 6; L. Poujol, *Quelques observations concernant les Juifs . . .* (Paris, 1806), p. 39; Véron-Reville, *Histoire de la Révolution française dans le Haut-Rhin* (Paris-Colmar, 1865), p. 21.

[278] J. Liblin, "Chronique du serrurier Dominique Schmutz de Colmar." *RA*, XXIV (1874), 394; *Briefe eines Reisenden über das Elsass . . .* (Frankfurt, 1790), see F.-C. Heitz, *La Contre-Révolution en Alsace de 1789 à 1793* (Stras-

cials tried to protect the creditor. In September 1790 the Upper Rhine *Directoire* complained in a memorandum to the National Assembly that creditors were ruined by accepting *assignats* from their debtors and urged that the value of *assignats* should be fixed according to their local Alsatian purchasing power. In a memorandum of December 14, 1791 the general council of Moselle referred to "evil minded debtors." A judge of Bitche (Moselle) wrote in the year IV (1795–1796) of his difficulties because creditors refused to accept paper money from their debtors. On July 9, 1795 the justice of the peace of Sélestat (Lower Rhine) complained of ungrateful debtors who grew rich with their creditors' help and then tried to repay them in *assignats*. The debtors of the city-hospital of Saint-Dié (Vosges) tried to pay off what they owed with paper money. On the other hand, the debtor Laurent Philippe of Rémiremont (Vosges), who borrowed *assignats* during the Revolution, was requested as late as 1810 to pay his debt in "good" money. On September 9, 1793 Rumpler of the Strasbourg *Bureau de paix* wrote to the Legislative Committee that he had entrusted all his assets valued in "good money" to a banker who wanted to repay him in *assignats*. In a petition of January 30, 1796 Xavier Tuleur of Orbey (Upper-Rhine) requested the Ministry of Justice to force his debtors to repay their debts not with *assignats* but with money of the same value which they had borrowed.[279] Even the Catholic Church took this position: morally a debtor could not repay his debt with *assignats*. At confessions priests warned the faithful to repay debts in good money.[280] In the Meurthe department as in other parts of France people tried to use paper money to pay revolutionary taxes. At the beginning of the Revolution Rouen

bourg, 1865), pp. 13–14; *Patriotische Litaney*... (n. p., 1792). 4 pp., cf. Heitz, *op. cit.*, pp. 251–55; *Je vous dirai vos vérités* (n. p., n. d.), p. 61; *Hirtz-Bähr an die drey Köninglein* [Strassburg, 1791.] 10 pp. ("gute Schulden mit schlechten Papier zu bezahlen").

[279] J. Joachim, "Le département du Haut-Rhin et l'inflation monétaire en 1790." *RA*, LXXII (1925), 389–90; *Mémoire sur le rétablissement du crédit public et particulier* (Metz, 1791), p. 5; AN, BB–16–496, 627, 635, 913–14, D–III–210, 213.

[280] *Documents pour servir à l'histoire religieuse en Alsace pendant la Révolution* (Mulhouse, 1859), p. 90; G. Hubrecht, *Les assignats dans le Haut-Rhin* (Strasbourg, 1932), p. 185.

706

(Seine-inférieure) suffered from a great number of bankruptcies, but their number fell sharply in 1791–1792, probably because debts were repaid with paper money. As a result the law of July 13, 1795 provided that before a debt had reached maturity a creditor could not be forced to accept repayment in *assignats*.[281]

Of course, Jewish debtors, too, tried to repay creditors with paper money. Such a case was related by the Alsatian anti-Jewish pamphleteer, François-Louis Rumpler (1730–1806), in a pamphlet against Isaac Lehman who presented *assignats* to a Basel creditor. A story was told about an Alsatian Jew named Bernheimer (or Bernhüter), who was imprisoned for trying to pay for a gold box with *assignats* after having shown gold coins in his possession.[282] Many sources refer to Jewish creditors' protests against repayment in *assignats*.[283] A register of debtors in the Colmar district, who in the years III and IV (September 22, 1794 — September 21, 1796) deposited *assignats* for repayment of debts owed by them, lists 237 names of creditors, including Jews who had made seventy-five loans.[284] It is impossible even to give an approximate number of Jewish creditors who were repaid with *assignats*. But their number was certainly large enough to enable us to conclude that the decree of September 28, 1791, which ordered the Jews of Alsace to present a list of the debts owed to them, was not put into effect because the debtors repaid their debts in *assignats*. Such was the conclusion of the lawyer Louis Poujol (1771–1848), whose anti-Jewish pamphlet of 1806 greatly influenced the character of

[281] A. Troux, *La vie politique dans le département de la Meurthe d'août 1792 à octobre 1795* (Nancy, 1936), II, 180–81; Pierre Dardel, "Crises et faillites à Rouen et dans la Haute-Normandie de 1740 à l'an V." *Revue d'Histoire économique et sociale.* XXVII (1948), 62; Hubrecht, *op. cit.*, p. 185; Poujol, *op. cit.*, p. 39.

[282] Louis Rumpler, *Lisez, ça ne coute rien* [Strasbourg, an IV.] 4 pp.; Idem, *Quelques pièces fugitives . . .* [Strasbourg, 1793,] p. 7; [Treit,] *Plaidoyer d'un défenseur officieux, déclaré inadmissible pour oser défendre un créancier bâlois . . .* [Strasbourg, an IV,] p. 12.

[283] *Réponses des sieurs Poinsignon au mémoires imprimés sous les noms du juifs Abraham-Isaac Brisac, et de Me. Guibal* (Nancy, n. d.), p. 27; AN, BB–16–496 (Leib Cahin against Pierre Rauch).

[284] AdHR, L 863.

Napoleon I's anti-Jewish decrees, and of another anti-Jewish lawyer and pamphleteer, Xavier Chauffour.[285]

Did Cerfberr try to use the inflation caused by the increase in the supply of paper-money in order to ease the financial problems of the Jewish communities? This is doubtful. Cerfberr paid their debts without consulting other Jewish leaders. By this investment he most probably sought to protect his 130,000 livres in *assignats*, which were later valued at 49,432 livres in specie. In fact, in 1793 the Alsatian Jewish leaders contested the debt owed to Cerfberr.[286]

Cerfberr's heirs sued for payment of the debt. On July 18, 1804 the civil court of Strasbourg ordered the commission for the liquidation of the debts to pay Cerfberr's heirs 49,432 livres in capital, plus interest (which totaled 23,348 livres for the period from 1793 to February 13, 1806). A decree of July 12, 1806 set the total debts at 182,645 francs.

The commission for the liquidation of the debts was dissolved by a decree of September 5, 1810 and its duties were turned over to the Jewish consistories of both Alsatian departments, created by the decree of March 17, 1808.

The debts owed by the Alsatian Jews were of three kinds: (1) Debts owed to the heirs of pre-1789 creditors who had won lawsuits. (2) Money owed to employees who had not received their salaries. (3) Debts incurred since 1791 by the Jews of both Rhine departments, but not by those who had since left Alsace.

The first category included debts owed to the heirs of the creditors Cerfberr (72,580 livres), Abraham Moch (5,550 livres), and Abraham Cahen (5,550 livres) — a total of 83,680 livres, interest included. On July 1, 1806 only 28,348 livres in interest had been paid. On September 29, 1817 the debt to the heirs of these three creditors amounted to 108,895 livres: 95,145 livres

---

[285] Poujol, *op. cit.*, p. 39; Chauffour cadet, *Réflexions sur l'application du décret impérial, du 17 Mars 1808, concernant les créances des juifs* (Colmar, [1808]), p. 3; Idem, *Observations sur le serment More Judaïco* ... (Colmar, [1844]), p. 25.

[286] According to the text of the sentence of July 18, 1804 and a petition addressed on July 10, 1865 by the Lower Rhine consistory to the prefect (Documents, Alsace, No. 57, fol. 184–85, No. 63, fol. 218, No. 68, fol. 226–35).

to the heirs of Cerfberr, of which 45,912 was interest; 6,875 respectively to the heirs of Abraham Cahen and Abraham Moch, of which 3,875 in each sum was interest. Of this huge debt, only 17,061 livres had been paid by the end of 1817.

The second category included debts owed to the rabbis Mathis Weyl of Rosheim, Michel Séligman, and heirs of Joseph Marx, who claimed 12,325 in unpaid salaries. In addition a debt of another 84,960 livres was owed to one hundred and one small creditors, mostly for unpaid salaries to rabbis, teachers, secretaries, lawyers, etc.

The third category included debts owed to the heirs of Aaron Meyer of Mutzig and Lehman Netter of Rosheim who had lent money for the purpose of supporting the *yeshivoth*.[287]

On January 30, 1811 both Alsatian departmental consistories made an agreement, according to which the Upper-Rhine was to supply two fifths of the funds necessary to pay the debts. This arrangement was subsequently changed, because the decree of September 5, 1810 provided that the consistorial tax of 1812 was to serve as a basis for levying the debt-tax. Prior to that date the government taxes of 1791 were used as the base for levying the debt-tax. But on February 8, 1803 F.-M. Hombourg and Samuel Séligmann Witersheim wrote to the prefect that since 1791 the economic status of the Jews had changed; Jews who were rich became poor and vice versa. Therefore, the 1791 rate for real estate taxes was inequitable as the base for the tax to discharge the Jewish debts. On January 4, 1806 the commission to liquidate the debts complained that the collection of the tax based on the rate of the regular government taxes was unjust because sometimes Jews with little property paid more than rich Jews. On December 14, 1806 the Lower Rhine Jews

---

[287] Abraham Moch was the first Jewish member of the general council of Lower Rhine. Mortgage archives and various other documents prove that Moch was one of the principal Jewish creditors of Jewish and Christian debtors in Alsace. Z. Szajkowski, *Agricultural Credit and Napoleon's Anti-Jewish Decrees* (New York, 1953), p. 95. Abraham Cahen of Saverne was a deputy to the Jewish Assembly called by Napoleon I in 1806. See D. Tama *Organisation civile et religieuse des Israélites de France* . . . (Paris, 1908), p. 115. A yeshiva existed in Mutzig, see M. Ginsburger, "Mutzig." *SS*, IV, No. 5 (1933), 10.

wrote to the Ministry of the Interior that those Jews who had
no real estate property and who did not even pay license taxes
because they did not have any ostensible business (stores) were
not required to pay any taxes at all — even if they had a considerable amount of cash and held many promissory notes. In
1807 the Jews of Quatzenheim stated that rich Jews were assessed
moderately, but the poor were forced to pay huge sums.[288] Similar
complaints were made on February 26, 1807 by the Jews of
Wissembourg and on March 2, 1807 by the Jews of Westhoffen.[289]
All these petitions were identical and written by the same person. It seems then that the poorer Jews in the Lower Rhine were
organized in opposition against paying the largest part of the
taxes for the liquidation of the debts.

In the Upper Rhine similar petitions were sent in 1808 by
large groups of Jews of Colmar, Bergheim, Horbourg, Wintzenheim, Herrlisheim, Voeglinshoffen, Hattstatt and many other
communities in connection with the tax to cover the expenses
incurred by the deputies to the Sanhedrin called by Napoleon I.[290]
On June 2, 1808 the Jews of Colmar submitted a list of twenty-
eight families residing there, of whom fifteen were designated
as "poor," twelve as possessing "mediocre fortunes" and only
one a "comfortable fortune." Fifty-two out of eighty-four
Jewish families of Bergheim were designated as "poor" and eleven
as possessing properties valued at 15,000 francs or more. Six out
of thirty families of Horbourg were described as possessing from
5,000 to 20,000 francs each; all the others did not own enough
even to feed their families. In Wintzenheim the Jews were classi-

[288] ". . . ceux qui ont le plus de fortune se trouvent taxés à des sommes
modiques, tandis que le moins fortunée qui par son petit commerce, ou son
industrie gagne à peine le plus nécessaire à son existence précaire y est impôsé
à des sommes considérables . . ." (Original copy of a petition addressed in
March 1807 to the Ministry of Finances. Documents, Alsace, No. 10, fol.
39–42).

[289] Documents, Alsace, No. 11, fol. 43–46, Nos. 28–29, fol. 76–83 (". . . de
la somme totale d'environ 2592 frs. 90 c., celle de 827 frs. 70 c. a été mise à
la seule charge de la veuve d'Emmanuel Dreyfus, et qu'on y a encore ajouté
41 frs. 40 c. pour frais de bureau. Cette veuve est chargée de dix enfants
vivants. Sa fortune, il est vrai, est en bien de fonds." From the Wissemburg
petition, *ibid.*)

[290] On the Sanhedrin-tax see Anchel, *op. cit.*, pp. 142–56.

fied in seven groups according to their wealth. Only one family
was included in the first class — the richest of the community,
four in the second class, sixteen in the third class, twelve in the
fourth class, fourteen in the fifth class, seven in the sixth class,
and fifty-six in the seventh class — all of them poor families
unable to pay any taxes. Thirty out of forty-three families of
Hattstatt were designated as "poor."[291]

The taxes that the Jews had to pay for the liquidation of the
debts were larger than the consistorial and government taxes
combined. Four hundred and twenty-eight Jewish heads of
family who had lived in Alsace in 1791 paid 10,781.64 francs in
government taxes in the year X (1801–1802). But in 1808 they
had to pay more than double — 25,889.55 francs — for the
liquidation of the debts. In the same year X, 261 Jewish families
who originally came from the pre-1789 territory controlled by
the city of Strasbourg paid 5,073.09 francs in general taxes and
in addition 4,065.05 francs for the liquidation of the debts.
According to a document of February 13, 1806 Jews of Alsatian
origin still residing in the Upper Rhine department paid 20,878.81
francs, in the Lower Rhine department 37,306.75 francs, and
in the Seine department 14,430.80 francs — a total of 72,616.36
francs in land, chattels and in license-taxes.[292] The regular
consistorial budgets of both Rhine departments for the year
1812 amounted to 20,834,84 francs. For the year 1814 both consistories were ordered to collect an additional tax of 54,402.67
francs for the liquidation of the debts.[293]

In accordance with the decree of September 5, 1810, repeated
by a prefectural order of Lower Rhine dated October 7, 1814 and
approved on December 7, 1814 by the government, the debt was
fixed — together with interest — at 217,610.67 francs. To repay
it a special tax in four yearly instalments was to be effective from
1814 to 1817. The share of the Lower Rhine was 117.261.04
francs and of the Upper Rhine 100,349.63 francs. (The regular
consistorial taxes were taken as the base for the new special tax.

[291] Documents, Alsace, Nos. 31–41, fol. 86–110.

[292] AN–F–19–1849; Documents, Alsace, No. 38, fol. 105–106; Z. Szajkowski,
Poverty and Social Welfare Among French Jews 1800–1880 (New York, 1954),
pp. 11–12.

[293] Documents, Alsace No. 79, fol. 272–73.

In 1812 the regular consistorial tax was 9.607.84 francs for the Upper Rhine and 11,227 francs for the Lower Rhine.)[294] By the end of 1819, only 110,764 francs had been collected of which the Lower Rhine contributed 42,271 francs.

The decrees of May 30, 1806 and March 17, 1808, directed against the Jewish creditors of Christian debtors, were an obstacle in liquidating the debts owed by the former Jewish communities. Many Jews stated that by reason of these decrees they were unable to receive payment of the debts owed them by Christian debtors, and hence were unable to pay heavy taxes.[295] The prefect of Upper Rhine convoked an assembly on October 8, 1806 of twenty-eight Jewish leaders of sixteen local consistories in order to impose a tax to cover the expenses of sending deputies to the Jewish Assembly of Paris. Nine out of the twenty eight leaders refused to pay the tax because the decree of May 30, 1808 declared a moratorium on debts for which Christians were liable to them.[296] The invasion of 1814 and economic crises in 1814 and 1815 also made it impossible to repay the debts.

In 1817 the debt still owed to the heirs of Cerfberr amounted to 90,002 livres 5 s. 3 d. Of this sum only 49,232 livres represented principal, the rest unpaid interest.[297] According to a document of 1819 the total sum owed to all creditors was 193,855 livres, of which only 68,622 livres had been repaid by the end of 1819.[298]

[294] *Ibid.*, No. 2, fol. 3–4.

The division of former provinces into departments often brought out significant demographic and economic differences among Jewish communities. Thus, the number of small Jewish communities was greater in the Lower Rhine than in the Upper Rhine. The Jews of the Upper Rhine were considered wealthier than those of the Lower Rhine. Likewise, in the Sephardic center of Southwestern France the Jews of Landes (most of whom lived in Saint-Esprit) were considered wealthier than those of Gironde (most of whom lived in Bordeaux). Only three of the Alsatian communities where Jews were listed for the first time in 1806–1808 were located in the Upper Rhine; all the others were in the Lower Rhine. S. Posener, "The Immediate Economic and Social Effects of the Emancipation of Jews in France." *JSS*, I (1939), 283, and Alsatian Jewish censuses of 1784 and 1806–1810. See also Szajkowski, "The Demographic Aspects . . ."

[295] *Ibid.*, No. 6, fol. 9. Letter from Hombourg, treasurer of the liquidation commission, to the prefect of Lower Rhine, June 12, 1809.

[296] Ad HR, V 87.

[297] Documents, Alsace, No. 16, fol. 258.   [298] *Ibid.*, No. 1, fol. 1–2.

In time, only the debt owed to the heirs of Cerfberr remained outstanding. A ruling of the court of Strasbourg issued on August 30, 1823 set the amount of this debt as of July 1, 1823 at 57,351.34 francs plus interest. On January 27, 1825 the consistory stated that the debt could be paid only through a special tax of 96,168.58 francs. However, new difficulties arose. On March 28 and July 25, 1825 the Minister of the Interior pointed out that the *Conseil d'Etat* considered such a special tax illegal. The heirs of Cerfberr, however, disputed this decision and continued to demand payment of the debt. The consistory expressed no opposition to this action, claiming that it could not protect the interests of the former Jewish communities of Alsace, and that the defense of a decision of the *Conseil d'Etat* was not among its duties. On January 3, 1827 the King issued a decree which nullified the decisions of March 28 and July 25, 1825 and turned the whole matter over to the prefect of Lower Rhine again, with instructions to act in accordance with the decree of September 5, 1810. The prefect then ordered the Jews to collect a special tax for repayment of the debt.

Forbin des Issarts, the deputy of the Vaucluse department who spoke out in favor of the Christian creditors of his department, stated that the government had rejected a demand by the Alsatian Jews for the nationalization of the debts owed by them.[299] But, if we are not mistaken, there was never any demand for the government to take over the debts of the Alsatian Jewish communities. Perhaps, this was due to the desire on the part of the Alsatian Jews to let nothing interfere with their struggle for emancipation and with their opposition to the decree of September 28, 1791 which stopped the regular repayment of the debts owed by peasants to them.[300] Or, perhaps it was because the creditor Cerfberr, to whom the largest debt was owed, and who was the principal Alsatian intermediary in the struggle for equal rights for Jews, had some reason of his own for not wanting the government to assume responsibility for the debts. The nationalization of these debts would clearly have

[299] Issarts, p. 4 (see Bibliography, No. 107).

[300] Z. Szajkowski, "The Law of September 28, 1791 on Jewish Creditors in France." *Zion*, XVII (1952), 84–100 (in Hebrew).

713

been a blow to the economic interests of the Cerfberr family. Much later the Alsatian Jewish consistories advocated not the nationalization of the debts but the rejection of their creditors' claims, on the ground that the Jewish *Nation* which had borrowed the money ceased to exist during the Revolution. This thesis was sustained in a brief submitted on November 11, 1834 by the three lawyers, E. Martin, L. Liechtenberger and L.-L. Michaux-Bellaire, and supported by the jurist J.-F. Rauter. They argued that Cerfberr's heirs could not ask for repayment of the debt because the loan was arranged through the Jewish *Nation* which had been legal before the Revolution, but had been dissolved thereafter, and hence no organization was legally responsible for its debts. Furthermore, the Jewish consistories in Alsace were associations founded in 1808 that dealt only with religious matters. According to the decrees of March 17, 1808 and 1810, the Alsatian consistories had taken over the work of the special commission for the liquidation of the debts, but the functions of the two departmental Alsatian consistories were specifically defined by the decree of March 17, 1808 and these did not include any of the functions of the *Nation Juive* as it existed before 1789. Therefore the consistories were not legally responsible for the affairs of the *Nation*. Neither could new taxes based on the decree of 1810 be levied, because this decree had a specific time limit. A similar position was taken by the attorney Paul Fabre in 1851, when he submitted a brief on the Cerfberr debt.[301]

---

[301] *Consultation*, pp. 18–19 (see Bibliography, No. 124); "Note Consultative. Pour le Consistoire israélite de la circonscription de Strasbourg. Créance Cerf Berr sur l'ancienne communauté juive d'Alsace. Paris, 15 août 1857." Signed: Paul Fabre, avocat au Conseil d'Etat et à la Cour de Cassation (ZS).

Edouard Martin was a well known Alsatian jurist and republican leader who defended the cause of revolutionaries. For his opposition to the regime of the Second Empire he was sentenced himself. Louis Liechtenberger was an Alsatian jurist and republican of the same school. During the Revolution of 1848 he became commissioner for the Lower-Rhine and was elected a deputy. In 1851 Louis-Léon Michaux-Bellaire became professor of law at Strasbourg University. Jacques-Frédéric Rauter was president of the Strasbourg bar association, professor of law from 1825 on and dean of the faculty from 1837 on (Sitzman, II, 169–70, 252, 296, 506).

Among other lawyers, who defended requests by Jews against paying taxes

In the 1850's the heirs of Cerfberr presented new requests for repayment. The position of the Jewish consistory was stated in a petition of December 23, 1855, addressed to the prefect: (1) Laws on financial matters are not abstract and do not apply to unlimited periods, but cover specific financial matters for a limited time. The decree of December 27, 1806 authorized a tax to liquidate the debt which was fixed precisely at 182,645 francs. The tax was paid and the decree then became void. No new taxes could be levied on the legal basis of this decree. (2) Nineteen Alsatian Jewish communities were taken away from France by the Treaties of 1814 and 1815. Since the Jews of these communities were now foreign nationals, they could not be expected to pay taxes in France, unless the French Ministry of Foreign Affairs could obtain from the nations of their residence promises to require them to do so. To force the remaining Jewish communities in France to pay the share of the tax of these nineteen communities would be contrary to the tradition of French jurisprudence in such matters. (3) Since the Alsatian Jewish *Nation* was dissolved during the Revolution, there was no collective Jewish responsibility for the debts.[302]

All this became even more complicated as a result of conflicts among Cerfberr's heirs themselves. Some heirs were converted to Catholicism,[303] others sold their claims to the debts. Most of the notes originally held by Cerfberr and his heirs were bought up by Louis and Achille Ratisbonne, two brothers who were

for the liquidation of the debts, were the famous republican leader Odilon Barrot and Jean-Baptiste Darrieux in a case of Avignon taxes (1821), De La Grange in a case of Metz taxes (1823), Lassis in a case of Alsatian taxes (1827), Bonjean, Dumont and Frignet in cases of Metz taxes (1845 and 1850). Halphen, pp. 356–80.

[302] Documents, Alsace, No. 50, fol. 140–71.

[303] Among the converted members of the Cerfberr family were: Louis-Marie-Théodore Ratisbonne (1802–1844) and Marie-Alphonse Ratisbonne (1812–1884), sons of the Jewish leader August Ratisbonne, himself a son-in-law of Cerfberr. Both became active anti-Jewish Catholic leaders. On August and Louis Ratisbonne see *Rég.*, I (1836), 93 and Benoît-Lévy, in *AI*, XVI (1855), 258. For a bibliography of pamphlets on the converted Ratisbonne brothers see Louis Wilhelm, *Bibliothèque Nationale et Universitaire de Strasbourg. Catalogue de la Section Alsacienne et Lorraine* (Strasbourg, 1912–23), II, 264.

leaders of the departmental consistory of Lower Rhine.[304] After Louis Ratisbonne died, his heirs, through the Strasburg attorney Meyer, demanded that they be paid the Cerfberr debt, which amounted to 222,168.58 francs (96,168 principal and the remainder, interest which had accumulated since January 6, 1824). The consistory accused the creditors of speculation (*spéculations des créanciers*) and proved that L. Ratisbonne had bought up notes for 56,468 francs in the name of one of his employees, and actually paid only 36,923 francs for them. The attorney Meyer could not deny the accusations and it raised a storm of protests. In 1859 Achille Ratisbonne gave up his claim to a share of the debt after setting certain conditions. According to one document, he relinquished his claim only to that money which the Jews of Lower Rhine would have had to pay him, but not to the money which the descendants of Lower Rhine who now lived in other departments would have to pay. He explained that the money he would get from these people, would be distributed as charity to Alsatian Jews.

In 1857 the consistory of Upper-Rhine called a conference of all communities. On March 26, 1858 the prefect of Upper Rhine permitted the consistory to initiate legal action against the Ratisbonne heirs. This action was to be based on three grounds: (1) That part of the debt which was due in 1814 from the Jews of the communities taken away from France in 1815 should be deducted. (2) In accordance with the Napoleonic code, interest need only be paid for five years. (3) The consistories were in a position to demand the nullification of the whole debt. The prefect of the Lower Rhine, however, did not permit the consistory in his department to take such action and in 1865 the council of the prefecture ruled that the Jews must pay 51,774.46 francs to the Ratisbonne heirs, interest not included. One year later the consistories agreed to accept these terms. Cerfberr's heirs, however, demanded a high rate of interest which would have doubled the amount. In a circular dated July 25, 1866 the consistory referred to the debt as amounting to 90,000 francs. *L' Univers Israélite* wrote that Cerfberr's heirs purposely did not accept payment of the whole debt, so that huge sums in interest

[304] On the Ratisbonne brothers see notes 241, 303.

could accumulate. The Alsatian debts were actually never paid. At the end of 1869, and the beginning of 1870, the Ministry of the Interior and the prefecture of Lower Rhine were still considering the organization of a new commission to liquidate the debts. On November 20, 1869 the prefect of Lower Rhine complained that the Jewish consistory of Upper Rhine refused to cooperate, and although the consistory of Lower Rhine was well-disposed, nothing was achieved because of the collective responsibility of all the Alsatian Jews. On February 10, 1870 the heirs of Louis Ratisbonne wrote to the Minister of the Interior about the collection of the debts owed to them. In 1871–72, after the annexation of Alsace by Germany, many Jews left the province. It became so difficult to collect community taxes from Jews whose ancestors had lived in Alsace at the beginning of the Revolution, that the whole matter of the debts was forgotten.[305]

[305] Documents, Alsace, No. 78, fol. 270 (a letter written on July 30, 1867 by the Upper Rhine consistory); Bibliography, Nos. 125–36. For the chapter on the Alsatian debts the author used also a collection in the Ad Lower Rhine, series V.

On the liquidation of the debts see also: J.-B.-A.-A.-Ch. Sirey, *Recueil général des lois et arrêts* . . . (Paris, 1812–1843), I–XLIII (1800–1843); Desiré, Armand et Edouard Dalloz, *Jurisprudence générale* . . . (Paris, 1825), and later publications; Félix Lebon et Germain Roche, *Recueil général des arrêts du Conseil d'Etat* . . . *depuis l'an 8 jusqu'à 1839* . . . (Paris, 1839–46). 7 vols.

XXIII. THE MIGRATION OF JEWS AND ITS EFFECT ON THE LIQUIDATION OF THE DEBTS OF THE COMMUNITIES THEY LEFT

The Jewish communities invariably took action against Jews who tried to emigrate without paying their share of the collective debts. To cope with attempts to evade fiscal responsibilities, in 1558 the Carpentras community forbade Jews to spend more than fifteen days out of town without special permission. As late as 1779 the Avignon community prohibited emigration, except to Palestine,[306] and tried to compel its former residents who had settled in Bordeaux to pay their share of the community's debt.[307] On April 18, 1789 the Jewish community of Avignon imposed a tax of $\frac{1}{2}$ per cent on the wealth of Manuel Astruc and Jonathan de Sozia, two Avignonese Jews of Bordeaux, which was estimated to be 50,000 and 12,000 livres respectively.[308]

[306] Baron, *op. cit.*, II, 15.

[307] Bibliography, Nos. 82–83. The Sephardic *Nation* of Bordeaux could not compel the Avignonese Jews of Bordeaux to pay the debts. On this occasion the *Nation* expressed its traditional hatred of "foreign Jews." In the *Nation*'s minutes of Dec. 31, 1724 it was noted: "Il a estte represantté que le deputté de la communautté des Jeuif davignon qui est a Bordeaux a la poursuitte d'un proces contre sertains particuliers establis dans cette ville natif du did avignon soistet estre soutenus par le Corps des portugais establis en cette ville, en conformitte des ansiens privilleges quil a pleu au Roy de confirmer dans la poursuitte du dit proces et les faire entrer dans les arrangements que la ditte communautte des Juifs davignon a pris pour obliger ces pretendeus debiteurs a leur payer, et comme il est sertain que les avinones nont jamais estte dans le Corps des portugais nous avos rejette l'idée qui a estte proposée, et nous prions les sindugs prepossez pour avoir soin des nos pauvres de faire savoir a ceux des portugais qui ne se sont paz trouves dans la presente assemblée qu'il est de nostre devoir, et de nostre interest de ne prandre aucune part dans les differents des ditz avignonez, et moins encore dans leurs pretendues arrangements, que nous regardons comme une chose estrangere et dans laquelle nous ne devevons entrer de paz unne facon . . ." (No. 33, fol. 12). On the conflicts between the Sephardim and the Avignonese Jews of Bordeaux see Z. Szajkowski, "Relations . . ."

[308] Ad Vaucluse, E, Gaudibert's notarial acts, 1789, fol. 558.

Still, many rich Jews emigrated and it became increasingly difficult for their old communities to collect enough taxes to repay collective debts. During the Revolution this situation became even more serious for the communities which were losing their population to other areas. Prior to the Revolution, when the Jews could not settle everywhere, they were restricted to a small number of communities. The Revolution authorized the Jews to move from one community to another and to settle freely in any part of the country.[309] In the first years of the Revolution a large number of Jews emigrated to other communities and the leaders of the communities they left were disturbed by the thought that the burden of the communal debt would have to be distributed among the remaining Jews only. Even earlier, when the Jewish community of Carpentras had to cover a part of the expenses of the Rome community, a city official wrote on September 5, 1788 that forty out of 226 Jewish families had already left for France.[310] Because of the persecutions against Jews prior to the Revolution and the bloody conflicts in Avignon and Comtat Venaissin in 1789–1793, a larger number of Jews, especially the rich, emigrated to France. Non-Jewish public opinion, because of fears of losing capital and commerce as a consequence of the Jewish emigration, favored an improvement of the status of Jews. On June 21, 1789 the city council of Carpentras rejected by a secret vote of twelve to eight a proposal to ask the Pope to ameliorate the Jews' status in order to discourage their emigration.[311] This sentiment in favor of keeping the Jews in Carpentras was even more openly expressed in public debates and pamphlets during the Revolution.[312]

[309] *Observations*, p. 17, see Bibliography, No. 104.

[310] Calvet, 5938, p. 464.

On the eve of the Revolution many rich Jews sold their houses. On Dec. 18, 1788 Abraham de Monteux (called Aron the elder) of Avignon announced the sale of his houses and apartments for 25,000 livres (Prévot, *op. cit.*, pp. 10–11). According to a census of May 19, 1789 forty-two Jewish families of Carpentras shared apartments with 2 persons per "house," thirty-two — with 3, thirty-one — with 4, thirty-four — with 5, twenty-one — with 6, fifteen — with 7, thirteen — with 8, five — with 9, two — with 9 or more (AIU, R 43, p. 144).

[311] Am Carpentras, BB 264, June 21, 1789.

[312] [J.-J-C-V. Raphaël, or Cottier-Julian,] *L'enfant du patriotisme* [Car-

The first important proposal for the annexation of the Papal province by France, which was made in 1789 by the deputy from Aix-en-Provence, Charles-François Bouche (1737–1795), contained a provision that no Jews should be allowed to leave the papal province before paying their part of the communal debts.[313] On March 22, 1791 a delegation of Carpentras requested that the city adopt measures to prevent rich Jews from leaving. The delegation was apprehensive that those remaining would have to bear the burden of supporting the poor and paying off the old debts. The rich Jews, however, left Carpentras in April, after selling their clothing and jewelry. On July 17, 1791 the Jews petitioned the city council for permission to arrange a meeting of Jews of Carpentras origin to be presided over by a member of the city council. The council granted the petition and requested the city councils of Montpellier, Beaucaire, Bagnol, Orange, Nîmes, Arles, Tarascon, Aix, Pont-Saint-Esprit, Carcasonne, Pézenas, Aramont and other places where Jews from Carpentras had settled to announce that such a meeting would take place in Carpentras on August 20, 1791. At the meeting it was decided that the Jewish community of Carpentras would organize itself in three sections (Carpentras, Aix and Nîmes) for the purpose of repaying its debts.[314]

pentras, 1789.] 13 pp.; F.-R.-Ch.-J. Cottier, *Dialogue*. [Carpentras, 1789.] 15 pp.; *Demandes et doléances de la ville de L'Isle* (n. p., n. d.), p. 10 (a pro-Jewish demand in connection with Jewish emigration); Ad BdR, L 1991 (statement by Barbeau on the Jewish emigration, July 11, 1793); Am Avignon, 1–II–40; "De l'état des Juifs dans le Comtat Venaissin, avant et après 1789." *AI*, I (1840), 290–91, 652.

[313] Charles-François Bouche, *De la restitution du Comté Venaissin* . . . (Paris, 1789), chap. X, pp. 39–40.

[314] *Copie de la Supplique*, see Bibliography, No. 84; Columbia, X893C–C22, vol. 2: "Voyant notre communauté se dissoudre par l'effet des lois qui les supprimaient toutes, la municipalité de Carpentras, par sa délibération du 17 juillet 1791, résolut de prendre des mesures pour que les membres puissent se libérer, avant d'être affranchis des obligations communales par l'entière dispersion du corps. En conséquence, elle fit une proclamation pour tous les juifs étrangers qui faisaient partie de la communauté, et la fit publier et afficher à Aix, Nîmes, à Montpellier, &c, &c, par le canal des autorités locales. Cette proclamation invitait les juifs résidant dans ces villes à se rendre à Carpentras, pour se concerter avec ceux qui étaient restés sur les moyens d'acquiter la dette commune. En conséquence des ces mesures, et

720

Abbot Maxime de Pazzis noted in his report of 1808 on the Vaucluse department, which was formed in 1791 from the former papal province of Avignon and Comtat Venaissin and the principality of Orange, that only the poorest Jews remained in the department.[315] Of about 2,000 Jews living in Vaucluse

d'après la direction donnée par l'autorité, il fut envoyé des députés de part et d'autre, et l'on conclut enfin un traité, d'après lequel la communauté se composait à l'avenir des trois sections de Carpentras, d'Aix, et de Nismes, qui avaient chacun un syndic et un trésorier, et qui devaient contribuer au paiement des pensions et arrérages dûs par la communauté, et successivement à l'extinction des capitaux, d'après une certaine proportion. Ce traité s'executa pendant quelques années, jusqu'à ce que les évènemens de la révolution eurent tout boulversé."

[315] Maxime Pazzis [Abbé Maxime de Séguin de Pazzis], *Mémoire statistique sur le département de Vaucluse* (Carpentras, 1808), pp. 186–87: "Le plus pauvres seulement sont restées dans le département de Vaucluse."
During the Revolution and in later periods, the poor Jews of the Carpentras ghetto moved to the upper floors of houses of rich Jews who had left the ghetto for other parts of France. According to a petition sent on November 7, 1797 by Escoffier the elder, commissioner of the *Directoire Exécutif* of the city council, Jewish thieves had plundered the ghetto, but the Jews refused to denounce them. Escoffier, whose petition was strongly anti-Jewish, proposed to destroy the upper three or four floors of the Jewish houses. Am Carpentras, Rév., No. 217, reg. 1, fol. 5–4. The petition was published as a pamphlet with an anti-Jewish introduction: *Le Commissaire du Directoire Exécutif près l'administration municipale du canton de Carpentras à ladite administration.* [Signé: Escoffier aîné] (n. p., n. d.). 8 pp. During the old regime the Jews of Carpentras found a means of expanding the restricted area of their ghetto by building the highest houses in town, most of them of nine and ten floors (Am Carpentras, Rév. 44, fol. 50). In 1786 the Jews were forbidden to send up supplies to upper floors by baskets attached to cords, because people were injured by accidental tumbling of the baskets (*Ibid.*, FF–19, fol. 27). Soon they were forbidden to build their houses higher than eight floors, so as not to exceed the heights of the cathedral. The ghetto became so crowded that a group of Carpentras Jews asked for permission to settle in a new ghetto in Avignon and to build their own synagogue there. On November 22, 1777 the City of Avignon rejected the demand by a vote of twenty-two to one, probably because of strong opposition by the Avignonese Jews. Am Avignon, minutes, 1776–1778, fol. 161–64 and G 23; J. Bauer, "Un projet d'établisssement d'un second ghetto à Avignon (1777)." *REJ*, LII (1906), 304–07; Chobaut, *op. cit.*, CI, 8. On Sept. 20 and Dec. 24, 1800 the city council of Carpentras wrote to Jassé Crémieu, Abraham Alphandéri, Salomon Haïn Crémieu, Joseph Mossé and Mardochée Mossé who had left Carpentras for Montpellier, Nîmes, Aix and Marseilles, that their houses in the ghetto must be

prior to the Revolution only 631 remained in 1808. The percentage of non-Jews who had left the department was smaller. From 1836 to 1881 Vaucluse registered 100,000 new settlers, but during the same period 111,200 emigrated.[316] Twenty six out of the hundred and nine Jews who settled in Marseille between 1789 and 1808 were of Comtadin origin. According to one source, 219 Jews of Carpentras origin settled outside the community prior to the 1820's. Of this number, 106 left Carpentras prior to the Revolution of 1789 and 113 after 1789. Forty settled in the Gard department (mostly in Nîmes) prior to 1789 and forty-seven later; twenty-four before and forty-four after, in the department of Bouches-du-Rhône; sixteen before and eight after in the Hérault department; three before and nine after in the Seine department, six before and one after in the Alpes-Maritimes, etc.[317] Only a few wealthy Jews remained. In 1786 one Jew of Carpentras left an estate of 600,000 livres; another Jew then owned 100,000 livres and a third one over 150,000 livres. One year later a Carpentras Jew estimated his wealth at 728,000 livres. According to a list of April 6, 1794, three of the richest twenty families of Carpentras were Jewish. But according to a list of March 14, 1812, not one Jew was among the one hundred highest tax payers of Carpentras. According to a census of 1809, the wealth of 359 Jews who had remained in Carpentras was estimated to be 991,800 francs; of 106 Jews in Avignon — 262,100 francs; of 52 Jews in Cavaillon — 56,000 francs; of 22 Jews in L'Isle-sur-Sorgue — 120,000 francs. On the other hand, the wealth of 169 Jews who had emigrated from these four communities to Aix-en-Provence was set at 1,047,000 francs.[318]

repaired or completely destroyed. The same situation prevailed in Cavaillon. On June 12, 1806 the Mayor wrote to the prefect that most Jews had left Cavaillon for the department of Bouches-du-Rhône and the houses of the ghetto were in ruins (Am Carpentras, Rév. 48, fol. 18, 42; Am Cavaillon, reg. corresp. June 12, 1806). Only after the Revolution of 1830 did Carpentras Jews start to settle in houses outside of the ghetto (Bm Carpentras, Barjavel's notes, ms. 1217, fol. 166).

[316] Z. Szajkowski, "The Growth . . .," 180–183.

[317] AN, F–19–11008; Anchel, *op. cit.*, p. 37.

[318] Census of Jews in the regional consistory of Marseilles, 1809 (Jerusalem); Chobaut, *op. cit.*, CI, 11, CII, 38.

As another example one could cite the cases of Abraham Vidal of Carpentras

In a petition of August 31, 1789 the Jewish deputies of Metz appealed to the National Assembly to prohibit the emigration of any Jew from the ghetto before he had paid his share of the tax for the liquidation of the debts.[319]

In his report to the Council of the Five Hundred H.-A.-J. Chappuis asked how the Jews who had left the ghettos of Metz and Avignon could be compelled to pay special taxes levied by their former communities.[320] The commissions to liquidate the debts were authorized to tax Jews who had left their communities. New problems connected with liquidating the debts resulted from this decision, which produced a series of conflicts. On the other hand it created new ties uniting Jews all over France through a complicated system of special taxes.

In 1809 the commission to liquidate the Avignon debts decided to levy ten yearly taxes of 24,040.27 francs. Of this sum the the Avignonese Jews who had settled in Bordeaux were assessed 16,500 francs and the Avignonese Jews of other parts of France — 7,440 francs. It would appear that the commission tried to make the Jews who had left the community pay the major part of the tax. The Avignonese Jews of Bordeaux protested strongly in a pamphlet of 1818. Following are a few cases cited in it. Jacob Waidll came from Switzerland to Bordeaux and married a girl of Avignonese origin named Perpignan living there, therefore he was asked to pay the tax. Jossué and Elie Perpignan, two brothers of Avignon, settled in Bordeaux in 1718, where Jossué married a Sephardic girl named Lopes Dias. In 1818 their descendants were requested to pay the special tax for the liquidation of the Avignonese debts.[321]

According to a register of Metz debt-taxes for the period March 23, 1795 — August 26, 1798, the sum of 37,785.75 francs was paid by 1,036 Jews of whom only 478 still lived in Metz

and Carcassonne (Colombe Crémieu) of Avignon, who settled in Ales (Gard). In 1813 and 1817 they were ordered by the sub-prefect to pay their taxes for the liquidation of the debts of Carpentras and Avignon (Am Ales, II–J2).

[319] *Adresse* . . . 31 Août 1789 . . ., pp. 17–18.

[320] Chappuis, p. 9 (see Bibliography, No. 32).

[321] Bordeaux pamphlet of 1818 (see Bibliography, No. 103). Jacob Lion of Bayonne did pay his taxes to the Carpentras commission (according to his letters of March 1 and 19, 1822, addressed to the commission. JTS, 01529).

proper, 558 in other communities of the former Metz province, or in new communities, including Paris (11), Nancy (10), Lunéville (14), and Strasbourg (9). Jews of Metz origin who were assessed resided in sixty different communities, according to a document of February 2, 1802.[322] By 1811, 730 Jewish family heads of Metz origin, who were then assessed 25,005 francs for the debts, resided in 122 towns and villages.[323] In 1816, 826 descendants of Jews of Metz, then living elsewhere in France, paid 20,906 francs. In Metz itself only 176 Jews paid 4,874 francs.[324]

One important conclusion can be drawn from these facts: the rich Jews lived in the large cities while the small communities were composed mostly of poor Jews. Of the eleven Jews who

[322] Documents, Metz, No. 51, fol. 518.

[323] A total of 385 Jews resided in forty-two places in the Moselle department; 157 in twenty-four places in Meurthe; 69 in eighteen places in Lower Rhine; 9 in six places in Upper Rhine; 25 in five places in Meuse; 2 in two places in the Ardennes; 5 in three places in Marne; 30 in Paris; 1 family each in the department of Aisne, Basses-Pyrénées, Charente-inf., Côte-d'Or, Pas-de-Calais and Rhône; 2 in the Gironde and 26 in ten places in occupied German States.

[324] AN, F–19–1948. The number of Jewish families of Metz origin includes those of the communities in the former province of Metz.

In Metz the number of Jews did not rise as a result of emancipation in the same proportion as in Strasbourg, Nancy and other large provincial centers. Only twenty-nine new Jewish families settled in Metz between 1793 and 1806. The total number of Jewish families there decreased from 550 (3,025 persons) in 1789 to 503 in 1800 and 456 (2,186 persons) in 1806. The number of marriages dropped: twenty-one in 1798–1800 against forty-four in 1787–1789; and the number of births to one hundred eighty-two in 1798–1800 against one hundred ninety-nine in 1787–1789. On the other hand the population of the Jewish communities in the district of Metz increased from 447 families in 1789 to 550 in 1800, in spite of a decrease in the number of marriages and births in the district (21 marriages and 85 births in 1789 against 25 marriages and 111 births in 1788), and the rise of mortality (62 in 1789 against 48 in 1788). We may then conclude that during the old regime many Jews lived in Metz because they were not permitted to reside elsewhere. After the emancipation more Jews settled in the smaller communities around Metz than in this departmental capital itself. V. Colchen, *Mémoire statistique du département de la Moselle* (Paris, an X), pp. 54–55; *AI*, IV (1843), 640, XXIX (1869), 196; S. Posener, "Les Juifs sous le Premier Empire." *REJ*, XCIV (1933), 161–63. See also Szajkowski, "The Demographic Aspects . . ."

in 1811 paid the highest tax — 500 francs or more — nine resided in Metz and two in Paris, but not one of them in the smaller communities.[325]

[325] JTS, 01565. Many Jews left the city of Metz, but few of those who remained settled outside the ghetto. In the year X only 89 Jews in Metz resided outside of the ghetto. M. Liber, "Napoléon I et les Juifs." *REJ*, LXXI (1922), 129. In 1806, the prefect of Moselle wrote that since 1793 only 29 Jewish families had left the ghetto and settled in other parts of the city. To the Jews the streets outside the ghetto was an alien and fabulous world, called *the town* (Abraham Cahen, "Règlements . . ." *ASEJ*, I [1881], 97). Even after 1830, the other parts of the city were called *Mâqôm*. Szajkowski, *Poverty . . .*, p. 26.

See also Z. Szajkowski, "The Decline and Fall of Provencal Jewry." *JSS*, VI (1944), 31–54.

XXIV. THE ECONOMIC RESULTS OF THE LIQUIDATION OF THE DEBTS

The historian, Robert Anchel, attributed the belated liquidation of the debts to the lack of cooperation on the part of the Jews.[326] He overlooked the fact that these debts did serious damage to the economic status of the Jewish community as a whole and of each Jew individually.

Taxes to repay the debts provide valuable information on the Jews' economic status. The first conclusion which we can draw is that only part of the Jewish population was able to pay the taxes, and that, of those who did pay, most were in the lowest tax brackets. According to one list, 590 Jews of Metz were assessed 61,573 livres in debt-taxes for the years 1792 and 1793. Only eighteen of them paid 500 livres or more each; twenty one — from 300 to 500 livres; eighty nine — from 100 to 300 livres; one hundred and sixty — from 40 to 100 livres and three hundred and two — less than 40 livres. As the tax was fixed at the yearly rate of 1/1000 of each Jew's wealth, the property of the Metz Jews then able to pay taxes was evaluated by themselves at over 60,000,000 livres. This was an enormous sum, but most of the wealth was concentrated in the hands of a small group of rich Jewish families.[327]

---

[326] *REJ*, CIII (1938), 115, R. Anchel's review of *Histoire des Juifs de France des origines à nos jours* (Paris, 1937), by Léon Berman (p. 273 — debts).

[327] The eighteen Jews who paid 500 livres or more were: Hayem Wolf — 2,175 livres, 8 s.; Cerf-Goudchaux Halphen — 2,154 livres, 17 s.; Joseph D'anguy — 1,857 livres, 12 s.; Garçon-Samuel Lévy — 1,117 livres; Joseph Gougenheim — 1,070 livres, 19 s., 6 d.; Jacob-Meyer Cahen — 1,021 livres, 10 s.; Daniel Samuel and Ely Trenel — 940 livres; Nathan-Séligman Marly — 729 livres, 16 s.; Olry-Lyon Schwabe — 744 livres, 16 s.; Cerf Worms — 715 livres, 2 s., 6 d.; Lazard-Lyon Nordon — 701 livres, 12 s.; Simon-Cerf Cahen — 678 livres; Isaïe-Berr Bing — 628 livres, 16 s.; Jacob Brisac — 628 livres; Vve Judat Lévy and heirs — 613 livres, 16 s.; Joseph Oulif — 568 livres, 1 s.; Lyon-Abram Berr — 508 livres; Mayer-Louis Schwabe — 506 livres (JTS, 01565). Isaïe-Berr Bing was one of the first and most active

726

The Metz tax of 37,784.75 francs for the period March 23, 1795 — August 26, 1798 was paid by 1,036 Jews. Of this number 524 paid less than 10 francs each, 347 from 10 to 50 francs, 88 from 50 to 100 francs, 66 from 100 to 500 francs and only 11 each paid 500 francs or more.[328] In a report of the year IX on these debts submitted by the prefect of Moselle, 90 per cent of the Jews were classified as poor.[329] For the year 1816 debt-taxes paid by 176 Jews still residing in Metz amounted to 4,874 francs. Of this number 12 paid 3 or 4 francs each, 68 paid 5–10 francs, 45 paid 11–25 francs, 37 paid 26–50 francs, 4 paid 51–100 francs and only 10 paid more than 100 francs each. In other parts of France 826 Jews of Metz origin paid the same tax.[330] A report submitted in 1839 by government tax officials on the economic status of 1,296 Jewish families who were required to pay the Metz debt-taxes described only 548 families as wealthy, 208 as fairly well to do, 170 as not well to do and 270 as without property or poor.[331]

In 1842–1843 a list of Jews of Metz was drawn up in order to impose on them a tax of 21,721 francs to liquidate the debts. Only those families who had material resources of 200 francs or more were required to pay this tax and it seems that strict control was exercised. The families on the list numbered 1,099, though the number that originated in Metz was much greater; the others were obviously too poor to pay the tax. One hundred four families were listed as having material resources of 200 francs, 251 from 250 to 400 francs, 104 — 500 francs, 144 from 600 to 900 francs, 377 from 1,000 to 3,000 francs, 91 from 3,500 to 9,000 francs. There were very few really wealthy Jews whose families originated in Metz: only twenty-one worth 10 to 25 thousand francs and seven worth more than 25,000 francs. In this connection we must emphasize that these wealthy Jews had

maskilim in France. See *Revue philosophique* (Thermidor, an VIII–4), 316–18; E. Tcherikower, "The Jewish Struggle for Right during the French Revolution." *JFrance*, II, 18–21.
[328] JTS, 01565.
[329] Ad Moselle, V 166.
[330] AN, F–19–1948.
[331] Ad Moselle, V 159; Szajkowski, *Poverty* . . ., p. 83.

all emigrated from Metz and settled in other parts of France. In Metz itself and the whole department of Moselle only 630 families were required to pay the tax. Here were concentrated the Jews of Metz origin who had little wealth; none of them was classified as having a wealth of 10,000 francs or more. The largest number of wealthy Jews from Metz lived in Paris, but Paris also had its share of poor Jews from Metz, since only 144 Parisian Jews were required to pay the tax. In 1853, a list was drawn up which included 1,662 families who originated in Metz. The wealth of all 1,662 families was estimated at 7,644,650 francs but the majority appeared to have modest holdings: 667 families — 1,000 francs and less; 751, from 1,200 to 5,000 francs; 135, from 6,000 to 10,000 francs, 96, from 11 to 50,000 francs; and 13, more than 50,000 francs. Paris alone, with 409 of the 1,662 families, had more wealthy Jews than all other parts of the country together. Thirteen families had material resources (2,205,000 francs) almost as great as 802 other families (2,419,750 francs).[332]

Seligman Birié, a poor religious teacher of Metz, paid a yearly tax of 39 livres. His mother, a widow without any resources, paid 21 livres 10 sols.[333] By way of comparison it should be noted that in 1831 the combined salaries of all the sixty-two rabbis and cantors in France amounted to 46,000 francs.[334]

A police document of 1808 on the debts of communities of Alsace estimated that there were 2,000 Jewish families in Lower Rhine. Of these, 650 were unable to pay taxes. The remaining 1,350 families were divided into four classes according to their wealth: 125 families in the first class, paying 4/10 of the tax; 270 families in the second class, paying 3/10; 405 families in the third class, paying 2/10 and 540 families in the fourth class, paying 1/10. In the village of Petit-Pierre, six Jewish families paid a total community tax of 20 francs in 1812, and for repayment of the debts 52.22 francs annually. In Hochfelden, 10 families paid 69 francs in community taxes, and 180.18 francs

[332] Ad Moselle, V 159, 166; AN, F–19–1948; Bibliography, Nos. 57, 72; Szajkowski, *Poverty* . . ., p. 10.

[333] Gerson-Lévy (see Bibliography, No. 139).

[334] Robert Anchel, *Notes sur les frais du culte juif en France de 1815 à 1831* (Paris, 1928), 60–62.

728

for the debts. There was a flood of petitions which asked relief from the tax for repayment of the debts. Most of them were from poor Jews, who submitted certificates from local mayors attesting that they were too poor to pay the tax. The commission for the liquidation of debts printed special forms, which, when filled out by the petitioners, certified that they were poor. Between February 22, 1816 and July 18, 1821, 298 Jews of Lower Rhine asked that their share of the tax to cover the debts be decreased or forgiven; of these requests only 98 were rejected.[335]

335 Szajkowski, *Poverty . . .*, pp. 56–57.

XXV. THE DEBTS OF THE SEPHARDIC
NATION OF BORDEAUX

The *Nation* of the Sephardic Jews of Bordeaux borrowed money not only for its normal budget of community activities, but also in order to buy protective Letters patent as a safeguard for the Sephardic Jews and to bribe high officials.[336] On July 11, 1758 Sara Mendes, the widow of Raphaël the elder requested repayment of a loan of 3,419 livres 19 s. 4 d. granted to the *Nation* by her late husband.[337] Jb. Pereire and his heirs were paid 400 livres in interest for a loan to the *Nation*.[338] On May 21, 1776 the *Nation* decided to seek a loan of 30,000 livres,[339] and on March 13, 1781 borrowed 12,000 livres from Abraham Pimentel, who on April 4, 1780 was elected one of its syndics. The following May 13 the *Nation* paid back 6,000 livres and the remaining 6,000 livres were converted into annuities of 525 livres to be paid to the syndic's daughter Esther Pimentel or to her heirs.[340] The annuities were insured by a mortgage on a parcel of land and a house near the Jewish cemetery (called Sablonat),

---

[336] On Dec. 14, 1693 the Marranos of Bordeaux, known as New Christians, presented the city 11,000 livres in bonds, with the proviso that their present would free them from paying special taxes for the hospital *St. André* (AmBx, BB, registre de la Jurade, 1693, fol. 29–30). In 1789 the *Nation* was taxed 9,406 livres 13 s. 4 d. for the city's *capitation* and militia taxes, which was paid by 160 of the richest Jews (AmBx, CC 1098). At the request of Jacob Rodrigue Pereire on Dec. 12, 1754 the Bordeaux *Nation* granted a loan of 6,690 livres to a person who could be useful to the *Nation* (Nation, fol. 45, (No. 444). In 1764, a group of fifty-two Sephardim of Bordeaux, who had opposed the financial and other activities of their *Nation*'s leaders, also protested against the various gifts: ". . . des pensions et des presens qu'ils font à qui bon leur semble" (Ad Gironde, Rauzan the elder's notarial minutes, 34, June 24, 1764).

[337] Ad Gironde, E, Rauzan's notarial minutes, July 11, 1758.

[338] Nation, No. 497, fol. 128, March 12, 1782.

[339] *Ibid.*, No. 441, fol. 114.

[340] Abraham Pimentel died on Jan. 20, 1787 (Am Bordeaux, GG 845, No. 1656).

which belonged to the *Nation*.[341] On November 2, 1781 the
Nation borrowed 8,000 livres from its syndic Jacob Rodrigues
Lima, subsequently converted into annuities of 640 livres, also
guaranteed by a mortgage on the Sablonat property.[342] From
1778 to 1786 the Bordeaux *Nation* had to repay 33,000 livres
for loans obtained in July 1777.[343]

As a result of the decree of January 28, 1790, which granted
full citizenship to the Sephardim, the Jews of Bordeaux and
Bayonne dissolved their *Nations* and most of the community's
religious and social functions were taken over by philanthropic
societies.[344] One of the duties of the Bordeaux *Société de Bienfaisance* was to pay annuities for debts owed by the former
Nation. The Society paid the Pimentel annuities until November
13, 1793 and the Lima annuities until November 2 of the same
year.

The Society was unable to maintain discipline within the community. In later years, when many Jews had forgotten the
benevolent attitude of the Revolution towards Jewish emancipation, the Jewish leaders of the Bordeaux Society blamed the
revolutionary events for the confusion in the community.[345] In
a report submitted at a meeting of December 16, 1804 it was
stated:

"Then came the Revolution, the religious groups were free,
the Jews received the name and privileges of free citizens. This

[341] Nation, Nos. 477, 486, 492, fol. 125, 127 (Apr. 4, 1780, March 13, May
13, 1781).

[342] *Ibid.*, No. 541, fol. 138, Nov. 2, 1781.

[343] *Ibid.*, No. 450, July 9, 1777.

[344] The Society of Bordeaux was founded in 1738 and existed officially only
until Apr. 13, 1809. J. Uhry, "Souvenirs israélites de Bordeaux." *AI*, LIII
(1892), 262–63. A few other Jewish societies existed in Bordeaux. On October
5, 1792 Abraham d'Elie Julian bequeathed 250 livres to the *confrèrie Tipheret
Bahurim* and 300 livres to the *confrèrie Gamilut Hazidim* (Am Bx, GG14,
p. 86). In 1803 another society was founded: *Règlement de la Société de bienfaisance de Tob-Lacol ou Bonne envers tous, fondée en 1803* (Bordeaux, 1851).
18 pp.

[345] This happened in many communities, e. g. in Carpentras. In 1816 the
Carpentras commission to liquidate the debts petitioned Louis XVI: "Dès
le commencement de cette révolution que S. M. a si heureusement terminé"
(Columbia, X893C–C22, vol. 1).

was an expensive benefit which was paid for by much suffering. From that moment on our taxes were abolished. This was a good thing for every one of us individually, but a misfortune for our institutions. The functions of the syndics diminished to activities of an internal character and they lost their authority. Taxes were not paid. Our institutions were disrupted and it became urgent to save everything through a free contribution for our philanthropic Society."

In 1792 J. Rodrigue, Alexandre jr., J. and J. Pereyre, and Rodrigues the elder were elected administrators of the Society. At the end of 1792 they called a general assembly of the Society, but only a few Jews were present. They demanded that the administrators perform their function and advance to the Society the funds necessary for the continuation of its normal activities. Rodrigues advanced 6,000 livres to the Society, mostly for charitable distribution to paupers. But then came the Terror:

"In vain did he [Rodrigues] try to collect taxes; few people paid their taxes. It seems that the political events occupied everybody's minds and closed their hearts. Soon came the storm of the Revolution [Terror]. All useful institutions were smashed by the events of the general struggle."[346]

The Society ceased its activities and became a debtor of 10,000 livres to Alexandre and of 600 livres in *assignats* to Pereyre. It also owed 300 livres to the druggist Cadilhon and 240 livres to a butcher for medicines and meat distributed to the poor,[347] 250 livres to the syndic Lévy, 800 to the syndic Pereyre. In 1804 the Society owed 5,180 livres in unpaid annuities to Pimentel's heirs and 4,964 livres to Lima's heirs. Pimentel's heirs accepted a settlement of 2,590 livres; Lima's heirs demanded the immediate payment of 1,964 livres and the remaining sum within four years. The Society also owed 1,500 livres to Fonseca, who went to Paris in order to fight the nationalization of the

---

[346] Minutes of the Society (Jerusalem); S. Szajkowski, "Notes on the History of French Jews," *Davke*, No. 24 (1955), 243–56 ("The First Assembly of the Bordeaux Jewish Community after the Revolution of 1789," in Yiddish).

[347] The name of Dominique Cadilhom, born in Mont-de-Marsan, is mentioned in the Bordeaux calendars from 1781 till 1800. He died on July 16, 1800 at the age of 75 (Am Bx, 3–E–56. No. 725).

Jewish cemetery.[348] Alexandre, Fonseca and Pereyre agreed to accept in repayment only half of the debts owed to them. But there was no income. In 1791 the Society had leased the Sablonat property to the Christian Avenel, who not only refused to pay the rent, but had, in 1803, asked the sum of 1,200 livres for guarding the house. After long preparation the Society held a meeting on June 29, 1803, at which the Sephardic and Avignonese Jews of Bordeaux were present. New by-laws were accepted with the principal aim of repaying the debts. Those able but refusing to pay a tax of 12 livres were denied burial in the Jewish cemetery. The minutes of the first meeting were signed by 155 family heads. At another meeting of December 16, 1804 it was announced that a tax of 7,296 livres had been collected. Only 9 families paid over 100 livres or more, 17 — from 65 to 100 livres, 112 — from 24 to 50 livres and 84 — from 12 to 20 livres.[349]

*   *
*

The Jewish communities in the occupied territories also had to pay debts. In 1810 the Community of Turin had debts amounting to more than 100,000 francs; the Community of Montferrat (department of Marengo), more than 170,000 francs. The Communities of Parme and Plaisance also had large debts.[350]

A large number of Jewish communities had to repay smaller debts dating from before the Revolution or from a later period.

[348] According to one document Fonseca spent 3,038 livres in the fight against the nationalization of the cemetery. Of this sum 362 livres was paid to lawyers, including 240 livres to Beaufleury (Jerusalem).

[349] See note 346.

[350] Decrees of Oct. 22, 1810 (on the liquidation of the Turin debts) and of Apr. 19, 1811 (on the liquidation of the Monferrat debts), AN, F–19–1847; Bibliography, No. 137.

In Piemont a privilege renewed every ten years, known as *Casaca*, protected the tenants of the ghetto against their landlords. The privilege was not renewed in 1806 and the Italian deputies to the Sanhedrin demanded the abrogation of the collective responsibility of the Jewish communities to landlords because the communities no longer existed. AN, F–19–1847.

According to a document of the Lower Rhine consistory dated March 18, 1831, sixteen Jewish communities owed 18,359.60 francs for debts contracted in order to construct their synagogues.[351] The Jews of Paris, too, had debts.[352]

[351] Bischheim owed 500 francs, Dettviller — 1,200, Epfig — 4,200, Gerstheim — 3,000, Haguenau — 60,670, Hochfelden — 1,100, Marckolsheim — 400, Mütersholz — 995, Mutzig — 1,027.65, Saarunion — 100, Saverne — 1,000, Schirhofen — 11,300, Soultz-sous-Forêts — 13,000, Schweighausen — 2,000, Schwindratzheim — 5,000, Wittersheim — 500. In the Upper Rhine in 1831 the community of Wintzenheim still owed 5,021 francs, Guebwiller — 1,700, Herrlisheim — 50, Wittersdorf — 300, according to a report of Jan. 16, 1831 (Documents, Alsace Nos. 4–5, fol. 7–8).

[352] "une des questions les plus importantes dont le Consistoire Central et Départemental ont eu à s'occuper depuis la révolution est, sans contredit, celle qui touche la libération des dettes du Temple." Leaflet of the Central Consistory, dated Dec. 15, 1837 and signed by M. Cerfberr, 1 p. (ZS). The central consistory owed a certain sum to rabbi David Sintzheim. On Nov. 28, 1816 the consistory paid 1,800 francs to his heirs (Documents, Alsace, Nos. 88–89).

XXVI. CONCLUSIONS

The debts owed by the Jewish communities were contracted to pay oppressive sums wrested from them under the old regime because of anti-Jewish restrictions. The creditors were Christians.

The autonomous Jewish communities, then largely agencies for collecting taxes, were carefully controlled by the authorities. However, through these communities the Jews were often able to defend themselves against encroachments upon their hard-won but limited rights. In the course of the fight for Jewish emancipation during the revolutionary period the autonomous Jewish communities were violently attacked as contrary to the spirit of the new regime. The Jews were granted full citizenship on condition of giving up all autonomous privileges and accordingly the Jewish communities were dissolved.

The Jews requested that the debts be nationalized and repaid by the government. This was a justifiable demand, because all other autonomous *corporations* had been dissolved, their properties confiscated and the debts owed by them assumed by the government. The Jewish communities were no different from other dissolved corporations. The Christian creditors of the Jews, fearful that the government would refuse to repay them, fought bitterly against the Jews' demand. They relied on a long complicated series of legal arguments which the legislative authorities of the revolutionary regime could easily have dismissed. In fact, many legislative leaders strongly favored the nationalization of the debts. However, the government's reluctance to repay the debts from public funds was reinforced by unfavorable and mistaken decisions of judicial bodies, to whom the matter was referred. The legislative authorities and the government had sound legal basis for ruling by decree that the Jewish communities were in the category of *corporations*, which were dissolved prior to the emancipation. However, it acted otherwise and thus forced the Jews to continue to exist as communal groups. The Jewish commissions appointed for the

734

purpose of liquidating the debts continued most communal activities of the dissolved communities.

The government's refusal to nationalize the debts saved over a million livres for the Republic's treasury, but at the cost of hardship to the Jews. Of course, the commissions to liquidate the debts helped to retain communal ties among the Jews and to preserve their group existence, until the official reconstitution of Jewish communities during the First Empire. However, historians and partisans of the Revolution must view the government's action as incompatible with the aspirations of the new regime. For this error only the authorities — and not the Jews — are blameworthy. The Jews argued eloquently for the nationalization of the debts and thus for the complete abolition of their officially dissolved communities. But they lost.

The Revolution thus followed the pattern of the old regime and of many other countries: on the one hand, it dissolved autonomous Jewish communities, and, on the other, it forced them to remain in existence for taxation and other administrative purposes.

APPENDIX I

DEBTS OF THE JEWISH COMMUNITIES IN FRANCE

A BIBLIOGRAPHY OF PAMPHLETS AND PRINTED DOCUMENTS

I. DEBTS OF THE JEWISH COMMUNITIES OF METZ AND THE METZ PROVINCE

1. *Monseigneur, le Conseil est informé qu'il a plu au Roi d'établir depuis peu sur chaque famille juive, un droit appelé de Manance . . .* (n. p., n. d.). 1 p. fol.
On the Brancas tax.

2. *Mémoire pour la communauté des Juifs établis en la ville de Metz. Contre les prétentions de Monsieur le Duc de Brancas* (n. p., n. d.). 3 pp. fol.

3. *Sur la Requeste presentée au Roy en son Conseil par la communauté des Juifs estably à Metz* (n. p., n. d.). 2 pp. fol.
Petition against the Brancas tax.

4. *A Monsieur l'Intendant. Supplient humblement les élus de la communauté des Juifs de cette ville* ([Metz], n. d.). 1 p. 4°.
Ordinance of Feb. 7, 1724 on the taxes to be paid by the provincial Jewish communities, signed by the Intendant [Jean-François] de Creil. See also Nos. 5, 7–10.

4a. *L'an mil sept cens cinquante-quatre le . . .* [Metz, 1740.] 1 p. 4°.
Formular for taxes.

5. *Etat de la taxe fait par les syndics de la communauté des Juifs de Metz, sur les Juifs habitans dans les lieux de la Généralité d'icelle pour le recouvrement des deniers à aider à la somme de vingt mille livres que ladite communauté est obligée chaque année*

736

à *Mrs. les Ducs de Brancas & Lauragois ou autres, par don du Roy du 4. Avril 1743* . . . (n. p., n. d.). 3 pp. fol.

See Nos. 4, 7–10.

6. *Au Roy.* [Signé: Me. de Serionne, avocat] (n. p., 1745). 3 pp. 4°.

Petition against the Brancas tax.

7. *Etat de la taxe faite par les syndics de la communauté des Juifs de la Ville de Metz, sur les Juifs habitans dans les lieux de la Généralité d'icelle, pour le recouvrement des deniers à aider à la somme de vingt mille liv.[res] que ladite communauté est obligée chaque année à Mr. le Duc de Brancas & autres; qu'il sera payé chaque quartier d'année par les collecteurs nommez* (n. p., n. d.). 2 pp. fol.

Together with an ordinance of Dec. 11, 1742 signed by the Intendant Jean-François de Creil. Was published periodically, see Nos. 4–5, 8–10.

8. *Etat de la taxe fait par les syndics de la communauté des Juifs de la Ville de Metz, sur les Juifs habitans dans les lieux de la Généralité d'icelle, pour le recouvrement des deniers à aider à la somme de vingt mille livres que ladite communauté est obligée chaque année à Mrs. les Ducs de Brancas & Lauragois ou autres, par don du Roy du 4. Avril 1743 à commencer le premier Janvier 1746* . . . (n. p., n. d.). 3 pp. fol.

Together with an ordinance signed by the Intendant Jean-François de Creil of Dec. 27, 1752. See Nos. 4–5, 7, 9–10.

9. *Etat de la taxe fait par les syndics de la communauté des Juifs de la Ville de Metz* . . . *lesquelles-dites taxes seront payées par les collecteurs préposés* . . . (n. p., n. d.). 3 pp. fol.

Together with an ordinance of Feb. 2, 1763 signed by the Intendant Jean-Louis de Bernage. See Nos. 4–5, 7–8, 10.

10. *Etat de répartition faite par la communauté des Juifs de la Ville de Metz, de la somme imposée aux Juifs établis dans l'étendue de la Généralité de ladite Ville, pour subvenir, conjointement avec ladite communité, à l'acquit des charges & impositions auxquelles elle est attenue* . . . (n. p., n. d.). 3 pp. fol.

Dated May 20, 1772 and signed by the syndics Joseph Lambert, Samuel-Jonas Lévy, Alexandre-Salomon Cahen, Cerf Godechaux, Judith Schwab,

Louis Trenel, Lyon de Mayence, Elie C[G]ompetz, Mayer-Godechaux Cahen.
Together with an ordinance of Nov. 9, 1772 signed by the Intendant Charles-
Alexandre de Calonne. See Nos. 4–5, 7–9.

10a. [Petition addressed to the King by the Jewish community
of Louvigny, on a conflict with the communities of Phalsbourg,
Mettebouné [?], etc. 1779. According to a petition of the Metz
community, 1792. JTS, 01528.]

11. [An approval of the tax of the Jewish community of Metz
for the period of four years. Dec. 24, 1789. Signed by Jean de
Pont [Depont.] (n. p., n. d.). 1 p. fol.
Without a title. See No. 20.

12. *Mémoire pour les Juifs de Metz, concernant une redevance
de 20,000 livres qu'ils payent annuellement au Duc de Brancas, sous
le titre de droit d'habitation, protection & tolérance.* [Signé: Louis
Wolff, Député des Juifs de Metz & des Trois Evêchés] (n. p.,
[1790]). 8 pp. 4°.

13. [Jacques-François-Laurent] de Visme [Devisme], *Rapport
fait au nom du Comité des Domaines, le 20 Juillet 1790, sur le
droit de protection levé sur les Juifs. Par M. de Visme, Député
du Vermandois. Et Décret rendu sur ce rapport. Imprimé par
ordre de l'Assemblée Nationale* (Paris, n. d.). 16 pp. 8°.

14. *Lettres patentes du Roi, sur le Décret de l'Assemblée Nationale, du 20 Juillet dernier, portant suppression des droits
d'habitation, de protection, de tolérance & de redevances semblables
sur les Juifs. Données à Saint-Cloud le 7 Août 1790. Transcrites
en Parlement, en vacations, le 17 Août dudit an* (Paris, 1790).
4 pp. 4°.
Another edition: Paris, 1790, 3 pp. 4°, without the registration.

15. ———, *Transcrites en Parlement, le 21 du même mois*
(Metz, 1790). 3 pp. 4°.

16. ———, (Bordeaux, 1790). 4 pp. 4°.
Together with "Déliberation du Directoire du Département de la Gironde"
of Aug. 4, 1790.

17. ———, (Nantes, 24 Août 1790). 4 pp. 4°.

18. ———, (n. p., n. d.). 3 pp. 4°.

Together with "Transcription . . . par le Directoire du Département du Puy-de-Dôme, en exécution de sa délibération du 20 Août 1790 . . .' '

19. *Loi qui renvoie au Directoire du District de Metz, les contestations nées & a naître du rôle de contribution fait par les Juifs de Metz. Donnée à Paris, le 27 Mai 1791* (Paris, 1791). 2 pp. 4°.

Decree of May 20, 1791.

20. ———, [Metz, 1791.] 4 pp. fol.

Together with the Jewish petition of Aug. 17, 1791 to the *Directoire* of Moselle and the *Directoire*'s decisions of Dec. 26, 1789 and Aug. 18, 1791; the Intendant's decision of Dec. 24, 1789 [see No. 11], and the Decree of May 20, 1791.

21. ———, *Transcrite sur les registres du département de la Meurthe le 20 Octobre 1791* (Nancy, 1791). 3 pp. 4°.

22. *Décret relatif à une pétition de plusieurs juifs de Nancy, au sujet de la loi du 20 Mai 1791, concernant les rôles de la ci-devant communauté des Juifs de Metz, du 1ᵉʳ Mai 1792* (Metz, [1792]). 2 pp. 4°.

23. *Pétition à la Convention Nationale, pour les ci-devant Syndics et élus de la ci-devant communauté des Juifs de Metz. Objet de la pétition. Les pétitionnaires demandent que les loix qui ont déclaré dettes nationales celles des communes, communautés et autres corporations politiques soient exécutées à l'égard de la ci-devant communauté des Juifs de Metz.* [Signé: Gaudchaux, Mayer Cahen, fondé de pouvoirs] (n. p., [1792]). 20 pp. 8°.

For a summary of the petition see No. 24. The correct name of the community leader who signed the items 23–24 was Goudchaux-Mayer Cahen.

24. *Sommaire.* [Signé: Gaudechaux-Mayer] (n. p., [1792]). 3 pp. 4°.

Summary of No. 23.

25. *A Messieurs, Messieurs les administrateurs du département de la Moselle.* [Signé: Nathan Cahen, Juif de Louvigny] (Metz, 1792). 14 pp. 4°.

Petition in the name of the smaller Jewish communities against the community of Metz and its role in the problem of debts.

26. Bernard Dalsace, *Pétition sur les affaires des Juifs. 1ᵉʳ Avril 1794* (n. p., 1794). 8°.

740

27. *Extrait des registres des délibérations du département de la Moselle, Séance publique du 5 Messidor an III [23 Juin 1795] de la République française, une et indivisible.* [Signé: (Claude) Lambert, secrétaire général, (Louis-Gabriel) Dupin, chef du bureau des contributions] (Metz, [1795]). 7 pp. 4°.

On the conflict between the Jews of Metz and the provincial communities.

28. *Précis pour les créanciers des Juifs de Metz, adressé au Corps législatif, sur la demande qui lui est faite de déclarer dettes nationales celles de la ci-devant communauté des Juifs* [Signé: "Deprille, un des créanciers, et au nom de tous, comme leur Syndic et procureur-fondé"] (Paris, [1794]). 21 pp. 4°.

29. *Consultation sur cette question: Si les dettes de la ci-devant communauté des Juifs de Metz doivent être considérées comme nationales; en réponse au Précis adressé par les créanciers des Juifs au Corps législatif.* [Signé: (Claude-François) Chauveau-Lagarde, Le Roy. 23 Floréal de l'an 5 (12 Mai 1797)] (Paris, an V). 8 pp. 4°.

30. *Réponse aux Juifs de Metz de la part de leurs créanciers.* [Signé: Puyproux aîné, l'un des créanciers et au nom de tous] (n. p., n. d.). 22 pp. 8°.

31. *Résumé pour les Juifs de Metz, contre leurs créanciers.* [Signé: (C.-F.) Chauveau-Lagarde, Jean-Jacques-Régis de Cambacérès] (Paris, [an V]). 12 pp. 4°.

Reply to No. 30.

32. Chappuis [Haycinthe-Adrien-Joseph Chapuy], *Corps législatif. Conseil des Cinq-Cents. Rapport fait par Chappuis, au nom d'une commission composée des Représentants du peuple Grégoire, [J-H.] Laurençot [Laurenceot] (du Jura), [J.-B.-M.] Saladin & Chappuis. Séance du 16 Germinal [an V — 5 Avril 1797]* (Paris, an V). 10 pp. 8°.

33. [Jean-Baptiste-Michel] Saladin, *Corps législatif. Conseil des Cinq-Cents. Rapport fait par Saladin, au nom d'une commission spéciale, composée des Représentans Grégoire, Chappuy [Chappuis], [C.-E.-J.] Louvet, [J.-F. baron de] Beyts & Saladin, sur les pétitions des Juifs de Metz & d'Avignon. Séance du 7 Fructidor an V [24 Août 1797]* (Paris, an V). 15 pp. 8°.

34. [François-Marie-Joseph Riou de Kersalaun,] *Corps législatif. Conseil des Cinq Cents. Rapport fait par Riou sur les pétitions des Juifs de Metz & d'Avignon, au nom d'une commission spéciale. Séance* du 4 Frimaire an 6 [24 Novembre 1797] (Paris, Frimaire an VI). 8 pp. 8°.

35. *Encore un mot pour les créanciers des Juifs de Metz.* [Signé: Puyproux aîné, un des créanciers"] (n. p., n. d.). 4 pp. 4°.
Reply to No. 34.

36. [Broadside announcing the sale of communal Jewish property, end of 1797.]

According to minutes of Jan. 8, 1798 (Documents, Metz, No. 66): "en conformité des affiches imprimés qui ont été placardés dans toutes les carefours et lieux."

37. [Broadside announcing the sale of communal Jewish properties on Jan. 6, 1799 (17 Nivose an 7).]

Signed by Jacques-François Adam, syndic of the Christian creditors. According to minutes (Documents, Metz, No. 66): "en conformité des affiches imprimés qui ont été placardés dans tous les carefours."

38. [*Arrêté du Préfet de la Moselle.*] *Du 15 Brumaire an X* [6 Nov. 1801] (n. p., n. d.). 2 pp. 4°.

39. *Compte que rendent au Citoyen Préfet du département de la Moselle les citoyens Mayer-Goudchaux Cahen; Moyse-Hayen Bing; Cerf-Alexandre Cahen; Nathan Oulif; Joseph Gougenheim; Goudchaux-Mayer Cahen; Marchand Mayence; Moyse Gompertz; Aron-Marx Lévy; Mayer-Louis Schwabe et Louis-Isaac Cahen, anciens syndics en exercice et Commissaires élus de la ci-devant Communauté des Juifs de Metz, de la gestion qu'ils ont eue des biens de ladite Communauté, ainsi que des recettes et dépenses qu'ils ont faites à compter du jour de sa suppression, en exécution de l'arrêté des Consuls, du 5 nivôse an 10 [26 décembre 1801]* (Metz, [an XI]). 18 pp. 4°.

P. 16: "Metz le 5 fructidor an 10 . . ." Together with: "Extrait des minutes de la Préfecture du département de la Moselle. Metz, le 17 Frimaire an XI."

40. *Arrêté relatif à la liquidation des dettes de la ci-devant communauté des Juifs de Metz. Du 5 Nivôse an X* [26 Décembre 1801] (Paris, an X). 3 pp. 4°.

742

41. ———, (Metz, [an X]). 3 pp. 4°.

42. ———, (n. p., n. d.). 2 pp. 8°.

43. *No. 1465. Bulletin des Lois, No. 145. Arrêté relatif à la liquidation des dettes de la ci-devant communauté des Juifs de Metz. Du 5 Nivôse an X [26 Décembre 1801]* (Paris, an X). 3 pp. 4°.

44. ———, (n. p., n. d.). 2 pp. 8°.

45. ———, (Metz, [an X]). 3 pp. 4°.

46. *Pétition aux citoyens, conseillers d'Etat, membres de la Section de l'Intérieur.* (n. p., [1801]). 15 pp. 4°.
Signed by "Mayer Lévy, l'un des pétitionnaires, fondé de pouvoir des autres pétitionnaires" and the lawyer Dumesnil [de] Merville. Petition by the Jews of the Thionville arrondissement against the community of Metz.

47. *Cotisation de* [Metz, 1810?]. 2 pp. 4°.
Circular, begins with: "Contrat décretée par le soussigné, receveur de la ci-devant communauté juive de Metz."

48. *Ancienne Communauté des Juifs de Metz. Rôles formés en vertu de l'Arrêté Consulaire du 5 Nivôse an dix [25 Dec. 1801], pour le paiement des rentes viagères dues par l'ancienne Communauté des Juifs de Metz. Ordonnance de —* [Metz, 181–]. 1 p. fol.

49. *Cotisation de l'an 1814. Le receveur de la ci-devant Communauté des Juifs de Metz, a M —* [Signé: Boucherat] (Metz, 1 Octobre 1814). 1 p. 4°.

50. *Analyse succinte de l'affaire de la communauté des Juifs de Metz, renvoyée au Conseil d'Etat. Faits* (Metz, 9 Février 1828). 3 pp. 4°.
Signed by the creditor Dubalay.

51. *Louis Philippe . . .* (Metz, 1838). 11 ff. 8°.
Verdict by the Tribunal of the 3rd Moselle arrondissement, Jan. 2, 1838. Affair of Marie Cochel, widow of Isaac Goudchaux, and Jean-Alexandre Tardif. 3 editions on stamped paper.

52. *Liquidation de l'Affaire Tardif* (Metz, n. d.). 3 pp. 4°.

53. *Commission de liquidation des dettes de l'ancienne communauté des Juifs de Metz* (Metz, 25 Juillet 1838). 2 pp. 4°.
Circular.

54. *Préfecture de la Moselle. Communauté juive de Metz. Recouvrement du rôle de répartition dressé le 19 Juillet 1842.* (Metz, 26 janvier 1846). 2 pp. 4°.
Circular by the Prefect of Moselle to the Prefects of other departments on the liquidation of the debts.

55. *Cotisation pour l'extinction des dettes de l'ancienne communauté des Juifs* [Metz, 184–]. 1 p. 4°.
Signed by Stoffels, collector of taxes.

56. *Mémoire pour M. Lion-Cerf Cahen, Cosman-Joseph Cahen, Isaac Schwabe et consorts, intervenants contre MM. Salzédo, Crémieux, Halphen et consorts.* [Signé: Dumont, Adrien] (Paris, 184–). 12 pp. 4°.

57. *Rôle de la répartition pour l'extinction des dettes de l'ancienne communauté des Juifs de Metz. Année 1842* (Metz, [1843]). 32 pp. 8°.

58. *Cotisation de l'an 1842. Le receveur de la ci-devant communauté des Juifs de Metz* (Metz, 24 Juillet 1843). 1 p. 4°.
Signed by Stoffels, collector of taxes. Not the same as No. 61.

59. *La Commission de la liquidation des dettes de l'ancienne communauté juive de Metz. 25 Juillet 1843* (Metz, 1843). 12 pp. 8°.
Report signed by Lion Goudchaux. See No. 144.

60. *Préfecture de la Moselle. Communauté juive de Metz. Recouvrement du rôle de répartition dressé le 19 juillet 1842* (Metz, 30 Juillet 1843). 2 pp. 4°.
Circular addressed to the tax-collectors. See also No. 66.

61. *Cotisation de l'an 1842. Le Receveur de la ci-devant Communauté des Juifs de Metz* (Metz, 24 Juillet 1843). 2 pp. 4°.
Circular signed by Stoffels. Not the same as No. 58.

62. [Circular against paying the tax for the liquidation of the Metz debts. Signed by Adolphe Crémieux, Halphen, Cahen, Fould and Max Cerfberr of Paris.]

According to the report of Jan. 3, 1844, see Nos. 62a, 63, 70–71.

62a. [An appeal by the same Jews of Paris for funds to fight against the taxes for the liquidation of the Metz debts.] n. p., n. d. 1 p. 4°.

Without a title. 1840's. See Nos. 62, 63, 70–71.

63. *Commission de liquidation des dettes de l'ancienne communauté juive de Metz* (Metz, 1844). 12 pp. 4°.

Report of Jan. 3, 1844.

64. *Conseil d'Etat. Extrait du registre des délibérations. Séance du 12 Avril 1845* (Metz, [1845]). 6 pp. 4°.

Affair Salzédo and the Metz debts.

65. *Mémoire présenté par M. le Préfet de la Moselle en exécution de l'Article du 1er Juin 1828, à l'effet de revendiquer, pour la juridiction administrative, l'examen des réclamations portées devant le Tribunal civil de Sarreguemines, par divers israélites de Frauenberg, contre leurs cotisations au rôle dressé en 1842, pour le paiement des dettes de l'ancienne communauté juive de Metz.* [Signé: Germeau] (Metz, 30 Juin 1845). 7 pp. 4°.

66. *Préfecture de la Moselle. Communauté juive de Metz. Recouvrement du rôle de répartition dressé le 19 Juillet 1842* (Metz, 20 Janvier 1846). 2 pp. 4°.

Circular addressed to the tax-collectors. See also No. 60.

67. *Ministère de l'Intérieur.* Paris, 4 Février 1846 (n. p., n. d.). 1 p. 4°.

Circular addressed to the Prefects on the lawsuit involving Dreyfus and the Metz debts.

68. *Préfecture de la Moselle. Liquidation des dettes de l'ancienne communauté juive de Metz* (Metz, avril 1847). 2 pp. 4°.

Circular addressed to the Mayors.

69. *Prefecture de la Moselle. Division des affaires militaires. Liquidation des dettes de l'ancienne communauté juive de Metz* (Metz, avril 1847). 2 pp. 4°.

Circular.

70. *Règlement des dettes de la communauté juive de Metz. Note pour MM. Fould, Halphen, Worms de Romilly, Dreyfus, Cahen etc. . . . contre MM. Bourqueney, Seitivaux, etc.* [Signé: E. Allou, Collin, M. Moulin.] (Paris, [1848]). 23 pp. 4°.

See also Nos. 62–63, 71.

71. *Consultation pour les Srs. Mourgues, Bourqueney et Seitivaux, contre les Srs. Worms de Romilly, Halphen et Fould.* [Signé: Stéphane Cuënot.] [Paris, 1850]. 10 pp. fol.

See also Nos. 62–63, 70.

72. *Liquidation des dettes de l'ancienne communauté juive de Metz. Mise en recouvrement du rôle de 1853. Compte de l'emploi du produit du rôle de 1843. Copie du rôle de 1853* (Metz, [1854]). 76 pp. 8°.

73. *Préfecture de la Moselle. Communauté juive de Metz. Recouvrement du rôle de répartition dressé le 27 mai 1855* (Metz, 6 Septembre 1855). 3 pp. 4°.

Circular addressed to the tax collectors. Not the same as No. 76.

74. *Rôle de l'année 1855. Le receveur de la ci-devant communauté des Juifs de Metz* (Metz, 1er september 185[5]). 2 pp. fol.

Together with: "Extrait de l'arrêté de M. le Préfet du département de la Moselle, en date du 21 août 1855."

75. *La Commission nommée par M. le Préfet du département de la Moselle, en exécution de l'arrêté des Consuls du 5 Nivôse an X, pour la liquidation des dettes de l'ancienne communauté Juive de Metz* (Metz, 3 septembre 1855). 4 pp. 8°.

Report.

76. *Préfecture de la Moselle. Communauté Juive de Metz. Recouvrement du rôle de répartition dressé le 27 mai 1855 . . .* (Metz, 6 septembre 1855). 4 pp. 4°.

Circular. Not the same as No. 73.

746

77. *Le Receveur de la ci-devant communauté des Juifs de Metz* (Metz, 1855). 6 pp. 4°.

Circular and report.

78. *Recette central du département de la Seine* (Paris, 20 février 1856). 2 pp. 4°.

Taxes for the liquidation of the Metz debts.

79.–80. *Liste nominative des Israélites qui paraissent devoir concourir au paiement des Dettes de l'ancienne communauté des Juifs de Metz, et sur la position desquels des renseignements sont demandés par la Comission de liquidation, à M.* (n. p., n. d.). 4 pp. fol.

Formular. Another formular was printed together with 1 p. of "Instructions sur la manière de remplir cet état."

81. *Metz, le —— —. Le Citoyen Boucherat, receveur de la ci-devant communauté des Juifs de Metz* (n. p., n. d.). 1 p. 4°.

Circular.

II. DEBTS OF THE JEWISH COMMUNITIES OF THE FORMER PAPAL PROVINCE OF AVIGNON AND COMTAT VENAISSIN

82. *Mémoire pour les Sieurs Marquis d'Alpuget & Consorts de la Ville d'Avignon, créanciers de la communauté des Juifs de la même ville, demandeurs contre quelques particuliers Juifs, aussi de la ville d'Avignon, réfugiéz à Bordeaux, deffendeurs* (n. p., n. d.). 7 pp. fol.

83. *Extrait des Registres de Parlement* [de Bordeaux, 1723]. fol.

Fragment in the City archives of Bordeaux, II 113. Annulment of sentences of March 19, 1717 and Dec. 20, 1723 by the papal authorities of Avignon in favor of the creditors of the Avignon Jews against L'Ange [Lange] Mossé and other Avignonese Jews of Bordeaux.

84. *Copie de la Supplique présentée par les Administrateurs de la Carrière des Juifs de la Commune de Carpentras, à MM. les Maire & Officiers Municipaux* (Carpentras, 1791). 6 pp. 4°.

On the emigration of the rich Jews from Carpentras and the debts. Dated July 17, 1791, and signed by Moyse de Milliaud aîné, Jacassuyé Alfanderic,

Ruben Crémieu. Together with "Extrait des registres de la Commune de Carpentras," July 10, 1791.

85. *Observations pour les Juifs d'Avignon, à la Convention Nationale* (n. p., an III). 19 pp. 8°.
Dated Sept. 26, 1794 and signed: "Aaron Ravel, chargé de pouvoir, Aaron Vidal, Milhaud." See No. 86.

86. *Nouvelles observations pour les Juifs d'Avignon* (n. p., an III). 15 pp. 8°.
Dated Nov. 14, 1794 and signed by "Aaron Ravel, chargé de pouvoir, Aaron Vidal, Millhaud." See No. 85.

87. *Extrait du registre des arrêtés du Comité de Législation. Séance du 19 Germinal l'an troisième [8 avril 1795]* (n. p., n. d.). 2 pp. 4°.
On the Avignon debts.

88. *Mémoire pour les citoyen Dominique Chambaud, de la commune d'Avignon; Jean Chaulet . . . demandeurs: contre le citoyen Jassé-Haïn Crémieu, de cette commune d'Aix, fils et héritier de Jassuda-David Crémieu, défendeur.* [Signé: Granet, homme de loi et defenseur officieux] (Aix, an VII). 34 pp. 4°.
On the Carpentras debts. See Nos. 89–90.

89. *Mémoire pour le citoyen Jassé Haïn Crémieu, naturalisé français, demeurant à Aix: contre les citoyens Dominique Chambaud . . ., et contre les membres de la ci-devant communauté des Juifs de Carpentras, en qualité au procès, appellés en garantie subsidaire.* [Signé: Chansaud, Homme de Loi] (Aix, an VII). 34 pp. 4°.
See Nos. 88, 90.

90. *Précis pour les citoyens Dominique Chambaud . . . demandeurs: contre le citoyen Jassé Haïn Crémieu, de cette commune d'Aix, fils et héritier de Jassuda-David Crémieu, défendeur.* [Signé: Granet, Homme de Loi] (Aix, an VII). 41 pp. 4°.
See Nos. 88–89.

91. *Extrait des Minutes de la Secrétairerie d'Etat. Au Quartier impérial de Posen, 12 décembre 1806* [Avignon, 1807]. Broadside.
On the debts of the communities of the former papal province.

92. *Extrait des registres de la Préfecture du département de Vaucluse. Arrêté du Préfet du département de Vaucluse* (Avignon, 26 juillet 1808). Broadside.

Appointment of a commission for the liquidation of the Carpentras debts.

93. *Arrêté de M. le Préfet de Vaucluse, en date du 4 mars 1811, qui approuve la liquidation de la dette des Juifs de l'ancienne communauté de Carpentras . . .* [Avignon, 1811.] 10 pp. 4°.

94. *Préfecture de Vaucluse. Arrêté portant nomination de la nouvelle commission de liquidation des dettes des communautés juives de Lille [L'Isle] et d'Avignon* [Avignon, 2 mai 1816.] Broadside.

95. *Département de Vaucluse. Acquittement des dettes de l'ancienne communauté des Juifs de Carpentras. Avertissement délivré pour le paiement des sommes portées aux rôles de répartition du dixième* à payer en 1816 . . . (n. p., n. d.). 1 p. 4°.

96. *Circulaire* (Carpentras, Septembre 1816). 3 pp. 4°.

96a. *La Commission formée pour la répartition de la dette de l'ancienne communauté israélite de Carpentras. Octobre 1816* (n. p., n. d.). 1 p. 4°.

97. *Avis.*

On the Carpentras debts. According to the manuscript 01529 at the JTS: "Coût d'impression des avis individuelles pour une assemblée générale . . . 17 octobre 1816."

98. *Préfecture de Vaucluse. Avis.* [Signé: Baron de St.-Chamans.] (Avignon, 9 novembre 1816). Broadside.

On the activities of the Commission for the liquidation of the debts.

99. *Avis. La Commission formée pour la répartition de la dette de l'ancienne Communauté Israélite de Carpentras, A M — —* [Carpentras, 1816.] 3 ff. 4°.

100. *Préfecture de Vaucluse. Arrêté concernant la liquidation des dettes des anciennes communautés israélites d'Avignon et de Lille* [L'Isle] (Avignon, 22 janvier 1817). Broadside.

101. *Avis. La Commission formée pour la répartition de la dette de l'ancienne communauté israélite de Carpentras.* [Signé:

Isaïe Valabrègue, Cadet Carcassonne, Cadet Naquet, Mossé Valabrègue, Isaac Alphandéry, Mordochée Monteux, Jo[h]anan Lisbonne.] (n. p., 29 avril 1817). 3 pp. 4° & broadside.

102. *Préfecture de Vaucluse. Ordonnance relative au recouvrement des dettes des anciennes communautés israélites d'Avignon et de Lisle [L'Isle] du 24 décembre 1817* [Avignon, 1818.] Broadside.

103. *Mémoire adressé à Son Excellence Monseigneur le Ministre Secrétaire d'Etat de l'Intérieur, par quelques israélites de Bordeaux* (Bordeaux, [1818]). 26 pp. 4°.
Petition by Bordeaux Jews of Avignon origin on the debts of Avignon.

103a. *Avis. Répartition de l'exercice. 1818* (Carpentras, 15 Avril 1818). 4 pp. 4°.

103b. *Avis . . . Exercice 1819* (n. p., n. d.). 3 pp. 4°.

104. *Observations de MM. les Syndics des créanciers des anciennes Carrières ou Communantés Juives, d'Avignon, de Carpentras, et de L'Isle, au département de Vaucluse, avec les pièces justificatives à l'appui de leur Pétition à la Chambre de MM les Députés, pour obtenir la révocation du rejet de l'amendement prononcé dans la séance du 6 juillet 1820.* [Signé: Roland, Vialla, Poncet, M. Paulun, Nery, J. Bertrand, Jonquieres] (n. p., n. d.). 51 pp. 4°.
The memorandum was analysed in "Les Juifs de Carpentras avant la Révolution." *Provence artistique et pittoresque*, Aug. 5, 1883.

105. *Ordonnance du Roi* (n. p., 30 Août 1820). 3 pp. 4°.
On the Carpentras debts.

106. *Impôts et budget. Communautés israélites. Mémoire à l'appui de la pétition adressée à la Chambre des Députés par les Israélites soumis au paiement des dettes des anciennes communautés juives du Comtat Venaissin . . .* [Signé: Isaac Alphandéry, cadet Naquet, M. Monteux, Johanan Lisbonne, Abraham Digne.] (Aix, 1821). 44 pp. 4°.

107. *Rapport de M. [Joseph-Charles-Louis-Henri] Marquis [de] Forbin des Issarts, député de Vaucluse, au nom de la commission des pétitions . . .* [Paris, 1821.] 8 pp. 8°.
Reprint from the *Moniteur*, Apr. 6, 1821. On the debts of the Jewish communities.

108. *Circulaire. La Commission formée pour la répartition de la dette de l'ancienne Communauté israélite de Carpentras.* [Signé: Jo[h]anan Lisbonne, vice-président; Isaac Alphandéry; Isaïe Valabrègue; Cadet Naquet; Mossé Valabrègue; Mardochée Monteux; Abraham Digne] (n. p., février 1822). 3 pp. 4°.

109. *Créances sur les anciennes communautés juives des villes d'Avignon et de L'Isle. Relevé des principales pièces établissant les droits des créanciers . . . Fin décembre 1827* [Avignon, 1827.] 38 pp. 8°.

On the debts of the communities in the former papal province see also Nos. 32–34.

III. THE DEBTS OF THE ALSATIAN JEWISH COMMUNITIES

110. Wittersheim, Seligman, *Messieurs les Commissaires des départements du Haut- et du Bas-Rhin pour la liquidation des dettes des Juifs domiciliés de la province ci-devant Alsace.* [Signé: Seligman Wittersheim] (n. p., 1792). 2 pp. 4°.

111. *Auszug aus der Berathschlagung der Nieder-Rheinschen Departments -Direktoriums vom 1. Jul. 1793, im 2ten Jahr der Frankischen Republik . . .* (n. p., n. d.). 4 pp. 4°.

"Zur General-Liquidation der Schulden."

112. [A Circular of 1793, addressed to the Mayors.]

According to a document of Oct. 17, 1793, (Documents, Alsace): "Payé au Sr. Heitz imprimeur pour impression des Etats [see No. 113] et circulaires en langue allemande adressées aux maires des communes du Haut et du Bas Rhin aux fins de remplir le montant des impositions foncière et mobiliaire à laquelle chaque Juif couché sur ces états et cotisé." See No. 113.

113. *Namens-Verzeichniss derjenigen Juden, welche in der letztern, durch die Juden vorsteher den ehemaligen Provinz Elsass, errichteten Roll der Anlage, in der Gemeinde — häuslich eigesessen waren, und in dem Gemeinen-Austheiler der Grund- und Mobiliar-Steuer gedachter Gemeinde pro 1791 angelegt worden sind folgt* [Strassburg, 1793.] 4 pp. fol.

See No. 112.

114. *Arrêté qui détermine la mode de répartition des sommes destinées à la liquidation des dettes passives des Juifs d'Alsace. Boulogne, le 18 brumaire an XII [10 novembre 1803]* ([Strasbourg?,] an XII). 3 pp. 4°.

115. *Préfecture du Bas-Rhin. Décret du 27 octobre 1806, extrait des Minutes de la Secrétairerie d'Etat. Au Palais de Berlin, le 27 octobre 1806* (Strasbourg, [1806]). Broadside.

116. *Liquidation générale des dettes de la ci-devant Nation juive d'Alsace. Indigence et non valeur. Avis de la commission de liquidation sur les pétitions suivantes* (n. p., [ca. 1806]). 2 pp. fol.

117. *Liquidation Gén.ᶫᵉ des dettes de la ci-dev. Nation juive d'Alsace. Les commissaire et caissier de la liquidation des dettes de la ci-devant Nation juive d'Alsace, à M — — * (n. p., [ca. 1806]). 1 p. 4°.

118. *Préfecture du département de la Seine. Ville de Paris. Premier arrondissement. Extrait du rôle de répartition pour la liquidation de la dette de la Nation juive, de la ci-devant Province d'Alsace, rendu exécutoire par M. le Conseiller d'Etat Préfet du Bas-Rhin, le 24 Février 1807* (n. p., n. d.). 1 p. 4°.
Similar documents were published at various periods and by more Paris arrondissements.

119. *Liquidation générale des dettes de la ci-devant Nation Juive d'Alsace. Avis de la Commission de liquidation, sur la réclamation . . .* (n. p., [1807?]). 1 p. fol.

120. *Décret impérial qui prescrit de nouvelles mesures pour faire acquitter la dette des Juifs de la ci-devant province d'Alsace. Au Palais de Saint-Cloud, le 5 septembre 1810* [Strasbourg, 1810.] 4 pp. 4°.

121. *Reçu de . . . Strasbourg, le — — 180 — —* (n. p., n. d.). 1 p. 32°.
Receipt for debt-taxes.

122. *L'an mil huit cent . . . en vertu d'une contrainte décernée par Mr. Benjamin-Moïse Bloch, receveur principal du consistoire des Israélites de la circonscription de Wintzenheim . . .* (n. p., [1814]). 1 p. 4°.
On the debt-tax.

123. *Consistoire israélite du département du Bas-Rhin. Dettes des Israélites d'Alsace. Etat des sommes dues aux créanciers ci-après denommés par la ci-devant communauté israélite d'Alsace, indiquant en même temps celles qui ont été remboursées jusqu'au –* (n. p., n. d.) 4 pp. fol.

124. *Consultation pour les Israélites habitant le département du Bas-Rhin contre les porteurs des créances de l'ancienne nation juive d'Alsace.* [Signé: Martin, L. Liechtenberger, Michaux-Bellaire, Rauter.] (Strasbourg, 1835). 20 pp. 4°.

125. *Consistoire israélite, circonscription de Colmar. Analyse.* Dette Cerf-Beer [Cerfberr] (Colmar, 23 Juillet 1857). 2 pp. 4°.

126. *Commission Cerf-Beer* [Cerfberr] (Strasbourg, 23 janvier 1859). 2 pp. 4°.

127. *Préfecture du Bas-Rhin. 1ʳᵉ division. Liquidation des dettes de l'ancienne communauté juive d'Alsace* (Strasbourg, 4 Août 1860). 1 p. 4°.
Circular addressed to the Mayors and signed by Reboul [L.-J. Reboul-Deneyrol], Secretary of the Prefecture.

128. *Département du Bas-Rhin. Liquidation des dettes de l'ancienne communauté juive d'Alsace. Etablissement d'une nouvelle matrice de rôle des redevables. Feuille de renseignements* (Strasbourg, [ca. 1860]). 3 pp. 4°.

129. *Département du Bas-Rhin. Liquidation des dettes de l'ancienne communauté juive d'Alsace. Etablissement d'une nouvelle matrice de rôle des redevables. Renseignements confidentiels* Strasbourg, [ca. 1860]). 4 pp. fol.

130. *Préfecture du Bas-Rhin. Culte israélite. Liquidation de la dette de l'ancienne communauté juive d'Alsace. Demande de renseignement* (Strasbourg, [ca. 1860]). 1 p. fol.
Circular addressed to the Prefects.

131. *Préfecture du Bas-Rhin. 1ʳᵉ division. Liquidation des dettes de l'ancienne communauté juive d'Alsace. Etat nominatif des redevables inscrits au rôle de recouvrement rendu exécutoire le 31 décembre 1814* (Strasbourg, [ca. 1860]). 4 pp. fol.

132. *Liquidation des dettes de l'ancienne communauté juive d'Alsace. Feuilles de renseignements. Commune d — — Nombre d'articles* (Strasbourg, 1860). fol.

Folder used for files of documents on tax payers.

133. *Consistoire israélite. Circonscription de Strasbourg, Extrait du registre des déliberations. Séance du Juillet 1866* (n. p., n. d.). 2 pp. 4°.

On the Cerfberr debt.

134. *Consistoire israélite. Circonscription de Strasbourg. Commission Cerf Beer* [Cerfberr] (Strasbourg, 25 Juillet 1866). 2 pp. 4°.

135. *Préfecture du Bas-Rhin. 1ʳᵉ division. Liquidation des dettes de l'ancienne communauté juive d'Alsace. A. M. le percepteur de la circonscription* (Strasbourg, le 31 Juillet 1867). 1 p. 4°.

136. *Préfecture du Bas-Rhin. Culte israélite. Liquidation de la dette de l'ancienne communauté juive d'Alsace. Demande de renseignement* (Strasbourg, 186[8]). 1 p. fol.

Not the same as No. 130.

IV. DEBTS OF OTHER JEWISH COMMUNITIES

137. *Décret impérial sur la mode de liquidation des dettes de la ci-devant communauté des Juifs du Montferrat. De notre Camp impérial d'Osterode, le 25 Mars 1807* (n. p., n. d.). 4 pp. 4°.

138. *Paris, le 15 Décembre 1837. Monsieur et cher Coreligionnaire* . . . [Signé: M[ax] Cerfberr.] [Paris, 1837.] 1 p. 4°.

Circulair on the liquidation of the debts of the Paris Synagogues.

V. LATER STUDIES ON THE DEBTS OF THE JEWISH COMMUNITIES

139. *G. L. Y.* [*Gerson-Lévy*], *Extinction de la dette de l'ancienne communauté de Metz* [Paris, 1843.] 8 pp. 8°.

Reprinted from *AI*, IV (1843), 636–43.

140. O[lry] Terquem, *Souvenirs historiques, concussions, dettes. Les ducs de Brancas et les Juifs de Metz* [Paris, 1844]. 30 pp. 8°.
Reprinted from *AI*, V (1844), 547–74.

141. Maurice Aron, *La liquidation des dettes de l'ancienne communaute juive de Metz* (Versailles, 1883). 29 pp. 8°.
Reprinted from *ASEJ*, II (1883), 109–35.

142. C. Wolf, "Les Juifs de Metz et la famille Brancas." *UI*, LIII — 2 (1898), 307, 405, 485, 535.

143. Dr. Nathan Netter, *Die Schuldennot der Metzer Gemeinde. 1789–1854. (Beitrag zur Geschichte der jüdischen Gemeinde Metz)* (Berlin, 1917). 139 pp. 8°.
Reprinted from *MGWJ*, LVII (1913), 591–619, LVIII (1914), 63–80.

144. Goudchaux Lion, "La Commission de liquidation des dettes de l'ancienne communauté juive de Metz." *RJL*, 1932, 8–13.
Report of July 25, 1843. See No. 59.

145. P. H[aguenauer], "Dette de l'ancienne communaute juive de Metz." *RJL*, 1934–35.
Documents of 1834–35.

146. Adrien Valabrègue, *Mémoire adressé à Monsieur le Ministre des Cultes par le Consistoire israélite de Marseille. En réponse à la délibération du Conseil municipal de Carpentras (août 1896), qui conteste l'existence légale de la Communauté Israélite de cette ville* (Lyon, 1896). 15 pp. 8°.
Mostly on the Carpentras debts.

147. M. Ginsburger, "Un emprunt de la Nation juive d'Alsace." *REJ*, LXXXI (1925), 83–86.
See also: [François-Balthazar] Darracq, *Opinion de Darracq dans l'affaire des Juifs de Bordeaux. Séance du 18 Floréal an 7* (Paris, an 7); Achille-Edmond Halphen, *Recueil des lois . . . concernant les israélites depuis la Révolution de 1789 . . .* (Paris, 1851), pp. 8, 11, 13, 16, 35, 218, 226, 233, 328; Robert Anchel, *Napoléon et les Juifs* (Paris, 1928), pp. 519–30; René Pacquet, *Bibliographie analytique de l'histoire de Metz pendant la Révolution 1789–1800* (Paris, 1926), I, 206–08, II, 1415–16; Nathan Netter, *Vingt siècles d'une communauté juive. Metz et son grand passé* (Paris, 1938), pp. 67–82, 179, 207–28; Z. Szajkowski, *The Economic Status of the Jews in Alsace, Metz and Lorraine, 1648–1789* (New York, 1954), pp. 62–67, 149–51; Idem, *Poverty and Social Welfare among French Jews* (New York, 1954), pp. 11–17, 83–84.

APPENDIX II

THE STATUTES OF THE JEWISH COMMUNITY OF METZ, 1742–1786

As an example of the statutes of a Jewish community we bring the contents of the statutes of the Jewish community of Metz, published in 1786. They present a real *code civil* of an autonomous body. The author is preparing for publication a bibliography of statutes of the Jewish communities in the eighteenth century France.

Recueil des loix, coutumes et usages observés par les Juifs de Metz, en ce qui concerne leurs contrats de mariage, tutelles, curatelles, majorités, successions, testamens, &c. rédigé & translaté en françois, en exécution des Lettres-patentes du 20 août 1742, registrées au Parlement de Metz, le 30 du même mois, &c. Auquel on a joint l'Extrait qui a été fait par feu Monsieur Lançon . . . (Metz, 1786). vj, 276 pp. 8°. Together with: *Coutumes et usages observés par les Juifs de Metz. Extrait du Cahier présenté le 2 mars 1743 au Parlement de Metz, en exécution des Lettres-patentes du 20 août précédent, lues en l'assemblée de Mrs. les Commissaires, le 20 février 1744. Ce extrait a été fait par feu Mr.* [Nicolas-François] *Lançon . . .* (n. p., 1786). 104 pp. 8°.

Part I contains: Préface (pp. j–vj); Lettres patentes du Roi . . . 20 août 1742 (pp. 1–13); Titre premier. Des juges & jugemens (pp. 16–24); Titre II. De la preuve testimoniale (pp. 25–37); Titre III. De la preuve littérale résultante des actes & contrats . . . (pp. 38–46); Titre IV. Des successions (pp. 47–62); Titre V. Des tutelles (pp. 63–75); Titre VI. Des mariages (pp. 75–85); Titre VII. Des testamens (pp. 86–103); Titre VIII. Des actions . . . (pp. 104–117); Titre IX. Des quittances & dépôts . . . (pp. 117–121); Titre X. Des demandes formées sans titres . . . & des sermons . . . (pp. 121–140); Titre XI. . . . Actes privés . . . (pp. 141–142); Titre XII. Des personnes qui peuvent, ou ne pouvant valablement contracter (pp. 143–146); Titre XIII. Des remises & quittances (pp. 147–148); Titre XIV. Des donations entre vifs . . . (pp. 148–163); Titre XV. Des ventes, achats . . . (pp. 163–175);

755

Titre XVI. De la nullité des ventes . . . (pp. 175–181); Titre XVII. *Ibid.* (pp. 181–185); Titre XVIII. De l'effet des protestations contre les ventes (pp. 186–189); Titre XIX. De la préférence promise . . . (pp. 190–192); Titre XX. Des conditions . . . (pp. 192–199); Titre XXI. Des causes qui peuvent . . . valider ou annuller (pp. 200–205); Titre XXII. Des dépôts (pp. 205–211); Titre XXIII. Des gages & nantissemens (pp. 211–217); Titre XXIV. Des cessions (pp. 218–222); Titre XXV. Des causes qui peuvent retarder l'exécution des débiteurs (pp. 222–225); Titre XXVI. Des exécutions (pp. 225–229); Titre XXVII. Des hypothèques . . . (pp. 229–234); Titre XXVIII. Des demandes en exécutions formées contre un débiteur absent (pp. 234–239); Titre XXIX. Des demandes formées par les héritiers d'un créancier décéde (pp. 240–241); Titre XXX. Des obligations qui ont en garde ce qui appartient à des autres (pp. 241–253); Titre XXXI. Des locations des maisons (pp. 253–258); Titre XXXII. Des cautions (pp. 258–266); Titre XXXIII. De ceux qui font les affaires des autres . . . (pp. 266–271); Table (pp. 273–276).

Part II contains: Titre premier. Des contestation: de Juif à Juif (pp. 1–2); Titre II. Des tutelles & de l'âge de majorité (pp. 3–8); Titre III. Des actes & des contrats (pp. 8–15); Titre IV. Des ventes & achats (pp. 15–20); Titre V. Des mariages, de la dot . . . (pp. 21–30); Titre VI. Des donations & testamens (pp. 31–38); Titre VII. Des successions (pp. 38–47); Titre VIII. Des substitutions (pp. 47–48); Titre IX. Des locations des maisons, servitudes & du paiement des ouvriers & domestiques (pp. 49–50); Titre X. Des exécutions sur les biens des débiteurs (pp. 51–56); Table (p. 57); Arrêts et règlemens, concernans les Juifs de la Synagogue de Metz. Du 23 janvier 1759 (pp. 58–67); Lettres patentes, qui confirment les privilèges ci-devant accordés aux Juifs établis dans la Ville de Metz [du 3 février 1777] (pp. 68–78); Extrait des registres de Parlement [du 17 mai 1777] (pp. 78–82); Arrêt de la Cour de parlement, portant règlement pour l'exécution des jugements rendus par le rabbin . . . Du 21 décembre 1782 (pp. 82–101); Approbation (pp. 102–104).

"Arrêts . . . Du 23 janvier 1759" (part II, pp. 58–67) contains analyses of the following acts of the Metz Parliament: June 28, 1693, on the right of converted Jews in questions of inheritance; June 31, 1758, on the conflict between Marie-Anne d'Alsace and the Jewish community of Metz; Jan. 30, 1759, on the rabbis' jurisdiction (affair Rosette d'Alsace); Jan. 23, 1759, affair Salomon Reicher and the rabbis' jurisdiction.

On this *Recueil* see also: *Lettres patentes du Roy, portant que par les chefs de la communauté des Juifs de Metz, il sera fait un Recueil en langue françoise des coutumes & usages qu'ils observent en ce qui concerne, &c. Données à Versailles le 20. août 1742. Registrés en Parlement [de Metz] le 30. dudit mois* (Metz, 1742). 8 pp. 4°; *Mémoire pour les Rabbins, Elus et les Syndics des Juifs de la ville de Metz.* [Signé: Me. de Sérionne] (Metz, [1745]). 8 pp. 4°; *Au Roi.* [Signé: Me. de Sérionne] (n. p., 1745). 3 pp. fol. An abbreviated edition of the statutes was published in 1853: *Lois des Juifs. Usages observés par les Juifs de Metz* (Colmar, 1853).

APPENDIX III

EXCERPTS FROM REPORTS ON GIFTS PRESENTED BY THE JEWISH COMMUNITY OF METZ TO HIGH OFFICIALS IN PARIS

On February 22, 1786 Moïse Weill, the Paris agent of the Jewish community of Metz, wrote in a letter addressed to the community:

"A Monsieur le Maréchal de Broglie j'ai remis, aussitôt après reception de votre ordre, ses 1000 livres contre quittance. Il a accepté cette somme très gracieusement." Two days later he wrote: "Le retard des 3 oies, lesquelles je n'ai reçu que le mercredi dernier, est la cause que je tardais d'aller chez Monsieur le Maréchal de Brol [Breuil]. J'ai fait celà le jeudi dernier et je lui ai remises deux oies dont il était très content. Il m'a reçu très gentilment et il vous a loué auprès de M. Allom, son secrétaire auquel j'ai également donné ses 96 livres contre sa quittance. Celui-ci me dit que la Communauté offre 1000 livres à Monsieur le Maréchal pour Novel-An. Lorsque je lui disait de n'en pas avoir obtenu votre ordre, il pensait que les syndics attendront l'arrivée de Monsieur le Maréchal à Metz, où il fera en été un voyage, pour les lui présenter personnellement. Si j'avais votre ordre, je les avais payés. Vous ne devez pas [vous] gêner dans des occasions pareilles, car je suis à même d'avancer des petites choses pareilles ... P. S. Je veux vous aussi informer que j'ai fait, le jeudi dernier, une visite auprès de Monsieur de Caraman en nom de la Communauté. Je connais ce Monsieur depuis très longtemps et il m'a très poliment reçu. Il vous a loué et il m'a demandé si j'avais quelque ordre de vous. Je lui ai répondu que n'en ai rien. Vous savez sans doute de quoi qu'il s'agit."

On March 29, 1789 Weill wrote to Metz: "En réponse à vos deux chères lettres du 24 et 25 Adar écoulé et aussi à [l'envoi] des 9 oies, lesquelles sont arrivées dans un très bon état! Je les ai remises aux Messieurs auxquels elles étaient destinées et l'ont accepté avec plaisir, car je les ai rémises personnelle-ment. Monsieur le Ministre de la Guerre m'a dit les mots suivants: 'Je vous prie de temoigner ma reconnaissance à ces Messieurs' Les autres Ministres m'ont remercié de la même façon, très poliment, surtout Monsieur Devildel. Il me manque encore 2 oies pour M. Necker, Ministre des Finances."

Following is the text of a receipt for 1,000 livres: "Je reconnois avoir reçu de la Communauté des Juifs de Metz par les mains du Sr. Viel [Weill], son agent, la somme de mille Livres, pour l'année mil sept cent quatre vingt huit,

757

758

comme d'usage, dont quittance. A Paris ce dix février mil sept cent quatre vingt neuf. [Signé:] Lemaal duc de Broglie."³⁵³

---

³⁵³ Documents, Metz, No. 120, fol. 695–702. Copies made by Salomon Landmann. However, Christian communities, too, were forced to present gifts to high officials. In 1781 de Servat, agent of the city of Bordeaux in Versailles, wrote to the *Jurats* of Bordeaux: "J'ai eu l'honneur de vous dire que M. Joly de Fleury était décidé à recevoir les présents que les villes sont dans l'usage de faire [aux ministres] et que j'avais été prévenu qu'une bourse de vos jetons le flatteroit infiniment" (Am Bordeaux, B, lettres received by the *Jurats*, Dec. 29, 1781, fol. 3).

APPENDIX IV

EXCERPTS FROM A BRIEF ON THE
ALSATIAN DEBTS (1835)

"... C'est contre *les représentans de la ci-devant nation juive d'Alsace,* que les héritiers Cerf Berr et leurs ayant droits ont dirigé leur pourvoi au Conseil d'état, et l'ordonnance qui y a statué et dont on provoque l'exécution relate elle-même qu'il s'agit de sommes dues *aux créanciers de l'ancienne communauté des juifs d'Alsace.*

Il ne peut donc y avoir aucun doute sur ce point. C'est le corps moral de l'ancienne communauté des juifs d'Alsace qui était le véritable débiteur. Mais ce corps moral n'existe plus depuis que la révolution de 1789 a confondu tous les Français quels que soient leur religion et leur culte, et depuis que la loi du 27 septembre 1791 a levé et aboli tous les privilèges et toutes les exceptions qui concernaient les juifs.

... Dans la règle le créancier d'une communauté, comme celui d'un individu, a pour gage de sa créance tous les biens du débiteur, de sorte qu'il semble que les droits du créancier doivent en première ligne s'exercer sur les biens de la communauté débritice, et que ce n'est que lorsque la communauté n'a plus aucun bien vaillant que les individus qui la composent peuvent être imposés pour le paiement des créanciers.

Mais cette loi de l'impôt n'est elle-même régulièrement admise qu'à l'égard des individus qui continuent à faire partie de la communauté débritice, et qui, partageant les avantages qu'elle peut leur procurer, doivent naturellement en partager aussi les charges; et c'était de tous tems une question controversée que de savoir si cet impôt pouvait également atteindre ceux des anciens communistes [membres des communautés] qui avaient quitté la communauté.

Ce n'est pas absolument là la position des individus qui faisaient partie de l'ancienne communauté juive d'Alsace, mais il y a pour chaque communiste en particulier beaucoup d'analogie entre sa sortie individuelle et l'extinction ou la dissolution de la communauté en général; et les conséquences pour chaque communiste personnellement doivent presqu'être les mêmes, quant à l'obligation de participer au paiement des dettes légitimement contractées par la communauté.

Rigoureusement le corps moral est une personne distincte et séparée; et ce qui est dû par la communauté n'est pas dû par les individus qui la composent: *Si quid universitati debetur, singulis non debetur: nec quod debet universitas singuli debent. L. 7. § 1. ff. Quod cuj. univers. nom.*

... Leur demande est en effet présentée comme s'ils ignoraient complétement l'extinction ou la dissolution de l'ancienne communaute juive d'Alsace, ou comme s'ils se trouvaient vis-à-vis d'une nouvelle communauté chargée de toutes les dettes et obligations de l'ancienne. Or, l'une et l'autre de ces deux opinions sont erronnées, puisque nous avons fait voir et, que l'ancienne com-

759

760

munauté a nécessairement été atteinte par l'effet de la loi du 27 septembre 1791, et qu'elle n'a été remplacée, ni pu être remplacée par aucune communauté nouvelle qui aurait succédé à toutes ses charges actives et passives.

Il existe dans doute encore aujourd'hui et dans une foule de villes ou villages de l'Alsace des communautés Israélites; mais celles-ci sont comme elles l'ont toujours été de simples associations pour l'entretien et l'exercice de leur culte. Ce sont de véritables paroisses, des communautés spéciales restreintes aux localités où elles se sont constituées; il existe aussi dans chaque département un Consistoire départemental, créé par le décret du 17 mars 1808, et ce sont ces deux Consistoires des Haut- et Bas-Rhin, que le décret de 1810 a substitués d'office à la Commission qui avait été nommée pour la liquidation de la dette juive.

Mais le but et les fonctions de ces Consistoires départementaux sont définis par le décret qui les a institués; ils se restreignent également à l'entretien et à l'exercice du culte, sauf la mission spéciale qui leur avait encore été attribuée à l'époque du décret, d'encourager les Israélites à l'exercice des professions utiles, et de donner chaque année à l'Autorité connaissance du nombre des conscrits Israélites de la circonscription.

... EN RÉSUMÉ, les prétentions des héritiers Cerf Berr et consors étaient une dette du corps moral de l'ancienne communauté juive d'Alsace.

Ce corps moral a cessé d'exister par l'effet de la révolution de 1789, et particulièrement en vertu de la loi du 27 septembre 1791; et puisqu'il n'a été remplacé par aucune communauté nouvelle qui ait succédé à ses charges, la dette restée étrangère aux autres Israélites, qui sont venus plus tard habiter les départemens des Haut- et Bas-Rhin, a dû se diviser entre les seuls membres de l'ancienne communauté ou leurs héritiers.

Cette division entre les communistes, consacrée par l'arrêté du Directoire du département de 1793, et par l'arrêté du gouvernement de l'an XII, s'est définitivement opéré par le décret de 1810, et par le rôle de répartition dressé en exécution de ce décret; et comme il n'y avait pas de solidarité entre les anciens communistes, chacun d'eux n'était personnellement tenu que pour le montant de sa cote aux rôles de 1814.

Ainsi ceux qui ont acquitté cette cote sont définitivement libérés, et les créanciers sont sans recours contre eux à raison des non-valeurs de quelque cause qu'elles puissent provenir.

C'est par erreur que les créanciers agissent comme si l'ancienne communauté, débitrice originaire, subsistait encore.

On ne pourrait d'ailleurs jamais faire une nouvelle répartition en vertu du décret de 1810, car ce serait lever un second impôt en vertu d'une loi dont l'autorité, essentiellement limitée à la répartition faite en 1814, se trouve épuisée.

Toute nouvelle répartition serait illégale, et chque Israélite touché d'une contrainte ou d'un avertissement pourrait, par son opposition, porter la question de légalité devant les juges civils, et prendre à partie les fonctionnaires qui auraient ordonné ou tenté le recouvrement."[354]

---

[354] *Consultation*, pp. 7–8, 11–12, 18–19 (see Bibliography, No. 124).

APPENDIX V

THE JEWISH COMMUNITIES OF THE
METZ PROVINCE

The author previously made an attempt to list the smaller communities in the Metz province. However, this list was incorrect because of difficulties in translating the Hebrew names of the communities shown in financial records of the Brancas-tax (*EcSt*, p. 38). Following is a corrected but incomplete list: Achâtel, Alincourt, Augny, Avricourt, Barst, Basse Yutz, Baudrecourt, Bionville, Bliesbrücken, Bourscheid, Budange, Buding, Budling, Chambrey, Chaté, [Achâtel?], Chicourt, Delme, Dieuze, Donlay, Ennery, Erstroff, Etting [or Etzling], Forbach, Frémestroff, Haute-Yutz, Hellering, Hellimer, Hombourg, Imeldange, Imling, Kédange, Koenisgsmacher, Lagrange, Lamersdroff, Les Etangs, Lixheim, Longeville [-les-Metz], Louvigny, Luttange, Marly, Manome [Manom], Metting, Metzervisse, Méy, Mittelbronn, Monner, Moulin[s-lès-Metz], Montenach, Morhange, Neunkirchen, Niedervisse, Phalsbourg, Pont pierre, Rédange, Rurange, Saint-Jean (a few communities with this name), Sierck, Solgne, Thionville, Tragny, Uckange, Vallières, Vantoux, Vic-sur-Seille, Viviers.

APPENDIX VI

EXCERPTS FROM NATHAN CAHEN'S PETITION AGAINST THE JEWISH COMMUNITY OF METZ

(1792)

"Nathan Cahen, juif, habitant de Louvigny, à lui joint les Juifs habitans les lieux de Marly, Augny, Ventoulx, Sansonnet, Haute-Iust, Basse-Iust, Sarrelouis, Herstroff, Niedervisse, Kédange, Metzervisse, Buding, Delme, Chambrey, Dolnay, Mézières près Vic, et autres villages compris dans les rôles d'aucuns des différens villages et lieux ci-dessus;

Après avoir pris communication de la requête présentée sous le nom des anciens syndics et élus de la ci-devant communauté des Juifs de Metz, notifiée le 31 mai 1792 . . .

Ont l'honneur de répondre, que le systême des adversaires conduit à des conséquences si révoltantes, qu'il n'est pas à craindre qu'aucun corps administratif, aucun tribunal, ni l'assemblée législative se port jamais à l'accueillir.

Il est, ce systême, de commencer par ruiner tous les juifs de la campagne, par réduire femmes et enfans à la mendicité, les chefs de familles à la désertion et tout ce qui y tient indistinctement aux tristes et violens effets du désespoir.

. . . Jamais, non jamais, les juifs de la campagne n'ont eu l'honneur d'être membres de la communauté des juifs de Metz; ils n'en étoient que les esclaves.

. . . les juifs de la campagne ont constamment, annuellement, sans distinction, sans interruption, exactement payé le montant de tous ces rôles, formés par les potentats de la synagogue [de Metz].

. . . A la différence des juifs de Metz, qui, après avoir attiré parmi eux, et dans la ville, ce qu'il y avait de juifs aisés dans les campagnes, ne payoient presque rien en raison de leur ascendant notoire, et savoient s'alléger sur les juifs du dehors.

. . . Il est de fait que jamais les juifs du dehors n'ont été membres de la communauté des juifs de Metz; que jamais ils n'ont concouru, ni été appellés aux élections de ses officiers; que jamais ils n'ont assisté, ni été appellés à aucune espece de comptabilité, à aucune espece de répartition, à aucune espece de délibération; que toujours ils sont demeurés esclaves du gouvernement, de l'administration et de l'autorité coactive.

Aujourd'hui, qu'on les honore du titre d'hommes, de celui de citoyens; qu'on les tire de la servitude, rien de mieux quant au moral, et rien en cela qui ne soit commun à tous les sujets françois.

L'on n'en a pas la moindre obligation aux juifs de Metz, et cela ne peut leur servir de titre, pour achever de ruiner les juifs de la campagne.''[355]

---

[355] *A Messieurs* . . . (see Bibliography, No. 25). It seems that the petition was written, or edited, by the lawyer Louis Petry (*Ibid.*, p. 14). In another document Petry is also mentioned as the "fondé de pouvoir" of the Metz community (Paquet, II, 1089).

APPENDIX VII

A 19th CENTURY OPINION ON THE JEWISH SYNDICS

In 1835 the Consistory of Paris appointed a commission to report on the reform of the communal Jewish life. On January 18, 1836 S. Mayer-Dalmbert made the following statement, which indicates the traditional attitude of the Jews to the syndics of the Jewish communities prior to the emancipation:

". . . je dois vous faire une première observation, qui porte sur la dénomination qu'on vous propose de donner aux personnes chargées de l'éxécution de vos bienfaisants projects, *on veut les appeler syndics.*

Certes, Messieurs, pour ceux qui feraient la part de l'époque, ce titre n'aurait rien de repoussant. C'est dira-t-on une centralisation de toutes les administrations existantes et il fallait trouver un nouveau nom : mais il est des hommes qui se souviennent encore d'un temps qui depuis longtemps n'existe plus, ils croiront voir reussisciter les institutions et l'administration des anciens syndics, ils croiront nous voir rétrograder.

Avant notre émancipation il y a 42 ans, lorsque nous n'étions qu'une secte tolérée, on nous faisait administrer par des syndics qui dans certaines circonstances seulement et à leur volonté, consultaient l'assemblée des anciens. N'est il pas à craindre qu'en voyant revivre ce titre, bien des esprits en soient choqués, ils s'imagineront que l'on veut faire revivre par lui d'anciens droits et des vieilles coutumes . . . pourquoi alors ne les appelerions nous pas sub-délégués[?]

Ce titre est fort honorable et n'aura pas le tort immense de rappeler un état de choses que nous devons nous efforcer d'oublier . . ."[356]

---

[356] The commission was composed of S. Alkan, E. Brandon, B. Cohen, Chief-Rabbi Marchand Ennery, E. Halphen, J. Lan, S. Mayer-Dalmbert, Ph. Simon, and Baruch Weil (ZS). Mayer-Dalmbert became in 1815 a member of the central consistory (L. Kahn, *op. cit.*, p. 195).

La vita intellettuale profana fra gli Ebrei nella Francia del XVIII secolo

Circa cinquant'anni dopo che agli Ebrei della Francia fu concessa la piena cittadinanza, un periodico ebreo-francese notava che gli Ebrei «entravano nella società attraverso tutte le porte che erano state aperte loro dalla Rivoluzione» (1). È perciò importante avere un'idea precisa intorno alla vita intellettuale profana degli Ebrei nella Francia del XVIII secolo, per poter valutare le differenze che distinsero quel periodo da quello successivo all'emancipazione.

La vita intellettuale profana era sviluppata di più fra gli Ebrei sefarditi. Più degli ashkenaziti e degli Ebrei della provincia papale si trovavano a contatto frequente coll'ambiente non ebraico. Tuttavia il numero degl'intellettuali Ebrei laici nella Francia del XVIII secolo era tanto piccolo, che è molto difficile se non impossibile indicare un centro in cui esercitassero una influenza qualsiasi.

Il più distinto per ingegno fra gli Ebrei sefarditi era probabilmente Abraham Furtado. Girondista attivo e Presidente del Sinedrio convocato da Napoleone I, Furtado scrisse molti notevoli studi rimasti però manoscritti. Sono stati pubblicati soltanto alcuni suoi opuscoli polemici e alcune traduzioni in francese di poesie ebraiche (2). Jacob Rodrigues Pereire era il noto pioniere dell'educazione dei sordo-muti (3). Se si osserva bene, il solo Ebreo sefardita che scelse la letteratura quale sua professione fu Isac de Pinto noto quale cronista di Bordeaux sotto lo pseudonimo di Pierre Bernardau. Però Pinto per quanto fosse nativo di Bordeaux, visse ad Amsterdam e non può quindi esser considerato Ebreo francese (4).

(1) Rap. *M. Ennery. La Paix*, 1846, 250.

(2) Z. Szajkowski, *The Sephardic Jews of France during the Revolution of 1789* « Proceedings of the American Academy for Jewish Research », XXIV (1955), 142-43, 151-52.

(3) Ernest La Rochelle, *Jacques Rodrigues Pereire* (Paris, 1882, pagg. 576).

(4) Bernardau ha sbagliato nello scrivere che Pinto viveva a Bordeaux. Biblioteca civica di Bordeaux, ms. 713-1, vol. IV, pag. 414. Su Pinto vedi Z. Szajkowski, *Relations among Sephardim, Ashkenazim and Avignonese Jews in France from the 16th to the 20th Centuries*, « Yivo Annual of Jewish Social Science », X (1955). 179-81.

Originally published in *Rassegna Mensile di Israel,* vol. XXVII (1961).

Louis-Francia de Beaufleury di Bordeaux, avvocato e primo storico ebraico moderno della Francia, fu autore d'un'eccellente storia degli Ebrei sefarditi di Francia, pubblicata nel 1799. Prima e durante la Rivoluzione pubblicò un volume di poesie e molti opuscoli sopra questioni municipali, sopra il credito, il vino e l'amore. Nel settembre del 1791 Beaufleury fu eletto secondo deputato-sostituto alla Convenzione ma non ebbe mai l'occasione di sedervi. Sembra che si fosse convertito al Cristianesimo (5).

La letteratura era allora di moda fra i ricchi Ebrei di Bordeaux. Durante la Rivoluzione l'abbiente capo della Comunità israelitica, David Gradis, pubblicò alcuni libri «filosofici» contro gli atei, che lo resero generalmente sospetto (6). Suo nipote, Benjamin Gradis (1782-1843), membro della *Société des Vaudevillistes* di Bordeaux, pubblicò nel 1799 diversi articoli firmati per lo più colle iniziali A. L. (7).

(5) L. F. B. [Louis-Francia de Beaufleury], *Histoire de l'établissement des Juifs à Bordeaux et à Bayonne, depuis 1550* (Paris, anno 8 [1799]), 198 pagg.) ; Z. SZAJ-KOWSKI, *Louis Francia de Beaufleury, un ebreo deputato sostituto durante la Rivoluzione francese*, « Davke » n. 20 (1954), 241-48 (in jiddish). Beaufleury era figlio del banchiere di Bordeaux Louis-David Francia de Beaufleury. Nel 1776 sposò una giovane di nome Veniere, molto probabilmente cristiana (Archivi dipartimentali di Gironda E. Famiglie, Francia. Testamento della madre di Francia, Rebecca-Maria, 20 marzo 1786). Secondo una fonte (Libreria municipale di Bordeaux, ms. 713-1, vol. 46, pag. 231 ; Cronaca di P. Bernardau) Beaufleury morì nel 1817 in età di 65 anni a Carbonblanc (Gironda), ma non si trova alcuna traccia della sua morte nei registri locali dello stato civile. Nella medesima cronaca di Bernardau (vol. 7, pag. 503, 26 gennaio 1800) Beaufleury è descritto come ebreo convertito (*ex-ebreo*).

(6) [DAVID GRADIS], *Courte dissertation sur l'origine du monde* ... (Parigi, Bordeaux, anno 7) 52 pagine ; IDEM, *Discussions philosophiques sur la préexistance de la matière* (Parigi, anno VIII) 208 pagine. Secondo la Cronaca di Bernardau (vol. 7, pag. 457, 17 marzo 1799) un certo Delesse pubblicò un opuscolo *Dieu créateur* contro i libri di Gradis. Intorno alle opere « filosofiche » di Gradis vedi pure le osservazioni satiriche di Pierre Bernardau. Z. SZAJKOWSKI : *I delegati degli Ebrei di Bordeaux alla Commissione Malesherbes (1788) e all'Assemblea nazionale (1790)* in *Zion*, XVIII (1953), 33-34 (in ebraico). Nel 1784 Gradis scrisse un *Mémoire sur le système des économistes* che non è stato mai pubblicato (Libreria municipale di Bordeaux n. 828). Durante il Primo Impero Gradis pubblicò : *Essai de philosophie rationnelle sur l'origine des choses* (Bordeaux, anno X) ; *Discussions philosophiques sur l'athéisme* (Parigi, 1803) ; *Observations critiques sur l'ouvrage de M. Lancelin, intitulé: Théorie physique de l'Organisation des mondes* (Bordeaux, 1805).

(7) H. CHAUVOT, *Le Barreau de Bordeau* (Parigi, 1856), pag. 531; *Diners de la Société littéraire de Bordeaux*, 1801-1802, N. 1, 48-50 ; N. 2, 26-28 ; N. 3, 14-16 ; N. 4, 28-29 ; N. 5, 33-35 ; N. 6, 18-20 ; N. 7, 24-25 ; N. 9, 16 ; N. 11, 9-13 ; E. FÉRET, *Statistique générale* ... *de la Gironde* (Bordeaux, 1889), III, 293. Nel 1845 fu pubblicata la sua novella *Zeidouna*.

Bordeaux, come altre grandi città, aveva la sua porzione d'ingenui dilettanti, che erano l'oggetto di pubblici scherzi, ma che rappresentavano spesso la spina dorsale di splendide imprese di cultura. Tale era il caso di Isaac Rodrigues (1754-1822), figlio di Abraham Rodrigues e di Judith Lopes Gonzales. Nel 1795, insieme colla moglie Ester Nugès e col suo amico cristiano Jean-Ignace-Joseph-Hyacinthe Goethals (1760-1841), fondò un museo di storia naturale (*Société d'histoire naturelle*). Bernardau notava il seguente epigramma per Rodrigues :

> « Quelle est cette laide femelle
> Courte, bossue et d'un teint espagnol,
> Qui caressant deux singes auprès d'elle
> Entre la loge du Mogol
> Et celle de Polichinelle
> . . . .
> Monsieur, c'est Judith Rodrigues
> Elle fait voir le serpent à sonnettes.

In un'altra occasione Bernardau scrisse su « quell'Ebreo ricamatore, decrepito campione che fa raccolta di conchiglie e di farfalle», notando che « il suo progetto non riuscirà, perchè è utile ». Rodrigues proponeva che al programma delle scuole pubbliche e private si aggiungesse la storia naturale. Il suo museo diventò la società locale dotta, la *Société des Sciences,* aggregata più tardi alla locale *Académie des Sciences* (8).

Autori ebrei, specialmente nella provincia papale, composero satire, commedie e consimili opere letterarie. Il migliore esempio fu la commedia di Purim di Carpentras, *La Reine Esther,* pubblicata nel 1774 (9), che non è però un esempio di seria attività intellettuale laica. Lo stesso si deve dire del gran numero di odi e di preghiere composte in onore della monarchia e d'altre pubbliche attività (10).

Durante il periodo rivoluzionario degli anni 1789-1800 autori ebrei pubblicarono in ebraico una diecina di opere originali e tradotte, di cui sei apparvero in Francia e le altre all'estero. Soltanto tre studi originali in francese sopra temi ebraici furono pubblicati nello stesso periodo da

(8) *Règlements de la Société d'histoire naturelle de Bordeaux* (Bordeaux, [1796]), 8 pagine ; La cronaca di Bernardau nella Libreria municipale di Bordeaux, ms. 713-1, vol. 4, pagg. 233-34 (27 ottobre 1808), vol. 7, pag. 378 ; Archivi della città di Bordeaux, D, 1822, n. 1534 ; *Tableau de Bordeaux,* n. 102 (20 novembre 1801), *Bulletin Polymatique de Bordeaux,* 1811, 113-25 ; E. CARMOLY, *Ester Nugès,* Archives Israélites, XXIII (1862), 206-07.

(9) Z. SZAJKOWSKI, *Motivi ebraici nella cultura popolare del Contado Venossino nel secolo XVII-XIX* (Yivo Bleter, XIX (1942), 335-36, in jiddish).

(10) Sarà argomento d'uno studio separato.

autori ebrei. Di essi due erano gli studi «filosofici» di David Gradis, già ricordato, che però non hanno nessun valore. Degna di menzione è la storia degli Ebrei di Bordeaux e Bayonne (pubblicata nel 1799) di Beaufleury. Quarantotto studi, opuscoli e documenti di soggetto non ebraico furono pubblicati da parte di autori ebrei in quello stesso periodo, tutti però senza valore. Più interessanti sono gli opuscoli pubblicati a favore dell'emancipazione ebraica che possono stare a paragone di analoghe opere di autori non ebrei. Una analisi dettagliata dimostra che son pochi gli autori ebrei di quegli opuscoli che possedevano le conoscenze e la capacità necessarie per la difesa degli Ebrei. Zalkind Hurwitz, Isaia-Berr Bing e Berr-Isaac Berr rappresentano il meglio in una diecina di autori. Dei numerosissimi opuscoli scritti in favore dell'emancipazione ebraica, ventuno sono di autori ebrei, ventiquattro di autori non ebrei, per lo più avvocati, che però portano nomi di ebrei. Solo undici dei primi e otto dei secondi trattano i massimi problemi della loro emancipazione. Dieci dei primi e sedici dei secondi trattano questioni secondarie (p. es. la liquidazione dei debiti dovuti dalle Comunità ebraiche, la confisca del cimitero israelitico di Bordeaux, le persecuzioni locali contro gli Ebrei, ecc.). La maggior parte della letteratura a favore dell'emancipazione ebraica era dunque scritta da autori non ebrei, spesso sotto la forma di rapporti presentati ad enti rappresentativi ufficiali e a club rivoluzionari, ed era in generale di prima grandezza. Questi Autori non-ebrei comprendevano Henri-Baptiste Grégoire, Jacques Godard, Adophe Thiéry, Richard-François-Philippe Brunck, Eulogious Schneider, Joseph-François Cheauveau de la Garde, Jacques-François Laurent de Visme, Hyacinthe-Adrien Chappuis, Jean-Baptiste Michel Saladan, François-Marie-Joseph Rion e molti altri (11).

Alcuni autori ebrei erano incapaci di afferrare l'importanza dei grandi fatti; p. es. Moïse Ensheim, amico di Mendelssohn, autore d'un inno patriotico per la vittoria degli eserciti francesi a Valmy nel 1792. I suoi articoli sulle vicende rivoluzionarie di Francia e sulla lotta per l'emancipazione ebraica, pubblicati in *Ha-meassef* di Berlino, dimostravano una mancanza assoluta di comprensione di quanto stava accadendo in Francia (12).

Gli autori ebrei non avevano capito neppure l'ultimo periodo del Primo Impero. Dal 1801 al 1815 alcuni Autori ebrei pubblicarono dodici

---

(11) Secondo Z. SZAJKOWSKI, *L'emancipazione degli Ebrei durante la Rivoluzione francese. Bibliografia di libri, opuscoli e documenti a stampa, 1789-1800.* «Studies in Bibliography and Booklore», IV-V (1958-1959).

(12) B. TCHERIKOWER, *La battaglia ebraica per i diritti durante la Rivoluzione francese*, 1789-1791 «The Jews in France», II (Nuova York, 1942) 14-16 (in jiddish).

libri in ebraico e tredici opere originali o tradotte in francese che tratta-
vano argomenti ebraici. Il tema di ventidue pubblicazioni di autori ebrei
era d'interesse generale non ebraico e nessuno possedeva alcun permanente
valore. Qualcuno soltanto dei numerosi ospucoli polemici era veramente
notevole ; il migliore fra tutti era l'*Appel* del 1801 di Michel Berr. Un
bellissimo studio sui decreti antiebraici di Napoleone I fu scritto da un
non-ebreo, Antoine Toussaint d'Esquiron [Desquiron] di Saint Agnan.
La specialità della produzione letteraria di quel periodo era rappresentata
da odi e preghiere in onore di Napoleone ; ma anche in questo campo
erano pochi gli autori che presentavano vero ingegno (13). Nel 1820
furono molte le opere profane prodotte da autori ebrei dotati di notevole
capacità. Erano uomini ed anche alcune donne, educati in parte nelle
scuole pubbliche, durante la cui giovinezza erano accadute le vicende
rivoluzionarie e quelle napoleoniche.

C'era pure un piccolo gruppo di pittori e di musicisti ebrei. Fra i
pittori eccelleva Antoine Gonzales (1741-1801) di Bordeaux che aveva
decorato alcuni pubblici edifici di Bordeaux e di Marsiglia (14). Fra i
musicisti va ricordato Isaac-Francis Dacosta (1778-1864). Figlio d'un
commerciante e violonista dilettante di Bordeaux, era stato alunno di
X. Lefèvre e nel 1798 aveva ottenuto il primo premio di clarinetto al
Conservatorio di musica di Parigi. Dacosta era stato uno dei fondatori,
nell'aprile del 1797, della *Société littéraire* di Bordeaux (15). Jacob Azevedo (?-1809). cantante di Bordeaux ed amico del famoso cantante
Dominique-Pierre-Jean Garat, partecipò al concerto privato di Maria
Antonietta. Era ebreo religioso e cantore occasionale della sinagoga di
Bordeaux (16).

Un ebreo di Bordeaux, David Mezes, fu autore d'un'opera intitolata

(13) Secondo Z. Szajkowski, *Judaica-Napoleonica. Bibliografia di libri, opuscoli e
documenti a stampa, 1801-1815.* « Studies in Bibliography and Booklore, II (1956),
107-152.

(14) *Journal de Bordeaux,* 12 decembre 1790, 1127-28 ; Ch. Marionneau, *Les
Salons bordelais . . . au XVIIIe siècle* (Bordeaux, 1883), 150-52 ; E. Bénézit, *Dictionnaire critique et documentaire des peintres* (Parigi, 1913), II, 455 : Féret, *op. cit.,*
III, 287 ; Archivi municipali di Bordeaux, fondo Laboubée, vol. 9, fol. 93. Intorno
ad altri Ebrei attivi in questo campo vedi L. Kahn, *Un graveur juif au XVIIIe siècle.*
« Univers israélite », LI (1895), 699-707, 735-39 ; Idem, *Les Juifs de Paris pendant
la Révolution* (Parigi, 1899), pag. 123.

(15) E. Fèret, *op. cit.,* III, 162 ; Libreria municipale di Bordeaux, note di Laboubée, 713, vol. 6, pag. 163 e P. Bernardau, *Tablettes,* 713, vol. 7, pagg. 64, 183,
713-2 ; vol. 3, pag. 37 ; Archivi municipali di Bordeaux, fondo Delpit, XXV.

(16) *Echo de Bordeaux,* 11 febbraio 1809 ; Féret, *op. cit.,* III, 30 ; Libreria municipale di Bordeaux, ms. 712, I, fol. 47.

Une sur mille, rappresentata per la prima volta a Bordeaux l'8 aprile 1802. Era direttore di *L'Abeille*, rivista locale di storia e letteratura che si pubblicò fra febbraio e ottobre del 1797 e fu stampata dalla vedova, Noë, di notissima famiglia ebraica (17). Mezes era il tipo dei sefarditi intellettuali della fine del XVIII secolo : di mediocre ingegno e di limitata cultura. Uno storico di Bordeaux scrisse che egli era *molto ignorante* e, secondo un'altra fonte, credeva che Enrico IV fosse il figlio di Enrico III (18).

A Metz viveva un attore ebreo di nome Cerf (19). Gli Ebrei sefarditi erano stati amanti del teatro anche prima. Nel 1749 la città di Bordeaux aveva vietato l'ingresso al teatro ad un ebreo di nome Francia (20). Nel 1755 l'ebreo di Bordeaux, Jacob Raphaël, aveva accordato alla città un prestito di 60 mila lire per ricostruire il suo teatro che era rimasto preda delle fiamme. Un cronista, M. V. A. Laboubée, notava che la casa di Raphaël era il convegno di tutte le persone distinte (21).

Nonostante le severe restrizioni contro i medici ebrei (22), alcuni ebrei esercitavano quella professione nella Francia del secolo XVIII. A Bordeaux David Anabia fu eletto il 6 aprile 1766 a succedere al padre defunto, Daniel Anabia, quale medico della *Nazione* sefardita. Il 26 febbraio 1786, *la corporazione* dei medici decise di procedere contro Bargue, *ebreo*, per pratica illegale della medicina. Bargue esercitava illegalmente l'arte medica in base alle leggi anti-ebraiche. (Poichè anni prima, il 13 aprile 1766, la *nazione* sefardita accordava 60 lire ad un certo medico

(17) Libreria municipale di Bordeaux, ms. 712, vol. 13, pag. 4 ; ms. 713-1, vol. 3, pag. 310 ; ERNEST LABADIE, *La presse bordelaise pendant la Révolution* (Bordeaux, 1910), pagg. 171-172. Mezes pubblicò alcune poesie nei *Diners de la Société littéraire de Bordeaux*, n. 1, 33-35 ; n. 2, 29-31 ; n. 3, 31-32 ; n. 4, 8-9 ; 39-50. Pubblicò pure articoli nel *Mercure de la Gironde* (LABADIE, *op. cit.*, pag. 171).

(18) H^te MINIER, *Les poêtes bordelais* in « Actes de l'Académie des Sciences . . . de Bordeaux » XXII (1860-61), 435 ; H. CHAUVOT, *op. cit.*, pag. 531.

(19) Archivi dipartimentali della Mosella, V, 149.

(20) Libreria municipale di Bordeaux, ms. 713-1, vol. I, pag. 86, 4 giugno 1759.

(21) *Ibid.*, ms. 712, vol. 15 ; BEAUFLEURY, *op. cit.*, pagg. 101-02. Il 6 gennaio 1796 due Ebrei di Bordeaux venivano condannati per aver turbato la pace del teatro locale : *Jugement du Tribunal de la commune de Bordeaux, qui condamne les citoyens Salzédo & Peixotto jeune, en 200 livres d'amende chacun, & en huit jours de détention, pour avoir causé du trouble au grand spectacle, du 16 nivôse, an 4me* (Bordeaux, n. d.).

(22) Il notissimo medico di Bordeaux e co-fondatore dell'Accademia di Bordeaux, Joseph Cardose, fu costretto a convertirsi al Cristianesimo. Però la vedova fu più tardi considerata ebrea e come tale tassata dalla *nazione* sefardita di Bordeaux. AD. DETCHEVERRY, *Histoire des Israélites de Bordeaux* (Bordeaux, 1850), pag. 66 ; T. MALVEZIN, *Histoire des Juifs à Bordeaux* (Bordeaux, 1875) pagg. 166-67 ; DR. G. PERY, *Histoire de la Faculté de médecine de Bordeaux* (Bordeaux, 1888), pag. 24.

Bargues, probabilmente suo parente) (23). A Parigi viveva un medico ebreo di nome Fonseca (24). A Nancy e a Metz era attivo medico Jacob Berr. Gli era stato negato il diploma di medico nel 1758 per la sua qualità di ebreo, ma l'ottenne nel 1793 durante la Rivoluzione (25). Jacques Aronsohn (1759-1845) di Metz, che nel 1790 ottenne il diploma di medicina, è considerato il pioniero della vaccinazione in Francia. Era figlio del *parnàs* della Comunità di Metz, Goudchaux-Mayer Cahen e padre del noto medico alsaziano Jacques-Léon Aronsohn (1793-1861) (26). Di tutti i medici ebrei soltanto Jacob Berr dimostrò, per breve tempo, un interesse per la vita ebraica della Comunità. È l'autore di un opuscolo contro le Comunità ebraiche autonome.

Ora si pone la domanda : chi dev'essere considerato intellettuale «ebreo» laico ? Secondo noi, per essere considerato intellettuale ebreo non basta essere scrittore, avvocato, medico, musicista o esercitare altre professioni intellettuali. Per essere considerato intellettuale ebreo, lo scrittore, l'avvocato, o il medico dev'essere anche attivo quale ebreo, vale a dire scrivere intorno ad argomenti ebraici o partecipare alla vita comunale ebraica ed esercitare qualche influenza sull'ambiente ebraico. Se è così molti intellettuali finora ricordati debbono essere esclusi, di modo che il quadro della vita intellettuale profana diventava ancora più povero.

Lo stesso si deve dire di molti ebrei che, durante la Rivoluzione, presero parte attiva alla cosa pubblica quali consiglieri municipali, quali

(23) Minute della *nazione* di Bordeaux (negli archivi dipartimentali della Gironda). nn. 346, 349 ; Archivi dipartimentali della Gironda, C, reg. 1696, minute della corporazione dei medici, n. 44. Il 4 luglio 1761 e il 7 giugno 1765, la stessa corporazione adottò alcuni provvedimenti contro un medico ebreo illegale di nome Chaves (*ibid.*, nn. 450, 463). Nel 1738 viveva a Saint-Esprit-les-Bayonne un farmacista ebreo di nome Jacob Silva. E. Duceré, *Histoire topographique et anecdotique des rues de Bayonne* (Bayonne, 1887), I, 226.

(24) L. Kahn, *Les Juifs à Paris depuis le VIe siècle* (Parigi, 1889), pag. 51.

(25) P. Delaunay, *La vie médicale....* (Parigi, 1935), pagg. 350-351 ; E. Carmoly, *Histoire des médecins juifs anciens et modernes* (Bruxelles, 1844), pag. 204 ; Idem, *Revue orientale*, II (1842), 392 ; *Annuaire du département de la Mozelle*, V anno (Metz, n. d.), pag. 85 (*Berr, médecin de l'Hôpital militaire*) ; Chr. Pfister, *Histoire de Nancy* (Parigi, 1909), III, 327. Léon Bultingaire, *Club des Jacobins de Metz* (Parigi-Metz, 1906), pag. 101 (Berr era un giacobino).

(26) M. Ginsburger, *Jüdische Aerzte im Elsass* (n. p., 1933), pag. 10 ; Paul Dorveaux, *Le Docteur Aronssohn* in «Cahiers Lorrains», 1931, 83-84 ; E. Carmoly, *Hist. des médecins...* pagg. 202-03. Vedi pure Richard Kohn, *L'activité scientifique des médecins juifs en France depuis 1789* in «Medécine hébraïque», n. 12-15 (1952). Cogli anni 1806-1809 il numero dei medici ebrei crebbe fortemente. A Metz, p. es., Albert Philipe fu medico dell'esercito ; Abraham Philippe, Lazare Terquem e B. Cahen furono studenti di medicina (Archivi dipartiment. della Moselle, V, 149).

funzionari di uffici civici e soci di club rivoluzionari. La maggior parte di costoro possedevano senza dubbio una qualche istruzione profana e parlavano correntemente il francese. Non si può pensare, p. es., che Jacob Goudchaux-Berr, *funzionario municipale* di Metz, che controfirmò il 7 luglio 1794 la sentenza di morte contro l'emigrato Antoine Pertschneider (27) non possedesse una cultura profana.

(*Continua*)

(27) R. PAQUET, *Bibliographie analytique de l'histoire de Metz pendant la Révolution* (Parigi, 1926), I, 476, 497. Sugli ufficiali ebrei durante i vari periodi della Rivoluzione vedi gli Studi seguenti dell'Autore : *Gli Ebrei Sefarditi di Francia durante la Rivoluzione del 1879* in « Proceedings of the American Academy for jewish Research », XXIV (1955), 157 ; *Gli Ebrei comtadini e l'annessione della provincia papale alla Francia, 1789-1791* in « Jewish Quarterly Review » XLVI (1955), 192-193 ; *L'Ebraismo francese durante la reazione del Termidoro* in « Historia judaica », XX (1958), 102-104 ; *Gli Ebrei nei club dei Giacobini durante la rivoluzione francese del 1789* in « Rassegna Mensile d'Israel » XXIV (1958), 296-304.

La vita intellettuale profana fra gli Ebrei nella Francia del XVIII secolo

(Continuazione e fine v. n. precedente)

II

Le aspirazioni degl'intellettuali laici fra gli Ebrei ashkenaziti erano analoghe a quelle dei pionieri del movimento della *Haskalà*. *L'Haskalà* cercava di rendere partecipi gli Ebrei alle idee laiche moderne e patrocinava, fra le altre cose, una riforma di alcuni riti religiosi tradizionali. *L'Haskalà* in Francia adottò il programma che questo movimento aveva presso gli Ebrei tedeschi e risentì grandemente dell'influenza di Mosè Mendelssohn e dei suoi amici di Berlino. Alcuni dei primi scritti che preparavano la opinione pubblica cristiana a un atteggiamento favorevole agli Ebrei furono il risultato dell'azione di Mendelssohn. Per sua iniziativa Christian Wilhelm von Dohm incluse nel suo libro, in cui proponeva la riforma dello statuto politico degli Ebrei, una memoria sulla condizione degli Ebrei alsaziani inviata dal capo degli Ebrei d'Alsazia, Cerfberr di Medelsheim. Nel 1787, H.-G. Conte de Mirabeau pubblicava il suo libro su Mendelssohn (28).

La personalità più nota del gruppo della *Haskalà* di Francia era Zalkind Hurwitz, ebreo polacco che aveva vissuto qualche tempo a Berlino prima di stabilirsi in Francia dove lottò strenuamente per l'emancipazione ebraica. In realtà Hurwitz era un estraneo alle Comunità ebraiche organizzate. Le sue idee intorno alla religione e alla vita comunale ebraica erano estremiste perfino per i *maskilìm* franco-ebrei, la maggior parte dei quali erano moderati in materia religiosa (29). Moïse Ensheim, ebreo stra-

---

(28) CHR. W. VON DOHM, *Ueber die bürgerliche Verbesserung der Juden* (Berlino-Stettino, 1781) Ediz. francese, tradotta da J. BERNOULLI, *De la réforme politique des Juifs* (Dessau, 1782). H. G. Cte DE MIRABEAU, *Sur Moses Mendelsohn . . .* (Londra, 1787).

(29) L. KAHN, *Les Juifs de Paris . . .* pagg. 130-50. ROBERT ANCHEL, *Un juif polonais en France, Zalkind Hourwitz* in « Univers israélite », XCII, n. 38 (1937).

niero che godeva il favore di Mendelssohn, faceva parte del gruppo di Francia, senz'essere però così estremista come Hurwitz (30).

I capi ufficiali ebrei che lottavano per l'emancipazione dell'Ebraismo ashkenazita di Francia furono Cerfberr di Strasburgo (1730-1793), Isaïe Berr-Bing (1759-1805) di Metz e Berr-Isaac Berr di Nancy (1744-1828). Tutti tre erano in intimi rapporti con Mendelssohn. Fra loro il vero intellettuale era Bing, uomo di grandi conoscenze storiche sui problemi ebraici. Egli dimostrò pure gran coraggio nel formulare la richiesta per il miglioramento della condizione ebraica, come Graetz notò alludendo alla replica che il Bing fece ad un libello antisemita del 1787 (31). Cerfberr non era un intellettuale, ma seppe organizzare con molto acume la lotta a favore dell'emancipazione ebraica. Berr-Isaac Berr possedeva facoltà intellettuali inferiori soltanto a quelle di Isaïe Berr Bing e capacità pratiche eguali a quelle di Cerfberr (32).

Lipmann-Berr, mercante e industriale, apparteneva pure a quel gruppo di *maskilim*. Nel 1792 offrì la somma di 150 franchi che doveva essere destinata dalla locale *Académie des sciences et belles lettres* all'autore del migliore studio sopra un tema di storia ebraica. Nel 1793 l'Accademia offriva altri 150 fr. per lo stesso scopo ; ma essa cessava di esistere prima della presentazione di quegli studi (33). Un altro membro del medesimo gruppo di Nancy era Michel Berr (1780-1843), giovane di forte ingegno. Era figlio del capo degli Ebrei di Lorena, Berr-Isaac Berr, e genero di Isaïe Berr-Bing. Michel Berr, più tardi avvocato, pubblicò nel 1801 il suo *Appel* rivolto alla Conferenza della Pace a Lunéville. Era l'opuscolo migliore in favore dell'emancipazione ebraica scritto da un ebreo francese sotto il Primo Impero. Michel Berr descrive se stesso come « più francese che ebreo ». Poi sciupò il suo giovane intelletto nella pubblicazione di una

---

(30) Vedi nota 12.

(31) *Revue philosophique* (Termidoro, anno VIII-4), 316-18 ; TCHERIKOWER, *op. cit.* (vedi nota 12), II, 18-21. Isaïe-Berr Bing era il suocero di due giovani *maskilim*, Michel Berr di Nancy e Hartog Sommerhausen (1781-1853) che si era stabilito nel Belgio. « Archives israélites » V (1844), 173 ; XIV (1853), 186. Bing, direttore delle Salines de l'Est, era uno degli Ebrei più ricchi di Metz. Durante la Rivoluzione fu uno dei 18 Ebrei che pagarono a Metz le più alte imposte comunali ebraiche (Jewish Theological Seminary, Nuova Jork, ms. 01565). A suo figlio, Charles Bing, si deve la fondazione di scuole ebraiche laiche. Tradusse in francese *L'Ami des jeunes demoiselles ou Conseils aux jeunes personnes* . . . (Parigi, 1835), 2 vol.

(32) L'autore di queste note prepara per la pubblicazione uno studio particolareggiato su Berr-Isaac Berr.

(33) *Quelle a été la distribution des trois pouvoirs chez les Juifs, depuis l'élévation de Saül au trône jusqu'à la conquête de la Judée par les Romains.* JUSTIN LAMOUREAUX *Mémoire.* . . . (Nancy, 1803).

quantità di opuscoli su temi senza importanza e in una serie di conflitti coi capi ebrei (34). Un altro membro del gruppo di Nancy era il matematico Jacques Schwab (c. 1767-1815) giunto in quella città dalla Germania nel 1791 (35). Merita pure di essere menzionato Israël-Hayemson Créhange (1769-1844) di Sedan, amico di Bing e fervido lettore di *Ha-Measef* (36). Questo gruppo di ammiratori francesi di Mendelssohn non era unito nella sua posizione per quanto si riferiva ad alcuni importanti problemi ebraici.

Al principio della Rivoluzione gli Ebrei ashkenaziti propugnavano il mantenimento delle Comunità autonome come esistevano sotto l'antico regime. Alcuni erano perfino disposti ad abbandonare completamente la lotta per l'emancipazione pur di preservare l'autonomia ebraica. Il deputato e rappresentante di Parigi nel dipartimento della Mosella, François-René-Augustin Mallarmé, riferiva che l'ebreo ortodosso Joseph Gugenheim, arrestato durante il Terrore, era un fanatico che si opponeva alle domande per l'immediata emancipazione ebraica (37). Secondo Zarfati [Olry Terquem], il capo degli Ebrei riformati del XIX secolo, Cefberr di Nancy, era pure contrario alla completa emancipazione degli Ebrei (38).

Però i più moderati fautori delle Comunità ebraiche autonome, sui quali la scuola berlinese esercitava una forte influenza, comprendevano i capi ebrei riconosciuti Cerfberr di Alsazia e Berr-Isaac Berr di Nancy.

Gli Ebrei ashkenaziti non ottennero la piena emancipazione fino

(34) MICHEL BERR, *Appel à la justice des nations et des rois.* . . . (Strasburgo, 1801) pag. 18 (*Devenu plus francais que juif*) ; D. DE C. *Extrait de l'Argus du 6 juillet 1824. Notices biographiques sur les littérateurs contemporains. Michel Berr* (Parigi) pagg. 109-216.

JEAN BETINET, sécrétaire perpétuel de l'Académie de Sciences de Montmartre, à Michel Berr (satira) ; ALBERT MONTEMONT, *Epître à Monsieur Michel Berr* (Parigi, 1822), 11 pagg. e seconda edizione (Parigi 1822), 12 pagg.; X. MARMIER, *Notice biographique sur Michel Beer* [Berr] (Strasburgo, 1834) 16 pagg. [Estratto dalla *Revue germanique*]. E. CARMOLY, *Revue orientale*, III (1843-44), 62-74, 122-34. *Archives israélites*, IV (1843), 721-27, V (1844), 109-116, 168-80.

(35) J. SCHILL, *Jacques Schwab*, in « Revue juive de Lorraine », 1934, 60-61. JOSEPH LOEB maestro di religione nella casa della famiglia Cerfberr a Strasburgo, era nel 1871 insegnante privato di matematica. ADOLPH SEYBOT, *Das alte Strassburg* (Strasburgo) pag. 173.

(36) *Archives israélites*, V (1844), 753-57.

(37) « Il s'etait opposé à ce que les Juifs ne demandèrent pas plutôt de jouir des droits de citoyens actifs ; que c'est un homme dangereux et fanatique » (PAQUET, *Bibliographie.* . . . 640, 759, 932, 1090, 1093). Mallarmé non era anti-ebreo. Fra i funzionari locali da lui nominati c'erano alcuni Ebrei (*Ibid,,* II, 1370).

(38) « Cerf Berr nel [17]89, era fra i malcontenti, macchinava contro la nostra emancipazione » (ZARFATI) MICHEL BERR « Archives Israélites » IV (1843), 725-26.

al 21 settembre 1791, non solo per effetto della forte opposizione anti-
ebraica ma anche a causa del desiderio degli Ebrei di conservare qualche
forma di autonomia comunale. Il primo voto dell'Assemblea Nazionale
di aggiornarsi prima di arrivare ad una decisione sullo stato degli Ebrei
era giustificato per il fatto che non era sicuro se gli Ebrei stessi desideravano di diventare cittadini francesi senza restrizioni, secondo una nota
del 24 dicembre 1789 del Diario di Adrien Duquesnoy, deputato di Bar-le-
Duc ed amico degli Ebrei (39).

I fautori dell'autonomia dovettero sostenere una dura battaglia.
Zalkind Hurwitz aveva già proposto che fuori della sinagoga i rabbini
e gli amministratori delle Comunità non avessero alcuna autorità sulla
vita ebraica. In verità Hurwitz chiedeva che i Rabbini fossero spogliati
interamente delle loro funzioni. Il 20 settembre 1789 metteva in guardia
il Comitato dei rapporti dell'Assemblea Nazionale contro i « fanatici della
mia nazione », contro « l'inquisizione rabbinica » e la « cloaca » della Comunità ebraica (40). Il nipote di Berr-Isaac Berr, Jacob Berr, medico a
Nancy, propugnava l'abolizione completa delle Comunità israelitiche.
In un opuscolo sosteneva che Berr-Isaac Berr voleva mantenere gli Ebrei
in uno stato di estraneità nei confronti dei non-ebrei, perpetuando così
il loro isolamento. Jacob Berr accusava il « regime dispotico » della
Comunità di essere responsabile di tanti mali e criticava Berr-Isaac Berr
per la sua richiesta « pericolosa » che fossero mantenute le Comunità
ebraiche autonome (41).

I debiti dovuti dalla Comunità ai creditori cristiani provocarono un
conflitto fra la vecchia e la nuova generazione della Comunità di Metz.
Dopo lo scoppio della Rivoluzione i « giovani ebrei » (jeunes juifs), da
poco ammogliati o da poco stabiliti a Metz, si rifiutarono di pagare le
tasse e di liquidare i loro debiti. Nel rifiuto di pagare le tasse era implicito
un conflitto ben più serio fra le due generazioni, quella vecchia degli
Ebrei ortodossi e quella più giovane dei fautori d'una riforma delle pratiche religiose ebraiche (42). Il rifiuto del governo di assumere quei debiti

(39) ROBERT DE CRÉVECOEUR, *Journal d'Adrien Duquemoy....* (Parigi, 1894),
II, 208.

(40) ZALKIND HURWITZ, *Apologie des Juifs* (Parigi, 1789), pagg. 38-39. Vedi anche
la nota 29.

(41) *Lettre du Sr. Jacob Berr, Juif, maître en chirurgie à Nancy, à Monseigneur
l'Evêque de Nancy* (1790). Su Jacob Berr vedi E. CARMOLY, *Histoire des médecins
juifs, anciens et modernes* (Bruxelles, 1844) pag. 204 ; IDEM, *Revue Orientale*, II (1842),
92 ; CH. PFISTER, *op. cit.*, III, 327.

(42) Un rapporto della Prefettura del 30 marzo 1801, scriveva su questo conflitto:
« La scission commença entre les Juifs de campagne et ceux de Metz, comme elle
existait déjà entre les villages qui s'étaient coalisés pour faire la loi aux villes. Elle

avrebbe costretto gli Ebrei a mantenere le loro Comunità e probabilmente avrebbe dato origine a idee superstiziose e bigotte, come la Comunità di Metz sosteneva in una petizione diretta alla Convenzione Nazionale (43).

III

Era cosa rara per gli Ebrei abbandonare pubblicamente la loro religione. I pochi casi occorsi possono essere classificati in quattro categorie differenti :

1) Ebrei convertiti ;

2) Ebrei che avevano sposato donne cristiane ma non si erano convertiti al Cristianesimo ;

3) Ebrei che avevano rigettato apertamente la tradizione e la religione ebraica sotto l'influsso delle vicende della Rivoluzione ;

4) Ebrei che avevano rallentato i loro legami colla vita religiosa ma non avevano abbandonato le Comunità.

Anche durante la Rivoluzione furono pubblicati da parte dei circoli cattolici opuscoli destinati a salvar gli Ebrei mediante la conversione. Basandosi sulle vecchie leggi, le Autorità alsaziane consegnavano alle istituzioni cattoliche i bambini ebrei illegittimi. I capi federali della Rivoluzione non avevano però alcun interesse a permettere che gli Ebrei aderissero alla Chiesa. Non è infatti noto alcun atto di conversione durante il periodo rivoluzionario. Gli Ebrei che desideravano abbandonare la loro Comunità potevano ora farlo senza convertirsi al Cristianesimo che non godeva le grazie dei circoli rivoluzionari (44). I matrimoni misti, patrocinati tanto dai protagonisti quanto dai nemici dell'emancipazione ebraica, erano diventati un simbolo della nuova era rivoluzionaria. Inoltre, grazie alle idee rivoluzionarie, l'Ebreo non era più costretto a convertirsi al Cristianesimo per sposare una ragazza cristiana. Solo più tardi, a comin-

---

s'étendit ensuite entre les anciens et les jeunes juifs. Les moteurs de ces discordes étoient de certains hommes qui croient au fanatisme contre quoionque tenoit à une religion. Beaucoup parmi les enfants de Moyse ont resisté aux efforts de ces sectaires fanatiques eux mêmes ; mais les jeunes gens voulant faire écho, se sont *mis au pas* en frondant les anciens. De là deux opinions opposées ont formé deux partis parmi eux. (*Mon opinion developpée et discutée sur la prétention des jeunes gens juifs contre les anciens*). Documenti sulle Comunità ebraiche di Francia durante la Rivoluzione del 1789. Metz, n. 6, fogli 31-36. Nella biblioteca dell'Hebrew Union College, Cincinnati.

(43) « reveiller dans beaucoup de têtes ... peut-être même des idées fanatiques et superstitieuses « (Jewish Theological Seminary, Nuova Jork, ms. 01530-1).

(44) Z. SZAJKOWSKI, *Matrimoni, matrimoni misti e conversioni fra gli Ebrei francesi durante la Rivoluzione del 1789. Historia judaica*, XIX (1917), 47-53.

ciare dal Primo Impero, allorchè il numero delle conversioni, cresciuto notevolmente, ebbe per conseguenza il rilasciarsi dei legami della religione ebraica, i matrimoni misti risaltarono visibilmente (45).

Il declinare della vita religiosa tanto fra i Cristiani quanto fra gli Ebrei fu notato in un opuscolo pubblicato nella provincia papale al principio della Rivoluzione (46). Singoli Ebrei e perfino capi di Comunità ebraiche manifestarono apertamente la loro mancanza di riguardo per la religione avita coll'offrire oggetti religiosi ebraici in dono a club rivoluzionari, ecc. Però in moltissimi casi gli Ebrei lo fecero non perchè attribuissero alla nuova religione rivoluzionaria la qualità di *Être suprème*, ma per salvare la loro libertà individuale e quella delle Comunità ebraiche (47).

Alcuni Ebrei influenti smisero di osservare la loro religione, ma continuarono a vivere in un ambiente ebraico ed a partecipare alla vita comunale ebraica. Jacob Lazard (Sarrelouis 1759-Parigi 1840), amico di Hurwitz e di Ensheim, rappresentava questo gruppo. Insieme con Berr-Isaac-Berr era membro della delegazione ebraica che fu ricevuta dall'Assemblea Nazionale. Fu più tardi ricco mercante di diamanti e deputato nel sinedrio convocato da Napoleone I. Avrebbe voluto che durante la Rivoluzione un gruppo di « missionari » emancipati preparassero la strada ad una generale emancipazione ebraica. In materia di religione era un libero pensatore (48).

IV

L'estensione della conoscenza della lingua francese da parte degli Ebrei è un criterio della loro vita intellettuale profana.

Mentre il francese era in uso fra i sefarditi, la maggior parte di questi Ebrei continuavano a parlare il locale giudeo-portoghese (49). Nel 1630,

---

(45) *Ibid*, 41-44.

(46) « La miséricorde divine retient encore la vengeance coeleste, prête à faire de vous un moins de moeurs, moins de bonne foi, moins de décence & de religion surtout dans les lieux saints, chez les Chrétiens que chez les Juifs ». *Avis plus que pressant*, pag. 7.

(47) Z. SZAJKOWSKI, *L'osservanza religiosa ebraica durante la Rivoluzione francese del 1789*. « S. Niger Memorial Volume » (N. Jork, 1958), 193-216 (in *jiddish*).

(48) *Archivies israélites*, I (1840), 469.

(49) Usiamo l'espressione giudeo-portoghese lasciando agli specialisti decidere se chiamare *ladino* o con altro nome la lingua parlata dai Sefardim di Francia sotto l'influenza dello spagnolo e del portoghese. Vedi su questo problema : G. CIROT, *Recherches sur les Juifs Espagnols et Portugais à Bordeaux* (Bordeaux, 1908), pagg. 3-20 (« Les vestiges de l'Espagnol et du Portugais dans le parler des Juifs bordelais »).

il marrano Diego D'Acosta, che era vissuto in Francia per il corso di 28 anni, non sapeva ancora parlare francese (50). Atti notarili contemporanei menzionano casi consimili oppure notano che una persona parlava francese, ciò che era, molto probabilmente, raro (51). I sefarditi usavano spesso lo spagnuolo e il portoghese nella corrispondenza (52) e nelle attività comunali (53). Abraham Furtado, essendosi nascosto durante il Terrore, scrisse un diario in francese, ma i commenti di un suo congiunto sono riportati da lui nell'originale portoghese (54). Non più tardi del 1817 un forestiero notava che i rabbini delle tre sinagoghe di Saint-Esprit - lès-Bayonne continuavano a predicare in spagnuolo. Il loro uditorio era però composto di vecchi : i giovani chiedevano discorsi in francese (55). Un monumento del 1834 del Cimitero di Bordeaux reca un'iscrizione spagnuola (56).

IDEM, *Notes sur les Juifs portugais de Bordeaux* (1930), 15 pagg. Estratto dalla *Miscelanea de estudios en honora de D. Carolina Michaëlis de Vasconcellos*, sulla lingua delle minute della *Nazione* di Bordeaux. J. LAMBERT, *Observations sur quelques particularités du parler bayonnais*. Biarritz Association, (maggio, 1911) ; ALBERT LÉVI, *Les vestiges de l'Espagnol et du Portugais chez les Israélites dé Bayonne* (Bayonne, 1930), 16 pagg. ; GABRIEL PEREYRE, *Traité pratique de la petite sacrificature* (Bayonne, 1892), pag. 3.

(50) CECIL ROTH, *Les Marranes à Rouen*. REJ, LXXXVIII (1929), 116. FRANÇOIS Paez de Léon, un marrano di Bordeaux, scrisse la sua *Nouvelle arithmétique mise en jour pour l'utilité des négocians* (Bordeaux, 1691), VIII, 368 pagg. nella sua lingua natia e tradotta poi da lui stesso in francese : « J'avois composé le présent ouvrage en ma langue maternelle ... je l'ay traduit en François, de mon mieux » (p. III). Nel 1712 pubblicava il suo secondo libro, *Le Miroir des negocians*.

(51) Archivi dipartimentali di Gironda, atti notarili di Rauzan il vecchio, 29 ottobre 1766, 2 gennaio 1769 ; 12 giugno 1770 (il testamento di Abraham Rodrigues Nunes fu scritto *en caractères* [lingua] *portugais*), minute di Gatellet, 13 giugno 1786 (testamento di Esther Henriques *parlant et entendant la langue française*).

(52) Rachel Dasylva scriveva a David Gradis in spagnolo. *Mémoire pour les sieurs David Gradis & fils. . . . Contre le sieur David Dasylva . . . .* [Bordeaux, 1799], pag. 50.

(53) Una parte delle minute del secolo XVIII della *Nazione* sefardita di Bordeaux sono scritte in giudeo-portoghese (negli archivi dipartimentali della Gironda). Pochissime delle domande d'aiuto dirette dai poveri alla *Nazione* di Bordeaux sono scritte in francese (biblioteca del Jewish Theological Seminary, Nuova Jork).

(54) Biblioteca civica di Bordeaux, ms. 1946.

(55) *L'Ermite de la Guyenne* [V. J. de Tony]. *L'Ermite en voyage* (Mercure de France, I, 22 marzo 1817, 580-81). Secondo una novella pubblicata nel 1925 il dialetto era usato in un periodo molto tardo nella Sinagoga di Bayonne. LILY JEAN TAVAL, *Noemi* (Parigi, 1925), pag. 23.

(56) CIROT, *Recherches . . .* pag. 152.

L'insegnamento del francese era vietato nel ghetto di Carpentras, secondo Th. Milhaud, biografo di suo padre, rabbi Mardochée Crémieu. La lingua francese non era ignota fra gli Ebrei delle quattro Comunità della provincia papale di Avignon e del Contado Venassino (Avignon, Carpentras, Cavaillon e L'Isle-sur-Sorgue). Gli alunni della *jeshivà* di Carpentras usavano libri francesi. Nel 1769 un Ebreo di Carpentras fu attaccato perchè fu veduto leggere un libro francese. Però gli Ebrei della provincia papale usavano nella vita quotidiana il loro idioma noto come *Chuadit*. Dal 1789 in poi questo idioma, di cui soltanto poche parole hanno sopravvissuto fino ad oggi, è decaduto : coll'emancipazione quegli Ebrei hanno cominciato a parlar francese (57).

Gli Ebrei ashkenaziti dell'Alsazia, di Metz e della Lorena parlavano *jiddish*. Solo un piccolo gruppo conosceva il francese ; a Strasburgo erano gli Ebrei ricchi, secondo J-L.-F. Fesquet che descrive i suoi viaggi attraverso l'Alsazia nel 1802. L'idea che gli Ebrei diffusero l'uso del francese nell'Alsazia è stata accolta da molti storici, ma questo è vero soltanto per il periodo post-rivoluzionario. La lingua letteraria tedesca era ignota agli Ebrei alsaziani, se si deve dar retta ad una memoria amministrativa del 1780. Uno degli scopi della Rivoluzione fu quello di abolire i dialetti provinciali e d'introdurre il francese come lingua generale. Per raggiungere questo scopo fu chiesto agli Ebrei di abbandonare lo *jiddish*, proposta fatta pure dai *maskilim*, i quali consideravano l'uso dello *jiddish* come l'ostacolo maggiore all'emancipazione sociale degli Ebrei e alla completa emancipazione politica. È però dubbio se l'amara denigrazione dello *jiddish* da parte dei *maskilim*, che molti storici datano dalla Rivoluzione, si verificò prima dell'inizio del XIX secolo (58). Berr-Isaac-Berr, che per molti anni combattè l'uso dell'*jiddish*, dovette più tardi deplorare la scomparsa di quella lingua e dell'ebraico dalla vita ebraica e con essa la scomparsa di molte altre tradizioni ebraiche. Quando il francese diventò la sola lingua ufficiale e usuale dei Concistori francesi, Berr-Isaac-Berr chiese che l'ebraico e lo *jiddish* fossero adoperati nelle riunioni concistoriali per i·verbali e per la corrispondenza (59).

(57) Z. SZAJKOWSKI, *La lingua degli Ebrei nelle quattro Comunità del Contado venosino*, Con una prefazione di MAX WEINREICH (Nuova York 1948), VII, 78, XI pagg. in *jiddish*.

(58) CHARLES HOFFMAN, *L'Alsace au XVIII siècle* (Colmar 1906), II, 65 ; Z. SZAJKOWSKI, *L'azione contro lo jiddish in Francia nei secoli XVIII e XIX*. « Yivo Bleter » XIV (1939), 54-74 (in jiddish). IDEM, *Osservanza ebraica religiosa* (vedi nota 47), 206-207 ; J.-L.-F. FESQUET, *Voyage à Strasbourg* (a. IX), pag. 8 ; PAUL LÉVY, *Histoire linguistique d'Alsace et de Lorraine* (Parigi 1929), II, 30-34.

(59) Z. SZAJKOWSKI, *Sulla storia degli Ebrei francesi* [gli ultimi anni di Berr-Isaac Berr]. « Davke » n. 24 (1955), 240-41. David Singer di Uffheim (1778-1846) fu uno

Anche durante il Primo Impero un gran numero di Ebrei non sapevano neppure fare la loro firma in caratteri latini, come è dimostrato dalle dichiarazioni dei nomi in base al decreto 20 luglio 1808 sui nomi ebraici. Di 10.178 Ebrei che fecero quelle dichiarazioni nel dipartimento dell'Alto Reno, 1.608 firmarono in caratteri ebraici. A Foussemagne, 166 su 177 firmarono in caratteri ebraici ; a Hagenbach, 87 su 90 ; a Hattstatt, 164 su 255 ; a Colmar, 66 su 190 ; a Wettolsheim 76 su 110 ecc. (60). A Nancy (Meurthe) 410 su 766 firme erano in francese, 200 in ebraico e 44 in ambedue le lingue o in tedesco con caratteri gotici. 99 Ebrei, per lo più donne, non firmarono. In realtà le 766 dichiarazioni furono fatte soltanto da 363 Ebrei per sè e per i propri figli. Di quelle 363 firme 161 erano in francese, 109 in ebraico, 10 in ambedue le lingue, 5 in tedesco, mentre 78 non fecero altro che il loro segno (61). Di 11 dichiarazioni a Nantes (Loira inferiore), sei erano firmate in francese, una in ebraico, un ebreo era analfabeta e gli altri 3 erano assenti (62). Uno studio più particolareggiato sulle firme dimostra che un gran numero di Ebrei erano analfabeti. A Rimbach (Alto Reno) 120 Ebrei dichiararono i loro nomi. Su 54 che firmarono in ebraico, la maggior parte delle firme mostrano chiaramente di essere state scritte con difficoltà. 48 non riuscirono a scrivere il proprio nome ma fecero il loro segno ; pochi soltanto firmarono in caratteri latini e gli altri non fecero nemmeno il loro segno (63). Pochi Ebrei scelsero nomi francesi. Uno solo dei 279 Ebrei di Bouxviller scelse un nome francese : *Cerf*, traduzione francese di *Hirsch* (64).

V

Gli Ebrei frequentarono scuole laiche nel primo tempo che seguì al periodo rivoluzionario. Nel 1798 Gabriel-Marq [Jassuda-Michael] Mossé di Carpentras, che ancora bambino fu convertito forzatamente al Cristianesimo, fu laureato alla *Ecole Polytechnique*. Durante la Rivoluzione, Abbot François-Valentin Mulot, rappresentante di Parigi, ottenne

---

dei primi ebrei a sostenere l'uso della lingua francese nelle preghiere. « Archives israélites » VII (1846), 100-01.

(60) « Archives Nationales » F 19-11012.

(61) A. GAIN, *La population juive de Nancy en 1808* « Revue juive de Lorraine », 1933, 293.

(62) L. BRUNSCHWIEG, *Les Juifs de Nantes*, REJ, XIX (1889), 305.

(63) Archivi dipartimentali dell'Alto Reno 5 E 246-2.

(64) PAUL LÉVY, *Histoire linguistique* . . . II, 91 : sui nomi degli Ebrei francesi, vedi PIERRE MENDEL, *Les noms des Juifs français modernes*. REJ, CX (1949-1950) 15-65.

contro le autorità locali il ritorno del giovane Mossé ai suoi genitori. Mossé divenne più tardi mediocre poeta (65).

Durante la Rivoluzione, Gerson-Lévy (1784-1864) era alunno dell'*Ecole centrale de la Moselle*, l'unica scuola moderna di Metz. Nel 1804 fu eletto presidente della locale società intellettuale (*société d'émulation*). Era uno dei capi nella lotta contro gli Ebrei ortodossi (66). Michel Goudchaux, durante la Rivoluzione alunno di una scuola pubblica a Nancy dove ottenne sempre i voti più alti, divenne Ministro di Francia durante la Rivoluzione del 1848 (67). Marx Wolf, che si iscrisse nel 1789 come studente all'Università di Strasburgo, fu attivo giacobino e presentò al club dei giacobini uno studio intitolato *Traité sur la morale de la République* (68). Alcuni Ebrei divennero maestri. L'ebreo giacobino, Lazard Zay di Metz, divenne nel 1792 maestro in una scuola pubblica di Strasburgo. Olry Terquem ed Ensheim furono professori al *liceo* francese di Magonza (69).

Il numero degli alunni ebrei delle scuole pubbliche crebbe rapidamente negli anni successivi. Secondo un rapporto concistoriale del 1810, 1.257 bambini ebrei frequentavano le scuole pubbliche o esercitavano «professioni utili». Il numero totale degli Ebrei di Francia era allora, secondo lo stesso rapporto, di 46.663. La maggior parte degli alunni della scuola ebraica venivano dalla Mosella (Metz compresa) e dalla Meurthe (inclusa Nancy) dove non vivevano che 10.683 Ebrei, ma non dai dipartimenti dell'Alsazia, dove ce n'erano 26.155 (70).

VI

Il possesso di librerie laiche private è un altro criterio della vita intellettuale civile degli Ebrei francesi.

(65) Z. SZAJKOWSKI, *Gli Ebrei comtadini* (v. nota 27), 191, n. 15.

(66) M. THIEL, *Notice biographique sur M. Gerson-Lévy* (Metz, 1865), pag. 7.

(67) MICHEL BERR, *Appel à la justice des nations. . . .* (Strasburgo, 1801), pag. 64. Mayer Anspach (1751-1844), genero del medico di Metz Philippe, fu uno dei primi Ebrei di Metz a mandare i suoi figliuoli ad una scuola pubblica. «Archives israélites », V (1844), 756-57. Uno dei suoi figli, Joel Anspach, divenne avvocato e membro del Concistoro centrale. Pubblicò il *Rituel des prières* (Metz, 1820) e *Paroles d'un croyant israélite* (Metz, 1842).

(68) E. BARTH, *Notes biographiques sur les hommes de la Révolution à Strasbourg* (Strasburgo, 1885) pag. 174.

(69) *Liste des membres composans la société populaire de Strasbourg . . . 25 vendemmiaio, anno III* [15 novembre 1794] ; « Archives israélites » V (1844), 69 ; XXIII (1862), 461-66.

(70) A. E. HALPHEN. *Recueil des lois . . . concernant les israélites . . .* (Parigi, 1851), pagg. 312-27.

Durante la Rivoluzione un mercante ebreo di Blâmont (Meurthe), Salomon Spire, possedeva l'*Histoire philosophique et politique des isles françaises dans les Indes occidentales* pubblicato nel 1784 (71). Nessun documento però si ha rispetto al possesso di librerie laiche fra gli Ashkenaziti. Erano pure rare ricche collezioni di libri religiosi. La più gran parte delle librerie ebraiche civili era proprietà dei sefarditi.

Abraham Rodrigues Pereyre (1728 ?-1784) di Bordeaux possedeva una libreria. Nel 1775 compilò un catalogo della sua libreria consistente allora in 800 opere. Il cronista di Bordeaux, Pierre Bernardau, notava che Pereyre viveva in un tempo in cui la gente di Bordeaux trovava strano il fatto che Montesquieu scriveva libri (72). Il banchiere ebreo di Bordeaux, Louis-David Francia de Beaufleury, padre dello storico Louis-Francia de Beaufleury, possedeva una ricca libreria privata. Nel 1795 Francia presentò un libro a Bernardau che in quell'occasione notava che Francia era « un uomo educato, per quanto ebreo » (73). Abraham Furtado pure possedeva una ricca collezione di libri. Nel suo diario ricordato sopra notava che leggeva opere di Buffon, La Fontaine, Corneille, Dante e molti altri (74). Una libreria di opere di storia naturale era stata raccolta dal naturalista Isaac Rodrigues già citato (75). Il fatto che gli Ebrei di Bordeaux dimostravano molto interesse negli affari della libreria pubblica è provato dalla petizione del 1790 firmata da 17 Ebrei, fra molti altri, che domandavano che la libreria rimanesse aperta in ore convenienti al pubblico (76).

(71) PAUL LANG, *Le citoyen Salomon Spire* « Revue juive de Lorraine » IV, n. 42 (1928), 31-33. Il titolo del libro di Raynal è citato in modo inesatto.

(72) *Catalogue des livres de la Bibliothèque de Pereyre junior. Avec le prix & volumes de chaque ouvrage, à Bordeaux, MDCCLV.* 16º (Biblioteca municipale di Bordeaux, ms. 836). *Cronaca di Bernardau (ibid.* ms. 713-1, vol. 14, foglio 12). CAM. COUDREC, *Catalogue des manuscrits de la Bibliothèque de Bordeaux* (Parigi, 1894) pag. 513 Secondo il registro GG 790 degli archivi municipali Pereyre morì il 26 febbraio 1784 a 56 anni.

(73) « Ce livre . . . m'a été donné, en 1795, par M. Francia, ancien banquier à Bordeaux, homme aimable et instruit, quoique juif de cette ville » (Biblioteca municipale di Bordeaux ms. 713-1, vol. 43). Sullo storico Beaufleury vedi : Z. SZAIKOWSKI, *Louis Francia de Beaufleury.* » Davke, n. 20 (1954), 241-48 (in *jiddish*).

(74) Z. SZAJKOWSKI, *Gli Ebrei sefarditi di Francia durante la Rivoluzione del 1789.* « Proceedings of the American Academy for Jewish Research » XXIV (1955), 147. La libreria di Furtado è pure ricordata da un cronista di Bordeaux (Biblioteca municipale di Bordeaux, ms. 712, vol. 8 : foglio 5).

(75) Nel 1796 Bernardau notava un acquisto di libri di Rodrigues. Ms. 713-1, vol. 3, pag. 98.

(76) G. DUCANNÈS-DUVAL, *Ville de Bordeaux. Inventaire sommaire des archives municipales. Période révolutionnaire. 1789-an VIII* (Bordeaux, 1929). IV, 528-31.

Israël-Bernard de Valabrègue (circa 1714-1779) di Avignon, che viveva a Parigi, possedeva una ricca biblioteca di 1.792 volumi. Era un merciaio, interprete per le lingue orientali, cioè conservatore di manoscritti e libri ebraici della Libreria reale e autore di opuscoli vari (77). Mardochée Venture, che veniva pure dalla provincia del papa, succedette a Valabrègue nella libreria reale. Tradusse libri di preghiera in francese per i sefarditi e pubblicò un calendario per gli ebrei delle provincie papali (78). Dopo la morte di Venture avvenuta il 12 marzo 1789, Moïse Ensheim, David Silveyra (contruttore d'un ponte nella Francia sud-ovest e poi agente a Parigi degli Ebrei sefarditi) e Zalkind Hurwitz optarono per la carica alla libreria. Il 13 maggio 1789 Hurwitz ebbe la nomina (79).

In conclusione si può dire che, al tempo dell'emancipazione degli Ebrei francesi, la loro vita intellettuale profana si trovava ad un grado basso. Forse la mancanza di cognizioni civili impedì a molti Ebrei di abbandonare il loro ambiente ebraico durante il procelloso periodo della Rivoluzione. Data l'assenza d'un forte nucleo di intellettuali ebrei capaci di guidare la lotta per l'emancipazione ebraica, l'atteggiamento della

(77) PAUL HILDENFINGER, *La bibliothèque de Bernard Valabrègue* (Parigi, 1911). 16 pagg. [Estratto dal *Bulletin du Bibliophile*, 1911, 421-32]. IDEM, *Documents sur les Juifs à Paris au XVIII siècle* (Parigi, 1913), 229-30. Valabrègue era l'autore delle *Lettres orientales*, tomo I (Tessalonica, 1754). *Précis de la prière que les Juifs Avignonois établis à Bordeaux, et ceux d'Avignon, actuellement à Paris ont faite pendant trois jours consécutifs pour obtenir de Dieu le rétablissement de la santé de Monseigneur le Dauphin ...* (1765), 4 pagg. *Odes prononcés par les Juifs d'Avignon et de Bordeaux résidants à Paris.... à l'occasion du Sacre de Louis XVI, le 11 juin 1775 ...* (Parigi, 1775), 24 pagg.; *Lettre ou réflexions d'un milord à son correspondant à Paris au sujet de la Requête des marchands des Six-Corps contre l'admission des Juifs aux brevets,* etc. [firmato: J. B. D. V. S. J. D. R.] (Londra [Parigi], 1767), 72 pagg.

(78) *Calendrier hébraïque, qui contient tous les roshodes....* (Amsterdam [?] 1745) 196 pagg. *Prières journalières à l'usage des Juifs portugais ou Espagnols....* (Nizza, 1772), 570 pagg.; (Bordeaux, 1838). 400 pagg. *Prières des Jours de Rosh-Hashana et du Jour de Kippour à l'usage del Juifs Portugais ou Espagnols.,...* (Nizza 1773), 752 pagg. *Prières des festes de Pessah.... Tome troisième* (Nizza 1774) 676 pagg. *Prières des Jours de jeûnes de Guedalya. Tome quatrième* (Nizza 1783) 532 pagg. *Cantique des Cantiques....* (Nizza 1774), 127 pagg. Nel 1765 pubblicò insieme con Isaïe Vidal il *Seder ha-Kontres.* Secondo alcune fonti, i *piutim* degli Ebrei della provincia papale furono composti da Venture. S. M. DOM PEDRO II. *Poésies hébraïco-provençales* (Avignon, 1841). Venture tradusse in francese le *Prières faites pour l'heureuse délivrance de la Reine, recitées en hébreu depuis le 15 fevrier 1785* (Parigi 1785).

(79) P. HILDENFINGER, *Documents ...* pagg. 79, 226. LEON KAHN, *Les Juifs de Paris pendant la Révolution* (Parigi, 1898) pagg. 132-137. Silveyra era l'autore del *Projet du Sieur Silveyra pour l'établissement d'un pont sur la rivière de Garonne, au passage ordinaire de Bordeaux à la Bastide, construit sur des bateaux au pontonl ...* (12 pagg.)

Rivoluzione nei confronti degli Ebrei può dirsi magnanimo. L'opposizione contro l'emancipazione ebraica era molto forte. Al principio della Rivoluzione gli Ebrei stessi non erano disposti ad accettare la piena cittadinanza. Nonostante quest'assenza di una forte guida civile ebraica, e la repugnanza a rinunziare, al principio della Rivoluzione, alla loro autonomia interna, la Rivoluzione accordò agli Ebrei la piena cittadinanza.

In generale, il livello intellettuale degli Ebrei francesi nel XVIII secolo era basso. Non c'erano, p. es., grandi dotti nelle discipline religiose fra i Rabbini francesi, eccettuati alcuni giunti di fuori. Ma questo sarà un argomento d'uno studio separato.

JEWISH RELIGIOUS OBSERVANCE DURING THE FRENCH REVOLUTION OF 1789

The struggle against religion was one of the most significant moments in the history of the French Revolution of 1789. Essentially, this was far more a struggle for the survival of the new regime and directed against the Roman Catholic Church, which openly sided with the counterrevolutionary elements, than an attack by revolutionary atheists on religion in general. This struggle also affected the attitude of the revolutionary powers toward Protestants and Jews, although these two groups of religious minorities were not involved in hostilities against the new regime. In most instances the attacks on the Protestant and Jewish religions were merely an echo of the storm that broke loose against the Catholic Church. Such attacks, of course, had their effect upon the workaday life of the Jewish communities insofar as the observance of Jewish laws and customs was concerned. In this study we wish to present a number of facts bearing on this problem and on the basis of these facts essay a conclusion.

SABBATHS AND JEWISH HOLIDAYS

The leaders of the French Revolution of 1789 regarded Sunday and the other religious holidays as relics of the old regime, hence a constant threat to the Revolution. Sunday was officially abolished as a day of rest and replaced by *décadi*, every tenth day in the French republican calendar. This change in the calendar strongly affected the observance of the Sabbath and the Jewish holidays. Many of the Jacobins, who formed the extreme left of the political spectrum, were strongly influenced in their attitude toward religion by the Encyclopedists, who regarded the Jewish religion unfavorably. The antipathy of both groups derived in part from the fact that they saw in Judaism the origin of their

Originally published in *YIVO Annual of Jewish Social Science*, vol. XII (1958–1959).

principal foe—Christianity. In the eyes of the Jacobins the observance of Sunday on the part of the Christians was merely the logical outcome of the observance of the Sabbath by the Jews.[1]

The problem of Sabbath observance was generally an important factor in the struggle for and against Jewish emancipation. In 1788 the administrative officials of the province of Alsace declared that Jews would never be able to become farmers because of the observance of the Sabbath and other Jewish holidays; because of Jewish and non-Jewish holidays they will miss 140 workdays each year. In 1790 an anti-Jewish pamphleteer attempted to demonstrate that because of their religion the Jews would be able to work no more than six months a year.[2] The anti-Jewish elements argued that on account of the Sabbath the Jews would not be able to serve in the army or in the national guard. To be sure, in 1792 the Jewish Community of Metz attempted to secure exemption from activities on the Sabbath for Jews serving in the national guard, and on November 7, 1792, seven Jews of Haguenau, Lower Rhine, presented a petition to the same effect. On December 3, 1792, the authorities of the Lower Rhine department rejected such a petition by several Jews of Niederroedern. Ultimately, Alsatian Jews had to perform their military duties also on the Sabbath, as was the case in Bordeaux, Avignon and in practically all Jewish communities in France.[3]

In Saint-Esprit-lès-Bayonne (a suburb of Bayonne), where the majority of the inhabitants were Jews, they also constituted a majority in the Jacobin Club and in the municipal council during the Reign of Terror. (The Reign of Terror began in July 1793 and ended with the arrest of Robespierre on July 27, 1794.) There the struggle against Sabbath observance was conducted with no less vehemence than in cities where the local authorities were predominantly non-Jewish. On March 18, 1794, the "Jewish" Jacobin Club of Saint-Esprit-lès-Bayonne resolved to confiscate all

[1] On the Jacobin attitude toward the Sabbath see: Engel, Matthias, *Meine Meinung über die Verlegung der Sonntags-Feyer auf den Decadi* (Strasbourg 1794) p. 10; Kammerer, J. J., *Die Religion der Jugent und der Vernunft über die Feier der Decaden* (Strasbourg 1793) pp. 14–20.

[2] *Les Juifs d'Alsace, doivent-ils être admis au droit de citoyens actifs?* (n.p. 1790) p. 118; Hoffmann, Charles, *L'Alsace au dix-huitième siècle* (Colmar 1907) IV, p. 369.

[3] Szajkowski, Z., "French Jews in the Armed Forces during the Revolution of 1789," *Proceedings of the American Academy for Jewish Research,* vol. XXVI (1957) pp. 142–43.

Sabbath candelabra. The Jews who did not surrender the candelabra voluntarily were regarded as fanatics and were frequently fined. On June 7, 1794, the Jew Montes was fined 15 livres for the benefit of the poor for refusal to sell laces on the Sabbath to the non-Jew Larré. Montes was also ordered to sell his wares on the Sabbath to all customers. Since the Jews of Saint-Esprit-lès-Bayonne continued to wear on the Sabbath their Sabbath garments the Jacobin Club on June 14, 1794, ordered the police to visit the public places and to arrest every "quondam Jew who flaunts his idleness." Jacob Silva, Andrade, Flores and Miranda were fined for appearing publicly in Sabbath garments. These measures led to sharp conflicts in the Jewish community. Some Jews maintained that the order of the Paris representative Monestier de la Lozère concerning the observance of *décadi* was aimed officially against Sunday observance and not the observance of the Sabbath. The Jewish Jacobins of the community complained to the Paris representatives on that score in a letter dated July 7, 1794. Three days later the Paris representatives issued an order praising the anti-Sabbath campaign of the Jacobins in Saint-Esprit-lès-Bayonne and urging them to continue the fight against "the spirit of superstition." The Jewish Jacobins there not only fought against Sabbath observance, but also against Sunday observance. The Jacobins—the majority of whom were Jews there—were sent on missions to the surrounding villages, which were under the administrative jurisdiction of the city to abolish Sunday observance and to replace it with *décadi,* as well as to urge the peasants to work in the fields on Sundays.[4]

The Hebrew teacher Jessel Lehman, of Ribeauvillé, recorded in his diary, which he kept in Yiddish cipher, that in Alsace the Jews had been forbidden to observe the Sabbath and had been compelled to assist the farmers in their chores on the Sabbath. Moreover, the kindling of Sabbath lights and the wearing of Sabbath garments were also forbidden. The Jews were compelled to keep their stores open on the Sabbath and the non-Jews, on Sun-

[4] *Guerre aux Tyrans. Paix au Peuple. Les Représentants du Peuple près l'Armée des Pyrénés Occidentales.* [Signed: Pinet aîné, Cavaignac] (Bayonne, n.d.) broadside; Ducéré, E., *Dictionnaire historique de Bayonne* (Bayonne 1911) I, p. 459; Ginsburger, Ernest, *Le Comité de Surveillance de Jean-Jacques Rousseau, Saint-Esprit-lès-Bayonne* (Paris 1934) pp. 28, 121–22, 195, 259, 265–66, 272, 284, 287–90; Darricau, Albert, *Scènes de la Terreur à Bayonne et aux environs, 1793–1794* (Bayonne-Biarritz 1903) p. 149.

day. In one community (Ribeauvillé?) where Jews conducted religious services clandestinely, two commissars assembled all the Jews on Friday night and lectured them severely on the evils of religion. On the following day they checked on clandestine Sabbath observance. A letter of December 6, 1793, from Mulhouse, stated that "even the Jews no longer observe the Sabbath." On July 12, 1794, the Jacobin Club of Colmar, which was anti-Jewish, complained that the Jews refuse to work on the Sabbath. The "Société Populaire" of Jacobins in Salins-Libre (formerly Château-Salins) demanded twice, on March 4 and on April 11, 1794, that the Jews be forbidden to kindle Sabbath lights because of a scarcity of oil. In many instances, the Sabbath candelabra were confiscated from their owners. In Haguenau Jews conducted religious services secretly in an oil factory. They entered through a side door, which led to the house of a Jewish neighbor, Samuel Ah. To divert the possible attention of the authorities, several Jews in working clothes walked up and down the street. Sabbath candles were klindled clandestinely in the ovens.[5]

On April 26, 1794, the "Société Populaire" of Nîmes resolved "to appeal to all quondam Jews" to reject their former holidays. Agricole Moureau, the leader of the Jacobins in Avignon during the Reign of Terror, later on complained in his anti-Jewish pamphlets that at the time of the Revolution the Jewish councilmen there refused to sign on the Sabbath the minutes of the council meetings. He stated that the Jews would rather see their homes consumed by the flames than extinguish the fire on the Sabbath. (Noteworthy is the fact that these are almost the identical words of the *maskil* Zalkind Hourwitz, a Polish Jew who fought for Jewish emancipation in France, in his book published in 1789. He argued that the Sabbath observance in the spirit of the Talmud could easily bring about the destruction of an entire city by conflagration.)[6]

[5] Lehman's Diary, pp. 27b, 29a (in the Alsace Museum, in Strasbourg). Jessel Lehman's brother, Issachar Ber was rabbi in Soultz (*Strassburger israelitische Wochenschrift. Wissenschaftliche Beilage.* Jan. 24, 1907); Adler, Simon, *Geschichte der Juden in Mülhausen i.E.*, (Mulhouse 1914) p. 64; Leuilliot, Paul, *Les Jacobins de Colmar* (Strasbourg 1923) p. 271; Haguenauer, Robert, "Les Juifs de Château-Salins," *Revue juive de Lorraine*, vol. II, no. 21 (1927) p. 17; Scheid, Elie, "Histoire des Juifs de Haguenau pendant la période française," *REJ*, vol. X (1885) pp. 230–231; *Idem*, "Histoire de la synagogue de Haguenau," *L'Univers israélite*, vol. XXXVII (1882–83) pp. 758–59.

[6] Bibliothèque municipale de Nîmes, ms. 362, 7 floréal an II; Moureau

Even during the period of the Thermidor, which came in the wake of the Reign of Terror, the Jews continued to be persecuted for their observance of the Sabbath. The *heder* of the *melamed* Isaac Bamberger, of Obernai, Lower Rhine, was ordered closed in July 1798 for observing the Sabbath instead of *décadi*.[7] Sabbath observance was forbidden even in cities where the number of Jewish residents was negligible, e.g. Troyes.[8] Noteworthy is the fact that even during the Reign of Terror the Metz community retained the services of the non-Jew Dominique as *shabes goy* (a non-Jew performing the services forbidden to Jews, such as kindling the fires and the like). Even the *shulklaper* (the beadle who summoned the worshippers to services in the morning by knocking at their doors) there remained in his office during that entire period.[9]

In Paris the Jews worshipped on the High Holidays during the Reign of Terror in a cellar converted into a synagogue secretly. To divert the attention of passers-by, several Jews were singing revolutionary songs in the courtyard. In Haguenau the Jews arranged the *seder* (the Passover festive meal) clandestinely in the aforementioned oil factory.[10]

In the days of the Old Regime many Jewish communities had

[Agricol], *De l'incompatibilité entre le Judaïsme et l'exercice des droits de cité* ..., (Paris 1818) p. 51; Hourwitz, Zalkind, *Apologie des Juifs* (Paris 1789) p. 19.

[7] Reuss, R., "Documents nouveaux sur l'antisémitisme dans le Bas-Rhin," *REJ*, vol. LIX (1910) p. 273. The Bordeaux chronicler, Pierre Bernadau, noted in his chronicle for March 2 and April 19, 1795, that for the time being only the Jews benefited by the decree on freedom of religion and they observed the Sabbath (Municipal Library of Bordeaux, vol. III, pp. 80 and 95).

[8] Graetz, H., *Popular History of the Jews* (New York 1919) V, p. 386. During the Revolution in all likelihood only a few Jews lived there. Cerf Lyon, a Jew, was arrested there for speculating in currency. See Kahn, L. *Les Juifs de Paris pendant la Révolution* (Paris 1898) p. 224. There is no mention of the Sabbath in the departmental and municipal archives or in the local histories of the Revolution. See Babeau, Albert, *Histoire de Troyes pendant la Révolution* (Paris 1873–74) 2 vols.; Prévost, Chanoine A. E., *Le Diocèse de Troyes pendant la Révolution* (Troyes 1908–1909) 3 vols.

[9] Based on receipts for wages paid by the Jewish community in Metz to the *shabes-goy* on December 30, 1792, and in 1793 to the *shulklapers* Joseph Olry and Cerf Birié (in the author's possession).

[10] Levi, G. Ben, "Mémoires d'un colporteur juif," *Archives isŗaélites*, vol. III (1842) p. 463; Prague, H. "Les Juifs de Paris sous la Terreur," *ibid.*, vol. XL (1879) pp. 121–122; Scheid, Elie, *op. cit.*, pp. 230–31; *L'Univers israélite*, vol. XXXVII (1882–83) pp. 758–59. The *melamed* Lehman entered in his diary for the year 1793 (p. 24a) that in his community (Ribeauvillé?) the rejoicing in the Passover holiday was marred by the drafting of seven Jews into the army.

special ovens for the baking of matzos, which were in most cases located in the courtyards or in the cellars of the synagogues. It seems that up to the Reign of Terror the Jews encountered no difficulties in the baking of matzos. On March 5, 1792, the municipal council of Nancy gave the Jews permission to use the municipal oven for one month for the baking of matzos. On April 22, 1792, the Jewish community of Metz paid to the baker Foull (or Fould) the sum of 440 livres for baking 400 pounds of matzos, which was indeed an exorbitant price. Later on, because of a flour shortage and the fight against religion it became increasingly difficult to obtain permission for the baking of matzos. On February 4, 1794, the Jewish baker and butcher Moïse Pimentel, of the Paris district of Marat, petitioned the municipal council for 24 measures of wheat, or 8 sacks of flour, to provide matzos for 220 Jews in Paris. He explained that in an ordinary week these 220 Jews would consume 2,517 pounds of bread. Thus, in granting his petition the city would save 1,253 pounds of flour. The council discussed Pimentel's petition, but arrived at no definite decision. According to one source, permission was granted in March 1794 (during the Reign of Terror) to the Jewess Rebecca Hadamard of Metz to bake matzos. On April 26, 1794, the heads of the Jewish community in Carpentras were ordered to surrender the two large pans in which the dough for the matzos was mixed to the munitions agency. They were promised compensation for the utensils. After the Reign of Terror Passover observance became easier. Thus in 1796 the Jews of Nice baked matzos. On February 10, 1798, the municipal council of Avignon granted permission to the baker Eléazard Carcassonne to use the synagogue oven for the baking of matzos. Since the synagogue was then nationalized, Carcassonne had to pay the municipality a certain sum for the use of the oven.[11]

[11] Archives municipales de Nancy. Délibérations, vol. VI, p. 82 (March 5, 1792); Archives départementales de la Moselle, V 166; *Le Journal de la Montagne*, vol. XI, no. 85 (Feb. 6, 1794); Kahn, L., *op. cit.*, pp. 192–93; "Notice sur Madame Rebeca Hadamard, née Lambert, de Metz," *Archives israélites*, vol. IV (1843) pp. 220–23; Archives Municipales de Carpentras, Révolution 23; Meiss, Honel, *A travers le ghetto; coup d'oeuil retrospectif sur l'Université israélite de Nice, 1648–1860* (Nice 1923) p. 53; Archives municipales d'Avignon. Délibérations, 22 pluviôse an 6.

Pursuant to a resolution of the prefecture of July 8, 1801, the synagogue in Avignon along with the matzos oven were torn down in order to build a road there. In 1794 seven families of Nîmes built a new synagogue and a new

In 1799, on the Feast of Tabernacles, the municipal authorities in Nice ordered agents to ascend a church steeple to see if the Jews have built *sukot*. Five offenders were taken and tried for publicly manifesting "signs of their Hebrew religion," which was in violation of the decree of March 29, 1795, prohibiting public manifestations of religion. However, they were not convicted.[12] It is also known that the Jews of Metz observed the Feast of Weeks.[13]

TRADITIONAL GARB AND TONSORIAL REGULATIONS

The Revolution brought about changes in all phases of workaday life even to the extent of the fashion of dress. The aforementioned Alsace *melamed*, Jessel Lehman, noted in 1789 in his diary: "The Revolution is gaining in all France. In all of Alsace and France [red-white-blue] cockades must be worn."[14]

We have spoken above of the fight against Sabbath garments. Noteworthy are several similar instances. In the early days of the Revolution a demand was put forth to forbid the traditional garments of the Jews so that they would not remain segregated from the rest of the population.[15]

Beard and side-locks (*peot*) were a favorite theme of ridicule of the Jew even at the time of the Revolution. A counterrevolutionary publication scoffed at the republican bishop and friend of the Jews, Henri Grégoire, that he allegedly called upon Christians to wear beards like Jews.[16] But in the eyes of the Jacobins beards and side-locks were symbols of religious fanaticism and the National Convention received a petition demanding the prohibition of the wearing of beards and side-locks. On March 14, 1794, the "Société Populaire" of Boulay, Department of Moselle, called for a prohibition of the wearing of beards by Jews and Anabaptists, since this constituted an expression of religious allegiance.

---

oven for matzos. See Archives nationales, F19–1847; Kahn, S., *Notice sur les Israélites de Nîmes* (Nîmes 1901) p. 9.

[12] Neiss, H., *op. cit.*, pp. 54– 60; "Succoth à Nice en 1799," *L'Univers israélite*, vol. LXXIX (1923) pp. 61–63.

[13] "Cedrons [sic] pour la fête des feuillage." (According to a receipt of the Jewish community of Metz, dated September 11, 1792, in the author's possession.)

[14] Lehman's Diary, pp. 14–14a.

[15] *Requête à Nosseigneurs les Etats-Généraux en faveur des Juifs* (Paris 1789) p. 8.

[16] *Journal général de la Cour et de la Ville* (1791) no. 52 ("Mandement de Mgr. Grégoire . . . exhortant à porter la barbe comme les Juifs").

In the Lower Rhine this prohibition went into effect against Jews still earlier, on November 23, 1793. On February 5, 1794, the "Société Populaire" of Jacobins in Salins-Libre called on the Jews "to shave off their beards, and the women to adopt the coiffure of the other republican women."[17] This fight against the external symbols of religious allegiance was continued during the period of the Thermidor. The *melamed* Jessel Lehman noted in 1795 in his diary several cases in which Jews had their beards and side-locks publicly cut off. They even had to pay barber's fees for this service. Among the victims was Lehman's father-in-law, who was aroused from his sleep in the middle of the night and publicly subjected to the revolutionary rite of having his beard and side-locks cut off. Incidentally, some Jews forestalled this public rite by shaving off their beards themselves. According to one source, the head of the yeshiva in Metz, Rabbi Aaron Worms, shaved off his long beard at the outbreak of the Revolution and enlisted in the national guard. When he was handed a lance, he called out in Hebrew, "This is the day that we looked for."[18]

In the Sephardic community of Peyrehorade the Jewish Jacobins were ordered to discontinue within 24 hours "the fanatical custom" of wearing *zizit* (fringed undergarments) under penalty of exclusion from the revolutionary club. One Jew, the younger Léon, declared that the Jews will not comply with this request unless the Christians will similarly discard their crosses and other religious emblems. In Alsace the wife of Abraham Auerbach (the daughter of Rabbi David Joseph Sintzheim) was tried for

---

[17] Ginsburger, M. and E., "Contribution à l'histoire des Juifs d'Alsace pendant la Terreur," *REJ*, vol. XLVII (1903) p. 203; Guir Frédéric, *Histoire de Boulay* (Boulay 1933) p. 53; Hilfendinger, P., "Actes du district de Strasbourg relatifs aux Juifs," *REJ*, vol. LXI (1911) p. 107; Reuss, R. *Séligman Alexandre . . .* (Strasbourg 1886) pp. 24–26; [Ulrich, André,] *Recueil des pièces servant à l'histoire de la Révolution à Strasbourg* (Strasbourg 1795) II, p. 199; Foesser, Js., *Meistratzheim* (Strasbourg 1939) p. 228; *La Révolution française,* vol. LII (1907) p. 554; Haguenauer, Robert, *op. cit.,* p. 17.

[18] Lehman's Diary, p. 296. Aaron Worms was rabbi of the communities in the district of Créhange up to 1786. In that year he moved to Metz, where he became head of the yeshiva and also a member of the religious tribunal. Immediately after the outbreak of the Revolution he called upon the Jews to take to productive callings. To provide the proper example, he had his son, Abraham, learn a trade. Later on this son conducted a school in Belfort. After the death of Rabbi Joseph Gougenheim, Aaron Worms became chief rabbi of Metz in 1815. His son-in-law, David Cohen, was rabbi in Marseilles. See Levy, Gerson, "Nécrologie de M. A. Worms . . . ," *La Régenération,* vol. I (1836) pp. 226–31.

wearing a hairdo (presumably a *sheytl,* a wig) that bespoke her allegiance to a religious and fanatical sect.[19]

Frequently public clashes occurred when Jews refused on certain occasions to doff their hats. In March 1792 the Jews in Bischheim encountered difficulties in taking the civilian oath of allegiance to the republic when they refused to doff their hats. On March 17, 1792, the district administration ruled that the Jews had a right to take the oath of allegiance in consonance with their religious practice. Nevertheless clashes continued and ultimately the departmental authorities had to take matters into their hands. The burgomaster was removed from his office and a special commissary was sent to administer the oath to the Jews. In December 1792 the Jews of Bischheim were not permitted to participate in the elections because they refused to doff their hats. Similar incidents occurred in the neighboring community of Schiltigheim and in other places. According to the historian Robert Anchel, Orthodox Jews occasionally refrained from taking the oath of allegiance for that reason. In some communities the rabbi, cantor or other Jewish representative took the oath in the name of all the Jews in the community. (In Soultz, for example, the oath in the name of the community was taken by the cantor, Jacob Joseph.) According to Robert Anchel, the Orthodox Jews thus found a way of taking the oath indirectly.[20]

SHEHITA

The problem of Jewish ritual slaughter (*shehita*) was always of paramount importance to the Jewish communities. In addition to its religious import it was also of economic significance in the life of the community. The Jewish butchers sold the non-kosher cuts to non-Jews at a reduced price. The non-Jewish butchers feared this competition and repeatedly demanded the expulsion of the Jews.[21]

In the early days of the Revolution some of the anti-Jewish

[19] Ginsburger, E., "Les Juifs des Peyrehorade," *REJ*, vol. CIV (1938) pp. 50–51; Ginsburger, M. and É., *op. cit.,* p. 287.

[20] Reuss, R., "L'Antisémitisme dans le Bas-Rhin pendant la Révolution," *REJ*, vol. LXVIII, p. 261; Hilfendinger, *op. cit.,* vol. XL, pp. 247–49; vol. LXI, pp. 103, 253–54; Anchel, R. *Napoléon et les Juifs* (Paris 1927) pp. 5–7.

[21] Hoffmann, *op. cit.,* vol. IV, pp. 344–45; Szajkowski, Z., *The Economic Status of the Jews in Alsace, Metz and Lorraine, 1648–1879* (New York 1954) pp. 23, 37.

elements began an anti-*shehita* campaign. The abbot F. M. Thiébault, who in the national Assembly opposed Jewish emancipation, argued that the dietary laws and Sabbath observance would
interfere with Jewish military service. However, it seems that before the Reign of Terror and later on, even during the Thermidor, the Jews had no difficulty in obtaining kosher meat. The municipal council of Ingwiller (Lower Rhine) provided kosher meat
for Jewish soldiers. On November 23, 1790, the municipal council of Bordeaux appointed a commission to regulate *shehita* in
the community. During the entire period of the Revolution the
Jewish community of Metz had a special item in its budget for
shehita.[22]

During the Reign of Terror, however, *shehita* was frequently
the subject of attack and in some places it was forbidden outright.
On December 2, 1793, the municipal council in Strasbourg assailed *shehita* not merely as a superstitious practice but also as a
health menace. Jewish butchers, the council argued, frequently
suffered from various skin ailments and thus jeopardized the
health of their customers, Jewish and non-Jewish alike. In 1794
the non-Jewish butcher J. Kempf had a cow ritually slaughtered
clandestinely for the Jewish trade. He was caught, and the meat
was confiscated and distributed to the poor. A group of Alsatian
cantors, who were arrested along with some Catholic and Protestant clergymen—as will be related below—were not permitted kosher
food. They subsisted on bread and wine and were grateful to their
non-Jewish fellow inmates for not denouncing them for observing the dietary laws.[23]

[22] Thiébault, F. M., *No. ou Récit IV* ... (Metz 1789) p. 6; Guggenbühl,
Willy, *Ingwiller* (Saverne 1951) p. 199; Ducaunnès-Duval, A., *Ville de Bordeaux, Inventaire sommaire des archives municipales. Période révolutionnaire,
1789–an VIII* (Bordeaux 1896) I, p. 133.

Toward the end of 1792 Bordeaux had two Jewish butchers, Isaac Pineda
and Michel (Municipal Archives, G8–9). The Jewish community of Metz paid
Nicolas and Etienne Petitjean for cleaning "the Jewish abattoir" on December
2, 1792, March 10, and May 5, 1793, March 31, 1796, and July 6, 1797 (receipts
in the author's possession). The *melamed* Lehman noted in his diary for 1793
(p. 26a) that his community had to provide kosher food for the Jewish soldiers
that were sent to the Wissembourg front. Lehman had to pay 5 livres in
assignats.

[23] Archives municipales de Strasbourg. Corps municipal. Délibérations,
vol. V, p. 1368; Werner, P., "Altkirch pendant la Terreur," *Revue d'Alsace,*
vol. LXXXI (1934) p. 236; Gerold, Johann Karl, *Bilder aus der Schreckenzeit,
Erlebnisse eines deportierten elsässischen Geistlichen* (Strasbourg 1883) pp. 13–
15, 45; Rumpler, F. L., *Quelques pièces fugitives* (n.p., n.d.) pp. 6–7.

CIRCUMCISION

In the early days of the Revolution circumcision was a frequent theme of ridicule and parody. The author of the popular poem "Déclaration des Droits de l'Homme et du Citoyen" (1789) wrote:

> Rien ô ma chère liberté
> Ne peut te circoncire.

One newspaper reported that the deputy Jean-Sylvain Bailly (1736–1793) went to the synagogue and had himself circumcised.[24]

No attempts to prohibit circumcision were made in the early days of the Revolution. Things were otherwise during the Reign of Terror. The district attorney of Strasbourg sharply inveighed against circumcision as a superstitious and barbarous act, ending up with a general attack on the Jews. In November 1793 a Jacobin publication called for the prohibition of circumcision not merely on the grounds of religion, but to prevent superstitious people from committing crimes unwittingly.[25]

Nevertheless the Jews continued to circumcise their male in-

During the Revolution the mayor of Issenheim prohibited the slaughter of more than one animal at a time. He also demanded that the tongues be given to him. The departmental directory of the Upper Rhine countermanded the order. The Jew Baruch of Niedernheim supplied meat for the Jewish community of Meistratzheim, Alsace, from 1794 to 1810. All sons of Jacob Alvarez Pereyre of Saint-Esprit-lès-Bayonne served in the army. One of them, Moses, ate nothing but kosher food, even when he was a prisoner of war in Spain. See Ginsburger, M., "Arrêtés du Directoire du département du Haut-Rhin relatifs aux Juifs," *REJ*, vol. LXXV (1992) pp. 61–63; Foesser, Js., *op. cit.*, p. 355; Léon, H., *Histoire des Juifs de Bayonne* (Paris 1893) pp. 417–18.

[24] Damade, Louis, *Histoire chantée de la République, 1789–1799* (Paris 1882) p. 25; *Le Courrier extraordinaire ou Le Premier arrivé*, vol. VII, no. 5 (1791); Kahn, L., *op. cit.*, p. 59.

[25] Reuss, R., *Séligman Alexandre . . .*, pp. 24–25; *Idem*, "Documents nouveaux sur l'antisémitisme . . . ," *REJ*, vol. LIX (1910) p. 252; Ginsburger, M. and E., *op. cit.*, p. 285; Mühlenbeck, E., "Il y a cent ans," *Revue d'Alsace*, vol. XLIV (1893) p. 439; *Feuille du Salut Public*, vol. I, no. 130 (Nov. 1793); Kahn, L., *op cit.*, p. 191.

Rabbi Zevi Benjamin Auerbach, in his book *Brit Avraham* (Frankfurt-on-the-Main 1860) thus memorializes his father: "The righteous shall be had in everlasting remembrance! / In honor of my father and my teacher, the excellent and pious, / Our teacher, Rabbi Abraham Auerbach, / The memory of the righteous shall be for a blessing, / Who risked his life for the sake of the commandment of circumcision in the city of Strasbourg in 1794, / When Robespierre and his associates prohibited circumcision and the practice of the other precepts and sought to obliterate their memory, / And God in His mercy saved us.

In the course of over sixty years he was a guide and father of the holy communities of Strasbourg, Forbach, Neuwied[?], Coblenz, Cologne, Bonn and their environs."

fants not only in the early days of the Revolution, but also during the Reign of Terror and the Thermidor.[26] Despite great difficulties, isolated Jewish families in the villages and small townships brought their newborn infants to the larger Jewish communities to be circumcised.[27] In many instances the ceremony had to be postponed.[28] Marranos who arrived from the French colonies[29] or from Spain and Portugal submitted to circumcision even during the Revolution.[30] Even during the Reign of Terror some *mohalim* (performers of circumcision) kept records of their operations.[31]

Heder, YESHIVA, *Mikve*

In many communities the *hadarim* and yeshivas continued in existence during the early days of the Revolution. They had to close, however, during the Reign of Terror and even during the Thermidor. The yeshiva of Mutzig, Alsace, headed by Rabbi La-

[26] On July 23, 1793, the *mohel* Isaac Schweich circumcised in Paris the son of Cantor Oury, David Lévi, afterward known as Feis Lévi. See Lambert, Mayer, "Liste de circoncisions opérées par le mohel Isaac Schweich (1775–1801)," *REJ,* vol. LII (1906) pp. 297–98.

[27] Meir Beny, born October 16, 1789, in Montauban, was brought on December 30, 1790, by his parents Juda and Sipora Beny (of Amsterdam) to Bordeaux to be circumcised (Bordeaux Municipal Archives, GG 70, fol. 77, no. 1691). On September 24, 1794, the *mohel* Mayer Weill circumcised a boy in a community in the Department of Meurthe three days after the eight-day period, because no *minyan* (the requisite ten males for congregational worship) could be assembled in those perilous days. See Schwab, Moïse, "Manuscrits hébreux de la Bibliothèque municipale du Havre," *REJ,* vol. LXVIII (1914) p. 265.

[28] On December 21, 1796, the *mohel* Isaac Schweich circumcised in Paris the eighteen-year-old Abraham Valari, who declared that his parents were Jewish (Lambert, *op. cit.,* p. 300).

[29] On September 20, 1792, Jacob Mendes Alvares Guimarlines and his wife, Rebecca d'Abraham Coën, had their two sons circumcised: Abraham, born November 23, 1786, in San Domingo, and Isaac, born there on October 29, 1788. David Astruc, born in San Domingo, the son of Daniel Astruc and of his Sephardic wife, of London, was circumcised in Bordeaux on January 7, 1792, at the age of 16 years and 12 days (Municipal Archives of Bordeaux, GG 70, fol. 89, no. 1892; fol. 90, no. 1893, 794; fol. 44, no. 196; 798, no. 33).

[30] Isaac Lopes Simoins, born in Spain, was circumcised in Bordeaux on June 29, 1791, at the age of 21. David Pareira, born in Portugal, was circumcised in Bordeaux on July 11, 1791, at the age of 16 (Municipal Archives of Bordeaux, GG 70, fol. 81, nos. 1726, 1729).

[31] Several Bordeaux circumcision registries, which were turned over during the Revolution to the municipal archives, contained entries made even during the Reign of Terror, such as the circumcision registry of the *mohel* Elie Astruc, which goes up to November 26, 1793 (*loc. cit.*). In their retreat from the Alsatian city of Trimbach the enemies destroyed the house of Rabbi Raphaël Feist, who also acted as *mohel.* In a protocol drawn up on February 14, 1796, the municipal council ascertained that of all his possessions the rabbi had saved nothing but his circumcision registry. See Reuss, R., "Documents . . . ," p. 263.

zare Aaron was still in existence on August 1, 1792. Rabbi David Joseph Sintzheim moved his yeshiva from Bischheim to Strasbourg. In Paris two *hadarim* functioned; one was conducted by the Polish *melamed,* Aron, and the other by J. Cahen. During the Reign of Terror both of these teachers took their pupils on *décadi* to the revolutionary Temple de la Raison, which was housed in the famous Notre Dame cathedral. In 1793 the yeshiva in Metz was ordered closed. The *melamdim* of Nancy were strongly criticized for teaching their pupils only Hebrew. In the last years of the Revolution Cerf Dessau conducted a yeshiva there. Quite some time after the Reign of Terror, in July 1798, the *heder* of Isaac Bamberger in Obernai, Alsace, was ordered closed for failure to observe the republican calendar, that is for observing the Sabbath.[32]

In 1790 there still existed in the Sephardic community of Bordeaux a yeshiva, maintained by the association Guemilût Hassadim. On December 21, 1792, David Lévy declared that he was "a teacher in the Jewish community." According to a document, dated December 9, 1797, he conducted a Jewish "educational establishment" (*maison d'éducation*). In 1797–98 Abraham Rodrigues and Moïze Vidal were registered as Jewish teachers. On January 31, 1799, Abraham Léal stated in a petition to the municipal council his readiness to instruct children in the Hebrew language. The authors of an anti-Jewish pamphlet in Bordeaux reported that an entire house then served as a Jewish school. In the second Sephardic community, in Saint-Esprit-lès-Bayonne there were nine Jewish teachers. On May 16, 1792, they took the oath of allegiance to the republic.[33]

Some Jews sent their children to yeshivas abroad. Mayer Charléville, who had been rabbi in Pinsk, Poland, and then rabbi in Metz, sent his sons during the Reign of Terror to study in a German yeshiva. For sending their children to yeshivas abroad the

[32] Reuss, R., "L'Antisémitisme dans le Bas-Rhin . . . ," p. 268; Cohn, Albert, "Lettres juives," *Archives israélites,* vol. XXV (1864) p. 1065; Archives nationales, F. 19–11026 (Metz); Floquet, G., "Le Culte de la Raison et de l'Etre Suprême et les fêtes civiques à Nancy pendant la Révolution," *Annales de l'Est,* vol. XIV (1900) f. 590; Reuss, "Documents . . . , " p. 273. Joseph David Sintzheim, *Yad David* (Offenbach 1799).

[33] Archives municipales de Bordeaux, GG 796, fol. 5, no. 16; G 9, Nov. 25, R 120, nos. 44, 59 and 71; Despiau et Pujol, *Réponse à un mémoire sous le nom des citoyens français professant le culte judaïque à Bordeaux* (Paris, an VII) p. 6; Ginsburger, E., *op. cit.,* p. 31.

parents and the children were placed on the lists of counterrevolutionary emigrés and their possessions were frequently confiscated.[34]

Practically every Jewish community had a *mikve* (ritual bathhouse). In Metz the *mikve* was open even during the Reign of
Terror. In 1794 the Jewish community of Nîmes was split. Seven
families seceded and built their own synagogue and *mikve*. In
Nice there was a *mikve* in 1796.[35]

NAMES, LANGUAGES

The Jews followed the revolutionary trend and gave their
children names in consonance with that trend. In Saint-Esprit-lès-
Bayonne Jewish children were given such names as Brutus, Virgil,
Delphine and Elodré. Even nicknames assumed a revolutionary
coloring. One Jew was nicknamed *Carabinier* because he had volunteered for military service.[36] Obligatory surnames for Jews, however, were introduced not during the Revolution, but under the
First Empire, in 1808.

Prior to the Revolution the Jews of France spoke diverse
tongues. The Ashkenazim spoke Yiddish, the Sephardim—Ladino,
and the Jews of the papal province of Avignon and Comtat Venaissin—Šuadit. Hebrew was used in worship and in other ritual
functions.

The Revolution attempted to abolish the various French dialects and other foreign languages spoken in France and to introduce standard French as a universal tongue. In many places, mainly in the border departments of Alsace, the French language became

---

[34] Szajkowski, Z., "Jewish Emigrés During the French Revolution," *Jewish Social Studies,* vol. XVI (1954) p. 329.

Among the *melandim* of Alsace and other parts there were a number of
foreigners, who during the Revolution encountered great difficulty in remaining in the country. Wolf David, of Berlin, who was a *melamed* in Mutzig
for 20 years, and Jacob Abraham, who hailed from Nordheim, Bavaria, were
ordered to leave the country. They appealed the order. See Hilferdinger, *op.
cit.,* p. 113.

The *melamed* Joseph Fabius, of Hellimer, Moselle Department, author
of *Bikure Yosef* conducted a *heder* in Lunéville. Later on he moved to Sarrebourg, where he continued his occupation. See *Archives israélites,* vol. VI
(1845) pp. 452–53.

[35] Kahn, S., *op. cit.* p. 9; Meiss, H., *op. cit.,* p. 53. Receipts of the Metz
community for work done in the ritual bathhouse (in the author's possession).

[36] Léon, H., *op. cit.,* pp. 256, 385, 397. At the time of the First Empire
Jews were named Napoléon. In Dijon Babette Bernheim was thus called in
1809 and in Saarunion, Lower Rhine area, there lived a Jew named Napoléon
Wolf (Municipal Archives, Registries of the *état civil*).

the external expression of revolutionary patriotism.[37] In this climate the local administrative organs frequently attempted to coerce the Jews to speak French. On January 11, 1792, the municipal council of Metz requested the federal authorities to compel the Jews to give up their language. On June 11, 1793, the authorities in the Lower Rhine prohibited the use of the Hebrew alphabet in letters sent abroad, under the pretext of guarding against espionage. On July 20, 1794, the Upper Rhine district of Colmar put forward a demand to prohibit the use of dialects.[38]

The Jews, like numerous other inhabitants, could not speak French. A traveller who visited Alsace in 1802 found that only the wealthy Jews there could speak French. As late as 1817 the rabbi of Bayonne delivered his sermons in Ladino, although the younger Sephardim began to demand French sermons. Among the Jews the use of Hebrew as well as the various vernaculars was also linked with religious practice. It is a well-known fact that in the last years of the Revolution the use of the vernacular was deemed absolutely necessary in the religious ceremonial. However, the *maskilim* fought the use of Yiddish and the Jewish intelligentsia became very soon an important segment of the disseminators of the French language and culture in Alsace and in the neighboring border departments. Noteworthy is the fact that the head of the Lorraine *maskilim,* Berr Isaac Berr, who during the Revolution had suggested that the Jews introduce into their worship the French language, later on changed his mind. In the last years of his life he came to the realization that Yiddish is an important factor in the preservation of the Jewish religion and tradition.[39]

[37] Grégoire, H., *Rapport sur la nécessité & les moyens d'anéantir le patois . . . . 16 prairial, l'an deuxième* (n.p. n.d.) 28 pp.; Campagnac, Edmond, *La langue française en Alsace sous la Révolution* (Paris 1928); Lévy, Paul, *Histoire linguistique d'Alsace et de Lorraine* (Paris 1929) II, p. 13.

[38] Archives nationales, D–III–174; *Délibération du Conseil général du département du Bas-Rhin, de Juin 1793* (Strasbourg n.d.) 4 pp.; *L'administrateurs composant le Directoire du district de Colmar à leurs concitoyens* (n.p. n.d.) 4 pp.

[39] Fesquet, J. L. F., *Voyage à Strasbourg* (n.p. [an IX]) p. 8; [Jouy, V. J. de] "L'Ermite en voyage, par l'Ermite de la Guyane," *Mercure de France,* vol. I (1817) pp. 580–81; Grégoire, H., *Réclamation des fidèles catholiques de France . . . . en faveur de l'usage primitif de la langue vulgaire dans l'administration des sacramens et la célébration de l'office divin* (Paris 1801); Szajkowski, Z., "Tsu der geshikhte fun di frantseyzishe yidn," *Davke,* no. 24, 1955, pp. 240–41.

Rabbis and Cantors

The account of the observance of Jewish laws and customs during the Revolution would be incomplete without some information on rabbis and other religious functionaries.[40]

In the early days of the Revolution, prior to the Reign of Terror, the rabbis were not exposed to persecution. On the contrary, in some departments the local authorities even made attempts to normalize rabbinical functions. Thus, for example, a Jewish young woman, Güttel Weyl, of Riedwihr, Upper Rhine, petitioned the local authorities to appoint a rabbi to judge her case against her fiancé, Joseph Briegert (Bigart), who broke his engagement. On October 21, 1790, the departmental directory assigned Rabbi Jacob Mayer, of Rixheim, to take charge of the case.[41] Otherwise, however, were things during the Reign of Terror. Rabbi Isaac Lunéeschutz, of Westhoffen, a grandson of Rabbi Shlomo Ephraim Lentshits, was imprisoned for several days.[42] Because a "liberty tree" (a symbol of the Revolution) was cut down, the *shohatim* (ritual slaughterers) and cantors of several smaller Alsace communities were arrested together with the priests. (There were no rabbis in these communities.) In Diebolsheim the cantor, a father of five children, was arrested because of this offense.[43] There was some relief in this respect during the period of the Thermidor, but even then rabbis and other religious functionaries were frequently persecuted. The aforementioned *melamed* Lehman recorded in his diary in 1795 the following: "The priest was arrested. We scholars live in great fear, for it is rumored that we, too, will be taken."[44]

Yet many rabbis continued in various communities and in all phases of the Revolution to fufill their official functions. Some of them even published their writings in France or abroad. In 1789 there appeared in Metz a new edition of *Shevut Yaacov,* responsa, by Rabbi Jacob Reysher and in 1790–91 the three parts of *Meore Or,* novellae, by Rabbi Aaron Worms. In 1793 there

---

[40] The same can be said about synagogues. See Szajkowski, Z., "Synagogues during the French Revolution of 1789–1800," *Jewish Social Studies,* vol. XX (1958) pp. 215–232.

[41] Archives départementales, Haut Rhin, L 645; Ginsburger, M., "Arrêtés . . . , " p. 48.

[42] See the preface to the book *Klilat Yofi* (Roedelheim 1813).

[43] Gerold, *op. cit.,* pp.13–15.

[44] Lehman's Diary, p. 296.

appeared in the same city the *Halakha Berura,* novellae and sermons, by Rabbi Oury Phoebus Cohen. In 1798 a new edition of
Likute Zevi, by Zevi Hirsh, son of Hayim, of Wilmersdorf, appeared in Lunéville. In the following year the printer Abraham
Friseck published there an edition of the *Selihot* (Penitential
Prayers). Other French rabbis at that time published their books
abroad. *Shomer Musar,* a moralistic tract, by the rabbi of Nice,
Raphaël Jehouda Israël, appeared in 1796 in Italy; *Shaar Naph-
tali,* novellae and responsa, by the rabbi of Haguenau, Naphtalie
Lazare Hirsh Katzenelenbogen, appeared in 1797 in Frankfurt-
on-the-Oder; *Yad David,* novellae and responsa, of Rabbi David
Joseph Sintzheim, appeared in 1799 in Offenbach. Some rabbis
wrote their works in those trying years, but left them in manuscript form. Michel Vidal was given in 1790 a pension by the
Jewish community of Avignon to enable him to complete his book
Dor holekh vedor ba. The Alsatian rabbi, Raphaël ben Nethanel
Widersheim, wrote a book in 1790–92.[45] To be sure, this entire
literary harvest was rather meager. It must be borne in mind,
however, that there were very few scholars among French rabbis
at the time of the Revolution.

Prior to the Revolution the rabbis in Alsace were appointed
by the king or the local sovereigns from a list of candidates submitted by the heads of the Jewish community. The nearly 180
Jewish communities in Alsace were entitled only to five or six
rabbis in the following communities: Haguenau and Ribeauvillé,
where the rabbis were appointed by the king; Mutzig, where the
appointment was by the bishop of Strasbourg; Bouxweiller, by the
landgrave of Hesse-Darmstadt; Niedernai, by the local nobility.
A resolution of the State Council, of August 19, 1739, gave also
the Free City of Strasbourg the right to appoint a rabbi for the
Jewish communities within its jurisdiction. In addition there were
assistant rabbis, officially designated as *demi-rabbins, commis-
rabbins* and *rabbins subalternes,* who were appointed by the Jewish communities. The census of 1784 indicated that the 19,707
Jews in Alsace (3,913 families) had 18 rabbis, 30 assistant rabbis
and 100 cantors. On the eve of the Revolution Alsace had the
following rabbis: Süssel Moyse Enusch, Ribeauvillé; Jacob Mayer,

---

[45] Bibliothèque Calvet (Avignon), ms. 2104, fol. 781; Bibliothèque Universitaire de Strasbourg, ms. 4010–4012.

Rixheim; Jacob Gougenheim, Haguenau; Wolf Reichshoffer, Bouxweiller; Simon (Moïse) Horchheim, Mutzig; Benjamin Hemerdinger, Niedernai. Süssel Moyse Enusch, a native of Frankfurt, who began to officiate as rabbi in Alsace in 1753, died in 1790. On May 14, 1790, Isaac Aaron Phalsbourg, of Mutzig, was elected rabbi of the Upper Rhine area, and the elections were confirmed by the department directory on April 18, 1791. Since Rabbi Phalsbourg could not immediately assume his position, Jacob Mayer, rabbi of Rixheim, took his place.[46]

During the Revolution Rabbi Joseph David Sintzheim, famous for the role he later played in the Napoleonic Sanhedrin, settled in Strasbourg. He was a grandson of Abraham Sintzheim, who had been rabbi in Mannheim, Germany, in 1710. Sintzheim married a sister of the Alsace communal leader Cerfberr and settled in Bischheim, where he conducted the yeshiva, established by his brother-in-law in 1778. During the Reign of Terror he was compelled to leave for Strasbourg and lost all his books. He did not become the official rabbi there for Rabbi Samuel was the incumbent of that office in 1795.[47] During the Revolution Haguenau had several rabbis, namely Jequil Gougenheim, who during the Reign of Terror was enjoined from using the title rabbi, and Naphtalie Lazare Hirsch Katzenelenbogen, author of *Shaar Naphtali*. He had been formerly rabbi in Frankfurt-on-the-Oder and at the time of the First Empire he was appointed chief rabbi of the Upper Rhine area. In the last years of the Revolution Moïse David Günzburger, assistant rabbi in Haguenau since 1772, was promoted to the position of rabbi. He remained in that community with brief interruptions to 1824. Earlier, in 1793, he took a rabbinical position in Hegenheim for a brief period, which he resumed

---

[46] Hoffmann, Ch., *op. cit.*, pp. 333–342; *Notice sur l'état des Israélites en France* (Paris 1821) p. 26; Hemerdinger, Gabriel, "Le dénombrement des Israélites d'Alsalce (1784)," *REJ*, vol. XLII, 1901, pp. 253–64; Oberlin, J. J., *Almanach d'Alsace* (1789) p. 230; Liber, M., "Les Juifs et la convocation des Etats Généraux," *REJ*, vol. LXIV (1912) p. 264.

To an inquiry of the Strasbourg Municipal Council, in May 1793, concerning the number of rabbis the Jewish leader Cerfberr furnished a list of names of such functionaries which was identical with the names of these functionaries at the beginning of the Revolution (Minutes of Strasbourg Municipal Council, vol. IV, pp. 513–14, May 11, 1793).

[47] See the introduction to Rabbi Joseph David Sintzheim's *Yad David* (Offenbach 1799); David, Max, "Josef David Sintzheim," *Das jüdische Blatt*, vol. III (1912) nos. 44 and 52; Ben-Ammi, "Le premier grand rabbin de France," *L'Univers israélite*, vol. LXIII (1907–1908) pp. 645–51; Archives dé-

JEWISH RELIGIOUS OBSERVANCE

again in 1810.[48] Jacob Moch, of Ettendorf was rabbi in Bischheim. Jacob Jequil Meyer, a disciple of Tebelé Scheuer, of Frankfurt-on-the-Main, was rabbi in Niedernai. During the Reign of Terror he was imprisoned for several days. In the period of the Thermidor Rabbi Jeger Meyer, who during the Reign of Terror was rabbi in Rixheim, was also rabbi there. Later on, he became rabbi in Strasbourg.[49]

During the Revolution Rabbi Moïse Wurmser was rabbi in Soultz. He was a son of Rabbi Isaac Aaron Phalzbourg, of Uffholz.

On April 5, 1796, however, Rabbi Jacob Joseph took there the civil oath in the name of all the Jews of Soultz. Seligmann, a *melamed* of Zillisheim, was in 1791 rabbi in Blotzheim. Mayer Rothschild, of Haguenau, was during the Revolution rabbi in Surbourg. In 1795 the sexagenarian Elias Moses of Metz, was rabbi in Westhoffen. In Marmoutier the rabbi was Menlé Wormser and in Uttenheim Moïse Bloch, known as "the sage of Uttenheim." Jacob Braunschweig was rabbi in Wintzenheim and Simeon Hachebourg, in Mutzig.[50]

Because of the hard times some communities had no funds for paying the rabbi's salary. Thus, for example, in Bouxweiller the community leader Solomon Benjamin petitioned the government to compel the Jews to pay the rabbi's salary. Other rabbis

---

partementales du Bas-Rhin, I-L, 1555; Spach, Louis, *Description du département du Bas-Rhin* (Paris 1872) III p. 73; *Idem, Die Israeliten im Elsass* (Strasbourg 1871) p. 2.

[48] Scheid, Elie, *Histoire des Juifs d'Alsace* (Paris 1877) p. 83; *Idem,* in *L'Univers israélite,* vol. LXIII–I, 1907–08, pp. 645–51; Bloch, Jos., *Le Cimetière juif de Haguenau* (Paris 1953) pp. 34–35; *Revue Orientale,* vol. 1 (1841) p. 33; *Strassburger israelitische Wochenschrift* (1906) no. 36; Nordmann, A., *Der israelitische Friedhof in Hegenheim* (Basel 1910) pp. 101–102.

[49] "Bischheim," *Bulletin de nos Communautés* (Sept. 16, 1955); "Jacob Jequil Meyer," *Souvenir et science,* vol. IV, no. 9 (1933) p. 12; Gide, Gustave, *Notice historique sur la commanderie de l'Ordre Teutonique à Rixheim* (Rixheim 1897) p. 75; Ginsburger, M., "Les mémoriaux alsaciens," *REJ,* vol. XLI (1900) pp. 128–29.

[50] Ginsburger, M., *Histoire de la communauté israélite de Soultz* (Strasbourg 1939) p. 64. *Idem.,* "Soultz," *Souvenir et Science,* vol. IV, no. 4 (1933) p. 13; *Idem.,* "Les familles juives de Soultz," *Revue d'Alsace,* vol. LXX (1923) p. 415; Nordmann, *op. cit.,* p. 108; Schwarz, "Das Rabbinat Suburg bis zu seiner Verlegung nach Sulz (1865)," *Soultz-sous-Forêts et ses environs* (Guebwiller 1924) pp. 76–77; Archives départementales du Bas-Rhin, I-L 1555 (Elias Moses); Gehler, Léon, "Les Juifs de Marmoutier," *Société d'Histoire et d'Archéologie de Saverne et environs,* nos. 3–4 (1954) pp. 25–28; Archives nationales, F 19–11004 (Jacob Braunschweig); Wickersheimer, Dr. E., *Catalogue général des manuscrits . . .* (Strasbourg-Paris 1923) p. 694 (Simeon Hachebourg).

left Alsace. Rabbi Moïse Cerf left his congregation in Alsace and became rabbi in Switzerland.[51]

Arye Leyb, son of Asher, author of *Shaagat Arye* and *Ture Even,* a former associate rabbi in Frankfurt-on-the-Main, was rabbi in Metz from 1766 to his death in 1795. After his death there was no rabbi, but a rabbinical *collegium,* consisting of Oury Phoebus Cahen, Mayer Charleville and Joseph Gougenheim, who during the Reign of Terror had been imprisoned for some time. One document indicates that in 1795 the leaders of the community drew up a set of regulations governing the election of a rabbi in 1796. In 1791 a central rabbinate was established in Sarreguemines for all the communities in the area.[52]

On the eve of the Revolution Jacob Schweich in Nancy was rabbi of the entire province of Lorraine. He was a native of Germany and was appointed rabbi in Nancy in 1786, after the death of Rabbi Jacob Perl. During the Reign of Terror his rabbinical diploma was publicly burned along with similar documents of priests, and he was compelled to leave the city.[53]

In the Sephardic community of Bordeaux David Athias, who had succeeded his father, Jacob Haïm Athias, to the rabbinical office in 1760, remained at his post during the entire Revolution. On October 19, 1795, he took an oath of allegiance to the republic. Three days later, Abraham H. Lévy, who apparently was a cantor, took the same oath. Abraham H. Lévy was the father of the Bordeaux cantor, Daniel Lévy, who delivered the eulogy on the death of Rabbi Athias in 1806.[54] In Saint-Esprit-lès-Bayonne

[51] Weill, J., "Contribution à l'histoire des Communautés alsaciens au XVIII siècle," *REJ,* vol. LXXXI (1925) p. 176; Ginsburger, M., "Histoire des Juifs de Carouge," *REJ,* vol. LXXVI (1923) p. 158.

[52] Archives départementales de la Moselle, L 532, V 152; Archives municipales de Metz, P 3–2; Anchel, R., *op. cit.,* p. 27; *Archives israélites,* vol. 1 (1840) p. 30; Landman, Salomon, Catalogue des archives consistoriales israélites de Metz (1934 Jug. 134; Cahen, Ab., *Le Rabbinat de Metz pendant la période française* (Paris 1886) p. 67; Netter, N., *Vingt siècles d'histoire . . .* (Paris 1938) pp. 230–31; Weill, Robert, "Les Juifs de la région de Sarreguemines," *Bulletin de nos communautés* (Sept. 30, 1955).

[53] Baumont, H., *Histoire de Lunéville* (Lunéville 1900) p. 361; Anchel, R., *op. cit.,* p. 19; Pfister, Ch., *Histoire de Nancy* (Paris-Nancy 1908) III, p. 333; Gain, A., "La population juive de Nancy en 1808," *Revue juive de Lorraine,* 1933 p. 270, 1934, pp. 132–33; Durival, N., *Description de la Lorraine et du Barrois* (Nancy 1774) I, p. 15; Lévy, Alfred, *Notice sur les Israélites du Duché de Lorraine* (Paris 1885) p. 15; Archives départementales de la Meurthe-et-Moselle, V. 10; *Archives israélites,* vol. III (1842) p. 598.

[54] Archives municipales de Bordeaux, I 41 & P8; p. 12; Cirot, G., *Recherches sur les Juifs Espagnols et Portugais à Bordeaux* (Bordeaux 1908) pp.

Jacob Athias was rabbi during that period. Above we have mentioned the fact that there during the Reign of Terror the Jews constituted a majority in the Jacobin Club and in the municipal council. On November 24, 1793, Rabbi Athias was confined for 24 hours to his house by the Jacobins for failure to reflect in his sermons in the synagogue the revolutionary spirit. He was ordered to preach in consonance with the current views of the time. For repeated failure to comply with this order he was imprisoned on November 30, 1793, for three days.[55] Another rabbi in Saint-Esprit-lès-Bayonne was Abraham Andrade, who collaborated with the Jacobins. In 1809 he was appointed rabbi in Bordeaux. After his death, in 1836, he was blamed for his enthusiasm for the new regime at the time of the Revolution. It is certain, however, that Rabbi Andrade helped liberalize the policies of the Jewish Jacobins in the community. It was largely owing to his efforts that no one was guillotined there during the Reign of Terror.[56]

On April 18, 1789, Elie Witte Ispir (Espir), of Prague, was reconfirmed in his position as rabbi of Avignon, which he had held since 1775, for another five years. Rabbi Espir was apparently inspired by the trends of the period. The Jewish community elections in Avignon, which took place on October 2, 1790, were conducted in a democratic spirit in consonance with the ideas of the revolutionary regime. Rabbi Espir declared in a sermon that the community leaders should no longer be elected along class lines, for this was against the spirit of equality. Pursuant to his sermon, Moïse Petit, the treasurer of the community, resigned and in his place Aaron Rouget was elected. On September 18, 1795, Rabbi Elie Gard took the oath of allegiance to the republic. On September 30, 1796, the following took the same oath: Michel Vidal, Manasses the younger, and Mardochée Valabrègue. One of these was undoubtedly the rabbi of the town. On September 10, 1798, Lyon Saint-Paul took the oath and on January 2,

80–81, 134, 152; Delvaille, L., *L'Indicateur* (Bordeaux, July 17, 1806) p. 4; Bibliothèque municipale de Bordeaux, ms. 712, I, fol. 65.

55 Ginsburger, E., *op. cit.*, pp. 106, 109. His son, Jacob Athias, was later a rabbi in Bayonne, where he died on March 23, 1842. See *Archives israélites*, vol. III (1842) pp. 194–98, 366.

56 Noë, N., *Oraison funèbre de feu Mr. Abraham Andrade, grand rabbin de Bordeaux* (Bordeaux [1837]) Prospectus; *Dominicale Bordelaise* (August 21, 1836) pp. 53–56; Léon, H., *Histoire des Juifs de Bayonne* (Paris 1893) pp. 262–64.

1801, Elie Gard again.[57] On October 3, 1797, Rabbis David Mey-
rargue and Samuel Baze took the oath in Carpentras and on September 26, 1800, Isaac Monteaux and David Haïn Mossé.[58] Rabbi
Mardochée Crémieu, of Carpentras, removed in 1790 to Aix-en-
Provence, where he apparently officiated as rabbi.[59] In Orange, in
the vicinity of Carpentras, Rabbi Isaïe Cavaillon renounced the
rabbinate on February 27, 1794, at the heights of the Reign of
Terror.[60]

On November 10, 1793, Rabbi Salomon Hesse, of Paris, publicly abjured his religion. In 1796 Michel Séligmann, a *melamed*
in the house of Berr Cerfberr, was appointed rabbi of Paris. Two
years later he became chief rabbi.[61]

On March 3, 1793, Rabbi Israel Cahen took the oath of allegiance to the new regime in Dijon. In Nice the position of rabbi
was held by the aforementioned Raphaël Jehouda Israël from
1788 to 1808.[62]

In those communities that had no rabbis, the authorities came
to regard the cantors and the *shohatim* as the representatives of
the Jewish religion. As mentioned above, they were arrested along
with rabbis and priests. During the Reign of Terror Cantor Mardochée Meyrargues publicly abjured his religion and worshipped
at the Temple of "the cult of reason" in Nîmes. On September
25, 1797, Cantor Salomon Samuel Lévy, of Fontainebléau, pledged
allegiance to the Revolution and hatred to the monarchy and
anarchy.[63]

[57] Chobaut, H., "Les Juifs d'Avignon et du Comtat et la Révolution Française," *REJ*, vol. CI (1937) p. 15, vol. CII (1937) p. 33; Prévot, Ph., *A travers
la carrière des Juifs d'Avignon* (Avignon 1702) pp. 33–36; Archives départementales de Vaucluse, actes notariales de Gaudibert, Apr. 18, 1789, ol. 560,
Oct. 2, 1790, fol. 1,094 (Espir); Bibliothèque Calvet, Avignon, ms. 2,104, Aug.
12, 1789 and I–2–29, 2 complément, an III, 9 vend., an V, I–II–10, 24 fruct.
an VI, 12 niv. an IX.
[58] Archives municipales de Carpentras, Révolution 26, 12 vendémiaire an
VI, 44, fol. 59, 4 vendémiaire an IX.
   In May 1789 Abraham Monteaux was *melamed* in Carpentras (Library
of the Alliance Israélite Universelle in Paris, R 43, p. 143).
[59] Milhaud, Th., "Notice biographique du rabbin Mardochée Crémieu,
d'Aix," *Archives israélites*, vol. II (1841) pp. 731–32.
[60] Archives départementales de Vaucluse, L–5, no. 5, district d'Orange.
[61] Kahn, L., *op. cit.*, p. 190; Anchel, R., *op. cit.*, p. 27.
[62] Archives municipales de Dijon. Délibérations, vol. VI, p. 202.
   He was rabbi in Dijon till 1841. See Gerson, A[ron], *Essai sur les Juifs
de Bourgogne . . . .* (Dijon 1893) pp. 64–65; Bauer, J., "L'Université israélite
de Nice de 1785 à 1803," *REJ*, vol. LXIII (1912) p. 272.
[63] Kahn, S., *op. cit.*, Rouvière, *Histoire de la Révolution Française dans*

CONCLUSIONS

In sum, despite the difficult times the Jews have found means of remaining loyal to their faith and tradition. But can we designate all these instances of persecution of the Jewish religion and tradition as anti-Jewish measures? Undoubtedly no. These were not measures by the revolutionary powers aimed specially against the Jews, but against all religious practice. If the Jews became victims of these measures, it was quite incidentally. Sunday observance was proscribed and along with it also Sabbath observance. Occasionally, the local authorities took advantage of these laws to settle accounts with the Jews. This was generally the case in Alsace and the neighboring departments where the tradition of Jew hatred was endemic. As late as 1790 the Jews in Niedernheim were not permitted in the streets at the time of church processions on Sundays and other holidays. Failure to observe this law was punishable by arrest.[64] When steps were taken against religious observance in these places, the Jews were the first victims. This, however, was no rule and the federal authorities were not involved. Several Jews were guillotined for speculation and espionage, but not one case is known of a Jew who was guillotined because of his religion. (Several such instances cited by various historians appear to rest on an error.)[65]

There were numerous instances of Jews who renounced the faith of their fathers. One periodical in its issue of April 1790 boasted of the fact that even the Jews were abandoning their religion. A Jew was the first speaker at the dedication of the temples of "the cult of reason," formerly Christian churches, in Bouxweiller and Ingwiller; the Sephardic community of Saint-Jean-de-Luz paid homage to the revolutionary "cult of reason." The Jew Alexandre Lambert sharply inveighed against the Jewish religion in a speech that was later published as a brochure. Earlier, we mentioned the case of the two *melamdim* that led their pupils to the temple of "the cult of reason." Rabbi Salomon Hesse declared on November 10, 1793, that he had "no other God than the God of Freedom and no other faith than the Religion

---

le *département du Gard* (Nîmes 1889) II, p. 395; Wogue, J., *L'Univers israélite*, vol. XVII (1862) pp. 367–68; *Archives israélites*, vol. V, 1844, p. 801.

[64] Foesser, Js., *op. cit.*, p. 363.

[65] Szajkowski, Z., "The Attitude of French Jacobins Toward Religion," *Historia Judaica*, vol. XVIII (1956) pp. 107–120.

of Equality." Jacob Benjamin, "of the faith of Moses, Abraham and Jacob," publicly declared that he was a French citizen and no longer an adherent of any sect. On June 28, 1794, the wealthy Alsatian merchant, Seligman Alexandre, sent out from his prison cell 100 livres for the propagation of the revolutionary religion of "the Supreme Being." This may have been an act of ingratiation with the authorities.[66]

Numerous similar instances could be cited. Frequently Jews acted thus not because of true revolutionary zeal, but because they were compelled to make public declarations against their religion. On the whole, there was no mass movement then among the Jews to break with the past. A noted exception was Saint-Esprit-lès-Bayonne, where the municipal council and the Jacobin Club were almost exclusively Jewish. And even there the matter was not quite so simple. There is enough evidence to warrant the conclusion that even there they acted the way they did for lack of choice. Their open fight against religion was in part a concession to the new regime, but also the result of a realization that they were responsible for the faith of the community and if they would not consent to conduct a moderate form of revolutionary propaganda others would do it in a more drastic fashion.

[66] *Le Journal général de France*, no. 92 (Apr. 2, 1790); *Le Batave, no.* 347 (Jan. 28, 1794); Lambert, Alexandre, *Discours de morale* .... (Rochefort n.d.) 23 pp:; *L'Univers israélite* (1864–65) p. 159; *Le Courrier républicain* (Nov. 13, 1793); *Affiches de la Commune de Paris,* no. 149 (Nov. 12, 1793); *Journal de la Montagne,* no. 1 (Nov. 1793); *Nouvelles politiques et étrangères,* no. 317 (Nov. 13, 1793); Reuss, R., *Seligman, Alexandre* ...., pp. 37–38; Kahn, L., *op. cit.,* pp. 180, 187, 189–90.

SYNAGOGUES DURING THE FRENCH REVOLUTION
of 1789-1800

ON THE EVE of the revolution of 1789 the number of synagogues in France was limited by various restrictions. In 1784 the 8,225 Jews (1,665 families) living in 58 communities of Upper Alsace were served by 53 synagogues, but only three of them were public synagogues — those in Ribeauvillé, Westhoffen, and Haguenau. All the others were rather barely tolerated conventicles. The Jews of Horburg were permitted to build a synagogue in 1773, but on condition that it be called *maison pour prier*.[1]

In the first years of the revolution, *i.e.* prior to the Terror of 1793-94, Jews were able to build synagogues openly in communities where formerly only conventicles existed. The synagogue of Buschwiller (Upper Rhine) was built in 1790; the synagogue of Pfaffenhoffen (Lower Rhine) — in 1791.[2] Prior to the revolution, the Jews in Paris unofficially had a few very small synagogues, more likely prayer rooms in private homes. In 1791 they demanded the right to open a synagogue.[3] In Versailles (Seine-et-Oise) Daniel Daniel founded a small synagogue in 1789.[4] Jews of Saint-Rémy (Bouches-du-Rhône) were permitted to open a synagogue on August 31, 1791, on condition that a non-sectarian inscription should be placed on the main entrance.[5]

The revolutionary civil authorities not only permitted synagogues but used them for various administrative purposes. As we shall see, some city councils notified their Jewish citizens of important matters through

---

The following abbreviations are being used in the notes and in the appendix: *AI—Archives israélites;* AN—Archives Nationales; CA—City archives of; Calvet—The Calvet Library of Avignon; DA—Departmental archives of; REJ—*Revue des Etudes juives; TJ—La Tribune juive* (Strasbourg); *UI—L'Univers israelite;* ZS—In the author's possession.

1. Hoffman, Charles, *L'Alsace au dix-huitième siècle,* vol. iv (Colmar 1907), p. 320.
2. AN, F[19] 11101; "Jüdische Gemeinden einst und jetzt: Pfaffenhoffen," in *TJ* (Aug. 10, 1934), p. 633.
3. *Moniteur universel* (réimpression) vol. viii (June 6, 1791), p. 628. In a document of Sept. 15, 1792, the following four synagogues are mentioned: on *rue Brisemiche, rue des Petits-Champs, rue Saint-Martin, rue du Renard.* Kahn, L., *le Comité de bienfaissance* (Paris 1886), p. 115.
4. CA, Versailles. Information furnished by the archivist Agnes Joly on Apr. 1, 1955.
5. DA, Bouches-du-Rhône, L-IV-8 bis. The Jews were represented by Jassuda de Millaud, Aron de Millaud and Carcassone. In the later part of the 19th century a synagogue existed also in Orange (Vaucluse) — on 15, *rue Victor Hugo* until April 2, 1897, when it moved to another building (Calvet, manuscript 5938, p. 115).

Originally published in *Jewish Social Studies,* vol. XX (1958).

the synagogues. The City Council of Carpentras demanded on November 27, 1792, that the rabbi announce in the synagogue that citizen Donnere was to register all births, marriages and deaths in accordance with the law of September 20, 1792, on the *état-civil*.[6] On March 9, 1793, the City Council of Bordeaux advised Rabbi David Athias that on the following day officials would read in the synagogue the appeal of the Convention to the French people.[7] On October 21, 1792, the synagogue of Metz was the scene of a patriotic celebration in honor of the military victory at Valmy on September 30. The mayor and representatives of the army which defended Thionville were invited. Rabbi Olry Cahen delivered the sermon, and Moise Ensheim wrote an ode in Hebrew which was published together with a French translation by Isaïe-Berr Bing.[8] This is the only known case of public prayers organized in a synagogue in honor of a victory of the revolutionary army. The Republic did not care much for such prayers by religious bodies and did not order them, precedents during the old regime and in the post-revolutionary years notwithstanding.

However, during the Terror of July 1793-July 27, 1794, many synagogues and other communal properties of Jewish communities were closed and nationalized. On December 7, 1793, the *Directoire* of the Lower Rhine issued a circular demanding that the confiscation of religious Jewish properties be accelerated. On February 1, 1794, the District of Strasbourg ordered the synagogues closed, and the rabbis were forced to surrender religious articles.[9] Beginning with April 11, 1794, the synagogue of Mutzig (Lower Rhine) served as a meeting hall of the local *société populaire* throughout the period of the Terror.[10] When the Jacobins of Quatzenheim (Lower Rhine) discovered that the Jews were prepared to continue holding services, all religious articles were removed from the synagogue. In Uttenheim and Westhoffen (Lower Rhine), the furniture and religious articles of the synagogues

6. CA, Carpentras, Rév. 25, Nov. 27, 1792.

7. CA, Bordeaux, P. 8.

8. *Cantique composé par le citoyen Moyse Ensheim à l'occasion de la fête civique célébré à Metz, le 21 Octobre l'an 1er de la République dans le temple des citoyens israélites* (Metz nd.), 7 pp.; AI, vol. i (1840), p. 35; "Une fête dans la synagogue de Metz en 1793," *ibid.*, vol. iii (1842), pp. 570-72; Cahen, Ab., "Le Rabbinat de Metz pendant la période française," REJ, vol. viii (1886), p. 108.

9. Reuss, R. "Antisémitisme dans le Bas-Rhin pendant la Révolution," *REJ*, vol. lxviii (1914), pp. 262-63; *L'Agent national du district de Strasbourg aux Communes* (Strasbourg 7 Messidor l'an second), 2 pp.; Reuss, R., *Séligmann Alexandre ou les Tribulations d'un israélite strasbourgeois pendant la Terreur* (Strasbourg 1880), p. 18; Hildenfinger, P., "Actes du district de Strasbourg relatifs aux Juifs," REJ, vol. lxi (1911), p. 107; Ginsburger, M., "Contributions à l'histoire des Juifs d'Alsace pendant la Terreur," *REJ*, vol. xlvii (1903), pp. 286-87.

10. Hildenfinger, *op. cit.*, vol. lx (1910), p. 236; *REJ*, vol. xlvii, pp. 286-87.

were nationalized and sold.[11] In Boulay (Moselle) crosses were burned publicly on December 17, 1793, together with religious articles taken from the synagogue.[12] The synagogue of Lunéville (Meurthe), which was built in 1785, remained open at the beginning of the Terror. At a meeting of the *société populaire* held March 14, 1794, the Jacobin Hallecourt demanded that the Jews be forced to discontinue their "grimaces(*singeries*)and illegal assemblies." They accepted his proposal that commissioners be sent at once to close the doors of the synagogue.[13] The civil authorities of Paris prohibited "rabbis, Greek pastors, Protestants, Catholics and others," to conduct religious services on the streets.[14] According to some sources the synagogue of L'Isle-sur-Sorgue was destroyed.[15]

For various reasons, however, nationalization of Jewish communal property was not as consistent or brutal as the nationalization of Catholic Church property. The closing and confiscation of synagogues and the seizure of religious articles should not be regarded as purely anti-Jewish acts, but as part of the general anti-religious policy. The above mentioned order of February 1, 1794, forbidding public prayers in the Strasbourg district was directed against churches as well as synagogues. In fact, the anti-religious policy was directed chiefly against the power-

11. Hildenfinger, *op. cit.,* vol. lxi, p. 115; "Sterbende jüdische Gemeinden: Quatzenheim," *TJ* (June 1, 1934), p. 437. Luntschuetz, Rabbi Abraham Isaac, *Kelilat Yofi* (Rödelheim 1813), preface; Reuss, R., "Documents nouveaux sur l'antisémitisme dans le Bas-Rhin 1794 a 1799," in *REJ,* vol. lix (1910), pp. 260-61.
12. Guir, Frédéric, *Histoire de Boulay* (Boulay 1933), pp. 53, 72.
13. *UI,* vol. xc (1934-35), p. 801; Lévy, Alfred, *Notice sur les israélites du Duché de Lorraine* (Paris 1885), p. 17; Parisot, Robert, *Histoire de Lorraine,* vol. iii (Paris 1924), p. 240; Beaumont, H., *La Société populaire de Lunéville, 1793-1795* (Nancy 1889); idem, *Histoire de Lunéville* (Lunéville 1900), p. 363; Lang, P., "Les Juifs de Lunéville et la petite histoire," *Revue juive de Lorraine,* vol. xi (1935), p. 154.
14. *Les Annales de la République Française,* vol. ii, no. 295 (Oct. 19, 1793); Kahn, Léon, *Les Juifs de Paris pendant la Révolution* (Paris 1898), p. 181.
15. "Le vandalisme révolutionnaire détruisit entièrement la synagogue et le ghetto" (minutes of a meeting of Jewish representaitves from the arrondissments of Avignon, Orange and Apt, Nov. 14, 1806 (ZS). But this is a much exaggerated statement which does not do justice to the events as they actually happened, although the religious silver articles were confiscated. In the beginning of 1791 most Jews had already left the community, and by July 1793 only a few families had remained there. In 1794, they turned over the keys to the civil authorities and the synagogue was nationalized. Soon the deserted houses of the ghetto started to fall apart, only the nationalized synagogue remaining intact. On April 2, 1797, the City Council wanted to return the key sof the synagogue to the few remaining Jewish families who, however, refused to take charge of the building, probably because of the outstanding old debts owed by the Jewish community to the Christian creditors. The civil authorities then impounded all valuables. But on September 25, 1798, the Jews Joseph Millaud, Moïse Carcassonne and Mardochée Millaud asked the civil authorities for permission to practice openly their religion (probably in a small synagogue in a private home). *CA,* L'Isle-sur-Sorgue; De Joannis, *Le Fédéralisme et la Terreur à L'Isle-sur-Sorgue* (Avignon 1884), p. 240; Chobaut, H., "Les Juifs d'Avignon et du Comtat et la Révolution française," *REJ,* vol. ci (1937), p. 32.

ful Catholic Church which helped organize the campaigns against the new regime. The action against the religious minorities of Protestants and Jews should be regarded only as small by-products of an uproar. Jews and Protestants were not as powerful or dangerous to the Republic as the Catholics were and, in most cases, they were considered friendly to the new regime. Still, there was the question of principle—the fight against all religious symbols, without exception. It was impossible to close churches and allow the Jews to keep their synagogues open. According to the historian Edourd Gézardin, the closing of the Lunéville synagogue by the Jacobins was a repressive act against Jewish "mercantilism." This can not be proven, although in some provincial centers, anti-Jewish feelings did prevail on such occasion. But this was not done as a result of federal anti-Jewish policy or by instructions from the central authorities in Paris. The synagogues were not as rich as the Catholic churches for they did not possess as many gold and silver articles and hence did not suffer as much. Yet most of their possessions were confiscated. The same can be said of the Protestants.[16]

In a few cases Jews willingly gave up religious articles, but in most instances they had to be forced to do by threats of severe repressive measures against the entire communities. On November 4, 1793, the City Council of Nancy decided to invite the Jews to surrender as had the Catholics, those religious articles of gold and silver which were not absolutely neded for religious ceremonies. This decision was made public in a circular dated November 13 (or 15) and addressed to the "republicans and philosophers of the former Jewish religion." The Jews had no choice, and on November 19, 1793, they gave up the religious articles. A short time later the synagogue was closed altogether.[17] On November 10, 1793, the *prêtre juif* [rabbi] of Paris, Salomon Hess, brought religious objects to the *section des amis de la patrie*. He stated: "The Jews, too had their superstitious toys. The nation, which was for such a long time oppressed, outlawed and banished from the society by fanatical priests, this nation regained her natural rights of citizens and men thanks to the enlightenment of reason and the French philosophy, thanks to the glorious Holy Constitution . . . We have no other God than the one of Liberty, no other faith than of Equality. This God and this faith do not ask for prayers but to be defended." It is not

16. Gérardin, Édouard, *Histoire de Lorraine* (Paris 1925), p. 79; Reuss, R. *Les églises protestantes d'Alsace pendant la Révolution* (Paris, 1906), pp. 183-84.
17. Lionnois, J. J., *Histoire des villes vieille and neuve de Nancy* . . . vol. ii (Nancy 1811), pp. 506-08. *CA*, Nancy, minutes, vol. 9, p. 275; vol. 10, p. 160; *AI*, vol. v (1844), pp. 415-16; *La Vérité israélite*, vol. vii (1862), p. 617; Pfister, Chr., *Histoire de Nancy*, vol. ii (Paris- Nancy 1908), p. 506, vol. iii, p. 333; Floquet, G., "Le Culte de la raison et de l'Etre Suprême et les fêtes civiques à Nancy pendant la Révolution," *Annales de l'Est*, vol. xiv. (1900), p. 544; Anchel, R., *Napoléon et les Juifs* (Paris 1928), p. 16.

known if he did this in his own name, or on behalf of a religious Jewish body but his gesture was praised as service to the "God of liberty and the religion of equality" and 1,200 copies of a pamphlet on this event were published. As this happened in many other localities, the Jews of Paris, too, thought it necessary to voluntarily give up some religious articles in order to save the Jewish community from anti-religious persecution. Thus, religious articles from the synagogues at *rue du Renard Méry, rue des Petits Champs* and No. 94 *rue des Boucheries* were turned over on November 11, 1793, and March 13, 1794. On this occasion, one Jew stated to the Convention: "Our fathers transmitted to us laws which came from the top of a mountain; the laws which you give to France come from a mountain which we venerate nonetheless. We have come to thank you." [18]

On October 15, 1790, the City Council of Avignon discussed a proposition made on October 5, by the local friends of the Constitution which demanded that the religious institutions should give up their religious silver articles. The proceeds were to be used to buy wheat for the winter. On the following December 30 the City Council decided to ask the Jews to give up their religious silver articles. Rabbi Elie Vitte Spire and the community leaders *(baylons)* were asked to state under oath which articles were absolutely necessary for the maintenance of religious services. During the Terror, on October 30, and on November 25, 1793, the Jews of Avignon "willingly" gave up a large number of religious articles; other articles were confiscated. Soon the synagogue was closed altogether and confiscated.[19] The synagogue of Carpentras was confiscated, and on November 30, 1793, the City Council presented it to the Jacobins as a place to hold their meetings. According to the diary of abbott F. C. Durand (1787-1818), the Jews tried to pay a large sum to prevent this profanation of their synagogue, but their application was rejected. In fact, the situation was so dangerous that the Jews thought it safer to give up the synagogue on their own accounts. On February 21, 1794, a Jewish delegation consistong of Milhaud Jr., David Mayrargues, Mossé Crémieux, Sabatheny Crémieux and

---

18. *Extrait des délibérations de l'assemblée générale de la section des Amis de la patrie, du 20 brumaire de la deuxiéme année républicaine et indivisible* (Paris an II), 4 pp.; Schwab, M., in *AI*, vol. xxix (1868), pp. 645-46; Kahn, *op. cit.*, pp. 158-59, 188, 190; *Le Journal de la Montagne*, vol. ii, no. 163 (Apr. 25, 1794); Grégoire, H., *Histoire des sectes religieuses*, vol. iii (Paris 1828), p. 421.

19. *CA*, Avignon, vol. xi, fol. 76, 112, Oct. 15 and Dec. 30, 1790. Calvet, ms. 4206, fol. 170, Oct. 30, 1793; *Courrier d'Avignon*, no. 261 (Nov. 27, 1793); *La Gazette française* no. 705 (an II); Moureau, [Agricol], *De l'incompatibilité entre le judaïsme et l'exercice des droits de cité* . . . (Paris 1819), p. 78. ("En 1793, les vases sacrés en argent de la synagogue d'Avignon, furent comme ceux de nos églises, envoyes à la trésorie nationale à Paris"); Chobaut, *op. cit.*, p. 31. According to Prévot, A., *A travers la carrière des Juifs d'Avignon*, I-II (Avignon 5701), p. 18, the synagogue was closed on September 20, 1791, which is not correct.

Samuel Baze turned over the keys of the synagogue to the City Council. A Jewish spokesman stated that to God they can pray everywhere and since the Jews were much interested in the Republican order they would comply with the national desire and be united with the other citizens in the Temple of Reason, "where all men are brothers." [20] The most valuable religious articles of the Carpentras synagogue were confiscated and sent to the national treasury. The National Agent for the District of Carpentras reported on February 15, 1794, that the sacred figures of the churches went into the national melting-pot in the good company of the synagogal objects in spite of the reported antipathy existing between them.[21] It appears that in Cavaillon the synagogue remained in the hands of the Jews. But on December 9, 1793, the General Council decided to inform the Jews of a request of the *société populaire* concerning the religious silver objects of the Jews, and asking the Jews that they should participate in helping the fatherland.[22] Before the revolution 170 Jews (37 families), most from the four communities of the Papal Province, lived in Nîmes (Gard). During the Terror they were the first to turn in (on December 8, 1793) 930 livres and seventeen religious articles made of silver, which were taken from the synagogue on *rue Carreterie*. The Jews were, most probably, forced to do so; still, they continued to pray in an unofficial synagogue.[23]

Whenever possible, Jews, secretly, and in many cases openly by legal means, fought against the nationalization of synagogues and reli-

20. City Library of Carpentras, manuscript 1186, Durand's diary written in the form of letters, 170th letter, fol. 115. Following is the text of the statement made by the Jewish representatives, as noted in the minutes of the City council, "Citoyens magistrats nous venons ici deposer dans le seing de votre assemblée les clefs de notre cy devant synagogue, nous somes trop interessés au maintien de l'ordre républicain pour ne nous pas conformer au bien public et au voeu national, le dieu que nous croyons le ciel de ciele ne pouvant le contenir on peut l'adorer par toute la terre, nous alons nous reunir tous ensemble au temple de la raison là où tous les hommes sont frères et nous prierons dieu ensemble en suhaitent la prosperité de la république une et indivisble." *CA* Carpentras, Rev. 51, 3 ventôse an II; Bauer, Jules, "Les Juifs comtadins pendant la Révolution," in *REJ*, vol. liv (1907), p. 284; Chobaut, *op. cit.*, vol. cii, p. 32.
21. ". . . tous les saints sont dans le creuzet national . . . on leur associe les joujoux et less grelets de la sinagogue de Carpentras, le tout part de compagnie et de très bon accord, malgré l'antipathie que l'on supossit entre eux." *DA*, Vaucluse 4 L 36, 27 pluviôse an II. On the confiscations see also:: Valagrègue, Adrien, *Mémoire addressé à monsieur le ministre des cultes par le consistoire israélite de Marseille en réponse à la délibération du conseil municipal de Carpentras (août 1896), qui conteste l'existence légale de la communauté israélite de cette ville* (Lyon 1896), 15 pp.
22. *CA*, Cavaillon, minutes, 19 Frimaire an II; Chobaut, *op. cit.*, p. 32.
23. At the end of 1794 seven Jewish families, who opposed the existing Jewish Community council, founded their own synagogue on *rue Roussy*, which was completed in 1796. *CA* Nîmes, Club populaire, 18 Frimaire, an II, Kahn, S., "Les Juifs à Nîmes . . . " in *REJ*, vol. lxvii (1911), p. 243; *idem, Notice sur les Israélites de Nîmes* (Nîmes 1901), p. 9; Rouvière, F., *Histoire de la Révolution dans le Gard*, vol. ii (Nîmes 1889), p. 104. In 1806 a synagogue existed also in Pont-Saint-Esprit, *DA*, Gard, 6-V-43.

gious articles. Of special interest is such a case in the community of Metz. During the Terror the Jacobins of Metz destroyed the religious symbols in the synagogue and on this occasion made a statement that the same thing was done with the churches. One newspaper wrote that the Scrolls of the Law in the Metz synagogue were destroyed. "The laws of this clever imposter, written on parchment, will serve to make drums to sound the charge and to throw down the walls of new Jericho." For a while the principal synagogue served as a stable for cattle. A large number of religious articles from the principal and smaller synagogues was confiscated. Various non-religious properties confiscated from a few hundred Jewish families, or items turned in by them voluntarily, were deposited in the synagogues where an inventory was made on October 24, 1793, and from there the articles—19,640 pounds of copper, as well as clothing and other items—were taken away to the warehouses.[24] According to an inventory of confiscated religious articles, on January 23 and 24, 1794, the following synagogues existed then in Metz: the Old Synagogue (with two synagogues for women), the main synagogue, called New Synagogue, the synagogue of Nathan Terquem, the synagogue established from the funds left in the will of Abraham Schwabe. The Old Synagogue was nationalized, but only later during the Thermidor, in the year IV, the authorities put it up for sale as a nationalized property; the Jews protested. In a petition to the departmental *Directoire* the Jews stated that the sale of the synagogue, which is a place of prayer, would be against the spirit of the laws on freedom of religious practice. They also put forward another very strong argument against the proposed sale. Prior to the Revolution the Jewish community had borrowed large sums from Christian creditors. During the Revolution the Jewish community asked the Government to take over its properties and also pay its debts, as was done with the debts owed by the Christian religious corporations abolished by the new regime. The Jews stated that as long as their debts were not yet nationalized, the synagogue could not be nationalized and sold. Anyway, the synagogue should be regarded as a piece of property mortgaged by the creditors of the Jews. The *Directoire* decided on April 23, 1796, not to sell the synagogue as long as the status of the Jewish community and the debts were not cleared up. This decision was later approved by the Ministry of Finances in charge of the sale of nationalized properties. The synagogue was returned to the Jews and reconditioned by the *parnesim* who

---

24. *Le Courrier républicain,* vol. ii, no. 100 (Jan. 29, 1794); *CA* Metz, I P 3 and I S 75, fonds Barbé, rue de l'Arsenal (on December 26, 1794, Ricard, Commissioner of War, sold 200 sheep which were penned up in the synagogue); Cahen, *op. cit.,* vol. xiii, pp. 107, 113; Anchel, *op. cit.,* p. 15, 17; *DA,* Moselle, L 532. According to one document, the following religious articles confiscated from the synagogues were depostied at the *Société populaire* of Metz: 46 Torah Scrolls, 88 other items and 2 sacs of birth certificates (*CA,* Metz, 3 P 1).

were elected at the assembly on September 3, 1795. The former Jewish community of Metz also possessed other properties, including many houses which were rented to private persons. Legally, the Christian creditors controlled all financial activities of the former Jewish community, not only the rent of the houses, but also the seats in the synagogues. Thus, on May 7 and 15, 1796, houses and synagogue seats were rented publicly: 68 seats for men and 139 for women of the main synagogue, 61 seats for men and 52 for women of the synagogue in the yard. The total income of the rent amounted to 1,244 livres 10 sols. In the year VII (1798-99) the Christian creditors put up for sale not only the houses of the Jewish community and the seats in the synagogues, but also religious articles, i.e., 17 Ten Commandments Tablets.[25]

Many Jewish communities maintained secret synagogues during the Terror. The synagogue of Haguenau (Lower Rhine) was closed in February 1794, but the Jews opened a secret synagogue in a factory of colza oil, to which they went through a neighboring house belonging to the Jew, Samuel Ah. In Westhoffen the Jews prayed secretly.[26] According to the testimonies of a Jewish peddler and rabbi, Mendel Prague, the Jews of Paris prayed secretly in a cellar. An Alsatian Jew named Baruch was the cantor. In order to avoid public attention, a Jew stood in the yard singing revolutionary songs.[27]

After the Terror, the Jews were able to reopen many of their synagogues, or even to build new synagogues where none had existed before, as the Christians did with churches. The Jews of Strasbourg were again able to open synagogues. There were four in all — to be considered more as conventicles — in February 1796, all in the private houses of Scheyen Netter, Abraham Auerbach, Moïse Isaac and Joseph

25. *CA*, Metz, 3 P 1-2, 4; *DA*, Moselle, V 166; *AN*, F^{19} 11014; Anchel, *op. cit.*, p. 27. It should be noted that the Sephardic Jews of Bordeaux used a very different legal argument against the nationalization and sale of their cemetery. They stated that they were never organized as a corporation, but only as a philantropic society and, therefore, their property should not be nationalized. This subject will be dealt with separately.

26. Sheid, Elie, "Histoire de la synagogue de Haguenau," in *UI*, vol. xxxviii (1883), pp. 758-61, vol. xxxix (1883), p. 26; *idem*, "Histoire des Juifs de Haguenau pendant la période française," in *REJ*, vol. x (1885), pp. 230-31. On Westoffen see note 11.

27. Ben Lévi, G., "Mémoires d'un colporteur juif", in *AI*, vol. iii (1842), p. 463; Prague, H., "Les Juifs de Paris sous la Terreur," *ibid.*, vol xl (1879), pp. 221-22.

Lehmann.[28] When the Decree of February 21, 1795, again permitted religious activities, the synagogue of Haguenau was reopened, but only as late as July 1795. As soon as the Terror was over, at the end of 1794, the Jews of Quatzenheim whose synagogue had been closed, built another.[29] The Departmental authorities of Upper Rhine granted the request of June 8, 1795, by Samuel Lévi, Michel Schwob, Jacques Brunschwig and Leib Brunschwig of Habsheim and turned over to the Jews the synagogue which during the Terror had been used as a military warehouse.[30] The synagogue of Boulay (Moselle) too, was reopened. As late as January 17, 1799, religious ceremonies in public were prohibited and — it is almost symbolical — the synagogue of Boulay was again transferred from *rue de Four-Banal* to the *rue des Juifs*.[31] In Epinal (Vosges) Michel Hess, Abraham Salomon and Joseph Israel signed a statement on April 21, 1797, to the effect that they intended to gather for prayers on Friday evenings and Saturdays in the house of Abraham Salomon located at 98, *rue de Petit Rualménil*.[32] After the Terror, the Jews of Paris had one or more small synagogues. In Fontainebleau (Seine-et-Marne) on August 4, 1795, the Jews demanded permission to open a synagogue in a house known as *La Synagogue*.[33] It seems that, when the Terror was over, the Jews of Avignon still owned some communal properties connected with the synagogue. They surely had unofficially one or more small synagogues in private

28. On September 12, 1797, Baruch Aaron notified the civil authorities that the Jews would pray in the house of the Wittersheim brothers on No. 8, *rue Burlée*. Similar notifications were made on September 21, 1797, by the Jews concerning a synagogue in a house of Léopold Samuel on No. 5, *rue de la Chaîne;* on November 22, 1797, by Issac Heyman Netter about the transfer of the above mentioned synagogue in the house of Joseph Lehman on No. 12, *rue du Jeu des Enfants* to No. 14, *rue du Vieux Marché au Vin.* Reuss, R., "Documents . . ." p. 265; Glaser, Alfred, *Geschichte der Juden in Strassburg* (Straussburg 1894), p. 57;CA, Strassbourg, minutes of the *Corps municipal*, vol. 12, p. 213, vol. 13, pp. 748, 811. On the Strasbourg synagogues of the 1800's-1830's see Seyboth, Ad., *Strasbourg historique et pittoresque* . . . (Strasbourg 1894), p. 200; *idem, Das alte Strassburg* (Strassburg 1890), p. 66.

29. Soon afterwards two conventicles were opened in Haguenau in the houses of Abraham Aron Moch and David Reims. On August 4, 1798, the Jewish tavern-keeper Jacob Abraham demanded permission to rent a house to a few Jews to be used as a synagogue. See note 26. On Quatzenheim see note 11.

30. DA, Upper Rhine, L645; Ginsburger, M., "Arrêtes du Directoire du département du Haut-Rhin relatifs aux Juifs (1790)," *REJ*, vol. lxxv (1922), p. 66.

31. See note 12.

32. *CA*, Epinal, minutes, D 40, 2 florécal an V.

33. *AI*, vol. L (1885), p. 362; *L'Abeille*, Fontainebleau (Oct. 25, 1889). Salomon-Samuel Lévy, who died in 1844, was over 50 years cantor in Fontainebleau, *AI*, vol. v (1844), p. 801; *UI*, vol. xvii (1862), pp. 367-68. On Paris see note 18.

homes.[34] But only from the year IX (1800) on do we find official documents concerning a synagogue in Avignon.[35] Soon after the Law of May 30, 1795, on the freedom of religion became known, the Jews of Carpentras requested that their synagogue should be returned to them. Their request was discussed by the City Council on September 10, 1795, and the matter was postponed until the next meeting where, most probably, it was not discussed either. Only in 1800 the matter was taken up again and as a result the synagogue was not given back to the Jews as their property, but rented to them. On May 12, 1800, the Jews paid the rent for one year, and on May 15, the City Council granted a petition signed by David Meirargues, Samuel Baze, Joseph Samuel, Moise Meyrargues, Abraham Mossé Lyon, David Valabrègue, Manuel Baze and Isaïe Valabrègue requesting the keys of the synagogues.[36] On September 18, 1795 the Jews of Dijon (Côte-d' Or) were

34. "Etat de situation d'une salle d'assemblée provenant des Juifs. L'An quatre et le troisiéme jour de germinal, nous Jean Baptiste Guérin, architecte des domaines nationaux, et Pierre Bremond, commissaire des propriétés nationales, nous nous sommes transportés à la Carrière des Juifs pour y prendre l'état de consistance d'une salle servant cy devant aux fêtes des juifs, étant présent le C^n Mardochée Valbrègue, Juif proposé pour occuper la d^{te} salle . . ." (ZS); Chobaut, op. cit., vol. cii, p. 35.

35. Thus, e.g., on January 2, 1801, Elie Gard stated to the Mayor his desire to exercise the functions of rabbi in a house [synagogue] of the Jewish ghetto and promised loyalty to the Constitution. CA, Avignon, S-2 & V (The Catholic priests made such statements on Dec. 24, 1800). When it became urgent for the city to demolish the synagogue in order to open a road from the ghetto to the Place Neuve the Prefect of Vaucluse decided, on July 8, 1801, to compensate the Jews by giving back to them their old synagogue which had been nationalized during the Revolution. On the previous day, on July 7, the Mayor Guillaume Puy fils wrote to the Prefect, that this would attract to the city Jews from communities having no synagogue and help to develop the city's commerce. Three days later, on July 10, 1801, the Mayor and his deputies came to the ghetto and officially installed the Jews in their old synagogue. In the presence of the city officials and the Jews' rabbi Michel Vidal took the oath of loyalty to the Constitution. Ibid., V; AN, F^{19}1847; Chobaut, op. cit., vol. cii, p. 32. Following is the minute of the act of July 10, 1801: "Aujourd'hui vingt un Mesidor an 9, à sept heures du Soir, nous Maire [Puy fils] & adjoints de cette ville d'Avignon en exécution de l'arrêté du préfet de ce dépt. en date du 19 duc^t nous sommes rendus dans un quartier de cetted d^{te} ville, habité depuis longues anns par des citoyens professant de la religion juive, à l'effet de les installer dans le Temple qu'ils ont destiné à l'exercice de la religion après avoir au préalable exigé du rabbin [Michel Vidal] la promesse de fidelité voulee par la loi, nous avons fait ouvrir le d. Temple en présence did. Rabbin & des principaux Juifs de la Carrière et l'avons nommément lui Rabbin mis en possession du d. Temple . . . "

36. CA, Carpentras, Rév. 42, 24 fructidor an iii; 24, 25 floréal an viii; Chobaut, op. cit., pp. 33-35.

granted permission to open a synagogue in the house of Scein Cahen, *rue du Tillot.*[37]

The Jews of Bordeaux even requested that the religious articles confiscated during the Terror should be returned to them. At the outbreak of the revolution the Bordeaux Jews possessed five or six synagogues.[38] Most of them continued to exist until the Terror. But even before the Terror, on September 12, 1792, the Jecobin Léveque, at a meeting of the *Société des Amis de la Liberté,* denounced a Christian who did not work on Saint Matthews' Day, and the Jews because they kept their silver articles in the synagogue.[39] During the Terror the synagogues were closed, and many valuable religious objects confiscated. On November 14, 1793, and the following days the commissioners Gaudric and Cocul of the departmental revolutionary committee visited six synagogues confiscating all religious articles they could find. They appointed Daniel Rophé, sexton of the private synagogue belonging to the rich merchant David Gradis, to collect the religious articles from all other synagogues. This probably explains the fact that very few articles were actually confiscated.[40] In Bordeaux, too, the Jews were forced to give up "willingly" religious articles. Thus, on November 12, 1794, they brought to the *Club National* a Scroll of the Law.[41] After the Terror, the Jews requested a building for a synagogue and on December 9 and 24, 1796, the synagogues of David Gradis on *rue Bouhaut* and of Jacob Escaramella on *rue des Augustins,* were registered with the municipal authorities.[42] Rabbi Athias again in the main synagogue made announcements of public interest, *e.g.,* about the election law

37. On September 24, 1795, they were given permission to move the synagogue to a house on *rue de la Maison Rouge.* On October 14, 1795, the City Council decided to investigate the molestation of Jews in their synagogue. It was probably because of this molestation that the synagogue was moved again to a house on *place du Morimond* by a permission given November 28, 1795. *CA,* Dijon, minutes, vol. x, p. 785, vol. xi, pp. 3, 26, 66; *DA,* Côte-d'Or, L 1195. On the Dijon synagogues of the 19th century see Gerson, A[ron], *Essai sur les Juifs de la Bourgogne* (Dijon 1893), pp. 65-67.

38. According to entries in the rgistries of births, circumcisions, marriages and deaths of the Bordeaux Jews. *CA,* Bordeaux, CG; Cirot, G., *Recherches sur les Juifs Espagnols et Portugais à Bordeaux* (Bordeaux 1908), p. 178; Leroux, Alfred, *La colonie germanique de Bordeaux,* I (Bordeaux 1918), p. 231.

39. *DA,* Gironde, L 2159.

40. *DA,* Gironde, L2106, 2144, 2177, 2183, 2188, 2199, 2203, 2214. The following six synagogues were visited: The synagogue of Payse Sciza (on No. 32 *rue Bouhaut*), of the Talmutora (on *rue Neuve des Enfants Trouvés*), of Cardoze *(rue Bouhaut),* [Jb.] Fernand (on the same street), the Cathedral of the Hebra *(Cathedralle hebra, rue des Augustins),* the little synagogue *(Petite synagogue,* on the same street).

41. *CA,* Bordeaux, 65 D 15.

42. Ducaunnès-Duval, G., *Ville de Bordeaux. Inventaire sommaire des Archives municipales. Periode revolutionnaire 1789- an VIII,* vol. iv (Bordeaux 1929), p. 495; *CA,* Bordeaux, P 8.

of August 12, 1796.[43] Already in the beginning of the Thermidor representatives of synagogues and private citizens sent petitions in which they requested the return of the religious articles confiscated during the Terror. Most of them stated that they turned over the religious articles to the above mentioned Daniel Rophé. Some jointly gave detailed descriptions of the confiscated objects. On June 29, 1795, eleven Jews signed a collective petition in which they requestd that the religious articles confiscated during the Terror, still intact, should be given back.[44]

This legal return to the open practice of religion after the Terror developed slowly.[45] In many communities synagogues which had been confiscated during the Terror were sold as national property during the Thermidor. Where final sales were not accomplished the Jews were able to recover their synagogues only as late as the beginning of the First Empire (*e.g.*, in Avignon).

In a few cases, nationalized churches were transformed into synagogues. On January 2, 1796, the Jews of Toulouse (Haute Garonne), about eighty in number demanded in a petition signed in their name by Abraham Moise, for permission to open a synagogoue in the nationalized church of *Saint-Rome*. Six months later they were granted permission to open a synagogue in the smaller nationalized church *des Pénitents*. We do not know if the project was realized. For in a memorandum of 1806 the Jews of Toulouse stated that they were poor and had no synagogue.[46] In most of those cases Jews probably did not even know the religious origin of the buildings bought by them for use as synagogues. But even if they did know, it could hardly be taken as an act of religious bigotry. In many more cases Christians purchased nationalized synagogues and, in fact, buying of nationalized property was then a patriotic act.[47] Even in the nineteenth century, church build-

43. On Aug. 12, 1796, the civil authorities of Bordeaux asked the rabbi to announce in the synagogue the regulations on the election law. On Aug. 21, rabbi Athias replied that he would post the announcement on the door of the synagogue and read its contents during the Sabbath prayer. Detcheverry, Ad., *Histoire des Israélites de Bordeaux* (Bordeaux 1850), p. 100; *UI*, vol. xviii (1862-63), p. 329.

44. Such petitions were sent by Moise Salom (Jan. 13, 1795); Isaac Lange (on the same date); Benjamin Petit in the name of his mother, the widow Jb Petit (Jan. 15, 1795); Elie Perpignan (Jan. 20, 1795), widow Rodrigues, her sons and brothers (Jan. 23, 1795); Alexandre jr. (Jan. 24, 1795); Vidal Lange and his son (Jan. 26, 1795); Abraham Alvarès de Leon (on the same date); and Abraham Moraes (a non-dated petition). DA, Gironde, L2177, 2203, 2214; Q 881.

45. The religious teacher and scribe Jessel Lehman of Ribeauvillé, the brother of Issachar Baer Lehmann, former rabbi of Soultz, noted on September 26, 1795, in his diary written in a ciphered Yiddish, that the Jews were praying again, but still without prayer shawls. (Diary in the Alsatian museum of Strasbourg, p. 30 B.)

46. Gros, J., "Les Juifs de Toulouse pendant la Révolution et l'Empire", in *Revue des Pyrénées,* vol. xviii (1906), pp. 250-251.

47. Szajkowski, Z., "Jewish Participation in the Sale of National Property During the French Revolution," Jewish Social Studies, vol. xiv (1952), pp. 291-316.

ings nationalized during the revolution were transformed into synagogues.[48]

Some synagogues suffered from attack by mobs; this, however, was not a direct result of the anti-religious policy. Thus, on March 21, 1798, the synagogue of Pfastatt was subject of a pogrom. A few Christian attackers were arrested, but freed when an indemnity of 2,400 francs was paid to the Jewish community. Earlier in 1792 soldiers entered the synagogue of Metz, their disorderly conduct interfering with the services. The Jews complained to the civil authorities and, on April 6, 1792, Lafayette, Commanding General of the Northern Army, wrote to the City Council of Metz that "the soldiers of the Constitution should know that religious freedom is one of the most sacred principles." A similar occurrence is reported in Nancy. (In 1788 the Jews were granted permission to build a synagogue there, which was inaugurated in 1790.) Prior to the Terror, the Jews of Nancy were not persecuted because of their religion, but in December 1791 and February 1792, crowds of non-Jews, civilians and military men invaded the synagogue, probably out of curiosity, and made a lot of noise. On December 26, 1791, the City Council forbade such visits to the synagogue but on February 29, 1792, the City Council had to discuss another complaint lodged by the Jews on the same subject.[49]

Of special interest are the events in Saint-Esprit-lès-Bayonne. Prior to the Revolution, the Jews of Saint-Esprit-lès-Bayonne had six synagogues.[50] During the Terror the Club of the Jacobins and the municipality of Saint-Esprit were composed mainly of Jews. It is, thus, of a

48. The church *Commanderie de Malte* of Dijon (Côte-d'Or), which was used as a warehouse during the Revolution, was bought in 1820 by the Jews and converted into a synagogue. *Journal politique et littéraire de la Côte d'Or* (Oct. 4, 1820), pp. 1003-04. The church of *Sainte- Marie-la-Petite* of Rouen (Seine infèrieure) which was nationalized in May 1791 and on May 1, 1792, sold to Nicolas Midy for the sum of 40,500 livres, was purchased by the Jewish community on August 25, 1865, for 28.000 francs and transformed into a synagogue. CA, Rouen, Q. The Jews of Verdun (Meuse) bought the nationalized *Eglise des Jacobins*, which was converted into a synagogue and inaugurated in October 1805. Chaize, Léon, *Histoire de Verdun*, 1789-1870 (Verdun, n.d.), p. 171. On the general religious problem of transforming former churches into synagogue in the older periods see Baron, Salo W., *The Jewish Community*, I (Philadelphia 1942), p. 230; on the same subject for the 19th century see Eisenstein, J. D., *Ozar Dinim u-Minhagim* (New York 1938), p. 41.

49. Ginsburger, M., *Aus der Zeit der Revolutionskriege* (Breslau, 1916), p. 4; CA, Metz, 3P2; [Barbé,] Jean-Julien, *La Fayette à Metz* (Metz, 1920), p. 29; CA, Nancy, minutes, vol. vi, p. 7.

50. (1) The synagogue of *Gueldes*, (2) the synagogue on *Rue des Jardins*, (3) the *Alexandre* synagogue, (4) the synagogue on the *Boulevard de Jean-d'Amou*, (5) the *Brandon* synagogue, (6) the synagogue of the *Yeshiba*, which was the official synagogue of the community. E. Ducéré, *Histoire topographique and anécdotique des rues de Bayonne*, vol. vi (Bayonne 1894), p. 137; Lévi, Albert "A propos du Temple israélite de Bayonne," in *Société des Sciences . . . de Bayonne. Bulletin*, n. s., No. 26 (1938), pp. 116-29.

special contest to see if the Jewish Jacobins tolerated synagogues. The synagogues there were not closed altogether, but the Jacobins, on many occasions, tried to control the synagogal activities and give them a revolutionary direction. Officials of the synagogues were arrested for counter-revolutionary acts or opinions. Gabriel de Jacob Gommes, syndic of a synagogue, was arrested by an order of December 26, 1793, because he deplored the fate of a "fanatic." Already earlier, on November 24, 1793, the Club decided to put rabbi Jack Athias under a 24 hours house arrest because he did not preach in a revolutionary vein. He was ordered to preach henceforth "on the great morale of Reason and the principles of the salutary Revolution which should bring happiness to all men." He was also ordered to make a public retraction of his previous opinions. On November 30, 1793, the Club ordered to place rabbi Athias under arrest for three days because he did not disown his opinions expressed in the synagogues. On the same day the Club arrested Benjamin Louis Nounes because he had discontinued to preach in his synagogue and did not use his talent and influence to direct the "fanatical" citizens toward the revolutionary spirit. On October 27, 1793, Pierre Armand Dartigoeyte, Commissioner to the Army of the Pyrénées, and the Paris representative S. B. Cavaignac, prohibited all religious manifestations. But it seems that this order was not fully carried out in Saint-Esprit, where not all synagogues were closed. On December 3, 1793, the two synagogues of B. L. Nounes and Tobias (formerly the Brandon synagogue) were ordered to close and the Jews of these synagogues were ordered to join the two synagogues established by Alexandre and Furtado. While later Alexandre's synagogue, too, was closed, the Furtado synagogue remained open. But on April 20, 1794, the Jacobins of Saint-Esprit criticized the Jacobins of Bayonne, who later attacked their colleagues of Saint-Esprit for tolerating synagogues and the observance of Sabbath by the Jews. Thus, the Jewish Jacobins of Saint Esprit were compelled to express their thanks to the Bayonne Jacobins for their criticism and it was decided to tighten the control over the remainder of religious activities still left to Jews. The last synagogue was then closed. Religious objects were confiscated and Jews were even forced to present them voluntarily. Thus, on June 20, 1794, the Jacobins of Saint-Esprit informed the collector of confiscated valuables in Dax that they were sending him four silver Torah ornaments taken from synagogues and placed by Jews on the altar of the fatherland, together with a calyx and a patent presented by a citizens of another religious group. "These offerings," they wrote "announce the triumph of Reason; there is still prejudice to root out; a few more moments and everything will be marvelous."

But on the other hand, the Jewish Jacobins themselves secretly helped to hide the religious objects.[54]

In the neighboring community of Peyrehorade the *Société populaire montagnarde,* which included Jewish members closed the synagogue during the Terror. But it seems that the Jews did not participate willingly in such manifestations of the new Religion of Reason. On April 21, 1794, a member of the Society requested that all Jewish members who would not give up within twenty four hours all external signs of their religious attachment should be expelled. The Jew Leon Jr. stated then that the Jews would not do so because the Christians did not give up their crosses and religious paintings. During the Thermidor the synagogue was again opened there. According to one source, the Jews of Bidache and La Bastide left for Peyrehorade and Saint-Esprit-lès-Bayonne, because their synagogues were closed.[52]

The problem of synagogues is closely connected with the status of the rabbis and cantors during the Revolution; this subject will be treated in a separate study.

In conclusion it should be repeated that the synagogue suffered during the Revolution, but this could not be regarded as result of an anti-Jewish policy.

51. Ginsburger, Ernest, *Le Comité de surveillance de Jean-Jacques Rousseau, Saint- Esprit-lès-Bayonne* (Paris 1934), pp. 25, 106, 109, 112, 129, 270; Léon, H., *Histoire des Juifs de Bayonne* (Paris 1893), p. 162.

52. Ginsburger, E., "Les Juifs de Peyrehorade," *REJ.* vol. civ (1938), pp. 50-51. On May 22, 1797, the Jewish community engaged Jacob Baiz Simon as cantor; on Nov. 12, 1797 Samuel Bernal was appointed as his successor (*ibid.*, 60-61); *The Jewish Encyclopedia,* vol. ii, (New York 1903), p. 606. According to another source, the Jews of Bidache "willingly" presented their synagogue and religious articles to the local *Temple de la Raison*: Léon, *op. cit.*, pp. 165-66.

APPENDIX

Information on Synagogues by Regions

The synagogues of the following communities in the department of Upper Rhine were built prior to the Revolution: Bergheim (1777), Biesheim (1760), Blotzheim (1750), Bollwiller (1740), Freminger (1776), Grussenheim (1770), Habsheim (1783), Hagenbach (1720), Hattstatt (1769), Herrlisheim (1760), Hirsingen (1787), Issenheim (1770), Jungholz (1754), Lumpschwiller (1780), Niederhagenthal (1765), Oberdorf (1787), Oberhangenthal (1763), Reginsheim (1757), Riedwihr (1768), Rixheim (1762), Seppois-le-bas (1762), Sierentz (1742), Soultzmatte (1767), Uffheim (1740), Uffholz (1785), Voegelinshoffen (1750), Wattwiller (1767), Wintzenheim (1752), Wittenheim (1757). According to a list prepared in the 1830's by the Lower Rhine consistory. *(ZS.)* In Wintzenheim the synagogue functioned normally prior to the Terror. In July 1791 Koshel Hirtz, cantor in the synagogue since 1754, asked the departmental authorities to force the community to pay him his salary in accordance with his contract of Oct. 2, 1782. His request was granted *(DA,* Upper Rhine, V97, p. 108). According to a census of August 15, 1806, there were 150 Jewish communities in the Lower Rhine, but only 120 of them possessed synagogues. *DA,* Lower Rhine, 7 M 190.

The synagogues in the following communities of the Moselle department were built prior to the Revolution: Boulay (1730), Buding (1757), Créhange (1756), Frobach (1778), Grossbliedersdorf (17-), Koenigsmacker (1750), Luttange (1768), Metz (1603), Metzervise (1748), Phalsbourg, Puttelange (1736), Sarranguemines (1755), Vantoux (1777). *AN,* F[19] 11101.

In 1792-1793, Moyse Zaye was sexton of the synagogue of Metz *(DA* Moselle, V 156 b). On Sept. 1, 1793, the treasurer of the synagogue, Michel Salomon Foulde, paid 9 livres for cleaning the synagogue and its yard; on November 19, 1793 — 20 livres for repairing candlesticks *(ibid.).* On Agust 30, 1795, 200 livres were paid to Meir ben Mendel Unrich for repairs in the yard and, on Nov. 1, 1797, an unspecified sum was paid for repairs of the roofs *(ZS).* In 1797 the Metz scribe Gerson Zanwill wrote a book of prayers for the cantor of the synagogue (in the Library of the Jewish Theological Seminary, New York). In the same year the society "Gomlé-Hassadim" bought back religious articles which had been confiscated during the Terror from the *Claus* synagogue. ("Procès-verbal, dressé par la confrérie Gomlé-Hassadim, concernant l'achat d'objets de culte de la communauté de Metz, racheté par la confrérie . . . 1799." Consistorial archives of Metz, Ci 6-7. According to Salomon Landmann's manuscript catalogue of the Archives, "Catalogue des Archives consistoriales israélites de Metz," 1934, 2 vols.) According to various documents, the following persons appear as cantors in Metz during the Revolution: Lion [Lyon] Bing, Emanuel Bing, Salomon Zay, Neheime, Bernard Aaron Bloch (appointed in Sept. 1795), Séligman *(DA* Moselle, V 156 B and documents in the author's possession). On April 11, 1803, the Mayor of Metz ordered all private synagogues to close down, and to use only the main synagogue (Printed broadside of Apr. 11, 1803).

In Phalsbourg (Moselle) the synagogue built long before the Revolution continued to function, but probably not during the Terror. The Jew Michel Aron benefited from the troubled period; he stored wood piles along one wall of the synagogue and started to build a stable beside the synagogue. Alexandre Aron in the name of the Jewish community demanded to force M. Aron to clean up the place and, on September 28, 1796, Alexandre Aron's demand was granted by the local judge. (According to a copy of the sentence, ZS.) The synagogue of Augny (Moselle) was enlarged in 1795. In 1797 the community of Sarreguemines bought the synagogue which was built in 1755 and had belonged to a private family. *AN,* F[19] 11101.

The synagogues of the following communities in the department of Meurthe were built before the Revolution: Burscheid, Charme (ca. 1770), Dieuze (ca. 1757), Etain (1788), Fénétrange (ca. 1770), Lixheim, Mittebronn (ca. 1774), Phalsbourg (1730), Raon-l'Etape (ca. 1780), Vergavile (ca. 1780). *AN,* F[19] 11101.

In Paris many religious articles were hidden during the Terror and thus escaped destruction. In 1809 the two main Paris synagogues possessed thirty-four Torah Scrolls; some of them, most probably, escaped destruction during the Terror; it is worthwhile to list the persons who donated these objects: 1) Le Grand Rabbin Michel Séligman, 2) Joseph Hinstein, 3. J. Javal aîné, 4) Abraham Lyon, 5) Moïse Joseph, 6) Baruch Weil, 7) Héritiers Cerf Berr, 8) Isaac Simon, 9) Mayer Simon, 10) Isaac Dreyfus, 11) Emanuel Dreyfus, 12) Héritiers de Jacob Trefous, 13) Cerf Heller, 14) Isaac Simon, 15) Abraham Lyon, 16) Samuel [de Dürmenach], 17) [Wolf] Javal jeune, 18) Emanuel Meyer Dalmbert, 19) Abraham Michel, 20) Héritiers Wolff Lévy, Hayem Bloc. 21) Aaron Schmoll, 22) Salom Alkan, 23-24) Lévy Calmer, 25) Mardoché Elie, and nine which had belonged to the community for a long time. (According to a document of 1809, ZS.)

Samuel Herzog, a trustee of a Paris synagogue in 1796, died in 1797 (according to the inscription on the grave of the Jewish cemetery of Montrouge). In 1810-1812 there were eight synagogues in Bordeaux. On May 14, 1812, the new main synagogue (destroyed by fire on June 27, 1873, rebuilt and inaugurated on Sept. 5, 1882) was dedicated, Leroux, *op. cit.,* p. 231; Detcheverry, *op. cit.,* p. 113; Malvezin, T., *Histoire des Juifs à Bordeaux* (Bordeaux 1875), p. 306; Uhry, Isaac, *Monographie du culte israélite à Bordeaux* (Bordeaux 1892), pp. 9-10; Cohen, J., "La Synagogue de Bordeaux," in *Le Judaisme Séphardi,* n.s., No. 11 (July 1956), pp. 485-89. Saint-Esprit had five synagogues in 1811: (1) of the *Hebera,* (2) the *Tobie* synagogue, (3) the *Dufort* synagogue, (4) the *Leon* synagogue, (5) the synagogue on the *Boulevard Jean d'Amou.* On Apr. 3, 1811, the Consistory decided to abolish the first two synagogues (according to the minutes of a meeting of the consistory, 1811. ZS.). The Jews of Nice (Alpes-Maritimes) most probably kept their synagogue during the entire revolutionary years. Meiss, H., *A travers le ghetto: coup d'oeuil rétrospectif sur l'Université israélite de Nice,* 1648-1860 (Nice 1923), p. 53.

MARRIAGES, MIXED MARRIAGES AND CONVERSIONS AMONG FRENCH JEWS DURING THE REVOLUTION OF 1789

I

RECOGNITION IN FRANCE OF THE JEWISH LAW OF MARRIAGE

PRIOR to the Revolution of 1789 the autonomous character of the Jewish communities played a very important role in the life of the French Jews. These communities were allowed to control the most important religious and civil events in the life of the Jews, and their autonomy was strengthened by the fact that the French courts of law recognized the validity of Jewish marriage law, not insisting on the application of French civil law to marriages among Jews. This was the attitude of the courts even in the first years of the Revolution of 1789, when both friends and foes of Jewish emancipation voiced their opposition to the existence of autonomously administered Jewish communities. In fact, the Jewish law on marriage was recognized by some French courts of law even after September 27, 1791, when the last group of French Jewry, the Ashkenazim, were granted full citizenship and, as a result, the Jewish communities ceased to exist in their pre-Revolutionary form. The discussions on problems of law enforcement were even more important as a factor helping to prepare the later and complete assimilation of the Jews to French civil law.

The Jewish marriage law was often debated publicly in connection with conversions of Jews. In 1713 the converted Jew Claude-Marie Eliézer of Thionville was forced

Originally published in *Historia Judaica*, vol. XIX (1957).

to surrender their child to his Jewish wife. But this was not always so. Kendel Moch, the daughter of Abraham Moch, the head of the Jewish community of Haguenau, was married to Bernard Hirtz in 1723. In 1731 Hirtz converted to Catholicism and requested his wife to do likewise with their two children. When she refused, Hirtz married a Christian woman. Abraham Moch defended his daughter's right to guard the children in a memorandum in which he recalled the case of Eliézer of Thionville. But Moch was forced by the law courts to surrender the children to Hirtz.[1]

There was in the seventeen-fifties the famous case of the Alsatian Jew Borach Lévi, who, after his conversion, was not permitted by Canon law (indissolubility of the marriage) to divorce his Jewish wife Mendel Cerf and to marry a Christian girl. Lévi argued with the Church authorities that in Alsace and other French provinces Jews who converted to Christianity were later allowed to remarry if they first sent to their Jewish wives a summons to join them in the Catholic faith. In this way the Jew Salomon Lambert of Metz, who was baptized on May 29, 1751 in Verdun, was able to marry on the following July 27 the Catholic girl Marguerite Renaud of Récicourt. Lambert's Jewish wife, Colombe Hadamart, refused to embrace Catholicism. The Catholic authorities of Metz testified that the summons sent by Lambert to his wife was recognized by the Jewish community of Metz as a divorce according to Jewish law. But this was impossible, and therefore incorrect. For, according to Jewish law, the wife of a converted Jew remained legally married as long as her husband, although converted, did not divorce her according to the formalities of Jewish law. He could not force her to accept the divorce. On the other hand, he was not allowed by Canon law to divorce her. It is possible that Lambert sent to his wife not only

[1] *Mémoire pour Louis Etienne Bernard juif baptizé demeurant à Haguenau intimé & demandeur en requête. Contre Kendel Moch sa femme* (no place given [= n.p.], [1730]); Elie Scheid, "Histoire des Juifs de Haguenau," *REJ.,* X (1885), 204-210.

the official summons to join him, but also a Jewish letter of
divorce without informing the Church authorities of this.
Lévi also cited the already mentioned case of Bernard Hirtz
and the case of Edel Bernheim, the wife of Aron Lévi of
Zillisheim.   In 1747 Edel Bernheim ran away with the Jew
Wolf Bacher.   Both were converted in Strasbourg.   Edel
summoned her husband to convert himself and to join her.
The husband replied by requesting her to join him.   Nevertheless, both fugitives were married on August 14, 1748.   On
March 29, 1749 the Sovereign Council of Alsace recognized
the marriage as valid and ordered Aron Lévi to return his
wife's dowry to her.   In spite of all this Borach Lévi could
not obtain the permission of the Church to remarry; he
appealed to the Parliament of Paris which ruled against his
request, on January 2, 1758.[2]

The Canon law, prohibiting converted Jews to remarry
unless they became widowers, was even mentioned officially
in the Letters Patent of 1784 on the Alsatian Jews.[3]   This
was probably a result of the Lévi case.

Another famous case of the 1760's-1780's involved the
Bordeaux banker Charles Peixotto of Bordeaux who had
married Sara Mendès Dacosta in 1762.   On December 30,
1778, Peixotto obtained from the *Châtelet* of Paris an annulment of the marriage in accordance with the French
civil law on marriage.   This was the beginning of a long
and famous litigation.   Sara Mendès Dacosta refused to accept the decision of the *Châtelet* of Paris.   She appealed to
the Parliament of Bordeaux, which voided the decision of
the *Châtelet* of Paris because Peixotto was a legal resident of
Bordeaux.   Peixotto then sent to his wife a letter of divorce
according to the Jewish law and requested the Parliament
of Paris to recognize the Jewish divorce as valid in accordance with French civil law.   The case was again argued

---

[2]   Isidore Loeb, "Borach Lévi," *Annuaire de la Société des Etudes
Juives*, III (1882), 273-334.
[3]   *Lettres patentes du Roi, portant Règlement concernant les Juifs. Du
10 Juillet 1784* . . . (Colmar, 1784), art. 24.

before the Judges of the *Châtelet*, who decided on May 10, 1779 to ask for the opinion of the syndics of the Jewish *Nation* (community) of Bordeaux. On July 20, 1779, the Parliament of Paris approved the new decision taken by the *Châtelet*. On August 22, 1780, the syndics of the Bordeaux *Nation* held their first meeting on this conflict. But before they were able to reach a decision Peixotto was baptized in Spain (on April 18, 1781). Already on March 31, 1781, and again on May 21, 1782, he requested his wife to join him in the Catholic faith, obviously with the intention to have this action recognized as an annulment of the marriage. But his wife died before the controversy came to a legal end through the courts of law. As a result of the Peixotto case the Jewish *Nation* of Bordeaux took steps against the possible repetition of such a situation. In a memorandum submitted in 1788 to the Malesherbes Commission, which was preparing a statute for the Jews of France, the *Nation* of Bordeaux proposed that divorce be forbidden among Jews. In extreme cases, however, Jews could appeal to the *Nation*, which could grant a divorce but only by a three-quarters majority of the votes. Should the *Nation* reject such a demand, the person could appeal to the French courts of law.[4]

Halitsah, the law according to which the brother of a man who died childless must marry the widow in a levirate marriage or release her, was also recognized by the French authorities. Thus, the Parliament of Bordeaux, on May 7, 1768, ordered Daniel Tellès Dacosta to release his sister-in-law, Blanche Silva, widow of Jacob Tellès Dacosta, in accordance with Jewish law.[5]

At the end of 1751 (or in the beginning of 1752)

---

[4] The author is preparing a complete bibliography on the Peixotto case.

[5] Minutes of the Bordeaux *Nation*, No. 367, fol. 91, Apr. 17, 1768 (in the departmental archives of Gironde); L.F.B. [Beaufleury], *Histoire de l'établissement des Juifs à Bordeaux et à Bayonne depuis 1550* (Paris, an 8 [1799]), pp. 138-140; T. Malvezin, *Histoire de Juifs à Bordeaux* (*Bordeaux*, 1875), p. 280; Cardozo de Bethencourt, "Le Trésor des Juifs Sephardim," *REJ.*, XXVI (1893), 242.

Daniel Nonez of Bordeaux married secretly and without parental consent. The syndics of the Bordeaux *Nation* asked the intendant to expel Benjamin Tudesco, a brother-in-law of Nonez, who had performed the marriage. Some of the witnesses to the marriage were excommunicated. The poor witnesses were deprived of the right to receive charity and expelled from the city.[6] But in an earlier case involving the marriage of a minor, the Bordeaux Parliament ruled contrariwise, always according to Jewish law. In Saint-Esprit-lès-Bayonne, an ordinance, renewed in 1700-1703, prohibited marriages without parental consent. In 1741, Abraham Robles of Saint-Esprit, a minor, married Sara Rodriges-Janic secretly and without the consent of his father Moyse Robles. In this case the Bordeaux Parliament ruled in favor of the Jewish law, permitting the marriage of minors and against the local tradition which became a rule.[7]

French jurisprudence also respected the Jewish tradition against breach of engagement. C. . . of Bordeaux was forced by the Bordeaux Parliament to marry the girl B. . . In the beginning of the eighteenth century Francis Francia of Bordeaux had to seek refuge in London for fear of being arrested for breach of promise.[8] The famous Paris revolutionary Jacob Pereyra, a Jew from Bayonne who, together with Anacharsis Cloots and other Hebertists, was guillotined on March 24, 1794, was compelled, in 1768, to flee to England because of an affair with the daughter of a Bordeaux Jewish banker.[9]

[6] Georges Cirot, *Recherches sur les Juifs espanols et portugais à Bordeaux* (Bordeaux, 1908), pp. 76-77.

[7] Salo W. Baron, *The Jewish Community*, III (Philadelphia, 1942), 204; Me Bouan, *A juger . . . pour Moyse Robles . . . contre Abraham Robles son fils, mineur de dix-neuf ans . . .* [Bordeaux, 1743], 21, 1 pp.; Graugeneuves, *A juger . . . pour Abraham Robles, Juif, du Faubourg Saint-Esprit . . . contre Moise Robles, son Père* [Bordeaux, 1743], 15 pp.; De Salviat, *La Jurisprudence du Parlement de Bordeaux* (Paris, 1787), pp. 23-30.

[8] *The case of Mr. Francis Francia, the reputed Jew, who was acquitted of high-treason, at the Sessions-House in the Old Baily, on Tuesday, Jan. 22, 1716* (London, 1716), 12 pp.

[9] Beaufleury, *op. cit.*, p. 127; Paul d'Estrée, *La vieillesse de Richelieu*

The Jewish laws pertaining to property rights in marriage were also recognized by the French authorities. Marriage contracts drawn up by rabbis had to be registered with the authorities, but this was done only in order to protect Christian creditors. Thus, the Alsatian Sovereign Council, on January 11, 1701, and September 27, 1717, ordered that such contracts were to be deposited within fifteen days in the notaries' offices, so that Jewish debtors could not keep secret from Christian creditors information regarding their dowries and their financial marriage settlements.[10] In legal cases involving inheritance the authorities in Alsace, Metz, and Lorraine favored the law of the Jewish community councils which denied the right to converts to benefit from property inherited from Jews.[11] That the Jews enjoyed considerable autonomy concerning marriage law is evidenced by an order issued by the Sovereign Council on September 1, 1784 regarding the property of married Jewish women. This order aimed at equalizing, in this respect, the rights of the Jews with other inhabitants of Alsace, and particularly at protecting the interests of the Jews' Christian creditors. Yet when it happened that the recognized rules of the Jewish

(Paris, 1921), pp. 223-225. Cf. Louis Finkelstein, *Jewish Self-Government in the Middle-Ages* (New York, 1924), pp. 145-147. This tradition prevailed even in the nineteenth century. When David Athias was to become rabbi of Saint-Esprit in 1825, he was strongly opposed by Jacob Gommez Silva for breaking his promise given fifteen years earlier to Sara Silva (according to documents in the author's possession).

[10] *Louis par la Grâce de Dieu* (Colmar, January 11, 1701), Broadside. According to N. de Corberon, *Recueil d'ordonnances du Roy et règlements du Conseil Souverain d'Alsace* (Colmar, 1738) p. 37; and de Boug, *Recueil des Edits . . .*, I (Colmar, 1775), 310, the above cited ordinance was of Jan. 21, 1701. *Extrait des registres du Conseil Souverain d'Alsace* (n.p., 27 Septembre 1717), 4 pp.; *Extrait des registres du Conseil Souverain d'Alsace* (n.p., n.d.), 4 pp. [The rabbi of Robeauville could not seal inheritences]. See Z. Szajkowski, *The Economic Status of the Jews in Alsace, Metz and Lorraine* 1648-1789 (New York, 1954), pp. 88-89.

[11] Verdicts of the Metz Parliament, Feb. 23, 1704, and of the Council of Alsace, Feb. 9, 1746; *Extraits des registres du Conseil Souverain d'Alsace. Du 8 Janvier 1785* (Colmar, 1785), 6 pp.; *Précis pour Salomon-David Alphen, contre M. Jean Pierre Pecheur. . . .* (Metz, n.d.), 42 pp.

communities regarding these matters differed from those enforced by this order, the order of September 1, 1784 was temporarily rescinded, as was Article XIX of the Letters Patent of July 10, 1784 concerning the same matter.[12]   On the eve of the Revolution, in 1788, the Jews of Bordeaux demanded in their memorandum to Malesherbes that the Jewish law on inheritance be maintained, as this was the custom among the Ashkenazic Jews.[13]

In the first years of the Revolution the Jewish law on marriage was still recognized by French jurisprudence as valid for Jews.

An illegitimate child named Moize Mendes was born in Bordeaux on May 22, 1780.   On July 18, 1780, he was circumcized by Abraham Burgues, who noted in his record of circumcisions that the boy was probably a son of David Mendes.   The father was married on March 31, 1761 to Judith Daigullard.   It is not known whether he divorced his wife and under what circumstances he married Rebecca Peixotto, after the birth of his son, on November 22, 1780.   However, through a notarial act of May 14, 1797, David Mendes acknowledged that Moize was his son, and he demanded of the civil court of Bordeaux that it legalize this notarial act.   On April 8, 1798, the court of law recognized Moize as David Mendes' son, because—as the judge argued in his decision—the Jewish law recognizes marriage by the simple act of presenting a ring and approves also polygamy. The court's ruling was then recorded in the register of circumcisions.[14]

Abraham Peixotto, Jr., of Bordeaux wanted during the Revolution to divorce his wife Rachel Rodrigues Monsante. He argued that at the time of his marriage he was a minor and was not married according to French law.   But the

[12]   *Extrait des registres du Conseil Souverain d'Alsace. Du 8 janvier 1785* (Colmar, 1785), 6 pp.

[13]   Henry Léon, *Histoire des juifs de Bayonne* (Paris, 1893), p. 153.

[14]   City Archives of Bordeaux, GG 794, f. 10, No. 41.

rabbinical tribunal of Bordeaux decided in favor of his wife. On May 14, 1792, the Court of Justice of the Bordeaux district, presided over by De Brézets, delivered judgment in favor of Rachel Rodrigues, and their child, born on December 13, 1791, was declared legitimate. In the opinion of the court the marriage of the couple was subject to Jewish law, because the Decree of January 28, 1790, which granted full citizenship to Sephardic Jews, maintained their former privileges. According to the court the Jews were now subject to all political laws, but they were entitled to continue to live according to their religious laws, including the law on marriage. As the National Assembly had not yet decided on the forms of marriage for the various religious groups, the court had to recognize Jewish law.[15]

Güttel Weyl of Riedwihr demanded of the *Directoire* of the Upper Rhine to nominate a rabbi to arbitrate her claim of breach of promise against Joseph Biegert. On October 21, 1790, the *Directoire* named rabbi Jaques Meyer to arbitrate the case.[16]

The practice of religious marriage ceremonies without previous civil marriage was common even during the Revolution. Thus, on March 23, 1796, Athias, the "sy devant Rabin" (former rabbi), delivered a certificate that on the same day he had married Mordochaï Molina and Ester Carrançe. The certificate was later confirmed by the city officials. In 1810 a Jew from Orléans tried to legalize his marriage which had been concluded in the year IV (1795-96) in Paris by a religious ceremony only.[17]

Commonly recognized also was the Jewish practice of divorce. But the Jewish Assembly, called in 1806 by Napoleon I, stated that since the Revolution rabbis granted religious divorces only if written proof of divorce already

15 *Ibid.*, GG 844, f. 89; Malvezin, *op. cit.*, pp. 276-77.
16 M. Ginsburger, "Arrêtés du Directoire du département du Haut-Rhin relatifs aux Juifs (1790)," *REJ.*, LXXV (1920), 48.
17 Cirot, *op. cit.*, p. 169; R. Anchel, *Napoléon et les Juifs* (Paris, 1928), p. 438.

granted by the French courts of law were submitted to them.[18] Not until May 21, 1802 did an order signed by Napoleon I direct rabbis to perform religious marriage ceremonies only for couples who had previously been married by a civil officer. On February 19, 1807, the French Jewish Sanhedrin convened by Napoleon I adopted decisions in the same spirit for marriage and divorce (Articles II and III). Thus, the French Jews became the first Jews in Europe to abandon their traditional religious law guarding important phases of Jewish life and to yield to the civil laws of the country in which they lived.[19]

II

MIXED MARRIAGES

In Revolutionary France mixed marriages became a symbol of the new era. With the advent of the revolutionary regime a Jew was no longer forced to convert to Christianity in order to marry a Christian woman. (Mixed marriages mostly took place between Jewish men and Christian women.)

Protagonists and foes of Jewish emancipation alike advocated mixed marriages. Abbé Henry Grégoire was much interested in this problem.[20] Professor Christian-Guillaume Koch, Protestant leader of Alsace and opponent of Jewish

---

[18]   Anchel, *op. cit.*, p. 171. In 1796, Isaac, son of Naphtali Hirzel Lévy, divorced his wife Leah, daughter of Aaron of Niedernai, in accordance with Jewish law. University Library of Strasbourg, manuscript 4047. Divorces for foreign Jews residing in France are still settled according to the divorce laws of Jews in their countries of origin. Renée Lévy, *Le Divorce juif et les conflits de lois qu'il peut engendrer* (Paris, n.d.), 189 pp.; bibliography on pp. 186-187.

[19]   A. E. Halphen, *Recueil des lois . . . concernant les Israélites . . .* (Paris, 1851), p. 15; G. Tama, *Collection des procès-verbaux et décisions du Grand Sanhédrin* (Paris, 1807), pp. 51-54.

[20]   According to information furnished to the author in 1955 by P. Gruenbaum-Balin, author of *Henri Grégoire, l'ami des hommes de toutes les couleurs* (Paris, 1948), 278 pp. Compare with H. Grégoire's *Motion en faveur des Juifs. . . .* (Paris, 1789), p. 18.

emancipation, wrote in an unpublished anti-Jewish memorandum of June, 1790 that the Jews should not be granted
full citizenship, noting as one of the reasons for such a
policy the fact that the Jews would never marry Christians.[21]
On November 18, 1793, a Jacobin of Nancy demanded that
Jewish men be forced to marry non-Jewish women, because
Jews and Christians should form one united family.[22]

The Jacobins did not force mixed marriages upon Jews,
but some Jews did marry Christian women. Thus, the
Jewish physician Jacob Berr, the only Jewish member of
the Jacobins Club in Metz during the Terror, who fought
the preservation of autonomous Jewish communities, was—
according to some sources—the first French Jew to marry
a Christian girl during the Revolution.[23] In one instance,
a Jew of Montagne-Seignanx (formerly Sainte-Marie de
Seignanx, in the Landes) made his mixed marriage a question of principle. On March 8, 1794, he invited the Paris
representative, B.-J.-B. Monestier, to attend his wedding to
a non-Jewish woman, this wedding being a symbol of "equality and brotherhood."[24] A few other cases of mixed marriages might be cited. Raphaël Dennery of Metz, who
served in the Legion of Nantes, married there during the
Terror the Christian woman Emilie Diot. Their children
were raised as Christians, but Dennery himself at the end
of his life (he died in 1841) became an orthodox Jew.[25] In
Bordeaux, Moyze Dacosta of Bayonne married Marie Charlat

21 Archives du Chapitre St.-Thomas, 148-b 77-6 (II-2) (in the City
archives of Strasbourg).

22 City archives of Nancy, minutes, vol. 10, p. 174; Massé, *Discours
prononcé à la Société populaire, dans sa séance du 17 fructidor, an II* . . .
[Metz, n.d.], p. 9; Anchel, *op. cit.*, p. 16.

23 E. Carmoly, *Histoire des médecins juifs, anciens et modernes* (Bruxelles,
1844), p. 204. *Idem, Revue Orientale*, II (1842), 92; Chr. Pfister, *Histoire
de Nancy*, III (Nancy, 1908), 327; Léon Bultingaire, *Le Club des Jacobins
de Metz* (Paris-Metz, 1906), p. 101.

24 A. Richard, *Le Gouvernment révolutionnaire dans les Basses-Pyrénées*
(Paris, 1927), p. 185; E. Ginsburger, *Le Comité de surveillance de Jean-
Jacques Rousseau, Saint-Esprit-lès-Bayonne* (Paris, 1934), p. 33.

25 *Archives israélites*, III (1842), 117, 337-39.

of Paris, baptized on May 25, 1772.[26]   The daughter of Isaac Marqfoy was married to Comte J. B. Treillard, a former attorney of the Paris Parliament, who later became a member of the State Council.[27]   The father of Joseph Salvador (born in 1796) married a Christian woman.[28]   Still, it would not be correct to speak of a large number of mixed marriages during the Revolution.

Instances of Jews breaking with the Jewish religion and tradition were then exceptional, and only very few Christian parents were ready to accept unconverted Jews as sons-in-law.   This was rather a subject for anti-Jewish jokes and stories.[29]   Most often mixed marriages provoked sharp family conflicts.   This happened, for example, to the son of Jacob Delvaille of Bordeaux who—with his father's consent—married in the year V (1796-97) the Christian girl Françoise Vaugon.   Only a civil marriage ceremony was performed. But later her parents-in-law requested her to become Jewish and when she refused, her husband left her and asked for a civil divorce.   Subsequently, he came back to his wife and died on July 28, 1802 when his wife was pregnant.   At first—while Françoise was still a minor—Jacob Delvaille was the legal guardian of his grandchildren, but when the mother came of age and demanded the guardianship of her own children, the father-in-law refused to recognize her. In the legal memoranda which were published on this affair came to light the tragedy of such a mixed marriage.[30]

[26]   Departmental archives of Gironde, 3E 2-1741, notarial acts of Rauzan, Nov. 18, 1794.

[27]   Léon, *op. cit.*, p. 420.

[28]   A. Spire, *Quelques Juifs et demi Juifs* (Paris, 1928), I, 208.

[29]   In Strasbourg an anti-Jewish satire on a Jew's love affair with a Christian woman was published: *Merkwürdige und seltsame Liebesgeschichte zwischen einem jungen verliebten Juden, und einer überschönen Büttners-Frau, welche sich am Rhein bey Strassburg zugetragen 1790* . . . (n.p., n.d.), 4 pp.   It is worth while to note the case of a Christian widow of Avignon who became pregnant by the Jew D. of Valabrèques.   Aimé Vincenti, *Le Tribunal Civil du département de Vaucluse de l'an IV à l'an VIII* (Avignon, 1928), p. 95.

[30]   Laine [Lainé], avocat, *Mémoire pour la dame veuve Delvaille contre le sieur Jacob Delvaille* (Bordeaux, [1803?]), 48 pp.; Duranteau, fils, avocat,

Did the loosening of the ties of the Jewish religion and the mixed marriages resulting from the Revolution influence Jews toward conversion? This is probable. Yet it was not visible during the Revolution, but only in the later years, beginning with the First Empire.

III

RESTRICTIONS OF JEWISH MARRIAGES

Prior to the Revolution Jews could not marry or settle everywhere in France. In Alsace and neighboring provinces the right of domicile did not apply to a Jew's entire family, but only to his first-born son, who could marry and settle where his father lived. According to the Letters Patent of July, 1784, which also aimed at reduction of the number of Jews, Alsatian Jews could not marry without the special permission of the King.[31] Rabbis and community leaders were not permitted to marry Jews without such a permit. Even during the first years of the Revolution the Christian population of Alsace and the neighboring provinces tried to

Réplique pour le Citoyen Jacob Delvaille contre la Dame Françoise Vaugon (Bordeaux, [1803?]), 78 pp.

Following are a few facts on the extent of mixed marriages in the first post-Revolutionary years. On June 30, 1806, the police prefect of the Seine department reported that several (*plusieurs*) Jews of both sexes married Christians. S. Posener, "Les Juifs de Paris . . .," *Univers israélite*, XCI (1935-1936), 762. In 1808, 6 out of 36 Jewish family heads of Brest were married to Christian women (Louis Bernard, Lyon Cahen, Lion Lion, Jahel Hirche, Philipe Lion, Joseph Brunsvick; according to a census in the author's possession). In 1808, 3 of 23 Jewish families of Toulouse were of mixed marriages. Archives nationales, F[19] 11023; J. Gross, "Les Juifs de Toulouse pendant la révolution et l'empire," *Revue des Pyrénées*, XVIII (1906), 257. In 1809, the Jewish peddler, "Burin (*ci devant Elias*) Thomas of Abbeville" (Somme), born in Hamburg, Germany, had a Christian wife. One woman of the Dijon Jewish community in 1809, Anne Crombach Sivry, was of Christian origin (censuses in the author's possession).

31 Charles Hoffmann, *L'Alsace au dix-huitième siècle*, IV (Colmar, 1907), 350-352; Z. Szajkowski, "The Jewish Problem in Alsace, Metz, and Lorraine on the Eve of the Revolution of 1789," *Jewish Quarterly Review*, XLIV (1954), 223-226; idem, *The Economic Status of the Jews in Alsace, Metz and Lorraine 1648-1789*, pp. 26-28.

maintain the old anti-Jewish restrictions, especially the prohibition against Jews freely marrying and taking up residence.[32]   Already in some of the memorials of grievances,
requests were made that control of Jewish marriages should
continue.[33]

The policy of the Alsatian departmental authorities was
to continue the old restrictions against the Jews, since the
National Assembly had not yet come to any decision on the
Jewish status.   Thus, Alsatian Jews were still forced to apply for permission to marry.   On September 27, 1790, and
February 22, March 3, and May 18, 1791, respectively,
Jacques Wolf of Obersteinbrun, Meyer Dreyfus and Marc
Dreyfus of Uffheim, and Jacques Dilisheim and Joseph
Schwob of Hegenheim applied for and obtained such permits.   But in many cases City Councils or districts prohibited the marriage of Jews.   Nathan Lazard of Fegersheim
on January 25, 1790 obtained the King's permit to marry,
but the City Council ordered the rabbi not to perform the
marriage ceremony.   It also prohibited the marriage of
Macholem Abraham and his fiancee Bessel of Mutzig.   N.
Lazard appealed to the *Directoire* of the Strasbourg district
and was granted permission to marry, but on July 31, 1791,
the same Directoire prohibited a Jew from Osthoffen from
marrying off and settling his third son there.   In September,
1790, Manuel Gerschen of Quatzenheim protested against
being forced to pay 120 livres for permission to marry off
his son.   In October, 1790, the City Council of Mutzig
forced Jacques Lévy to pay 60 livres for such permission.
On February 15, 1791, the City Council of Odratzheim
protested against permitting Jewish marriages.   Samson
Isaac of Uttenheim, who had obtained the King's permit
to marry on February 25, 1789, was refused in June, 1791

---

[32] Z. Szajkowski, "The Discussion and Struggle over Jewish Emancipation
in Alsace in the Early Years of the French Revolution," *Historia Judaica*,
XVII (1955), 124-126.

[33] M. Liber, "Juifs et la convocation des États-Généraux," *REJ.*, LXIII
(1912), 188.

permission to marry a girl of Fegersheim and settle there.[34] There were so many conflicts between city councils and Jews who were refused permission to marry that on January 25, 1791 the *Directoire* of Lower Rhine asked the National Assembly to decide the question of Jewish status in connection with the subject of marriage.[35] Only after Alsatian Jews were granted full citizenship on September 27, 1791, were they free to marry without restriction. But these anti-Catholic "Malthusanian convictions" continued to be a basic part of the anti-Jewish policy of the Catholics, among them L.G.A. de Bonald (1767-1840), who helped, with his anti-Jewish propaganda, to prepare Napoleon's anti-Jewish decrees of 1806 and 1808.[36]

It seems worth while to present some statistical data on Jewish marriages during the Revolution. Among the Jews of Metz there were 194 marriages in the year 1789— year VIII (September 23, 1799-September 22, 1800)— against 168 in the previous years 1777-1787. In the arrondissement of Metz 26 marriages were registered in 1789 against 25 in 1788. In Carpentras 73 marriages were registered in 1789-1791 against 71 in 1786-1788; in Avignon, 3 marriages in 1788 and the same number in 1789; in Cavaillon, 6 marriages in 1789-1791 against 1 in 1786-1788; in L'Isle-sur Sorgue, 3 marriages in 1789-1791 against 5 in 1786-1788. In Bordeaux, 35 Jewish marriages were registered in 1789-1791 against 34 in 1786-1788.[37] It seems that the number of marriages among Jews did not diminish in spite of the fact that many emigrated during the Revolution

34 M. Ginsburger, "Arrêtés . . .," *REJ.*, LXXV (1922), 47, 53, 55, 60-61; R. Reuss, "L'Antisémitisme dans le Bas-Rhin pendant la révolution," *REJ.*, LXVIII (1914), 238, 250-251, 253-255; P. Hildefinger, "Actes du district de Strasbourg relatifs aux Juifs (1790)," *REJ.*, LX (1910), 238-239, 241-243.

35 Archives nationales, D-IV-56, No. 1638; Hildenfinger, *op. cit.*, p. 242.

36 J. Hours, "Un Précurseur oublié de l'antisémitisme français: le vicomte de Bonald," *Cahiers sioniens*, IV, No. 11 (1950), 165-169.

37 According to the registries of the Jewish population in the departmental archives of Moselle and the city archives of Metz, Carpentras, Avignon, Cavaillon, L'Isle-sur-Sorgue and Bordeaux; Cirot, *op. cit.*, p. 183; S. Posener, "Les Juifs sous le Premier Empire," *REJ.*, XCIV (1933), 161-162.

from the former papal province of Avignon and Comtat Venaissin as well as from Metz. This, however, is a subject for a separate study.

IV

FORCED CONVERSIONS OF ILLEGITIMATE CHILDREN

Missionary propaganda among Jews, voluntary conversions of Jews, and forced conversions of Jewish children were frequent. From 1695 until 1789, 23 Sephardic Jews were converted, including 16 girls.[38] In Alsace and other provinces converted Jews were exempt from paying taxes and lodging soldiers for a period of three years.[39] Jews were often forced to pay annuities to their converted children.[40]

In time, however, forced conversions of children were prohibited. An ordinance of July 15, 1728 forbade such conversions in Bordeaux. In 1735, after a cousin of Samuel Lévy of Sierc was converted by force, the Jews of Metz petitioned the King, asking that, as was done in Bordeaux, all Jewish child-converts of Metz below the age of fourteen be returned to their parents. The priest of Donnelay attempted to convert by force a child of Simon Jacob (1743?). In 1752 the Alsatian Council ordered the priest Kellerman of Oberlauterbach to return to the Jew Gerson Kaufmann

[38] On conversions in Bordeaux and Saint-Esprit-lès-Bayonne, see Malvezin, *op. cit.*, pp. 151-169; Léon, *op. cit.*, pp. 135-139; Cirot, *op. cit.*, pp. 170-173. On conversions in the four communities of the papal province, see notes 41-45. The number of 23 converted Jews seems to be much underestimated.

[39] A Broadside of Aug., 1683. There is no general study on conversions among the Jews of Alsace and neighboring provinces. Pierre Paul Neofid, converted in 1723 in Lorraine, was exempt from paying taxes: L. Vanson, "Curieuses requêtes des Juifs . . .," *Revue juive de Lorraine*, X (1934), 233-234. The converted Jew Jean Rodrigue of Nantes asked for exemption from taxes: city archives of Nantes, HH 182.

[40] Malvezin, *op. cit.*, Joseph Alphonse Albarès, who converted to Catholicism, was refused his heritage by his family in 1720. Me Caillavet, avocat, *A nosseigneurs de Parlement* [Bordeaux, 1720], 5 pp.

his child which had been snatched from him. In 1763 a Jewish child of Fenetrange was converted by force. After a protracted intervention and subsequent to a case where the child of Feiss Lévy of Zellviller was stolen from his parents, the Maréchal de Ségur promulgated in the name of the King an order forbidding the conversion of Jewish minors. This order, however, did not apply to Jewish children born out of wedlock. In 1769 the Parliament of Havre prohibited the forced conversion of the eleven-year-old Rebecca Gentilhomme and the thirteen-year-old Esther Pimentel. On September 7, 1776, the Parliament of Nancy forbade forced conversions of Jewish children under thirteen years of age and ordered the return to Hayem Elias and Cerf Isaïe Oulmann of their children who had been converted against their parents' will. On June 30, 1789, and on earlier dates, the Bishop of Carpentras, too, forbade conversion of Jewish children by force, thus repeating earlier prohibitions.[41]

However, every Jew of Avignon had to pay a fine of one hundred écus for failure to attend missionary sermons. The Jews of L'Isle-sur-Sorgue, too, were forced to listen to such sermons.[42] As late as May, 1790, the Jews of Carpentras were compelled to be present at the Abbé Pierre-François Boudin Justin's missionary sermons. At the meeting of the General Council of Carpentras on November 7,

---

[41] *Ordonnance du Roy. Du quinzième juillet* 1728 (Bordeaux, n.d.), 3 pp.; *Privilèges dont les Juifs portugais jouissent en France depuis* 1550 (Paris, 1777), p. 4; *Lettre de Mgr. le Duc de Choiseul à M. le Procureur General du Roi au Conseil Souverain d'Alsace.* A Compiègne, le 24 juillet 1767 (Colmar, 1767), 7 pp.; [*Arrêt du Parlement de Rouen. Du* 11 *Mars* 1769] (Rouen, 1769); *Archives israélites*, XX (1859), 170; Moïse Schwab, *Histoire des Israélites* (Paris, 1895), p. 285; *Edit de St. Office en exécution des ordres de Clément XIII, à nous adressés par lettre du C^{al} Cavalechini, en date de Rome,* 18 *février, défendant de baptiser les enfants juifs ou de menacer de les baptiser* (Avignon, mars 1767), Broadside; [*Edit contre le baptême forcé des enfants*] (Avignon, 20 mars 1773), Broadside; [*Edit du 20 mars 1776*] (Avignon, 1776), Broadside; *Ordonnance de Monseigneur l'évêque de Carpentras concernant le baptême des enfants juifs,* 30 juin 1789 (Carpentras, 1789), Broadside & 3 pp.

[42] City archives of Avignon, FF, 1612-1613; Calvet, Library of Avignon, manuscript 5938, f. 00561 (Apr. 6, 1607).

1790, Flandrin demanded improvement in the status of the Jews, beginning with suppression of the sermons. But the procurator argued that this could be decided only by the *Assemblée représentative* of Comtat, and Flandrin's proposition was rejected.[43] In 1792 the Jews demanded that the pulpit from which Justin made his sermons and for which they were forced to pay should be given back to them.[44] During the Revolution the Abbé François-Valentin Mulot (1749-1804), one of the Paris mediators in the conflict between Avignon and Comtat, forced the authorities of Carpentras to return to his parents ("au nom des droits sacrés de l'homme") young Jassuda Michael Mossé, who had been forcibly converted to Christianity in 1784.[45]

A royal edict of April 13, 1682 permitted the Catholic Church to take charge of non-Catholic illegitimate children. But in 1762 the Duc de Choiseul prohibited the conversion

[43]   City archives of Carpentras, Rév 49, fol. 15 & 21 (minutes).

[44]   Jules Bauer, "Les Conversions juives dans le Comtat Venaissin," *REJ.*, L (1905), 93; H. Chobaut, "Les Juifs d'Avignon et du Comtat et la révolution française," *REJ.*, CII (1938), 25; Armand Lunel, "Du temps des ghettos comtadins," *Les Oeuvres libres,* no. 130 (Apr., 1932), 374. In Oct., 1789 and May, 1790, Abbé Justin still penned conversion sermons and other anti-Jewish writings (Bauer, *op. cit.,* 93). The Jewish request on the chair, signed by Joseph Samuel, Samuel de Baze, Mossé Crémieux, Samuel Lyon, City archives of Carpentras, Rev. 305. On conversions in the papal province, see also: Armand Lunel, *Nicolo Peccavi* (Paris, 1926); A. Spire, *Quelques Juifs . . .*, II (Paris, 1928), 24; Michel Mollo, *Les Mystères du Comtat, chronique d'une grande histoire* (Carpentras, 1856). (A novel on the Revolutionary period. Roboam, a converted Jew, who became a Dominican monk to seek revenge for the persecution of the Jews by undermining the Church. He appeals to the Jews to fight for their full emancipation.)

[45]   *Compte rendu par M. l'Abbé Mulot, à l'Assemblée Nationale, comme commissaire du Roi à Avignon le 19 Novembre 1791* (n.p., n.d.), p. 41; departmental archives of Vaucluse, fonds Lapeyre, no. 310, ff. 193-195 (statement by the child's father, Jacob Joseph Mossé, "citoyen actif de la ville d'Aix"). On Mulot's friendly attitude toward Jews see: *Recueil des pièces relatives à l'admission des juifs à l'état civil* (Paris, 1790), pp. 9, 18. On the Mossé case and other forced conversions of children in the papal province prior to its annexation by France in 1791, see: Chobaut, "Les Juifs d'Avignon et du Comtat et la révolution," *REJ.,* CI (1937), 27-28; E. Carmoly, "Joseph-Marq Mossé," *Archives israélites,* XXIII (1862), 461-466; Leopold Stein, *Der Knabenraub von Carpentras* (Berlin, 1863; Prague, 1897); Z. Szajkowski, "The Conversion of Zemah Carmi in Carpentras," *Yivo Bletter,* XXIV (1944), 123-130; Bauer, *op. cit.,* C. Roth, "Une Mission des communautés du Comtat Venaissin à Rome," *REJ.,* LXXXIV (1927), 1-14.

in Alsace of illegitimate children under five years of age who were recognized by their parents after the latter's marriage. This was later repeated in a royal order of July 24, 1767, but it applied only to Lutherans and not to Jews, with the additional provision that the children could not be removed from the convent after the parents had been married. On the other hand, children born to the parents less than nine months after their marriage were to remain with their parents.[46]

In 1790 the author of a pamphlet on Jews asked that Jewish mothers be allowed to choose the religion of their illegitimate children,[47] but officially the Edict of 1682 was not revoked. Abbé Henry Grégoire himself, then President of the Committee of Reports, wrote in April, 1790 to the priest of Dettwiller that the Edict was still in force. This was used by the Alsatian authorities as an excuse to continue the practice of forced conversions of illegitimate children. On the basis of Grégoire's letters, Alsatian Protestants were compelled to send their illegitimate children to the Catholic schools of Geudertheim and Candel.[48]

In October, 1790 the authorities of Obernai (Lower Rhine) arrested the Jewish girl Judel (Jédélé) of Osthoffen, an expectant mother. Her fiancé, Elias Salomon, asked for permission to marry her immediately and the departmental *Directoire* granted his request. But so many conditions were attached that the child was born in prison and forcibly baptized and kept in a Catholic institution. Eight days later Elias and Judel were married by the Rabbi Feishel Hirsch of Obernai, but the child was not given back to his parents. In April, 1792 the departmental *Directoire* decided

[46] On the other hand two brothers, Sephardic Jews of Bordeaux, denounced their sister as a prostitute in order to avoid payment of a dowry of thousand livres to her fiancé. Her illegitimate child was taken to Saint-Louis, a Catholic institution for foundlings; Cirot, *op. cit.*, pp. 56-57.

[47] *Sur les Juifs en France* (n.p., 1790), pp. 17-18.

[48] R. Reuss, *Notes sur l'instruction primaire en Alsace pendant la révolution* (Paris-Nancy, 1910), pp. 32-33. Should this be considered another proof of H. Grégoire's already known hopes for the conversion of Jews?

that the child should be raised at the *Directoire's* expenses in the Catholic foundling home in Strasbourg. Later, on April 27, 1792, the same authorities took a more liberal position and decided to return the child to his parents. But the Catholic Church refused to abide by the decision, and we do not know how this affair ended.[49]

The child of Jédélé of Krautergersheim was baptized in similar circumstances, and on May 5, 1792 the *Directoire* ordered that the child be returned to its parents. In June, 1791, the Jewish girl Hanne of Zellwiller, fiancée of Judel Veil, asked the authorities to forbid the forced conversion of her future child, but her request was not granted; in November, 1792 the child was still in Catholic hands. On May 21, 1779 an illegitimate Jewish child of Bischofsheim was forcibly baptized. On July 4, 1791, the departmental authorities decided to bring the child to the Strasbourg foundling institution. However, after the full emancipation of the Jews, the same authorities, on April 29, 1792, granted the request of Moyse Elias of Itterswiller for prohibition of the forced baptism of the child to be born to his daughter Marianne Moyse, fiancée of Jacob of Balbronn. A similar request of October 1, 1792 by Wolf Meyer of Obernai was also granted. The *Directoire* of Lower Rhine decided on October 29, 1791—over a month after the Jewish emancipation—to pay a pension of 24 livres from the funds of the pensions committee to the converted Jewess Marie-Elénore Bernheim.[50]

[49] R. Reuss, "Un Chapitre de l'histoire des persécutions religieuses. Le clergé catholique et les enfants illégitimes protestants et israélites en Alsace au XVIIIᵉ siècle et au debut de la révolution," *Société de l'histoire du protestantisme français. Bulletin*, LII (1903), 6-31; idem, "L'Histoire d'Elias Salomon de Dauendorf et de Jédélé d'Obernai (1790-1792)," *REJ.*, LXVIII (1914), 235-245; idem, *La Constitution civile du clergé et la crise religieuse en Alsace, 1790-1795*, I (Strasbourg, 1922), 108, 113; *Geschichte der gegenwärtigen Zeit* (Strassburg, Dec. 2, 1790) (published by the Protestant *André Meyer*).

[50] Reuss, "Histoire d'Elias Salomon . . .," *op. cit.*, p. 12; idem, "L'Antisémitisme dans le Bas-Rhin pendant la révolution," *op. cit.*, pp. 254-255, 257-259.

V

MISSIONARY ACTIVITIES

The federal leaders of the Revolution were not concerned with gaining Jewish children for the Church, but some local authorities and pamphleteers could not forget their own Christian past and anti-Jewish feelings. Thus, an Alsatian anti-Jewish pamphleteer of 1790 demanded that Jews who might want to embrace Christianity should be protected against persecution by their former co-religionists.[51] An Alsatian revolutionary not only called upon Jews to forget the Messiah, because they now lived in a state of equality and liberty, but he also expressed his hope that some day they would accept the teachings of Christ.[52] As for official Catholic circles, they still continued to dream of saving the Jews through conversion and in this spirit many pamphlets were published even during the Revolution.[53]

[51] *Sur les Juifs en France* (n.p., 1790), p. 17.

[52] *Johann Friedrich Riecher in der Gesellschaft der Jacobiner an seine Mitbürger. Strassburg den 14 October 1792. . . . Erste und zweite Rede* (n.p., n.d.), p. 39.

[53] *Réflexions sur la liberté du culte* (Paris, 1790), p. 9; [Franc de Pomignan], *Lettres à un juif converti* (Paris, 1790), 310 pp.; *Warnung für alle Nationen und Menschen aus dem traurigen Schicksale der jüdischen Nation hergleitet* (n.p., 1790), 4 pp.; François-Guillaume, *Sermonce générale de paix et de réunion à l'Eglise et à sa chaire apostolique adressée à toute la nation des juifs* (Riom, 1795), 116 pp. [First edition—Avignon, 1765, 110 pp.]; [Cl.-F. Des Fours de la Genetière], *Avis aux catholiques sur le caractère et les signes du temps où nous vivons, ou de la conversion des Juifs . . .* [Lyon], 1795);*Discours adressé aux Juifs et utile aux Chrétiens pour les confirmer dans leur foi* (Lyon, 1788), 141 pp. [with a letter of the Carpentras bishop. The sermon was probably delivered in the presence of *chers Israelites*]. André Gairal mentions in *La Question juive en 1789. Extrait de la controverse et le contemporain* (Lyon, 1886), p. 18, an appeal of 1793 for the conversion of Jews. On Oct. 22, 1791, a woman named Marguerite Lefèvre was arrested for insulting Alphée de Gravende, *juive d'origine*, while returning from the *messe du roi*. A. Tuetey, *Répertoire général des sources manuscrites de l'histoire de Paris pendant la révolution française*, V (Paris, 1900), p. 351. In a petition of October, 1792, the "citoyenne Salomon, fille du grand Salomon, chef de la tribu de la nation juive, nouvelle convertie" asked the Convention to pay her annuities out of the funds from the properties of the *émigrés*, her

On a few occasions missionary activity took on the characteristic form of the re-establishment of the Jewish people —a converted one, of course—in Palestine. In this spirit should also be understood a project of 1798 for the restoration of the Jews in Palestine[54] and Napoleon I's appeal of 1799 to the Jews, well publicized by historians, in which he promised to restore Jerusalem to them. It seems now that Napoleon got this idea from Thomas Corbet, a brother of the Irish General William Corbet (1779-1872) of a Protestant family which was, most probably, influenced by such re-establishment projects in England.[55] But Napoleon himself later persecuted the sincere supporters of the restoration of a Christian-Jewish state. In the year XIII a group foretelling the revival of Judaism was discovered in Nantes (Loire-inférieure). Its leader, François Bonjour, a former priest of Fareins (Ain), and a few of his followers were arrested; his twelve-year-old son Elie Daniel was put in a hospital for the insane. After being released they emigrated to Switzerland.[56] In 1806-1807, a pamphlet was circulated in Paris in which the author called upon the Jews to enlist in the army because Napoleon would liberate Jerusalem. The police forbade the circulation of the pamphlet pending an investigation of the author's intentions.[57]

godfather Antoine-René Le Voyer, former governor of the Arsenal, and her godmother the duchesse Adelaide-Geneviève de Montmorency, Archives nationales, C 238, no. 248; Tuetey, *op. cit.*, VIII, 35; *Archives parlementaires*, LIII, 5.

[54] *Lettres adressées aux Juifs*, par deux auteurs anglois . . . (Paris, 1789); *Re-Establishment of the Jewish Government, an extract from a French Journal* [*Courier*, June 19, 1798] . . . *with a letter from a Jew to his brethren.* Translated from the Italian [London, 1798], 11 pp.; I. Bicheno, *Restoration of the Jews . . .*, 2nd edition (London, 1807), pp. 60-62.

[55] A. S. Yahuda, "Conception d'un état juif par Napoléon," *Evidences*, No. 19 (mai-juin 1951), 3-8.

[56] "Un nouveau Messie en l'an XIII," *Archives israélites*, LVIII (1897), 293.

[57] Samuel Yessite (Chrétien) Paly-Rasch, de la Maison de David, *Qu'est-ce qu'un Israélite chrétien?* (Paris, 1806), 15 pp.; E. d'Hauterive, *La Police secrète du Premier Empire*, III (Paris, 1908), 142.

In conclusion, it should be said that there was a great deal of confusion in the judicial status of the Jews during the Revolution. While the new regime advocated the complete abolition of autonomous Jewish communities, the French Law courts still recognized Jewish religious law on marriage as valid for the Jews. Many local administrations continued to restrict the freedom of the Jews even after the latter were granted full citizenship.

The Emancipation of
Jews During the French Revolution

A Bibliography of Books, Pamphlets and Printed Documents, 1789–1800

IT IS HARDLY NECESSARY to discuss the importance of a bibliography on Jews during the French Revolution of 1789–1800. The facts on the glorious fight for Jewish emancipation are well known through an endless amount of already published material. The author is not making an attempt to recount these or new facts, or to present new conclusions. The bibliography is also limited to contemporary historical material, books, pamphlets and printed documents published between 1789 and 1800. Contemporary articles from periodicals, books, pamphlets and printed documents containing important information on Jews, and later studies will be the subject of another very large bibliography.

The largest group in the bibliography consists of pamphlets in favor of or against Jewish emancipation. Unlike the later period of Napoleon's First Empire[1] there are almost no odes and prayers for the new regime. In order to complete the picture of Jewish life and Jewish influence during those years, the bibliography also contains writings by Jews and non-Jews on general problems and items of Christian Hebrew scholarship. We did not include in the bibliography a very large number of official publications on general matters signed by Jewish Mayors (of Saint-Esprit-lès-Bayonne and Cavaillon), Jewish members of city councils, Jewish leaders of various municipal commissions etc. In division XXIX (Jewish writers on non-Jewish subjects) we did not include a large number of items by authors of Jewish origin, mostly Marranos, who had no contact with Jewish life and should be considered as non-Jews.[2]

The bibliography is arranged in 38 divisions according to subjects and periods. The arrangement was done largely according to the author's conception of the history of Jews during the French Revolution and the major problems to be outlined in such a history. But then it should be noted that for many other problems on Jews during the Revolution we could not find any material other than archival sources, periodicals and later studies. It has been difficult to determine into which division some items should be included. Because of this there are no separate divisions for some important subjects [e. g. Jews of Metz,

---

[1] Napoleonica. For abbreviations and sources see pp. [3]–[8].
[2] E. g., four pamphlets published in 1789–1791 by Telles d'Acosta. See MW, IV, 407.

Originally published in *Studies in Bibliography and Booklore* (1959).

Émigrés, *Assignats* (paper money), etc.]. But in such cases the indexes could be of much help. With a few exceptions each division is arranged chronologically. The material of each year is then arranged in a more detailed chronological order of months and days, or in an alphabetical order of authors, titles or parties.

Of previous attempts to compile such a bibliography S. Posener's is the most complete (87 items). Special divisions in various catalogues should also be mentioned (Ln[184] in the National Library of Paris, Mi vi in the National and University Library of Strasbourg). Some items noted by bibliographers of the Revolutionary period were not included because they were really published later.[3]

Of course, our bibliography with 589 items is not complete and the author will be grateful for additions and remarks. We have noted the library or archives where each item may be found. The author would like to express his sincere gratitude to the librarians and archivists for their help.

CONTENTS

---

[3] E. g.: Poujol, Louis, *Quelques observations concernant les Juifs* . . . Paris, 1790, according to Mongland, I, p. 839; but it was really published in 1806. Joseph Mayer-Dalmbert, *Mémoire concernant les approvisionnemens de la ville de Paris*, according to MW, III, p. 346, is really dated March 19, 1830.

ABBREVIATIONS, ARCHIVES, LIBRARIES, CATALOGUES AND OTHER SOURCES

AdBR.   Archives départementales, Bas-Rhin (Strasbourg).

AdG.   Archives départementales, Gironde (Bordeaux).

AdGard.   Archives départementales, Gard (Nîmes).

AdHR.   Archives départementales, Haut-Rhin (Colmar).

AdM.   Archives départementales, Moselle (Metz).

AdMM.   Archives départementales, Meurthe-et-Moselle (Nancy).

AIU.   Bibliothèque de l'Alliance Israélite Universelle (Paris).

AmBa.   Archives municipales, Bayonne.

AmBx.   Archives municipales, Bordeaux.

AmCarp.   Archives municipales, Carpentras.

AmM.   Archives municipales, Metz.

Amsterd.   The Royal Library of Amsterdam.

AN.   Archives Nationales (Paris).

AnAI   Annuaire des Archives Israélites, Paris.

Arsenal.   Bibliothèque de l'Arsenal (Paris).

BAPR.   Bibliothèque des Amis de Port-Royal (Paris).

Barbier, A.-A. *Dictionnaire des ouvrages anonymes* . . . Paris, 1872–79. 4 vols.

Basel.   Staatsarchiv, Basel.

Benjacob, I. A.   *Ozar ha-Sepharim.* Wilna, 1880.

Benoît, A. *Lunéville et ses environs.* Lunéville, 1878–1880. 2 vols.

Berlin.   Freie Universität, Berlin. Universitätsbibliothek.

Bernardau.   Manuscript of the Bordeaux chronicler, Pierre Bernardau, in the BmBx.

Bernheim, Dr. A.   "Les Tables de la Loi." *UI*, LXXXVIII (1939), 877.

Berlinische Monatschrift.

Bibl. Als.   *Bibliographie alsacienne*, Strasbourg, 1922–1938. 6 vols.

Bibliographie der Schweizerischen Landeskunde. Jüdische Konfession und die Judenfrage. Bern, 1907.

Bibliothèque de la ville de Marseille. Catalogue du Fonds de Provence. Marseille, 1890–94. 4 vols.

Bibliothèque du Musée Calvet d'Avignon. Catalogue des ouvrages concernant Avignon et le département de Vaucluse. Avignon, 1912–21.

BLiège.   Bibliothèque municipale, Liège.

BM.   British Museum (London).

BmBx.   Bibliothèque municipale, Bordeaux.

BmC.   Bibliothèque municipale, Colmar.

BmCarp.   Bibliothèque municipale, Carpentras.

BmHavre.   Bibliothèque municipale, Le Havre.

BmLille.   Bibliothèque municipale, Lille.

BmLyon.   Bibliothèque municipale, Lyon.

BmM.   Bibliothèque municipale, Metz.

BmMs.   Bibliothèque municipale, Marseille.

BmN.   Bibliothèque municipale, Nancy.

BmNt.   Bibliothèque municipale, Nantes.

BmStg.   Bibliothèque municipale, Strasbourg.

Bonn.   Universitätsbibliothek, Bonn.

Bordeaux Delegates.   Szajkowski, Z. "The Diaries of the Bordeaux Jews to the Malesherbes Commission (1788) and the National Assembly (1790)." *Zion*, XVIII (1953), 31–79.

BuStg.   Bibliothèque Nationale et Universitaire, Strasbourg.

Cabinet des Estampes.   Palais Rohan, Strasbourg.

Cahen, A. "Bibliographie Judaïco-Française. Théâtre." *AnAI*, 5652. Paris, 1891, 58–63; 5653. Paris, 1892, 55–63.

Cahen, A. "L'Emancipation des Juifs devant la Société royale des arts et des sciences de Metz en 1787, et M. de Roderer." *REJ*, I (1880).

Cahen, S. "De la littérature hébraïque et juive en France." *Archives israélites*, I (1840), 33–52.

Calendars. Szajkowski, Z. "Two Republican Calendars of 1795–1796." *The Jews in France*, edited by E. Tcherikower. New York, 1942, II, 309–310.

Calvet. Bibliothèque du Musée Calvet, Avignon.

Carmoly, E., *Biographie des israélites de France*. Frankfurt-sur-le-Mein, 1868.

———. "De la Typographie hébraïque à Metz." *Revue Orientale*, III (1843–44), 209–215, 282–289.

———. *La France israélite*. Paris-Leipzig, 1855.

Carnavalet. Musée Carnavalet, Paris.

Catalogue de l'Histoire de France. Paris, 1855–79. 11 vols.

Catalogue général des livres imprimés de la Bibliothèque Nationale. Auteurs. Paris, 1897–1955. Vols. I–CLXXXIII.

Challamel, A. *Les Clubs contre-Révolutionnaires*. Paris, 1895.

Charavary, E. "Un appel pour charger les Juifs de l'approvisionnement de Paris." *La Révolution française*, XXIV (1893), 62–68.

Chassin, Ch. L. *Les élections et les cahiers de Paris en 1789*. Paris, 1888–89. 4 vols.

Chauffour. Waltz, André. *Catalogue de la Bibliothèque Chauffour*. Colmar, 1889.

ChD. Bibliothèque de la Chambre des Députés, Paris.

Chobaut, H. "Les Juifs d'Avignon et du Comtat et la Révolution française." *REJ*, CI–CII (1937–38).

CJ. Le Cahier jaune. Paris, 1942.

Courrier d'Avignon, 1790.

Degerman. *Catalogue de la collection d'Alsatiques . . . de Jules Degerman.* n. p., n. d.

Drumont, E. *La France juive*. Paris, 1886. 2 vols.

Dt. Dutch.

Economic Status. Szajkowski, Z. *The Economic Status of the Jews in Alsace, Metz and Lorraine, 1688–1789*. New York, 1954.

Engl. English.

Eichstädt, Wolkmar. *Bibliographie zur Geschichte der Judenfrage*. Band I. 1750–1848. Hamburg, 1938.

Estreicher, Karl. *Bibliografia Polska*. Kraków, 1882–1939, Series 2–3.

Favier, J. *Catalogue des livres et documents imprimés du Fonds Lorrain de la Bibliothèque municipale de Nancy*. Nancy, 1898.

Féret, E. *Statistique du département de la Gironde*. Bordeaux, 1889. Vol. III.

Fombusque, J. de. "Comment les Juifs ont acquis la citoyenneté française en 1791." *La question juive en France et dans le monde*, No. 8 (1943), 11–70.

Fr. French.

Frankfurt a. M. Stadt- und Universitätsbibliothek, Frankfurt am Main.

Fürst, Julius. *Biblioteca Judaica.* Leipzig, 1849. 2 vols.

Gairal, A. *La Question juive en 1789.* Lyon, 1886.

Ger. German.

Ginsburger, M. *Jüdische Ärzte im Elsass.* [Reprint from the *Annuaire . . . du Club Vosgien*, 1 (1933.)] n. p., n. d. 13 pp.

Goizet, J. et Burtal, M. A. *Dictionnaire universel du Théâtre en France.* Paris, 1867.

Göttingen. Universitäsbibliothek, Göttingen.

Gradis Archives. Private archives of the Gradis family, Bordeaux.

Gregoriana. A bibliography of H. Grégoire's works, by S. Posener, in manuscript. Arsenal.

Guerber, Joseph. *Bruno Franz Léopold Liebermann.* Freiburg, 1880.

H. Hebrew.

Halphen, A. E. *Recueil des lois . . . concernant les israélites . . .* Paris, 1851.

Ha-Measef, 1789–1790.

Hatin, H. E. *Bibliographie . . . de la presse périodique française.* Paris, 1866.

Heckmann, Paul. *Félix de Wimpffen et le siège de Thionville.* Paris, 1926.

Heitz, F. C. *La Contre Révolution en Alsace de 1789 à 1793.* Strasbourg, 1865.

———. *Les Sociétés politiques de Strasbourg pendant les années 1790 à 1795.* Strasbourg, 1865.

Hildenfinger, P. A. "L'Adresse de la Commune de Strasbourg à l'Assemblée Nationale contre les Juifs (Avril 1790)." *REJ*, LVIII (1909) 112–28.

Hubrecht, Georges. *Les Assignats dans le Haut-Rhin.* Strasbourg, 1931.

HUC. The Library, Hebrew Union College - Jewish Institute of Religion, Cincinnati, Ohio.

HUJ. The Library of the Hebrew University, Jerusalem.

It. Italian.

Jerusalem. Archives of The Jewish Historical Society of Israel, Jerusalem.

JHSE. *The Jewish Historical Society of England. Transactions.*

Journal général de la Cour et de la Ville, 1791.

JTS. The Library, Jewish Theological Seminary of America, New York, N. Y.

Kahn, Léon. *Les Juifs de Paris pendant la Révolution.* Paris, 1898.

Knuttel, W. P. C. *Catalogues van de Pamflettenverzameling berustende in de Koninklijke Bibliotheek.* 's Gravenhage, 1905–1910. Vols. 5–6.

Labadie, Ernest. *La Presse bordelaise pendant la Révolution.* Bordeaux, 1910.

Lacroix, Sigismond. *Actes de la Commune de Paris pendant la Révolution.* Paris, 1884–1914. 7 & 8 vols.

———. "Ce qu'on pensait des Juifs à Paris en 1790." *Revue politique et littéraire*, XXXV (1898), 417–24.

Lechevalier, A. *Bio-bibliographie des écrivains de l'arrondissement du Havre.* Le Havre, 1902–03.

[Lévylier, R.] *Notes et documents concernant la famille Cerfberr*. Paris, 1902–06. 3 vols.

Liber, M. "Les Juifs et la convocation des Etats-généraux." *REJ*, LXV–LXVI (1913).

Lille. Danchin, Fernand. *Les imprimés lillois*. Lille, 1931. 2 vols.

Marburg. Universitätsbibliothek, Marburg / Lahn.

Mercure de France.

Mistère. Rothschild, Bᵒⁿ N. J. E. de. *Mistère du Viel Testament*. Paris, 1878–91. 6 vols.

Mongland, Andrè. *La France révolutionnaire et impériale*. Grenoble, 1930–38. 5 vols.

München. Universitätsbibliothek, München.

MW. Martin, Andrè et Walter, Gèrard. *Catalogue de l'histoire de la Révolution française*. Paris, 1936–54. 4 vols.

Napoleonica. Szajkowski, Z. "Judaica-Napoleonica. A Bibliography of Books, Pamphlets and Printed Documents. 1801–1815." *Studies in Bibliography and Booklore*, II (1956), 107–52.

Nordmann, A. *Geschichte der Juden in Basel*. Basel, 1913.

NYPL. The New York Public Library.

OBL. *Catalogue des Alsatica de la Bibliothèque de Oscar Berger-Levrault*. Nancy, 1886. 7 vols.

Paquet, René. *Bibliographie analytique de l'histoire de Metz pendant la Révolution, 1789–1800*. Paris, 1926. 2 vols.

Patriote (Le) français, 1790.

PC. Private collection.

Pfister, Chr. *Histoire de Nancy*. Paris, 1902–09. 3 vols.

Posener, S. "A Bibliography of French Works on Jews in the Second Half of the 18th Century." *The Jews in France*. New York, 1942, II, 56–72.

RA. Revue d'Alsace.

Reinach, T. *Les Juifs et la Révolution française*. Paris, 1909.

REJ. Revue des Etudes Juives.

Revue (La) Rhénane, 1923.

RJL. Revue Juive de Lorraine.

Robinet, J. F. E. *Le Mouvement religieux à Paris pendant la Révolution*. Paris, 1896–98. 2 vols.

Rocambole (La) des journaux, 1791.

Rôdeur (Le) français, 1790–1791.

Rosenbach, A. S. W. *An American Jewish Bibliography*. Philadelphia, 1926. Vol. XXX of *PAJHS*.

Rosent. Rosenthaliana Library, Amsterdam.

Roth, Cecil. *Magna Bibliotheca Anglo-Judaica*. London, 1937.

——— . "The Liturgies of Avignon and the Comtat Venaissin." *Journal of Jewish Bibliography*, I (1939), 99–105.

Rubens, A. *A Jewish Iconography*. London, 1954.

Saintonge. Bulletin de la Société . . . de la Saintonge.

Shatzky, J. "A Yiddish Weekly in the Times of the French Revolution." *Yivobleter*, ii (1931), 49–72; iii.(1932), 285.

Szajkowski, Z. *Agricultural Credit and Napoleon's Anti-Jewish Decrees*. New York, 1953.

———. "Anti-Jewish Riots during the Revolutions of 1789, 1830 and 1848." *Zion*, xx (1955), 82–102.

———. "The Attitude of French Jacobins Toward Jewish Religion." *Historia Judaica*, xviii (1956), 107–120.

———. "The Comtadin Jews and the Annexation of the Papal Province by France, 1789–1791." *JQR*, xlvi (1955), 181–93.

———. "The Discussion and Struggle over Jewish Emancipation in the Early Years of the French Revolution." *Historia Judaica*, xvii (1955), 129–32.

———. "Jewish Participation in the Sale of National Property During the French Revolution." *Jewish Social Studies*, xiv (1952), 291–316.

———. "The Law of September 28, 1791, on Jewish Creditors in France." *Zion*, xvii (1952), 84–100.

———. "Louis-Francia de Beaufleury, a Substitute Deputy during the French Revolution," *Davke*, xx (1954), 241–48.

———. "The Sephardic Jews of France during the Revolution of 1789." *Proceedings of the American Academy for Jewish Research*, xxiv (1955), 137–64.

SIW. *Strassburger israelitische Wochenschrift*.

Teissier, G. U. *Essai philologique sur les commencements de la typographie à Metz*. Metz, 1828, pp. 143–54, 222–231. (Hebrew publications of Metz.)

Tourneux, Maurice. *Bibliographie de l'histoire de Paris pendant la Révolution française*. Paris, 1890–1913. 5 vols.

UI. *L'Univers israélite*.

Véron-Réville. *Histoire de la Révolution française dans le Département du Haut-Rhin*. Colmar, 1865.

Vivie, Aurélien. Dictionnaire de Bibliographie Girondine. 62 vols., in manuscript. AmBx.

———. Documents. AmBx.

Walter, Gérard. *Répertoire de l'histoire de la Révolution française*. Paris, 1941–51. 2 vols.

Waltz, A. *Bibliographie de la ville de Colmar*. Colmar, 1902.

Wilhelm, L. *Bibliothèque Nationale et Universitaire de Strasbourg. Catalogue de la Section alsacienne et Lorraine*. Strasbourg, 1908–1929. 5 vols.

Yid. Yiddish.

Yivo. Yivo Institute for Jewish Research, New York, N. Y.

Zeitlin, William. *Bibliotheca Hebraica Post-Mendelssohniana*. Leipzig, 1891–95. 2 vols.

I. General Subjects, Periodicals, Calendars

1. Spire, Abraham. בעשרייבונג פון דער פערענדרונג, אודר אויף רואהר אין פראנקרייך, וואו מאן נעט רעוואליסיאהן פון פאריז דיא קאפיטאל, אויך דיא פע[ר]זאמעלונג דיא דעפי־ טיהרטע אויז דעם נאנצען ... קעניגרייך. דיע פע[ר]זאמעלונג נעט מאן עטא שענערא. Metz, 1789. 110 pp. 16°.

A Chronicle of the revolutionary events. Yid. Followed by No. 2. See Shatzky. JTS.

2. צייטונג. Nos. 1–19. Metz, Nov. 5, 1789–Apr. 1790. 2 pp. 16°.

A Weekly published by Abraham Spire. Two numbers contained 4 pages each and one number, 8 pages. Yid. See note to No. 1. JTS.

3. ... לוח משנת. Metz. 32°.

Published since 1768. The title for the year IV (1795–1796) is: קאלענדר דעם 4־טן יאהר דער רעפובליק פראנסעז לוח משנה תקנה לפ'ק. Metz, 1795. 16 pp. Contains revolutionary dates and slogans. During the Revolution the calendar was published by the printer Abraham Spire. H. & Yid. See Calendars. JTS. See also Nos. 4 & 5.

4. דעקאט קאלנדר פר דש דריטי יאהר דר רעפופליג. Strasbourg, 1794. 12 pp. 32°.

Calendar for the year III (1794–1795), published by the book binder Lebel b. Gabriel of Detweiler. The inside title is: לוח משנת תקנ'ה לפ'ק ווי אויך דר בייא דעקאטער נייאר קאלענדר דר פראנקן פר דש דריטי יאהר דר רעפופליג נדרוקט בייא יאנס לארעינ. See note to No. 3. See also No. 5.

5. ... לוח משנת. Lunéville. 16 pp. 32°.

Published from 1793 until 1815 by the printer Abraham Friseck. See also Nos. 3–4.

6–6a. [Beaufleury, Louis Francia de.] *Histoire de l'établissement des Juifs à Bordeaux et à Bayonne, depuis 1550.* Par le Citoyen L. F. B., Jurisconsulte du Département de la Seine. Paris, an 8 [1799]. 198 pp. 8°.

JTS, NYPL. Pp. 161–195: "Mémoire à consulter..." (see No. 302). According to Bernardau (ms. 712, vol. 6, f. 15) Beaufleury published a *Prospectus* of his history. It seems that Beaufleury also prepared the publication of a second volume on the history of the Alsatian Jewry: "Les journaux annoncent sous presse à Bordeaux une Histoire des Juifs de Bordeaux, de Bayonne et d'Alsace, par un jurisconsulte du Département de la Seine, 2 vol. in 8°." Bernardau, ms. 713-I, vol. 3, p. 503, Jan. 26, 1800. On the author see: Szajkowski, "Louis-Francia de Beaufleury."

II. General Polemics on Jews, 1789

7. [Hell, François Joseph Antoine de. Project of a *cahier des doléances*.] n. p., Février 1789. 9 pp. 4°.

With a project of requests on the Jews. AN (BA-II, 6, dr. 1).

8. Hourwitz, Zalkind, Juif Polonois. *Apologie des Juifs, en réponse à la question: Est-il des moyens de rendre les Juifs plus heureux et plus utiles en France?* Paris, 1789. 94 pp. 8°.

BN, JTS, HUJ. Published in May, 1789, according to Chassin (III, 257–58) and Lacroix (III, 605). One of three Studies rewarded by the Academy of Metz. See Cahen, "L'Emancipation." For Grégoire's study see No. 9. The third study, by

[Adolphe] Thiéry, *Dissertation sur cette question: Est-il des moyens de rendre les Juifs plus heureux et plus utiles en France?* Paris, 1788. IV, 105 pp. 8°. As the *Dissertation* was reviewed by the *Mercure de France* of Jan. 2 and Apr. 3, 1790, Monglond (I, 840) thinks that another edition was probably published in 1789 or 1790. To only one of the two copies in the BN is added a catalogue of the publisher.

9. Grégoire, [Henri Baptiste], curé du diocèse de Metz. *Essai sur la régénération physique, morale et politique des Juifs.* Ouvrage couroné par la Société royale des sciences et des arts de Metz, le 23 août 1788. Metz-Paris, 1789. 262 pp. 8°.

BN, HUC, JTS. See No. 9. For the English edition see No. 10.

10. Grégoire, [Henry Baptiste]. *An Essay on the Physical, Moral, and Political Reformation of the Jews.* Translated from the French. London, [1791]. VIII, 288 pp. 8°.

JTS. English edition of No. 9.

11. *Mémoire pour les Juifs de Lunéville et de Sarreguemines. A Nosseigneurs de l'Assemblée Nationale. 3 Août 1789.* n. p., [1789]. 8 pp. 8°.

BN. Reprinted by Benoît and A. Lévy. See also No. 80. For a Ger. translation see No. 20.

12. *Adresse présentée à l'Assemblée Nationale, le 31 Août 1789, par les Députés réunis des Juifs, établis à Metz, dans les Trois Evêchés, en Alsace & en Lorraine.* n. p., [1789]. I, 18 pp. 8°.

Signed by: "Louis Wolff, Gandchaux [Goudchaux-] Mayer-Cahen, Députés de Metz & des Trois-Evêchés. D. Sintzheim, S. Seligman Wittersheim, Députés d'Alsace. Mayer-Marx, Ber [Berr] Isaac Ber [Berr], Députés de Lorraine." pp. 17–18: "Demande particulière adressée à l'Assemblée Nationale par les Députés des Juifs de Metz" on the debts owed by the Jewish communities. BN. For It. & Dut. editions see Nos. 13 & 14. For Ger. translation see No. 20.

13. *Stato constituzionale degli Ebrei in Francia e suo esame.* n. p., n. d. 14 pp. 8°.

Inside title: "Supplica degli Ebrei Francesi presentata dai loro deputati all' Assemblea Nazionale, riserita dalla Gazzetta di Lugerno in Ottobre 1798." It. edition of No. 12. BN.

14. *Gelijkhed, Vrijheid, Broederschap. J. C. Hespe aan't Volk van Holland, en bijzonder aan de burgerij van Amsterdam. Ten geleide van het allerinterssantst Adres der Jooden in Vrankrijk aan de Nationale Vergaadering overgegeven.* Amsterdam, 1795. 16 pp. 8°.

Dut. edition of No. 12. Rosent.

15. Bing, Isaac Ber [Berr]. *Mémoire particulier pour la Communauté des Juifs établis à Metz.* Rédigé par Isaac Ber-Bing, l'un des Membres de la Communauté. [Signé:

Goudchau-Mayer-Cahen, Louis Wolf, Députés de la Communauté.] n. p., [1789]. 30 pp. 8°.

BN. Written by a brother of Isaïe=Berr Bing, or by himself. Published at the end of September or in October 1789. For a Ger. translation see No. 20.

16–16b. Berr, Berr Isaac. *Discours des Députés des Juifs des provinces des Evêchés, d'Alsace et de Lorraine, prononcés à la barre de l'Assemblée Nationale, par le sieur Berr Isaac Berr, l'un des Députés de la Lorraine, et l'extrait du procès-verbal de l'Assemblée Nationale y relatifs.* Paris, 1789. 7 pp. 8°.

Oct. 14, 1789. BN. The original in: AN, C 33 dr. 285 b, p. 17. H. translation in *Ha-Meassef* (1790), 30–32. Carmoly mentions also Ger. & Dut. editions (*La France israélite,* 60).

17. Grégoire, [Henri Baptiste], curé d'Eberménil, député de Nancy. *Motion en faveur des Juifs, précédée d'une Notice historique sur les persécutions qu'ils viennent d'essuyer en divers lieux, notamment en Alsace, et sur l'admission de leurs Députés à la barre de l'Assemblée Nationale.* Paris, 1789. XVI, 47 pp. 8°.

Published after the National Assembly's meeting of Oct. 11, 1789. JTS, Printed also in vol. I (1789) of *Procès-verbal de l'Assemblée Nationale.* Reprinted also in Paris, 1939. For a Polish edition see No. 18. Published in 1914 by S. Posener in a Russian translation. For a Ger. translation see No. 20.

18. ———. *Mowa J. X. Gregorza, plebana Embermenilskiego, deputata nantskiego [sic] za Żydami, z francuskiego na polski język przełożona z dodatkiem projectu Reformy Żydów polskich i potrzebnemi notatami objaśnione przez Imci Pana Salomona Polonusa, doctora medycyny, konsyliarza JK Mości w Wilnie.* Roku, 1792.

According to Grégoriana, no. 14. Polish edition of No. 17, together with a project on the reform of Polish Jews, by Salomon Polonus.

19. H . . . [Hell, F. J. A.], député de H . . . [Haguenau]. *Mon opinion sur les Juifs; ex-

trait des cahiers dont je suis porteur. Paris, [1789]. 12 pp. 4°.

Dated from Haguenau, Dec. 25, 1789. BN.

20. B. L. [Bendavid, Lazarus]. *Sammlung der Schriften an die Nationalversammlung, die Juden und ihre bürgerliche Verbesserung betreffend.* Aus d. Französischen. Berlin, 1789. 134 pp. 8°.

Contains an undated introduction "Nachricht" and nine chapters: I, Bittschrift der Juden zu Lunéville und Sarreguemines, an die Nationalversammlung; II, Schreiben der Deputirten der portugisischen Judenschaft zu Bordeaux an Herrn Gregor...; III, Adresse der Juden zu Paris an die Nationalversammlung; IV, Addresse, die der Nationalversammlung von den vereinigten Deputirten der Judenschaft zu Metz, den dreien Bisthümern zu Elsass und Lothringen zm 31. August 1789 überreicht worden ist; V, Bonsedore Bittschrift der Deputirten der Metzger Judenschaft an die Nationalversammlung; VI, Memoire... von Isaac Ber-

Bing...; VII, Zusatz zu der Adresse, die der Nationalversammlung von den Juden zu Lunéville und Sarreguemines überreicht worden; VIII, Vortrag des Herrn Grafen Stanislaus von Clermont-Tonnere, über die Verfolgung welche die Juden im Elsass bedrohet; IX, Vorstellung zum Besten der Juden von Herrn Gregor... nebst vorangeschikten historischen Nachrichten... Frankfurt a. M.

21. *Requête à Nosseigneurs les Etats généraux en faveur des Juifs.* [Paris, 1789.] 15 pp. 8°.

Not signed. Was probably published before the *Adresse* (No. 12). BN.

22. Thiébault [François Martin], curé de Sainte-Croix, député du bailliage de Metz. *No. ou Récit IV, et suite du compte rendu à ses commettans... Sa discussion de la demande des Juifs, d'avoir désormais droit de cité indéfini.* Metz, 1789. 18 pp. 8°.

Published after Oct. 14, 1789. BN.

III. Anti-Jewish Riots of Alsace, 1789

As soon as the news of the fall of the Bastille reached Alsace, the people attacked a large number of Alsatian Jewish communities, plundered property and destroyed Jewish houses. Many Jews took refuge in Basle and Mulhouse, where they were well treated, although not allowed to remain there. (On these riots see Szajkowski, "Anti-Jewish Riots.")

23. *Gebett, welches wir an jedem Sabbat für die Wolfart der Stadt Mülhausen absprechen...* תפלה שאנו מתפללין בעד שלום העיר מילהויזן בכל שבת קדש אחר הנותן תשועה שאנו מתפללין בעד אדונינו המלך. Basel, 1789. 2 ff. 4°.

H. & Ger. JTS, BuStg. Basel (Kirchenarchiv, S 4, 1789, Q, No. 71) possesses also another prayer in manuscript: תפלה להתפלל כל שליח צבור עבור בכונה בעד שלום העיר המפארה באסיליא ואופיה בכל ש"ק אחר הנותן תשועה. For Naftali Hirz Wessely's ode on this subject see *Ha-Meassef*, Sept. 1789; For a Ger. translation see Nordmann, pp. 181–82.

24. *Extrait des registres du Conseil Souverain d'Alsace. Du 1er Août 1789.* Colmar, 1789. 4 pp. 4°.

On the transfer of the guilty to the prison of Sélestat. Fr. & Ger. AdBR.

25. *Nous Maréchal des Camps & Armées du Roi, Inspecteur divisionnaire employé en Alsace.* n. p. n. d. Broadside.

Warning against the pogroms. Dated Aug. 1, 1789 and signed by Cte de Castéja. Fr. & Ger., without a Ger. title. JTS.

26. *Sébastien Etienne Nacquard, Chevalier de l'Ordre Royal & Militaire de St. Louis, Ecuyer, Conseiller du Roi, Lieutenant-Colonel de Cavalerie, Prévôt-général de la Maréchaussée d'Alsace. Jugement prévotal. Prevotal = Urtheil... n. p., n. d.* Broadside.

Dated Aug. 13, 1789. Fr. & Ger. Sentence against participants in the riots. JTS.

27–27a. *Sébastien Etienne Nacquard, Chevalier de l'Ordre Royal & Militaire de St.*

Louis, Ecuyer, Conseiller du Roi, Lieutenant-Colonel de Cavalerie, Prévôt général de la Maréchausée d'Alsace. n. p., n. d. Broadside.

Sentence dated Aug. 20, 1789. According to the text the same sentence was published also in Ger. JTS.

28–28a. *Sébast. Etienne Nacquard, Con.ᵉʳ du Roi, Lieut.ᵗ Col.ˡ de Cavalerie, Chev.ᵉʳ de l'Ordre de St. Louis, Ecuyer, Prévôt gén.ᵃˡ de la Maréchaussée d'Alsace. Jugement prévôtal.* n. p., n. d. Broadside.

Dated Aug. 20, 1789. According to the text the same sentence was published also in Ger. JTS.

29–29a. *Sebastian Stephan Nacquard. Ritter des Königl. und Militärischen St. Ludwigs-Ordens, Ecuyer, Köningl. Rath, Obrist = Lieutenant der Reiteren, Prévôt-général der Maréchaussée im Elsass. Prevotal = Urtheil.* n. p., n. d. Broadside.

Dated Aug. 26, 1789. According to the text the same sentence was published also in Fr. JTS.

30. *De par le Roi. 26 août 1789.* Strasbourg, 1789. Broadside.

Order against the pogroms. Fr. & Ger. The JTS possesses a fragment with the Fr. text only.

31. *Extrait du Procès-verbal des Séances de la Commission intermédiaire provinciale d'Alsace. Du vingt-huit Août 1789. Auszug aus dem Protokoll der Zwischenkommission der Provinz Elsass . . .* n. p., n. d. Broadside.

Warning against the pogroms. Signed by Hoffmann, "Secrét. prov. adj." Fr. & Ger. JTS, AdHR.

32. [An order of the same Commission against the pogroms, Sept. 1789.] 4°.

According to OBL, IV, 30.

33–33a. *Sébastien Etienne Nacquard . . . Jugement prévostal . . . à Altkirch le 6 Octobre 1789 par M. Antoine Célestin Weinborn.* n. p., n. d. Broadside.

According to the text the same sentence was also published in Ger. JTS.

33b. *Sébast. Etienne Nacquard . . . Jugement prévôtal et en dernier ressort, rendu à Altkirch le six octobre mil sept cent quatre — vingt — neuf, par M. Antoine-Célestin Weinborn . . . Prevotal = Urtheil . . . Strasbourg, n.d.* Broadside.

Fr. & Ger. HUC.

34. *Sébastien Etienne Nacquard . . . Jugement prévôtal et en dernier resort, rendu à Altkirch le sept octobre mil sept cent quatre-vingt-neuf, par M. Antoine-Célestin Weinborn . . . Prevotal-Urtheil, und in letzter Instanz . . .* Strasbourg, n. d. Broadside.

Fr. & Ger. JTS.

35. *Sébastien Etienne Nacquard . . . Jugement prévôtal et en dernier ressort, rendu à Altkirch le neuf octobre mil sept cent quatre-vingt-neuf . . . Prevotal-Urtheil, und in Letzter Instanz . . . Strasbourg, n. d.* Broadside.

Fr. & Ger. JTS.

[It is worth while to note a few broadsides and pamphlets which do not especially mention the Jewish aspect of these events:

1. *Liebe Mitbürger.* Colmar, den 27 Julii 1789. Broadside.

2. *Liebe Mitbürger.* Hüningen, den 30sten Julii 1789. Broadside.

3. *Nous, Jean-Baptiste-Donatien de Vimeur, Chevalier, comte de Rochambeau . . . Commandant en chef de la Haute & Basse Alsace.* Strasbourg, 6 Août 1789. Broadside.

4. *Ordonnance de M. le Cᵗᵉ de Rochambeau . . . Verordnung . . .* Strasbourg, 2 Août 1789. Broadside.

5. *Warnungs-Patent des Löbl. Oberrheinischen Kreises gegen die Störer der öffentlichen Ruhe. Traduction des Lettres Patentes d'admonition de la part du louable Cercle du Haut-Rhin, contre les perturbateurs du repos public.* [*Frankfurt, 9 Novembre*] *1789.* Porrentruy, 14 Décembre 1789. 11 pp. fol. Ger. & Fr.

6. *Extrait des registres du Conseil Souverain d'Alsace. Du 25 Janvier 1790. Auszug aus der Hohen Elsässischen Raths Protocoll. Vom 25ten Jenner 1790.* Colmar, n. d. Broadside.]

IV. The Decree of Dec. 24, 1789, on Non-Catholics

On Dec. 21–24, 1789, the National Assembly discussed a proposal to grant equal rights to Protestants, Jews and actors. But the anti-Jewish fraction was so strong that on Dec. 24, 1789 the Assembly adopted an evasive resolution separating the Jewish question from that of the other groups. The Assembly reserved for itself the right to decide about the Jews later. The fight for Jewish emancipation was thus not concluded.

36. Brunet de Latuque, [Pierre]. *Motion faite dans la séance de l'Assemblée Nationale, du Lundi 21 Décembre 1789, concernant les non-Catholiques,* par M. Brunet de Latuque, Député de Nérac. [Paris], n. d. 7 pp. 8°.
BN.

37. Clermont-Tonnerre, Comte Stanislas de. *Opinion de M. le Comte Stanislas de Clermont-Tonnerre, député de Paris; le 23 décembre 1789.* [Paris], n. d. 16 pp. 8°.
BN.

38–38c. Rabaut, Jean Paul [called Rabaut Saint-Etienne]. *Opinion de M. Rabaut de Saint-Etienne, sur la motion de M. le Comte [Boniface Louis André] de Castellane: Nul homme ne peut être inquiété pour ses opinions, ni troublé dans l'exercice dans sa religion.* Paris, 1789, 15 pp. 8°.
Aug. 23, 1789. Four editions. BN.

39. Broglie, [Charles Louis Victor] Prince de. *Opinion de M. le Prince de Broglie, Député de Colmar, sur l'admission des Juifs à l'état civil.* [Paris], n. d. 8 pp. 8°.
BN, BuStg.

40. Thiébault, [F. M.] *Discussion de cette proposition de M. [Adam-Philippe] de Custine: La Liberté de l'exercice public de toutes les religions doit être prononcée dans l'Assemblée Nationale, par son Co-Député M. Thiébault, Curé de Sainte Croix à Metz.* Metz, 1789. 51 pp. 8°.
BN.

41. *Nouvelle adresse des Juifs à l'Assemblée Nationale. 24 Décembre 1789.* Paris, 1789. 4 pp. 4°.
Not signed. BN.

42. *Lettres patentes du Roi sur le Décret de l'Assemblée Nationale pour l'admission des non-Catholiques dans l'administration et dans tous les emplois civils et militaires. Données à Paris au mois de Décembre 1789.* Paris, 1790. 2 pp. 4°.
BN.

43. ———. *Transcrites en Parlement, en vacations, le 29 Décembre audit an.* Paris, 1789. 3 pp. 4°.
BN.

44. ———. [Strasbourg, 1790.] 2 pp. 4°.

Together with "Extrait du Procès-verbal des séances de la Commission Intermédiaire provinciale d'Alsace, du 2 Janvier 1790." BuStg. For the Ger. edition see No. 45.

45. *Offene Briefe des Königs, ueber einen Schluss der National* = *Versamlung, die Zulassung der Nichtkatholischen zur Verwaltung und zu allen bürgerlichen und militärischen Stellen, Aemtern und Würden betreffend. Gegeben zu Paris im Monat Dezember 1789.* Strassburg, n. d. 2 pp. 4°.

Ger. edition of No. 44. BuStg.

46. ———. [Strasbourg, 1789.] 4 pp. 4°.

A combined edition of Nos. 44 & 45. BuStg.

47. *Lettres patentes* . . . [Strasbourg, 1790.] Broadside.

Fr. & Ger. The JTS possesses only a fragment with the Fr. text.

48. ———. Bordeaux, 1789, 3 pp. 4°.

BmBx.

49. ———. Nîmes, 1789. 3 pp. 4°.

AdGard.

50. ———. Aix 1790. 3 pp. 4°.

PC.

51. ———. Lille, n. d. [1790].

According to Lille, II, no. 5199. Not in the possession of the BmLille.

52. [Godard, Jacques?.] *Pétition des Juifs établis en France, adressée à l'Assemblée Nationale, le 28 janvier 1790, sur l'ajournement du 24 Décembre 1789.* Paris, 1790. IV, 107 pp. 8°.

Signed by Mayer-Marx, Berr Isaac-Berr, David Sintzheim, Théodore Cerf-Berr, Lazare Jacob, Trenelle père, Cerf-Berr. Pp. 3–4: "Nous sommes

instruits qu'une adresse des Juifs de Bordeaux vient d'être présentée à l'Assemblée nationale [see No. 61] . . . & elle nous a déterminés à précipiter le mémoire que nous avons l'honneur de vous adresser, afin que notre sort puisse être décidé en même temps que celui de nos frères de Bordeaux." BN, For Ger. & Dt. editions see Nos. 53 & 54. HUC. has an edition with the following pagination: vi [7] – 111 pp.

53. *Unterthänige Vorstellung der in Frankreich ansässigen Juden veranlast durch die Verlegung der Streitfrage über ihr bürgerliches schiksal vom 24 December 1789, und der Nationalversammlung zugeschrieben den 28 Jänner 1790. Aus dem Französischen.* Strassburg, 1790. 74 pp. 8°.

BuStg, BN, JTS. See Nos. 52.

54. *Adres der Jooden in Frankryk woonende, ingeleverd bij de Nationale Vergadering.* [Amsterdam, 1791.] 72 pp. 8°.

Rosent. See Nos. 52 & 53.

55. [Thiéry, Adolphe.] *Réflexions impartiales d'un citoyen sur la question de l'éligibilité des Juifs proposé et discutée dans les séances de l'Assemblée Nationale les 23 et 24 Décembre [1789] et ajournée par la même assemblée.* [Paris, Janvier 1790.] 8°.

See Bordeaux Delegates, 65 ("l'auteur était Mr. Thiéry, avocat à Nancy"). PC.

56. [Servan, Joseph Michel Antoine.] *Evénements remarquables et intéressants, à l'occasion des décrets de l'auguste Assemblée Nationale, concernant l'éligibilité de MM. les comédiens, le bourreaux et les juifs.* [Paris], 1790. I, 37 pp. 8°.

Inside title: "Extrait de la séance de l'Assemblée nationale du lundi 24 Décembre 1789." A parody against the Jews being defended at the Assembly by Honoré Gabriel de Riqueti comte de Mirabeau. Was often erroneously cited as a pro-Jewish pamphlet. BN.

(*To be continued*)

The Emancipation of
Jews During the French Revolution

A Bibliography of Books, Pamphlets and
Printed Ducuments, 1789–1800

(Continued)

V. THE SEPHARDIC JEWS

The Sephardic Jews of France were concentrated in Bordeaux, Saint-Esprit-lès-Bayonne and a few other small communities of Southwestern France. They were the first of the Jews in France to gain full emancipation by the decree of Jan. 28, 1790. A major aim, thenceforth, of the Sephardic leaders was to prevent the immediate grant of full citizenship to the Ashkenazim. The Sephardim participated, much more than the Ashkenazim in all events of the Revolution. In Saint-Esprit the Club of Jacobins was composed mostly of Jews and in Bordeaux Jews were even active federalists.

57. *Tableau de l'Assemblée primaire du Bourg Saint-Esprit et de sa jurisdiction, vers le chef-lieu du département.* Bayonne, [1789.] Broadside.

A list of the residents. AmBa.

58. *Essai sur la tolérance des non-Catholiques en France. Poème adressé à MM. les Députés des Trois Ordres.* [Bordeaux?,] 1789. 12 pp. 8°.

On Protestants and Jews. BmBx.

59. *Protestation en forme de lettres des nobles Cohens aux gentilshommes soi disant les Nobles de la Sénéchausée de Bordeaux induement assemblées le 10 février 1789.* Bordeaux, 1 Mai 1789. 8 pp. 8°.

An anti-Jewish parody, particularly against Jewish participation in the elections. BN, JTS.

60. *Lettre adressée à M. Grégoire . . . par les députés de la nation juive portugaise de Bordeaux, le 14 août 1789.* Versailles, [1789.] 4 pp. 8°.

Signed by [Abraham] Furtado, [David] Azévédo, David Gradis, électeur, Lopes Du Bec [Dubec]. BN, JTS. See No. 20.

61. *Adresse à l'Assemblée Nationale.* Paris, 1789 [1790]. 8 pp. 4°.

Petition of the Bordeaux Jews, dated Dec. 31, 1789, but published in January 1790. See: Bordeaux Delegates, 72. P. 5: signatures; p. 6: Meeting of the Bordeaux Jews, Dec. 24, 1789; p. 7: "Etat des pièces remises au Comité de Constitution qui établissent la possession où sont les Juifs de Bordeaux, de Bayonne, etc. de la qualité de Citoyens actifs." BM. See note to No. 52.

62. Silveyra, [David], agent et député. *Adresse présentée à l'Assemblée Nationale par*

le député des Juifs espagnols et portugais établis au bourg Saint-Esprit-lès-Bayonne. Paris, janvier 1790. 8 pp. 4°.

According to MW (iv, 361) the petition was published in June 1790, which is not correct. BN.

63. *Lettres patentes du Roi, sur un Décret de l'Assemblée Nationale, portant que les Juifs, connus en France sous le nom de Juifs portugais, espagnols et avignonais, y jouiront des droits de citoyen actif. Transcrites en Parlement, en vacations, le 9 Février dudit an.* Paris, 1790. 3 pp. 4°.

BN. See also Nos. 64–70.

64–64a–b. ———. Bordeaux, 1790. 3 pp. 4°.

Two Bordeaux editions, published by the printers Michel Rade and Pierre Phillipot. A third edition, published by Rade, is mistakenly dated 1789. JTS, AdG, PC.

65. ———. *Transcrites sur les registres des Cours supérieurs.* Aix, 1790. 3 pp. 4°.

BmMs.

66. ———. Nantes, 13 Février 1790. 3 pp. 4°.

BmNT.

67. ———. Lille, 1790. 2 pp. 4°.

BmLi.

68. ———. Metz, [1790.] 2 pp. 4°.

JTS, BuStg.

69. ———. *Enrégistrées le 18 Février suivant.* Colmar, 1790. 2 pp. 4°.

BmC.

70. ———. *Registrées en Parlement le 15 Février suivant.* Nancy, [1790.] 3 pp. 4°.

BmN, HUC.

70a. [A printed letter, signed by Comte de Saint Priest, sent together with copies of the decree on the emancipation of the Sephardim.] Paris, 17 février 1790. 1 p. 4°

Departmental archives of Hérault, C 2748.

71–71a. *Décision du Comité de Constitution requise par David Silveyra, syndic, agent des Juifs patentés. 28 Octobre 1790.* Paris, 1790. 1 p. 4°.

Another edition: . . . *donné à la requisition de David Silveyra, sindic & agent des Juifs français.* Jews with individual Letters patent could benefit from the Decree of Jan. 28. BN, JTS, PC.

72. *La Nouvelle du jour ou Lettre à un politique x.* Bordeaux, 1790. 8 pp. 8°.

BmBx. See Vivie's Documents (AmBx, v, 101). Louis XVI, who granted full rights to the Jews, was considered by the Jews as their Messiah.

73. Gergerez fils, M. *Adresse aux défenseurs de l'humanité, sur le Décret rendu par l'Assemblée Nationale, en faveur des Juifs.* [Bordeaux,] 1790. 8 pp. 8°.

In favor of the Jews. BmBx.

74. De Laissac, capitaine au Régiment de Limousin. *Lettre à M. [Isaac René Guy] Le Chapellier, Membre de l'Assemblée Nationale.* Paris, 1790. 48 pp. 8°.

Against the Jews and the Decree of Jan. 28. JTS.

74a. *Impromptu d'un espagnol [D. Joseph Marchena] admis par acclamation et l'unanimité au Club des Amis de la Constitution à Bayonne.* Bayonne, 1792, 1 p. 8°.

According to a document of the Spanish Inquisition Marchena was a Jew. See A. Paz y Mélia. *Papeles de Inquisición. Catalaga y Extractos.* Madrid, 1947, p. 174.

See also Nos. 6, 20, 275–76, 300–305.

VI. General Polemics, 1790–1791

75. Godard, Jacques, avocat au Parlement. *Lettre des Juifs établis en France à M. le Président de l'Assemblée nationale.* Paris, 1790.

According to Posener (No. 93) in the BmM (No. 363), where such an item does not exist. It is possible that Posener mistook the introduction to the *Petition* of Jan. 28, 1790 (*Lettre au Président de l'Assemblée*), by Godard (see No. 52) as the title of another pamphlet.

76. Vasse, La Baronne de [Baroness Cornélie de Wouters?], Angloise. *Mémoire à l'Assemblée Nationale, pour démontrer aux Français, les raisons qui doivent les déterminer à admettre les Juifs indistinctement aux droits de citoyens.* Paris, 1790. 1 f., 9 pp. 8°.

Published after Jan. 28, 1790. JTS, BN. Robinet (I, 328) mentioned the pamphlet without the author's name.

77. L., Abbé [Lamourette, Abbé Antoine Adrien]. *Observations sur l'état civil des Juifs, adressées à l'Assemblée Nationale.* n. p., [1790]. 1, 20 pp. 8°.

Published after Jan. 28, 1790. On p. 18 the author announced another study, which was not published: "Nous nous proposons de traiter dans un autre Ecrit, de l'état civil des Juifs, considéré dans son rapport avec les Loix." BN.

78. Berr, Berr Isaac. *Lettre à l'abbé [Jean Sifrein] Maury et la Réponse de celui-ci.* Paris, 1790. 4 pp. 8°.

Maury's letter is dated Jan. 1790. BmN. See also No. 79

79. Wessely, Naftali Hirtz. *Instruction salutaire adressée aux Communautés juives de l'Empire; par le célèbre Hartwic Weisly, Juif de Berlin; traduite en françois en l'année 1782. Nouvelle édition, augmentée de notes, d'une Lettre à M. l'abbé Maury, Député à l'Assemblée Nationale, par l'éditeur, & de la réponse de M. l'abbé Maury.* Paris, 1790. 101 pp. 8°.

BN. Translated and edited by Berr Isaac Berr from דברי שלום ואמת. Berlin, 1782. 1st Fr. edition:

Instructions salutaires adressées aux Communautés juives de l'empire de Joseph II. Paris, 1782. Maury's letter is dated Jan. 1790. BN. See No. 78.

80. *Nouveau mémoire pour les Juifs de Lunéville & de Sarreguemines; présenté à l'Assemblée Nationale, le 26 Février 1790.* [Paris,] 1790. 8 pp. 8°.

For the first memorandum see No. 11. BN.

81. *Lettres patentes du Roi, sur un Décret de l'Assemblée Nationale, concernant les conditions requises pour être réputé Français, et admis à l'exercice des droits de citoyen actif. Données à Paris le 2 Mai 1790* . . . [Paris,] 1790. 2 pp. 4°.

Decree of Apr. 30, 1790, on aliens, "sans . . . rien préjuger sur la question des Juifs, qui a été et demeure ajournée." BN. For a Ger. edition see No. 82.

82. ———. Strasbourg, [1790]. Broadside.

Fr. & Ger. Ger. title: *Offener Brief des Königs* . . . Together with the minutes of the meeting of the Strasbourg City Council, May 22, 1790. See No. 81. BuStg.

83. Lambert, Abraham. *Lettre à M. [Jean François] Reubell, Député d'Alsace, à l'Assemblée Nationale.* n. p., [1790]. 8 pp.

Dated from Metz, May 10, 1790. PC.

84. [Sanchamau, J. B.]. *L'Ecole des Peuples et des Rois, ou Essai philosophique sur la liberté, le pouvoir arbitraire, les Juifs et les noirs; avec des notes historiques et critiques.* Paris, Mai 1790, 170 pp. 8°.

The author's name appears on p. 10. In favor of Jews. JTS, BN.

85. *Proclamation du Roi, sur une instruction de l'Assemblée nationale, concernant les function des Assemblées administratives du 20 oûta 1790.* [Paris, 1790.] 2 pp. 4°.

On the "éligibilité des citoyens." As of Jews, only those mentioned in the Decree of Jan. 28, 1790, could profit from the new law. BN.

86. ———. Bordeaux, 1790. 2 pp. 4°.

BmBx. The Decree was published by many other departmental and municipal authorities.

87. *Proclamation du Roi, sur le Décret de l'Assemblée Nationale, faisant suite au Décret concernant l'organisation judiciare. Du 11 Septembre 1790.* [Paris,] 1790. 2 pp. 4°.

"L'Assemblée nationale n'entend encore rien pré-juger par rapport aux Juifs." BN.

88. [Fare, Anne Louis Henri de La.] *Opinion de M. l'évêque de Nancy, Député de Lorraine, sur l'admissibilité des Juifs à la plenitude de l'état civil, et des droits de citoyens actifs.* ["Signé: A. L. H. Evêque de Nancy, Député de Lorraine.] Paris, 1790. 14 pp. 8°.

Published before Apr. 22, 1790. Against the Jews. See No. 89. BmN, BN, HUC.

89. Berr, Isaac Berr. *Lettre du sieur Berr-Isaac-Berr, négociant à Nancy, Juif, naturalisé en vertu des Lettres-patentes du Roi, enrigis-trées au Parlement de Nancy, député des Juifs de la Lorraine; à Monseigneur l'évêque de Nancy, Député a l'Assemblée Natioanle.* Paris, 1790. 20 pp. 8°.

Dated Apr. 22, 1790. See Nos. 88 & 219. BmN, BN, HUC.

90. Goudchaux, Lion. *Lettre du Sr Lion Goudchaux, Juif de Nancy, à M. l'Abbé Maury, député à l'Assemblée Nationale, sur sa motion pour l'inadmission des Juifs au droit de Cité.* Nancy, 1790. 16 pp. 8°.

Dated May 5, 1790. BmN.

91–92. Foissac, de [Général Philippe François de Latour-Foissac]. *Plaidoyer contre l'usure des Juifs des évêchés, de l'Alsace et de la Lorraine.* [Strasbourg, 1790.] 109 pp. 8°.

Title on p. 1: "Plaidoyer pour plus d'un million de citoyens contre le fléau de l'usure des Juifs par Mr. de Foissac, capitaine au Corps Royal de génie, commandant la Garde Nationale de la ville de Phalsbourg." BN, BuStg. Another edition without the title on p. 1, PC.

93. *Sur les Juifs en France.* n. p., 1790. 23 pp. 8°.

Against the Jews. Probably by an Alsatian author. AIU, HUJ.

94. *Lettre à M. [Charles Maurice de] Talleyrand [-Périgord], ancien évêque d'Autun, chef de la communion des Talleyrandistes, sur son rapport concernant l'admission égale et indéfinie de tous les cultes religieux,* Paris, 1791. 8°.

Dated June 20. BN.

VII. ALSATIAN POLEMICS, 1789

Alsace, with almost half of the French Jews living there, was the main center of anti-Jewish polemics. Here originated the principal fight against Jewish emancipation. For other publications of the year 1789 see also Nos. 23–35.

95. Clermont-Tonnerre, Cte Stanislas [Marie Adélaïde de]. *Opinion relativement aux persécutions qui menacent les Juifs d'Alsace.* Versailles, [1789]. 4 pp. 8°.

Dated Sept. 28, 1789. BN.

96. *Avis aux catholiques. An die Katoliken. Strasbourg, le 13 Décembre 1789.* [Stras-bourg], n. d. 2 pp. 4°.

For equal rights "pour les individus de toutes les religions sans distinction," without mentioning the Jews. BuStg.

97. *Warum das Kräussel-Horn auf dem Münster zu Strassburg geblasen wird.* [Stras-bourg, 1789, or 1790.] 1 p. 4°.

BuStg.

VIII. The Anti-Jewish Campaign of Strasbourg, 1790

Strasbourg, with its traditional anti-Jewish restrictions, led the Alsatian fight against Jewish emancipation. It was almost impossible for a Strasbourg Jacobin to defend Jews. The Strasbourg Society of the Friends of the Constitution published a report in favor of Jewish emancipation. This drew furious attacks against the Jews and their few Jacobin friends, and was the excuse for a well organized campaign against Jews in the entire province. See Hildenfinger, "L'Adresse de la Commune de Strasbourg," and Szajkowski, "The Discussion and Struggle."

98. *A la Garnison de Strasbourg.* [Strasbourg, 1790.] 3 pp. 4°.

"Par un Strasbourgeois qui a voyagé vingt-quatre ans. Strasbourg, ce 11 Février 1790." For peace between the Catholics, Protestants and Jews. NYPL.

99. [Brunck, Richard François Philippe.] *Rapport lu à l'Assemblée de la Société des Amis de la Constitution le 27 Février mil sept cent quatre-vingt-dix sur la question de l'état civil des Juifs d'Alsace.* [Strasbourg, 1790.] 31 pp. 8°.

Prepared by Brunck and signed by Jean Jacques Thédore Le Barbier de Tinan, President of the Society, Genthon and François Laurent Xavier Levrault, secretaries. Another edition was signed by Levrault (see No. 100). P. 31: Extrait du procès-verbal de la Société . . . du 27 février 1790." The same Extrait is dated March 2, 1790, in the Ger. edition (see No. 101). For the German edition and later reprints see No. 101. BuStg, BN, HUJ. See OBL, I, 33.

100. Levrault, [F. L. X.]. *Rapport de l'Assemblée de la Société des Amis de la Constitution, le 27 Février mil sept cent quatre-vingt-dix sur la question de l'état civil des Juifs d'Alsace.* [Strasbourg, 1790.] 32 pp. 8°.

According to OBL, I, 32. See No. 99.

101. [Brunck, R. F. P.] *Bericht welcher in der Gesellschaft der Freunde der Konstitution über die Frage vorgelesen wurde: Können die Juden in Elsasse des Bürgerrrecht theilhaftig werden.* [Strassburg, 1790.] 38 pp. 8°.

Ger. edition of No. 99. Signed by de Tinan, Genthon, and Levrault. P. 30: "Auszug aus dem Protokoll der Gesellschaft . . .," March 2, 1790. Pp. 31–38: "Nachtrg." Reprinted as "Noch ein Beytrag zu den Vorschlägen über die bürgerliche Verbesserung der Juden. Bericht . . . ," *Der neue deutscher Zuschauer*, VII (1791), 296–316. Reprinted also in *Allgemeine Zeitung des Judenthums*, II (1842), 185–92, 215–31. BuStg.

102. *Reproche faite à M. Levrault d'avoir signé, comme secrétaire de la Société des Amis de la Constitution, le rapport sur l'état civil des Juifs.* [Strasbourg, Mars 1790.] 2 pp. 4°.

OBL, I, 32.

103. Foissac, De. [Latour Foissac, Général Philippe François de]. *Observations sur un Ecrit en faveur des Juifs de l'Alsace, présenté au Comité des amis de la Constitution de Strasbourg, le 27 Février dernier.* n. p., n. d. 29 pp. 8°.

Dated from Phaltzbourg [Phalsbourg], Apr. 1, 1790. BN, BuStg, HUJ.

104. *Extrait des Registres du Corps Municipal de la ville de Strasbourg du 3 Avril 1790. Auszug aus den Registern des Municipal-Korps der Stadt Strassburg, vom 3ten April 1790.* [Strasbourg, 1790.] 2 pp. 4°.

Fr. & Ger. Signed by "Rumpler, secrétaire-greffier." Convocation of a meeting on Apr. 7 on Levrault's Report. Reprinted in No. 105. BmStg.

105. *Assemblée de la Commune. Extrait des Registres du Conseil général de la Commune de la ville de Strabsourg. Du 3 Avril 1790.*

Versammlung der Commune. Auszug aus den Registern des Gesammten Raths der Gemeinde der Stadt Strassburg vom 3ten April 1790. [Strasbourg, 1790.] Broadside.

Fr. & Ger. Signed by "Rumpler, secrétaire-greffier." Contains also the text of No. 104. BuStg.

106. Levrault, [F. L. X.]. *Lettre écrite par le Substitut du Procureur de la Commune de Strasbourg à M.* [*François Xavier Alexis*] *Poirot, Président de l'Assemblée du District des Récollets, le mercredi 7 avril 1790. Schreiben des Substituten des Gemeinde-Prokurators an Hrn Poirot, Präsidenten der Versammlung bei den Franziskanern, Mittwoch den 7ten April 1790.* [Strasbourg, 1790.] 2 pp. fol.

Fr. & Ger. BuStg, JTS.

107. *Lettre écrite à M.* [*Etienne François Joseph*] *Schwendt, Député à l'Assemblée Nationale par MM. les Maire & Officiers Municipaux de la Ville de Strasbourg, le 8 Avril 1790. Schreiben der Herren Maire und Municipal-Beamten der Stadt Strassburg an Herrn Schwendt, Abgeordneten bey der Nationalversammlung, den achten April 1790.* [Strasbourg, 1790]. Broadside.

Signed by "Rumpler, secrétaire-greffier." Contains also "Lettre de MM. les Maire & Officiers Municipaux de la ville de Strasbourg, à M. le Président de l'Assemblée Nationale en date du 8 Avril 1790." Against the Jewish emancipation. BuStg, BN, HUC, JTS.

108. *Bürger zu Strasburg, gebt Acht auf Euere Freyheit.* [Strassburg, 11ten April 1790.] 4 pp. 4°.

On the Levrault affair. On pp. 3–4: "Sehr erbaulicher Bericht, als Nachruf, von dem, was gestern Nachmitags den 10ten April 1790, auf den Rathause vorgefallen." BuStg. Heitz (*Les Sociétés*, p. 30) mentioned a Fr. title: "Citoyens de Strasbourg, soyez sur votre garde pour votre liberté," but there was, probably, no Fr. edition.

109–109a. *Très humble et très respectueuse Adresse que présente à l'Assemblée nationale* *la commune toute entière de la ville de Strasbourg.* Strasbourg, [Avril 1790]. 14 pp. 4° & Paris, [Avril 1790.] 20 pp. 4°.

Against Jewish emancipation. The Paris edition was published by E. F. J. Schwendt, who presented it to the National Assembly on Apr. 20, 1791. BN, BuStg. For the Ger. edition see No. 110.

110. *Unterthänigste-gehorsamste Vorstellung der gesamten Gemeinde der Stadt Strassburg an die National-Versammlung.* Strassburg, [1790]. 11 pp. 4°.

Ger. edition of No. 109. BuStg.

111. *Très-humble adresse présenté à l'Assemblée Nationale par la Commune de Strasbourg duement assemblée, contre la pétition du droit de citoyens actifs faite le 28 Janvier dernier au nom de 20,000 Juifs répandus en Alsace et contre un écrit intitulé: Rapport . . . sur la question de l'état civil des Juifs de ladite Province.* [Strasbourg, 1790.] 11 pp. 4°.

Against No. 99. BuStg, BN. For the Ger. edition see No. 112. The title given by Posener (No. 126) is not correct.

112. *Unterthänigste Vorstelung der Gemeinde von Strasburg über eine Bittschrift, welche den 28ten Jänner dieses Jahr im Namen der Juden des Elsasses der National-Versammlung vorgelegt worden und über ein Werk betitelt: "Abhandlung der Frage über den Bürgerstand der Juden eben derselben Provinz.* [Strassburg, 1790.] 11 pp. 4°.

Ger. edition of No. 111. BuStg.

113. *Réponse des Juifs de la province de Lorraine à l'Adresse présentée à l'Assemblée Nationale par la Commune toute entière de la ville de Strasbourg.* n. p., 1790. 24 pp. 4°.

Apr. 13, 1790. Probably written by Berr Isaac Berr (see Liber, LXV, 104). BN. Ger. translation: "Antwort der Juden in der Provinz Lothringen, auf die der Nationalversammlung von der sämmtlichen Stadtgemeinde zu Strasburg überreichte Bittschrift," *Berlinische Monatschrift* (Oct., 1791), 351–92, translated by David Friedländer.

114. *Avis aux Alsaciens*, [Strasbourg, 1790.] 28 pp. 8°.

Against the Jews. BuStg. For the Ger. edition see No. 115. See also No. 116.

115. *Warnung an die Elsässer*. [Strassburg, 1790.] 28 pp. 8°.

Ger. edition of No. 18. BmStg.

116. *Warnung an die Elsässer gegen die Judenemancipation*. Mai 1790.

According to Guerber, p. 83. Possibly a mistaken transcription of the title of No. 114.

117. Ginzrot, Sohn. *Antwort über eine Schrift, betitelt: Bericht, welcher in der Gesellschaft der Freunde der Constitution über die Frage vorgelesen wurde: "Können die Juden im Elsass des Bürgerrechts theilhaftig werden"? und zur widerlegung der darinn* vorkommenden Stellen eine, Biedermanns unwürdig, den der edle Name Bürgerfreund zieren sollte. [Strassburg,] 1790. 15 pp. 8°.

BuStg, BN.

118. *Observations sur la possibilité et l'utilité de l'admission des Juifs en Alsace aux droits de citoyens adressées à un Membre de la Société des Amis de la Constitution à Strasbourg, par un ami de l'homme.* [Strasbourg, 1790.] 20 pp. 8°.

BN.

119. *Amis de la Constitution, Réflexions sur la Société des Amis de la Constitution.* [Strasbourg,] 1790. 4 pp. 4°.

According to OBL, I, 32. According to Heitz (*Les Sociétés*, p. 29) the *Réflexions* were published by the Society in connection with the Levrault affair.

IX. ALSATIAN POLEMICS, 1790–1791

120. *Adresse des Juifs alsaciens au peuple d'Alsace.* n. p. [1790]. 6 pp. 8°.

Probably of Feb., 1790, because on p. 4 is mentioned the preparation of the petition for the Paris Jews (see No. 152). For the Ger. edition see No. 121. BN, BuStg.

121. *Zuschrift der Elsassischen Juden an die übrigen Einwohner Elsasses*, n. p., [1790]. 8 pp. 8°.

Ger. edition of No. 120. BuStg.

122–123. [Two anti Jewish leaflets, Feb. 1790.]

"Le 23 Février [1790] le Bureau intermédiaire d'Huningue en Alsace a denoncé à M. le P^t du Comité des recherches un prospectus en libelle signé Wilz ou Vist et l'envoy d'un lettre annonçant des craintes sur l'effet d'un décret qui atendroit aux juifs d'Alszace la plénitude des droits de Citoyen actif. Les imprimés ont été envoyés à toutes les communautés du ressort du district d'Huningue ..." AN, D–xxix bis 3 (41/20).

124. *Observation intéressante, relative à la demande du droit de citoyens actifs, faite au nom des Juifs d'Alsace.* n. p., n. d. 2 pp. 4°.

By the City Councils of Bischheim, Lingolsheim and Daugendorf, after the discussion on Jews at the National Assembly on Apr. 15, 1790. Against the Jews, BN.

125. *Proclamation du Roi, sur un Décret de l'Assemblée Nationale concernant les Juifs. Du 18 Avril 1790.* Paris, 1790. 2 pp. 4°.

Decree of Apr. 16, 1790, for the protection of the Alsatian Jews. For the Ger. text see Nos. 126 & 130. BN.

126. ——— . Strasbourg, [1790]. Broadside.

Fr. & Ger. See No. 125. Ger. title: *Proklamation des Königs*. BuStg.

127. *Très humble et très-respectueuse Adresse à l'Assemblée Nationale, exprimant le voeu*

unanime de la Commune de Colmar. Arrête à l'Assemblée de MM. les Commissaires le 25 Avril 1790. n. p., n. d. 4 pp. 8°.

Published as a result of the anti-Jewish action by Strasbourg. For the Ger. edition see No. 128. BmC.

128. *Unterthänigste, ehrerbietigste Adresse an die Nationalversammlung, welche den einmüthingen Wunch der Gemeinde von Colmar erthält . . . 25ten April 1790.* n. p., n. d. 4 pp. 8°.

Ger. edition of No. 127. BmC.

129. *Demüthigste und ehrerbietigste Bittschrift an die National-Versammlung.* n. p., n. d. 8 pp. 8°.

Petition of the City Council of Huningue against Jewish emancipation, Apr., 1790. Published as a result of the anti-Jewish action of Strasbourg. BuStg.

130. [Limburg-Wehlen Stirum, Dermian August Carl, Graf von.] *Auguste par la grâce de Dieu, Prince évêque de Spire . . . comte de Limbourg-Stirum &c. &c. à tous les curés de Nôtre Diocèse en Alsace, salut! Von Gottes Gnaden Wir August Bischof zu Speier . . . An alle Pfarrer Unserer Diözes im Elsass, Unsern Gruss.* n. p., n. d. 3 pp. fol.

Fr. & Ger. Request of May 4, 1790, to respect the Decree of Apr. 16, 1790. See No. 125. BN, BuStg.

131. [Scaramuza.] *Les Juifs d'Alsace doivent-ils être admis au droit de citoyens.* n. p., 1790. VIII, 208, 46 pp. 8°.

According to Barbier (II, 1051) this anti-Jewish book is written by Scaramuza; or by Hell, according to Chauffour, No. 2313; or possibly by Reubell, according to Degerman, p. 94. HUC, JTS, BN.

132. *Proclamation de par les Maire et Officiers municipaux de la ville de Strasbourg.* [Strasbourg, 1790.] Broadside.

Dicision of Sept. 4, 1790. "Fait également défense aux dits Juifs de se tenir ensemble sur les places

devant les cafés et autres lieux publics, surtout les jours de fêtes et dimanches . . ." See also No. 133. BuStg.

133. *Proclamation de par les Maire et Officiers municipaux. Proclamation auf Befehl des Maire und der Munizipal-Beamten. 25 Septembre 1790.* [Strasbourg, 1790.] Broadside.

Fr. & Ger. On the same subject as No. 132. BuStg, AdBR.

134. Pflieger, [Jean Adam]. *Réflexions sur les Juifs d'Alsace . . .* Paris, 1790. 20 pp. 8°.

Against the Jews. For the Ger. edition see No. 135. According to one source the pamphlet was not written by Pflieger, a Deputy to the National Assembly, himself. See *Suite de dénonciation . . . contre . . . Phliéger & Rewbell.* Paris, 1790, p. 21. BuStg, BN.

135. ———. *Bemerkungen über die Elsässischer Juden . . .* n. p., [1790]. 16 pp. 8°.

Ger. edition of No. 134. BuStg.

136. [Hell, F. J. A. de.] *Observations d'un Alsacien sur l'Affaire présente des Juifs d'Alsace.* Seconde édition (la première a paru en 1779). Neuchatel [Strasbourg], 1790. 23, 123 pp. 8°.

The first edition of 136 pp. was published in 1779. With a new introduction "Avis des Editeurs," pp. iii–xxiii. On the affair of counterfeited receipts. See Szajkowski, *Economic Status*, pp. 123–140. BuStg.

137. J. *Die Juden-Verfolgungen.* [Strassburg,] 1790. 16 pp. 12°.

BuStg.

138. *Lettre d'un Alsacien sur les Juifs d'Alsace.* Paris, 1790. 24 pp. 8°.

Title on p. 2: "Lettre d'un Alsacien, sur les Juifs d'Alsace, à M. Reubell, Député de cette Province, à l'Assemblée Nationale." BN, HUC.

139. [Seybold, David Christoph.] *Erfreuliche Nachricht für die Juden von einem bald zu erwartenden Hohenpriester oder Brief des*

Rabbiners zu Rappoltsweiler an den Rabbiner zu Metz. Aus dem Jüdischteutschen Original treulich übersetzt. [Strassburg,] 1790. 8 pp. 8°.

A parody against Jews, some Protestant circles and the idea of centralizing the Protestant Church of Strasbourg. See also Nos. 142–143. BuStg.

140. *Ueber die Vertreibung der Juden.* n. p., 1790. 16 pp. 8°.

Against the Jews. BuStg.

141. *Zuschrift an die Landleute im Elsass über den Verkauf der National-Guter.* Strassburg, 1790. 8°.

Against the sale of nationalized property and the prospective Jewish buyers. BuStg.

142. *Cerf-Behr [Cerfberr] aux trois Rois.* [Strasbourg, 1791.] 10 pp. 8°.

An anti-Jewish parody in connection with the election of the constitutional Bishop François Antoine Brendel, March 6, 1791. The "three Kings" were the Commissioners Mathieu Dumas, Jean Jacques Foissey and Marie Jean Hérault de Sécheles. For the Ger. edition see No. 143. See also No. 139. BuStg.

143. *Hirtz-Bähr an die drey Königlein.* [Strassburg, 1791.] 10 pp. 8°.

Ger. edition of No. 142. BuStg.

144. Rumpler, [Abbé François Louis]. *A mes amis de tous les cultes. 15 Juin 1791.* [Strasbourg, 1791.] 12 pp. 8°.

Against the Jews. BuStg.

X. The Jews of Paris

In Paris the Jews found many sincere friends among the revolutionary leaders who openly favored and fought for Jewish emancipation. Only one of all Parisian Districts did not follow this pro-Jewish trend. For an analysis of the emancipation of the Paris Jews see Lacroix, *Actes,* VII (1898), 551–560, "Ce qu'on pensait des Juifs à Paris en 1790," and Kahn.

145. [Godard, Jacques.] *Adresse présentée à l'Assemblée Nationale le 26 Août 1789, par les Juifs résidant à Paris.* [Paris,] 1789. 9 pp. 8°.

According to *Oraison funèbre de Charles Michel de l'Eppée . . . 23 Février 1790,* by Abbé Fauchet. Paris, 1790, p. 48, the *Adresse* was written by J. Godard. The copy at the BN bears a manuscript date "3 Septembre 1789." Signed by "J[acob] Goldschmit, Président. Abraham Lopes Lagouna, Vice-Président. M. Weil, Electeur. J. Benjamin, Electeur. Mardoché[e] Lévi, Député. Lazard Jacob, Député. Trenelle père, Député. Mardoché[e] Elie, Député. Joseph Pereyra Brandon, Député. Delcamps fils, Député." H. translation in *Ha-Meassef,* 1789.

146. Godard, Jacques. *Discours prononcé le 28 Janvier 1790, par M. Godard, avocat au Parlement, l'un des Représentans de la Commune, en présentant à l'Assemblée générale de la Commune une députation des Juifs de*

Paris. Imprimé par ordre de l'Assemblée. [Paris,] 1790. 12 pp. 8°.

BN. Reprinted in No. 147.

147. *Recueil de pièces relatives à l'admission des Juifs à l'état civil (28–30 Janvier 1790).* Paris, 1790. 1 f., 34 pp. 8°.

Another edition of No. 146. Contains: Discours de Godard [28 Janvier 1790, see No. 146; La réponse de l'abbé Mulot, président de la commune; Discours . . . le 30 Janvier 1790, par M. Cahier de Gerville . . . chef d'une députation du district des Carmélites; Extrait du procès-verbal des délibérations . . . du district des Carmélites . . . du 29 Janvier 1790; La Réponse de M. l'abbé [François Valentin] Mulot; Opinion de M. l'abbé [Antoine René Constance de] Bertolio . . . le 30 Janvier 1790; Arrêté de la même assemblée . . .; Discours de M. Godard. BN, HUC.

148. Debourg [de Bourge, Jean Claude Antoine], l'un des Représentans de la

Commune. *Discours prononcé le 30 Janvier [1790] dans l'assemblée générale des Représentans de la Commune de Paris, à l'occasion de la demande faite, le 27, par les Juifs de Paris.* [Paris, 1790.] 15 pp. 4°.

In favor of the Jews. See No. 149. BN.

149. *Arrêté de l'Assemblée générale des Représentans de la Commune. Du samedi 30 janvier 1790.* [Paris,] 1790. 3 pp. 8°.

In favor of the Jews. See No. 148. BN.

150. *Voeu de l'Assemblée partielle de la Commune de Paris, district des Petits-Pères, sur la pétition des Juifs de Paris. En l'assemblée générale du 5 Février 1790.* [Paris, 1790.] 6 pp. 4°.

In favor of the Jews. BN.

151. *Extrait du procès-verbal du district des Mathurins. 20 Février 1790.* [Paris, 1790.] 4 pp. 4°.

Against the Jews. BN.

152. *Adresse de l'Assemblée des Représentans de la Commune de Paris, à l'Assemblée Nationale, sur l'admission des Juifs à l'Etat civil. Suivie d'un Arrêté des Représentans de la Commune sur le même objet et de la Réponse de M. le Président de l'Assemblée Nationale à la Députation de la Commune.* [Paris,] 1790. 15 pp. 8°.

Written by Jacques Godard and revised by the abbot Claude Fauchet and Honoré Marie Nicolas Duveyrier. The *Adresse* was read by Godard at the National Assembly on Feb. 24, 1790. The "Adresse" is signed by Godard, Fauchet, Bertolio and Duveyrier. The "Arrêté" is signed by the Mayor Bailly, Mulot, Bertoliam, Charpentier, Broussonet and Améilhon. P. 15: Reply by the Bishop of Autun, the Assembly's President. BN, HUC.

153. Vion. *Rapport fait par M. Vion, Conseiller-Référendaire en la Chancellerie du Palais, & Membre du Comité du District de Saint-Germain l'Auxerrois, sur les diverses adresses & pétitions des Juifs de Paris.* Paris, 1790. 24 pp. 8°.

The copy at the BN bears a manuscript note "Mars 1790." In favor of Jews.

154. Bourge, Jean Claude Antoine de. *Lettre au Comité de Constitution sur l'affaire des Juifs.* Paris, 1790. 45 pp. 8°.

May 19, 1790. In favor of Jews, directed against the Strasbourg petition (see No. 109). BN.

155. Brissot de Warville, [Jean Pierre]. *Rapport sur la Lettre de M. de Bourge au Comité de Constitution, concernant l'affaire des Juifs . . . le 29 Mai 1790.* [Paris, 1790.] 8 pp. 8°.

Reprinted in *Le Patriote français*, No. 311, June 15, 1790. BN.

156. [Goulleau, Mᵉ.] *Requête des marchands et négocians de Paris, contre l'admission des Juifs.* [Paris, 1790.] 27 pp. 4°.

1ˢᵗ edition: 1767, 2ⁿᵈ edition: 1775. Reprinted with an introduction and notes by Hell, according to a note on the copy at the JTS.

157. Vieillard, [Philippe], ancien consul de France à la Chine, Commissaire du Comité de Saint-Roch. *Dissertation sur la demande des Juifs de Paris, tendante à être admis au rang de citoyens actifs, lue à l'Assemblée de la Commune de Paris le ———— .* [Paris, 1791?]. 15 pp. 8°.

BN.

158. *Adresse présentée à l'Assemblée Nationale par les Juifs domiciliés à Paris.* Paris, [1791.] 3 pp. 4°.

Signed by "Mardoché[e] Elie, Député, David Silveyra, Agent." See No. 159. BN.

159. *Municipalité de Paris. Par les Maire et les Officiers municipaux. Extrait du registre des délibérations du Corps Municipal. Du vingt-six Mai 1791.* [Signé: [Jean Sylvain] Bailly, Maire; Dejoy, Secrétaire.) [Paris, 1791.] 2 pp. 4°.

In favor of the *Adresse* (see No. 158). BN, JTS.

XI. The Jews in the Four Communities of Avignon, Carpentras, Cavaillon and L'Isle-sur-Sorgue of the Former Papal Province

About 2,000 Jews lived in the four communities of the papal province of Avignon and Comtat Venaissin (Avignon, Carpentras, Cavaillon, L'Isle-sur-Sorgue). The first impressive request for the annexation of the papal province by France, made in 1789 by the deputy Ch. F. Bouche, contained the projection of a status for Jews. Avignon, which fought for the annexation, favored the emancipation of the Jews, while Comtat Venaissin, which was against annexation, continued the old anti-Jewish policy. Both factions used the Jewish problem for propaganda purposes. The Jews supported the movement for a reunion with France. Ultimately the Jews became citizens, but this they owed to the local pro-French patriots and to the support of the Paris representatives. On this problem see Chobaut and Szajkowski, "The Comtadin Jews."

160. [Cottier, François Régis Charles Joseph.] *Dialogue.* [Carpentras,] 22 Juin 1789. 15 pp. 8°.

A dialogue between "Mr. D**, Citoyen de Carpentras" and "Isaac Foresta, Juif domicilié de la même ville" on the emigration of the Carpentras Jews. BmCarp, Calvet, BN. See also No. 161.

161. *L'Enfant du Patriotisme.* [Carpentras, 1789.] 13 pp. 8°.

By Jean Joseph Claude Vincent Raphel (called Raphael aîné), or Cottier-Julian. On the same subject as No. 160. Mistakenly catalogued in *Bibliothèque du Musée Calvet* (p. 282) as published in 1788. BmCarp, Calvet, BN.

162–163. Martin, ex-consul de la ville d'Avignon. *La Révolte des Juifs à Avignon, ou le noir complot contre le Vice-légat suivi de ce qui s'est passé dans cette ville le 15 de Septembre* [1789], *écrit par un notable bourgeois de la ville.* n. p., 1789. 8 pp. 8°.

Calvet, BN, JTS. According to the BN (Lb³⁹2353) the pamphlet was published in Paris. The City Council of Paris published a broadside denouncing the pamphlet. See H. Grégoire, *Motion* (see No. 17), pp. XI–XII and Kahn, p. 24.

164–164a. Bouche, Charles François. *De la Restitution du Comté Venaissin, des villes et état d'Avignon . . .* Paris, 1789. 40 pp. 8°.

2d edition: 46 pp. pp. 31–40: on the Jews. BN, Calvet.

165. *Extrait du Procès-verbal de l'Assemblée Représentative du Comté Venaissin. Du 28 Octobre 1790.* Carpentras, n. d. Broadside.

Signed by: Moulin, président, Vidal chanoine, Bertrand, le Chevalier de Taulignan, Bayle, secrétaires. Together with "Du Mandement de M. le Maire et de MM. les Officiers municipaux" of Nov. 10, 1790. On the abolition of the yellow hat. See also No. 167. PC.

166. *Préliminaire d'un projet d'arrangement.* [Carpentras, 1790?] 8 pp. 8°.

Proposed by-laws for a new Jewish community council of Carpentras. Probably by a non-Jewish author. BN.

167. *Proclamation.* [Signés: D'Aurel, maire, Damian, Barjavel, Flandrin, J. Escoffier, Allié l'aîné, Durand, J. J. Esclangon, Ayme fils, Barjavel le jeune, Achard, Eydoux, André.] Carpentras, [1791.] 1 p. 4°.

On the abolition of the yellow hat, Jan. 25, 1791. See No. 165. AmCarp, PC.

168. *Proclamation de l'administration du département de Vaucluse relative à l'agiotage.* Avignon, 1793. 3 pp. 4°.

JTS.

169. *Le Commissaire du Directoire Exécutif près l'administration municipale du canton de*

Carpentras. Du 17 Brumaire an 6 républicain [*17 Nov. 1797*]. [Signé: Escoffier aîné, commissaire du Directoire Exécutif.] n. p., n. d. 8 pp. 8°.

Against thieves in the Jewish Ghetto. Proposition to demolish the three upper floors of the Jewish houses. With an anti-Jewish introduc-

tion, probably by the same [Antoine?] Escoffier. PC.

170. *Chanson nouvelle contre Musca fils cadet, Juif* . . . [Carpentras, 179– .] 1 p. 4°.

Calvet.

See also Nos. 255–57, 261–67, 395–96.

XII. NANCY POLEMICS

The Jewish community of Nancy was of special importance because its leader was Berr Isaac Berr, whose role in the fight for Jewish emancipation is well known. Nancy also became known for the refusal of the National Guard there to accept Jews, and this caused the publication of a series of pamphlets.

171. **Lettre de M*** Garde-citoyen, à M**** [Nancy, 1789.]

On the enlistment of Jews in the National Guard. See also Nos. 172–177.

172. Valois. *Appel aux Gardes-citoyens de la Ville de Nancy, sur la Lettre anonyme à eux adressée.* [Nancy, 1789.] 7 pp. 8°.

Dated Sept. 23, 1789. BmN. See also Nos. 171, 173–177.

173. Valois, M., Garde citoyen de la Compagnie de Nicolas le jeune. *Apologie de l'opinion de M.* [J. J.] *Ranxin, sur cette question: Les Juifs doivent-ils être admis dans la Milice Nationale?* [Nancy or Metz, 1790.] 3 pp. 12°.

BN. See also Nos. 171–172, 174–177.

174. *Lettre d'un citoyen, aux Gardes-citoyens de la ville de Nancy, en réponse à la question: Les Juifs doivent-ils être admis dans la Milice Nationale?* [Nancy, 1790.] 6 pp. 8°.

BmN. See also Nos. 171–173, 175–177.

175. [Berr Jacob.] *Réflexions sur la Lettre d'un ⟨ aux Gardes citoyens de la ville de Nan y, en réponse à la question: les juifs doivent-ils être admis dans la Garde Nationale?* [Nancy, 1790.] 8°.

See also Nos. 171–174, 176–177. Carmoly, *Biographie.*

176. *Ma façon de penser sur l'inadmission des comédiens à la garde citoyenne de la ville de Nancy.* [Nancy, 1790.] 6 pp. 8°.

Also on the enlistment of Jews. BmN. See No. 177.

177. *Adresse de remerciement, de la part des comédiens de la ville de Nancy, à l'auteur enroué, borgne et bossu de l'écrit intitulé: Ma façon de penser sur l'inadmission des comédiens dans la Garde citoyenne de cette ville.* [Nancy, 1790.] 7 pp. 8°.

On the same subject. See No. 176. BmN.

178. Sonnini de Manoncourt, Charles Nicolas Sigisbert. *De l'admission des juifs à l'état civil. Adresse à mes compatriotes, par un citoyen du Nord de la France.* Nancy, 1790. 16 pp. 8°.

In favor of Jews. PC.

179. Berr, Berr Isaac. *Discours de la communauté des juifs à MM. les municipaux et notables de la ville de Nancy, réunis en assemblée générale le 12 avril 1790; prononcé par le Sr Berr-Isaac Berr, l'un des syndics de ladite communauté.* [Nancy, 1790.] 3 pp. 4°.

According to Pfister, III, 332.

XIII. The Decree of Sept. 27, 1791

The Decree of Sept. 27, 1791, granted citizenship to the Ashkenazic Jews, and thus ended the fight for their legal emancipation.

180. *Loi relative aux Juifs. Donnée à Paris, le 13 Novembre 1791.* Paris, 1791. 2 pp. 4°.

The title is the same as of No. 187, but not the text.

181. ———. *Gesetz die Juden betreffend.* Strasbourg, n. d. Broadside.

Fr. & Ger. See No. 180. BuStg.

182. [Decision of the Directoire of Lower Rhine on the formalities of the civic oath

by Jews, Dec. 27, 1791.] Strasbourg, 1791. 4 pp. 4°.

According to OBL, v, 56.

183. [Berr, Berr Isaac.] *Lettre d'un citoyen, membre de la ci-devant communauté des Juifs de Lorraine, à ses confrères, à l'occasion du droit de Citoyen actif, rendu aux Juifs par le Décret du 28 [27] Septembre 1791.* [Signé: ***. Juif, Citoyen Actif.] Nancy, 1791. 22 pp. 8°.

Reprinted in Berr's *Lettre* to Grégoire of 1806. See Napoleonica, No. 11.

XIV. The Decree of Sept. 28, 1791.

In 1777 and 1778 Alsace was inundated by a mass of counterfeit receipts signed in Hebrew characters, purportedly by Jewish creditors. When the Jews requested the payment of debts owed them by Gentile debtors, they were presented with these falsified receipts. The counterfeiting of the receipts was accompanied by anti-Jewish riots and well organized anti-Jewish propaganda. A series of decrees ordered the liquidation of these receipts and fixed the manner for repaying the debts. At the outbreak of the Revolution the debts were not yet paid off. This became the major propaganda-slogan for denying citizenship to the Alsatian Jews. When the National Assembly granted citizenship to all Ashkenazic Jews on September 27, 1791, the anti-Jewish deputies from Alsace obtained on the next day the vote of a decree ordering the Alsatian Jews to submit within one month a list of all debts owed them by Christian creditors; and the Alsatian authorities were requested to study the debtors' abilities to repay the debts. In fact, emancipation was given to the Jews on the condition that they liquidate the debts on terms favorable to Christian debtors but ruinous to the Jews themselves. The Jews, however, refused to submit the list, and the decree of September 28 was never put into effect. See Szajkowski, "The Law of September 28, 1791."

184. *Extrait du Procès-verbal des délibérations intervenues en la session du Conseil-Général des administrateurs du Département du Haut-Rhin, dont l'ouverture a eu lieu le 3 Novembre 1790. Du 8 Novembre 1790.* n. p., n. d. 2 pp. 4°.

JTS, AdHR. See No. 185.

185. *Auszug aus dem Proces-verbal der Berathschlagungen, so in der den 3ten Wintermonat 1790 eröfneten Sitzung der allgemeinen Rathversammlung, durch die Verwalter oberreinischen Department, genommen worden. Vom 8ten Wintermonat 1790.* n. p., n. d. 2 pp. 4°.

Ger. edition of No. 184. AdHR.

186. *Extrait du registre des séances du Directoire du département du Haut-Rhin du 7e du mois de janvier 1791. Arrêté No. 1078. Auszug aus dem Register der Sitzungen des oberrheinischen Departements - Direktoriums. Vom 7ten Jenner 1791. Schluss No. 1078.* [Signé: Jourdin, secrétaire-général.] n. p., n. d. 8 pp. 4°.

Fr. & Ger. BuStg, JTS.

187. *Loi relative aux Juifs de la ci-devant province d'Alsace. Donnée à Paris le 13 Novembre 1791.* Paris, 1792. 2 pp. 4°.

BN. See Nos. 188–190.

188. *Loi relative aux Juifs de la ci-devant Province d'Alsace. Donnée à Paris, le 13 Novembre 1791. Transcrite le 3 Décembre suivant.* [Signé: M. L. L. Duport.] [Colmar, 1791.] 2 pp. 4°.

For the Ger. edition see No. 189. BuStg, JTS.

189. *Gesetz, die Juden ehmaligen Provinz Elsass betreffend. Geben zu Paris den 13ten Wintermonat 1791. Protokollirt den 3ten Christmonat.* Colmar, 1791. 2 pp. 4°.

Ger. edition of No. 188. JTS.

190. *Loi relative aux Juifs de la ci-devant Province d'Alsace. Paris, 13 Novembre 1791. Gesetz der Juden der ehemaligen Provinz Elsass betreffent.* [Strasbourg, 1791.] 4 pp. 4°.

Registered with the *Directoire* of Lower Rhine on Dec. 5, 1791. Fr. & Ger. BuStg. See also Nos. 187–189.

191. *Extrait de deux lettres de MM.* [Etienne François Joseph] *Schwendt et* [Christophe Guillaume] *Koch, Députés à l'Assemblée Nationale, à M.* [Philippe Frédéric baron de] *Dietrich, Maire de Strasbourg, datées de Paris 28 et 29 Septembre 1791.* [Strasbourg, 1791.] 4 pp. 4°.

On the Decrees of Sept. 27 & 28, 1791. BuStg. For the Ger. & other editions see Nos. 192–193.

192. *Auszug aus zwey Briefen der Herren Schwendt und Koch, Deputirten bey der National-Versammlung, an Hrn. Dietrich Maire zu Strassburg, unter des Tagesanzeigen von Paris den 28 und 29ten September 1791.* [Strasbourg, 1791.] 4 pp. 4°.

Ger. edition of No. 191. BuStg.

193. *Extrait de deux lettres ... Auszug ...* [Strasbourg, 1791.] 8 pp. 4°.

Combined Fr. & Ger. edition of Nos. 191 & 192. BuStg.

194–194a. ———— . [Strasbourg, 1791.] 1 p. fol. and Colmar, n. d. 4 pp. 4°.

Fr. & Ger. BN, BmC.

195. *Extrait du Procès verbal des délibérations intervenues en la session du Conseil Général du Département du Haut-Rhin, dont l'ouverture a eu lieu le 24 Novembre 1791. Du 7 Décembre 1791. No. 51.* [Signé: Jourdain, secrétaire général.] [Colmar, 1791.] 2 pp. 4°.

JTS. For other editions see Nos. 196–197.

196. *Auszug aus dem Prozes-Verbal der Berathschlagungen, so in der den 24ten Wintermonat 1791 eröfneten Sitzung der allgemeinen Rathsversammlung der oberrheinischen Departments ergangen. Vom 9ten Christmonat 1791. No. 51* [Colmar, 1791.] 2 pp. 4°.

German edition of No. 195. See also No. 197. JTS.

197. *Extrait ... Auszug ...* [Colmar, 1791.] 4 pp. 4°.

Combined Fr. & Ger. edition of Nos. 195–196. BuStg, BmC.

198. Bronchving [sic!], Joseph, Vormser, A., députés par les Juifs, Cheauveau de la Garde, M. [Joseph François], homme de loi, défenseur officieux. *Pétition de Messieurs les Juifs du Haut-Rhin, à l'Assemblée Nationale.* Paris, [1792.] 7 pp. 4°.

Against the Decree of Sept. 28, 1791. BmC.

199. *Délibération du Directoire du département du Bas-Rhin, du 2 Novembre 1792. Berathschlagung der Nieder-Rheinischen Departement-Direktoriums, von 2ten November 1792.* [Signé: F. Dessolliers, Vice-Président, Jean Frédéric Burger, Elie Stoeber, F. Neumann, Antoine Joseph Dorsch, Antoine Teterd, F. Ant. Sidel, F. C. Greuhm, Administr.; P. F. Monet, Procureur-Général-Syndic; Hoffmann, Secrétaire général.] [Strasbourg, 1792.] 4 pp. 4°.

BuStg, JTS. Only the title is the same as that of No. 278, but not the text.

200. Chauveau-Lagarde, [Joseph François], *Défenseur officieux des Juifs du Département du Haut-Rhin. Dénonciation du Département du Haut-Rhin à la Convention Nationale.* Paris, 1793. 4 pp. 4°.

Against the decision of the Upper Rhine General Council of Dec. 7, 1791. JTS.

201. *Pétition de [Cent] soixante Citoyens François du Département du haut-Rhin, classés par quelques malveillans, sous la dénomination de Juifs de la ci-devant Province d'Alsace, représentés par leurs fondés de pouvoirs, les Citoyens [Joseph] Bronchvig, [Emanuel] Treyfous et [Daniel] Cahen.* n. p., n. d. 12 pp. 4°.

Against the Decree of Sept. 28, 1791. *Cent* is handwritten. At the end is reprinted Foussedoire's defense of the Jews (see No. 215). AN. André Foussedoire sent the petition to the National Convention. On March 4, 1792, the Convention permitted an Alsatian Jewish delegation itself to present the *Petition* (AN, D-III-213-14).

XV. ALSATIAN POLEMICS AFTER THE EMANCIPATION, 1792 — THE YEAR
V (— SEPTEMBER 1796)

202. *Extrait du registre des séances du Directoire du département du Haut-Rhin, séant à Colmar. Du 19 Janvier 1792. L'an 4e de la Liberté, No. 595. Auszug aus dem Register der Sitzungen des oberrheinischen Departements-Direktorium zu Colmar . . .* [Signé: Jourdain, Secrétaire général.] n. p., n. d. 8 pp. 4°.

BuStg, JTS. Fr. & Ger. Attack against Jews in connection with the *assignats*.

203. *Avis . . . Délibération du Directoire du département du Bas-Rhin. Du lundi 21 mai 1792.* [Strasbourg, 1792.] 4 pp. 4°.

On the situation of the Jews in Bischheim. Order given in April, 1792, to A. M. Laurent to accept their civil oath. BuStg.

204. *Je vous dirai vos vérités.* n. p., 1792. 102 pp. 8°.

BmC. Against the Revolution and the Jews.

205. *Opinion d'un Membre du Département du Haut-Rhin, sur les individus juifs de ce Département. Lue à la séance publique du Conseil général dudit Département, le 12 Janvier 1793, & ajournée à la discussion du mardi 22 dudit mois.* n. p., n. d. 14 pp. 8°.

Against the Jews. BAPR, BuStg, BmC. For the German edition see No. 206.

206. *Meinung eines Mitglieds des oberrheinischen Departments über die Juden desselben. Vorgelesen in der öffentlichen Sitzung des Gemeinderaths des obgedachten Departments, den 12. Jenner 1793 . . .* n. p., n. d. 12 pp. 8°.

Ger. edition of No. 205. BAPR, BmC.

207. *Délibération du Conseil général du département du Bas-Rhin. Du 11 Juin 1793, l'an deuxième . . . Beratschlagung des Nieder-Rheinischen Departement-Raths . . .* Strasbourg, n. d. 4 pp. 4°.

Fr. & Ger. Against the use of Hebrew characters in correspondence with foreign countries. BuStg.

208. Schneider, [Jean Georges, called Eulogius]. *Ueber die Juden. Eine Beilage.* Strassburg, 1793. 8 pp. 16°.

In favor of Jews. A Supplement to the *Argos, oder der Mann mit hundert Augen,* of July 16, 1793. BN, BuStg. Reprinted in *RA* (1891), 131–36 and as a reprint *Ein Urteil über die Juden,* by Dr. M. Ginsburger, n. p. n. d. Heitz (pp. 76–77) mentions a French title, *Des juifs,* but there was, probably, no French edition.

209. *Au Peuple. An das Volk.* [Signé: Le Maire de Strasbourg, P. F. [Pierre François] Monet.] 29 Brumaire an II [19 Novembre 1793]. Broadside.

Fr. & Ger. For fraternity among Jews, Protestants and Catholics. JTS.

210. *Merkwürdige und seltsame Liebsgeschichte zwischen einen jungen verliebten Juden, und einer überauschönen Büttners Frau, welche sich am Rhein bey Strassburg zugetragen, 1793* . . . n. p., n. d. 4 pp. 4°. JTS.

211. *Invitation de l'accusateur public près le Tribunal criminel du département du Bas-Rhin, à ses frères les sans-culottes. Strasbourg, 22 Floréal an II [11 Mai 1794]. Einladung des öffentlichen Anklägers bey dem Peinlichen Gericht des Nieder-Rheinischen Departments an seine Brüder die Sansculottes.* [Signé: F[rançois] Neuman[n].] Strasbourg, n. d. Broadside.

Fr. & Ger. Against speculators and Jews. BuStg.

212. *Accusatuer (L') public près le Tribunal criminel du Département du Haut-Rhin, à tous les bons patriotes du même Département. 24 Prairial an 2 [21 Juin 1794]. Der öffentliche Ankläger bey dem peinlichen Gericht des oberreinischen Departments an alle gutdenkende Patrioten des nämlichen Departments.* [Signé: Yves.] Colmar, n. d. Broadside.

Fr. & Ger. Against speculators and Jews. BuStg.

213. ["Circulaire de l'Agent National du District de Strasbourg aux Communes . . .

du 26 Prairial [14 Juin 1794] . . . des abus commis par des citoyens nommés Juifs qui munis de fausses requisitions osent enlever les . . . en les payant en numéraire."]

AmStg, Minutes of the *Corps municipal,* vol. 5, 15 Messidor an II.

214. *Délibération du corps municipal de la Commune de Strasbourg. Séance publique du 6 Thermidor de l'an second [24 Juillet 1794]* . . . Strasbourg, [1794.] 3 pp. 8°.

The Jews are ordered to respect the laws of Sept. 20 and Dec. 19, 1792, on the recording of births of children in the registries of the *état civil.* BN.

215. *[André] Foussedoire, Représentant du Peuple dans les Départemens des Haut- et Bas-Rhin. Foussedoire, Volks-Repräsentant in der ober- und unterrheinischen Departementen.* Colmar, [1794]. 4 pp. 4°.

BuS g, JTS. Fr. & Ger. Against the persecution of Jews. Of Aug. 19, 1794, according to OBL, I, 33. See No. 201.

216. *Extrait du registre des arrêtés du Comité de Législation. Séance du 11 Brumaire, l'an troisième [1 Octobre 1794] de la République française, une & indivisible. Auszug aus dem Protokolle des Komités der Gesetzgebung* . . . Strasbourg, [1794]. 4 pp. 4°.

Fr. & Ger. Order to protect the Alsatian Jews. Together with "Délibération du Directoire du Département du Bas-Rhin. Du 2 Frimaire, l'an troisième." BuStg.

217. *Copie de la pétition par plusieurs Citoyens du Bas-Rhin, à la Convention Nationale.* Colmar, [1794]. 7 pp. 4°.

A Jewish petition against persecutions. Together with the order of Oct. 1, 1794. See No. 216. BmC.

218. *Schreiben eines Nicht-Juden an den Verfasser der Republikanischen Chronik, des Judenthum betreffend. Der Asche Moses Mendelssohns gewidmet.* [Strassburg, 1796?.] 54 pp. 8°.

BuStg.

XVI. Jewish Community Problems. The Revolutionary Fight Against
the Jewish Religion

Fraternization between all religious groups was sincerely advocated at the beginning of the Revolution. Later the Jacobins considered the Jewish religion as dangerous as all other "old" religions. But the Jacobins were not ideological atheists. They did not fight religion on principle, but only the Catholic Church for its association with the counter-revolution. Persecution of the Jewish religion by Jacobins should not be understood as an ideological struggle for the abolition of the Jewish faith, or as action of an anti-Jewish character. Where Jews suffered, it was because of general anti-religious acts. The new regime created among Jews themselves a tendency toward the abolition of autonomous communities. See Z. Szajkowski, "The Attitude of French Jacobins Toward Jewish Religion."

219. Berr, Jacob. *Lettre du Sr. Jacob Berr, juif, maître en chirurgie à Nancy, à Monseigneur l'Evêque de Nancy, député à l'Assemblée Nationale, pour servir de réfutation de quelques erreurs qui se trouvent dans celle adressée à ce prélat, par le Sr. Berr-Isaac Berr.* [Nancy,] 1790. II, 10 pp. 8°.

Dated Apr. 25, 1790. Against autonomous Jewish communities. P. II: "J'ai été si étonné de voir le Sieur [Berr] Isaac-Berr réclamer l'existence de notre régime particulier, demander que l'Assemblée Nationale conservât le pouvoir civil de nos Rabbins et de nos Syndics, que j'ai cru devoir bien vite m'élever contre une si dangereuse proposition." See No. 89. BmN.

220. *Adresse de la Société des Amis de la Constitution à ses frères les habitans des campagnes, le 20 Mai 1792.* Epinal, 1792. 15 pp. 8°.

On the fraternity between Catholics, Protestants and Jews and the secularization of the *état-civil*. BuStg.

221. *Proclamation du Conseil de guerre.* Metz, 9 Septembre 1792. 8 pp. 4°.

BN. Art. 5: abolition of the Jewish cemeteries for reason of military defense.

222. Schneinder, Eulogius. *Jesus und die Pharisäeer. Zwei Fastenpredigten . . .* Strassburg, 1792. 14 pp. 8°.
BuStg.

223. Kammerer, J. J. *Die Religion der Jugent und der Vernunft über die Feier der Dekaden.* Strassburg, 1793.

A Jacobin analysis of the Jewish Sabbath. The copy at the BuStg was lost.

224–224a. *Extrait des délibérations de l'Assemblée générale de la Section des Amis de la Patrie, du 20 Brumaire de la seconde année Républicaine, une et indivisible [10 Novembre 1793].* [Signé: Fortenfant, Président; Fournier, Deshaye, Guilbert l'aîné, et Vanbromeurs, secrétaires.] [Paris,] n. d. 4 pp. 4°.

"Salomon Hesse, Juif, renonçant le judaïsme." BN. The *Section* decided to publish Hesse's speech in 1200 copies, including 400 in broadside form.

225. *Aux républicains et philosophes de la ci-devant religion juive.* Nancy, le 23 Brumaire l'an 2 de la République [Nov. 13, 1793]. 2 pp. 4°.

Contains a decision of Nov. 12, 1793, by the *Conseil général de la commune* requesting the Jews to "abjure sur l'autel de la Patrie les erreurs antiques de la superstition avec les ministres des autres cultes." Signed by Bigerot, *officier municipal.* PC.

226. *Extrait du registre des délibérations du Directoire du District de Strasbourg. Séance publique du deuxième jour du mois de Frimaire, deuxième année de la République*

française [*22 Novembre 1793*]. Strasbourg, an II. 3 pp. 4°.

Against Jewish religious practices. PC

227. Lambert, Alexandre. *Discours de morale, prononcé le 2 décadi, 20 Frimaire l'an 2e de la République une et indivisible* [*10 Décembre, 1793*], *au Temple de la Vérité, ci-devant l'église des Bénédictins, à Angély-Boutonne, ci-devant Saint-Jean-d'Angély, fait par le citoyen Alexandre Lambert fils, Juif et élevé dans les préjugés du culte judaïque.* Rochefort, n. d. 23 pp. 8°.

PC. See *Saintonge*, III (1881), 164.

228. *Délibération du Directoire de Strasbourg. Du 13 Pluviôse l'an second* [*1 Février 1794*]. Strasbourg, n. d. Broadside.

Against Jewish religious gatherings. BN.

229. *L'Agent national du District de Strasbourg aux communes. Der National-Agent des Strassburger Distriktes an die Gemeinden. 7 Messidor l'an second* . . . [25 Juin 1794]. [Signé: (Joseph-Antoine) Mainoni.] [Strasbourg,] n. d. Broadside.

Fr. & Ger. Against Jewish religious gatherings. BuStg.

230–230a. *Délibération du Directoire du District de Strasbourg. Du 9 Messidor, l'an second* . . . [*27 Juin 1794*]. *Berathschlagung des Strassburger Distrikt-Direktoriums* . . . [Signé: Fraudel, Président, Didierjean,

Bury, Braendlé, Agent-national-suppléant, Christmann, secrétaire.] Strasbourg, n. d. 7 pp. 4°.

Fr. & Ger. Against the practice of Jewish religious burials. BN, BuStg. Was published also as a broadside.

231. [*Jacques*] *Pinet,* [*Jean Baptiste*] *Cavaignac, les Représentants du Peuple près l'armée des Pyrénées-Occidentales. Bayonne, le 21 Messidor an 2* [*9 Juillet 1794*]. Bayonne, n. d. Broadside.

Against the observance of Sabbath by the Jews of Saint-Esprit-lès-Bayonne. JTS.

232. *Extrait des jugements de la Police municipale de la Commune de Metz. Du 8 Frimaire an III* [*28 Novembre 1794*]. [Signé: (Jacques François) Adam, secrétaire.] Metz, n. d. Broadside.

Sentences against Alexandre Halphen and Aaron Picquard for the practice of Jewish religious burials. AmM.

233. *Liberté, Egalité, Fraternité. Extrait du registre des Jugements du Tribunal Correctionnel de l'Arrondissement de Nice, département des Alpes-Maritimes* . . . *Du 8 Brumaire an VII* [*29 Octobre 1798*]. [Signé: Crabalona, président, Sanier, juge de paix, Bonifassi, assesseur.] [Nice] n. d. Broadside.

Sentences against Abraham Joseph Foa, Sabato Viterbo (called Sabadaï), Hananen Cohen (called Salvador), Simon Bensoussan, and Auziel Vita Maquis, for building tabernacles. PC.

XVII. Debts Owed by the Jewish Communities

The Jewish communities had to pay so much in taxes that they were forced to borrow from Christians, and they thus became collective debtors to Christian creditors. During the Revolution the Jews demanded that their debts be taken over by the government, as had been done with all debts of religious and other bodies which were dissolved by the new regime. The Christian creditors fought against the nationalization of these debts. In spite of the fact that all reports by the commissions of the Council of Five Hundred favored the Jewish demand, these debts were never taken over by the government.

A. DEBTS OF THE JEWISH COMMUNITIES OF METZ AND THE METZ PROVINCE

234. [An approval of the tax of the Jewish Community of Metz for the period of four years. Dec. 24, 1789.] [Signé: Depont [Jean de Pont.]. n. p., n. d. 1 p. fol.

Without a title. PC. See No. 243.

235. *Mémoire pour les Juifs de Metz, concernant une redevance de 20,000 livres qu'ils payent annuellement au Duc de Brancas, sous le titre de droit d'habitation, protection & tolérance.* [Signé: Louis Wolf, Député des Juifs de Metz & des Trois Evêchés.] n. p., n. d. 8 pp. 4°.

BN. See Nos. 236–237.

236. Visme, [Devisme, Jacques François Laurent] de. *Rapport fait au nom du Comité des Domaines, le 20 Juillet 1790, sur le droit de protection, levé sur les Juifs, par M. De Visme, député du Vermandois et décret rendu sur ce rapport.* Paris, [1790]. 16 pp. 8°.

P. 15: "Décret du 20 juillet 1790." BN. See Nos. 235, 237.

237–237a. *Lettres patentes du Roi, sur le Décret de l'Assemblée Nationale, du 20 Juillet dernier, portant suppression des droits d'habitation, de protection, de tolérance & de redevances semblables sur les Juifs. Données à Saint-Claud le 7 Août 1790. Transcrites en Parlement, en vacations, le 17 Août dudit an.* Paris, 1790. 4 pp. 4°.

Another edition: Paris, 1790. 3 pp. 4°, without the registration. See Nos. 235–236, 238–241. BN.

238. ———. *Transcrites en Parlement, le 21 du même mois.* Metz, 1790. 3 pp. 4°.

BuStg. See Nos. 237, 239–241.

239. ———. *Bordeaux, 1790. 4 pp. 4°.

Together with "Délibération du Directoire du Département de la Gironde" of Aug. 4, 1790. BmBx. See Nos. 237–238, 240–241.

240. ———. Nantes, 24 Août 1790. 4 pp. 4°.

BmNt. See Nos. 237–239, 241.

241. ———. n. p. n. d. 3 pp. 4°.

Together with "Transcription . . . par le Directoire du Département du Puy-de Dôme, en exécution de sa délibération du 20 Août 1790 . . .". See Nos. 237–240. JTS.

242. *Loi qui renvoi au Directoire du District de Metz, les contestations nées & à naître du rôle de contributions fait par les Juifs de Metz. Donnée à Paris, le 27 Mai 1791.* Paris, 1791. 2 pp. 4°.

Decree of May 20, 1791. JTS. See Nos. 243–244.

243. ———. [Metz, 1791.] 3 pp. fol.

Together with the Jewish petition of Aug. 17, 1791 to the *Directoire* of Moselle and the *Directoire's* decisions of Dec. 24, 1789 [See No. 234] and Aug. 18, 1791. See Nos. 242 & 244. AdM, HUC.

244. ———. *Transcrite sur les registres du Département de la Meurthe, le 20 Octobre 1791.* Nancy, 1791. 3 pp. 4°.

JTS. See Nos. 242–243.

245. *Décret relatif à une pétition de plusieurs Juifs de Nancy, au sujet de la loi du 20 Mai 1791, concernant les rôles de la ci-devant communauté des Juifs de Metz, du 1er Mai 1792.* Metz, [1792]. 2 pp. 4°.

PC. See No. 242.

246. *Pétition à la Convention Nationale, pour les ci-devant syndics et élus de la ci-devant Communauté des Juifs de Metz.* [Signé: Gaudchaux, Mayer-Cahen, fondé de pouvoirs.] n. p., [1792]. 20 pp. 8°.

BN. For a summary of the petition see No. 247. The correct name of the community leader who signed the items 246–47 was Goudchaux Mayer Cahen.

247. *Sommaire.* [Signé:Gaudchaux-Mayer.]
n. p., [1792]. 3 pp. 4°.

Summary of No. 246. BN.

248. *A Messieurs, Messieurs les administrateurs du département de la Moselle.* [Signé: Nathan Cahen, Juif de Louvigny.] [Metz, 1792.] 14 pp. 4°.

Petition in the name of the smaller Jewish communities against the community of Metz and its role in the problem of debts. JTS.

249. Dalsace, Bernard. *Pétition sur les affaires des Juifs. 1er Avril 1794.* n. p., n. d. 8°.

BN.

250. *Extrait des registres des délibérations du départément de la Moselle. Séance publique du 5 Messidor 3e année [23 Juin 1795] de la République française, une et indivisible.* [Signé: (Claude) Lambert, secrétaire général, (Louis Gabriel) Dupin, chef du bureau des contributions.] Metz, [1795]. 7 pp. 4°.

Paquet, pp. 1088–1090. HUC.

251. *Précis pour les créanciers des Juifs de Metz, adressé au Corps législatif, sur la demande qui lui est faite de déclarer dettes nationales celles de la ci-devant Communauté des Juifs.* [Signé: Deprille, un des créanciers, et au nom de tous, comme leur syndic et procureur-fondé.] Paris, [1794]. 21 pp. 4°.

BN. See No. 252.

252. *Consultation sur cette question: Si les dettes de la ci-devant communauté des Juifs de Metz doivent être considérés comme nationales; en réponse au Précis par les créanciers des Juifs au Corps Législatif.* [Signé: (Claude François) Chauveau-Lagarde, Le Roy. 23 Floréal de l'an 5 (12 Mai 1797).] Paris, n. d. 8 pp. 4°.

BN. See Nos. 251 & 253.

253. *Réponse aux Juifs de Metz de la part de leurs créanciers.* [Signé: Puyproux aîné, l'un des créanciers et au nom de tous.] n. p., n. d. 22 pp. 8°.

Reply to No. 252. BN. See also No. 254.

254. *Résumé pour les Juifs de Metz; contre leurs créanciers.* [Signé: [C. F.] Chauveau-Lagarde, Jean Jacques Régis de Cambacérès.] Paris, [an v]. 12 pp. 4°.

Reply to No. 253. BN.

255. Chappuis [Chapuy, Haycinthe Adrien Joseph]. *Rapport fait par Chappuis, au nom d'une commission composée des Représentants du peuple Grégoire, [Jacques Henri] Laurençot [Laurenceot] (du Jura), [J. B. M.] Saladin & Chappuis. Séance du 16 Germinal [an v — 5 Avril 1797].* Paris, an v. 10 pp. 8°.

BN.

256. Saladin, [Jean Baptiste Michel]. *Rapport fait par Saladin, au nom d'une commission spéciale, composée des Représentants Grégoire, Chappuy [Chappuis], [Claude Etienne Joseph] Louvot, [Joseph François baron de] Beyts et Saladin sur les pétitions des Juifs de Metz & d'Avignon. Séance du 7 Fructidor an v [24 Août 1797].* Paris, an v. 15 pp. 8°.

BN.

257. Riou [de Kersalaun, François Marie Joseph]. *Rapport fait par Riou sur les pétitions des Juifs de Metz & d'Avignon, au nom d'une commission spéciale. Séance du 4 Frimaire an 6 [24 Novembre 1797].* Paris, Frimaire an vi. 8 pp. 8°.

BN. The commission consisted of de Riou, Beyts, Chappuis, Louvot, Grégoire.

258. *Encore un mot pour les créanciers des Juifs de Metz.* [Signé: Puyproux aîné, un des créanciers.] n. p., n. d. 4 pp. 4°.

Reply to No. 257. BN.

259. [Broadside announcing the sale of communal Jewish properties, end of 1797.]

According to minutes of Jan. 8, 1798 in the author's possession: "en conformité des affiches imprimés qui ont été placardés dans toutes les carefours et lieux."

260. [Broadside announcing the sale of communal Jewish properties on Jan. 6, 1799.]

According to minutes in the author's possession: "en conformité des affiches imprimés qui ont été placardés dans tous les carefours."

B. THE DEBTS OF THE AVIGNON AND COMTADIN JEWISH COMMUNITIES

261. *Copie de la Supplique présentée par les Administrateurs de la Carrière des Juifs de la Commune de Carpentras, à MM. les Maire & Officiers municipaux.* Carpentras, 1791. 6 pp. 4°.

On the emigration of the rich Jews from Carpentras and on the debts owed by the Jews. Dated July 17, 1791, and signed by Moyse de Milliaud aîné, Jacassye Alfanderic, Ruben Crémieu. Together with "Extrait des registres de la Commune de Carpentras," July 17, 1791. Calvet, BN.

262. *Observations pour les Juifs d'Avignon, à la Convention Nationale.* n. p., an 3. 19 pp. 8°.

Dated Sept. 24, 1794, and signed by Aaron Ravel, Aaron Vidal, Milhaud. See No. 263 Calvet, BN.

263. *Nouvelles observations pour les Juifs d'Avignon.* n. p., an 3. 15 pp. 8°.

Dated Nov. 14, 1794 and signed by Aaron, Vidal, Milhaud. See No. 262, Calvet, BN.

264. *Extrait du registre des arrêtés du Comité de Législation. Séance du 19 Germinal l'an troisième [8 Avril 1795.]* [Avignon, 1795.] 2 pp. 4°.

265. *Mémoire pour le citoyen Dominique*

Chambaud, de la Commune d'Avignon; Jean Chaulet, Vannier . . . demandeurs: contre le citoyen Jassé Haïn Crémieu, de cette commune d'Aix, fils et héritier de Jassuda-David Crémieu, défendeur. [Signé: Granet, homme de loi et défenseur officieux.] Aix, an VII. 34 pp. 4°.

On the Carpentras debts. JTS. See Nos. 266–267.

266. *Mémoire pour le citoyen Jassé Haïn Crémieu, naturalisé Français, demeurant à Aix: contre les citoyens Dominique Chambaud . . . et contre les membres de la ci-devant Communauté des Juifs de Carpentras, en qualité au procès, appellés en garantie subsidaire.* [Signé: Chansaud, homme de loi.] Aix, an VII. 34 pp. 4°.

JTS. See Nos. 265, 267.

267. *Précis pour les citoyens Dominique Chambaud . . . contre le citoyen Jassé Haïn Crémieu, de cette commune d'Aix, fils et héritier de Jassuda David Crémieu, défendeur.* [Signé: Granet, homme de loi.] Aix, an VII. 41 pp. 4°.

JTS. See Nos. 265–266.

See also Nos. 255–57.

C. THE DEBTS OF THE ALSATIAN JEWISH COMMUNITIES

268. *Messieurs les Commissaires des Départents du Haut- et du Bas-Rhin pour la liquidation des dettes des Juifs domiciliés de la province ci-devant Alsace.* [Signé: Seligman Wittersheim.] n. p., 1792. 2 pp. 4°.

BuStg.

269. *Auszug aus der Berathschlagung der Nieder-Rheinischen Departments-Direktoriums vom 1. Jul. 1793, im 2ten Jahr der Frankischen Republik . . .* n. p., n. d. 4 pp. 4°.

"Zur General-Liquidation der Schulden." JTS.

270. *Namens-Verzeichniss derjenigen Juden, welche in der letztern, durch die Juden vorsteher den ehemaligen Provinz Elsass, errichteten Roll der Anlage, in der Gemeinde ——— häuslich eingessen waren, und in dem Gemeinen-Austheiler der Grund- und Mobiliar-Steuer gedachter Gemeinde pro 1791 angelegt worden sind folgt.* [Strassburg, 1793.] 4 pp. fol.

JTS. See No. 271.

271. [A circular of 1793.]

According to a treasurer's report in the author's possession: "1793. 17 8bre. Payé au Sr. Heitz imprimeur pour impression des Etats [see No. 270] et circulaires en langue allemande addressées aux maires des communes du Haut et Bas Rhin aux fins de remplir le montent des impositions foncière et mobiliaire à laquelle chaque Juif couché sur ces états est cotisé."

XVIII. TAXES

The financial policies of the Revolution present one of the most complicated problems of that period. The new regime looked for money and it became urgent to find it among bankers, merchants, persons suspected of speculation and counter-revolutionary acts, or wealthy people in general, who could be taxed, fined and arrested. Jews were often found among them. In many cases local revolutionary leaders were influenced by traditional anti-Jewish feelings in handling the financial affairs of the Revolution, and Jews were singled out in the drive to save the Republic's finances through compulsory high taxes and fines. In the beginning of the Revolution the Jews still continued to pay taxes not as individuals, but as a collective body through their communities. In Alsace the Jews were included in the general tax system at the end of 1790.

272. *Extrait du procès-verbal des séances de la Commission intermédiaire provinciale l'Alsace, du premier Juin 1790. Auszug aus dem Protokoll der Zwischen-Kommission der Provinz Elsass, vom 1ten Junius 1790.* [Signé: Hoffman, secrétaire prov. adj.] n. p., n. d. 3 pp. 4°.

Fr. & Ger. On the tax "vingtième d'industrie" to be paid by the Jews. JTS, BuStg.

273. *Délibération du Directoire du Département du Bas-Rhin, du Samedi onzième du mois de Juin 1791. Berathschlagung . . .* n. p., n. d. 4 pp. 4°.

Fr. & Ger. On the taxes for 1789–1790 to be paid by the Jews. BN.

274. Gradis, David. *Réclamation. 24 Mars 1792, l'an quatrième de la Liberté.* Bordeaux, n. d. 3 pp. 8°.

On taxes paid by Gradis. Together with a decision of the *Directoire* of March 24, 1792. JTS.

275. *Liste de toutes les personnes domiciliées*

et résidantes dans la ville de Bordeaux. Quartier du Mirail.* [Bordeaux,] n. d. Broadside.

List of tax payers in the Jewish section of the city. See No. 276. AmBx.

276. *Liste . . . Quartier de l'Hôtel de Ville.* [Bordeaux,] n. d. Broadside.

See No. 275. AmBx.

277. *Contribution patriotique. Liste de toutes les personnes domiciliées et résidantes sur la paroisse Saint-Ferroy, de la ville de Metz.* Metz, n. d. Broadside.

Contains: "Etat des contribuables de la Communauté des Juifs." [Nov. 1790.] Paquet, 1, 55–58.

278. *Délibération du Directoire du Département du Bas Rhin. Du 2 Novembre 1792, l'an Ier . . . Beratschlagung des Nieder-Rheinischen Departement-Directorium.* Strasbourg, n. d. 4 pp. 4°

Fr. & Ger. Abolition of obligatory communal Jewish taxes. BuStg.

XIX. Jewish Army Purveyors

Jewish army provisionaries were of great importance to the government, but they were also much disliked and were accused of causing all sorts of evils. During the Revolution the number of Jewish financiers was small. But the tradition of the economic usefulness of the Jews, the idea that the Jews could accomplish great things in this field still persisted. The most important event of the Jewish participation in the army purveyance was the role of Max Berr [Cerfberr] in the *Directoire des Achats* (Purchasing Directory).

279. *Arrêt de la Cour de Parlement, qui ordonne qu'à la diligence du Procureur général du Roi, il sera incessamment informé, par devant M. de Roguier, conseiller, commissaire, nommé, lequel se transportera sur les lieux, à l'occasion de l'émeute populaire arrivé à Bouleuj, le 19 Janvier 1789. Du 27 Janvier 1789.* Metz, n. d., 4 pp. 4°.

Pillage of wheat imported by C e r f - B e r r from abroad. BmM, Paquet, I, 486.

280. *Anciens (Les) Directeurs des Achats au Public.* [Signé: [Jacques] Biedermann, Marx [Max] Berr [C e r f b e r r], 6 Mars 1793.]

Lévylier, II, 23–24.

281. [Broadside against Biedermann and C e r f b e r r.]

According to *Avis* (see No. 282): "Des affiches placardées."

282. *Avis. Subsistances militaires.* Paris, 1793. 2 pp. 4°.

The Convention on Biedermann and C e r f b e r r. ChD.

283. Boissy d'Anglas, [François Antoine Cᵗᵉ de]. *Convention Nationale. Rapport sur l'arrestation des citoyens Bidermann & M a x B e r r [Cerfberr], membres du Directoire des Achats, et sur les plaintes portées contre cette administration,* Paris, 1793. 23 pp. 8°.

BN.

284. *Conditions du Marché passé par les Comités de Salut Public et des Finances réunis, à la compagnie Lanchère père et fils aîné et Cerf Berr frères, pour la levée et l'entretien des chevaux nécessaires aux armées de la République, pendant deux années qui commenceront au premier Germinal prochaine.* Paris, Ventôse an III. 4°.

AN (AD–VI–44).

285. *Décret de la Convention Nationale, du 11 Juin 1793, qui ordonne la mise en liberté de Baruch C e r f b e r r, régisseur des Achat de l'armée du Rhin. Dekret des National Konvents.* [Strasbourg, 1793.] 4 pp. 4°.

Fr. & Ger. BuStg.

286. *Observations pour le citoyen C e r f - B e r r, régisseur des Achats des subsistances militaires, à l'armée du Rhin, en réponse au Général* [Adam-Philippe de] Custines. n. p., 1793. 30 pp. 4°.

BN, ChD.

287. *Observations pour le citoyen L i p m a n- C e r f b e r r, en réponse au rapport fait, le 25 Janvier, par les Commissaires de la Convention nationale, à l'armée de la Belgique.* Paris, 1793. 19 pp. 4° & charts.

BN, ChD.

288. *Entreprise des équipages d'artillerie des Armées de Rhin et Moselle, des Alpes, d'Italie et du Midi. C e r f - B e r r, Frères.*

Extrait du règlement général d'administration et de police. Pour les conducteurs et chefs de division. Strasbourg, 179– . iv, 62 pp. 8°.

OBL, I, 99.

289. *Réponse des Directeurs des Achats généraux de subsistances, aux questions du Comité de la Guerre, sur leur administration.* [Signé: Biedermann, M a r x [M a x] B e r r.] [Paris,] 1792. 103 pp. 4° & 6 charts.

BN, ChD.

290. [Arrêté du Représentant Merlin sur le complétement du Service des chevaux d'artillerie, suivi d'une lettre à Baruch C e r f B e r r.] Strasbourg, an III. 16 pp. 8°.

OBL, I, 99.

291. *Femme (La) de Benjamin J a c o b à la Convention Nationale.* n. p., [1792]. 32 pp. 8°.

Petition for the liberation of Jacob. BN.

292. *Police. De par les Maire et les Officiers municipaux de la ville de Metz. Sentence concernant les amidonniers, boulangers, marchands de farine, j u i f s et autres,* [Signé: Blondin.] Metz, 9 Octobre 1790. Broadside.

AmM. Paquet, I, 488.

293. *Précis pour la citoyenne Henriette Sommervogel . . . contre Salomon et Michel L é v y , Frères de Bischheim-au-Saum . . .* [Signé: Mueg, Simon.] Colmar, [179–]. 15 pp. 4°.

BuStg. See No. 294.

294. *Errata du Précis imprimé pour . . . Sommervogel . . . contre Salomon et Michel Lévy frères . . .* n. p., [179–]. 1 p. 4°.

BuStg. See No. 293.

295. *Pierre Seigneur, de la Section de la Butte des Moulins, à mes concitoyens les Parisiens.* n. p., n. d. Broadside.

Proposal to ask the Jews to import to Paris wheat from abroad. AN (AF–II–357). See Charavary. Printed on a proof of another Broadside.

XX. Jewish Participation in the Sale of National Property

The sale of *biens nationaux* (national property, confiscated from the Church, émigrés and counter-revolutionaries) was one of the most important events of the Revolution. Speculation in such properties was frequent and this served as useful anti-Jewish propaganda. The anti-revolutionary circles tried to frighten Catholics into thinking that Jews and Protestants would desecrate the nationalized holy places and that peasants would be expropriated by Jews. Jews were attacked by reactionaries for wanting to buy national property and by revolutionaries for not buying it. Very few Jews bought national property for farming purposes; most Jewish buyers purchased such properties for resale or trade. But by granting loans to peasants of Alsace and neighboring departments they played an important role in the parcelization of land. See Szajkowski, "Jewish Participation."

296. *Le Meuilleur des Amen à l'usage des juifs et des chrétiens.* n. p., [1789 or 1790.[7 pp. 8°.

In favor of the nationalization of Church property and against speculation. BN.

297. *Observations du citoyen Hayem Worms, négociant, et membre du Conseil-Général de la Commune de Sarre-Libre, Département de la Moselle; pour servir de réponse à la pétition du citoyen Joseph René Bassigny, se disant*

cultivateur à Sarreguemines. n. p., [an 3.] 14 pp. 4°.

Against the annulment of a purchase of nationalized property by Worms. BN.

298. *No. LXXXI. District de Bordeaux. Etat d'Estimation du domaine national, ci-devant Hôtel de l'Intendance.* [Signé: Peixotto, soumissionnaire des objet ci-dessus.] Bordeaux, 23 Octobre 1791. Broadside.

With a map. JTS.

299. *Vilvot, Jacques Hardel, de Haguenau, département du Bas-Rhin en sa qualité de co-acquéreur du ci-devant couvent de Annonciats de la même commune au citoyen, président et membre du Directoire exécutive.* n. p., n. d. 12 pp. 4°.

On a sale of nationalized property to Jews. JTS.

See also No. 423.

XXI. The Conflict over the Nationalization of the Jewish Cemetery
of Bordeaux

The revolutionary regime tried to abolish separate religious cemeteries and replace them with general cemeteries for the entire population. The Jews of Bordeaux fought stubbornly against the nationalization of their cemetery. They demanded that the sale of their cemetery to two Gentiles be declared null and void, because the cemetery was not officially communal property but represented a philanthropic undertaking. The administration acceded to the Jewish demand, but an open conflict with the buyers and enemies of the Jews could not be avoided.

300. *Extrait de l'Arrêté de l'Administration départementale de la Gironde, du 11 Messidor, an IV de la République française une et indivisible* [29 Juin 1796. Signé: Duplantier, président, Planthion, secrétaire d'office.] n. p., n. d. 4 pp. 4°.

Annulment of the sale of the Jewish cemetery. PC.

301. *Mémoire pour les citoyens [Pierre] Despiau et Poujos [Pujol], de Bordeaux.* Bordeaux, n. d. 32 pp. 4°.

Columbia University Libraries, N. Y., PC.

302. *Mémoire à consulter et consultation, pour les citoyens Français, professant le culte Judaïque à Bordeaux, connus sous le nom de Juifs Portugais et Avignonais.* n. p., n. d. 7, 47 pp. 8°.

The "Consultation," dated Nov. 29, 1798, is signed by: [Louis] Francia [de] Beaufleury, Ferey, [François Placide Nicolas?]/[J. J. R. de Camba-

cérès, [A. J. B.] Debonnières. Reprinted in Beaufleury's *Histoire* (see No. 6).

BN, JTS.

303. Despiau, [Pierre] et Pujol, [Augustin]. *Réponse à un Mémoire imprimé sous le nom des Citoyens français, professant le culte judaïque à Bordeaux,* n. p. n. d.

According to No. 304.

304. Prévot, [Marc Florent.] *Rapport fait par Prévot, sur une pétition des citoyens Pujol & Despiau, habitans de la commune de Bordeaux, soumissionnaires de biens appartenans aux Juifs établis en cette commune. Séance du 21 Germinal an 7 [10 Avril 1799].* Paris, an 7. 7 pp. 8°.

BN.

305. Darracq, [François Balthazar.] *Opinion de Darracq dans l'affaire des Juifs de Bordeaux. Séance du 18 Floréal an 7 [7 Mai 1799].* Paris, an 7. 31 pp. 8°.

Against the Jews, BN, JTS.

XXII. Jewish Agents for France and Other States

Jews, with their knowledge of the German language and family contacts with Germany were often in a position to supply the French with valuable information about enemy positions. Some Jews served as spies, e. g. Joseph Godchaux of Thionville, who refused to betray France. On the other hand, some Jews did serve as spies for the émigrés or as foreign agents.

306. *Le messie Ephraïm. Lettre de Binjamin Benoni, juif de Pou, à Elias Lévi, juif d'Allemagne.* n. p., [1791.] 7 pp. 8°.

Against Benjamin Veitel Ephraïm, agent of Prussia. See Léon Kahn, "Un agent du Roi de Prusse à Paris," *AnAI, 5658* (Paris, 1897). BN. See also No. 307.

307. *Lettre d'Ephraïm à [P. A. F. Choderlos de] Laclos.* n. p., n. d. 4 pp. 8°.

An apocryphal letter, dated Paris, Apr. 22, 1791. The author writes on the "intentions de Frédéric-Guillaume, mon maître" and "roi de Prusse, mon maître." BN. See also No. 306.

308. Goudchaux, Joseph. *Pétition adressée à*

la Convention Nationale par Joseph Goudchaux. Paris, [1792.] 8 pp. 4°.

Against Général Georges Félix Baron de Wimpffen. BN. See Heckmann, pp. 112–17. See also Nos. 309–310.

309. Wimpffen, Georges Félix Baron de. *Lettre au Ministre Pache.* Caen, 1793. 11 pp. 4°.

Against Goudchaux. BN. See No. 308.

310. ———. *Lettres du général Félix Wimpffen, commandant de Thionville.* Paris, n. d. 23 pp. 4°.

BN. See Nos. 308–309.

See also No. 342.

XXIII. Juridical Documents: Political & Economic

The Terror and the dissension of the leaders of the Revolution also influenced the situation of the Jews. The degree of Jewish participation in the factional struggles defined the attitude of the revolutionary leaders toward them. A few Jews were guillotined for their federalist activities. Others were arrested or fined and many of them were innocent victims of the tragic period. But the Revolution did not persecute the Jews as such and no Jew lost his life because of his religion.

311. A l e x a n d r e , Séligmann. *Dénonciation à mes concitoyens des vexations que m'ont fait éprouver les fidèles suppôts du traître Robespierre, lors du système de Terreur établi dans la République.* Par Séligmann A l e x a n d r e , manufacturier et citoyen de Strasbourg. Strasbourg, an III. 38 pp. 8°.

Motto on the title page: "Par eux tout est en sang, par eux tout est en poudre, / Et ils n'avaient du ciel imité que la foudre." Pp. 23–38: "Pièces justificatives." BN, JTS, BuStg. See Reuss, Rod.

Souvenirs historiques. Séligmann Alexandre, ou Les Tribulations d'un Israélite Strasbourgeois pendant la Terreur. Strasbourg, 1880; Löwenstein, Dr. L. "Die Juden im Elsass vor und während der Schreckensherrschaft," *Blätter f. Jüdische Geschichte und Literatur,* I (1900), 33–34, 49–50, 65–69, II (1901), 1–3.

312. *Jugement rendu par la Commission militaire, séante à Bordeaux, qui condamne Samuel A s t r u c , marchand d'étoffes de soie, natif et domicilié à Bordeaux, comme*

égoïste et n'ayant point eu de confiance aux assignats, à une amende de 30,000 livres, dont 10,000 pour les Sans-Culottes de Bordeaux, et le restant pour la République, et ordonne qu'il sera sur le champ mis en liberté. Du 14 Pluviôse, l'an deuxième [2 Février 1794] . . . Bordeaux, 1794. Broadside.

BN, AdG, JTS. Signed by [Jean Baptiste Marie] Lacombe, president, Morel, Barreau, Marguerié, Lacroix, Albert and Giffey, secretary, who also signed the items 313, 316–18, 321–22, 324–25, 327, 329–33.

313. *Jugement rendu par la Commission militaire, séante a Bordeaux, qui ordonne que David A z e v e d o, agent-de-change, sera sur le champ mis en liberté. Du 14 Pluviôse, l'an second [2 Février 1794]*. Bordeaux, [1794]. Broadside.

BN, AdG, JTS.

314. *Pétition. Le citoyen Raphaël B l o c h, habitant de la commune de Ventzenheimb, district de Colmar, département du Haut-Rhin, au Comité de Législation.* [Colmar, an II.] 4 pp. fol.

Signed by [Joseph] "Bonchvig [Bronchvig], fondé de pouvoir." Appeal against a forced contribution of 25,000 livres. AN CD–III–215).

315. *Jugement rendu par le Tribunal révolutionnaire établi à Nismes, qui condamne les nommées* . . . *Jassé C a r c a s s o n n e* . . . *membre de la municipalité à l'époque du fédéralisme* . . . *à la peine de mort* . . . *Du 1er Thermidor an second [1 Juillet 1794]* . . . Nismes, [1794]. Broadside.

AdGard, JTS.

316. *Jugement rendu par la Commission militaire* . . . *Du 17 nivôse an II [6 Janvier 1794]*. Bordeaux, 1794. Broadside.

Liberation of a group of actors, including Samuel Franco D a c o s t a. AdG.

317. *Jugement rendu par la Commission militaire, séante à Bordeaux, qui condamne*

Jean D a v i d, marchand drapier, âgé de 70, natif et domicilié de Bordeaux, à une amende de 15,000 livres . . . *Du 1er Germind, l'an deuxième [21 Mars 1794]*. Bordeaux, [1794]. Broadside.

BN, AdG.

318. *Jugement rendu par la Commission militaire, séante à Bordeaux, qui condamne Moyse-Marc F o i, natif de Bayonne, domicilié à Bordeaux, à une amende de 50,000 livres* . . . *acquite Daniel Errera fils, natif de Saint-Esprit, près Bayonne, domicilié à Bordeaux; Michel Delaunay, natif de May* . . .*; ordonne que Léon F o i et Abraham G u a s t a l l a seront reintégrés dans les prisons pour qu'il soit pris sur leur compte des renseignements. Du 5 Ventôse, l'an deuxième [23 Février 1794]*. Bordeaux, [1794]. Broadside.

BN, AdG, JTS.

319. [Sentence of six years in prison and a fine of 50,000 livres imposed upon Samuel H i r t z of Ribeauvillé for speculation. June 2, 1793.] Broadside.

According to Véron-Réville, 114; Hubrecht, 78. See No. 320.

320. [Last two pages (7–8) of a petition by Samuel H i r t z . See No. 319.]

BmStg.

321. *Jugement* . . . *qui acquite Joseph J u - l i a n, ancien négociant, natif de Bayonne, domicilié à Bordeaux. Du 17 Ventôse an II [7 Mars 1794]*. Bordeaux, [1794]. Broadside.

AdG.

322. *Jugement* . . . *qui condamne Moyse L a n g e, dit l'Américain* . . . *en 80,000 livres d'amende* . . . *Du 11 Ventôse, l'an deuxième [1 Février 1794]*. Bordeaux, [1794]. Broadside.

BN, AdG.

323. [A circular denouncing Léopold L é v y as the "principal agent de l'exportation du numéraire à l'étranger." 1792.]

According to Hubrecht, 48.

324. *Jugement qui condamne Aaron L o - p e s . . . à une amende de 50,000 livres . . . ordonne qu'il sera sur le champ mis en liberté. Du 23 Ventôse, l'an deuxième [13 Mars 1794].* Bordeaux, [1794]. Broadside. BN, AdG.

325. *Jugement . . . Séance du 2 Thermidor, an second [20 Juillet 1794].* Bordeaux, 1794. Broadside.

Sentence of death against Jean M e n d e s (called Blondin) and others. According to most historians Mendes died because of his Jewish faith, but he was converted to Christianity. See Szajkowski, in *Historia Judaica,* XVIII (1956), 113.

326. *Les Représentants du Peuple près l'Armée des Pyrénées Occidentales et les départements environnants.* Bayonne, 18 Pluviôse an 2 [6 Février 1794]. 3 pp. 4°.

BN. Signed by Jacques Pinet. Recognition of the falsehood of the charges against Abraham N u n e z of Saint-Esprit-lès-Bayonne.

327. *Jugement rendu par la Commission militaire, séante à Bordeaux, qui condamne Charles P e i x o t t o , banquier, âgé de 53 ans . . . à une amende de 1,200,000 livres . . . Du 26 Frimaire, l'an second [16 Décembre 1793].* Bordeaux, n. d. Broadside.

A converted Jew, although still considered by most historians of the period and in item No. 328 as a Jew. BN, AdG. See also No. 18.

328. Goupilleau, [Philippe Charles Aîné]. *Rapport . . . sur la pétition du citoyen Charles P e i x o t t o , banquier, contre un jugement de la Commission militaire de Bordeaux, du 26 Frimaire an II, qui le condamne à une amende de 1,200,000 fr. [livres]. Séance du 24 Vendémiaire an VII [15 Octobre 1798].* Paris, n. d. 6 pp. 8°.

BN. See No. 17.

329. *Jugement rendu par la Commission militaire, séante à Bordeaux, qui ordonne qu'Isaac P e r e y r e , agent de change, sera sur le champ mis en liberté. Du 13 Nivôse l'an second [2 Janvier 1794].* Bordeaux, [1794]. Broadside.

JTS, BN.

330. *Jugement . . . 11 Pluviôse an l'an second [30 Janvier 1794].* Bordeaux, [1794]. Broadside.

Detention of Jean P e r p i g n a n until the end of War and imposition of a fine of 50,000 livres. AdG.

331. *Jugement . . . qui acquite Jacob P i - m e n t e l , négociant . . . natif de Portugal . . . Du 1er Ventôse l'an II [19 Février 1794].* Bordeaux, [1794]. Broadside.

BN, AdG.

332. *Jugement . . . qui condamne les Frères R a b a , négocians à Bordeaux, en une amende de cinq cens mille livres . . . Du neuvième our de la première décade du deuxième mois de la seconde année [30 Octobre 1793].* Bordeaux, [1793]. Broadside.

JTS, BN, AmBx. Against the five brothers Jacob Henri, Abraham Henrique, Gabriel Salomon Henrique, Aaron Henrique, and Moïse Antoine Rodrigue Raba.

333. *Jugement . . . qui acquitte Moyse S a - l o m ci-devant marchand à Paris . . . Du 17 Pluviôse, l'an deuxième [5 Février 1794].* Bordeaux, 1794. Broadside.

JTS, BN.

334. *Au nom de la République française une et indivisible.* Strasbourg, an II.

Sentence of Dec. 27, 1793, ordering the liberation of Raissel Soe [S é e] of Oberbergheim. According to *SIW,* x (1913), No. 33.

335. [Fragment of a broadside announcing the death sentence of Azaria V i d a l , guillotined in Lyon on Dec. 9, 1793.]

PC.

(*To be continued*)

The Emancipation of
Jews During the French Revolution

A Bibliography of Books, Pamphlets and
Printed Documents, 1789–1800

BY ZOSA SZAJKOWSKI, *New York*

(Continued)

XXIV. JURIDICAL DOCUMENTS: CIVIL & CRIMINAL

The printed sentences and juridical pamphlets (briefs, known in French bibliographies as *Factums*) are a very important source for the history of the Jews of France during this, or any other period. These *factums* contain much information on the economic and other activities of the Jews. Above all, the *factums* containing information on the legal status of marriage and divorce according to Jewish law are of great importance. Such lawsuits involved individuals, but were always of much importance for the entire Jewish community. These *factums* indicate the effectiveness with which the Jews used the law courts in order to defend their economic and other positions. Without the force of the law, without the possibility of legal recourse against anti-Jewish discrimination, the privileges obtained by the Jews often would have been without value. Of course, only a small number of lawsuits were publicized in printed *factums*, which involved large expenses. So, the *factums* are mostly the record of lawsuits involving rich people. Some of the *factums* in this bibliography were preceded by such documents published during the old regime.

336. [Sentence against "Lazare A b r a - h a m juif [de Nancy] accusé de vol." 21 Décembre 1791.] Broadside.

AdMM (L 104).

337. *Mémoire pour le Sieur Daniel A s t r u c, négociant de cette ville. Contre le Sieur Thomas, négociant, et le Sieur Peyrony Morepos.* [Signé: J. Fs. Cornu, Laumond.] Bordeaux. [1791?]. 24 pp. 4°.

BmBx. Affair of a debt.

338. *Réflexions pour les Citoyens Passade & Compagnie, négociants à Bordeaux contre la citoyenne Bataillard, veuve du citoyen Duperier.* [Signé: (Thomas) Lumière.] Bordeaux, n. d. 56 pp. 4°.

Affair involving A s t r u c. BmBx.

339. *Mémoire au Roi, pour le sieur [Louis Francia] de Beaufleury, auteur des Mémoires & des Calculs relatifs à l'établissement d'une Compagnie d'Assurances sur la vie des*

homes, les premiers & les seuls qui aient été accueillis par le Gouvernement, les premiers & les seuls qui aient eu la sanction de l'Académie Royale des Sciences. [Paris, janvier 1793.] 1, 18 pp. 8°.

BmBx. See also No. 340.

340. *Précis pour le sieur de Beaufleury.* n. p., n. d. 31 pp. 8°.

With the title of No. 339 as sub-title. PC.

341. *Jugement du Tribunal criminal du Département de la Moselle qui condamne Isaac B e h r à la peine de dix années de fers, provisoirement remplacée par celle des galères et ordonne qu'il sera préalablement conduit sur la place publique de la Commune de Sarreguemines, pour y être attaché à un poteau l'espace de six heures, pour avoir fait sortir du territoire de la République des suifs |en branches; déclare, en outre, acquis et confisqués au profit des citoyens Stakre et héritiers de Michel Pion les suifs qui ont été arrêtés, du 22 Mesidor, l'an deux . . . [10 Juillet 1794].* [Signé: Delattre, Président et Dauphin, Greffier en chef.] Metz, [1794]. Broadside.

AV, D^{III} 173 (Forbach).

342. [Sentence of death against Léopold B e r n h e i m of Kembs, suspected of being a foreign spy. Sept. 9, 1795.] Broadside.

Fr. & Ger. Only a fragment of the broadside in BmStg.

343. *Mémoire pour Cerf B l i e n , contre Goudchaux-Mayer Cahen.* Metz, IVe année républicaine. 18 pp. 4°.

BmM.

344. *Arrêt du Parlement qui condamne Joseph B l o c k , Juif sans asyle & déjà repris de iustice, aux galères pour neuf ans . . . pour crimes du vol. Du 5 octobre 1789.* Metz, 1789. Broadside.

AdM, JTS.

345. *Précis pour la veuve et les enfans de Jacques Fabre, contre une partie des héritiers collatéraux de Pierre-David B o n a f o u s . . .* [Signé: Auguste Ravez, défenseur officieux.] Bordeaux, n. d. 36 pp. 4°.

JTS, BmBx.

346. *Réponses des sieurs Poinsignon aux mémoires imprimés sous les noms du juif Abraham-Isaac B r i s a c .* Nancy, [179-]. 44 pp. 4°.

BmN.

347. *Mémoire pour le sieur Jean Aubertin, juge-consul des marchands, à Metz, contre le sieur Godchaux-Mayer C a h e n , juif, négociant de la même ville, et Moyse Salomon Emmericque [sic!], aussi juif de Metz, intimés.* [Signé: M^e. Lemaire.] Metz, [1790]. 30 pp. 4°.

Commercial conflict. JTS, AmM. See Paquet, I, 416. See No. 348.

348. *Supplément au Mémoire pour le Sieur Jean Aubertin, juge consul, contre les sieur Godchaux-Mayer C a h e n et Moyse Salomon Emmericque [sic!].* [Signé: M^e. Lemaire] Metz, [1790]. 8 pp. 4°.

AmM. See Paquet, I, 416. See No. 347.

349. *Jugement du Tribunal criminel du département de la Moselle, qui d'après les déclarations des jurés spéciaux de jugement condamne Michel C a h e n , marchand boucher, domicilié à Guinglange, à la peine de quinze années de fers, comme convaincu d'avoir sciemment, méchamment et à dessein distribué et voulu distribuer des écus de six livres et des pièces de trente sols, tous reconnus faux, et déclare ses biens acquis à la République. Metz, Du 24 Floréal, an III [13 Ma 1795].* [Signé: Chaufin, président, Dauphin,^i greffier en Chef.] Metz, n. d. Broadside.

AdM. Paquet, I, 424.

350. *Extrait des registres des délibérations du département de la Moselle. Séance publique du 1ᵉʳ Vendémiaire, an IV [23 Septembre 1795]* . . . Metz, n. d. Broadside.

Reprint of a decision of the Legislative Committee of Paris. Annulment of a decision by the City Council of Metz concerning the rent of the house of Suzanne Salomon Cerf, the wife of Jacob-David May, involving the rent to Jews and Christians. JTS, AmM. Paquet, I, 428.

351. [Death sentence against Feitz C e r f of Niederwisse, by the Criminal Tribunal of Moselle, for the distribution of false *assignats*. October 6, 1794. The same sentence liberated another Jew, Bourig-Cerf.] Broadside.

Fragment in AmM.

352. [Sentence of Sept. 21, 1790, forcing the Bishop de Rohan to repay to C e r f-b e r r a debt of 267,880 livres 2 s. 7d.] Broadside.

A fragment in BmStg.

353. *Justice de Paix du troisième arrondissement de la Commune Strasbourg. Au nom de la République française. Séance publique. L'an quatre de la République française, le quatorze Pluviôse [3 Février 1796], par Nous Jean Géofroi Wild, Juge-de-paix* . . . *a été rendu le jugement qui suit, entre le citoyen Baruch C e r f - B e r r* . . . *demandeur, contre le citoyen Cotta, rédacteur de la Gazette du Rhin [Rheinische Zeitung], défendeur.* n. p., n. d. 7 pp. 4°.

BuStg, JTS. Cotta accused Cerf Berr of anti-Republican feelings.

354. *Jugement de la justice de paix de la deuxième section de la commune de Metz, qui condamne Israel C h o u d i c k, boucher, résidant en cette commune, à l'amende du quadruple droit de patente, indépendamment du prix de celle dont il a négligé de se pourvoir dans les delais fixés par les lois du 6 Fructidor an IV et 25 Vendémiaire an V. Extrait des minutes du greffe* . . . *Audience du 18 Frimaire an V [8 Décembre 1796] de la République française* . . . Metz, n. d. Broadside.

Paquet, I, 429.

355. *Précis pour le citoyen Jassé Hain [Haïm] C r é m i e u, d'Aix; contre le citoyen Jean-Baptiste Rocamus, de la Tour-d'Aigues.* [Signé: Jassé Haïn Crémieu et Chansaud, Homme de loi.] Aix, an VI. 7 pp. 4°.

A conflict over debts. JTS.

356. *Dernier mot pour le citoyen Salomon-Haïn C r é m i e u : contre les frères Bédarride.* [Signé: Crémieu & Chansaud, Homme de loi.] Aix, an VI. 7 pp. 4°.

A conflict over debts. JTS.

357. *Extrait des registres des audiences de Parlement.* Bordeaux, 1790, 20 pp. 4°.

A conflict between B. Plantevigné and G. Feuilherade, involving Antoine D a c o s t a. BmBx.

358. [Death sentence against Moyse D a - v i d, a Jew of Uckange, for the distribution of false assignats. September 4, 1794.] 4 pp. 4°.

Only the last two of four pages in AmM.

359. *Mémoire pour Louis F r a n c i a, Benjamain [sic] Francia, et les cohéritiers de feu François Francia, attestans conjointement avec Abraham et Jacob de George Francia. Contre Antoinette Sara, Dalpujet, femme Cousin.* Bordeaux, 1796. 72 pp. 4°.

PC.

360. *Consultation pour Joseph Fenwick, consul des Etats-Unis d'Amérique, contre* . . . *F u r t a d o et Texier, négocians à Bordeaux.* [Signé: Champion-Villeneuve, H. Duveyrier, Dejoly. Paris, le 10 Brumaire an 5.] 4°. [Bordeaux, an V.] 26 pp. 4°.

PC.

361. *Observation pour le citoyen Vond'horen, armateur du corsaire Le Spartiate... Contre... le citoyen F u r t a d o , tous appelans d'un iugement ... le 12 Brumaire an 7 ...* [Signé: (Marc Pierre Marie) Emérigon, homme de loi, Laumond, fondé de pouvoir.] Bordeaux, n. d. 23 pp. 4°.
PC.

362. *Précis pour Stephen Lée, capitaine du navire Le Charles, de Neu-Yorck, appelant, et le citoyen Peter-Apoix, répresenté par le cit. Lévy F u r t a d o ... contre le citoyen Vond'horen...* [Signé: Buhan (Jean Laurent, or one of his two sons).] Bordeaux, 179– · 37 pp. 4°.
PC.

363. *Mémoire pour les sieurs David G r a d i s & Fils, négocians à Bordeaux, défendeurs à la demande en homolgation du rapport arbitral des sieurs Tavernier & Boiteau, du 22 Octobre 1789 ... Contre le sieur David Dasylva ...* [Signé: (M. P. M.) Emérigon.] [Bordeaux, 1789.] 153 pp. 4°.
PC.

364. [Sentence on the Affair of the theft of the diamonds at the *garde-meuble.* Aaron H u m b e r q u e to be set free. Aug. 17, 1792]. [Paris, 1792.] 2 pp. 4°.
AN, W 250.

365. *Au nom de la Nation. Le Tribunal criminel du Département du Bas-Rhin a rendu le jugement suivant. Im Namen der Nation.* [Signé: Schwingdenhammer.] Strasbourg, n. d. Broadside.
Fr. & Ger. Sentence against the thieves "Moise I s a a c & Jacques A a r o n , citoyens juifs." BuStg, HUC.

366. [Death sentence against Joseph J a - c o b , a Jew of Pirmasens, by the Criminal Tribunal of Paris for the distribution of "faux assignats." May 6, 1795.] Broadside.
PC., title missing.

367. *Mémoire pour les citoyens Sorbé et fils, L a n g e , F o n s e c a neveu, R o b l e s ...Assureurs...* [Signé: Duranteau (N., or his son André), Drouet.] Bordeaux, an VIII. 72 pp. 4°.
PC.

368. *Uebersetzung des Briefes den Hr. Duport, Justiz-Minister, an die HHn. Handels-Richter zu Strassburg, den 7 August 1791 von Paris aus, geschriben hat.* n. p., n. d. 3 pp. 12°.
A conflict between Joseph L e h m a n n und Sohn and Baron de Harsch on a question of credit, an IV. BuStg.

369–369a. Rumpler, [Chanoine François Louis]. *Lisez! Ça ne coute rien... A l'accusateur public, près le Tribunal criminel du département du Bas-Rhin ... l'Histoire véritable de l'honnête [Joseph] Lehmann ... de la race d'Israël ... 16 Nivôse an IV [6 Janvier 1796].* [Strasbourg, 1796.] 4 pp. 8°.
Distributed also as a reprint of a larger book with the pp. numbered 41–44. For other of Rumpler's pamphlets against Lehmann see No. 370 and Napoleonica, Nos. 3–5. BuStg.

370. ———. *Plaidoyer d'un défenseur officieux, déclaré inadmissible pour oser défendre un créancier bâlois, contre les brigands Strasbourgeois, qui veulent le dévaliser en forme.* n. p., n. d. 16 pp. 8°.
For Faesch against Joseph and Isaac L e h m a n n . See No. 369. BuStg.

371. *Mémoire et consultation d'avocats de Paris et de Colmar, pour le Baron de Haindel ...* [Strasbourg, 1789?] 8 pp. 4°.
Against his creditor Volf L é v y . See Nos. 372–374. BN.

372. *Précis pour le Baron de Haindel ... contre Volf L é v y , le Marquis de Belloy, & autres créanciers ...* [Paris, 1789.] 17 pp. 4°.
BuStg. See Nos. 371 & 374.

373. *Mémoire pour Wolf L é v y, banquier à Strasbourg; contre le Baron de Haindel* . . . n. p., n. d. 81 pp. 4°.

BuStg. See Nos. 371–372 & 374.

374. *Réponse pour le Baron de Haindel au Mémoire des Sieurs Volf L é v i & Consorts* . . . [Paris,] n. d. 94 pp. 4°.

BuStg. See Nos. 371–373.

375. *Mémoire pour le citoyen Dudon père, demeurant à Bordeaux, contre les citoyens Lameza* . . . *en présence des citoyens Roux et L o p e s* . . . [Signé: Devios.] Bordeaux, [an VII]. 40 pp. 4°.

PC.

376. *Parere et consultation, pour les citoyens Goudal, Laforcade et Comp^e., négocians, à Bordeaux, sur l'appel interjetté par Bernard M e d o u s* . . . [Signé: (Guillaume, or Jean Baptiste) Brochon, (Leonard Gaye de) Martignac, Auguste Ravez. Bordeaux, le 1er Vendémiaire, an 5.] Bordeaux, n. d. 16 pp. 4°.

Conflict over a debt. See No. 377. PC.

377. *Extrait du jugement du Tribunal civil du département de la Charente, séant à Angoulême. Du 25 Fructidor, an quatrième. Rendu contre les citoyens Goudal* . . . [Signé: Bernard M e d o u s, 5 Frimaire an 5.] Bordeaux, n. d. 20 pp. 4°.

PC. See No. 376.

378. *Précis dans la cause pendante au Tribunal civil séant à Strasbourg, entre Abraham-Aaron M o c h, négociant à Strasbourg, défendeur; contre Catherine-Dorothee Eschenauer* . . . Strasbourg, [179–]. 10 pp. 8°.

Conflict over a debt. BuStg.

379. *Requête du sieur M o ï s e, Juif Avignonois & citoyen actif du royaume de France.*

A Messeigneurs de l'Assemblée nationale, contre M. Honoré de Riquet, comte de Mirabeau, député à la susdite Assemblée Nationale.

According to *Courrier d'Avignon*, no. 87, Apr. 12, 1790, p. 348.

380. *Mémoire pour les citoyens Abraham, Jacob et Moïse O x e d a frères* . . . *contre les citoyens Joseph Oxeda et Daniel Silva.* [Signé: Abraham Oxeda, Jacob Oxeda, Moïse Oxeda, (N.) Albespy, homme de loi, Marion, avoué.] [Bordeaux, an IX.] 36 pp. 4°.

PC.

381. *A Monsieur le Grand Sénéchal* . . . *supplie* . . . *Charles Paul Joseph P e i x o t t o de Beaulieu* . . . *contre Dame Alexandre* . . . Bordeaux, 1789. 21 pp. fol.

AmBx.

382. [Marie de Saint-Georges de Montmerci, François Jacques Thomas.] *Généalogie curieuse et remarquable de M. P e i x o t t o, juif d'origine, chrétien de profession & banquier de Bordeaux. Ouvrage destiné a prouver aux mécréans que M. Peixotto descend en ligne directe d'Adam, de Noé et de tous les Cohens de l'univers.* Avignon, 1789. IV, 40 pp. 4°.

BN. See No. 383.

383. *Mémoire pour M^e. François-Jacques-Thomas, Marie de Saint-Georges, avocat* . . . *sur l'Appel fait par sieur P e i x o t t o, de l'appointement des Jurats de Bordeaux, du 2 Avril 1789, & de son chef* . . . *contre sieur Paul Joseph Peixotto, Juif de naissance* . . . [Bordeaux, 1789.] 47 pp. 4°.

BN. See No. 382.

384. Tourton. *A l'Assemblée Nationale.* Paris, n. d. 4 pp. 4°.

On his and his partner R a v e l' s situation during the old regime. BN.

385. *Arrêt du Parlement qui condamne le nommé Lyon R e n a r d , Juif, natif de Soultz . . . pour crime de vol. Du 17 avril 1789.* Metz, 1789. Broadside.

AdM.

386. *Jugement du Tribunal Criminel du Département de la Gironde, qui condamne Etienne Perreau, natif de Dijon, tailleur d'habits, a huit années de fers . . .* Bordeaux, [1795]. Broadside.

A swindle against a Jew named R o d r i g u e s. AmBx.

387. *Jugement du Tribunal de Commerce de Bordeaux, rendu par défaut, ordonnant la nouvelle assignation de R o d r i g u e s fils, marchand à Bordeaux, pour le paiement d'un billet de 450 fr., souscrit par lui en faveur de Painchaud, marchand à Limoges.* [Bordeaux,] n. d. 4°.

A fragment at AmBx.

388. *Jugement du Tribunal criminel du Département de la Gironde, qui sur la déclaration du Jury de Jugement, condamne Etienne Perreau, convaincu de vol . . . Du 27 Frimaire, quatrième année [18 Décembre 1795].* Bordeaux, [1795]. Broadside.

Acquittal of R o d r i g u e, alias Rodrigues Moran. PC.

389. *Courts apperçus sur la réplique des sieurs Perès-Duvivier, Jean-Jacques Muller &*

R o d r i g u e s; *pour le sieur Ganseford.* [Signé: Mᵉ Dufort.] Bordeaux, 1789. 30 pp. 4°.

PC.

390. *Jugement du Tribunal de la police de la commune de Bordeaux, qui condamne les citoyens S a l z e d o & P e i x o t t o jeune, en 200 livres d'amende chacun, & en huit jours de détention, pour avoir causé du trouble au grand spectacle: Du 16 Nivose, an 4me . . . [6 Janvier 1796].* [Signé: Bouillon, officier municipal, président . . .] Bordeaux, n. d. Broadside.

AmG.

391. *Mémoire* [Signé: Aaron Castro S o l - l a r , 24 Janvier 1794.] Bordeaux, n.d. 63 pp. fol.

A conflict between Sollar and Benjamin Nunes Taverez. See No. 392. PC.

392. *Dénonciation à ses concitoyens.* Bordeaux, n. d. 4°.

T a v a r e z against Sollar. See No. 391 PC.

393. *Moyens d'appel pour le citoyen Benjamin Dubois, armateur du corsaire Le Bougainville . . .* [Signé: Buhan, Mauzé.] Bordeaux, [an v?]. 89 pp. 4°.

A conflict involving Levi & Moïse W a r b u r g , G o t s c h a l c k and others. PC.

XXV. Prayers, Hymns

394. Ensheim, Moyse. *Cantique composé par le citoyen Moyse Ensheim, à l'occasion de la fête civique célébrée à Metz, le 21 octobre, l'an 1ᵉʳ de la République [1792], dans le Temple des citoyens Israëlites.* למנצח שיר למשה עונסהיים. הושר ביום נברה יד יושבי ארץ מולדתנו על כל אויבנו מסביב. [Metz], n. d. 8 pp. 4°.

Fr. & H. Translated into French by Isaïe Berr Bing. BmN, HUC. This is the only item of this type. For hymns of a non-Jewish character by Jewish authors see Nos. 547, 559-60, 564, 570. For hymns of foreign countries see Nos. 546-48, 556, 559-63, 566.

XXVI. Missionary Activity — Restoration

Missionary propaganda among Jews, voluntary conversions of Jews, and forced conversions of Jewish children were frequent prior to the Revolution. As late as May, 1790, the Jews of Carpentras were compelled to be present at missionary sermons. In Alsace Jewish illegitimate children were taken away from their mothers by the Church even during the Revolution. The federal leaders of the Revolution were not concerned with gaining Jews for the Church, but some local authorities and pamphleteers could not forget their own Christian past and they became involved in missionary activities. As for official Catholic circles, they still continued to dream of saving the Jews through conversion, and in this spirit many pamphlets were published even during the Revolution. On a few occasions missionary activity took on the characteristic form of the re-establishment of the Jewish people, converted, in Palestine. In this spirit Napoleon I's appeal of 1799 to the Jews, in which he promised to restore Jerusalem to them should also be understood. See Z. Szajkowski, "Marriages, Mixed Marriages and Conversions Among French Jews During the Revolution of 1789," *Historia Judaica*, XIX (1957), 47–54.

395. *Ordonnance de Monseigneur l'évêque de Carpentras, concernant le baptême des enfants juifs*. Carpentras, 30 juin 1789. 3 pp. 4°.

BmCarp.

396. [Edict of Aug. 12, 1789, against the forced conversion of Jewish children and interdiction of use of Christian midwives and nurses by Jews.] [Avignon, 1789.] Broadisde.

Without a title, Calvet.

397. *Lettres adressées aux Juifs, par deux auteurs anglais*. Traduit en Français, par un Anglais. Paris, 1789. xiv, 61 pp. 8°.

BmCarp.

398. [An appeal for the conversion of Jews.] 1789.

According to Gairal, p. 18.

399. [Pompignan, Le Franc de.] *Lettres à un Juif converti*. Paris, 1790. 310 pp. 16°.

BN.

400. *Warnung für alle Nationen und Menschen, aus dem traurigen Schicksale der jüdischen Nation hergleitet*. n. p., [1790.] 4 pp. 8°.

BmC.

401. [Desfours de la Génetière, Charles François.] *Avis aux catholiques sur le caractère et les signes des temps ou nous vivons, ou De la conversion des Juifs, de l'avènement intermédiaire de Jésus-Christ et de son règne visible sur la terre*. Ouvrage dédié à M. l'évêque de Lescar. Lyon, 1794. 12°.

BN.

402. François-Guillaume.***. *Sermonce générale de paix et de réunion à l'Eglise et à sa chaire apostolique adressée à toute la nation des Juifs*. Riom, 1795. 116 pp. 8°.

JTS. 1st edition: Avignon, 1765. 110 pp.

403. *Re-Establishment of the Jewish Government, an extract from a French Journal [The Courier, June 17, 1798] ...With a Letter*

from a Jew to his brethren. Translated from
the Italian. [London, 1798.] 11 pp. 8°.

BM.

404. [Napoleon's appeal of 1799 for the
Restoration of a Jewish state.]

The original text in printed form was never found.

XXVII. HEBREW PUBLICATIONS — GENERAL SUBJECTS

A. PUBLICATIONS PRINTED IN FRANCE

405. Reischer, Jacob. ספר שאלות ותשובות
שבות יעקב מהרב מהו' יעקב זאב בן הרב מהו'
יוסף רישר . . . חלק שלישי. Metz, 1789. 112 ff.
4°.

Vol. III. JTS.

406. Worms, Aaron. מאורי אור. Metz,
1790. 4°.

Vol. I; vol. II: 1791; vol. III, 1817; vol. IV, 1822;
vol. V, 1827; vol. VI, 1831. JTS.

407. Kohen, Oury Phoebus. הלכה ברורה,
. . . חדושי הלכות . . . ואגדות ודרשות. Metz,
1793. 39 ff. fol.

JTS.

408. Zebi Hirsch b. Chajjim. לקוטי צבי
[מלוקט ע"י צבי הירש בן חיים מווילהרמש-
דארף] . . . ותיקון חצות מספ' שערי ציון [ע"י
נתן נטע הנובר]. Lunéville, 1798. 90, 18,
91–120 ff. 16°.

JTS.

409. סליחות, מנהג פוליניא אשכנז וצרפת עתי"א.
Lunéville, 1799. 4°.

NYPL.

410. Nieto, David. מטה דן וכוזרי, חלק שני.
Metz, 1800. 89 ff. 8°.

NYPL. 1st edition: London, 1714.

B. HEBREW PUBLICATIONS PRINTED ABROAD

411. Raphaël Jehouda Israel. שומר מוסר.
Leghorn, 1796. fol.

By the rabbi of Nice.

412. Katzenellenbogen, Naft. H. שו"ת שער
נפתלי. Frankfurt a. M., 1797. 60 ff. fol.

By the rabbi of Haguenau.

413. סליחות, מנהג עלואס. Frankfurt a. M.,
1798. 8°.

414. Sintzheim, Joseph David. יד דוד.

חלק ראשון. והוא חיבור כולל על התלמוד . . .
Offenbach, 1799. 2, 288 ff. fol.

415. Mendelssohn, Moses, פעדאן . . .
Brünn, 1798. 8°.

Translated by Isaïe Berr Bing of Metz.

For Hebrew publications of Metz prior to the
Revolution see S. Cahen; "De la littérature . . .;"
G. U. Teissier, *Essai . . .*, pp. 143–54, 222–31;
E. Carmoly, "De la typographie . . ." There were
no Hebrew publications of the four communities
in the former papal province during the Revolution.
For Hebrew publications of these communities
prior to the Revolution see C. Roth, "The
Liturgies . . ."

XXVIII. WORKS IN FRENCH BY JEWISH AUTHORS ON JEWISH SUBJECTS

416. [Gradis, David.] *Courte dissertation sur
l'origine du monde, ou Réfutation du système
de la création. Par un Négociant dont le nom
et la maison de commerce sont très anciens à
Bordeaux.* Paris – Bordeaux, an sept. 52 pp.
8°.

Printed in Bordeaux. With a few Hebrew words
of a "non-mobile" type (words cast as one, not
letter by letter). On p. 2 D. G. is named as the
author. BmBx. See also No. 417.

417. ———— . *Discussions philosophiques sur la préexistence de la matière* . . . Paris, an VIII. 208 pp. 8°.

BmBx. See also Nos. 416 & 418. For the author's later publications see Napoleonica, Nos. 381–82.

418. Delesse. *Dieu créateur.*

Against No. 417. According to Bernardau: "Un nommé Delesse, espèce de soi disant encyclopédiste, vient dep ublier une réfutation du panflet [sic!]

spinosiste du juif Gradis dans une brochure métaphysique, intitulé Dieu créateur" (BmBx, manuscript 713–1, vol. 7, p. 457, March 17, 1799).

419. Penini, Jedaiah. *Bechinat 'Olam.* Metz, 1795. 4°.

Only the fifth chapter, translated from H. into Fr. by Isaïe Berr Bing, according to Fürst, III, 73 ("Abgedruckt in diessen Traductions Françaises").

Beaufleury, *Histoire* . . . See No. 6.

XXIX. Jewish Writers on Non-Jewish Subjects

420. Aronssohn, Jacques, *De Phrenitide symptomatica quasdam observationes cum epicrisi* . . . Giessen, 1790. 32 pp. 8°.

The author was then a physician of Saarunion. See Ginsburger, p. 10.

421. Azévédo, David. *Projet d'établissement d'une Caisse patriotique d'échange d'assignats, présenté par la Société des Amis de la Constitution à ses concitoyens.* Bordeaux, n. d. 15 pp. 8°.

BmBx.

422. [Beaufleury, Louis Francia.] *Convention nationale. Mémoire relatif aux moyens qu'on pourrait employer pour retirer quatre milliards d'assignats de la circulation.* Par un citoyen du département de la Seine & Oise. Imprimé par ordre du Comité des Finances. Paris, Pluviôse an III. 14 pp., 1 f. 8°.

BmBx.

423. ———— . *Mémoire sur les biens et les revenus du clergé; précédé d'observations impartiales, sur une note insérée dans le Mercure du Samedi 29 Août 1789, no. XXXV* . . . n. p., n. d. 13 pp. 8°.

BmBx.

424. ———— . *Mémoire sur les élections, sur leurs inconvéniens, et sur leurs dangers; présenté à la Convention Nationale, par un*

Juge du Tribunal du District de Corbeil & du Tribunal Criminel du Département de la Seine & Oise. n. p., n. d. 40 pp. 8°.

BN, BmBx.

425. ———— . *Observations.* n. p., n. d. 3 pp. 8°.

On M. Blondel's report concerning the author. BmBx.

426. ———— . *Projets de bienfaisance et de patriotisme pour toutes les villes du royaume, et applicables dans toutes les villes de l'Europe* . . . Paris, 1789. 95 pp. 8°.

BmBx. 1st edition: Paris 1785. 96 pp. 8°.

427. ———— . *Projet d'une tontine perpétuelle, approuvé par l'Académie royale des Sciences. Adressé à Nosseigneurs les Etats-Généraux.* n. p., n. d. [1789] 30 pp. 1 f. 8°.

BmBx.

428. ———— . *Qu'est-ce que l'amour.* 1790.

According to Féret, (III, 30), a note by B[orde] de F[ortages] who probably mistook *Usure* (see No. 429) for *amour.*

429. ———— . *Qu'est-ce que l'usure, et quels sont les moyens de l'arrêter sans recourir aux lois pénales* . . . Par M***, Député-suppléant à l'Assemblée Nationale Législative.* n. p., n. d. viiij, 53 pp., 1 f. 8°.

BmBx, BN.

430. ———. *Recueil de poésies ou Les Loisirs du Citoyen L. F. B.* . . . Paris, n. d. 48 pp. 8°.

BmBx.

431–431b. Bloch, Marcus Elieser. *Ichtylogie, ou Histoire naturelle, générale et particulière des poissons.* Berlin, 1785–1795. 6 vols. fol.

1st edition: 1785–88. 6 vols. Other editions: Berlin, 1795. 5 vols; 1795. 6 vols.

432. Bonfils. *La Morale du citoyen.* Strasbourg, 1791. 2 vols. 8°.

According to Fürst, II, 126, who, probably, mistook the author as a Jew, was published not in Strasbourg, but in Lausanne. BN.

433. Carvallo. *Réclamation du Citoyen Carvallo* . . . Bordeaux, 1793. Broadside.

Proclamation of his honesty. AdG.

434. Cohen, Francis, [later Sir Francis Palgrave]. *Omphoy batraxomyomaxia. La guerre des grenouilles et des souris d'Homère. Traduite* . . . *de la version latine d'E. Berglère* . . . *par M. F. Cohen.* Londres, 1797. 57 pp. 4°.

BM. See Roth, p. 415.

435. Coupé, M. L. *Sentences de Théognis et Poème moral de Procylice* [sic!]. *Traduction nouvelle par M. L. Coupé.* Paris, 1796. 198 pp. 12°.

Vol. IV of *Collection des poètes grecs.* According to Fürst (III, 98) the title is: *Oeuvres de Theognis et Phocylide.*

436. Dacosta, [Isaac François Franco]. [Circular on the foundation of the Bordeaux "Société littéraire et des sciences."] Bordeaux, 2 Avril 1797. 1 p. 4°.

Signed by Dacosta and others. BmBx, ms. 713-2, vol. 3, No. 37.

437. *Extrait des registres de la Section du Bon*

Accord, No. 19. Séance du 25 du premier mois de la deuxième année. [Bordeaux, Octobre 1793.] 2 pp. 4°.

Signed by Azévédo, Bonfin fils and Fonséca neveu. In favor of Lopes Dubec, suspected of Girondist activities. JTS.

438–438a. [Frey, Lucien, called Junius.] *Les aventures politiques du Père Nicasse, ou L'Anti-fédéraliste.* Paris, 1793. 72 pp. 8°.

BN. 2nd edition: 71 pp.

439. ———. *Philosophie sociale.* Paris, 1793. 236 pp. 8°.

BN.

440. [Furtado, Abraham.] *Considérations sur les dissensions civiles et les révolutions.* n. p., n. d. 31 pp. 8°.

JTS. See Szajkowski, "The Sephardic Jews," 151–52.

441. ———. *De l'utilité des Clubs.* Bordeaux, 179– .

According to Bernardau (ms 713-3, vol. 4, p. 140).

442. ——— and others. *Lettres aux Commissaires du Musée.* [Bordeaux,] n. d. 4 pp. 8°.

Signed by Furtado, P. V. Vergniaud, J. F. Ducos and J. B. Boyer Fonfrède. The BmBx possesses also a reply to this pamphlet: *Le Musée aux citoyens de Bordeaux,* n. p., n. d. 16 pp. 12°.

443. Goldschmid. *De l'utilité des eaux minérales factices et de   -référence qu'elles méritent sur les eaux de sources.* Paris, [an VII.] 12 pp. 8°.

Reprint from the *Journal de médecine,* Ventôse, an VII. BN.

444. [Gradis, David.] *Proposition d'une pétition à l'Assemblée Nationale.* [Bordeaux, 1791]. 4 pp. 8°.

According to a note on the copy of the Gradis Archives (12-150) Gradis was the author.

445. Henriques, Emmanuel, *Journal de la Convention Nationale*. Paris, No. 1, 23 Septembre 1792. 12 pp. 8°.

BN.

446. Homberg, E. le jeune. *Lettre adressée à M. le président de l'Assemblée Nationale.* Le Havre, 30 Août 1791. 8 pp. 8°.

Together with: "Adresse des citoyens, négociants et capitaines de navire du Havre, à l'Assemblée Nationale," signed by E. Homberg le jeune. Against the Decree of May 15, 1791 on the emancipation of slaves. BmHavre. For the Jewish origin of the author see: *Lettres-patentes du Roi qui accordent aux sieurs [Lion, Gerson et Eliezer] Homberg frères et [Joseph] Lallemant, négocians du Havre-de-Grâce, les droits de régnicoles et naturels français, du mois de Septembre 1775*. Paris, 1776. 4°. A Jewish woman of Le Havre named Homberg wrote revolutionary poetry; see Kahn, p. 123. See No. 447.

447. Hombert, Eug. Fils. *Avis au peuple. Couplets chantés au théâtre du Havre.* Le Havre, 6 Prairial an III [25 juin 1795]. 3 pp. 8°.

According to Lechevalier, No. 4610. Against the regime of the Terror. Hombert is, probably, the same author as Homberg, see No. 446.

448. Jacobson, G. J. *Bydragen tot de algemeene zaken van de Marine . . .* Rotterdam, 1799. xxviii, 36 pp. 8°.

Amsterd.

449. Julian, Louis. *Adresse présentée à la Convention nationale . . . au nom de la Section des Tuilleries, le 10 germinal an III [30 mars 1795]*. [Paris, 1795.] 4 pp. 8°.

On the "assemblées primaires." BN.

450. Mendes, Abraham. *Observations sur deux imprimés qui viennent de paroître; le premier ayant pour titre: Projet pour l'établissement d'une Caisse d'Escompte à Bordeaux, & le second: Vues relatives à la Caisse d'escompte . . . et Moyens proposés pour secourir l'Etat, par M. Abraham Mendes, teneur de livres, & officier-lieutenant au Corps patri-* otique du Génie à Bordeaux. Bordeaux, 1791. 32 pp. 8°.

BN, JTS.

451. *Abeille (L'), journal historique et littéraire . . .* Bordeaux, Février — Octobre 1797. 4 vols. 4°.

Published by David Mezes. See Labadie, pp. 190–92.

452. Moline, Pierre Louis. *La Colonne de la Grande Armée, cantate héroïque . . .* musique de Ferdinand Paer. Paris, n. d. 4 pp. 8°.

According to Kahn (p. 122) Moline was a Jew. BN. See also Nos. 453–61.

453. ———. *Hymne dédié au Temple de la Raison et de la Vérité de la section de l'Observatoire.* [Paris,] n. d. 4 pp. 8°.

BN.

454. ———. *Idille sur la liberté, dédiée à l'Assemblée Nationale, pour être chanté au Champ de Mars, le 14 Juillet 1790, jour de la Fédération des citoyens français.* Musique de M. Philidor. [Bourg,] 1790. 4 pp. 8°.

BN.

455. ———. *Mémoire historique et politique sur les Indes Orientales, ou L'Exposé succint des grands avantages que la République française pourrait retirer . . .* Paris, an III. 35 pp. 8°.

BN.

456. ———. *Michelin, ou L'Humanité récompensée*, mélodrame en 1 acte, représentée à l'Orient, pour la première fois le 10 Janvier, 1790 . . . Lorient, 1790, iv, 31 pp. 8°.

BN.

457. ———. *Le Neufrage héroïque du vaisseau Le Vengeur*, opéra en 3 actes, par

les citoyens Moline et Pagès . . . Paris, an iii. 38 pp. 8°.

BN.

458. ———— . *Orphée et Eurecide*, opéra en 3 actes . . . Paris, an vi. 22 pp. 8°.

BN. 4th edition, 5th edition: Paris, 1809.

459. ———— . *Recueil des morceaux de musique qui seront exécutés par les aveugles travailleurs à la fête de l'Etre-Suprême, le 20 Prairial l'an ii* . . . Paris, n. d. 12 pp. 8°.

Texts by Moline and others. BN.

460. ———— . *La Réunion du dix août, ou L'Inauguration de la République française, sanculotide dramatique en 5 actes* . . . Paris, an ii. 42 pp. 8°.

By Moline and Gabriel Bouquier. BN.

461. ———— . *Le Tombeau des imposteurs et l'inauguration du Temple de la Vérité, sanculotide dramatique en 3 actes* . . . Paris, an ii. x, 100 pp. 8°.

By Moline and others. BN.

462. Peixotto, Charles, colonel commandant du régiment patriotique de Talanse [Talence], à Bordeaux. *Observations sur les assignats.* [Bordeaux, 179– .] 14 pp. 8°.

BN.

463. Rodrigues, J[acques, i. e. Isaac]. *Règlemens de la Société d'Histoire naturelle de Bordeaux.* Bordeaux, 1796. 8 pp. 4°.

Signed by Rodrigues and others. BmBx, ms. 713–2, vol. 3.

464. Schwab, Jacques. *Le système métrique et ses rapport à l'usage du département de la Meurthe.* Nancy, an viii [1799]. 96 pp. & charts. 8°.

BmN. The *Supplément à l'ouvrage*: *Le Système métrique* was published in the year x. iv, 52 pp. On the author see Schill J., "Jacques Schwab," *RJL* (1934), 60–61.

465. Wolff. *Société populaire séante en la salle électorale.* [Discours prononcé à la séance du 2 Fructidor an ii: 19 Août 1794.] [Paris,] n. d. 14 pp. 8°.

On the revolutionary clubs. BN.

466. Wolff fils Marx. *Discours sur la morale publique et domestique. Prononcé à la Société populaire de Strasbourg, dans sa séance du 11. Floréal de l'an 2. de la République française [30 Avril 1794].* [Strasbourg, 1794.] 8°.

BuStg.

467. Zadig, Abr. *Geist der neusten medizinischen Literatur in Frankreich.* Breslau, 1799. 8°.

Fürst, iii, 540.

XXX. Non-Jewish Writers on General Jewish Subjects

468. [Bonnaud, J. J.] *Hérodote historien du peuple hébreu sans le savoir.* Liège, 1790. vii, 278 pp. 12°.

BLiège. 1st edition: 1786.

469. C***, Abbé de [Pernin des Chavanettes]. *Discours sur l'histoire des Juifs, depuis le commencement du monde jusqu'à la destruction de Jérusalem par les Romains.*

Nouvelle édition. Prato, 1789. 148, 4 pp. 8°.

BM.

470. [Collins, Anthony.] *Der Geist des Judenthums.* Cairo, im 8ten republikanischen Jahre [1799]. 306 pp. 8°.

Marburg, Frankfurt a-M. The French translation was published in London, 1770: *L'Esprit du*

Judaïsme, ou Examen raisonné de la loi de Moyse, et de son influence sur la religion chrétienne. Traduit de l'anglais de A. Collins, par le B^{on} [P.H.D.] d'Holbach. With a revolutionary date of publication.

471. [Guénée, Antoine.] *Letters of Certain Jews to Monsieur Voltaire. Containing an Apology for Their Own People, and for the Old Testament* . . . Translated by the Rev. Philip Lefann. Philadelphia, 1795. 2 vols. in one. 519 pp. 8°.

1st French edition: Paris, 1769; first English edition: Dublin, 1777. See Rosenbach, p. 104.

472. Laborde, J. B. de. *Abrégé des principaux faits arrivés depuis la naissance d'Enoch jusqu'à celle de Jésus-Christ.* Paris, 1789. 2 vols. 4°.

Part two of *Essai sur l'histoire chronologique de quatre-vingt peoples de l'antiquité.*

473. L'Hospital, [Jean Eléazar]. *[Lettre à]* Gonzalès. Bordeaux, an VII. 8°.

According to Vivie, vol. 29.

474. ———. *Notice littéraire sur Rodrigues*

Pereire, éducateur des sourds-muets. Bordeaux, an II. 12 pp. 8°. BN.

475. Mentelle, Edme. *Précis de l'histoire des Hébreux, depuis Moyse jusqu'à la prise de Jérusalem par les Romains* . . . Paris, an VI. xvi, 108 pp. 12°.

BN, BmBx.

476. Schwind, Karl Franz. *Ueber die ältesten heiligen Semitischen Denkmäler* . . . Strassburg, 1792. VIII, 143 pp. 8°.

BuStg.

477. Villeneuve, L. P. Couret de. *Les Lyriques sacrés* . . . *précédés d'une dissertation sur la poésie des Hébreux, traduit de l'anglais du Dr. Blair.* 2me édition. Paris, 1789. xlviii, 405 pp. 12°.

BN.

478-478a. Wahl, S. F. G. *Magasin pour la littérature ancienne et principalement la littérature biblique.* Casel, 1787–1789; Halle, 1790. 8°.

According to Barbier.

XXXI. THE BIBLE

479. Berthier, Le P. Guillaume François. *Isaie, traduit en français avec des notes et des réflexions.* Paris, 1788–89. 5 vols. 12°.

Published by P. de Querbeuf. BN.

480. [Bohineux, Le.] *Psaumes de David* . . . Paris, 1789. xvi, 507 pp. 8°.

BN.

481. Maistre de Sacy, Isaac-Louis Le. *La Sainte Bible, contenant l'Ancien et le Nouveau Testament. Traduite en français sur la Vulgate* . . . *Nouvelle édition, ornée de 300 dessins de M. Marillier [et Monsiau].* Paris, 1789 — an XII. 12 vols. 4°.

BM.

482. *Paraphrase du Venite exultemus Domino, ou Premier Psaume de l'Office du Peuple pour la vigile de la fête des Etats Généraux.* [Paris, 1789.] 7 p. 8°.

BM.

483. Rondet, Laurent Etienne. *Explication de la Sainte Bible, selon le sens littéral et selon le sens spirituel;* nouvelle édition . . . Nismes, 1781–89. 19 vols. 8°.

BmBx.

484. Mothe-Guyon, Madame J. M. B. de la. *La Sainte Bible, avec des explications & réflexions qui regardant la vie intérieure* . . .

Nouvelle édition exactement corrigée. Paris, 1790. 20 vols. 8°.

1ˢᵗ edition: 1715.

485–485a. *Les Psaumes de David mis en vers* . . . Vevey, 1790. 624 pp.; Guernesey, 1791. 620 pp. 12°.

BM.

486. *Recueil de Psaumes, d'Hymnes et de Cantiques.* Berlin, 1791. 8°.

XVI, 364 pp. in the incomplete copy of the JTS.

487. *Grundliche Beweise erstlich dass die heilige Schrift des Alt- und Neuen Testaments, warhaftig Gottes Wort* . . . [Strassburg,?], 1792. 8°.

BmStg. 1ˢᵗ edition: Strassburg, 1787.

488. *Extrait de l'écriture sainte à l'usage des aveugles.* Paris, 1794. 124 ff. 4°.

Published by Valentin Haüy? BM.

489. *La Sainte Bible* . . . Amsterdam-La Haye, 1794. Unpaged. 12°.

Reprint of the 1731 edition. BM.

490. *Les Psaumes de David* . . . Amsterdam, 1796. 12°.

Bound with *Canticles* . . ., pp. 1–275. BM.

491. *La Sainte Bible* . . . Amsterdam, 1797, Unpaged. 12°.

BM. Reprint of the 1693 edition of Geneva.

492. Boisgelin, Jean de Dieu Raimond de. *Le Psalmiste. Précédé d'un discours préliminaire sur la poésie sacrée.* Londres, 1799. XXXI, 119 pp. 8°.

BM.

XXXII. Biblical Themes in Drama and Belles Lettres

Biblical and other historical Jewish subjects, which were very popular among Christian scholars and in the dramatic literature prior to 1789, were neglected during the Revolution. Biblical heroes were replaced by Greek and Roman legendary figures. Still, some authors did use Biblical themes, and in many cases adapted them to the revolutionary slogans. For Biblical subjects in the dramatic literature prior to the Revolution see Cahen, "Bibliographie Judaïco-Française. Théâtre."

493. Bonneville, Nicolas. *La Ruine de Jérusalem, chants lyriques à plusieurs interlocuteurs, en vers.* Paris, an II. 8°.

BN.

494. *Chaste (La) Suzanne.* Avignon, 1793. 26 pp. 8°.

According to Goizet, p. 470.

495. *Charlotte Corday, ou la Judith moderne, tragédie en 3 actes et en vers.* Caen 1797. XI, 59 pp. 18°.

A biblical subject used for a political pamphlet. BN.

496. Dugat, Pierre Denis. *La mort d'Azaël, ou Le Rapt de Dina, poëme en six livres.* Paris, an VII. iv, 516 pp. 8°.

BN.

497. Genlis, Mᵐᵉ de. *Josif uznannyi bratjami svojmi, komedija v 2 dêsistvijak. Soîinenie Žanlisa; perevod s francuzkego Matneeva.* Moskva, 1799. 12°.

Russian edition of *Joseph reconnu par ses frères*, in *Théâtre saint à l'usage des jeunes personnes.* Paris, 1785. I, 201–251. According to *Mistère*, III, xlix.

498. Gassier, J. M. [Jean Marie] & Le-

maire, Henri. *Joseph. Drame en cinq actes, a grand spectacle, mêlée de pantomime,* chants et dances. Musique du cit. Gillet; ballets du cit. Eugène Hus, décors du cit. Gillet, représentée, pour la première fois, à Paris, sur le Théatre des Jeunes-Artistes, au mois de Floréal au 8. Paris, an VIII. 40 pp. 8°.

BM, BmLyon. By Gassier-Saint-Amand according to the catalogue of the BM.

499. Guilet, curé constitutionnel. *Mort d'Abel (La), tragédie en 5 actes et en vers.* Blois, 1792. 8°.

BN.

500. *Herbsttext, 1790. Nach dem patriotischen Sinne des hebräischen Originales.* Psalm 106. 1–5 . . . n. p., 1790. 1 f. 8°.

BuStg. See also No. 510.

501–501b. Legouvé, [Gabriel Marie Jean Baptiste]. *La Mort d'Abel, tragédie en trois actes et en vers, par le citoyen Le Gouvé.* Paris, 1793, X, 47 pp. 8°.

Represented at the Théâtre de la Nation on March 6, 1792. BN. 2nd edition: XXIV, 64 pp., and a counterfeited edition of 1793, 47 pp.

502. Martainville, A. L. A. [Alphonse Louis Dieudonné]. *Noé, ou Le Monde repeuplé, vaudeville en un acte, tiré de l'Ancien Testament* . . . Paris, an VI. 30 pp. 8°.

Represented at the Théâtre des Jeunes Artistes on May 14, 1798. Arsenal.

503. Penancier. *La Chaste Suzanne, ou Le Triomphe de la vertu, pantomime en deux actes,* par le citoyen Penancier. Bordeaux, 1793. 10 pp. 8°.

Represented at the Bordeaux theater. According to Goizet, 470.

504. Racine, Jean. *Oeuvres.* Paris, an VII. 12°.

Vol. III contains Iphigénie, Phèdre, Esther, and Athalie.

505. Rapdé, J. B. Augustin, *Arlequin Jacob et Gilles Essaü, ou le Droit d'aînesse, folie-vaudéville en un acte, en prose; sujet tiré de l'Ancien Testament.* Paris, an VII. 8°.

BN.

506. Ségur, Joseph A. *La Création du monde, oratorio en trois parties, traduit de l'allemand, mis en vers français par Joseph A. Ségur, musique d'Haydem* . . . Paris, an IX. 2 ff.. 24 pp. 4°.

Represented at the Théâtre des Arts on Dec. 24. 1800. BN.

507. Tasso, Torquato. *La Jérusalem délivrée,* traduite en vers par Baour-Lormian. Paris, 1796. 2 vols. 4°.

BN.

508. ———— . *Jérusalem délivrée,* traduite en vers par J. M. B. Clément. Paris, 1800. XXVIII, 387 pp. 8°.

BN.

509. ———— . *La Jérusalem délivrée,* traduit en vers par Antoine Renou. Paris, 1800. 8°.

BN.

510. *Zweite (Der) Herbsttext des Jahres 1790.* Psalm 67. Mel. "Ihr Töchter Zions kommt herbei." n. p., 1790. 1 f. 8°.

Ger. & Fr. BuStg. See also No. 500.

XXXIII. Publications with Biblical Titles, Dates, or Places of Publication

511. *Jérémiade des fermiers généraux (11 mars 1790).* [Paris,] 1790. 8 pp. 8°.

BN.

512. Testard, *La Bible à ma tante, folie en un acte.* n. p. n. d. 31 pp. 8°.

"Théâtre d'Emulation," March 7, 1798. BN.

513. *Tableau des officiers et des membres de la T∴ R∴ loge de St-Jean d'Ecosse du Patriotisme . . . pour l'année 5786* [sic!]. Lyon, n. d. 11 pp. 8°.

BmLyon.

514. *Tableau des frères composant la loge de la Sincère-Union . . . pour l'année maçonique 5787* [sic!]. Lyon, n. d. 8°.

BmLyon.

515. *Tableau des frères composant la respectable Loge de la Bienfaisance, à l'Orient de Lyon . . . pour l'année 5791* [sic!]. Lyon. 4 pp. fol.

BmLyon. With a manuscript note: "B. Caillat, secrétaire."

515a. Firmin, Abraham. *Tableau général des LL . . . de l'an de la V.: 5800.* [sic!] [Paris, 1800.] 16 pp. 8°.

BN.

516. *La Passion, la mort et la résurection du Peuple.* Imprimé à Jérusalem [Paris], 1789. 23 pp. 8°.

BN.

XXXIV. JEWISH SUBJECTS IN NON-BIBLICAL WRITINGS

517. *Histoire admirable du Juif-errant* [errant] *lequel depuis l'an 1033 jusqu'à l'heure présente ne fait que marcher . . .* Lion [1800?]. 22 pp. 8°.

BmLyon.

518. *Juif n'être pas si tiaple. Air de Confédération du Parnasse. Avec accompᵗ de guittare.* Paris, [1790?.] 8°.

Adopted to "Oui noir mais pas si diable," from Grétry's "L'Amitié à l'épreuve." BM.

519. [Cumberland, Richard.] *Le Juif,* drame en 5 actes, traduit librement de l'anglais. Hambourg, 1797. 109 pp. 8°.

BN.

520. Lessing, Gotthold Ephraim. *Nathan le Sage. Cinquième, sixième et septième scènes du III acte.* Traduit par J. B. [Isaïe Berr] Bing aîné. Paris, an v.

L'Historien, no. 550, May 24, 1797. BN.

521. Walker, Georges, auteur de Cinthelia. *Théodore Cyphon et le Juif bienfaisant. Traduit par Lebas.* Paris, an VIII. 2 vols. 12°.

BN.

XXXV. HOAXES, MISLEADING NAMES OF AUTHORS, TITLES, ETC.

In order to attract the attention of the public, pamphlets were often published with titles of Jewish interest, with Jewish names of authors, or purporting to be published in Jerusalem. This was still being done in a much later period, e. g.: [Roisselet des Sanchères.] *Bibliothèque historique du Juif-Errant. Histoire de la captivité, du jugement et de l'exécution de Louis XVI, par le Juif Errant.* Paris, 1858. 2, 157 pp. 18°.

522. *Ascension (L') de Louis XVI, roi des Juifs et des Français, au ciel même, de l'imprimerie des S. S. archanges . . .* [Paris,] mai 1790 [sic!]. 24 pp. 8°.

BN.

523. Astaroth, Juif de Nation [Caron, Philippe]. *Confession faite au diable par les ex-directeurs Merlin . . . Dispute du diable avec les fournisseurs des armées . . .* [Paris,] n. d. 8 pp. 8°.

BN.

524. ———. *Pétition du diable aux deux*

Conseils, demandant l'établissement d'une ménagérie dans la cour du palais du Directoire . . . [Paris,] n. d. 8 pp. 8°.
BN.

525. ————. *Visite du diable aux deux Conseils, au Directoire, et chez quelques ministres de la République française . . .* Paris, n. d. 8 pp. 8°.
BN.

526. ————. *Visite du diable au Manège, et grand détail de l'événement malheureux arrivé hier 24 Messidor à 10 heures du soir aux Tuileries . . .* Traduit de l'hébreu, par Isaac Nathan. Paris, n. d. 8 pp. 8°.
BN.

527-527a. [Bonnay, Mis Charles François de.] *Le Prophète Jonas, Juillet 1793*, par un émigré. Maestricht, 1793. 42 pp. 8°.

Anti-revolutionary pamphlet with a biblical subject as title. BN. 2d edition: La Haye, n. d. 42 pp.

528. *Conseils de Salomon, au meilleur et au plus chéri des rois*. Paris, 1789. 8 pp. 8°.

A political pamphlet with a biblical subject as title. BN.

529. *Dissertation sur l'excellence du lard et du boudin, dédiée aux Juifs*, par M. Cochon.

According to *La Rocambole des journaux*, I, No. 3 (June, 1791).

530. *Jugement (Le) de Salomon.* n. p., 1789. 8 pp. 8°.

A political pamphlet with a biblical subject as title. BN.

531. *Juif (Le) errant.* Paris, Avril 1790. 8 pp. 8°.

Three Nos., 4 Nos. according to Hatin. Published by "M. Sabalias, fils de Nephtin, qui fut fils de Gerboal." BN.

532. *Juif (Le) errant, journal politique et littéraire, ou Relation véridique de tous les*

événéments relatifs à la République française. [Paris, 1799.] 2 pp. 8°.

Prospectus of the newspaper published by Clément Hémery, see No. 533. BN.

533. *Juif (Le) errant, journal politique et littéraire*, rédigé par la citoyenne Clément Hémery. Paris, No. 1, 3 Février 1799. 4°.

No. 33: March 5, 1799. Arsenal. See No. 532.

533a. Keleph-ben-Nathan, *La philosophie divine, appliquée aux lumières naturelle, magique . . .* n. p. 1793. 3 vols. 8°.

By Marc Philippe Dutoit-Mambrin. First published in 1790 without mention of "Keleph-ben-Nathan": *De l'origine . . .* Paris, 1790. 2 vols. 8°. BN.

534. *Mandement de Mgr. [Henri] Grégoire . . . prescrivant la coëfure jacobite, et exhortant à porter la barbe comme les Juifs.*

According to *Journal général de la Cour et de la Ville*, No. 52 (1791).

535. *Passion (La) du Jésus des vrais catholiques crucifié par les Juifs schismatiques du département et de la municipalité de Nevers.*

According to Drumont, I, 277.

536-536a-b. *Passion (La) et la mort de Louis XVI, roi des juifs et des chrétiens.* Jérusalem [Paris], 1790 [sic!] 27 pp. 8°.

"N. B. Le lecteur est prié de ne pas confondre cet écrit patriotique avec une rapsodie aussi plate que ridicule, qu'on a affublée du même titre que le nôtre." BN. Third edition: Jérausalem, 1790. 27 pp. 8°. 63 editions according to Drumont, I, 276. According to Challamel (p. 132) the title is *Mort et passion de Louis XVI, roi des Juifs et des Français*.

537. *Pentecôte (La), ou Descente de l'esprit de Louis XVI, roi des Juifs et des Français, sur ses fidèles apôtres.* A Jérusalem, de l'imprimérie des apôtres, 1790. 29 pp. 8°.
BN.

538. *Reproches de Louis XVI à son peuple. Ces reproches sont calques sur ceux que le*

Messie fait aux Juifs par l'organe des ses prophètes, et qui, sous le nom d'Impropres, se trouvent dans l'Office de la semaine sainte. Paris, 1792. 16 pp. 8°.

BN.

539. *Résurection de Louis XVI, roi des Juifs et des Français.* A Jérusalem [Paris], Mai 1790 [sic!.] 8°.

BN.

540. Richard [Richart, Charles Louis] le Père, Dominicain. *Parallèle des Juifs, qui*

ont crucifié Jésus-Christ, leur Messie, et des Français qui ont guillotiné Louis XVIᵉ, leur roi. [Mons,] 1794. 89 pp. 8°.

See Pichauld, Anatole. *Une exécution révolutionnaire à, Mons, en 1794 . . .* Gard 1842. BN.

541. *Trois (Les) rois, ou le partage du gâteau. Se trouve partout.* n. p. 5 janvier 1790. 20 pp. 8°.

Title on p. 3: "Epître d'Ariste aux Crates, peuple errant, comme les Juifs, sur les bords de la Seine."

BN.

XXXVI. Jewish Place Names

The revolutionary events brought many changes in the daily life of the people. Thus, the use of the word *Jew* for names of streets and places was regarded as contrary to the new regime and the names of many such streets and places were changed. However, the word *Jew* continued to be used in some localities.

542. Collandière. *Discours sur l'existence de l'Etre Suprême et l'immortalite de l'âme, prononcé . . . en présence des autorités constitués et de la commune de V i l l e j u i f, le 20 Prairial de l'an* II [*8 Juin 1794*]. n. p., n. d. 28 pp. 8°.

BN.

543. *Epreuves de la fonderie de F. G.*

Levrault, rue des J u i f s, no. 33 à Strasbourg. Strasbourg, n. d. 8°.

BuStg.

544. *Catalogue des livres français qui se trouvent chez les Frères Levrault . . . imprimeurs-libraires à Strasbourg, rue des J u i f s, no. 33 . . .* Strasbourg, an VIII. 396 pp. 8°.

BuStg.

XXXVII. Jews in Other Countries

The victorious French troops brought into many lands the ideas of liberty and the emancipation of the Jews. In this division are included only publications dealing directly with the French Revolution, but not the great number of publications of a local character.

A. ENGLAND

545. Gordon, Lord George. *Memorial . . . written in the Prison of Newgate, and distributed among the friends of liberty in France and England . . .* [London, 1789?] 18 pp. 8°.

BM.

546–546a. *A Form of Prayer and Supplication for . . . Success of the British Arms . . . Portuguese Synagogue in Bevis Marks, London. On Friday the 19th of April 1793 . . . Composed in Hebrew by the Rabbis of the Said Synagogue; and translated into Eng-*

lish . . . *by David Levi.* סדר תפלה ותחנה.
London, 1793. 27 pp. 8°.

Eng. & H. Another edition of the H. text only:
London, n. d. 8 pp. 8°. *JHSE*, IX (1922), 126;
Roth, p. 227.

547. סדר שבח והודאה לאל עליון גואלנו במאמר
המלך אדוננו אשר דן כן.

H. Service in the Bevis Marks Synagogue for the
Naval victories of Jervis and Duncan. See H.
Lowe, in *The Jewish Guardian*, Dec. 23, 1921, p. 5.

548. Myers, Moses. *A Form of Prayer,
Praise, Thanksgiving and Laud, to be chanted
in the German Jews Synagogue in London . . .
On Thursday the 29th day of November
1798. Being the day that His Majesty our*

*gracious Sovereign, hath commanded us to
give thanks and praise to the Almighty God,
who is tremendous in works, for the great
socces of Admiral Nelson . . . Composed in
Hebrew by the Rev. Moses Myers; and
translated into English . . . by David Levi*
סדר תפלה שבח והודאה ותהלה לזמר בבתי
כנסיות של ק״ק אשכנזים בלונדון . . . London,
n. d. 20 pp. 8°.

JTS. See *JHSE*, IX (1922), 127; Roth, p. 314.

549. Adolphus, John. *Biographical memoirs
of the French Revolution.* London, 1799.
2 vols. 8°.

BM.

B. GERMAN STATES

550. [Kahle, Friedrich Ludwig.] *Anmerkungen zu dem Buche: Über die bürgerliche
Verbesserung der Juden vom Herrn Geheim-
den Rath von Dohm . . .* Berlin, 1789.
112 pp. 8°.

München, Frankfurt a. M. Dohm's book, first pub⁻
lished in 1781, contains a chapter on the Jews of
Alsace. See also No. 553.

551. [Grattenauer, K. W. F.] *Ueber die
physische und moralische Verfassung der
heutigen Juden, Stimme eines Kosmopoliten.*
Germanien, 1791. 8°.

Frankfurt a. M. Influenced by the French Revolution.

552. Brandes, Ernst. *Über einige bisherige
Folgen der Französischen Revolution in
Rücksicht auf Deutschland.* Hannover, 1792.
160 pp. 8°.

Frankfurt a. M. Also on the Jews.

553-553a. Dohm, Christian Wilhelm von.
Ueber die bürgerliche Verbesserung der Juden.
Berlin, 1789. 8°.

With notes by F. L. Kahle. Another edition was

published in 1793 in Berlin, together with Moses
Mendelssohn's "Ritualgesetze der Juden." According to Fürst, I, 210. The first editions were
published in 1781 and 1783.

554. Pappenheimer, Heymann Salomon.
*Die Pariser Jacobiner in ihren Sitzungen. Ein
Auszug aus ihrem Tagebuch, veranstaltet von.
H. S. Pappenheimer und mit Anmerkungen
versehen von Johann Wilhelm von Archen-
holz.* Hamburg, 1793. XII, 460 pp. 8°.

Berlin.

555-555a. [Fichte, Johann Gottlieb.] *Beitrag zur Berichtigung der Urtheile des Publi-
kums über die französische Revolution.* [Jena,]
1793, XXIII, 435 pp.; n. p., 1795. 438 pp. 8°.

Bonn, Göttingen. Against the Jews.

556. Höchheimer, Moses. *Preissgesang bem
zwischen Sr. Königlichen Maiestät von Preusen
und der französischen Republic zu Basel am
5. April 1795. geschlossenem Frieden, gesun-
gen von Moses Höchheimer, Rabbiner in
Anschbach.* Erlangen, [1795.] 9 pp. fol.

Ger. & H., without a Hebrew title. The Hebrew
text begins with הריעו כל יושבי הארץ זמרו. Yivo.

557. Courtois, J. B. [Pappenheimer, H. S.]. *Robespierre's und seiner Mitschuldigen Zweck* ... Altona, 1796. 2 vols. 8°.

Frankfurt a. M.

558. Luc, Johann André de. *Lettre aux*

auteurs juifs d'un mémoire adressé à Mr. [*Wilhelm Abraham*] *Teller.* Berlin, 1799. 99 pp. 8°.

Frankfurt a. M. Translated from: *An die Hausväter jüdischer Religion* ... Berlin, 1799. See Eichstädt, pp. 28–29.

C. HOLLAND

559. תפלה נכונה לשאלת רחמים ולהתפלל אל השם יתברך בעת צרה ולדרוש ממנו תשועת והצלחת חיילי המדינות האלו. Amsterdam, 1793. 8 pp. 16°.

H. & Dut., without a Dut. title. Reprint of a 1782 edition and other editions.

560. תפלות ובקשות ... להתפלל בכל י"ד יום כאשר החלה המלחמה עם הצרפתים Amsterdam, 1793. 8 pp. 4°.

561. תפלה נכונה ... והצלחת חיילי המדינות האלו. Amsterdam, 1793. 8 pp. 8°.

Rosent.

562. *Dank-Altaar, opgerigt op Neerlands Purim-feest, op de bepaalde vierde Bede-Stond, den 10 April 1793. Maar nu* ...

veranderd in een Dank-stond. Amsterdam, 1793. 16 pp. 8°.

Poeme. Amst.

563. *Plegtige gebeden voor de Joodsche gemeente te Rotterdam, ter geleegenheid der veertiendaagsche Bedestonden in den oorlog met de Franschen, begonnen den 27sten February 1793. In de Hebreeuwsche taal opgesteld dor Levij Heimann van Breslau, opperrabibijn der Joodsche Gemeente te Rotterdam. In het Nederduitsch vertaald dor geleerde Joodsche mannen, en, op nun vezoek, nader overzien, vebeeterd, en met woorkennis van Rabij Levij, uitgegeeven, door van Scharp, Predikant te Rotterdam.* Rotterdam, 1793. x, 24 pp. 8°.

H. & Dut. Amst.

D. ITALY

564. *Uguaglianza. Libertà. In Nome della Republica Francese. Il Commissario del Direttorio Esecutivo presso l'Armata d'Italia.* Ferrara, 1796. 1 p. fol.

"Decreta che gli Ebrei in Ferrara ci goderanno li medesimi diritti che gli altri Cittadini di questa Legazione." Signed: Hamelin, Agente Militare. Jerusalem.

565. Fano, Marco da. *Ritratto d'una città*

aristocratica, con un elogio alla nation francese ed al general Bonaparte. Venezia, [1797.] 14 pp. 8°.

By a Jewish author. BN.

566. תפלה ובקשות להצלחת המלך פראינץ השני. Montova, 1799.

Benjacob.

E. POLAND

567–567a. Calmanson, Jakób. *Essai sur l'état actuel des Juifs de Pologne, et de leur perfectibilité* ... Varsovie, 1796. 31, 16 pp. 4°.

Polish edition: *Uwagi nad niniejszym stanem Żydów polskich y ich wydoskonaleniem* ... Z francuskiego przez J. C. W Warszawie, 1797. 71 pp. 4°.

568. *Essai d'un plan de réforme ayant pour objet d'éclairer la Nation Juive en Pologne et de redresser par la ses moeurs.* Varsovie, n. d. 34 pp. 8°.

569. Bernard, A. *Observation sur l'enterrement prématuré des Juifs.* Mitau, 1799. 31 pp. 8°.

See also No. 18.

F. PRAGUE

570. לודוויק דער xvi קעניגס פאן פראנקרייך. אורטייל אונד טאד אדר דעם דענקמאהל דער אוננערעכטינקייט און עפּענטליכען נאכריכטן אונד אורגינאל בריפן אויז דעם דייטשן אינס

העברעשע איבר זעצט. [Prague,] 1793. 18 ff. 8°.

JTS. Ode on the execution of Louis xvi.

G. SWITZERLAND

571. [An order of September 1790 against Jewish peddlers.] Basel. Broadside.

Basel. Ger. Directed against the Jews of Alsace.

572. [An order of October 13, 1790, against Jewish peddlers.] Basel. Broadside.

See note to No. 571.

XXXVIII. Iconographical Material

573. A lithograph showing a Frenchman appealing to three Jews to take up agriculture. With the legend: "Quittez un vil trafic, renoncez à l'usure, / Aux arts et aux métiers, joignez l'agriculture. / Stellt Wucher und Betrug, und schnödes Schachern rin, / handwerck, Kunst, Ackerbau, mus euer Nahrung sein. / In No. 131.

574. "Le crime rituel tache indélébile au front d'Israël," by C. E. Duguet. "Un enfant saigné est rétiré de la Seine, sous le Directoire." Reproduced in *CJ*, no. 9 (Oct. 1942), 13. No such drawing is to be found in the *Cabinet des Estampes* of the BN.

575. "L'un de ces Messieurs [secrétaires de l'Assemblée Nationale] s'est avisé dernièrement à dessiner une caricature représentant M. l'évêque d'Autun [Charles Maurice de Talleyrand-Périgord, évêque d'Autun] . . . au bas de l'habit duquel on lit: "Motion pour faire accorder la liberté civile aux juifs, Devant est un israélite qui lui porte une bourse d'or sous le nez et le prélat s'écrie: Roi des juifs, tu l'emportes.

L'auteur de cette caricature l'a présentée lui-même au prélat, qui en a beaucoup ri." *Rôdeur français*, No. 26, Feb. 6, 1790; Kahn, pp. 58–59. "Une caricature du temps représente Talleyrand à qui un juif porte une bourse d'or sous le nez, et l'évêque s'écrie: Roi des Juifs, tu l'emportes." Reinach, p. 6.

576. An anti Jewish caricature of Strasbourg, ca. 1800. Cabinet des Estampes, Strasbourg. See Szajkowski, *Agricultural Credit*, p. 20.

577. A satire on the forbidden sale of worn ecclesiastical clothing. Conversation between a priest and an old-clothes dealer. "Mr. le Juif voulez vous faire un emplette / de cet habit de Capucin / Gardez le, reverend pour faire une brayette / Car il ne vaut pas un Carlin." Etching, 8 3/8 x 5 5/8. JTS. See Rubens, No. 1572.

578. A satire of Bordeaux showing the dwarf Richefort and the Jewish giant Cordova, by [Philippe Gustave Cte de]

Galard. Reproduced in Barraud, Jean. *Vieux papiers bordelais* (Paris, 1910), 290–91.

579. A portrait of Léopoldine Frey, engraved by Chrétien from a portrait by S. Fouquet. Carnavet.

580. Gespräch eines Juden zu Kassel bey Mäitz mit einem eingebildeten Freÿheits-Mann über den Freÿheitsbaum, im Jänuer 1793." Reproduced in many encyclopedias.

581. The destruction of the Ghetto wall of Mainz by Moïse Cahn with the help of French soldiers. Mentioned in *La Revue Rhénane*, March 1923 and *UI*, LXXVIII (1923), 239–40.

582. תפלה מכל השנה. An illuminated prayer book, by Gershoni. Metz, 1797. JTS.

583. On Biblical subjects in the revolutionary iconography see Bernheim.

584. For illustrations of the Bible see Division XXI.

585. Le Juif errant. For an illustration of this subject see No. 533.

586. Maps of synagogues and cemeteries. See: Ginsburger, M. *Histoire de la communauté israélite de Bischheim au Saum* (Strasbourg, 1937), p. 50 (a map of the synagogue, 1789) and *Der israelitische Friedhof in Jungholz* (Gebweiler, 1904), "Schloss Jungholz . . . Aeltester Juden-Friedhof des OElsass. Aufgestellt nach einem Plane vom 28 Germinal, 5me année . . . 1905" and "Plan géometrique du Château et dépendance de Jungholz . . . le 28 Germinal an v."

587. Armorial bearings. For such bearings of the Cerfberr's during the Revolutionary period see Lévylier, I, 140, III, 6–7.

588. Jewish printers of iconographical material on non-Jewish subjects. Jacob Lévy of Bischheim au Saum wrote in a petition of 2 Fructior an II (March 2, 1794) to the City Council of Strasbourg that he printed and distributed "pièces patriotiques et républicaines dont il peut se flatter qu'elles ont beaucoup contribuées [sic!] à corriger l'esprit publique [sic!]." AN(D–III–210-5).

589. Jewish painters and designers of the Revolutionary period. Antoine Gonzales of Bordeaux [see Maronneau, Ch. *Les Salons bordelais* (Bordeaux, 1883), pp. 150–52]; Jean-Henry Simon [see Kahn, L. "Un graveur juif au XVIIIe siècle," *UI*, LI (1895), 699–702, 735–739]; Arnold, a Jewish painter of Paris (see Kahn, p. 123).

INDEX OF AUTHORS, EDITORS AND TRANSLATORS

INDEX OF TITLES

INDEX OF HEBREW TITLES

CHRONOLOGICAL INDEX

INDEX OF PLACES OF PUBLICATION

AGRICULTURAL CREDIT

AND

NAPOLEON'S
ANTI-JEWISH DECREES

———

V. THE ANTI-JEWISH DECREES OF 1806 AND 1808
AND THE LAW OF SEPT. 3, 1807

For a number of juridical reasons the Decree of May 30, 1806, was illegal. In the first place it was not enacted by the *Corps Législatif*. But Napoleon did many illegal things. Still the question arises, whether there existed as a matter of course in France a legally established rate of interest and a definition of usury settled by law, at the time Napoleon promulgated the anti-Jewish Decree of May 30, 1806, for usury. The answer is definitely in the negative: there existed no law to settle a legal rate of interest, hence this was merely one more proof that the Decree of May 30, 1806, was an exceptional law against the Jews alone. The anti-Jewish pamphletists and historians strove to prove the contrary, but let us analyze the situation.

On Oct. 12, 1789, the National Assembly permitted loaning money at interest, the rate of which was still to be settled by law. As the law did not forthwith establish how high the rate of interest should be, it immediately left the gate ajar for usurious operations." In Lower Rhine the Administration paid in 1790-1797 two per cent per month for loans, merchants paid 5, 6, and 7% per month. Gradually, the interest-rate was normalized at 8-9% per year in commerce and at 1% monthly for the military administration. Already as early as in 1800 a prominent merchant could obtain loans at 6, 7 and 8% per annum, which was considered a loan on favorable terms. The Prefect of Upper Rhine wrote in 1802 of the need of a legal rate of interest, although in practice there was a rate which could not be exactly regulated by a precise law." Nor was there a legal interest-rate in Napoleon's Civil Code, it merely mentioned that the legal rate would be settled by a law and that it did not forbid (Article 1907) that the conventional rate could exceed the legal in every case not prohibited by law." The Notarial Association of Lower Rhine wrote to the Minister of Justice (on

---

4365,5103;S7-8620;S2-9421); AI, vol. XVI (1855) p. 422; 466a, XIV, p. 295, 309, 311, 321, 331-33.
" A few remarks about Jews in the play "The Pawnbroker" evoked a storm of protests in 1829. In 1860 such words were not uttered any longer. In "A Village Usurer", the best and most popular play about usury in the country-side, which had its première in Paris, May 14, 1859, nothing is said about Jews at all. In Madame Bovary", L'Heureux, a non-Jew, is the classical example of a respectable usurer. The modern usurers of Balzac are Parisian stock-exchange speculators rather than village-usurers. Even Gobseck (in "Comédie humaine" whom Balzac pictures as the son of a Jewess and a Dutchman, is not the sort of usurer who would engage in such petty "jobs" as ruining the peasants. In Balzac the classical example of a village usurer is the Mayor Grégoire Rigou. (Les Paysans). 74; 461; 443; 167; 431; 441, p. 57-63.
" 264; 231, p. 76; 466a, XIV, p. 288.
" 414, p. 42; 400, p. 192.
" 442, vol. XIV, p. 433-76. There is no mention of Jews in the discussion on the Civil Code in 1804.

Excerpts from the book published in 1953.

Apr. 17, 1805) that one of the causes of usury was the lack of clarity in Article 1907 of the Civil Code, which lends itself to such interpretation that the conventional rate of interest on loans may be as high as is voluntarily determined by the creditor and the borrower. True, it remains at the discretion of some jurists to apply the Law of 1725 which did, indeed, determine the rate of interest, but the whole matter is not clear and is utilized for usury. On May 20, 1806, the General Council of Meurthe proposed that Article 1907 should be rounded out by settling at 6% the maximum of the conventional rate of interest not for Jews alone, but for everybody. A. Rendu, author of a tract on loans, wrote in 1806 that the law did not determine any rate. Also de Bonald, author of an anti-Jewish pamphlet, wrote that since the days of the Revolution usury had been legalized. Masson, a Paris attorney, wrote on May 6, 1806, that the Civil Code permitted usury (at the same time he voiced apprehension lest the Protestants be next turned against, after the Decree aimed especially at the Jews)." During the preparation of the anti-Jewish Decree the situation was also referred to in the Government circles. In Theihard's (of the Council of State) Report to the Minister of Justice Regnier, as well as in the Justice-Secretary's Report to Napoleon (March-April 1805) we read that charges of usury were not being filed against Jews only. Theilhard wrote that in the State Council the attitude was still hostile to setting a legal rate of interest, that the time for changing the Civil Code on this point had not yet arrived. The Minister of Justice asked Napoleon to take steps against all and not Jewish usurers only, althought the Civil Code had not determined any legal rate of interest. In a discussion about Jews (May 17, 1806) Napoleon mentioned setting a legal rate of interest. On Aug. 20, 1806, the Minister of Interior wrote Napoleon that Christians, too, and not Jews alone were usurers. Before taking any measures against the Jewish usurers, a legal rate of interest ought to be determined, what usury is — defined, penalties provided and the law applied also against the Jews. He reiterated the same in a Report of Apr. 9, 1807."

Only as late as Sept. 3, 1807, i.e. 15 months after the exceptional anti-Jewish Decree of May 30, 1806, a Law was promulgated which confirmed that the conventional and legal rate of interest should not exceed 5% in private credit and 6% in commercial credit. Penalties were also provided for not-observing the legal rate. But even thereafter many circles still kept pointing out that prior to Sept. 3, 1807, there had existed no legal rate. This argument often cropped up in lawsuits; in the writings of famous jurists

" AN.BB16-628&F19-11004; "Que permet la loi civile à l'égard du prêt à intérêt ? La réponse sera courte. La loi civile permet tout", Rendu, 280, p. 38, 212; "l'usure fut regardée comme une pratique légitime" (de Bonald, 429, vol. I, p. 436); "On a présenté au gouvernement l'idée de priver les Juifs des droits de citoyens... cette idée est dangereuse et impolitique... Après les Juifs, les Protestants seraient ou pourraient être inquiétés... Peut-on leur faire un crime de l'usure, quand le Code civil la permet, au moins implicitement ? (titre du Prêt)... et d'ailleurs, t o u s les usuriers ne sont pas juifs" (Masson, 53).
" AN.BB16-758(5288), AFIV300(2151)&F20-102; Fenet, 442, p. 433-34; 452, p. 217.

(M. Petit, Merlin, J. Nachet): also of a number of historians of French Jews." Jews, too, frequently set forth this argument. The Jewish Consistory of Metz wrote on March 2, 1818, in a letter to the First President of the Royal Tribunal that a number of Jews, indeed, kept on practicing usury even after the Revolution, but Jews were not alone in doing so. This speculation was as almost "legalized" by the Civil Code and the Law of Sept. 3, 1807, was merely a proof of it."

Did the preparations for the anti-Jewish exceptional Decree of May 30, 1806, move Napoleon also to prepare the Law of Sept. 3, 1807? This is not an impossibility and certain historians hold this view. In T. Hallez's opinion, the Law of Sept. 3, 1807, as well, was possibly "made somewhat against the Jews"; the historian A. Lemoine wrote so with complete certainity in 1900; likewise, the French-Jewish historian M. Liber is inclined to believe it, and R. Anchel writes about the Law of Sept. 3, 1807, as a supplement to the anti-Jewish Decree of March 17, 1808.'"" In the documents preserved from the discussions around the preparation of the Law of Sept. 3, no mention whatever was made about Jews (a part of the documents of the Council of State were destroyed) hence the whole theory is no more than a conjecture, and the Decrees of May 30, 1806, of Sept. 3, 1807, and March 17, 1808, cannot be treated *en bloc*. Indeed the historian E. Driault wonders how R. Anchel could have done so. In the eyes of the historian A. Mathiez, the Law of 1807 was indispensable to Napoleon in order to be able to lay the ground for trying Jewish usurers under the provisions of the Decree of March 17, 1808." It is true that the Law of Sept. 3, 1807, would have sufficed for suppressing usury also among Jews, the penalties provided for were very rigorous, and this is another proof that Napoleon wanted an exceptional anti-Jewish Law. Yet it is rather difficult to suspect Napoleon of such a Machiavellian scheme as the promulgation (on Sept. 3, 1807) of a Law which should set a legal rate of interest, to have to combat at the same time a strong opposition in the Council of State, in order to provide the courts with a basis for prosecuting the Jews under the terms

---

" "C'est dans la loi du 3 septembre 1807 qu'il faut aller puiser les dispositions législatives annoncées par le Code civil [article 1987]... C'est donc par cette loi que l'usure a pris place parmi les délits. Le genre de crime n'existait pas avant la loi du 3 septembre" (349, p. 40-41); 103, p. 194; 348, p. 5; 249, p. 164; 278, p. 23-24; 455, vol. XXXV, p. 435; 457, p. 133; 60, p. 54.

" "Cette odieuse spéculation, autorisée en quelque sorte, par le Code civil, avait généralement fait en France des prógrès effrayants; témoin la loi du 3 Sept. 1807." 30, p. 17. The Anglo-Jewish anonymous author of an open letter to the Sanhedrin also wrote that in France there was no law against usury. 49, pp. 11-13. 21. The same was attested by the editor of the English translation of the Sanhedrin minutes. 64, p. V. In the same sense should be understood the Sanhedrin's reply to Napoleon that n e c h e c h meant any rate of interest, but not a usurious one, because there was no legal rate established in the Jewish religious code (104, p. 32; 109, p. 1083-84).

" "L'on sait, par exemple, que la loi qui fixe le taux des intérêts n'est que du 3 septembre 1807. N'était-elle pas, elle aussi, faite un peu contre les Juifs." Hallez, 103, p. 194; Lémoine, 48, p. 303; Liber, 51, vol. LXXII, p. 13; "nous la considérons [la loi du 3 sept.] ici comme un complément du décret du 17 mars 1808." Anchel, 16, p. 431. In their brief in behalf of the Upper Rhine Jewish Consistory (ca. 1809), four attorneys declared that the Decree of March 17, 1808, was a continuation of the Law of Sept. 3, 1807, aimed at all French citizens. 21, p. 9.

" AN,C701(14),C*I-189; Driault, 35, p. 293; Mathiez, 54, p. 380.

of an anti-Jewish Decree which was still being prepared and was to be promulgated only 6 months later. The three Decrees, issued in the same season were perhaps no more than an accidental result of office-preparations, but it clearly shows that usury was a plague that existed throughout the land, that it was no specifically Jewish problem, but Napoleon would not admit it.

To issue an anti-usury law was not sufficient to make credit sounder. As a matter of fact, the Law of September 1807 could never operate in the framework of its original drafting. There were many partisans, but still more opponents of the Law and successive decrees were necessary that temporarily guaranteed free credit, built fences around the old Law or made it even stronger. Two Decrees were issued during the invasion of 1814: Jan. 15, 1814, about loans on pledges, and Jan. 18, 1814, which suspended the Law of 1807 for one year. On March 9, 1836, the full abolishment of the Law was discussed in Parliament. Immediately after 1848 the socialists demanded that the legal rate of interest be reduced to 3% and even less. Proudhon demanded credit without interest altogether. After protracted debates Parliament passed in June 1850 a law which enabled the judges to penalize not only "habitual usury," but also isolated cases of usury. But in 1857 an exception was made for the *Banque de France* to charge more than 6%. This was the result of the growth of finance-capital, of France's relations with foreign capitals. Some economists went so far as to declare that usury was nothing but an "imaginary offense," that Napoleon I had as a matter of fact exaggerated the evils of usury. With the Law of 1807 Napoleon sought to draw capital away from private to public credit. But was not this Napoleonic policy really contrary to the interests of the peasants in whose name Napoleon put through the anti-Jewish Decrees? The Catholic attorney J. Liégeois wrote in 1858 and 1863 that the peasant could not gain by the Law of 1807, because it was a monopoly for usurers, since the peasant was not a good security at 5%. Similar declarations were made during the credit investigations. The Strasbourg Chamber of Commerce demanded that the Law should be repealed. The theory gained strength enormously that the magnitude of the interest-rate was not conclusive as to usury. In his well-known commentary on the Law of 1807, E. Detourbet wrote in 1866 that the risk the creditor runs must be taken into consideration. Man is so created that if in getting a loan he calculates badly and loses in the speculation, he blames his creditor before all else. Even if he makes a profit of 20% he still thinks that 8% is too much to pay the creditor. The economist Paul Leroy-Beaulieu wrote as late as in 1881 that charging even as high a rate as 50% did not mean usury, but to give a loan to a minor, a demented person, etc. was usury. As a matter of fact, the Law of 1807 was rarely applied in practice. Between 1871 and 1884 only some 15 persons were convicted for usury annually." It is worthy of note that the well-known Fourierist

---

" 109, p. 83; 246, p. 84; 90; 249, p. 219; 250, vol. I, p. 6, 79; 267, p. 27-28; 268, p. 210-211; 436, vol. II, p. 790.

924

antisemite A. Toussenel who raged against the Jewish monopoly in usury, was opposed to the Law of 1807. He wrote: Nothing else, but some friend of the Jews framed the Law which drives the petty debtors to resort to usurers, because granting a loan involves the lender in a risk.[3] On the other hand the economist M. Batbie wrote in 1866 that, along with other causes (antagonism of the socialists), the anti-Jewish riots, for instance setting free the guilty of the anti-Jewish pogroms in the Upper Rhine (1848) helped creating a public sentiment against annulling the legal rate of interest.[4]

[3] Toussenel, 169, p. 167-69.
[4] 425, p. 81. The eminent French-Jewish historian and jurist I. Bédarride defended the Law of September 3, 1807. 426, vol. II, p. 437, cf. 266, p. 181-84. The French Jewish author Alexandre Weill wrote in 1860 that in the Revolution of 1848 the Red Flag meant "Down with usury!" He dreamt of the coming time when the worker will not have to skimp in order not to starve in his old age; when there will be rest-homes for invalids and poor people—then usury will disappear (291). After 1871, he continued to demand the enforcement of the legal rate of interest (468). The famous Jewish banker Isaac Pereire was opposed to the increased rate of interest granted only to privileged banks (277). That was a part not only of his Saint-Simonian ideas, but also of his struggle with the Banque de France controlled by his enemy Rothschild. The Jew Maurice Hess wrote in 1869: "la Banque de France favorise... les tripotages de la Bourse et quelque chose de pire... La démocratie n'a pas de pire ennemi que le monopole financier" (255-1,p.31,45). (Hess translated into French Sinai et Golgotha... (P 1876), published by the "Société scientifique littéraire israélite".) The Hungarian Jewish émigré Ignace Einhorn Horn wrote in 1869: "l'abondance et le bon marché de l'argent de la Banque [de France] ne profitent qu'à un cercle limité de clients... Les... centaines de mille de commerçants, d'industriels et d'artisans n'arrivent, à puiser dans les ressources de la Banque [de France], s'ils y arrivent, que par de nombreux et coûteux intermédiaires" (Horn, in L'Avenir national, cf. 255-1, p. 30-31).

Left: Detail of a Metz Image printed by Gangel, 1854, with the legende: "Mémoire du boulanger, misère, désespoir, bagne. Plus de crédit". *Right:* The usurer, detail of an Epinal Image, printed by Pellerin, 1850.

(Bibliothèque Nationale, Paris.)

VI. AGRICULTURAL CREDIT IN FRANCE

At the time Napoleon I issued his anti-Jewish Decrees, nobody as yet had even dreamed of organizing credit for the peasant. Agricultural credit, banks in general in Alsace, came to be considered seriously much later. As a rule, the historians of Napoleon's anti-Jewish Decrees have taken no notice of it, hence it is worth while to consider the matter a bit more thoroughly."

Like France as a whole, The Upper and Lower Rhine and the adjacent Departments suffered from the scarcity of credit. In 1805, the town-council of Nancy reported on this state of affairs; the Strasbourg Chamber of Commerce confirmed this in 1811; Louis Ratisbonne, a Jewish merchant of Strasbourg, reiterated it in 1826; the ex-judge P. J. Chedaux of Metz declared in 1830, that credit was scantier than it had been at the time of the Revolution of 1789." The anonymous author of a song-collection in mongrel Judaeo-German and Hebrew (1830 or 1831) bewails the fact that: "truth has been long-buried and credit has become stupid."" A loan could be gotten only from a private lender, oft-times from the usurer. In 1850, a Deputy from Alsace stated that usury was the only source of credit for peasants and if this, too, would disappear, the peasant's condition might grow still worse. Subsequently one historian wrote that usury would vanish, if the demand for credit could be satisfied." But there was neither a possibility nor any desire to meet the demand for credit.

One point is plain after all, the discussions about agricultural credit were started in France for the sake of neither Alsace alone, nor because of the Jews alone. Agriculture in the whole land suffered from the scarcity of credit, and nothing was being done to improve the situation. During the First Empire the bankers did more

---

⁹⁵ The only attempt was made not in Alsace, but in the Southern Department of Gironde, where a special fund was organized to provide credit for viticulturists. In 1808-1812 only 100 persons took loans, and in all cases they were not poor peasants in need of small loans, but big viticulturists, who pawned their wine-harvest and speculated with the obtained money. AN,F10-437; Dr. G. Martin, 271. In this study we do not consider at all the role of "big" Jewish capital. A great deal of abuse has been heaped at Jewish capitalists and some pro-Jewish sentiments were also voiced by Jews and non-Jews. The Jewish leader, Adolphe Crémieux, once expressed himself in a court of law to the effect that suffering as it did from financial chaos France viewed the name of Rothschild as a synonym of honor, order, and loyalty (S. Cahen, 86). In 1846, in reply to an article by Henry de la Madeléne who called the Jews "men of money", the Christian writer Aurélien Scholl declared that the Jewish bankers and merchants inspire the greatest confidence (N a i n   J a u n e , Aug. 31, 1864). But Jewish "big" capital— just as the non-Jewish— was not interested in offering small loans to the Alsatian peasants. Accordingly, this question lies outside our theme.
⁹⁶ AdMM,M(report from Nancy, 1805); 405, p. 50; 176, p. 13, 15.
⁹⁷ ‏"די וואָרהייט איז שוין לאַנגסט בעגראַבען, אונד דער קרעדיט איז נאַרריש געוואָרדען"‎
Before World war II, this manuscript was in the Library of the Paris Rabbinical School. On the popular slogan "Le crédit est mort" see R. Saulnier et Van der Zee, 284-1.
⁹⁸ Brants, 229, p. 42; Metz, 205, p. 14.

925

speculating than giving loans even to merchants and industrialists and until the 1850's it is altogether impossible to speak of agricultural credit. The economist Wolowski's proposal in 1839, to organize a land-credit bank was treated as utopian. Only in 1848 more serious discussions of this matter were begun, and at that time, such land-credit banks existed already in some European countries: in Russia (since 1818), Poland (since 1825), Belgium (1835), Germany and other countries. An organized credit with state control was by no means welcomed by all groups of people. The economist Charles Barre wrote in 1849 that a large part of the Public Treasury must not, indeed, be risked for the organization of credit at so restless a time, when revolutions break out and governments change every 15 years. Credit needs times of tranquility and confidence, hence it is better merely to promote private credit institutions. The situation was such that the lower the rank one occupied in the social scale, the higher was the rate or interest he paid for a loan; the merchant paid more than the government, the artisan and laborer — more than the merchant, the peasant — more than the laborer, the petty peasant — more than the big one. Whoever had little capital could not enlarge his factory or commerce, and whoever had no capital at all was altogether hard up in undertaking anything, unless he paid usurious interest for a loan. The transactions of the *Banque de France* were limited. The Bank and the Government had no interest whatever for letting develop departmental branch banks. This was part of the struggle of the great capital against other initiatives, among them the notorious feud between the Rothschilds and Pereire Bros. As a rule, the Government and the large banks favored industry and had no desire to advance capital to countryfolk."

The agricultural credit (*Crédit agricole*) and the land-credit (*Crédit foncier*) were created quite late, the *Crédit foncier* by the Decree of March 28, 1852, parenthetically the Decree spoke only of giving loans to owners of houses within the jurisdiction of the Paris Court of Appeals, i. e. 7 Departments, all remote from Alsace. There was also the additional complication of making a distinction between land-credit (which required that the borrower gave a mortgage security of his land) and agricultural credit (which required mainly personal, moral guarantees of the debtor). Practically the land-credit completely controlled the operations of the agricultural credit. During the first 12 years, the land-credit lent the City of Paris 450 million frs., the communities 150 million, the Departments 114 million, and only 50 million to agriculture. This credit-institution

---

" Beaudonnat, 223, p. 41; Levasseur, 451, vol. II, p. 476; Barre, 221, p. 91-92; Carey, 233, p 15; D'Esterno, 252. The Fourierist François Vidal was elected in 1848 as Deputy from Lower Rhine. His book on credit (288), dedicated to the Lower Rhine, was written from the standpoint of France as a whole and does not emphasize Alsace. Perhaps it is worth while noting that the Hungarian Jewish emigré Edouard Horn was the first to write in France on the popular credit institutions in Germany (Batbie, 222, preface); Horn, 257-1. Horn published many books on credit, e.g., La Liberté des banques (P 1866), German edition — Bankfreiheit (Leipzig 1867); Das Creditwesen in Frankreich (Leipzig 1857); Le Credit populaire (P 1864); Caisses syndicales (P 1867), etc.

for assisting agriculture was so organized that only the great centers but not the villages could benefit by it. In this way the most important effort to organize credit for agriculture turned out a mere illusion. Much study, discussion, writing and planning was devoted to agricultural credit, but other countries had learned, from all of that, much more than France herself had. As late as in 1901 the historian Camille Bloch wrote that the organization of credit had brought no expected results whatever."[']

The utopian socialists linked all agricultural credit and credit in general with the realization of socialism. Charles Fourier was opposed to the creation of free agricultural banks without any collectivist control. Their ideas came nowhere near being able to help the peasants immediately and were often contrary to the peasants' interests. Curious was the theory of the Fourierist anti-semite Alphonse Toussenel. In his anti-Jewish book he proposed that the Government should take over the agricultural credit and grant the peasants loans to the full value of the property. The Government could afford to do so, being richer than the Jews, and through taxation the Government would incur no losses, the interest on the loans should be added to the taxes and collected simultaneously with these latter. The Government should thus give to the peasant with one hand and take back with the other."[']

The truth is that all opponents of organized agricultural credit — Charles Fourier and other socialists among them — opposed the parcelization of land and feared that agricultural credit might make the number of petty peasants still greater.

[']	C. Bloch, 225, p. 3; H. Sagnier, 283; Jossau, 258, 260, p. 1313-16; F. Granié, 254, p. 66-67; Roche, 281, p. 2; Flaxland, 309, p. 4; de Chevert, 338, p. 460-61; M o n i t e u r (1866) p. 275; Beaudonnat, 223; A. Chirac, 234, p. 51-58. It should be noted that loans in land credit were extended by intermediaries who deducted their percentage fee (308, p 10). In a comedy of P. Ponsard (459, p. 284), first produced in June 1856, a peasant complains as follows:
"Messieurs, ces beaux projets, qui vous semblent plaisants,
Ne nous arrangent pas, nous autres, paysans;
Tout l'argent va chez vous, et les propriétaires
N'en peuvent plus trouver pour cultiver leurs terres.
...Ah ! oui ! — le capital, à nos champs infidèles,
S'envole vers la Bourse où la prime l'appelle,
Et chez les étrangers fait pleuvoir des milliards.
Sans qu'il en tombe un sou parmi nos campagnards."
The Socialist B. Malon wrote that for this reason the play was a failure (269, p. 217).
[']	Proudhon, 460, p. 237-38; F. Vidal, 288; Fourier, 331, p. 135-36; Toussenel. 169, vol. II, p. 141. It is worth while to mention the views of a few Jewish writers on credit. In 1848, the orthodox Jewish leader Alexandre Ben-Baruch Créhange demanded the establishment of free loans for indigents and lauded the government for ordering that all pawned articles up to 10 frs. in value be returned to the owners (95, p. 15-16). In the '40s and in 1861 Alexandre Weill wrote against' the Rotschilds and in favor of nationalizing credit. He asked what the Jewish bankers had done for the Jewish ideal of brotherhood:
"Ainsi nos financiers, frelons de nos abeilles,
Cueillant dans leurs hôtels le fruit mûr de nos veilles
...Million du juif, qui sers-tu?
L'Esclavage est-il abattu?
Tes pauvres frères sont-ils libres?
A l'oppresseur tu tends les bras,
Esclave d'hier...
Des travailleurs de toute foi,
Ruissellent de sueur, pour toi
...Dis-moi! de quel droit est-tu riche?!!"
A. Weill, 290. I did not see his pamphlet of the '40s, which he mentioned in the preface to his booklet of 1861.

Banks in Upper and Lower Rhine and adjacent Departments came into existence at a much later era. There were only 2 branches of Paris banks in the Upper Rhine in 1839; local banks were founded in Colmar in 1848, 1857, 1859 and 1863; In the Lower Rhine there were but 2 branches of Paris banks and one local Strasbourg bank in 1843; a branch of the *Banque de France* was opened in Strasbourg only in 1846.[102]

These were all banks of limited compass, with incredibly small circulation and almost no ties with the village. Most of the banks in Alsace were organized on the principle of mutuality and closed their doors very soon: the Strasbourg *Banque Populaire* existed in 1865-1869; the *Banque Populaire* of Ribauvillé existed but one year, 1867-1868; and the Cooperative Bank (*Caisse coopérative*) of Gueb-viller — only several months in 1867; the *Banque Populaire* of Beblenheim, the mutual banks of Sundhausen and Reschwoog — also a short while. Only in Mulhouse the *Crédit Populaire* bank led a normal existence since its founding in 1865, because that city was the largest industrial center in Alsace. In Metz (Moselle) there were in 1841 seven banks (among them one belonging to the two Jewish partners Lévy and Worms). The Jewish banker and historian Justin Worms, was director of the *Comptoir National d'Escompte* of Metz, founded in 1848 in Metz by a group of merchants, who were threatened with ruin owing to the lack of credit; after the German annexation of Metz he evacuated the bank to France. One of the early managers of the Metz branch of the *Banque de France* (opened only in 1848) was the Jew, Isaïe Schwabe, formerly a manufacturer of dress-goods, and for a time the mayor ad interim of the city. In 1863 the Jewish banker Isaac Mayer (1833-1897) took over the failed bank of Moralis which had been opened with a capital of 1,000,000 frs.; subsequently Mayer increased its capital to 2,500,000 frs. In Lorraine modern banks were first founded after 1871, with the exception of the *Comptoir d'Escompte* of Nancy, founded in 1848.[103] Agricultural Credit and Land Credit accomplished

---

[102] Banque philantropique de Paris and the Banque mutuelle de Paris in the Upper Rhine; Caisse de libération des dettes hypothécaires de Paris, Banque de prévoyance de Paris, and the Strasbourg Cabinet d'affaires d'intérêt et de famille in the Lower Rhine; Comptoir national d'escompte de Colmar (1848); Compagnie générale des caisses d'escompte (1857), remplaced in January 1859 by the Comptoir commercial du Haut-Rhin (existed till 1863); Banque populaire à Colmar (1865). 171; 184, p. 445-60; 201, p. 8, 21; 214; 238, p. 342; 370, p. 318; 372, p. 386; 422, Nº 2544-53, 2558, 2561. The notary Thurman tried to establish in 1818 a branch of the Caisse hypothécaire (C B R, Feb. 26, 1818).

[103] 317, p. 140-42; 318; 388, p. 163; 377, p. 313; 100, p. 51-56; 101, p. 305-6; 194, p. 41-42; A I, vol. XXVI (1865) p. 365. In Nancy, there existed for a

nothing in Alsace. At an inquest of credit in 1856, the Strasbourg
Notaries Association's representative, Wasmer, stated that the two
credit-institutions had never aclimatized in Alsace. Since its founding until 1865, the Land Credit (*Crédit Foncier*) granted 398,250 frs.
of loans in Upper Rhine, a trifling sum, and 300,000 frs. of those
were used in building homes for workingmen at the factories in
Mulhouse. As industry grew, capital kept withdrawing ever more
away from villages; the city credit offered the capitalists more
advantageous terms. During the Fifties complaints were heard in
Alsace that from the endeavors made by the Government to ease
credit only industry and commerce had reaped the benefits at the
expense of agriculture."

It was the same with all sorts of other institutions that could
have helped the peasant to obtain loans on easy terms, such as,
e.g., loan-and-savings banks, pawnshops, etc. Savings-banks in
general sprang up late in France, the first — in Paris in 1818.
Such a loan-office was opened in Metz in 1819, and it was one
of the best in France; in Mulhouse — in 1832; in Strasbourg —
in 1834; Belfort and Altkirch — in 1835; Sainte-Marie-aux-Mines —
in 1836; Thann and Colmar — in 1837. But all of these were
city savings-banks which did mighty little for agriculture. The
capital of such a savings-bank consisted altogether of 6,000 to
40,000 frs. The Metz savings-bank, the best of them all, had 71
depositors per 1,000 inhabitants, but non-peasants exclusively. Only
5 of the 331 depositors in the savings-bank of Nancy in 1834 were
peasants. In Alsace-Lorraine there were in 1872 only 22 savings-
banks and 4.8 depositors per 1,000 inhabitants, and in 1883 only
8 savings-banks in Upper Rhine, 16 in the Lower Rhine and 6 in
Lorraine. Altogether the peasant disliked to keep his savings in
savings-banks or banks." Discussions went on constantly about
the need of organizing loan-offices in order to combat usury by
aiding peasants to buy horses and livestock. This was a particularly
sore problem of the peasant because many peasants owned land-
parcels so tiny that the livestock were their most important source
of nourishment. Not only the purchase of cows on credit but even

time a small private Jewish bank of the family of Michel Goudchaux, who
became Minister of Finance in 1848. In the same city there also was the
small private bank of Lévy-Bing. On the whole, Jews of Metz and Nancy
showed more initiative in modern banking than the Alsatian Jews.
    [104] 209, p. 2; 210, p. 3, 30-34; 250, vol. I. p. 286; 322, p. 227; 329, vol. XIII,
p. 203.
    [105] 175; 177, p. 11; 181; 183, p. 27; 185; 188; 199; 206; 212; 217; 247, p.
13; 263, p. 1-17; 282. In 1856, an agricultural committee of the Somme Department complained that the savings banks were only a hindrance to agricultural
credit. Formerly, a peasant could obtain a loan from a wealthier relative;
now the relative puts his money in the savings banks or he buys bonds with
an assured annual income (287). J. F. Flaxland wrote on the problem of
savings in Northeastern France: "Il n'y a, en effet, point de village dans nos
départements du Nord-Est, où l'on ne trouve pas quelques familles qui ne
tiennent soigneusement des épargnes, d'une valeur plus ou moins grande,
cachées au fond d'une armoire ou dans tout autre lieu de sûreté. Ces familles... n'accordent leur confiance ni au Crédit foncier ni au Crédit agricole
de France" (306, p. 9). In an essay submitted in 1825 for the Lower Rhine
Agricultural Society's contest, Louis Blanchard, author of an anti-Jewish
booklet about Jewish usury in Alsace (1818) wrote that for combating Jewish
usury it was necessary to develop cantonal loan offices (81). Later on he
incorporated this study in a missionary book (82).

930

the lease of a cow for a certain time (*cheptel*) was very widespread, and this was often a way of usuriously skinning the peasant. Such a savings bank was established in Sélestat in 1848. But prior to 1870 these savings-banks were never widely developed.[166] Lombard houses did exist, but they also were founded at a later period (in Metz — 1813, in Strasbourg — 1826). But here also, just as all through France, this institution was a disguised net of legal usury. All over France the average rate of interest charged in the pawnshops was 12%, later on 9%. In Besançon this institution was called *banque usuraire* ("usurer bank"). Husson, secretary of the Lower Rhine Association of Sciences, Agriculture and Arts declared in 1852 that as much as 25% was charged in the state controlled pawnshops, by means of various combinations. Moreover, the pawnshops existed chiefly for the city element. The peasant seldom had anything to pawn; the interest rate was higher than any demanded by the worst usurer; in certain cases the *commissionnaire* (pawnbroker) gave loans for 24 hours only, and the loan had to be constantly renewed, for 20 francs the charge was 60 centimes per 24 hours, which, together with other fees amounted to 1,095% (219 francs) of interest per year.[167] Nor did the Alsatian peasant know sick-benefit insurance and other such sorts of social insurance. Something was done in this direction in Alsace, as early as in 1818, but only among the workingmen, not among the peasants; sick-benefit-funds existed in 1868 in 48 of the 59 Upper Rhine factories, thanks chiefly to the Protestant industrialists.[168]

---

[166] AdBR,M11-33: 301, p. 3-4, 17 18. Incidentally, this was a sore problem for all of France. In the Seine-et-Oise Department usury was ascertained as late as 1881 in the buying of cattle and agricultural implements (239, p. 6).
The Jewish horse and cattle-dealers were of a very great importance for the economy of Northeastern France. On June 17, 1833, the Alsatian Deputy André declared that Alsace was not a good place for cattle breeding and, for this reason, cattle has to be imported (369a, p. 4). According to the Lunéville sub-prefect's report dated Apr. 20, 1807, horses, cattle, and grain were imported from the neighboring Vosges (AdMM,M). Naturally, there were many complaints against Jewish horse and cattle-dealers; but, as a matter of fact, they were always looked upon with much distrust. Maquignonnerie derived from m a q u i g n o n (horse-dealer) and was an old French synonym for swindling (444a, p. 467). But even so, horse-dealers were regarded by peasants as indispensable men. During the Revolution of 1789 pro-government priests often posed as horse-dealers in order to get into the peasants' confidence (377a, p. 236).
[167] 246, p. 68; 252, p. 112-28; 280, p. 215; 328, p. 25-26; 386, p. 70-88.
[168] 186, p. 210-11.

"Credit is dead". Image of Metz, printed
by Dembour, 1840.
(Bibliothèque Nationale, Paris.)

VIII. AGRICULTURAL CREDIT AND THE PARCELLIZATION
OF LAND

The truth is that agricultural credit was unwanted, not only because industry and speculation were favored, but because it was feared that agricultural credit might advance the parcellization of land still more.' The government, the Church, the local authorities, even the socialists combated the cutting up of land into small parcels, which was a revolutionary event in the eyes of the reactionist and a reactionary event in the eyes of the leftist circles. The division of land into parcels was widespread in France as a whole,'" but particularly so just in Alsace. In 1861 there were in Alsace alone nearly as many petty peasant owners of land parcels as there were in all England. Since those desirous of buying land-parcels annually exceeded by 24% the number of those willing to sell land, the prices were greatly boosted. In 1866 there were in Lower Rhine: 1% of large land properties (up to 120 hectares); 29% of medium-sized estates (6 hectares or more); 70% of small properties (under 6 hectares). In 1866, 495,638 persons engaged in agriculture in the two Rhine-Departments owned only 107,075 estates.'"

There were also partisans of land-parcellization. The Prefect of Moselle, himself an opponent of small estates, nevertheless wrote in 1803 that the parcellization of land made life easier in the village; the Prefect of Meurthe wrote in a similar vein. It goes without saying that the peasants themselves were happy over the realization of their dream — of not having to work for some one else, of being a husbandman for oneself. The Alsatian author of a pamphlet in honor of the King's visit to Alsace in 1831 wrote that the Province had to thank the parcellization of land for its prosperous condition. In Upper Rhine matters came to a clash between the Agricultural Association of Colmar (founded in 1842) and the Ministry. The Colmar Association held to the principle of favoring middle and petty peasants in agricultural contests, whereas the Government demanded that only large agricultural enterprises should be forested. For this democratic attitude on its part the association's subsidy was cut by half. In 1851, André Cohut wrote in an Alsatian paper that land-parcellization would, indeed, result in insufficient productivity, but if the large estate should swallow up the small ones that would mean running counter to the democratic trends,

---

[169] In all of France (in 1862), 56.29% of all peasants possessed less than 5 hectares, 19.19% possessed from 5 to 10 hectares, and only 4.77% possessed 40 hectares or more. 450, p. 173; 279, p. 96.

[110] Tisserand & Lefébure, 322, p. 123, 128, 213; AdBR,XIM138,p.3; 329, vol. XIII, p. 63. As late as 1907, 59.68% out of 94,128 Lower Rhine properties contained less than 2 hectares, 27.01% 2-5 hectares, 12.199% 6-20 hectares, 0.33% 21-100 hectares, 0.02% over 100 hectares. 402, p. 165.

and therefore a middle road must be found. But the majority held to a different view.[111] The truth is that, even if at certain times the petty-peasant was exploited by the reactionaries, in many cases the petty peasantry was a force of the liberal circles. Thus, e. g. at the time of the post-Napoleonic Restoration, the Bourbon Government did not venture to annul the purchase of nationalized land (*Biens nationaux*) during the Revolution, because it had to take into account the peasants who had bought these estates and thus the re-creation of a feudal class was avoided. One must not forget that the real aim of the billion francs paid out to the former owners of the nationalized properties was to try to halt the land-parcellization and re-establish large estates, but that object was never attained. The economist Paul Leroy-Beaulieu wrote in 1881: "It is difficult for us now to grasp the prejudices against land-parcellization that held sway in the first two decades of the XIX Century; there was a universal conviction that this would ruin agriculture."[112]

These sentiments inimical to a large class of petty peasants had foredoomed the fate of agricultural credit with the Government help. It was feared that a credit within the reach of rural folk would fractionalize the land still further. Such was also the conclusion reached by the Parliamentary inquest (in 1866) which was against placing credit-opportunities at the peasant's disposal, because the peasant might use it to buy new land parcels, whereas its main purpose was to "humanize" the credit, to teach the peasant how to employ the money obtained, not to buy land with it. From Northern France only 16% of replies to this inquest demanded an organized form of credit; from Southern France 25% were for and 75% against; from Central France — 30% for and 33% against; from the West — only 4% for and from Eastern France only 3%. From France as a whole 84% replies rejected any and all organized credit for agriculture. The Parliament's Commission of the inquiry, in its report, was in favor of private initiative and not of Government efforts to organize agricultural credit.[113] Similar was also the sentiment in Alsace and the adjacent Departments. In 1802, the Prefect of Vosges was against the division of land and even the Prefect of Moselle who had written himself that this had made the village more prosperous, stood for favoring industry at the express disadvantage of agriculture, so as to put a stop to the breaking up of land. In 1831, the Council General of the Meurthe passed a resolution against small estates. Such a view was also current in Moselle ; it was also held by the agricultural economist J. N. Schwertz; in the Lower Rhine the building of railway lines

[111] Colchen, 383, p. 114; Marquis, 408, p. 107-8; "un pays qui a dû une longue prospérité à la division des terres." 369, p. 5; Kaeppelin, 397, p. 290; A. Cohut, in: CBR, Jan. 10, 1851.
[112] Capéfigue, 232, vol. III, p. 153. The sub-prefect of Sélestat (Lower Rhine) wrote on June 5, 1832, that the widespread parcellization of land is a guarantee against both, the reactionary and the extreme left opposition to the government. AdBR,IIIM28-29; 450, p. 163; 330, p. 24; 439, vol. I, p. 82.
[113] 259, p. LI; 336; 447, p. 30; 329, vol. XIII, p. 130, 145, 148, 173, 203; 329a, p. 19-20; 332.

was opposed among other things because it would help fragmentize the land. In the early Forties the attorney Chauffour wrote that Jewish usury had increased thanks to the apportioning of land. The wealthy Alsatian peasant J. J. Maritz, once himself a champion of small estates, wrote in the Fifties that many opposed the organizing of credit and that in reality the Alsatian peasant sought loans in order to buy new parcels of land, hence the ability to obtain loans easily was a misfortune for him. In 1852, the Belfort Consultative Chamber of Agriculture demanded that agricultural credit should be organized, but care should be taken not to give the peasants anything wherewith to buy parcels of land. In November 1856, Trautmann of the Strasbourg Agricultural Chamber stated that small estates had drawn creditors away from the village, because bankers placed no trust in small borrowers.[114] The matter was so pressing that in 1857 the Agricultural society of the Lower Rhine instituted a prize-contest on whether the wide distribution of land was a positive or a negative event. There are 5 replies in the contest. In the opinion of Rohmer of Hoenheim, a teacher, the result of the large land distribution was negative and if agriculture was in good shape it was merely a result of working till now the cultivated plots of land and applying new methods. The author of another memorandum saw in the large number of petty peasantry but the result of the peasant's basest instincts. This was also the view of the third memorandum's author. He related that the peasants rushed to buy land-parcels in cantons where they did not even reside, and he suggested that in registering the purchases in connection with the land-parcellization the fees should be double. The authors of the last two memorandums were in favor of distributing the land. As the motto for his essay, one of them chose the sentence: "To improve agriculture means to improve the lot of all." The author of a book for the prize-contest of the Association of Agriculture and of the four cattle-fairs of the Lower Rhine voiced in 1858 in favor of centralizing estates through exchange; Rigaut, a justice of Wissembourg urged in 1858 a law against land-parcellization. In this spirit M. Stoltz spoke at an agricultural convention in Lower Rhine in 1859. The Metz Agricultural Association, in its reply to an inquiry in the Sixties wrote that peasants obtained loans to repay old loans and bought with this money new land-plots.[115]

All discussions about expanding agricultural credit aimed first of all at providing more security to the creditor by changing the existing laws in that direction.[116] Now, too, just as in the XVIII

[114] AdBR,XIM11; Desgouttes, 385, p. 27-31; Colchen, 383, p. 114, 119; Chauffour, 93, p. 13; Maritz, 202. p. 75, 78 and 203, p. 4; de Viville, 216, p. 16; 293; 300, p. 75-76; Schwertz, 319, p. 20, 25; 324; Lefèvre, 403, p. 11.
[115] AdBR. Documents of the Agricultural Society and XIM31; 295, Apr. 1859, p. 92; 307, p. 6; 305, p. 4, 9-10.
[116] 304, p. 9. The two anti-Jewish Alsatian authors, A. Heilmann and A. Hertzog, wrote in the same spirit (190, p. 164; 191). The French jurisdiction on mortgages was as follows: (1) There were no absolutely guaranteed mortgages; (2) The guarantee of the loan by a mortgage entailed large expenses; (3) Obtaining payment of the debt by juridical expropriation of the mortgaged property involved very long litigation and heavy expenses. The law did not permit the debtor to mortgage cattle, the crops, furniture, and other chattels. According to d'Esterno (251, p. 21), French agriculture produced in the '60s

Century, they strove in Alsace to "moralize" the credit for the
peasant, to tell the peasant for what purpose and how much he may
borrow."[7] But all these parlor discussions were feebler than the
peasant's urgent need and his urge to buy land. The masses
demanded organized credit in order to fight usury.[118] When the
masses were needed, a fight was waged in favor of credit for them.
Election-time every candidate promised the voters to wage war on
usury, and demaned loan-banks. At such times the candidates
did not mention concentration of land as pre-condition for organized
credit.[119] Did the Alsatian authorities sincerely believe, even in
midnineteenth Century, that the great partitioning of land was
interlinked with usury? L. J. Reboul-Deneyrol, Secretary-General
of the Lower Rhine prefecture, wrote in 1858 that even among "the
best minds" in Alsace the opinion was widespread that usury and
small estates were interlinked; but in the Administration they did
not side with this view, even if they did believe that in Alsace
usury was more strongly enrooted than in other parts of France.[120]

an annual crop valued at over 6 billion in cattle, houses, implements, reserves
of wine, lumber, etc. And yet agriculture could not find credit facilities,
partly because the law did not allow mortgage on the 12 billion worth of
movable goods. 226, p. 1-3; 253, p. 2
[117] In a petition of July 27, 1806, the notaries of the Altkirch canton
proposed to combat usury by not allowing a debtor to mortgage more than
1/3 of his property (AN,BB16-639). In his proposal of 1825 for the creation
of cantonal loan banks the above mentioned Louis Blanchard wrote that the
loans must not exceed 100 francs (81, p. 72).
[118] In the industrial and agricultural inquest of 1849, 12 of 29 replies
from the Upper Rhine contained complaints against usury and demands for
agricultural banks; in only 4 of these replies Jews were mentioned. The replies
from the Lower Rhine also demanded agricultural credit. 312, p. 49, 54, 56,
62, 66, 78, 95, 106, 179, 190, 201, 227; 306, preface.
[119] In a campaign speech of April 22, 1848, the candidate Heinrich Rosen-
tiel stormed against those "whose religion is usury" (AdBR,IIM96, a printed
leaflet). The Democratic Committee of Lower Rhine had a slogan: "Weiss
oder Roth; Wucher oder Ackerbaubanken?" (BuStg,7658-5). The Lower Rhine
candidate J. B. Schaller of Haguenau advanced in May 1849 the slogan of
organizing in each canton agricultural banks in order to combat usury
(AdBR,IIM96,a printed leaflet). The Democratic Committee of Strasbourg advanced the same demand (Ibidem). Victor Elbel, of the Central Napoleonic
Committee wrote in an election leaflet that this Committee would abolish
usury, but it could be done only with the help of agricultural banks (Ibidem).
In the 1848 elections in the Upper Rhine, the periodical R é p u b l i q u e d u
P e u p l e wrote that "a revolutionary is he, who wants to liberate the worker
from the usurious oppression of the capital and is in favor of creating agricultural banks" (420). The candidate Frédéric Titot demanded the enforcement
of the anti-usury laws (AdHR,E,coll.A.Waltz,M3). The candidate George Klem,
mayor of Gundolsheim (Upper Rhine) also demanded the organization of
agricultural credit (I b i d e m). In 1849, the Central Democratic Club of
Upper Rhine put forth the demand for a law against usury (I b i d e m).
A Democratic Club ("Der demokratische Verein des Oberrheins") supporting
the candidate Ledru Rollin against Prince Napoléon (the future Napoléon III)
stormed against usury (ZS, a printed leaflet). In 1848, the Upper Rhine Deputy
J. Chauffour put forth the same demands (382, p. 9). In 1849, the same
slogans were advanced by the candidates J. J. Maritz and G. Dauphin (AdHR,
M5/2, printed leaflets). The same occured in later years. The candidate Mirand,
an Upper Rhine peasant, complained in 1870: "There is a lack of money;
there is a lack of credit" (AdHR,E,coll.Waltz,M8).
[120] Reboul-Deneyrol, 416, p. 182.

IX. THE PEASANT'S LAND-CRAVING

The peasant was reproached on all sides for his traditional craving to purchase ever more land-plots, above his powers, even negotiating usurious loans only to buy again and again more than his neighbor, even if he was unable to till that land. The Strasbourg jurist Flaxland wrote in 1808 a memorandum on the appalling need of the peasants chiefly as a result of taking on loans to buy ever more and more land-parcels. And he wrote that Napoleon's Decree of March 17, 1808, brought aid "to the evil elements among the peasants." The Council-General of Moselle wrote that the peasant's desire of property exceeded his craving to improve his lot. In his booklet (about Alsatian peasants and usury) filled with hate of the Jews (1853), A. Heilmann wrote that the peasant's vanity and jealousy bring agriculture to ruin. The acreage of a peasant's farm, the number of cows and horses determine his influence and his chances to obtain credit and hence the race to buy ever more and more land. Owing to the emigration from the villages to the city, agriculture suffered sorely from the scarcity of working-hands, but still the peasants rather rented plots of land if in no position to buy them, but he would not help a neighbor, as the Alsatian economist E. A. Oppermann proved in the Sixties.[121] Jews, too, occasionally mentioned that peasants contracted debts above their means to buy land.[122]

Surely there was a good deal of truth in the censure of this psychology of the peasant and it is proper to observe that the reproaches came mainly from anti-Jewish sources. By-the-way, Northeastern France was no exception. The same held true before the Revolution not in Alsace only, but in France as a whole, also at the time of the Revolution and not in France alone: the same *Landhunger* among the peasants existed in Germany.[123] The peasant's misfortune did not lie in the huge interest-rate as in the borrowed principal itself often invested in still more land-parcels or in liquidating old debts and the peasant wanted to repay the borrowed capital, without selling the land he had bought, whereas a merchant who borrowed money to buy merchandise with it could refund

---

[121] Colchen, 383, p. 119; Ponteil, 414, p. 45; Riegert, 23, p. 53; Gravier, 310, p. 5, 7; Maritz, 202, p. 75 and 203, p. 5; Barre, 221, p. 114; Stolz, 295, p. 91; Castex, 296, p. 12; Tisserand & Lefébure, 322, p. 213; H. Contamine, 384, vol. I, p. 139; AdHR,E.Wendl.48/16,p.25 ("avidité de s'arrondir": notary Wendling of Landser, 1806); Liber, 51, p. 152; Bonnemère, 325, vol. II, p. 353; CBR, 1/27/1865 ("Cette nécessité d'acquérir et de s'arrondir"); AdBR,XIM138,p.13 ([le crédit] servant ordinairement à payer des dettes ou à acquérir des terres avoisinantes"); Leuilliot 108, p. 261; Heilmann, 190, p. 22, Oppermann, 317, p. 15.
[122] Furtado, 37; Lipman Cerf-Berr, 52.
[123] Sagnac, 462, p. 261 and 462a, vol. II, p. 190; 463, p. 5b. The author of an Alsatian counter-revolutionary pamphlet (1792) predicted that the peasants buying nationalized properties would be unable to pay their debts and, consequently, have to resort to Jewish usurers. 394 p. 19.

936

the capital by the sale of the merchandise. The best counsel that could be given the peasant was: borrow nothing or small sums that you will be able to repay. If necessary, sell a piece of land and pay back the loan. Gone were the years 1806-1818 when the peasant of Alsace and neighboring provinces held his Jewish creditor by the throat and hoped never to have to repay his debt. The professional anti-Semites campaigned for the prolongation of the Decree of March 17, 1808, but deep down in their hearts they knew that the source of evil did not lie in the Jew and that Alsace was in no worse condition that the parts of the country where no Jews happened to live altogether. In order to obtain credit easily the peasant had to be in a position to enlarge the borrowed capital by work and be able to repay the principal and interest from the products of his toil. But the French peasant was in no position to do this and little by little the idea took root everywhere that farming brought a return smaller than what negotiating a loan cost. And indeed it held true of Alsace and the neighboring provinces where the income from land was lower than the interest the peasant had to pay for a loan, even at the legal 5% rates of interest which were never observed. A traveler, J. L. Fesquet related in 1802 that in Lower Rhine land brought only 2 1/2%-3% of income and only 4 1/4-4 1/2% around Toul (Lorraine). According to the memorandum of a Lower Rhine Deputy of Oct. 8, 1807, a peasant owning an estate of 28 acres — such a peasant was considered a wealthy man — had an annual income of 3,440 frs. and 3,030 frs. expenses (900 frs. — food, 300 frs. — taxes, 890 frs. — laborers' pay, etc.), so he could not allow himself the luxury of loans. In 1808, the Prefect of Upper Rhine wrote that peasants borrow at 12, 15 and 20%, where his land gives him only 4% or at most 6% of income, — in this way the peasants come to ruin. A. Heilmann wrote that the Alsatian peasants who had obtained loans in 1836-1847 at 7-20% interest and bought land derived but 2% income from the land. In 1848, in reply to an inquiry, there came from the arrondissement of Ensisheim (Upper Rhine) very bitter words against Jews and it was added that even the legal rate of 5% on loans was too high for the peasant, the net income from land cannot permit him to pay such a rate. Of 20 inventories of the estates of deceased peasants there were 14 with liabilities exceeding the assets. The Consultative Chamber of Agriculture of Belfort (Upper Rhine) ascertained in 1852 that the Land Credit can do nothing for agriculture. The peasant who will seek a loan there is on the road to ruin, since the rate of interest plus the expenses will be 7% and not 5%. In one situation only must he allow himself such a loan, when he must repay a loan which he had obtained at usurious rates: in that case it is a question of merely gaining time, and even so it is almost positive that he will be ruined."[124] Indeed, only rarely

[124] Batbie, 425, p. 111; Durif, 249, p. 228; Seneuil, 237, p. 354-5; Hiernaux, 256, p. 165-6; ArchMM,M (Report of the Lunéville sub-prefect, 1805): Contamine, 384, vol. I, p. 139; Fesquet, 390, p. 23, 39; AN,F19-11011 (Report of a Lower Rhine Deputy); AdBR,M42/1,p.33 (Report of the Lower Rhine Prefect, 1808); Heilmann, 190, p. 13; K.-Rabecq, 300, p. 74-75 and 312, p. 179.

could a peasant normally pay up his debt. About 1830, the Jewish creditor Isaac Sée of Sélestat was condemned to pay a fine of 25,870 frs. for 63 cases of usury. Isaac Sée defended himself in a brief prepared by the well-known attorney de Neyremand which analyzed in detail all the 63 cases, every one a loan obtained by a peasant. It turned out that the debtors were never in a position to pay off the loans, after a few years they had to approach the creditor he should take back a piece of land, etc., but meantime new interest had accumulated. In the majority of cases the debt was never paid off during the borrower's lifetime and passed on by inheritance, together with the mortgaged property, to the children who hated the creditor all the more, because, after all they had not borrowed the money of him. At times the peasant was himself responsible for his wretched plight. It happened that he even borrowed for speculation.[125] It must be admitted that if the situation had greatly improved after 1871, that, too, was due to the fact that the peasant had grown more calculating in his work, more intelligent, used more modern implements and had planned some time in advance to be able to pay off the loan. But, in addition to the peasant's hunger for still more land, there were still other causes which the "moralizers" of credit had not noticed. For instance, there was also tradition. In Alsace, there was an ancient custom that after the death of a family's head the estate did not pass to the oldest son but was divided in equal shares among all the heirs. In this particular case the tradition of inheritance played an important role and affected the general state of agriculture. After the peasant's death, the oldest son took the entire parcel of land and gave his brothers money wherewith to purchase new land-plots, the money he could obtain only from a usurer and frequently he had to come to ruin.[126]

But whether the peasant really contracted loans exclusively in order to increase his property still remains an open question. Even though Alsace really was among the Departments with the least number of large estates, the farming inquest of 1862 ascertained that the total of landless peasants there was no smaller than in other Departments. Only rarely a peasant had a horse of his own or a cow. The poorer families raised goats, and when as much as an orchard

[125] 362. R. Krzymowski confirms the same for the arrondissement of Altkirch as late as 1905 (313, p. 63). In June 1831, the peasant Jean Kueny of Pfaffenheim (Upper Rhine) wanted to buy the small factory in Hattstatt at auction. He neither had money, nor could he obtain a loan immediately, because he was already in debt. So, he had to apply to the Jewish real estate merchant Nephtaly Bloch of Herrlisheim (342). In 1815, the Gentile Raymond Fonrouge entered into a military contractor partnership with the two eminent Jewish brothers Ratisbonne of Strasbourg, but as Fonrouge had no money of his own, so he borrowed from the Gentile physican Ostertag a large sum to be reimbursed by 20% of the profits in his share in the business. But Ostertag, too, had no money, so he, in his turn, took a loan from the Gentile banker Mennet who was to get 50% of the physician's income from the agreement with R. Fonrouge (358). The richest peasant in Lampertheim, André Lobstein, was a debtor of the Strasbourg Jewish creditor Elie Schnéeberger. In his turn he lent money to non-Jewish and Jewish debtors, at high rates of interests. He over-reached himself so greatly in his loan operations that he could not pay the debts to his own creditor; so he made the Jews the scapegoats of his troubles (354).
[126] 329, vol. XIII, p. 74; 395, p. 45-46; 396, p. 384.

or, still more, a larger parcel of land was bought, the thought of buying a cow came up. A large percentage of peasants tilled rented land-parcels and they had to pay the rentals in produce or in cash. During the Revolution of 1789 nearly 50,000 Alsatian peasants fled abroad, and were as a rule poverty-stricken when they returned. The villages had suffered from the invasions and deprivation, even though in historical works, for a time, there was current the legend of prosperity and social tranquility in the country during the Restoration.[127] The rural areas suffered from poor crops, inundations and phylloxera in the vineyards, from competition in rye that was imported from Russia and Hungary, from competition of the city which took the workers away from the village.[128] The taxes were always high. The mayor of Huningue (Upper Rhine) wrote on Aug. 12, 1805, to the Prefect that attacks on the Jews are in preparation, that the Jews were taking to Basel their jewelry and their loan-receipts (I.O.U.s). As one of the causes of the anti-Jewish sentiments he mentioned the too high taxes. The two peasants Jean Dubac and F. Krafft of Marlenheim (Lower Rhine) wrote in their petition of 1805 to Napoleon I that the peasants were suffering from the delays in litigation and must resort to the Jews for loans. About 1848 it was computed in Soultz that after paying all taxes the landless farm-laborer had 37 centimes for food, rent and clothing per day. Bread cost 20-55 centimes per kilogram, varying from one year to another. For the purchase of one's own piece of land, a horse, a cow, work-tools; to pay rent, taxes; to conduct a litigation, for hundreds of other things, the peasant had to have money. And withal the Alsatian peasant was by no means the most unfortunate in France. The peasant of the Landes who knew nothing about Jewish creditors was still in a much worse situation. As a rule he was a sharecropper (*métayer*) who had to hire a piece of land from the land-owner and give him a share of his crop, mostly also to pay high interest for the cows and plough which he had rented from the proprietor, and as a result he led a primitive indigent existence.[129]

---

[127] 321, p. C. The German economist J. N. Schwertz, a strong opponent of the parcellization of land, wrote in 1816 that in the Lower Rhine on the average a peasant owned one horse per every 15 1/2 acres (320, p. 47) "Au XIXᵉ siècle, en Lorraine, les familles les plus pauvres de la campagne nourrissaient une chèvre. Quand elles avaient acheté avec le fruit de leur travail deux ou trois parcelles de terrain, elles remplaçaient la chèvre par une vache. Beaucoup s'arrêteraient là... L'argent était rare, très rare" (302, p. 49). "Le manœuvre, pour peu qu'il ait de facultés, ambitionne d'avoir à lui soit son logement, soit un jardin à cultiver", AdMM,M (Statistique agricole, rapport de Dieuze). "Beaucoup de biens ruraux appartiennent aux habitants des villes, qui les afferment aux paysans" (374, vol. II, p. 229). In 1849, more than half the income of the "Œuvre Notre-Dame" of Strasbourg, 55,823 frs. of 94,081 frs., was derived from renting land to peasants (f e r m a g e s   d e s   b i e n s   r u r a u x), C B R   1/25/1849; 418, p. 230; 454, p. 421-460; 464, p. 155. On account of the entry of the occupation armies in June 1815, the 21 communities of Landser sustained a loss of 1.431 heads of cattle, 104 wagons, houses valued at 287,861 frs., produce valued at 119,148 frs. The loss totalled 555,451 frs. (AdHR,coll.Wendl.99/14.)
[128] In 1790, 80% of the Lower Rhine population was composed of peasants, in 1861 only 52% (298, p. 8, 12; 419, p. 4-5). Prompted by competition between industry and agriculture, the Colmar arrondissement Council protested in 1821 against child labor in factories. AN,FIcIIIHt-Rhin12.
[129] 401. p. 519, 521; AdHR,M54-3 (report of the Huningue Mayor); AN,BB16-629 (petition of Duboc & Krafft); 396, p. 384; 448, p. 8.

X. THE PEASANT AND THE BANK

The peasant's entire psychology was such that he wanted to get a loan in secret, so that none of his neighbors might know his situation and his plans. A. Heilmann wrote (1853) that the peasant would rather have many debts unbeknown than one debt known openly. The Vicomte T. de Castex, mayor of Thanvillé wrote in 1866 about agricultural credit in Alsace that the minute people learned about a peasant that he was looking for a loan his reputation was destroyed. The same was written at the time by A. de Türckheim of Neuwiller, himself a champion of small estates. During an inquiry about agricultural banks in Lower Rhine, it was proven that the peasant would rather have recourse to a usurer than make his loan known to the world. An anonymous correspondent of the anti-Semitic Alsatian newspaper *Volksbote* complained that the Alsatian peasant would never go to his neighbor to sell a piece of land, when in need of money. His heart cannot bear that his neighbor should enlarge his property: he would rather go to *Schmulen,* the Jewish speculator, who will cheat him.[130] Jews, too, have themselves often pointed out this psychology of the peasant. Under the Decree of March 17, 1808, the Jewish loan-giver had to prove through witnesses that he really had given the borrower the full sum. But however well-justified this may be from the purely-juridical point of view — the Jewish Consistory of Wintzenheim (Upper Rhine) wrote in 1809 — it is impracticable, because it runs counter to the psychology of the peasant who wishes to keep the loan in secret — and consequently the creditor cannot produce any witnesses.[131]

If there did exist anywhere a bank or a loan-office — and that was a rarity — the peasant had first of all to rid himself of the age-long tradition of doing everything in secret, in order to make up his mind to apply to a bank for a loan. Frequently this was really beyond his powers. The justice of the peace of Marckolsheim assessed himself with the sum of 200 frs. to aid in developing agricultural credit, so that the peasants should not have to get loans from Jews. In a letter of May 3, 1850, to the Prefect of Lower Rhine, he related by the way that in order to obtain a loan from a bank the peasant must come "with his entire family" to the bank and then everybody would know his secret.

---

[130] Heilmann, 190, p. 22; de Castex, 296, p. 15 AdBR,XIM33,137; 250, vol. I, p. 284. The manufacturers were just as eager as the peasants to keep their dealings with creditors a secret. The desire of the industrialists to obtain loans without publicity was one of the reasons of the failure of the project of a governmental bank of credit for industry during the First Empire (Ballot. 219, p. 51); P I, vol. I (1869) p. 625-28.
[131] A letter of the Wintzenheim Consistory (ZS).

In the proposed by-laws of an agricultural bank at Geispolsheim (Lower Rhine) of 1853 it was stipulated that every borrower must have a second person as security and his status must be personally investigated by the director of the bank, the judge and the tax-collector![132] The terms of obtaining a loan from a bank were such that the peasant could but rarely comply with them. In 1832, there was a plan to establish at Strasbourg a central cooperative bank with local branches. According to the draft of the by-laws a member trying to get a loan could not have his property mortgaged and the property had to be worth three times as much as the sum he wished to borrow from the bank.[133] For a time there was in Alsace a scheme to create an association with a capital of 12-13 million frs. to save the bankrupt debtors. The plan was to buy in the property of a ruined debtor and resell back to him the same property on part-payments in the course of 20 years, secured by a mortgage and all other guarantees. For instance, the peasant owned land and a home valued at 6,000 frs. which was mortgaged for 4,000 frs. The association would purchase this property not at its actual value, but for the mortgage-sum which the peasant must pay back and would resell the property to him for 20 yearly instalments of 400 frs. each. There would be expenses of 800 frs. (actually 942 frs. because registry fees (*droits d'enregistrement*) would be for the full 6,000 frs. and not for 4,000 frs. only). This meant that the peasant would get only 3,200 frs., not enough even to repay the loan and he would have to pay annually 480 frs. and not 400 frs., in addition to several hundred frs. of interest. In the course of the first 10 years he would have to pay out 7,000 frs. for the 3,200 frs. No peasant would have taken a loan in a bank on such terms. By the way, the whole project was not acted upon, because it was realized that the association could not get sufficient securities from the borrowers. In the projected by-laws of a land-credit association in Strasbourg (1852) the following terms for granting loans were provided: the borrower can get a loan only on a first mortgage, the mortgaged property must have an assured income; the loan cannot exceed one half of the mortgaged property; no less than 200 frs. is loaned and the loan cannot be repaid before 5 or later than 50 years, the borrower paying all costs. As it was, such credit-offices extended loans only to members.[134]

---

[132] AdBR,XIM33.

[133] Jung, 195. The rule of the Colmar B a n q u e p o p u l a i r e (founded in 1864) was that every member was entitled to a loan only three times his holdings in the bank (173, p. 6-7). In 1865, the S o c i é t é de c r é d i t m u t u e l of Beblenheim (Upper Rhine) granted loans amounting to twice the applicant's investment in the bank. The first 70 members of the bank had a total investment of 4,425 frs., so large loans were out of question (213). In 1852, the notary Grandjean proposed that the C r é d i t F o n-c i e r should charge 7.6% on loans in St Dié and 6% in Epinal (AdVosges, 39M11). The projected C r é d i t F o n c i e r of Epinal (Vosges) was to grant loans on unmortgaged real property; only after having been evaluated by two respected expert commissioners and verified by a notary (179).

[134] 204; 210, p. 30-34; Tisserand & Lefébure, 322, p. 230. In 1842, the Fourierist Just Muiron proposed to the Agricultural Society of Besançon to establish communal banks, which would extend loans secured by the harvest. But when examined more closely this arrangement would leave very little for the peasant; the peasant would get only one quarter of the income from the harvest. In the '40s, a similar project was advocated by M. Kampmann

The banks of Land Credit (*Crédit foncier*) granted loans only on condition that the borrower should present: an accurate detailed list (of the property he wanted to mortgage) drawn up by a notary; a statement of income; proofs that the property is unmortgaged; tax-certificates; be insured against fire, etc. The by-laws of the *Crédit foncier* were so changed in 1856 that without much ado the debtor's property could be sold for non-payment of one semi-annual rate of interest.[135] On Aug. 16, 1852, the Council of the Sélestat arrondissement expressed a desire that whereas the terms of getting loans at the *Crédit foncier* were complicated for Alsace, where the land was minutely parceled, the terms should be eased. The Prefect of Lower Rhine wrote to Senator Marchand in 1853 that the *Crédit foncier* could bring only negative results for the Alsatian peasant who could not comply with the conditions of obtaining a loan. In short: the peasant after all, would not have much use from the banks. The banks required that the peasant's property should be free from a previous mortgage.[136] The peasant had to prove that the land indeed belonged to him, and that he could not always do. Until the middle of the XIX Century the registry of land-surveying in Alsace had not yet been completed. The Agricultural Council of Landser (Upper Rhine) had established on Aug. 2, 1852, that peasants could not prove the genealogy of their property in the last 30 years, which the credit-agents demanded. The Consultative Chamber of Agriculture of Saverne (Lower Rhine) had ascertained on Nov. 7, 1853, that peasants owing 5 to 20 hectares that stemmed from some 10 or 20 land pieces of various former land owners, each parcel, in its turn, having in the 30 years belonged to 10-15 different proprietors, peasants of this kind could not furnish absolute proofs that the entire land had been free of debts. The same was proven in 1853 by the director of the *Crédit foncier* at Strasbourg at a meeting of the Consultative Chamber of Agriculture.[137] As a rule, banks required that the peasants should carry insurance against frost, inundations, fire and epidemics among cows. But in all of France few peasants had such insurance and still fewer had it in the Northeastern Departments.[138] Some banks

---

of Colmar (247a; 196). The B a n q u e a g r i c o l e et h y p o t h é c a i r e of Mulhouse (founded in 1868) extended loans on first mortgages only. The loan-applicant was required to take out fire-insurance on the house which was to be mortgaged. He also had to use a notary's services and present eight different documents (182, p. 2, 12-14). In 1838, a Metz project for a Departmental bank was also conceived in terms of granting loans on first mortgages only (216, p. 6). During a trial in Colmar in 1842, it was revealed that a loan at the legal rate of 6% together with commission, amounted to 9% (340, p. 15-16).

[135] 240; 241, p. 20, 22; 254, p. 68-71. A decision of the Supreme Court of Appeal (C o u r d e C a s s a t i o n) of Aug. 23, 1808, clearly pointed out that for a mortgage to be valid it is not sufficient to specify in the deed of mortgage that it is on the mortgagor's entire property; it is essential to enumerate specifically all items in the mortgagor's property (351, p. 14).

[136] AdBR,XIM33andIIIM128; Cetty, 298, p. 35.

[137] AdHR,E,coll.Wendl.99/11; AdBR,XIM11; 299, p. 34; 416a, p. 58 ("Le notaire doit être soigneux pour constater les titres de propriété..."). At the end of 1834, some 20% of the land in both parts of Alsace was not as yet registered in the cadastral survey (465, ol. II, p. 102-03). But in 1853, the official yearbook of Lower Rhine indicated that the cadastral survey had been completed, 373 (1853) p. 213.

[138] In 1871-1885, French agriculture suffered an annual loss of 214 million frs. owing to frost, floods, and cattle-epidemics (255, p. 62). In Upper

942

required that the debtor should pay back the entire debt by single payment.[139]

The submission of so many official documents involved great outlays and, in order to escape outlays, the peasant sought to obtain loans purposely on simple I.O.U.s, not certified by any public official, as was proved by the Consultative Chamber of Agriculture of Metz at the time of the agricultural inquiry in 1866. A. Heilmann wrote in 1853 that usury would cause much less evil, if the high costs of legalizing the documents would not deter the peasants from legalizing them. For the same reason the peasants shied at legalizing the purchases of land, houses and cattle. About 1853, the registry-fees in buying something for 500 frs. amounted to 69.55 frs., exclusive of the fees to the notary, the keeper of mortgage-deeds, the traveling-costs, etc. The Alsatian economist J. F. Flaxland had ascertained that if the peasant buying a piece of land wished to enjoy all the guarantees granted him by the law, he must pay more heavily. In buying a piece of land for 150 frs. he had to pay 100 frs. for notarial acts and various other office-fees, and even more than that in selling a piece of land in case of death. And the Alsatian economist Eug. Ad. Oppermann wrote in 1869 that lower amounts were entered in registering transactions, — in order to avoid the high costs. In the arrondissement of Mulhouse (Upper Rhine) between January 1850 and September 1866 there were recorded mortgages for 11,980,909 frs. for loans obtained by peasants. In 1861, there were there 4,713 purchases of land-parcels totaling 714 hectares averaging 1,357 frs. per hectare. These land-pieces were not sold through notaries, because the sellers did not possess any regular documents to establish their ownership. During the same period 1,514 purchases were made through public notaries (996 hectares at 2,414 frs. average per hectare). In the canton of Cernay in 1865, there were 997 purchases through notaries and 675 privately.[140]

Rhine industrialists and merchants founded in 1818 a fire insurance society (the General Council tried to establish such a society in 1812). People set fire to their own houses in order to harvest insurance benefits greater than the value of the destroyed property (198, p. 351-52). In Strasbourg such a fire insurance society was founded in 1820 (207). In 1831, the Upper Rhine fire insurance society numbered some 15,000 members, but most of them were city dwellers (412, p. 48-49). In the important Alsatian agricultural center of Altkirch a society insuring cattle against epidemics was founded only as late as 1888 (388, p. 40). It appears that the insurance movement among Alsatian Jews was not as popular as among the Jews in the interior of France, where they played a rather important role in the insurance business. Among the 1842-1846 Upper Rhine subscribers to the C o m p a n i e r o y a l e d ' a s - s u r a n c e s s u r l a v i e (founded in 1830, with Baron J. de Rothschild as one of the administrators) there was only one Jew— A. Lévy of Bergheim (178).

[139] "...il [le paysan] n'aime pas recourir à un emprunt en forme, c'est-à-dire par obligation; le remboursement du capital ne se fractionne ordinairement pas; il faut donner le capital d'une fois et à la première réquisition..." (L'Abbé Obrist, 208). In 1832, the Jew E. Lévy and his partners purchased a debt of 6,000 frs. from Ch. B. Tourneisen, a Basel creditor of S. Beck and M. A. Abtey of Hattstadt. It was revealed that the whole debt had to be repaid in a lump sum (351, p. 4).

[140] AmM,F3-33; Heilmann, 190, p. 9-11, 163; Flaxland, 308, p. 30; Oppermann, 317, p. 75; 329, sér. 2, vol. XIII, p. 332-333. About 1850, to obtain a legal loan of 300 frs. entailed administrative expenses of 48.50 frs. on the borrower, of course, plus interest (Polonius, 279, p. 10, 172). To guarantee by mortgage a loan of 500 frs., the debtor had to pay 14% for a year (but only 9.5% for two years) in administrative expenses and interest. The smaller the

The problem of loans on I.O.U.s had been a sore problem even before 1789, but just in Alsace this sort of loans was in great vogue.[141] To be sure the credit had its faults, but it had excellences as well, because where this sort of credit did not exist, the peasant could not get any loans, as e.g. in Pas-de-Calais.[142] It was a natural occurence for a debtor to acknowledge and thereby juridically legalize a loan which had not been legalized until then. Under the Civil Code (Article 1322) an I.O.U. acknowledged by the borrower must be recognized also by the court. But when a debtor did not want to pay a loan, he exploited the legal distrust of simple I.O.U.s. By the way, here an important part was played by the notaries who fought against such uncertified I.O.U.s, because these reduced their incomes. On Jan. 21, 1864, Jules Favre stated in the Senate that the villages were being doomed to a sort of legal usury. The best means of encouraging free circulation of money in the villages was to use I.O.U.s and not mortgages, i.e. to accustom the peasant to honor and hold his signature on an I.O.U. as a guarantee and a proof of confidence in him.[143]

---

loan, the larger were proportionately the expenses, because some administrative fees did not vary according to the capital. Only in the second half of the 19th Century the expenses for mortgaging declined (Piogey, 336, p. 113-117). The account book of an Alsatian Jewish merchant show that in 1842 the sale of a land-parcel for 14,000 frs. entailed expenses of 1,100 frs., and the cost of recording a sale of a land parcel for 1,200 frs. was 53.25 frs. (Library of the Alliance Israélite Universelle, ms. No 192). In 1826, in canceling a mortgage in the Wissembourg arrondissement, the debtor had to pay one fr. per debt. If the mortgage had more than one mortgagee, the mortgagor had to pay one fr. for each mortgagee. The legal price for the notary's visit to the peasant's home was 0.96 fr. per kilometer for a notary from the city and 0.64 fr. per kilometer for a country notary (420a, p. 8, 18-19, 22). In 1850, a loan of 100 frs. to be guaranteed by a mortgage involved the following expenses in Alsace: fees to the notary-9.30 frs.; stamps-5.60 frs.; mortgaging expenses-2.21 frs.; renewal for the mortgage after 10 years-5.97 frs.; renewal after 30 years-22.57 frs.; nullification of the mortgage-19.15 frs. (Maritz, 202, p. 88).

[141] According to a report of the district of Sarre-Union dated August 16, 1795, three different ways of granting loans existed before 1789 in Alsace: (1) For a fixed term (à term préfixe); (2) To be repaid on the first term; (3) Granted on mortgaged properties, to be repaid not— as in the rest of France— on a fixed date, but on a date announced three months in advance by the creditor or the debtor. The first two types of loan were not made on the basis of legal documents, but only on the debtor's word or simple I.O.U. (AN,DIII212). Thus, simple I.O.U.s and receipts were a common practice in Alsace. But in order to fight usury this was often prohibited.

[142] 335, vol. IV, p. 391.

[143] Detourbet, 246, p. 160. In 1808, the debtor Schmittbourg sought to prove that it was common for a debtor to admit his debt by a simple I.O.U., but with Jewish creditors it was necessary to be more careful (357). On August 31, 1807, the notaries of the Delemont canton protested against loans on simple I.O.U.s, because this led to chicanery (Jews were not mentioned in this protest). But the Ministry of Justice observed that such documents were still legal, although the law did not favor them, as they decreased the income of mortgage offices. They were made at the creditors' own risk and in order to have a standing in the courts they had to be registered. Similar petitions sent by the notaries of the canton of Porrentruy and, on May 19, 1808, by the notaries of the canton of Simmern (Rhin-et-Moselle) prove that this was an organized campaign of the notaries, seeking a greater income from legalized I.O.U.s (AN,BB16-639,645).

XI. THE JEWS, AGRICULTURAL CREDIT, AND LAND-PARCELLIZATION

In connection with the various projects of agricultural credit the Jewish question was involved very often. In 1825, the Association for Sciences, Agriculture and Arts of Lower Rhine announced a contest on the subject of how to make the Jews of Alsace share in the benefits of "civilization", etc. M. Tourette, a member of the Association published his essay for the contest wherein he criticized the entire approach to the inquiry which sought an answer to the problem of how to force the Jews into "civilization" without thought of changing at the same time the negative attitude of Gentiles toward the Jews. His plan was, with the help of Jewish funds, to establish a loan and savings office which should not only assist Jews in turning to land-tilling, but also grant loans on mortgages to Gentiles. But he admitted that this required a great deal of enlightenment not among Jews alone, but among the Gentile peasants as well. He wrote that at first tne Alsatian peasant would not borrow money at this loan-office, because he was just as conservative in his ways as the Jew in his Jewish customs. For a long time the peasant would still have recourse to usurious loans rather than sell even one small tract of his land in order to improve his circumstances. The populace will have no confidence in the Jews until a good example has been set.'"

But the Jewish side of the problem was not always treated so idyllically as by M. Tourette. In reality, since there was no organized agricultural credit at all in Alsace, Moselle and Lorraine, the Jewish creditor was quite often the only person from whom the peasant could get a loan. Often the Jews were the only ones ready to grant the peasants very small and short-termed loans, because it did not pay the city's Gentile creditors to do so. For the peasant to be able to enjoy the benfits of a local credit it would be necessary to decentralize the credit system. Not the peasant should have had to come to the banker, in the city, but (rather) the bank should be situated in the very midst of the peasantry. Also, the

---

¹⁴⁴ Tourette, 125. By "civilization" was understood forcing Jews to abandon many of their customs and accept modern ways of life among Gentiles. To Gentiles, even to Gentile peasants who could not even read and write, the Jews were externally uncivilized because of their customs and language. They did not understand the great Jewish culture unseen by them. But even modern "scholars" approach the Jewish aspect the same way, e.g., the study L i f e w i t h P e o p l e. The J e w i s h L i t t l e - T o w n of E a s t e r n E u r o p e, by M. Zborowski and E Hertzog (New York 1952), where Jews are studied by the same method as "primitive peoples of the world" are.

The following happened in a small town of Lorraine in 1864: In collecting a debt from a Jewish woman, a priest's mother charged 4 more francs than she was entitled to. The Jewish woman complained to the priest, who replied in a letter that he is ready to return the 4 francs adding: "My mother is not a Jewess" (A I, vol. XXV, 1864, p. 280).

local credit system, which was totally unfamiliar to the peasant, should have been popularized and both of these elements were lacking. The Alsatian peasant felt lost when he had to make a trip to the big city. The city was far away, the trip entailed expenses, the peasant could not always leave his work. So he called in the Jew — the *Schmouser*, as they called the Jewish intermediary — and asked him to market his crop. In 1856, M. Eschbach, a professor of Law, wrote that frequently the Jewish *Schmouser*, sold the peasant's produce at a higher price than the peasant would have gotten himself.[145] Only the Jew who had not yet shaken loose of his wretched existence prior to 1789 could adjust himself to the peasant's difficult circumstances, to the long terms of repayment, without good securities, etc. Therewith the Jews enabled the peasants to acquire little plots of land and become proprietors on their own. This was proved by the Parliament's inquiry in

---

[145] L. Durand, 248, p. 642 43; Eschbach, 440, p. 471-72. In the year XII, the peasant Jean Sirquel of Phalsbourg (Moselle) lost his cattle in an epidemic and had to ask the Jew M.A. for a loan. In 1807, in a petition to the Minister of Justice, he wrote that he had to turn to a Jew, because "the pockets of decent people were closed to debtors" (AN,BB16-467). When a traveller in Alsace in 1806 asked why people came for loans to Jews who are usurers, the answer was that only Jews were willing to grant loans (401, p. 536). The same was said by the antisemitic lawyer X. Chauffour in 1852 (92, p. 8). "Il ne faut point perdre de vue que les Israélites sont presque seuls à prêter par sommes de 100, 200 ou 300 frs., et que de là résulte, en grande partie, le monopole exercé par eux" (322, p. 217). On small and short-term debts higher interest rates were charged; up to 20%, according to an inquiry of 1845 (261, p. XIV, note 2). Even the Colmar notary M. Renker, who declared that Jews ruined the peasants, also admitted that in giving credits the Jews adapted themselves to all situations and, so, helped proletarian peasants to become landowners.

Often, peddlers were intermediaries between peasants and their Jewish creditors. Gentile merchants had a grudge against Jewish peddlers because they sold their merchandise cheaper. They were particularly bitter against those Jewish peddlers who auctioned off their merchandise. This was legal, but found very little favor among the city merchants. During one auction in Strasbourg (1827) the Jewish peddler Marx Lajeunesse of Nancy sold 30,000 frs. worth of merchandise to 4,000 clients. The Strasbourg merchants saw to it that he was sentenced for selling merchandise of an inferior quality (350a). In the year XI, the Mayor of Colmar forbade peddlers to sell merchandise otherwise than in open market. Two years later, the Gentile merchants of Colmar complained against the competition of the Jewish peddlers (AmC,H14-14b). In June 1814, the merchants of Haguenau complained against their competitors, the Jewish and foreign peddlers. A similar petition of the Saverne merchants (June 1814) did not mention Jewish peddlers. The Prefect of Lower Rhine sought the opinion of the Strasbourg Chamber of Commerce, which declared that the city merchants were seeking to abolish free competition (AdBR,3M923). On Dec. 30, 1816, the Minister of the Interior warned the Prefects that the restriction of licensed peddling would abolish free competition (AdBR,3M923). On Dec. 30, 1816, the Minister of the Interior wrote to the Minister of Justice that the city merchants were only trying to abolish free competition; at first they attacked foreign peddlers, now they were complaining against Jews (AN,BB16-791,dr.8901). On Apr. 1, 1828, four Jewish peddlers of Obernai protested against an order of the Mayor of Barr prohibiting peddling (AdBR,3M923). All over France Jewish peddlers were often attacked in pamphlets as usurers, etc. The author of one pamphlet (ca. 1830) made a Jewish peddler speak French with a would be Alsatian Yiddish accent. (The d changes into t; the v into f; the j and g into s h (c h); the q into g; the p into b; the c into z; etc.): "Vous tites que vous n'afez bas tarchantu... fulez fus que ché fus brète dix-huit cents francs, fus allez me suscrire une lettre de change payable tans ine an... sans auguine interet... ché ne veux que mon archant. Chez fus tonnerai teux zents francs en écus tut suite... tans un mois, et ché fus enfoye, au-chourd'hui pour huite cents francs de vieille feraille... et pour les ternières huit cents francs, che fus tonnerai tes sangsus..." (106a). But were Jewish peddlers really disliked? On the contrary; according to Reboul-Deneyrol, the Jewish peddlers were very popular in Alsace (416, p. 416-72).

946

1866.[146] Not infrequently a single Jewish creditor gave more loans
than all the Alsatian banks together. When the Jew Daniel Sée
of Ribeauvillé died (in the 1830's) he left behind an inheritance
of over 2,000 debtors in the arrondissement of Colmar alone, as
his heirs wrote in a factum against J. Rudinger, one out of 2,000
debtors, the only one that did not want to acknowledge his indebtedness.[147] This opportunity which the Jew afforded the landless
peasant to become a proprietor on his own, — that could never be
forgiven the Jew. The reactionary Catholic circles especially could
not excuse the Jew for his role in democratizing agriculture. The
well known economist Léonce de Lavergne, who opposed small
estates, painted in the blackest colors the state of agriculture in
Alsace in 1860. "Every one accuses the Jew," he wrote. "Even
if one should grant that the Jew makes conditions of the village
worse, he still does not create this state of affairs, the responsibility
lies primarily in the chase after land and the results springing
therefrom." He proposed to reestablish large estates by creating
cooperatives of small inheritances.[148] By the way, the Jews themselves have often stated that they purchased large estates and
resold piecemeal to peasants and the peasants could even pay on
the installment plan.[149] As early as in the XVIII Century the Jews
were reproved for their role in fragmentizing the land.[150] At that
time, — just as later, in the XIX Century — it was a reaction
against "individualism", which had already set in in agriculture.[151]
Some of the anti-Jewish pamphleteers of the XIX Century, such as
Betting de Lancastel, even strove to prove that the price of land
had fallen in Alsace, ergo the Jew's usury was responsible for the
peasant's downfall. This is part of a wider propaganda that the
Jew had always urged the peasant to take a loan, had shoved
money into his hand, and how could the peasant get rid of him?
The truth is that, on the contrary, the price of land had constantly
risen even in later years, and in all of France. To be sure there
were also many cases of usury among Jews and that was unavoidable.
At a meeting of the Municipal Council of Nancy, Nov. 7, 1808, the
report-maker stated that everybody was practicing usury and that
in this respect no reproach could be cast against Jews alone, when
they granted loans for purchasing land to such insecure borrowers

[146] 329, 2e sér., vol. XIII, p. 121-26. The same conclusions were reached
in their book on Alsatian agriculture (1869) by E. Tisserand, director of agricultural schools in France, and L. Lefébure, Deputy from Upper Rhine (322,
p. 215-217, 223-225).

[147] "L'inventaire de la succession Sée avait révélé l'existence de plus de
deux mille débiteurs dans le seul arrondissement de Colmar" (362, p. 32).

[148] De Lavergne, 333, p. 36, 125, 165-171. Frequently, peasants did not
wish to do business with non-Jews. "The old Moses," a character in a novel
of Erckmann-Chatrian, suffered at the hands of a Gentile competitor, because the peasants wanted to deal only with him (389, p. 54).

[149] Mayer Séligman of Ribeauvillé wrote in a petition of 1806 that he
never practiced usury; he only bought large estates and resold them in parcels to peasants who paid by installments after harvest time, with the income
from land which they had bought on credit from him (AN,BB16-639).

[150] Hoffmann, 392, vol. I, p. 83.

[151] M. Bloch, 428.

wild propaganda against the Jews, although the Catholic clergy did not spare the Protestants as well. This propaganda bore fruit: pogroms at the outbreak of the Revolution in 1789, Napoleon I's Decrees against the Jews in 1806 and 1808, pogroms in 1830-1832, and at the outbreak of the Revolution in 1848. Behind the propaganda against Jewish usury — only against Jewish usury — there was, besides the traditional hatred of the Jewish people, the grudge and nostalgic yearning for the large feudal estates that had been nationalized during the Revolution of 1789, the interests of the big peasant as against the petty peasant and the landless peasant.[152]

[152] De Lancastel, 80, p. 87; Obrist, 208; Goutzwiller, 391, p. 362-63; Anchel, 16, p. 318. In 1806, the price of land in the area of Nancy was three times what it had once been (Germain, 316, p. 3). The Jewish real estate dealer of Nancy, Lippmann, wrote in 1837 that the large parcellization of land increased the price of large estates (353, p. 7). In 1836, the sale value of a hectare in the arrondissement of Strasbourg was 2,969 frs. and 4,196 frs. in 1866; in the arrondissement of Mulhouse 940 frs. in 1836 and 2,005 frs. in 1866. Each year the number of prospective land purchasers exceeded by 24% the number of those willing to sell. For this reason prices became inflated (329, 2e sér., vol. XIII, p. 57, 65-71, 75, 120). In Moselle land values started to drop only by 1850, after a series of crises (384, vol. I, p. 139). In the village of Hüttenheim 1,739 parcels of land were sold or exchanged in 1881-86. Out of 406 parcels in 1885-86, 222 parcels were divided into smaller ones. How this could be caused by the Jews is difficult to understand, but Dr. A. Hertzog tried to do just that. He did not even attempt to adduce any evidence that this parcellization resulted from obligations to pay old debts or incur new ones. In effect, he referred to several facts unrelated to Jews: the urge to enlarge the estates (Arrondirung), migration to th. city, etc. (311, p. 106-11). Of the 426 parcels sold in 1885-86 there were o n l y f o u r dispossession cases for unpaid debts to Jewish creditors. A loan fund could not be organized in the village because there was no organized drive for it. At any rate, at that time the peasants could not easily get loans. During the agricultural inquiry of 1885 one of those testifying stated that peasants drove land prices up so high that their neighbors could not buy new parcels of land. About Jews he wrote in the same vein as others had done before him: Jews adjust themselves to the difficult desires of the peasant debtors, such as long terms, small loans and secrecy (Bodenheimer, 294, p. 6). Land values rose in all of France (326, p. 49).

[153] Strikes only against Protestant and Republican industrialists were organized in 1869-70 jointly with the Bonapartists by Catholic priests who grouped themselves around the V o l k s b o t e (417, p. 211-12 and 417-2, p. 13). Propaganda against Jews and Protestants was not new in Alsace. In 1859-60 such a propaganda went on in connection with the conflict between France and the Pope ("Die Juden siend böse, dass sie noch keinen Messias haben, und wollen, das die Katholiken keinen Papst haben. Sie haben den Spectakel angefangen", 379, p. 6). The Catholic circles tried to represent the R a i f f e i s e n loan offices in Alsace as a triumph of the Catholic Church; that not only were the Catholic priests the initiators of these loan societies, but also that for the Catholic peasants the societies were twice as important as for te Protestants (Danzas, 180, p. 116). One could write much more about the role of the Catholic clergy in the villages but this would take us astray from our theme. When F. W. Toussaint dared to write in 1875 that the large landowner finds help among the notaries and clergy, a storm of protest arose, and in the French edition of this book (1876) this statement had been eliminated (323, p. 87 in the German edition, p. 57 in the French edition).

On the anti-Protestant and even anti-French attitude of the Alsatian Catholic leaders in the 19th Century see Julien Sée's [C. Julien's] pamphlet (417-1) and the bibliography on the same subject in his diary of 1870-71 (417-2, p. 239-40, 246-54). Sée translated into French " La Vallée des pleurs, chronique des souffrances d'Israël" (P 1881).

XII. WERE THE LISTS OF MORTGAGES TO JEWS RELIABLE?

In preparing the Decrees against Jews Napoleon I and his Ministers relied on the rosters of mortgages to Jews which had been supplied by the mortgage-offices not only of Northeast, but of the entire country. The amounts of debts outstanding from debtors — mainly peasants — to Jewish creditors truly looked very large, occasionally fantastically large. On the basis of the administrative reports, the Minister Champagny wrote in his report of Apr. 9, 1807, to Napoleon I, that since the beginning of the Year VII (Sept. 22, 1798) until Jan. 1, 1806, there had been recorded mortgages to Jews in the amount of 21,199,286 frs. in the Upper Rhine. Even if a portion of the recorded mortgages had already been paid up, there must be added at least 10 million frs. of debts on simple I.O.U.s which had not been recorded in the mortgages. Most of the mortgages are against peasants, a part of the peasants' properties had already passed into Jewish hands for non-payment of debts, etc. A similar report had also been supplied from Lower Rhine. Metz, the Deputy from Lower Rhine had named the total of 30 million frs. of mortgages to Jews in all Alsace. In 1808, a pamphleteer from Metz asserted that one-half of Alsatian land already belonged to Jewish money-lenders.[154] In 1808, a list of mortgages for 3,140,087 frs. in favor of Jews was sent in from the Moselle Department.[155] On July 16, 1808, a list of mortgages for 1,546,756 frs. in favor of Jews was sent from the arrondissement of Toul (Meurthe); from the arrondissement of Lunéville (January 1808) for 1,112,126 frs., etc.[156] The same happened in later years, when a fight for the prolongation of the Decree of 1808 was waged. The Prefect of the Upper Rhine wrote on Dec. 9, 1823, of mortages to Jews in the amount of 7,053,000 frs. in the arrondissement of Altkirch. From this arrondissement there was submitted in October 1823 a list of 3.668 mortgages to Jews, in the amount of 7,053,181 frs. recorded in the period between Oct. 1, 1813, and Sept. 30, 1823.

---

[154] AN,AFIV-300dr.2151&F19-11011; Lemoine, 48, p. 41-42; Anchel, 16, p. 122; 68, p. 3.

[155] AN,F19-11009;AdM,V149. Of this sum mortgages for 2,252,008 frs. were held by Jews of the Moselle Department and the rest by Jews from other Departments. There were mortgages for 844,754 frs. in the arrondissement of Metz (778,194 frs. in the city of Metz itself); 849,839 frs. in the arrondissement of Sarreguemines, 557,415 frs. of Thionville. In the arrondissement of Briey mortgages for 443,372 frs. were in favor of Jews, however only in favor of Jews residing in neighboring Departments. In the arrondissement of Sarreguemines there were for 444,707 frs. additional mortgages in favor of Jews residing in neighboring departments (for 260,877 frs. in favor of Jews of Lower Rhine). It should be pointed out that generally different official reports presented different figures.

[156] AN,F19-11009. From the Department of Vaucluse was sent in 1811 a list of 542 mortgages (529,310 frs.) held by Jews. From the arrondissement of Aix (Bouches-du-Rhône) was sent in a list of over 1,000 mortgages (2,239,655 frs.) held by Jews. AN,F19-11008,11010.

From the arrondissement of Belfort there was sent in a list of 1,217 mortages for 953,371 frs., for the same period. The pamphleteer Betting de Lancastel specified the amount of mortgages in favor of Jews in 1813-1823 in the Upper Rhine as 16,489,781 frs. and in Lower Rhine as 18,000,000 frs.[137] The figures produced the effect: they determined the attitude toward the Jews.

But were the rosters of mortgages in favor of Jews really trustworthy? Particularly characteristic is the following case related by the Prefect of Moselle in his report of Oct. 13, 1808, to the Minister: the first transcript of mortgages in favor of Jews in Metz, gave the amount of 5,000,000 frs. The Jews protested and, upon investigation, the amount was reduced to 778,000 frs. Later, the registrar of mortgages increased the total to 1,483,700 frs., but the Jews declared that only 778,194 frs. were owed them on mortgages. According to the notes to the Thionville sub-prefect's report for 1808 there were 1,657,415 frs. of mortgages in favor of Jews, but from this were to be deducted: in the amount of 200,000 frs. mortgages which were positively non-usurious; uncanceled mortgages — 600,000 frs.; mortgages of Jewish wives held against their husbands — 50,000 frs.; surety mortgages etc. — 250,000 frs. In the official report of the sub-prefect there was, accordingly, specified the sum of 557,415 frs. The sub-prefect of Sarrebourg wrote on June 8, 1808, to the Prefect of the Meurthe that seemingly the truth had not been adhered to everywhere in making up the lists. The prefect of the Bouches-du-Rhône, in Southern France, wrote that the amount of 4,591,721 frs. of mortgages in favor of Jews in his Department was exaggerated.[138] The whole method of wishing to prove Jewish usury with the aid of lists of mortgages in favor of Jews was adventurous and dishonest. An exaggerated picture of Jewish usury was needed and they sought to give the picture the character of utmost authenticity, and surely there was no better material than the mortgage-registers. All documents prove hat at the time it was immediately known that the registers of morgages in favor of Jews were unreliable, and yet the entire structure of anti-Jewish propaganda and anti-Jewish decrees was reared on the basis of these registers. Let us try to analyze why the registers were not reliable. It is important to stress again that already in 1806-1808 and later, in the fight for the renewal of the Decree of 1808, both Jews and non-Jews immediately pointed out that the registers did not give a faithful picture of debts to Jews, of the Jews' share in honest private credit and in usury.

I. There is no way whatever of ascertaining from the mortgages, which loan is honest and which usurious. On Sept. 1, 1806, the Jews declared that usury was jumbled with debts for commercial

---

[137] AN,F7-9533;AdHR,V109. It is to be noted that nearly half of these mortgages were registered prior to 1819, when the Decree of March 17, 1808, was still in force.
[138] 80, p. 62. AdM,V149;AN,F19-11007&11009. Already in 1790 the Society of Friends of the Constitution in Strasbourg declared that from the total 10,757,161 [francs] of mortgages held by Jews should be subtracted the lapsed and doubtful mortgages and passive debts (4, p. 14).

transactions. On Jan. 12, 1809, the members of the Disciplinary Chamber of Notaries of the arrondissement of Marseille wrote to the Minister about the enormous difficulties encountered in determining which notarial acts in favor of Jews were of a usurious nature, that it was in general impossible to decide it, that in a domain such as usury, it was dangerous to introduce the supplanting of facts with sophistry. In its petition to the Minister of the Interior, the Jewish Consistory of the Upper Rhine declared in 1824, that it was impossible to find out whether a mortgaged loan was usurious. The mayor of Ensisheim, himself a Jew-baiter, wrote on Sept. 2, 1823, to the Prefect of Upper Rhine that it was wellnigh impossible to determine the volume of debts owed to Jews, that not much would be learned from the transcripts of mortgages. It would be necessary to delve also into the court-archives in order to familiarize oneself with the arbitration-transactions which entitle creditors to mortgage the debts owed them; in the registry-offices (*bureaux d'enregistrement*) there ought to be searched the daily purchases (*transcriptions*) because whenever a Jew bought a house he almost surely had already in mind a prospective purchaser of the house. In Dec. 1845, the Minister of Agriculture declared that the mortgages could not give the exact status of the village, since a large part of the loans was registered as a result of commercial and industrial transactions.[159]

2. A very large number of mortgaged-loans had already been repaid to the creditors by the debtors, but were not stricken off the mortgage books, and this enormously magnified the true volume of recorded debts to Jews. Attention was called to this in 1808 by the Prefects and mortgage-officers of nearly all Departments which sent in lists of mortgages in favor of Jews. The Prefects of the occupied regions wrote in the same vein.[160] The Jewish leader Furtado pointed out the same in 1806 and the Alsatian Jews — in 1818 and 1824 and on many other occasions.[161] This did not happen exclusively with debts to Jews. In 1840 there were in all France registered mortgages totaling 12 billion frs., inclusive of 500,000,000 frs. on those of wich the terms had run out. This came about simply because the debtor wanted to avoid an additional expense. Under the law the debtor had to pay for the striking off a mortgage of the books. In 1850 the fees for striking out a debt of 100 frs.

---

[159] AN,BB16-758(5288); "Ce serait ébranler les plus solides fondements de la société, que d'induire en pareille matière, la fraude de l'usure, par conjecture et par raisonnement, en droit la France ne se présume jamais. (Dolus non praesumitur.) En fait il faut en avoir la conviction intime, et cette conviction ne peut être que le résultat de preuves évidentes. La voix de la renommée ne saurait même être un guide fidèle; elle est trop souvent mensongère, elle est presque toujours l'écho de la mauvaise foi, et de la malveillance" (AN,F19-11008); "rien dans ces registres publics ne peut indiquer qu'une créance soit usuraire." (31, p. 15); AdHR,V108; "le relevé que l'on prendrait au bureau des hypothèques n'offriroit aucun résultat: il faudrait encore aller scruter dans les greffes des Justices de Paix, pour connaitre les transactions par conciliation qui leur donne droit d'hypothèques, et dans les bureaux d'Enregistrement, pour les ventes et reventes journalières qui ont lieu; car quand un juif acquiert un immeuble, il est presque sûr d'avoir déjà son nouvel acquéreur." (AdHR,V108); Wolowski, 292, p. 122.
[160] AN,F19-11007-8-9&1837.
[161] AN,F19-11005,11007; 31.

amounted to 18-15 frs. This was an enormous sum for a debtor-peasant. In March 1818, the Alsatian Jewish Consistories wrote to the Central Jewish Consistory that peasants deleted records of debts only when they had to get new loans. In 1823 the Jewish Consistory of the Lower Rhine wrote to the Attorney-General of Colmar that the mortgageors did not delete the mortgage records, because they knew that, under the law, after 10 years all unrenewed mortgages would automatically be stricken off the rolls. On July 2, 1808, the Prefect of Meurthe wrote to the Minister of the Interior that at the end of the year 1808 all mortages would be stricken off if uncancelled or unrenewed by the debtors or creditors. But the lists of mortgages in favor of Jews were drawn up shortly before that term, and as a matter of course, in the lists sent to Paris, there were included all the debts which had been paid up but the debtors had not stricken them out.[162] As already said, according to the notes to the sub-prefects report of 1808, there were in the arrondissement of Thionville mortgages to Jews in the amount of 1,657,415 frs. Of this 200,000 frs. were deducted for mortgages that had already been paid up, but the debtors had not the mortgages stricken off the rolls. (Moselle was the only Department in Northeastern France, where the Prefect had taken pains to present an objective report.) On Jan. 1, 1808, there were registered in the mortgage-office of Sarreguemines uncancelled mortgages (to Jews) amounting to 1,294,246.53 frs. and stricken off the rolls — totaling 486,073.34 frs. (see Table X).[163] In some mortgages folios not even 5% of the mortgages were stricken out. Only in the Strasbourg mortgage-office and in Lorraine were the numbers of cancelled mortgages high, because there were there numerous loans among merchants who strictly observed the formalities (see **Table XI**).

3. The Minister of the Interior's Circular of May 9, 1808, to the Prefects, concerning the drawing up of rosters of mortgages to Jews, explicitly ordered to list mortgages that were registered for adjudicated estates of peasants.[164] But at the time and in rosters of later years also mortgages of non-peasants were included. The Prefect of Moselle wrote so specifically to the Minister on July 25, 1808.[165] In Folio IV of the mortgage-office (June 20, 1799-June 23, 1800) of Lunéville we have found 39 mortgages to Jews,

---

[162]   292, p. 117; 202, p. 88-89; AN,F19-11007; "se contentent d'attendre que les dix années qui suivent l'inscription, éteignent l'hypothèque de droit" (ZS). "Nous sommes dans l'année à l'expiration de laquelle les premières inscriptions s'éteindront par le fait seul de leur non renouvellement. Beaucoup de créances appartenant à des Juifs ont été remboursées à l'aide d'autres emprunts, et les inscriptions prises par les Juifs, créanciers originaires, subsistent toujours sous leurs noms, mais au profit des nouveaux prêteurs." (AN,F19-11009).

[163]   AdM,V149; AN,F19-11009.   The same occured in later years.   In 1884, the Metz office of mortgages declared that the mortgages did not represent a true picture of the debts. The debts on simple I.O.U.s were not recorded there and in order to save expenses the paid up mortgages were not stircken off the records.   315, p. 184-85.   A. Hertzog noted in 1886 about one village in the Upper Rhine that the mortgage statistics were not reliable and they did not give an accurate picture of the peasants' indebtedness.   311, p. 111.

[164]   "...Le relevé des créances hypothécaires établies par les Juifs sur les propriétés rurales." AN,F19-11007.

[165]   AN,F19-11009.

only 21 of them from peasants-debtors. In the roster of mortgages to Jews forwarded to Paris in 1808, 23 of Folio IV were set down in favor of Jews in the amount of 42,329.78 frs. When the 1808 roster was compared by us with the original Folio IV, it was clearly seen that 5 mortgages to Jews in the amounts of 127 frs., 232.50 frs., 355.50 frs., 254.30 frs., and 1,666.67 frs. are from non-peasant mortgageors, and one mortgage for 1.987.25 frs. turns out to be a mortgage by a Jew to a Jew. In Folio 8 of Lunéville we found 52 mortgages to Jews, 23 of them from peasants: in the list of 1808, sent to Paris, 38 of the Folio are specified, but of this list mortgage No. 253 (11,200 frs.) is of a resident of Paris, the Nos. 257, 469 and 471 are from merchants, No. 378 — from a director of taxes, No. 546 from a beer-brewer, No. 596 from a man of means, No. 660 from a shoemaker, etc. In Folio 19 of Lunéville (Years XIII-XIV) we found 80 mortgages to Jews, 43 of them from peasants: in the roster of 1808, — 54 mortgages (78,555.07 frs.) were specified, but among these 54 mortgages appear the Nos. 73 and 659 from a saloon-keeper, No. 185 of a baker, No. 374 of an attorney, No. 472 from a merchant, No. 608 from the proprietor of a cabaret, No. 617 from a Paris cook. In Folio 21 (1806) we found 48 mortgages to Jews, 32 of them from peasants: in the roster of 1808 only 35 are mentioned, but of these No. 106 is from a controller of taxes, No. 162 from a leather-merchant, etc.[166] From the Neufchâteau (Vosges) mortgage-office there was sent in in 1806 a roster of 211 debts to Jews from peasants (270,820 frs.). In truth, at the Prefecture of the Department it was immediately admitted that a number of the debtors did not seem to be peasants, but likewise that according to the local authorities, they possessed also the qualifications of peasants (probably they owned land, too). After a thorough comparison of the roster with the original mortgages in Folios 1-13 of the 211 mortgages we found 93 (for 133,226.29 frs.) to be of debtors who are considered in the original Folios as merchants, attorneys, wives of officers, mill owners, saloon-keepers, manufacturers, shoemakers, cabinetmakers, printers, tailors, bakers, etc.[167] For instance, in the roster sent to Paris from the arrondissement of Epinal (Vosges) in 1806, there appears the creditor Michel Lazard with a loan of 2,980 frs. against the debtor J. B. Richard. In the mortgage Folio the debtor is termed a building-contractor.[168] In another part of France, in Narbonne, mortgages amounting to 52,000 frs. were recorded to Jews, but the Prefect explicitly wrote in 1808 that the sum was the result of a mortgage against a voucher of a business transaction and of a debt for a sold estate. From the mortgage-

[166] AN,F19-11009; HypLunéville.

[167] AN,F19-11011; HypNeufchâteau: vol. 1 (No. 142, 233, 317, 367, 539); vol. 3 (No. 614, 682); vol. 4 (No. 354, 519, 584); vol. 5 (No 79, 91, 241, 293, 463, 559, 573, 665); vol. 6 (No. 1, 83, 84, 188, 226, 386, 511, 593); vol. 7 (No. 515); vol. 8 (No. 163, 211, 245, 261, 263, 294, 447, 547, 564, 595); vol. 9 (No. 4, 262, 291, 474, 608); vol. 10 (No. 116, 225, 409, 442, 463, 567); vol. 11 (No. 8, 23, 31, 45, 48, 73, 92, 163, 186, 217, 293, 344, 391, 422, 506, 565); vol. 12 (No. 302, 313, 322, 358, 383, 410 422, 451, 520, 527, 539); vol. 13 (No. 3, 5, 52, 67, 72, 102, 126, 138, 191, 254, 267, 285, 371, 442, 463, 478, 479, 496).

[168] AN,F19-11011, HypEpinal, vol. 9, No. 306 (Feb. 1, 1806).

office of Vercil (occupied region of Sesia) a roster of 225 mortgages (352,823 frs.) to Jews was set down in 1808. But it was stated in the accompanying report that few of the mortgages are from plain peasants, most of them are mortgages obtained in commercial transactions."

4. Many of the mortgages are for large sums, enormous sums for that period. In such cases they represent loans granted by Jews not to peasants (who always sought only small loans), but loans to capitalists, large land-owners and men of industry. Cases of this sort should not have appeared in the rosters of mortgages to Jews sent in 1806 and 1808 to Paris. Herewith a few examples: On July 5, 1806, the Prefect of the Vosges forwarded to Paris a roster of mortgages "to Jews from peasants" of his Department, in the amount of 672,229 frs. An examination of the roster discloses the following cases: Samuel Alcan appears in the roster with a mortgage for 43,000 frs. from the Jew Abraham Alcan and two Gentiles of Paris and Nancy; Marx Ely of Nancy appears with two mortgages for 14,798 frs. from Demarets and other men of means. On the roster there are listed mortgages for as large sums as 18,000 frs., 10,725 frs., 16,500 frs., 12,000 frs., etc., about which there may be doubt whether such large loans were really made to peasants. About a number of debtors on the roster there are distinctly specified such professions as merchants, inn-keepers, etc. In the Metz transcript of mortgages to Jews (1,391,500 frs.) there are debtors for such high amounts as 47,184 frs., 106,000 frs., etc. The mortgage-office of Briey (Moselle) forwarded a roster of mortgages to Jews, totaling 599,250 frs. (besides cancelled mortgages for 118,354 frs.). There, too, one finds loans such as for 18,920 frs., 10,608 frs., etc. Among the mortgages to Jews on the roster sent in from the arrondissement of Lunéville (Meurthe) there appear borrowers with such debts as 54,300 frs., 11,200 frs., 16,150 frs., 14,500 frs., 10,236 frs., 39,240 frs., etc. From Upper Rhine, where efforts were made to have the Decree of 1808 renewed, a list of mortgages totaling 15,986,410 frs. in 1813-1823 was forwarded to the Government. In it is recorded a mortgage as follows: on Apr. 11, 1822, Javal Brothers, two well-known Jewish bankers of Paris, gave a loan of 112,000 frs. (an enormous sum at that time) to G. Schoen of Mulhouse who was a large-scale merchant and industrialist. But the mortgage appears in the roster of mortgages to Jews, no doubt just in order to swell the sum-total. Even though we have it from all sources that peasants took small loans, yet in the roster there are such sums as 17,000; 22,000; 24,000; 29,000; 19,048; 18,134; 11,895 frs., etc. The story was the same in other parts of France. In the arrondissement of Aix (Bouches-du-Rhône) there appear (in July 1808) among the mortgages to Jews for a total of 2,239,655 frs., 52 mortgages for sums ranging from 4,000 to 200,000 frs. (in a total of 1,222,318 frs.): 2 mortgages are for 200,000 frs. each, 3 range from 50,000 to 94,000 frs. and 47 range from 4,000 to 40,000 frs. each)."

[169] AN,F19-11008&1837.
[170] AN,F19-11008-09&11011;AdHR,V109-10; HypLunéville, vol. 6, No. 581;

5. In March 1808 the Alsatian Consistories called attention to the fact that from the rosters of mortgages to Jews there should also be eliminated the mortgages to Jews possessing licenses: Article 11 of the Decree of March 1808 speaks explicitly of Jews without licenses.[171]

6. The Prefect of Gard pointed out that many debts to Jews had already been partly repaid, but the total debts were still carried on record in the mortgages. The following are a few similar examples from Moselle: the Jewish creditor Isaac Deitz stated that he held mortgages on Gentiles to the amount of 4,862.70 frs., but had already received payment of 299.50 frs., on account; Garçon [Jr.?] Isaac held 12 mortgages totaling 7,555.13 frs., but on these he had already been paid 1,469 frs.; Samuel Isaac held 10 mortgages for 5,422 frs. on which he had been paid 813 frs.[172]

7. The same mortgage was very often registered in several or even all arrondissements of a Department and the grand total of mortgages became larger in the number of items. Furtado had stressed this in 1806 in a memorandum submitted to the Minister of the Interior. The Prefect of Meurthe, where 3,277,931 frs. was as the total of mortgages to Jews, wrote that one of the reasons of this excessive total was that the juridical mortgages were recorded as adjudicated in all mortgage-offices for the total amount in each. The Prefect of Alpes-Maritimes wrote similarly how out of a total 220,780 frs. of mortgages to Jews there were fictitious mortgages amounting to 77,591 frs., because recorded in more than one arrondissement. In Nice and the arrondissement of Nice a 700 fr. mortgage to a Jew was recorded twice. In 1824 the Jewish Consistory of Upper Rhine wrote that in case of estates mortgaged by the debtor in several arrondissements the creditor will take mortgages for the full amount of the debt in each arrondissement. The following are several concrete cases from the mortgage-offices of Lower Rhine. In the year V the same mortgages for 280 frs. are recorded to Benjamin Bernheim from a non-Jewish debtor in the mortgage-office of Bouxviller (Nos. 12 and 13) and of Brumath (No. 2). A mortgage for 7,800 frs. to the Jew Jacob Löwel by a Jewish debtor in the Year IV is recorded in the office of Saverne (Nos. 174, 175, 176) and of Brumath (Nos. 130, 131, 132, 133). In all France there were, in 1840, mortgages recorded for 12 billion frs., but of these 500,000 frs. were for recordings of the same mortgages in more than one office.[173]

8. Frequently security-mortgages were also taken out in the name of wives of the borrowers and also of other relatives. Attention had already been called to this from the occupied Department of

---

vol. 8, No 253; vol. 9, No 175; vol. 10, No 325; vol. 16, No 286; vol. 18, No 490; vol. 24, No 585.
    [171]   AN,F19-11007.
    [172]   AN,F19-11008-09.   The Department of Gard reported mortgages for 870,667 frs. held by Jews.
    [173]   AN,F19-1837,11005,11007&11009;   HypBouxwiller &   Brumath;   31;   292, p. 117.

Stura (921,856 frs. mortgages to Jews); the Alsatian Jews, too, called attention to this in March 1818. The following is a concrete example: in 1810 there was recorded a mortgage of a Gentile woman to a Jewish creditor, but this was merely a fictitious mortgage, a security mortgage, the real debtor was her husband, and when they divorced, it became necessary, in dividing the estate, also to strike out the fictitious mortgage standing in the wife's name.[174]

9. Because the debtors did not strike out the mortgages — the Alsatian Jews wrote in 1818 — the practice is that buyers of houses take security-mortgages for various other properties of the sellers. The same is repeated by the Jewish Consistory of the Upper Rhine in its memorandum of 1824.[175]

10. The same memorandum pointed out that in cases where the creditors held only a special mortgage on a part of the debtor's properties, he sought a court-permit to register a general mortgage on all the properties of the debtor. In such a case he did not strike out the particular mortgage.[176]

11. The same memorandum likewise pointed out that if the creditor sold a mortgaged loan, the purchaser should take a mortgage from the seller and his original borrower. This was also affirmed in 1824 by the anti-Jewish pamphleteer Betting de Lancastel.[177]

12. Furthermore, the memorandum related that in the case of a group of creditors where the court would decide in which order they were to be paid (*collocation*) or would delegate another creditor (*délégation*), each of the creditors or representatives would register a mortgage in his own name, even if there already existed a general mortgage.[178]

13. The same memorandum pointed out that in case of several debtors and vouchers appearing on one document; mortgages were taken from each of them. Even earlier (June 21, 1808) the sub-prefect of Thionville wrote that owing to this practice the same amount was often registered three times. The same was affirmed by Betting de Lancastel in 1824.[179]

14. In order not to forget and particularly not to lose the right to interest, the creditor frequently renewed the mortgage a few years before the expiration of the legal 10 years and thus the mortgage appears duplicated for a time. From the occupied Department of Rhine-and-Moselle a roster of 1,439 mortgages (for 1,315,204 frs.), to Jews was sent in in 1808. The accompanying report related that in 1806 the old mortgages were hastily renewed, although there still remained several years before the striking out of the first mortgages which would not have been renewed. For this reason nearly all mortgages to Jews on the left bank of the Rhine

[174] AN,F19-1837,11007&BB16-631(666).
[175] AN,F19-11007; 31.
[176] 31.
[177] 80.
[178] 31.
[179] AN,F19-11009; 80, p. 89.

were recorded twice, as clearly shown by their dates, and, accordingly, the sum-total must be reduced to 657,602 frs.[1]

15. In transferring a mortgage-secured debt to a new creditor, the latter takes a new mortgage, but the old one is not cancelled by the debtor (as he should), and thus there are two mortgages on record.[2]

16. A purchaser of an estate (which had been mortgaged) does not cancel the mortgages recorded against the estate.[3]

17. The Prefect of Gard pointed out that in the rosters of mortgages the principals as well as the interest were included in the figures.[4]

18. The Consistory of the Lower Rhine wrote in 1823 to the district-attorney of the Colmar Court that the majority of debts to Jews were for sold houses for which the buyers did not pay up all the money by single payment. The houses were sold on the instalment plan to pay up in from 5 to 6 or 8 years. The total price remained recorded in the mortgage records until the entire indebtness was wiped out, i .e. the actual value of such a mortgage was by far smaller than the sum recorded.[5]

19. In the mortgage-offices, when drawing up the lists of mortgages to Jews, it was not always possible to be guided by the creditors' names. In 1808 it was reported from the Alpes-Maritimes that the lists had been drawn up insofar as Jewish names could be identified. The Alsatian Jews pointed out in 1808 that Protestants bore the same names as Jews and Protestant creditors might have been counted in as Jews.[6]

20. Later on we shall see that many mortgages were from Jews to Jews. But also these mortgages were included in drawing up the lists. In 1808 this was pointed out by the Prefect of the Alpes-Maritimes and the mortgage-office of Marseille. From Folio 4 of the Lunéville mortgage-office (1799-1800) 23 mortgages were set down in favor of Jews on the list forwarded to Paris in 1808. On the roster there appears even a mortgage of 1,987.25 frs. of a Jew to a Jew. In the list from Folio 19 there is a mortgage No. 752 which is from a Jew to a Jew. In the roster of mortgages to Jews in Upper Rhine for the years 1813-1823, which was drawn up in 1823, the following names appeared among the debtors: Emanuel Lévy, Simon Lévy, Joseph Meyer, Joseph Singer, Xavier Meyer, George Meyer, Nicolas Bloch, Salome Meyer, Bernheim, Bloch, Netter, Gross, Meyer, Fuchs, Schneider, Gerspach, Kauffmann, Wormser, Fischmann, Blum, Lang, Hirtz, Buchman, Fessler, Vogel, Klein, Franck, Mooss, Singer, Strudel, Lang, Bloch,

[1] AdHR,V108; AN,F19-1838.
[2] 31.
[3] 31.
[4] AN,F19-11008.
[5] "On y remontre plus souvent les ventes d'immeubles, quand les acquéreurs n'en payent pas entièrement les prix d'achat. Les ventes des biens par lots à 5-6 jusqu'à 8 années de termes y sont portées également & subsistent en entier tandis que plus ou moins de termes sont déjà acquittés" (ZS).
[6] AN,F19-1837&11007.

Werth and many others which are without any doubt Jewish
names. These debts, too, were included in order to swell the indebtedness to Jews. If one should search it is possible to find information concerning every one of the debtors. Let us take one
illustration: in 1813 there appeared a debtor Joseph Lazarus of
Altkirch with two debts to the creditor Jacques Wolf. Joseph
Lazarus was a well-known Jewish businessman, his name is
constantly met with on the list of tax-payers of the Jewish Consistory.[146]

21. Some mortgages were recorded merely as a formality,
as a security for the future. Here is such a case: on Dec. 31, 1804,
the judge of the canton of Soultz rendered a verdict in favor of
the Jewish merchant Elie Marx of Wissembourg against the peasant
Fr. Reiland of Oberssebach on the case of a debt of 100 frs., of
which 32 frs. principal, 9 frs. interest, and the balance judicial
and other costs. The mortgage was recorded on March 3, 1808,
with the proviso that the verdict could not be executed as long as
the Decree of May 30, 1806, would be in force.[147]

22. In comparing the lists of mortgages to Jews sent in 1806-
1808 to Paris with the original mortgage Folios it is as a rule
difficult to grasp which was the (reliable) principle guiding the
mortgage-officers in making up the rosters. More likely they had
no principle and the rosters were indeed unreliable. From Folio 10
(Year XI) of the Lunéville mortgage-office 31 mortgages from Jews
were enumerated on the list: we have found in that Folio 54 mortgages to Jews, 35 of these from peasants. Even in Metz where
they strove to be careful in making the lists they could not find
the modus operandi in making up the lists: 28 mortgages are
credited to Jews in the transcript from Folio 2 of the arrondissement
of Metz; we found in that Folio 46 mortgages to Jews, of which
11 were from peasants. Among these 11 we found 5 mortgages
from peasants who do not appear in the list which had been
forwarded to Paris. On the other hand there were set down
10 mortgages (for 55,127.50 frs.) which were distinctly from merchants, army-officers, men of industry and other non-peasants, and
even the mortgage No. 454 (for 47,187.70 frs.) of a Jewish creditor
from the Jewish debtor Jacob Goudchaux. On the roster sent
to Paris 26 mortgages to Jews are recorded from Folio 7; in that
Folio we found 78, among them 52 that were not mentioned
in the roster for Paris, and 18 of these 52 are from peasants. On
the other hand, among the 26 mortgages are enumerated 16 mortgages to Jews (22,920.90 frs.) which are not from peasants, 7 of them
from merchants, and the occupations of 9 are not mentioned at
all. From the Folios 31-32, 34 mortgages are enumerated on the
Paris roster; we found 97 mortgages in the 2 Folios, but in the
roster sent to Paris, also 23 mortgages are enumerated (18,725.47 frs.)
which are explicitly from non-peasants, while 16 of the 27 mort-

[146] AN,F19-11007-8-9; HypLunéville, vol. 4; AdHR,V109-110;ArchCC,10.
[147] HypWissembourg, vol. 37, No. 477.

958

gages to Jews (which we have found but they do not appear in the list) are indeed from peasants (see Table XII). Apparently some mortgages even from peasants were deemed positively non-usurious and, therefore, were not incorporated in the lists for Paris, or the lists were made up in no serious manner whatever."'

23. The mortgage-lists which were drawn up in 1806-1808 and in later years concerned exclusively mortgages in favor of Jewish creditors. In no single case was such a list accompanied by a roster of a report on mortgages in favor of non-Jews. Hence it was impossible to know how large in reality was "the Jewish usury", whether by combatting "Jewish usury" the problem would already have been solved. And nobody in general had asked himself the question.

The Jews argued that the amount of debts to Jews was exaggerated in the transcripts from the mortgages. The Jews even submitted corrected rosters which had been compiled on the basis of individual declarations of every Jewish creditor. Under date of July 20, 1808, the Jewish Consistory of Metz had such individual declarations printed which were filled out by all Jews. In the declaration every Jew named the sum of land-secured mortgages he held and stated that any sum exceeding that given in his declaration was not recognized by him. In 1808 a revised list of mortgages to Jews (for 1,657,405 frs.) was submitted from the Moselle Department, the Jews protested and asserted that they held mortgages in favor of Jews of Metz only in the amount of 778,194 frs. and for 70,045 frs. in favor of Jews of other parts of Moselle. For the arrondissement of Sarreguemines the Jews rejected the sum of 849,839 frs. and acknowledged mortgages for only 337,200 frs. In a declaration of Oct. 20, 1808, signed by Rabbi Salomon Samuel, the Jews of the Lower Rhine acknowledged only debts of 3,779,773 frs. thereof 2,988,792 frs. for monetary loans and 790,981 frs. for commercial transactions (see Table XIII). In 1807 the Jewish Consistory of the Upper Rhine ascertained that all in all the Jews of the Upper Rhine held mortgages for only 5,100,809 frs., together with the debts in this Department in favor of Jews in other regions 5,673,209 frs., but 2 years later the Consistory wrote that one-half of the debts were for debts resulting from commercial transactions and 25 per cent of these loans had already been lost prior to the Decree of 1808, because the debts could in no way be collected from the borrowers."'

Many present-day historians have espoused without any modification this method of citing only the mortgages to Jews and thereby justifying Napoleon's anti-Jewish Decrees and "understanding" the Alsatian anti-Semitism. Let us take one illustration: the historian Fernand L'Huillier cursorily perused a few mortgage-folios in the arrondissement of Saverne (Lower Rhine) for the Years VII-VIII and wrote in 1947 that the majority of mortgages

AN,F19-11009; HypLunéville & HypMetz.
AN,F19-11009;ArchCC9 (a letter dated Apr. 17, 1810). See p. 111. The individual declarations of the Lower Rhine Jews were destroyed.

were to Jews and hence the rise of Alsatian anti-Semitism was normal. How many mortgages and for what amounts they were given to Jews as compared with non-Jews, that the author does not state. Per contra he merely gives a list of Jewish creditors. But our analysis of the mortgages in that same arrondissement distinctly proves that only a small percentage of mortgages were registered to Jews (see Tables I and II). Exactly the same pseudo-scientific methods are applied by the Marxist historian Leuilliot and even by his teacher, the great historian Mathiez.[190] But as for writing about Jews in Northeastern France anything may be expected on the part of the historians, even the most fantastic falsifications. Here is such a case: the historian André Gain analyzed a list of creditors of Emigrés from Lower Rhin during the Revolution, whose properties had been nationalized. On the basis of this document Gain wrote that "almost always when the principal of a debt was floated with interest, it turns out that the creditors are Aarons, Lévys, or Séligmanns of Strasbourg," in other words Jewish creditors. But in the document which Gain describes there is set down only one general total which is due to the creditor. The roster comprises 819 debts and not even in one single case is it possible to say how much of the amount is principal and how much is interest. Only 58 out of the 819 debts are to Jewish creditors and, at that, not those for large amounts.[191] What other conclusion can be drawn save that the historian André Gain had falsified in his analysis of a document.

In 1901-1902 the historian Ph. Sagnac wrote that we know the total of mortgages to Jews only from administrative reports. They ought to be compared with the original mortgage-folios and that would be a long and delicate task, perhaps no longer possible to perform.[192] From the few illustrations we have already given, it is clear that the rosters of mortgages to Jews were put together in 1806-1823 without any system whatever, with a malicious intention to exaggerate the volume of mortgages to Jews. In the next chapter we shall relate our attempt to analyze the mortgage-folios.

---

[190]   401, p. 519-20; 54; 108.
[191]   "Liquidation des dettes d'émigrés" (AdBR,Q; Gain, 445, vol. II, p. 265). During world war II, Gain became an open partisan of the German racist ideas and was nominated by the Pétain Government as rector of a large University.
[192]   59, p. 477.

MORT EPOUVANTABLE D'UN AVARE

An anti-usury Image of Metz, 1840
(Bibliothèque Nationale, Paris.)

XIII. AN ANALYSIS OF THE MORTGAGES

In 1949-50 the author carried on a survey of the mortgages in both Departments of Alsace, Moselle, Meurthe-and-Moselle and Vosges. (See Tables I-XIV). The following conclusions were arrived at on the basis of that survey.

1. First and foremost, in his survey the author had to take into account the fact that a large number of registry-folios in the mortgage-archives of Northeastern France had already been lost or destroyed.[193] The number of registry-folios is so large (in Lower Rhine alone there are approximately 2,000 volumes, in the series *Inscriptions* alone), that the author had to limit himself to examining only a selection from the registry-folios. The survey comprises 107 registry-folios of the series *Inscriptions*; vith 62,149 mortgages and a smaller selection from other register-series. At all events it is by far the largest number of mortgages ever analyzed in this part of France not only in connection with the Jewish phase of mortgages but *per se* as well. In rare cases the mortgage-registers mention that the mortgagee is a Jew (*Juif*).[194] In his survey the author bore in mind the characteristic Jewish names of that section of France and compared them with the Jewish inhabitants of records of that period. In a small number of uncertain cases Jewish-sounding names were counted as Jewish. In selecting the registry-folios for the survey the author took several volumes from each arrondissement and from different periods. Unfortunately most of the mortgage-archives of the Upper Rhine were no longer in existence. In this Department there have been preserved only the registers of the Colmar arrondissement beginning with the 1850's, and of the Belfort arrondissement beginning with the 1830's.[195] The author cannot be suspected of having picked

---

[193] For the Lower Rhine we found the mortgage registries of the arrondissements of Strasbourg, Saverne, and Wissembourg; for Sélestat only the registries of a later period. For Sélestat we utilized the registries of fees for registration, but they, too, belong to a later period. For the Upper Rhine we found registries of Colmar and Belfort only— all of a later period. The mortgage archives are much more complete in the Departments of Moselle, Meurthe, and Vosges. The Departmental position of the arrondissements in the Departments of Moselle and Meurthe were arranged according to their former location. In Meuse the mortgage archives had been lost. Under the law, copies of mortgage registries were to be sent to a central location for security. But in 1951 we could not locate them. In some cases several mortgages are registered under the same number. For this reason, the number of mortgages in our tables sometimes exceeds the current enumeration in the original mortgage-registers. The number of mortgages of indeterminate amounts are cited in parenthesis. They are also included in the general number of mortgages of each volume. See notes 195, 196, 212, 215.
[194] HypWissembourg, I n s c r i p t i o n s , vol. 77, No. 115, 224; HypSaverne, vol. 117; HypNancy, vol. 19, No. 203, 418.
[195] In 1939, a number of mortgage registers were evacuated to Altkirch, from there to Huningue, where the author saw them in a half decayed condition in the cellar of the law court. It was impossible to handle them in that state. They were mainly t r a n s c r i p t i o n registers from Mulhouse.

particular registers with fewer mortgages to Jews, because in the arrondissements where he noticed a large number of mortgages to Jews (Saverne, Sarreguemines), he analyzed a larger number of folios than for other regions. About this survey many of the forewarnings may be reiterated which we already made in the preceding chapter about the reliability of the rosters of mortgages to Jews which had been sent in to the Government in 1806-1823. However, in our analysis the object is not so much to find out the number of mortgages and the size of the sums, or the state of credit in general.[196] We sought chiefly to ascertain the percentage of mortgages to Jewish creditors, whether the assertion that the largest part of debts was to Jewish creditors was correct, and prior to our study, nobody had tried to do that.

2. The number of mortgages to Jewish creditors was quite large, considering that the Jews constitued a small minority of the population (in Alsace-2.64% in 1871), but in this case one must not take into consideration the absolute number of Jews, but rather the much higher percentage the Jews constituted in buying and selling land, cows and horses, in countryside commerce in general, — all that had to do with village credit. At any rate it turns out that the administration's allegations during he First Empire, and later, as well as those of modern historians, to the effect that the majority of morgages were recorded as granted to Jewish creditors are untrue. From Table I one can see that out of 62,149 mortgages of a certain type that we scrutinized (*Inscriptions*) only 9,125 (a little under 14.7%) are to Jewish mortgagees; 339 are to Gentile mortgagees from Jewish mortgagors; 52,371 are to non-Jewish mortgagees from Gentile mortgagors; 314 to Jewish mortgagees from Jewish mortgagors. The picture becomes still more striking when the amounts are examined. The 62,149 mortgages total 115,543,561 frs., but the Jews are not credited with mortgages for 14.7% of this amount, but with 7,395,563 francs which is only 6.4%. For the Lower Rhine we have examined 20,512 mortgages amounting to 34,192,543 francs, of these only 3,877 totaling 2,991,305 francs were to Jewish creditors from Gentiles.

3. In the period from 1799 to approximately 1805, a great number of mortgages were registered to the Government for sold nationalized properties (*Biens nationaux*), for non-payment of taxes, fines, etc. In the Folios 2-8 of Sarreguemines, 698 out of approximately 6,000 mortgages are credited to the Government; in Folio 7 of Metz, 138 out of 748; in Folio 6 of Thionville, 108 out of 791. Hence, for these years it turns out that the percentage of Jews among the private creditors was somewhat higher. But that was

---

[196] The best preserved series of mortgage registers are the mortgagors' indexes (R é p e r t o i r e   d e s   f o r m a l i t é s   h y p o t h é c a i r e s), with mortgagors' names, dates, sums and the nature of the mortgages (juridical, for sales, etc.), dates of repayment, cancellations, etc. This series of registers is an excellent source for the study of credit conditions. However, we could not make use of this series because the mortgagees' names are not given. whether there ever existed registers containing mortgagees' indexes, we do not know; probably not. The mortgagors' indexes were necessary in order to learn the mortgagors' status.

so only during the first years. The sums in the mortgages to the Goverment are as a rule very small.

4. In the regions close to the Departmental Capitals (Strasbourg, Colmar, Metz, Nancy) the percentage of debts to Jews is lower than in the smaller centers.

5. In the early mortgage-folios, a large percentage of mortgages is recorded on the basis of documents antedating 1789, even on the basis of documents of the early XVth Century. In Folio I of Saverne 51 of the 741 mortgages are based on acts prior to 1789; in Folio X of Saverne, most of the 808 mortgages, some from the years 1446, 1469, 1523, 1597, 1619, etc.; in Folio IV of Bouxwiller such are 263 of the 432 mortgages. This is characteristic mainly of both. parts of Alsace, but is a much rarer phenomenon in Moselle, Meurthe and the Vosges. An attempt to analyze this curious circumstance would take us too far astray from our subject. There can be no doubt that we are dealing with the heritage of *rentes* from before 1789. The Revolution of 1789 abolished the feudal *rentes*, but other *rentes* remained in force (*rentes rachetables*) and this left room for all sorts of complications. A large number of such *rentes* was exchanged for mortgage-secured debts, and that, in our opinion, is the origin of most mortgages based on acts previous to 1789. In a large proportion of such mortgages it is expressly stated that they are recorded on the basis of documents which had constitued *rentes*. Parenthetically, this is one more definite proof that until 1789 the peasants had owned no land. But for our theme it is particularly important that, with numerically rare exceptions, the mortgages to Jewish creditors from Gentile debtors are based on notarial and other acts subsequent to 1789. The majority of former debts were paid up by the Gentile debtors to their Jewish creditors in the early years of the Revolution, usually in paper money (*assignats*). The mortgages from the year VII onward are nearly all for fresh loans contracted after 1789, their largest part in order to enable the peasants to purchase nationalized properties, communal lands and land-parcels of private owners. Administrative reports, the Jews themselves, as well as most historians, do indeed state that peasants borrowed from Jews in order to be able to purchase parcels of land. The Revolution and the First Empire fought the concentration of land in the hands of great magnates, and were in favor of the individualistic movement in agriculture, the peasant's urge to possess a piece of land of his own. However, the Revolution and the First Empire did not give the peasant the financial resources for it; the peasant had to find a loan himself. In Norteastern France he found a loan most easily through the Jewish creditor. By no means all administrations, chroniclers and historians were pleased with the role of the Jews, but that is another matter."

¹⁷⁷ "Le cultivateur, qui a beaucoup de paiements à faire, parce que dans le cours de la Révolution, il a fait beaucoup d'acquisitions, ou qui est poursuivi par le percepteur des contributions, est forcé de recourir à l'emprunt" (AdBR, 3M3, a letter of the Prefect, year X); "Les Juifs distribuaient à loca-

6. A very large percentage of mortgages in Alsace is registered in favor of Catholic and Protestant ecclesiastical institutions as well as of clergymen privately. Nearly all debtors of this sort are peasants. In Folio 19 of the Wissembourg mortgage-office (1804) there are mortgages Nos. 45-49 and 54-55 recorded in favor of the Catholic Church of Billigheim; the Nos. 162-195, 197-199, 210-242 and 318-319 to the Church of Hayna; the Nos. 255-258, 365, 390-394, 413, 505-507, 534-535, 548-550, 597, 699-701 to the Wissembourg Catholic Church of St. Jean; the Nos. 384-387 to the Catholic Church of Schweigen; the Nos. 588-589 to the Church of St. Jacques of Rüdselz; the Nos. 439-444, 458, 462-466, 473-485 to the Church of Schleichal. In Folio 20 of the same mortgage-office (1804) the mortgages Nos. 238-264 are recorded to the Catholic Church of Rohrbach; the mortgages Nos. 441-458, 463-468 to the Church of Schlüthal and approximately 100 more mortgages to other various ecclesiastical institutions. In Folio 37 (1808) of the same mortgage-office the Nos. 613-623 are to an ecclesiastical institution of Herxheim. In Folio 48 (1810-1811) of the same mortgage-office the Nos. 96-107, 109-114, 123-128, 140-143 are to the Catholic Churches of Rohrbach and Wissembourg. In Folio 77 (1819) five priests are creditors, two on court-mortgages. In Folio 193 (1849) of the same mortgage-office the mortgages Nos. 24-25, 122, 164, 190, 207, 237, 253 and many others, are to the Catholic Churches of Nieder-betschdorf, Sourbourg, Wissembourg, Slundweiller and Hegeney. In Folio 26 of the Saverne mortgage-office (1809) the Nos. 67-184 are to the Protestant Church of Ingwiller. In Folio 128 (1819) of the Strasbourg mortgage-office the Nos. 231-241, 243-244, 281-296, 328-334, — to the Catholic Church of Wantzenau. On December 23, 1851, in the Colmar mortgage-office (Folio 625, Nos. 129-153), there were recorded 25 mortgages to ecclesiastical institutions of Wiedens-hollen. (Exactly in the same way many mortgages are recorded to secular institutions formerly of ecclesiastical origin. In Folio 3 of the Strasbourg mortgage-office the Nos. 139-189 — to the Foundation of St. Thomas of Strasbourg, and in Folio 128 the Nos. 41-57, 264-266, 374-383, 436-443, 463-472, 498-508, 561-567, 573-576, 585-587, 609-617, 659-675 are recorded to the same institution.) It will be no exaggeration to assert that in Alsace there were recorded to ecclesiastical institutions no fewer mortgages than to Jewish creditors. Our object is not to pass judgment but merely to establish a fact which deserves to be explored a bit more thoroughly. For the benefit of those who will want to pass judgment, we shall merely observe that the Jews were individual creditors and not

---

tion leurs nouveaux domaines à de pauvres laboureurs" (AN,AFIV300-2150); L'Huillier, 401, p. 520-51; Fauchille, 36, p. 8-9; Anchel, 16, p. 121-22; Lemoine, 48, p. 38; Lambla, 398, p. 190; Halphen, 104, p. 325; Anchel, 70, p. 500; Szyster, 15, p. 129; Spaer, 60, p. 53-4; Baumont, 376, p. 468; Léfébure, 334, p. 9; Hoffmann, 392, vol. I, p. 183.

A 1790 report of the Strasbourg Friends of the Constitution (4) related that in Sundgau (Upper Alsace, where there were pogroms against the Jews in 1789), the peasants have much confidence in their priests to whom they confess, who often drink with the peasants and offer them resources enabling their children to begin a life of their own. Are we to understand that the priests rented land to peasants or that they gave them monetary loans in order to enable young people to get married?

an organized Jewish body, whereas the Church-institutions as creditors were indeed organized religious bodies. A few remarks are in order about this kind of mortgages. In many cases the principal as well as the interest is given in the Folios. A large number of mortgages of this type is recorded on the basis of documents antedating 1789. Alsatian clergymen I talked with about mortgages of this kind, strove to show me that these are mortgages for contributions to Church institutions, pledges which the donors could not pay up at once, and were, accordingly, mortgaged. This is not so. Of the 1,556 mortgages recorded in the receipt-book (*recettes*), vol. 85 of the Sélestat mortgage-office in 1851-1852 (see Table VIII), ninety-three are to Catholic and Protestant church institutions. Of the ninety-three mortgages, two represent sales (*vente*), one is a court-mortgage, only one is on a donation basis, and all others are mortgaged obligations.[188]

7. The mortgages to Jewish creditors from Gentile borrowers are for sums smaller than the mortgages to non-Jews from non-Jews. Examination of the 62,149 mortgages (in the series *Inscriptions*) has shown (see Table I), that every mortgage to non-Jews from non-Jews averages 231 francs and every mortgage to a Jew from a Gentile is only 81 francs on the average. Mortgages for large amounts to Jews are quite rare, particularly from peasants. In the Folios 31-32 of the Metz arrondissement there are 23 mortgages from Gentiles to Gentiles for 10,000 francs and over, and not a single one for such an amount from Gentiles to Jews. Of the 97 mortgages to Jews from Gentiles in those two Folios, three are for 51-100 frs., thirty for 101-250 frs., forty-eight for 251-1,000 frs., eight for 1,001-2,000 frs., six for 2,001-3,000 frs., and two for 3,001 frs. or more. In Folio 267 of the Thionville arrondissement there are eighteen mortgages from Gentiles to Gentiles, for 3,001 frs. and over, and not a single one from Gentiles to Jews for such a sum. If a large mortgage turns up, it is from a banker or large-scale industrialist. In Folio 1 (years IV-VII) of Wasselone only twenty-two out of 319 mortgages are to Jews, one is to Daniel Lévy for 72,500 frs., but the borrower was the well-known banker Jean Dietrich. This conclusion accords with data from other documents. In 1808 the Jews of Moselle declared that actually they held mortgage-secured loans for 848,239.70 frs. The number of Jewish creditors of Moselle was only 103. Of these, forty-seven had given loans of less than 3,000 frs. (all the debts to the creditors). Only three granted loans for 50,000 frs. and over.[189] The Departmental Archives of the Vosges contain a summary of the mortgage-secured debts to Jews on the basis of the creditors' names (1808); the number of Jewish creditors of Vosges and the adjacent Departments, even of Paris, reaches 108 and the sum of mortgage-secured loans,

---

[188] We found only a few cases of Jewish loans to Christian clergymen. Such a case is to be found in the year XII in the arrondissement of Vic where Etienne Bonneval, priest of Blanche-Eglise, was a mortgagor for 555 frs. to the Jew Lazard Lévy (HypVic, vol. 5, No. 697).

[189] AN,F19-11009.

667,909.93 frs.; forty of the creditors are listed for mortgages under 1,000 francs. Many inferences can be drawn from these facts, among them the conclusion already arrived in mid-nineteenth Century by the historian I. Bédarride, that since the wealth of many Alsatian Jews consists of mortgage-secured debts, a Jew's property is much smaller than that of a non-Jew.[200] For us the conclusion is particularly important that as a rule the mortgage-secured debts of peasants were for purchases of small parcels of land, cows, horses and small loans, — hence the small sums of mortgages to Jews. As a matter of fact, this is in keeping with the general picture of mortgages in the entire country. In 1841 there were registered 329,576 mortgages for 491,575,820 frs. in all France; 155,220 of these mortgages (36,640,928 frs.) for sums under 400 frs.; 89,803 (62,421,262 frs.) at 400-1,000 frs., and 84,553 (392,513,625 frs.) over 1,000 frs. each. A preponderant part of the mortgages was through sale of real estate for which the purchasers did not pay on the spot.[201]

8. A small percentage of Jews were creditors. In Folio I of the mortgage-office of Saverne the mortgages to Jews were as a rule to the heirs of Lehman Hirtzel of Bouxwiller; most of the mortgages to Jews in Folio 11 of Saverne are to Daniel Lévy of Strasbourg and the two partners Schmulen Elias and Cochel Simon of Saverne; the bulk of mortgages to Jews in Folio 19 of Nancy are to Lazard Michel; most of the mortgages to Jews in Folio 100 of Lunéville are to Alexandre and Godchaux Gompert. This is in accord with the lists of Jewish creditors which had been sent in in 1806 and 1808. The number of Jews who were engaged in granting loans to peasants, in selling them land, cows and merchandise on credit was by far greater, but the majority of these Jews were poor middlemen for a small number of wealthy Jewish money-lenders, as stated in an anti-Jewish yearbook of Upper Rhine in 1846.[202]

9. The fact cannot be denied that most mortgages to Jews were from peasants (see Tables I-III). Of 9,125 mortgages for 7,395,563 frs., to Jews from Gentiles, 4,300 (for 3,116,469 frs.) were from peasants; 2,702 (for 2,525,761 frs.) were from non-peasants; in the mortgage-books there are no precise data concerning the occupations of the debtors in 2,123 mortgage-secured loans of 1,753,332 frs., but it may be supposed that a part of them were peasants. In Moselle, where there were no anti-Jewish pogroms, the proportion of mortgages to Jews from peasants was higher than in Alsace. A more thorough comparison of mortgages to Jews from peasants and those to Gentiles from peasants (see Table III) shows that the ratio of mortgages from peasants to Jewish creditors is larger than to non-Jews. This is natural in view of the Jewish business dealings with the peasants. Nevertheless the number of

---

[200]   158, p. 397.
[201]   336, p. 113-17; 427, p. 381; 446, p. 395.
[202]   371, 1846.

mortgages to non-Jews from peasants was quite considerable, particularly in later years.

10. In some folios more mortgages are recorded to Gentiles from Jews than the other way around (Saverne, Vols. 26, 113; Wissembourg, Vol. 186; Sélestat, Vol. 217; Colmar, Vols. 621-628; Belfort, Vol. 86; Sarreguemines, Vols. 155, 174; Lunéville, Vol. 50; Vic, Vol. 10; see Table I). In Folio 5 of Saverne, out of 725 mortgages 295 are recorded to Jews from Gentiles (327,093 frs. out of 1,788,032 frs.). A large number of these 295 mortgages are to the Jewish partners Léon Auscher and Henri Halff, but they, in turn, were at the same time debtors to a Gentile for a very large sum.

11. Our analysis shows what we already have said several times, that only a part of mortgages to Jews was for money-loans. Most mortgages were on sales of real estate, cattle, horses and merchandise on credit. Of 3,453 mortgages in the arrondissement of Sélestat in 1846-1847 and 1851-1852, which we have investigated (see Table VIII), 1,435 were recorded on the basis of *obligations*, 3,123 to Gentiles, 120 to Jews and the balance to Jews from Jews; 790 mortgages were recorded on the basis of court decisions; 824 mortgages were recorded as results of sales, among these 160 to Jews from non-Jews; 286 mortgages were recorded as a result of auction-sales, none of them from Gentiles (in former years the role of Jews in auctions was, indeed, large); the remaining mortgages were for *donations,* will cases, marriage contracts, etc. Since it must be assumed that some of the court-mortgages, too, were for sales, it is clear that the majority of mortgages were not recorded as a result of monetary-loans. As a matter of fact the official reports had arrived at the same conclusions even before this. Of the ninety-four mortgages (for 1,546,756.69 frs.) to Jews in the arrondissement of Toul (Meurthe) thirty-four (for 1,007,285.75 frs.) were based on notary obligations, fifty-seven (for 516,284.37 frs.) were court-mortgages and three (for 23,186.54 frs.) for houses sold. Of the 701 mortgages (778,558.16 frs.) to Jews in the arrondissement of Vic 429 (for 412,278 frs.) were for *obligations*, 129 (165,765.20 frs.) through court and 153 (for 200,514.48 frs.) for houses sold.[111]

12. One of the strongest anti-Jewish slogans was that the majority of compulsory surrenders of real estate for non-payment of debts were to Jewish creditors. The large number of litigations between Jews and Gentiles in the courts of Northeastern France cannot be denied. Of the 273 lawsuits before the *Tribunal Civil* of the arrondissement of Altkirch between July 27, 1800, and April 27, 1808, 232 were of Gentiles against Gentiles, nineteen of Gentiles against Jews, nineteen of Jews against Gentiles and three of Jews, against Jews. Of the 837 lawsuits before the *Tribunal Civil* of Colmar between July 14, 1800, and May 12, 1801, 471 were between Gentiles, fifty-five of Gentiles against Jews, 197 of Jews against Gentiles and fourteen between Jews. Of the fifty-eight cases before the *Tribunal de Commerce* of Colmar between January 16, 1793, and

---

[111] AN,F19-11009.

October 15, 1794, twenty-seven were between Gentiles, eight of Gentiles against Jews, eleven between Jews and twelve of Jews against Gentiles. Of the 1,413 lawsuits before the same tribunal between June 6, 1823, and February 13, 1828, 665 dealt with formalities (oath-taking, registration of documents, etc.) and only 748 were lawsuits between two parties; of these, 528 between Gentiles, seventy-seven of Jews against Gentiles, sixty-nine of Gentiles against Jews and seventy-four between Jews.[264] According to the anti-Semitic attorney Chauffour there were 465 suits before the same tribunal in the course of twelve months in 1843-1844; in 307 of them Jews were either plaintiffs or defendants. During the same period there were in Mulhouse before the *Tribunal de Commerce* 1,295 litigations, of them 652 involved Jews, while before the *Tribunal Civil* of Colmar there were 782 lawsuits, 214 of them between Jews and Gentiles and twelve between Jews and Jews.[265] The *Tribunal de Commerce* of Metz rendered fifty-eight verdicts for a total of 28,774.95 frs. in favor of Jews against Gentiles in the period from May 1791 to June 1808. In the arrondissement o Sarreguemines there were 487 lawsuits of Jews against Gentiles and 155 of Gentiles against Jews between September 23, 1799, and January 1, 1808.[266] In the district of Colmar alone, during the years IX, X and XI there were dispossessions for non-payment of debts totaling 1,480,000 frs. (we do not know how many were in favor of Jews). According to a report of September 1823, in the Upper Rhine there were executed in 1818, 114 dispossessions in favor of Jews for unpaid debts amounting to 195,750 frs., about one-eighth of all dispossessions. During that period there were in the arrondissement of Belfort 381 dispossessions, only forty of them in favor of Jews.[267] Of the 299 dispossessions recorded in the Nancy mortgage-office between November 4, 1807, and April 21, 1823, only nine were in favor of Jews.[268] The number of mortgages recorded as a result of court-verdicts in favor of creditors was quite large—proportionately larger in favor of Jewish creditors (see Table IV). Of the 3,453 mortgages in the arrondissement of Sélestat which we have examined (see Table VIII), 790 are judicial; 2,733 are of Gentiles against Jews, 454 of them through court order; 593 are of Jews against Gentiles, 317 by court order. Of the 8,852 mortgages in the arrondissement of Nancy, which we have examined (see Table VII), 438 are judicial; 8,735 are between Gentiles, 395 of them judicial; 117 are of Jews against Gentiles, forty-three of them judicial. According to a report of July 16, 1808, of the mortages to Jews in the arrondissement of Toul (Meurthe) totaling 1,546,756 frs. the judicial mortages amounted

[264]   AdHR,U (1vol.).
[265]   AN,F19-11030.
[266]   AN,F19-11009; AdM,V149.
[267]   AdHR,M54-2 and V108.
[268]   "Registre de formalité. Transcription des saisies immobilières", vols. 1-5. In vol. 1, I did not include the numbers 1-14, because the mortgagees' names are missing. The Jewish mortgagees were: Mathieu Simon, Jacob Jacob, Isaac Jacob, Sara Berr, Joseph Caïen (dit Lajeunesse), Oury Schwab and Samuel Caïen-Neymarck, vol. I, No. 17, 57; vol. 2, No 9; vol. 3; vol. 4, No. 79, 125; vol. 5, No. 50, 64, 67.

to 516,284 frs."' A more detailed study especially of the Jews
vis-à-vis the courts would be necessary for a more accurate conclusion. Yet it must be remarked that on the eve of 1806 they
had already accumulated a large number of unpaid debts, an
inheritance of former years,²'' which was bound to lead to crisis
and end in litigations. Lawsuits and dispossessions on the basis
of court-sentences show that the peasants were debt-ridden, but
not that the creditors were usurers. The courts were most severe
on the creditors, especially Jews, and quite so during the years
1806-1818. A large percentage of judicial mortgages to Jews can
also demonstrate that Gentile debtors ventured to harass Jewish
creditors and in such cases the Jews had no alternative but to go
to court. However, the number of judicial mortgages to Gentiles
is also large. Of 1,586 mortgages in Folios 2-3 (1799-1803) of Sarreguemines, 330 are judicial; 427 to Jews from Gentiles, 104 of them
judicial (see Table IV). In some mortgage-offices there have been
preserved registry-books of judiciary acts (*Actes judiciaires*). Of 3,107
such writs in Meurthe of the years 1799-1803 which we have
examined (see Table XIV) only 79 are in favor of Jews. However,
the registers are not a good source for ascertaining the proportion
of Jews in court actions, because in addition to loan-matters there
are recorded all sorts of acts, such as adoptions, and even a verdict
that the Jew David Isaac Salomon is the son of a Polish Jew, Isaac
Caen.

13. We have already mentioned at various times that in the
course of time the number of mortgages to Jews — both absolute
and relative — fell considerably, and this is clear also from our
investigation. The size of the mortgages to Jewish creditors likewise
falls, and as a rule there are recorded mortgages to Jews on sales
of real estate and not for loans. A large number of mortgages,
particularly from about 1820 on are but renewals (*renouvellements*)
of old unpaid mortgage-secured loans, often ten years old and over.
Frequently the creditors had already lost any hope of ever collecting
the debts. Of 319 mortgages of Gentiles to Jews in the Folios
623-627 (1851-1852) of the Colmar arrondissement, twenty-eight are
renewed mortgages. Such practice was attested for the arrondissement of Belfort in an official report of September 1, 1923."'

14. There has been a constant tendency to seek justification
for the anti-Jewish pogroms of 1789, 1830-1831, and 1848, in Alsace,
on the basis of the large file of mortgage-secured loans of Jews
to peasants. However, our investigation (Tables I-II) shows that
the percentage of mortgages to Jews, even absolutely, was in Alsace

²'' AN,F19-11009. Juridical mortgages always involved heavy expenditures
and swelled the debts. Here are a few samples from vol. 628 of Colmar:
mortgage No. 21-110 frs. principal, 201.50 frs. including interest and expenses;
No. 22-60 and 129 frs.; No. 23-89 and 189 frs.; No. 24-195.57 and 360 frs.; No.
34-600 and 1,100 frs.; No. 83-413.65 and 1,022.67 frs. In vol. 625 of Colmar
(1852) we find the mortgage No. 285 of the Gentile J. J. Kiener against his
Jewish mortgagor Joseph Daniel Sée for 3.20 frs., but the interest and expenses
amounted to 50 frs.
²'° 401. p. 529.
²'' AdHR,V108.

neither higher than in Moselle where the number of Jews was smaller, nor much larger than in Meurthe. Yet there were no pogroms against Jews in Meurthe and Moselle. Further on we shall endeavor to make it clear that the reactionary groups with their anti-Jewish agitations were more responsible for these pogroms than the peasants' indebtedness to Jews.

15. The large number of mortgages to peasant-creditors from peasant-debtors is probably for the sale of parcels of land.

16. The mortgage-archives contain two series of volumes recording mortgages: A.- *Inscriptions*, of which we have examined 114 Folios with 62,149 mortgages (see Table I); B.- *Transcriptions* (transcripts, copies), where the entire documents were transcribed; whereas in series A the mortgage is merely entered on the basis of an act. The second series is particularly important in investigating mortgages recorded as a result of real estate transactions. Some mortgages but not all, appear in both series. Of the 1,556 mortgages in the cash-book (fee-registers, *recettes*)[212] 85 of Sélestat, 1,192 appear in the series *Inscriptions*, 187 in the series *Transcriptions*, and 177 in both. Of the 188 mortgages in *Transcriptions* Folio 244, of Sélestat, seventy-seven are also in *Inscriptions* Folios 117-118 (see Tables V and VI). From this we see that the series *Inscriptions* is the more important for our study, but it is necessary to examine the other series, even though the work involved is very complicated. This work would be much facilitated by an investigation of the cash-books (*recettes*) of the mortgages, but unfortunately few volumes of this series prior to 1860 have survived. We have inspected several such volumes (see Tables V-VIII), from which it has once more become clear that only a small number of mortgages have been recorded to Jews. Of the 188 mortgages in Folio 244 *Transcriptions* of the arrondissement of Sélestat in 1847, for 284,957 frs., only five of them (1,290 frs.) are to Jews. Of 154 mortgages in both series (for 1,673,429 frs.) in the cash-book 67 of Sélestat (1846), only 237 mortgages totaling 136,854 frs. were from Gentiles to Jews. Of 1,556 mortgages of both series in the cash-book 85 (1851-1852) of the Sélestat arrondissement for 1,733,487 frs., only 283 (amounting to 179,612 frs.) were to Jews from Gentiles. Out of 8,852 mortgages in the cash-books 15-16 (1826-1827) and 24-25 (1832-1833) of the arrondissement of Nancy, only 117 were from Gentiles to Jews.

17. We have already mentioned on several occasions the problem of loans on simple I.O.U.s (*actes sous seing privé*). According to a number of statements this type of debts to Jews was still larger than the mortgage-secured loans.[213] Of 642 legal decisions in the arrondissement of Sarreguemines in 1807-1808 rendered in favor of Jews residing in Departments other than Moselle, forty-three

verdicts (for a total of 18,038 frs.) were delivered on the basis of I.O.U.s.[214] An investigation of such loans (in some localities, the Folios in which I.O.U.s and other *actes sous seing privé* were recorded have been preserved)[215] is most complicated and will not always be reliable. Under the Law of December 12, 1798, the courts had no right to recognise such unregistered private contracts; but at present it is certainly impossible to settle what percentage of private contracts had been recorded—even then it had become impossible to settle this question. Accordingly no examination whatsoever of acts of this type will give a complete picture of credit on I.O.U.s. For that purpose it would be necessary to analyze the *actes* and find a criterion which would determine which recorded I.O.U.s were for loans. Indeed, not only such contracts for loans, but also for sales, transfer of property and profits, contracts on house-rents, protocols about examining the general condition of a horse or cow to be sold, etc. are registered. Owing to the Jews' large share in the commerce of Northeastern France the percentage of such recorded contracts to Jews would have been especially high, possibly higher than found in the Folios of mortgage-secured loans, but as a matter of act the percentage is not higher. Of the 4,950 registered *actes sous seing privé* in the Meurthe Department which we have examined (see Table IX) only 230 are to Jews. In Lower Rhine we found a still smaller percentage.

---

[214] AN,F19-11009.
[215] "Registre de recette des droits d'Enregistrement des Actes sous signature privée."

Left: Image of Epinal, 1870. *Right:* "Usurer", detail of an Epinal Image, 1850.
(Bibliothèque Nationale, Paris.)

Judaica-Napoleonica

A Bibliography of Books, Pamphlets and Printed Documents, 1801–1815.

O NE HUNDRED AND FIFTY years ago — on May 30, 1806, Napoleon 1 promulgated his first anti-Jewish Decree and convoked the Jewish Assembly (*Assemblée des Israélites*), which began its sessions on July 26, 1806. Later he convoked the Sanhedrin, which ended its sessions in April, 1807. On March 17, 1808, Napoleon promulgated his "ignominious decree" (*décret infâme*), which practically deprived the majority of French Jews of their rights for a period of ten years.

An endless amount of material has already been written on the subject of Napoleon and the Jews and we are not making an attempt at presenting new conclusions with the publication of this bibliography. In fact, the bibliography has been limited to books, pamphlets and printed documents published between 1801 and 1815; contemporary articles from periodicals, iconographical material, and later studies on the subject have not been included. A complete bibliography showing all phases of Napoleon's attitude towards Jews and the reaction of the Jews thereto would fill, at least, one very thick volume.

Our present bibliography shows rather the poor intellectual state of French Jewry in the time of the First Empire. The number of the French Jews — not including those living in the occupied countries — was small, only about 40,000. Already before the Revolution of 1789, the French Jews did not have much of an intellectual life of their own but drew heavily on the intellectually richer communities of Eastern and Central Europe. During the Revolutionary years of 1789 to 1800 the French Jews lost their communal organizations and this state of French Jewry can be seen from our present bibliography. Most of the important pamphlets on Napoleon's policy toward Jews were published by non-Jews or by Jews residing outside of France. Even the anti-Jewish publications, which paved the way for Napoleon's anti-Jewish policy, were not large in number. Most of the anti-Jewish activities were conducted not in public, but within the central and local administrations.

This was, indeed, a tragic period for France, and for its small number of Jews, too. The Jews did not or could not fight openly Napoleon's anti-Jewish policy. They had to wait for the end of the ten years' validity of the Decree of March 17, 1808. Of course, the Assembly and the Sanhedrin could be regarded as shameful bending by the Jewish leaders to Napoleon's will. But such was also the attitude of the entire French nation which accepted the Emperor's dictatorship. With all its weakness the Sanhedrin did accomplish

Originally published in *Studies in Bibliography and Booklore* (1956).

Myth-retrospective

something — the unification of the Ashkenazic and Sephardic Jews within the newly created Consistories. Later a pro-Napoleonic legend was created among the Jews. This was a response to the later reactionary campaigns of the Catholics and also a result of the Jews' capacity to forget wrongs done to them. To the Jews Napoleon remained the creator of the Consistories which gave them a legal basis to remain organized as a religious minority. There can also be no doubt that the Napoleonic Wars helped greatly to emancipate the Jews outside of France.

The largest group in the bibliography consists of odes and prayers in honor of Napoleon.[1] But this should not surprise us and does not always give a true picture of Jewish sentiments. The ceremonies in honor of Napoleon and other regimes were almost always organized upon orders by the governments.[2] Jews always chanted — willingly or forcibly — in honor of all regimes. Some Jewish leaders and authors who praised Napoleon were later eager to praise the Restoration. Abraham de Cologna, who, at many occasions, praised Napoleon, did the same thing for the Monarchy.[3] This was not a purely Jewish attitude. Non-Jews, too, followed the established practice of praising the respective regime in power.[4]

In order to complete the picture the bibliography contains also writings by Jews and non-Jews on general Jewish problems; this gives us a more complete picture of Jewish life in France during those years. As the fight against Napoleon's anti-Jewish policy ended only in 1818, we included the publications on this problem during the Restoration years.

Items of Christian Hebrew scholarship were not always included, because they can easily be found in already existing bibliographies.

The bibliography is arranged in 25 divisions according to subjects. Each division is arranged chronologically. The material of each year is then arranged alphabetically, or in a more detailed chronological order of months and days.

Of course, the bibliography is not complete, especially in material of the occupied countries. The author will be grateful for additions and remarks.

The items mentioned in the present bibliography are to be found in the following libraries and archives: Alliance Israélite Universelle (Paris), Archives Nationales (Paris), Biblio-

---

[1] Carmoly's "Napoléon et les panégyristes hébreux," in *Revue orientale*, II, 25–33, contains only a few odes.

[2] "Monsieur l'Ancien, dans des temps calamiteux, on commandait aux Ministres des cultes, des actions, de grâces pour le gain de telle ou telle bataille: ces Ministres obéissaient en tremblant; mais ils faisaient mentalement, pour la paix, des voeux qu'il ne leur était pas permis de manifester . . . La paix est faite, Monsieur . . . Empressez-vous, Monsieur, d'annoncer ce bienfait de la Providence aux fidèles de votre communion": A circular by the French Ministry of Interior, June 15, 1814. 2 pp. 4°.

[3] A. de Cologna, "De l'obligation de prier pour l'autorité qui gouverne," in *L'Israélite français* (1817), pp. 145–150, with a prayer for Louis XVIII.

[4] Michā'il ibn Niqūlā ibn Ibr. Sabbāg published odes in honor of Napoleon and Louis XVIII: *Poème à louange de l'Empereur Napoléon Bonaparte*, n. p., [1804] 6 pp.; *Cantique à S. M. Napoléon* . . . Paris, 1811. 35 pp.; *Cantique . . . à Sa Majesté . . . Louis le Désiré* . . . Paris, 1814. 23 pp. See: Anchel, Robert, *La Commémoration des Rois de France à Paris pendant la Restauration* (Paris, 1924), 40 pp.

thèque Nationale (Paris), British Museum (London), Calvet Museum and Library (Avignon), Hebrew Union College (Cincinnati), Hebrew University (Jerusalem), Jewish Theological Seminary (New York), Rosenthaliana Library (Amsterdam), University Library of Strasbourg, the Municipal Libraries of Bordeaux, Carpentras, Marseille, Metz, Nancy and Strasbourg, Departmental Archives of Meurthe-et-Moselle, Moselle, Lower and Upper Rhine, and Vaucluse, and private collections.

ABBREVIATIONS: Engl., English; Dut., Dutch; Fr., French; Ger., German; H., Hebrew; It., Italian; Lat., Latin.

I. GENERAL POLEMICS ON JEWS, NOT RELATED TO NAPOLEON'S ATTITUDE TOWARD JEWS

1. Berr, Michel. *Appel à la justice des nations et des rois; ou, Adresse d'un citoyen français au congrès qui devait avoir lieu à Lunéville, au nom de tous les habitans de l'Europe qui professent la religion juive.* Strasbourg, 1801. 72 pp. 8°.

German translation: Levy Rubens, "Bruchstücke aus der Schrift: Zuruf an die Gerechtigkeit der Nationen und Könige ... von Michel Berr. 1801." *Sulamith,* II, 1 (1808), 320–35, 382–96, II, 2 (1809), 27–41.

2. [Ligne, Charles Joseph Prince de.] *Mélanges militaires, littéraires et sentimentaires,* t. 21. Dresde, 1801. 357 pp. 8°.

Pages 173–92: "Mémoire sur les Juifs."

3. Rumpler, [Chanoine François Louis]. *Joseph Lehmann, Baruch Joseph, escrocs avérés, fripons avoués ... 30 floréal an 9 [20 mai 1801].* [Strasbourg], an IX. 26 pp. 8°.

The same as No. 4.

4. ———. *Au Ministre de la Justice.* [Strasbourg, 1801]. 26 pp. 8°.

Against Lehman; the same as No. 3.

5. ———. *Catastrophe terrible. Extrait du nécrologue de la sinagogue de Strasbourg, du 3 du mois Nisan, l'an 5561 (16 ventôse l'an 9 rép. [7 mars 1801]), traduit littéralement,* de l'hébreu en langue française, par le frère et ami Joseph Lehmann, fils d'Issac.* [Strasbourg], an IX. 2 pp. 8°.

6. ———. *Ecce Homo ... de la Momie à face judaïque, Seigneur de Hohenbourg ...* Barr, an XI. 40 pp. 8°.

7. Schottin, Maria Salomea. *Ueber Juden und Judengenossen im Niederrhein, an Bürger Bonaparte, ersten Konsul der Franken-Republik, und an die ganze Menscheit.* Strassburg, im eilften Jahr der Franken-Republik. 16 pp. 8°.

Against usurers.

8. [Valabrègue, Israel B(ernard) de.] *Schreiben eines Lords an seinen Correspondenten zu Paris. Zur Vertheidigung der Juden.* Aus dem Französischen übersetzt, und mit einer Vorrede nebst Anmerkungen begleitet von B**.** Breslau, 1804. XXX, 62 pp. 16°.

First published in 1768: J. B. D. V. S. J. D. R. *Lettre, ou Réflexions d'un milord ... Londres* [Paris], 1768. 83 pp. 8°.

9. [Bing], Isaïe Berr. *Lettre du S. I. B. B., Juif de Metz, à l'auteur anonyme d'un écrit intitulé: "Le Cri d'un citoyen contre les Juifs."* n. p., [1805]. 34 pp. 8°.

Published by Bing's son-in-law, Michel Berr. First edition, 1787. 57 pp. 8°.

10–10a. [Guénée, Abbé Antoine]. *Lettres de quelques Juifs portugais, allemands et polonais à M. de Voltaire.* 6ᵉ édition; Paris, 1805, 3 vols. 12°; 7ᵉ édition, Paris, 1815, 4 vols. 12°.

First edition, 1769.

11. Berr, Isaac Berr. *Lettre ... à M. Grégoire, sénateur, à Paris.* Nancy, 1806. 48 pp. 8°.

12. ———. *Réflexions sur la régénération complète des Juifs en France* ... [Paris, 1806.] 30 pp. 8°.

Dutch translation in: *Bijdragen betrekkelijk de verbetering van maatschappelijken staat der Joden,* Vol. 1 (1806), No. 29, pp. 250–63.

13–13a–d. Grégoire, Abbé Henri. *Observations nouvelles sur les Juifs et spécialement sur ceux d'Allemagne.* n. p., 1806. 22 pp. 8°.

Another edition was published as a reprint from the *Magasin encyclopédique*, 1 (1806), 109–128; it was published also in two other editions with the title: *Quelques observations concernant les Juifs en général et particulièrement ceux d'Alsace pour fixer l'attention du gouvernement sur la législation des différentes peuples à leur égard* ... Paris, [1806]. 22 pp. and [Paris, 1806.] 22 pp. Italian edition: *Osservazione sullo stato degli ebrei in Francia ed in Germania* ... Tradotte in italiano da Salomon Isac Luzatti Cosalese. Paris, n. d. 24 pp. 4°. According to Grégoire's *Mémoires*, 1, 336, another Italian edition was translated by the Bishop Gamboni of Venice.

14. ———. *Pièces officielles sur la réforme politique des Juifs, dans l'Empire français, pouvant être ajoutées aux Observations nouvelles sur les Juifs.* n. p., 1806. 8 pp. 8°.

15. *Les Juifs de la Lorraine, de Metz et d'Alsace.* [Paris, 1806.] 10 pp. 8°.

Reprinted from the *Moniteur universel* (July 25, 1806). Later reprinted by A. E. Halphen, *Recueil* ... (Paris, 1851), pp. 169–78.

16. Reinhard. *Ueber die Juden.* [Strassburg], 1806. 112 pp. 8°.

17. Dohm, Christian Wilhelm. *Riforma politica degli Ebrei;* versione dal Tedesco ... Mantova, 1807. 12°.

First edition, in German — 1781, in French — 1782.

18–18a–b. Grégoire, Abbé Henri. *Observations nouvelles sur les Juifs, et spécialement sur ceux d'Amsterdam et de Francfort.*

Extrait de la *Revue philosophique, littéraire et politique.* [Paris, 1807.] 18 pp. 8°.
Dutch edition, translated by Belinfante: *Nieuwe bedenkingen over de Joden* ... Haag, 1807. IV, 30 pp. 8°. Italian edition: *Nuove osservazioni sopra gli ebrei in generale e particolarmente su quelli d'Amsterdam e di Francfort, versione italiano corredata di note riguardanti specialmente gli ebrei d'Italia.* Milano, 1807. 24 pp. 8°. German edition: "Neue Betrachtungen über die Juden ..." *Magazin für Religion-, Moral- u. Kirchengeschichte*, IV (1806), 523–43.

19. Desquiron, [Antoine Toussaint d'Esquiron de Saint Agnan]. *Considérations sur l'existence civile et politique des Israélites.* Mayence, [1808]. 43 pp. 8°.

20. Dufriche de Foulaines, F. N., *Harmonie des cultes catholique, protestant et mosaïque, avec les constitutions de l'Empire français* ... Paris, 1808. 460 pp. 8°.

21. Berr, Michel. *Sur la liberté des cultes et sur le project de décret relatif à l'observance des fêtes et dimanches.* [Paris, 1814.] 11 pp. 8°.

Reprinted from the *Mercure de France*, Sept., 1814.

22. D ... t, B. *La boîte à perrette des Protestans et des Israélites.* [Paris, 1815.] 8 pp. 8°.

22a. *Réflexions relatives à un acte de notre législation politique.* Paris, avril 1815. 10 pp. 8°.

Demand to cover the religious budgets of Jewish Consistories by the Government; p. 9: "on nous a promis la liberté entière."

II. Polemics in Connection with Napoleon's Policy toward Jews

23. Bicheno, J. *The Restoration of the Jews, the Crisis of all Nations; or an Arrangement of the Scripture Prophecies, which relate to the Restoration of the Jews, from their First Dispersion, to the Calling of their Grand Sanhedrin at Paris, October 6th, 1806 . . .* London, 1807. II, 235 pp. 8°.

First edition, London, 1800. 115 pp. 8°.

24. Bonald, Louis Gabriel Ambroise. "Sur les Juifs." *Mercure de France*, XXIII (1806), 249–67.

Also distributed as a reprint without title page, with same pagination.

25. [Jacobsohn, Israel.] *Les premiers pas de la nation juive vers son bonheur sous les auspices du Grand Monarque Napoléon. Annoncés aux amis de l'humanité* par C., ami de M. B. Schottlaender. Paris, [1806]. 47 pp. 8°.

26. Lamoureux, [Jean Baptiste] Justin, *De la régénération définitive des Juifs.* [Paris, 1806.] 9 pp. 8°.

Extrait de la *Revue philosophique, littéraire et historique*, 10 juillet 1806.

27. Masson, avocat. *Sur les Juifs.* Paris, 6 mai 1806. 3 pp. 8°.

28. *Napoléon le Grand rétablit le culte des Israélites, le 30 Mai 1806.* Paris, [1806]. 1 p. fol.

Text, with a lithograph by Couché fils.

29. Paly-Rasch, Samuel Yessite (Chrétien), de la Maison de David, Lieutenant à l'Hôtel Imperial des Invalides. *Qu'est-ce qu'un Israélite chrétien?* Paris, 1806. 15 pp. 8°.

Fr. & H. The author, who signs in Hebrew ראש לבית דוד — שמואל ישועי פליה states that God chose "the Corsican" in order to reconstruct Christian Jewry in Jerusalem.

30–30a-b. Poujol, [Louis]. *Quelques observations concernant les Juifs en général et plus particulièrement d'Alsace . . .* Paris, 1806. 156 pp. 8°. Another edition: 1806. x, 156 pp. German edition: *Einige Bemerkungen über die Juden . . .* Strassburg, 1806. 116 pp. 8°.

31. P . . . [Peixotto], Moyse, de Bordeaux. *Réponse à un article sur les Juifs, de M. de Bonald, inséré dans le Mercure de France, du 8 février 1806.* Bordeaux, 1806. 39 pp. 16°.

32. Rodrigues, J., fils. *Observations sur un article de M. de Bonald, sur les Juifs, inséré dans le Mercure de France du 8 février 1806.* [Paris, 1806.] 14 pp. 8°.

Extrait de la *Revue philosophique, littéraire et politique*, Nos. 19–21 (Mars, 1806).

33. *Brief van eenen verlichten Jood, die gelijktijdig geleefd heeft met Jezus van Nazareth, en waarschijnlijk een van zijne Apostelen geweest is; gevonden in de nagelaten Papieren en Geschriften van een lid van het Joodsche Sanhedrin te Parijs. Vertaald naar het Hebreeuwsche afschrift van eenen voornamen Huogleeraar . . .* Amsterdam, 1807. 46 pp. 8°.

34. Fränkel, Levi Schauelsohn. *Sendschreiben eines jüdischen Rabbiners in Betreff der neuesten merkwürdigsten Ereignisse in der Christenwelt . . .* Breslau, 1807. 16 pp.

Includes eulogy: [Papenheim, Salomon.] *Nachruf an den Rabbiner Levi Schauelsohn Fränkel in Angelegenheit seiner unternommenen Reise nach Paris.* Breslau, 1807.

35. *Lettre & adresse par une société d'Israélites à Francfort s/M. qui a pour but de contribuer au bonheur des Israélites. A Monsieur Furtado, Président de l'assemblée des députés des Israélites à Paris.* n. p., 1807. 8 pp. 8°.

36. *Pièces concernant la Députation de la communauté israélite sous le nom d'Adath Jeszurum* [sic] *d'Amsterdam, au Grand Sanhédrin de Paris.* Paris, 1807. 32 pp. 8°.

37. [Reid, William Hamilton.] סנהדרין חדשה *And Causes and Consequences of the French Emperor's Conduct Towards the Jews* ... London, 1807. XII, 190 pp. 8°.

38. Ascher, Saul, *Napoleon oder über den Fortschritt der Regierung.* Berlin, 1808. XII, 140 pp. 8°.

Pp. 90–92 on Jews.

39. Badin, avocat au Conseil d'Etat et à la Cour de Cassation. *Résumé pour les Israélites du département du Bas-Rhin.* [Paris, 1808.] 21 pp. 4°.

40–40a. Bamberger, Joseph. *Ein Wort zu seiner Zeit. Oder: Betrachtungen bei Gelegenheit des grossen Sanhedrin in Paris.* [Frankfurt a/M.], 1808. 93 pp. 8°.

Second edition, 1817.

41. B[aquet], avoué. *Dialogue entre un avoué et un Juif de Metz ou Brève dissertation sur le Décret du 17 mars 1808.* Metz, 1808. 14 pp. 8°.

42. Becquey-Beaupré, Perignon, Champion et Laforie. *Consultation sur la question de savoir si les dispositions de la loi du 17 mars 1808, sont applicables aux jugemens passés en force de chose jugée, obtenus par ceux qui professent la Religion de Moïse.* [Paris, 1808.] 16 pp. 4°.

43. C., M., *L'Usurier, ou Le Juif confondu. Comédie en un acte et en prose.* Metz, 1808. 48 pp. 8°.

44. Cerfberr, B[aruch]. *Réflexions d'un député de l'Assemblée des Juifs,* Paris, 1808. 8°.

45–45a. Chauffour le Cadet, [Ignace]. *Réflexions sur l'application du Décret impérial, du 17 Mars 1808, concernant les créances des Juifs.* ["Plaidoyer fait à Metz le 9 novembre 1808"]. [Metz, 1808.]. 12 pp. 4°.

German edition: *Betrachtungen über die Anwendung des Kaiserlichen Dekrets vom 17ten März 1808 in Betreff der Schuldforderungen der Juden.* Aus dem Französichen übersetzt und mit einer Nachschrift begleitet von Friedrich Bucholz. Berlin, 1809. IV, 89 pp.

46. Cohen, L., of Exeter. תורת אמת. *Sacred truths addressed to the Children of Israel ... on the book entitled the New Sanhedrin ...* Exeter, [1808]. II, 51 pp. 12°.

47. *Eclaircissement sur les prétentions que le Sieur Herz-Loeb Lorch a à former contre Mr.* [Fr. J.] *de Schmittburg, ci-devant échanson héréditaire de l'électeur de Trêves.* Mayence, [1808]. 4°.

48. *Réponse aux Eclaircissemens sur les prétentions que forment les Sieurs Herz-Loeb Lorch, Mayer-Herz Reinach et Abraham Kahn, négocians à Mayence, contre M. Schmitburg, propriétaire à Gemunden, département de Rhin-et-Moselle.* Coblentz, octobre 1808. 4°.

49. Jacobsohn, Israel, Conseiller privé de finances à Brunswic. *Très humble remontrance adressée à Son Altesse Eminentissime le Prince Primat de la Confédération du Rhin sur la nouvelle constitution des habitans juifs établis à Francfort.* Brunswic, 1808. 134 pp. 8°.

Contains also remarks on Napoleon's policy towards Jews.

50. *Letter to the Parisian Sanhedrin, containing reflections on their recent proceedings ... with observations on the conduct of Buonaparte, relative to his projected subversion ... of Judaism, in France.* By an English Israelite. London, 1808. VIII, 46 pp. 8°.

51. P., J., de N*** [J. P. Pons, de Nîmes]. *Réflexions philosophiques et politiques sur la tolérance religieuse, sur le libre exercice de tous les cultes* . . . Paris, 1808. 8°.

52. Sharp, Granville, *Jerusalem, or an Answer to the following enquiries: What is the Etymology of the word Jerusalem? and is there any connection between Salem and Jerusalem* . . . London, 1808. 72 pp. 8°.

With remarks on Napoleon.

53. Tadini, Placido. *Notizie politico-storiche sul Sinedrio degli Ebrei,* opuscolo di Placido Tadini, directorre delle Scuole . . . Allessandria, 1807. 76 pp. 4°.

54. V . . . [Vivien, Jean-Baptiste], Me, avocat à la Cour d'Appel de Metz. *Recherches historiques pour servir d'appendice aux Réflexions sur l'application du Décret impérial du 17 mars 1808, concernant les créances des Juifs.* [Metz, 1808.] 10 pp. 8°.

See No. 55.

55. A., J. *Lettre à M. V., avocat à la Cour d'Appel de Metz, auteur de l'écrit intitulé: Recherches historiques pour servir d'appendice aux Réflexions sur l'application du Décret impérial du 17 mars 1808 concernant les créances des Juifs.* [Metz], 1809. 8°.

See No. 54.

56–56a. Desquiron, [Antoine Toussaint d'Esquiron de Saint Agnan], M. *Commentaire sur le Décret impérial du 17 mars 1808 précédé d'une notice historique sur l'existence civile et politique de la nation juive, depuis sa dispersion, jusqu'à nos jours.* Mayence, 1809. 86 pp. 8°.

Second edition, Paris, 1810. 166 pp. 8°.

57. *Mémoire et consultation sur pourvoi en grâce, pour Baer Abraham, commis-marchand; Abraham Isaac, son père, marchand mercier, et Samuel Joseph, marchand boucher, tous trois Juifs, demeurans à Strasbourg.* [Strasbourg, 1810.] 4°.

III. Minutes of the Jewish Assembly and Sanhedrin (Collections)

58. *Procès-verbal des séances de l'Assemblée des Députés français professant la religion juive.* Imprimé d'après le manuscrit communiqué par M. le Président. Paris, 1806. VIII, 92 pp. 8°.

Minutes of the meetings of July 26 — Sept. 18, 1806. See No. 59.

59. *Procès-verbal des séances de l'Assemblée des Députés français professant la religion juive.* Imprimé d'après le manuscrit communiqué par M. le Président. Paris, 1806 [1807]. VIII, 230 pp. 8°.

See No. 58. The title page and the first 92 pp. are the same as No. 58, with pp. 93–230 added and containing the minutes of Sept. 18, 1806 — Feb. 5, 1807 and March 25 — April 6, 1807. Between p. 184 and 185 is bound a 112 pp. section "Actes du Grand Sanhédrin"; see No. 60.

60. *Actes du Grand Sanhédrin.* [Paris, 1807]. 112 pp.

No title page, contains the minutes of Feb. 4 — March 9, 1807 and the "Préambule des Décrets." Printed as an addition to the [1807] edition of 230 pp. See No. 59.

61. Tama, Diogène. *Prospectus de la Collection générale des écrits et des actes relatifs aux individus professant la religion hébraïque.* [Paris, 1806]. 4 pp. 8°.

See Nos. 62–67.

62. ———. *Collection des écrits et des actes relatifs au dernier état des individus professant la religion hébraïque* . . . Paris, 1806. 328 pp. 8°.

Twelve issues. The same text as in part 2 of No. 65; cf. Nos. 61, 63–67.

63. ———— . *Collection des actes de l'Assem-blée des Israélites de France et du Royaume d'Italie, convoquée à Paris, par décret de Sa Majesté impériale et royale du 30 mai 1806.* Paris, [1807]. xii, 328 pp. 8°.

The same as No. 62, 12 issues.

64. ———— . *Collection des procès-verbaux et décisions du Grand Sanhédrin, convoqué à Paris, par ordre de Sa Majesté l'Empereur et Roi, dans le mois de février et mars 1807.* Paris, 1807. 132 pp. 8°.

Twelve issues. Minutes of Feb. 9—March 9, 1807. The same text as in the last part of *Organisation*; cf. Nos. 62 & 65.

65. [————.] *Organisation civile et religi-euse des Israélites de France et du Royaume d'Italie, décretée par Sa Majesté l'Empereur et Roi, le 17 mars 1808; Suivie de la Collec-tion des Actes de l'Assemblée des Israélites . . . et de celle des Procès-verbaux et Décisions du Grand Sanhédrin . . .* Paris, 1808. 16, xii, 328, 132 pp. 8°.

Collection of Nos. 63–64 and a 16 pp. introduction consisting of Napoleon's decrees.

66. ———— . *Raccolta degli atti dell' assem-blea degli Israeliti di Francia e del regno d'Italia. Convocata a Parigi con decreto di S. M. I. e R. del 30 Maggio 1806. Publicata dal Signor Tama . . . e seguita dai processi verbali e decisioni del Gran Sinedrio.* Milano, 1807. 316, 116, 4 pp. 8°.

67. ———— . *Raccolta degli atti dell' Assem-blea degli Israeli di Francia e del regno d'Italia . . .* Livorno, [1807]. 3 vols. 272, 237, 148 pp. 24°.

Vol. iii, pp. 91–148: "Supplemento agli atti del Gran Sinedrio Ebraico."

68. *Supplemento agli atti del Gran Sinedrio Ebraico.* Milano, 1807. 40 pp. 8°.

Cf. No. 67.

69. *Raccolta dei documenti ufficiali ed auten-tici e di altri scritti . . . relativi alla deputazione ebraica convocatasi in Parigi, cominciando dall' invito di Sua Maestà alla deputazione italiana a concorrere alla creazione del Sinedrio.* Mantova, 1807. 84 pp. 8°.

70. *Continuazione della Raccolta dei docu-menti ufficiali ed autentici e di altri scritti e squarci storici . . . alla Deputazione Ebraica convocatasi in Parigi . . .* Mantova, 1807. 84 pp. 8°.

71. Tama, Diogène. *Transaction of the Paris Sanhedrin . . .*, Translated from the French . . . by F. D. Kirwan. London, 1807. xvi, 334 pp. 8°.

72. Cassel, Salomon, זאמלונג דער וויכטיגסטען פערהאנדלונגען בייא דער דורך איין קייסערליכעס דעקרעט פאם 30 מייא 1806 אין פאריס צוזאמען בערופענען גראסען פערזאמלונג דער יודען נעבסט אללען דאריוף באצוג האבענדען נעגענשטאאנדרען. נעזאמלעט נעדרוקט אונד הערויס נעגעבען אין באסעל בייא וויללהעלם האאס. [פארבעריכט — שלמה קאסיל. [באסעל, תקס"ז. [Basel, 1807.] 80 pp. 16°.

73. *Bijdragen betrekkelijk de verbetering van den maatschappelijken staat der Joden.* Den Haag, 1806–07. 12, viii, 544 pp. (12°).

Periodical.

74–74a. Bran, Alexander. *Gesammelte Ac-tenstücke und öffentliche Verhandlungen über die Verbesserung der Juden in Frankreich.* Hamburg, 18[06]–07.

Eight Nos., 2 vols.; 2d edition, 1806. 96 pp.

75. *Recueil contenant le règlement organique du culte judaïque, et les décrets impériaux y relatifs; les réponses de l'Assemblée Générale des Israélites tenue à Paris, aux questions lui proposées; et les décisions doctrinales du Grand Sanhédrin. Précédé d'un précis des faits et*

cérémonies, et des procès-verbaux de l'élection, nomination et installation du consistoire israélite du département de Rhin-et-Moselle, avec les discours prononcés à cette occasion. Coblentz, 1809. IV, 128 pp. 8°.

Fr. & Ger.

76. Lopez Cancelada, Juan. *Decreto de Napoleon, Emperador de los Franceses, sobre los judios residentes en Francia, y deliberaciones que tomaron éstos en su cumplimiento, con un resúmen de otros sucesos interesantes.* Mexico, 1807. 134 pp. 4°.

With lithographs, and preceded by a sketch of the history of the Jews.

77. *Décisions doctrinales du Grand Sanhédrin qui s'est tenu à Paris au mois d'Adar premier, . . . 5567 (Février 1807), sous les auspices de Napoléon-le-Grand. Avec la traduction littérale du texte Français en Hébreu*

תקנות אשר יסדו אנשי שם סנהדרין . . . בעיר
ואם פאריש בחדש אדר ראשון . . . התקס"ז
תחת . . . נאפוליאון. Paris, 1812. 72 pp. 4°

Fr. & H. Pp. 68–72: "Liste des Membres . . ."

78. *Decisien van den Grooten Sanhedrin, in 1807 te Parijs vergaderd geweest . . .* Amsterdam, 1813.

See also Nos. 79–112.

IV. Minutes of and other Publications on the Jewish Assembly and Sanhedrin (Details)

79–79a. *L'Assemblée des Députés des Israélites de France et du royaume d'Italie à leurs coreligionnaires.* Paris, 6 octobre 1806. [Paris, 1806.] 4 pp. fol.

Fr. & H. Published also with the title: *Déclaration de l'Assemblée des Députés des Israélites . . . à leurs co-religionnaires.* n. p., n. d. 4 pp. 4°. See also Nos. 80–82.

80. . . . מאסיפת פקידי בני ישראל יושבי צרפת
ואיטליה . . . לבני אמונתם . . . [Paris, 1806.]
4 pp.

H. & It. Signed: J. Rodrigues. See also Nos. 79, 81–82.

81. אל ראשי עם קדש בני ישראל יושבי צרפת
ואיטליה מאת אחיהם רבני וחכמי העדה הנקהלת
במצות אדונינו הקיסר והמלך הגדול יר"ה פ"ה
פאריס קרית מלך רב לכלכם כנהר שלום וברכה
מאת ה'. Paris, 1806. 3 pp. 4°.

See also Nos. 79–80, 82.

82. *Die Versammlung der Abgeordneten der französischen und italienischen Israeliten an ihre Glaubensgenossen.* ה' דבר טוב על ישראל.
מאסיפת פקידי בני ישראל יושבי צרפת ואיטליה

הנקהלת בעיר פאריס לבני אמונתם ולשומרי
תורתם עתרת שלום אמת, n. p., n. d. 4 pp. fol.

H. & Ger. See also Nos. 79–81.

83. [Furtado, Abraham.] *Exhortation aux Israélites de France et du Royaume d'Italie.* [Paris, 1806.] 4 pp. 4°.

84. Cerfberr, Lipman. *Discours pour l'ouverture de l'Assemblée générale des Juifs, prononcé le 26 juillet 1806.* Paris, 1806. 7 pp. 8°.

85. *Extrait de l'Histoire philosophique de la nation juive. Assemblée légale séante à Paris. Questions faites par le Gouvernement français à l'assemblée hébraïque le 29 juillet 1806 et réponses faites par ladite assemblée.* Nancy, [1807?] 16 pp. 8°.

86. Homberg, Herz. *Zwölf Fragen, vom Minister des Innern in Frankreich der Israelitischen Deputation in Paris vorgelegt und von ihr beantwortet. Aus dem Französischen übersetzt.* Wien, 1808. 92 pp. 8°.

87. *Détail officiel de tout ce qui s'est passé à la première et deuxième séances de l'Assemblée des Juifs . . . Paris, 30 juillet 1806.* n. p., n. d., 4 pp. 4°.

88. *Discours de MM. les Commissaires de S. M. Impériale et Royale, prononcé à l'assemblée des Français professant le culte de Moïse, dans la séance du 18 septembre.* [Paris, 1806.] 12 pp. 8°.

See also Nos. 89–92.

89–89a. [Furtado, Abraham.] *Réponse. Détail officiel de la séance de l'assemblée des Juifs . . . A. Furtado. Discours prononcé à cette assemblée par MM. les commissaires de S. M. Impériale et Royale . . .* Paris [1806.] 4°.

Published also with the title: *Détail officiel de la Séance de l'Assemblée des Juifs,* (*Séance du 18 de ce mois.*) n. p., n. d. 4 pp. 4°. See also Nos. 88, 90–92.

90. *Discorso d'sig. commisarii di S.M.I.E.R. indicizzato all'assemblea de' Francesi professanti il culto di Mosè (18 settembre 1806).* Torino, 1806. 21 pp. 8°.

With: "Riposta del signor Furtado." See also Nos. 88–89, 91–92.

91. מקרא העדה הדברים אשר דברו שרי הקיסר הגדול המלך האדיר נאפאלעאן בהתאספ ראשי העם עדת ישורון אשר בצרפת ואיטליא, בעיר פאריש . . . n. p., 1806. 8°.

See also Nos. 88–90, 92.

92. *Denkwürdige Rede gehalten am 18ten Sept. 1806 von den . . . Commissarien . . . des Napoleon, in der Versammlung zu Paris.* Nach dem Französischen in Hebräische und Deutsche übersetzt מקרא העדה הדברים אשר דברו שרי הקיסר הגדול המלך האדיר נאפאלעאן... בששי לחדש תשרי שנת תקפ"ז n. p. [Kjobenhavn?, 1806]. 16°.

H. & Ger. See also Nos. 88–91.

93. Berr, Isaac Berr. *Discours du S*ʳ*. Berr, Fabricant de Tabac, Membre du Conseil muni-*

cipal de Nancy . . . *Député à l'Assemblée des Français professant la religion juive . . .* [Paris, 1806.] 8 pp. 8°.

94. Berman, Wolf, *Motion faite . . . dans la séance de l'Assemblée des Israélites du 24 novembre 1806 . . . sur les articles* XXII, XXIII, XXIV *et* XXV *du projet de règlement du culte judaïque proposé à son adoption.* [Paris, 1806.] 6 pp. 4°.

95. *Extrait des procès-verbaux de l'Assemblée des Israélites convoquée et tenue à Paris en 1806 . . . Délibération et arrêté du 23 décembre 1806, en faveur d'Abraham Cohen et son épouse . . .* [Paris, 1806.] 4 pp. 4°.

Marriage and divorce according to Jewish jurisdiction.

96. Marqfoy, aîné de Baïonne [Bayonne], M. [Marc Foi, or Marc Foy]. *Discours prononcé . . . sur la nature des réponses à faire aux 4ᵉ, 5ᵉ et 6ᵉ questions proposées à ladite Assemblée par les Commissaires de Sa Majesté Impériale et Royale.* Paris, septembre 1806. 4 pp. 12°.

97. *Réclamation des Juifs portugais, espagnols et avignonais, de Paris, de Bordeaux et du Midi de la France.* [Paris, 1806.] 1 p. 4°.

98. *Liste des Membres composant le Grand Sanhédrin.* Paris, 1807. 15 pp. 8°.

99. *Programme* [de l'ouverture du Grand Sanhédrin]. [Paris, 1807]. 2 pp. 4°.

100. *Prière des Membres du Sanhédrin, récitée dans leur assemblée convoqué à Paris le 1ᵉʳ jour d'Adar de l'année 5567* [9 Février 1807] ב"ה תפלת ישרים קריאי העדה אנשי שם סנהדרין בהתאספ יחדיו בעיר ואם פאריס המהוללה מטעם אדוננו הקיסר . . . נאפוליאון הראשון. Paris, 1807. 15 pp. 8°.

Fr. & H.

101. *Reden gesprochen in der Versammlung des grossen Sanhedrins, am 2ten und 9ten März 1807, uebersetzt auf Veranstaltung der Herren Daniel Levi, August Ratisbonne und R. Picard, aus Strassburg, Deputirte bey dieser Versammlung.* Strassburg, n. d. 24 pp. 4°.

102. Avigdor, Jacob Samuel. *Discours prononcé à l'Assemblée des Israélites de l'Empire Français et du Royaume d'Italie; par J. S. Avigdor (de Nice), secrétaire de l'Assemblée, Membre du Comité des Neuf et du Grand Sanhédrin,* Paris, 1807. 16 pp. 8°.

103. Bondi, Zamorani. *Die quo in Parisiensi civitate sedem suam habuit Synedrium Populi Israelis, jubente Maximo Napoleonione . . . In occasione della prima tenutasi dal gran Sinedrio . . .* יום אשר הוקם על מכונו בית ועד גדול . . . שר את סנהדרין לבני ישראל בעיר פאריסי . . . השירה הזאת אסיא דמן שויא טוב צאמוראני מפקידי עיר פירארא. Paris, 1807. 6 pp. 4°.

Lat., H. & It.

104. Cerf-Berr [Cerfberr], Lipman. *Discours de . . . Député du Haut-Rhin, à l'Assemblée Générale des Israélites, prononcé le 25 Mars 1807.* [Paris, 1807.] 13 pp. 8°.

105. Cologna, Abraham de. *Discorso pronunziato nella grande Sinagoga di Parigi, all' occasione dell' apertura del Gran Sanedrin. Discours prononcé à la grande Synagogue de Paris, à l'occasion de l'ouverture du Grand Sanhédrin.* Traduit en français par M. le Président Furtado. Paris, 1807. 27 pp. 8°.

It. & Fr.

106. Cracovie [Cracovia], Jacob Samuel. *Discours à l'occasion de l'installation du Grand Sanhédrin . . .* Traduit par Lion-Jacob Goudchaux de Metz. *Discorso all' occasione dell' istallazione del Gran Sanhedrin . . .* Paris, 1807. 32 pp. 8°.

It., Fr. & H.; pp. 28–32: "Ode hébraique par M. le Rabbin Cracovie . . . qui a été chanté dans la grande Synagogue de Paris, le jour de l'anniversaire de la naissance de S. M. L'Empereur et Roi שיר חדש ליום . . . הולדת . . . נאפוליאן . . . מאת יעקב מנחם קראקוביא . . . ונעתק ללשון צרפתי מאת ליב בן כהרר יעקב סילני ממיץ.

107. Furtado, Abraham. *Rapport de M. Furtado au Grand Sanhédrin, en lui proposant les trois premières décisions doctrinales.* [Paris, 1807.] 16 pp. 8°.

108. *Opinion de MM. Rodrigues* [Isaac et J. fils] *de Bordeaux et de Paris, sur l'Arrêté proposé par la Commission des Neuf, et prononcée par celui de Paris, à la Séance du 25 mars 1807, dans l'Assemblée des Israélites de France et du Royaume d'Italie.* [Paris, 1807.] 3 pp. 4°.

109. *Article* VII. *Professions utiles.* Paris, 1807. 3 pp. 4°.

See No. 65, pp. 79–82.

110. Romanelli, Samuele. זמרת עריצים *Ossia Raccolta di inni ed Ode di Parecchi Rabbini dell' Assemblea degli Ebrei e del Gran Sanedrio.* Con la versione Italiana di Samuele Romanelli. Mantova, 1807. 43 pp. 8°.

H. & It. Circolare dell' Assemblea alle Universita Israelitiche; Preghiera dei Rabini del Sinedrio; Abramo Cologna. Ode per il giorno della nascita di Napoleonie . . . Elia Aron Latis. מזמור לדוד Inno . . . Ode del Signor Bondi Zamorani . . . Ode del Signor J. Meyer, per il giorno natalizio di S.M.I. et R. Inno des Sig. Bonaventura Modena . . . Inno del Sig. [Samuel] Witersheim.

111. [Sintzheim, Joseph David.] *Discours prononcé par le chef du Grand Sanhédrin à la clôture des séances.* Traduit par A. Furtado. Paris, [1807]. 4°.

112. Furtado, Abraham, ex-Président. *Mémoire sur les projets de décret presentés au Conseil d'Etat concernant les Israélites.* [Paris, 1807.] 16 pp. 4°.

See also Nos. 58–78.

V. Circulars on Expenses of the Deputies to the Jewish Assembly
and Sanhedrin

113. *Le Ministre de l'Intérieur, à M* . . .
Député juif du département d . . . *Paris, 23
juillet 1806.* 2 pp. 4°.

114. *Assemblée des Députés des Israélites de
France et du Royaume d'Italie.* [Paris, 1806.]
1 p. 4°.

Decision of Sept. 24, 1806, on the expenses.

115. *Le Président de l'Assemblée des Députés
des Israélites de France et du Royaume d'Italie.
A ses Coreligionnaires.* Paris, 30 septembre
1806. 1 p. 4°.

116. *Le Préfet du département du Haut-Rhin,
membre de la Légion d'honneur, à Monsieur* ――― . *Colmar, le 12 novembre 1806.*
Colmar, [1806]. 4 pp.

Fr. & Ger.

117. [Formulaire de sommation par le
Préfet du Haut-Rhin aux Juifs pour payer
l'indemnité des députés composant l'Assemblée et le Sanhédrin.] Colmar, Février 1807.
2 pp. fol.

Fr. & Ger.

VI. Decrees on the Jews

118. *Arrêté relatif à la bénédiction nuptiale
par les rabbins, du 1er prairial an x de
la République française, une et indivisible*
[21 mai 1802]. [Strasbourg], an x. 2 pp.
4°.

119. *Extrait des délibérations de la Mairie de
la Commune de Metz. Du 21 germinal an* ii . . .
Maetz [Metz], n. d. Broadside.

Order by the Mayor Goussaud to close all private
synagogues.

120-120a. *Décret impérial qui déclare deux
articles de celui du 23 prairial an* xii [*12 juin
1804*] *sur les sépultures, non applicables aux
personnes qui professent en France la religion
juive. Au Palais des Tuilleries, le 10 février
1806.* [Paris, 1806.] 2 pp. 4°. Also [Bor-
deaux?], n. d. 1 p. 8°.

121. *Rapport et projet de décret* [No.] *1274
de la Section de l'Intérieur, sur une réclamation
des Juifs de Bordeaux. M. de Ségur, rapporteur, 1re Rédaction. Paris, 29 janvier 1806.*
n. p., n. d. 3 pp. 4°.

Cemeteries.

122. *Avis sur des questions touchant les
Juifs* [No. *1341*]. *Paris, 30 avril 1806.* n. p.,
n. d. 3 pp. 4°.

123. *Projet de Décret sur la convocation d'une
Assemblée d'individus professant la religion
juive* [No.] *1355.* M. Regnaud [*de Saint-
Jean-d'Angély*], Rapporteur. *Paris, 21 mai
1806.* n. p., n. d. 6 pp. 4°.

124-124a. *Décret impérial portant sursis à
l'exécution de jugemens rendus en faveur des
Juifs contre des cultivateurs non négocians de
plusieurs départemens de l'Empire. Au Palais
de Saint-Cloud, le 30 mai 1806.* Paris, 1806.
4 pp. 4°.

No. 334. *Bulletin des Lois*, No. 94; also No. 1631,
Bulletin, No. 94, and other editions.

125-125a-b. *Projets de décrets et avis relatifs aux Juifs. Section de l'Intérieur.* M.
Regnaud, Rapporteur. *1re Rédaction,* [No.]
1502. Paris, 30 mai 1807. n. p., n. d. 15 pp.
4°; *2e Rédaction. Paris, 6 juin 1807.* n. p.,
n. d. 10 pp. 4°; *3e Rédaction. Paris, 9 juin
1807.* n. p., n. d. 12 pp. 4°.

126. *I^(re) Division . . . Circulaire. Mesures contre l'usure des Juifs. Paris, le 10 juin 1806.* [Paris, 1806.] 4 pp. 4°.

Together with the Decree of May 30, 1806.

127–127a–c. *Décret impérial, qui prescrit des mesures pour l'exécution du règlement du 10 décembre 1806 concernat les Juifs. Du Palais des Tuileries, le 17 mars 1808.* [Paris,] 1808. 3 pp. 4°. Paris, [1808]. 7 pp. 4°.

No. 545. *Bulletin des Lois,* No. 187, also No. 3237, *Bulletin,* No. 187. 4 pp. 8° and No. 3238, *Bulletin,* No. 187.

128–128a. *Décret impérial concernant les Juifs. Au Palais des Tuileries, le 17 mars 1808.* Paris, [1808]. 4 pp. 4°.

No. 541. *Bulletin des Lois,* No. 186; also No. 3210, *Bulletin,* No. 186.

129. *Projet d'avis tendant à interpréter l'article 4 du Décret du 17 mars 1808, concernant les obligations souscrites par un Français non-commerçant au profit d'un Juif. Section de Législation. M. le Comte Treilhard, Rapporteur. I^(re) Rédaction.* [No.] *1752.* Paris, 1808. 3 pp. 4°.

130. *Ministère des cultes. 2e Division. Bureau des Israélites. Circulaire. Paris, le 29 mars 1808.* 1 p. fol.

Preparation of "tableau des synagogues consistoriales à établir dans l'Empire."

131. *Décret impérial, qui excepte les Juifs établis à Libourne des dispositions du Décret du 17 mars 1808. A Bayonne, le 16 juin 1808.* n. p. n. d. 2 pp. 4°.

132. *Der Unter-Präfekt des Bezirks an Herrn Maire zu* ———. *Zabern, den seksten Julius 1808.* n. p., n. d. 1 p. fol.

Signed: Reiss; on the Decree of March 17, 1808.

133. *Décret impérial sur l'installation des Membres du Consistoire central des Juifs établi à Paris. Au palais de Saint-Cloud, le 19 octobre 1808.* Paris, n. d. 2 pp. 4°.

134. *Décret sur l'organisation des synagogues consistoriales. Au camp impérial de Madrid, le 11 décembre 1808.* n. p., n. d. 3 pp. 4°.

135. *Section de l'Intérieur. M. Le Comte R. de Saint-Jean d'Angély, Rapporteur. I^(re) Rédaction. No. 24,724. Rapport et projet de Décret tendant à prononcer en faveur des Juifs de plusieurs départemens, l'exemption portée par l'article 9 du Décret du 6 [17] mars 1808.* Paris, 21 mars 1809. 8 pp., 2 charts. 4°.

136. *Das Israelitische Consistorium des Nieder-Rheinischen Departements. An Herrn Aufsichts-Commissar des Tempels zu* ———. [Strassburg, 1810.] 1 p. 4°.

Article 7 of the Decree of March 17, 1808.

137. *Décret impérial portant que les Juifs du département des Alpes-Maritimes et de quatorze autres départemens sont compris dans l'exception portée par l'article 19 du Décret du 17 mars 1808. Au Palais de Compiègne, le 11 avril 1810.* [Paris, 1810.] 2 pp. 4°.

Bulletin des Lois, No. 279.

138. *Projet de Décret relatif aux Juifs de Livourne,* M. le Comte Berlier, Rapporteur. Paris, 4 février 1811. 2 pp. 4°.

139. *Ministère des Cultes. Division de la comptabilité. Objet: Recouvrement des sommes comprises dans les rôles de répartition pour les Israélites. Circulaire. Paris, le* ——— *juillet 1812.* n. p., n. d. 1 p. fol.

140. *Rapport et projet d'avis sur la question de savoir si les Juifs de la Capitale sont exempts du Décret du 17 mars 1808 sur la Police des Juifs. Rapport du Ministre de l'Intérieur. Du 27 octobre 1813.* M. le Comte Boulay, Rapporteur. I^(re) rédaction. Paris, 10 décembre 1813. 5 pp. 4°.

141. *Décret impérial portant que les Juifs de Paris sont compris dans l'exception portée par l'art. 19 du décret impérial du 17 mars 1808,* sur la police des Juifs. Au palais des Tuilleries, le 26 décembre 1813. Paris, [1814]. 3 pp. 4°.

VII. Names of Jews

142–142a–d. *Décret impérial concernant les Juifs qui n'ont pas de nom de famille et de prénoms fixes. À Bayonne, le 20 juillet 1808.* [Paris, 1808.] 2 pp. 4° [*Bulletin des Lois,* No. 198]; [Paris, 1808.] 3 pp. 8° [No. 3589, *Bulletin,* No. 198]; Nancy, 1808. 8 pp. 8°; Saint-Lô, [1808]. Broadside. Signed by the Prefect L. Costaz and dated Sept. 30, 1808; Pau, n. d. Broadside. [With: "Arrêté du Préfet des Basses-Pyrénées, 6 octobre 1808".]

143. *Le Ministre de l'Intérieur, Comte de l'Empire, à Messieurs les Préfets des départemens. Circulaire. Noms et Prénoms des Juifs.* Paris, le 8 septembre 1808. 2 pp. 4°.

144. *Préfecture des Bouches-du-Rhône. Arrêté relatif à l'exécution du Décret concernant les Juifs qui n'ont pas de nom de famille et de prénoms fixes. Du 23 septembre 1808.* Marseille. Broadside.

145. *Le Consistoire israélite de la circonscription de Paris.* [Paris, 1808.] 1 p. 4°.

Art. 4 of the Decree of July 20, 1808.

146. *Noms et Prénoms des Juifs. Décret impérial concernant les Juifs qui n'ont pas de nom de famille et de prénom fixes. Nahmen und Vornahmen der Juden . . .* Strasbourg, n. d. Broadside.

Together with: "Arrêté du . . . Préfet," Sept. 13, 1808. Fr. & Ger.

147. [Lettre du Préfet de la Moselle sur l'exécution du Décret du 20 juillet 1808.] Metz, 13 sept. 1808. 3 pp. 8°.

148. *Exécution du Décret du 20 juillet 1808, relatif aux noms et prénoms des Juifs. Metz, le 13 septembre 1808.* n. p., n. d. 3 pp. 8°.

Circular to the mayors signed by the prefect Vaublanc.

149. *Décret impérial concernant les Juifs qui n'ont pas de nom de famille et de prénom fixes. Du 20 juillet 1808.* Nancy, n. d. 8 pp. 8°.

Together with "Arrêté du Préfet de la Meurthe du 14 septembre 1808."

150. *Consistoire central des Israélites. Extrait des registres des délibérations. Séance du 8 mars 1810. Central-Consistorium der Israeliten, Auszug aus den Registern der Deliberationen. Sitzung von 8ten März 1810.* Strasbourg, n. d. Broadside.

With a decision by the Lower Rhine Consistory of March 26, 1808, forbidding the use in the Synagogues of other than the newly adopted names.

151. *Le Consistoire israélite de la circonscription de Nancy. A MM. les Commissaires par lui délégués dans le département de la Meurthe,* Nancy, 28 mars 1810. [Nancy, 1810.] 7 pp. 4°.

On the Decree of July 20, 1808.

152. [Circulaire du Consistoire de Paris invitant les Juifs de vérifier leurs déclarations des noms.] Paris, [1809]. 1 p. 4°.

153. *Le Ministre de l'Intérieur, Comte de l'Empire, à MM. les Préfets des départements. Les prénoms des Israélites peuvent être des noms de personnages connus dans la Bible. Circulaire.* Paris, le 28 septembre 1813. 1 p. 4°.

VIII. Debts of the Former Jewish Communities of Metz, Alsace, the Comtadin Communities and Montferrat

154. *Pétition aux citoyens, conseillers d'Etta, membres de la Section de l'Intérieur.* n. p., [1801]. 15 pp. 4°.

Petition by the Thionville community against the community of Metz, signed by Mayer Lévy and the lawyer Dumesnil-Merville.

155. [Arrêté du Préfet de la Moselle,] du 15 brumaire an x [6 Nov. 1801]. 2 pp. 4°.

156–156a–b. *Arrêté relatif à la liquidation des dettes de la ci-devant communauté des Juifs de Metz. Du 5 nivôse an x [26 décembre 1801].* Paris, an x. 3 pp. 4°. [No. 1465. *Bulletin des Lois,* No. 145]. Metz, [an x]. 3 pp. 4°; n. p., n. d. 2 pp. 8°.

157. *Comptes que rendent au Citoyen Préfet du département de la Moselle . . . anciens Syndics en exercice, et Commissaire élus de la ci-devant Communauté des Juifs de Metz, de la gestion qu'ils ont eue des biens de ladite Communauté, ainsi que des recettes et dépenses qu'ils ont faites, à compter du jour de sa suppression, en exécution de l'arrêté des Consuls, du 5 nivôse an 10.* Metz, 17 frimaire an xi [8 décembre 1802]. 18 pp. 4°.

158. *Arrêté qui détermine le mode de répartition des sommes destinées à la liquidation des dettes passives des Juifs d'Alsace.* Boulogne, le 18 brumaire an xii [10 novembre 1803]. [Strasbourg?] an xii. 3 pp. 4°.

159. *Préfecture du Bas-Rhin. Décret du 27 octobre 1806, extrait des Minutes de la Secrétairerie d'Etat. Au Palais de Berlin, le 27 octobre 1806.* Strasbourg, [1806]. Broadside.

On the debts of the former Alsatian communities.

160. *Décret impérial qui prescrit de nouvelles mesures pour faire acquitter la dette des Juifs de la ci-devant province d'Alsace. Au Palais de Saint-Cloud, le 5 septembre 1810.* [Strasbourg, 1810.] 4 pp. 4°.

161. *Extrait des Minutes de la Secrétairerie d'Etat. Au Quartier impérial de Posen, 12 décembre 1806.* [Avignon, 1807.] Broadside.

On the debts of the former Avignon and Comtadin communities.

162. *Arrêté de M. le Préfet de Vaucluse, en date du 4 mars 1811, qui approuve la liquidation de la dette des Juifs de l'ancienne Communauté de Carpentras . . .* [Avignon, 1811.] 10 pp. 4°.

163. *Décret impérial sur le mode de liquidation des dettes de la ci-devant communauté des Juifs du Montferrat. De notre Camp impérial d'Osterode, le 25 mars 1807.* 4 pp. 4°.

We did not include in the bibliography a large collection of tax summonses in order to repay the debts. Some of these summonses contain elaborate texts.

IX. Hymns, Prayers, and Addresses

A. IN HONOR OF NAPOLEON'S CORONATION

164. Crosnic, Josef. *Louange à l'Eternel qui a partagé de Sa Majesté à un mortel, en mettant la couronne impériale sur la tête de Napoléon Bonaparte.* Par un Juif polonais Josef Crosnic תהילה לאל אשר חלק מכבודו לבשר ודם כתר על ראש נאפאליאן באנאפאארטע

להיות קיסר הצרפתים. n. p., [1804]. 2 pp. 4°. Fr. & H.

165. Hirsch, Lazar[e]. *Rede des Bürgers Hirsch Lazar, Rabbiners zu Hagenau und der umliegenden Gegend, gehalten den 29.*

Thermidor Jahr 12 [17 Aug. 1804] bey Gelegenheit der Dank- und Lob-Lieder, welche die jüdische Gemeinde für die dem mächtigen Helden Napoleon Bonaparte ertheilte Kaiser-Krone in der dasigen Synagoge absang. [Strassburg, 1804]. 14 pp. 8°.

166. *Hymne à l'occasion de l'avènement de Sa Majesté Impériale Napoléon au trône de l'Empire des Français. Pour être chanté dans la grande Synagogue de Metz, vendredi, 3 messidor, an 12 [22 juin 1804], à six heures du soir.* Traduite de l'hébreu.

167. Mayer, Jacob. *Ode pour célébrer le jour immortel de l'élévation de Sa Majesté Napoléon à la dignité impériale*; composée en hébreu par J. Mayer. מזמור שיר על יום משיחת אדוננו נאפאלעאן האדיר קיסר פראנצע. Paris, an XII — 1804. 15 pp. 8°.

Fr. & H. Some bibliographers note the Hebrew title מזמור לתודה, see No. 170. "Cette Ode dont M. Jadin, membre du Conservatoire, a fait la musique, a été chanté solennellement par M. Lecerf, artiste dramatique, dans la grande Synagogue . . . 4 thermidor an XII (23 juillet 1804)."

168. Zay, Bernard. *Hymne pour célébrer solennellement le jour immortel du couronnement de Sa Majesté Napoléon . . . Pour être chantée en hébreu, dans la grande Synagogue de Metz, le ——— frimaire an 13 [Nov.–Dec. 1804], 1re du règne de l'Empereur Napoléon 1er.* Composée en hébreu par Bernard Zay, et traduite par Gerson Lévy. Metz, n. d. 7 pp. 4°.

Fr. & H.

169. *Hymne pour être chanté en l'honneur de couronnement de S. M. Napoléon, Empereur des Français et l'inauguration de la Synagogue de Thionville, le vendredi, 28 nivôse an XIII [18 janvier 1805].* Metz, an XIII. 4°.

Translated from the Hebrew by Gerson Lévy.

170. *Fête religieuse célébrée à Paris, le 10 pluviôse an XIII [30 janvier 1805], par les*

Français du culte judaïque, à l'occasion du couronnement de Napoléon שיר ומזמור אשר שרו בני ישראל על יום משיחת נאפאלעאן האדיר קיסר פראנצע . . . פה פאריס יום ד"א של ר"ח אדר ראשון ה' " תק"סה, Paris, 1805. 31 pp. 4°.

Fr. & H. Lazare Chailly, Ouverture de la fête; Hymne, par Mendel Kargeau מאת שיר ומזמור, מענדל קארנואי, traduit par Michel Berr; Cantique, par J. Mayer, מזמור לתודה, מאת מאיר במ"י מבערנהיים, traduit par Michel Berr.

171. Kargeau, Mendel. *Hymne* שיר ומזמור . . . Paris, 1805. 4°.

Reprint: No. 170.

172. יום יום מלכים ימלכו, שיר עת הכתר .נאפוליון למלך, טריאסטי, תקס"ה. 8°.

173. *Nella partenza per Milano all' incoronazione dell' augusto Napoleone I*, sonetti in musa ebraica colla versione italiana del Matasia Levi. Alessandria, 1805.

174. Carcassonne d'Avignon, J. R. *Discours prononcé le 7 décembre 1806, avant le Te Deum, dans le Temple des Israélites portugais, à l'occasion de l'anniversaire du Sacre de S. M. Napoléon Ier . . .* Paris, [1806]. 7 pp. 4°.

175. Milliaud, Moïse. *Cantique adressé à Napoléon le Grand, Empereur des François et Roi d'Italie.* משה מיליאב, מזמור שיר .לנפולאון הגדול הקיסר והמלך. Paris, 1806. 13 pp. 8°.

Fr. & H.

176. Sintzheim, Joseph David. *Discours prononcé par M. le Grand Rabbin D. Sintzheim . . . 4 décembre 1808, anniversaire du jour du couronnement de S. M. I. et R.* Traduit de l'hébreu par M. Elie Halévy. Paris, 1808. 8 pp. 14°.

177. Cologna, Abraham de. *Discours prononcé dans le Temple de la rue Ste Avoyé . . .*

le dimanche 3 décembre 1809, à l'occasion de la cérémonie célébrée en actions de grâces pour l'anniversaire du couronnement de Sa Majesté

l'Empereur et Roi, et pour la conclusion de la Paix entre la France et l'Autriche. Paris, [1809]. 6 pp. 4°.

B. WAR AND PEACE

178. [Büschenthal,] Lipmann Moses. *Ein Psalm der Judengemeinde in Strassburg, für das Glück der fränkischen Waffen im Kriege gegen England.* Aus dem Hebräischen. n. p., n. d. 4 pp. 8°.

179. Lévy, Elie. *Hymne à l'occasion de la Paix, chantée en hébreu et lue en français, dans la grande Synagogue, à Paris, le 17 brumaire an x [8 Nov. 1801]* . . . אליהו חלפן הלוי, השלום שיר ליום הושב חרב אל נדנה יום א' ג' כסליו תקס"ב. Paris, an x. 46 pp. 4°.

H., Fr. & Ger., without German title page.

180. מזמור לתודה על כריתת השלום בין ממלכת ענגלאנד וצרפת *Dankfeyer beym Frieden zwischen England und Frankreich, gehalten von der jüdischen Gemeinde in der Synagoge zu Hannover am ersten Januari 1802.* [Hannover, 1802.] fol.

H., Ger. & Fr.

181. Friedrichsfeld, David b. Zebi Hirsch. קול מבשר משמיע שלום והוא שיר על השלום הנעשה בעיר אמיענס במדינת צרפת בין ממשלת ארצה ובין מלך ארץ אנגלי ומלך ארץ שפאני . . . כ"ג לחודש אדר הסמוך לניסן והוא הו' כמבשר לפ"ק . . . ע"י דוד פרידריכספעלד מילדי ברלין. Amsterdam, 1802. 16 pp. 16°.

182. Sintzheim, Joseph David. *Sermon prononcé dans la grande Synagogue à Strasbourg, le 2 brumaire an 14 [24 oct. 1805] pour célébrer les glorieuses victoires de S. M., l'Empereur des Français* . . . Strasbourg, [1805]. 7 pp. 4°.

183. אל ראשי עם . . . בני ישראל יושבי צרפת ואיטליא. [Paris, 1806.] 2 ff. 8°.

Circular letter advising to pray for the welfare of Napoleon and his victory. Dated Paris, 9 Heshwan, 1806.

184. תפלה לבני ישראל יושבי צרפת ואיטליא על הצלחת צבאות חיל אדונינו הקיסר והמלך נפוליאון הגדול . . . [Paris, 1806.] 2 ff. 12°.

See No. 183.

185-185a. Carcassone d'Avignon, J. R. *Discours prononcé avant le Te Deum, le 25 janvier 1807, dans le Temple des Israélites portugais et avignonais, sis rue Cimetière-St.-André-des-Arcs, à l'occasion des brillantes victoires remportées par la Grande Armée sur les Russes.* Paris, [1807]. 7 pp. 8°.

Another edition of the same place and year. 4 pp. 8°.

186. Cahen, Aaron. *Ode à l'occasion de la paix, chantée dans la grande Synagogue, à Metz, le 15 août 1807, jour de la naissance de Sa Majesté* . . . traduite par Gerson-Lévy, Metz, [1807]. 8 pp. 8°.

Fr. & H.

187. תפלה לבני ישראל יושבי צרפת ואיטליא על הצלחת צבאות חיל אדונינו הקיסר והמלך נפוליאון הגדול, תקנה בחדש מרחשון תקס"ז, ויניציאה, תקס"ז. 12°.

See No. 185.

188. *Ode. Adressée à Sa Majesté Napoléon le Grand, Empereur de France et Roi d'Italie. Par la communauté juive de Francfort à Son passage par cette ville après Son nouveau triomphe* שיר למנצח נאפאליאן הגדול. Francfort, juillet 1807. 8 pp. 4°.

Fr., H. & Ger. Without German title page.

189. Sintzheim, Joseph David, Cologna, Abraham de. *Discours prononcé dans le Temple de la rue Ste-Avoye, le dimanche 25 décembre 1808, lors de la célébration de la fête de la réddition de la ville de Madrid. Suivie d'une prière composée en hébreu, par M. D. Sintzheim . . . et d'une prière et d'un hymne composés en hébreu par M. A. de Cologna.* Traduits en français par M. Elie Halévy. Paris, 1808. 16 pp. 4°.

Fr. & H.

190. Nuñez Vaes, Jacob. קול אומרים הודו, שיר על הצלחת נאפוליאון וחיל צבאו, ה'ר יעקב נוניס ואיס. Livorno, 1808. 4°.

191. Cologna, Abraham de. *Discours prononcé le 13 mai 1809 . . . à l'occasion des victoires remportées par l'armée française aux champs de Tann, Eckmühl, Ratisbonne . . . suivi d'une prière composée en hébreu par . . . D. Sintzheim,* traduite par M. Elie Halévy. Paris, [1809]. 11 pp. 4°.

Fr. & H.

192. *Le Consistoire israélite de la circonscription de Paris.* [Paris, 1809.] 1 p. 8°.

Invitation to the prayers of July 30, 1809, on the occasion of the victories of Engendorf and Wagram.

193. *Le Consistoire israélite à Monsieur —— Notable israélite . . . .* Créveld, 2 août 1809. n. p., n. d. 1 p. 4°.

Fr. & Ger. "Chargés par S. E. le Ministre des Cultes de publier dans les Synagogues de notre circonscription la brillante victoire remportée par notre Grand-Empereur sur nos ennemis près d'Engendorf et de Vagram . . . nous ordonnons . . . de faire chanter dans votre Synagogue . . ."

194. Mayer, Jacques. *Cantique en actions de grâces, pour célébrer les trois immortelles*

batailles de Thann, Eckmühl et Ratisbonne. Composé en hébreu et traduit en français par Jacques Mayer. Strasbourg, 1809. 4 pp. 8°.

Fr. only. "Ce cantique a été chanté en hébreu et lu en français dans la grande Synagogue à Strasbourg, le 21 mai 1809."

195. Mossé, J. M. [Jassuda Michal]. *Ode sur la guerre présente.* Paris, 1809. 9 pp. 8°.

196. ——. *Ode aux insurgés d'Espagne (12 décembre 1809). Ode sur la guerre d'Autriche (15 mai 1809), et chant guerrier aux Français (26 août 1809).* [Paris, 1810.] 24 pp.

197. Séligmann, Michel. *Prière récitée en hébreu dans le Temple de la Rue Ste Avoye, le dimanche 30 juillet 1809, lors de la célébration de la victoire remportée par les armées de S. M. I. et R., aux champs d'Engendorf et de Wagram.* Traduit en Français par M. Elie Halévy . . . Paris, 1809. 7 pp. 4°.

Fr. & H.

198. Cologna, Abraham de. *Discours prononcé le 23 mai 1813, à l'occasion des actions de grâces rendues à l'Eternel, pour la grande victoire remportée par l'armée française au camp Lützen.* Paris, 1813. 8 pp. 4°.

199. *Königreich Westphalen. Konsistorium der Israeliten. Nr. 7844. U. B. An die sämtlichen Israelitischen Gemeinden im Königreich Westphalen.* Kassel, am 12ten Mai 1813. 1 p. 4°.

Prayer in honor of the victory of Luetzen.

200. *Consistoire israélite. Circulaire relative à la paix.* [Strasbourg], 1814. 4 pp. 4°.

C. IN HONOR OF NAPOLEON'S ESCAPING DEATH

201. Schaller, Geofroy Jacques. *Ode à Bonaparte, Premier Consul, conservé pour la troi-*

sième fois à la France. Composé en Latin, et traduite en Français et en Allemand, par Geofroy Jacques Schaller. Nouvelle édition enrichie d'une traduction en [vers] hébreux par Lipmann Moyse [Büschenthal]. מזמור שיר לבאנאפּארט אחרי הציל ה' אותו ג' פעמים מיד מבקשי נפשו. חובר בלשון לאטיני ונעתק אל לשון צרפת ואשכנזי מאת המשורר שאללער ונעתק עתה אל שפת עבר ע"י ליפמאן בן כ"ה משה בישעגטהאל. Strasbourg, [1802]. 16 pp. 8°.

Lat., Fr., Ger. & H. False title: Ode an den Helden Bonaparte. . . . First edition without the Hebrew translation: *Psaume à Bonaparte. Quand Jehova l'eut sauvé des assassins . . . Ein Psalm an Bonaparte* . . . Strasbourg, an IX.

202. Hirsch, Lazar[e]. *Rede des Bürgers Lazar Hirsch, Rabbiners in Hagenau, gehalten den verflossenen 18. Ventose 12, bey Gelegenheit des Dankfestes, welches die jüdische Gemeinde, für die Erhaltung des theuren Lebens des Ersten Konsuls Bonaparte, in der dasigen Synagoge beging.* Strassburg, [1804]. 8 pp. 8°.

203. Isaac, Simon. *Rede gehalten . . . den 20ten Ventos Jahr 12 [March 11, 1804] aus Anlass des verrichteten Dankfests wegen der Rettung des ersten Konsuls.* Mainz, [1804].

D. IN HONOR OF NAPOLEON'S BIRTHDAY

204. Cologna, Abraham de. *Ode pour le jour de la naissance de Napoléon le Grand* . . . Traduite en français par Michel Berr . . . avec un avertissement du traducteur ביום התקדש חג הולדת האדיר נאפוליאוני . . . השירה . . . הזאת שר אברהם חי קולוניא, Paris, 1806. 23 pp. 16°.

Fr. & H. See no. 206.

205–205a. Lattes, Elie Aaron. *Sollennizzandosi dal Popolo d'Israele l'Anniversario della nascita di S. S. M. Napoleone il Grande . . . nel giorno 15 Agosto 1806* . . . dedicato al Signor Furtado. Parigi, 1806. 7 pp. 8°.

It. & H. Another 1, 3 pp. edition in Hebrew with an Italian title page.

206. Mayer, J., and Cologna, Abraham de. *Odes hébraïques pour la célébration de l'anniversaire de la naissance de S. M. L'Empereur des Français et Roi d'Italie*, par J. Mayer et Abraham de Cologna, traduites en français par Michel Berr . . . avec un avertissement du traducteur. Paris, 1806. 37 pp. 8°.

Fr. & H. J. Mayer, Ode מזמור שיר על יום הלדת אדוננו נאפאלעאן; A. Cologna, Ode . . . התקדש ביום חג הולדת האדיר נאפוליאוני. See Nos. 204, 207.

207. Mayer, Jacques. *Ode pour célébrer le jour de l'anniversaire de la naissance de*

Napoléon . . . Composée en hébreu par J. Mayer et traduite en français par M. Berr . . . מזמור שיר על יום הלדת אדוננו נאפאלעאן . . . מאת מאיר במ"י מבערגהיים ונעתק אל לשון צרפת מאת אהבו מנחם בן מ"הורר בער אור'של נרו'. Paris, [1806.] 13 pp. 8°.

See No. 206. Page 12: "Cette Ode a été chantée par les Israélites de l'Empire français, convoqués et assemblés par décret impérial. Paris, le 15 août 1806."

208. Modena, Buonaventura. *L'Augusto anniversario della nascita di S. M. Napoleone il Grande . . . celebrando, li 15 agosto 1806.* Al Signor Furtado . . . canta e dedica למנצח שיר מזמור ביום הלדת הקיסר ומלך נפולאון ראשון. אלה דברי הקטן מזל טוב מודינא. לכבוד ראש האסיפה כמה"ר אברהם פורטאדו, י"צו. Parigi, 1806. 9 pp. 8°.

It. & H.

209. Sègrè, J. B. *Discorso pronunziato . . . all' occasione del giorno anniversaria della nascita di S. M. l'Imperatore dei Francesi . . . Discours prononcé en italien à Paris, le 15 août 1806, dans le Temple hébraïque . . . à l'occasion du jour anniversaire de la naissance de S. M. l'Empereur des François et Roi d'Italie*; traduit en François par Mlle Julie Théodore Cerf-Berr. Paris, 1806. 15 pp. 8°.

It. & Fr.

210. Sintzheim, Joseph David. *Sermon prononcé dans la grande synagogue de Paris, le xv août 1806.* Paris, [1806]. 4°.

Translated by Lyon Marx.

211. Wittersheim, [Nathanael?]. *Hymne chanté par les Députés français professant le culte de Moïse, dans leur Temple à Paris, le 15 août 1806, jour de la naissance de notre auguste Empereur et Roi*; composé en langue hébraïque et traduit par [Samuel] Wittersheim l'aîné, Député du Bas-Rhin. Dédié à M. Furtado מזמור שיר יום הולדת הקיסר ומלך נאפולעאן ... Paris 1806. 13 pp. 8°.

H. & F.

212. Fiorentino, Salomone. *Preghiere recitate, e cantate nel Tempio degli Ebrei di Livorno il di 15. agosto 1808. Ricorrendo il faustissimo giorno natalizio di S. M. I., e R. l'Augustissimo Napoleone I* ... שפ"ר הוד

213. Levi, Matasia. *Per il fausto anniversario della felicissima nascita di S. M. I. E. R. Napoleone Il Grande ... Sabbato giorno ... 15. agosto 1812* ... Alessandria, [1812]. 12 pp. 4°.

214. Landau, David. *Hymne pour célébrer l'anniversaire de la naissance de Sa Majesté Napoléon Ier ... Chanté solennellement par la Communauté israélite ... Le 15 août 1813* מזמור לתודה ליום הולדת נאפאלעאן הגדול הקיסר ומלך אשר אמרו עדת ישראל ... דרעזדען יום ג' י"ד אב שנת תקע"ג לפ"ק. Dresde, [1813]. 4 pp. 8°.

Reprinted in *L'Univers israélite*, VIII, 155.

מלכות קול תפלה קול תחנה לצור שוכן מעונה לכבוד ולתפארת גפן ... נאפוליאני. Livorno, 1808. 16, 6 pp. 4°.

It. & H.

E. IN HONOR OF NAPOLEON'S VISITS TO OCCUPIED CITIES

215. Büschenthal, Lippmann Moses. *Ode an Se. Majestät Kaiser der Franzosen, auf seiner Reise durch die Niederrheinischen Departements, von der Judengemeinde zu Coblenz,* ... תהלת לעדת ישורון. Rödelheim, n. d. 8°.

Ger. & H. Celebration in honor of Napoleon's arrival on Sept. 17, 1804. Published by Wolf Heidenheim with his introduction in German.

216. *Prières prononcées par les Israélites à l'occasion de l'entrée solennelle de Sa Majesté Napoléon le Grand, et de Son Auguste Campagne dans la bonne ville d'Amsterdam* שיר ותפלה אשר שרו והתפללו היהודים ביום בוא הוד הקיסר נאפאלעאן עירו הטובה אמשטרדאם הבירה. n. p., [1804]. 18 pp. 16°.

Fr. & H. With: "Prière prononcée par le Grand-Rabbin, le Sieur Moïse Saul."

217. Scheyer, Herz David, Grand Rabbin. *Sermon en réjouissance et action de grâces des Israélites mayençais, à l'occasion du séjour de Sa Majesté Impériale Napoléon ... traduit en allemand par Moyse Emmanuel Wihl. Rede am Dank- und Freudenfeste der Mainzer Jüdischen Gemeinde bei Gelegenheit des Aufenthaltes unseres theuersten allergnädigsten Kaisers Napoleon in Mainz* ... אמירה נעימה ביום החדוה, בראות תוך חומותינו, מחמד עינינו, אדונינו החכם האדיר גבור חיל קיסר יר"ה. נאפאלעאן באנגעפערט ... אשר חבר ודרש הירץ שייאר. Mayence, Fructidor an XII [1804]. 47, 18 pp. 4°.

H., Fr. & Ger.

218. Aron, Joseph Philippe. *Psaume pour louer l'Eternel qui nous a fait la grâce de conduir dans nos murs ... Napoléon le Grand ... le 17 juillet 1807, chanté à la congrégation d'Israélites* ... Dresde, 1807. fol.

Fr., Ger. & H.

219. שיר למנצח נאפאלעאן הגדול קיסר צרפת
ומלך איטאליא יר"ה הובא לי מעדת ישורון,
יושבי קרית פראנקפורט בשובו שער עירם משדי
חיל המערכה אשר בו נבר ועשה *Traduction de
l'Ode adressée à Sa Majesté Napoléon le
Grand . . . par la communauté juive de Francfort à Son passage par cette ville après son
nouveau triomphe.* Francfort a/M., 1807.
16 pp. 4°.

Fr. & H.

220. שיר הוד לכבוד אדונינו הקיסר האדיר
וההסיד. ה' ירום הודו וירשום וגבה ונישא נאפאלעאן
קיסר צרפת ומלך אטליה ושאר ארצות ביום זרחה
השמש לנו פה וואַרשויא יום לירח שנת התקס"ז
ליצירה אז ישיר ישראל את השירה הזאת.
[Warsaw, 1807.]

Fr. & H. Ode in honor of Napoleon's arrival at
Warsaw in December, 1806. Reprinted in: .ע ;נ
פרענק, יהודי פולין בימי מלחמות נפוליון. Warsaw, 1912,
and in: *Kwartalnik*, II (1913), 121–27.

221. *Hymne, louanges et prières, prononcés
par le Révérend Grand-Rabbin des Israélites
portugais à Amsterdam; à l'occasion de ce que
Leurs Majestés Impériales et Royales l'Em-*
pereur et Roi, Napoléon le Grand, et l'Impératrice Reine, Marie Louise, daignèrent honorer
de Leur Auguste présence le Temple de la
susdite Communauté, au mois d'octobre 1811
קול תודה רנה ותפלה קול זמרה ששון ושמחה.
קול אומרים הודו ל"ה בצלצלי שמע. ביום האדיר
הזה בימי שנה. יום אשר ראינו את המאור הגדול
בתוך המקדש המעוֹן, בית תפלת הספרדים יע"א
פה העיר . . . אמשטרדם יע"א. הקיסר העצום.
והמלך האדיר . . . נאפוליאון הגדול קיסר
הצרפתים ומלך איטאליא יר"ה עם נות בית. אשת
חקו כל כבודה בת קיסר ומלך מראיה לואיזה יר"ה.
Amsterdam, 1811. 22 pp. 4°.

Fr. & H.

222. *Prières et cantiques de la Communauté
des Israélites chantés à l'occasion de l'heureuse
arrivée de L. L. M. M. Impériales et Royales
Napoléon le Grand, et de Son Auguste Epouse
Marie Louise dans la bonne ville de Rotterdam,*
ליהודים היתה אורה שמחה וגילה. שירי כבוד
ותפלה ביום עבור הקיסר נפליון ונבירתו פה
ראטרדאם. n. p., [1812]. II, 11 pp. 4°.

Fr. & H.

F. IN HONOR OF NAPOLEON AND HIS FAMILY

223. Bardi, Joseph, *In nuptias Napoleonis
magni . . . et Mariae-Aloysiae Austriacae . . .*
carmen hebraïcum נדול ורב ורם נאפוליאון,
אזמרה שמך משמן טוב. Pisa, 1810. 1 p. fol.

224. *Le Consistoire israélite à MM. les
Commissaires-surveillants des Synagogues.
Créveld, 3 décembre 1810.* n. p., n. d. 4 pp. 4°.

Fr. & Ger. Prayer for Napoleon's wife.

225. *Das Konsistorium der Israëliten des
Bezirkes von Winzenheim, an die bei den
Synagogen angestellten Aufsichts-Kommissa-
rien. Winzenheim, 18ᵗᵉⁿ April 1810.* n. p.,
n. d. 2 pp. 4°.

Fr. & Ger. Prayer for Napoleon and Marie
Louise.

226. Löw, Jehuda Ben Seeb. יהודה ליב בן
זאב, קול רנה. Wien, [1810]. 8°.

Odes in honor of the peace with Austria and
Napoleon's marriage.

227. *Prière pour Sa Majesté l'Impératrice et
Reine, adoptée par le Consistoire Central pour
être récitée dans tous les Temples des Israélites
de l'Empire.* Paris, 1810. 7 pp. 4°.

228. Rocque Martine [Rocquemartine, or
Rocca Martino], Mardochée. *Mandement
du Grand Rabbin du Consistoire des Israélites
de la circonscription des Bouches-du-Rhône,
séant à Marseille. Prière . . . à l'occasion de la
grossesse de S. M. l'Impératrice Reine. Marseille, 26 novembre 1810.* n. p., n. d. 3 pp. 4°.

229. שיר כלולות, להג אפריון נאפוליון הראשון
עם מריה לואיזה בת הקיסר מאוסטריה, מקהלת
היהודים בווינא. Wien, 1810. 11 pp. 8°.

230. Ro[c]quemartine [Rocquemartine, or
Rocca Martino], Mardochée. *Mandement
de Mardochée Roquemartine, Grand Rabbin,
du Consistoire israélite de la circonscription de
Marseille, au sujet de l'heureux accouchement
de S. M. l'Impératrice Reine.* Marseille, 24
Mars 1811. 4 pp. 4°.

231. Mossé, J. M. [Jassuda Michal]. *La
France consolée. Ode sur la naissance de S.*

M. le Roi de Rome. Paris, 1811. 6 pp.
8°.

232. Sintzheim, Joseph David. *Discours
prononcé le 9 juin 1811, dans le Temple de la
rue Saint-Avoye, à l'occasion de la naissance
de Sa Majesté le Roi de Rome.* Paris, 1811.
6 pp. 4°.

233. שיר ותפלה, ליום הלדת מלך רומא. Hamburg, 1811. 4°.

234. שירים, בעת נולד בן לנפוליון. Amsterdam, 1811. 15 pp. 8°.

G. MISCELLANEOUS

235. Latzar [Lazare], Hirsch. *Prière pour
la conservation des jours et la prospérité de
S. M. l'Empereur des Français. Composée en
langue hébraïque par M. Hirsch Latzar,
Rabbin à Haguenau et arrondissement.* n. p.,
n. d.

Fr. & Ger.

236. Moline, Chéry. *Poème sur le rétablissement d'Israël.* Paris, 1807. 11 pp. 8°.

Napoleon will re-establish the Jewish nation;
missionary tendency.

237. *Culte de Moïse. Traduction de l'hébreu
des prières récités par les Israélites de Lyon à
l'ouverture de leur temple.* Lyon, n. d. 4 ff. 8°.

"Prières . . . le 7 mars 1807 . . . fait par Abraham
Mayer, Ministre du culte judaïque de Lyon."
With a prayer for Napoleon.

238. Cohen, Salomon Jacob. *Über den
wahren Geist der mosaischen Gesetzgebung.
Eine Predigt, am ersten Tage der jüdischen
Pfingsten in der Synagoge zu Cassel gehalten.*
Cassel, 1808. 20 pp.

With a prayer for Napoleon.

239. Nuñez Vaes, Jacob, הוד מלכות, ה"ר
יעקב נונים ואיס. Livorno, 1808. 24 pp. 4°.

H. & It. Prayer for Napoleon.

240. Carlburg, Löb. *Rede des Herrn Löb
Carlburg, Grossrabbiners der Consistorial-
Synagoge zu Crefeld, gehalten den 26ten May,
bey Einweihung gedachter Synagoge . . .* Crefeld, 1809. 8 pp. 16°.

With a prayer for Napoleon.

241. *Consistoire Central des Israélites. Extrait des Registres des Délibérations. Séance
du 30 août 1809.* [Paris, 1809]. Broadside.

H. & Fr. Text of a prayer for Napoleon.

242. Monteux [Montaux], Moyse. *Discours prononcé à la Synagogue de Carpentras . . . le 23 décembre 1809, jour de
l'installation du Chantre de la Synagogue.*
n. p., n. d. 15 pp. 8°.

With a prayer for Napoleon.

243. *Procès-verbal de l'installation suivie, le
jour 25 mai 1809, du Consistoire départemental des Israélites établi à Casal . . . et discours prononcé à cette occasion par M. le
sous-préfet [Fauzon] et par M. le Grand
rabbin [Trèves Michel Vita].* Casal, [1809].
4°.

With a prayer for Napoleon.

244. Roque-Martine [Rocquemartine, or
Rocca Martino], Mardochée. *Discours pro-*

noncé le jour de l'Installation du Consistoire israélite, de la circonscription de Marseille [*le 24 mai 1809*], par Mardochée Roque-Martine, Grand-Rabbin, ex-membre du Grand Sanhédrin. n. p., n. d. 8 pp. 8°.

With a prayer for Napoleon.

245. *Le Consistoire du Département du Bas-Rhin, Au Sieur Commissaire surveillant de la Synagogue à* ———. *Mars 1810.* [Strasbourg, 1810.] 1 p. 4°.

Fr. & Ger. With the Central Consistory's decision of Aug. 30, 1809 (see No. 241) and the "nouvelle formule de prière pour notre auguste Souverain."

246. *Benedizione che dalla Nazione Ebrea si da in ogni festiva solennita' all' Augusto Nostro Imperatore e Re coll'esposizione del Sacro Pentateuco. Bénédiction que la nation juive donne à S. M. l'Empereur et Roi dans toutes les fêtes avec l'exposition de la Sainte Ecriture.* Mantova, 1810. 10 pp. 8°.

It. & Fr.

247. Bridel, Louis. *Traité de l'année juive, antique et moderne. Suivi d'une ode hébraïque à la louange de Sa Majesté Impériale et Royale Napoléon le Grand . . . avec sa traduction en vers français,* Basle, 1810. 4, xxx, 196 pp. 8°.

Page 183: "Ode."

248. *Le Consistoire israélite à Monsieur . . .* Créveld, 20 Mars 1810. n. p., n. d. 3 pp. 4°.

Fr. & Ger. The Central Consistory's decision of Aug. 30, 1809; see No. 241.

249. *Notice sur la fondation, en cette ville, d'une Synagogue consistoriale, pour l'exercice du Culte juif.* Bordeaux, n. d. 4 pp. 4°.

Contains Rabbi Abraham Andrade's sermon of June 7, 1810, in honor of Napoleon.

250. *Descrizione della solenne istallazione del Concistoro israelitico eseguita in Roma il di 1 agosto 1811.* Roma, 1811. 27 pp. 8°.

With a prayer for Napoleon.

251. [Extrait des délibérations du Consistoire central du 8 avril 1812, rendant grâces à Napoléon 1er au sujet de l'instruction religieuse de la jeunesse juive.] n. p., n. d. Broadside.

252. *Inauguration du Temple. Programme.* [Bordeaux, 1812.] 2 ff. fol.

Contains: "Prière pour Sa Majesté l'Empereur et Roi, et la Famille Impériale," by Rabbi Abraham Andrade.

253. *A Messieurs les membres du Consistoire de* ———. Bordeaux, 1812. 2 pp. 4°.

Prospectus for the *Te Deum* composed by J. B. Auvray for the inauguration of the Bordeaux Synagogue, with Abraham de Cologna's ode "qui contient une invocation pour la famille impériale."

254. Helft, Isaac. *Discours prononcé par M. Isaac Helft, commissaire délégué de la Synagogue Consistoriale de Marseille, à l'occasion de l'inauguration du Temple Israélite de la Ville de Lyon, le 13 avril 1813.* Lyon, 1813. 5 pp. 8°.

With a eulogy for Napoleon.

255. Roque-Martine [Rocquemartine, or Rocca Martino], Mardochée, *Prière composée . . . pour être récitée à l'occasion de l'inauguration du nouveau Temple israélite de la ville de Lyon* [*mars 1813*] . . . Traduite en français par M. Elie Halévy . . . Paris, 1813. 5 pp. 4°.

Fr. & H. With a prayer for Napoleon.

256. Cracovia, Jacob Samuel. נא שומרי . . . היכל אפול. n. p., n. d.

Ode in honor of Napoleon.

257. מזמור שיר, מקהלת ישראל בקליוא לכבוד נאפוליון. n. p. n. d. 4 pp. fol.

H. & Ger.

H. IN HONOR OF LOUIS AND JÉRÔME NAPOLEON

258. Saul, Moses. *Lofzangen en gebeden ter dank en feestvierung binnen de groote kerk der Hoogduitsche Joodsche Gemeente te Amsterdam. Ter gelegheid der plegtige intrede van . . . Lodevyk Napoleon . . . en uit 't Hebreuwsch vertaald dor Ephraïm Lion Davids* שירים ותשבחות להשמיע בקול רנה ותודה בבה"כ הגדולה דק"ק אשכנזים באמשטרדם יע"א ביום בא לעיר הזאת אדונינו מלכינו המלך החסד לודוויג נאפאעלעאן . . . יוסדו ע"י אדמ"ו . . . יעקב משה . . . והועתק ללשון הולאנדיא ע"י כ"ה אפרים בן כ"ה ליב. Amsterdam, [1807]. 32 pp. 8°.

Dut. & H.

259. קול תודה וקול שמחה ותפילה. Amsterdam, 1807. 16 pp. 8°.

Prayers and order of service for the birthday of Louis Napoleon, published by Aaron Belinfante and Abraham Gomes de Mesquita.

260. Amersport, Benjamin. שיר, ה"ר בנימין אמרספורט. Amsterdam, [1808.] 16 pp. 8°.

Fr. & H. Ode in honor of Louis Napoleon, translated by Moïse Lehmans.

261. ——— . שיר נמסר למלכנו לואיס נאפוליאון בעת בואו לעיר אמשטרדם לקבוע שם

1808 סיפטימבר ב' הולדו ביום מלכותו. Amsterdam, 1808.

Fr. & H. Translated into Hebrew by Moïse ben Treitel.

262. Berlin, Aryeh Leib. דבר בעתו מה טוב, ה"ר אריה ליב ברלין. Cassel [Roedelheim, 1807].

Sermon in honor of Jérôme Napoleon's coronation.

263. שיר לכבוד הירונימוס באנאפארטע, Roedelheim, n. d. fol.

H., Ger. & Fr.

264. Jacobsohn, Israel. *Rede am Dankfeste wegen des von Seiner Majestät dem Könige von Westphalen den Unterthanen jüdischer Nation ertheilten Bürgerrechts, gehalten in der Synagoge zu Cassel den 11. Februar 1808.* Cassel, [1808]. 15 pp.

265. ——— . *Discours prononcé dans la Synagogue de Cassel, le 15 Novembre 1810, anniversaire de la naissance de S. M. le Roi de Westphalie.* Traduit de l'allemand par C. D. Casel, 1810. 14 pp.

X. VARIOUS DOCUMENTS OF JEWISH COMMUNITIES

266. *Sendschreiben des R. [Joseph] David Sinzheim an seine jüdischen Mitbrüder im Niederrheinischen Departement.* Aus dem hebräischen übersetzt von B. Lipmann Moses. Strassburg, [1803]. 15 pp. 16°.

Against usury. See No. 267.

267. *Dank-Adresse mehrerer jüdischen Bürger an Herrn David Sinzheim, Rabbiner zu Strassburg. 16 Messidor an XI [5 July 1803].* Strassburg. 3 pp. 16°.

See No. 266.

268. *Le Consistoire central des Israélites, à Messieurs les membres du Consistoire départemental de la circonscription d ———— . Paris, ce ——— [8 mai 1809].* n. p., n. d. 3 pp. fol.

Founding of schools.

269. *Le Consistoire central des Israélites, A Messieurs les Membres du Consistoire départemental de la circonscription d ——— . Paris, ce [mai 1809].* n. p., n. d. 3 pp. fol.

Organisation of the Consistories.

270. *Procès-verbal de l'installation, suivie le 25 mai 1809 du Consistoire général des Israélites établi à Casal.* Casal, n. d. 4°.

271. *Empire Français. Extrait des registres des délibérations du Consistoire des Israelites de la circonscription de Wintzenheim, du 29ᵉ juin 1809. Auszug aus den Registern der Berathschlagungen des Consistorium der Israeliten des Wintzenheimer-Bezirks. Arrêté* No. —. Colmar, n. d. 7 pp. 4°.

Fr. & Ger. On the nomination and duties of the Synagogue commissioners.

272. *La Conservation de la vie.* Paris, *18 octobre 1809.* Paris, [1809]. 6 pp. 4°.

Appeal of the Central Consistory for vaccination of children; see No. 273.

273. *A MM. les Membres du Consistoire départementale de la circonscription de ——.* n. p., [1809]. 6 pp. 4°.

Appeal of the Central Consistory for the vaccination of children, Oct. 18, 1809. "C'est ainsi que nous parviendrons à mériter la confiance et la continuation de la bienveillance que le plus grand des Monarques nous accorde." See No. 272.

274. *Les Membres du Consistoire israélite de la circonscription de Marseille, à M ——. Marseille, le 2 novembre 1809.* n. p., n. d. 1 p. 4°.

For the vaccination of children; see No. 272.

275. *Solution donnée par le Consistoire Central des Israélites de l'Empire à diverses questions qui lui ont été proposées par la Synagogue de Coblentz; accompagnée de pièces y relatives et suivie de la décision de S. E. le Ministre des Cultes.* Paris, 1809. 31 pp. 4°.

276. *Le Consistoire de Trèves, aux habitans de sa circonscription, professant la Religion mosaïque. Das Consistorium zu Trier an die Einwohner seines Bezirks, welche sich zur Mosaischen Religion bekennen.* n. p., [1809]. 7 pp. 4°.

Fr. & Ger. Appeal for morality.

277. *Le Consistoire Israélite du Bas-Rhin, A M. le Commissaire.* Strasbourg, *le* [24] *janvier 1810.* n. p., n. d. 1 p. 4°

"Recensement des mendians."

278. *Le Consistoire israélite à —— commissaire surveillant de la Synagogue. Créveld, 7 février 1810.* n. p., n. d. 3 pp. 4°.

Mendicity.

279. *Das Consistorium der Israeliten des Nieder-Rheinischen Departements, An Herrn —— Aufssichts-Commissär der Synagoge zu ——.* Strassburg, *den 10 Hornung 1810.* n. p., n. d. 2 pp. 4°.

Mendicity.

280. *Le Consistoire Israëlite de Trèves à ses co-religionnaires. Trèves, le 15 février 1810.* n. p., n. d. 4 pp. 4°.

Fr. & Ger. Against mendicity.

281. *Le Consistoire israélite du département du Bas-Rhin, à M ——, Commissaire surveillant de la Synagogue à ——. Das Consistorium der Israeliten des Nieder-Rheinischen Departements, An Herrn Aufsichts-Commissär der Synagoge zu ——. Strasbourg, le 19 février 1810.* n. p., n. d. 2 pp. 4°.

Fr. & Ger. Against mendicity.

282. *Le Grand Rabbin du Consistoire de Nancy, aux Israélites de la circonscription.* Nancy, *le 22 février 1810.* n. p., n. d. Broadside.

Signed: Jacob Schweich. Against mendicity.

283. *Le Consistoire de Nancy à MM. les Commissaires par lui désignés.* Nancy, 1810. 4°.

Signed: J. Schweich. On consistorial administration.

284. *Auszug aus dem Register der Berathschlagungen des Konsistoriums der Israeliten*

des Bezirks von Winzenheim. Sitzung vom 12ten März 1810. Beschluss No. 23. n. p., n. d. 4 pp. 4°.

Organization of the Synagogues.

285. *Le Consistoire israélite de la circonscription de Winzenheim. A Messieurs les Commissaires surveillans de son ressort. 15 mars 1810.* Colmar, n. d. 4 pp. 4°.

Fr. & Ger. Appeal for the vaccination of children; see No. 273.

286. *Le Consistoire israélite de la circonscription de Nancy, à MM. les Commissaires par lui délégués dans le Département de la Meurthe. Nancy, le 28 mars 1810.* 7 pp. 4°.

Census of the Jews and their economic and cultural status, with a letter from the prefect dated Jan. 30' 1810. See No. 308.

287. *Le Consistoire israélite de la circonscription de Nancy. A ses co-religionnaires. 9 avril 1810.* n. p., n. d. Broadside.

Mendicity.

288. *Le Consistoire des Israélites à Messieurs les Commissaires surveillants des Synagogues. 7 mai 1810.* Créveld, n. d. Broadside.

Fr. & Ger. Appeal to profit from the amnesty of March 25, 1810, for deserters.

289. *Adresse du Consistoire israélite de Marseille . . . Marseille, 15 mai 1810.* n. p., n. d. 4 pp. 4°.

290. *Le Consistoire israélite du département du Bas-Rhin, Au Sr Commissaire surveillant de la Synagogue à ———— . Juin 1810.* [Strasbourg, 1810]. 2 pp. 4°.

"Livraison des cèdres et palmes pour la fête de Tabernacle."

291. *Extrait des registres des délibérations du Consistoire israélite de la circonscription de Wintzenheim du 8 juillet 1810.* n. p., n. d. 4°.

Mendicity.

292. *Auszug aus den Registern der Berathschlagungen des Konsistoriums der Israeliten des Winzenheimer-Bezirks. Vom 8ten Heumonat 1810.* Colmar, n. d. 10 pp. 4°.

293. *Extrait des registres des délibérations du Consistoire israélite de la circonscription de Wintzenheim. Délibération du 24 juillet 1810.* n. p., n. d.

Mendicity.

294. *Le Consistoire israélite du Bas-Rhin à M ———— Commissaire surveillant du Temple mosaïque de ———— . Strasbourg, ce ———— juillet 1810.* n. p., n. d. 4°.

Fr. & Ger. Against religious ceremonies on the streets.

295. *Consistoire Central. Extrait des registres des délibérations. Séance du dix-sept septembre 1810.* [Paris, 1810]. 3 pp. fol.

"Taxes forcées pour cause de bienfaisance."

296. *Consistoire Central. Extrait des registres des délibérations. Séance du 17 septembre 1810. Central-Consistorium. Auszug aus den Berathschlagungs-Registern. Sitzung an dem 17ten September 1810.* Strasbourg, n. d. 3 pp. fol.

Fr. & Ger. A Strasbourg edition of Nos. 295, 299.

297. *Le Consistoire Central des Israélites de l'Empire, à ses coreligionnaires du Bas-Rhin. Paris, le 22 octobre 1810. Das Central-Consistorium der Israeliten des Reichs, An seine Mitreligions-Verwandten des Nieder-Rheins.* Strasbourg, n. d. 3 pp. fol.

Fr. & Ger. Against the internal conflicts and for morality in the Jewish communities.

298. *Le Consistoire du Culte israélite de la Circonscription de Trèves, à Monsieur le Maire de ———— . Trèves, le 29 octobre 1810.* n. p., n. d. 2 pp. 4°.

Circular of May 30, 1809, demanding information on the situation of the Jewish communities.

299. *Extrait des registres des délibérations du Consistoire des Israëlites de la circonscription de Wintzenheim. Du 13 novembre 1810. Arrêté.* Colmar, n. d. 14 pp. 4°.

Fr. & Ger. With the Central Consistory's decision of Sept. 1810; see No. 295.

300. *Empire Français. Extrait des registres des délibérations du Consistoire des Israëlites de la circonscription de Wintzenheim. Du 13 novembre 1810 Arrêté No. —. Auszug aus den Berathschlagungsregistern des Consistoriums der Israeliten des Wintzenheimer-Bezirks.* Colmar, 1810. 14 pp. 4°.

With the Central Consistory's letter of Oct. 22, 1810; see No. 297.

301. *Arrêté du Consistoire israélite de la circonscription de Strasbourg. Strasbourg, le 6 décembre 1810. Schluss des Israelitischen Consistoriums der Strassburger Circonscription.* n. p., n. d. 2 pp. fol.

Fr. & Ger. Morality, charity, founding of a theological school in the department, etc.

302. *Le Consistoire israélite du département du Bas-Rhin, A M. —— Commissaire surveillant de la Synagogue de —— . Das Consistorium der Israeliten des Nieder-Rheinischen Departements, An Herrn Aufsichts-Commissär der Synagoge zu ——.* Strasbourg, 1810. 2 pp. 4°.

Fr. & Ger. Against mendicity.

303. *Le Consistoire central des Israélites, A Messieurs les Membres du Consistoire départemental de la circonscription d ——.* [Paris, 1810?] 3 pp. fol.

Election of the members of the Consistories.

304. *Das Consistorium des israelitischen Cultes vom Departement des Donnersbergs. An die Herren Rabbinen . . . Circulaire No. 426. Mainz, 18ten April 1811.* n. p., n. d. 4 pp. 4°.

Appeal to serve in the army.

305. *Le Commissaire général de Police à Strasbourg, Au Consistoire israélite du Bas-Rhin. Der General-Polizey-Commissär, An das israelitische Consistorium des Nieder-Rheins. Strasbourg, le 19 juin 1811.* 2 pp. 4°.

Fr. & Ger. Against Jewish beggars.

306. *Le Ministre de l'Intérieur, Comte de l'Empire, A Messieurs les Préfets des départemens. Circulaire. Réclamations en matière de contributions pour frais du culte israélite. Paris, le 12 décembre, 1811.* 1 p. fol.

307. דברי אגרת. Rödelheim, 1812. 16 pp. 4°.

Statutes of the Westphalian Consistories.

308. *Das Consistorium der Israeliten des Winzenheimer-Bezirks an die Auffsichts-Kommissarien seines Gebiets. Winzenheim, den 31ten Jenner 1812.* Colmar, n. d. 7 pp. 4°.

Census of the Jews, their economic and social status; see No. 286.

309. *Das Consistorium der Israeliten des Nieder-Rheinischen Departement, An Herrn-Aufsichts-Commissär der Synagoge zu ——.* Strassburg, den 19ten Hornung 1812. 2 pp. 4°.

Against beggars.

310. *Le Consistoire des Israélites de la circonscription de Wintzenheim, A Messieurs les Commissaires surveillans près les synagogues des communes de son ressort. Wintzenheim, le 20 avril 1812. Französisches Reich. Das Consistorium der Israeliten des Winzenheimer Bezirks an die Herren — Aufsichtskommissarien der Gemeindesynagogen.* Colmar, n. d. 15 pp. 4°.

Fr. & Ger. Founding of schools, with the Central Consistory's letter of March 22, 1812.

311. צירקולאר שרייבען לנדיבי לב ומחזיקי תורה בני עמינו שי' מהנבאים דבית המדרש אים

נידערדרהיינישען דעפאַרטעמענט. Strasbourg, n. d. 4°.

May 27, 1812. On the founding of theological schools, with praises for Napoleon.

312. *Le Consistoire israélite du département du Bas-Rhin, à Monsieur le Commissaire surveillant près le Temple mosaïque de la commune d'* ——— . *Strasbourg, ce 2 juin 1814.* Strasbourg, 1814.

Fr. & Ger.

313. *Les membres du Comité de la Société israélite d'encouragement et de secours à leurs co-religionnaires.* [Paris, 1815.] 1 p. fol.

Appeal for charity and report of activities since 1811.

314. *Culte de Moyse. Répartition des frais. Exercice 181–. Strasbourg, le* ——— *181–. A Monsieur.* n. p., n. d. 2 pp. 4°.

We did not include in the bibliography a large collection of tax summonses. Some of these summonses contain elaborate texts.

XI. The Invasion and the Hundred Days

315. *La Délivrace d'Israël. Coeur imité de l'écriture, à Son Altesse Royale Madame Duchesse d'Angoulême.* Provins, [1814]. 8 pp. 8°.

The non-Jewish author uses a historical Jewish subject for the expression of his political ideas. See No. 317.

316. Jacob, Meyer [Mayer, Jacob]. *Rede des Herrn Meyer Jacob, Ober Rabbiner Beym Consistorium der Israeliten des Nieder-Rheins, gehalten den 4ten Juny 1814, in der Consistorial-Synagoge zu Strassburg, bey Gelegenheit der Widerherstellung des Burbon'schen Hauses.* n. p., 1814. 11 pp. 4°.

317. Leroy, Joseph. *Israelitarum epinicium in occasum regis regnique Babylonici.* (Isaïe, prophet, chap. xiv.) — *Chant de joie des Israélites, sur la chute du roi et du royaume de Babylone,* traduction libre. Paris, 1814. 15 pp.

See note on No. 315.

318. *Par ordonnance de Son Excellence le Général en Chef de l'armée, Mr. le Comte de Wrede.* [Colmar, 1814.] 7 pp. 4°.

Forced contribution to be paid by the Jews. See Nos. 319–320 and Anchel, R., "Contribution levée en 1813–14 sur les Juifs du Haut-Rhin," *REJ,* lxxxii (1928), 494–501.

319. *Extrait des registres de la Préfecture du Département du Haut-Rhin, du 26 juillet 1814.* Arrêté No. 400. 4 pp. 4°.

See Nos. 318, 320.

320. *Ordonnance de Son Excellence le Général en Chef de l'armée, Mr. le Comte de Wrede.* [Colmar, 1814.] 7 pp. 4°.

See Nos. 318–319.

321. Mossé, J. M. *Le Cri du peuple français.* Paris, 1814. 4 pp. 4°.

322. Cologna, Abraham de. *Discours religieux, prononcé le 21 janvier 1815, à l'occasion de la cérémonie funèbre célébrée dans le Temple israélite, rue Sainte-Avoye* [Paris, 1815.] 9 pp. 4°.

In memory of Louis xvi.

323. Mayer, Joseph. *Qu'ils viennent! nous les attendons! voilà comment nous les recevrons.* Paris, [1815]. 4°.

324. B[err], M[ichel]. *Lettre à M. le Comte Lanjuinais, membre du Sénat . . .* n. p., avril 1814. 53 pp. 8°.

On the political events.

325. B.[err], M.[ichel]. *Observations sur l'Acte additionnel aux constitutions de l'Empire et sur notre situation politique.* Paris, 1815. 40 pp. 8°.

In favor of the Acte.

326. Dalmbert, M[ath]ias M., et M[ie] L[s]

Giraudeau. *Observations sur l'Acte additionnel aux constitutions de l'Empire du 22 avril 1815.* ¯aris, avril 1815. 41 pp. 4°.

In favor of the Acte.

See Nos. 21–22a.

XII. JEWS OF FOREIGN COUNTRIES FOR THEIR GOVERNMENTS AGAINST NAPOLEON

327. *Form of Prayer . . . the success of His Majesty's arms, and the spreading of . . . peace over us. To be read in the Portuguese Synagogue . . . on Friday, the 13th of February, 1801 . . .* London, 1801. 20 pp. 8°.

Engl. & H.

328. Luria, Isaac. *A penitential sermon, preached in the Spanish and Portuguese Jewish Synagogue . . . 19th of October, 1803 . . . success to His Majesty's arms . . .* London, 1803. 8°.

329. Herschel, Solomon. *Sermon preached . . . success of His Majesty's Fleet under Lord Nelson, off Trafalgar.* London, 1805. 16 pp. 4°.

330. Weil, Meyer Simon. *Hoffnung u. Vertrauen. Predigt wegen des Ausmarsches des vaterländischen Heeres, gehalten am 28sten März 1813 in Gegenwart mehrerer freiwilligen Jäger jüdischen Glaubens in d. grossen Synagoge zu Berlin.* Aus d. Hebräischen übersetzt v. Isaac Levin Auerbach. [Berlin, 1813.] 16 pp.

Second edition, Berlin, 1918.

331. Eisenstadt, Michael. שיר תהילה. Schklow, 1814. 8°.

Ode in honor of Russia's victory over Napoleon.

332. Feder, Tobias Gutmann. הצלחת אלכסנדר. Berdyczew, 1814. 16 pp. 16°.

Ode in honor of Russia's victory over Napoleon.

333. —— . קול שמחה וששון. Berdyczew, 1814. 8°.

Ode in honor of Russia's victory over Napoleon.

334. Jeitteles, Juda. *Worte des Friedens, der Wahrheit u. der Religion, vorgetragen am 7. Juli 1814 in der sogenannten Altneu-Synagoge zu Prag, in Gegenwart der daselbst zu Feyer wegen erkämpften Friedens u. glücklicher Rückkehr Sr. glorreichen Majestät unsers Kaisers u. Königs versammelten Israelitengemeinde.* Prag, [1814].

335–335a. Kronik, Moses. תפלה ותודה. Breslau, 1814. 8°.

H. Ode and prayer by the Jewish community of Glogau on the occasion of the blockade of Apr. 24, 1814. Another edition with a German translation.

336. Levi, Abraham. *Rede in der Synagoge zu Rödelheim am 1ten May 1814, bei Gelegenheit der Siegesfeyer der Hohen Alliirten.* [Rödelheim, 1814.]

337. Meldola, Raphael. *Form of Prayer . . . to be used in the Portuguese Synagogue . . . 7th day of July, 1814 . . . for having put an end to . . . warfare, and blessed us with peace.* London, 1814. 12 pp. 8°.

Engl. & H.

338. תודה וקול זמרה. Altona, 1814. 8°.

H. & Ger. Ode in honor of Hamburg's liberation.

339. [Ode in honor of Holland's liberation from France.] Amsterdam, 1814. 12°.

See *Archives israélites*, XIV (1853), 288.

340. Fraenkel, Seckel Isaack. חבלי המוניא
 וקנאת אל. Altona, 1815. 4°.

Ode on the French in Hamburg.

341. *Rede und Gebet zur Einweihungsfeier der Synagoge und zur Einsegnung der freiwilligen Krieger der israelitischen Gemeinde zu Königsberg, gehalten am 19. April 1815.* [Königsberg, 1815.] 13 pp.

342. Büschenthal, Lipman Moses. *Rede zur Erinnerungsfeier des siegreichen Einzugs des verbündeten Heeres in Frankreichs Hauptstadt. Gehalten in d. Synagoge Breslau, d. 6ten April 1817.* [Breslau,] 1817.

343. Löwenstamm, Abraham Levy. *Dank u. Erbauungs-Predigt an dem, auf Höchsten Königl. Befehl zum religiösen Danktage bestimmten 22. Juny 1817, wegen dem durch die Alliirten am 18ten Juny 1816 erhaltenen glorreichen Sieg von Waterloo, gehalten in der israelitischen Synagoge zu Emden, u. in die deutsche Sprache übertragen.* Emden, 1817.

344. רנה ותפלה לאל בכל שנה ושנה על הישועה הגדולה אשר עשה לארץ הזאת, בהפילו שונאיו ביום הרג רב בבקעת וואטר״לא ושפת שלום לכל יושביה. בחודש יוני תקע״ה. Amsterdam, 1815. 8 pp. 8°.

XIII. Jewish Authors of non-Jewish Works on Napoleon

345-345a. Goldsmith, Lewis. *Crimes of Cabinets; or a Review of their Plans and Aggressions for the Annihilation of the Liberties of France* . . . London, 1801. VIII, 315 pp. 8°. French edition: *Crimes des cabinets* . . . Hambourg, 1801. XII, 230 pp. 8°.

346. ———. Napoléon Ier, empereur. *Recueil des manifestes, proclamations* . . ., édité par Lewis Goldsmith. Londres, 1810. 8°.

347-347a-b. ———. *Secret History of the Cabinet of Bonaparte* . . . London, 1810. XXX, 607 pp. 8°. Portuguese edition: *Historia secreta* . . . London, 1811. XVI, 438 pp. French editions: *Histoire secrète du cabinet de Napoléon* . . . Londres-Paris, 1814. 2 parts in 1 vol. 8°; 3d French edition, 1814. 312 pp. 8°.

348-348a. ———. *Address to the Sovereigns of Europe, as to the manner of treating Napoleon Bonaparte.* London, 1815. French editions: *Adresse à tous les souverains de l'Europe* . . . Paris, 1815. 198 pp. 8°; *Procès de Buonaparte, ou Adresse à tous les souverains de l'Europe* . . . Paris, 1815. 198 pp. 8°; 2^d edition, [Paris], 1816. 188 pp. 8°.

349. ———. *The Anti-Gallican Monitor and Anti-Corsican Chronicle for the year 1811* [-1817]. London, 1818 [-1825]. 14 vols. fol.

XIV. Periodicals, Calendars

350. *Annales historique et littéraires du Peuple juif. Paris, novembre 1813.* Paris, n. d. 12 pp. 8°.

Only the prospectus signed: L. Setier.

351. . . . לוח משנת. Metz. 32°.

Published since 1768.

352. . . . לוח משנת. Lunéville. 32°.

Published from 1793 until 1815.

353. Monsanto, J. Rodrigues. *Calendrier hébraïque . . . pour 50 ans.* Bordeaux, 1814. 16°.

XV. Bible, Prayer Books, Haggadot

354. תפלות ובקשות לימים נוראים. Lunéville, 1806. 32 ff. 8°.

355. Venture, Mardochée. *Prières journalières à l'usage des Juifs portugais ou espagnols* ... Marseille-Paris, 1807. 5 vols. 8°.

First edition: Nice-Paris, 1772–73.

356. ———. *Prières des Hébreux en français.* Paris, 1807. 5 vols. 12°.

357. Prisac, Abraham. ... 'חמשה ספרי ... ובראשם ... הקדמה דברי מוסרי' בס' תיקון השלחן הם קבועי' שחיבר ר'ו ... ליב במהר'ו ... סנ'ל. Lunéville, 1807. 4, 47, 1, 88 ff. 16°.

358. סדר תפלות כמנהג הקהילות הקדושות ... ספרדים. [Paris,] 1808. 226 pp. 32°.

359. ... חמשה חומשי תורה גם תרגום אונקלס ... וביאור ... רש"י ... חמש מגלות והפטרות ... Lunéville, 1807–1809. 5 vols. 8°.

360. Valabrègue, Isaac de, editor. חמשה חומשי תורה. Paris, 1809. 2 vols. 8°.

361–361a. סידור מנחת תמיד והוא תפלה מכל השנה. 228 ff. 8°.

German rite. Four other editions in 36°.

362. סדר ברכת המזון. Metz, 1813. 8°.

363. תפלה מכל השנה כמנהג אשכנז ופולין. Metz, 1814. 8°; another edition: 179, 190–313 pp. 48°.

364. ספר תהלים עם מעמדות. Metz, 1814. 128 pp. 8°.

365. סדר הגדה של פסח. Lunéville, 1805. 64 pp. 16°.

366. סדר הגדה לפסח. Lunéville, [1806]. 32 pp. 12°.

367. הגדה בית חולין. Metz, 1807. 4°.

368–368a–b. הגדה של פסח אופס נייא אינס דייטשע איבר זעצט אונד מיט ניטצליכע אונגמער־ קונגען פרזעהן. Metz, 1814. 14 pp. 12°; Metz, 1814. 76 pp. 8°; Metz, 1814. 44ff.

XVI. Various Hebrew Publications of Metz and Lunéville

369. Gabirol, Salomon ibn. גורן נכון תקון מדות הנפש ... עם ספר מוסרי הפילוסופים .... Lunéville, 1804.

370. בקשה, על ההרונים בשנות ת"ח-ט'. Lunéville, 1806. 31 pp. 8°.

371. Tyrnau, Isaac. מנהגים של כל המדינות האלו פולין ... שחבר אייק טירנא. Lunéville, 1806. 68 ff. 8°.

372. Klausner, Abraham. מנהגים. Lunéville, 1806. 79 pp.

373. Luzatto, Moses Chayyim. מסלת ס' ישרים. כולל כל ענייני מוסר ויראת ה' חברו ... משה חיים לוצאטו. Lunéville, 1806. 66 ff. 12°.

374. Frankfurter, Wolf ha-Levi. לקוטי בנימין הלכות שחיטות. Lunéville, 1807. 8°.

375. Gabirol, Salomon ibn. גורן נכון. 2d edition. Lunéville, 1807. 19, 27, 4, 2 ff. 8°.

Three parts in one vol.: מוסרי, תקון מדת הנפש הפלסופים, ספר התפוח לאריסטוטוליס.

[Eliakim ben Jacob, of Komarno.]

376. שער לימוד ללמד בני יהודה קשו'ת הנה
כתובה על ספר מלמד שיח. Lunéville, 1806.
67 ff. pp. 16°.

377. Bidinge, Moise Israël. דרוש לבר מצוה.
Metz, 1811. 17 pp. 8°. 2ᵈ edition: Metz,
1821.

378. סדר ברכת המזון. Metz, 1813. 24 pp. 8°.

379. Bidinge, Moïse Israël, ספר אם למקרא.
Metz, 1815. 3 parts in 1 vol. 8°.

380. Oppenheim, Gumprecht. ספר לקוטי
אפרים [חידושי תורה ופשטים]. Metz, 1815. 8°.

XVII. Various Jewish Works in French

381. [Gradis, David.] *Essai de philosophie
rationnelle sur l'origine des choses.* Bordeaux,
an x. 431 pp. 8°.

382. ———. *Discussions philosophiques
sur l'athéisme* . . . Paris, 1803. 146 pp.
8°.

383. Lessing, G. E. *Nathan le Sage; ou Le
Juif philosophe, comédie héroïque en 3 actes,
en prose, ornée de ballets et de spectacles,* par
M. C. [Cubières de] Palmèzeaux. Paris,
an xiv. viii, 53 pp. 8°.
See No. 460.

384. Berr, Michel, *Notice littéraire et historique sur le livre de Job.* n. p., [1806].
27 pp. 8°.
Reprint: *Magasin encyclopédique.*

385. Penini, Jedaiah. *L'Appréciation du
monde,* traduit par Michel Berr. Metz,
1808. 8°.

386. Gabirol, Salomon ibn, dit Avicebron.
La Création, poème traduit en vers français de

l'hébreu, par J. C. Moline. Paris, 1809.
40 pp. 8°.

387. [Noé, Noé.] *Tableau synoptique de
l'application de la méthode de l'enseignement
mutuel aux principes de la langue hébraïque* . . .
[Bordeaux, 1810?] fol.

388. B[err], M[ichel]. *Notices et essais.*
n. p., [1811]. 12 pp. 8°.
Reprint.

389. ———. *Notices biographiques* . . . Paris, [1814?] 8 pp. 8°.

390. ———. *Notice sur Maymonide* . . .
Paris, [1815]. 12 pp. 8°.

391. ———. *Notice sur Vessely, poëte hébraïque du* xviii. *siècle, avec quelques passages
de son poëme de la Mosaïde.* Paris, 1815. 8°.
Reprint: *Mercure étranger.*

392. Carcassonne, Dr. David. *Essai historique sur la médecine des Hébreux anciens
et modernes.* Montpellier, 1815. 83 pp. 8°.

XVIII. Jewish Authors of non-Jewish Subjects

393. Schwab, Jacques. *Supplement à l'ouvrage: Le Système métrique* . . . Nancy, an x.
iv, 52 pp.

Le Système . . . was published in 1799; see No.
413.

394. Hourwitz, Zalkind. *Origine des
langues* . . . Paris, n. d. xii, 166, 8 pp. 8°.

395. ———. *Polygraphie* . . . Paris, an x.
viii+114 pp. 8°.

396. Rodrigues, Isaac. *Plan d'organisation du Muséum d'Instruction publique, établi à Bordeaux, par les soins des cit. Rodrigues et Gothals.* Bordeaux, 1801. 10 pp. 4°.

397. Mendes, Abraham. *Examen d'un ouvrage ayant pour titre: Méthode simplifié de la tenue des livres par E. T. . . . Jones.* Bordeaux, an XII. 59 pp. 8°.

On bookkeeping, see No. 398.

398. Rodrigues, J., fils. *Observations sommaires et critiques, sur la méthode simplifiée . . . de E. T. Jones.* Paris, 1804. 20 pp. 8°.

See Nos. 397, 407-408.

399. Berr, Michel. *Lettre à Mr. Millin . . .* Paris, 1805. 16 pp. 8°.

On Baron de Dalberg's *Les beaux arts et leurs écoles,* translated by M. Berr.

400. ———. *Notice sur Baggesen, poète danois.* Paris 1805. 8°.

401 ———. *Eloge de Gesner.* Paris, 1806. 8°.

402. Gradis, David. *Observations critiques sur l'ouvrage de M. Lancelin, intitulé: Théorie physique de l'organisation des mondes.* Bordeaux, 1805. 8°.

403. Mossé, J. M. [Jassuda Michal]. *La Caninéide, ou Turc et Miton, poëme-épi-philosophi-tragi-satyri-héroï-comique, orné de tout son spectacle.* Caniséis [Paris], 1808. 138 pp. 8°.

404. ———. *Quelques mots sur le beau sexe, et sur les détracteurs, suivis des Prémices poétiques.* Paris, 1808. 146 pp. 16°.

405. ———. *Poésies, dédiées au comte Regnault de Saint-Jean-d'Angély.* Nouvelle édition; Paris, 1809. 143 pp. 16°.

406. ———. *Le Délire poétique, ode; L'Abandon généraux, élégie; Le Printemps, idylle.* Paris, 1810. 14 pp. 8°.

407. Rodrigues, J. *La tenue des livres théorique et pratique . . .* Bordeaux, 1810. 4, 4, 331 pp. 8°.

See Nos. 396-397, 408.

408. ———. *Observations adressés à M. le Conseiller d'Etat, directeur général de l'imprimerie . . . sur son ouvrage comparé avec celui de M. Edmond Degrange, intitulé: la Tenue des livres rendue facile . . .* Bordeaux, 1811. 58 pp. 8°.

See Nos. 396-397, 407.

409. Hourwitz, Zalkind, *Lacographie, ou Ecriture laconique, aussi vite que la parole . . .* Paris, 1811. XI, 76 pp. 8°.

410. Mossé, J. M. [Jassuda Michal]. *Dernier chant et dernier printems d'un cygne.* Paris, 1811. 8 pp. 8°.

411. ———. *Chronique de Paris. . . .* Paris, 1812. 3, 192 pp. 8°.

412. Halphen, Cerf Michel. *Jeux de cartes harmoniques . . .* Metz, 1812, 4 pp. & 59 maps.

413. Schwab, Jacques. *Elements de géometrie,* 1re partie. Nancy, 1813. VIII, 107 pp.

Only the first part was published; see No. 393.

414. Berr, Michel. *Langue allemande. Traduction de deux odes de Schiller.* Paris, [1814]. 8 pp. 8°.

415. ———. *Notice sur M. Charles Villers . . .* [Paris, 1815.] 7 pp. 8°.

Reprint: *Mercure de France.*

XIX. Juridical Documents

416. *Second mémoire pour le cit.* [*Louis*] *Francia B e a u f l e u r y . . . contre le cit. Abraham D a c o s t a . . .* [Bordeaux, an ix.] 80 pp. 8°.

417. *Griefs d'Appel.* Bordeaux, n. d. 18 pp. 4°.

L. Francia B e a u f l e u r y against J. Lamothe; signed: Beaufleury and Secondal.

418. *Plaidoyer prononcé devant Messieurs les Juges de la Cour d'Appel séante à Bordeaux, par M. L. Francia-B e a u f l e u r y, Jurisconsulte, dans sa cause, contre M. J. Lamothe, propriétaire.* n. p., n. d. 12 pp. 4°.

419. *Jugement rendu par le Tribunal civil de l'arrondissement d'Altkirch, le 10 messidor an x* [*29 mars 1802*] *contre Abraham et Fromel L é v y de Kembs, par suite de la saisie faite à leur domicile, le 22 et 23 ventôse, an x, de marchandises . . .* Strasbourg, an x. 10 pp. 4°.

420. *Mémoire pour Jacob I s r a ë l, à Oberbrounn (Bas-Rhin) appelant d'un jug* rendu à Sarreguemines, an x, contre François Cetto . . .* Metz, n. d. 32, 17 pp. 4°.

421. *Supplément au Mémoire pour le citoyen Jacob I s r a ë l, anc. propriétaire, dem. à Oberbronn . . . contre les cit. François Cetto . . .* Metz, n. d. 17 pp. 4°.

422. *Précis dans la cause pendante au tribunal civil séant à Strasbourg entre Abraham-Aaron M o c h . . . contre Catherine-Dorothée Eschenauer . . .* Strasbourg, [1801]. 10 pp. 4°.

423. *Précis pour la citoyenne Henriette Sommervogel . . . contre Salomon et Michel L é v y . . .* Colmar, [1802].

424. *Extrait des registres du Tribunal d'Appel, séant à Bordeaux. Du 5 fructidor an xi* [*23 mars 1803*]. Bordeaux, n. d. 15 pp. 4°.

A civil lawsuit involving the G r a d i s family.

424a. *Mémoire pour la dame veuve Delvaille contre le sieur Jacob Delvaille.* Bordeaux, [1803?]. 48 pp. 4°.

Signed: Laine [Lainé], avocat. Conflict about a mixed marriage between the son of Jacob Delvaille and the Christian woman Françoise Vaugan. See No. 424b.

424b. *Réplique pour le citoyen Jacob Delvaille contre la Dame Françoise Vaugan.* Bordeaux, [1803?]. 78 pp. 4°.

Signed: Durandeau fils, avocat. On the same subject as No. 424a.

425. *Mémoire à consulter et consultation pour Abraham I s a a c, Baer A b r a h a m et Samuel J o s e p h, condamnés par Jugement du Tribunal spécial de Strasbourg.* Paris, an xii. 29 pp. 4°.

Signed: Chauveau-Lagarde, Beryer, Bellard, March 27, 1804. See No. 426.

426. *Mémoire et consultation sur pourvoi en grâce contre un jugement du Tribunal spécial de Strasbourg.* Paris, 1804. 54 pp. 4°.

Signed: "Mayer Daniel, fondé de pouvoir," "Consultation," by Poirier, Fournel, Chas, May 24, 1804. See No. 425.

427. [Arrêté rendu contre Jacques B e e r, Meyer M o s è s, Gomprich B e e r, V e r t h e i m e r, S c h u m a c h e r, David et Aaron G o e t z et consorts, dans une affaire des faux billets de banque.] Strasbourg, 1806. 64 pp. 8°.

428. [Arrêté rendu contre Baruch L e v i, David Aaron S t r a s b u r g e r et les frères Trapet, dans une affaire des faux billets de banque.] Strasbourg, 1806. 60 pp. 8°.

429. [Arrêté rendu contre François Grimm . . ., Raphaël J o s e p h, F i - s c h e l, Aaron et Moses G o e t z, Jacques et Gomprich B e e r, dans l'affaire de contrefaçon des faux billets de banque de Vienne.] Strasbourg, 1806. 88 pp. 8°.

430. *Arrêt de la cour de justice criminelle du département de Vaucluse, qui condamne, pour fait d'escroquerie, Elie C r é m i e u x, Juif, tailleur d'habits, natif de Carpentras, domicilié à Apt . . .*, Carpentras, [12 avril 1806]. Broadside.

431. *Précis pour le Sieur . . . Pelissier contre le Sieur Mardochée V i d a l, Juif.* [Carpentras], 1806. 4°.

432. *Le Réveil trompeur de la Judée.* Trèves, [1807]. 2, 88 pp. 8°.

"Précis pour Charles Théodore et Alexandre Warsberg . . . contre G o t t s c h a l k et Isaac M a y e r, Juifs, domiciliés à Mannheim." Signed: Fritsch, Georgel, July 20, 1807.

433. *Requête en conclusions pour MM. les Administrateurs de la Régie de l'Enregistrement et du Domaine, poursuites et diligences de M. Magnan, directeur à Bordeaux, demandeurs en main-levée, Contre les Sieurs Jacob P e i x o t o, et Isaac P e i x o t o, tuteur de Daniel P e i x o t o, interdit, pris comme héritiers de leur père [Charles Peixoto], et en cette qualité débiteurs . . .* Bordeaux, juillet 1808. 35, 1 pp. 4°.

Signed: Duvergier, Lerraillat. See No. 438.

434. *Consultation. Pour Joseph Fenwick, Consul des Etats-Unis d'Amérique . . . Contre l'agent du trésor public, stipulant pour les citoyens Emmerth, F u r t a d o, & Texier, négociants à Bordeaux.* n. p., [1809]. 39 pp. 4°.

Signed: Bellart, Delamalle, Lacalprade, Pérignon, Paris, Jan. 28, 1809.

435. *Etude de M. Drouhard . . . Tribunal civil de première instance de Besançon. Juge-ment du 24 janvier 1809.* Besançon, [1809]. 8°.

Affaire Benoît B l o c h fils and Auguste Balois.

436. *A Messieurs les Juges de la Cour d'Appel de Bordeaux.* Bordeaux, [1810]. 33 pp. 4°.

Signed: L. Baissel, Hugues. Conflict involving d e L a m e n a u d e, N u n è s - P e r e y r a, Mlle B r a n d o n, David R a p h a ë l, and others.

437. *Arrêts de la Cour d'Appel de Dijon, 1809 et 1810. Entre les Srs. Samuel B l u m et Hub.-Michel Bardousse . . .* Paris, 1810. 16 pp. 4°.

438. *De par Sa Majesté l'Empereur et Roi. A Vendre successivement et par la voie des enchères qui seront reçues en l'étude de M. Meilléres, notaire impérial à Bordeaux, à ces fins commis, les immeubles dépendans de la succession de feu Charles-Joseph-Paul (ci devant Samuel) P e i x o t t o -de-Beaulieu, ayant autrefois exercé la profession de banquier à Bordeaux.* Bordeaux, [1810]. Broadside.

See No. 433.

439. *Mémoire et consultation . . . pour Baer A b r a h a m . . .* [Strasbourg, 1810.]

440. *Réplique pour les S.rs Bosc, Louvet et Froger, contre la D.me de Cascq, V.ve de N u n e s - P e r e y r a.* Bordeaux, [1810]. 63 pp. 4°.

Signed: Cassaignes, Dupré.

441. *Seconde consultation pour les S.rs Froger, Louvet et Bosc, intimés, contre la D.me V.ve P e r e y r a - Lamenaude, appelante.* n. p., n. d. 63 pp. 4°.

Signed: Brochon, Martignac, Cassaignes, Denucé. Bordeaux, Apr. 5, 1810.

442. [Jugement rendu par le Tribunal correctionnel de Strasbourg, contre le Sieur Moïse K l e i n. Strasbourg, 1813.]

443. *Mémoire pour les enfants et héritiers de la D.ᵐᵉ Rocaute . . . contre les S.ʳˢ Pierre et Hector P e t i t . . .* Bordeaux, 1813. 69 pp. 4°.

Signed: Roullet.

444. *Conclusions motivées, pour Jacob Goudchaux B e e r . . . à Metz . . . contre Mathias Geib, marchand de chevaux . . . faillite des Frères A r o n . . .* Metz, n. d. 16 pp. 4°.

445. *Mémoire pour Lion C e r f, marchand, dém. à St. Avold, poursuivi pour détention d'armes de guerre.* Metz, n. d. 22 pp. 4°.

446. *Mémoire pour Philippine W e i l, femme d'Olry Abraham C a h e n, intimée, contre Isaïe G o m p e r t z.* Metz, n. d. 2 pp. 4°.

447. *Précis pour le Sieur B e r r et la Dame G o u d e c h a u x . . . contre . . . Demouzay . . .* n. p., n. d. 17 pp. 4°.

448. *Précis pour le Sieur Cerf C a h e n, marchand de chevaux . . . contre la veuve et les héritiers de Cerf F r i b o u r g dit Bénédic . . .* Metz, n. d. 11 pp. 4°.

See also Nos. 47–48, 57.

XX. Non-Jewish Authors on General Jewish Subjects

449. Bucher, P. B. *Histoire de l'usure chez les Egyptiens, les Juifs, les Grecs, les Romains, nos anciens et les Chinois . . .* Paris, 1806. 215 pp. 8°.

450. Fleury, Abbé Claude. *Abrégé des moeurs des Israélites et des Chrétiens . . .* Paris, 1806. IV, 156 pp. 12°.

Many editions were published before 1789.

451. Volney, Constantin François Chassebeuf comte de. *Recherches nouvelles sur l'histoire ancienne. I. Examen de l'histoire des Juifs jusqu'à la captivité de Babylone.* Paris, 1814.

XXI. Biblical Subjects in Drama

452. Caigniez, Louis Charles. *Le Jugement de Salomon,* mélodrame en 3 actes . . . Musique de C. Quaisin. Paris, 1802. 39 pp. 8°.

Two editions. Dutch edition: *Salomons eerste gericht . . .* Amsterdam, 1807. 60 pp. German editions: Wien, 1804; München, 1808. First represented at the Ambigu-Comique, Jan. 18, 1802.

453. [Plancher de Valcour, P.A.L.P. et Leblanc.] *Esther,* mélodrame en trois actes à grand spectacle mêlé de chants et de dances, par les citoyens . . . Paris, an XI. 44 pp. 8°.

Ambigu-Comique, Nov. 18, 1802. Italian edition: *Ester . . .* Roma, 1806. 60 pp.

454. Deschamps, J. M., D . . . [Després, J. B. D.] et Morel [Morel de Chédeville], Etienne. *Saül,* Oratorio mis en action. Musique de Lachnitz et Kalkbrenner. Paris, 1803. IV, 22 pp. 4°.

Théâtre des Arts, Apr. 7, 1803.

455. Chevalier, P. E. *Rachel ou la Belle Juive,* mélodrame en trois actes . . . Paris, an XII. 28 pp.

Théâtre de la Gaîté, Oct. 15, 1803.

456. Nogaret, François Félix. *Jérémiade d'Aristénète sur la mort prématurée d'un poème de sa façon intitulé: "Le Réveil*

d'Adam," hiéro-drame en 3 actes. Paris, 1804. 57 pp. 8°; Paris, 1804. 14 pp. 8°.

457. Deschamps, J. M., Desprès, J. B. D. et Morel de Chédeville, Etienne. *La Prise de Jéricho.* Musique de Lachnitz et Kalkbrenner. Paris, 1805. IV, 36 pp. 4°.

Académie impériale de musique, Apr. 11, 1805.

458. Aignan, Etienne. *Nephtali ou les Ammonites* . . . Paris, 1806. 8°.

459. Caigniez, Louis Charles. *Le Triomphe de David*, mélodrame en 3 actes. Musique de Leblanc . . . Paris, 1806. 39 pp. 8°.

Théâtre de la Gaîté, Nov. 6, 1805.

460. Palmézaux, M. C. [Cubières de Palmézeaux, Michel de]. *Nathan le sage; ou, le Juif philosophe*, comédie héroïque en 3 actes et en prose. Paris, an XIV. VIII, 53 pp. 8°.

The same as No. 383, but with biblical couplets, and without Lessing being mentioned as the author.

461. Lefranc. *Pharaon, ou Joseph en Egypte*, mélodrame en 3 actes, en prose. Paris, 1806. 8°.

462. Romagnesi. *Samson, ou la Destruction des Philistins*, mélodrame . . . arrangé et mis par César Ribié. Paris, 1806. 8°.

Théâtre de la Gaîté, Feb. 20, 1806.

463. Baour-Lormian, P. M. F. L. *Omasis, ou Joseph en Egypte*, tragédie en 5 actes. Paris, 1807. 48 pp. 8°.

Théâtre Français, Sept. 14, 1806, and in St.-Cloud before Napoleon on Sept. 18, 1806.

464. Pineu Duval, A. V. *Joseph*, drame en 3 actes. Paris, 1807. 8°.

Music by Méhul. Many later editions. Opéra Comique, Feb. 17, 1807.

465. Lan . . ., L. D. *Joseph*, poëme en huit chants. Paris, 1807. 12°.

466. [Peignot, Etienne Gabriel.] *La Création et le Paradis perdu*, par un Bourguignon. Bagdad, [1807?]. 20 pp. 12°.

467. C*** [Cercueil], J. H. *Daniel, ou l'Imposture dévoilée*, tragédie . . . Mantes, 1809. I, 56 pp. 12°.

468. Guillard, N. F. *La Mort d'Adam.* Paris, 1809. 8°; Lyon, 1857. 12 pp. 12°.

469. Hoffmann, François Benoît. *Abel*, tragédie . . . Paris, 1810. 8°.

470. Colau, Pierre. *L'Egypte sauvé, ou Joseph vendu par ses frères (— Esther, ou la Belle Juive).* Paris, 1812. 2 parts in 1 vol. 12°.

471. ———— . *Suzanne, ou le Triomphe de l'innocence, suivie de l'Egypte sauvée, ou Joseph vendue par ses frères* . . . Paris, n. d. 108 pp. 12°.

472. [———— .] *Tobie, Esther, et Ruth, suivis de diverses autres pièces, tirées de l'Ecriture sainte.* Paris, n. d. 88 pp. 12°.

473. Florian, J. P. Claris de. *Eliezer et Nephtaly*, poème traduit de l'hébreu. Suivi d'un Dialogue entre deux chiens. Nouvelle imitée de Cervantes . . . Paris, 1810. 16°; 1812. (16°).

474. Baour-Lormian, P. M. F. L. *Jérusalem délivrée*, opéra en 5 actes. Paris, 1812. XII, 60 pp. 8°; 1812; 1813.

Music by Persuy. Académie impériale de Musique, Sept. 8, 1812. Dutch edition: '*T velost Jeruzalem* . . . Haarlem, 1813. VIII, 53 pp. 8°.

475. [Friedelle], Mme Alexandre. *Le Lévite d'Ephraïm ou la Destruction des Benjamites* . . . Paris, 1813. 30 pp. 8°.

Paris, Gaîté, July 29, 1813.

476. Laborie, M. *Esther, ou le Triomphe de Mardochée,* ballet . . . Lyon, 1813. 8°.

Music by Dreuilh. June 1813.

XXII. Jews in non-Biblical Subjects

477. Mosneron de Launay, Bon Jean-Baptiste. *Memnon, ou la Jeune israélite.* Paris, 1806. 319 pp. 8°.

Historical novel.

478. Caigniez, L. Ch. *Le Juif errant,* mélodrame en 3 actes . . . Musique de M. Alexandre. Paris, 1812. 59 pp. 8°.

Théâtre de la Gaîté, Jan. 7, 1812.

479. Pompigny, Maurin de. *La Princesse de Jérusalem, ou le Juif reconnaissant,* mélodrame en 3 actes. Paris, 1812. 56 pp. 8°.

Music by Quaisain and Lanusse. Ambigu-Comique, Jan. 1812.

XXIII. Varia

480. Bernardau, Pierre. *Promenade à Talence, ou Description de la maison de campagne de MM. Raba frères* . . . Bordeaux, 1803. 14 pp. 8°.

Reprint.

481. *Extrait des minutes de la Mairie de Metz. Du 23 fructidor de l'an 13.* Metz, n. d. Broadside.

"Les habitans de la rue de l'Arsenal sont chargés du logement de neuf cents militaires."

482. Büschenthal, Lipman Moses. שיר ליום הולדת. Rödelheim, 1805. 12°.

Ode in honor of David Sintzheim.

483. *Service funèbre célébrée dans la synagogue des Juifs de Thionville, le 22 janvier 1807, en l'honneur de feu M. Dondeine, maire de cette ville* . . . Traduit de l'hébreu. Metz, n. d. 4°.

484. *Certificats délivrés, par les autorités militaires et civiles, à Messieurs Lippmann (Frères) entrepreneurs généraux du service des convois militaires et vivres-viande des 2e et*

3e Div.^ons territoriales, propriétaires domiciliés à Verdun. Verdun, [1808].

Obtained by the brothers Lippmann in order to be excepted from the Decree of March 17, 1808.

485. *Bittazion,* n. p., n. d. 4 pp. 4°.

Ger. Anti-Jewish parody written in the form of a petition by Aronel Busswiller to the sub-prefect.

486. *Le Chant du Coq.* קרית הגבר. *Le Chant de Minuit. 1re Parabole adressée aux Enfants d'Israël.* n. p., n. d. 12 pp. 8°.

Page 12: "Extrait de l'Eclaireur. Receuil de Pièces destinées à concourir au Rétablissement du Règne de Dieu sur toute la terre." Catholic conversion propaganda.

487. *Minerva ad Furtado.* n. p., n. d. 1 p. 4°.

Lat. Ode in honor of Furtado.

488. Soubia, [Jacob Abraham]. *L'Espoir d'Israël. Suivi d'une satire contre l'Abbé Geoffroy. Poésies.* 2e partie. Paris, 1813. 16, 8 pp. 8°.

Ode for Napoleon and Catholic conversion propaganda

XXIV. Later Effects of Napoleon's anti-Jewish Decrees

489. Guichard. *Consultation sur le Décret du 17 Mars 1808 . . . Paris, 3 janvier 1816.* n. p., n. d. 16 pp. 4°.

490. Cerfberr, Alphonse Théodore. *Observations sur les voeux émis par les conseils généraux des départemens du Haut et du Bas-Rhin, relativement aux mesures à prendre contre les Juifs par suite du décret du 17 Mars 1808.* Paris, 1817. 16 pp. 8°.

491. [Blanchard, Louis.] *Quelques idées sur l'usure des Juifs dans les départemens du Haut et du Bas-Rhin,* par un Sundganien. Paris, 1818. 223 pp. 8°.

Fr. & Ger.

492. *Requête adressée au Roi par le Consistoire Central des Israélites, contre la prorogation du Décret du 17 Mars 1808, qui soumet les Juifs à une législation spéciale.* Paris, 1818. 4°.

493. *Lettre pastorale adressée par le Consistoire Central aux . . . affranchis des dispositions du Décret du 17 Mars 1808. Paris, 1818.* 4°.

See Nos. 494–496.

494. *Hirtenbrief des Central-Consistoriums der Israeliten in Frankreich, den Consistorien, in deren Bezirk sich eins oder mehrere Departemente befinden, die von den Verfügungen des Dekrets vom 17ten März 1808 neulich befreit worden sind, zugeschrieben.* Colmar, 1818. 12 pp. 4°.

See Nos. 493, 495.

495. *Consistorium der Israeliten des Nieder-Rheins. Hirten-Brief des Central-Consistoriums der Israeliten in Frankreich, an diejenigen Consistorien, unter deren Circonscription sich ein oder mehrere Departemente befinden, welche von den Verfolgungen des Dekrets*

vom 17ten März 1808 befreit worden. Strasbourg, 1818. 10 pp. 4°.

See Nos. 493–494, 496.

496. *Circulaire de M. le Grand Rabbin . . . et du Consistoire israélite. Metz, 6 avril 1818.* n. p., n. d. 24 pp. 4°.

See Nos. 493–495.

497. *Le Consistoire israélite de la circonscription de Wintzenheim, le 3 novembre 1820.* Colmar, 1820. 4 pp. 4°.

Fr. & Ger. Decision of Oct. 4, 1820, against usury.

498. Gortan, C. J. *La Chute de l'usure, ou le Miroir de l'âme pour la conversion du Juif usurier.* n. p., [1821]. 8°.

Prospectus; see Nos. 499–500.

499. ———. *Prospektus einer Zeitschrift . . . Der Sturz des Wuchers oder belehrende Seelenspiegel des wucherenden Juden.* Colmar, 1821. 8 pp. 8°.

See Nos. 498, 500.

500. ———. *Der Sturz des Wuchers, oder der belehrende Seelenspiegel des wucherenden Juden.* No. 1. Colmar, 1822. 16 pp. 8°.

See Nos. 489–490.

501. *Le Consistoire israélite de la circonscription de Strasbourg. Aux Israélites du Département du Bas-Rhin. Strasbourg, le 13 octobre 1823.* Broadside.

Fr. & Ger. Against usury.

502. *A Son Excellence Monseigneur le Ministre secrétaire d'Etat au département de l'intérieur.* Colmar, 1824. 4°.

Against projected anti-Jewish decrees because of usury.

503. *Sociéte israélite des Amis du travail fondée à Colmar.* Colmar, le 8 août 1839. 2 pp. 4°.

Circular against usury.

504. *Consistoire israélite. Circonscription de Colmar. Extrait des registres des arrêtés [du 20 juillet 1851].* Colmar, n. d. fol.

Against usury.

505. [Guerber, Joseph.] *Hülfsbüchlein gegen viele Wucherjuden etwelche Wucherchristen. Ein Freund des Elsässer Bauern-*standes. Herissau, 1852; 2d edition, 1853. 8°.

506. *Département du Haut-Rhin. Consistoire israélite. Circonscription de Colmar. Circulaire, A Messieurs les Rabbins et Commissaires-Administrateurs. Colmar, le 18 Mars 1853.* n. p., n. d. 3 pp. 4°.

Against newly projected anti-Jewish decrees because of usury.

507. Heilmann, A. *Les Paysans d'Alsace. L'Impôt et l'usure.* Strasbourg, 1853. 164 pp. 8°.

XXV. Later Works on Napoleon and the Jews

508. Rapoport, Salomo Jehuda. תכונת עיר פֿאריז ואי עלבא. Lemberg, 1814. 8°.

509. Heydeck, Don Juan Joseph [baptized Jew,] Profesor de Lenguas orientales. *La Fe Triunfante, o carta a la junta llamada el Gran Sanhedrin de los Judios de Paris, y a todo el pueblo hebreo esparcido por el mundo.* Madrid, 1815. 4, VIII, 404 pp. 4°.

510. S., C. H. *Beleuchtung der in dem Jahre 1807 von dem grossen israelitischen Sanhedrin in Paris erfolgten Antworten der ihr vorgelegten 12 Fragen . . .* Mainz, 1817. 44 pp. 4°.

511. Weissen-Becker. *Die Christen und die Juden . . . Mit Nachrichten vom grossen Sanhedrin, welcher auf Befehl Napoleons in Paris 1806 gehalten wurde.* Frankfurt a/M., [1819]. 110 pp. 8°.

512. *Décision prise en 1807 dans le Grand Sanhédrin convoqué à Paris . . . et règlement du temple et du bureaux de bienfaisance des Israélites de Lyon.* Lyon, 1840. 61 pp. 8°.

No. 512 is given as an example only. The number of 19th century publications containing such material on the Sanhedrin is very large.

513. Ginzburg, Mordecai Abraham. הצרפתים ברוסיא הוא דברי ימי שנת תקע"ב, תקע"ג . . . Wilno, 1842. 115 pp. 8°.

514. *Zsidó valláselvek. Megállapítva a nagy Sanhedrin által, mely 1807ik évi februarban Párisban tartatott.* Franciából magyarra fordítva s jegyzetekkel felvilágosítva Löv Lipot . . . Pápa, 1848. 44 pp. 12°.

515. Mohr, Abraham Mendel. דגל מרבה, ספר תולדות מלך רב, נאפאלעאן הראשון קיסר ארץ צרפת . . . Czernowicz, 1855. 2, 228 pp. 12°.

516. ———. נאפאלעאן הראשון והשלישי ותקפם וגבורתם. Lwów, 1855. 8°.

517. Shiper, Fajwl. . . . תולדות נאפאלעאן, מיום לדתו עד יום מותו. Warsaw, 1857. 67, 72, 59 pp. 8°.

518. Ginzburg, Mordecai Abraham. ספר ימי הדור, הוא תולדות הימים החדשים, מראשית ימי השנוים בצרפת בשנת תק"ל עד ימי מסע

נאפאלעאן לארץ רוסיא בשנת תקע"ב על פי
סופרי אמונים. Wilno, 1860. 132 pp. 8°.

519. [Neufeld, Daniel.] *Wielki Sanhedryn
paryzki w roku 1806 przez Napoleona I.
zwołany. Przyczynek historyczny do rozjaś-
nienia kwestyi żydowskiéj.* Warsaw, 1861.
60 pp. 8°.

520. Kestin, Duber. מסע מצרים, ספור
קורות נאפוליון הראשון במסעו למצרים. Warsaw, 1861. 118 pp. 8°.

521. Halphen, E. דברי הימים, לבני ישראל
באר ץ צרפת גם סנהדרין גדולה . . . כתוב
צרפתית מה"ר אליה חלפן ומתרגם חפשי מה"ר
שמואל אהרן ב"ר יצחק ראזענבלאטט. Warsaw,
1863. 72 pp. 8°.

522. Tchugaevitch, Peter. Рѣшеніе еврей-
скаго вопроса во Франціи . . . Kiev, 1874.
50 pp. 16°.

On the Sanhedrin.

523. Декреты Великаго Синедріона со-
биравшагося въ Парижѣ перваго Адара
мѣсяца 5567 года отъ сотворенія міра
(въ Февралѣ 1867) подъ покровитель-
ствомъ Наполеона Великаго תקנות אשר
וסדו [יסדו] אנשי שם סנ־הדריך. [Kiev, 1874?]
39 pp. 16°.

524. Ginzburg, Mordecai Abraham. פי
החירות, ספור מלחמות האשכנזים והרוסים
בצרפת בשנות תקע"ג. Wilno, 1884. 167 pp.
8°.

INDEX OF AUTHORS

INDEX OF TITLES

INDEX OF HEBREW TITLES

FRENCH JEWS DURING THE REVOLUTION OF 1830 AND THE JULY MONARCHY

I

JEWISH PARTICIPATION IN THE EVENTS OF JULY, 1830

ON July 25, 1830, Charles X dissolved the French parliament. Thereupon the deputies and the people rose in open resistance against the regime of the Restoration, and during the "three glorious days" of July 27, 28, and 29, the future of France was once again decided upon the barricades. On August 2 Charles X abdicated, and Louis Philippe (1773-1850) was proclaimed *Lieutenant général* and a week later King of France. Thus the Revolution of 1830 abolished the absolute monarchy and instituted a monarchy by election. Very soon, however, Louis Philippe was driven to oppose liberal and revolutionary forces, and in his foreign policy he tried to make the great powers forget that he had acceded to the throne as the result of a popular uprising.

Although Jews are known to have participated in the revolutionary events, the lack of a documentary record,

Note: The following abbreviations are used in the notes: *AI* — *Les Archives israélites*; AN — Archives Nationales; *BAL* — A. Cerfberr de Médelsheim, *Biographie Alsacienne-Lorraine* (Paris, 1879); *Crémieux* — S. Posener, *Adolphe Crémieux (1796-1880)*, 2 vols. (Paris, 1933); *DBF* — *Dictionnaire de biographie française*, I-IX (Paris, 1929-60); Halphen — Achille Edmond Halphen, *Recueil des lois . . . concernant les Israélites . . .* (Paris, 1851); Jerusalem — The Jewish Historical General Archives in Jerusalem; *JSS* — *Jewish Social Studies*; Lower Rhine — Departmental Archives of Lower Rhine; *Opposition* — Felix Ponteil, *L'Opposition politique à Strasbourg sous la monarchie de juillet* (Paris, 1932); *Rév. 1848* — *La Révolution de 1848 et les révolutions du XIX siècle, 1830-1848-1870*; *UI* — *L'Univers israélite*; *YB* — *Yivo Bleter* (in Yiddish).

Originally published in *Historia Judaica*, vol. XXII (1960).

such as a contemporary Franco-Jewish periodical might have provided, makes it hard to determine the exact extent of their activity. To begin with, we may note the reference by the Central Jewish consistory, in a petition of August, 1830, to the fact that "the French Jews shared the dangers incurred by their fellow citizens."[1] And accounts of specific cases do exist, a few of which follow.

Michel Goudchaux (1797-1862) was wounded while leading a large group that stormed the Tuileries on July 29. The son of a Jewish banker of Nancy, he helped to organize a Jewish public school there. In 1827 he went to Paris to direct a branch of his father's banking business and continued to be active in the Jewish community. He quickly became interested in politics and in 1829 helped to publish the liberal republican newspaper *National,* which played an important role in preparing the revolutionary events of 1830. After the July uprising Goudchaux became mayor of a Paris district. Anticipating that he would be forced into the ranks of the opposition, he refused to accept a higher post and was appointed paymaster in the department of Lower Rhine.[2]

For his role in the July events Philippe Anspach (1805-1875), a lawyer from Metz, was rewarded with a high position in the administration of law. In Metz he had been one of the founders and leaders of the first Jewish public school (1818). His brother, Joël Anspach, was the editor of the first French translation of the Hebrew prayerbook for Ashkenazic Jews. Philippe Anspach, who became a member of the Central Consistory, was the father-in-law of two well-known Jewish personalities, Gustave de Rothschild and Emile Dreyfus.[3]

Michel Alcan (1811-1877), the son of a Jewish soldier

[1] S. Posener, "La Révolution de juillet et les israélites de France," *UI,* LXXXV (1930), 586. This short study of a few pages is the only one concerning the Jews and the July Revolution published until now.

[2] Achille de Vaulabelle, *Chute de l'Empire* . . . , VII (Paris, 1854), 400; *AI,* XXIV (1863), 56-61; E. Carmoly, in *AI,* XXIV (1863), 608-12, 752-55, 806-14; Raymond Lazard, *Michel Goudchaux* (1797-1862): *son oeuvre et sa vie politique* (Paris, 1907), pp. 3-5.

[3] *AI,* XXXVI (1875), 747-48.

of the days of 1789, fought on the barricades and was decorated with the Croix de Juillet. As a child he had attended a Jewish trade school. As an adult he organized educational courses for workers, became a well-known engineer, and contributed significantly to the development of the French textile industry. In 1848 he was elected deputy from the department of Eure.[4]

Olinde Rodrigues (1795-1851), a Jewish Saint-Simonian, also fought on the barricades.[5]

Adolphe Crémieux (1796-1880) took an active part in the July events in Nîmes, where great animosity existed between the Catholic adherents of the Restoration and the Protestant partisans of the new revolution. As is well known Crémieux later settled in Paris, playing an important role in politics, first as a cautious partisan of the July Monarchy and later in the republican opposition.[6]

In Bordeaux two Jews, Benjamin Lopès-Dubec (1783-1851) and Joseph Rodrigues (1784-1858), were among the members of the new municipal administration elected on August 3, 1830. However, these offices may possibly not have been conferred as a reward for political activities.

In Bayonne, Josué Léon (1749-1834), who was active in the revolutionary clubs of the 1789 Revolution, became deputy-mayor during the Restoration, a position he held until his death. It was in Léon's summer-house that the prefect of the department of Landes during the Restoration found a safe hiding-place in July, 1830.[7]

The Jewish communities everywhere in France took part in the solemn celebrations in honor of the new regime.

---

[4] *DBF*, I (Paris, 1933), 1328-29; *BAL*, pp. 85-86.

[5] Sébastien Charléty, *Histoire du Saint-Simonisme* (Paris, 1931), p. 81.

[6] S. Posener, "La Révolution du juillet et le Département du Gard," *Mercure de France*, CCXXI (1930), 612-13; *Crémieux* I, 88-149. Moïse Monteux (1792-1832) of Carpentras, a lawyer of Nîmes and a friend of A. Thiers, was invited, at the beginning of the July regime, to come to Paris (*AI*, I, 1840, 615-17). According to the anti-Jewish writer Robert Launay, the Revolution of 1830 attracted to Paris many "barefoot" people, who looked for a chance to profit from events in that city. Among them was the peddler family of the famous actress Rachel; *Figures juives* (Paris, 1921), p. 38.

[7] Th. Malvezin, *Histoire des juifs de Bordeaux* (Bordeaux, 1875), pp. 319-20; Henry Léon, *Histoire des juifs de Bayonne* (Paris, 1893), p. 258.

In Mulhouse, a center of liberal Protestant industrialists, the 1830 Revolution was greeted enthusiastically. Many Jews made donations for the victims of the July events in Paris and for the erection of a local monument in their honor.[8] The Revolution, or, to be more accurate, Louis Philippe, was praised by Jewish communities in hymns and sermons and by individual Jewish authors of odes. Of course, such panegyrics were produced in France during every regime, often by the same authors. This time, however, Eliakim Carmoly was able to take as a motto for his *Ode* the words of Ecclesiastes: "Happy are you o land, when your king is the son of free men." In 1833, the rabbi of Lille spoke of Louis Philippe as "the King who emerged from the barricades." The same sentiment was repeated in later sermons. Rabbi Michel A. Weill of Alger remarked in 1847 that the King "ascended the throne through the triumph of free institutions." In Saint-Esprit the mayor announced with broadsides a *Te Deum* for the new regime in the church and in the synagogue. This was indeed a singular occurrence in a city in which in 1816 the priest had refused to allow Jews to be present in the church at a ceremony in memory of Louis XVI, and where in 1838 the Catholics protested strongly against the election of a Jew, Isaac Rodrigues, as deputy mayor. To evaluate such episodes properly, one should bear in mind the fact that in many places the Catholic clergy ignored the new regime and refused to celebrate the event in the churches.[9]

Alexandre Weill related how the news of the Paris events was greeted in Frankfurt, where a group of French youths were studying in the *yeshivoth*: "The news of the Revolution of 1830 sounded like a trumpet of Jericho in

[8] *Affiches de Mülhausen* No. 30, Sept. 4, 1930 (D. Wahl, Moïse Wahl, Cléman Lévy, M. Lévy, M. Paraf, etc.); André Brandt, "Mulhouse et la Révolution de 1830," *Bulletin de la Société Industrielle de Mulhouse,* CII (1936), 437-52.

[9] E. Carmoly, *Ode en l'honneur de S. M. Louis Philippe 1er, roi des français, à son avènement au trône* (Metz, 1830), 12 pp. (French and Hebrew). *La Paix,* II (1847), 413; Léon, *op. cit.,* pp. 318-319, 339-40, 342; Paul Raphaël, "Le Clergé et la fête de Louis Philippe en 1831," *Rèv.* 1848, XIII (1917), 17-23; H. Contamine, *Metz et la Moselle de 1814 à 1870,* I (Metz, 1931), 369-70.

the hearts of all the Jews of the universe. We, the Alsatian and French Jews, ran through the streets of Frankfurt, drunk with pride and happiness, singing, shouting, gesticulating like demented prisoners who had just been liberated."[10]

In their praise of the new regime Jewish leaders were careful enough to follow the line of Louis Philippe's policy, since the latter was well established in power. In a sermon delivered in 1833 in memory of the victims of the events of July, 1830, the rabbi of Lille attacked the revolutionary opposition to Louis Philippe: "Is then not ingratitude even today the vice of the masses? Do we not see insatiable men dedicated to revolutions, unsatisfied with the benefits procured by the three days of July, exaggerating the claims of liberty even to the point of pushing toward anarchy?" The rabbi then compared Louis Philippe to King Samuel and continued: "Well, my brothers, we have our King chosen by the Nation, the King who emerged from the barricades, who gave us a real *charte*, who enlarged our freedom; this citizen king who tries to make us happy, who finds his happiness only in the welfare of his peoples. Under his reign we enjoy a profound peace with all the nations. Industry is more active than ever, without precedent in the annals of our history, and commerce prospers more and more. Yet all this is disregarded, and his government is being subjected to insults and slander. Do we not have to fear, my brothers, that God will be irritated by so much wickedness and that in anger he will punish such malice? It is true that the Lord promised not to destroy us anymore by a deluge, but the revolutions toward which it is desired to push us, are they not an equally terrible calamity? This is why, my brothers, we should plead with Our Lord, as our father Abraham pleaded for the inhabitants of Sodom, and ask Him not to destroy the righteous men together with the wicked. And now, my brothers, wrap yourselves up in meditation; we shall pray for the King and all the royal family and also

[10] A. Weill, *Ma jeunesse* (Paris, n.d.), p. 266; A. Weill, *Introduction à mes mémoires* . . . (Paris, 1890), pp. 60-62. On the French Jews in Frankfurt, see also Weill, "Les Juifs de Paris: il y cinquante ans," *La Gerbe* (Paris, 1890), p. 51.

for the peace of the souls of the victims and martyrs of the Revolution of July." This was, indeed, a sermon of a purely political character, directed against the labor movement, an unprecedented occurrence in the annals of Jewish communities at this early period. Lille was then a revolutionary center, and there the July Revolution was supported by workers against the industrialists.[11]

There is no doubt that many Jews held radical political opinions. However, from all the facts known it seems that, except for a few individual cases, the Jews as a group participated neither in the republican opposition of the eighteen-twenties, nor in the Revolution of July, 1830, nor in the republican opposition to the July Monarchy. In spite of many anti-Jewish acts during the Restoration, the mass of Jews did not oppose it actively, for they remembered the anti-Jewish restrictions of Napoleon I.

There were other, more indirect reasons for the limited political engagement of the Jews through 1830. Most of the republican and liberal secret societies were in effect closed circles of friends who knew each other well, and with few exceptions Jews were not as yet accepted on equal terms by the Christian population, even by liberals. Even after July, 1830, Jews were not admitted into the societies that were founded thanks to the liberties newly won by the French.[12] Moreover, Jews were not attracted by the semi-religious, mystical character of many such opposition societies, for romanticism was not a strong trait of the first generations of emancipated Jews.[13] It was during the following regime,

---

[11] The rabbi's sermon is taken from a detached page of a Lille newspaper (Jerusalem, Inv. 994); Octave Festy, *Le Mouvement ouvrier au début de la monarchie de juillet* (Paris, 1908), p. 132. The Jewish community of Lille was founded after the emancipation.

[12] Alexandre Weill was of the opinion that Jews were accepted in the academies provided that they would not exercise any social or direct influence; *Mes batailles* (Paris, 1867), p. 291. "Depuis juillet 1830, des cercles se sont formés à Carpentras, des bals, des soirées ont eu lieu, les israélites n'y ont jamais été admis"; *AI*, I (1840), 683. In 1893 the Carpentras salon of the sub-prefect, Ladreit de la Chartière, was barred to Jews. But neighboring Aix-en-Provence, which professed to be the spiritual capital of Provence, also had a Jewish mayor, City Library of Carpentras, MS 16587; Z. Szajkowski, "The Decline and Fall of Provençal Jewry," *JSS*, VI (1944), 52-53.

[13] S. Posener, "La Première Génération d'Israélites français après

the July Monarchy, that the Jews played a role as a political force, of significance mainly during the Revolution of 1848 and the Second Empire. In 1845, the number of Jewish notables who had the right to vote was 965 (there were 73,975 Jews in France in 1851). Among them, 380 were merchants and industrialists, 36 army officers, 60 members of city councils, 4 mayors, 17 judges and lawyers, and so on. A large proportion of them was actively interested in Jewish life (667 out of the 965 took part in the consistorial elections). This was the narrow base of suffrage achieved by Jews at the start of their participation in the political life of France. Yet the prefect of Lower Rhine wrote in 1843 that the extent of the progress by Jews since 1789 was unbelievable.[14]

The only exception to the minor political role of Jews was the movement of Saint-Simonism, in which Olinde Rodrigues, Léon Halévy, Gustave d'Eichthal, Isaac and Emile Péreire, and others were very active. The school of Saint-Simonism consisted essentially of utopian aristocrats, but though these Jews were of key importance to the movement, no large Jewish group was among its devoted followers; the Saint-Simonian philosophy remained completely alien to the mass of French Jewry. Also, most Jewish Saint-Simonians became estranged from Jewish life and were more Christian than Jewish in belief. Upon the outbreak of the July Revolution, which gave the Saint-Simonians an opportunity to come in contact with the masses, the leaders of the movement advised their friends not to take part in the revolutionary events, partly because of indecision and partly

l'émancipation," *UI*, LXXXVC (1930), 456; Z. Szajkowski, "The Jews in the Post-Napoleonic Restoration in France (1814-1815)," *The Jews in France*, I (New York, 1942), 190-204 (in Yiddish). Alexandre Weill wrote in his memoirs: "En 1830, elle s'appela: Romantisme et émancipation de la chair. . . . Ma foi ne fut expulsée que par la raison philosophique. Je ne croyais plus à la Révélation, mais aussi non plus à la différence des nations et des religions. . . . Moi aussi, je devais payer mon tribut aux erreurs matérielles de mon siècle. Moi aussi, je m'enivrais du vin du vertige de l'athéiste et du crapuleux Romantisme," *Mes années de Bohème* (Paris, 1888), p. 471.
    [14] *AI*, VI (1845), 831-36: "Sans doute, il y a plus de calcul que de sincérité dans ces changements. Comment expérait-on la régénération aussi subite d'une nation si longtemps abâtardie?" Lower Rhine, V-149, No. 758.

because of uncertainty as to its outcome. Opposed to a
government run by workers, they preferred a regime based
on the ideology of 1789. True, Olinde Rodrigues was mentioned above as one of the revolutionary fighters of July,
1830, but his was an exceptional case among the Saint-
Simonians. In a few places members of the movement tried
without success to attract the masses. In Alsace the liberal
newspaper *L'Alsacien,* of which Michel Goudchaux was an
editor, fought the Saint-Simonians as an "oligarchy" that
would abolish individual freedom if it achieved its ends.
Saint-Simonians gave up the idea of becoming a political
party, resigning themselves to the role of a philosophical,
semi-religious school. In connection with the revolutionary
events of Lyon in April, 1834, they called upon the people
not to revolt, but to wait for God's will to express itself.[15]

II

THE LAW CONCERNING THE JEWISH CLERGY

From the Jewish point of view the most important act
of the new regime was the law of February 8, 1831, declaring that members of the Jewish clergy were civil servants
and should be salaried by the government.

The Charter of the Restoration regime had given equal
rights to all religious groups. Article 6, however, excluded
the Jewish clergy from the category of civil servants; the
salaries of rabbis and cantors were paid from special taxes
collected by the Jewish consistories. The Jews rightly
viewed this treatment as evidence that they were second-
class citizens who still had to achieve full emancipation. I.
Berr, a Jewish lawyer of Metz, asserted that during the

---

[15] Georges Weill, "Les Juifs et le Saint-Simonisme," *Revue des études
juives,* XXXI (1895), 261-80; G. Weill, *L'Ecole Saint-Simonienne* (Paris,
1896), pp. 191-93; Z. Szajkowski, "The Jewish Saint-Simonians and Socialist
Antisemites in France," JSS, IX (1947), 33-60; Charléty, *Histoire* . . . , pp.
79-85, 115; Festy, *op. cit.,* pp. 61, 80-84; *L'Alsacien,* Aug. 28, 1831; [Jean]
Terson, *Un St.-Simonien au peuple de Lyon, à l'occasion des événements d'avril
1834* (Lyon, 1834), p. 15.

Restoration "the future of the Jews was gloomy and uncertain, and they were fearful that the gains of 1789 would be contested some day." The Restoration's Charter left open the possibility of adverse interpretations with reference to the Jews.[16]

At the beginning of the new regime, on August 3, 1830, the Central Consistory held a special meeting for the purpose of demanding the abolition of Article 6 of the Charter, which made civil servants of the Catholic and Protestant clergy alone (*seuls*). The meeting recognized it as a "duty not to let the opportunity escape to solicit, in favor of the Jewish religion, the benefit of the system of equality which had just been proclaimed at the price of the blood of such noble victims from all communions." They decided, however, against an outright demand for the abolition of Article 6 of the Charter, favoring instead a milder request that the government recognize rabbis as civil servants. But the Central Consistory was not active enough in following the developments in the parliament, and a private group of Jews took it upon themselves to press the issue. Javal, Fould, Michel Goudchaux, Jacob Lazard, and Alphonse-Théodore Cerfberr petitioned the parliament and the duc d'Orléans, the future King Louis Philippe,[17] while at the same time Israël Bédarride (1798-1869), a Jewish lawyer, solicited the help of his friend Benjamin Constant, leader of the left-wing opposition.[18] As a result of these interventions, the word *seuls* (alone) was omitted from the article on the clergy in the new version of the Charter adopted by the parliament,

---

[16] *AI*, II (1842), 238.

[17] Goudchaux has been mentionel before; Javal's first name is not given. Fould was probably Benoît Fould; (*AI*, III, 1842, 362). Alphonse-Théodore Cerfberr (1797-1859), a captain in the army and author, was a member of the Central Consistory. On him see S. Cahen, *AI*, XXI (1860), 12-13. Jacob Lazard (1759-1840) was a well-known merchant, who actively participated in the fight for Jewish emancipation in 1789; he was a deputy to the Sanhedrin convoked by Napoleon I; *AI*, I (1840), 467-71.

[18] On Bédarride, see J. Félix, in *AI*, XXX (1869), 717; M. Lisbonne, *Etude nécrologique sur Israël Bédarride* (Montpellier, 1870), reprinted from *Revue judiciaire des cours impériales*; *AI*, XXXI (1870), 202-03. In 1833 Michel Berr published a eulogy in memory of Constant: *Eloge de Benjamin Constant, prononcé le 12 juin 1833, dans la chaire de l'Athénée royal de Paris* . . . (Paris, 1836).

thus—as Constant wrote to Bédarride on August 17, 1830—
leaving the door open for the next step directly in favor of
the Jewish clergy.[19] The duc d'Orléans also promised such
action in the near future. In fact, on December 4, 1830,
the parliament resolved that the Jewish clergy should be
salaried by the government, and on February 1, 1831, the
same resolution was adopted by the Chambre des Pairs and
became law on February 8.[20]

   This new act in favor of the Jews was an outgrowth of
new republican ideas, as the historian, Robert Anchel, has
correctly noted; it was not voted "in a moment of enthusiasm" but after a sharp discussion. The vote in the parliament was 211 in favor of the law and 71 against; in the
Chambre des Pairs, 57 in favor and 32 against with 2 ab-
stentions. Another historian, Léon Bermann, commented
on this event, not in connection with the Revolution of
1830, but with the general devolopment of the French
rabbinate. For a long time the new act was interpreted
strictly with no deviation from the letter of the law. Thus,
in 1832 the Mayor of Lyon rejected a request for a subsidy
for the synagogue to provide housing for the rabbi because
the law of February 8, 1831, referred only to rabbis'
salaries.[21]

   Nevertheless, most contemporary Jewish leaders and
later historians hailed this act as a great event in Jewish
history. Thus, the unknown Alsatian author of a contemporary Yiddish description of the Revolution reported that
Louis Philippe was very favorably disposed toward the Jews
and ordered that all rabbis should be paid by the Government.[22] In 1831, Samuel Cahen dedicated his French trans-

   [19] Michel Berr, *Du passé* . . . (see note 58), p. 21.
   [20] Posener, *"La Révolution"* (*supra*, n. 6), 87-89; *Crémieux*, I, 157-58;
Lazard, *Michel Goudchaux* . . . , p. 568; Robert Anchel, *Notes sur les frais du
culte juif en France de 1815 à 1831* (Paris, 1928), pp. 32-45; Halphen, pp. xliii-
xlv, 88-90, 92-94, 103-105, 386-450.
   [21] Anchel, *Notes* . . . , p. 33; Léon Berman, *Histoire des juifs de France
des origines à nos jours* (Paris, 1937), p. 399; Alfred Lévy, *Notice sur les
israélites de Lyon* (Paris, 1894), pp. 37-38.
   [22] Jerusalem, Inv. 992: "Diser melech Louis Philippe is uns Jahudim,
Boruch-Hashem, sehr ginstig und ot glaich ordenirt, dos alle rabonim fun
guverneman colt virth."

lation of the Bible to Louis Philippe. Cahen, a teacher in the Jewish public school in Paris, emphasized the fact that his translation was being published during "the reign of the first constitutional King of France, when tolerance too became a truth." A similar view was expressed by a Jewish delegation on June 10, 1831, during Louis Philippe's visit to Metz. At a reception given by the King in 1835 Adolphe Crémieux declared that the Revolution of 1789 had proclaimed the principle of liberty of conscience, but until the July Monarchy people had feared the consequences. Rabbi L. M. Lambert of Metz stated in 1840 that this was "the greatest act of justice in favor of the Jews since the destruction of the Second Temple." According to M. Th. Milhaud of the Jewish community of Aix-en-Provence, the July Monarchy destroyed all administrative barriers between the Jewish and other religions. The lawyer and historian Achille Edmond Halphen stated in 1851 that the Jews would always bless the memory of Louis Philippe, who brought them complete civil equality both in law and in fact. The Franco-Jewish poet and co-founder (in 1860) of the Alliance Israélite Universelle, Eugène Manuel, wrote that Judaism "was protected by the law, by [public] opinion, and by the liberal sympathies of the Monarchy of 1830."[23] The same opinion was expressed by non-Jewish officials. The prefect of Lower Rhine wrote in 1843 that the real Jewish emancipation dated, not from 1791, but from February 8, 1831.[24] Even more important than such utterances was the fact that as a consequence of the law in favor of the Jewish clergy Catholicism ceased to be the exclusive official religion and became only the religion of the majority of Frenchmen.

[23] *La Bible, traduction nouvelle . . . dédiée à Louis-Philippe 1er, roi des français,* par S. Cahen, I (Paris, 1831), v; *Discours adressés au roi, et de Sa Majesté. Metz, ce 10 juin 1831* (Metz, 1831), pp. 15-16; *Crémieux,* I, 155-56; L. M. Lambert, *Précis de l'histoire des hébreux, depuis le Patriarch Abraham jusqu'en* 1840 (Metz, 1840), p. 416; M. Th. Milhaud, *Discours . . .* (Aix, 1846), p. 7; *AI,* II (1841), 238-39; Halphen, p. xliii; Eugène Manuel, "Souvenirs intimes, un coin du passé," *La Gerbe* (Paris, 1890), p. 46; cf. N. Leven, *Cinquante ans d'histoire: L'Alliance Israélite Universelle,* I (Paris, 1911), 53.

[24] Lower Rhine, V-149, No. 758.

Anchel's comment, noted above, that the law of February 8, 1831, was not a gracious concession to Jews but was hard-won, is confirmed by other developments in the life of French Jewry during the July Monarchy. It was in this period that the oath *more judaico* was abolished, not by the action of the King or the legislature, but in the courts[25] after a long-drawn battle going back to the Restoration. But the July Monarchy did not solve other important problems of the Jewish communities, such as the debts they had accumulated before 1789 and still owed. The Jews persistently requested the nationalization or annulment of these debts as a remnant of the old regime, but the July Monarchy followed the line of its predecessors and refused to modify the obligation of the Jews to repay the debts.[26]

III

ANTI-JEWISH RIOTS IN ALSACE

According to many sources, anti-Jewish riots broke out in Alsace at the beginning of the Revolution of 1830, a repetition of similar occurrences in 1789 and a forecast of later incidents, in 1848. Anti-Jewish riots became a kind of tradition which the Alsatian people observed upon the outbreak of any revolution in France.[27]

In 1830 the Jews of Wintzheim demanded protection from the prefect; according to one source anti-Jewish riots also broke out in 1830 in the communities around Phals-

---

[25] Cf. Ed. Martin, *Mémoire amplicatif pour le sieur Lazare Cerf . . . à Saverne contre Isaïe Gougenhém . . . à Haguenau. Question: les israélites français peuvent-ils, en matière civile, être assujettis à un serment spécial, différent au serment imposé aux autres citoyens* (Paris, 1842), 24 pp.

[26] Z. Szajkowski, *Autonomy and Communal Jewish Debts during the French Revolution of 1789* (New York, 1959), pp. 115, 155, No. 124.

[27] M. Ginsburger, *Encyclopaedia Judaica*, VI (1930), 553; Christian Pfister, *Pages alsaciennes* (Paris, 1927), p. 216; Gabriel Daty, "Les Juifs en Alsace et en Lorraine," *La Question juive vue par vingt-six èminents personalités* (Paris, 1934), p. 40; Paul Leuilliot, "L'Usure judaïque . . .," *Annales historiques de la Révolution Française*, VII (1930), 250; *UI*, II (1845), 131, 231, 250; Z. Szajkowski, "Pogroms in Alsace during the Revolutions of 1789, 1830 and 1848," *Zion*, XX (1955), 82-102 (in Hebrew).

bourg (Moselle).[28] But the most serious riots associated
with the Revolution of July, 1830, occurred almost two
years later, in the Upper Rhine community of Bergheim
where, on June 12, 1832, peasants and workers of the local
factories attacked the Jews with casualties of two dead and
eighteen or twenty wounded.[29] Two days later the sub-
prefect of Seléstat (Lower Rhine), near Bergheim, reported
that a mob had fired on an army unit that was trying to
disperse anti-Jewish attackers. Fearing that the anti-Jewish
riots might spread to the neighboring communities of Lower
Rhine, the sub-prefect ordered the gendarmes and mayors
to defend the Jews. In a second report, written later on
the same day (June 14) after a personal visit to Bergheim,
he gave the following description of the aftermath of the
pogrom: "The streets were full of broken furniture thrown
out by the rioters from Jewish homes; roofs and other parts
of Jewish houses were destroyed; Christians who were apprehensive that they might be subjected to a search, were returning various effects from looted Jewish houses. Jews
who had tried to escape to Seléstat found the roads blocked
by Christians."

Very soon mobs tried to attack other Jewish communities. On June 17, 1832, the same sub-prefect reported
that the inhabitants of Châtenais were preparing that very
evening to attack the Lower Rhine Jewish community of
Schervillé (Scherviller). Since he could not depend upon
the National Guard, the sub-prefect sent a regular army
unit to defend the Jews of that community. Believing that
information on what had taken place in the Upper Rhine

[28] Leuilliot, "L'Usure judaïque . . ." (supra, note 27), VII, 250; L.
Schoumacher, Erckman-Chatrian (Paris, 1933), p. 32. During the dearth riots
that broke out in June, 1832, in Metz, a Jewish storehouse of wheat was looted.
"Souvenirs du Baron André Sers . . . ," Annales de l'est, Series 2, I (1905),
517-19.
[29] Mémoire pour la commune de Bergheim appelante; contre le sieur
Israël-Gabriel Sée, intimé. [Signé: Yves, avocat,] n. p., n. d. 32 pp.; Réfutation
par un israélite du Haut-Rhin, de plusieurs articles calomnieux, publiés contre
le Consistoire Israélite de Colmar (Strasbourg, 1841), p. 13; M. Ginsburger,
Les Juifs à Ribeauville et à Belgheim (Strasbourg, 1939), pp. 12-14; idem.,
"Les Troubles de Bergheim en 1832," Strassburger israelitische Wochenschrift,
IV (1907), No. 1.

would deter the mob from attacking the Jews of Schervillé,
he ordered the mayor to give maximum publicity to the
riots in Bergheim, where three attackers were killed and
twenty-five arrested. On June 20, 1832, an officer of the
gendarmerie reported the following incident that had taken
place in Ittersviller (Lower Rhine): On June 4, the Jews
of that community organized a procession in honor of the
opening of their synagogue. They carried the republican
tricolor flag and a tablet bearing the Ten Commandments.
The Jews had hired four National Guardsmen from Andlau
(Lower Rhine) to protect their festivities, for the local
National Guard was unreliable. Provocatively, the Christians
drove their cattle into the line of march of the Jewish procession, and a scuffle followed. The priest in his sermon
the following Sunday inveighed against the Jews, warning
that they might retaliate by driving their cattle into the
line of march of the next Catholic procession.[30]

Who was responsible for the anti-Jewish incidents in
Alsace? According to the local authorities, it was the
Catholic priests. In 1836 the Jewish physician Michel Levy
(1809-1872) wrote: "The emancipation of the Jews was
an anti-Catholic act."[31] Christian inhabitants of Ittersviller
(Lower Rhine) were among the attackers in Bergheim, and
the mayor of the community reported on June 20, 1832,
that the local priest, named Kern, warned while preaching
in church on June 17, 1832, that the Jews who killed Christ
would attack the Catholic procession. Then the priest said:
"We now possess the liberty of July," and "We must show
that we are Christians . . . fight in the name of Jesus Christ
for our religion." On June 21 the sub-prefect declared
that Kern was a dangerous man who had been responsible
for many riots and was the probable author of two articles
against the Jews and the Revolution of July published in a
local newspaper.

30 Lower Rhine, 3 M 39.
31 Michel Lévy, *Coup d'oeil historique sur l'état des israélites en France
et particuliérement en Alsace* (Strasbourg, 1836), p. 27. On Lévy, a physician
and consistorial leading figure, see Rap., "Les médecins israélites de Paris," *La
Paix*, I (1846), 198-205; H. Barouk, "Le Grand Hygièniste Michel-Lévy,"
Revue d'histoire de la médecine hébraïque, No. 3 (1849), 4-8.

On June 13 and 24, 1832, the sub-prefect reported that hatred of the Jews and incitement to loot were being stirred up as the basis for a broader action against the regime inaugurated by the Revolution of July. In fact, the Alsatian leaders of the Catholic Church were then working hand-in-hand with the Legitimist party. As the Protestants and the Jews were among the most dedicated adherents of the new regime, the Catholics' slogan was that their Church was in danger. On June 6, 1832, the sub-prefect of Selestat reported to his superior, the prefect of the Lower Rhine, that agitators had tried to foment a revolt of the people against the July regime by playing up the high cost of living and hard times. When this maneuver failed, the age-old incitement of the people against the Jews was resorted to. At first, the sub-prefect wrote, he believed that the riots were directed by the "red flag," meaning left-wing elements. However, he soon became convinced that the leadership came from the "white flag." At confessions the priests asked their communicants to attack the Jews. In the opinion of the sub-prefect, as long as the clergy were independent of the government, they would provoke such attacks, and he added that a large-scale uprising against the government was being prepared in Alsace. Two years later, on October 15, 1834, the same sub-prefect reported similar preparations in Alsace, which the Catholic clergy were abetting, this time in the hope of support by a foreign invasion. The priests were again active in the villages, where they agitated against the Jews. "The Jews are always the excuse the agitators use for provoking uprisings in Alsace."[32]

Not only peasants but factory workers as well took part in the Alsatian anti-Jewish riots of 1830, as they had done earlier and would do again in later years. Was labor's participation in anti-Jewish riots a result of organized anti-

[32] Lower Rhine, 3 M 28-29; *Courrier du Bas-Rhin*, Feb. 17, 1843. In 1841, 491 Jews were living in Bergheim, only 439 in 1846; in Itterswiller there were 212 Jews in 1846; in Scherswiller 339 in 1846.

Jewish propaganda by a labor movement or of anti-Jewish sentiment aroused by reactionary circles? According to some historians, a well-organized labor movement then existed in Alsace, an opinion to which this author can adhere only with many reservations.[33] In any event, it is impossible to say that the leadership of the Alsatian labor movement was anti-Jewish. In fact, Jonas Ennery, a teacher in the Strasbourg Jewish school, who was well known as a Jew, was elected in 1848 as a Socialist deputy from the Lower Rhine and this in spite of violent anti-Jewish pogroms in the neighboring communities of Upper Rhine at that time.[34]

Was usury the reason for the anti-Jewish riots? This was the usual contemporary explanation and it is also the opinion of many historians. Let us see. In the arrondissement of Saverne (the home district of many of the Christians who attacked the Jews of Bergheim), 331 mortgages in the amount of 421,679 francs were registered between May 4 and June 25, 1825; only 63 in the amount of 56,314.30 francs were in favor of Jewish mortgagees. In the same region 635 mortgages in the amount of 367,632.72 francs were registered between March 8 and April 13, 1832; only 151 in the amount of 55,436.14 francs were in favor of Jews.[35] In M. M. Kahan-Rabecq's view, the fact that the Jews were the well-to-do class of the population in the villages was an invitation to pogroms. The great poverty of the French Jews, especially in the Alsatian villages, which has been described in detail elsewhere,[36] is usually ignored by the French historians.

[33] M. M. Kahan-Rabecq, L'Alsace économique et sociale sous le régne de Louis-Philippe (Paris, 1939), 2 vols.

[34] Szajkowski, "Pogroms . . . ," Zion, XX, 98.

[35] Ponteil, "L'Usure . . . ," 231-51; Opposition, p. 284; Kahan-Rabecq, La Classe ouvrière en Alsace pendant la monarchie de juillet . . . (Paris, 1939), p. 78; Z. Szajkowski, Agricultural Credit and Napoleon's Anti-Jewish Decrees (New York, 1953), Table I.

[36] M. M. Kahan-Rabecq, La Classe . . . , p. 78; Z. Szajkowski, Poverty and Social Welfare among French Jews, 1800-1880 (New York, 1954).

IV

THE PROBLEMS OF ALGERIA AND FOREIGN COUNTRIES

Many other events of this period have a bearing upon Jewish life in France; some of them still require detailed study. One of these is the occupation of Algeria in 1830.

For Charles X this campaign was a well calculated diversion from domestic political troubles. Alger capitulated on July 5, 1830, and the King used this moment of popular rejoicing over the French victory to curb the freedom of the press, to dissolve the parliament, and to institute other restrictive measures. The official excuse for the French occupation of Algeria was an old conflict between the two countries over debts involving two Algerian Jewish families named Bacri and Busnach. For the French conquerors their role was most important.[37]

In France enthusiasm over the victory in Algeria continued even after the abdication of Charles X. Michel Berr, in a pamphlet published in 1830, predicted that Algeria would mean for all peoples the same as the discovery of America and that the Jews there would gain their liberty. Indeed, under French occupation a new era did begin for the Jews of Algeria. Actually, the leaders of the French Jews looked upon the Algerian Jews as an uncivilized horde. But they were nevertheless Jews of a French colony, and something had to be done on their behalf in order not to impair the prestige of French Jewry. Hence, this was a turning-point, not only in the annals of the colonial Algerian Jews, but also for the emancipated Jews of France, who without preparation became the protectors and guides of a large number of Jews outside France. The Central Consistory, for example, helped to organize the Jewish consistories of Algeria.[38] In 1838, Gustave d'Eichthal, a leading

---

[37] Morton Rosenstock, "The House of Bacri and Busnach: A Chapter from Algeria's Commercial History," *JSS*, XIV (1952), 343-64; "Les Origines de l'expedition d'Alger en 1830," *La Revue libérale*, XXV (1959), 42-58.

[38] M. Berr, *Du passé* . . . (see *infra*, note 58), pp. 27-28; Morton Rosenstock, "The Establishment of the Consistorial System in Algeria," *JSS*, XVIII (1956), 41-54; Z. Szajkowski, "The Struggle for Jewish Emancipation in Algeria after the French Occupation," *Historia Judaica*, XVIII (1956), 27-40.

Jewish Saint-Simonian, prepared a detailed project on how to organize Algerian Jewish consistories.[39]

In 1844 the *Archives israélites* published an appeal for the establishment of a *Comité européen de colonization israélite* as a post-script to an article on the situation of Jews in Poland by Jan Czynski, who was interested in the Fourierist ideas on Algerian colonization. The Saint-Simonians also developed a program for Algerian colonization. But anti-Jewish feelings were strong among the military leaders in Algeria and also colored the attitude of the civil and military authorities in Paris, who were responsible for the newly occupied territory. It was mainly because of this attitude that Jean-Jacques Altaras, the Jewish leader of Marseille, failed in his project to colonize Russian Jews in Algeria.[40]

The Revolution of July, 1830, greatly influenced the fight for Jewish emancipation in other countries, at the same time creating new problems for French Jews, who developed a consciousness of their ties with Jews the world over. As a result they also grew more mature in strictly Franco-Jewish matters.[41]

The Polish insurrection of 1830 was enthusiastically greeted by the republicans of France, who saw in it a logical result of the July Revolution. They demanded France's help for the Poles and the slogans for a French democracy and Polish independence became associated. Soon however, it became clear that France would not wish a war for Polish freedom or for the freedom of any other country. Many French republicans tried to use Polish, German and Italian

---

[39]   *AI*, V (1844), 142-43; J. Czynski, *La Colonisation militaire sous Bugeaud* (Paris-Alger, 1839); Szajkowski, "The Struggle . . . ," *Historia Judaica*, XVIII, 28-29. In 1842 there existed a society of European Jews in Algeria for the help of the native Jews, *AI*, III (1892), 301.

[40]   Z. Szajkowski, "New Materials on Altaras and His Colonization Plan," *YB*, XXI (1943), 47-70 (in Yiddish).

[41]   "La Révolution de 1830 avait fait tresailler l'Europe, amené le soulévement de la Pologne contre le tsar, de la Belgique contre la Hollande, du peuple contre les princes dans quelques petits Etats de l'Italie et de l'Allemagne, donné des espérances aux libéraux d toute l'Europe. N'allait-elle pas rendre aux Juifs tout ce que la réaction de 1815 leur avait enlevé? Ils espéraient . . ."; Leven, *Cinquante ans* . . . , I, 53.

political groups in France in the fight against the French Monarchy and also in preparation for revolutions in their home countries. At first the Polish National Committee (Komitet Narodowy) in France refused to adopt a policy of involvement in French politics. This was one of the reasons for the founding on March 17, 1832, of an opposition group (*Towarzystwo Demokratyczne Polskie*). Joachim Lelevel, one of the leaders of the Polish refugees, favored a united front with the French republicans, and so did Jan Czynski, a protagonist in the fight for the emancipation of Polish Jewry.[42]

Some French Jews were active in the movement for Poland's freedom, among them Adolphe Crémieux and Alphonse-Théodore Cerfberr. It was Crémieux who was appointed by the Franco-Polish Committee to write the text of the Committee's pathetic declaration of February 12, 1831, in support of the Polish insurrection.[43] The financial transactions of the National Polish Mission were conducted through the bank of Fould-Oppenheim.[44] Jewish participation in the Polish insurrection was enthusiastically greeted in Paris. Eugène Manuel, the Franco-Jewish leader and poet, relates that his grandfather, the cantor Israél Lövy (1773-1832), conducted the services in the Paris synagogue on the very day in September, 1831, that news reached Paris of the fall of Warsaw. He "loved Poland as a fatherland." D. Levi-Alvarez, a well-known educator, called the Polish insurrection "a great poem in action."[45] Many Jews were among the Polish refugees who came to France, where they greatly influenced French Politics.[46]

[42] *Echo Miast Polskich*, I (1843), 11; *Pólnoc*, I (1835), 59; A. Lewak, *Od zwiazków weglarskich do mlodej Polski* (Warszawa, 1920), pp. 17-18.

[43] "Manifeste du Comité Central Français en faveur des polonais," *La Pologne et la France en 1830-31* (Paris, 1831), 19-33; *Crémieux*, I, 116. Cerfberr's role in the Committee was noted in *Pólnoc*, I (1835), 24.

[44] "Akta misji polskej," vol. 5, part 10, No. 354, etc. (in the Mickiewicz Library of Paris).

[45] L. Börne, *Lettres écrites de Paris*, 1830-31 (Paris, 1832), pp. 172-73; Eugène Manuel, "Israel Lövy, hazan de Paris," *AI*, XI (1850), 349; D. Levi-Alvarez, *Esquisses littéraires* (Paris, 1858), p. 474.

[46] *AI*, IX (1848), 289. The Jewish author of a pamphlet made an appeal for aid to Polish refugees: Joseph Mayer, *Opinion . . .* (Paris, 1832), p. 19.

In 1833 "The Philanthropic Society for the Advancement of Jewish Emancipation throughout the World" was established in Paris to fight for Jewish rights and Polish interests. Among the leading members of the society, presided over by General Marie-Joseph Lafayette and known as the Lafayette Committee, were Adolphe Crémieux, James Mayer de Rothschild, and Alphonse-Théodore Cerfberr. Jan Czynski and others tried to involve this society in French political issues. Crémieux and Rothschild, however, did not wish it to have "a political character," considering it unwise to associate the fight for Jewish emancipation in other countries with a liberal political opposition in France. They were also afraid that such a step might result in anti-Jewish reprisals in Russia-Poland and in other countries. Thus, at the beginning of the July Monarchy, the leaders of French Jewry laid down principles for a Jewish "foreign policy" that were followed in succeeding years by the French Jews. The society had a brief life. In 1833 Czynski and others of its influential Polish members were expelled from France, and it was to this that Czynski attributed the dissolution of the society. Later Léon Hollaenderski, a leading figure among the Polish Jews in France placed the blame for his expulsion on Czynski himself. "Czynski committed a great error; he treated the question of the emancipation of the Israelites as a political question. Attributing all the evil to the aristocracy, he made common cause with democrats exclusively."[47]

Alexandre Weill, an eccentric writer, was active in the "Young Germany" movement, and many fighters for

The author of another 1831 pamphlet wrote that "if the Jews would have been strong enough in Poland . . . to raise the banner against the Tsar we could speak of progress of the human spirit in this century," [J. A. de Fonseca?,] *La Cannemagique ou le libéralisme dévoilé. Roman politique* (La Haye [Paris], 1831), p. 41. See also [Mayer,] *La Pologne et la Russie,* par M., ancien officier français . . . (Paris, 1831), XIX, 24 pp.

[47] Jan Czynski; *Questions des juifs polonais* (Paris, 1833), pp. 21-22; Léon Hollaenderski, *Les Israélites de Pologne* (Paris, 1846), p. 136; Antoni Oskowski, *Pomysly o potrzebie reformy towarzyskiej etc.* (Paris, 1834), pp. 1-5; Z. Szajkowski, "The Founding of the Alliance Israélite Universelle," *YB,* XVIII (1941), 2; Abraham Duker, "The Lafayette Committee for Jewish Emancipation," *Essays on Jewish Life and Thought in Honor of Salo Baron* (New York, 1959), pp. 169-76.

a German republic were among his friends.[48] At a liberal banquet held on March 20, 1834, in Strasbourg the Jewish stockbroker G. Wurmser addressed the German patriots, and on May 27 he read an address by the German patriots at a demonstration in honor of Lafayette's memory. An Alsatian Jew named Weil, brother of a Jewish teacher, died while on a mission in Germany for German refugees in Strasbourg.[49] German refugees in France influenced Jews not only there but in other countries as well.[50]

During the July Monarchy the climate was favorable for a showdown on restrictions against French Jews in Switzerland. The French Jews had tried unsuccessfully to solve this problem during the previous regime. Adolphe Crémieux intervened in 1835, but the question was soon shelved by the government of Louis Philippe, probably in retaliation for his having shifted from passive acceptance of the July regime to support of the republican opposition. Even the Central Consistory, recognizing the government's new attitude, gave up insisting on safeguards for the rights of French Jews in Switzerland. Instead, the fight was left to the Alsatian Jews under the able leadership of M. Nordmann, rabbi of Hegenheim, who continued to press for free entry into Switzerland for French Jews. Nordmann did not plead for the rights of French citizens solely as a question of French principle abroad. He insisted on the emancipation of the Jews of Switzerland as well. This was finally won during the Second Empire of Napoleon III.[51]

[48] A. Weill, *Briefe hervorragender verstorbener Männer Deutschlands* (Zürich, 1899); J. Dresch, "Une Correspondence inédite de Karl Gutzkow de Madame d'Agoult (comtesse de Charnacé) et d'Alexndre Weill," *Revue germanique*, II (1906), 63-95. See also Weill, *Staatsentwürfe über Preussen und Deutschland* (Stuttgart, 1843; also Darmstadt, 1845).

[49] *Opposition*, pp. 390, 405; L. Spach, "Le Grand Duché de Bade en 1848," *Revue d'Alsace*, XVI (1865), 109-11.

[50] Cf. Gustav Freytag, *Karl Mathy* (Leipzig, 1870), p. 127; Otto Wittberger, *Die deutschen politischen Flüchtlinge in Strassburg von 1830-1849* (Berlin-Leipzig, 1910), p. 14.

[51] Halphen, pp. 109, 456-69; Sol M. Stroock, "Switzerland and American Jews," *Publications of the American Jewish Historical Society*, XI (1903), 7-52; Félix Neher, "Une Carte antisémite de la Suisse au XIX⁰ siecle," *Evidences*, IV, No. 27 (1952), 40-44; *idem*, "L'Emancipation des juifs en Suisse au XIX⁰ siècle et les Israélites d'Alsace," *L'Alsace et la Suisse à travers les*

The voice of French Jews was also raised in favor of Jews of other countries.[52] During the years 1830-1847 the Jews of England, Germany, and other countries were no less zealous in their efforts for less privileged Jews the world over.

V

THE POLITICAL ATTITUDE OF VARIOUS JEWISH GROUPS

The eighteen-thirties saw large-scale participation by French Jews in finance, commerce, and industry. What was the political attitude of the Jewish upper bourgeosie? The Rothschild family clearly favored the Bourbons, but they quickly began to court the new ruler, and J. M. de Rothschild became Louis Philippe's banker. Benjamin Gradis (1789-1858), of the well-known Bordeaux family, was opposed to a parliamentary regime. In various pamphlets he defended a monarchy based, not on the rising bourgeoisie, but on the aristocracy of landowners and also—for reasons of propaganda—on the proletariat. Among the shareholders of the Bordeaux newspaper *Courrier,* founded in 1837, which defended the government and became the organ of the local upper-income class, were the Jewish families Gradis, Perpignan, Raba, and Rodrigues; Bordeaux did not possess any real republican press during the July Monarchy. In another part of France, in Moselle, the *Courrier de la Moselle* followed the republican line of the Paris *National,* while the *L'Indépendant de la Moselle* favored the government. Gerson Lévy (1784-1864), a Jewish author and champion of reform of the Jewish religion, directed *L'Indépendant* from 1830 until 1855.[53]

---

siècles (Strasbourg, 1952), pp. 385-193; Jacques Brisac, *Ce que les israélites de la Suisse doivent à la France* (Lausanne, 1916).

[52] *E.g.,* Eugen Dalmeyda, *Lettre d'un juif à S. S. le pape Grègoire XVI sur l'édit de l'inquisition d'Ancône contre les juifs . . .* (Paris, 1843), 15 pp.

[53] Count Egon Caesar Corti, *The Rise of the House of Rothschild* (New York, 1928), pp. 391-407; *idem, The Reign of the House of Rothschild* (New York, 1928), pp. 1-33. On Gradis, see E. Carmoly, *AI,* XXIII (1862), 29-34; Z. Szajkowski, "The Struggle over the Election System in the Jewish Com-

From the Jewish community of Bordeaux came a few leaders of the Saint-Simonian school. Thus, Jewishness clearly did not determine the philosophical or political attitude of French Jews. Although A. Crémieux in 1840 spoke in London in the name of "the emancipated Jews in France" in favor of the abolition of slavery, the Gradis family of Bordeaux was against the emancipation of Negroes even in 1848.[54] It is also impossible to clarify the political attitudes of Jews according to their economic and social status. Michel Goudchaux and Marx Théodore Cerfberr were both rich, both came from eminent Jewish families of the same milieu, and both were in the Jewish communities, yet their political affiliations were far apart. While Goudchaux fought as a republican leader, Cerfberr was elected in Alsace a conservative deputy.

There were Jews in the liberal opposition of Alsace. In 1832, G. Wurmser was among the leaders of the Alsatian association for freedom of the press. He, May junior, Léon Bicart, and Michel Goudchaux were active in the *Circle patriotique* of Strasbourg. A Jew named Bloch of Weitersweiler was involved in the importation of contraband arms from Germany in January, 1832. In 1840, when there was a threat of a war because of Germany's attitude against France, Alsatian Jewish horse dealers were sent to Paris in order to negotiate with the Ministry of War on the purchase of horses. They were unable to accomplish anything, and for this the government was blamed by the Alsatian liberals.[55] The most prominent Jewish leader of the Alsatian liberals was the aforementioned Michel Goudchaux, editor of the liberal *Alsacien*. It was he, who, in December, 1831, made

munities of France, 1850-80," *YB*, XXXV (1951), 143-44; A. Charles, *La Révolution de 1858* . . . [Bordeaux, 1945], p. 49; M. Thiel, *Notice bigraphique sur M. Gerson-Lévy* (Metz, 1865), p. 14; Contamine, *Metz* . . . , I, 371; also the book by the Jewish leader David Singer (1778-1846), *Miroir politique de la France,* par un homme du peuple (Paris, 1841), (on Singer, *AI*, VII (1846), 100-02).

[54] *AI*, I (1840), 383-85; Z. Szajkowski, "Bordeaux et l'abolition de l'esclavage dans les colonies en 1848," *Revue historique de Bordeaux* . . . XXXXVII (1954), 113-41.

[55] *Opposition*, pp. 247, 302, 305, 624-25, 938-41; *AI*, I (1840), 322-23.

a welcoming speech to the Polish refugees in the name of
the national guard, and he was the official host to the Polish
generals. Later, Goudchaux went back to Paris where he
continued to be among the leading figures of the republican
opposition.[56]

Yet Jewish liberals did not follow blindly all republican
movements. Thus, while some disappointed Alsatian republicans favored German contacts, the Jews of the province
were the strongest pro-French element there. According
to the editor of *Les Archives israélites,* the German character
of the Alsatian people was responsible for local anti-Jewish
action.[57] Neither were all Jewish politicians active republicans, Cerfberr being a case in point.

VI

INTELLECTUALS WITHOUT A CAUSE

The first generations of emancipated Jews in a country
of frequent revolutions and changes in regime included
men of talent whose accomplishments were small because
of their eccentricities. Some of them were active during
the July Monarchy.

Michel Berr (1781-1843), the son of Berr-Isaac Berr
of Nancy, was the author of *Appel* (1801), an important
pamphlet on Jews written by an emancipated French Jew.
Another pamphlet, published by him after the events of
July, 1830, which was sold for the benefit of the victims
of the so-called glorious three July days, was touching
stylistically, but the opinions expressed revealed an amateur
politician.[58] Berr hoped to secure some high position through

---

[56] *Opposition,* pp. 100-01, 221-22, 239, 241, 244, 293; A. Gourevitch,
"Le Mouvement pour la réforme électorale (1838-1841)," *Rév.* 1848, XI
(1914), III, 119.

[57] A. Weill, *Introduction à mes mémoires* (Paris, 1890), pp. 63, 184;
George Weill, "L'Alsace de 1815 à 1848," *Revue de Paris,* XXIII — I (1916),
383 ("les juifs . . . une élite instruite . . . entièrement française"); R. [S.
Cahen], *AI,* V (1844), 464.

[58] Cf. the following pamphlets by M. B. [Michel Berr], *Observations
sur l'acte additionnel ux Constitutions de l'Empire et sur notre situation po-*

the help of his many friends who became leading figures in the new regime, but he was doomed to disappointment, for his extraordinary political ideas made it impossible for his republican friends to trust him. Though he became notorious for his attacks on various personalities and for other eccentricities, he was described as one of the "eminent men amongst us."[59]

Alexandre Weill (1811-1899) was another eccentric, vacillating constantly between various moods and philosophical and political doctrines. He was active as a Fourierist in spite of the anti-Jewish character of this movement. When H. Balzac published an article against the socialists in the *Corsaire-Satan* (1847), the editor of *La Démocratie Pacifique* commissioned Weill to reply. At the same time he was closely associated with the Saint-Simonians. Karl Gutzkow has characterized Weill thus: "Depending on his mood, he is a German or a Frenchman, a follower of Pierre Leroux or his foe. He has thousands of ideas that evaporate even before he has a chance to express them." He attacked Victor Hugo and others for their atheistic influence on the youth of 1830, while he himself at one time considered baptism. It may be that Weill was not sincere. He is said to have been paid by the government for his articles in a Stuttgart newspaper, while his friend, Heinrich Heine, was paid for his correspondence sent from Paris to Augsburg.[60]

The arrest of the Duchess of Berry, who was plotting a Legitimist insurrection, saved France from civil war. One of the most sensational events of this period, it was made

litique (Paris, 1815); *Notice sur les Benjamites rétablies en Israël, par M. de Maleville* (Paris, 1816); *Lettre à Monsieur le Comte Languinais, membre du Sénat* . . . (Paris, 1814) (with praise for Louis XVIII); *Du rabbinisme et des traditions juives* . . . (Paris, 1832), p. viiJ ("notre glorieuse revolution de juillet"); *Du passé, du présent et de l'avenir* (Paris, 1830); *Encore du présent, du passé et de l'avenir* (Nancy, [1834]).

[59] G. Ben Levi, *Moral and Religious Tales* (London, [1846], p. xv.

[60] A. Weill, *Introduction à mes mémoires*, pp. 38, 43-45, 65; *Mes batailles* (Paris, 1867), pp. 182, 195, 236; *Feu contre feu! Réponse à un ultramontain* (Paris, 1845); *Le Nouveau Cordelier. 1789, 1830, 1848* [Paris, 1848]; *Briefe* . . . (Zürich, 1889), p. 212; Karl Gutzkow, *Gesammelte Werke*, VII (Jena, n.d.), 282; L. Veuillot, *Oeuvres complètes*, 1st séries, X (Paris, n.d.), 485; Launay, *Figures* . . . , p. 92.

possible only through her denunciation by Simon Deutz, a converted Jew, son of Emmanuel Deutz, the Chief Rabbi of France. This episode provoked much anti-Jewish propaganda; it deserves a separate study.

Among the young men of talent—although liberals did not participate in the events of 1830—Joseph Salvador is to be mentioned. His books had a great influence upon liberal opinion. His study of the constitution of the Jewish people was regarded as an attack upon the French Monarchy and as a justification of the trial of Louis XVI as a legal, constitutional act. There is a question whether Salvador should be considered a Jew. But even if we conclude that he should not, it must be noted that at this time he was known and criticized as a Jewish author. His attitude toward the Revolution of July, 1830, was one of indifference; he was shut up in his world of studies.[61]

In conclusion it should be said that the small world of French Jewry during the July regime was a microcosm of the life of the country, without any sharply defined political attitudes. There were many liberals, many opportunists, some confused people, and they were to be found among Jews, too. There was one exception to this generalization: French Jewry had few outright monarchistic reactionaries. This political inclination was reserved mostly for Catholics.

---

[61] Gabriel Salvador, *J. Salvador, sa vie, ses oeuvres et ses critiques* (Paris, 1881), pp. 2, 7, 10, 15-16, 22, 33, 39, 56, 70.

Simon Deutz: Traitor or French Patriot?

The Jewish aspect of the arrest of the Duchesse de Berry

THE arrest of the Duchess de Berry—one of the most important events at the beginning of the July Monarchy—revealed a tragic picture of the lack of religious and moral balance of certain Jews after the emancipation, and of the lack of political conviction of the Jewish community in France as an organised body.

On November 7, 1832, Mané-Caroline-Ferdinande-Louise de Bourbon, Duchesse de Berry (1798-1870) was arrested in Nantes by the police acting under the orders of Adolphe Thiers, the new Minister of the Interior. She was the widow of Charles Ferdinand de Bourbon (the second son of Charles X), who had been assassinated in 1820. The Duchess was actively engaged in a conspiracy of the Legitimists against Louis-Philippe and his regime of the July Monarchy. She even favoured, and besought, an invasion by British and Russian armies and she was, in fact, on the verge of provoking a civil war in France. Her arrest was the signal for a hysterical public outcry not only by the Legitimists, but even by a very large number of liberals and sincere republicans. Many did not clearly perceive the dangerous path chosen by the Duchess, and they looked with contempt upon the manner of her arrest. She was denounced to Thiers by Simon Deutz, who, according to the Legitimists, received a considerable sum for his pains. Deutz was a converted Jew, the son of the Chief Rabbi of France, and the press, pamphleteers, chroniclers and later historians repeatedly asserted that the Duchess was sold to the police by a Jewish traitor. In order to present Deutz's crime in an even more lurid light, the Duchess was described as Deutz's benefactress.[1] This was Victor Hugo's argument in his poem, *A l'homme qui a livré une femme*:

> "C'est l'honneur, c'est la foi, la pitié, le serment,

---

[1] Simon Deutz, *Arrestation de Madame* (Paris, 1835). 82 pp. Edited by L. H. MOULIN; Tv . . . Morel, *La Verité sur l'arrestation de Madame, duchesse de Berry, ou Les mensonges de Deutz dévoilés . . . avec portrait du traître* (Paris, 1836). xv+215 pp.; S. POSENER, *Adolphe Crémieux* (Paris, 1933), i, pp. 169-75; PAUL KLEIN, *Mauvais juif, mauvais chrétien*, *Revue de la pensée juive*, no. 7 (1950), pp. 83-87; On Jews during the Revolution of July 1830 see SZAJKOWSKI, *French Jews during the Revolution of* 1830 *and the July Monarchy*, *Historia Judaica*, 21 (1960), pp. 105-130.

Originally published in *The Journal of Jewish Studies*, vol. XVI (1965).

> Voit ce que le Juif a vendu lâchement.
> Juif! les impurs traitans à qui l'on vend son âme.
> ....
> Ce n'est pas même un Juif! c'est un paien immonde,
> Un renégat, l'opprobre et le rebut du monde.
> ....
> Marche, autre Juif errant! marche avec l'oi qu'on voit
> Luire à travers les doigts de tes mains mal fermées!"

Alexandre Dumas wrote: "Deutz, there are names that become mortal injuries, Deutz was the name of this Jew." A woman wrote:

> "Il a donc reparu l'infâme!
> A qui Judas légua son âme!
> ....
> Il n'est ni Français ni chrétien."

Some pamphleteers stated that even Deutz's conversion to Catholicism was done only in order to save appearances. A story was told how the Duchess cried out after being arrested: "At least, this miserable Deutz is not a Frenchman!" One pamphleteer wrote that "in betraying God he [Deutz] practised betraying men." In some accounts Deutz was described as "probably" a Jew. The *Nouvelle Sentinelle*, a government newspaper of Niort, on November 18, 1832, referred to "a Jew drawn to the Catholic religion, a renegate, a favourite of the Roman Clergy, one of those devout converts who became affiliated with the Revolution."[2]

Simon Deutz, born in 1802 in Koblenz, was the son of Emmanuel (Menachem) Deutz (1763-1842), who was a member of the Sanhedrin convened by Napoleon I, and Deputy-Chief Rabbi of France from 1810 onwards. When the Chief Rabbi, Abraham de Cologna, left France in 1826, Deutz became his successor.[3] Simon Deutz

---

[2] ALEXANDRE DUMAS, *Histoire de dix-huit-ans* (Paris, 1853), ii, p. 63; Morel, *op. cit.*, p. 185; Guibourg, *La Relation fidèle et détaille de l'arrestation de Madame* (Nantes, 1832), appendix ("converti en apparence du moins, à la religion catholique"); *Deutz, ou Imposture, ingratitude et trahision*; par l'auteur de la Vendée et Madame [général P. F. S. Dermoncourt] (Paris, 1836), p. 131; Dermoncourt, Général [P. F. S.], *La Vendée et Madame* (Paris, 1834), p. 330. The first edition appeared in 1833. According to some sources this book was written by Alexandre Dumas; IMBERT DE SAINT-AMAND, *La captivité de la duchesse de Berry* (Paris, 1890), pp. 35-45.

[3] On Emmanuel Deutz see *Les Archives israélites*, iii (1842), pp. 65-72.

was a pupil in the *yeshivoth* of Wintzenheim and Metz. Later he was an apprentice in the printing shop of Sétier, official printer for the Central Jewish Consistory. However, the young Deutz showed a complete lack of character. He left for Rome, where he was converted to Catholicism in 1828, and adopted the name of Haycinthe de Gonzague. This was but one of the many tragedies in the life of the Chief Rabbi, who had plenty of domestic troubles: an unhappy first marriage, and the earlier conversion (in 1823) of his son-in-law, David Drach, a brilliant young author and teacher at the first public school for Jewish children which was established in Paris in 1819, and later the author of many anti-Jewish books. Soon after his conversion Drach came back to Judaism, but only for a very short while. It was a ruse to gain the confidence of his wife who refused to join him in Catholicism, and to find out the whereabouts of his two children. In fact, he soon joined the Church again and even converted his children.[4]

There is no doubt that Simon Deutz was greatly influenced by the conversion of his brother-in-law, although he later wrote that he was, possibly, also driven to Rome by the hope of vengeance against Drach, who had ruined the happy life of his sister.[5] Drach wrote, in a pamphlet on the conversion of his brother-in-law, that before being converted to Christianity, Deutz was influenced by the 18th-century philosophers. He had lost his Jewish faith, became a confused young man without any faith at all. Only later did he join the Catholic Church.[6] Indeed, this was characteristic of many young men of the first generation of emancipated Jews in France who had lost their faith and were not ripe yet for compromises with the existing Jewish environment, or for the idea of remaining a secular Jew. Even after joining the Catholic Church Deutz remained, for a time, a very confused man.[7]

[4] P. L. B. Drach, *Lettre d'un rabbin converti . . .* (Paris, 1827): iii+334 pp.; *Idem, De l'Harmonie entre l'église et la synagogue . . .* (Paris, 1844). 2 vols.; Morel, Ignace Xavier (ci-devant Lévy-Gumpel), de Mutzig, en Alsace, docteur-médécin. Extrait du *Mémorial Catholique.* (*March,* 1826.) *Renseignements relatifs à la persécution dont M. Drach, rabbin converti a été objet* (n.p., n.d.). 13 pp.; Deutz, *op. cit.,* pp. 66-69; Klein, *op. cit.* For a list of Drach's other publications before and after his conversion see *Catalogue général des livres imprimés de la Bibliothèque Nationale,* xli (1910), pp. 935-40.

[5] Deutz, *op. cit.,* p. 7.

[6] P. L. B. Drach, *Relation de la conversion de M. Hyacinthe Deutz, baptisé à Rome le 3 février 1828 . . .* (Paris, 1828), pp. 11-12.

[7] *Ibid.,* pp. 21-22: "A présent M. Deutz est tranquille; mais cette tranquilité est le prix de bien des efforts."

Because Deutz was the son of France's Chief Rabbi, his conversion caused a sensation and he became a favoured son of the Church. He was entrusted by the Pope with many delicate missions.[8] Later, in his pamphlet of 1835, Simon Deutz described himself as a converted Jew who, while in Rome, tried constantly to ameliorate the situation of the persecuted Jews of Rome. Leo XII (1823-1829) asked Deutz to prepare a memorandum on the Jews of Rome and his successor, Pope Pius VIII (1829-1830) appointed a special commission to prepare a statute dealing with the Jews, with cardinal Bartolommeo Alberto (Mauro) Cappellari as chairman and Deutz as secretary. However, Cappellari was well known for his anti-Jewish feelings, and Deutz's memoranda were constantly ignored. In 1830, Deutz complained in a letter written to Borély, who later became attorney-general in Aix-en-Provence and was well known for his friendly attitude towards Jews: "Rome will never do anything in order to improve the temporal status of the Jews. However, Rome will do anything for the salvation of their souls." Being unable to accomplish anything in favour of the Jews, Deutz left Rome in 1830 for the United States, *via* Marseilles and London. In the United States he tried to organize a Catholic printing house, but in this he failed. Seeing the tolerant attitude towards Jews in the New World, his dissatisfaction with Rome became even greater.[9]

At the end of 1830 Simon Deutz found himself again in London, which was then a centre of Legitimist intrigues against Louis-Philippe and the July Monarchy. From London Deutz went to Rome. He met the Duchesse de Berry at the beginning of February 1832, by which date Cardinal Cappellari had become Pope Gregory XVI. Deutz was asked by the new Pope to make a stand for the Duchess against Louis-Philippe, in order to fight the new regime of France and "serve the faith." Deutz was sent on a mission to Portugal and Spain in order to obtain arms and men for the Duchess. He was entrusted with the delicate mission of securing a promise of military assistance from Russia. Tsar Nicolas I told him, that he could not embark on a war against France. However, he promised that should the Duchess be able to provoke a civil

---

[8] M. Fortuné de Cholet, *Madame, Nantes, Blaye* (Paris 1833), p. 143: "Sa Sainteté emploie Deutz dans plusieurs missions délicates, et Deutz les accomplit au-delà de ses souhaits."

[9] Deutz, *op. cit.*, pp. 7-14.

war in France, Russia would intervene in a pacificatory capacity. According to Deutz, this Russian promise influenced the Duchess' decision to leave for France and start a civil war there.[10]

In April 1832, Deutz took the oath of allegiance to the Duchess and to the cause of promoting a civil war. Later he was to state that already then he had started to think of saving France from such a catastrophe. In fact, on June 1, 1832, Deutz wrote from Spain to the Minister of Interior, M. C. B. de Montalivet, denouncing the Duchess' intrigues and her preparations of a civil war. The minister did not reply, and when he was back in France Deutz repeated his denunciation during a visit to Montalivet and later to his successor, Adolphe Thiers, who was less embarassed to use a "traitor" in order to find out the Duchess' whereabouts.[11]

It was thanks to Deutz alone that Thiers was able to arrest the Duchess, but he and his subordinates hated Deutz. They did not believe in his patriotic motives. Their attitude towards Deutz was characteristic of the police's attitude towards all informers.[12] Le Constitutionnel, Le National, and other newspapers inclined favorably towards the July Monarchy, wrote on November 9, 1832, that the arrest had saved France from a civil war. However, almost everyone, including a large number of sincere republicans, was shocked by the arrest, and particularly by the circumstance of a traitor having been used for this job. And—as it always happened in such cases—Deutz was of course accused of having received a very large sum (half a million Francs, according to some sources).

Did Deutz receive money from Thiers? This question was never satisfactorily answered. No archival sources were found to prove such an accusation. Later, Deutz declared, in defending himself, that his only desire was to prevent civil war in France. Deutz

[10] Ibid., pp. 15, 24-25.
[11] Ibid., p. 26.
[12] Joly, the special police commissioner who was charged by Thiers with the arrest of the Duchess, noted the following opinion of Deutz given by him to Thiers: "La vie d'un grand scélerat qui allait encore vendre et livrer une femme qui était restée sa bienfaitrice et celle de ses enfans [sic]. Le Ministre, tout en applaudissant à mes sentimens philantropiques, répondit que la sureté du pays & celle du Roi, étaient de plus haute consideration; que d'ailleurs le contract avec cet homme, dans cette occasion, ne pouvait en rien m'atteindre ni m'attribuer une participation à son crime." AN [= Archives Nationales] F⁷12171. See also L. Guibourg, Relation fidèle et détaillée de l'arrestation de S. A. R. Madame, duchesse de Berry (Nantes, November 1832), p. 40 ("les agents de la police sont d'accord avec toute la France, pour lancer anathême contre ce malheureux").

himself wrote that, while engaged in discussion with Thiers, he requested only a promise that the Duchess would never be persecuted. However, this patriotic motive was disregarded in the hysterical outcry against the Jewish traitor. In *La Quotidienne* of November 29, 1832, Drach attacked his former brother-in-law and friend for his treachery, and in effect invited an attack upon Deutz by publishing a full description of his physical appearance. Since 1827, the Church had gratified Drach by giving him the post of librarian to the Duke of Bordeaux and since then Drach had cherished his legitimist loyalty. In fact almost all converted Jews of his generation were sympathetic towards the anti-republican regimes.[13]

A legitimist insurrection in the Vendée had failed even before the Duchess' arrest. On May 10, 1833, while still under arrest, she gave birth to an illegitimate child whose father was an Italian nobleman (whom she later married). The legitimist idol then fell from glory in the eyes of many of her followers and this helped to normalise the political situation.

Deutz stated, in a memorandum written in order to defend himself, that with the arrest of the Duchess France shook off a family of the enemies of her liberties. He promised to publish his memoirs some day, if God and his enemies, the Carlists, would let him live long enough. He concluded the memorandum with the following words: "I did my duty, my conscience is undisturbed. I die contented. Long live France! Long live Louis-Philippe!"[14]

A few years later, in 1835, Simon Deutz published an apologetic memorandum, edited by Louis Henri Moulin, a well-known lawyer. In this memorandum Deutz told the story of how, after being converted, he tried to influence a change in the Vatican's attitude towards the Jews of Rome. This endeavour became a

---

[13] Deutz, *op. cit.*, p. 42; Klein, *op. cit.*, p. 91.

[14] "Madame Duchesse de Berry fut arrêté et la France fut délivrée pour toujours d'une famille ennemie de ses libertés. Depuis cette époque une ère de persécution, méritée par l'immensité du service que je venais de rendre, commença pour moi. Cette persécution ne se terminera probablement que lorsque mes ennemis auront vengé dans mon sang l'injure irréparable que j'ai faite à leur odieux parti. Mais avant de mourir je dois à la France et surtout à la vérité de donner quelques éclaircissemens sur les rapports qui ont existé entre Madame et moi et sur les motifs qui m'ont inclut d'agir ainsi que je l'ai fait. Un jour peut-être, si Dieu et les Carlistes me laissent la vie, mes mémoires seront publiés . . . J'ai fait mon devoir, ma conscience est tranquille. Je meurs satisfait. Vive la France! Vive Louis Philippe!" ("Notes de S.D.," in AN, F⁷12173. These Notes were the basis for Deutz's later pamphlet.)

monomania with him. Deutz also wrote that he knew the post-Napoleonic Restoration only from its anti-Jewish persecutions, and he had never participated in any political activities. He again maintained that his only desire was to save France from civil war, and that there was no doubt in his mind that the Duchess did everything possible "to stir up the still lukewarm ashes of the civil war." "That by choking the civil war that was ready to break out even more actively and more ravenously than ever, by saving the blood of so many generous citizens, by dealing a mortal blow to a party which is an irreconcilable enemy of our liberties, he [Deutz] rendered to his country an immense service."[15]

One year later, in 1836, another converted Jew, Ignace Xavier Morel (formerly Lévy Gumpel), a childhood friend of Deutz, published a violent pamphlet against him, with repeated references to the Jewish aspect of this affair. Morel's pamphlet was full of hate, malignant slogans and accusations against Deutz. Morel compared Deutz to Judas and his denouncement of the Duchess as a result of the "rabbis' hatred against the Church." He accused the Chief Rabbi of France of having kept for his son his German citizenship in order to avoid his serving in the French army. "He is not a Frenchman!"—Morel wrote. Thus, Morel tried to prove the veracity of the popular slogan that the French people were not responsible for the action of this Jew against the Duchess, because the Jewish traitor was not even a French citizen.[16]

From the first moment of the Duchess' arrest an anti-Jewish campaign was started. Deutz was attacked as a Jew and many were shocked by the fact that his father, the Chief Rabbi of France, did not turn his back on his son when they met.[17]

How to halt this dangerous popular anti-Jewish campaign, which according to the historian S. Posener, might have compromised for a long time the situation of French Jewry, became the concern of Adolphe Crémieux, then already a well-known lawyer, republican and also a leading member of the Central Jewish Consistory. After an interview with Simon Deutz, Crémieux asked his father, the Chief Rabbi, to publish in the press, in the interest of the Jews, a protest against the "shameful" act

---

[15] Deutz, op. cit.
[16] Morel, op. cit.
[17] AN, F^{19}11038. A letter by the Minister of Justice to the Minister of Religious Affairs, Jan. 22, 1835.

committed by his son Simon. Such a protest in the name of the
Chief Rabbi was never published. Crémieux, for his part, refused
to prepare a memorandum in defence of Simon Deutz. Later,
Deutz charged Crémieux with having yielded to the public outcry.
Crémieux wrote to Simon Deutz that all relations between them
must cease and he would not defend him: "If you will try to defend
yourself in the eyes of the public, France will be deaf to the justification of an act of cowardice; it is necessary to be put to shame
after having consumed the treachery . . . if you counted on me as
your co-religionist, then you should forget it: you do not now
belong to any religion, you renounced the religion of your ancestors
and you are not any more a Catholic: none of the religions will
accept you and you cannot call upon anyone; because Moses
invoked total abhorrence of anyone perpetrating such a crime as
yours, and Jesus Christ, delivered by the treachery of his apostles,
represents the same eloquent position in the eyes of the Christian
religion." Somehow, probably with the knowledge of Crémieux
himself, this sharp letter was published first in *La Quotidienne* of
November 23, 1832, and later in other newspapers. On the next
day Deutz protested in the *Courrier Français* against the publication of the Crémieux letter, but to no avail. The letter did more
harm to Deutz and to his family than all the legitimist pamphlets,
as Deutz himself wrote later (on June 26, 1835) to Crémieux.
However, later attacks on Deutz were less often accompanied by
anti-Jewish remarks.[18]

A violent campaign was conducted against the "traitor's"
father, Chief Rabbi Emmanuel Deutz. In order to disembarrass
itself of the now elderly Deutz, and to be cleared of the suspicion
of being sympathetic towards his son, the Central Consistory was
ready to abolish completely the Chief Rabbi's office. At first, on
May 14, 1833, the Central Consistory proposed to create one office
for both functions, the Chief Rabbinate of Paris and of the Central
Consistory, with Rabbi Marchand Ennery of Paris as the new
Chief Rabbi. On this occasion the Central Consistory complained
against Deutz's practice of preaching in Yiddish, this being
contrary to the spirit of "regeneration" prevailing then among
French Jews. In fact, Deutz never learned enough of the French
language in order to be able to preach in French. However, he
wrote on June 28, 1833, to the Minister of Religious Affairs that

[18] See Appendix; Deutz, *op. cit.*; POSENER, *op. cit.*

more Jews in Paris speak Yiddish than French. He stated in a letter written to the Minister two weeks later (July 12, 1833), that he would never voluntarily give up his position as Chief Rabbi.[19]

On September 8, 1833, a violent incident occurred in the Synagogue of rue Notre-Dame-de-Nazareth, where the Jews protested against the Chief Rabbi's presence. The next day the police comissioner of the Saint-Martin-des-Champs district reported to the Prefect of Police the result of his investigation on this and similar incidents, *viz.*, that the protests against the Chief Rabbi were not motivated by any political, pro-Carlist sentiments. On the contrary, the Jews were in general sympathetically inclined towards the July Government. However, they experienced a natural sentiment of indignation against a man who sold both his God and the Duchess.[20]

The Chief of the division for non-Catholics in the Ministry of Religious Affairs assured Deutz, that if the position of Chief Rabbi were not to be abolished, all members of the Central Consistory would submit their resignation. Deutz was of course promised a respectable allowance. The Central Consistory even asked the Ministry to grant him the *Légion d'honneur*, a highly appreciated decoration often given to people before degrading them. On October 11, 1833, the Minister required Deutz to refrain from preaching in the synagogue on the following day, as he had planned to do. Then the Central Consistory demanded that the Minister completely reorganize this body in such a manner, that Deutz would be excluded. However, the Minister avoided taking such a drastic position right away. He preferred to let both parties cool off. In fact, peace soon reigned again in the Central

---

[19] AN, F[19]11038.

[20] *Ibid.*: "Depuis que le fils Deutz a apostasié sa religion, et surtout depuis qu'on l'a signalé comme ayant livré la Duchesse de Berry, qui l'avait pris à son service, la plupart des Israélites ne l'ont vu qu'avec mepris. Ces divers renseignemens que j'ai recueillis m'ont appris que ce sentiment n'est excité chez eux par aucune impulsion politique; le Carlisme ne peut y avoir aucune part; car en général tous les Juifs savent apprécier les avantages que leur procure le Gouvernement de Juillet. Mais ils éprouvent ce sentiment naturel d'indignation contre un homme qui a vendu son Dieu et sa bienfaitrice. Il parait que, des le principe, on avait engagé M. Deutz, Grand-Rabbin, à laver l'espèce de tache qui rejaillisait sur la croyance israélite, et à rompre tutes relations avec son fils. Malgré celà, M. Deutz l'a reçu et logé chez lui. Depuis lors il y a eu scission entre le grand-Rabbin et les membres des deux consistoires. On dit que le 1er Janvier dernier, la plupart des notables de ces deux conseils, se disposant à complimenter le Roi, se sont retirés pour ne pas se trouver avec le père protecteur de l'apostat."

Consistory. Deutz took part again in most of its activities and on December 30, 1834, he asked the Minister to disregard all his previous protests against the Central Consistory.[21] In a statement addressed in February 1835[?] to the Minister of Religious Affairs the Chief Rabbi defended himself for having been friendly towards his son. He wrote that on several occasions his son expressed a desire to come back to the Jewish faith. On his arrival to Paris on Nov. 9, 1832, Simon Deutz formally made such a request to the Chief Rabbi of Paris. A few days later, on Nov. 12 or 13, Adolphe Crémieux, after speaking to Simon Deutz, requested the Chief Rabbi to repudiate publicly the arrest of the Duchess, in spite of the fact that his own son was responsible for this event. To this the Chief Rabbi, at first gave his consent. However, after having spoken to his son, Rabbi Deutz asked Crémieux not to publish such a statement. On the following December 23, the Central Consistory held a meeting without inviting the Chief Rabbi. This proved—wrote the Chief Rabbi—that the Central Consistory's action was directed by political rather than religious motives. Much later, at the end of 1834, a delegation of the Consistory visited Deutz. He was assured of the Consistory's desire to find a peaceful solution to the conflict, provided that the Chief Rabbi would be willing to omit the name Deutz from his signature.[22]

It was most probably Adolphe Crémieux who was instrumental in arranging this settlement. He knew the text of Simon Deutz's memorandum before its publication, and the change in his attitude had a great influence upon the members of the Central Consistory. The memorandum published by Deutz also contained a letter from Deutz to Crémieux, dated June 26, 1836, and a reply in which the Jewish leader expressed a different opinion from the one made public in November 1832. Crémieux, by the later date, had become convinced that Deutz did not accept any money from Thiers and that he had acted only in order to "save France from a civil war and a foreign war."[23]

Simon Deutz later returned to the Jewish faith, married a Jewish girl in London, resided for a time in the United States and finally settled in France.[24]

[21] AN, F¹⁹11038.
[22] *Ibid.*, see Appendix.
[23] Deutz, *op. cit.*; POSENER, *op. cit.*, vol. i, pp. 172-73.
[24] Klein, *op. cit.* See also JEAN-ROBERT COLLE, *La Chouannerie de 1832 dans les deux Sèvres et la Vendée orientale* (Lezay 1948), pp. 115, 134 ("Il adopta

The affair, with its police activity, religious, political and private intrigues is a touchstone for the confusion which reigned in the minds of some young and able French Jews of the first generations after the emancipation. Politically, the Franco-Jewish community as a whole was also confused, as Crémieux's first statement against Deutz demonstrated. Even more so was the reaction of the Central Consistory, which demanded Emanuel Deutz's resignation from the Chief Rabbinate. All kind of excuses were put forward in support of this demand: his age, his imperfect knowledge of the French language, his domestic troubles, etc. Had the Central Consistory requested Emanuel Deutz's retirement from the Chief Rabbinate at the time of the two conversions, of his son-in-law and his son, its action could have been justified, but the Consistory did not do so until much later, as a result of his son's "treachery".

The Central Consistory's persecution of its Chief Rabbi was a political action, and a striking example of the lack of independent political opinion on the part of this organised body representing French Jews. It was very natural to panegyrise Charles X[25] in liturgical and poetical compositions, and the family of the

l'enfant abandonné d'un de ses coreligionnaires, qui deviendra l'écrivain Catulle Mendes").

[25] The following is a list of prayers and odes in the memory of Louis XVIII and in honour of the new King Charles X: תפלה בעבור נשמת אדוננו המלך Louis XVIII roi de France, et de Navarre (n.p., n.d.). 1 p.; Abraham Belaïs, Ode en l'honneur de Sa Majesté Louis XVIIIᵉ (Paris, 1824). 15 pp. In French and Hebrew; A. de Cologna, Discours prononcé dans le temple israélite de Paris, rue Notre Dame de Nazareth, le 7 novembre 1824, etc. (Paris, 1824). 8 pp.; M. Goudchaux, fils, Discours prononcé à la Synagogue de Strasbourg ... Le 12 Octobre 1824 à l'occasion du service funèbre de Sa Majesté Louis XVIIIᵉ, de glorieuse mémoire. [Avec: Discours par Marchand Ennery, L.-M. Lambert et Charleville] (Strasbourg 1824). 12 pp.; Lettre pastorale adressée par le Consistoire Central des Israélites de France, aux Consistoires des circonscriptions isrélites du Royaume. [Mort de Louis XVIII et avénément de Charles X, signés: de Cologna, Em. Deutz, Aron Schmolle, J. S. Polack, 19 sept. 1824] (Paris 1824). 2 pp.; D. Lévi [David E. Lévi-Alvarès] Le Roi est mort! vive le Roi!!! stances sur la mort de Louis XVIII et sur l'avènement de Charles X ... (Paris 1824). 8 pp.; Louis Nettre, Discours sur la mort de Louis XVIII, prononcé à la Synagogue de Colmar le 12 octobre 1824 ... Traduit de l'hebreu (Colmar 1824). 7 pp.; Salomon Roos, Discours sur la mort de S. M. Louis XVIII ... Trauer Rede auf den Tod S. M. Ludwigs XVIII gehalten in der Synagoge in Colmar, den 12. Oktober 1824, von S. R., Jugendlehrer in Colmar, Discours sur la mort de S. M. Louis XVIII ... Trauerrede ... par Judas Lévy (Colmar 1824). 15 pp.; Service funèbre pour Sa Majesté Louis XVIII, roi de France et de Navarre, de glorieuse mémoire, célébré à la synagogue consistoriale de Strasbourg, le 12 Octobre 1824 (Strasbourg, 1824). 12 pp.

Duchess de Berry during the Restoration.[26] All organised bodies did so either spontaneously or by order, and such hymns and other expressions of loyalty to the regime in power were rarely taken seriously. However, after July 1830, the Jewish leaders were under no compulsion to join in the popular outcry against the "traitor" who delivered to the police the legitimist formenter of a civil war. The Jews, as such, had nothing to gain from a victory of the Duchess' circle. The patriotism generated in 1830 was fresh, and so linked to the events of 1789 which granted the Jews their emancipation, that it would have been only natural to expect from them strong distrust of anti-revolutionary elements. In fact,

[26] *Consistoire israélite de la circonscription de Paris. Temple de la rue Sainte-Avoye. Dimanche 8 octobre* 1820 (n.p., n.d.). 1 p. [Billet pour la cérémonie religieuse "en actions de gânces de l'heureuse délivrance de ... la Duchesse de Berry"]; *Le Consistoire israélite de la circonscription de Strasbourg. A Monsieur le Commissaire surveillant de la Synagogue,* 2 octobre 1820 (Strasbourg 1820). 3 pp. French, German and Hebrew. [Cérémonie religieuse pour la naissance du Duc de Bordeaux, avec prière]; Drach, D., מזמור שיר *Ode hébraïque sur la naissance de S. A. R. Mgr le duc de Bordeaux ...*, présentée à S. M. Louis XVIII par l'auteur dans l'audience du 23 octobre 1820 (Paris, 1820). 15 pp., Hebrew and French; D. Lévy [David E. Lévi-Alvarès], of Bordeaux, *Nous t'a entendons! Stances composées le jour des obsèques de S. A. R. Mgr le duc de Berry* (n.p., n.d.). 2 pp.; *Idem, Rounde adréssade a les damès de Bourdéou, en l'haounou de la néchènse d'aou duc dé Bourdéou. Ronde dédiée aux dames de Bordeaux, en l'honneur de la naissance de S. A. R. le Duc de Bordeaux. Chanté au Tuileries, le 29 sept.* 1820 (n.p., n.d.). 3 pp.; [Prière, en date du 29 mars 1820, par le Consistoire de Metz à l'occasion de la mort du duc de Berry] (n.p., n.d.). 1 p.; *Traduction d'une Complainte et Prière composée par M. le Grand-Rabbin, membre du Consistoire israélite de Nancy, à l'occasion de la cérémonie funèbre de S. A. R. Mgr Le Duc de Berry, qui doit avoir lieu le 24 de ce mois. Laquelle prière et complainte, ainsi que la traduction en français, a été adoptée en séance du Consistoire, du 19 mars* 1820 (n.p., n.d.). 1 p.; *Prière pour le Roi et S. A. R. M^{gneur} Le Duc de Bordeaux, composée et recitée par M. le Grand-Rabbin dans la Synagogue consistoriale, à l'occasion de la Fête 29 Nissan,* תפלה על משפחת אדונינו . . . . המלך יר''ה ועל הצלחת 5581, 1er *Mai* 1821 הבן היקיר (Metz 1821). Broadside. Hebrew and French; *Programe de la cérémonie religieuse en actions de grâces, qui aura lieu dans le Temple israélite (rue N.-D. de Nazareth) le 7 Décembre* 1823, *à l'occasion de la rentrée triomphante de S. A. R. Monseigneur le Duc d'Angoulême* (Paris 1823). 1 p.; *Administration du Temple Israélite. Paris, le* 1er *décembre* 1823. [Signed: Polack and E. Mayer Dalmbert] (n.p., n.d.). 1 p. [Convocation à la cérémonie religieuse à l'occasion de la rentrée du Duc d'Angoulême dans la Capitale]; Ab. de Cologna, משדי קרב ברשרד שיר ביד השר דיאנגולענע עם שובו (Paris, 1823). 8 pp.

The Duchess de Berry's knowledge of Jewish life was, probably, very limited. Her large library contained seven histories of the Jews, including M. Rabelleau's *Histoire des Hebreux* (Paris, 1825), 2 vols., probably because the book was dedicated to the Duke of Bordeaux: *Catalogue de la riche bibliothèque de Rosny* ... (Paris, 1837), p. 127.

we have already noted that a Paris police commissioner reported on September 9, 1833, that Jewish sentiments against Emmanuel Deutz did not involve any political Carlist sympathies, because the Jews were faithful to the July government. If the Consistory joined in denouncing the Jewish betrayer of the Duchess, so also did most French leaders, who treated this affair superficially and without discernment; for Deutz at that time was neither a traitor nor a Jew.

Should this paper be regarded as a reappraisal of the events, and as an attempt to whitewash Simon Deutz—to represent him not as a traitor, but as a patriot who saved France from civil war? The answer is probably yes, especially in view of the fact that the anti-Deutz attitude has remained unchanged up to date,[27] and that the entire Affair of the Duchess' arrest has been treated with preconceived ideas and a refusal to fall back on a well established opinion—as the historian, S. Posener, has noted correctly.[28]

APPENDIX

Exposé addressed by Chief Rabbi Emmanuel Deutz to the Minister of Religious Affairs. February, 1835 [?][29]

Je croit, qu'il est de mon devoir de repondre au reproche que l'on m'a fait pour avoir eu des relations avec mon fils qui avoit abjuré sa religion il y a cinq ans. Pour me justifier d'un tel reproche il suffit de rapporter les faits tels qu'ils se sont passés. Peu de tems après avoir abjuré il m'écrivit une lettre dans laquelle il me marqua, en manifestant son repentir d'avoir commis une faute de cette nature dans un moment d'aveuglement, qu'il desiroit vivement à rentrer dans le sein de notre religion. A Rome même il étoit connu comme un homme qui n'ajoutait pas foi aux dogmes chrétiens,

[27] The well-known historian, PIERRE DE GORCE, wrote that the Duchess "was betrayed by a Jew called Deutz": *Louis Philippe* 1830-1848 (Paris 1931, 8th édition), p. 99. In 1932, a historian wrote that Louis Philippe's act of arresting the Duchess "by a Jew and a traitor" instead of expelling her, lacked the characteristic French elegance and generosity: J. SENOT DE LA LOUDE, *A propos du Centenaire de l'arrestation de la Duchesse de Berry à Nantes. 7 novembre 1832. Bulletin de la Société archéologique et historique de Nantes . . .*, lxxi (1932), p. 229. A Jewish historian, writing about Deutz, refers to him as the "bad Jew and the bad Christian" (KLEIN, *op. cit.*).
[28] POSENER, *op. cit.*, i, p. 175.
[29] AN, F¹⁹11038, quoted without changes in the original spelling.

c'est ce qui est encore attesté par Mr. Drach dans sa lettre inserée dans la *Quotidienne* du 12 X^{bre} dernier. Il a quitté Rome il y a deux ans et me demanda ce qu'il avoit à faire pour redevenir Israëlite. Je lui repondit donc qu'il n'avait qu'a le declarer ouvertement au Rabbin de l'endroit qu'il habitoit et d'en suivre les préceptes.

En arrivant à Paris le 9 9bre dernier il faisoit de suite au grand Rabbin de cette ville la déclaration suivante: qu'il étoit résolu d'après de mûres refflexions à rentrer dans la religion de ses pères et de donner toutes les satisfactions qu'on désiroit aux communautés d'Israël pour le scandale qu'il leur avoit causé. Des lors, quoiqu'il ne fût pas encore venu chez moi, j'avois avec lui des relations verbales pour le confirmer dans ses bonnes dispositions. Car quoique notre religion ne nous preserve pas à faire des proselites, elle nous impose néamoins comme un devoir sacré de chercher à y ramener tout enfant de Jacob qui s'en serait écarte, surtout quand celui-ci en manifeste son repentir sincère, surtout s'il s'agit d'un père vis a vis de son fils, c'est là une verité que tous les Rabbins attesteront. Bien loin qu'alors aucun Israélite ni aucun de mes collègues M^{rs} les Membres du Consistoire Central m'en ait fait le moindre reproche, bien au contraire, Mr Crémieux est venu chez moi le 12 ou 13 9bre et manifesta le desir de voir mon fils. Etant présse pour aller au Tribunal il me pria de le faire chercher et de lui dire de l'attendre. Tous les deux vinrent peu de temps après, et s'entretenoient ensemble. Après cet entretien Mr Crémieux m'observa, que pour reprimer les clameurs de la Quotidienne sur le sujet de l'arrestation de la Duchesse de Berry il seroit utile au bien des Israélites hors de France d'inserer une protestation et de blamer publiquement cette trahison quand même ce seroit l'oeuvre de mon fils et j'y consentis.

Le même soir mon fils étant revenu il allégua des forts raisons pour ne pas publier le dit circulaire. J'allai de suite trouver Mr. Crémieux, qui trouvant mes raisons fondées, me promis qu'il ne paraitra pas.

Le 17 9bre mon fils partit pour Londres. Dès lors jusqu'au le 9 X^{bre}, j'étois toujours en parfaite harmonie avec mes collegues et invité à toutes les séances. Ce n'est que le 23 X^{bre} (environ six semaines après le départ de mon fils) que le Consistoire Central s'assemblea pour la prmière fois sans m'inviter et sans m'indiquer les motifs de cette exclusion. De tous ces faits resulte evidemment que l'exasperation du Consistoire Central étoit plutôt fondé sur des motifs politiques que Religieux. En effet M^{rs} le membres du consistoire sont revenus de leurs premières resolutions à mon égard. Ils m'ont envoyé Dimanche le 10 c^{nt} une députation de deux membres pour m'assurer de leurs sentiments d'amitié, en y ajoutant qu'ils desireroient sincèrement sièger avec moi si je pouvois me resoudre à supprimer le surnom Deutz de ma signature. J'ai demandé du tems pour y réfléchir en les assurant que je ferai tous les sacrifices convenables pour m'accorder avec eux.

INTERNAL CONFLICTS IN FRENCH JEWRY AT THE TIME OF THE REVOLUTION OF 1848

Originally published in Volume I of *Yidn in Frankraykh* ("Jews in France"), New York, Yivo, 1942

The Revolution of 1848 was received by French Jewry with mixed feelings. In the circles of the wealthy we find adherents of various political tendencies, monarchists as well as republicans. Hence the Jews played a heterogeneous role in the Revolution, too.

The house of Rothschild, which already occupied a prominent position in French Jewry, was at the outbreak of the Revolution completely disoriented. Its rise in France had been associated with the old monarchical regime. In Paris a rumor was spread that Rothschild wanted to take all his gold abroad, and that the police kept the head of the house, Baron James Rothschild, under surveillance. However, notwithstanding his monarchical convictions, James Rothschild decided to adapt himself to the new regime and become a loyal republican, just as he had previously been a loyal friend of the royal house. When the right wing got the upper hand in French politics, and Prince Louis Napoleon was elected president of the Second Republic, Rothschild became apprehensive lest the new ruler avenge Napoleon's fall, to which the Rothschild house, as is well known, had contributed in large measure; and he became, in the words of his biographer, "an ardent republican."[1] Another well-known Jewish banker, Achille Fould, a member of Parliament, received the Revolution with little enthusiasm.

Due to the Revolution, two Jews were appointed to the Ministry of the Provisional Government for the first time: Adolphe Crémieux (Justice) and Michel Goudchaux (Finance). Besides the *Démocratie Pacifique,* organ of the Fourierists, who were slightly inclined to anti-Semitism, French public opinion as a whole expressed no opposi-

---

[1] Egon César Comte Corti, *La Maison Rothschild*, Paris, 1930, Vol. II, Chaps. VI-VII.

Originally published in *YIVO Annual of Jewish Social Science*, vol. II–III (1947–1948).

tion to this measure.[2] Michel Goudchaux (1797-1862), son-in-law of Berr-Isaac Berr of Nancy—the famous *shtadlen* (intercessor) of the revolutionary period of 1789—and a prominent banker, had first fought on the republican side during the Revolution of 1830 (for a time Goudchaux was an adherent of St. Simon); later he went over to the monarchists, and still later to the republicans. He inveighed sharply against the monarchist regime, however, only in discourses and articles, keeping aloof from revolutionary conspiracies. Goudchaux was appointed to the provisional government to appease the financial circles, who saw in him "a hope of anti-revolutionary influences in the government."[3] He actually opposed vigorously the left wing of Louis Blanc and Ledru-Rollin. He asserted that he was ready to resign in the event of a rise in the influence of the radicals, and Louis Blanc in turn threatened him with death.[4] Adolphe Crémieux, a sincere republican since the days of the restoration, was a moderate. His role was to maintain the balance between the right and the left in the government; he opposed socialist-communist ideas in the interests of individual liberty, which he prized above all.[5]

Later, in 1849, a discussion was carried on in the columns of the periodical *Archives Israélites* as to whether French Jewry should prefer a republican or a monarchical order.[6] But entering the Consistory and the synagogue, the leading circles in French Jewry set aside all political differences; politics dared not enter into religious affairs. On one point both sides, republicans and monarchists, were united: in their struggle against socialist theories. Among the Jewish population one could also find adherents of modern revolutionary ideas. At the head of the St. Simon movement were several Jews. But the official leaders of French Jewry were bitter enemies of the new social theories and combated them, as was done throughout those social strata to which they belonged. Thus for instance Adolphe Franck, the well-known Franco-Jewish philosopher and student of the Kabbalah, one of the most prominent persons in French Jewry, inveighed sharply against communism, which, in his opinion, could

[2] S. Posener, *Adolphe Crémieux*, Paris, 1933, Vol. II, pp. 63-64.
[3] Raymond Lazar, *Michel Goudchaux*, Paris, 1907, p. 6; Felix Ponteuil, *L'Opposition politique à Strasbourg sous la monarchie de Juillet*, Paris, 1932.
[4] *Ibid.*, pp. 7-10.
[5] Posener, *op. cit.*, Vol. II, p. 99. His sincere republican convictions occasionally moved him to refuse the favor of influential Jews hostile to the republican regime. De Circourt, diplomatic agent of the Provisional Government, tells in his memoirs that Crémieux declined on that account to act as attorney for Rothschild in a certain case. A. de Circourt, *Souvenirs d'une mission à Berlin en 1848*, Paris, 1909, Vol. II, p. 414.
[6] *Archives Israélites*, 1848, p. 342.

lead only "to a life of misery, of want, in an environment of ignorance, to a return to barbarism."[7] After the Revolution of 1848 had
set out on opportunistic paths, and protest demonstrations favoring
the maintenance of the achievements of the revolutionary February
days took place, the periodical *Archives Israélites* wrote that if any
Jews had participated in those demonstrations, they were people
"without a conscience."[8] The periodical published a pamphlet *A Small
Catechism of a Practical Socialist* to prove that socialism saw the holy
principle of the family "in the brothel and among bastards" and
with its principles of equality aimed at an "equality of misery."[9]

Those few people in the Jewish circles, such as Armand Lévy,
who saw clearly what path the revolution was taking had as yet no
influence on Jewish public opinion in France, or they were, like
Alexandre Weil, caught in a maelstrom of inner conflicts and con-
fusions.

Armand Lévy, one of the most consistent French champions of
democracy of the 1848 period, appeared in the front rank of political
fighters, to which belonged Barbès, Raspail, and Blanqui. Born in
1827 to a converted father, he went to Paris at the age of 17 to
study law, already imbued with socialist ideas.[10] In the Collège de
France he was a close friend of his teacher Michelet and the exiled
Polish poet Adam Mickiewicz. With the latter he subsequently maintained an intimate friendship, aiding him in his activities and accompanying him on his journeys to Italy and Constantinople. At the
bidding of Michelet, Armand Lévy organized in the Collège de
France a secular student organization, in opposition to the Catholic
student organization. As early as 1847 he was penalized for his
republican ideas and disqualified from the bar. In February, 1848,
he was a member of a revolutionary student organization and after
the pro-Polish demonstrations of May 15, he was imprisoned for a
while in the Vincennes tower. During the presidential elections of
the Second Republic, he was entrusted with the responsible task of
editing the proclamation of the committee sponsoring the candidacy
of Raspail in the Panthéon district. Upon the election of Louis

[7] Adolphe Franck, *Le communisme, jugé par l'histoire*, Paris, 1849 (2nd ed.), p. 97.
[8] *Archives Israélites*, 1848, p. 342.
[9] *Ibid.*, p. 354.
[10] J. Gaumont, "Un républicain revolutionnaire romantique," *Revue d'Histoire économique et sociale*, 1931, pp. 395-467. Pierre et Paul, "Armand Lévy," *Les Hommes
d'aujourd'hui*, Vol. II, No. 190. Among the manuscripts of the Polish Mickiewicz Museum
in Paris (No. 1034) are a number of letters of Armand Lévy to his family and friends
written in 1848.

Napoleon to the presidency, Armand Lévy was forced to flee to Belgium, whence, however, he was deported. From then on he constantly fought for a democratic order in France. He was one of the pioneers of the French labor movement. In 1848 he was still entirely unknown in Jewish circles, but he rose to an influential position in the sixties and seventies because of his struggle on behalf of the Jews of Rumania. Together with Armand Lévy, another Jew, Nathan Lévy, inveighed in the republican Club du Casino against "treason to the February Revolution." [11]

Michel Alcan (1811-77), who in 1848 was elected deputy to Parliament, was also opposed to the policies of Louis Napoleon. Alcan was the son of a Jewish soldier of the days of the French Revolution. He worked hard in his youth and acquired an education. He then dedicated himself to the organization of educational courses for workers. [12] Alexandre Weil, a Franco-Jewish writer, was of a different type. His ideas on the February events were permeated with the revolutionary spirit, but he was drowned in a sea of contradictions, so characteristic of the man. [13] He early attempted to play the role of a "prophet"; affecting a biblical style, he compared himself to Moses, wherefore his abilities were overlooked, and he was not taken seriously. In 1848 he fought the socialist-communist circles, because of their atheism. Later, in 1871, he wrote of himself that combating "anarchy, active in the name of atheism," he found himself suddenly "in the arms of the Jesuits." [14] Among the Jewish deputies in Parliament after February, 1848, was also Jonas Ennery, who was compelled to leave France in 1851 because of his republican views. The Jewish mathematician I. A. Blum, who as early as 1844 had been a contributor to the workers' publication *Journal des Travailleurs* [15] (1812-77), also spent some time in prison in 1848 for his republican opinions.

Early during the Revolution, the central Consistory, which had accommodated itself to all regimes in France, this time, too, declared its allegiance to the new powers. On February 26, a procession of the

[11] J. Tchernoff, *Associations et sociétés secrètes sous la deuxième République*, Paris, 1905, p. 213.
[12] A. Cerfberr, *Biographie Alsacienne-Lorraine*, Paris, 1879, pp. 85-86.
[13] Alexandre Weil, *Ce Que j'aurais dit à l'assemblée nationale*, Paris, 1848, *Dix mois de Revolution 1848*, Paris, 1869.
[14] Alexandre Weil, *Lettres de vengeance d'un Alsacien*, Paris, 1871.
[15] On Jonas Ennery, see *L'Univers Israélite*, Vol. XXXV, p. 727; on I. A. Blum, *La Grande Encyclopédie*, Vol. VI, p. 1182.

spiritual heads of Catholics, Protestants and Jews (Chief Rabbi Ennery) marched to the City Council of Paris, carrying an inscription "unity of worship, universal brotherhood." [16] On April 21, the president of the Council of Paris received the rabbi of that city, and the latter at that time asserted that "the year 1848 would complete the two revolutions, of 1789 and 1830." [17] The sentiment of the Jewish population was in favor of the Revolution, and in some localities the rabbis too shared in that enthusiasm. There were also instances in which Jews fought with arms. On April 16, as Rabbi Isidor, the new Chief Rabbi of Paris, was about to deliver his inaugural sermon to the large audience assembled in the synagogue, a pro-government demonstration took place, in which many Jews joined; the Rabbi could not deliver his sermon. [18] In the battles in the streets of Paris a fifteen-year-old Jewish lad was wounded. [19] The press was lavish in its praises of the heroic bearing of the Jewish captain Moïse, friend of the famous sergeants of La Rochelle, at the seizure of the police headquarters. [20] There were also Jewish casualties, for instance, Sergeant Marx of Metz. [21] In some revolutionary clubs Jews, because of their merits, were selected to be the standard bearers. [22] The synagogues conducted memorial services in honor of the victims. The Consistories collected money for the benefit of those affected by the Revolution, the sufferers in the disorders; [23] and a delegation of Jewish societies, headed by Rabbi Isidor, on April 1 handed over to the government a gift of 1,275 francs. [24]

Very impressive was the Jewish participation in the planting of liberty-trees, which in every city was turned into a festive revolutionary demonstration. In Alsace-Lorraine the Jewish part in the planting of liberty-trees was particularly prominent, despite the anti-Jewish excesses of the first days of the Revolution. [25] At the celebration in Strasbourg, sixty Jewish emigrés from Poland, insurrectionists of 1831, were present. After the celebration, the rabbi mentioned this fact in the synagogue, and since it happened to be on Passover, the Jews of Strasbourg deemed it an honor to invite the Jewish "insur-

[16] *Archives Israélites*, 1848.
[17] *L'Univers Israélite*, Oct. 1, 1890.
[18] *La Vérité*, May 5, 1848, p. 3.
[19] *Archives Israélites*, 1848, p. 380.
[20] *Ibid.*, p. 287.
[21] *Ibid.*, p. 282.
[22] *Loc. cit.*
[23] *Loc. cit.*
[24] *La Vérité*, 1848.
[25] M. Ginsburger, "Troubles contre les Juifs d'Alsace en 1848," *Revue des Etudes Juives*, Vol. LXIV, pp. 109-117.

rectionists" to the *Seder* (the festive meal).[25] The sixty Jewish insurrectionists undoubtedly were members of the Polish Legion, formed
at that time in Paris and preparing to march upon Poland to free
the fatherland. The Legion set out for its destination by way of
Alsace. The liberty-tree was planted in Strasbourg a day after the
arrival of the Polish legionnaires, and they were received with enthusiasm by the population of Strasbourg.[27] Aron, the Chief Rabbi of
Strasbourg, in a circular of March 1, 1848, requested all rabbis of
the neighboring communities to conduct services in their synagogues
in memory of the martyrs of the "heroic battle" of Paris,[28] and during the celebration of the liberty-tree invoked blessings on the
"monument to our joy and hopes," closing with the exclamation:
"Long live the universal Republic."[29] A powerful sermon against
the "disgraceful regime of corruption, which God's breath had destroyed"[30] was delivered by the rabbi at the celebration in Mulhouse.
In Luneville an address was delivered by the Jew Katz,[31] and in
Colmar Chief Rabbi Goudchaud delivered a sermon.[32] The students
of the rabbinical school in Metz donated to the government 25 francs
collected among themselves, and the *Khevra Kadisha* (honorary
burial society) gave 200 francs.[33] The renowned Franco-Jewish actress,
Rachel, thrilled French audiences with her singing of the "Marseillaise."[34]

In the first days of the revolution a group of Parisian orthodox
Jews founded a Jewish democratic club, modeled after the countless
popular clubs that sprang up in those days. Paris alone counted, by
the end of March, 1848, 140 such clubs, whose influence upon
political life was enormous. In one of them, in Raspail's "Ami du
Peuple," 6,000 people met daily.[35]

Concerning the leaders of the Jewish democratic club, we possess
the most detailed information about Alexandre (Ben-Baruch) Créhange (b. in 1791 in Etain, near Nancy; d. May 13, 1896, in Paris).

---

[26] *Archives Israélites*, 1848, p. 289. Jan Czynski tells in *Le Reveil d'Israel*, 1848, that
all Polish-Jewish emigrants in Paris offered their services to the French Provisional Government.
[27] Colonel Louis Blaisou, *Un passage de vive force du Rhin français en 1848*, Paris,
1933, p. 70.
[28] Paul Muller, *La Révolution de 1848 en Alsace*, Paris, 1912, p. 54.
[29] *Elsaesser Republikaner* (Republicain Alsacien), Strasbourg, Supplement to No. 26
(1848).
[30] *Archives Israélites*, 1848, p. 237.
[31] *Ibid.*, p. 228.
[32] *Discours prononcé le 30 avril 1848 par Monsieur le Grand-Rabbin Goudchaud*,
Colmar, 1848, 4 pp.
[33] *L'Ami du Peuple*, Metz, May 4, 1848.
[34] *Le Temps*, April 5, 1915.
[35] G. D. Weil, *Le droit d'association et le droit de réunion*, Paris, 1893, p. 178.

Créhange was one of the leaders of the orthodox circles in Paris; he subsequently became one of the founders of the Alliance Israélite Universelle. He was a bookkeeper by profession,[36] but devoted most of his time to literature. He translated the *Ts'eno U'reno* (a Yiddish paraphrase of the Pentateuch dating from the 17th century) into French, published several periodicals and calendars, a dozen or so religious and ethical manuals in French, as well as pamphlets against the Jewish religious reformists, and was also active in a number of Jewish organizations. In his religious views he was orthodox, although not an extremist, and in his political convictions a republican, an adherent of a democratic regime in the country and in the Jewish communities. At the time of the Revolution of 1848 he published a booklet, a discourse between a teacher and his disciples, in which he developed his religious and democratic views.[37] The booklet was recommended by the Ministry of Public Instruction and Religion of the Provisional Government as a textbook for Jewish schools.[38] Créhange also wrote and published with his friend Wague a worker's hymn, "The Marseillaise of Labor," and had it sold in the streets.[39]

The previously mentioned club was named "Club Démocratique des Fidèles" (Democratic Club of the Faithful), which was to imply: faithful to the Jewish religion. The meetings of the club were open to the public; its protocols appeared in the periodical *La Vérité*, published by Créhange.[40] It is worth while remarking that although the protocols of the club appeared in this periodical, which was fairly well known, they have hitherto been ignored by the Franco-Jewish

---

[36] In a pamphlet against his employers he includes a few interesting autobiographical details; see Créhange. *A MM. les membres de la Soc. Industrielle et Commerciale à Paris*, Paris, 1835, 16 pp. (Bibl. Nat. Ln 27 31732). Créhange died May 13, 1896, and not in 1872 as erroneously stated in the *Jewish Encyclopedia* and in the *Encyclopaedia Judaica;* see *L'Univers Israélite*, Vol. LI, p. 249; *Archives Israélites*, Vol. LVII, p. 173. In 1863 Créhange became a member of the Paris Consistory. He was then even more popular than before, for he was among the founders of the "Alliance." Whether or not, upon his joining the Consistory, Créhange attempted to realize those reforms for which he had fought in 1848, is a subject that merits investigation.
[37] [Créhange] A. Ben-Baruch. *Des droits et des devoirs du Citoyen, instruction tirée de l'Histoire Sainte ou entretiens d'un maître d'école avec ses élèves*, Paris, 1848 (Bibl. Nat. Lb 53 125).
[38] *Moniteur*, March 25, 1848.
[39] Créhange, *La Marseillaise du travail*, Paris, 1848, 4 pp., (Bibl. Nat. Ve 55471 [659]). Also, a Jewish laborer of Lyon published a Republican song; A. Lévy, *Trio républicain, dédié aux électeurs*, Lyon, 1848, 1 p. Other Jewish publications of 1848-49 worth mentioning are: David Milland, *Vérités historiques sur la royauté suivées d'un Dialogue entre un Ouvrier Républicain et un Ouvrier Légitimiste*, Marseilles, 1849; in which he pleads for a check on Republican advances; and Maurice Block, *Lettres à mon ami Jacques* (1-3), Paris, 1849, in which the author, later a well-known economist, speaks against the abolition of private property.
[40] *La Vérité*, journal des intêrets israélites. Redacteur-gérant: A. Créhange, Paris, No. 1, Apr. 17, 1848, 16 pp. — the first six numbers of that periodical are in the possession of the library of the "Alliánce"; also the Paris "Bibliothèque Nationale" has an incomplete collection (LC 3 63). In the Jewish press outside of France I find mention of the club only in the *Allgemeine Zeitung des Judentums* (1848, p. 264).

historians—in all probability not intentionally—and we examine them here for the first time. This applies also to the club, which we here study for the first time on the basis of materials found in the National Archives in Paris.

Première année. — N° 2. — Lundi 17 Avril 1848.

LA VERITE

JOURNAL DES INTÉRÊTS ISRAÉLITES.

PRIX DE L'ABONNEMENT
Pour la France & l'Étranger.

Un mois....... 1 fr.
Trois mois.....
Six mois.......
Un an ....

LA VÉRITÉ paraîtra
tous les huit jours.

PARIS,
6, rue des Petites-Écuries.
(Les lettres taxées seront refusées.)

Union et Paix.

SOMMAIRE.

A nos lecteurs.—Club démocratique des Fidèles.--Pétition.—Dons patriotiques. —De l'organisation du travail.—La charitable Mercière juive.—Troubles dans le Haut-Rhin. M. Klein. M. Hemerdurger.— Mandement.—Correspondance. Non Cerisier.—Bibliographie.—Annonces.

A NOS LECTEURS.

En octobre dernier, à l'expiration de la première année de *la Paix*, nous voulions nous retirer du journalisme. Nous avions dit quelques vérités, l'on nous a intenté un procès. Nous avions signalé des abus, l'on a voulu nous faire condamner à l'amende et à la prison. Nous en avons conclu que, pour plaire, il fallait mentir et flatter : nous ne voulions

The first public meeting of the club took place on April 2, 1848, in a house at 95, Rue St. Martin. According to the published report, the attendance was so large that the hall could not accommodate all the people, and Dr. Trèves, one of the founders of the club, moved to postpone the meeting and to seek larger quarters. The assembled group, however, resolved to go through with the meeting. The first address, delivered by Henry, a co-founder of the club, clearly indicated the intentions of its founders: they wanted to take advantage of the revolutionary enthusiasm abroad to conduct elections to the Consistory on a general democratic principle, in accordance with the general elections that had been held throughout the country on March 5, 1848. In his address Henry stated: "We demand the dissolution of the Consistories in France and their reorganization on the basis of general elections, the only method that is in accord with our

Republican institutions." These words were enthusiastically received by the audience. Dr. Trèves on the same day addressed an appeal to the Provisional Government in that spirit, proposing to create "a commission of Jews, devoted to the task of restoring to us our rights, of which we have been deprived." [41]

The "Club Démocratique des Fidèles" also printed a petition with these demands to the Provisional Government, [42] secured signatures, and transmitted it to the authorities on May 3, 1848. [43] The petition, addressed to the "citizen members of the French Republic," stated that the Consistory, embracing the Jewish population of ten departments (states), was elected by 220 notables (voters to the Consistory) and that in the elections of December, 1847, only 111 notables participated. "A Consistory formed in this manner is not the expression of the masses of the Jews in the election districts, since these very masses are not permitted to vote," the petition continued.

The events of February, 1848, had their influence not merely on the Jews of Paris. From the outlying districts began to come demands for a change of the election system and the Consistory. The Central Consistory of Paris notified the Minister of Religion, in a letter dated April 17, 1848, that a number of local consistories had directed attention to the fact that the decree of 1844 "was not in accord with the principles of equality, which had gained the upper hand as a result of the February events." It happened to be time then for the re-election of some members of the Consistory, and according to the law the lists of the "notables" had to be posted in the synagogues. This time, some of the Consistories refrained from posting the lists, for they saw in the old election methods a contradiction to the new spirit of the Revolution.

> Although we are in full agreement with the measures taken by the Consistories [wrote the Central Consistory in the above-mentioned letter of April 17], we are unable on our initiative alone to change the election laws with reference to our religion, concerning which the new government has as yet had no opportunity to express itself. [44]

On May 17, 1848, the "Club Démocratique des Fidèles" ratified its statutes. As far back as the first number of his periodical *La Vérité*,

---

[41] In the Paris Archives Nationales F 19 11015.
[42] It is worth remarking here that in the Catholic and Protestant parishes we find no corresponding movement, which indicates that Jewish communal life in France long after the emancipation was more than merely a matter of religion.
[43] Several such petitions, dated April 16, 1848, containing over a hundred signatures, are in the Paris Archives Nationales (F 19 11015). They are written in the style of Dr. Trèves' petition of April 2, 1848.
[44] Archives Nationales, F 19 11015.

Créhange characterized the spirit of the club in these words: "faithful to the country, faithful to the Republic, faithful to the principles of our religion, faithful to the motto: liberty, equality, fraternity." The entire program of Créhange was to be found in the words he had written back in 1846: "Conservative in religion, progressive in social life." [45] "The club," the first clause of the statutes states, "will bring about reforms in the synagogue, will call attention to shortcomings, will indicate the way to economy." The officers of the club were: Henry, president; Wahl, vice-president; Créhange, secretary; Mayer, treasurer. The "commissaries," as they were called, were: Cosman, David, Gaffré, Nettre, and Sophar. The meetings of the club—usually stormy—were very well attended. Thus, on April 19, 1848, according to *La Vérité*, 300 men assembled and listened to stirring addresses exhorting them to the observance of the Jewish traditions, and the democratization of the Jewish congregations. Créhange in particular distinguished himself by his oratory. Here is an example of one of his addresses, delivered at a previous meeting, on April 9:

> Moved by the breath of God, the stones of February arose and crushed the privileged voters, the proud upholders of despotism. A throne was reduced to ashes, but our leaders still cling to their pathetic system. For them nothing has changed.

For the first time a group of French Jews proclaimed their political motto thus openly. As we shall see later, the club did not hesitate, in a petition to the Ministry concerning the tax on kosher meat, to accuse the Consistory of persecuting Jews for their patriotic (republican) sentiments.

The Consistory was not accustomed to such vigorous opposition. Because of the new spirit abroad it could not overtly combat the club, but attempted to avenge itself on some of its leaders; they were attacked in the synagogue, one of them was deprived of the privilege of officiating in the synagogue in the capacity of cantor; it exerted pressure upon people to discontinue their membership in the club, and strove by other means to undermine it.

In addition to the demands for instituting democratic elections, the club put forward a number of other demands, over which a controversy had been raging for years among the orthodox and the reformers in the congregation. The club expressed the opinions and the interests of the poor orthodox masses. Whether it was a question of

45 *La Paix,* Paris. 1846. p. 24.

a tax on kosher meat or matzos, or "honors" in the synagogue, or burial rites—essentially it was a struggle of the poor orthodox against the wealthy reformers.

Especially distressing and important to the poorer Jewish population was the problem of kosher meat.[46] The Jewish population of Paris consumed, proportionately, more meat than the non-Jewish. According to the figures of the Ministry of Commerce, every Parisian consumed on the average 47 kilograms (119.5 lbs.) of meat a year, and according to the figures of the Consistory in Paris, every Jew in Paris consumed 50 kilograms (125 lbs.), besides fowl. The kosher meat in Paris was sold by four butchers, and the tax on this meat brought into the coffers of the Consistory an annual income of some 15,000 francs, which enraged the poorer Jewish population. As early as 1840, a delegation of 70 Parisian Jews, representing the congregations, had appeared before the Consistory and had demanded the reduction of the tax on kosher meat. Créhange then complained that "the burden of these taxes falls exclusively upon the middle and poorer classes" — "the more expensive meats destined for the tables of the rich were tax-free." [47] In Metz a sharp conflict broke out between the Consistory and the Jewish community on account of the tax. The local butchers complained that the poorer Jews could not pay such taxes, and submitted a memorandum to the chief of police, taking for their motto . . . the democratic law of October 7, 1789: "All public taxes, whatever their nature, should be paid by all citizens and proprietors in proportion to their wealth and their means." [48]

At a meeting of the "Club Démocratique des Fidèles" (April 9, 1848), Créhange exclaimed:

> We do not want charity to be given at our expense. We do not want the middle class to be taxed so that charity might be given to the poor. And you all know, gentlemen, that the tax on kosher meat affects primarily the middle class, since the expensive meats are not taxed.

On May 26, 1848, the club sent a petition to the government against the tax [49] and complained about the Consistory that "does not

---

[46] The data on the controversy over the tax are taken from the following sources: Archives of the Central Consistory; Archives Nationales, F 19 11030; a printed memorandum of the Paris Consistory about kosher meat: Consistoire Israélite de Paris, *A MM. les Membres du Consistoire Central*, Paris, 1846, 44 p. (Library of the "Alliance," J-3388). See also R. Anchel, *Notes sur les frais du Culte Juif en France*, Paris, 1928; *La Sentinelle Juive*, Paris, 1840, p. 70; *La Vérité*, Paris, 1848.
[47] *La Sentinelle Juive*, 1848, p. 70.
[48] *Mémoire à préfet du département de la Moselle*. Par Louis Rottembourg, etc. tous Bouchers Israélites à Metz, 1830, 26 pp. (4º). The Metz Consistory replied to this memorandum with a brochure: *Observations du Consistoire Israélite de Metz, en Réponse à la pétition addressée à M. le Préfet de la Moselle par les Sieurs Louis Rottembourg, etc.* Metz (1830), 23 pp. (4º). Both brochures are in the Archives Nationales F 19 110 30.
[49] Archives Nationales F 19 110 30.

defend the interests of the people, but, on the contrary, imposes upon the middle and the poorer classes the burden of taxes and suppresses the religious and patriotic sentiments of the faithful." The petition further related that as a result of the revolutionary events of February the hold of the tax was already partly broken: "*Shokhtim* (ritual slaughterers) minister to the needs of butchers who sell meat 10 or 15 centimes cheaper than the Consistory butchers." In reply to the petition, the Consistory defended its position by stating that some of the meat was declared ritually unfit for consumption, hence the butchers had to charge a higher price to recoup their loss; the Consistory had to maintain supervisors of the butcher shops; it had to dispense charity; and, above all, it had to cover with the income from the taxes the debts incurred in building (in 1820-21) the synagogue on Notre Dame de Nazareth Street. The Ministry took the side of the Consistory and discharged its obligation to the "Club Démocratique des Fidèles" with a reply, stating that permission will be granted to increase the number of Jewish butcher shops and "this will take care of the interests of the poorer Jews in Paris." [50] It is not impossible that this laconic answer of the Ministry was dictated by the fear that, should the tax be abolished, it would have to increase the amount of the government subsidy allotted for Jewish religious purposes. The permission to open additional butcher shops signalized a partial victory. However, the members of the club were not satisfied. They replied that the synagogue was maintained by the poorer elements, who did not benefit by it, since the synagogue contained only 500 seats, which were rented for the holidays to the wealthy, and the poor had no place for worship.

The members of the "Club Démocratique des Fidèles" wanted to utilize the seat situation in the synagogue in order to raise once more the question of private chapels, a subject of controversy for several decades in all communities of France. [51] In order to assure its income, the Consistory prevailed upon the government to rule that without the Consistory's consent no private services could be held. Besides the material significance, still another consideration entered into this question. In the private chapels the traditional Jewish customs were observed, and the power was in the hands of the orthodox. The club

[50] *Loc. cit.*
[51] In 1839 Creháge delivered an address on that subject, which was later published: *Discours prononcé le 24 juin 1839 dans la séance du Consistoire du dép. de la Seine en faveur des réunions religieuses des sociétés de secours mutuels*, Paris, 1839, 15 pp. (8°). See also L. Kahn, *Les Sociétés*, etc., Paris, 1887.

therefore demanded the construction of an additional large synagogue and the authorization of private chapels. On May 24, 1848, the club chose a committee of eight, whose task it was to create a central association for mutual aid, which was to include all the smaller associations. This planned central association, which was an attempt to create, besides the Consistory, another central Jewish body in the spirit of democratic orthodoxy, was to be the answer to the politics of the Consistory "that possesses the ability to elicit in us a feeling of disgust toward charity." Club circles also protested against the excessive taxes on matzos.[61]

The Club meetings also touched on another moot question of Parisian Jewry: the problem of the burial plot in the Jewish section of the Montmartre cemetery.[62] The Consistory, together with the city administration, had decided to set up there two temporary burial plots. The victims of this decision were only the poorer Jews, since the wealthy had provided themselves in advance with family plots. The orthodox regarded this decision concerning temporary burial a disgrace to the dead, since to exhume the dead is against Jewish usage. Créhange, in 1841, even wrote a special brochure on that subject, in conjunction with a certain Bolvillier.[64] In the synagogue this subject of burial plots not infrequently led to arguments and even blows. On May 4, 1848, a meeting of the "Club Démocratique des Fidèles" elected a committee of nine to settle the controversy over the burial plots.

The Club also protested the inauguration of the sale of "aliyos" (synagogue honors) in connection with the lections in the Scriptures. In principle, the reformers, too, had agreed to abolish the sale of "aliyos," since, in their opinion, this transformed the synagogue into a market. But the "aliyos" were a source of income for the Consistory that could not be easily replaced. The poorer groups, for their part, were dissatisfied because the wealthier would generally procure all the "aliyos" and leave none for the poor.

Of all the demands put forth by the "Club Démocratique des Fidèles," such as the demand for democratic elections, the abolition of the tax on kosher meat, the demands in reference to the seats and

---

[61] *Archives Israélites,* 1848, p. 193; *La Pure Vérité,* May 20, 1846.
[62] Since 1810 the Jews of Paris have had no cemetery of their own, and the Jewish dead are buried in the municipal cemeteries, where the Jewish plots were concentrated in a separate section; see L. Kahn, *Le Comité de Bienfaisance . . . les cimetières,* Paris, 1886, p. 119.
[64] Créhange et Bolvillier, *Aux Israélites de Paris, au sujet de changements proposés pour le cimetière de Montmartre,* Paris, 1841, 15 pp.

honors in the synagogue, private chapels and burial plots, only the first was realized. The government was ready to yield to that demand, which appeared to it to be in accord with the spirit of the time. The other demands hinged upon internal problems of Jewish community life, of which the government officials understood but little.

The result of the various petitions and appeals was a decision by the Ministry of Public Instruction and Religion to change the election system of the Jewish Consistories: in place of a group of "notables," all the Jews 25 years and over were granted suffrage. In an official letter[55] of June 7, 1848, which was subsequently given the force of a decree, the Minister ordered the Central Consistory to transfer automatically the names of all Jewish voters in the general election lists (for the city councils and Parliament) to the election lists of the Consistories. The letter added that this decision was the only course possible after the events of the last days in the country. "The extension of suffrage in a political sense to its final limits calls for an analogous expansion of the Jewish notability."[56]

The Paris Consistory issued a printed proclamation, in French (July 10, 1848), calling upon the Jews to register for the election lists. The proclamation also stated that as far back as the first days of the Revolution, the Paris Consistory had applied to the Central Consistory for a change in the election lists.[57] From existing documents one can see that various Jewish circles attempted to delay the inaugurated reforms. In general, the Central Consistory manifested little energy and initiative. At the session of the Consistory, on December 3, 1848, Hemerdinger[58] introduced a drastic resolution to dissolve the Consistories and re-elect them according to the new election system, but it was not accepted.[59] Government circles were ready, in the spirit of the time, to embark upon further democratization of the election laws of the Consistories.[60]

[55] Reprinted in A. E. Halphen, *Recueil des lois concernant les Israélites*, Paris, 1851, p. 150.
[56] Archives Nationales F 19 11015.
[57] The proclamation is in the Archives Nationales F 19 11015.
[58] Hemerdinger was sent by the Provisional Government as commissioner to investigate the pogroms on Jews in Alsace. A relative of his was a member of the "Club Démocratique des Fidèles." On his mission to Alsace see Léon Kahn, "Un commissaire de la Republique en 1848." *Annuaire des Archives Israélites*, 1890.
[59] Archives of the Central Consistory, protocol of Dec. 3, 1848.
[60] A letter of the Ministry of Religion to the Consistory, preserved in the Paris Archives Nationales, reads that "the Jewish representation must be normal and complete and more suited to the spirit of our constitution." For that purpose, the letter further states, it would be necessary to increase the number of secular representatives in the Consistory (on June 15, 1850, a decree to that effect was actually issued, see Halphen, *op. cit.*, p. 160). The letter is not dated but is most probably of Sept. 3, 1848. In another letter of the Ministry, cognizance is taken of the need to make the number of provincial representatives in the Central Consistory proportionate to the number of Jews in the respective provinces (according to the decree of 1844, all provinces sent an equal number of "notables").

Number of Consistory Notables and Voters before and after June 7, 1848 *

Consistories		Number of Notables and Actual Voters in the Elections Before June, 1848			Number of Notables and Actual Voters in the Elections After June, 1848		
Departments	Number of Jews in the Department	Date of Elections	Number of Actual Voters	Number of Notables	Date of Elections	Number of Actual Voters	Number of Notables
Paris	17,000	9-XI-1847	154	224	26-XII-1852	602	2,295
Strasbourg	23,531	18-III-1846	69	152	2-IX-1850	2,732	4,790
Metz	8,071	6-X-1847	40	72	29-V-1850	746	?
Nancy	10,479	1847	70	97	16-I-1853	860	1,683
Colmar	16,871	3-XI-1847	67	133	18-XII-1850	504	3,631
Marseilles	3,958	19-XI-1847	55	138	19-X-1854	528	711
Bordeaux	3,500	24-X-1847	46	89	6-I-1850	238	408
Saint Esprit	2,500	18-X-1847	31	65	17-II-1850	171	341
Total	85,910		532	910		6,381	13,859 (exclusive of Metz)

The table is compiled on the basis of the lists of notables A. N.—Fig. 11,050; 11,051. The number of notables in Metz, after June, 1848, is missing. The figures on the total Jewish population is taken from *L'Univers Israélite* (1848), p. 40.

The democratic elections suddenly brought upon the area of active public life a large number of Jews who up to that time had had no voice in the affairs of the community. The figures as to the numbers of those eligible to vote before and after June 7, 1848, appended here, give us a clear picture of this democratization. As can be seen, the number of eligible Jewish notables (voters) rose after the reform of 1848 from 910 to 13,859 (exclusive of the city of Metz); in reality, however, not quite one-half of those eligible to vote (6,381 of the 13,859) participated in the elections. Possibly, this was due to the fact that the first elections to the Consistories after the change in the election methods had gone into effect took place considerably later, at a time when the enthusiasm had already cooled off. This same phenomenon was manifest in the general political life of the country. In the first elections to Parliament in 1848, after the introduction of general suffrage, out of 9,360,000 voters 7,893,000 voted, which is a very small absenteeism. Later, with the drop in the enthusiasm there was also a drop in the number of voters, and absenteeism became quite pronounced.[61]

The new voters to the Jewish Consistories came exclusively from the poorer classes: peddlers, farmers, artisans, employees and workingmen, the lower classes of religious functionaries (sextons, cantors), etc. Particularly noticeable was the number of peddlers among the voters: whereas previously this class had not furnished a single "notable" to the Consistories, after June 7, 1848, their number in the Consistory of the Department of Nancy alone reached 157, in Marseilles, 42. Also the number of merchant voters increased enormously: employees in industry and handicraft: in Nancy, 115; Marseilles, 73; Bordeaux, 59; Saint Esprit, 50. Clerks: Marseilles, 61; Bordeaux, 68. The Marseilles Consistory added to its voters a large number of Jewish carpenters and shoemakers; Nancy, 28 laborers; Bordeaux, a blacksmith.[62]

It is interesting, however, to note that the new democratic election reforms, upon becoming law, brought some uneasiness into Jewish circles. After the first moments of enthusiasm, it appeared that even the orthodox had no uniform attitude to the problem. They became somewhat apprehensive over the unexpected results that such a change might bring about into the life of the Jewish communities. The dissatisfaction with the new election system derived from various causes. Some were suspicious of the new authorities: the orthodox from the more progressive districts feared a victory of the reformers, while the reformers from districts predominantly orthodox dreaded an orthodox victory. The reformers were also alarmed at the possibility of the separation of state and religion, which was then seriously discussed. *Archives Israélites*, their organ, wrote openly that declaring religion a private affair might lead to a victory of the orthodox, who would then—in the absence of state control—be in a position to act on their accord, appoint their own rabbis, a state of affairs which would bring about an inevitable schism in French Jewry.[63] *L'Univers Israélite*, organ of the moderate orthodox, published in 1849 (in 1848 it had temporarily discontinued publication) several articles against the new

---

[61] G. D. Weil, *Les élections depuis 1789.*
[62] On the basis of the lists of "notables," Archives Nationales F 19 11050, 11951.
[63] *Archives Israélites*, 1849, pp. 42-141, 205-210, 250. Among those demanding a separation of state and religion was also Armand Lévy. His first public appearance in a revolutionary club in 1848 was to protest against the religious ceremonies of the funeral of the victims of the February disorders (Pierre et Paul, *op. cit.*). In the election platform of Raspail's committee in the Panthéon district, which Lévy edited, he included the demand for the separation of state and religion. The Mickiewicz Museum in Paris has an interesting letter on that subject by d'Alton-Shée to Armand Lévy.

election system, which might transfer political events from the streets into the synagogue.[64] There was also some apprehension lest the new election system undermine the "patriarchal rights." The new election system, wrote the *Archives Israélites,* may be good for politics, but dangerous to religion, where authority plays such a prominent role.[65] Some concern was also expressed for the "sacred principle of the family," since the son could voice, in the synagogue, a different opinion from that of his father.[66] Furthermore, there was a danger of "harmful" elements finding their way into the Consistory and introducing political tendencies.[67]

In the last analysis, the events of 1848 brought about no great changes in French Jewry. The new election system was not sufficiently utilized by the democratic elements in the communities. The internal struggles of the communities did not transcend the bounds of synagogue interests. If there came into being a revolutionary element among the Jewish population, it generally withdrew from communal affairs, and devoted itself to the general political struggles of the country. The contests in the congregations over issues of tax, burial plots, seats and "honors" in the synagogue, could not satisfy such an element. The orthodox, too, underwent some changes in the course of time; the winds of assimilation found their way into their ranks. Like the reformists, they, too, saw their entire Jewishness in the synagogue only. The controversy between the orthodox and the reformers in the Jewish communities still revolved about one problem: to modernize the Jewish religion. The other struggles, social and political, were waged outside the congregation, along with the non-Jewish population.

The Consistories remained the same as before 1848. Even the one achievement of the revolutionary days, the democratic election system, did not succeed in really democratizing the regime in the Consistories, and the rulers of the congregations and Consistories remained the same, or practically the same, as heretofore. The Consistory went the way of the entire regime in the country. After the enthusiasm of the first days of the Revolution of 1848 came political opportunism; the Second Republic was succeeded by the Second Empire and the

[64] *L'Univers Israélite,* 1849, p. 58.
[65] *Archives Israélites,* 1849, p. 207.
[66] *Ibid.,* p. 162.
[67] *Ibid.,* p. 99. Benjamin Wahl, the public leader of Mulhouse, wrote to the ministry (Feb. 20, 1853) a letter protesting against the general elections, since there was a possibility that the adherents of the "rationalist system" might be victorious (Archives Nationales F 19 11050).

monarchist regime of Napoleon III. Jewish life was and remained a miniature of the general political life in the country.

A few final words on the effect of the February Revolution upon the Jews in the French colony of Algeria:

Soon after the events of February, a group of Algerian Jews began a movement calling for suffrage, and secured 600 signatures to a petition. It seems that at the head of this group stood a Polish Jew, named Rubinstein, said to have been an "insurrectionist" in Poland, who had fled and settled in Algeria. Together with the local rabbi, Dalitz, also an East European (from Białystok), Rubinstein for some time led the opposition to the Algerian Consistory, and flooded government offices with memoranda. In one of these memoranda, dated April 8, 1850, he writes that the emissary who had been charged with submitting the petition with the 600 signatures to the government in 1848, under pressure from the Consistory, failed to carry out his mission, and that petition never reached the authorities.[68]

> The attention of the reader is called to related studies by the author on the French Jews in the post-Napoleonic restoration, and in the Paris commune of 1871, in *Yidn in Frankraykh*, I.

[68] Archives Nationales F 19 11117.

BORDEAUX
ET L'ABOLITION DE L'ESCLAVAGE
DANS LES COLONIES EN 1848

    Un décret du 4 mars 1848 a institué une commission sous la présidence de Victor Schoelcher, pour préparer l'émancipation des esclaves dans les colonies françaises. Aux termes des treize décrets et des deux arrêts du 27 avril 1848, l'esclavage devait être aboli dans deux mois, afin que la récolte pût être terminée. Les propriétaires des esclaves ont mené une lutte secrète contre l'émancipation des noirs. L'abolition de l'esclavage était une des raisons de l'impopularité du gouvernement à Bordeaux, spécialement parmi les armateurs et négociants qui tiraient leurs profits du fret du sucre.

    De cette attitude bordelaise nous trouvons un tableau très exact et détaillé dans la correspondance de la maison Gradis, l'armateur bordelais, dont nous publions ici des extraits. Ce sont les copies de lettres adressées aux agents de la maison Gradis, principalement à la Martinique[a].

    Nous avons omis seulement les parties traitant diverses affaires commerciales, bateaux, etc., qui ne sont pas sans un grand intérêt pour l'histoire du commerce bordelais au XIXe siècle, mais qui ne touchent pas directement la question de l'esclavage et autres problèmes politiques de l'époque.

Originally published in *Revue Historique de Bordeaux et du Département de la Gironde* (1954). Excerpt.

Michel Berr *

The Failure of an Intellectual among the First Generation of
Emancipated Jews in France

THE first generation of emancipated Jews in France—a country with changes of regime, frequent revolutionary as well as constitutional—included some men of talent whose achievements were small because of their eccentricities: somehow they lost their way. One of them was Michel Berr (1780-1843), son of Berr-Isaac Berr (1744-1828) [1].

Michel Berr was born into the rich Berr family of Nancy nine years before the Revolution of 1789. His youth was thus crowded with impressions of a most important period in the history of Jews and of France in general. As private tutor to his son, his father Berr-Isaac Berr engaged Benjamin Wolf (Louis Germain), a *maskil* from Breslau [2]. Later on the younger Berr studied law at the University of Strasbourg and became the first lawyer among the Ashkenazic Jews of France. For a short time he practised law in Nancy [3]. He then married Minette Bing, daughter of Isaïe Berr Bing (1759-1805), one of the earliest French *maskilim* [4]. He soon

* The following abbreviations of studies on Michel Berr are used in the notes: CARMOLY = E. CARMOLY, *Notice sur Michel Berr, Revue Orientale*, iii (1843), pp. 62-74, 122-31; TSARPHATI = OLRY TERQUEM, *Michel Berr, Archives israélites*, iv (1843), pp. 721-27, v (1844), pp. 109-16, 168-80. On Michel Berr see also: *Notices et essais de M. Michel Berr* [Signed M. B. (MICHEL BERR)] n.p., n.d., 17 pp. (reprinted from *Précis analytique des travaux de la Société académique . . . de Nancy*, 1811); D. DE C., *Extrait de l'Argus, du 6 juillet 1824. Notices biographiques sur les littératures contemporains. Michel Berr.* n.p., n.d. pp. 209-16; X. MARMIER, *Notice biographique sur Michel Berr,* Strasbourg, 1834. 16 pp. (reprinted from *Revue Germanique*); *Dictionnaire de Biographie française,* vi (Paris, 1954), p. 141.

[1] Berr Isaac Berr and his wife Catherine Karche had nine children: (1) Isidore (1768-May 7, 1840), married to Agathe Simon (1765-Febr. 1, 1837); (2) Cécile (1765-Dec. 8, 1853), married to Isaac Mayer Marx, son of Mayer Marx; (3) Sara (?-Febr. 27, 1847), married to Hippolyte Cerf (called Cerfberr); (4) Babet (1774-Dec. 9, 1860), married to Samuel Wolf, a German Jew; (5) Minette (?-1832), married to the Nancy banker Garçon-Jacob Goudchaux (1768-1818), see note 11; (6) Françoise, married to Lazare Garçon Lévy (their daughter was married to her uncle Lippman Berr); (7) Lippman Berr, married his niece Caroline Lévy; (8) Michel Berr (1780-July 14, 1843), married Minette Bing; (9) Merley, married to Amsel Mass (according to registries of the *état-civil* in the departmental archives of Meurthe-et-Moselle).

[2] M. BERR, *Discours* (see note 25), p. 7; *L'Espérance, Courrier de Nancy,* July 20, 1843; TSARPHATI, pp. 110-12; CARMOLY, pp. 64, 122.

[3] *Notice sur M. Berr, Argus,* July 1824, p. 109; TSARPHATI, p. 169; CARMOLY, p. 64. On Bing see *Revue philosophique,* xiii, 4, pp. 316-18.

[4] Another daughter of Bing was married to Hartog Sommerhausen (1781-

Originally published in *The Journal of Jewish Studies,* vol. XIV (1963).

left for Paris, where he served as deputy for the Seine department at the Jewish Assembly convened by Napoleon I [5]. In the following years Michel Berr occupied many positions. His tenure was, however, brief in each case, and he did not make friends of his chiefs and employees. While serving as secretary of the Sanhedrin convened by Napoleon I he came into conflict with Abraham Furtado. For a while he was employed by the Ministry of Interior in the administration of Westphalia. (According to one source, Berr had obtained this job in recognition of his translations into French of a few Hebrew odes in honour of Napoleon.) Back in Nancy, he was employed at the departmental Prefecture, but he soon left again for Paris. He was for a short time a translator in the Ministry of Interior concerned with the foreign press, but lost his job. For some while he was a professor of German literature. From 1826 he lived for a short time in Belgium with his sister-in-law. There he was given the task of editing a French edition of the *Conversations Lexicon*; but after being strongly attacked for his participation in local political discussions, he lost this job too. Michel Berr did not hesitate to attribute to anti-Jewish feeling the motives of those who dismissed him. He returned to Paris, and later (in 1839) to Nancy, where he remained until his death [6]. In 1801, while a law student at Strasbourg, Michel Berr had published his *Appel* addressed to the peace conference which was supposed to be convened in Lunéville. A booklet of 72 pages, the *Appel* was dedicated to H. Grégoire, and was an appeal to defend the Jews in countries where they were still persecuted. It is written in the traditional style of Mirabeau, Dohm and Grégoire, and is full of apologetic arguments, used by others many times before him, in regard to usury, the Sabbath, ideal Jewish family life, the paucity of criminals among Jews, etc. Of himself Michel Berr wrote in this pamphlet that he had become "more French than Jewish". Despite all its weaknesses, Berr's

1853); see *Archives israélites*, xiv (1853), p. 186. Bing was also the father of J. Bing, an army officer, and of Charles Bing (1793-1836), a lawyer of Metz' author of *l'Ami des jeunes demoiselles*, Paris, 1835, 2 vols, and a leader of the first public Jewish school in Metz; see G-LY [GERSON LÉVY], in *La Régénération*, i (1836), p. 329.

[5] D. TAMA, *Organisation civile et religieuse des Israélites*, Paris, 1808, p. 117.
[6] *L'Espérance*, July 20, 1843; CARMOLY, pp. 66, 124-28.

For Michel Berr's translations of Hebrew odes in honour of Napoleon I see Z. SZAJKOWSKI, *Judaica-Napoleonica*, etc., *Studies in Bibliography and Booklore*, ii (1956), Nos. 170, 204, 206-207.

Appel was one of the best French pamphlets in defence of Jews published at the time. It was a promising start by a young Jewish intellectual of the first generation of emancipated Jews [7].

But Berr's *Appel* of 1801 already evince some of the characteristics of all his later writings: seventeen out of the seventy pages of this pamphlet consist of notes, often not related to the main subject. In later years this became a mania with the author. He published, in the form of pamphlets, his published or unpublished letters addressed to editors of various periodicals to which he added many pages of notes and notes on notes. This was supposed to enhance the scientific value of the pamphlets, but most often the notes consisted of attacks against leaders of the Central Jewish Consistory and of naive descriptions of his friendship with many important personalities. After Berr's name on the title pages of his pamphlets, there appears a long list of his functions and memberships in various local academies [8]. His studies (or, to be more exact, letters to the editors), were published in many periodicals and encyclopedias [9]. He sent his pamphlets to many friends and well-known personages. While he had no reputation as an author, his name was known, and he was accepted in many *salons*.

Berr wrote on Jewish historical and other problems [10]; obituary

[7] Michel Berr, *Appel à la justice des nations et des rois; ou, Adresse d'un citoyen français au congrès qui devait avoir lieu à Lunéville, au nom de tous les habitans de l'Europe qui professent la religion juive.* Strasbourg, 1801. 72 pp., 8°. German translation: LEVY RUBENS, *Bruchstücke aus der Schrift: Zuruf an die Gerechtigkeit der Nationen und Könige ... von Michel Berr.* 1801. *Sulamith*, ii, 1 (1808), pp. 320-35, 382-96, ii, 2 (1809), pp. 27-41.

[8] The following is such a list, printed on the title page of *Extrait du Journal de la Meurthe des* 20 et 26 *Juin* 1834. *Encore du présent, du passé et de l'avenir*, par Michel Berr. Nancy, n.d. 4 pp. "Membre de la Société royale des Antiquaires de France, de la Société Philotechnique de Paris, des Sociétés Académiques de Nancy, Metz et Strasbourg, de Gueting et de Mayence, de Nantes, Caen, Cambray, Niort et Poitiers, l'un des collaborateurs de l'Encyclopédie des Gens du Monde, ancien Professeur à l'Athénée royal de Paris et traducteur au Ministère de l'Intérieur, député de Paris à l'Assemblée israélite et secrétaire du Sanhédrin en 1807, candidat présenté par les Collèges des notables Israélites de Metz et de Colmar pour le Consistoire central de Paris."

[9] For example, in the *Argus, Biographie universelle* (MICHAUD), *Bulletin des sciences philologiques et historiques, Constitutionnel, Constitutionel des Pays-Bas, Contemporains célèbres, Courrier des spectacles, Décade philosophique, Encyclopédie des gens du monde, Galerie des contemporains, Journal de la Belgique, Mercure de France, Mercure étranger, Minerve littéraire, Le Pilote.*

[10] *Notice littéraire et historique sur le livre de Job.* n.p., n.d. 27 pp. (reprinted from *Magasin encyclopédique*, Oct. 1806); *L'Appréciation du monde* [by PENINI], *traduite par Michel Berr.* Metz, 1808 (the translation was included in ARTHUR

notices and biographies of Jews [11] and also of non-Jews [12]. He published literary reviews [13] and translations [14]. He also began a

BEUGNOT'S *Les Juifs d'Occident*, Paris, 1824, pp. 169 ff.); *Lettre au rédacteur de "l'Argus" sur l'ouvrage intitulé: "Les Juifs d'Occident"*, Paris, n.d. 7 pp.; *Langue hébraique*, [Paris, 1815.] 8 pp. (reprinted from *Mercure étranger*, No. xviii (1815), on L. P. Sétier's *Grammaire hébraique*. Paris, 1814); *Sur le divorce considéré chez les Israélites. Au rédacteurs du "Mercure de France"*, Paris, [1815.] 8 pp.; *Notice sur Maymonide (lue dans une séance de l'Académie . . . de Nancy)*, Paris, 1815. 12 pp.; *Notice sur les Benjamites, rétablis en Israël; par M. de Maleville. Extrait du Mercure étranger*, No. xxi (1816). Paris, 1816. 19 pp. (see note 46); *De la littérature hébraique et de la religion juive*. Paris, n.d. 8 pp. (reprinted from *Revue encyclopédique*, July 1822); *Lettre sur les Israélites et le Judaïsme, au directeur du "Panorama des nouveautés Parisiennes . . ."* [Paris, 1823.] 3 parts in one vol.; *Littérature hébraique . . .* Paris, 1823. 12 pp. (reprinted from *Journal asiatique*); *De la fête du nouvel an et du jeûne des expiations ou grand pardon chez les Juifs*. Paris, n.d. 6 pp. (reprinted from *Gazette des cultes*, Oct. 13, 1829); *Du Rabbinisme et des traditions juives, pour faire suite à l'article "Christianisme" de Benjamin Constant, et à l'article "Judaisme" de M. de Kératy, dans l'Encyclopédie moderne . . .* Paris, 1832, xix, 50 pp. *Rite et règlement pour le culte israélite français de Metz*, Nancy, 1842.

[11] *Notice sur Vezelise (Vessely)*. Paris, 1815 (reprinted from *Mercure étranger*); *Eloge de M. Abraham Furtado . . .* Paris, 1817. 34 pp. Another edition: *Eloge de M. Abraham Furtado . . . Discours qui devait être prononcé dans la grande synagogue de la rue Saint-Avoie, à Paris, à la cérémonie funèbre célébrée en l'honneur de la mémoire de M. Furtado . . .* Paris, 1817. 47 pp.; *Extrait des Annales de l'Honneur en France . . .*, n.p., [1818.] 4 pp. (on Garçon-Jacob Godechaux of Nancy, son-in-law of Berr-Isaac Berr); *Nécrologie de M. Baruch Weil*. n.p., n.d. (reprinted from *Le Philantrope*, Apr. 20, 1828).

[12] *Notice sur Bagessen, poéte danois*. Paris, 1805; *Essai sur la vie et les ouvrages de Paul-Jérémi Bitaubé*. Nancy, 1809. 19 pp.; *Notice sur M. le Baron Riouffe, préfet de la Meurthe*. Paris, 1813. 17 pp. (reprinted from *Mémoires of the Nancy Adademy*); *Notice sur M. Charles Villers*. Paris, n.d. 7 pp. (reprinted from *Mercure de France*, Apr. 3, 1815); *Notice biographique sur Campe*. Paris, 1819. 6 pp. (reprinted from *Revue encyclopédique*, Aug. 1818); *Nécrologie. Le Comte Lambrecht membre de la Chambre des Députés . . .* Paris, n.d. 4 pp. (reprinted from *Pilote*, Aug. 15, 1823); *Notice sur le comte Lanjuinais . . .* Bruxelles, n.d. 20 pp. (reprinted from *Constitutionnel du Pays-Bas*, Jan. 22-23, 1827); *Eloge de Benjamin-Constant, prononcé le 12 juin 1833, dans la Chaire de l'Athénée Royal de Paris*, Paris, 1836. 168 pp.; *Extrait du "Journal de la Meurthe" des 18, 20 et 22 octobre* 1832. Nancy, n.d. 4 pp. (biography of the duke of Broglio).

[13] *Des poésies et autres ouvrages de M. Molirat*, Paris, 1814; *Examen de l'Histoire des sectes religieuses de M. Grégoire*, Paris, 1815; *Extrait de la soixante-quatrième livraison de "l'Abeille"*. Paris, 1821. 10 pp. (collective review); *"Résumé de l'histoire de la Lorraine", par M. Etienne fils*. Paris, n.d. 3 pp. (reprinted from *Bulletin universel des sciences et de l'industrie*, Jan. 1826).

[14] *Lettre à M. Millin . . . rédacteur du "Magasin Encyclopédique"*. Paris, 1805, 16 pp. (reprinted from *Magasin Encyclopédique*, ii, Apr.; 1805, on Baron Dalberg's study on art schools, translated by Berr); *Langue allemande. Traduction de deux odes de Schiller*. Paris, n.d. (reprinted from *Mercure étranger*, No. xvi, 1814); *Luther, tragédie en 5 actes*, par le P. Friedrich Ludwig Zacharias Werner. Paris, 1823 (translated by Berr and published as vol. vi of *Chefs-d'oeuvre des théâtres étrangers*); *Extrait du "Courrier des spectacles"*

book on the Revolution of 1789 and a history of Lorraine [15]. Above all, Berr took up the defence of Jews on every occasion. The author of an epistle addressed to Berr wrote: "Porsuis, défend les droits des tribus d'Israël" [16]. During the first Restoration Berr strongly upheld the Jews' rights [17], and also the rights of German Jews in 1817 [18]. In 1819, he attacked Abbot Pradt's unsympathetic remarks about the Jewish religion [19]. Although the *Nouvelle Biographie* included a friendly biography of Berr, he disliked the tenor of the comments about Jews in general and he replied in 1821 with an apologetic pamphlet [20]. Berr ridiculed anti-Jewish statements in a review of his translation of Werner's tragedy *Luther* [21], and criticized remarks against Jewish tradition made in connection with a competition for the best study on Alsatian Jewry [22]. In a review of a book he attacked L. G. A. de Bonald's well-known anti-Jewish attitude [23]. In 1828 Berr considered that the Jewish clergy ought to become employees of the French government [24].

As we shall see, Berr did not participate actively in communal Jewish life. One of the exceptions was his participation for a while in the direction of public schools for Jews. He was the author of the first Franco-Jewish catechism for Jewish children [25]. This was

---

du 3 mars 1823. n.p., n.d. 1 p. (on unfriendly reviews of his translation of *Luther*).

[15] *Eloge de Benjamin-Constant* (see note 12); CARMOLY, p. 67.

[16] *Jean Betinet, secrétaire perpétuel de l'Académie ... de Montmartre ... à M. Michel Berr, seigneur de Turique, marchand privilégié du roi ...*, [Paris, 1824.]

[17] Michel Berr, *Sur la liberté des cultes et sur le projet de décret relatif à l'observance des fêtes et dimanches.* Paris, n.d. 11 pp. (reprinted from *Mercure de France*, Sept. 1814).

[18] M. Berr, *Sur une décision du Sénat de Francfort, à l'égard des Israélites de cette ville.* n.p., n.d. (reprinted from *Journal du commerce*, Nov. 9, 1817).

[19] *Des quatre concordats, de M. De Pradt, ou Observations sur un passage de cet ouvrage.* Paris, 1819. 40 pp.

[20] *Observations sur un article du second volume de la Nouvelle Biographie des contemporains.* Paris, 1821. 15 pp.

[21] M. Berr, in *Courrier des Spectacles*, March 3, 1823 (see note 14).

[22] *Lettre au rédacteur de l'Argus, sur le programme d'un sujet de prix, relatif aux moyens d'améliorer l'état des Juifs en Alsace, proposé par la société académique de Strasbourg.* Paris, [1824.] 7 pp.

[23] *Extrait du Panorama des Nouveautés Parisiennes*, Livraison du 25 juin 1825. n.p., n.d. 8 pp. (In Honoré Torombert's *Principe du Droit politique mis en opposition avec le Contrat social de J. J. Rousseau.* (Paris, 1825).

[24] *Extrait du Corsaire du 4 Août* 1828. [Signed Michel Berr.] [Paris, 1828.] 4 pp. 4°.

[25] [Michel Berr,] *Abrégé de la Bible et choix de morceaux de piété et de*

probably the best such catechism at the time [26]. He published it at his own expense and without the official approval of the Central Consistory. Teaching Jewish children "useful" professions, and the founding of vocational schools was the basic educational philosophy of nineteenth century French Jews [27]. Berr, too, followed this line. In fact, he thought that this "productivisation" of the Jews' economic status was even more important than complete social emancipation, such as for example the giving to the Jewish clergy the status of salaried employees of the state [28]. He violently attacked the founding of a Jewish *lycée* (high-school), since he favoured Jewish elementary schools only, where children would be taught the basic ideas of Judaism. A high school, according to him, would only perpetuate the division between Jews and Christians [29]. In this respect he followed the position taken by many other Jewish leaders.

As early as 1801, Berr broached the idea of the fusion of the Jewish and the Christian religions. Such a result could be achieved, he wrote, by ending all Jewish persecution [30]. After his death, a Nancy newspaper gave the following description of the influence of Parisian society on Berr's attitude towards religion. In the first

morale à l'usage des Israélites de France, par un Israélite français. Paris, 1819. xlv, 344, xii pp. 12; *Idem, Préface de l'ouvrage intitulé "Abrégé de la Bible ..."* Paris, 1819. xli pp. 12°; *Idem, Nouveau Précis élémentaire d'instruction religieuse et morale ...* Nancy, 1839. xli, 104 pp. Another edition: Pont-à-Mousson, 1842. xii, 96 pp. See also *Extrait de Journal de la Meurthe. Nouveau précis élémentaire d'instruction morale et religieuse ... par M. Michel Berr.* [Signed H.L.] Nancy, n.d. 4 pp. 4°; Michel Berr, *Discours prononcé le ... 21 juillet 1827, dans une séance publique du Comité des écoles israélites de Nancy.* Nancy, n.d. 22 pp.

[26] Other catechisms published in 1818-1821: Lion Mayer Lambert, *Catéchisme du culte judaïque ...* Metz, 1818. 144 pp.; Samuel Cahen, *Précis élémentaire d'instruction religieuse ...* Paris, 1820. 59 pp.; Elie Halévy, *Instruction religieuse ...* Metz, 1820. 142, 10 pp. Dr. S. L., *Court enseignement élémentaire religieux et moral pour la jeunesse israélite française.* Paris, 1821.

[27] Z. SZAJKOWSKI, *Jewish Trade Schools in France in the 19th Century, Yivo Bleter*, xlii (1962), pp. 81-120 (in Yiddish).

[28] Michel Berr, *Lettre au Rédacteur du Progresseur, sur la Loi d'élection municipale en rapport avec le culte israélite, avec des notes sur les Pays-Bas, la peine de mort, le duel, etc.* Paris, 1829, 19 pp., p. 8: "le voeu le plus ardent et prononcé de nos familles israélites est moins actuellement cette entière égalité de rang et d'influence sociale de leur culte qui, en ce moment, est réclamée pour lui dans des intentions diverses, mais bien que nos familles soient encouragées dans toutes les voies nobles et utiles que leur ouvre la justice des lois, et dans lesquelles il est de leur devoir de marcher".

[29] M. B[err], *Lettre sur les premières livraisons ...* (see note 42), p. 5; *Idem, Observations sur un article ...* (see note 20), p. 14.

[30] *Appel ...* (see note 7), p. 48.

years of the 19th century, when Berr came to Paris, it was unusual
to meet a Jew who was well educated in the secular schools.
Michel Berr was consequently well received by such personalities
as Benjamin Constant, Henri Grégoire, Madame de Staël, and
many others. From them he acquired ideas on religious and other
matters which he could not easily digest. Above all, his influential
new friends tried to convince him that Judaism belonged to the
past. He began to lose his faith in traditional Judaism but gained
only a vague sentiment of respect for Christianity. This sentiment
was not strong enough to induce him to join the Church, but made
him dream of becoming the leader of a modernized Judaism [31].
But his dream was doomed to complete failure. According to
Michel Berr's religious philosophy, the Jewish religion is essentially
progressive and never stationary. All non-sesential elements should
be thrown out of the Talmud, and only the purely prophetical,
moral ideas should be retained. In Judaism all moral ideas are
Jewish, while mystical aspects are like foreign bodies. The same
pruning should be applied to the religious values of Christianity.
Christ's ideas contain prophetic elements which should be adopted
by Jews. According to the reform leader Tsarphati (Olry Terquem),
Berr's idea of fusion was misunderstood by both Jews and Christians. He wrongly proposed his idea on fusion as an end, when in
reality it was supposed to be only a means to the reform of existing
religions. Because of this he was hated by Jews, and missionaries
considered him an associate [32]. Berr sharply attacked Anspach's
Paroles d'un croyant (1842), for not being sufficiently tolerant of
Christians [33]. He criticized Salvàdor's book *La Loi de Moïse* (1822)
as inspired by fanaticism and written by a man of poor erudition [34].
He seconded the attack in *Journal des Débats* by Chief Rabbi
Abraham de Cologna against Noah's idea of founding a Jewish
state. Such a project—Berr wrote— was anti-social. The existence
of Jews as a dispersed people among other nations should be
considered as a definite condition. The only possible and acceptable
modification of such a condition and of the Jewish messianic idea
of the future would be the establishment of a centre for universal

[31] *L'Espérance, Courrier de Nancy.* July 20, 1843.
[32] TSARPHATI, pp. 175, 724.
[33] *Archives israélites*, iv, (1843), 228-29.
[34] Michel Berr, *Lettre adressée au Courrier des tribunaux, sur l'ouvrage de
Salvator et les articles de M. Dupin sur cet ouvrage.* n.p., n.d.; *Un mot de M.
Michel Berr* ... (see note 44), p. 17.

worship at the place of the ancient and divine revelation [35].

Although he was an admirer of Christianity, Michel Berr was never converted. He remained an active Jew all his life at a time when many of his generation did become Christians. Those he disliked and attacked openly, as, for example, the convert Drach [36]. Nevertheless he was viewed with suspicion by most Jews, who attributed to him pro-Christian sentiments.

Berr's inconsistency led him to defend conservative Jews and to criticize the leaders of the reform movement, such as a member of the Committee of the first Jewish public school in Paris, who dared to attack the orthodox elements. In 1824, Berr did not approve of a competition for the best study of Alsatian Jewry because the rules contained an attack on Jewish traditions and customs. He was critical of Tsarphati (Olry Terquem), leader of the French reform Jews and author of the *Lettres tsarpatiques*, for the latter's attacking the use of Hebrew in prayers and other Jewish traditions [37].

It is difficult to reconcile Michel Berr's views on assimilation with his criticism of Olry Terquem's ideas for the reform of religious practices. Berr's own explanation of this inconsistency was to recall Mme de Staël's warning to those, who after Brumaire 18th were afraid of a Jacobin comeback: "The Jacobins! we will fight them, and you too" [38].

Possibly the inconsistency in his position on reform of Jewish customs was a result of his father's influence. The old leader of the Lorraine Jews was one of the first *maskilim* in France. However, in the last years of his life he changed his views on many problems connected with the reform movement. Thus although he had earlier favored prayers in the French language, in his latter years he urged that "the language of the Jews in the Hebrew alphabet" be used in administration matters in order to safeguard Jewish traditions [39].

---

[35] Michel Berr, *Lettre sur les Israélites et le Judaïsme* . . . Paris, 1825, p. 6.

[36] *Ibid.*, p. 3; *L'Espérance*, July 20, 1843.

[37] See Berr's *Un mot* . . ., pp. 9-10; *Lettre au rédacteur de l'Argus* . . .; *Lettre sur les premières livraisons* . . ., p. 9 (see notes 10, 42). On the general aspect of Reform movement in France see Z. SZAJKOWSKI, *Conflicts between Orthodox and Reformers in France. Horev*, xiv-xv, (1960), pp. 253-92 (in Hebrew)

[38] Michel Berr, *Lettre sur les Israélites et le Judaïsme, au directeur du Panorama des Nouveautés Parisienne.* [Paris,] 1825, 4, 6, 4 pp.

[39] "Dès mon installation comme membre du Consistoire, j'ai remarqué avec étonnement que dans aucuns arrêtés ni procès-verbaux des séances, il

The fact that he was the son of Berr-Isaac Berr possibly deterred him from conversion. In any case, the idea of conversion did not fit Berr's notion of his own destiny. He sincerely believed that he was superior to all other Jewish leaders of his generation and that it was his appointed *rôle* to direct the Central Jewish Consistory. Berr considered himself a great literary talent. He was sure of his ability to reform the Jewish religion, and to make it more poetical.

ne se trouve pas une seule citation hebraïque. Il m'a paru que les membres composant alors l'administration ne s'attachent qu'à la exécution scrupulante des décisions sanhédrinales comme une nouvelle loi modifiée, et comme la seule à suivre. Et par conséquence le texte sacré de la Sainte Bible devait être exclu de l'administion du Consistoire, et bien plus encore, un autre caractère hébraïque qui nous a été transmis par nos ancêtres, et qui souvent faisoit la consolation des pères, mères et enfants qui se trouvaut éloignés les uns des autres épanchoient mutuellement leurs peines, leurs espoirs enfin, se communiquient reciproquement les secrets de famille dans un idiome au caratère particulier non connu par tout le monde. Depuis quelques mois seulement que j'ai l'avantage de présider les séances du Consistoire, j'ai remarqué que plusieurs lettres écrites en langue et caratères hebraïques par des vieillards de nos coreligionnaires ou par d'autres qui ne savent pas écrire en français, étant de notre circonscription, se trouverent entre les mains du secrétaire, non Israélite, et auxquelles cependant on devoit répondre. J'en ai fait l'observation à MM. mes collègues, qui m'ont répondu que lorsque Mr. le Grand-Rabbin voudra bien leur faire connoitre le contenu ils feront la réponse en français. Celà m'a paru comme si les fonctions essentielles du Consistoire étoient de faire oublier parmi nous cette langue sacrée de laquelle cependant nous trouvons la croyance de notre sainte religion. Heureusement pour moi et pour mes co-religionnaires qui pensent comme moi, en commencant par M. le Grand-Rabbin, qui sans doute a fait inutilément les mêmes remarques avant moi, heureusement dis-je pour nous, nous possedons la lettre ministrielle du 14 Mars 1820, relative à l'horrible attentat commis sur S. A. R. Mgr le Duc du Berry. Son Exc. le Ministre de l'Intérieur, en nous transmettant les ordres et les volontés du Roi nous prescrit spécialement de faire la cérémonie funèbre pour le repos de l'àme de ce prince Royal que toute la France pleure *selon nos rites et usages*. Le mode de cette triste cérémonie que j'avois proposé en déposant cette lettre sur le Bureau ayant été adoptés unanimémant et Mr. le Grand-Rabbin s'étant empressé de répondre à notre invitation en composant une complainte et une prière en hébreu, nous avons eu l'honneur d'en informer le ministre en lui adressant un exemplaire, écrit à la main en caractères hébraïques, tel que nous l'avons obtenu sur le mont Sinaï par les mains de Moïse, fidèle serviteur de Dieu, à côté d'une traduction imprimée en langue françoise. Qu'en est-il resulte? Un article flatteur pour nous dans le Journal de Paris du 30 mars dernier [1820], que nous devons regarder comme une approbation encore plus flateuse de la part de son Exc. le ministre de l'Intérieur. Le procès-verbal de notre séance extraordinaire du 19 mars [1820], devant indispensablement contenir le texte de la complainte-prière en hébreu ainsi que la traduction en françois, comment donc MM. les collègues peuvent-ils persister à ne pas admettre, non seulement un secrétaire rédacteur israélite, selon mon premier amendement, mais encore mon second amendement concernant l'établissement d'un 4me registre pour le texte hébraïque. Je persiste donc dans mon amendement" (in the General Historical Archives of Israel, Jerusalem. See also SZAJKOWSKI (see note 45), pp. 240-41).

He wanted to be at once the Châteaubriand and the Luther of Judaism. His obsession was to occupy a high administrative position. He was under the illusion that one day he would be called to occupy a seat in some highly respected body, as for example, the *Académie des Inscriptions* [40]. He anticipated the fulfillment of his dream not as a converted Jew, but as leader of a vigorous representative body. (Berr expressed the belief that one day the Sanhedrin convened by Napoleon I would be revitalized [41].)

Although he failed in his efforts to become a member of the Central Consistory, Berr was not satisfied to accept lesser positions and, as a result, did not belong to any important organised Jewish body. He did not hesitate to publish frequent attacks in non-Jewish periodicals on Jewish leaders and in connection with matters relating to purely religious and social problems of communal Jewish life. Thus, he sent to the editor of a non-Jewish periodical a long letter against the editors of *L'Israélite français*, the first Franco-Jewish periodical, published in 1817-1818. He then reprinted his letter with notes, as a pamphlet. The editors of *L'Israélite français* issued a pamphlet in reply, and Berr in turn replied in a second. According to Carmoly, Berr's hatred of the editors of *L'Israélite français* was the result of their decision to make some changes in an article he had submitted for publication [42]. A few years later, Berr and a group of other Jews, planned another Franco-Jewish periodical, *Annales israélites*. However, Berr antagonized so many leaders of the project that nothing but a prospectus was published [43]. Berr's attacks against the Jewish Consistories often exposed him to public ridicule. The anonymous author of a pamphlet published in 1824 wrote that Berr's fame as a scientist was based only on the large number of local academies

[40] TSARPHATI, pp. 171-74. One of his friends publicly demanded the granting to Michel Michel of a high position in the Ministry of Religious Affairs. *Extrait du Corsaire du 8 mars* 1828. Paris, le 6 mars 1828. [Signed J. Raphaël, de Lyon, artiste.] [Paris, 1828.] 3 pp. 8°.

[41] Berr, *Eloge de Benjamin-Constant* . . . (see note 12), pp. 166-67 (note 14).

[42] *L'Israélite français. Ouvrage moral et littéraire; rédigé par une Société de gens de lettres.* Paris, 1817-1818; Michel Berr, *Lettre sur les premières livraisons de "l'Israélite français", adressée à M. Villenave, rédacteur en chef des "Annales politiques".* Paris, 1818, 31 pp.; *Réponse à la Lettre imprimée de M. Michel Berr, adressé à M. Villenave* . . ., Paris, 1818, 35 pp.: Michel Berr, *Sur une réponse à la brochure intitulée: Lettre sur les premières livraisons de l'Israélite Français.* Paris, 1818. 4 pp.; CARMOLY, p. 25.

[43] *Annales israélites. Ouvrage de morale, d'éducation et de littérature*, Paris, septembre 1823. 4 pp.; *Un mot à Michel Berr* . . . (see note 44), p. 17; M. Berr, *Lettre sur les Israélites* . . . (see note 38).

of which he was a member—in reality he was the *Garbet de la Littérature*; that he pretended to have an illegible handwriting so that nobody could detect his orthographic mistakes; that he was unable to hold any position for long; that he was denied membership in Jewish societies where his "presence provokes trouble and division"; etc. [44].

In his attacks on Franco-Jewish leaders Michel Berr was, most probably, influenced by the example of his aged father. In the last years of his life Berr-Isaac Berr was in constant conflict with the Jewish Consistory of Nancy. Until his last days, Berr-Isaac Berr, formerly recognized as leader of the Lorraine Jews, called himself the elder (*ancien*) of the Nancy community and he so signed his letters and petitions. But this was only a title. The real leaders of the Nancy community were the merchant Lipman Lipman (1771-1843) and Rabbi Baruch Gougenheim (1752-1842). The elder Berr's attempts to aggrandize his position in the community and to control its activities provoked constant conflicts [45].

Michel Berr's inconsistency in political matters was sharply exposed during the Restoration and the July Monarchy. During the Hundred Days of Napoleon I's reign in 1815 (March 20-June 22), Berr published his memorable pamphlet in support of the *Acte additonnel*. The object of this legislation was to give Napoleon's new regime the appearance of parliamentary govenmernt. Berr's pamphlet was, undoubtedly, one of the best and notable of those published in favour of that important piece of legislation. Berr signed the pamphlet with his initials only, as if afraid of possible reprisals in the event of Napoleon's defeat. In fact, right at the beginning of the second Restoration he declared himself in favour of Louis XVIII, in a characteristic expression of opinion on important political and social matters, in a note to a critic on a study by Pierre Joseph Maleville (1778-1832). Maleville had advocated the restoration of Louis XVIII and had been rewarded with many honours and high official posts. Berr praised Maleville for favoring the Restoration of Louis XVIII, and predicted that

[44] *Un mot à Michel Berr*. Paris, 1824. 18 pp. Berr replied with the following pamphlet: *Un mot de Michel Berr, avec des notes; En réponse à un Pamphlet anonyme, intitulé: Un mot à Michel Berr, publié par des Juifs de Paris*. Paris, 1824. 64 pp. For Berr's attacks against the Central Consistory see also Michel Berr, *Extrait du "Corsaire" du 24 juillet* 1828. n.p., n.d. 4 pp.; *Idem, Extrait du "Corsaire" du 4 août* 1828. Paris, n.d. 4 pp.

[45] Z. SZAJKOWSKI, *Berr-Isaac Berr's last Years, Davke*, No. xxiv, pp. 238-40 (in Yiddish).

the King would follow in the path of Henry IV and Louis XVI [46].
(Another Jew, Mathias Mayer Dalmbert, expressed in a pamphlet
the attitude of the liberal middle-class toward the *Acte additionnel*.[47])

A pamphlet, published by Michel Berr after the events of July
1830, and sold for the benefit of the victims of the glorious three
days of July, again revealed the author as an inconsistent and
amateur politician. The following is a characteristic passage:
"The dreams of my youth are realized! Justice and liberty, glory,
wisdom, virtue, national and protective laws, a throne protecting
the laws of the people, an undissolved pact between the government
and the nation . . . " He praised Napoleon I's genius as a soldier
as well as his good intentions on behalf of France, but saw no
merit in him as a legislator and politician. Berr readily aknowledged
that he favoured Louis XVIII. He did not extol the Restoration's
Charter, but hoped for improvements in its character. Only Louis
Philippe had all the qualities of a liberator, a man who carried
"the national colours, the banner of freedom, glory, laws and
liberty." In addition, Berr advocated all sorts of ideas that indicated
the politically immature bent of his mind: He defended the memory
of General Charles François Dumoriez, Louis Philippe's commander in the field during the Revolution, whose conspiratorial activities drove him into exile along with Louis Philippe [48]. Berr
praised the "noble and unfortunate" Girondists. According to
him, the Bourbon dynasty fell because it tried to rule by divine
right, instead of with the consent of the representatives of the
people. Berr was even ready to accord hereditary power to Louis

[46] M.B. [Michel Berr], *Observations sur l'acte additionnel aux Constitutions
de l'Empire et sur notre situation politique.* Paris, 1815. 44 pp.; *Idem, Notice
sur les Benjamites rétablis en Israël, par M. de Maleville.* Paris, 1816, p. 19
(reprinted from *Mercure Etranger*, No. xxi, 1816); *Idem, Lettre à Monsieur
le Comte Lanjuinais, membre du Sénat* . . . Paris, 1814. 53 pp. (contains praises
of Louis XVIII); Emile Le Gallo, *Les Cent Jours.* Paris, 1924, p. 233 (on
Michel Berr's pamphlet, *libéral aux inclinations bonapartistes*). See also PIERRE
JOSEPH DE MALEVILLE, *Les Benjamites rétablis en Israël, poéme traduit de
l'hébreu.* Paris, 1816. xxxiv, 302 pp.; *Idem, Au gouvernement provisoire et aux
deux Chambres.* Paris, 27 juin 1815; *Défense de M. de Maleville* . . . n.p., 1
juillet 1815. 11 pp.

[47] MIAS M. [MATHIAS MAYER] DALMBERT, ancien élève de l'Ecole Polytechnique, et Ls [Louis] Giraudeau, ex-chef des diverses Administrations,
Observations sur l'Acte additionnel aux constitutions de l'Empire. Paris, avril
1815. 41 pp.; E. LE GALO, *op. cit.*, pp. 232-33.

[48] On the attitude of Dumouriez towards Jews see Z. SZAJKOWSKI, *French
Jews in the Armed Forces during the Revolution of* 1789, *Proceedings of the
American Academy for Jewish Research*, xxvi (1957), pp. 157-58.

Philippe and his family—a view which drew sharp criticism from the republicans. He favoured an indirect "double vote" through electoral bodies. Thus, a mayor would be appointed by the King from among municipal councillors chosen by an electoral body. The mayor would then represent both the people and the government. Only those paying not less than 300 francs in taxes would be eligible to serve as deputies; the right of the *pair* would be hereditary, etc. He proposed the erection of many monuments to commemorate even living heroes: Louis XVI, who granted rights to Protestants and Jews; Louis XVIII, in recognition of his Charter; the Girondist Vergniaud, a great orator; Benjamin Constant, J. J. R. de Cambacérès, J. E. M. Portalis, General L. L. Hoche; Napoleon himself, "not to the sovereign, not even to the Consul, but to the conqueror of Europe, the hero of Egypt, the defender of the invaded fatherland and to the victim of Saint Helena"; but most of all to General Lafayette; and also to A. M. C. de Lamartine, F. G. P. Guizot, Victor Cousin, F. A. Châteaubriand. This would have been, indeed, an extraordinary gallery of monuments, capable of satisfying all social, religious, philosophical and political views. Michel Berr hoped in vain for some high position in the new regime through the help of his many friends who became leading figures. Disappointed, he left Paris for his native Nancy. In view of his extravagant ideas, Berr's republican friends could hardly have supported him [49].

Shortly before his death, Michel Berr entertained some expectations that the government would allow him a pension as a writer. He even dreamed of obtaining the distinguished *Légion d'honneur*. But these hopes, too, were unfulfilled [50]. In the last years of his life he was isolated from all influential Jews, ridiculed by many of them, and made himself ridiculous by adding to his name a long list of titles, and unable to forget his grudge against the recognized leaders of French Jewry. In this period Berr's only joy was his son, Isaïe (Charles), who became a well known

[49] Michel Berr, *Du passé, du présent et de l'avenir*. Paris, 1830. 30 pp.; *Idem, Encore . . .* (see note 8); *Idem, Du rabbinisme . . .* (see note 8), p. viii ("notre glorieuse révolution de Juillet"); TSARPHATI, p. 178.

Other political pamphlets by Berr: *Lettre à Monsieur le Comte Lanjuinais sur des sujets politiques*. Paris, 1814. 53 pp.; *Le Hibou et les oiseaux, apologue politique*. Paris, 1815; *Au Rédacteur de "l'Indépendant de la Moselle", sur le dernier attentat à la vie du roi des Français et de ses fils*. Nancy, n.d. 3 pp.

[50] *L'Espérance*, July 20, 1843.

lawyer of Metz and who sometimes also wrote on Jewish problems. Later, the son was procurator in Riom and other cities [51].

After Michel Berr's death, a Nancy newspaper summed up his influence on the social and religious life of the Jews in France as *nil* [52]. Of course, Michel Berr's actions and writings were always impractical [53]. Yet, in spite of his eccentricity and his exaggerated seeking of public attention, Berr could be described by Gerson Ben Levi as one of the "eminent men amongst us" [54].

[51] *Archives israélites*, v (1844), pp. 288-89; J. BERR, *ibid.*, i (1840), pp. 617-19 (on *more judaico*).

[52] *L'Espérance*, July 20, 1843.

[53] "C'était de l'agitation et non de l'activité" (TSARPHATI, p. 172).

[54] G. Ben Levi, *Moral and Religious Tales for the Young . . .* London, [1846,] p. xv (translated from the original French edition).

THE JEWISH SAINT-SIMONIANS AND SOCIALIST
ANTISEMITES IN FRANCE*

> *"Le socialisme, un jour, s'étant oublie,*
> *l' antisemitisme fut. Il n'est pas de sottes*
> *origines."* (Tabarant, 1898)

The movement inspired by Claude-Henri Saint-Simon and the views of its opponents regarding the Jews are significant phases of the anti-Jewish trend in 19th-century France. Since the publication of Georges Weill's article on Saint-Simonism and the Jews in 1895,[1] a number of valuable studies relating to the subject have appeared. A study of the Jewish adherents of Saint-Simonism and of the part played by the opponents of the movement will reveal the significant contribution of the early French socialists to the background of Edouard Drumont. The essay presented here is intended to analyze the political current which gave birth to Drumont's first antisemitic book in 1886. Claude Henri Saint-Simon (1760-1825) founded his movement in the post-Napoleonic years, when France was striving for economic recovery. This process, however, was hampered by the lack of enterprising business-men particularly men with substantial capital at their disposal. The masses, it is true, looked with a hostile eye at the manufacturers and the bankers and yet the man in the street had the naive belief that "capital" was capable of achieving miracles. The prevailing type of French capitalist, however, was at that time the small businessman, who had to borrow from others of the same class, a state of affairs which led to the emergence of small co-operative enterprises. The government was not in position to lend any substantial assistance.

This was the situation in France, when Saint-Simonism emerged, pro-

---

* Read before a meeting of the Yiddish Scientific Institute on May 26, 1946.

[1] Weill, Georges, "Les Juifs et le Saint-Simonisme," in *Revue des études juives*, vol. xxxi (1895) 261-80.

Originally published in *Jewish Social Studies*, vol. IX (1947).

claiming that politics must become a social science. The Saint-Simonians never mentioned the exploitation of the workers, nor did they put forward the demand for social equality. They did talk a great deal, however, about improving the lot of the poor, about the need for organizing in order to master and exploit the natural resources and the machines, and about centralized enterprises and big markets, serving not only individuals, but the masses as well. These ideas were draped in the cloak of a new religion, announced by the "prophet," Saint-Simon. The adherents of Saint-Simonism were to be found mainly among the students of the Polytechnicum, the young bankers and businessmen.[2] What Léon Halévy said about Emile Péreire, a Jewish Saint-Simonian, applies to other followers of the new gospel as well: all firmly believed that the moment was close at hand, when man would conquer nature and matter.[3] This school consisted essentially of utopian aristocrats with far-reaching ideals; Saint-Simonism never became a mass movement. While the Saint-Simonist dream of a new religion was stillborn, the practical aspects of the movement proved more lasting: the activities of its adherents had a considerable share in the industrialization of the country and in the strengthening of the structure of French capitalism.

Saint-Simon had never studied Jewish problems, although this did not deter him from having an unfavorable opinion of the Jews.[4] This, however, is of little consequence here. As Sebastien Charléty, one of the best historians of Saint-Simonism, has rightly pointed out, the history of the movement began after Saint-Simon's death.[5] The real founder was a Jewish youth, Benjamin Olinde Rodrigues (1795-1851); it was from him that Enfantin, who was to become the "father" of the Saint-Simonian temple, received Saint-Simon's ideological heritage.[6] Rodrigues was born in Bordeaux in a merchant's family, which moved to Paris, where the father was for a time secretary of the Sanhedrin.[7] Rodrigues spent his

[2] Pinet, G., "L'Ecole polytechnique et les Saint-Simoniens," in *Revue de Paris,* vol. iii (1894) 73-96.

[3] Halévy, Léon, *F. Halévy* (Paris 1863) p. 17.

[4] "Ce peuple sombre, concentré, devoré de l'orgueil," in *Oeuvres de Saint-Simon et d'Enfantin* (Paris 1865-78) vol. xix, p. 178.

[5] Charléty, Sebastian, *Histoire du Saint-Simonisme* (Paris 1931) p. 25.

[6] *Globe* (April 20, 1832).

[7] Courtéault, Paul, "Un Bordelais Saint-Simonien," in *Revue philomathique de Bordeaux et du Sud-Ouest,* vol. xxviii (1925) 152; Hildenfinger, P., "Un Ami des juifs en 1810," in *Univers Israélite,* vol. xcvii (1904) 304.

youth in a Jewish milieu, which soon became emancipated and even assimilated, but nevertheless remained exposed to antisemitism.[8] Although Rodrigues was an exceptionally able young man, he was not admitted, because of his Jewish descent, to the Ecole Normale Supérieure and, therefore, shifted to banking and to the Polytechnicum, where he met Saint-Simon and became his intimate friend, associate and counselor. Another young friend of Saint-Simon's was a neighbor of Rodrigues, Léon Halévy, who was for a time Saint-Simon's secretary and who became during the years following the master's death in 1825 one of his most active disciples.

Léon Halévy was a son of Elie Halévy (Halphen) (1760-1826), who came from Germany to Paris as a young man and was known as the author of a poem dedicated to Napoleon I (1801).[9] Elie Halévy worked as a clerk in the Jewish consistory; he was the author of a Jewish catechism[10] and edited the first French-Jewish periodical, *L'Israelite Francais*.[11] He sent his children, Léon and Fromenthal, to the Charlemagne lyceum, a step which had considerable repercussion among the Parisian Jews.[12] According to the testimony of Léon, the father had no direct influence on the education of his children; both sons grew up to be well-educated men. Léon Halévy became a professor of the Polytechnicum, secretary to Saint-Simon and a noted writer and his brother achieved prominence in music and literature.[13] Léon Halévy also suffered on account of his Jewish descent,[14] though he wrote once that the French Jews have no reason to fear intolerance any more. Michel Berr, a former secretary of the San-

[8] Posener, S., "La Première génération d'Israélites français après l'émancipation," in *Univers Israélite* (1903) no. 42-44; Bloch, Maurice, "La Société juive en France depuis la Révolution," in *Revue des études juives*, vol. xxxvi (1904); Berman, Léon, *Histoire des juifs en France* (Paris 1937) p. 397, 413-14.

[9] *Archives Israélites*, vol xliv (1883) 296-97; *Allgemeine Zeitung des Judentums*, Beiblatt no. 1; Graetz, H., *Geschichte der Juden*, vol. xi, p. 217-18.

[10] Halévy, Elie, *Instruction religieuse et moral à l'usage de la jeunesse israélite* (Metz 1820); cf. *Catalogue général de livres imprimés*. vol. lxvii p. 1014; Halévy, *op. cit.*, p. 7.

[11] *L'Israelite français, ouvrage moral et littéraire, rédigé par une société de gens de lettres* (Paris 1817-18); cf. B[err], M[ichel], *Lettre sur les premières livraisons de L'Israélite Français, addressée à M. Villenave* (Paris 1818); Posener, S., in *Parizer Haint* (January 23, 1931).

[12] *Archives Israélites*, vol. xxxiv (1883) 296-97.

[13] Halévy, *op. cit.*, p. 8. Some have erroneously made Fromenthal also a Saint-Simonian: cf. Malon, Benoit, *Histoire du Socialisme* (Paris 1883) vol. ii, p. 35.

[14] I. M., "Four generations," (Yiddish) in *Paris* (August 30, 1935); cf. Kahan, Daniel, in *Revue juive de Lorraine* (July 1935).

hedrin, in 1825 pointed out in answer to Halévy that the position of French Jewry was still far from satisfactory.[15]

The parents of Olinde Rodrigues and of Léon Halévy lived in the same house and were good friends;[16] the young men used to meet very often. The apartments of Halévy and Rodrigues became literary "salons" where well-educated Jewish youth of Paris and their non-Jewish friends used to meet to discuss literature, art and politics. It was at these gatherings that Rodrigues recruited new followers of Saint-Simonism — his own brother, Eugène, who died prematurely in 1830, Baron d'Eichthal and the Péreire brothers, Isaac and Emile, who were related to the Rodrigues.[17] Baron Gustave d'Eichthal was born in a family of Jewish bankers from Bavaria named Seligmann.[18] The Seligmanns migrated to Paris and after some time their bank was taken over by the Mirabeaux.[19] According to some sources, when d'Eichthal was born, his parents were already baptised, but Weill contends that Gustave embraced the Christian faith as a young man.[20] D'Eichthal himself once confessed to "Father" Enfantin that at the age of fourteen he had become a Christian and at nineteen a Saint-Simonian.[21] D'Eichthal said later, in the preface to a pamphlet, which he published together with a negro Saint-Simonian, Ismail Urbain, that in his childhood he had often suffered because of his Jewish name. He wrote, at that period, to a friend: Urbain and I, a negro and a Jew, are "two outcasts, two prophets."[22]

The brothers Jacob Emile (1800-74) and Isaac Péreire (1806-80) came from an old Sephardic family which had settled in Bordeaux. Their grandfather was the famous Jacob Rodrigues Péreire (1715-80), the first teacher of deaf mutes in France.[23] The Péreire brothers too were students

[15] Berr, Michel, *Lettre sur les israélites et le judaisme au Directeur du Panorama des nouveautés parisiennes* (Paris 1825) p. 2.

[16] Halévy, *op. cit.*, p. 17.

[17] Malzévin, T., *Histoire des juifs à Bordeaux* (Bordeaux 1875) p. 328-29.

[18] Michaud and Villenave, *Histoire du Saint-Simonisme et de la famille de Rothschild* (Paris 1847) p. 47.

[19] Hamon, Augustin (F. A.), and X. Y. Z., *Les Maîtres de la France* (Paris 1936) p. 241.

[20] Weill, Georges, *L'Ecole Saint-Simonienne* (Paris 1896) p. 122.

[21] Charléty, *op. cit.* p. 73. He was, nevertheless, identified as one of the Jewish Saint-Simonians by Lazare, Bernard, *L'Antisémitisme, son histoire et ses causes*, 2nd edition (Paris 1934) vol. ii, p. 199 and Posener, S., in *Univers Israélite* (1930) no. 42-43.

[22] D'Eichtal, Gustave, and Urban, Ismail, *Lettres sur la race noire et la race blanche* (Paris 1839) p. 12-13.

[23] Séguin, E., *J. R. Péreire* (Paris 1847); Léon, Henry, *Histoire des juifs de Bordeaux* (Paris 1893) p. 406.

at the Polytechnicum and thus found themselves within the orbit of Saint-Simonism. Of the other Jewish Saint-Simonians who joined the group at a somewhat later date mention may be made of Sareles[24] and the physician Léon Simon; the latter was noted for advocating homeopathy on the ground that it is a cheap method of curing diseases and, therefore, of particular value to the workers.[25]

II

The number of active and prominent Jewish Saint-Simonians at no time exceed a dozen. One must, however, bear in mind that the Saint-Simonians were, in general, a small sect and that it was precisely the few Jewish members who play the major part in the practical realization of Saint-Simonian teachings. Thus the participation of Jews in this movement was very conspicuous, a fact of which both Jews and antisemites have made much. Jewish apologetic writers used to exclaim: "Look at the immediate results of Jewish emancipation! A handful of Jews have played an important part in the economic reconstruction of France!" The historian Léon Berman, for instance, rightly asserts that Rothschild and the Péreire brothers helped France to make up for the delay in her industrial development.[26] Alexander Weill, a Jewish writer, of whom we shall speak at length later, wrote (1867) that "since the death of the [Second] Republic the Jews, together with the Saint-Simonians, played a leading part in the country's financial, industrial and commercial development."[27] The famous Jewish anarchist, Bernard Lazare, an active participant in the campaign to exonerate Dreyfus, declared likewise that the Jews were instrumental in realizing the Saint-Simonian slogans of the rising bourgeoisie. Lazare believed that in this instance, too, the Jews acted as exponents of bourgeois philosophy and proved the most reliable allies of the bourgeoisie; this was, to Lazare, the main reason why the conservative elements were largely anti-Jewish. It is, indeed, a fact that the Catholic Church had looked for some time upon the growth of industry with considerable apprehension. The French Revolution, maintained Lazare, emancipated the Jews, because the bourgeoisie was vitally inter-

---

[24] Posener, loc. cit., p. 456.

[25] Cf. Lorenz, Otto, Catalogue général de la librairie française, vol. iv, p. 402, vol. vi, p. 572.

[26] Berman, op. cit., p. 405.

[27] Weill, Alexandre, Mes Batailles (Paris 1867) p. 291.

ested in liberating those who were particularly fitted for the role of pioneers of industry and finance.[28] As we shall see later, Eugène Rodrigues expressed a similar opinion at an even earlier date.

Various wits used to call the Saint-Simonians "new Christians," or even "new Jews."[29] Others observed good-naturedly that Saint-Simonians and Jews had one quality in common — both helped each other.[30] The noted republican journalist and historian, Taxile Delord (1815-77), told the following story: A Frenchman wanted to open a store; his friend, however, tried to dissuade him from this plan, as the would-be shopkeeper did not have a Jewish partner. The former answered: "Never mind, I have two Saint-Simonians."[31] On the other hand, in view of the strong ideological opposition to Saint-Simonism on the part of Fourierists, Proudhonists and adherents of other socialist schools, the active participation of Jews in the Saint-Simonist movement gave the impetus to a new "socialist" brand of antisemitism.

The Fourierists, the Proudhonists and the plain Jew-baiters regarded Saint-Simonism as a Jewish venture. Not only — thus ran the consensus — did a few able Jews take an active part in the Saint-Simonist movement; the point is that they did it precisely *because* they were Jews. Thus the Jewish share in Saint-Simonism assumed the proportions of spiritual hegemony. Even some Jewish scholars seem inclined at times to accept this version. The late S. Posener wrote that the participation of Jews in the movement was a form of protest against the persecution of their people. It was his distinguished Jewish origin, according to Posener, that induced Baron D'Eichthal to espouse the Saint-Simonist gospel, for in his childhood he had suffered because of his Jewish descent.[32] Olinde Rodrigues declared at a Saint-Simonist meeting in 1832 that on the day a Jew met Saint-Simon and found in him his new father, he became a member of a new universal family. "The feudal Christian gave a paternal kiss to the persecuted Jew who had crucified Jesus."[33] An interesting and sound assertion was made by an active socialist, who wrote in 1899 that the particularly conspicuous part played by the Jews in the development of

[28] Lazare, *op cit.*, p. 48-51.

[29] Rodrigues, Eugène, *Lettres sur la religion et la politique* (Paris 1832) p. 272.

[30] Castille, Hippolyte, *Lè Père Enfantin* (Paris 1859) p. 4-5.

[31] Delord, Taxile, *Les Troisièmes pages du journal "Le Siècle", portraits modernes* (Paris 1861) p. 110.

[32] Posener, *loc. cit.*, p. 526.

[33] *Globe* (January 16, 1832).

French trade and finance was due not so much to specific Jewish features, as to the fact that the non-Jewish population was for a time rather backward in this respect, while the Jews took the initiative.[34] Eugène Rodrigues argued in his *Lettres sur la réligion et la politique,* in which he set forth the basic tenets of the Saint-Simonist religion, that the Jews had been by nature an industrial people. This trait became even more pronounced as the result of the Jewish dispersion: in the diaspora it was the function of the Jews to promote industry.[35]

At first the Saint-Simonians dreamed of a complete emancipation of the Jews and tried to do something in order to further it. For some time d'Eichthal, Enfantin and others believed that it would be possible to enlist Austria's aid in liberating the Jewish people. At the beginning of 1837 d'Eichthal went to Austria, where he sought an audience with Prince Charles in order to persuade him that the Jewish people had a new religious mission to fulfill and that it was, therefore, Austria's sacred duty to undertake the task of emancipating the Jews. Enfantin felt at the time very hopeful about d'Eichthal's trip, although only a few years earler (1831) he had gone on record, in his pronouncements on European politics, as a bitter foe of Austria. Perhaps in 1837 Enfantin toyed with the idea of enlisting the support of the foreign statesman, and he obviously gave credence to the rumours about Metternich's friendly attitude toward Saint-Simonism. D'Eichthal's trip, however, proved a complete failure.[36] Enfantin wrote in a letter to Heinrich Heine, who had at that time Saint-Simonist leanings:[37] "The Orient is calling upon God's chosen people; here is the wandering Jew, he is more than an individual, his name is Israel."[38] Enfantin, the "Father" of the sect, prophesied that the liberation would come through the Father and the Mother; the latter was about to appear in the guise of a Jewish woman from Turkey. "A society for welcoming the Mother" came into being, and the Saint-Simonians issued an appeal to Jewish women, urging them to participate in the welcome.[39]

[34] Rouanet, Gustave, "La Question juive," in *Revue Socialiste,* vol. xxix (1889) 29.

[35] Rodrigues, Eugéne, *op. cit.,* p. 118.

[36] D'Allemagne, H. R., *Les Saint-Simoniens* (Paris 1930) p. 196; *idem, Prosper Enfant et les grandes entreprises du XIXe siècle* (Paris 1935) p. 8-9, 118; Charléty, *op. cit.,* p. 247.

[37] Butler, E. M., "Heine and St. Simonism," in *The Saint Simonian Religion in Germany* (Cambridge 1926); Clarke, Margaret A., *Heine et la Monarchie de Juillet* (Paris 1927).

[38] D'Allemagne, *Prosper Enfant,* p. 8-9.

[39] Colin, Auguste, *Aux femmes juives et à toutes celles qui liront cette parole, salut, au nom de Dieu, Père et Mère* (Lyon, July 1833).

On Rosh Hashana, after the funeral of a Saint-Simonian, d'Eichthal and four other adherents of the "new religion" went to the synagogue, dressed in Saint-Simonist costumes.[40] Always so practical and down-to-earth, the Saint-Simonians became singularly vague and confused whenever they were faced with Jewish problems. All their plans concerning the emancipation of the Jews used to dissolve into that fog of mystery, with which the Saint-Simonians liked to surround themselves.

The only Jewish Saint-Simonian who exhibited some common sense in his approach to the Jewish question was Jules Carvallo (1820-1916), who played, however, no important part in the movement. Carvallo's proclamation advocating an international Jewish Congress, published in the *Univers Israélite* of February 1851, contributed substantially toward the establishment, in 1860, of the Alliance Israelite Universelle.[41] Like many other Saint-Simonians, Carvallo had graduated from the Polytechnicum, and two years later from a school for road-building. He worked for a time as a road-builder for the Péreire brothers, chiefly abroad, where he became interested in the position of the local Jewish community, and felt that it was his duty to make an effort to improve the lot of his co-religionists. In Carvallo's appeal of 1851 we find an echo of the Saint-Simonist theory that the Jewish people were given to the world in order to improve it, that the Jews have a historic mission to fulfill. In order, however, to be able to live up to this gigantic task, argues Carvallo, the Jewish people must, first of all, unite in order to defend themselves and "to protect the life of those whom God has entrusted with the task of carrying out His great plans." Carvallo's call for a Jewish congress was the only practical step taken by a Saint-Simonian in order to relieve the sufferings of the Jews. In spite of his adherence to that sect, however, Carvallo remained essentially a devout Jew; his appeal appeared in an orthodox publication that had nothing to do with Saint-Simonism. One should add that by the time Carvallo's statement was published, Saint-Simonism was already on the decline and the only tangible effects of the active participation of Jews in the movement were the big fortunes, made by a few Jewish businessmen, such as the Péreire brothers, in the process of realizing the Saint-Simonist program of industralization.

The only prominent Saint-Simonian who was actively interested in

[40] "Les Souvenirs de Lambert-Bey," in *Archives Israélites* (1864) 211-15.
[41] Szajkowski, Z., "The Founding of the Alliance Israélite Universelle," (Yiddish) in *Yivo Bleter*, vol. xviii (1941) 4-5.

the emancipation of Jews, was the baptised Jew, d'Eichthal. The non-Jewish Saint-Simonians never took him seriously; they looked upon him as a sort of a quixotic dreamer. Michel Chévallier used to call him "the Jewish Tyrtaeus."[42]

At a later stage of Saint-Simonism it was not too difficult to find among its adherents evidence of some anti-Jewish feeling. Emile Barrault, the same Saint-Simonian who, in speaking of the mystical concept of the Jewish "Mother" from Turkey, asserted that "Jews provide the industrial and political link between various people, they are the bankers of the angels, they hold in their hands the clue to war and peace,"[43] the same Barrault, who, together with d'Eichthal, went to a synagogue after the funeral of a comrade, carried on in 1848 violent antisemitic propaganda.[44] Even Pierre Leroux had written a number of articles against the Jews,[45] and the gifted Saint-Simonist writer, George Sand, who cannot be accused of antisemitism, wrote to a friend in April 1857 that she saw in the Jew the type of man who aspires to become the king of the world and threatens to murder Jesus Christ, i.e. the ideal. George Sand expressed the fear lest within fifty years France become Jewish.[46] One exception ought to be mentioned, Adolphe Guéroult, a friend of Carvallo's, who later became the editor of a Saint-Simonist organ with a Bonapartist tinge, *L'Opinion Nationale,* in which he often published sympathetic articles about the Jews.[47] In 1847, as French consul in one of the Central European countries, Guéroult urged the French government and French Jewry to do something for the local Jews, for example, to set up a school for Jewish children with French as the language of instruction. The government, however, received this suggestion rather coldly and the French Jews "did not even bother to answer."[48]

III

Saint Simonism was a neutral terrain where people of various faiths

[42] Charléty, *op. city.* p. 247 (The poet Tyrtaeus is noted for inspiring the Spartans *ca.* 600 B.C.E. to subdue the Messenian rebels.)

[43] Barrault, Emile, *Aux Femmes juives* (1833?); cf. Charléty, *op. cit.,* p. 247.

[44] Barrault, Emile, *Lettres contemporaines, 3e livraison. Lettre à M. Rothschild (Paris* [August] 1848); Czynski, J., *Le Réveil d'Israél* (Paris 1848) p. 136, 155; Drumont, E., *La France juive* (Paris 1886) vol. i, p. 370.

[45] Czynski, *op. cit.,* p. 155.

[46] "George Sand antisémite," in *Univers Israélite,* vol. xxxviii (1882-83) 438-39.

[47] Guéroult, Adolphe, *Etudes de politique et philosophie religieuse* (Paris 1863) .

[48] *L'Opinion Nationale* (July 15, 1860).

could meet and fraternize particularly if they had not been previously more closely knit together by their respective religions. The Saint-Simonist philosophy was basically incompatible with Jewish religious tradition. Saint-Simonism attempted to effect a synthesis of all existing religious faiths, but it was Christianity that was to form the core of the new doctrine. In fact, as recent historical studies have clearly shown, it was not long before the Saint-Simonist apparatus started working full blast for the Catholic Church. Indeed, many of the members eventually developed into conventional Catholic propagandists,[49] while, with the exception of Carvallo, none of the Jewish Saint-Simonians was ever active in any sphere whatever of Jewish communal life. Willy-nilly the Jewish followers of Saint-Simonism were moving farther and farther away from Jewish tradition, as they proceeded down the path of the new religion, whose basis was Catholic.

Long after he had left the movement and had become engrossed in research, Gustave d'Eichthal wrote that he had learned from Saint-Simonism one important truth: that the final organization of modern society can be achieved only through the regeneration of Christianity. "I use, however, the word 'Christianity'," he added, "in the broadest possible sense in connection with Judaism from which Christianity has separated."[50] His son, Eugène d'Eichthal (1844-1936), an avowed foe of socialism,[51] wrote in the introduction to the collection of his father's writings that Gustave d'Eichthal tried to combine modern civilization with the Christian-Jewish tradition.[52] The historian Weill believed that d'Eichthal's active participation in the Saint-Simonist religious services, celebrated at their temple at Menilmontant and his zeal in learning the ways of the "new religion" and in studying the Bible were motivated by the ardent desire "to build a bridge of common religious tradition between Saint-Simonism and Judaism."[53] In reality, however, Gustave d'Eichthal was a fervent Christian, much more so than the other Saint-Simonians. In 1832 he confided to a friend that he had had a vision in which he had seen the Virgin and that Jesus Christ dwelled in his bosom.

[49] Brunet, George, Le Mysticisme social de Saint-Simon (Paris 1925) p. 123-25.

[50] D'Eichthal, Gustave, Mémoire sur le texte primitif du premier récit det la création (Paris 1875) p. 3-4.

[51] D'Eichthal, Eugène, Mes Griefs contre le Socialisme (Paris 1888) p. 12; cf. Tirard, Paul, in Revue des sciences politiques, vol. lix, p. 5-7.

[52] D'Eichthal, Gustave, Mélanges de critique biblique (Paris 1886) vol. ii.

[53] Weill, in Revue des études juives, vol. xxxi (1895) 266-67.

Some time earlier he had tried to make Enfantin a better Catholic.[54] The only vestige of d'Eichthal's ideas on Jews and Judaism was his persistent interest in Bible study, a subject on which he wrote several books.[55]

Léon Halévy, who left the Saint-Simonist movement at an early date, also became estranged from Jewish life, although he occasionally wrote on Jewish affairs[56] and published two booklets on ancient and modern Jewish history.[57] Halévy married a gentile girl[58] and was strongly influenced, through the medium of Saint-Simonism, by Christian ideas, although the Saint-Simonist concept of a new, regenerated Christianity deterred him from conversion. In his history of the Jewish people Halévy wrote that Judaism was intended to become eventually a universal religion, but it could not fulfill this mission without returning to the purity of the primitive Jewish faith, as Jesus had done.[59] The Jewish religion, argued Halévy, must be reformed, since it is an Asiatic religion.[60] The "father" of Saint-Simonism, Enfantin, praised Halévy's history highly and quoted with approval the passage dealing with the role of Jesus.[61] Halévy's history suggested to Enfantin the idea that the Jews were not living up to the standards set by the religion which they had given to the world. Similarly, another writer in a periodical with strong Saint-Simonist leanings, remarked that Halévy was no ordinary Jew but a philosopher.[62] In his preface to the credo of the first Saint-Simonians Halévy wrote that "Christianity as realized by the French Revolution has finally torn to shreds the curtain which obstructed our view."[63] Halévy later parted with the Saint-Simonians. He claimed that Saint-Simon did not want to be a God, that Saint-Simonism was intended to be a school, rather than a religion.[64] Halévy did not return, however, to Jewish tradition; he

[54] Allemagne, *St. Simonisme*, p. 264.

[55] Vernes, Maurice, *M. Gustave d'Eichthal et ses travaux sur l'Ancien Testament* (Paris 1887); Loeb, Isidore, in *Revue des études juives*, vol. xv (1887) 153-55.

[56] Halévy, Léon, "Egée, scène lyrique," in *L'Israélite Français* (1817) 137; "Les Juifs d'Afrique Centrale, Arabie, Chine, Malabar," in *Annales Critiques* (1856); "Sur un Arrêté de M. Cousin," in *Archives Israélites*, vol. i, p. 449.

[57] Halévy, Léon; *Résumé de l'histoire des juifs anciens* (Paris 1825); *Résumé de l'histoire des juifs modernes* (Paris 1828).

[58] *Archives Israélites*, vol. xxxxiv (1883) 206; Halévy, *F. Halévy*, p. 22.

[59] Halévy, *Résumé de l'histoire des juifs anciens*, p. 336-37.

[60] *Ibid*, p. 385.

[61] E[nfantin], in *Le Producteur*, vol. i (1825) 280-84.

[62] *Le Globe* (1825) 828.

[63] *Opinions littéraires, philosophiques et industrielles* (Paris 1825) p. 19.

[64] Halévy, Léon, *Saint Simon, ode* (Paris 1831).

never lived as a Jew, although he was buried in the Jewish cemetery. After his death an orthodox French-Jewish magazine wrote that "in general Léon Halévy does not belong to Judaism, except for his cradle and his grave."[65]

Spurred on by their Saint-Simonist philosophy, the Péreire brothers grew very rich, particularly during the reign of Napoleon III (1852-70); the Second Empire and Saint-Simonism seemed to have been made for each other.[66] In 1868 the property of the Péreire brothers was estimated as 160,000,000 francs.[67] Emile Péreire was the pioneer of railroad building in France.[68] The bankers, including Rothschild, came into the picture only after Emile Péreire had been granted by parliament the concession for the first railroad in France, from Paris to Saint-Germain (1835). Later the Péreire brothers initiated and founded new credit enterprises;[69] theirs was not an insignificant share in the growth of Paris.

The Péreire brothers eventually moved away from Jewish tradition (this is particularly true of the younger brother).[70] After the death of Emile Péreire the organ of the conservative French Jews wrote: "Let it be known that today a great Jew has fallen."[71] There is a story that when Emile Péreire was engaged in building the Bordeaux-Madrid railroad, arriving in Spain for the first time from which his ancestors had been banished, he exclaimed: *"Shema Israel!"*[72] When his brother, Isaac, died he was buried in accordance with Jewish rites but the above-quoted Jewish magazine wrote that his death was a loss for finance, but not for Jewry.[73] His son Eugène (1831-1907) was brought up in a fashion that had little in common with Jewish tradition. A biographer of the Péreire brothers states that when Eugène Péreire decided to marry the daughter of a Jewish notary, it transpired that Eugène was a man without a religion,

[65] *Univers Israélite,* vol xxxix (1884) 34.
[66] Weill, Georges, "Les Saint-Simioniens sous Napoléon III," in *Revue des études napoléoniennes,* vol. iii (1913).
[67] Allemagne, *Enfantin,* p. 205.
[68] Péreire, *La Question des chemins de fer* (Paris 1879) p. 69 ff.; Levasseur, E., *Histoire des classes ouvrières et de l'industrie en France de 1789 à 1870* (Paris 1904) vol. ii, p. 93-117.
[69] Stakic, V. D., *La Doctrine française du Crédit Mutuel* (Paris 1924).
[70] Cf. Posener, *loc. cit.,* p. 526, who exaggerates the Péreires interest in Judaism.
[71] *Univers Israélite,* vol. xxx (1874) 39.
[72] *Ibid.,* p. 310.
[73] *Ibid.,* vol. xxxv (1880) 698.

neither a Jew nor a Christian. His father told him, therefore, that he was free to choose his religion and Eugène, out of consideration for his fiancée, chose the Jewish faith and remained a Jew until the end of his life.[74]

In his book concerning religious problems[75] Isaac Péreire made no reference to the Saint-Simonist religion, but neither did he revert to the faith of his ancestors. He attempted rather to persuade the Church to conclude an alliance with freedom, science and industry and thus make possible the betterment of mankind.

To the bulk of French Jewry the Saint-Simonist philosophy remained completely alien; it was in fact vigorously opposed in some Jewish circles. Among its ardent opponents was Joseph Cohen (1817-1899), a lawyer from Aix-en Provence, who as a young man showed great interest in the situation of the Jews in Algeria.[76] Later he became the editor of the weekly *Verité Israélite* (1860-63) and wrote a number of articles and books, in which he not only defended the Jews but ventured to criticise Christianity.[77] For some time Joseph Cohen worked on the staff of the daily *La Liberté*, which was owned by Isaac Péreire in 1876-80. In a series of articles, published in his weekly and dealing with Enfantin's book, Joseph Cohen sharply attacked the religious concepts of Saint-Simonism. The philosophical and socio-economic teachings of Saint-Simon, he conceded, had an effect on the social development of France but had otherwise left no traces. The religious ideas of Saint-Simonism had withered away, since there was no genuine faith in God to keep them alive, and without such a faith no religion could long exist. The Jews believe in God and freedom, maintained Cohen; consequently they must believe in the moral responsibility of man. Enfantin pretends to be God's prophet; in fact, however, he is merely a philosopher, who with the limited resources of the mortal mind tries to penetrate the mystery of creation and eternity.[78]

One of the most articulate political opponents of Saint-Simonism among

[74] Castille, Hippolyte, *Les Frères Péreire* (Paris 1861) p. 56; *Archives Israélites*, vol. lxix (1908) 101.

[75] Péreire, Isaac, *La Question religieuse* (Paris 1878).

[76] Szajkowski, Z., "The founding of the Alliance Israélite Universelle," (Yiddish) in *Yivo Bleter*, vol. xxi (1943) 55, 57.

[77] Cohen, Joseph, *Les Déicides* (Paris 1864; 2nd edition 1886; English edition, Baltimore 1873); *Les Pharisiens* (Paris 1877) vol. i-ii.

[78] *Ibid.*, "La Vie éternelle, lettres à P. Enfantin," in *Vérité Israélite*, vol. iv (1862) 769-74, 773-99, 817-25.

the prominent French Jews was Adolphe Franck, (1809-93), a noted scholar and author of a book on Kabbala. Franck on several occasions harshly criticised the materialist school. His violent attacks on "socialist-communist" ideas gained him admission to the Academy of Moral and Political Sciences (1844), to the College de France (1854) and finally to the Institute de France. One of the most influential members of the Jewish Consistory,[79] Franck often expressed the official viewpoint of French Jewry, particularly of its "reformed" segment. In his philosophical dictionary he characterized the various socialist schools in the following manner: the Fourierists aim to destroy the family and all moral discipline; the communists are bent on destroying private property; the Saint-Simonians want to annihilate the individual by depriving him of his very conscience, to make of pantheism a religion and to create a new cult, dedicated equally to matter and spirit. This sect seeks to establish a universal tyranny from which one man only would profit.[80]

IV

In the heyday of Saint-Simonism its most bitter opponents were Charles Fourier and his disciples. The Fourierists, whose ideal was "God, matter and justice," loathed and vigorously opposed the materialistic aims of Saint-Simonism. The active participation of Jews in the Saint-Simonist movement induced Fourier and his followers to join the ranks of the Jew-haters. To be sure, Fourier's writings contain a few seemingly kind words about the Jews which may mislead the unsuspicious reader. Thus, Fourier proposed that Rothschild should buy Palestine and establish the Jewish national home there.[81] There is, however, no dearth of such "pro-Jewish" statements by avowed antisemites, the obvious motive behind these pronouncements being the desire to get rid of the Jews. One should, furthermore, be wary of classifying Fourier as a utopian Zionist. Fourier himself dispels all possible doubt as to his actual stand by inserting into

---

[79] Szajkowski, Z., "The founding of the Alliance Israélite Universelle," (Yiddish) in *Yivo Bleter*, vol. xviii (1941) 16.

[80] Franck, Adolphe, *Dictionnaire des sciences philosophiques* (Paris 1875) p. 1625, 1629; cf. idem, *Le Communisme jugé par l'histoire* (Paris 1848; 3rd edition 1871).

[81] Fourier, Charles, *La Fausse industrie* (Paris 1836) p. G 3,224; cf. Silberner, Edmund, "Charles Fourier on the Jewish Question," in JEWISH SOCIAL STUDIES, vol. viii (1946) 245-66.

the passage dealing with Palestine the ironic remark that, after establishing the Jewish national home, Rothschild will certainly emancipate the Christians too.[82] Fourier's writings abound in violent attacks on the Jews and Alphonse Toussenel, (1803-85), the most rabid Jew-baiter among the Fourierists, claimed that his antisemitism was in complete harmony with the teachings of his master.[83] Toussenel's hatred derived both from the Fourier school and from Catholic circles. During the thirties Toussenel worked on the staff of the ultra-conservative paper, *La Paix*,[84] where he met Louis Veuillot, who later became the leader of the Catholic antisemites, who undoubtedly exerted a strong influence on Fourier's most prominent disciple.

In 1845 the Fourierist Librairie de l'Ecole Sociétaire published a book castigating Jews and Saint-Simonians, destined to achieve great notoriety, Toussenel's *Les Juifs rois de l'epoque. Histoire de la féodalité financière.*[85] The main thesis of the book was the Jewish domination of France; "The dispersed remnants of the Saint-Simonian tribe joined hands with the dispersed remnants of the Jewish tribe. . . . This alliance was quite natural in view of the fact that a good many followers of the Saint-Simonist temple were circumcised." (Vol. 1, p. 223) Toussenel warned that Jews can grow rich only at the price of the country's general ruin *(ibid.,* p. 7); all the railroad owners were Jews (p. 9); the Saint-Simonians are merely the Jew's lackeys. (p. 10)

Before Toussenel the bulk of the antisemitic literature published in France had been sponsored by the Catholics. These writings charged that Jews were responsible for the French Revolution and that they were

---

[82] Fourier, *ibid.,* p. H 3.

[83] Toussenel, *Les Juifs Rois De L'Epoque* (Paris 1847) p. xiv; cf. Schapira, Israél, *Der Antisemitismus in der französischen Literatur. Edouard Drumont und seine Quellen* (1934) p. 66-67; Muckle, F., *Geschichte der sozialistische Ideen im 19.Jhdt.,* vol. i, p. 110-111; *idem, Die grossen Sozialisten* (Berlin 1920) vol. i, p. 82-83; *Encyclopädia Judaica,* vol. ii, p. 1078-88; Grabski, W. I., *Karol Fourier* (Warsaw 1928) p. 68, 94, 144-45.

[84] Fernessole, Abbé Pierre, *Les Origines littéraires des Louis Veuillot* (Paris 1922) p. 169.

[85] An impossible edition of 1836 (!) is mentioned in Le Groupe des E.S.R.I., *Antisémitisme et Sionisme* (Paris 1900) p. 2; an impossible edition of 1841 (!) is mentioned by Guérin, Jules, *Les Trafiquants de l'antisémitisme,* p. 265. Later editions: 1847 (2 vol.) ; 1863 (cf. Lambélin, Roger, *L'impérialisme d'Israél* [Paris 1924] p. 306) ; 1886 and 1887 (cf. Lorenz, O., *op. cit.,* vol. xii p. 987) ; German edition, *Das Königthum der Juden in Frankreich, oder Geschichte der Finanz-Feudalherrschaft. Ertes Heft. Constitutioneller Staatshaushalt* (Erfurt 1851) .

bent on dominating the world.[86] Another group of propagandists claimed that the Jews had made no progress since their emancipation but had remained a foreign body in the national organism; typical of this brand of antisemitism is the book of the historian Theophile Hallez.[87] A third group openly attacked Jewish orthodoxy; they had no objection to "the Jewish God" but blamed all evils on the Talmud. They urged the Jews to repudiate the Talmud and the rabbis,[88] a view which was, incidentally, very popular among the Jewish reformers in France.

Fourier and his disciples, particularly Toussenel, aligned socialism with the antisemitic forces. It seems, however, that in the beginning socialist circles were not particularly satisfied with Toussenel's book. The editors of the Fourierist journal, *La Démocratie pacifique*, on whose staff Toussenel occupied the leading place, intentionally ignored the book.[89] A rumor circulated in Jewish circles that Victor Considerant, a prominent Fourierist, had ousted Toussenel from the editorial staff but this was untrue. Toussenel continued his anti-Jewish diatribes in this journal.[90] A Polish emigre and sincere friend of the Jews, Jan Czyniski, who was a noted Fourierist, protested against Toussenel and was followed by the Jewish emigre, Fraenkel, who had strong Fourierist leanings.[91] The Fourierist journals, however, praised Toussenel's work; even the socialist organ of the well-known Etienne Cabet published favorable reviews of Toussenel's book.[92]

The second and third editions of this book (1847) were prefaced by an intensified attack on the Jews, full of coarse invectives and abuse. At the same time Toussenel continued to vilify the Jews in the Fourierist press. In 1847 there also appeared a pamphlet directed against Rothschild and the Saint-Simonians. This consisted of the biographies of Saint-Simón

[86] Malet, Chevalier, *Recherches historiques et politiques qui prouvent l'existence d'une secte révolutionnaire, son antique origine* . . .(Paris 1817); Becourt, Rénault, *Conspiration universelle du judaisme*. . . . (1835, preface only); Clavel, *Histoire pittoresque de la franc-maçonnerie* (Paris 1843).

[87] Hallez [Théophile], *Les Juifs en France, leur état moral et politique* (Paris 1845).

[88] See the publications of Louis Veuillot, and Chiarini, Abbé Louis A., *Théorie du judaisme* (Paris 1830); *Idem, Le Talmud de Babylonie* (Leipzig 1831).

[89] *Le Travail Affranchi* (February 4, 1849) 5.

[90] *Archives Israélites* (1864) 804.

[91] Czynski, *op. cit.,* p. 130, 136, 155.

[92] *Le Populaire de 1841* (August 16, 1845, supplément; September 27, 1846, p. 4).

and Rothschild reprinted from the *Biographie Universelle* with a brief introduction attacking the Jews much more than the Saint-Simonians. There are many analogies, asserted the author, between Saint-Simonism and Judaism; indeed, Saint-Simonism had disintegrated and most of its followers had returned to their original group, the Jewish sect.[93]

Toussenel set the pattern subsequently followed by all French antisemites. His charges were repeated in the 1850s by the historian, M. Capéfigue, who contended that the Jews and the Saint-Simonians had one trait in common, namely, that the Saint-Simonians make speculation more colorful and attractive by adding to it some romantic glamor.[94] The influence of Fourier and Toussenel during the 1860s was reflected in the writings of Gougenot de Mousseau.[95]

At a later date Toussenel's arguments were repeated by Edouard Drumont, whose writings have overshadowed those of all his forerunners. Discussing the Jewish influence on Saint-Simonism, Drumont asserted that it was merely an attempt on the part of the Jews to extricate themselves from their moral ghetto; since the Jews refused to adopt Christianity, they found it necessary to create the Saint-Simonist religion.[96] Israel Schapira was unquestionably right in stating that Toussenel was the "immediate forerunner" and master of Drumont.[97] The latter hailed Toussenel as the harbinger of antisemitism [98] and his book as a great work of lasting value.[99] Jules Guérin, one of Drumont's associates, likewise asserted that Toussenel's book "was the first anti-Jewish work that drew the attention of the public to the Jews and to their role in the past and present;" Drumont simply copied Toussenel.[100] When the struggle raging around the Dreyfus affair was nearing its climax, the foes of Dreyfus, at the instance of the antisemitic leader, Grandmaison, honored Toussenel's

---

[93] Michaud and Villenave, *op. cit.*

[94] Capéfigue, M. (I.B.H.), *Histoire des grandes opérations financières* (Paris 1855-1860) vol. iv, p. 132-33.

[95] Mousseau, Gougenot de, *Le Juif et judaisme et la judaisation des peuples chrétiens* (Paris 1863) p. 181. Drumont published the second edition of this book.

[96] Drumont, Edouard, *La France juive* (Paris 1886) vol. i, p. 350-51.

[97] Schapira, *op. cit.*, p. 32-33.

[98] Drumont, E., "Toussenel," in his *Les Héros et les pitres* (Paris [1901]) p. 267.

[99] *Idem, La France juive*, vol. i, p. 346.

[100] Guérin, *Les Trafiquants de l'antisémitisme*, p. 265; Yvert, Le Comte (G.I.E.), *Les Juifs et la propiété* (Paris 1884); 2nd edition, 1901, p. 14-15; Drumont, E., *La France juive devant l'opinion* (Paris 1886) p. 15, 71.

memory by erecting a monument in his native village of Montreuil-Bellay.[101]

It is, moreover, noteworthy that certain socialists endorsed Toussenel's antisemitism. The socialist Auguste Chirac, of whom we shall speak later, used as the motto for his antisemitic pamphlet an excerpt from Toussenel's book.[102] The editors of the *Revue Socialiste* wrote in an obituary of Toussenel that his book "is a valuable work that ought to be reprinted."[102a]

In 1886 Benoit Malon, a prominent socialist (1814-93), asserted, in connection with Drumont's *La France Juive,* that there is in general no antisemitism in France; Toussenel's "excellent work" is, in Malon's opinion, simply an anti-capitalist pamphlet, without any anti-Jewish tinge. In fact, the first antisemitic daily in France, *L'antisemitique* (1881), was for Malon just another anti-capitalist organ.[103] Malon's remarks, however, are comparable to those found occasionally even in Jewish apologetic writings, which regarded Toussenel's attacks on the Jews as no more than a form of "protest and resistance against the Jewish bankers."[104] The naivete of such a view is obvious to any open-minded reader of Toussenel.

V

Toussenel's book paved the way for a new series of anti-Jewish writings.[105] As was noted above, through the Péreire brothers, Rothschild became interested in the Saint-Simonist plan of building railroads. However, he never associated himself with the Saint-Simonist ideology but simply invested in new and profitable enterprises. On July 8, 1846 there occurred on Rothschild's northern railroad (Chemin de Fer du Nord) a catastrophe that resulted in a number of casualties; the public was incensed. The man in the street had regarded the railroads even before the catastrophe with considerable distrust and apprehension. To some respectable statesmen the railroads seemed to be either a plaything or an

---

[101] Drumont, *Les Héros et les pitres,* p. 273.

[102] Chirac, Auguste, *Les Rois de la République. Histoires des juiveries* (Paris 1886) 2 vols.

[102a] *La Revue Socialiste* (1885), no. vi, p. 478-79.

[103] Malon, "La Question juive," in *La Revue Socialiste* (June 1886) p. 506.

[104] Levaillant, M. I., *La Genèse de l'antisémitisme sous la Troisième République* (Paris 1907).

[105] *Guerre aux fripons* (Paris 1845 (cf. "Satan," *Histoire édifiante,* p. 17); *Les Juifs rois de l'Europe* (cf. Mirecourt, E. de *Rothschild* [Paris 1856] p. 65) ; *Les Juifs rois de l'Espagne* (cf. *Archives Israélites* [1857] p. 317); R. B. de L., *Law et les chemins de fer . . . pour servir à l'instruction des agioteurs de la bourse en 1845* (Paris 1845).

unduly complicated invention. Adolphe Thiers advocated the building of a railroad so that the Parisians would have something to play with, but he was quite sure that this toy would be of little use to the population of the capital.[106] A distinguished scholar like Dominique-Francois Arago could argue that the moment the train entered a tunnel the passengers were bound to suffocate.[107] It goes without saying that the socialists bitterly attacked the railroad company. "Money is all that matters here," wrote Cabet after the railroad catastrophe, "human life is of no importance."[108] In addition the crop failed in 1846 and there was a widespread fear of hunger. Rothschild imported a large transport of corn and organized the free distribution of bread among the poor. However, the effects of his philanthropy proved to be the very opposite of what he had expected. People started whispering that Rothschild had stored up huge reserves of corn for speculation and that his bread was poisoned.[109]

Toussenel's book had already broken the ground and there began to appear various leaflets scolding the railroads owners, the Jews and Rothschild I, their King. Most of these were written by a journalist, Mathieu (Georges Marie) Dairnvaell, who signed his first pamphlets "Satan."[110] The anti-Rothschild pamphleteers concocted a story about a lawsuit against the author of the first pamphlet to attack the Jewish banker and even published a series of faked "reports" regarding this lawsuit.[111] There appeared also some pro-Rothschild pamphlets, which had a certain effect

[106] Clapham, J. H., *The Economic Development of France and Germany, 1815-1914* (Cambridge 1928) p. 144.

[107] Levasseur, *op. cit.*, vol. ii, p. 108.

[108] *Le Populaire de 1841* (July 26 and August 28, 1846).

[109] Schwab, M., "Vie, oeuvres et obsèques du Baron James de Rothschild," in *Archives Israélites*, vol. xxix (1868) 1083.

[110] Other pamphlets by the same author: *Histoire édifiante et curieuse de Rothschild Ier, roi des Juifs, suivie du récit de la catastrophe du 8 juillet, par un témoin oculaire* (Paris 1846) 15 editions; German translation: *Erbauliche und seltsame Historia von Rothschild I König der Juden*, von Satan (Berlin 1846); *Rothschild Ier, ses valets et son peuple* . . . (Paris 1845) 5 editions; *Guerre aux fripons, chronique sécrète de la bourse et des chemins de fer* . . . (Paris 1846) 4 editions; *Histoire de Rothschild Ier, roi des Juifs* (Paris 1846) , of which only the preface was published.

[111] *Grand procès entre Rothschild Ier, roi des Juifs et Satan* . . . (Paris 1846) ; *Jugement rendu contre J. Rothschild et contre Georges Dainwaell* . . . (Paris 1846) ; other anti-Jewish pamphlets: *Tu dors Rothschild, et tes actions baissent!* . . . (Paris 1846); St.-Paul Robert, *La Vérité sur la maison Rothschild* (Paris 1846); *Premier traitement désopilatif* . . . *traduit de l'hébreu* . . . *Guérison radicale de l'épidémie des actions de chemins de fer* . . . (Paris 1846); Mesnard, Jean Baptiste, *Dix jours de règne de Rothschild Ier* . . . (Paris 1846) ; *Les Entrennes à Rothschild, almanach des mille et un* (cf. Drumont, *La France juive*, vol. i, p. 354).

on public opinion, in spite of the fact that they were rather poorly written.[112] Some of these pamphlets came, allegedly, from the pen of C. L. Marle, author of several good textbooks and the publisher of the paper, *La Constitution* (February 28-August 11, 1849). Several of Marle's textbooks were produced in collaboration with a Jewish educator, David E. Levi Alvarez.[113]

At first it was generally assumed that the author of the anti-Rothschild pamphlet, published in 1846, was the noted Jewish journalist, Alexandre Weill (1811-1898), undoubtedly one of the most colorful Jewish personalities in 19th-century France.[114] Writer of prose and verse, philosopher, linguist, a politician and historian, the prolific Weill achieved prominence in none of these fields.[115] Much of what he has written is worthless or even silly, and yet there was something attractive about him. For a time Weill was in vogue; the newsboys used to shout the titles of his articles. He was often very sincere and always a real Puritan. Weill was perhaps the only French writer of his time who believed that a married man should not have mistresses. He idolized Victor Hugo and it was his devotion to the novelist that accounts to a large extent for Hugo's friendly attitude toward the Jews but Weill could not forgive the great poet for having a mistress and severely criticised his immoral life.

Weill was after a fashion attached to Jewish tradition but, if one may

[112] *Réponse de Rothschild Ier, roi des Juifs, à Satain, rois des imposteurs* (Paris 1846.) Another edition (Brussels 1846) is signed by Frissard; *Erwiderung Rothschilds I, Königs der Juden, auf das von "Satan" an ihn gerichtete Pamphlet, nach dam französischen* (Berlin 1847) ; M. P. de R. . . ., *Nouvelle réponse du prince des Israélites, Rothschild Ier, à un pamphlétaire* . . . (Paris 1846) ; *Première réponse officielle de M. la Baron James de Rothschild* . . . (Brussels 1846) . The publisher promised another pamphlet: *Que nous veut-on avec ce Rothschild Ier, par un Banquier;* A. D. . ., avocat, *Guerre aux Juifs* . . . (Paris 1846) ; cf. *Archives Israélites* 1846) , 638-40; Goudchaux, Eugène, *Un Juif au peuple français* . . . *Deuxième partie: à M. Georges Dainwael* (Paris 1846) ; *Importantes révélations sur la lutte engagée par les Jésuites contre les Juifs, par un farfadet humanitaire* (Paris 1846) .

[113] *Catalogue général des livres imprimés,* vol. cvii, p. 147-150.

[114] Bloch, M., *Alexandre Weill, sa vie et ses oeuvres* (Paris 1905); Dreyfus, R., *A. Weill, ou le prophète du Faubourg St. Honoré* (Paris 1908, *Cahiers de la Quinzaine,* série ix, cahier 9); Berret, Paul, "Alexandre Weill et Victor Hugo," in *Revue juive de Genève,* vol. ii (1933-34) no. iv, p. 150-55, no. v, p. 195-98; Saurat, Denis, "A. Weill et Balzac," in *Revue juive de Genève,* vol. i, no. vi, p. 256-61; Cahen, Isidore, "Alexandre Weill," in *Archives Israélites* (1899) p. 133-35; Praag, Siegfried van, "Alexandre Weill," in *Der Jude* (Berlin 1923) p. 681-91; Dresch, I., "Une correspondance de Karl Gutzkow, de Mme d'Agoult et d'Alexandre Weill," in *Revue Germanique* vol. ii (1906) 93-95; Kahn, Sylvain, "La Vie d'un juif d'Alsace," in *Menorah* (Paris 1925) 59-60.

[115] British Museum, *Catalogue of printed books,* vol. lxxxvi, p. 223-25; *Supplement,* p. 350-51.

believe the Catholic leader and antisemite, Louis Veuillot, in 1849 he proposed to embrace the Christian faith.[116] Perhaps, this was, however, but one of his whims, or perhaps a trick he played on Veuillot. At the time when he was supposedly contemplating conversion, Weill violently attacked the Catholic Church; at a later date he wrote in a poem that of all the plagues of the world the greatest calamity for the Jews proved to be the so-called Christian God of love.[117] He accepted the Bible but denounced the Talmud.[118]

Full of contradictions, oscillating constantly between various moods and philosophical and political doctrines, Weill was for a time one of the most popular Fourierist journalists; he used to set the tone of political journalism and of creative writing in various Fourierist publications. It was undoubtedly Weill whom the editors of the *Archives Israélites* (1846, p. 496) had in mind when they ruefully observed that although *La Démocratie Pacifique* featured Toussenel's vicious attacks upon the Jews, some of its contributors are Jewish. When Balzac published an article against the socialists in the *Corsaire-Satan* (1847), the editor of *La Démocratie Pacifique* commissioned Weill to reply to this famous writer. Weill, who had previously contributed to the *Corsaire-Satan,* violently attacked Balzac and set the tone of all the subsequent polemics.[119] The versatile Jewish Fourierist never liked Balzac who, as Weill stated, used to wind up his discussion of every social problem with an apology for Catholicism.[120] At the same time Weill was closely associated with the Saint-Simonians, contributed to Leroux's *Revue Indépendente,* admired Saint-Simon as an historian and even tried to imitate his stye.[121]

Veuillot who did not take too seriously Weill's alleged intention of becoming a Christian, wrote: "Essentially he is a Christian, but as to the form he is thoroughly confused: he was already in, and then out and then in again; he left once more and once more returned."[122] Karl Gutzkow

---

[116] Veuillot, L., *D'après Nature. Oeuvres complètes* (Paris 1929) 1st series, vol. x, p. 475.

[117] Weill, A., *Agathina, ma femme* (Paris 1879) p. 98.

[118] *Idem, Les Livres de Dieu, Moise et le Talmud* (Paris 1864); cf. Bloch, S., in *Univers Israélite,* vol. xx (1864-65) 33-38; Rabbinowicz, M., in *Archives Israélites,* vol, xxvi (1865) 214-17, 258-63.

[119] Hunt, H. J., *Le Socialisme et le Romantisme en France* (Oxford 1935) p. 214-15, 172.

[120] Weill, A., *Introduction à mes mémoires* (Paris 1890) p. 145.

[121] *Ibid.*, p. 14, 16; Berret, *op. cit.*, p. 150-51.

[122] Veuillot, *op. cit.*, p. 475.

characterized Weill thus: "Depending on his mood he is a German or a Frenchman, a follower of Pierre Leroux or his foe. He has thousands of ideas that evaporate even before he has a chance to express them."[123] Weill often attacked the Jewish Consistory and the Rothschilds; the non-Jews made good use of his jibes at the Jewish bankers. Two years before the railroad catastrophe (1844) there appeared in Stuttgart a pamphlet by Weill, castigating in violent terms the financial despotism and the oligarchy of the Rothschilds.[124] In Germany it was in general easier for a Jew to criticize a Jewish millionaire. There one could afford the luxury of poking fun at the *Univers Israélite* for calling the Rothschilds "the royal family."[125] Jewish communal life in Germany did not depend on the Jewish bankers, whereas in France the Jewish community was small and poor and the influence of the Rothschilds was strong enough to block any outspoken criticism of their activities. Thus it seemed natural to assume that the anti-Rothschild pamphlets of 1846 were written by Weill. However, in a letter to the *Archives Israélites* (1846, p. 536) Weill, avowing that he had attacked the Rothschilds and would continue to do so, emphatically denied any association with the anti-Jewish pamphlet; its author, according to Weill, was Georges Dairnvaell.

The first reaction in Jewish circles to the antisemitic pamphlets was not particularly strong. Samuel Cohen, editor of the *Archives Israélites*, the organ of the reformed Jews, answered the attack on Rothschild in *La Réforme*.[126] He abstained, however, from criticizing sharply the first edition of Toussenel's book (1845); Cohen's article on Toussenel in the *Archives Israélites* was mild and evasive. Toussenel exaggerates quite a bit, he writes, in his views on the role of commerce, but his book contains some excellent passages, which are at times vitiated by a rich imagination but almost invariably bear the imprint of honesty and intelligence.[127] Cohen obviously could not believe that the Fourierists had become antisemitic.

Eugène de Mirecourt, author of a popular series of biographies of

[123] Gutzkow, Karl, *Werke*, vol. vii, p. 282.
[124] Weill, A., *Rothschild und die europäischen Staaten* (Stuttgart 1884).
[125] *Allgemeine Zeitung des Judentums* (1846) 688.
[126] *The Jewish Chronicle*, vol. ii (London 1945) no. ix, p. 77.
[127] R. (= S. Cohen), in *Archives Israélites*, vol. vi (1845) 753.

famous men, relates, in a popular biography of the Rothschilds, that Salomon Rothschild remarked with reference to a pamphlet directed against him: "Only a Jew could have written this book."[128] The popular series of anti-Rothschild pamphlets, published in 1846, made a considerable stir even beyond the French borders.[129] The Vienna Rothschilds urged the Prussian government to suppress these pamphlets, which were being distributed in Germany too.[130] It is possible that the pamphleteers, of the anti-Rothschild as well as of the pro-Rothschild variety, were simply after the bankers' money, but Rothschild persisted in ignoring both groups.[131] In connection with pamphlet published after the railroad catastrophe, the *Archives Israélites* wrote that it was certainly very regrettable, but at the same time pointed out that at the first stage of a big enterprise, such as a railroad company, accidents are bound to occur.[132]

VI

Under the July monarchy, the Fourierists had led French socialism into the antisemitic camp. In the period of the Second Empire Proudhon and his friends played this role. Pierre-Joseph Proudhon (1809-1865) never concealed his anti-Jewish feelings and gave vent to them on several occasions, while speaking about the revolution of 1848, about Poland, Napoleon III, the Saint-Simonians, etc.[133] Almost all the Jew-baiters of the more recent period have praised Proudhon highly.[134] Edmond

[128] Mirecourt, Eugène de, *Rothschild* (Paris 1856) p. 65-66.

[129] *Archives Israélites* (1864) p. 644.

[130] Corti, Egon, *Der Aufstieg des Hauses Rothschild* (Leipzig 1927) vol. ii, p. 265-67.

[131] *Ibid.*, p. 265.

[132] B. L. (= G. Ben-Lévi), "M. de Rothschild et les pamphlétaires à 30 centimes," in *Archives Israélites* (1864) 561-66; *Idem*, "Les Chemins de fer et la tolérance religieuse," *loc. cit.* p. 421-24.

[133] Proudhon, P.-J., "Mélanges," in *Oeuvres complètes*, vol, xvii, p. 31; *idem, Résumé de la question sociale* (Paris 1848) p. 36; *idem, Si les traités ont cessé d'exister?* p. 9; *idem, Correspondance,* September 7, 1853; October 20, 1858; January 29 and December 14, 1862. Cf. the Nazi writer, Schulze, Willibald, "War Proudhon Anarchist?" in *Deutschlands Erneuerung* (January 1939) 14-21; cf. also Schapiro, J. S., "Pierre Joseph Proudhon, Harbinger of Fascism," in *American Historical Review* vol. 1 (1945) 714-37; Lázare, B., *op. cit.*, (1934), p. 66-67; Czynski, J., *op. cit.*, p. 155; Bernard, Louis, *L'Antisémitisme démasqué* (Paris 1894) p. 93, 156.

[134] Drumont, E., *La France juive*, vol. i, p. 366-67; *idem, La France juive devant l'opinion* p. 72; *idem*, "Proudhon et Karl Marx," in *Figures de bronze ou statues de neige*, p. 317-32; *idem*, in *La Grande Revue*, vol. liii (1909) 140; Maurras, Charles, in *Action Française* (August 13, 1910); *Dictionnaire politique et critique* (1933) vol. iv; Lambélin, Roger, *L'Impérialisme d'Israël* (Paris 1924) p. 29.

Picard maintained that it was Proudhon, rather than Marx, who should have been considered the leader of international socialism; according to Picard, Marx achieved his status solely by means of Jewish intrigues and by the Jewish passion for self-aggrandizement.[135] In the office of the monarchist and antisemitic newspaper *Action Francaise,* the portrait of Proudhon was prominently displayed.[136]

Proudhon had all the qualities of the antisemite of his generation (1840-60). He was undoubtedly a sincere socialist and yet his political philosophy was full of contradictory reactionary ideas. It is enough to recall his pronouncements in favor of the Southern states during the American Civil War and his hostile attitude toward Poland's struggle for independence.[137] Proudhon fought bitterly against the Catholic Church. He was, consequently, also an avowed foe of Saint-Simonist mysticism. Even more revolting to Proudhon were the practical precepts of Saint-Simonism; herein lies, as a matter of fact, one of the main causes of Proudhon's antisemitism. Proudhon, however, never indulged in vicious Jew-baiting a la Toussenel, as Léon Daudet, the well-known antisemitic writer, has rightly pointed out.[138] Proudhon's slogan was "property is theft;" he consequently vigorously opposed the "feudal industrialism" of the Saint-Simonians, among whom a few Jews played so prominent a part. One of Proudhon's closest friends, George Duchène (1824-76), nevertheless followed in Toussenel's footsteps. His writings, which contain some of the most violent attacks to be found in French antisemitic literature, were highly praised by the anti-Jewish socialists and by other antisemites.[139]

[135] Picard, Edmond, in *La Grande Revue,* vol. liii (1909) 143.

[136] Bouglé, *La sociologie de Proudhon* (Paris 1911), viii; Schapiro, *loc. cit.,* p. 732.

[137] Proudhon, *La guerre et la paix* (Paris 1861) p. 179; *idem, Si les traités de 1815 ont cessé d'exister?;* cf. Abensour, Léon, "P.-J. Proudhon et la Pologne," in *Grande Revue* vol. ciii (1920) 3-15.

[138] Daudet, Léon, *Flammes* (Paris 1930) p. 74.

[139] Duchène, Georges, *L'Empire industriel . . .* (Paris 1869); *idem, La Spéculation devant les tribuneaux . . .* (Paris 1866); *idem, Etudes sur la féodalité financière* (Paris 1867). Other anti-Jewish books by non-socialists: Rupert, L[ouis], *L'Eglise et la Synagogue* (Paris-Tournai 1859); Crétineau-Joly, J.[A. M.], *Histoire du Sonderbund* (Paris 1850); *L'Eglise romaine avant la révolution* (Paris 1863); Kauffmann and Cherpin, *Histoire philosophique de la Franc-Maçonnerie* (Lyon 1854).

VII

The antisemites, socialists and anti-socialists, saw in Rothschild the personification of Jewry; the Jew was *ipso facto* a swindler and capitalist. *Figaro* wrote: "A Jew is one who can prove that 2 x 2 = 3."[140] Other papers (*Journal de Havre, Le Siècle*) maintained that in Paris non-Jews had an average income of 300 francs, and the average Jew 12,500 francs.[141] During the pogroms in Alsace (1848), after having settled their accounts with the Jews, the hoodlums started spreading a hoax that the rich gentiles were merely Jews in disguise; it was only then that the authorities took steps to suppress the riots.[142] The synagogue was looked upon as a nest of social corruption.[143]

Fourier, Toussenel, Proudhon, Duchène and other antisemitic socialists were undoubtedly devoted fighters for a better world and very often keen analysts of the situation of the French masses; they were unable, however, to overcome their anti-Jewish prejudice and to recognize that there were poor as well as prosperous Jews.[144] If the Socialist antisemites were blind to the existence of poor Jews, the Jewish socialists, who were more often than not assimilated, never tried to open their eyes to the reality. There was, however, one noteworthy exception, Armand Lévy, who headed the pro-Napoleon socialist faction. Lévy's keen interest in Jewish life was largely due to the influence of his Polish friend, Adam Mickiewicz.

[140] *Figaro* (December 6, 1857); cf. *Archives Israélites,* vol. xix (1858) 35.

[141] *Archives Israélites,* vol. xviii (1857) 322.

[142] Ephraim, Armand, "La Question juive en 1848," in *La Gerbe* (supplément au no. 3 des *Archives Israélites* du 13 Février 1890) p. 32.

[143] *Archives Israélites,* vol. viii (1847) 32.

[144] Anchel, Robert, "Sur l'histoire des juifs en France," in *Cahiers Juifs* (1936) no. xix, p. 33, has depicted the Jews of this period as a farily prosperous group. There is, however, considerable evidence of a great degree of poverty; see Szajkowski, Z., "The Growth of the Jewish Population of France," in JEWISH SOCIAL STUDIES, vol. viii (1946) 314-15; *Archives Israélites* (1840) 89-96; Reboul-Deneyrol, *Paupérisme dans le Bas-Rhin;* Boudin, M., in *Journal de la Société de Statistique de Paris,* vol. i, (1860) 55; *Le Lien d'Israël,* vol. iii (1857) 139-46; Bloch, M.. "L'Oeuvre scolaire des juifs français depuis 1789," in *Revue des études juives,* vol. xxvi; Szajowski in *Yidn in Frankreich* (New York 1942) vol. i, p. 210; *Extrait du registre des délibérations du Consistoire Israélite de la circonscription de Strasbourg, 24 Octobre 1822;* Lévy, J., "Les Mendiants juifs en Alsace et en Lorraine," in *Le Lien d'Israél,* vol. iv (1858) 435-39; *Archives Israélites,* vol. i (1840) 315-17; Szajowski, "The Decline and Fall of Provençal Jewry," in JEWISH SOCIAL STUDIES, vol. vi (1944) 45-47.

VIII

In the first years of the Third Republic the most important anti-semitic publications were those written by socialists. Albert Regnard, a prominent socialist, maintains that "the hatred of Semitism was wide-spread among the young revolutionaries at the end of the Second Empire, particularly among the Hébertists with whom Tridon was associated." The latter group, it is true, was opposed to Christianity as well but chiefly on the ground that it was "a product of Semitism." This was, incidentally, the language employed by the Hébertists in denouncing the capitalist system too.[145] G. Tridon, a member of the central committee of the Paris Commune, (1871), was the author of one of the most vicious antisemitic books ever published in French.[146] The nature of Tridon's antisemitism is revealed by the very title of his book, *Le Molochisme Juif*. The author sets out to prove that the Jews have always been savages; they have offered human sacrifices, etc. The Jews, he declares, are a black stain on civiliza-tion, the curse of mankind. It is, therefore, the sacred duty of the Aryan race to fight the Semitic spirit and ideology. Tridon's ideas were exploited by his friend, Regnard, who praised Tridon's book in *La Revue Socialiste*. Regnard published a study on the inequality of races, in which he not only expanded the theory of Gobineau and other pioneers of racism, but in-jected a strong antisemitic flavor; this study was reprinted in book form by a socialist publishing firm.[147] Gobineau's theory was regarded in France as purely academic speculation and Regnard was the first to apply it for the purpose of antisemitic agitation.

Auguste Chirac became the leader of French antisemitism during the early years of the Third Republic.[148] Chirac gained a reputation as a socialist economist as the author of a number of anti-Jewish pamphlets, full of violent invectives and abuse (reprinted from *La Revue Socialiste*).[149] Drumont said later that Chirac had espoused socialism in protest against

---

[145] Regnard, A., in *Revue Socialiste* vol. v (1887) 499-500.
[146] Tridon, G., *Le Molochisme juif* (Brussels 1885); published posthumously.
[147] Regnard, Albert, *Aryens et Sémites. Le bilan du Judaisme et du Christianisme* (Paris 1890).
[148] Savine, Albert, "Auguste Chirac," in *Revue d'art dramatique*, vol. xviii (1903) 334-55.
[149] Chirac, Auguste, *Les Rois de la république. Histoire des Juiveries* (Paris 1883, 1887-89) 3 vols.; *idem, La Haute banque et les révolutions* (Paris 1876); *idem, L'Agiotage sous la Troisième République* (Paris 1888). Chirac promised another book: *Les Rois de la République, probita (épopée)*.

the Jewish bankers and declared that when the people will put the financiers on trial, Chirac would come forth as the prosecutor.[150] Malon, editor of *La Revue Socialiste,* wrote that after the time of Toussenel, Proudhon and Duchène, Chirac was the most vigorous opponent of big finance.[151] Malon, a member of the First International, an active participant in the Paris Commune and one of the most articulate and sincere champions of French socialism was not quite free from anti-Jewish bias;[152] it was Malon who, as editor of *La Revue Socialiste,* the theoretical organ of "integral" socialism, sponsored Chirac's journalistic activity.

In 1886, three years after Chirac's first book and one year after Tridon's pamphlet had been published, there appeared *La France Juive* by Edouard Drumont (1844-1917), a work destined to have a powerful effect on the development of French antisemitism. Without Drumont there would probably have been no Dreyfus affair; but whether this view can be borne out or not, Drumont's best-known forerunners in the field of antisemitic propaganda were socialists. The writings cited above were his principal sources; the motto of *La France Juive* is a quotation from the Fourierist Toussenel.

Drumont himself at times attempted to sound like a socialist; it goes without saying that his "socialism" was directed exclusively against Jewish capitalists. Some socialist circles accorded *La France Juive* a warm reception. Malon personally introduced Drumont to his friends in the labor movement who cordially welcomed the new antisemite with socialist leanings.[153] Tabaran, author of a series of popular socialist pamphlets and an avowed foe of Drumont, stated that the socialists had urged Drumont to join their movement.[154] It was not until antisemitism had joined hands with the "Boulangist" reaction (1889) that some socialist groups have become aware of the danger and started to fight against antisemitism.

It was a well-known fact that the "integral" faction of French socialism refused to participate in the campaign to exonerate Dreyfus. It is less known that some other socialists, such as Bakunin or the poet Clovis

---

[150] Drumont, E., *La Fin d'un monde* (Paris 1889) p. 159-60.

[151] *Revue Socialiste,* vol. iii (1886) 192.

[152] Drumont, *La Fin d'un monde* p. 72, 81, 91, 122-130, 135; *idem,* "Bénoit Malon," in *Figures de bronzes ou statues de neige* (Paris 1901) p. 349-358.

[153] Drumont, *La Fin d'un monde,* p. 125.

[154] Tabarant, *Socialisme et antisémitisme* (Paris 1889).

Hugues, had antisemtic leanings. These, however, are problems that call for separate study. It is perhaps no accident that the contemporary novelist, Louis Ferdinand Céline, author of several pornographic books attacking the Jews with a viciousness that surpasses even Streicher's, was in a position to use as mottoes for the chapters of his books excerpts from the writings of great pioneers of French Socialism, Fourier, Toussenel, Proudhon, Timon, Bakunin and others.[155]

*   *   *

In quoting only the antisemitic pronouncements of the French socialists, before Edouard Drumont, the writer may be suspected of having ignored the pro-Jewish statements. In order to allay any such suspicion, the writer wishes therefore to say explicitly that his efforts to find sympathetic references to the Jews in the French socialist literature, from Saint-Simon to the date of Drumont's first appearance, have been futile. It is consequently doubtful whether any such statements were ever recorded.

[155] Céline, Louis-Ferdinand, *Bagatelles pour un massacre* (Paris 1928) p. 74, 80, 98, 191.

THE STRUGGLE FOR JEWISH EMANCIPATION
IN ALGERIA AFTER THE FRENCH OCCUPATION

AFTER the occupation of Algeria in 1830 by France the new authorities introduced many changes in the administration of the Jewish communities. All these changes were established in such a way as not to destroy the old communities system, but rather to modernize it and to leave within the jurisdiction of lay leaders and rabbis only purely religious and philanthropic matters. Civil matters (birth, marriage, and death registers, etc.) the French subordinated to their own jurisdiction, which also applied to all non-French Europeans living in Algeria. The religious court of the Jews (*Beth-din*) found its powers increasingly restricted by various decrees (of October 28, 1830; October 8, 1832; August 10, 1834; February 28, 1841; and September 26, 1842), which deprived it of jurisdiction over criminal cases and permitted Jews to appeal from its decisions to the French administration. In the end, the *Beth-din* was permitted to judge only religious matters; all other affairs had to be submitted to the French judicial bodies.[1] On November 16, 1830, the French authorities nominated for the city of Algiers a *Mokdem* (*chef de la nation juive*), who exercised some police powers over the community and was also an official assistant to the mayor. On June 21, 1831, a council of three laymen was nominated to assist the *Mokdem* in his duties and to collect taxes. On March 28, 1836, the *Mokdem's* title was changed to *Adjoint Israélite*, and an ordinance of January 6, 1836, transformed him into a regular French official with a yearly salary of 2,000 francs.

---

[1] Situation des Israélites en Algérie. Rapport général, par M. [Michel A.] Weill, Grand Rabbin, 1850," AN (=Archives Nationales), F^{19}11143; André Chouraqui, *Marche vers l'Occident. Les Juifs d'Afrique du Nord* (Paris, 1952), pp. 100-101.

Originally published in *Historia Judaica*, vol. XVIII (1956).

The French Jews early became interested in the situation of Algerian Jewry. Basically, they considered the Algerian Jews as an uncivilized horde. In 1840, the *Archives Israélites,* at that time the influential Jewish journal, wrote: "It is an abominable race, greedy . . . incapable of gratitude and generous sentiments."[2] But, as they were nevertheless Jews of a French colony, something had to be done in their behalf in order not to harm the prestige of French Jewry. As early as November, 1833, the Central Consistory of French Jewry requested that the Government create a consistory in Algeria modeled after those of France. On December 12, 1836, the Central Consistory wrote to the Ministry of Justice and Religious Affairs: ". . . some advantage to the Government could result from the establishment of a Jewish Consistory in Algeria placed, as all departmental consistories, under the direction of the Central Consistory. It appears to us that this would attach to France an important part of the African population and accelerate the moral regeneration of these new fellow-citizens."[3]

The request was not granted. The Central Consistory then asked the regional consistory of Marseille to make a survey of the situation of Algerian Jewry. At the same time various private persons became interested in helping the Jews of Algeria. One of them was the well-known Jewish Saint-Simonian, Gustave d'Eichthal, who visited Algeria and prepared a project on how to organize Jewish consistories there. In a long letter dated September 28, 1838, D'Eichthal proposed to replace the old *Beth-din* with French-type consistories, which should, first of all, function as an institution of enlightenment. According to his letter, such a proposal had been made before by Tama, a Jewish merchant from Marseille who lived in Algeria already before 1830. In order not to destroy too rapidly the old communities administration, D'Eichthal proposed that the *Mokdem* should become a member of the modern consistories; he should even continue to keep his title. He further proposed

2 *Les Archives Israélites,* I (1840), 476-80, 537-48.
3 AN, F[19]11143.

that the Algerian Jews should accept the resolutions of the Sanhedrin, that had been convened by Napoleon I in 1807; a Judaeo-Arabic translation of them together with a historical introduction, should be circulated. The rabbis should become government officials, and young Jewish men from Algeria should study at the rabbinical school in France. G. d'Eichthal cautioned that the French jurisdiction over divorces be not forced upon the Algerian Jews before they became French citizens. One of the very first tasks should be the establishment of modern schools for children, not only for boys, but also for girls. D'Eichthal even foresaw the formation of special Jewish army units commanded by Jewish officers. And he asked the Central Consistory of France to send a delegate to Algeria. According to his letter he had already had earlier talks on these subjects with Jewish leaders in France.[4]

The Moslems were against any statute that would take away from them their separate administration, and the French Government did not touch their complete separatism. The Catholics of Algeria already had their legal statute, and another one was being prepared for the Protestants. Finally on April 3, 1839, the Ministry of War, which controlled Algeria's administration, instructed the Governor to prepare a statute for the Jews. But the Governor failed to act, and after a new intervention from the Central Consistory dated September 4, 1839, the Minister on that same day asked the Governor of Algeria to carry out the instruction of April 3. In the beginning of 1840, a commission for the preparation of a Jewish statute was created in Algiers. It was composed of Mayor Clément, Chief Rabbi Gionda di David Amano, the leader of the Algiers Jewish Community, Mardoché Amar, and other Algerian and French Jews. Because of the inaction of this commission the Paris Central Consistory intervened yet again on January 7, 1841, asking once more for the creation of Algerian Jewish consistories.[5]

---

[4] In the author's possession.
[5] AN[19]11143; *Les Archives Israélites*, I (1840), 270; Archives of the Paris Central Consistory, Minutes of December 24, 1837, April 8, 1838,

As a result of all these efforts, the Algerian Administration, in a report of June 7, 1841, proposed to the Minister of War that the separatist character of the Algerian
Jewish communal administration be changed and that it
be replaced by consistories to be formed in accordance with
the system of the French consistories created by Napolon I
in 1808 and controlled by the French administration. This,
the report stated, would help to emancipate the Algerian
Jews, who would then serve as intermediaries between France
and the Moslem population. If the Jews were granted civil
rights, they would abolish polygamy and accept French
jurisdiction over divorces. In 1841, the Government again
named a commission to settle the Jewish problem. As this
commission was not successful either, Jaques-Isaac Altaras
(1786-1873), President of the regional Marseille Consistory,
went to Algeria in 1842 together with the young lawyer
Joseph Cohen (1817-1899). Their intention was to create
Jewish consistories on the pattern of those in France. Their
journey alerted the Government in favor of Algerian Jewry.
In a report submitted to the Minister of War, they proposed: (1) Algerian Jews should be forced to abandon
their traditional garments and dress in the European manner[6] (but the Ministry was opposed to such a drastic step);
(2) civil rights should be granted to the Jews, who should
serve in the militia (the Ministry was disposed to grant
such rights only to the rich Jews); (3) Jews should be
permitted to become colonists (the Ministry was in favor
of this proposal since Jews were not barred from agriculture
anyway); (4) the French civil laws governing births, marriages, and deaths should be introduced for Jews; (5) the
Beth-din should be deprived of jurisdiction not only over
civil, but also over religious matters, and the laws valid
for the Europeans living in Algeria should be adopted for
the Jews (the Ministry was in favor of this step); (6) the
Jewish ministers should become government functionaries

November 24, 1839; Claude Martin, *Les Israélites algériens de* 1830 *à* 1902
(Alger, 1922), pp. 19-21.
    [6] On the clothing of Algerian Jews see J. Hanoune, *Aperçu sur les
Israélites Algériens et sur la Communauté d'Alger* (Alger, 1922), pp. 19-21.

(this was accepted by the Ministry); (7) schools should be organized for children; (8) the old system of *Mokdems* should be replaced by the introduction of French consistories (this, too, was approved by the Ministry). Many of these recommendations had been made earlier by various persons and, in 1840, in the *Archives Israélites.*[7]

As a result of the report submitted by Altaras and Cohen, the Ministry of War, on February 17, 1843, appointed a commission to prepare a draft of a statute for the Algerian Jews. The Deputy, Eugène Janvier, was named as the commission's president. Its members were Cuvier, of the non-Catholic office at the Ministry of Justice and Religious Affairs; Artaud, Inspector General of the universities; the deputies Max Cerfberr, Adolphe Crémieux, and the attorney Anspach, all three of the Central Consistory; Fellmann, of the Algerian office of the Ministry of War. Maurice Meyer, who had lost his professorship in Rouen because he was a Jew, was appointed the commission's secretary. On March 3, 1843, the Minister of War, the Maréchal Nicolas Soult Duc de Dalmatie, instructed the Commission to investigate the civil statute of the Algerian Jews (especially the problems of marriage, divorce, polygamy, etc.), the statute of the *Beth-din* and of the communal rabbis, the organization of schools, and the possibility of replacing the old communal administration by consistories. [8]

Altaras and Cohen had intended to initiate emancipation of the Algerian Jews by establishing schools. The new commission to a large extent discussed the situation of the existing religious schools and decided that the Government should finance and establish modern schools with a combined

[7] "Rapport sur la formation d'une Commission qui serait chargée d'examiner diverses questions relatives aux Israëlites Algériens d'aprés les Mémoires de M. M. Altaras et Cohen qui ont eté en mission en Algérie," in the author's possession; *Les Archives Israélites*, I (1840), 476-80, 537-48; Zosa Szajkowski, "New Materials on Altaras and His Colonization Plan," *Yivo-Bleter*, XXI (1943), 55-57 (Yiddish).
[8] AN, F[19]11143. The minutes of the Commission are in the author's possession. They were, for some reason, originally sent to Altaras by the *Conseil d'État* and thus escaped destruction with the archives of the *Conseil* in 1871. The Commissioin held the first meeting on March 27, 1843 and the last on June 2, 1843.

secular and religious curriculum stressing the teaching of the
French language. On this occasion, Adolphe Crémieux told
how he founded Jewish schools in Egypt during his 1840
visit there in connection with his intervention in the Damas-
cus blood-accusation.[9]

The organization of consistories was planned by the
Commission in such a way as to give to the advocates of
emancipation the upper hand over the orthodox elements.
The three representatives of the Central Consistory, assisted
by Artaud and Janvier, asked for the establishment of three
separate regional consistories for Algiers, Oran, and Constantine respectively, which were to be controlled by the
Paris Central Consistory. They maintained that this would
speed up the assimilation of the Algerian Jews. This example
and influence, they felt, should come from France. Their suggestion was accepted by the Commission, although Cuvier,
representing the point of view of the anti-Jewish military
administration in Algeria, demanded the formation of local
Algerian consistories dependent, not on Paris, but rather on
a Central Consistory in Algiers.

Because of the lack of enlightened local Jews capable
of influencing their communities, it was decided to appoint
a small number of consistorial leaders. Half of these, including the president, were to be taken from among the French

---

[9] "Mr. Crémieux développe le plan qu'il a suivi; dans l'organisation des
écoles juives d'Egypte, qui avant celà étaient dans un état pareil à celui ou
on voit aujourd'hui les écoles juives de l'Algérie. . . . Mr. Crémieux a fait
disparaitre cette organisation vicieuse, en établissant une Commission l'Instruction Publique, en mettant à la tête de l'école des garçons un chef capable,
assez versé dans la langue française, et israélite d'origine; à la tête de l'école
des filles une chrétienne, femme instruite et distinguée. Au-dessus de cette
Commission, il a placé l'autorité et l'inspection du Grand Rabbin et de deux
Comités, l'un composé de 12 Juifs des plus notables du pays, l'autre des Consuls
de divers pays et de quelques Français de distinction. Les professeurs juifs qui
exerçaient antérieurement ont eté conservés pour enseigner l'hébreu. Les enfants
pauvres ne payent pas la rétribution. Les enfants riches sont obligés de la payer
et d'apporter en outre le déjeuner quotidien de leurs condisciples pauvres. Les
écoles diverses ont été fondues en une seule pour les garçons et une seule pour
les filles, et ces établissements aujourd'hui sont dans un état si florissant que
les Catholiques ont demandé comme une faveur et obtenu d'y être admis.
L'école française des Israélites d'Alexandrie compte aujourd'hui 300 eléves,
celle du Caire 200 environ." From the Commission's minutes, April 3, 1843.

Jews living in Algeria, and the *Beth-din* was to be controlled by the French administration.

It seems that even at that time various circles advocated the granting of full French citizenship to the Jews. This was the idea underlying all projects aimed at the assimilation of the Algerian Jews and at the basis of many of the Commission's discussions. But Cuvier, from the first meeting of the Commission, fought against any decision that would allow the Algerian Jews to profit from French jurisdiction. He argued that they themselves had not made such a request; that they would accept French jurisdiction but not French civilization. Cuvier asserted that, in the eyes of the Algerian Jews, religious principles and civil jurisdiction were part of one indivisible principle, and it was too early to introduce to them principles of civil law, which were only then beginning to be understood even in European France. And he bolstered his case with examples from the report of Altaras and Cohen who, with their enlightened approach and firm opposition to orthodoxy, sharply and uncompromisingly attacked the rabbis, the *Beth-din,* and the religious schools. Cuvier did favor the granting of French citizenship to individual Algerian Jews who might deserve it, but—resorting to a well-worn argument—said that in France itself not all Jews were granted citizenship at once. However, the Jewish members of the Commission fought Cuvier's position. At the meeting of March 29, 1843, Anspach made a statement, which was very characteristic of the French Jewish leaders:

"Even in the spirit of those who brought us together there exists the possibility of a reform. Wheresoever France has laid her hand, she has transformed and succeeded. The small difficulties of details will be overcome. The Jews are not a nation; they are an assembly of individuals, without political links, united only in the Synagogue. In assimilating them we shall not come down to them—as it has been said— we shall lift them up to us. They will gain the respect of the local population when the Moslems see among them the French organization. It has been said that the Jews have not asked for assimilation. They desire it with all their hopes, and even if they have not asked for it, we should take up this problem. They do not know all our civil customs, they ignore the use of family names and instead call themselves son of . . . son of . . . [The Jews of France] were formerly in the same frame of mind in France and they willingly exposed themselves to the new

conditions. There will be no obstacle to a similar measure in Algeria . . .
It has been said that in France the distinction between Jews and [other]
citizens still exists in some provinces. It is true that some still prefer
their religion to obligations under the French law; but they do give
up without murmuring. The same principle could be applied to Algeria,
because Jews are everywhere the same."

The other French members of the Commission approved
Anspach's ideas. Janvier declared that the time had come
for a full and fundamental reform and not for temporary
measures. The majority of the Commission were for applying French jurisdiction to the Algerian Jews.

But already in his instructions to the Commission of
February 17, 1843, the Minister of War had asserted that the
Commission should not decide to grant full French citizenship to the Algerian Jews because the Arabs would dislike
such a step and, besides, the Jews were not prepared for it,
in any case. Consequently, the Jewish members of the Commission acted carefully, demanding only the assimilation
of the Algerian Jews within the French sphere of jurisdiction.

It is worth while to note that, in connection with the
Commission's activities, the Minister of Justice, in a letter to
the Minister of War dated August 16, 1843, envisioned the
establishment of Jewish consistories in other French colonies.

At first the Ministry of War was disposed to accept the
Commission's project. In a letter of June 28, 1843, to the
Minister of Justice, the Minister of War did not express any
opposition to it. On February 19, 1844, the Commission's
proposal for a statute for the Algerian Jews was examined
by the *Conseil d'Etat,* France's highest juridical body. But
on the same day the Legislative Commissions of the Army and
the Navy decided to obtain first the opinion of the military
administration in Algeria itself. This was a routine course of
action whenever a measure concerning Algeria was being
prepared, but it greatly complicated and dragged out matters. Finally, the Ministry of War categorically decided
against the application of French jurisdiction in matters concerning the Algerian Jews even though this would not have

been tantamount to granting them French citizenship.

Algeria was administered by the military authorities, and no statute in favor of Algerian Jewry could have been adopted against their will. The military authorities of Algeria were strongly anti-Jewish, and the Governor of Algeria, Maréchal Bugeaud, was an open anti-Semite. On October 24, 1845, the Director-General of Algerian Civil Affairs Blondel wrote to Albert Cohn: "It is a pity to see a man of Maréchal Bugeaud's talent unwittingly carried away by miserable passions. . . . I cover my head with my coat in deploring the errors of a man who, in contradistinction to his excellent military abilities and his devotion to his counry, has so little understanding for governmental and administrative issues."[10]

On September 9, 1843, Bugeaud intervened at the Ministry against the prompt voting of a statute for the Algerian Jews. He wrote: "I found Oran much more beautiful since my last visit. Unfortunately, the largest part of its population consists of rapacious Jews who have become insolent because we emancipated them too soon." On November 30, 1843, he wrote again: "The insolence of the Jews who were emancipated too soon has given a new impetus to the discontent of the Moslems and it is no exaggeration to attribute the Moslems' aversion to this resentment. Would it then be wise now to sanction this state of affairs by legislative action resulting from too great tolerance? I do not think so. . . . They [the Jews] are still far away from human dignity." In Paris the Maréchal's protest was taken very seriously. On December 12, 1843, the Minister of War assured the Maréchal that the projected statute would not imply the emancipation of the Jews.[11]

The military Governor of Algeria also opposed granting to the Paris Central Consistory any right to check the activities of the Algerian consistories. He demanded that the Jewish problem of Algeria remain a purely colonial matter, for he was afraid that in the future French Jews might intervene

[10] AN, F¹⁹11143 (Report of July, 1845).
[11] *L'Univers israélite*, XX (1865), 535.

in favor of their Algerian co-religionists. His demand was granted.[12]

On November 9, 1845, an ordinance on the organization of the Algerian Jewish consistories was published. This document contained not even a trace of the Commission's original proposition to apply French jurisdiction to Algerian Jewish matters and to give the French Jews a certain amount of control over the Algerian consistories. In the spirit of the ordinance, the newly created consistories had only educational functions: establishing schools; seeing to it that the rabbis kept reminding the Jews that they should be faithful to France; reminding the Jews to abide by the moral principles of the decisions voted by the Sanhedrin and so on.

This ordinance represented a victory for the anti-Jewish elements within Algeria's military administration. The fight for Jewish emancipation had to continue. It was carried on by strengthening the anti-Orthodox elements in the Algerian consistories. Of course, this strategy pleased the French authorities. On May 26, 1846, the authorities of Algeria insisted that the Chief Rabbi of Algeria, the President and the majority of the consistorial leaders should be French Jews living in Algeria. On November 22, 1846, the Government acted in accordance with this request and appointed to the consistorial leadership of Algeria the Rabbi Michel A. Weill, Director of Algerian Jewish schools, the attorney Joseph Cohen, and the merchant Marx Gougenheim—all of them French Jews. The two other appointees were Dr. Messaoudo Miguères and Lazare Lévi Bram of the Chamber of Commerce, (both Algerian Jews).[13]

The Ordinance of November 9, 1845 became law a year later and the Algerian Consistory was officially installed on January 31, 1847. No one was satisfied with the results obtained, and there were many reasons for such dissatisfaction.

Algeria at that time, was suffering from severe eco-

[12] AN, F19 11143; Z. Szajkowski, loc. cit., pp. 54, 64-65.
[13] AN, F19 11143.

nomic depression. After the occupation in 1830, the Algerian Jews took up many new occupations: They traded with Europeans; wealthy Jews became very active in the real-estate business, building many houses and helping greatly to develop Algiers and other cities. Poor Jews worked for the French. But the depression which began in real-estate and other business fields at the end of 1846 ruined many Jews economically and the newly established consistories had to sacrifice many important activities in order to help these Jews to survive the hard times. In 1849 the Consistory of Algiers had an income of 54,540 francs (including 45,000 francs from ritual slaughtering). Of this sum, 42,000 francs were spent in weekly assistance to the poor, 2,200 francs for additional Passover help, and 3,500 francs for the distribution of meat and clothing.[14]

The proponents of rapid civil and religious reform were dissatisfied with the consistorial activities, and the orthodox element was scandalized by the demands of the reformists, who were mostly French Jews. The consistories were kept in a state of agitation by the numerous conflicts between these two factions, by dissensions between the rabbis and the lay members, by a strong antagonism between the rich and the poor, and by a multitude of conflicts of a purely private character.[15]

---

[14] AN, $F^{19}11143$, $F^{80}1631$.

[15] Following are a few instances of such factional conflicts: During the consistorial elections of 1847 in Constantine, the Consistory stated that the candidate Messaoud Ghozlan understood well the French spirit and the value of assimilation, while his adversary, the cantor Jacob Simon Ben Amour, was an enemy of progress with little knowledge of the French language. The Constantine Director of Civil Affairs warned that Ghozlan's victory would stir up trouble; nevertheless, he was appointed "in order to avoid a majority of the strictly religious elements." On January 21, 1848, the orthodox Jews of Mostaganem protested against the appointment of Salom Sarfati to the city council becuse he was born in Morocco. The French authorities of Oran reported to the Governor that "the fight . . . against Sarfati is one of old ideas and old influences against the civilizing movement and the educated people." Abraham Benaim [Ben Haim] was a leader of the Oran Jewish Community from 1835 to 1845. In 1848 he was elected to the Consistory, but later on being rejected, he wrote to the Governor that he was already "a partisan of progress and civilization," while his opponent, Kanoui, "was sowing wheat on the cemetery," that "the salary of the rabbi's servant was paid by the community," and so forth (AN, $F^{80}1631$).

The Revolution of 1848, through the introduction of *universel suffrage,* strengthened the orthodox element in the consistories. Control over the Algerian consistories was transferred from the military authorities to the Ministry of Justice and Religious Affairs. Rabbi Weill of Algiers, in a report to the Ministry, wrote that the Revolution found followers among the fanatical orthodox and the "demoralized" youth, for whom the word "Revolution" was a synonym for rejection of all authority and order. Before the Revolution the Government had appointed the consistorial members from a number of whealthy Jewish notables, but the Revolution brought into consistorial activities representatives of various Jewish classes. In his report Rabbi Weill strongly attacked *le titre pompeux de suffrage universel.* And he asked that the right to vote be taken away from the large number of poor as well as from the "foreigners and adventurers," that is, the immigrant Jews from Tunisia and Morocco, who were orthodox.[16]

Rabbi Weill's report was followed by two similar reports from Constantine and Oran, and these three were used as the basis for a draft of a new ordinance, which was at once supported by the Paris Central Consistory. This project revived the 1841-1843 proposals to speed up the emancipation of the Algerian Jews by placing their consistories under the control of the Central Consistory and appointing a leadership with a majority of French Jews living in Algeria. On October 19, 1850, the Minister of War expressed his opposition to these revived proposals, but the matter was held under discussion for another few years. On May

[16] Among the leaders of the orthodox opposition was a Jewish immigrant from Poland called Rubenstein, who was often denounced by the reformed Jews. Rubenstein and another Polish Jew, Dolilietz [Dolicky], in 1850 sent petitions to the Government against Rabbi Weill. Among the Jews who then lived in Algeria was a group of Jewish participants in the Polish revolution against Russia, among them Abraham Rogozinsky and his son Abraham, Moïse Fraedlinger [Feitlinger], Gottlieb Kruger, Isidore Pratkowsky, and others (AN, F^{80}607, 608, 630, 1631; F^{19}11144).

4, 1856, Rabbi Weill and his reform followers again renewed their old proposals, now supplemented by a number of additional demands: replacement of the numerous small synagogues (over 25 in Algiers, 10 in Constantine, 17 in Oran) by a few large ones; reduction of the influence of the rabbis, and the like. On July 8, 1857, the orthodox majority of Algerian Jewry sent a petition to the Government denouncing the proposals of Rabbi Weill and his friends, but these were nevertheless supported by the Central Consistory and in an official Government project of 1858.[17]

A decree of August 29, 1862 placed the Algerian consistories under the supervision of the Central Consistory (Article XI), which also had to mediate between the Algerian Jews and the Government. A representative of the Algerian Jews, who had to be a resident of Paris, became a member of the Central Consistory.[18] This was a great victory for the reform elements, whose aspirations were furthered still more by a Decree issued September 16, 1867, which abolished the special Central Consistory of Algeria and placed the three regional consistories of Algiers, Constantine, and Oran under the direct control of Paris.[19]

All these discussions and conflicts had one major positive point: They helped to draw the Government's attention to the problems of Algerian Jewry. Indirectly they also influenced the opinion of the *Senatus-Consult* of July 14, 1865, which stated that Algerian Jews were Frenchmen who had the right to demand individual French citizenship. But only a few Jews took advantage of this prerogative.

---

[17] "Situation des Israélites en Algérie. Rapport général," by Rabbi Michel A. Weill (AN, F¹⁹11143); AN, F⁸⁰1631; F¹⁹11144; *Organisation du Culte israélite en Algérie*, Rapport au Conseil de Gouvernement par M. Bequet, Conseiller-Rapporteur (Alger, 1858), 16 pp.; *Ministère de l'Instruction et des Cultes. Epreuve. Culte israélite* [Paris, April 1857, Second project of the Decree], 18 pp.; *L'Univers israélite*, May, 1857; Jaques Cohen, *Les Israélites de l'Algérie et le Décret Crémieux* (Paris 1900), p. 88.

[18] Isaac Uhry, *Recueil des Lois . . . concernant les Israélites depuis 1850 . . . 2me édition* (Bordeaux, 1887), pp. 44-47.

[19] *Ibid.*, p. 63.

All the discussions and decisions in favor of the Jews would probably have remained only half-successful attempts in the fight for Jewish emancipation if the Decree of October 24, 1870 had not granted collective French citizenship to the Algerian Jews.

POVERTY AND SOCIAL WELFARE AMONG FRENCH JEWS

(1800-1880)

2. WEALTH AND POVERTY ACCORDING TO OFFICIAL ESTIMATES

The government and Consistory taxes paid by Jews can give us some idea of their economic status, although we should take some precautions when we consider them; but the same precautions should also be taken in an approach to Gentile tax returns. Since French taxpayers have tried to evade paying large taxes, taxes are not always a very exact indication of the economic condition of France, and the same also applies to Jews. On Jan. 4, 1806, the commission to liquidate the debts of former Alsatian Jewish

---

Excerpts from the book published in 1954.

communities complained that the collection of the special tax to cover the debts based on the rate of the regular government taxes was unjust because sometimes the Jews with little property paid more than the rich Jews. In the city, e.g., more was paid for licences than in the rural areas. On Dec. 14, 1806, the Lower Rhine Jews wrote to the Ministry of the Interior that those Jews who had no real estate property and who did not even pay license taxes because they did not have any ostensible business (stores) were not required to pay any taxes at all—even if they had a considerable amount of cash and hold many promissary notes. The general condition was subject to constant change. On Feb. 8, 1803, Antoine-M. Hombourg of the Strasbourg Commercial Court and Séligman Witersheim, former receiver (*syndic*) of the Alsace Jews to liquidate the debts, wrote to the Prefect that since 1791 the economic status of the Jews had changed; Jews who were rich became poor, and vice versa. Therefore, the 1791 rate for real estate taxes could not serve as the base for the tax to cover the Jewish debts. The regional Nancy Consistory often repeated that the Jews who did have real estate property were poorer than the Jewish capitalists (money lenders)." But one cannot completely disregard this material, especially since we are interested primarily not in the amount of taxes collected but in the classes which the Jewish population was divided into for purposes of taxation. (In addition to the direct tax there was a hidden or secret tax in some Jewish Communities. Every Jew who thought his property worth more than the official valuation, placed an amount equivalent to the difference in tax caused by the undervaluation into a collection box.)²⁰

---

¹⁹ AdBR,V,dettes. "La petite fortune de M. May consiste en bien fonds, qui ne rapportent pas autant que de l'argent placé et que ces biens fonds payent déjà les Contributions au Gouvernement." Minutes of the regional Nancy Consistory, October 4, 1820. "Le consistoire ne peut suivre la base des contributions foncières, puisqu'il en résulterait, surtout pour les Israélites, que le propriétaire se trouverait lésé et surchargé, tandis que le très grand nombre d'individus se livrant à un commerce ou à des spéculations quelconques, et ayant une fortune mobilière pour laquelle ils ne paient que très peu de chose, seraient exclusivement avantagés; que c'est aussi ce qu'ont voulu prévenir les décrets et ordonnances, en ne fixant aucune base de répartition au consistoire, autres que la notoriété qu'il se procure." Idem, Nov. 10, 1820. "On est fort heureux de pouvoir retirer 3 % des capitaux placés en biens, de quelque nature qu'ils soient, et que, pour ces biens, les propriétaires en payant déjà à l'Etat des contributions très élevées auxquelles se soustrait le pétitionnaire en conservant sa fortune en portefeuille". Idem, Aug. 12, 1823. "La qualité d'Electeur n'est pas toujours le signe ni d'une grande fortune, ni même d'une fortune réelle; et au cas présent cela n'annonce rien autre chose qu'un plus grand nombre d'individus qui, dans la Meurthe, ont acquis des propriétés foncières; c'est-à-dire qui ont mieux aimé consolider leur avoir que d'en tirer un plus fort revenu. Ils ont aussi par là mis leur fortune à découvert, tandis que les capitalistes au contraire ne livrent pas le secret de leur situation et qu'ils retirent 5 et 6 pour cent nets de leurs fonds et ne sont atteins que par de faibles contributions personnelles". Idem, Aug. 6, 1827.
²⁰ When one of these boxes of the Committee to liquidate the debts of the former Carpentras Jewish Community was opened in Aix-en-Provence in June, 1822, it was found to contain 1,731.82 frs. In 1823, Aix collected 17,670 frs. from the direct tax to liquidate the debts and 2,031.82 frs. from the collection box. In appraising Jewish property the following items were included: furniture, metals, merchandise, debts owed to them,

In the year X (1801-1802), Alsatian Jews who had lived in Alsace in 1791 paid 73,618 frs. in taxes to the government (17,351 frs. in taxes on chattels, 21,872 frs. in taxes on real estate and 33,392 frs. in license fees). The Jews from Upper Rhine paid 20,878 frs. the Jews from Lower Rhine 37,307 frs. and Alsatian Jews who had settled in Paris after 1791, 15,432 frs.; but most Jews were in the lower tax brackets. According to one tax list which included 424 Jews (10,781 frs.) only 308 paid taxes on chattels. Of these 308 Jews, 11 paid less than 1 fr., 85—from 1 to 1.99 fr., 76—from 2 to 2.99 frs., 85—from 3 to 4.99 frs., 40—from 5 to 9.99 frs., 10—from 10 to 25 frs. and only one Jew paid more than 25 frs. Of the 424 Jews, only 246 paid license fees: 67—less than 5 frs., 22 from 5 to 10 frs., 148 from 11 to 25 frs., 8 from 26 to 50 frs. and only one Jew paid more than 100 frs.[21] The tax of 23,646 frs. to cower the expenses of the Jewish Assembly in Paris, called by Napoleon I, was based on the amount of government taxes paid by Jews. From the list drawn up to collect this tax, we learn that 2,407 Jews paid 48,217 frs.; 1,005 Jews paid less than 10 frs. each and only 22 paid 100 frs. or more.[22]

In a report dated April 29, 1806, the Prefect of Lower Rhine stated that on the list of 600 inhabitants who paid the largest taxes, there were only 2 Jews, while proportionately (22,000 Jews [?] among 455,427 Gentiles) there should have been 28 Jews on the list. There was not one Jew among the 30 wealthiest inhabitants of Lower Rhine who paid the highest taxes in 1816 (from 1,392 frs. to 3,997 frs.). In 1829, Jews from Gougenheim were too poor to pay taxes altogether, and in Alsatian communities such as Illkirch, Molsheim, Dupingheim, Haguenau, etc., there was not one Jew who paid 50 frs. in taxes. In 1829, there were only 154 Jews in Lower Rhine who paid 50 frs., or more, in direct taxes.[23] On a list of 550 inhabitants of Upper Rhine, who were in the highest tax brackets, in the year XI, there were only two or three Jews. In

---

jewelry, dishes, pensions of more than 500 frs., and dowries. The only things not included were bad debts, and linens. In 1816, the committee levied a tax of 6.87 1/2 frs. on every thousand frs. in the possession of the Jews, and in 1822, a 2 % tax. Letters from Mardoché Crémieux Jr. of Aix to the Committee; *Avis. La Commission formée pour la Répartition de la Dette de l'ancienne comis de Carpentras* (Ca 29 avril 1817); *Circulaire. La Commission...* (Ca février 1822). JTS.

[21] These figures are taken from the lists drawn up by tax officials in connection with dividing a tax to be levied on Jews, which was to pay the debts of the former Jewish Communities of Alsace. AN,F19-1849-I;AdBR,V dettes.

[22] This register (ZS) comprises three different kinds of government taxes; here only the total sum is given.

[23] AdBR,V.Plan du culte juif, 1829; M-VII-190;AN,FICIII (Bas-Rhin 4). In 1807, the following Jews of Lower Rhine paid 200 frs. or more in government taxes: Salomon Samuel, Lazard Meyer (of Paris), Samuel Marx, Israël Relous, Samuel Mayeo, Daniel Lévey, Léopold (Vve de Samuel). The total number of Lower Rhine Jews who paid 48,217 frs. government taxes, was 2,407. In 1826, the following Jews of Lower Rhine paid 100 frs. or more in Consistorial taxes: Moyse Lévy (*Ingwiller*), Isaac Vve Lévy, Jacob Loebel (*Marmoutier*), Isaac Weill le jeune, Isaac Weill le moyen (*Müttersholtz*), Auguste Ratisbonne, L. Ratisbonne (*Strasbourg*). A total number of 1,256 Jews in 109 communities of Lower Rhine paid 13,347 frs.

1806, only 114 Upper Rhine Jews paid license fees; 410 paid personal and house taxes, but no land tax. 489 Jews paid less than 2 frs. land tax each and less than 4 frs. personal and house tax; 1,186 Jews paid less than 8 frs. land tax and the same amount for personal tax and chattel tax. A report of the Prefecture of Upper Rhine, dated June 2, 1808, stated that 15 of 28 Jewish families in Colmar were poor; that 52 of the 84 Jewish families in Bergheim were poor, 8 possessed less than 300 frs., 11 from 300 to 2,000 frs., 10 up to 25,000 frs. and 2 more than 25,000 frs. An official document about the Jews of Horbourg, dated June 10, 1808, stated that of 30 Jewish families 6 were worth from 5,000 to 20,000 frs. and the other 24 were barely able to subsist. On May 5, 1808, the government classified the Wintzenheim Jews according to their economic status as follows: the first 5 classes consisted of 1, 4, 16, 12 and 14 families; 7 families in the 6th class and 56 families in the 7th class (Jews who were too poor to pay any taxes at all). Of 19 families who lived in Wellosheim, only one Jew possessed as much as 7,000 frs. 1—2,000 frs., 5—from 400 to 800 frs., 7—100 frs. and 5—nothing. A report on the 47 Jewish families of Herrlisheim stated that 24 owned nothing, though they did pay some nominal taxes; three families had the notation "ruined" after their names. On April 22, 1808, the mayor of Woeglenshoffen reported that all 8 Jewish families of this town were poor and without means of support. Of the 43 families of Hallstat, 29 were listed as "poor" and 9 as possessing from 500 to 5,000 frs.; two families possessed from 30 to 40,000 frs."

According to a report of 1823, the Jews of Upper Rhine owned 1,127 hectares of land and horses, valued at 2,160,000 frs. The 1,127 hectares were divided as follows: 557 hectares valued at 800,000 frs. in the Altkirch arrondissement, 70 valued at 360,000 frs. in Belfort arrondissement and 500 valued at 1,000,000 frs. in Colmar arrondissement. In the Altkirch arrondissement, Jews owned houses valued at 300,000 frs., 100 hectares of woodland valued at 50,000 frs.; the remainder consisted of farmland. Of the 320 Jewish families in the canton of Wintzenheim (arrondissement of Colmar) 110 owned houses valued at 231,000 frs., 72 owned land valued at 180,000 frs.; Jews living outside of the canton had real property valued at 120,000 frs. Mortgages held by Jews were valued at 600,000 frs. Jewish property in the canton was valued at 1,131,000 frs.; two-thirds of the property was owned by Jews who lived in Wintzenheim." The whole estimate, however, is subject to review. Of the

" *Département du Haut-Rhin. Liste de cinq cent cinquante plus imposés...* (P an XI); AdBR,V,dettes. In 1825-26, the following Jews of the regional Colmar Consistory paid 100 frs. or more in Consistorial taxes: *Wintzenheim:* Benjamin Moyse Bloch. *Colmar:* Léon Rueff. *Bergheim:* Salomon Sée, Israél Gabriel Sée. *Grussenheim:* Lévy Nathan Schoengrun. *Ribeauvillé:* J. Daniel Sée. *Soultzmatt:* Leopold Dreyfus. *Uffholtz:* Mayer Beer Manheimer. *Thann:* Paul Lévy. *Mulhouse:* Elie Lantz. *Dürmenach:* Raphaël Lang, Emanuel Hauser. *Altkirch:* Jacques Wolf. *Belfort:* Constant Picard, Lazard Mayer. A total of 947 Jews from 57 communities paid 16,447 frs.
" AdHR,V108. According to Lancastel, the Jews of Upper Rhine owned

000,000 frs. in mortgages held by Jews, a considerable amount consisted of mortgages already paid off and not recorded as paid, guarantee mortgages, etc.

In 1829, the Jewish Consistory of Metz stated that in all of Metz there was not even one rich Jew whose annual *rente* amounted to 15,000 frs. In a petition dated the same year, the Consistory declared that in the whole Moselle Department, there was not one Jew who had an annual income of 15-20 thousand frs.; 20-25 families possessed 100-200 thousand frs.; the rest lived in poverty."

In the Departmental archives of Moselle, there is an interesting inquiry dated 1839, on the economic status of 1,296 Jewish families who lived in Metz or came from Metz and lived elsewhere, and who were required to pay a tax to repay the debts of the former Jewish community of Metz. The government tax officials reported on all Jewish families as to whether they were wealthy, well to do, poor, etc. (see Table I). Only 548 families were considered wealthy and well to do, 208 fairly well to do, 170 not well to do, and 270 without possessions, or poor. We must remember that tax officials have always had a tendency to overestimate Jewish property, and yet they stated that the majority was not rich. An official wrote about Raphaël Cerf of Colmar that he considered him a rich man because in comparison with the other Jews of Colmar he was wealthy. Another official wrote about Théodore Lévy of Lower Rhine, who was also considered wealthy, that he was "riddled with debts." According to same questionary 1,189 families paid government tax of 103,132 frs.; i.e., an average of less than 100 frs. per family: 264 paid 100 frs. or more; 499 from 26 to 99 frs.; 118 from 6 to 10 frs. and 87, five or less."

It is more than a hypothesis that Jews paid heavier taxes than non-Jews. In 1813, the Prefect of Upper Rhine ordered that the approximate 10,000 Jews of the Department should pay a special defense contribution of 53,000 frs., and the 404,000 non-Jews should pay only 29,000 frs. From the Jews he demanded another 300,000 frs. in the form of a loan. When Jews protested and declared they were unable to pay such a sum, he answered with threats, which he could not carry out only because he had to escape from the invading army. During the invasion the French administration of the Department continued to persecute the Jews economically. Not only were the Jews required to pay a disproportionate part of the general contribution of 620,000 frs., but also had to pay a special contribution of 304,000 frs.; out of this special sum levied, the administration succeeded in wresting 50,839 frs. from the Jews."

1,127 hectares valued at 1,262,000 frs. Betting de Lancastel, *Considérations sur l'état des Juifs* (S 1824) p. 87.
²⁶ *Observations du ci de Metz, en réponse à la pétition... par le Sieur Louis Rottembourg* (M [1830]) p. 16 (AN,F19-11030); Lettre du Consistoire de la Moselle au Ministre, 29 mars 1829 (ZS).
²⁷ AdM,V159.
²⁸ In July 1815, all the merchants, manufacturers, and capitalists of the Altkirch arrondissement were required to pay a total sum of 253,915 frs.; but 40.000 frs. of this sum was to be paid collectively by the Jewish

In 1842-1843, a list of Jews of Metz origin was drawn up in order to impose on them a tax of 21,721 frs. to liquidate the debts of the former Jewish community. Only those families who had material resources of 200 frs. or more were required to pay this tax, and it seems that strict control was exercised. Only 1,099 families were on the list, though the number of families that originated in Metz was much greater; it seems, however, that the others were too poor to pay the tax. 104 families were listed as having material resources of 200 frs., 251 from 250 to 400 frs., 104—500 frs., 144 from 600 to 900 frs., 377 from 1,000 to 3,000 frs., 91 from 3,500 to 9,000. There were very few really wealthy Jews whose families originated in Metz: only 21 worth 10 to 25 thousand frs. and 7 worth more than 25,000 frs. In connection with this, we must further emphasize that these wealthy Jews had all emigrated from Metz and settled in other parts of France. In Metz, itself, and in the whole Department of Moselle only 630 families were required to pay the tax. Here, were concentrated the Jews of Metz origin who had little wealth, and none of them were classified as having a property of 10,000 frs. or more. The largest number of wealthy Jews from Metz lived in Paris, but Paris also had its share of poor Jews from Metz, since only 144 Parisian Jews were required to pay the tax." In 1853, a similar list was drawn up which included 1,662 families who originated in Metz. The property of all 1,662 families was estimated at 7,644,650 frs. (see Table II), but the majority appeared to possess small properties: 667 families 1,000 frs. and less; 751 from 1,200 to 5,000 frs.; 135 from 6,000 to 10,000 frs.; 96 from 11 to 50,000 frs. and 13 more than 50,000 frs. Paris alone with 409 of the 1,662 families had more wealthy Jews than all other parts of the country together. 13 families had material resources (2,205,000 frs.) almost as great as 802 other families (2.419,750 frs.)."

In 1825, a total of 553 Jewish families of the regional Nancy Consistory paid 8,871 frs. in Consistorial taxes, but only 14 paid 100 frs. or more." In a prefectural report on the canton of Toul (Meurthe), dated April 7, 1808, it was stated that in the Northern and Southern portions of the canton there were 49 Jewish families (285 persons) of which seven earned their living from money-lending

---

community, in addition to 200 bed sheets, 200 shirts, 100 mattresses, 2 wooden bathtubs, 30 large jars of vinegar, grain, etc. for the occupation armies. AN,F7-9819(63956); *Extrait des registres de la Préfecture du Département du Haut-Rhin, du 26 juillet 1814. Arrêté No. 400,* 4 p.; *Par ordonnance de son Excellence le Général en Chef de l'armée, Mr. le Comte de Wrede* [C 1914] 7 p. AN,7-9819(63956); R. Anchel Contribution levée en 1813-14 sur les Juifs du Haut-Rhin. *REJ,* vol. LXXXII (1926) p. 494-501; Am Altkirch.

 ²⁹ *Rôle de répartition pour l'extinction des dettes de l'ancienne communauté des Juifs de Metz. Année* 1842 [M 1843] 32 p. BN,Ld185-23;JTS.

³⁰ *Liquidation des dettes de l'ancienne communauté juive de Metz. Mise en recouvrement du rôle de 1853* (M 1853). 76 p. BN,Ld185-34;JTS.

³¹ *Nancy:* Elie Marx, Jules Godfray, Salomon Moise Lévy, Lippmann Lippmann, Lambert Lévi, Joseph Lévi, Auguste Lévisthal, Salomon Lévi, Berr de Turique (père). *Pont-à-Mousson:* Joseph Cain dit Lajeunesse. *Verdun:* David Daniel, Mayer Lippmann. *Etain:* Aaron Cain. *Neufchâteau:* B.d. May.

and the rest from work. The 49 families paid 1,167 frs. in government taxes (not including the door and window tax), but only 6 paid more than 50 frs. each. Their possessions were estimatted as follows: six families at 300 frs. each; 25 from 1,000 to 2,500 frs.; 5 from 4,000 to 6,000 frs.; 8 from 15,000 to 30,000 frs. One Jew's fortune was valued at 200,000 frs., and 4 had no possessions at all. In the arrondissement of Château-Salins (in the same Department), there were, according to a report dated May 15, 1808, 136 Jewish families (702 persons); of these, only 15 families possessed more than 5,000 frs. each. On June 2, 1808, Lunéville reported on 83 Jewish families in the arrondissement. Of these, 29 possessed a combined total of 807,000 frs.; 17 were paupers, and the others also had no possessions. There was one wealthy Jew there, whose fortune amounted to 200,000 frs. According to another report (of the same date) 84 Jewish families (488 persons) lived in the arrondissement. Their combined direct tax amounted to 8,328 frs.: 29 paid less than 5 frs.; 30 from 5 to 25 frs.; 19 from 25 to 100 frs. and only 6, 100 frs. each; 1/3 were listed as paupers and 13 as possessing nothing. The report also stated that the wealth of one family was unknown; 16 possessed 2,400 frs. or less each, 28 from 3,000 to 10,000 frs.; 17 from 8,000 to 40,000 frs. and 12, 50,000 frs. or more.[32] In 1828, 33 Jewish families of Besançon (Doubs) paid from 5.05 to 457.38 frs. in direct taxes; the total tax of these families was 2,735 frs., but only 6 paid more than 100 frs. each.[33]

3. JEWISH POVERTY IN THE LOWER RHINE IN THE '50s

In 1858, L. J. Reboul-Deneyrol, secretary of the Prefecture of Lower Rhine, published the results of a questionary on poverty and charity in the Department.[34] The results of the questionary showed that in the whole Department of Lower Rhine, there were 46,317 paupers of a total population of 587,793, i.e., 1 of every 12 inhabitants was a pauper. Among the 22,008 Jews in Lower Rhine 2,814 were paupers; i.e. 13%; 4% more than among Catholics, 8% more than among Protestants, 6% more than among Calvinists (see Table III). There were Jewish paupers in 90 of the 130 communities where Jews lived: in 3 communities from 101 to 282

[32] AN,F19-11009;AdMM,V.
[33] AdDoubs,V. "Quatorze Israélites du Doubs peuvent seuls supporter une cotisation, que tous les autres sont dans la misère et n'existent, pour la plupart, qu'au moyen des sacrifices journaliers que ceux aisés font pour les soutenir." Minutes of the regional Nancy Consistory, Feb. 24, 1819.
[34] Camille Granier, who compiled a bibliography of publications dealing with charity and philanthropy in France, considered this questionary a masterpiece of official statistics in France. This questionary was also utilized later by the Alsatian economist F. Bernahrd. L.-J. Reboul-Deneyrol, *Paupérisme et bienfaisance dans le Bas-Rhin* (P-S 1858) p. 469, 482; Boudin, in *JSSP*, vol. I (1860), p. 55; *AI*, vol. XIX (1858) p. 731; *La Presse* (P), 18 XI 185;8 Camille Garnier, *Essai de bibliographie charitable* (P 1891) p. 508; F. Bernhard, *Moralité publique, paupérisme et bienfaisance publique et privée,* p. 391, 546, 564 [vol. III de la *Description du département du Bas-Rhin* (P 1871).]

paupers each (the greatest number in Strasbourg), in 11 communities from 51 to 100 paupers, in 17 communities from 31 to 50 paupers, in 20 communities from 11 to 20 paupers and in 22 communities 10 or less. Bueswiller had a population of 75 Jews, 34 of them were paupers; 18 of the 152 Jews in Schweinheim were paupers; 131 of the 759 Jews in Bischeim; 48 of the 390 Jews in Brumath; 23 of the 150 Jews in Wittersheim; 35 of the 163 Jews in Herrlisheim; 47 of the 125 Jews in Dauendorf; 50 of the 93 Jews in Gunstett; 282 of the 2,387 Jews in Strasbourg; 162 of the 262 Jews in Lingolsheim; 53 of the 334 Jews in Lauterbourg; 66 of the 184 Jews in Trimbach; 79 of the 280 Jews in Surbourg; 19 of the 42 Jews in Drachenbronn. Jewish poverty stands out more clearly when considered in proportion to the poverty of the rest of the population. 128 Jews of every 1,000 were paupers as compared with 88 per 1,000 Catholics and 52 per 1,000 Lutherans.

Jews gave the following reasons for their poverty: hard times and the high cost of living—22 communities (out of 187 of all the religious parishes), low wages—8 communities (out of 83), unemployment—12 communities (out of 74), inherited poverty—1 community (out of 111). All these are conditions for which the pauper was not responsible. Reasons for poverty which show the pauper to be responsible were hardly applicable to Jewish communities: bad marriages—1 community (out of 31), recklessness—0 (out of 93), wild parties and cabarets—0 (out of 131), luxury—0 (out of 61), estrangement from religion—0 (out of 49), miscellaneous reasons—0 (out of 128). Here, we are dealing with settled Jews who were unable to earn a livelihood and had to have recourse to charity. Deneyrol characterized the Jews as a very industrious people, if anything a little too industrious because their industry affected their health adversely. A Jew had to exert every effort to get by, for if he failed, his position was catastrophic. With small savings, the Jew was able to get by, but in order to be able to save, he had to deny himself necessities such as food. If he was, however, unable to save some money, he was lost and found himself in dire need. In this instance, the Jew was in a worse position than the Gentile.[25] In some communities, Deneyrol wrote, poverty reached the stage of a catastrophe. The Mayor of Mommenheim stated in his reply to the questionary that the Jews were very poor. For several years, business in the villages was very bad, and Jews were getting poorer all the time; more than 65 of the 300 Jews were outright paupers.

In summarizing the results of the questionary, the author made a statement which has often been made in reports on Alsatian Jews; that the Jewish population of Alsace consisted primarily of two classes: a wealthy class, and a poor class which lived by serving the wealthy. The middle class which was being created through industry and agriculture was not as numerous or important

---

[25] The historian A. Gasser wrote that the Jews acquired their property by work and thrift. *RA*, vol. LVI (1905) p. 220.

among Jews as it was among Gentiles. Jewish workers who graduated from trade schools as skilled mechanics (the French Jews had a few very good trade schools) seldom became first class factory employees. For the most part they emigrated to other sections of France, or got into a business which was related to their trade. It is, however, not correct that among the Jews there were only the very rich and the poor. All the figures on taxation and Jewish property used in this study demonstrate that there did exist a Jewish middle class, that transition from poor to rich was not abrupt."

The results of this questionary might lead to the conclusion that because of the greater development of Jewish charity, and the resultant better care of Jewish paupers as compared with Gentiles, more accurate figures of the number of Jewish poor were available, and so more Jewish paupers were listed than Gentiles. Actually, this is not the case. Among Jews, there were more paupers than among Gentiles, but the percentage of Jewish paupers who received aid from organized charitable institutions was smaller than the percentage of Gentile paupers. Of 2,814 Jewish paupers, 705 received no assistance at all. In 27 out of 90 communities, Jewish paupers received no official assistance. In the whole Department, 83% of the paupers received aid, but only 75% of the Jewish paupers were given assistance in comparison to 83% of the Catholic paupers, and 85% and 89% of the Lutherans and Reformed paupers (see **Table III**); this despite the fact that the Jewish philanthropic societies functioned better than the Gentile. In 1856, 5 Jewish philanthropic societies in Lower Rhine had an income of 31,845 frs., while 28 Protestant societies had an income of 182,305 frs. Certainly, private charity was better developed among Jews," but Deneyrol's study was based on information reecived from organized, rather than private charities. Had private charities been included, the number of Jewish paupers, in the results, would have been greater, because many poor Jews were ashamed to ask for assistance openly. Nor were most of the poor Jews aged (see Table III), or people who had no occupations at all, but they were Jews who simply could not earn enough to live on (as we shall see, the same was true of the Jewish paupers of Paris).

[36] The orthodox leader Créhange wrote satirically on the Jewish Consistories: "La richesse aura son représentant, la pauvreté aura le sien, et la classe moyenne, qui est la plus nombreuse, en aura deux." *UI*, vol. II (1845) p. 71.
[27] In 1843, the sub-prefect of Château-Salins (Meurthe) wrote that the Jews donated much more to charity than their fortunes warranted (AdMM,V); "La charité israélite cherche avant tout à faire le bien en secret". *UI*, vol. XII (1857), p. 415 (reprinted from the *Jüdisches Folksblatt*); "Mattoné besseisser'. H. Meiss, *Traditions populaires alsaciennes* (Ni 1928) p. 66. Of 15 Jewish charity institutions existing in Strasbourg in 1922, 11 were founded prior to 1870. Of 19 Protestant institutions 8 were founded before 1870: A. Hermann—Laure Weil, Les œuvres sociales israélites à Strasbourg; A. Hermann—E. Hertzog, Les œuvres sociales protestantes à Strasbourg. *Collection d'études économiques médicales et sociales*, cahiers 8 B-C (S 1922).

8. SOME STATISTICS ON JEWISH POVERTY IN PARIS

We can get some idea of Jewish poverty in Paris from the activities of the Jewish Philanthropic Committee (*Comité de Bienfaisance*) founded in 1809." Paris at that time had a Jewish population of 2,908 (840 families), and there were 300 (92 families) registered with the Committee. A report dated October 18, 1827, dealing with the attempt to establish a Jewish hospital, estimated that there were 1,500 to 1,600 Jewish paupers divided into four classes: 1) 250 families (750 persons) that were members of mutual-aid societies, and received aid when they were ill; 2) 120 families (350 persons), who did not live in the city, and were not members of societies; 3) servants; 4) foreigners. The last two classes may have consisted of 400-500 individuals; they were entirely without means of support in case of illness. In 1835, a special committee determined that 451 families regularly accepted charity; if each family consisted of 4 persons, and the whole Jewish population of Paris of 8,000 Jews, one out of five Jews in the city was a pauper. In 1840, the periodical *Les Archives Israélites* estimated that there were 7,000 Jews in Paris, and 1,636 (660 families) were registered with the Jewish Philanthropic Committee and receiving aid. The number of paupers registered with the Committee continued to increase much more rapidly than the general Jewish population of the capital. In 1836, 469 families (1,414 persons) were registered; in 1851, 876 families (2,271 persons, of which 98 were soldiers and persons under arrest)." In 1841, only 228 families were provided with bread, but

---

VI, suppl., 1861, pp. 22-23. Such an insurance policy against house begging was organized in the '90s by the Jewish Philanthropical Committee. Printed report of the Committee, May 7, 1896, p. XIV.

According to the printed annual reports of the Paris Consistory and of the philanthropic Committee. These reports were printed under different titles, mostly under the title of *Consistoire Israélite de la circonscription de Paris. Compte rendu général...* In 1861, was published a report for the years 1858-1860; in 1873, for the years 1866-1871. The reports of the Philanthropic Committee appeared for the first few years under the title of *Comité Consistorial Israélite de secours et d'encouragement*. Later, the title was changed to *Comité de bienfaisance israélite*. Some reports were published without any title, as for instance the important report of May 10, 1847. These reports are very rare, and I was unable to see a complete collection. The archives of the Philanthropic Committee were destroyed during World War II.

In the very first years of the Nineteenth century, there were seven Jewish mutual aid societies with 212 members in Paris. In 1809, the Consistory decided to merge the seven societies into one charity society. After long discussions and internal struggles, the society was formed under the name of *Comité de la Société Israélite d'encouragement et de secours*. Later the society changed its name to *Comité de bienfaisance*. L. Kahn, *Le Comité de bienfaisance* (P 1886) p. 5-11 ; Ibid, *Les Sociétés de secours mutuels philanthropiques et de prévoyance* (P 1887) p. 13.

" In 1838, 491 families (1,384 persons) were registered; in 1840, 660

10 years later, in 1851, 506 families received 17,354 kilos. In 1841, 237 families were provided with meat (583 1/2 kilos), in 1851, 441 families received 3,429 kilos. In 1841, 417 families were provided with fire wood, in 1851, 531. In 1841, 53 families were provided with matzoth (4,688 kilos), in 1851, 820 families received 5,910 kilos. In 1847, when the price of grain rose, the Consistory not only had to increase the amount of free matzoth that it distributed, but sell some matzoth at cost. Altogether, the Consistory purchased 225 sacks of flour for matzoth; 165 were sold and 60, i.e. more than 1/3, were distributed without charge to 2,602 persons (815 families and 215 single persons). In addition, 368 families applied to the Rabbi for permission to purchase matzoth at cost, and it was granted. This means that in 1847, 1,183 families were aided by the Philanthropic Committee in obtaining matzoth. In 1857, *Les Archives Israélites* estimated the Jewish population of Paris at 18,000 and that 1/6, i.e. 3,000, was supported by charity. (According to the government census of 1861, there were 14,867 Jews in Paris, and according to the census of 1872, 23,434 Jews.)"

Another good source of information on the poverty of Parisian Jews are the reports of the Jewish hospital" As early as June 1, 1826, an appeal was made to establish a 12 bed Jewish hospital. This hospital was established in 1842 especially for poor Jews, but

---

families (1,636 persons); in 1845, 683 families (1,683 persons, of these, 117 were soldiers and persons under arrest); in 1847, 816 families (2,293 persons); in 1848, 870 families (2,320 persons, of which 134 were soldiers and persons under arrest).

" *AI*, vol. II (1841) p. 24; vol. XVIII (1857) p. 323; L. Kahn, *Le Comité*, p. 30-31; Ibid, *Les professions*, p. 69-73; Ibid, *Les Juifs à Paris*, p. 139; Ibid, *Histoire des écoles*, p. 61; A printed report of the Philanthropic Committee June I, 1826, 3 p.; Printed report of the Paris Consistory for the years 1858-1860, p. 4.

"Considérant qu'ayant à répartir pour 1809 une somme de 17,000 francs... la majeure partie des taxes a dû nécessairement retomber sur un petit nombre de personnes aisées attendu que la très grande partie des Israélites du département de la Seine se compose de gens peu fortunés et d'indigènes." Decisions of the Paris Consistory, November 18, 1810.

"451 familles! Songez, Messieurs, l'abîme effrayant que ce mot découvre; en comptant la population israélite de Paris à 8,000 âmes et ces indigènes à 4 individus par famille on trouve qu'il y a un indigent sur cinq israélites à Paris... En Angleterre où la plaie du paupérisme est la plus horrible de l'Europe civilisée, on ne compte qu'un pauvre sur 17 individus" (ZS).

In 1862, the Paris Consistory wrote on the economic status of its members in the '20s—'40s: "A une époque où les fortunes particulières étaient si médiocres et où l'aisance ne se recontrait que chez un nombre très restreint d'Israélites". *Rapport... l'édification de deux Temples* (P 1862), p. 3. "Nous ne nous occuperons donc pas des enfants des grandes familles, nous ne nous occuperons que de la classe moyenne et pauvre, de cette dernière surtout, car c'est la plus nombreuse et la plus malheureuse". A. Créhange, *Projet... pour l'établissement à Paris d'une école de commerce, d'arts et métiers pour les jeunes israélites* [P 1844] p. 4.

" According to the printed reports of the Consistory and the Hospital. The reports of the hospital were published under the title *Consistoire Israélite de Paris. Maisons de secours et de retraite jondes par M. le Baron James de Rothschild, Compte moral et financier;* L. Kahn, *Le Comité*, p. 80, 83; *Paris, charitable et prévoyant* (P 1897) p. 461, 466; *Statistique de France*, 2⁰ série, vol. VI,.p. 168. One of the reasons for the founding of a Jewish hospital was the proselyting propaganda in the city hospitals. The hospital (*Maison de secours*) was opened in 1842; during a 10 years 3 months period, 1,400 patients were admitted there. (In 1861, the number of Jewish patients in the 7 general hospitals of Paris had been reduced to 14.)

not all the patients were registered with the Philanthropic Committee. This is further proof that poverty among the Parisian Jews was greater than the Philanthropic Committee's records show (of 86 patients hospitalized up to December 1842, only 18 were registered with the Committee). May 26, 1852, marked the opening of the Rothschild Hospital, which was built from funds contributed by Baron James de Rothschild.[92] The Rothschild Hospital admitted: 8,673 patients from 1852 to 1864, and 20,980 from 1865 to 1884. The number of patients constantly increased: an average of 745 a year between 1861 and 1865, 1,160 between 1866 and 1871. In the Nineties, the number of patients decreased: only 7,294 in 1889-95, but this was due to the decision to admit tubercular patients only in exceptional cases. In the whole Seine Department, there were 20 hospitals (of these, 19 were in Paris) which had 94,745 patients. Of all the private hospitals, the Jewish Hospital had the most patients, the second largest was a Catholic hospital with 612 patients in 1895 (the Rothschild Hospital had then 1,012).[93]

9. LIFE WAS MISERABLE AND DEATH EVEN MORE SO

The mortality rate and the figures on graves and funerals give us a tragic picture of poverty among Parisian Jews.[94] The Jews of Paris had no more painful problem than that of burial. Every Jew, whether he was rich or poor, aspired to have a grave of his

---

[92] *Inauguration de l'Hôpital Israélite fondé par M. James de Roth-schild. Le 26 mai* 1852 (P 1852) 38 p.; *Règlement de la Maison de Secours fondée par M. le Baron James de Rothschild, rue de Picpus, No. 76, à Paris* [P, 1852] 58 p. (litho.); *UI*, vol. VII (1852) p. 377-382. In 1864, Baron de Rothschild donated 30,000 frs. to the Paris Consistory for the foundation of a children's hospital. The Consistory had to cover the yearly budget of 10,000 frs. *Souscription en faveur de l'hospice des enfants* [1864] 3 p. In 1899, a society of Jewish nurses (*Œuvre israélite de garde-malades*) was formed in Paris (according to a printed leaflet).
[93] On the whole, patients in the Rothschild Hospital were treated well. The food was good, and the physicians were well qualified. Of an expenditure of 64,928 frs. from July 1852 to June 1855, 24,868 frs. went for meat, 15,036 frs. for wine, and 10,903 frs. for bread (see note 91). It is worth while to present some facts about Jewish hospitals outside of Paris. The Metz Jewish hospital was an old institution, dating from the Seventeenth century. In 1841, the author of a Metz guide wrote that food in the Jewish hospital was better than in the Christian. The hospital had 24 beds. The Jewish physician O. Terquem received an annual salary of 300 frs., but for that sum he was also required to visit the sick Jewish poor in their homes. The Lunéville Jewish hospital and home for the aged (founded in 1856) also distributed soup among poor Jews. In the Mulhouse Jewish hospital and home for aged, 137 patients were treated in July 1867-December 1872. The expenses reached 104,782 frs. From 1835 on there existed in Bordeaux a committee to help sick Jews at home. For that reason, the number of Jewish patients in the city hospital was small. In Marseille, there was also a Jewish hospital, 16 patients were treated there in 1862, 9 in 1867, 7 in 1870. Dr. N. Netter, *Geschichte des israelitischen Hospizes in Metz* (M 1910); Ibid, Das Hospiz in Metz. *SIW*, vol. VIII, No. 10 (1911); Maurice Aron, L'Asile des vieillards israélites de Lunéville. *Annuaire des AI...* 5668 (P 1907) p. 46-53; *Cr du Comité de l'Hospice — Hôpital israélite de Mulhouse* (Ml, 1867, 1869, 1872); Isaac Uhry, *Monographie du culte israélite à Bordeaux* (B 1892) p. 16. According to a survey of 1904, Jewish hospitals existed then in Paris, Bayonne, Lyon, and Marseille.
[94] Statistical data on Jewish and general mortality, burials, etc. were

own after he had passed on." The poor had to depend on the generosity of the charity organizations. In Paris, however, matters were not so simple. Until 1809 or 1810, Jews were buried on two small cemeteries of Montrouge and La Villette. After 1810, interment commenced in Jewish corners of general city cemeteries."

If the family was too poor to pay for a cemetery plot, the deceased pauper was buried temporarily in a common grave (*fosse commune*) and after 5 years the bones were exhumed and disposed of." Only the poor Jews suffered from this practice; the wealthier ones usually provided family plots for themselves, while they were still alive. (In 1847, the price of a permanent grave was 550 frs. and a grave for 5 years—50 frs.) People used to say that "one cannot die in Paris" (*on ne peut pas mourir à Paris*), and feared burial in a common grave for 5 years. In 1868, Rabbi Benoît Lévy wrote: "I know Parisian Jews who visit their ancestors' graves in Alsace and Lorraine, but in Paris there is no sign of their parents' graves after five years". In a petition of 1841, the Jews of Paris protested against the practice of reclaiming the ground (*la reprise des terrains*) of temporary Jewish graves. That same year, the orthodox Jewish leaders A. Créhange and M. Bolviller published a brochure in which they protested against the practice of exhuming and disposing of the bones from Jewish paupers' graves. The walthy—they wrote—will be able to visit the graves of their ancestors, erect fine tombstones, and decorate the gravesite, but the citizens of the middle and poor classes will not be able to pray at the grave of a loved one; the son will no longer be able to visit his father's grave, and pray for his sick mother or sister; a young girl will no longer be able to visit the grave of her mother. who passed away just at the time that her advice and help were most needed. This situation gave rise to considerable friction during the revolutionary days of 1848. In 1856, a certain Léopold Riess complained in a letter to the Paris Consistory that the Rabbi

obtained from the following sources: printed reports of the Consistory and the Philanthropic Committee; documents in the author's possession; ArchCParis,1840-1844,1855,1866; AdSeine,V31; AN,F19-11032(Inhumations et taxes, 1894-1896); *AI*, vol. XVIII (1857), p. 263-264; L. Kahn, *Le Comité*, p. 129; A. Husson, De la population indigente... *JSSP*, vol. V (1864) p. 293; T. Loua, De la mortalité à Paris dans ses rapports avec la transformation de la ville. *JSSP*, vol. VI (1865) p. 51, 83; *Documents relatifs au service des pompes funèbres de la ville de Paris pendant l'année* 1865 (—1866, 1868, 1869); *Recherches statistiques sur la ville de Paris et le département de la Seine*, vol. III (1860) p. 317; E. Buret, *oc*. p. 159-160.
⁹⁵ On January 6, 1791, Berr-Isaac Berr of Nancy wrote to the Jewish Community of Metz, that he had paid it 75 pounds annually for the privilege of being buried on the Metz Cemetery. AN,F19-1849-I.
⁹⁶ At first on Père-Lachaise; after 1825, on the Montmartre Cemetery (at first only for paupers in temporary graves); after 1828, on the Montparnasse Cemetery; from 1863 to 1865 on the Eastern Cemetery of Paris; after 1874, on the Ivry Cemetery; after 1875, on the Southern Cemetery of Paris. L. Kahn, *Le Comité* p. 94-125.
⁹⁷ It is worth while to mention the itemized expenses of a poor man's burial in July 1823, which amounted to 40 frs.: "Détail des frais d'inhumation pour les pauvres (1823); habillements mortuaires—16 [francs], la bière—6, fossoyeurs—2, quatre porteurs—10, pour garder le corps—6, total —40 frs." ArchCParis, a letter dated July. 1823.

often attended rich funerals on Père Lachaise, or Monmartre, but
seldom came to Montparnasse, where most poor Jews were buried.
The Prefect of Paris estimated in a letter to the Jewish Consistory,
dated August 10, 1852, that in the coming 5 years 1,250 Jews would
die. Of these, 1,000 would be buried free, 150 in temporary graves,
and 100 in permanent graves. In the '60s, it was estimated (according to Jules Lion) that 300 Jews a year died in Paris, of which
100 were children under 10. The burial of one deceased person
in a permanent grave cost 700 frs.; children were buried for half
price. This means that the private and communal burial budget
amounted to approximately 175,000 frs. annually. Parisian Jews
were, however, too poor to provide for such expenditures. According
to an estimate of the Consistory made in the '60s, 550 deaths
occured annually among Parisian Jews (325 adults and 225 children).
The families of 275 deceased were too poor to be able to pay even
the smallest fee, 135 paid the minimum, 365 were buried in temporary
common graves. Only 50 deceased Jews were provided with permanent graves at their families expense. In 1868, the Paris Consistory stated that of approximately 550 deceased Jews who died
in Paris every year, 2/3 were buried in common graves, where
they lied in one big hodge-podge (*Pêle-mêle*)."

From Table 1V, we see that during the years 1837, 1841-42,
1854-55, 1858 and 1861-84, 16,315 Parisian Jews died. Of these, only
7,837 came from families who were able to pay for permanent or
temporary individual graves. The families of 8,478 (more than
half) had to ask for assistance from the Philanthropic Committee.
These poor deceased were buried in temporary common graves,
and in most cases, the bones were thrown out five years after
their interment. Beginning with the '60s, the number of deceased
poor was actually greater because burial societies interred some
of them in permanent common graves.

Special organizations were founded to provide graves for the

"   ArchCParis,1855-56 and "Lettre du Préfet," 10.VIII.1852; P. Lunel,
Sociétés de bienfaisance et mutuelles, *UI*, vol. XVI (1861), p. 362; Benoit
Lévy, in *AI*, vol. XXIX (1868) p. 306; [Ci de Paris], *A Monsieur le Pair de
France, Préfet du département de la Seine* [P 1841] 6 p. (BN,Ld183-56); A.
Créhange et M. Bollviler, *Aux Israélites de Paris* [P 1841]. 15 p. (BN,Ld185-
55); Ibid, *Lettre au Rédacteur des Archives Israélites de France, sur la défense du Consistoire de Paris, par Ben Levi, dans l'affaire des cimetieres de
Paris* (P 1841) 7 p.; Benoît Lévy, La Fosse commune, *PI*, vol. I (1869) p.
198 ("cette hideuse fosse commune que notre administration israélite laisse
subsister pour les israélites pauvres qui meurent à Paris"); Ibid, Question
des cimetières parisiens. *AI*, vol. XXXV (1874) p. 268-269; Cimetières israélites de Paris. *AI*, suppl. au No. 5 (Mai 1841) p. 317-334; "Infortunés qui
ne pouvez vous engager à payer 500 francs à la ville, préparez vous à voir
mutiler cette pierre sur laquelle vous aviez déposé un baiser d'adieu; rési-
gnez-vous à voir remuer, bouleverser, disperser ces cendres chéries". Ben-
Baruch [Créhange], in *UI*, vol. I (1844), p. 316; S. Dreyfuss, De l'unifor-
mité des convois funèbres. *LI*, vol. IV, No. 1 (1858), p. 33-36; "l'horrible
fosse commune." *VI*, suppl. 21.II.1861; S. Frydman (Z. Szajkowski), The
Revolution of 1848 and the Internal Conflicts among French Jewry; *The
Jews in France*, edited by E. Tcherikower (NY 1942) vol. I, p. 228-229; Jules
Lion, Les sociétés israélites de Paris, *AI*, vol. XXVII (1866) p. 154-155; E. de
Rothschild, *Rapport au Comité de bienfaisance sur un projet de suppres-
sion de la fosse commune* [P 186-] p. 2 (Litho); [Appel lithographié du
Consistoire de Paris sur les inhumations], 5 avril 1868, 3 p.

Jewish dead. In 1861, "La Terre Promise" (a burial society founded
in 1854) expended 2,552 frs. for graves for 13 deceased members.
In the estimate of the '60s, the Consistory further stated that
the burial society "La Terre Promise" provided 12 or 15 free graves,
but this was far from a solution of the problem of what to do
with the more than 360 paupers who died annually. The receipts
for dues of the burial society "Le Repos Eternel" bore the motto:
"For the abolition of the common grave" (*Pour la suppression de
la fosse commune*). In 1867-68, earnest discussions began to take
place on developing burial societies, where for a small annual fee
members could be burried in permanent common graves (*caveaux*).
A report of "Le Repos Eternel" of 1878 stated that as late as 1870
the bones of 200-300 Jewish dead were scattered to the winds, after
only five years in a common grave. (Between 1870 and 1885, this
society burried 2,192 Jews in permanent collective graves. Of 1,703
deceased interred from 1873 to 1883, 446 were handled at reduced
rates, 132 free, 299 with subsidies from the Philanthropic Committee,
and 812 at the full rate paid by their families.) In the '90s, another
society was organized to save Jews from being buried in the temporary 5 year graves; the motto of this society was taken from
Ruth: "May the Lord deal kindly with ye as ye have dealt with the
dead"."

" But even so, a great part of the Paris Consistory budget was covered
by incomes from burials. In 1853-1872, the city bureau of burials repaid to
the Jewish Consistory 295,918 frs. In 1894-1903, the total income of the
Paris Consistory amounted to 4,382,090 frs., of which 412,940 frs. came
from the city bureau of burials, i.e. 41,294 annually. For the same period,
the Consistory had only 248,730 frs. expenses for burials, i.e. 24,873 frs.
annually. When the monopoly of religious Consistories on burials was
abolished by the Law of December 28, 1904, the Jewish Consistory had to
look for other sources of income. According to a lithographed memorandum
by the Paris Consistory dated September 15, 1904, 11 p. (fol.) and *Documents relatifs au service des pompes funèbres...* 1868 and 1872, p. 26-27 and
14-15. Edmond Benoit-Lévy wrote on the founding of the Society "Repos
Eternel": "Le corbillard ou pauvre et une concession pour cinq ans, voilà
tout ce que les malheureux peuvent demander... après cinq ans, au vent
la poussière !..., au brasier, les ossements ! Un jour, c'était en 1869, plusieurs
personnes se trouvaient au cimetière Montparnasse, réunies devant une
fosse en laquelle on venait d'enterrer un ami peu aisé; on était devant la
fosse commune. Tous étaient plongés dans les plus tristes pensées, à l'idée
qu'au bout de cinq ans il ne resterait plus rien de cet homme qu'ils avaient
accompagné là..., et cela uniquement parce que sa famille n'avait pas eu
les moyens d'acheter une concession à perpétuité pour y construire un
caveau. Cette constatation faite en commun... engendra aussitôt... la fer-
me intention de faire tout ce qui dépendrait d'eux pour supprimer la fosse
commune. *Le Repos Eternel* était né." *Rapport de l'administration du Repos
Eternel. Gestion de 1887-1888* (Vi 1888) p. 2-3. *Société de prévoyance israélite La Terre Promise. Rapport présenté par Mr. M. Léon, trésorier* (P
1861); *Le Repos Eternel. Rapport au Comité de Bienfaisance Israélite de
Paris par la Section des Inhumations* (P 25 mai 1870) 4 p.; *AI*, vol. XXIX;
(1868) p. 306-307: *Rapport de l'Administration du Repos Eternel. Gestion
de 1877-1878* (P 1878); L. Kahn, *Les Sociétés*, p. 123-124. The Jewish tailor
and song-writer Lyon-Cahen wrote:

"Toutes les phases de la vie
Viennent réclamer du comptant;
Déjà la bourse se délie
A la naissance de l'enfant...
Pour son dernier voyage,
On paye un corbillard."

Recueil de chansons de Lyon Caen 1854-1870 (P 1870).

In 1838, the mortality rate was 1 per 100 among Jewish paupers, and 1 per 150 among the rest of the Jewish population of Paris.[**] A considerable percentage of Jews died in hospitals. In 1874, 402 of 494 (526 including those outside of Paris) died at home and 92 in various hospitals and old age homes. When we consider the mortality rate among Parisian Jews according to arrondisments (Paris was divided into 12 arrondissements until 1859, after which the suburbs were included, making 20 arrondissements) we see clearly that the mortality rate fluctuated with the number of paupers. Incidentally, this was not only characteristic of Jews. In 1861, according to the new division of Paris, the rich 9th arrondissement ranked 5th in population, but 20th (last) in deaths. The 13th arrondissement had half as many inhabitants as the 9th, but ranked first in the number of paupers, and 4th in the number of deaths. The greatest number of Jewish paupers in the first half of the 19th century (according to the old division of Paris) was concentrated in the 6th, 7th, 8th, and 9th arrondissements. That was where the greatest number of registrants of the Philanthropic Committee, the city charity offices, and patients of the Rothschild Hospital lived. The well-to-do Jews lived in the 1st, 2nd, 3rd, 4th, and 5th arrondissements. When the question of the establishment of a Jewish shelter for school children came up for consideration, it was decided to place this institution in the 7th arrondissement, because of the many paupers to be found in this and in neighboring sections. There are no accurate statistics on the Jewish population of Paris according to arrondissements for this period, but from a comparison of the number of Jewish paupers and the Jewish mortality rate, it becomes clear that the most deaths occurred in neighborhoods which had the most paupers (see Table V).[***]

Here, it is deemed necessary to note that the number of deaths among Jewish paupers was not especially the result of a high mortality rate among children and the aged. In 1845, 699 persons 16 years of age, and younger, and 898 persons over 16, took charity (this does not include soldiers and persons under arrest). The

---

Even in 1907 the society *Union de la Jeunesse israélite pour la suppression de la fosse commune* wrote: "Sans notre intervention, il [le juif] serait enterré *pour cinq ans dans la fosse commune.* Ce court délai écoulé, son corps *serait déterré, puis jeté aux catacombes !*". Rabbi Raphael Lévy, chaplain of the Paris hospitals and prisons wrote: "Il [le juif malade] songe à ce qu'il adviendra de sa dépouille mortelle... de pouvoir dormir son dernier sommeil dans un coin de terre qui soit bien à lui". F. Aron, director of the Rothschild hospital wrote: "Pour éviter la fosse commune à un parent, à un ami, j'ai vu chez nos coreligionnaires une solidarité digne d'éloges: ils engageaient leurs effets au Mont-de-Piété." *Union de la Jeunesse Israélite pour la suppression de la fosse commune* (Vi, déc. 1896) and *Années 1902—1903—1904—1905—1906* [P 1907] 20 p.

[**] A lithographed letter from the Paris Consistory to the Prefect of the Seine Department, December 10, 1843, 3 p. (ZS).

[***] Statistical data on the relationship between poverty and mortality were obtained from the following sources: reports of the Consistory, the Philanthropic Committee, and the Rothschild hospital; *AI,* vol. I (1840) p. 94, vol. IX (1848) p. 580; Paul Boiteau, Curiosités de la statistique parisienne. *JSSP,* vol. XV (1874) p. 238.

same year, there were 107 deaths of persons under 16, 104 deaths of persons over 16, and 31 stillborn infants. In 1849, there were 891 recipients of charity under 16 years of age and 1,295 over 16. The same year, there were 189 deaths of persons under 16, 232 over 16, and 29 stillborn babies. The high infant mortality rate was another indication of poverty. In 1859-1871, there were 655 stillborn children among Parisian Jews; this was a large percentage of the Jewish mortality rate. Of 3,567 deaths among Parisian Jews in 1866-71, 316 were stillborn infants. In 1874-83, there were 416 stillborn babies included in the total of 6,471 deaths. But the same proportion applies to non-Jews.[102]

Even families who paid for gravesites, could not afford to buy permanent plots (concessions perpétuelles). The majority rented temporary plots (concessions temporaires), which were preferable to the common graves because tenure could be renewed. In 1854-55, 670 of 884 deceased Jews in Paris were interred at the expense of the Philanthropic Committee, 123 were interred in permanent graves at the expense of their families, and 91 in temporary graves at their families' expense. Funerals at families' expense were classified. This also gives us some idea of the economic status of Parisian Jews. In 1856, there were 7 classes (12, 28, 50, 100, 200, 300 frs. and up); but most funerals paid for by the families of the deceased were in the cheaper classes. In the same year, 1856, there were 2 in class 2, 7 in class 3, 8 in class 4, 22 in class 5, 60 in class 6, 63 in class 7 and not one funeral in class 1; the same is true of later years. There were almost no fancy funerals. In 1865, there was one where the synagogue was decorated, and in 1868 another, but it is possible that this custom of decorating synagogues and the gates of the deceased's home had not become popular among Parisian Jews. Not only did the Philanthropic Committee have to provide graves and coffins, but in a great many cases shrouds also had to be provided. In 1858, the Committee expended 17,504 frs. for burials, of which 4,814 frs. were spent for shrouds. In 1873, of 20,215 frs. for burials of the indigent, 2,500 frs. were spent for shrouds.[103]

Jews were not the only ones among whom there was such great poverty at death.[104] We are, however, not trying to prove that Jews were poorer than Gentiles. They were probably neither richer

---

[102] See notes 94 and 101.

[103] Between 1884 and 1886, there were 1,282 funerals at the deceased's families' expense. Of these, 1 was in class 1, 20 in class 2, 68 in class 3, 199 in class 4, 306 in class 5, 266 in class 6, 360 in class 7 and 62 in the cheapest class 8. In the '80s, Jewish poverty had already settled mainly in the 3rd and 4th arrondissements (according to the new division of Paris). These were also the sections which had the largest Jewish population, but not the greatest number of funerals paid for by the families of the deceased (119 and 149). The 9th arrondissement which was even then a rich Jewish section had most of these (222). In the three year period, 1894-96, there were 2,276 funerals in Paris. Of these, 914 were free, 1 in class 1, 22 in class 2, 66 in class 3, 205 in class 4, 410 in class 5, 554 in classes 6 and 7 and 104 in class 8. See notes 94 and 101.

[104] In the whole of France, one of every 28.43 people who died was a

nor poorer. Morally, however, we must take cognizance of the greater suffering among Jewish families who had to appeal to charity for a temporary common grave for their dead, because among Gentiles religious tradition was not against the exhumation and disposal of the bones of the deceased. When one visits the three oldest 19th century cemeteries of Paris today, one can see how few permanent Jewish graves there are, which antedate the '80s. A few graves of the rich, officers, lawyers, bankers, writers can be seen; but the great mass of Jewish dead were exhumed after only five years in the grave, and their bones cast out. Only the remains of the poor Jews interred by burial societies in later years rest in their permanent common graves.

With regard to burial, conditions were much better outside of Paris (see Appendix V).

10. MISCELLANEOUS FACTS PERTAINING TO JEWISH POVERTY IN PARIS

Jews were not better housed than Gentiles; housing conditions among Jewish paupers were even somewhat worse. In 1844, the Philanthropic Committee aided 618 Jewish families; we have information about the housing of 555 of them. Of these, 335 paid a combined total of 43,881 frs. in rent, an average of 130.99 frs. per family; 171 paid a combined total of 23,879 frs., or an average of 133.65 frs. per family. The combined total of rent payments of 506 families was 67,760.50 frs., an average of 133.99 frs. per family; 49 families lived rent free because they were watchmen, or lived with relatives.[163] In the '50s, Sephardic Jews of Paris moved into the St. Victor Quarter on the left bank because rents were too high in the other sections. They opened a small synagogue at 33 Maubert Place. By 1858, this synagogue had become too small for the increasing Sephardic Jewish population of this quarter, but the officers of the synagogue were unable to raise the 500-600 frs. necessary to enlarge it because the members of the congregation were too poor to make contributions.[164]

---

pauper and had to be buried at the expense of a charity society. In 1839, of the 25,597 people who died in Paris (the 20 arrondissements of the later division), 20,244 were buried in temporary common graves, 4,081 in temporary graves at their families' expense and 1,272 in permanent graves at their families' expense. In 1868, 66.92 % of all those who died in Paris, were buried in free temporary common graves. Between 1876 and 1879, 547 of every thousand people who died, were buried without charge. In 1868, of 19,352 funerals in Paris, paid for by the relatives of the deceased, only 1,418 were in the first four classes (most expensive). See notes 94 and 101.

[163] ArchCParis,1844. In 1838, 26,936 poor families (58,500 persons) in Paris (Jews and Gentiles) paid the following rents: 16,894 paid not more than 100 frs., 4,666 paid from 101 to 200 frs. and the remainder paid from 201 to 300 frs.; 5,222 lived rent free. *Etat numérique de la population indigente de Paris...* 1838, 2 p. It is worth while to note Alexandre Weill's pamphlets of 1860 on the general housing situation in Paris: *Lettre à S.M. l'Empereur sur la Ville de Paris* (P 1860) 36 p.; *Paris inhabitable* (P 1860) 46 p. and *Qu'est-ce que le propriétaire d'une maison à Paris?* (P 1860) 24 p.

[164] A letter from Constant Cahen, president of the synagogue, 1858 (ZS).

The rite of the Spanish Jews was used in the Synagogues of Bayonne,

Jews did not eat better than Gentiles; they often skimped all week in order to have good Sabbath food, and the sight of Sabbath food often made an erroneous impression on non-Jews, making them think Jews eat well.[07] In the '40s, each inhabitant consumed an average of 47 kilos of meat annually; according to some sources, 50 kilos. Parisian Jews, whose number was estimated at 7,000 in 1846, consumed 350,000 kilos of meat and 12,000 kilos of poultry annually, an average of 50 kilos per person. This, however, can be attributed to the fact that Jews did not eat no-kosher *charcuterie* meats, which the Gentiles consumed in great quantities, but which were not included in the general meat consumption figures. Actually, Jewish meat sales decreased because a few butchers had a virtual monopoly of kosher meat.[08] Bouillon was the basic food of the poor, but not every poor person could order bouillon, even in the cheapest restaurant, because of the dietary laws. On August 31, 1840, the private firm of Van Coppenaal applied to the Consistory for permission to manufacture kosher bouillon for poor Jews. The Consistory refused to become involved with a private firm, but the application proved that Jews were in need of this basic food of the poor. Beginning with the end of 1853, the Jewish Philanthropic Committee distributed free bouillon to the pupils of Jewish schools (44,149 in the school year 1871-72, 150,000 in 1875-76, 166,350 in 1883-84). In the Committee's soup kitchen (*Fourneau Economique*, called Rothschild's Kitchen after 1881 because it was believed that Rothschild maintained it, which was not true), one could, in 1856, buy a meal which cost 0.10 fr., and consited of 1/2 liter of bouillon, vegetables and 100 grams of meat.[09]

There must have been some professional beggars among the Jewish charity cases, but they were only a very small minority; the majority were employed workers whose earnings were too low. Of the 491 families (1,384 persons) who were on the Philanthropic Committee's rolls in 1838, 304 heads of family had trades, and 187 did not (mostly because of old age), 272 were too young to

Bordeaux, Pau, Perpignan, Toulouse, and in Paris; the rite of the Comtadin Jews in the Synagogues of Aix, Avignon, Carpentras, Cavaillon, and Nimes; the rite of the Livorno Jews in the Synagogues of Marseille and Nice; the rite of the German Jews was used in Paris and in all the other Synagogues of France.

[07] "Wenn Yontef herum ess, hot mer 'Haufess oun schwarzi Wäsch"; "Lomp nouf, daiyess mounter"; "Mar der Schawess defônn?" Meiss, *oc,* p. 86, 125, 202; "Le char des soucis... s'arrête le vendredi à l'entrée de chaque village." Stauben, *oc.* p. 9.

[08] ArchCParis,1840-1844; A leaflet on kosher meat published by the Paris Consistory, October 16, 1855; *Cic de Paris, A Messieurs les Membres du Consistoire Central des Israélites de France à Paris* (P 1846) 44 p. BN,Ld 185-57.

[09] In 1866, the soup kitchen provided 117,575 meals; 1867—124,400; 1868—106,751; 1869—99,984; in the War years 1870-71—393,332; 1876—112,804; 1877—113,802; 1879—144,001; 1880—153,977. The number of meals served increased with the first immigration of Russian Jews: in 1881—180,940 meals, in 1882—326,054, in 1883—296,072. A small number of meals were served free. Printed reports of the Paris Consistory and the Philanthropic Committee; L. Kahn, *Le Comité,* p. 62; *AI,* vol. XVII (1856) p. 177. In 1851, there were four kosher restaurants in Paris. B.-B. Créhange, *Almanach...* 5612 (P 1851).

work, and 343 children attended trade and other schools. Most of the patients in the Jewish Hospital had professions. Of 354 patients between April 1842 and December 1844, 92 were maids and servants, 223 had various occupations, and 39 had no occupations. Between July 1852 and June 1856, July 1857 and June 1859, and July 1861 and June 1863, 5,471 patients were admitted to the Rothschild Hospital. Of these, 4,703 had professions and only 768 did not.[110]

The Jews who had to ask for charity were not old people who could no longer work. Of the 1,636 persons who applied for assistance for Passover of 1840, we know the ages of 1,532. Of these, only 280 were more than 50 years of age.[111]

The Parisian Jews who were in need of charity were not wandering beggars, or immigrants from Eastern Europe who became a burden on French Jewry; the majority were French Jews. For a time, evil tongues argued that the foreign beggars (*mendiants étrangers*) were devouring the finances of the Philanthropic Committee. However, this was due to the fact that for some time the Committee failed to publish reports, and it was not clear where the poor Jews originated. According to the 1836 report, only 1/11 of the indigent heads of family was born in Paris; but also among the donors for Jewish charity only 1/11 was born in Paris. Between April 1842 and December 1844, 354 patients were admitted

---

[110] Of 599 families (1,569 persons) who received charity between April 1841 and April 1842, 409 heads of family had trades, and 171 did not (mainly, because of old age), 296 women worked at home, and 301 children attended school. Of the 409 heads of families who had trades and received charity in 1843, 226 were peddlers, and small merchants, 44 were day laborers. 29 were tailors, and of the rest, more than half had trades of one kind or another. Of the 618 heads of families who received charity in 1844, 443 were employed at 70 various trades. (Of 26,936 indigent families in Paris, in 1838, only 1,184 male heads of families and 3,307 female heads of families had trades.) Of the 4,703 patients in the Rothschild Hospital with occupations, 874 were maids and servants, 1,198 merchants (mostly peddlers), 238 tailors, 183 clerks, a large number were needle workers, capmakers, etc. Of 988 patients in 1883, 613 had professions, 209 had no professions, or were aged, and 166 were children. (The same proportion is applicable to gentile patients in City hospitals.) The statistical data on the age, descent, and occupational composition of the poor are taken from: the printed reports of the Paris Consistory, the philanthropic committee, and the hospital; ArchC Paris; L. Kahn, *Les professions manuelles et les institutions de patronage* (P 1885); *Etat numérique...* 1838; A. Husson, oc, p. 291.

Léon Lyon-Caen wrote on the life of a Jewish tailor in the 1840's: "Mon père était marchand tailleur... On travaillait du matin au soir, sans trève ni repos. Mes parents prenaient tout juste le temps de déjeuner sur une petite table dite à portefeuille, dont les deux côtés se rabattaient et qu'on dressait dans l'antichambre, la salle à manger étant réservée aux affaires." L[éon] Lyon-Caen, *Souvenirs du jeune âge* (P 1912) p. 8-9.

In his book *Les Juifs de Paris* (P 1952) p. 61, Michel Roblin misrepresented the statistical data on the professional status of Jewish paupers as typical for the entire Jewish population of Paris. His book is full of such unexcusable misstatements.

[111] Of 2,360 patients in the Rothschild Hospital (between July 1852 and June 1856) there were: 490 less than 20 years of age, 867 between 20 and 30 years of age, 495 between 31 and 50 years of age, and 508—51 years and older. Between July 1852—June 1856, July 1857—June 1859, and July 1861—June 1863, there were 5,471 patients, of which 1,081 were under 20 years of age and 676 were 61 years of age or older. See note 110.

to the Jewish Hospital. Of these, 263 were born in France, and 91 abroad. Of 5,471 patients in the Rothschild Hospital, between July 1852-June 1856, July 1857-June 1859, and July 1861-June 1863, 555 were born in the Seine Department (including Paris), 3.026 in Alsace, Moselle and Lorraine (2,123 in Alsace), 275 in various other parts of France and 1,555 abroad. Even in 1883, 2 years after the beginning of the large immigration from Russia and Poland, 532 of 988 patients were born in France.[112]

Some Jewish paupers received aid in the City philanthropic bureaus, too.[113] The number of paupers was actually much greater than the rolls of the Philanthropic Committee indicated because only some of the paupers were aided by the Committee. On July 25, 1836, the Committee compiled a list of 500 paupers, and decided not to aid anyone not on the list, except those who had lived at least two years in Paris. There was strict adherence to this decision. In 1839, 491 families received aid in Paris; each family was thoroughly investigated, and yet only two families were found who were not entitled to aid. Not even all the patients in the Jewish Hospital (and they were far from well to do) took charity. Of 354 patients between April 1842 and December 1844, only 125 received aid from the Philanthropic Committee. A great many poor Jews did not take charity because they were too ashamed. In the Franco-Jewish periodical *La Paix* of 1847, a story was printed which told about the suffering of a poor Jewish family because it had to apply for aid. The decrease in the number of Jewish families registered with the Philanthropic Committee was no indication that the lot of Parisian Jews had improved. As a matter of fact, between 1881-1883, the number of registrants decreased, despite the greater poverty caused by the influx of immigrants from Russia (383 registered families in 1880, 322 in 1883). This was due to the Committee's policy of helping only a limited number of paupers. But the expenditures of the Committee for special purposes rose from 288,710 frs. in 1880, to 337,386 frs. in 1883.[114]

How does the picture of poverty among Parisian Jews compare with that of poverty among Gentiles? In 1829, there were 62,705 registered paupers for 816,466 inhabitants, i.e. one pauper per 13.02 inhabitants; in 1838, 1 per 15.37; in 1841, 1 per 13.30; in 1850, 1 per 16.38 and in 1856, one per 16.59. In 1861, there were 90,287 paupers for 1,667.841 inhabitants; that is 1 per 18 inhabitants. These figures

[112] See note 110. Among Gentiles the figures were proportionately similar: 75 % of all the paupers in Paris, in 1863, came from other sections of France or from abroad.
[113] Sometimes they received aid from the city bureaus and in the Jewish Committee as well. In 1842, 551 families received aid from the Jewish Committee; of these, 229 were also aided by the city bureaus. In 1843, 288 out of 545 and 1844, 249 out of 555. ArchCParis; *AI*, vol. XXIV (1863) p. 283-84. In Lyon, there existed a special city bureau for the assistance of the Protestant and Jewish poor. *UI*, vol. III (1846) p. 10. In the '90s, a similar bureau existed in Bordeaux ("A Bordeaux il y a une section spéciale pour les Israélites". Rapport sur la situation religieuse, 1904. ZS).
[114] ArchCParis,1842-1844; Printed reports of the Philanthropic Committee; L. Kahn, *Le Comité*, p. 30; A., Les deux riches. *La Paix* (P 1847) p. 640-50.

include only registered paupers who were entitled to receive aid from the city. Actually, poverty in Paris was much greater. However, when we consider these figures in comparison to the figures on registered Jewish paupers, we see that proportionately, there were many more Jewish paupers.[115]

11. JEWISH CHARITY IN PARIS

The need for Jewish charity increased much more rapidly than the Jewish population of Paris, despite the minimal aid afforded the poor Jews by the Philanthropic Committee. In 1836, 50 old people received 0.13 1/2 fr. each daily as a regular grant. This, of course, was not even enough to provide for the bare necessities. Even the distribution of matzoth for Passover was so minimal that it amounted to less than a third of a franc per pauper. In 1812-1817, the Paris Jewish Community consumed 80 sacks of flour annually for matzoth. Of this, 13 sacks were consumed by the poor in 1812, and 15 in 1815. In 1825, paupers received 22 1/2 sacks of the 117 for the whole community. A poor family received on the average 20 lbs. of matzoth. Matzoth was distributed to the poor as follows: in 1810—approximately 2,000 kilos, in 1839—4,759 kilos, in 1842—4,988 kilos, in 1843—5,160 kilos, in 1844—5,368 kilos, in 1845—5,554 kilos, in 1846—6,300 kilos, in 1847—8,994 kilos, in 1855—12,000 kilos and 1865—13,000 kilos. In 1840, the committee distributed only 1,924 kilos of bread, and 399 kilos of meat, in 1845—9,768 kilos of bread, and 2,280 kilos of meat. For Passover of 1840, 660 families applied for assistance; for Passover of 1847—815 families. In 1840-43, the Committee expended 229,209 frs.; between 1861 and 1865—935,702 frs.; between 1866 and 1871, the expenditures rose to 1,203,184 frs. This is how the expenditures continued to increase: 1809-1819—100,449; 15,918 frs. in the single year of 1839; 1842—37.622; 1852—136,328; 1862—176,273; 1872—244,609; 1879—269,344 frs. In the ten year period between 1805 and 1815, the experditures were 63,819 frs. and in a similar ten year period, 1861-1871, 2,138,999 frs. In 1809-1899, the Committee expended 12,621,854 frs.[116]

---

[115] A. Husson, oc, p. 288-292; *Documents statistiques sur la France;* série I, vol. I (P 1835) p. 98-99; *Etat numérique...* 1838; Maxime du Camp, L'Indigence à Paris et l'assistance publique. *Revue des deux Mondes,* vol. LXXXVII (1870) p. 926; Ibid, La Bienfaisance Israélite à Paris. *Ibidem* (15 août 1887), p. 721-753; 15 sept. 1887, p. 275-311.

[116] In 1836, 190 medical cases received only 0.15 fr. a day; the support of 11 orphans amounted only to 95.11 frs. annually, or 0.26 1/2 per day. The 1866-71 expenditures were divided as follows: money grants for regular recipients of aid—194,471 frs., special grants—133,231 frs., partial rent grants—34,513 frs., whole rent grants—43,268 frs., grants to mothers of newly born babies—26,673 frs., matzoth and money grants for Passover—63,575 frs., medicine—3,896 frs., soup kitchen—109,354 frs., cemeteries—114,025 frs., childrens' clothing—110,267 frs., schools—227,216. "Il y a à Paris des familles israélites qui ont toutes les peines du monde à soutenir leur existence de tous les jours, et quand Pâque arrive elles sont forcées

In 1819, the fortunes of the 32 wealthiest Jews of Gironde were estimated at 15,620,000 frs., that of the 32 wealthiest Jews of the Basses-Pyrénées and Landes at 5,830,000 frs.; one family possessed 4 million frs.; 2—1,800,000 frs. each; 1—1,200,000 frs.; 6—500-700,000 frs. each; 16—400,000 frs. each; 13—80-100,000 frs. each and 19 less than 100,000 frs. each. In 1826, a community tax of 1,656 frs. in Bayonne was, however, paid by only 26 families; and a tax of 3,010 frs. in St.-Esprit by 120 families (58 paid less than 10 frs.; 9 from 50 to 100 frs. and only 7 more than 100 frs.). Of a total expenditure of 8,327 frs. in 1825, the Jewish community of Bayonne disbursed 1,100 frs. for bouillon for the poor. This community also had a special school for poor children (*école des pauvres*). In 1877, the French Academy awarded its prize for devotion to the Jewess, Judith Maintasie Lopès of St.-Esprit-Bayonne, a city which had many rich Jews. Orphaned at the age of 12, she had to care for a sick father, her brothers and sisters; at 30, she married a poor widowed shomemaker, who had four children. She had 5 children of her own, and had to care for 3 children of a stepdaughter who had died. At 65, she had to work very hard to support her two sisters, and twelve children.[119]

During the Revolution, most of the wealthy Jews left the Four Communities of Southeastern France (Avignon, Carpentras, Cavaillon and Isle-sur-Sorgue) and mostly poor Jews remained. However, the wealthy Jews were not the only ones who left. Of the 12 Jewish families from Carpentras who settled in Paris around 1812, only two were required to pay community taxes; the remainder were too poor.[120]

In 1809, the possessions of the 794 Jewish families (2,609 persons) in the regional Marseille Consistory (8 Departments, with such cities as Marseille, Lyon, the four Communities) was estimated to be worth 8,935,100 frs. This amount, however, belonged to only 304 families; an average of 29,361 frs. per family (see Table VI). 74 families possessed between 300 and 500 frs.; 53 families between 6,000 and 10,000 frs.; 66 families between 12,000 and 25,000 frs.; 45 families between 25,000 and 50,000 frs.; 30 families between 60,000 and 100,000 frs.; 13 families between 125,000 and 200,000 frs. and 3 families between 290,000 and 300,000 frs. Of 603 tax-payers, 92 were in the highest tax bracket, 79 in the second, 115 in the third and 317 in the fourth. 305 heads of family were employed, but had no property and 115 heads of family were unemployed and owned nothing. 63 were officially considered paupers and lived

[119] According to a document dated August 31, 1819, Budget of the Bayonne-Saint-Esprit communities, 1826 (ZS); H. Léon, *oc*, p. 167-69, 251-252, 269-270.
[120] *Publiciste*, 17 mars 1801; Aulard, *Paris... sous le Consulat* (P 1898-99) vol. II, p. 211-212; "la misère des Juifs demeurés dans leur domicile fut au comble". *Rapport de M. le Marquis des Issarts* (Extr. du *Moniteur*, 6 avril 1821) p. 3; Pamphlets were published by non-Jews against Jewish migration for fear lest city finances suffer: [Jullian Cottier], *L'Enfant du patriotisme* [Ca 1789] 13 p.; F. R. Cottier, *Dialogue* [Ca 1789] 15 p. BN, 8Lk2-4650,vol.I,No.3-4.

When we discussed poverty in Alsace, we pointed out that the large number of poor Jews did not indicate a well developed philanthropic apparatus, the same is true of Paris. We might think that in Paris Jews made more or greater charitable contributions; therefore, the greater number of recipients of charity among Jews accounted for the larger figures on Jewish paupers. This, however, is not so. The Philanthropic Committee's budget was indeed somewhat larger than that of similar general city bureaus. In 1852, the combined budget of 92 philanthropic city bureaus in the Seine Department amounted to 2,187,766 frs. The income of the Jewish committee for the same year amounted to 133,274 frs.; but on the average, the needy Jewish family did not receive more in aid from Jews that the needy Gentile family received from the city bureau. In 1861, each needy Jewish family received aid valued at 86 frs. on the average; i.e. an average of 34 frs. per person. We should also keep in mind that the Jewish Committee had expenses which were not covered by philanthropic agencies among Gentiles.[117]

de s'endetter, d'empirer leur position pour pouvoir acheter les matzoth". *UI*, vol. III (1846) p. 46.

Printed reports of the Paris Consistory and the Committee; L. Kahn, *Le Comité*, p. 31, 40, 152; *AI*, vol. II (1841) p. 623, vol. VIII (1847) p. 421, vol. LXI (1900) p. 886; *Les membres du Comité de la Société Israélite d'encouragement et de secours. A leurs co-religionnaires* [P 1815] 1 p.; *Etat des recettes et des dépenses faites à l'occasion des fêtes des Pâques* (Avril 1847) 3 p.; *Statistique de France*, 2e sér., vol. VI, p. 23; A. Husson, *oc*, p. 293.
    [117] See note 116.

APPENDICES

APPENDIX I. THE JEWISH POPULATION OF PARIS, 1872.

Before 1881, the number of Eastern European Jews in France was negligible. Almost all of the foreign Jews lived in Paris, but their number was a puzzle. In 1950, we found a census of the Parisian Jewish population made in 1872 by the Paris Jewish Consistory. 19 volumes of this census are now to be found in the Paris Consistory. Unfortunately, the important vol. 4, containing the census of the 4th arrondissement is missing. According to an official government census of 1872, there were in Paris 23,434 Jews (23,424 according to other sources), or 1.26% of the general population. The Consistorial census of 1872 indicates 16,535 Jews in the arrondissements 1-3 and 5-20—a sufficient proportion to enable us to analyze the composition of the Paris Jewish community in 1872. According to the government census, the 4th arrondissement, missing in the Consistorial census, had 4,687 Jews, the largest number of Jews in any Paris arrondissement. The Consistorial census gives the place of birth of 10,185 Jews (see Table IX). Of these, 7,875 were born in France, including the provinces occupied in 1871 by Germany. 2,333 were born abroad: 913 in German States, only 327 in Poland-Russia.

The census gives the birthplaces of the husband and wife of 2,488 families. Of these, there were 1,633 couples where both spouses were born in France; 448 couples where both spouses were born abroad; 407 couples were mixed, i.e. either the husband of wife was born abroad. In these "mixed" marriages, 91 French-born Jews married Jews from Germany, 49 from Holland, 40 from Poland-Russia, 31 from Belgium, 14 from Switzerland, 21 from England, 11 from Austria, 10 from Italy, 5 from the United States, etc. 109 couples were composed of Jews from Alsace or neighboring communities, who married German Jews. There were 243 couples where both, husband and wife, were born in Paris; 115 couples of mixed Parisian and non-Parisian birth, excluding Alsace and the neighboring Departments; 250 couples where one spouse was born in Paris, and the other in Alsace or neighboring Departments; 128 couples where both spouses came from Alsace and neighboring Departments; 125 Jews from Alsace and neighboring Departments married Jews from other parts of France, excluding Paris.[148]

---

[148] A Society of Polish Jews (" Société de Secours mutuel des Juifs polo-

TABLE I

The Economic Status of 1,296 Jewish Families originating in Metz, 1839

Residence	Rich	Well to do	Fairly Well to do	Moderate means	Poor and Without property	Total
Metz	48	64	26	42	24	204
Moselle*	12	245	144	117	161	679
Meurthe	9	64	14	5	23	115
B.-Rhin	13	26	—	6	10	55
H.-Rhin	8	7	4	—	10	29
Meuse	5	12	5	—	7	29
Vosges	—	6	8	—	6	20
Paris	71	21	—	—	17	109
Other depts.**	1	36	7	—	12	56
Total	167	481	208	170	270	1,296

* Except Metz. **Except Paris.

TABLE V

Mortality and poverty of Jews in Paris

arrondissements	Poor families registered with the Jewish charity commitee, 1838, 1840—41, April 1845 — April 1846, 1849, 1851.*	Poor families registered with the city's charity offices, 1840.	Patients in the Jewish hospital July 1852 - June 1856, July 1857 - June 1858, July 1861 - June 1863.*	Deceased, 1838—1844
I	29	1	115	46
II	21	—	196	60
III	45	3	459	77
IV	34	5	627	24
V	90	1	250	104
VI	465	26	498	250
VII	2321	171	1249	448
VIII	192	10	517	62
IX	809	55	722	164
X	35	3	109	33
XI	27	4	162	23
XII	67	—	280	46
Suborbs***	11	—	312	105
Total	4,146	279	5,496	1,482

* Exclusive of prisoners. ** Only newly admitted patients.
*** The later arrondissements 13-20.